MANN ON THE LEGAL ASPECT OF MONEY

MANN ON THE LEGAL ASPECT OF MONEY

SIXTH EDITION

Charles Proctor, LLD (*B'ham*)

Solicitor of the Supreme Court
England and Wales

OXFORD

UNIVERSITY PRESS

OXFORD
UNIVERSITY PRESS

Great Clarendon Street, Oxford OX2 6DP

Oxford University Press is a department of the University of Oxford.
It furthers the University's objective of excellence in research, scholarship,
and education by publishing worldwide in

Oxford New York

Auckland Cape Town Dar es Salaam Hong Kong Karachi
Kuala Lumpur Madrid Melbourne Mexico City Nairobi
New Delhi Shanghai Taipei Toronto

With offices in

Argentina Austria Brazil Chile Czech Republic France Greece
Guatemala Hungary Italy Japan South Korea Poland Portugal
Singapore Switzerland Thailand Turkey Ukraine Vietnam

Oxford is a registered trade mark of Oxford University Press
in the UK and in certain other countries

Published in the United States
by Oxford University Press Inc., New York

British Library Cataloguing in Publication Data

Data available

Library of Congress Cataloging in Publication Data

Data available

ISBN 0–19–826055–5   978–0–19–826055–4

1 3 5 7 9 10 8 6 4 2

Typeset by RefineCatch Limited, Bungay, Suffolk
Printed in Great Britain
on acid-free paper by
Antony Rowe, Chippenham

FOREWORD

My father never said what or who actually inspired him to write *The Legal Aspect of Money*. His formation, including his doctoral thesis "Die Sachgrundung in Aktienrecht" (The payment for shares in kind) at Berlin University, was in the field of company law. However, he must have had a latent awareness of problems of monetary law and practice. He was the grandson of a banker, partner of Mann and Loeb in Frankenthal in the Palatinate, which was sold to a predecessor bank of the Deutsche Bank in 1913. His father was concerned in liquidating some of the bank's affairs after 1918 and my father was a trainee for a short time in the successor bank. He grew up amid the uncertainties of currency exchange rates and restrictions in the French zone of occupation and during the great inflation in Germany. An intimate friend of his father since schooldays was Karl Hellferich, a pupil of Georg Friederich Knapp and author of the well-known book on money, whose dazzling bureaucratic and business career, as well as his extreme political views, must have meant that his name was frequently mentioned. Two of his professors at Berlin University, Martin Wolff and Arthur Nussbaum, each wrote on the law of money and would have discussed the legal consequences of the stabilisation of the mark in 1924. Finally the famous case of *Adelaide Electric Supply Co v Prudential Assurance Co* in 1934 was at the right moment for someone of his background, anxious to establish himself. My father wrote, "in the summer of 1936 I had decided to write a book on the law of money: a number of cases which were before the courts in those years appeared to make a systematic investigation and presentation of the subject necessary, particularly since no work on it in the English language was available".

Since my father's death on 16 September 1991, correspondence has been found in the archives of Oxford University Press (OUP). In particular the readers of the original manuscript are revealed, about whom my father often asked, but never discovered. His letter of 15 December 1937 addressed to OUP reads: "I write to ask whether you would be prepared to publish a book which I have just completed . . . the questions dealt with in the book are at the present moment of great practical importance." On 18 December my father was requested "to be good enough to forward us your MSS . . ." and a further letter on 7 January 1938 states "We are having your manuscript read but fear that there will be a little delay before we can come to a decision." An internal memorandum to Sir Humphrey Milford, the publisher, refers to a previous proposal from my father in January 1934 (he had arrived in England in October 1933), to translate and explain the new German company law, which had been declined, and goes on to say that "there is a considerable risk that the [book] would either be too much a book of the moment or too vague to be useful. Unfortunately Cheshire who would have advised is just leaving for a tour of Malaya."

On 30 December 1937, Kenneth Sisam of OUP asked Albert Feaveryear, author of *The Pound Sterling* (1931) to read the manuscript. Feaveryear replied on 10 January "I have no hesitation in saying that it [the book] should be most carefully considered for publication . . . Dr. Mann must be regarded as having written, I think, a pioneer work." In order to obtain an opinion on the international law, on the advice of Professor J.L. Brierly, the manuscript was sent to Professor D.J. Llewellyn Davies at Birmingham University. He answered on 22 March 1938: "I find that Dr. Mann does his work with extraordinary thoroughness and I do not believe that there can be any questions as to his accuracy. This is entirely in keeping with the opinion which I found of his work when I was a member of the staff of London University when he used to attend my seminars in Private International Law . . .".

Mr J. Mulgar, of OUP, made an offer for the publication of the book on 29 March, but felt that the work "might benefit by a certain polish in its English style". My father accepted the terms on 30 March and asked for an early date of publication in view of the number of relevant international conferences in the late summer. The manuscript was read by Sir Paul Harvey, compiler of *The Oxford Companion to English Literature*, as an expert editor, with suggestions for improvement and corrections. Final revisions were completed on 29 July; the order to print 750 copies was given on 5 September; my father's preface was dated 12 October, his wedding anniversary, the date of the prefaces of all subsequent editions. Judging by the dates on the letters of thanks for complimentary copies, the book of 334 pages must have been published at the end of November 1938, at a price of 21 shillings per copy.

Meanwhile, on 22 June 1938, the Senate of the University of London agreed that upon receipt by the Senate of four published copies of the thesis, the degree of Doctor of Laws be conferred upon my father as an internal student at the London School of Economics. After this there was correspondence between the University and OUP as to whether the title page should bear an inscription that the thesis had been approved for the degree. A compromise was agreed that the preface should state that the book had been accepted for the LLD degree. The Senate resolved on 18 December that all conditions had been met and to confer the degree.

In his preface, my father extended thanks for reading the manuscript to Mr L.C.B. Gower, later Professor Gower, the well-known expert on company law and subsequently Vice-Chancellor of Southampton University; and to

Dr K. Wolff of Paris, son of Martin Wolff, my father's fellow student in Berlin and subsequently a distinguished concert pianist. The preface to the Fifth Edition, 1992, referred to the "remarkable . . . Kenneth Sisam" who accepted the book and to the "unfailing help and courtesy which his publishers have at all times extended to him".

The book was started in the summer of 1936, written in a foreign language and completed when my father was aged thirty. By then he had established a law practice; completed the LLM degree in 1936 at the London School of Economics; had children in 1935 and 1937; and conceived and written the book.

In thanking Charles Proctor for completing the Sixth Edition of *Mann on the Legal Aspect of Money*, one must be pleased that my father's work and spirit will continue. Just as my father dated his prefaces on October 12, this foreword commemorates the seventieth anniversary of the wedding of my parents.

David Mann
12 October 2004

(With thanks to the Oxford University Press, for making their archives available.)

PREFACE TO THE SIXTH EDITION

Dr Mann completed work on the Fifth Edition of *The Legal Aspect of Money* shortly before his death in 1991. The present edition is therefore the first to be prepared by a different author. The quality of Dr Mann's own work is well known and, as a result, the present writer assumed the task of revising this text only after considerable hesitation. Nevertheless, it seemed appropriate to attempt a further edition, partly in view of the international prominence and unique character of *The Legal Aspect of Money*, and partly in recognition of Dr Mann's enormous contribution to the law over a period of some six decades.

Every attempt has been made to preserve Dr Mann's original work where possible, but it will be appreciated that some fourteen years have elapsed since the previous edition was published. The intervening period has witnessed a number of important developments in the monetary field, and these have required detailed consideration. In addition, some new material has been added to reflect the present writer's own views and particular fields of interest. Whilst the list cannot be exhaustive, it is appropriate to provide a list of some of the main areas of revision.

First of all, whilst the expression 'State theory of money' continues to be used in this work, it has been felt necessary to revise the underlying content of that theory in certain material respects. The subject is discussed in Chapter 1.

Secondly, whilst Dr Mann insisted on a careful distinction between domestic and foreign money obligations, this approach becomes more difficult to maintain in the light of the Court of Appeal decision in *Camdex International Ltd v Bank of Zambia (No. 3)* [1997] CLC 714. Materials dealing with the performance of monetary obligations and the principle of nominalism have been reorganised and revised to reflect the impact of that decision.

Thirdly, it was thought to be helpful to include a commentary on certain specific questions of private international law as they affect monetary obligations. Chapter 4 has been inserted for that purpose.

Fourthly, events affecting the former Republic of Yugoslavia and the division of Czechoslovakia shed new light on some of the difficulties which arise when the territorial scope of a monetary area is altered. The subject is considered in Chapter 6.

Fifthly, the continuing use of sanctions as an instrument of foreign policy led to the decision to include Chapter 17, dealing with the implications of such action for monetary obligations.

Sixthly, it is no longer felt possible to complete a work on money without at least some consideration of the institutional framework which underpins its creation. This statement can perhaps best be justified by the structures which were put in place for the creation of the euro and which are considered in Chapter 27. More general institutional questions are also addressed in Chapter 21.

Finally, there can be no doubt that the establishment of the eurozone has been the major monetary achievement of the last few years. This subject plainly required detailed treatment in a work of this kind. Part VI therefore reviews the major legal aspects of this development, and also considers the other forms of monetary organisation which a State may adopt.

The manuscript for this edition was substantially completed on 31 July 2004, although it has been possible to take account of a few subsequent developments.

Whilst the content of this work is, of course, the responsibility of the present writer, he is very glad to acknowledge the assistance which he has received from a number of different sources. Professor Dominique Carreau and Professor Tullio Treves were kind enough to review and comment on parts of the text, and to allow me to benefit from their extensive experience in this specialised field. Dr Jan von Hein likewise reviewed sections of the text and provided a most useful note on German legislative and case law developments since the Fifth Edition was completed. Antonio Sáinz de Vicuña and Erwin Nierop, respectively General Counsel and Deputy General Counsel at the European Central Bank, were kind enough to make available their time to discuss Part VI of this work; William Blair QC reviewed the manuscript at the request of Oxford University Press; Martin Thomas of the Financial Markets Law Committee helpfully responded to the many queries which I raised with him.

The present edition would not have appeared without the support of Dr Mann's family, in particular David Mann, who worked hard to ensure that his father's work was continued; the many at Oxford University Press who were involved with this work and who demonstrated considerable patience and restraint in the face of the inevitable delays at various stages of the publication process.

As will always be the case, however, my greatest debt of gratitude is owed to my wife, Martina, and to our children. Apart from the time, patience, and tolerance which this project has demanded over an extended period, my wife has made a very special contribution to the completion of this work. Aided by her Master's degrees in both law and business, she undertook an enormous amount of research and located vast amounts of material which would not otherwise have been included in this edition. It is no exaggeration to say that this book would not have appeared without her untiring efforts and support.

Charles Proctor
London
January 2005

PREFACE TO THE FIRST EDITION

'Although the civil law is not of itself authority in an English Court it affords great assistance in investigating the principles on which the law is grounded.'—
Blackburn J in *Taylor v Caldwell* (1863), 3 B. & S. 826

In general words, the object of this work is to treat the legal aspects of money in a systematic and comprehensive manner. There were, however, so many obstacles on the way to this goal which the author was unable to overcome in their entirety, that he must ask for the reader's indulgence. In support of this plea for leniency a few observations may perhaps be offered.

The first cause of the difficulties lies in the fact that there does not seem to exist any English (or American[1]) work dealing with the subject as defined above. The century from the end of the Bank Restriction period to the outbreak of the Great War in 1914, which witnessed so rich a development in the field of law, was marked by an unheard-of stability of economic and, consequently, of monetary conditions. It is, therefore, not surprising that lawyers were led to regard money, not as a problem of paramount importance, but as an established fact. This security was not shaken until the great and sometimes even chaotic disturbances of the monetary systems with which every country has been visited since 1914,[2] and which deeply imprinted themselves on the economic situation and the law not only of foreign countries but also of this country. Though it was never doubted that, whatever happened, the pound sterling remained the same in character and (internal) value, business men and courts were confronted with many intricate questions which originated from the depreciation or collapse of foreign currencies or from the changes in the international value of the pound. Thus, many important decisions of the English courts came into being, and yet it is probably no exaggeration to say that, in so far as the fundamental legal problems of money are concerned, the observations of Sir John Davis on the *Case de Mixt Moneys*[3] still were the only English source of information, and that in respect of many questions of detail there was no guidance at all in the

---

[1] The book by Bakewell, *Past and Present Facts about Money in the United States* (New York, 1936), is only of very limited value.

[2] A survey is given by Griziotti, "L'Évolution monétaire dans le monde depuis Ia guerre de 1914", *Rec* 1934 (48), pp. 1 sqq.

[3] (1604) Davis's Rep. (Ireland) 18.

otherwise rich treasures of the common law. There is obviously a gap to be filled, but, in view of the lack of preliminary studies on the one hand, and the immense number of problems and foreign material on the other, this gap is so great that it could not be attempted to give more than a first introduction on the lines of a general survey of and a guide to an inaccessible, though theoretically fascinating and practically vital, part of the law.

The choice of problems suitable for and requiring discussion has been restricted to three groups. In the first place, all those questions have been included which, for the sake of systematical elucidation, had to be answered; for it is believed that the subject demands particular care in putting and arranging the questions, in drawing clear distinctions and demarcations, and in working a way through the labyrinth of material. Secondly, all those questions have been dealt with which have been raised or answered in the cases decided by English courts; it is hoped that all, or at least all important, cases have been considered, but as some have been hunted up which hitherto have escaped the attention due to them, the suspicion is justified that there are many more either hidden in the reports or known but treated under the head of other than purely monetary problems. Thirdly, only those problems have been treated which had been, or might reasonably be expected to be, of practical importance from the point of view of English (municipal or private international) law; mere theory and speculation have in general been eliminated, though in the first part it was necessary to give a certain amount of space to theory; the question of which problems might become important for the law of this country is naturally a difficult one, but in such connections judgment has been based on the experiences of foreign countries.

Within these limits the legal aspects of money will be discussed from a purely legal point of view. Though economic theory will not be disregarded, it is no disparagement of it to say that its usefulness for legal research is not very great. Anglo-American monetary science has undoubtedly neglected the problem which from the point of view of the law is the vital one, namely nominalism and its various phenomena. In this respect it has therefore been necessary to have resort to the research of continental economists. Nevertheless, the lawyer's gratitude is due to those economists who have dealt with the economic and, more particularly, the monetary history of Great Britain, to which the law will have to attribute considerable importance. Mr Feavearyear's short but excellent book on *The Pound Sterling* (1931) is of particular assistance.

Though this book is devoted to the discussion of English law, an extensive space has been conceded to comparative research. The usual argument that comparative studies are necessary and useful because they place a wealth of experience at our disposal, and show what is right and what is wrong with us, is fortified by many circumstances. When Sir John Davis wrote more than 300 years ago, he largely drew on continental scholars, and if his observations have been accepted by the common law, as in the absence of other material they seem to have been, it follows that the sources of the English law of money are to a great extent of foreign origin. This may perhaps also be regarded as a justification for the fact that it is a lawyer originally trained under a foreign legal system who now ventures to revive the study of the law of money. Furthermore, the developments since 1914 have given rise to an abundance of foreign decisions and legal literature to which international value may justly be ascribed. In France, Italy, and Germany three important works have been published by Mater, Ascarelli, and Nussbaum respectively. The writer is particularly indebted to Professor Nussbaum,[4] who by his indispensable treatise as well as by many other publications dealing with various monetary problems paved the way for further research to a greater extent than any one of his contemporaries. Finally, it appears that in many foreign laws monetary problems have not been regulated by legislative measures, but left to be moulded and solved by judge-made law. This is a further reason why a comparison with English law is interesting.

The foreign material is so vast that the selection presented to the English reader is bound to be incomplete. Paramount importance has been attributed to the decisions of Supreme Courts; decisions of courts of first and second instance have generally been disregarded, because it is believed that decisions of such courts are very often unsuitable for comparative research, as their authority, under no circumstances binding, is especially assailable, and as the picture they convey can, therefore, too easily become misleading. Legal literature will be referred to rather eclectically, though a much greater quantity of books and articles have been consulted. All available decisions of the Supreme Court of the United States which "are always considered with great respect in the courts of this country"[5] and many decisions of American State Courts have been used. Otherwise, comparative research has chiefly been directed to French and German law. The method of dealing with comparative material will vary. Sometimes it will be used as a mere illustration; in other connections it will be referred to as a persuasive, or at least supporting, authority; in a third group of cases it will serve as a contrast to elucidate a rule of English law or to test its soundness.

---

[4] Formerly Professor at Berlin University, now visiting Professor at Columbia University in New York. Professor Nussbaum has announced that he is engaged in preparing a comprehensive study of the legal aspects of monetary theory and practice which, prepared under the auspices of the Columbia Council for Research in the Social Sciences, will "primarily rest on Anglo-American law and will consider as well important developments which have occurred since the publication of the German volume". See the article in 35 (1937) *Mich. L.R.* 865, which constitutes the first chapter of the forthcoming volume.

[5] *Beresford v Royal Insurance Co*, [1937] 2 All ER 243 (CA), at p 252 B *per* Lord Wright.

Within these limits and on these foundations an attempt has been made to investigate the legal aspects of money, the subject being divided into two distinct parts the difference between which needs emphasis: the first part deals almost exclusively with English money in English municipal law, and comparative material is used for the single purpose of showing the position of a given domestic currency within the frame of the given domestic law. Where questions connected with a currency other than the domestic one are considered in the first part, this is due to the necessity of elaborating certain connections between both. But otherwise, all questions relating to foreign currency, ie to the position of a currency within the ambit of a municipal or private international law of a country other than that to which the currency belongs (eg American money in England, German currency in France), have been reserved for the second part. It is the present writer's experience and conviction that this separation between domestic and foreign money obligations is absolutely essential for a clear exposition of the subject although it cannot be carried through without exceptions, and although it may sometimes cause inconvenience or overlapping. There is in each case not only a difference of problems, but there are also many differences of approach to the problems, which make it impossible to apply to the one case, without qualification, considerations operative in, or decisions relating to, the other.

The final revisions of the manuscript were completed on 29 July 1938; decisions and literature which appeared after that date could not be taken into consideration.

F. A. M.

London
12 October 1938

CONTENTS—SUMMARY

IV. EXCHANGE CONTROLS, EXCHANGE RATES, AND SANCTIONS

V. PUBLIC INTERNATIONAL LAW OF MONEY

VI. MONETARY UNIONS AND OTHER FORMS OF MONETARY ORGANISATION

CONTENTS

II. THE PRIVATE LAW OF MONETARY OBLIGATIONS

Introduction

3. The Character of Monetary Obligations

4. Monetary Obligations and the Conflict of Laws

5. The Interpretation of Monetary Obligations—Initial Uncertainty

6. The Interpretation of Monetary Obligations—Subsequent Uncertainty

III. THE PRINCIPLE OF NOMINALISM

Introduction

V. PUBLIC INTERNATIONAL LAW OF MONEY

Introduction

VI. MONETARY UNIONS AND OTHER FORMS OF MONETARY ORGANISATION

Introduction

TABLE OF STATUTES

TABLE OF ENGLISH CASES

TABLES OF SCOTTISH AND COMMONWEALTH CASES

CYPRUS

MALAYSIA

NEW ZEALAND

TABLE OF CASES FROM THE EUROPEAN COURT OF JUSTICE

TABLE OF INTERNATIONAL CASES

TABLE OF UNITED STATES OF AMERICA CASES

LIST OF ABBREVIATIONS

General

CHAPS	Clearing House Automated Payments System
CHIPS	Clearing House Interbank Payments System
EBRD	European Bank for Reconstruction and Development
ECB	European Central Bank
ECJ	European Court of Justice
ECOFIN	Council of Ministers of the European Union (Economic and Finance)
ECtHR	European Court of Human Rights
ECU	European currency unit
EMS	European Monetary System
ERM	Exchange Rate Mechanism
ESCB	European System of Central Banks
GCC	Gulf Co-operation Council
ILC	International Law Commission
IMF	International Monetary Fund
LIBOR	London Interbank Offered Rate
OECD	Organisation for Economic Co-operation and Development
SDR	Special Drawing Right
TARGET	Trans European Automated Real-time Gross Settlement Express Transfer System
WTO	World Trade Organisation

Reports/periodicals

AJCL	American Journal of Comparative Law
AJIL	American Journal of International Law
BFH	*Amtliche Sammlung von Entscheidungen des Bundesfinanzhofs* (Official Reports of Decisions of the Federal Tax Court, Germany)
BGE	*Entscheidungen des Bundesgerichts* (Collection of decisions of the Swiss Federal Tribunal)
BGHSt	*Amtliche Sammlung von Entscheidungen des Bundesgerichthofs in Strafsachen* (Official Reports on Criminal Law Cases of the Federal Supreme Court, Germany)
BGHZ	*Amtliche Sammlung von Entscheidungen des Bundesgerichtshofs in Zivilsachen* (Official Reports on Civil Law Cases of the Federal Supreme Court, Germany)

BIJI	*Bulletin de l'Institut juridique international*
BVerfGE	*Amtliche Sammlung von Entscheidungen des Bundesverfassungsgerichts*
BYIL	British Yearbook of International Law
Clunet	*Journal du droit international privé*, founded by Clunet
D	*Recueil périodique de jurisprudence de Dalloz*
DH	*Receuil hebdomadaire de jurisprudence de Dalloz*
ELR	European Law Review
ICLQ	International Comparative Law Quarterly
IPRspr	*Deutsche Rechtsprechung auf dem Gebeite des internationalen Privatrechts* (Collection of German decisions relating to conflict of Laws)
JIBFL	Journal of International Banking and Financial Law
JIFM	Journal of International Financial Management and Accounting
JW	*Juristische Wochenschrift*
LQR	Law Quarterly Review
MLR	Modern Law Review
NJW	*Neue Juristische Wochenschrift*
OJLS	Oxford Journal of Legal Studies
RabelZ	*Zeitschrift für ausländiches und internationales Privatrecht*, edited by Rabel and others
Rec	*Receuil des Cours de l'Academie de droit international* (La Haye)
Rev Crit	*Revue Critique de Droit Internationale Privé*
RGZ	*Amtliche Sammlung von Entscheidungen des Reichsgerichts in Zivilsachen* (Official Reports on Civil Law Cases of the German Supreme Court)
RIAA	Reports of International Arbitral Awards
RzW	*Rechtsprechung zum Wiedergutmachungsrecht*
S	*Recueil de jurisprudence de Sirey*
WM	*Wertpapiermitteilungen*

Part I

THE CONCEPT OF MONEY AND MONETARY SYSTEMS

INTRODUCTION

The first part of this text considers both the concept of money and the nature and organisation of a monetary system.

Intro.I.01

Chapter 1 considers the general concept of "money", and examines the attempts which have been made to formulate a satisfactory legal definition of this elusive term. As will be seen, it is the view of the present writer that such a definition serves only a limited value in a *private law* context, where the notion of "payment" is likely to be of far more practical importance. Nevertheless, it remains necessary to formulate a definition because the term "money" is also used in broader contexts. For example, public international law bestows upon the State the power to create and to regulate its monetary system; such a right can only be meaningful if the expression "money" has a meaning which is recognised for the purposes of defining the monetary sovereignty of the State. Considerations of this kind have led the present writer to reformulate certain aspects of the State theory of money adopted in the earlier editions of this work.

Intro.I.02

Chapter 2 examines the organisation of the monetary system, the role of domestic currencies and the nature of the legislation which is required to create a monetary system. Chapter 2 also considers the nature of the unit of account, the manner in which a monetary system may be varied or replaced, and the difficulties which may periodically arise in identifying the existence of an independent monetary system.

Intro.I.03

1

THE CONCEPT OF MONEY

Words are the tokens current and accepted for conceits as moneys are
for values

Francis Bacon (1561–1626), *The Advancement of Learning* (1605)

A. Introduction

The troublesome question, What is money? has so frequently engaged the minds   **1.01**
of economists that a lawyer might hesitate to join in the attempt to solve it. Yet
the true answer must, if possible, be determined. For "money answers everything".[1] Money is a fundamental notion, not only in the economic life of mankind,[2] but also in many spheres of law. It therefore seems appropriate for the

---

[1] Ecclesiastes, 10:19 See also *Grotius, De Jure Belli ac Pacis, ii* 12.17. It has been said that
"Next to language, money is the most important medium through which modern societies communicate"—see Widdig, *Culture and Inflation in Weimar Germany* (University of California,
2001) 79. Further, as the US Supreme Court noted in *Briscoe v Bank of Kentucky* (1837) 11 Peters
255, "there is no principle on which the sensibilities of communities are so easily excited, as that
which acts upon the currency".

[2] The significance of money for the evolution of modern society can scarcely be overstated. A
society could not have moved from subsistence production to specialised production and distribution of goods and services unless a medium of exchange had been created—see Silard, *International
Encyclopaedia of Comparative Law*, Vol XVII (1975) ch 20 and sources there noted. In a

lawyer to seek a definition of money, given the frequent use which is made both of the term itself and its many derivatives, including debt, damages, payment, price, capital, interest, tax, pecuniary legacy, and doubtless many others. All of this terminology may have further consequences; for example, only an obligation expressed in money can involve any obligation of payment or repayment, or carry any right to interest. Money is a term so frequently used and of such importance that one is apt to overlook its inherent difficulties, and to forget that the multitude of its functions necessarily connotes a multitude of meanings in different legal situations.[3] The universality of money and monetary systems no doubt also contributes to a certain complacency in seeking to identify a working definition.[4]

1.02   The following examples may provide an initial outline of some of the difficulties caused by this elusive term:

(a)   If a contract is to fall within the scope of the Sale of Goods Act 1979 then it must involve a transfer of goods "to the buyer for a money consideration, called the price".[5] If the consideration moving from the buyer is not "money", then the contract is one of barter, which in many respects differs from a contract for the sale of goods.[6]

(b)   Likewise, a contract for the transfer of land only involves the "sale" of that if the buyer is to pay a consideration in money.[7]

(c)   For the purposes of the Bills of Exchange Act 1882, a bill of exchange must require the drawee to pay "a sum certain in money".[8] An instrument requiring the transfer of something other than "money" is thus not a negotiable instrument for the purposes of that Act.

(d)   In the United Kingdom, the taking of deposits in the course of a

---

work of this kind, it is not possible to consider the history of money in any detail, although the general subject is a fascinating one. For interesting surveys, see Davies, *A History of Money from Ancient Times to the Present Day* (University of Wales, 1994); Chown, *A History of Money from 300 AD* (Routledge, 1994); Sinclair, *The Pound—A Biography* (Arrow Books, 2001). A major work in this area is Simmel, *The Philosophy of Money* (Routledge, 2nd edn, 1990).

[3] This state of affairs necessarily complicates the search for a single and comprehensive definition of "money".

[4] The general statements made in this opening paragraph are subject to various reservations expressed below. As will be seen, some have doubted the value or purpose of a definition of "money".

[5] See s 2(1) of the 1979 Act. The term "goods" therefore necessarily excludes money—see s 61(1) of the 1979 Act.

[6] See *Chitty on Contracts* (Sweet & Maxwell, 29th edn, 2004) para 43-013; Goode, *Commercial Law* (Penguin, 2nd edn, 1995) 209; *Simpson v Connolly* [1953] 1 WLR 911, 915 and *Robshaw v Mayer* [1957] 1 Ch 125. Similar distinctions are recognised in the German Civil Code—see Markesinis, *The German Law of Obligations* (Clarendon, 1997) 35.

[7] There is thus no "sale" if the land is to be transferred in order to extinguish some other, pre-existing obligation of the transferor—*Simpson v Connolly* [1953] 1 WLR 911.

[8] Bills of Exchange Act 1882, s 3(1).

deposit-taking business is prohibited, in the absence of appropriate author-isation. For these purposes, a "deposit" is a "sum of money" paid on terms that it will be repaid at a later date, whether with or without interest.[9] Clearly, in determining whether authorisation is required (or an offence has been committed), it is important to establish the precise meaning of "money" in this context.

(e) The terms of a given statute may create an obligation to pay "money" and it may be necessary to decide in what manner the obligation is to be per-formed. Thus, where a statute required payment "in current coin of the realm" it was held that only payment in cash would suffice—payment in goods or in other manner would not discharge the obligation.[10]

The instances just noted suggest a narrow and technical approach to the mean- **1.03** ing of "money", perhaps because each of them has a statutory derivation. But a much broader approach is adopted in other cases. For example:

(1) The action for "money had and received" can be brought when the subject matter is not money itself but some form of security therefor or other equivalent.[11]

(2) Whilst an individual may claim to have "money in the bank", it is clear that he no longer owns physical notes and coins which he handed over to the bank, for property in those items will have passed to the bank itself. Instead, he has become a creditor who can recover his debt by action. He does not "own" anything at the bank, nor is the bank a trustee of the money deposited with it.[12] Yet, as will be seen, the credit balance standing at his disposal may be used as a means of discharging financial obligations, and thus may be regarded as "money" to that extent.

(3) Equally, for the purposes of the equitable doctrine of tracing the term, "money" is by no means confined to physical cash—it extends to all assets capable of being identified in or disentangled from a mixed fund.[13]

---

[9] For the relevant legislation and the detailed definition of "deposit" see the Financial Services and Markets Act 2000 (Regulated Activities) Order 2001 (SI 2001/544), art 5.

[10] See *Hewlett v Allen* [1892] 2 QB 662, 666 approved in *Williams v North's Navigation Collieries (1899) Ltd* [1906] AC 136 and *Penman v The Fife Coal Co* [1936] AC 45. An obligation requiring payment "in current coin" includes banknotes—see Currency and Bank Notes Act 1954, s 1.

[11] *MacLachlan v Evans* (1827) 1 Y & J 380; *Pickard v Bankes* (1810) 13 East 20. See also *Spratt v Hobhouse* (1827) 4 Bing 173, where it was stated (at 179) that, in the context of an action for money had and received, everything may be treated as money "that may be readily turned into money".

[12] *Foley v Hill* (1848) 2 HL Cas 28; *R v Davenport* [1954] 1 WLR 569; *Grant v The Queen* (1981) 147 CLR 501.

[13] A point established in *Re Diplock* [1948] Ch 465, 517 et seq. The meaning of "money" is specifically discussed at 521. The decision was affirmed by the House of Lords (*Ministry of Health v Simpson* [1951] AC 251) but without reference to this specific point.

(4) In the context of a will, the term "money" will generally carry a rather broader meaning. At any rate, it has no fixed meaning, and it is the duty of the court to ascertain the testator's intention upon a reading of the document as a whole. Thus, "money" could include the whole of the personal estate and a reference to "all my money" could in some cases extend to the testator's entire real and personal estate.[14]

1.04 These few examples have, however, merely reinforced the original assertion, namely that "money" has a variety of different meanings in different situations, and individual cases require separate scrutiny; no hard and fast rule exists in this area. As a result, it becomes tempting to ask at this point whether the search for a general definition of money serves any useful purpose. As with so many legal expressions, all may depend upon the language which accompanies the term and the circumstances under which it is used. That the ease of recognition may be contrasted with the difficulty of definition is emphasised by the evidence of a London accountant given to the Committee on the Resumption of Cash Payments in 1819. When asked to explain a "pound", he said "I find it difficult to explain it, but every gentleman in England knows it . . . It is something which has existed in this country for eight hundred years—three hundred years before the introduction of gold."[15] It may be objected that this evidence is now of some antiquity. Yet even today, it is difficult to provide a more satisfactory response. Equally, differences of emphasis may occur depending upon the location in which the question arises; for example, in less developed societies, a definition of "money" may adhere more closely to traditional interpretations associated with bank notes and coins, whilst a broader approach (perhaps comprising government securities, bank money, and other instruments) may have to be adopted in the context of more advanced economies.[16] Further, as will be seen at a later stage, an obligation expressed in money will generally be discharged provided that the creditor receives the "commercial equivalent" of cash or money, and this formulation by itself tends to suggest that a precise definition of money will be both elusive and perhaps even unhelpful.[17] Finally Professor Goode has asserted that "much of the debate on what constitutes money in law is rather sterile and

---

[14] *Perrin v Morgan* [1943] AC 399; *Re Taylor* [1923] Ch 920. Thus, notwithstanding the authorities mentioned in n 10 above, the terms "cash" and "money" will, in this particular context, frequently include credit balances with banks and building societies, and may extend to holdings of government bonds: *Re Collings* [1933] Ch 920; *Re Stonham* [1963] 1 All ER 377; *Re Barnes Will Trusts* [1972] 1 WLR 587.

[15] The episode is noted by Silard (n 2 above).

[16] This statement is made for the purposes of illustration. However, it will later be suggested that government securities cannot constitute "money"; they are merely evidence of indebtedness, or of an obligation which is itself payable at a later date.

[17] On the "commercial equivalent" of cash and the performance of monetary obligations, see *The Brimnes* [1975] QB 929, considered at para 7.10 below.

has few implications for the rights of parties to commercial transactions, where payment by bank transfer is the almost universal method of settlement";[18] in his view, the notion of payment is a far more important legal concept. Given the work upon which he is engaged, the present writer has searched diligently for grounds to disagree with this view; but at least in the context of commercial and financial transactions, it is necessary to admit that the notion of payment is of more practical importance. As will be seen, there is much case law which deals directly with the concept of payment, but there have been very few occasions on which the court has been directly concerned with the meaning of money or has attempted to address that subject in a meaningful way. Can one therefore conclude that a generally applicable definition of "money" would have to be so broadly written that it would serve no real purpose and that, in any event, a satisfactory definition of "payment" would be far more useful in practical terms? Alternatively, is it preferable to avoid a definition of "money" altogether, and simply deal with practical problems on a case-by-case basis?

Tempting though this approach may be, it is plainly inappropriate simply to abandon the search, at least in the context of a book of this kind. One cannot complete a work on the subject of money without at least attempting a definition, even if both the discussion and the conclusion are in some respects inconclusive or unrewarding. It must also be recognised that the concept of money does not only arise for consideration in commercial transactions. For example, many references will be made to the sovereignty which a State enjoys over its monetary system;[19] it would be odd if that discussion were to proceed without any attempt at a definition of "money". **1.05**

It has already been noted that money is a fundamental notion within the economic life and activities of mankind. It seems to follow that an attempt to formulate a *legal* definition of "money" cannot proceed in isolation, but must take at least some account of economic theory. In addition, as will be seen, technological and other developments over recent years do have consequences for an attempt to formulate a legal definition of "money"—as the available means of payment multiply, the meaning of "money" must correspondingly broaden. **1.06**

B. The Meaning of "Money"—A Functional Approach

As noted above, a legal definition of "money" requires at least some consideration of its economic functions. Without attempting a detailed review of a **1.07**

---

[18] See Goode, *Commercial Law* (Penguin, 2nd edn, 1995) 492.
[19] See in particular Ch 19 below.

complex area, it may be noted that economists have tended to define money by reference to some of its functions, namely:[20]

(a) as a medium of exchange;[21]
(b) as a measure of value or as a standard for contractual obligations;[22]
(c) as a store of value or wealth;[23] and
(d) as a unit of account.[24]

1.08 The emphasis placed by economists on each aspect of this definition has tended to vary at different times[25] but it seems that the role of money as a medium of exchange is now regarded as its key feature.[26] As will be seen, the proposed legal definition of "money" reflects some of these economic considerations. Nevertheless, it is necessary to proceed with caution in this area because, as noted earlier, "money" can have very different meanings in different contexts. The law must provide a framework within which money has a role and its use has specified legal consequences. It is for this reason that bank deposits may be "money" to the economist,[27] but they have not always been regarded as such by the lawyer,

---

[20] eg see Crockett, *Money, Theory, Policy and Institutions* (Nelson, 2nd edn, 1979) 6; Lewis and Mizen, *Monetary Economics* (Oxford University Press, 2000) 5–6; Lipsey, Purvis and Steiner, *Economics* (Harper Collins, 7th edn, 1991) 695–8. Miskin, *The Economics of Money, Banking and the Financial Markets* (Little Brown & Co, 1986) 9, defines money as "anything that has a fixed and unvarying price in terms of the unit of account and is generally accepted within a given society in payment of debt or for goods and services rendered".

[21] That is to say, as a convenient proxy or method to facilitate the effective exchange of goods and services—see, eg, Jevons, *Money and the Mechanism of Exchange* (Kegan Paul, 14th edn, 2002) 1875; Bannock and Mansor, *International Dictionary of Finance* (S. Wiley & Sons, 2000) 181.

[22] See Crockett, *Money, Theory, Policy and Institutions* (Nelson, 2nd edn, 1979) 6; Macesich, *Issues in Money and Banking* (Praeger, 2000) ch 3.

[23] That is to say, it acts as a store of value between its original receipt and its subsequent utilisation by the holder as a means of payment—see, eg, Butler, *Milton Friedman: A Guide to this Economic Thought* (Gower, 1985) 67, and Lewis and Mizen, *Monetary Economics* (Oxford University Press, 2000) 10–11.

[24] It may be noted that these criteria are to some extent reflected in Art 10(1) of the Treaty between the Federal Republic of Germany and the German Democratic Republic dated 18 May 1990, which states that (in consequence of the currency union and subsequent unification of the two States), the Deutsche mark would be the "means of payment, unit of account and means of storing value".

[25] See Lewis and Mizen, *Monetary Economics* (Oxford University Press, 2000) 4.

[26] See, eg, Robertson, *Money* (London, 1927)—"money is anything that is widely accepted in payment for goods or in discharge of other kinds of business obligations"; Brunner, "Money Supply" in J. Eatwell, M. Milgate, and P. Newman (eds) *The New Palgrave: Money* (W.W. Norton & Co, 1989) 263—"money is still best defined in the classical tradition to refer to any object generally accepted and used as a medium of exchange". For an alternative formulation, see Friedrich Hayek, *The Denationalisation of Money* (1976) 46—"to serve as a widely accepted medium of exchange is the only function which an object must perform to qualify as money, though a generally accepted medium of exchange will generally acquire also the further functions of unit of account, store of value and standard of deferred payment".

[27] See, eg, F.E. Perry, *Elements of Banking* (Methuen, 4th edn, 1984) 22; see also F.S. Mishkin, *The Economics of Money and Banking and the Financial Markets* (Little Brown & Co, 1986) 21:

who may see them as a debt or an obligation on the part of the bank to repay money.[28] It is, of course, unsurprising that economists and lawyers should differ in their approaches to questions of this kind, for their areas of concern and objectives are also entirely different. The economist may be concerned with such matters as monetary policy, exchange rate policy, and the supply and soundness of money within an economic area as a whole. Lawyers, on the other hand, tend to be more concerned with the protection of the purely private rights of contracting parties and the discharge of monetary obligations.[29] The lack of common objective between the two disciplines inevitably results in the lack of a common approach or definition.[30] In other words, the lawyer must take account of the functional and economic purposes of money, but he will not alight upon a legal definition which is wholly derived from economic considerations. On the contrary, he must necessarily focus upon money as a means of performance of obligations which have legal force.

So where does the lawyer begin his search for a definition of "money"? The **1.09** following starting points are suggested:

(1) First of all, the role of money as a medium of exchange has already been emphasised. If a country's system of trade and commerce is to be based on money as a means of exchange, then the law must buttress that position and allow for the assured discharge of monetary debts by payment in that medium. Thus, the law must require that creditors accept payment

---

"to define money as currency is too limited for economists, because travellers cheques and savings deposits can be used to pay for goods and services [and] they can be converted quickly into currency".

[28] For reasons discussed later in this chapter, it is submitted that the lawyer's former caution in this area is no longer sustainable or realistic.

[29] Thus, whilst a bank deposit may be "money" so far as the economist is concerned, to the lawyer the arrangement creates an obligation to pay money—see *Foley v Hill* (1848) 2 HL Cas 28; *Universal Adjustment Corp v Midland Bank Ltd* (1933) 184 NE 152, *Richardson v Passumpto Savings Bank* 13 A 2d 184 (1940). Yet, as will be shown below, this does not necessarily disqualify a bank deposit from the status of money.

[30] That legal and economic definitions of money cannot be uniform was noted by von Mises, *The Theory of Money and Credit* (translated by H.E. Batson, Jonathan Cape, 1953) 69: "The fact that the law regards money only as a means of cancelling outstanding obligations has important consequences for the legal definition of money. What the law understands by money is in fact not the common medium of exchange but the legal medium of payment. It does not come within the scope of the legislator or the jurist to define the economic concept of money." This statement reinforces a point which has already been made, namely that the lawyer's preoccupation with private and commercial rights and the performance of financial obligations tends to diminish the importance of "money" as an independent legal concept, because the notion of "payment" usually plays a greater role in those cases in which a dispute does arise.

through that medium—in other words, the creditor must accept payment in legal tender.[31]

(2) Equally, it has been shown that money functions as a unit of account. Money could only discharge this function if the unit of account is uniform throughout the monetary area concerned. The required uniformity can only be achieved with any degree of permanence if the unit of account is prescribed by law. The essential features of money as a medium of exchange and as a unit of account thus require the underpinning of the law, or the State.

(3) The requirement that money should act as a "store of value" is perhaps less easily reflected in a purely legal definition of "money". And yet it may be possible (or even necessary) to accommodate this aspect in various ways. If money is to act as a store of value, then that value must be identified in a manner which the law can recognise and support. This, again leads to the conclusion that money must, with the support of the law, be denominated or expressed by reference to an identified unit of account.[32]

With these initial thoughts in mind, it is now appropriate to consider the formulations attempted in decided cases and other legal sources.

1.10 Blackstone[33] defined money as "the medium of commerce . . . a universal medium, or common standard, by comparison with which the value of all merchandise may be ascertained, or it is a sign which represents the respective values of all commodities". Perhaps the best known judicial definition in England is that used in *Moss v Hancock*[34]—money is "that which passes freely from hand to hand throughout the community in final discharge of debts and full payment for commodities, being accepted equally without reference to the character or credit of the person who offers it and without the intention of the person who receives it to consume it or apply it to any other use than in turn to tender it to others in discharge of debts or payment for commodities".

---

[31] This is inherent in the very notion of legal tender and is beyond doubt—see, eg, *Chitty On Contracts* (Sweet & Maxwell, 29th edn, 2004) paras 21-083–21-096. However, for reasons which will be discussed at a later stage, the importance of legal tender rules is now very limited.

[32] The view that the "store of value" feature must be recognised in a legal definition of money may also have additional consequences, eg it may support the view that the formal demonetisations of a currency may only occur as a result of legislative action in the State of issue—a proposition discussed at para 1.25 below. Furthermore, it may support the view that a State which substitutes its currency is obliged to provide for a "recurrent link" between debts expressed in the old and the new currencies; this point is considered at para 2.34 below.

[33] i, 276. Blackstone did, however, add that the coining of money also represented an act of sovereign power (i, 277).

[34] [1899] 2 QB III, 116, drawing upon F.A. Walker, *Money, Trade and Industry* (London, 1882). The latter part of this definition both describes and emphasises the character of money as a means of exchange, even though the term itself is not used. The phrase quoted in the text is perhaps more of a functional description, rather than a definition.

The Supreme Court of Canada has, in some respects, adopted an even broader definition, describing money as "any medium which, by practice, fulfils the function of money which everyone will accept in payment of a debt is money in the ordinary sense of the words, even though it may not be legal tender".[35]

These definitions have not strayed very far from the economists' view of money; they tend to adopt a purely functional approach. Moreover, they do not emphasise the legal framework within which money must exist if it is to be used as a final and complete means of discharging financial obligations; indeed, the Canadian Supreme Court appears to have taken the view that "money" could exist without any such legal support. By contrast, however, the definitions employed in the Uniform Commercial Code of the United States describe money as "a medium of exchange authorised or adopted by a domestic or foreign government as part of its currency". This language clearly indicates that the authority of the State is a necessary ingredient of the definition of money.[36] The point is reinforced by Article 1 (section 8, paragraph 5) of the Constitution, which reserves to the Federal Government the exclusive right to issue money. Moreover, even some economic commentaries have suggested that money must exist within a legally defined framework, or else it is not money at all—Keynes noted that "money is simply that which the State declares from time to time to be a good discharge of money contracts".[37] It seems fair to note that more modern definitions of "money" have tended to adopt a broader approach by including not only bank deposits but even government debt securities, which can readily be converted into cash. Thus Article XIX(d) of the Articles of Agreement of the International Monetary Fund states that the term "currency . . . includes without limitation, coins, paper money, bank balances, bank acceptances and government obligations issued with a maturity not exceeding twelve months".[38]

1.11

---

[35] *Reference Re Alberta Statutes* [1938] SCR 100,116. The final part of this statement recognises the undoubted truth that "money" is a much broader concept than "legal tender"—see para 2.25 below.

[36] See s 1-201(2.4) and the comment on s 3-107.

[37] See *Social Consequences of Changes in the Value of Money* (1923) reprinted in *Collected Writings*, ix, 63. Adam Smith also noted that money required a "public stamp" although this remark seems to have been directed at the need to protect the integrity of money by preventing forgery; he therefore contemplated the State as the guardian of the quality of money, not necessarily as the exclusive issuer—see *The Wealth of Nations*, Vol 1 (reprinted 1904) 27.

[38] Even this already broad definition is stated to be non-exclusive. Yet foreign government securities would not generally be regarded as "money" in a legal sense, for their value in terms of the domestic currency will vary according to prevailing interest rates and other factors. Further, as noted previously, even domestic currency securities represent an obligation to pay money at a later date; it is therefore difficult to see how, in law, such securities could themselves be regarded as "money".

1.12 It must also be said that monetary sovereignty is one of the attributes of a modern State under international law.[39] The right to regulate the monetary system resides with the State; and the obligation of other States to recognise that monetary system can only apply where the relevant money has been created under the legal authority of the first State. Now, the notion of State sovereignty implies the right to legislate in specific fields falling within the ascertained scope of that sovereignty.[40] Considerations of this kind suggest that, whilst a *legal* definition of money must necessarily contain or reflect at least some of the elements of the functional approach (and, hence, the realities of commercial and economic life), it must also include an element which reflects the international law requirement just noted—namely that "money" must exist within some form of legal framework, because it reflects an exercise of sovereignty by the State in question.

1.13 With these considerations in mind, it becomes attractive to adopt a functional approach—money is that which serves as a means of exchange—subject to the crucial proviso that its functions must have the formal and mandatory backing of the domestic legal system in the State or area in which it circulates. For anything which is treated as "money" purely in consequence of local custom or the consent of the parties does not represent or reflect an exercise of monetary sovereignty by the State concerned, and thus cannot be considered as "money" in a legal sense.

1.14 It is necessary to conclude that a definition of "money" in law must recognise both the functions of money and the legal framework within which it must be created. Against that background, it is possible to turn to theories of money which have previously been formulated.

---

[39] See the discussion at Ch 19 below, and see Carreau and Juillard, *Droit international économique* (Dalloz, 2003), who describe money as "L'un des éléments essentiels de la souveraineté de l'Etat moderne" (para 1428). In the light of points which will be made later, it is suggested that this assertion remains accurate notwithstanding the transfer of sovereignty involved in the creation of a monetary union—see para 31.03 below.

[40] See, eg, Brownlie, *Principles of Public International Law* (Oxford University Press, 6th edn, 2003) ch 15. If international law is to provide, at least in part, the source of a definition of money, then it must not be forgotten that such a sovereignty can be restricted, delegated, or transferred by treaty. This point is relevant in the context of economic and monetary union, and is discussed in Ch 31 below.

C. Legal Theories of Money

The State theory of money

The role of the State in the establishment of the monetary system and in the creation of physical money led Dr Mann to conclude[41] that, in law, the quality of money is to be attributed to all chattels: **1.15**

(a) which are issued under the authority of the law in force within the State of issue;

(b) which under the terms of that law, are denominated by reference to a unit of account; and

(c) which, under the terms of that law, are to serve as the universal means of exchange in the State of issue.

It is apparent that the definition relies heavily upon the role of the State in establishing a monetary system and in authorising the issue of notes and coins. It is thus necessary at the outset to review this approach in broad terms, and to consider a competing theory. It will then be appropriate to return to Dr Mann's definition in a little more detail.[42]

Under the definition just outlined, money must be issued under the central authority of the State concerned. This approach reflects the State (or Chartalist) theory of money developed by G.F. Knapp,[43] who opined that only chattels **1.16**

---

[41] See the Fifth Edition of this work, 8.

[42] If this definition is accepted then there can be no difference between money and the legal tender of any particular State. Money, therefore, would exist as a result of a direct exercise of sovereign power, and thus could readily be distinguished from other forms of payment such as cheques and letters of credit and which function as such by consent of the parties. The point is made by Gleeson, *Personal Property Law* (FT Tax & Law, 1997) 142–3, noted by Brindle and Cox (eds) *The Law of Bank Payments* (Sweet & Maxwell, 2004) para 2.1. For reasons discussed below, the emphasis on the *physical* aspects of money must now be discarded.

[43] *Staatliche Theorie des Geldes* (4th edn, 1923), translated by Lucas and Bonar, *State Theory of Money* (1924; abridged edition, A.M. Kelley, 1973). Knapp's theory provoked both strong support and vehement criticism—for discussion and further materials, see Hirschberg, *The Nominalistic Principle, A Legal Approach to Inflation, Deflation, Devaluation and Revaluation* (Bar-Ilan University, 1971) 11–30. The State theory was subjected to withering criticism by Ludwig von Mises in *The Theory of Money and Credit* (translation by H.E. Batson, Jonathan Cape, 1953)—eg, he states (at 69) that "the concept of money as a creature of law and the State is clearly untenable. It is not justified by a single phenomenon of the market. To ascribe to the State the power of dictating the laws of exchange is to ignore the fundamental principles of money—using society". Against this, one may quote the judgment of Strong J in the *Legal Tender Cases* (see n 64 below): "Every contract for the payment of money, simply, is necessarily subject to the constitutional power of the government over the currency, whatever that power may be, and the obligation of the parties is, therefore, assumed with reference to that power . . ." For a discussion of the evolution of the State's modern monopoly over money, see Glassner, *Money and the Nation State: The Financial Revolution, Government and the World Monetary System*, Dowd and Timberlake (eds) (Transaction Publishers, 1997) ch 1.

issued by the legal authority of the State could acquire the character of "money", and that the value to be attributed thereto is fixed by law, rather than by reference to the value of the materials employed in the process of production. Dr Mann supported this approach partly in the light of the universal acceptance of the principle of nominalism.[44] The State theory of money is the necessary consequence of the sovereign power or the monopoly over currency which States have assumed over a long period and which is almost invariably established by modern constitutional law.[45] It cannot be open to doubt that the United Kingdom currently retains and exercises sovereignty in monetary matters;[46] accordingly, the State theory of money may be regarded as a part of English law.[47] The right of coinage had for many centuries been recognised as a part of the Crown's prerogative, and was thus exercisable without parliamentary or other sanction.[48] Whilst the right to issue coinage has now been placed on a statutory basis, the exclusivity of the privilege to issue coins has been specifically preserved.[49] It should be added that the introduction of the euro does not detract from the State theory of money; on the contrary, it is an illustration of that theory, for the creation of the single currency is directly traceable to an exercise of monetary sovereignty by the individual participating Member

---

[44] The principle of nominalism is discussed in detail in Part III below.

[45] The powers of the State in currency matters plainly include the right to issue money, but also include a number of other matters affecting the regulation of money—eg the right to introduce exchange controls. The extent of State sovereignty in monetary matters and its recognition under customary international law are discussed in Ch 19 below. On the long-standing historical nexus between the monetary system and the State, see Carreau, *Souveraineté et coopération monétaire international* (Cujas, Paris, 1970) 23–47. In terms of history and chronology, however, it must be noted that forms of money came into use before the State had legislated for a monetary system and that, in many respects, the law merely provided a juristic imprimatur to that which had already become common practice. On the whole subject, see Kemp, *The Legal Qualities of Money* (Pageant Press, 1956) 131. The State theory thus cannot explain the meaning of money against a historical background. It may be that the Societary theory of money, considered below, is of greater assistance in that respect.

[46] For certain limitations imposed upon that sovereignty as a result of the United Kingdom's membership of the European Community and the introduction of the euro, see Ch 31 below. But these factors do not affect the general principle described in the main text.

[47] The point is implicit in decisions such as *Adelaide Electric Supply Co Ltd v Prudential Assurance Co Ltd* [1934] AC 122.

[48] For cases on this point, see *Case de Mixt Moneys* (1604) Davis 18; *Dixon v Willows* 3 Salkeld 238; *Pope v St Leiger* (1694) 5 Mod 1. The coins issued pursuant to an exercise of the royal prerogative thus constituted legal tender for the settlement of debts in this country. Only later did the courts accept that only Parliament had the right to ascribe the quality of legal tender—*Grigby v Oakes* (1801) 2 Bos & Pul 527. Parliament considered that its control over the monetary system extended to the American Colonies and, in 1751, passed "An act to regulate and restrain paper bills of credit in His Majesty's Colonies or Plantations of Rhode Island and Providence, Connecticut, the Massachusettes Bay and New Hampshire in America and to prevent the same being legal tender in Payments for Money" (24 Geo II, c 503, 1751).

[49] See the Coinage Act 1971, s 3 (as amended). Section 9(1) of that Act (as amended) renders it an offence to make or to issue any piece of metal as a token for money, unless the authority of the Treasury has been given for that purpose.

States.[50] The State theory thus does not prevent a group of States from introducing a common currency. Likewise, it does not prevent a single State from introducing more than one currency. Examples of the latter phenomenon tend to have something of a historical flavour, but China affords a modern example; the currency of mainland China is the yuan, but Hong Kong continues to issue the Hong Kong dollar, which is an entirely independent monetary unit.[51]

It should be appreciated that the law relating to bank notes, or paper money, **1.17** developed in a rather different way, for their history is connected with that of bills of exchange and banking. Banknotes in the modern sense were not always distinguishable from other negotiable instruments although even in an early case, it had been held that banknotes would usually be regarded as "money" in a legal context.[52] When the Bank of England was established in 1694,[53] it was not a bank of issue in the modern sense. The legislation did not even state whether the Bank was intended to issue notes at all, still less did it seek to confer upon it an exclusive, note-issuing monopoly which would have been consistent with the State theory of money.[54] Nevertheless, the Bank began to act as a bank of issue and circulation immediately after its incorporation. But in addition, many country banks continued to issue notes without government control.

As a result, the growth of money in circulation was not subject to any effective **1.18** form of regulation and the quality of money could clearly be affected by the solvency of the particular issuer.[55] This state of affairs in turn became the chief topic of discussion between the Currency and Banking Schools during the early part of the nineteenth century. The former school considered that the term "money" should be ascribed only to notes and coin, and that the issue of money should be undertaken directly by the Government or under its control.[56] As a result, the *creation* of money would rest in official hands, whilst the *distribution*

---

[50] This point is discussed in more detail in Ch 31 below.

[51] Furthermore, China and some other countries have in the past issued two separate units of account—one for use by nationals, and the other for use by foreign visitors.

[52] *Wright v Reed* (1790) 3 TR 554. In *R v Hill* (1811) Russ & Ry 191, it was held that banknotes were not "money, goods, wares etc" for the purposes of a criminal statute which created the crime of obtaining property by false pretences. Whatever may have been the position in the early 19th century, such a view is plainly unacceptable in the modern context. See also *Klauber v Biggerstaff* (1879) 47 Wis 551, 3 NW 357 and *Woodruff v State of Mississippi* (1895) 162 US 292, 300.

[53] Bank of England Act, 1694.

[54] *Bank of England v Anderson* (1837) 3 Bing NC 590, 652.

[55] This factor must have influenced the decision in *Ontario Bank v Lightbody* (1834) 13 Wend (NY) 108 where Lightbody had tendered notes in payment of a debt due to the Ontario Bank. Unknown to both parties, the issuer of the notes had become insolvent. Lightbody's argument that payment had both been tendered and accepted was dismissed by the court; notes could not form the subject matter of a valid tender where the issuer was insolvent. See also *Ward v Smith* (1868) 7 Wall 447.

[56] The Currency School held that the regulation of money supply was the key to sound economic policies.

of money would occur through banks and through private transactions.[57] This approach was endorsed by the Bank Charter Act 1844 which established the modern position. Subject to certain transitional arrangements, the privilege of issuing notes constituting "money" and enjoying the status of legal tender in England and Wales was made exclusive to the Bank of England.[58]

1.19   The Bank Charter Act appears rapidly to have pushed the English courts towards the State theory of money. Less than twenty years later, the Court in *Emperor of Austria v Day* said that the right of a foreign government to issue notes as paper money followed from powers vested in the State itself.[59] The same theory was also applied in twentieth-century cases decided by the House of Lords and the Privy Council, and to which it will be necessary to return at a later point.[60]

1.20   If the State theory of money appears to have gathered early momentum in England, matters took a slightly more tortuous course in the United States of America. The Constitution[61] confers upon Congress the power "to coin money, regulate the value thereof, and of foreign coin". Thus, the Supreme Court has noted that "to determine what shall be lawful money and a legal tender is in its nature and of necessity a governmental power. It is in all countries exercised by the governments."[62] It followed that Congress had the power (and, it may be added, the *sole* power) "to issue obligations of the United States in such form, and to impress upon them such qualities as money . . . as accord with the usage of sovereign governments. The power . . . was a power universally understood to

---

[57] The Banking School took a much broader view of the nature of money, holding that the unrestricted creation of money by means of bank credit was acceptable provided that it was linked with the genuine needs of trade.

[58] For the current legislation in this area, see Currency and Bank Notes Act 1954, s 1(2). On the status of the Bank of England see Bank of England Act 1946, s 4 and Currency and Bank Notes Act 1928, s 3. The amount of the notes issued by the Bank of England must be covered by securities as directed by the Treasury, and is subject to such limit as the Treasury may from time to time prescribe—Currency Act 1983, s 2.

[59] (1861) 3 DeG F & J 217; see in particular 234 and 251. Although the case is useful in many respects, the actual decision was criticised by Dr Mann, *Transactions of the Grotius Society* 40 (1955) 25, or *Studies in International Law* (1973) 505.

[60] See in particular *Adelaide Electric Supply Co Ltd v Prudential Assurance Co Ltd* [1934] AC 122 (HL) and *Bonython v Commonwealth of Australia* [1950] AC 201 (PC), discussed in Ch 2 below.

[61] See Art I, s 8, para 5.

[62] *Hepburn v Griswold* (1869) 75 US 603, 615. This case nevertheless held the legal tender legislation to be unconstitutional on the grounds that it required creditors to accept payment in a depreciated medium of exchange and thus constituted a deprivation of property "without due process of the law", contrary to the relevant provision of the Fifth Amendment. The case held that the constitutional power "to coin money" meant precisely what it said; coins could be made legal tender, but notes could not. This followed the similar decision in Indiana in *Thayer v Hayes* (1864) 22 Ind 282. The effect of these decisions was reversed by *Knox v Lee* and *Parker v Davies* (below).

belong to sovereignty."[63] In view of these considerations, the power of Congress to "coin" money was held to extend to the issue of greenbacks, or paper money.[64] Under these circumstances, it will be appreciated that the circulation of any other chattels claimed to have the quality of money would be inconsistent with the established monetary prerogative of the Federal Government. The first "greenbacks" were issued as part of the Government's efforts to finance the Civil War; for this purpose, Abraham Lincoln signed the first Legal Tender Act in February 1862. The Act authorised the issue of notes which were "lawful money and legal tender in payment of all debts, public and private within the United States". Until that time, the issue of banknotes had essentially been a function of private issuers.[65] If the Federal Government had now established the exclusive right to issue notes, then it was necessary to decide whether action by the individual States might infringe the monopoly. By Article 1, section 10 of the Constitution, individual States could not "coin money, emit Bills of Credit, make any Thing but gold and silver Coin a Tender in Payment of Debts". The Court in *Craig v Missouri*[66] held that "the emission of any paper medium by a State government for the purpose of common circulation" would be caught by the prohibition. But a few years later, paper "money" issued by a State-owned banking corporation was held to fall outside the prohibition—it was not issued by the State and on the faith of the State.[67] Later cases held that notes and

---

[63] See *Juilliard v Greenman* (1883) 110 US 421, 447 relying on the decision of the English court in *Emperor of Austria v Day* (1861) 3 DeG F & J 217, discussed at para 20.04 below. It may be said that the State theory of money became firmly entrenched as a part of federal law as a result of the *Juilliard* decision. The case arose from an Act of Congress in 1878, which had provided for the reissue of greenbacks in peacetime, and confirmed their quality as legal tender. The Supreme Court held that the power to issue such notes was an extension of the powers of Congress to borrow money—an interesting approach which equates the public law concept of money with the essentially private law of obligations which flow from a bill of exchange.

[64] *Knox v Lee* and *Parker v Davis* (1870) 79 US 457. It is perhaps unsurprising that issues surrounding national monetary sovereignty have tended to arise in the context of a federal State. Thus, in the Federal Republic of Germany, the Constitutional Court held (20 July 1954, *BVerfGE* 60) that an enactment by a *Land* which, "in its economic result" allowed revalorisation of executed obligations in order to adjust the effects of a *national* currency reform, related to the monetary system of the State as a whole and thus fell within the exclusive jurisdiction of the Federal Government.

[65] Such banknotes could be put into circulation without any official authorisation—see *Bank of Augusta v Earle* (1839) 38 US 519.

[66] (1830) 4 Peters 410.

[67] See *Briscoe v Bank of Kentucky* (1837) 11 Peters 255. In part, the decision relies on the fact that the issuing bank had set aside funds to meet its obligations under the notes in question, constituting obligations of that institution which could be enforced by action. They were not currency notes, where in many respects the promise to pay is in effect illusory—see in particular p 328 of the judgment. The main decision was followed in *Darrington v The Bank of the State of Alabama* (1851) 13 Harvard 12. It was later decided that a State did not contravene the provisions of Art 1, s 10 by passing legislation which stipulated that the holders of certain cheques could be paid by means of drafts drawn on another bank, because this did not have the effect of converting the drafts into a form of legal tender—see *Farmers and Merchants Bank of Monroe, North Carolina*

coupons issued by State banks—which were essentially departments of State governments—were not "bills of credit" for these purposes even though they could be accepted in payment of taxes and other sums owing to the State.[68] Of course, the exclusive right to issue banknotes enjoying legal tender status is now vested in the Federal Reserve although the notes represent obligations of the Federal Government, rather than the Federal Reserve.[69] In a series of cases, the Supreme Court further held that the power to determine the value or convertibility of legal tender[70] likewise rested with the State. The State theory of money may thus be regarded as a part of the law of that country.[71]

1.21 If one accepts the State theory of money as formulated by Dr Mann, then it becomes necessary to consider its practical consequences. Two points should be made in this context.

1.22 First of all, circulating media of exchange in law only constitute "money" if (a) they are created by or with the supreme legislative authority of the State and (b) the relevant law confers upon those circulating media a nominal value which is independent of the intrinsic value of the paper/metal from which they are made, of their actual purchasing power, and of their external value measured against other currencies. It follows that gift vouchers, tokens, and similar items—even though exchangeable against the provision of goods or services by their issuers—do not constitute "money" because they lack the support of the supreme legislative authority within the State concerned. For the same reason, promissory notes issued by a commercial or industrial company are not "money", even if they were to circulate and to be accepted as such throughout the community. Likewise, where a statute, without further definition, refers to "gold coin", it must be taken to refer to coin issued under the authority of the State and not to some privately produced replica.[72]

---

v Federal Reserve Bank of Richmond, Virginia (1923) 262 US 649. These cases throw light not only on the prerogative of issuing banknotes, but also on the problem of separate legal persons within the structure of a State. See generally, J.W. Hurst, *A Legal History of Money in the United States* (University of Nebraska Press, 1976); *From Rags to Riches: An Illustrated History of Coins and Currency* (Federal Reserve Bank of New York, 1992).

[68] See the *Virginia Coupon Cases, Poindexter v Greenhow* (1884) 114 US 270 and *Houston & Texas CR Co v State of Texas* (1900) 177 US 66. The cases are discussed by Nussbaum, *Money in the Law, National and International* (The Press Foundation, 2nd edn, 1950) 90.

[69] Federal Reserve Act 1913, s 16.

[70] See *Perry v US* (1935) 294 US 330; *Nortz v US* (1935) 294 US 317 and *Norman v Baltimore & Ohio Railroad* (1935) 294 US 240. It may be added in passing that the exclusive powers of the Federal Government to issue money necessarily implies the further power to punish counterfeiting of the currency—*US v Marigold* (1850) 50 US 560.

[71] For further support for this proposition, see *Stephens v Commonwealth* (1920) 224 SW 364, where reference is made to money as the "circulating medium by the authority of the United States".

[72] *Freed v DPP* [1969] 2 QB 115, a case arising under the Exchange Control Act 1947.

A currency issued by an insurgent authority and forcibly imposed upon the local **1.23** population in the course of a civil war is to be regarded as lawful money in the geographical area concerned, because the insurgents exercise *de facto* supreme authority in governmental matters, which makes obedience to their authority not only a necessity but a positive duty. This position is established by a number of decisions of the Supreme Court of the United States[73] which held, amongst other things, that a contract could not be rendered void or unenforceable on public policy grounds merely because the consideration had been expressed in the Confederate dollar. In the present context, this approach has the merit of consistency with the State theory of money, as formulated earlier. It is, however, not entirely clear that the English courts would adopt a similar approach; on occasion, they have refused to recognise the legislative or official acts of an insurgent government.[74] However, the English courts have indicated a willingness to apply laws made by unrecognised governments to the extent to which these deal with private rights and there are no countervailing considerations of public policy.[75] It is suggested that the English courts could, on this basis, recognise such a monetary law under appropriate circumstances, even though the relevant State or government is not formally recognised by the United Kingdom.

Similar questions may arise where the conflict is of an international nature, as **1.24** opposed to a civil war. Notes issued and made legal tender by a belligerent occupant in the course of an international war are "money" because they are imposed by the body which *de facto* (and even if only temporarily) exercises supreme authority and is responsible for public order and administration.[76] As a consequence, a debt contracted in the national currency prior to the onset of hostilities can subsequently be discharged in the occupation currency by payment of so many occupation currency notes as are—under the occupant's legal tender legislation—equivalent to the nominal value of the debt.[77]

---

[73] See *Thorington v Smith* (1869) 75 US 1; *Hannauer v Woodruff* (1872) 82 US 439; *Effinger v Kenney* (1995) 115 US 566; *New Orleans Waterworks v Louisiana Sugar Co* (1888) 125 US 18; *Baldy v Hunter* (1898) 171 US 388; *Houston and Texas CR Co v Texas* (1900) 177 US 66, but see (to different effect) *Thomas v Richmond* (1871) 79 US 453.

[74] See in particular *Madzimbamuto v Lardner-Burke* [1969] 1 AC 645 (PC); *Adams v Adams* [1971] P 188; and *Re James* [1977] Ch 41 (CA). All of these cases arose from Rhodesia's unilateral declaration of independence in 1964. More specific to the present context is the decision in *Lindsay, Gracie & Co v Russian Bank for Foreign Trade* (1918) 34 TLR 443, where it was suggested that notes issued by the Soviet Government could not be treated as "money" by the English courts, because that Government was not then recognised by the UK.

[75] *Carl Zeiss Stiftung v Rayner and Keeler (No. 2)* [1967] 1 AC 853 (HL).

[76] It is doubtful whether the international renunciation of the use of force could be taken to affect the rule stated in the text. On the subject generally, see Jennings and Watts (eds), *Oppenheim's International Law* (Longman, 9th edn, 1991) para 268.

[77] Supreme Court of the Philippine Republic in *Haw Pia v China Banking Corp* (1948) 13 The Lawyer's Journal (Manila) 173. This decision was discussed and followed in *Madlambayon v*

1.25   The second consequence of the State theory is that, in law, money cannot lose its character except by virtue of formal demonetisation—that is to say, the introduction of a subsequent law which deprives the earlier money of its character as such.[78] The statement just made implies that money cannot lose its character by custom, or by any other means. As a matter of law, it is suggested that this proposition remains accurate, even though history supplies many examples of the operation of Gresham's Law, where bad money drove good money out of circulation.[79] Gresham's Law has usually been applied to coins which were perceived to have a nominal value below the intrinsic value of their metallic (gold or silver) content. Inevitably, holders of the undervalued coins would tend to withhold them. But they retained their status as "money", for they were still legal tender for the number of units of account by reference to which they were denominated; and coins do not lose their legal tender status merely because some of the holders elect to save, rather than spend. If a coin—such as a gold sovereign[80]—can be sold for a price in excess of its nominal value, then it is being sold in the character of a commodity, and not as money.[81] Apart from such "commodity" cases, however, the courts will apply their national legal tender laws and will ignore any premium which the market may happen to place on particular coins.[82] Equally, the courts will generally ignore the fact that a long-term monetary obligation may lose its effective value over a period. Thus, the annual rental of three shillings a year payable under a 1,000-year lease from 1607, now has very little value, but it remains a money obligation which can be

---

Aquino [1955] Int LR 994 and *Aboitz & Co v Price* 99 F Supp 602 (District Court, Utah, 1951). These points are discussed in more detail at para 20.08 below.

  [78] See *Marrache v Ashton* [1943] AC 311, 318 (PC). The statement in the text does, of course, presuppose that the issuing State itself continues to exist. If a State ceases to exist or to enjoy independent status, then its notes and coin will thereby lose the necessary legal authority necessary to apply the State theory, and will thus cease to be money—*US v Gertz* (1957) 249 F 2d 662.

  [79] For a description of Gresham's Law, see J.K. Galbraith, *Money* (Bantam, 1975). As will be seen, Gresham's Law applies to coins because they can have a metallic value which exceeds their face value. It cannot apply to notes, which have virtually no intrinsic value.

  [80] Gold coins are legal tender in this country—see The Currency Act 1983, s 1(3).

  [81] On this subject, see para 1.43 below. For a discussion of a law which demonetised gold coins, thus leaving them to be treated as a commodity by reference to their intrinsic metallic value, see *Ottoman Bank v Menni* [1939] 4 All ER 9, 13.

  [82] See in particular *Treseder-Griffin v Co-operative Insurance Society* [1956] 2 QB 127, 146 (CA). The statement in the text is reinforced by the practice of the American courts during the "greenback" period (1861–79). Gold dollars were at a premium to notes, but the courts insisted on treating them as legal tender for equivalent units. See in particular *Thompson v Butler* (1877) 5 Otto (95 US) 694; *Stanwood v Flagg* (1867) 98 Mass 124; *Start v Coffin* (1870) 105 Mass 328; *Hancock v Franklin Insurance Co* (1873) 114 Mass 155. A particular example is *Frothingham v Morse* (1864) 45 NH 545, where the plaintiff had deposited $50 in gold coin as bail. It was held that the return of $50 in currency was sufficient to discharge the debt owed to him; he could not claim more on the grounds that the gold dollar commanded a market premium.

discharged at its nominal value.[83] These rules flow in part from the principle of nominalism which will be considered at a later stage.[84]

It may be added that States have occasionally minted gold coins without ascribing to them a specific value in terms of the local monetary unit—the South African Krugerrand is a case in point. Whilst it was (indirectly) described as legal tender, no specific monetary value was placed upon it.[85] It follows that such coins are not "money", and must be regarded as a commodity. This aspect of definition can be important and is considered later.[86]

1.26

The Societary theory of money

Although it is not adopted as the key starting point in the present work,[87] reference must be made to the "societary theory of money" which holds that it is the usage of commercial life or the confidence of the people which has the power to create or recognise "money". In other words, it is the attitude of society—rather than the State itself—which is relevant in identifying money. Now, to the economist, there is no doubt that public acceptance and confidence are important criteria within the definition of money; people will enter into contracts in terms of money and accept payment in it, because they are confident that other members of the same society will behave in like manner.[88] This, in turn, leads to the view that anything is money if it functions as such; taken by itself this definition is unsatisfactory in seeking to define the attributes of money from a legal perspective. As demonstrated earlier in this chapter, a purely functional approach to money cannot of itself provide an adequate basis for a legal definition; the Societary theory cannot be reconciled with the undeniable monopoly of modern States over their currencies[89] and the effective recognition of that monopoly by international law. Whether in situations of crisis or otherwise, money cannot be created—or lose its character—purely by

1.27

---

[83] *Re Smith & Stott* (1883) 29 Ch D 1009n. This may be contrasted with *Re Chapman & Hobbs* (1885) 29 Ch D 1007, which involved a 500-year lease from 1646 at an annual rent of one silver penny. The lease was found to have no value in money—a silver penny may have had a market (or commodity) value, but was no longer money.

[84] See Part III below.

[85] See The Mint and Coinage Act (No. 78 of 1964).

[86] See "Money as a Commodity" (para 1.43 below).

[87] The Societary theory does have some value in defining money by reference to its function as a means of payment—see "The Modern Meaning of Money" (para 1.49 below). It has also been shown that the theory is of some value when money is viewed in its historical context.

[88] See, eg, Lewis and Mizen, *Monetary Economics* (Oxford University Press, 2000) 22.

[89] It may well be that the Societary theory of money could claim a greater importance when banks began to issue notes and put them into circulation at a time when their legal status was not settled—see para 1.17 above. That point is now of purely historical interest, although it should be said that support for the societary theory can be drawn from some of the cases decided during that period—see, eg, *Griffin v Thompson* (1884) 2 How 249.

the will of the community;[90] legal sanction is required for that purpose. The recognition of Confederate notes as "money" by the US Supreme Court does not lend support to the Societary theory; on the contrary, the Court recognised that the acts of the insurgent Government within its territory could not be questioned, for it represented the *de facto* supreme authority at that time.[91] The Supreme Court was thus giving effect to the State theory in that case. Nevertheless, the usefulness of the Societary theory cannot be denied. It has already been seen that the theory is of some value in the context of money as a means of payment and, as will be shown below, it is also of some assistance in the context of eurocurrencies. It must be borne in mind that, especially in the modern world, States are frequently unable to control the external value of their currencies and that,[92] as will be seen, the sovereignty of the State over its own monetary system is now a relatively limited concept.[93] Under these circumstances, there is no doubt that the Societary theory of money plays a greater role than the adherents of the State theory would wish to admit.

---

[90] It is submitted that this statement is true as a purely legal proposition, but inflation and other factors may erode that principle in practical terms. It has been pointed out that, under conditions of rampant inflation, money "ceases to be an instrument to work or to produce; it loses its most important quality of being respected as a value in itself for future use. Distrust of the currency leads to hoarding by the farmer, and disinclination to deliver his agricultural products for money . . . It leads to disinclination on the part of the manufacturer to sell his goods for money unless he receives other tangible goods in return"—Nussbaum, *Money in the Law, National and International* (The Press Foundation, 2nd edn, 1950) 194, quoting the *Monthly Report of the Military Governor US Zone*, No. 77 (1945–6), published by the Military Government of Germany, Trade and Commerce.

[91] *Thorington v Smith* (1869) 75 US 11.

[92] Resort to systems of exchange control of the kind described in Part IV below is an increasingly rare phenomenon.

[93] The full force of the State theory is necessarily diminished by the factors just described. The point is made by Sáinz de Vicuña, in "The Concept of Money in the 21st Century" (April 2004). In the same paper, the writer discusses a new "institutional theory of money" under which the amount of money in circulation is under the control of the central bank. That control is essential, since the central bank cannot otherwise fulfil its functions—usually, the assurance of price stability. The theory reflects the undoubted realities that the external value of a major currency can now only be managed by means of market operations, as opposed to legislative instruments, and that its internal value or purchasing power will in large measure depend upon the amount of money in circulation; this will, in turn, depend upon the monetary policy of the central bank. In other words, if money is to serve as a stable measure of value, then it must exist within a sound institutional framework. The Institutional theory draws upon the State theory in recognising that the definition of a monetary system remains the prerogative of the State; it also draws upon the Societary theory in recognising that the value of money in terms of its purchasing power can only be determined by market forces, and not by the law. It will be apparent that the Institutional theory considers "money" in an institutional and macro-economic environment, and it is to be hoped that further work will be done on the development of this theory. As will be seen, the present edition adopts a variant of the State theory as its working model, largely because this deals more closely with the use of money in a private law context.

D. Money as a Chattel

Following this theoretical detour, it is necessary to return to some of the details **1.28** of the definition of money put forward by Dr Mann—in particular to his fundamental starting point that money could only exist as some form of chattel, in physical form. In the past, these chattels would consist of commodities or quantities of metal; in modern times they consist of coins and banknotes of the kind now familiar in all countries.

Both coins and notes are chattels in possession, in the sense of the rights which **1.29** may be exercised over them. The consequences of this position will be discussed shortly.[94] But it must be appreciated that banknotes additionally constitute a chose in action. In the case of the United Kingdom, they express a "promise to pay the bearer on demand the sum of . . . pounds"; in the case of other countries, a similar promise will be implied.[95] In other words, banknotes are promissory notes within the meaning of section 83 of the Bills of Exchange Act 1882.[96] But it must not be overlooked that a banknote "is not an ordinary commercial contract to pay money. It is in one sense a promissory note in terms, but no one can describe it simply as a promissory note. It is part of the currency of the country".[97]

The precise features of banknotes and coins in circulation within a particular **1.30** country will be defined by the legislation which establishes the monetary system. It therefore seemed more appropriate to deal with those details in a separate context.[98] But it is necessary to consider whether the existence of a chattel issued by or under the authority of the State is a necessary feature of the definition of

---

[94] See "The Status of Money as a Means of Payment" (para 1.54 below).

[95] See *Banco de Portugal v Waterlow & Sons* [1932] AC 452, 487; but see German Supreme Court, 20 May 1926, *RGZ* 1926, 114, 27; 20 June 1929, *JW* 1929, 3491.

[96] In similar vein, Currency and Bank Notes Act 1954, s 3 defines banknotes as "notes of the Bank of England payable to bearer on demand".

[97] *Suffel v Bank of England* (1882) 9 QBD 555, 563 and 567; see also *The Guardians of the Poor of the Lichfield Union v Greene* (1857) 26 LJ Ex 140. A Bank of England note thus embodies a promise to pay which could only be discharged by proffering a replacement note or equivalent coins in exchange. This curious state of affairs—the note is at the same time both a promise to pay and "money"—is perhaps the most eloquent confirmation of a view expressed earlier, namely that the concept of "payment" may be more important than the definition of "money" itself. A Bank of England note only constitutes *money* because it incorporates a promise of payment. The point was neatly expressed by the observation that "paradoxically enough, the claims on the central bank are always good because they can never be honoured. Payment does not come into question, since there are no media of payment available"—see Olivecrona, "The Problem of the Monetary Unit", 62–3, quoted by Goode, *Commercial Law* (Penguin, 2nd edn, 1995) 491. In other words, a central bank discharges its own monetary obligations by delivering a further obligation to pay.

[98] See Ch 2 below.

"money". In the light of the development of the financial markets and modern experience, it is submitted that this aspect of the definition can no longer be supported. One of the principal purposes of money is, of course, to serve as a means of discharging obligations which are expressed in that money. It may well be that, in formal terms, the *public* law of a State will only compel a creditor to accept payment in notes and coins in compliance with its legal tender laws. But laws of this kind are of ever-diminishing importance. They tend to invoke an image of a creditor who, for his own reasons, is keen to avoid receiving payment on highly technical grounds or who wishes to place tiresome legal obstacles in the path of his debtor. Of course, the reality is entirely different; creditors will often accept large numbers of small denomination coins or notes which do not strictly comply with legal tender requirements, for they will always be in a position to re-use the money so offered to them. Likewise, creditors will frequently accept cheques, bank transfers, credit cards, and any other form of payment which is commercially reasonable in the circumstances. Instruments of this kind are readily accepted in payment of monetary obligations, even though they are issued, arranged, and administered by private entities, as opposed to the State itself. As a technical matter, it may well be that the express or implied consent of the creditor will be required as to the selection of such a means of payment, but that consent will be forthcoming in almost every case; it seems unrealistic to impose any further, legally relevant distinctions based solely upon the requirement for a consent which will almost invariably be forthcoming as a matter of course. In one sense, therefore, the focus ceases to be the legal tender laws, which have a *public* character. Rather, it becomes necessary to consider issues of *private* law; under the circumstances of the case, had the creditor expressly or impliedly[99] undertaken to accept payment in the manner proffered to him? If so, and if the means of payment does not fundamentally alter the monetary character of the obligations,[100] then the instrument tendered to him with a view to discharging the debt must be regarded as "money" for the purposes of that transaction.[101]

---

[99] In many cases, the point will be obvious. If a creditor sues on a dishonoured cheque, then it is plain that he had originally accepted it as the method of payment. Equally, if the beneficiary of a letter of credit seeks to present compliant documents under its terms, then it is clear that the credit was the accepted means of payment.

[100] This condition should not be overlooked; if the essential character of the consideration is altered then the contract may cease to involve a monetary obligation at all.

[101] Once again, it is necessary to observe that any discussion of the legal definition of money tends unavoidably to veer towards the notion of payment. As noted earlier, traditional legal theory has refused to ascribe the title of "money" to bank deposits, largely on the ground that bank deposits are to be categorised as a debt of the institution concerned. This approach is unrealistic in practical terms, because a bank deposit and transfer may be used as a means of payment. In the view of the present writer, it is also unattractive as a matter of legal theory; that a particular relationship can be classified as a "debt" does not necessarily exclude it from other categories of

Money thus continues to exist within a legal framework, and, to that extent, the **1.31**
State theory of money remains valid. However, it is submitted that the creation
and existence of money cannot be dependent upon its issue in physical form by
or on behalf of the State.[102]

E. Denomination and the Unit of Account

Under the terms of the traditional State theory, only those chattels issued by the **1.32**
State which are denominated by reference to a distinct unit of account can, in
law, be regarded as "money". The requirement that money be denominated in
this way appears long established—Blackstone noted[103] that denomination is
"the value for which the coin is to pass current". Such distinct unit of account is
peculiar to the State which creates it and is therefore the characteristic feature of
a national currency system. The unit of account provides a standard of value
against which the value of commodites can be measured.[104]

While denomination with reference to a specific unit of account is necessary to **1.33**
confer the quality of money, it should be appreciated that not everything which
is so denominated is money. Thus, Treasury bills are expressed in terms of a unit
of account, but they represent merely claims to money, and their use of the unit
of account is simply a reference to the monetary system. The same general
remark may be made in the context of certificates of deposit issued by banks,
and many other debt instruments.[105] In contrast, a Bank of England note is

---

legal relationship, if it meets the relevant criteria. As has already been shown, banknotes themselves are an illustration of this kind of dual classification. There can be no doubt that notes issued
by the Bank of England constitute "money"; yet they also incorporate a promise to pay a sum
certain in money and thus also constitute promissory notes within the meaning of the Bills of
Exchange Act 1882. Those chattels which constitute "money" in this country even according to
the strictest definition of that term thus exhibit the form of dual characterisation which has just
been described. Support for this approach may be found in *Bank v Supervisors* (1868) 74 US 26
where the court regarded US banknotes as both "certificate of indebtedness" and as "currency".
In similar vein, see *Howard Savings Institute v City of Newark* (1899) 44 A 654.

[102] This apparently technical departure does, of course, mean that a far wider range of instruments may now fall to be treated as "money", where they would not have been so treated under
the more traditional State theory. It may be objected that a claim on a financial institution may be
lost in the event of the insolvency of that institution, and that it is thus inappropriate to treat its
deposit obligations as "money". This is, of course, true, but the holder of physical money also
accepts risks of loss (eg through fire or theft).

[103] i. 278.

[104] For a discussion of this principle from an economic perspective, see Simmel, *The Philosophy
of Money* (Routledge, 2nd edn, 1990) ch 2.

[105] These general remarks must be treated with some caution, for even instruments of this kind
can be treated as "money" if the parties so agree. The importance of private law in this context has
already been discussed above. Yet it is unattractive to treat as "money" an instrument which has a
deferred maturity date, which bears interest and the value of which may vary over time according
to prevailing interest rates and other factors.

nothing but the corporeal form, the embodiment of the unit of account, its fraction, or its multiple; further, and in contrast to the forms of instrument just described, a banknote represents an *immediate* right to payment. Herein lies the distinction between Treasury bills and similar instruments (on the one hand) and banknotes and coin (on the other). The former *represents* or *evidences* a claim to money; the latter *is* money.[106]

1.34 The definition of the unit of account (pound, dollar, euro, yen) is supplied by the various monetary systems and will thus be discussed elsewhere.[107] Here, it must suffice to say that a chattel cannot in law be regarded as money if it represents anything more than the simple embodiment of a unit of account, its fraction, or its multiple.[108] Despite their history within national monetary systems, neither gold nor silver can be regarded as "money" for their value may fluctuate in terms of money and is determined according to market demand; neither commodity is denominated by reference to a unit of account.

F. Universal Means of Exchange

1.35 Money can only serve its required function if it is intended to serve as the universal means of exchange in the State of issue.[109] It is this aspect of the legal definition which is perhaps closest to that adopted by economists; this is necessarily the case, for neither discipline can adopt a definition of money without reference to its cardinal function. Indeed, the English courts have occasionally felt this aspect of the definition to be sufficient on its own, without reference to the other criteria noted in the text.[110]

---

[106] Thus the possession of a £20 note is not evidence of entitlement to £20; it is £20; see *Hill v R* [1945] KB 329, 334. In another sense, however, the note is evidence, eg that the owner is entitled to have a new note issued to him by the Bank of England in the event that the original note is damaged.

[107] See Ch 2 below.

[108] Knapp's State theory of money has been criticised on the grounds that it does not take account of one of the essential functions of money, ie to serve as a measure of value—see, eg, Hirschberg, *The Nominalistic Principle, A Legal Approach to Inflation, Deflation, Devaluation and Revaluation* (Bar-Ilan University, 1971) 20–4, and sources there noted. Yet this may not be entirely fair, for the unit of account is itself the independent measure of value established by a monetary system. Mr Justice Holmes touched upon the point in *Deutsche Bank Filiale Nürnberg v Humphrey* (1926) 272 US 517, 519: "Obviously, in effect, a dollar or mark may have different values at different times. But to the law which establishes it, it is always the same."

[109] It should be appreciated that references to the "State of issue" may include (as in the case of the euro) a group of States participating within a single currency area. But the State theory of money is not undermined by this qualification, for the authority for the existence of the currency is ultimately still derived from the monetary sovereignty of the States within the zone.

[110] See the discussion of *Moss v Hancock*, at para 1.10 above.

Now, if money is the *medium* of exchange, it cannot be an *object* of exchange; in **1.36**
other words, money is not generally to be regarded as a commodity.[111] This is
not to say that money is immune from the economic rules relating to supply and
demand; but the quality of serving as the universal means of exchange within a
given economic area is an essential and indispensable requirement of money. For
this reason, let it be repeated, bills of exchange, cheques, Treasury bills, and
similar instruments cannot of themselves be described as money in the public
law sense which has been discussed earlier. Rather, they *represent* or *evidence* a
claim to money.[112] Likewise, gold may be an object of exchange by reference to
its prevailing value, but it is an *object* of exchange rather than a *medium* of it;
gold is thus not "money". Gambling chips represent money in specific circumstances but plainly lack the universal acceptance necessary to clothe them with
the quality of money.[113]

G. Money as a Store of Value

That money is to be regarded as a store of value or measure of wealth perhaps **1.37**
reflects the economic view of money, rather than its purely legal aspects. Nevertheless, it is suggested that this particular aspect of money does find some
support with the case authorities.

In this context, it may be recalled that money functions as a medium of **1.38**
exchange. But a person in possession of money is not legally bound to buy
anything, or to exchange his money for goods or services. In such a case, money
does not become valueless merely because it is not in use as a medium
of exchange; on the contrary, it serves as a store of value, representing the wealth
of the holder and his abstract purchasing power.[114]

This definition of money in its abstract sense—as a store or representation of **1.39**
value or wealth—can usefully be borne in mind in considering the very unusual
case of *Banco de Portugal v Waterlow & Sons Ltd*.[115] In that case, the Portuguese

---

[111] For those particular occasions on which money may be regarded as a commodity, see para
1.43 below.
[112] cf discussion in *Hill v R* (n 106 above).
[113] *CHT Ltd v Wood* [1965] 2 QB 63, followed in *Lipkin Gorman v Karpnale Ltd* [1991] 3
WLR 10 (HL).
[114] See Lewis and Mizen, *Monetary Economics* (Oxford University Press, 2000) 11–13; Savigny,
Obligationenrecht, i, 405.
[115] [1932] AC 452. For discussions of this case from an economic viewpoint, see Sir Cecil
Kirsch, *The Portuguese Bank Note Case* (London, 1932); R.G. Hawtry (1932) 52 Economic Journal
391; M.T. Holland (1932) 5 Cambridge LJ 91. For a case in which the owner of a patent in relation
to security paper issued proceedings against a commercial bank in England which held stocks of
foreign currency allegedly infringing the patent, see *A Ltd v B Bank* [1997] 6 Bank LR 85 (CA).

central bank commissioned the defendant printers to produce 600,000 bank-notes, known as Vasco da Gama 500 escudo notes. This was duly done and the notes were put into circulation in Portugal. Subsequently, a criminal group succeeded in fraudulently obtaining from the defendants a further 580,000 notes of the same type, printed from the original plates and indistinguishable from the first set. The fraudster managed to put a large number of these notes into circulation in Portugal. Upon discovery of the fraud, Banco de Portugal found themselves compelled to withdraw from circulation the entire issue of Vasco da Gama notes, and to replace both the genuine and fraudulent notes with a new issue.

1.40 When Banco de Portugal succeeded in its claim for breach of contract against the printers,[116] it was necessary for the court to determine the appropriate measure of damages. In particular:

(a) was the central bank entitled to damages calculated by reference to the face value of the new notes which they were obliged to issue in order to replace the fraudulent notes; or

(b) was it entitled only to recover the cost of the physical printing and production of the new notes?

1.41 The minority in both the Court of Appeal and the House of Lords believed that only the cost of reprinting the necessary stationery could be recovered. In each case, however, the majority opined that the face value of the notes in money could be recovered. When issuing notes, the central bank was effectively parting with, or putting into circulation, a portion of its wealth or was parting with money. The new notes, when issued, became legal tender for their face value and represented purchasing power in terms of commodities; they had to be accepted by the Portuguese Government in payment of taxes and other debts due to it, and the notes thus represented the credit or obligations of the central bank.[117] In other words, the notes constituted a monetary *asset* of the holder; they must correspondingly constitute a monetary *liability* of the central bank or other issuing authority. Waterlow's breach of contract had thus resulted in the creation of further liabilities on the part of the central bank, and it was entitled to be indemnified against those liabilities.[118]

The claimant was allowed to proceed because the defendant was a commercial bank. Had the proceedings been commenced against the issuing bank then—notwithstanding suggestions to the contrary in the judgment—the court would have lacked jurisdiction on grounds of State immunity.

[116] It was, of course, a term of the contract that notes should only be printed with due authority from Banco de Portugal itself.

[117] On these points, see the speeches of Lord Atkin at 487–9; Lord Macmillan at 507–8.

[118] For a different view of this case and for criticism of the outcome, see Nussbaum, *Money in the Law, National and International* (The Press Foundation, 2nd edn, 1950) 84–9.

The decision in this case accordingly leads to the conclusion that—in legal **1.42**
terms—money represents both purchasing power and a store of wealth or value.
In modern times, the value of money in terms of its purchasing power is prescribed by law and is wholly unrelated to the cost of materials involved in its
production.

H. Money as a Commodity

It was noted above that money is not generally to be regarded as a commodity.[119] **1.43**
Expressions such as "goods, wares and merchandise" and "goods and chattels"
will therefore usually be construed so as to exclude money, whether in a physical
or in any other form,[120] although the general principle must give way if the
explicit terms of the relevant statute or other instrument so require.[121] Since the
rule is not absolute, it is necessary to examine those few occasions on which
money *will* be treated as a commodity.[122] This will usually arise where coins are

---

[119] Yet this was not always so; it was often stated that foreign currencies generally fell to be
treated as commodities, rather than money—see the discussion under "Status of Foreign Money"
(para 1.60 below). Some of the confusion in this area might have been avoided had more
attention been paid to the decision in *Acceptance Corp v Bennett* (1992) 189 NW 901, 904, where
it was noted that money as a medium of exchange "is not an article of commerce".

[120] Note to *John Howard's Case* (1751) Foster CC 77; *R v Leigh* (1764) 1 Leach 52; *R v Guy*
(1782) 1 Leach 241; *R v Hill* (1811) Russ & Ry 191. Similarly, at common law, nothing could be
taken in execution unless it was capable of being *sold*, with the result that money could not be
seized for these purposes—see *Knight v Criddle* (1807) 9 East 48 and *Francis v Nash* (1734) Hard
53. Given the purpose of execution of a judgment, this position was anomalous and was remedied
by s 12 of the Judgments Act 1838—see *Wood v Wood* (1843) 4 QB 397. But the analysis does
support the conclusion that money and commodities have legal characteristics which are separate
and distinct. Thus, eg, "goods" has been found not to include currency filled into wage packets
for the purposes of s 7(1)(e) of the Capital Allowances Act 1968—see *Buckingham v Securitas
Properties Ltd* [1980] 1 WLR 380.

[121] See, eg, Theft Act 1968, s 34 (2)(b) where the term "goods" is specifically defined to include
money. The meaning of the term "goods" will, of course, depend upon the statutory context in
which it is used—see *The Noordam (No. 2)* [1920] AC 909. In the US, a package of gold coins
were held to be "goods, wares and merchandise" for the purposes of the statute at issue in that
case: *Gay's Gold* (1872)13 Wall 358; the New York courts have likewise held that, in certain
circumstances, gold coins could form the subject matter of a sale requiring the application of the
Statute of Frauds—*Peabody v Speyers* (1874) 56 NY 230; *Fowler v New York Gold Exchange Bank*
(1867) 67 NY 138, 146. Further, in Germany, the Federal Administrative Court, 5 March 1985,
held that a law restricting the sale of commodities included a *bureau de change* because the term
"commodities" applied to banknotes and coins "in so far as they are not the means, but the subject
matter of the turnover of goods".

[122] The theory that money should be regarded as a commodity was pressed by Mater, *Traité
Juridique de la Monnaie at du Change* (Dalloz, Paris, 1925). As others have pointed out, this was a
very difficult exercise given that a sharp distinction between money and commodities lies at the
very core of monetary legal analysis—see Nussbaum, *Money in the Law, National and International* (The Press Foundation, 2nd edn, 1950) 23. It should, however, be emphasised that
the starkness of this legal distinction does not necessarily find acceptance in other disciplines.

being traded or used for their rarity value, or where coins are sold by reference to their intrinsic metallic (as opposed to monetary) value. Money may thus be regarded as a commodity in the following instances:

(1) The decision in *R v Dickinson*[123] concerned Regulation 30E of the Defence of the Realm Regulations, which made it an offence to "melt down, break up, or use otherwise than as currency any gold coin which is for the time being current in the United Kingdom". Regulation 58 allowed the Court to "order that any *goods* in respect of which the offence has been committed shall be forfeited". The defendant was found to have committed an offence under Regulation 30E, and a forfeiture order was made in respect of £1,800 of gold sovereigns to which the offence related. The Court appears to have accepted that, in principle, gold coin—as legal tender—could not be regarded as "goods" for these purposes. However, the forfeiture order was upheld on the grounds that the sovereigns had been acquired with a view to melting them down. They had thus been acquired as a commodity, and not in the character of money.

(2) Coin sold "per weight" is being sold by reference to its metallic value—it is not being used as a medium of exchange. It thus cannot be described as "money" for the purpose of the transaction at hand, even though it may later be used as money for the purposes of a subsequent transaction.[124] If the purchaser pays an amount in excess of the legal tender value of the coin in question, then this would plainly indicate that it is the metallic content (rather than the money) which is the subject matter of the transaction.[125]

(3) Equally, a coin purchased for its rarity or curiosity value cannot be regarded as "money" in relation to that specific transaction, even though it may otherwise retain its formal status as legal tender.[126] Indeed, the very fact that one would refer to the *purchase* of a coin in such circumstances will indicate that the coin is being treated as an *object*—and not a *medium*—of exchange.

(4) There may be cases in which the surrounding circumstances make it plain that money is in fact being deployed as a commodity. If an employer distributes gold sovereigns to his employees by way of bonus, it may be inferred that they are intended to acquire the market (rather than

---

In economic terms, money is amenable to the law of supply and demand, and may thus be regarded as a commodity in that sense.

[123] [1920] 3 KB 533. See also *R v Goswani* [1968] 2 WLR 1163. For a New Zealand decision to similar effect, see *Morris v Ritchie* [1934] NZLR 196.

[124] See *Taylor v Plumer* (1815) 3 M & S 562 and *Banque Belge v Hambrouck* [1921] 1 KB 321, 326.

[125] This point is very clearly illustrated by the decision of the New Zealand court in *Morris v Ritchie* [1934] NZLR 196.

[126] *Moss v Hancock* [1899] 2 QB 111.

the nominal) value of these coins, and they will be liable to income tax accordingly.[127]

(5) It is perhaps legitimate to infer from the above cases that money will generally be treated as a commodity where this reflects the intention of the parties concerned.[128]

In more recent times, the distinction between money as "money" and money as **1.44** a "commodity" has engaged the attention of both the European Court of Justice and the Court of Appeal. The decisions arose in connection with coins minted in South Africa and in this country. Given that South African Krugerrands were only indirectly described as legal tender, and were not stated to have a specific value by reference to a unit of account expressed in rand,[129] it must follow that they were traded by reference to their metallic value; as a result, they should be regarded as "goods" (or a commodity) and not as money. Likewise, British silver alloy coins—such as a half-crown—should not be regarded as money because they have ceased to be a means of payment. In *R v Thompson*,[130] the European Court of Justice held that Krugerrands were "treated as being equivalent to money". This statement was of very doubtful factual accuracy and in any event the wrong test was applied. The wording just quoted virtually amounts to an application of the Societary theory of money and, as noted earlier,[131] this is not by itself an adequate *legal* definition of money. Applying the State theory, Krugerrands could not be "money" because they were not denominated by reference to a unit of account. In contrast, the Court was correct in finding that half-crowns were not legal tender and thus had to be regarded as "goods" for the purposes of Article 30 of the EC Treaty, which prohibited quantitative restrictions on imports and measures having equivalent effect. In view of this line of reasoning:

(a) the Court wrongly held that Krugerrands were a form of money, and fell outside the provisions of Article 30 of the Treaty;

(b) the Court correctly held that half-crowns were "goods" for the purposes of the Treaty, and restrictions on their transfer were, in principle, incompatible with the provisions of the Treaty guaranteeing the free movement of goods. However, British rules restricting the export of these coins could nevertheless be upheld on public policy grounds, because the national right

---

[127] *Jenkins v Horn (Inspector of Taxes)* [1979] 2 All ER 1141.

[128] This point is neatly illustrated by the decision of the Quebec Court of Appeal which draws a clear distinction between silver coins as a means of exchange and their metallic content: *R v Behm* (1970) 12 DLR (3d) 260 and a New Zealand decision, where gold coins were traded at a price in excess of their legal tender value: *Morris v Ritchie* [1934] NZLR 196.

[129] See the South African Mint and Coinage Act (No. 78 of 1964).

[130] [1978] ECR 2247.

[131] See para 1.27 above.

to mint coinage was traditionally regarded as involving the fundamental interests of the State.

1.45 The Krugerrands at issue in this case should have been treated on the same basis as the silver alloy coins.[132] In each instance, it was the intrinsic value of the coins (rather than their value as legal tender) which should have been at issue.

1.46 Subsequently, matters became a little clearer when the Court of Appeal, in a case arising from the same facts[133] found that the Krugerrands mentioned above were "goods" for the purposes of section 52 of the Customs and Excise Act 1952, and were thus liable to forfeiture following an attempt to smuggle them into this country. In the circumstances, it was plain that the smugglers had handled and used the Krugerrands by reference to their metallic value, and not by reference to their value as a form of currency. The judgment of the Court of Appeal was thus clearly right notwithstanding the difficulties posed by the unsatisfactory decision of the European Court of Justice.

1.47 There may be other specialised cases in which money ought properly to be treated as a commodity. For example, a security printer who contracts to produce a quantity of notes and to deliver them to a foreign central bank would be liable in damages for its subsequent failure to produce the notes or for any defect in their design. But the loss suffered by the central bank is the cost of obtaining notes from an alternative source, not for the face amount of the notes themselves.[134] But cases of this type will clearly be the exception, rather than the rule. Where the question has arisen in recent times, courts have refused to categorise money as goods or commodities.[135]

1.48 It may be concluded that notes and coins are being handled as money where—as in the vast majority of situations—these are being used by reference to their legal tender value. Where, however, notes and coins are sold by reference to their curiosity or rarity value, or by reference to their metallic value, then they are

---

[132] Relying on similar views expressed in earlier editions of this book, the Federal Supreme Court of Germany (8 December 1983) *BGHStr* 32, 198 or *NJW* 1984, 311 and the Supreme Court of Zimbabwe (*Bennett-Cohen v The State* 1985 (1) ZLR 46 or 1985 (2) SA 465) have decided that Krugerrands are not money, but goods or commodities. As a consequence, a sale of a Krugerrand should attract VAT in appropriate cases.

[133] *Allgemeine Gold & Silberscheidanstalt v Commissioners of Customs & Excise* [1980] QB 390.

[134] That the contract to produce such notes involves money as a commodity was suggested by Simon Brown LJ in the *Camdex* case. This must be carefully distinguished from the situation which arose in *Banco de Portugal v Waterlow & Sons* [1932] AC 452, which was discussed in paras 1.39–1.42 above.

[135] Thus, the ECJ has held that trading in foreign currencies with counterparties must be regarded as a provision of *services*, rather than *goods*, since the money is not "tangible property": see Case C–172/96, *First National Bank of Chicago v Commissioners of Customs & Excise* [1998] ECR I–4387.

being traded as goods or commodities. It will be apparent that this distinction will depend largely upon the intention of the parties concerned, as drawn from the circumstances surrounding the transaction in question. The cases in which money will be regarded as a commodity will necessarily be exceptional.[136]

I. The Modern Meaning of Money

The foregoing analysis has examined a number of aspects of money and it is clear that the State retains a major role in the creation of a monetary system; only the State can define the unit of account and provide it with legal backing in contractual situations. But it can no longer be accepted that money can exist only in a physical form or that the State has the monopoly over its creation.[137] It therefore seems to be plain that the State theory of money can no longer be accepted in terms of the formulation proposed by Knapp and those who accepted his views. The role of private institutions in the creation of money is now so great that the original theory has an air of unreality about it. However, changing circumstances rarely create new wisdom; they merely provide new insights into ideas which may have been current for many years. The State theory does not necessarily have to be discarded in its entirety; it may be sufficient to modify it to reflect developments which have occurred since it was originally formulated.

1.49

If the requirement that money should exist in the form of a chattel is no longer tenable, then it must follow that the expression "money" is an essentially abstract rather than a physical concept. Looking at the State theory of money in the round, it seems that the essential legal characteristics of "money" are as follows:

1.50

(a) it must be expressed by reference to a name and denominated by reference to a unit of account which, in each case, is prescribed by the law of the State concerned;[138] and

---

[136] This comment would appear to be further justified by reference to *Camdex International Ltd v Bank of Zambia (No. 3)* [1997] 6 Bank LR 43 (CA); the case will be discussed below in the context of foreign money.

[137] See "Money as a Chattel" (para 1.28 above). The statement in the text draws some support from von Mises, *The Theory of Money and Credit* (translated by H.E. Batson, Jonathan Cape, 1953) 69: "In determining how monetary debts may be effectively paid off, there is no reason for being too exclusive. It is customary in business to tender and accept payment in certain money-substitutes instead of money itself."

[138] The monetary sovereignty of a State thus involves the right to create and to define a monetary system in the manner just described. This subject is discussed generally in Ch 19 below. Although not explicitly stated as part of the definition of "money", it will invariably be the case that a central bank or similar authority will be established for the purpose of implementing monetary policy. It may be that the role of such institutions deserves more prominence in the

(b) the currency and unit so prescribed must be intended to serve as the generally accepted measure of value and medium of exchange within the State concerned.[139]

1.51 This revised definition does not in any sense deny the undoubted fact that the issue of *physical* currency is usually a monopoly of the State or the central bank; it merely recognises the fact that such physical notes and coins can no longer be recognised as the *sole* form of money in use within a particular country.[140] It follows that the definition of "money" offered above is in some respects true to the State theory, but now defines money in a purely abstract manner. Thus, while monetary laws can define the monetary system and define the unit of account, they cannot now readily limit the definition of "money" itself nor can they directly limit the amount of money in circulation. Such matters can be influenced, rather than be controlled through the conduct of monetary policy, but that is an entirely different matter. Whether a particular asset or instrument constitutes "money" in the sense that it can be used as a *means of payment* must be determined on a case-by-case basis and may in part depend upon changes in banking practice and technological developments; the nature of the instruments which fall within this definition may thus change from time to time. New forms of money may emerge as a means of payment as they gain a sufficient level of acceptance within the business world or the community generally.[141]

---

definition of "money" itself—see generally Sáinz de Vicuña, in "The Concept of Money in the 21st Century" (April 2004).

[139] The expression "generally accepted measure of value" has been adopted to emphasise the fact that foreign currencies are now freely used and accepted in many countries. The definition previously adopted in this work used the term "universal means of exchange" in the State of issue but for reasons just given, this would appear to overstate the position. It hardly needs to be said that the State can only prescribe that the specified unit of account is to be the usual medium of exchange *within the boundaries of the State itself*, for no State can require that another State allow the circulation of its currency within the territory of the latter State: *A Ltd v B Bank* [1997] 6 Bank LR 85 (CA). Nevertheless, the point is noted here because it assumes a certain relevance in relation to the eurocurrency market—see "Eurocurrencies", para 1.67 below.

[140] For a different approach, see Crawford and Sookman, "Electronic Money: A North American Perspective" in Giovanoli (ed) *International Monetary Law: Issues for the New Millennium* (Oxford University Press, 2000) 373–4. The authors hold that money must "(i) be commonly accepted as a medium of exchange in an area; (ii) be accepted as final payment, requiring no links with the credit of the transferor; (iii) pass freely and be fully transferred by delivery; and (iv) be self-contained, requiring no collection, clearing or settlement". This definition obviously differs from that in the text, partly because of its greater emphasis on money as a means of payment and partly because it does not focus on the role of the State in defining the monetary system. It must, however, be said that the authors were discussing the rise of electronic money as a *new* medium of payment, and the State's underpinning of the basic monetary system was therefore perhaps presupposed. Further, the authors rightly point out that private forms of money (such as travellers' cheques) are not new, and thus apparently accept the view that rules of private law dealing with questions of payment may now be of greater practical importance than the public law of money.

[141] See Crawford and Sookman (n 140 above) 375.

It would follow that a bank deposit could be regarded as "money" in the legal **1.52** sense because payment by means of a bank transfer is now a widely accepted medium of payment; as has been shown, a bank deposit is not disqualified as "money" merely because it represents a debt obligation of a private institution.[142] On the other hand, government bonds or other securities do not constitute "money"—and thus their transfer cannot constitute "payment"—because the creditor does not thereby acquire a right to the use of the money or its commercial equivalent;[143] he merely acquires the right to payment at a later date with interest in the meantime.[144]

In conclusion, it may be said that the State theory—in the somewhat attenuated **1.53** form proposed above—provides the definition of money in its abstract sense, whilst the Societary theory contributes to a description of money as a means of payment, and to the development of new forms of "money".

J. The Status of Money as a Means of Payment

It has already been noted that "private" forms of money may be used as a means **1.54** of payment, and may thus be regarded as "money" in a legal sense. But what characteristics must an instrument display if it is to qualify for this title? In this context it may be helpful to have regard to some of the special attributes of physical cash, for if an instrument is to qualify as "money", then the law must surely attribute to it characteristics which will enable it effectively to fulfil functions which are similar to those performed by notes and coins. If money is to exist in several different forms, then the law should certainly ensure that the rights of a person who receives "money" are essentially the same, irrespective of the precise form in which that money is received.[145] If new means of payment are to constitute "money", then consistency and the lawyer's respect for

---

[142] It is, however, probably fair to say that a bank deposit can only represent "money" in a legal sense if the deposit has matured or is payable on demand. Otherwise, it is not available as a means of immediate payment. A similar point is made by Sáinz de Vicuña, in "The Concept of Money in the 21st Century" (April 2004). Given that most banks will allow retail depositors to "break" deposits in return for a fee, so that funds become immediately available, the point may be regarded as marginal. If the practice of financial institutions in this area is, or were to become, sufficiently uniform, then it may well be that term deposits of this kind could likewise be characterised as "money".

[143] *The Brimnes* [1973] 1 WLR 386; *The Chikuma* [1981] 1 WLR 314.

[144] The concept of payment connotes the discharge of a monetary obligation rather than the receipt of an instrument which might lead to its discharge at a later date.

[145] That this should be the case was also recognised at a much earlier stage of monetary development. In 1820, in a case involving the use of banknotes, an English court remarked that "the representation of money which is made transferable by delivery only must be subject to the same rules as the money which it represents": *Wookey v Poole* (1820) 4 B & Ald 1.

precedent demand that those new means must display characteristics which are in most respects similar to the more traditional, physical form of money. It thus becomes necessary to seek to draw parallels between the legal attributes of the two forms of money. Against that background, it is proposed to consider some of the special attributes of cash, and to examine the extent to which money in a non-cash form can be treated on the same basis.

1.55 First of all, the doctrine *nemo dat quod non habet* has apparently never been applied to notes and coins; these always passed by delivery and thus could not be specifically recovered from a person who had obtained possession of them honestly and in good faith.[146] The reason for this is that, "by the use of money, the interchange of all other forms of property is most readily accomplished. To fit it for its purpose, the stamp denotes its value and possession alone must decide to whom it belongs."[147] or, in the words of Lord Mansfield, "the true reason is upon account of the currency of it".[148] The same rule was applied to banknotes, on the grounds that they constituted "cash", as opposed to goods or securities.[149] Thus, banknotes and coins came to be treated as negotiable chattels; if they "were received in good faith and for valuable consideration, the transferee got property though the transferor had none".[150] The position was summarised by Lord Haldane LC:[151]

---

[146] *Higgs v Holiday* Cro Eliz 746; *Miller v Race* (1758) 1 Burr 452; *Wookey v Poole* (1820) 4 B & Ald 1; cf also s 935, para 2 of the German Civil Code. The rule should also apply where notes and coins have originally been stolen from the issuing authority for they are indistinguishable from currency which has lawfully been released into circulation. However, a District of Tennessee court held to the contrary in *US v Barnard* (1947) 72 F Supp 531; the State could recover a gold coin stolen from the Mint, on the grounds that it was merely a chattel and had not acquired the character of money. There is some justification for this view, in that physical cash only acquires the status of "money" once it has been issued by the central bank concerned and delivered to a holder. This view is consistent with the status of a banknote as a promissory note under the Bills of Exchange Act 1882—see below.

[147] *Wookey v Poole* (1820) 4 B & Ald 1 at 7.

[148] *Miller v Race* (1758) 1 Burr 452, 457. It was formerly said that money could not be recovered because it was not separately identifiable, ie it had no "earmark"—see *Moss v Hancock* [1899] 2 QB 111 and the decision of the Supreme Court of Missouri in n 149 below. This approach does not seem to have any grounding in principle and is of no modern relevance.

[149] *Miller v Race* (1758) 1 Burr 452, 457. The same rule developed in the US. In *Newco Rand Co v Martin* (1948) 213 S W 2nd, 504, 509, the Supreme Court of Missouri said "money is currency, is not earmarked and passes from hand to hand. There is no obligation on a transferee to investigate a transferor's title or source of acquisition of money when accepted honestly and in good faith. One may give a bona fide transferee for value a better title to money than he has himself."

[150] *Banque Belge v Hambrouck* [1921] 1 KB 321, 329 *per* Scrutton LJ. The requirement of good faith is, of course, essential and should not be overlooked. Bad faith in a *general* sense will not defeat the transferee's title to him; the bad faith must relate specifically to the receipt of the notes at issue: *R v Curtis, ex p A-G* (1988) 1 Qd R 546; see also *Grant v The Queen* (1981) 147 CLR 503.

[151] *Sinclair v Brougham* [1941] AC 398, 418.

In most cases money cannot be followed. When sovereigns or bank notes are paid over as currency, so far as the payer is concerned, they cease *ipso facto* to be the subject of specific title, as chattels. If a sovereign or bank note be offered in payment, it is, under ordinary circumstances, no part of the duty of the person receiving it to inquire into title. The reason for this is that chattels of such kind form part of what the law recognises as currency and treats as passing from hand to hand in point, not merely of possession, but of property.

Money is, however, capable of being recovered specifically from a holder who received it in bad faith or for no consideration.[152] The common law remedy of tracing allowed the recovery of assets acquired with the money, provided that their identity could be ascertained.[153] The common law remedy stopped short of the point where the relationship of creditor and debtor suppressed the right *in rem*.[154] At this stage the equitable doctrine of tracing intervened,[155] allowing money to be followed *in rem* against a holder who acted in bad faith or gave no consideration, if it could be identified in or disentangled from a mixed fund.[156]

---

[152] *Clarke v Shee* (1774) 1 Cowp 197, followed by the House of Lords in *Lipkin Gorman v Karpnale Ltd* [1991] 3 WLR 10. In so far as banknotes are concerned, these constitute promissory notes for the purposes of the Bills of Exchange Act 1882, so that both good faith and the provision of value are presumed—see ss 30 and 90. Mere possession of a banknote is thus *prima facie* evidence of ownership: *King v Milson* (1809) 2 Camp 7; *Solomons v Bank of England* (1810) 13 East 136; *Wyer v The Dorchester and Milton Bank* (1833) 11 Cush (65 Mass) 51. Money cannot be recovered by means of an action for wrongful interference with goods, unless the specific notes and coins can be identified: *Banks v Wheston* (1596) Cro Eliz 457; *Orton v Butler* (1822) 5 B & Ald 652; *Lipkin Gorman v Karpnale Ltd* (above) at 15.

[153] *Golightly v Reynolds* Lofft 88; *Taylor v Plumer* (1815) 3 M & S 652; whether or not a particular asset can be said to be derived from a particular fund can plainly be a difficult question: *R v Cuthbertson* [1981] AC 470. *Taylor v Plumer* was followed in *Lipkin Gorman v Karpnale Ltd* [1991] 3 WLR 10, where it was held that the defendant is relieved if he has so changed his position that it would be inequitable to allow the claimant to succeed.

[154] See the explanation of Lord Haldane in *Sinclair v Brougham* [1914] AC 398, 419.

[155] *Re Hallet's Estate* (1880) 13 Ch D 696, overruling *Re West of England and South Wales District Bank, ex p Dale* (1879) 11 Ch D 772, where the earlier cases are discussed.

[156] The principal authorities are: *Sinclair v Brougham* [1914] AC 398; *Banque Belge v Hambrouck* [1921] 1 KB 321; *Re Diplock* [1948] Ch 465, 517, affirmed on other grounds *sub nom Ministry of Health v Simpson* [1951] AC 251. See now *Agip (Africa) Ltd v Jackson* [1991] 3 WLR 116 and see Millet, (1991) 107 LQR 71. The ability of a claimant to recover moneys from or to obtain restitutionary remedies against a third party who has received or dealt with money or property in which the claimant had an equitable interest has been the subject of significant judicial activity in recent years—see in particular *Royal Brunei Airlines Sdn Bhd v Tan* [1995] 2 AC 378; *Bank of Credit and Commerce International (Overseas) Ltd v Akindele* [2002] AC 164. The decision in the *Akindele* case was recently criticised by the House of Lords in *Criterion Properties plc v Stratford UK Properties LLC* [2004] UKHL 28. On the subject generally, see *Chitty on Contracts* (Sweet & Maxwell, 29th edn, 2004) ch 29. It is not proposed to pursue the subject here, partly because a very detailed discussion would be required in order to do justice to the subject matter. It does, however, seem to be clear that the modern remedies in tracing and restitution would apply equally to the funds received in physical form and to funds received by any other means. Thus, for the purposes of the present discussion, it is sufficient to note that the owner of money in a non-physical form enjoys the same legal protection as would be available to a holder of physical notes and coins under corresponding circumstances.

1.56   Secondly, banknotes import a promise to pay a stated sum in money and are thus promissory notes for the purposes of the Bills of Exchange Act 1882, although the Act only applies to promissory notes "with the necessary modifications".[157] Thus, a note stolen from the central bank prior to its issue is not a valid banknote because it remains inchoate until delivery to a person who takes it as a holder.[158] Yet it seems likely that a holder in due course of a Bank of England note, which is genuine but which has unlawfully been put into circulation will be protected.[159] It would also appear to follow from sections 69 and 89(2) that an owner who loses a banknote is entitled to have a new one issued to him against appropriate security;[160] but a banknote destroyed by fire has to be replaced unconditionally.[161] A forged banknote will, in the absence of estoppel, be inoperative.[162] On the other hand, it is well established that, where a bill or note is given by way of payment, the payment is presumed to be conditional;[163] this plainly cannot apply to the Bank of England notes, for their delivery will constitute a final and unconditional payment.[164] Further, a bill of exchange may be reissued only in certain cases,[165] but a Bank of England note may always be reissued after payment in due course.[166] In the case of *accidental* alteration to a bill or banknote, the treatment in each case appears to be uniform; the holder

---

[157] See Bills of Exchange Act 1882, s 89. On payment of banknotes see s 1(4) Currency and Bank Notes Act 1954.

[158] ibid s 84 and see the remarks of Lord Atkin in *Banco de Portugal v Waterlow & Sons* [1932] AC 452, 490. See also *Baxendale v Bennet* (1878) 3 QBD 525.

[159] See ss 20 and 21 of the 1882 Act and authorities such as *Smith v Prosser* [1907] 2 KB 735 and cf *Cooke v US* (1875) 91 US 389. The bank of issue is *entitled* to honour suspicious notes of this kind—see *Banco de Portugal v Waterlow & Sons* [1932] AC 452; the case did not, however, decide whether the central bank was *obliged* to do so.

[160] In this sense, see *Gillet v Bank of England* 6 (1889–1890) TLR 9. See also *Mayor v Johnson* (1813) 3 Camp 324: the owner of half a note cannot obtain payment without the other half, but Lord Ellenborough seemed to think that if the owner had lost both halves, then payment upon indemnity could be demanded.

[161] This was decided by the Court of Appeal in Ontario in *Bank of Canada v Bank of Montreal* (1972) 30 DLR (3d) 24, 1972 OR 881 and the decision was affirmed by a four-to-four decision of the Supreme Court of Canada: (1977) 76 DLR (3d) 385; for detailed commentary, see Mann (1978) 2 Canadian Business LJ 471. The effect of this decision was subsequently reversed by an amendment to the Bank of Canada Act.

[162] See Bills of Exchange Act 1882, s 24, which must apply equally to banknotes. Whilst payment in forged banknotes will thus usually be ineffective, this does not apply to a payment made in good faith to the bank of issue in its own notes, even though later found to be forged: *Bank of the United States v Bank of the State of Georgia* (1825) 10 Wheat (23 US) 333.

[163] On this presumption, see the discussion at para 7.13 below.

[164] Perhaps one can rely on the authority of MacKinnon LJ, who remarked that even though "Bank of England notes, if subjected to the unusual treatment of being read, will be found to be promises by a third party to pay", nevertheless they are "the best form of payment in the world": *Cross v London & Provincial Trust Ltd* [1938] 1 KB 792, 803.

[165] See Bills of Exchange Act 1882, ss 37 and 39.

[166] Pending its reissue, a bank retains the character of money—see *R v West* (1856) Deans & Bell 109; cf *R v Ranson* (1812) 2 Leach 1090.

will be entitled to payment if the content of the document can be proved.[167] But different treatment is accorded to the two instruments in the event of deliberate alteration. If the alteration is immaterial or latent, the holder of the bill may still be entitled to enforce it by virtue of the provisions of the Bills of Exchange Act 1882[168] but Bank of England notes have been held to fall outside these provisions.[169] As a result, banknotes are subject to the common law rule that any material alteration[170] is a complete defence, even against a holder in due course who could not have detected the alteration. Finally, in the conflict of laws, the transfer of banknotes and bills is governed by the law of the place in which the asset is situate,[171] and the rules relating to the identification of that place differ in each case. The debt represented by an ordinary bill of exchange may sometimes have to be treated as situate at the place where the debtor has bound himself to pay. Indeed, it has been held that bills drawn in India and payable in London and which, at the time of the holder's death were on-board a ship on the high seas were assets situate in England and therefore subject to English death duty, because "they represent, but they do not constitute, the asset".[172] But this reasoning cannot apply to modern banknotes; they are situate where they are actually found, rather than where they can be enforced.

The principles just discussed were, of course, established at a time when physical money was really the only recognised form of "money". It was thus a happy chance that a number of the questions which might arise with respect to banknotes could be answered with reference to the Bills of Exchange Act 1882 or the principles which it sought to codify. However, the 1882 Act relates to promissory notes which are in writing and signed by the obligor.[173] Consequently, the

1.57

---

[167] See *Hong Kong & Shanghai Bank v Lo Lee Shi* [1928] AC 181 where Lord Buckmaster said (at 182) that the notes issued by the appellant bank "are not legal currency, but owing to the high credit of the appellants, they are used as if they were".

[168] See the protection afforded to the holder by s 64 of the 1882 Act.

[169] *Leeds & County Bank Ltd v Walker* (1883) 11 QBD 84. The reasoning of Denman J (at 90) is perhaps not altogether convincing; that banknotes are in many respects different from ordinary promissory notes, that they do not require endorsement and that they constitute legal tender, is quite certain, but this hardly demonstrates that s 64 should be regarded as inapplicable. Doubts about this decision may be inferred from Lord Buckmaster's opinion in the *Hong Kong & Shanghai Bank* case (n 167 above).

[170] The alteration of the number is material: *Suffel v Bank of England* (1882) 9 QBD 555.

[171] See Dicey and Morris, *The Conflict of Laws* (Sweet & Maxwell, 13th edn, 2000) para 33-349.

[172] *Pratt v A-G* (1874) LR 9 Ex 140. In *Popham v Lady Aylesbury* (1748) Amb 69, Lord Hardwicke held that banknotes passed under the provisions of a will disposing of a house "with all that should be in it at his death", the reason being that banknotes are ready money, not bonds or securities which are only evidence of the moneys due. It is suggested that this decision is plainly correct, notwithstanding the doubts expressed in *Stuart v Bute* (1813) 11 Ves 657. See also *Southcot v Watson* (1745) 3 Atk 228, 232, where banknotes were held to be cash, and not securities within the meaning of the will.

[173] See Bills of Exchange Act 1882, s 83(1).

1882 Act can be of no real assistance in dealing with bank deposits or other, non-documentary means of payment as forms of "money". This state of affairs inevitably hinders the present attempt to draw parallels between traditional and more modern forms of payment. Nevertheless, having regard to some of the attributes of physical cash which have just been discussed, a few comparisons may be made:

(a) In the case of physical cash, a transfer of possession generally connotes a transfer of ownership, at least provided that the transferee has acted in good faith and given value, and will constitute "payment" in respect of the debt obligation concerned.[174] If funds have been transferred to the payee by means of a bank transfer or through electronic means,[175] then the credit to the transferee's account will generally be irrevocable[176] and the credit to his account will constitute his possession of, and thus his *prima facie* entitlement to the funds concerned.

(b) If the transferee received the funds in good faith and for value, then he is entitled to retain them by way of payment and he is not required to enquire as to the transferor's original source of funds, or any other matter.[177]

(c) Non-physical forms of cash may constitute "payment", so long as the transferee is immediately able to dispose of the full amount of the funds concerned and to apply them in discharge of his own obligations.[178] Payment in this form is, to this extent, equated with payment in physical cash.

(d) The recipient of a bank transfer acting in good faith would appear to acquire good title to the funds free of any prior equities.[179] In other words, the bank transfer enjoys some of the features, if not the formalities, of negotiability.

(e) A creditor who receives payment by means of a bank transfer is not in any sense concerned with the credit-standing of his debtor, nor will he usually be concerned with any error, mistake, or want of authority on the part of the bank which remits the funds to him.[180]

---

[174] This point has been discussed at para 1.55 above.

[175] On e-money, see para 1.59 below.

[176] See *The Brimnes* [1973] 1 WLR 386; *Tayeb v HSBC Bank* [2004] EWHC 1529 (Comm).

[177] At least, this is the position so far as the private law of monetary obligations is concerned. Legislation designed to counteract money laundering may require the transferee to ask questions in certain cases, but this regulatory requirement does not affect the general principle stated in the text.

[178] *The Chikuma* [1981] 1 WLR 314.

[179] This view is reinforced by the rule that having credited the relevant account, the bank can only reverse that entry—ie unilaterally cancel its own debt to the customer—under very limited circumstances. A particularly compelling example of this rule is offered by the decision in *Tayeb v HSBC Bank* [2004] EWHC 1529 (Comm).

[180] In broad terms, this would seem to be the effect of the decision in *Lloyds Bank plc v Independent Insurance Co Ltd* [1999] Lloyds Rep, Bank 1 (CA). The case is considered by Brindle and Cox (eds) *The Law of Bank Payments* (Sweet & Maxwell, 2nd edn, 1999). For a New York

(f) In a private international law context, the ability to obtain a good title to notes and coins appears to be governed by the law of the place in which the transaction occurs and the moneys are physically handed over to the creditor. Likewise, in the case of a bank transfer, the creditor's entitlement to the funds and the validity of his title to them will be governed by the law of the place to which the funds are remitted to the account of the creditor.[181]

The foregoing analysis demonstrates that payment by means of a bank transfer **1.58** shares many of the legal characteristics of a payment in physical money. This would seem to justify the earlier conclusion that funds standing to the credit of a bank account should be regarded as "money" for legal purposes. It is also appropriate to conclude that a new form of payment may be regarded as "money" if it broadly meets the criteria noted above.[182]

Although it is not proposed to examine the subject in any depth, it is likely that **1.59** "e-money" should also qualify for the label of "money" in the light of the points noted above. E-money has been defined as monetary value represented by a claim on the issuer which is stored in an electronic device and accepted as a means of payment by undertakings other than the issuer.[183] E-money may be

---

decision which considers the effect of art 4A of the Uniform Commercial Code (relating to electronic fund transfers), see *Sheenbonnet Ltd v American Express Bank* (1995) 951 F Supp 403.

[181] This follows from the rule that the law applicable to a bank account is the law of the country in which the relevant branch is situate, and the property, represented by the remitted funds, will be located in that country—see *Joachimson v Swiss Bank Corp* [1921] 3 KB 110 and other cases noted by Dicey & Morris, *The Conflict of Laws* (Sweet & Maxwell, 13th edn, 2000) para 22-029.

[182] It may be added that credit cards are a very convenient form of payment, but they do not constitute "money" within the criteria described above. Apart from other considerations, the creditor does not receive immediate access to the funds concerned; he merely acquires the right to payment from the card issuer at a later date: *Re Charge Card Services Ltd* [1989] Ch 497. In a sense, therefore, the use of a credit card involves the *novation* of a debt, rather than its payment; actual payment occurs at a later date. Furthermore, it would seem that interest-bearing securities would not be treated as "money", even though they may have been issued by a State or by a central bank. If money is to operate as a medium of exchange, then it must have "a uniform and unchanging value, otherwise it becomes the subject of exchange, and not the medium". Whilst this statement is derived from an old decision of the US Supreme Court the point remains valid; money must have a constant and unchanging value under the law of the State of issue, and the existence of an interest coupon necessarily deprives an instrument of this essential feature: see *Craig v Missouri* (1830) 4 Peters 410.

[183] Directive 2000/46/EC on the taking up, pursuit and prudential supervision of electronic money institutions, [2000] OJ L275/39. For the provisions which implemented this Directive in the United Kingdom, see the Financial Services and Markets Act 2000 (Regulated Authorities) (Amendment) Order 2002, SI 2002/682 and the Electronic Money (Miscellaneous Amendments) Regulations 2002, SI 2002/765. The general scheme of the legislation is to ensure that issuers of e-money are regulated institutions, thus ensuring the integrity of this new form of payment, and perhaps, to ensure that the conduct of monetary policy is not prejudiced by the increased use of private forms of money. For a general discussion of the subject, see the Committee on Payment and Settlement Systems, *Survey of Electronic Money Developments* (Bank for International Settlements, 2001).

stored on a card which may not disclose the name of the holder; the use of the card entails an immediate transfer of funds to the creditor's bank account, and he can thus accept e-money without reference either to the identity or the credit standing of the holder. Likewise, it would appear that, in the absence of bad faith, the creditor would obtain an unimpeachable title to the funds transferred to him. To this extent, e-money exhibits some of the characteristics of physical cash, and may thus qualify for the label of "money".[184] The fact that both bank deposits and e-money constitute obligations of, or are issued by, private organisations does, of course, further undermine the more traditional State theory of money.

K. The Status of Foreign Money

1.60 Thus far, the discussion has proceeded in relatively general terms and, broadly, has assumed that the currency under consideration was the pound sterling. It is now necessary to broaden this approach, and to discuss the position of foreign money under English law.

1.61 It is appropriate at the outset to make a few general points concerning the treatment of foreign currency and foreign money obligations in the present edition of this work. In earlier editions, Dr Mann was careful to draw clear distinctions between obligations expressed in sterling and those expressed in other currencies; he stated[185] that it was his "experience and conviction that this separation between domestic and foreign currency obligations is absolutely essential for a clear exposition of the subject". The need for this distinction rested in part upon the commodity theory of foreign money—ie that where foreign money constituted an object (as opposed to a medium) of a commercial transaction, then it should be regarded as a commodity, rather than a means of payment.[186] It may well be thought by some that the distinction remains

---

[184] For further discussion of this subject, including an analysis of the legal character of e-money and its monetary law consequences, see Crawford and Sookman, "Electronic Money: A North American Perspective" and Kanda, "Electronic Money in Japan" both in Giovanoli (ed) *International Monetary Law: Issues for the New Millennium* (Oxford University Press, 2000) chs 19 and 20; Effros, "Electronic Payment Systems Legal Aspects" in Hom (ed), *Legal Issues in Electronic Banking* (Kluwer, 2002).

[185] See the preface to the First Edition of this work.

[186] Foreign money could be the "object" of a transaction where it was purchased under the terms of a foreign exchange contract. In other words, a party could be obliged to "deliver" a foreign currency under circumstances which were not equivalent to "payment". The commodity theory was developed by Dr Mann, see the Fifth Edition of this work, 196–202. Whilst quoting various sources in support of the theory, Dr Mann did note that the validity of the distinction between *payment* and *delivery* of foreign money was "not unquestioned"—see the Fifth Edition, 196—and that although it had been accepted in a number of courts in the US, it had been rejected in *Matter of Lendle* (1929) 250 NY Supp 502, 166 NE 182.

valuable, but (at least so far as English law is concerned) the commodity theory of foreign money can no longer stand in the face of the Court of Appeal decision in *Camdex International Ltd v Bank of Zambia*.[187] It will be necessary to return to this decision in other contexts, but for the present, it must suffice to note some of the points made by the Court of Appeal in relation to the commodity theory. Phillips LJ accepted that coins or notes may be transferred by reference to a value attributable to their physical properties (for example, their metallic content or rarity value) and that an obligation to deliver such items should not be described as a "debt"; rather, the transaction should be treated as a transfer of commodities.[188] He then went on to say:[189]

> Beyond this, however, I do not think it helpful, or even possible, to differentiate between money as a commodity and money as a means of exchange by reference to the nature of the transaction under which it falls to be transferred . . . It seems to me that whether money is lent or borrowed, whether it is used to buy goods or services, or whether it is exchanged against a different currency, it retains its character as a medium of exchange. In each case, the transaction will involve a particular specified currency or currencies. This reflects the fact that there exist different media of exchange, that their relative values fluctuate over time and that for this reason parties to a transaction may be concerned to stipulate for a particular currency. The fact that the identity of the currency may be a material feature of the transaction does not translate the currency into a commodity, whatever the nature of the transaction.

In view of these remarks[190] and the attitude of the English courts to foreign currency obligations following the decision in *Miliangos v George Frank*

1.62

---

[187] [1997] CLC 714. It is also right to point out that Dr Mann did state (Fifth Edition of this work, 195–6) that in the vast majority of cases, foreign money would fall to be regarded as "money" and he approved of the statement of Brandon J to the effect that the term "money" includes "money in foreign currency as well as in sterling": *The Halcyon The Great* [1975] 1 WLR 515, 520.

[188] ie to this extent, endorsing the substance of the decision in *Moss v Hancock* (para 1.10 above).

[189] In *Marrache v Ashton* [1943] AC 311, Lord Macmillan remarked (at 317) that since Spanish banknotes were not currency in Gibraltar "they must be regarded in Gibraltar as commodities". Similarly in *Moll v Royal Packet Navigation Ltd* (1952) 52 SRNSW 187, the court held that an obligation to pay in a foreign currency was in law an obligation to deliver a foreign currency, with the result that a breach of the obligation gave rise to an action in damages, rather than in debt. In 1985, the Court of Appeals (2nd Cir) noted that, in an action "brought to recover sums expressed in foreign money the obligation—whether characterised as an unpaid debt or a breach of contract—is treated as a promise to deliver a commodity": *Vishipco Lines v Chase Manhattan Bank* (1985) 754 F 2d 452, 458. Even as recently as 1996, the Court of Appeal said that foreign banknotes which had already been issued by a foreign central bank but which were held in England "are not to be regarded here as legal tender, but as commodities or objects of commerce": *A Ltd v B Bank* [1997] 6 Bank LR 85 (CA). Statements of this kind were of uncertain validity when they were made, but in any event, they cannot now stand in the face of the *Camdex* decision.

[190] It should be said that Simon Brown LJ made very similar remarks, and Otton LJ agreed with both judgments.

(Textiles) Ltd,[191] the requirement for an entirely separate treatment of sterling and foreign currency obligations is—in the view of the present writer—much less compelling. As a result, the present edition seeks to deal with money and monetary obligations in a broad sense, with appropriate commentary where any remaining practical or theoretical distinctions between domestic and foreign money throw up specific points requiring discussion.

1.63 Returning now to the main theme, what can be said about the status of foreign money in England? The following, general propositions are suggested:

(1) First of all, foreign money is to be regarded as "money" under precisely the same circumstances as sterling is to be so regarded—ie it is always to be regarded as "money" except where delivered for its intrinsic metallic, rarity, or curiosity value. This parity of treatment flows inexorably from the Court of Appeal judgment in *Camdex*, to which reference has just been made. It must also be said that the decision in the *Miliangos* case and the dismantling of exchange controls in the United Kingdom[192] have tended progressively to diminish the importance of a sharp distinction between sterling and foreign currency obligations.[193] In some respects, it may be said that *Camdex* was a natural development following the decision in *Miliangos*. The latter decision was to be welcomed on pragmatic grounds whilst the former perhaps explained some of the more theoretical consequences of the *Miliangos* case.

(2) Whilst foreign money may be "money" under English law, it cannot constitute legal tender for sterling debts in this country.[194] Anything which is legal tender must be money, but not all money is legal tender. Legal tender is such money as is "current coin of the realm". But this merely means that foreign money cannot be tendered in discharge of an obligation to pay pounds sterling; it does not touch the question of the manner of discharging in England a debt expressed to be payable in a foreign currency.[195]

(3) It is submitted that foreign money is negotiable in England. Negotiability merely means that an instrument is capable of being transferred by endorsement or delivery (rather than by assignment), and such transfer takes effect free from prior equities or claims, even where the note

---

[191] [1976] AC 443. The consequences of that decision are considered in Ch 8 below.

[192] On this subject, see Ch 14 below.

[193] For reasons given at para 1.64 below, the key area of distinction now lies in the field of taxation.

[194] For an unsuccessful attempt to introduce an exemption to this rule, see The Euro and Sterling Choice Bill, which is considered in Ch 2 below.

[195] On the discharge or performance of monetary obligations generally, see Ch 7 below. As will be noted in Ch 2 below, the identification of legal tender remains a feature of all legislation which creates a monetary system, but the concept of legal tender is of ever diminishing importance.

concerned has previously been stolen. Banknotes and coins are, of course, invariably transferred by delivery and the negotiability of such instruments in England should be accepted by a court without further evidence.[196] It is true that, in a case involving the negotiability of Prussian State bonds, evidence that those bonds were negotiable in Prussia was not sufficient to confer upon them negotiable status in England. To hold otherwise would, according to the Court of Appeal, mean that German currency would be identical to its equivalent in English money.[197] This approach to the problem is, it is suggested, flawed; at least in the modern context, the only material distinction (in England) between sterling and foreign currency is that the former serves as legal tender for debts expressed in sterling, whilst the latter currency plainly does not fulfil that function.

(4) A number of statutory instances may be cited which confirm that foreign money is to be regarded as "money" within the United Kingdom. Many Acts of Parliament include specific provision to this effect. For example, the Companies Act 1985 allows that shares which are to be paid up in "cash" may be paid for in foreign currency.[198] For stamp duty purposes, "money" is again stated to include foreign currency,[199] and rules which criminalise the forgery of money in the United Kingdom apply equally to foreign money as they do to sterling.[200] It is perhaps fair to say that, if statutory references to "money" are given their ordinary and natural meaning, then the term will usually include foreign money, as well as sterling.[201] Following the *Camdex* decision which has already been noted, references to "money" will perhaps more generally be taken to include both the domestic unit and foreign money.[202]

---

[196] This is the position in New York—see *Brown v Pereira* (1918)182 App Div 992; 176 NY Supp 215 (Supreme Court of New York).

[197] *Picker v London & County Banking Co* (1887) 18 QB 515, 510, approved in *Williams v Colonial Bank* (1888) 38 CR D 388, 404, affirmed (1890) 15 AC 267.

[198] See ss 738(4) and 739(1) of the 1985 Act and the discussion of this subject in *Re Scandinavian Bank plc* [1987] 2 All ER 70.

[199] Stamp Act 1891, s 122.

[200] See Forgery and Counterfeiting Act 1981, s 27(i)(b) and Counterfeit (Currency) Convention Act 1935, s 1. In Australia, it was held that the words "currency, coinage and legal tender" in s 51(xii) of the Australian Constitution include foreign money. See *Watson v Lee* (1979) 144 CLR 374, 396. The practice of punishing the falsification of foreign money is well established and reflects an obligation arising under international law. In this context, see the interesting decision of the US Supreme Court in *US v Arjona* (1887) 120 US 479 and the general discussion on this subject in Ch 20 below.

[201] *The Halcyon The Great* [1975] 1 WLR 515.

[202] In many cases, the relevant legislation will make the point clear. For a recent example, see Art 3 of the Financial Collateral Arrangements (No. 2) Regulations 2003, SI 3226/2003, where "cash" is defined to mean "money in any currency credited to an account, or a similar claim for repayment of money and includes money market deposits".

(5) An action for money had and received can be brought regardless of the currency in which the relevant funds were received, and it follows that foreign currency is "money" for the purposes of this type of action.[203]

1.64 Of course, the fact that an obligation is expressed or payable in a foreign currency may have specific consequences before the English courts. For example, sterling must be regarded as a constant measure of value because that is the role which a currency performs within the context of its domestic legal system[204] but a foreign currency may appreciate or depreciate in value as against sterling. Such movements clearly have commercial consequences and may also have legal implications. Issues of a legal character have tended to arise in the context of taxation matters. For example:

(a) In one case,[205] a company was obliged to pay interest in respect of debentures issued by it. Bondholders could either accept the sterling amount of interest payable in London or (alternatively) they could present their warrants for payment in New York, receiving payment in US dollars at a preset exchange rate of US$4.86 to one pound. Under what is now section 349(2) of the Income and Corporation Taxes Act 1988, the company was obliged to withhold 25 per cent of the interest payable to bondholders and to despatch these sums to the Revenue on account of the tax liability of the holder. On despatching the warrants, the company thus paid to the Revenue 5 shillings per pound. When some of the warrants were cashed in New York at the fixed rate of exchange, the holders in fact received significantly more than the equivalent of one pound because, by that time, only US$3.39 was required to purchase one pound sterling. As a consequence, the Revenue argued that the amount deducted should have been 25 per cent of the larger sum received by the bondholders concerned. At first instance, the Revenue's claim was dismissed on the grounds that foreign money was a commodity and thus could not be regarded as "interest of money" for the purposes of the statutory rule.[206] Given that US dollars were being used as a means of payment, this view was not sustainable even by reference to the broader, commodity theory discussed earlier in this section; it is even less sustainable in the light of the *Camdex* case. The Court of Appeal reversed this ruling, mainly on the grounds that the phrase

---

[203] See, eg, *Harrington v MacMorris* (1813) 5 Taunt 228 and *Ehrensperger v Anderson* (1848) 3 Exch 148, where actions for money had and received were allowed to proceed even though the moneys concerned had been advanced in India in the local currency (and not in sterling). The contrary decision in *McLachlan v Evans* (1827) 1 Y & J 380 cannot stand.
[204] See *Treseder-Griffin v Co-operative Insurance Society* [1956] 2 QB 127 (CA). See also para 8.10 below.
[205] *Rhokana Corp Ltd v IRC* [1938] AC 380 (HL).
[206] [1936] 2 All ER 678.

"interest of money" was apt to include foreign currency obligations and everything which, in a commercial sense, could be said to constitute a "payment".[207]

(b) The Court of Appeal has rightly held that—for income tax purposes— profits arising from the sale of US dollars were to be treated as a trading profit and taxable accordingly.[208]

(c) Foreign currency (but not sterling) is a chargeable asset for capital gains tax purposes—one may gain or lose as a result of disposing of foreign currency.[209] This is consistent with the strict legal view expressed earlier, namely that (so far as English law is concerned) the pound does not gain or lose value,[210] but other currencies can gain or lose value in relation to it, thus creating a taxable gain or profit.

It is perhaps fair to say that these instances do not really reflect upon the status **1.65** of foreign currencies before the English courts. They merely illustrate the incontrovertible facts that (1) in the United Kingdom, taxation will usually be assessed in or by reference to sterling amounts; (2) so far as English law is concerned, sterling is a uniform and unchanging measure of value;[211] and (3) transactions in foreign currencies and fluctuations in their value (relative to sterling) may create profits, gains, or losses which may have an impact upon the ultimate sterling tax liabilities.

Apart from these relatively specialist cases, it is suggested that—so far as the **1.66** English courts are concerned—sterling and foreign currency obligations fall to be treated in an essentially similar manner, for example as regards the payment of interest, performance,[212] the consequences of breach, and other matters.[213]

---

[207] [1937] 1 KB 788 (CA).

[208] *Landes Brothers v Simpson* (1934) TC 62; *Imperial Tobacco Co Ltd v Kelly* [1943] 2 All ER 119. But a different view was taken in *McKinlay v HT Jenkins & Sons* (1926) 10 TC 372 and *Davies v The Shell Company of China* (1951) 32 TC 133. See Anon, "Taxation of Foreign Currency Transactions" (1952) 61 Yale LJ 1181.

[209] Taxation of Chargeable Gains Act 1922, s 21(1)(b).

[210] See the opening comments in this para.

[211] *Treseder-Griffin v Co-operative Insurance Society* [1956] 2 QB 127 (CA).

[212] It should be noted that so far as the English courts are concerned, a sterling obligation must be performed by payment in sterling. Where a foreign currency obligation is payable in England, the debtor has the option to pay either in the stipulated currency or in sterling—see para 7.30 below.

[213] Of course, transactions involving foreign currencies may raise specific conflict of law issues. But that is equally true of other factors which may affect a transaction such as the place of payment or the residence of the parties. It should also be emphasised that the view expressed in the text is by no means universally held. For example, although the conclusions to be drawn from the *Camdex* decision are stated in similar terms in Brindle & Cox (eds) *The Law of Bank Payments* (Sweet & Maxwell, 3rd edn, 2004) para 2-009, the authors do doubt some of the reasons for the decision and maintain that foreign currency could helpfully be treated as a commodity in a variety of cases and for different purposes. In particular, they argue that: (a) if a contract to exchange one foreign currency for another is treated as two parallel obligations to pay money, then one party could insist that the obligations be set off, so that only a net amount would be payable by one

L. Eurocurrencies

1.67   The enormous growth of the eurocurrency market over recent decades requires that a section should be devoted to a discussion of its characteristics.[214]

1.68   The term, "eurocurrency" is generally taken to refer to a deposit denominated in a currency other than that of the country in which the deposit holding branch is situate.[215] Eurodollars are thus US dollars deposited with and payable by a bank outside the United States.[216]

---

party. As the authors rightly point out, such a result would usually be absurd, because the object of the transaction is to make available to each party the *gross* amount of the required currency in order to meet with some other obligation expressed in that currency. But it is submitted that, in such a case, it will not be difficult to imply into the contract a term which excludes any right of set-off, if that reflects both the obvious intention of the parties and the custom of the market in which their contract is made. It is true that the *Camdex* case involved a statutory (rather than a contractual) obligation to pay over foreign currency in exchange for Zambian kwatcha. But the purpose of such laws is to ensure that foreign exchange resources are made over to the State; again, the exclusion of a right of set-off should therefore be a relatively straightforward matter of statutory interpretation; (b) relying upon the decision in *Richard v American Union Bank* (1930) 253 NY 166, 170 NE 532, the authors also point out that, in the context of a breach of a foreign exchange contract, it would be easier to recover damages for a fall in the value of the relevant currency if it were viewed as an obligation to deliver a currency, rather than as a simple debt obligation. Following the decision in the *Camdex* case, and as a result of the decision in *President of India v La Pintada* [1985] 1 AC 104, damages for a reduction in the value of a currency would only be recoverable under the second limb of the rule in *Hadley v Baxendale* [1854] 9 Exch 341, ie where the loss would only have been in the contemplation of the parties as at the date of the contract. This line of argument is plainly right and, in the view of the present writer, represents one of the best arguments in favour of preserving the "commodity" treatment of foreign money under these circumstances. As a practical matter, however, it may be hoped that the courts would resolve the problem by allowing claims for monetary depreciation. If, eg, a business customer asks a bank to provide a set amount of US dollars against sterling on a specific date, the bank will know that the customer requires those dollars on that day to meet a dollar obligation to a third party; it will likewise know that the customer will have to obtain those dollars from elsewhere if the bank fails to provide them and that the sterling cost of doing so may have increased. It should not therefore be too difficult to bring such losses within the second "limb" of *Hadley v Baxendale*. The possibility of recovering such losses was noted in *Barclays Bank (International) Ltd v Levin Bros (Bradford) Ltd* [1977] QB 270.

[214] On the origin of the eurocurrency market, see Stigum, *The Money Market* (McGraw Hill, 3rd edn, 1989); Carreau and Juillard, *Droit international économique* (Dalloz, 2003) paras 1564–1582. As the writers point out, no work exists which seeks to provide a comprehensive legal analysis of the eurocurrency market. However, much valuable material and commentary is to be found in Robinson, *Multinational Banking* (Sijthoff, 1972). See also Carreau, "Deposit Contracts" in *International Contracts* (materials reprinted from the proceedings at the Columbia Law School Symposium on International Contracts, Matthew Bender & Co, 1981).

[215] See Smedresman and Lowenfeld, *Eurodollars, Multinational Banks and National Laws* 64 NY University LR 733 (October 1989).

[216] The US Supreme Court defined eurodollars as "United States dollars that have been deposited with a banking institution located outside the United States with a corresponding obligation on the part of the banking institution to repay the deposit in United States dollars":

In order to assist in a consideration of the legal nature of eurocurrencies, it may be as well to provide some historical background. The creation of the eurodollar market[217] is a fascinating and complex subject, but a brief discussion must suffice for the present purposes. The eurodollar market originally came into being for essentially economic reasons. During the course of the 1960s and 1970s, the United States spent heavily overseas for defence, investments and imports. The United States thus began to incur substantial trade and payment deficits and, as a result, substantial quantities of US dollars accumulated in foreign hands abroad.

1.69

The eurodollar market thus has its origins in US trade deficits, but the growth of the market was fuelled by a combination of regulatory factors. First of all, regulatory policy in the US prohibited the payment of interest on current accounts and limited the rates payable on time deposits. Furthermore, reserve requirements were imposed on US dollar liabilities of banks within the US itself; federal deposit insurance premiums were assessed with reference to the domestic base of dollar liabilities but the corresponding liabilities of overseas branches were excluded from this calculation. As a result, it was possible to obtain a higher rate of return on eurodollars than was available on its purely domestic counterpart. Developments in 1964 and 1965 then led to massive growth in this market. In 1964, the United States enacted its interest equalisation tax; this amounted to a tax on the export of capital and effectively barred both American and foreign companies from using the financial markets in the United States to finance their operations outside that country. In 1965, the effect of this tax was reinforced by new regulations on foreign direct investment and by the Federal Reserve Board's Voluntary Foreign Credit Restraint Program. Borrowers seeking to fund their overseas activities in US dollars were thus pushed towards the eurodollar market.[218] The eurodollar market thus

1.70

Citibank NA v Wells Fargo Asia (1990) 495 US 660. The expression "eurocurrency" results from the original growth of the eurodollar market in London, but the definition is of general application. A more complete definition is given by Carreau and Juillard, *Droit international économique* (Dalloz, 2003) para 1585:

> un dépôt international de monnaie étrangère peut être simplement défini comme l'opération selon laquelle une personne (le déposant) place (dépose) pour une durée limitée (le terme) une somme d'argent, exprimée en une monnaie nationale donnée, dans une banque (le dépositaire) située en dehors du pays d'émission de celle-ci, à charge pour la banque de payer un intérêt et de restituer le principal à l'échéance convenue.

[217] Reference will be made throughout to the eurodollar market since it is obviously the predominant one, but any currency can be a "eurocurrency" if it is deposited with a bank outside the currency of issue. As will be noted below, however, participation in the eurodollar market is confined to financial institutions.

[218] On the points just made, see Pigott, "The Historical Development of Syndicated Eurocurrency Loan Agreements" in *Selected Legal Issues for Finance Lawyers* (Lexis Nexis UK, 2003) 247. For discussion of the eurodollar market and the reasons for its growth in London, see

developed in order to allow transactions in US dollars outside the regulatory framework of the issuing State.

1.71 The eurodollar market itself is principally a market which subsists between large banks and financial institutions. These banks will place deposits with each other for relatively short periods[219] and they will carry interest at the market rate prevailing when the deposit arrangement is agreed. The recipient institution will then use the deposit as a means of funding a transaction for a customer. Apart from eurocurrency loans, the existence of such large pools of dollar deposits also led to the growth of the eurobond market. Since eurobonds are bearer instruments, it has not always been easy for governments to ensure that interest paid on such instruments is declared and assessed for taxation purposes.[220]

1.72 It may also be instructive to consider how a "eurodollar" comes into existence. Suppose that A holds a dollar deposit with B Bank in the United States. A decides to transfer that deposit to C Bank, which is located outside the United States. As a result, A has a US dollar deposit with (or claim against) C Bank whilst C Bank has a corresponding claim against B Bank. At this point, A's eurodollar deposit is in many ways merely an indirect means of holding a dollar deposit with a bank within the United States.[221] At this point, however, one can begin to grasp the "multiplier" effect of the eurodollar market. C Bank has an asset in the form of proceeds of the deposit which has been placed with it. C Bank could thus lend those dollar funds to a borrower. He may in turn use them to acquire assets or investments. The seller may then elect to deposit those dollar proceeds with another bank outside the United States, D Bank. It will be seen that the first deposit originating within the United States has spawned a whole series of assets and liabilities, each of which are equivalent in amount to the first deposit. To this extent, it may be said that the operation of the banking system actually *creates* eurodollars. The eurodollar market is in many respects unregulated and, of course, this is one of the main attractions to those involved in the market. As will be seen below, this state of affairs has consequences for the status of eurodollars as "money".

Schenk, "The Origins of the Eurodollar Market in London 1955–1963" [1998] 35 (2) Explorations in Economic History 221.

[219] One, three or six months would be typical maturities but the precise period would be subject to agreement between the institutions concerned.

[220] The difficulty is well illustrated by a decision of the ECJ. The Kingdom of Belgium issued bearer bonds in the euromarket. In an effort to ensure that these were not used as a means of avoiding Belgian taxation, the terms of the bonds specifically prohibited their acquisition by residents of that country, but the Court held that this was an insufficient justification for a restraint on the free movement of capital: Case C–478/98 *Commission v Belgium* [2000] ECR I 7857. See also Case C–242/03 *Ministre des Finances v Weidert* (15 July 2004).

[221] It is appreciated that this analysis is not attractive from a legal perspective, but it perhaps reflects the financial realities of the position.

This very brief introductory survey provides the factual matrix against which to **1.73** answer a question which must be considered in a monetary law context, namely, what is the legal nature of the eurodollar?

It is very clear that eurodollars could not be treated as "money" under the **1.74** former State theory of money, for such dollars do not exist in physical form. But the revised State theory merely attributes to the legislature the power to define the unit of account which is intended to form the domestic medium of exchange. Eurodollars are clearly denominated by reference to a domestic unit of account which is intended to serve as the general medium of exchange in the United States. If, as they plainly do, dollars serve that purpose in the United States then they constitute "money"; and dollars cannot forfeit their character-isation as "money" merely because they are held outside the country of origin. This formulation, however, gives rise to a further conceptual difficulty because of the "multiplier" effect which was described earlier—eurodollars are created by the banking system outside the United States, and it is thus difficult to describe the United States as the country of origin at all. This state of affairs has led some writers to conclude that money may exist both in a *public* and *national* form, and also in a *private* and *international* form.[222] If this distinction is accepted, then it is plain that it is the location of the deposit-holding bank which is key to the existence of the eurodollar; that bank must be situate outside the United States. A deposit with a US bank at one of its branches within the United States is simply a deposit in the national currency; an inter-bank deposit in dollars with the London branch of the same bank is a eurodollar deposit. It is possible to identify other characteristics which distinguish eurodollar from national currency obligations. For example, because of the amounts involved, payment will be made by means of a bank transfer, rather than through any other medium.[223] Equally, a bank which accepts a eurodollar deposit will receive the proceeds of that deposit by means of a credit to its own account with an institution within the United States and, as has been shown, that is a "national dollar" credit rather than a "eurodollar" credit. Every eurodollar deposit is thus ultimately "mirrored" by a national currency deposit held through the correspondent banking network.[224]

---

[222] Once again, the increasing role of private law in the monetary field should be noted. For the suggestion made in the text, see, Carreau and Juillard, *Droit international économique* (Dalloz, 2003) para 1567, where the authors speak of "deux 'monnaies' différentes, l'une publique et nationale qui est la monnaie support (ou sous-jacente) et l'autre privée et transnationale qui est la monnaie 'dérivée'". For further discussion on this subject, see Carreau, *Le Systéme monétaire international privé* (1998) 274 *Receuil* 313.

[223] Although see the situation which arose in *Libyan Arab Foreign Bank v Bankers Trust Co* [1989] QB 728. The case is discussed below.

[224] On these and other points, see Carreau and Juillard, *Droit international économique* (Dalloz, 2003) paras 1586–1587.

1.75   In terms of their legal analysis, both a eurodollar deposit and a national deposit
involve a debt claim against the institution which has accepted the deposit.[225]
Furthermore, the eurodollar claim, as much as the national currency, is subject
to the laws of the country which issues that currency—the *lex monetae*—in two
particular aspects.[226] First of all, the issuing State is at liberty to redefine its
monetary system and to change the unit of account. Even in the context of a
eurodollar (international) deposit, the parties have inescapably contracted by
reference to the US dollar. Any change in that unit of account would thus be
applied to the eurodollar contract, for a monetary obligation implies an obligation to pay in whatever is the lawful currency of the issuing State *when the
payment falls due*.[227] Secondly, it has been noted above that a eurodollar deposit
is ultimately mirrored by a corresponding national deposit. Partly, as a consequence of that position, the reciprocal payments involved in a eurodollar
deposit contract ultimately involve a transfer through or affecting the clearing
system of the issuing State.[228] Fundamental questions of performance may thus
in practice be affected by the laws of the issuing State, even though the contract
itself may be governed by a different system of law.[229] At least in theory, therefore, a eurodollar deposit involves a greater degree of legal risk for it is at the
mercy of both the *lex monetae* in the extended manner just described, and the
law applicable to the contract.[230]

1.76   Is it possible to draw any meaningful conclusions from this general discussion?
One is left with the impression of a currency which lacks a "country of issue" in
the sense in which that expression was understood in the context of the more

---

[225] See Carreau and Juillard, *Droit international économique* (Dalloz, 2003) paras 1586–1587.
The position is the same in England—see *Foley v Hill* (1848) 2 HLC 28; *Joachimson v Swiss Bank
Corp* [1921] 3 KB 110; *Rowlandson v National Westminster Bank Ltd* [1978] 1 WLR 803.
[226] On the *lex monetae* principle generally, see Ch 13 below.
[227] On this subject, see para 9.03 below.
[228] In part, this is because the settlement of dollar transactions involves sizeable overdrafts
among participants on any given day, and these can only safely be undertaken in the context of the
Federal Reserve's function as lender of last resort—see Smedresman and Lowenfeld, "Eurodollars,
Multinational Banks and National Laws" (October 1989) 64 NY University LR 733. Further, the
effect of a wholesale eurodollar transaction is to transfer dollars from the reserve account of the
Federal Reserve to the reserve account of another bank. Evidence to that effect was given by
Dr Marcia Stigum in *Libyan Arab Foreign Bank v Bankers Trust Co* [1989] QB 728 but was
rejected by the Court.
[229] The contract would usually be governed by a different system of law because, by definition,
eurodollar deposits are held with banks outside the US, and such deposit contracts will usually be
governed by the law of the place in which the account is held.
[230] On the points made in this paragraph, see Carreau and Juillard, *Droit international
économique* (Dalloz, 2003) paras 1603 and 1609. It must, however, be said that, where the
contract creating the eurodollar deposit is governed by English law, the exposure to the *lex
monetae* is limited because English law does not recognise the transfer through the US clearing
system as the fundamental feature of performance—see *Libyan Arab Foreign Bank v Bankers Trust
Co* [1989] QB 728.

traditional State theory of money. To the extent to which eurodollars can be regarded as "money",[231] it may be said that they exhibit features of both the State and the Societary theories of money. The connection with the State theory stems from the inescapable link to the *lex monetae* and the unit of account prescribed by it. On the other hand, the eurodollar market came into being and enjoyed its massive growth outside the country which issues that currency and without the formal or official sanction which may be regarded as an implicit requirement of the traditional State theory. Thus, if eurodollars are "money", they owe their existence, at least in part, to their acceptance as a means of payment by financial institutions executing transactions within a private law framework—in other words, to the Societary theory of money.[232]

It is fair to conclude that, whilst the State theory remains dominant within the **1.77** field of monetary law,[233] the growth of the eurodollar market has breathed some new life into the Societary theory.

---

[231] For the reasons discussed at para 1.57 above in relation to bank deposits generally, it is submitted that eurodollars can be regarded as "money" at least once the maturity date has arrived.

[232] It must, however, be said that English law does not at present accept any distinction between eurodollars and other foreign currency claims, and thus affords no special status to eurocurrencies. This conclusion is a necessary consequence of the decision in *Libyan Arab Foreign Bank v Bankers Trust Co* [1989] QB 728, where the court rejected the suggestion of an implied term depriving the creditor of the right to receive payment in cash. See also the discussion at pp 63–4 of the Fifth Edition of this work. It should be added for completeness that the US Supreme Court likewise had an opportunity to consider the eurodollar market in *Citibank NA v Wells Fargo Asia* (1990) 495 US 660. The court below apparently tended to the view that— wherever they were made—eurodollar deposit contracts should be governed by New York law, since they were ultimately to be settled there. This reflects the greater importance which US courts have tended to ascribe to the place of performance as a feature in identifying the governing law of the contract. The case was, however, principally concerned with the liability of the head office of a bank for deposits placed with its overseas branches. For an illuminating discussion of the earlier stages of this litigation, see Smedresman and Lowenfeld, "Eurodollars, Multinational Banks and National Laws" (October 1989) 64 NY University LR 733.

[233] It is submitted that this must be so, given that the creation of the euro is both a very recent and very important illustration of that theory. On the whole subject, see Chs 29 and 30 below, where the legal framework for the euro is considered.

2

THE ORGANISATION OF THE MONETARY SYSTEM

A. Introduction

Chiefly in the course of the nineteenth century, almost all States enacted legislation with a view to organising their respective currencies. This led to the creation of national monetary systems as they are familiar to the modern world. **2.01**

In relation to the monetary system as a concept, the relevant laws all define the unit of account by reference to its name and any applicable subdivisions of the unit.[1] In relation to physical money, the applicable national law will lay down rules on legal tender,[2] the technical specifications for notes and coins including, for example, their metallic content, standard of fineness, security features, and other matters. **2.02**

At an institutional level, the monetary system usually comprises a central bank or similar authority which enjoys the exclusive privilege of issuing national banknotes. That institution will usually also be responsible for the creation and holding of monetary reserves, including foreign currencies and—to a diminishing extent—gold. It was formerly possible to say that issues of this kind properly **2.03**

---

[1] See para 2.30 below.
[2] See para 2.24 below.

fell within the scope of constitutional (rather than monetary) law[3] and that they should therefore be excluded from consideration in a work of this kind. Regrettably, it is no longer felt appropriate to take this view, and questions touching central banks and their role within the monetary system will therefore have to be considered at a later stage.[4]

2.04 Against that very brief, introductory background, it is proposed to consider the role of sterling within the international and domestic legal orders, the relevance of the unit of account and legal tender legislation, and various other matters.[5]

B. Sterling within the International Monetary System

2.05 In a text which focuses upon English law, it is naturally of some importance to explain some of the history of the British monetary system and the manner in which it is organised. This must be so even though sterling may now be regarded as a relatively minor player on the international currency markets. This survey will also help to explain, in a very general sense, the various means which have from time to time been adopted to ensure the credibility of a national currency.

2.06 The gold standard, in its historically older function of the regulator or stabiliser of the international value of money in general and of sterling in particular, originated in England in the eighteenth century. On the basis of the Proclamation of 1717 fixing the price of one guinea weighing 129.4 grammes at 21 schillings or at a mint price of £3 17s 10½d an ounce, it came to be recognised that gold had supplanted silver as the standard by reference to which money was to derive its value.[6] By 1819, the figure of £3 17s 10½d an ounce had come "to be regarded as a magic price for gold from which we ought never to stray and to which, if we do, we must always return".[7] When Peel's Act[8] put an end to the Bank Restriction Period under which the country had laboured since 1797, this was achieved by providing that the Bank of England was to pay its notes at par, ie at £3 17s 10½d per ounce. This, then, was the gold specie

---

[3] A point made by Dr Mann in the Fifth Edition of this work, 32.

[4] See Ch 21 below.

[5] The present chapter deals with the organisation of the monetary system in general terms. It was felt more appropriate to deal with other, more specific forms of monetary organisation in Ch 33 below.

[6] See Feavearyear, *The Pound Sterling* (Clarendon Press, 2nd edn, 1963) 154.

[7] Feavearyear, 148. It is interesting to note that, as early as 1791, Edmund Burke said: "So soon as a nation compels a creditor to take paper currency in discharge of his debt, there is a bankruptcy"—see *The Writings and Speeches of Edmund Burke* (Oxford University Press, 1989) VIII, 362.

[8] 59 Geo III, Ch 49.

standard in the classical sense of that term; it put the Bank of England under a statutory obligation to pay for all its notes in specie.[9] These arrangements continued until 1914, when they ceased to exist *de facto*.[10] When the Government attempted to deal with the disturbances of the First World War by returning to the gold standard,[11] the legislation introduced the gold bullion standard by providing that only the Bank of England would be entitled to bring gold to the mint and to have it coined, and that the Bank should be required to sell gold bars of 400 ounces of fine gold to any purchaser who tendered £3 17s 10½d an ounce. Subsequently, the Bank was relieved of the obligation to sell gold in return for its own notes, and the gold standard was thus abandoned in England.[12] For a period, England lived under a monetary system which lacked any connecting link with gold for the purposes of valuing the pound. Its value was maintained and controlled by the operations of the Exchange Equalisation Fund.[13]

After the end of the Second World War, the British monetary system rested **2.07** upon this country's membership of the International Monetary Fund.[14] Under Article IV, section 1 of the Articles of Agreement concluded at Bretton Woods, the "par value" of the currency of each member country was to be expressed in terms of gold as a common denominator or in terms of the US dollar of the weight and fineness in effect on 1 July 1944.[15] On 18 December 1946, the par value of sterling was fixed at 3.58134 grammes of fine gold or US$4.03 per pound sterling. Sterling was devalued twice within the framework of this system. On 18 September 1949, it was reduced to 2.48828 grammes of fine gold (US$2.80); on 18 November 1967, it was further reduced to 2.13281 grammes (or US$2.40). The par value determined the price of gold sold and bought by its members,[16] and required them to ensure that foreign exchange

---

[9] See s 6 of the Bank of England Act 1833, repealed by s 4 of the Currency and Bank Notes Act 1954.

[10] The Currency and Bank Notes Act 1914 permitted the issue of currency notes of one pound and of ten schillings without imposing any quantitative limitations or any duty to keep a reserve. The notes were legal tender and *de jure* convertible, but gold disappeared from circulation. See, generally, Pierre Vilar, *Or et Monnaie dans l'histoire 1450–1920* (Paris, 1974) or, in German translation, *Geld und Gold in der Geschichte* (Munich, 1984); for an English translation, see Vilar and White, *A History of Gold and Money, 1450–1920* (Humanities Press, 1976).

[11] Gold Standard Act 1925, s 1.

[12] Gold Standard Amendment Act 1931, s 1.

[13] See Finance Act 1932, ss 24 and 25 (as amended).

[14] The role of the Articles of Agreement of the IMF in the context of exchange controls will be considered in Ch 15 below. As a result of the Second Amendment to the Agreement, which will be considered later in this chapter, much of the enormous literature about the Fund became obsolete. For a more recent and very helpful description of the Fund and its history, see Carreau and Juillard, *Droit international économique* (Dalloz, 2003) paras 1439–1452.

[15] This was 0.888671 grammes per dollar.

[16] Article IV, s 2 required that member countries should only buy or sell gold at prices within ranges defined by the Fund. The precise scope of the provision was open to some doubt, but the point no longer requires discussion.

dealings within their territories occurred only within narrow limits based on parity.[17] Further, a member could not propose a change in the par value of its currency except to correct a "fundamental disequilibrium"; a change in excess of 10 per cent of the original par value required the Fund's authority, but that authority could not be withheld if the proposed change arose from such a fundamental disequilibrium.[18]

2.08 These arrangements have been aptly described as a gold parity standard. Although banknotes were inconvertible, a large part of the Bank of England's purchases and sales of gold was subject to the fixed pricing provisions of the Articles of Agreement. Accordingly, the value of sterling (or any other currency with a par value) was no less tied to gold than was the US dollar, the weight of which was fixed at 15 grains of gold fine or at US$35 per ounce.[19] That the gold or par value could in certain circumstances be changed affected the firmness of the tie, rather than its existence as a matter of principle. It could certainly be less freely changed than in earlier times.[20]

2.09 What then, was the legal significance of the fact that the pound had a par value of 2.13281 grammes of gold, which this country was not at liberty to vary in its sole discretion? The pound could not be said to *mean* 2.13281 grammes of gold. On the other hand, the Bretton Woods system involved far more than a mere programme or general policy. Rather, it defined the price which, subject to marginal variations, the Bank of England had to pay or receive if it agreed to deal in gold with other Fund members, and on which all foreign exchange transactions had to be based. It was the existence of a treaty obligation to maintain the par value that in law was the essential ingredient of the gold parity

---

[17] Article IV, s 3. The UK secured compliance with this obligation through its administration of the Exchange Control Act 1947, on which see Ch 14 below. From the 1950s onwards, certain countries allowed their currencies to "float" and thus be traded outside the limits stated in Article IV, s 2, and it seems plain that this conduct amounted to a breach of the Articles of Agreement.

[18] Article IV, s 5. The concept of "fundamental disequilibrium" is at the same time both elusive and highly subjective; it would be difficult for the Fund to withhold its approval on the basis that no disequilibrium had occurred and, so far as is known, approval was never withheld on this basis. Although it is impossible to suggest that the Bretton Woods Agreement did not derogate from the monetary sovereignty of its members, it should be realised that the system was not wholly effective in practice.

[19] Proclamation of 31 January 1934 (No. 2072, 48 Statutes at Large 1730).

[20] Lord Keynes denied that the Bretton Woods Agreement involved any type of gold standard, because "the use of gold merely as a common denominator by means of which the relative values of national currencies—these being free to change—are expressed, is obviously quite another matter", Parliamentary Debates, HL Vol cxxxi, col 845 (23 May 1944). Yet, as has been shown, the Agreement required member countries to effect transactions in gold and foreign currencies within pre-set margins; this must be indicative of a gold standard even if the central bank is not under a positive obligation to buy or sell gold.

standard.[21] The primary function of the gold standard was thus to support the system of parities established by the Bretton Woods Agreement.

The original Bretton Woods system broke down when, on 15 August 1971, President Nixon abolished the convertibility of dollars into gold.[22] From that time, the par value system established by the Agreement was necessarily and universally disregarded. By the Smithsonian Agreement of 18 December 1971, the International Monetary Fund sought to establish a system of central rates and "practices that members may wish to follow in the present circumstances".[23] It is clear that these arrangements were irreconcilable with the specific terms of the Fund Agreement itself, and thus could not be regarded as having any binding force under international law.[24] In any event, all currencies, including sterling, began to float, in the sense that dealings in gold and foreign currencies ceased to observe the system of fixed parities; the attempt to rescue a form of par value system by means of the Smithsonian Agreement thus proved to be wholly futile. The details of these developments are described by Kerr J in *Lively & Co v City of Munich*,[25] where it was held that, regardless of the formal position, no par value system was "in force" in any real sense.

2.10

Eventually, as a result of the Second Amendment of the Articles of Agreement,[26] which came into force on 1 April 1978, the International Monetary Fund became primarily a credit institution in that it retained the function to provide or procure international credit or liquidity for the benefit of member countries by transactions under Article V and the use of Special drawing Rights under Articles XVI to XXV of the Article of Agreement. The Fund's powers and tasks as a monetary

2.11

---

[21] An unauthorised change in the par value would plainly have constituted a breach of the Bretton Woods Agreement—see Mann, "The Binding Character of the Gold Parity Standard" (1969) I Jus Privatum Gentium (Festschrift für Max Rheinstein) 483.

[22] This is likely to have involved a breach of the Bretton Woods Agreement—see Jackson (1972) AJIL 110. This was, however, the perhaps inevitable result of the use of the US dollar as the primary medium of international trade since the 1950s. As the US began to run substantial deficits, the number of dollars in circulation far exceeded the amount of gold available for their exchange.

[23] The arrangements substituted a fluctuation margin of 2.25% for the US dollar in place of the 1% margin which had prevailed under the Articles of Agreement. For the text of the Smithsonian Agreement, see *Selected Decisions of the International Monetary Fund* (Eighth Issue, 1978) 14–21.

[24] This much seems to be apparent from the decision of the European Court in *Fratelli Zerbone v Amministrazione delle Finanze* [1978] ECR 99, where the status of "international rules" was attributed to the Articles of Agreement of the Fund but not to the Smithsonian Agreement. The Smithsonian Agreement represented a decision only of certain of the major Fund members, and thus it plainly could not operate as a revision to the Fund's Articles of Agreement. The point is not material because the Smithsonian Agreement failed to bring any order to the international monetary system.

[25] [1976] 1 WLR 1004.

[26] Cmnd 7311. On the Second Amendment, see Edwards (1976) AJIL, 722; Gold, *The Second Amendment and the Fund's Articles of Agreement* (IMF Pamphlet No. 25, 1978) and *The Conversion and Exchange of Currency under the Second Amendment* (IMF Pamphlet No. 23, 1978).

institution are now—at least in legal terms—little more than nominal in effect. Article IV of the Articles Agreement now contains obligations on the part of member countries "to collaborate with the Fund and other members to assure orderly exchange arrangements and to promote a stable system of exchange rates". Similar provisions require each member to "endeavour to direct its economic and financial policies towards the objective of fostering orderly economic growth" and to "seek to promote stability by fostering orderly underlying economic and financial conditions". It is only necessary to read these provisions in order to realise that they do not create any obligations of a character which are meaningful in law.[27] Nevertheless, Article IV provides a basis upon which the Fund consults with member countries on their exchange rate and other policies on a regular basis; reports on these consultation and surveillance procedures are published from time to time. If Article IV contains limited legal content, it should not thereby be assumed that it has no purpose in a wider context.

2.12 The Second Amendment also deprived gold of its former monetary status.[28] The par value system has been abolished and can only be reintroduced by an 85 per cent majority of the Fund's total voting power; further, the use of gold as a means of supporting exchange arrangements is now explicitly prohibited.[29]

2.13 It follows from this discussion that, from 1971 onwards, the Articles of Agreement of the Fund did not provide any fixed standard to which sterling was linked. As a result the external value of sterling depended upon the market forces of supply and demand and on the confidence of investors holding sterling assets. Governmental intervention in the market was also possible where thought appropriate; for that purpose, an exchange equalisation fund was established,[30] the primary purpose of which is "checking undue fluctuations in the exchange value of sterling".[31] In spite of the comments made in the last

---

[27] Perhaps the only provision in Art IV which might have any formal effect is to be found in s 1 (iii), which prohibits the manipulation of exchange rates or of the international monetary system with a view to obtaining an unfair competitive advantage. Even then, however, it would plainly be very difficult to achieve or to prove activities of this kind. The provisions discussed in this paragraph are considered in more detail in Ch 22 below.

[28] This statement is certainly true in the formal sense; ie currencies are no longer linked in value to a particular quantity of gold. Nevertheless, it remains the case that central banks hold significant stocks of gold, and producers have expressed concern that disposals of these stocks will have an impact on the market price of this particular commodity. Central banks within the eurozone have thus agreed to regulate their sales of gold, and have confirmed that gold "will remain an important element of global reserves"—see the "Joint Statement on Gold following the renewal of the Gold Agreement", ECB Press Release dated 8 March 2004. For a discussion of the continuing importance of gold held by the IMF itself, see Dick Ware, *The IMF and Gold* (World Gold Council Research Study 26, rev edn, May 2001).

[29] Article IV, s 2(b).   [30] See Exchange Equalisation Fund Account Act 1979.
[31] ibid, s 1(3)(a).

paragraph, it is interesting to note that these funds may be invested not only in foreign currency assets and Special Drawing Rights, but also in the purchase of gold.[32]

With effect from 8 October 1990, the United Kingdom joined the exchange rate mechanism of the European Monetary System. This involved an obligation to maintain the external value of sterling at levels which were based upon a central rate of DM2.95 to £1. The return to a fixed rate regime was, of course, a radical departure from the previous twenty years of floating rates. It proved, however, to be a short-lived experiment; sterling departed from the system as a result of the events of "Black Wednesday" (16 September 1992), and since that time, the external value of the currency has, once again, depended on market forces.[33]   **2.14**

C. Sterling within the Domestic Legal Order

The second function of the gold standard was to regulate and limit the volume of money in circulation by the requirement that notes should be backed by a quantity of gold held in reserve as security. The gold standard in this sense has also disappeared and is therefore of historical interest only.   **2.15**

As a consequence, sterling—and indeed all other currencies—is now properly to be described as fiduciary money;[34] ie it is accepted to have a certain value in terms of its purchasing power which is unrelated to the value of the material from which the physical money is made[35] or the value of any cover which the bank may be required to hold. Thus, the Bank of England can now issue notes up to limits set by the Treasury;[36] these notes are secured by the Bank's duty to hold in the Issue Department securities of an amount sufficient to cover the issue.[37]   **2.16**

Where provisions for the tangible cover of a fiduciary issue exist, it is necessary to ask whether they afford any protection for the holder of the banknote. It is submitted that this question must be answered in the negative. It is true that, in the United Kingdom, notes must be backed by securities held within the Issue   **2.17**

---

[32] ibid, s 3.

[33] On this episode and the exchange rate mechanism in general, see para 25.11 below.

[34] The same may be said of all other currencies.

[35] See Helleiner, *The Making of National Money* (Cornell, 2003) 21. From a legal perspective, the "acceptance" that money has a certain value in this sense requires that such value should also be ascribed by law.

[36] Currency Act 1983, s 2.

[37] Currency and Bank Notes Act 1928, s 3(1). The expression "securities" includes government paper.

Department; equally, in the United States, the Gold Standard Act 1900[38] provided that the reserves "shall be used for the redemption of the notes and certificates for which they are respectively pledged and shall be used for no other purpose, the same being held as trust funds". Yet these formulations are in the nature of administrative directions to the monetary authorities; they do not seek to confer any rights upon the holder of a banknote. That this is the true legal position was made clear by the remarkable case of *Marshall v Grinbaum*.[39] The Russian currency reform of 1897 had included a decree requiring that notes must be secured by gold. Under Russian law, the notes were legal tender and were exchangeable at the State Bank for equivalent amounts of gold. A holder of notes claimed a charge upon gold which belonged to the State Bank but which was physically held by the defendant. Petersen J rejected the existence of a charge. In relation to the Russian decrees, he said[40] that their objective:

> . . . was to maintain the value of the notes by making them exchangeable for gold and, in order to make this right of exchange effective, the Minister of Finance, as custodian of the State Bank was prohibited from issuing notes without keeping the gold reserve up to the prescribed amount. Where the ukase speaks of the notes being "secured by gold" or of the issue of notes "against a gold security" or of "the amount of gold securing the notes", it does not contemplate the creation of a charge or mortgage in favour of the holders of credit notes, it is merely making regulations for the issue of notes with the object of insuring that any holder who brings a note to the State Bank may receive the nominal amount of the note in gold . . .

2.18   Thus, the government or the central bank retained full control over the issue of notes even when it was backed by gold; this must be even more so in the case of a fiduciary currency. Yet it would be easy to overstate the extent or value of the degree of control which the government enjoys in this area. In particular, it does not directly control the amount or growth of bank deposits.[41]

2.19   It follows that requirements as to "cover" or "backing" for the issue of banknotes have only a very limited impact on the overall supply of money within the economy. Furthermore, such requirements confer no legal rights upon the holder of physical money.

---

[38] US Gold Standard Act 1900, s 4 (31 Statutes at Large 45).

[39] (1921) 37 TLR 913.

[40] At 915.

[41] The Government may, of course, influence such matters in a variety of ways, principally through interest rate adjustments but also through fiscal and taxation policies, and the imposition of reserve ratios or special deposits on financial institutions. Physical money in issue represents a decreasing proportion of the overall supply of money.

D. Types of Currencies

Since sterling is no longer backed by physical assets such as gold, it is obvious **2.20**
that notes issued by the Bank of England are "inconvertible"; yet such banknotes are equally obviously legal tender. It is necessary briefly to examine these
features.

Convertible and inconvertible currencies

Convertibility was a feature of those currency systems in which the standard **2.21**
currency consisted of gold, and in which any paper money in issue could always
be exchanged for the standard money.[42] The function of such convertibility was
therefore to ensure that paper money maintained its nominal value; this objective would be achieved so long as paper money was genuinely redeemable in
accordance with the procedure just described.

It has been shown that convertibility is very closely connected with the existence **2.22**
of a gold or other metallic standard. Convertibility in this sense had been an
essential feature of the Bank of England Act 1833, but it was modified by the
Gold Standard Act 1925, which exempted the Bank of England from liability to
redeem its notes with gold coin and merely placed it under the obligation to sell
gold bullion at a fixed price and, moreover, granted to the Bank of England the
exclusive right of obtaining coined gold from the Mint. This limited convertibility was abolished by the Gold Standard (Amendment) Act 1931, and sterling
has been an inconvertible currency since that time.

Inconvertibility exonerates the bank of issue from paying its own notes in gold **2.23**
and merely puts it under an obligation to pay them in currency, ie in its own
notes. If legislation is passed which renders notes inconvertible, then this will
apply (a) to all notes, whether issued before or after the inconvertibility rules
were introduced;[43] and (b) to all notes, even if held abroad.[44] Therefore, in the

---

[42] The term "freely convertible" is frequently used to refer to the ability to exchange one
currency for another without restriction. The term may properly be used where there are no
exchange control restrictions which would prevent such an exchange. In the present context, the
term "convertible" is used in the different sense described in the text.

[43] In Germany, holders of "old" mark notes sought to assert their right to payment in gold on
the basis that their notes had been issued before the war legislation which suspended convertibility. The Supreme Court disposed of this contention in two lengthy judgments: 20 May 1926
RGZ 114, 27; 20 June 1929 *RGZ* 125, 273; see also 18 February 1929 *JW* 1929, 1967.

[44] The law of the country in which the bank of issue is situate governs the obligations arising
under banknotes: *Marshall v Grinbaum* (1921) 37 TLR 913, 915 with regard to Russian banknotes. In the same sense, with regard to German banknotes, Italian Supreme Court, 28 February
1939, AD 1938–40 No. 56 and BIJI (1940) No. 11029 (affirming Court of Appeal Milan,

case of inconvertible currencies the promise "to pay" which banknotes express or imply is of limited significance. Nevertheless, inconvertibility does not deprive banknotes of their character as "money" or as negotiable instruments, nor does it deprive them of their intrinsic monetary value.[45].

E. Legal Tender

2.24 One of the functions of the monetary system is to define those chattels or other assets which are to constitute legal tender within the State concerned.[46] It thus becomes necessary to ascertain the meaning of legal tender and the consequences of this concept.

2.25 Legal tender is such money[47] in the legal sense as the legislator has so defined in the statutes which organise the monetary system. Chattels which are legal tender therefore necessarily have the quality of money but the converse is not true—not all money is necessarily legal tender.

2.26 In earlier times, the status of banknotes caused no small difficulty in this context. Section 11 of the Restriction Bill 1797 had merely provided that banknotes should be "deemed to be payments in cash, if made and accepted as such"[48] and it was thus possible to decide that, in the absence of an agreement to

---

18 February 1938, BIJI (1939) or *Clunet* 1939, 171) and Dutch Supreme Court BIJI 41 (1940) No. 10948. It has on occasion been maintained that the introduction of inconvertibility does not affect the position of foreign holders; but the view is fallacious, since in this sense monetary laws are not limited in their territorial application. A foreign bank of issue would, in any event, be immune from proceedings before the English courts to enforce any right to convertibility—see Mann (1979) BYIL 60, n 2 with further references.

[45] This is a necessary consequence of the decision in *Banco de Portugal v Waterlow & Sons* [1932] AC 452.

[46] Inevitably, however, as the importance of cash as a means of payment diminishes, the importance of this particular function is correspondingly reduced. As has already been shown, the diminishing importance of physical money has consequences for the very definition of "money" itself (see para 1.50 above).

[47] In 1923 in *Vick v Howard* 136 Va 101, 109, a Virginia court said that "the authorities . . . clearly recognise the distinction between money which is, and money which is not, legal tender. In other words, all legal tender is money, but not all money is legal tender." The latter part of this statement, on which the formulation in the text is based, is theoretically sound, as was earlier recognised in *Emperor of Austria v Day* (1861) 3 DeG F & J 217, 234; foreign notes and coins "might pass as money without being legal tender". Physical money in circulation in this country and accepted in the discharge of financial obligations qualifies for the title "money" regardless of its State of issue; it only qualifies for the title of "legal tender" if this country is the State of issue.

[48] This language may be treated as early confirmation of the fact that payment requires not merely a tender by the debtor but also acceptance by the creditor. The point is discussed at para 7.09 below.

that effect between the parties, banknotes were not legal tender.[49] Subsequently, it was provided that Bank of England notes were legal tender for all sums above £5 "so long as the Bank of England shall continue to pay on demand their said notes in legal coin".[50] The present situation is derived from the Currency and Bank Notes Act 1954; all Bank of England notes are now legal tender in England and Wales for the payment of any amount.[51] The legal tender quality of coins is defined by section 2 of the Coinage Act 1971, as amended by section 1(3) of the Currency Act 1983. Coins of denominations of more than 10 pence are legal tender for amounts not exceeding £10, coins of smaller denomination are legal tender for payment of amounts not exceeding £5 and bronze coins for amounts not exceeding 20 pence. Gold coins remain legal tender for any amount, provided that they remain of the required weight.[52]

Whilst foreign currencies may in practice be accepted in many transactions in this country, it is clear that this state of affairs is derived from the consent of the parties, rather than any formal obligation on the part of the creditor.[53] It may, however, be noted in passing that an unsuccessful attempt was made to confer upon the euro the status of legal tender within the United Kingdom. The Euro and Sterling Choice Bill was introduced in the House of Commons at the end of 2001, shortly before euro notes and coins were put into circulation in the euro-zone itself. Subject to certain limits, clause 1 of the Bill would have conferred upon the debtor the unilateral right to discharge a sterling obligation by payment in euros.[54] To confer the formal status of legal tender upon a foreign currency would have represented a radical departure from established practice, and it is perhaps unsurprising that the Bill made no further progress. But even apart from the issue of principle, it is apparent that the proposed arrangements would have operated unfairly to the creditor. It was clearly necessary to establish a rate of exchange, and it was provided[55] that the debtor could discharge his sterling debt in euro "according to the closing rate determined by the Bank of England at the

2.27

---

[49] *Grigby v Oakes* (1801) 2 Bos & Pul 527; *Lockyer v Jones* (1976) Peake's NPC 239, 240. As to an agreement to accept notes, see *Brown v Saul* 4 Esp 267. Notes issued by country banks were only legal tender if so agreed—see *Lockyer v Jones* above; *Tiley v Courtier* (1813), not reported but referred to and approved in *Polyglass v Oliver* (1813) 2 Cr & J 15.

[50] Bank of England Act 1833, s 6.

[51] Currency and Bank Notes Act 1954, s 1(2) and s 1(6).

[52] Coinage Act 1971, s 2(1) as amended.

[53] If a debt is expressed in a foreign currency but is payable in this country, then it is possible to make a valid *tender* in respect of the debt by proffering the requisite amount of foreign currency to the creditor, but the foreign currency plainly does not acquire the status of *legal tender* in this country.

[54] Clause 1 of the Bill provided that "payment in euros of an amount equivalent to the amount due in sterling shall have the same effect as if it were made in pounds sterling". Clause 7 of the Bill expressly preserved the effect of the Coinage Act 1970, s 2 and stated that "euro coins shall not be legal tender above the sterling values referred to in that section".

[55] Clause 4 of the Bill.

close of business on the day previous to the day on which any debt or obligation under a contract falls due"—with the inevitable result that a fall in sterling value of the euro on the day of payment itself would leave the creditor out of pocket. Further, the burden and cost of converting the euro amounts into sterling would presumably have fallen upon the creditor. However, the failure of the Bill renders it unnecessary to pursue this subject in further depth.

2.28 In modern times, all legal tender is inconvertible in the sense described above. It therefore constitutes what has been called forced issue or compulsory tender or fiat money (cours forcé, Zwangskurs). If a creditor refuses to accept payment of a debt when the necessary quantity of legal tender is proffered to him, then he will be disadvantaged in any subsequent proceedings relating to that debt.[56]

2.29 It should be emphasised that the foregoing discussion has something of a formal character. In particular, it will be appreciated that cash payments tend only to be made in transactions involving relatively small amounts of money and which only very rarely give rise to legal proceedings in the context of tender or payment.[57] In the modern context, questions concerning tender and payment have usually arisen in the context of payment through the banking system, no doubt because higher value transactions tend to be settled in this way. Such cases do not involve "legal tender" in its formal sense, because cash is not used as the medium of payment. Instead, the courts have asked whether the creditor has received the "commercial equivalent" of payment, in the sense that he has received a credit of the required amount upon which he is unconditionally entitled to draw.[58] This leads to a natural and inescapable conclusion; in a world in which the use of cash as a means of payment is steadily decreasing, the importance of the formal concept of legal tender necessarily diminishes at the same rate.[59]

F. The Definition of the Unit of Account

2.30 It is now necessary briefly to consider the unit of account[60]—such as the pound sterling, the dollar, or the yen—which constitutes the basic feature of every monetary system.[61] What can be said of this unit?

---

[56] On the subject of tender and payment, see generally Ch 7 below.

[57] Large scale payments in cash are now mostly associated with activities which are likely to be illegal, and which, for that reason, are perhaps unlikely to give rise to civil proceedings.

[58] The whole subject is discussed at para 7.10 below.

[59] It has already been noted that the diminishing importance of physical cash has consequences for the definition of "money" itself. See generally Ch 1 above.

[60] One of the first judicial uses of this expression is to be found in *Re Chesterman's Trust* [1923] 2 Ch 466, 477.

[61] In relation to the euro as the unit of account of the eurozone, see Ch 29 below.

First of all, money is both an abstract and a quantitative conception. Like other **2.31** quantitative conceptions such as length and weight, a reference to a unit of account only becomes meaningful if a reference to it includes a statement as to the *number* of units of account in question. A reference to a debt expressed in sterling lacks any material legal content unless the relevant *amount* is also stated.

Secondly, it is also necessary to ask whether the unit of account is itself a **2.32** measure of value, or whether the value of the unit is itself measured by reference to something else. In other words, does the unit of account exist independently or does there exist some link between the unit and some other substance or measure of value?

When paper money was convertible into gold, it was reasonable to suppose that **2.33** banknotes were merely representative of the value of the relevant quantity of gold. Indeed, the names chosen to designate the unit of account—"pound", "livre", "peso",[62] and others—frequently referred to a certain weight of metal. In relation to the pound sterling, it should not be forgotten that the unit of account had a par value of 2.13281 grammes of fine gold until the collapse of the Bretton Woods system in 1971. That the pound was nothing but a quantity of gold was the general view which prevailed throughout the nineteenth century.[63] However that may be, the metallistic doctrine just described has long been discredited. After Britain abandoned the gold standard in 1931, the paper pound existed and proved workable in the absence of any link to any other substance or measure of value. Further, even when the pound had a par value based on gold during the Bretton Woods era, this was a measure rather than a synonym of the currency unit.[64] Sterling and other currencies are now inconvertible and thus depend entirely upon the credit of the bank of issue. There is therefore no doubt that the unit of account is now an independent measure of value.[65]

These propositions may appear to be self-evident, yet it remains difficult to **2.34** provide a positive definition of the unit of account. G.F. Knapp[66] held that the

---

[62] See the remarks made in *St Pierre v South American Stores (Gath & Chaves) Ltd* [1937] 3 All ER 349, 357.

[63] This was in effect the conclusion reached by the Report of the Bullion Committee (1810). The same principle may be seen in the Bank Charter Act 1844. See generally, David Laidler, "The Bullionist Controversy in Money" in Eatwell *et al* (eds) *Extracts from the New Palgrave* (W.W. Norton & Co, 1989) 60.

[64] For a more detailed discussion of the history of this debate, see the Fifth Edition of this work, 43–6.

[65] It is difficult to see how any other view could be adopted. It is consistent with the principle of nominalism (see in particular Ch 9 below), and with the rule that the domestic currency is represented by a unit of account which does not change, regardless of external events which may affect its purchasing power: *Treseder-Griffin v. Co-operative Insurance Society* [1956] 2 QB 127 (CA).

[66] *The State Theory of Money*, 21. Knapp's approach was broadly approved by Dr Mann—see the Fifth Edition of this work, 46–7.

unit of account could only be defined historically, by reference to its "recurrent link" to some previous unit of account.[67] According to Knapp, such recurrent linking is effected by the rate of conversion which the State establishes for the payment of debts denominated with reference to a former monetary standard. Experience, no doubt, suggests that this approach is both practical and workable; most countries have a unit of account which can be traced by reference to its link with a former such unit. However that may be, Knapp's approach seems to avoid the problem of definition, rather than to solve it; if one cannot define the unit of account, then it seems unattractive to define it by reference to previous units of account which, necessarily, one is equally unable to define.[68] Further, Knapp's historical approach does not assist in England, because the history of the pound is a continuous one.[69] Legislation refers to the currency as the "pound sterling" but does not seek to provide a formal definition of that expression.[70] Ultimately, the unit of account is whatever the national legislator states it to be and, if this is unattractive as a definition, it is at least consistent with the State theory of money.[71] It also reflects the formulation provided by Nussbaum:[72] "the dollar concept existing at any given time is as little susceptible of definition as, say the concept of 'blue'. No more can be said than that 'dollar'

---

[67] As will be noted in the present paragraph, the theory of the recurrent link is perhaps of limited *theoretical* value in defining an existing unit of account. It is, however, of significant *practical* value for the lawyer who has to deal with impending changes affecting the legal structure of a monetary system. Where a State elects to change its national currency—eg by substituting the euro for the French franc—there must be some legislative act which prescribes the substitution rate in relation to obligations contracted prior to the changeover. That legislation thus provides the connection, or recurrent link, between the old unit of account and its replacement. The theory of the recurrent link forms a part of the *lex monetae* principle and must thus be applied regardless of the law applicable to the obligation as a whole. On this subject see, generally, para 13.04 below.

[68] As will be seen in paras 2.48–2.58, however, Knapp's approach to this problem may be of value in a negative sense. If the legislator has not found it necessary to establish a recurrent link, then this may demonstrate that there has been no change to the unit of account and no alteration in the monetary system as a whole. It should be emphasised that the comments in the text cast doubt on the value of the recurrent link theory *as a means of defining the unit of account*. It is not intended to impugn the importance of that theory as a part of the broader *lex monetae* principle.

[69] According to Feavearyear, *The Pound Sterling* (Clarendon Press, 2nd edn, 1963) 2, "The pound sterling came into existence in Anglo Saxon times. There has been no break in sequence of contracts in which pounds, shillings and pence have been the consideration from those times to the present day." The continuing identity of the pound was not affected by the introduction of decimal coinage. The legislation adjusted the subdivision of the pound by introducing new pence, but left the pound intact—see the Decimal Currency Acts 1967 and 1969 and the Currency Act 1982. The last Act substituted "penny" for "new pence".

[70] Currency Act 1982 s 1(1), formerly Decimal Currency Act 1967, s 1(1).

[71] On the State theory of money, see para 1.15 above. The exclusive right of the State to define the monetary system includes the right to define the unit of account. This remains the position even in relation to the more limited version of the State theory which has been proposed in this work.

[72] *Money in the Law, National and International* (The Press Foundation, 2nd edn, 1950) 13.

70

is the name for a value which, at any definite moment, is understood in the same sense throughout the community, and since goods and services are evaluated in terms of the dollar, that unit is a standard or measure of value."

It follows that the unit of account is an entirely abstract and independent concept, which cannot be further elucidated by relating it to some other concept or measure of value. **2.35**

G. Changes in the Monetary System

Whilst a satisfactory definition of the unit of account has proved to be elusive, there is no doubt that the concept is one of the essential characteristics of a monetary system. **2.36**

The independence of the unit of account has a variety of consequences. For example, neither the identity of the unit of account nor the existence of the monetary system is affected by measures or events which touch merely the value or purchasing power of money; inflation may erode the purchasing power of the unit but does not affect its essential character.[73] Equally, in legal terms, the monetary system is not affected by a rise or fall in the international value of the currency, the introduction of exchange controls, or any similar measure. Thus the identity of the pound sterling did not change when this country abandoned the gold standard in 1931, by relieving the Bank of England of the obligation to sell gold bullion against notes.[74] Likewise, when the United States declared gold clauses to be irreconcilable with public policy, and enacted that every obligation could be discharged dollar-for-dollar in notes which were legal tender, the character of the US dollar as a unit of account was not affected.[75] Equally, the pound as a unit of account did not change when its par value in terms of gold was devalued in 1949 and 1967, nor did the unit change when the currency was decimalised in 1971.[76] These points should be obvious in the sense that the unit of account as an abstract measure was not adjusted as a result of any of these **2.37**

---

[73] Once again, see *Treseder-Griffin v Co-operative Insurance Society* [1956] 2 QB 127 (CA).

[74] Gold Standard (Amendment) Act 1931. That the status of the pound sterling was not affected by these events was recognised by the German Supreme Court (21 June 1933, *RGZ* 141, 212, 214) and by the Czechoslovakian Supreme Court *RabelZ* 1934, 484.

[75] See the Joint Resolution of Congress, 5 June 1933. However, the Austrian Supreme Court held that the Joint Resolution resulted in a change of monetary system—26 November 1935, *RabelZ* 1935, 891, 895. This decision must be regarded as mistaken. The English courts had occasion to consider the Joint Resolution in *International Trustee for the Protection of Bondholders AG v The King* [1937] AC 500.

[76] The decimalisation of the currency affected the sub-divisions of the pound but not the pound itself.

steps.[77] In these cases, the monetary system remains the same even though the events described had major consequences for the national and international value of the currency.

2.38   The foregoing discussion has highlighted the type of events and occurrences which do not lead to any kind of change in the monetary system. Such changes will only be taken to occur where the developments at issue strike at the identity of the unit of account and thus of the monetary system itself.[78] Generally speaking, such alterations are due to two causes, either to territorial or political changes or to a complete collapse of the monetary system.[79]

2.39   A decision of the German Supreme Court[80] affords an interesting illustration of the view that only alterations in the constitution of the unit of account as evidenced by a rate of conversion affect the identity of a monetary system, and that other modifications of a monetary system relate merely to the value of money, unless they have consequences so disastrous as to amount to a destruction and thus to an alteration of the system. On 21 May 1931, the plaintiff bank discounted with the defendants, the German Reichsbank, a bill of exchange for 100,000 Mexican gold pesos, payable on 15 August 1931. On 27 July 1931 a new Monetary Law came into force in Mexico by which the currency was moved off the gold standard. It was provided that, though the unit of account was of 75 centigrams fine gold, the token money consisted of notes, silver, and bronze only, that any payment of Mexican money had to be effected by tendering silver or bronze coins at the nominal value, and that this applied to debts previously incurred. In view of this law, the acceptor of the bill paid at maturity the nominal amount of 100,000 Mexican gold pesos in silver coins. The defendants therefore received an amount less by 74,013.45 reichsmarks than they would have received had the bill been paid before the law of 27 July 1931. They debited the plaintiff's account accordingly, relying, *inter alia*, on a clause in their agreement with them which read as follows: "If bills of exchange or

---

[77] In this limited sense, Knapp's historical approach to the recurrent link may be of some assistance. In none of these cases described in the text did the legislator find it necessary to establish a recurrent link, and this supports the view that there had been no alteration in the monetary system.

[78] A change in the monetary system may thus occur even if the events concerned have not had any impact upon the *value* of the unit of account, in the sense of its purchasing power.

[79] Hyperinflation in Germany led to the creation of a new currency which was distinct from the former monetary system—German Supreme Court, 13 October 1933, *RGZ* 142, 23, 30, 31; the same point was implicitly recognised by the English courts in *Franklin v Westminster Bank* (1931) (CA) reproduced in the Fifth Edition of this work, 561. For English cases which consider the collapse of the Russian currency, see *Buerger v New York Life Insurance Co* (1927) 43 TLR 601, 605 and *Perry v Equitable Life Assurance Society* (1929) 45 TLR 468, 473.

[80] 13 Oct 1933, *RGZ* 142, 23.

cheques are not paid in the currency with reference to which they are denominated, the Reichsbank reserves the right to recover subsequently any eventual balances arising from the variation of the rates of exchange." Applying German law, the Supreme Court held that this clause was inapplicable, because the currency in which the bill was paid did not differ from that in which it was denominated. The court took the view:

> . . . that the various reasons which combine to produce the international value of a currency system cannot be distinguished, and that, on the other hand, the question whether a currency has collapsed, does not depend on an examination of the circumstances which have led to a different valuation. The valuation of a monetary system can at the most indicate that an alteration of the currency has perhaps occurred. For the decision whether such an alteration in fact exists, the Court of Appeal was right in holding it to be necessary to go down to the basis of the individual monetary system, and this basis is the ideal unit on which the system is founded (Nussbaum, *Das Geld*, p 44) or "the value represented by the unit of account which is the basis of the system".[81] An alteration of the currency only exists, if its basis is altered, whether this is due to the legislator consciously building up a new monetary system on a new unit of account, or to the events of economic life completely destroying that legal basis in disregard of the law.

It follows from the State theory of money that, generally, extrinsic alterations of **2.40** currency can only be effected by legislative measures. As regards the question under what circumstances intrinsic alterations may destroy the identity of the currency, a hard-and-fast rule cannot be laid down. With respect to depreciation of money, the working principle will probably have to be adopted that a "collapse",[82] or a catastrophic depreciation is required, or that the money must have become worthless[83] or "fantastically depreciated"[84] or, as was said in an American case,[85] so depreciated as to "shock the conscience and produce an exclamation".

H. Revaluation and Devaluation

As has been shown[86] the value of sterling or any other unit of account may be **2.41** established by governmental acts such as legislation or treaties, or by market

---

[81] Helfferich, *Das Geld* (Hirschfeld, Leipzig, 6th edn, 1923) 413.

[82] Expression of Sankey J (as he then was) in *Ivor An Christensen v Furness Withy & Co* (1922) 12 Ll LR 288.

[83] This was the basis upon which the German Supreme Court founded its revalorisation doctrines: see para 9.28 (c) below, and see *Franklin v Westminster Bank Ltd* (1931) (CA) (reproduced in the Fifth Edition of this work, 561) *per* Lord Hanworth MR.

[84] *Franklin v Westminster Bank Ltd* (1931) (CA) (reproduced in the Fifth Edition of this work, 561) *per* Mackinnon J.

[85] *Seymour v Delancy* (1824) 3 Cowen (NY) 445.

[86] See paras 2.05–2.14 above.

forces; further, the unit of account may have varying significance for domestic and international purposes.

2.42   The unit of account may be fixed or "pegged" by reference to another standard of value; in the past, this was usually gold used either directly or, under the former Bretton Woods par value system, indirectly. Other currencies could also be used as the standard of value.[87] If the relationship between the currency and the standard of value is formally changed by governmental action, one speaks of a devaluation or a revaluation, depending on whether the currency is reduced or increased in value as against the standard measure.[88]

2.43   Far more frequently, the currency will be "floating", such that its external value is determined by the laws of supply and demand.[89] A "floating" currency cannot be devalued or revalued in the technical sense, because its external value depends on market forces rather than an officially prescribed standard of value. Where the external value of a floating currency moves upwards or downwards, it is more appropriate to speak of an appreciation or depreciation (as opposed to a revaluation or devaluation). Thus, a depreciation of the Italian lira did not trigger a contractual clause requiring the revision of payments in the event of an official devaluation.[90]

2.44   It should be appreciated that the values just described relate to international relationships and thus influence the rate of exchange, ie the price of one currency in terms of another. They do not necessarily affect the unit of account's domestic purchasing power. Thus when sterling was allowed to float on 23 June 1972, the external value of the currency fell but this did not immediately reduce

---

[87] On currency pegging arrangements generally, see Ch 33 below.

[88] In *Federal Maritime Commission v Australian/US Atlantic and Gulf Conference* (1972) 337 F Supp 1032, it was held (on 4 February 1972) that "the United States dollar has not been officially devalued, an action which can only be effected by Congress which has not acted". The report does not make it clear whether the court was made aware that, on 15 August 1971 the President, acting alone, had abrogated the convertibility of the dollar into gold. But it is quite possible that this did not bring about a devaluation in the technical sense.

[89] Governments or central banks may intervene in the financial markets by buying or selling their own currency. This may have an impact on the market value of the currency but it does not affect the validity of the general statement in the text.

[90] See Decision No. 173, of the Italian Corte di Cassazione, 8 January 1981 [1981] I Giur Ital i, 1450. On the other hand, see the Arbitration Award in *Philip Morris International Finance Corp v Overseas Private Investment Corp* [1988] Int LM 488: in 1970 the holder of shares in a company in the Dominican Republic took out insurance against the "inconvertibility" of his investment earnings. In 1982, an official and a free foreign exchange market developed and in 1984 the dividend could only be remitted at the inferior official rate. The claim for the difference was rejected on the ground that the Dominican currency had become devalued rather than inconvertible. However, the decisive question—the meaning to be attributed to "inconvertibility" in 1970 when the policy was issued—was not considered.

the internal value of the pound; it only became less when imports became more expensive and other developments reduced its domestic purchasing power.[91] Further, it seems that there is no necessary or direct connection between the domestic and the international values of the unit of account; in the late 1970s and the early 1980s, significant rates of inflation eroded the domestic value of the pound, yet its value in terms of the US dollar remained broadly stable.

Where a unit of account is devalued or depreciates, the rate of exchange with other currencies is modified, but none of these currencies can be said to be revalued or to appreciate. Conversely, where a unit of account is revalued or appreciates in relation to other currencies, none of the latter is devalued or depreciated. Their value in terms of the particular unit of account affected by the change differs, but their value amongst themselves and their domestic values remain the same. In other words, the difference is relative, rather than absolute.

2.45

This is one of the principal lessons taught by the *Young Loan Case* (*Belgium and others v Federal Republic of Germany*) which was decided by an independent arbitral tribunal in 1980.[92] The relevant clause, introduced by the London Agreement on German External Debts of 1953, provided that in the event of the rates of exchange of any of the nine currencies of issue altering after 1 August 1952 by more than 5 per cent the amounts due were to be recalculated "on the basis of the least depreciated currency". The French version referred to recalculation "sur la base de la devise la moins dépréciée", whilst the German text required it "auf der Grundlage der Währung mit der geringsten Abwertung". When the German mark was revalued in 1961 and 1969, the creditor governments demanded an adjustment on the ground that, while the German text referred to *devaluation* in the formal or official sense (*Abwertung*), the English and French texts merely referred to *depreciation*, ie mere reduction in value; as a result, the German mark should be treated as "the least depreciated currency" and the adjustment clause should thus be brought into effect. The majority of the Arbitral Tribunal rejected this contention, primarily because under the Bretton Woods system which was in force at the time of the 1953 Agreement, there

2.46

---

[91] In the context of an official devaluation, it may be apt to recall the words of the Prime Minister, Harold Wilson, at the time of the last official devaluation of sterling. On 18 November 1967, shortly after the pound had been devalued, he said: "From here on, the pound abroad is worth 14 per cent or so less in terms of other currencies. It does not mean that the pound here in Britain, in your pocket or purse or in your bank has been devalued . . .".

[92] 59 Int LR 494. The majority decision broadly accepted the oral arguments of Dr Mann. The case has been much discussed—see Bathurst (1980) Texas Int LJ 519; Gianviti [1980] *Annuaire Français de Droit International 250*; Gold [1981] IMF Staff Papers 411; Hahn [1983] Netherlands Yearbook of International Law 3; Seidl-Hohenveldern [1980] German Yearbook of International Law 401.

could be no depreciation beyond the permitted "spread" of 2 per cent unless that depreciation was also adopted as a formal devaluation;[93] therefore the English and the French texts should be construed so as to refer to a devaluation (ie the equivalent of the *Abwertung* referred to in the German text) even though the language of *depreciation* had actually been employed.[94] Moreover, even had this not been so, the revaluation of one currency does not involve the devaluation of another; the latter remains unchanged, even though the rate of exchange between it and the former currency changes, so that in a strictly relative sense it becomes less valuable.

2.47 It should, however, be made clear that the terms "devaluation" and "depreciation" are frequently used interchangeably. It will frequently be an important guide to remember that the fate of one unit of account does not directly affect any other unit of account: it is merely the relative value of one currency in terms of other currencies that changes, but the latter currencies do not change.[95] The point must nevertheless now be of diminishing importance. The system of par values has ceased to operate since the early 1970s. Consequently, in order to give effect to the intentions of the contracting parties, any modern contractual reference to "devaluation" of a currency would now have to be read as a reference to the depreciation of that currency in terms of another; the parties cannot be

---

[93] The need to distinguish between depreciation (*Abwertung*) and depreciation (*Entwertung*) is also emphasised in Nussbaum, *Money in the Law, National and International* (The Press Foundation, 2nd edn, 1950) 171.

[94] The award demonstrates the difficulties which may arise where an agreement has been concluded in a number of different languages. It also illustrates the importance of construing a contract with reference to the circumstances prevailing as at the date on which the contract was made, rather than as at the date of the proceedings.

[95] Whether a particular enactment or contract refers to revaluation to devaluation or both, and whether a revaluation or devaluation has in fact occurred should not normally cause any difficulty. Both questions arose in *Fratelli Zerbone v Amministrazione delle Finanze* [1978] ECR 99. Article 1(1) of Regulation 974/71 provided for the payment of monetary compensation amounts in respect of imports if "a Member State allows the exchange rate of its currency to fluctuate by a margin wider than the one permitted by international rules". Although the word "fluctuate" would appear to cover both upward and downward movements, it was generally accepted that only revaluations were contemplated (pp 121–2). The Court found that the par value of the lira had been established at 625 lire to the dollar and that, in December 1971, Italy had adopted a new "central rate" of 581.50 lire to the dollar; Italy had therefore accepted a rate of exchange higher than the par value plus the permitted fluctuation margin of 1%. Accordingly, there had been a revaluation and the monetary compensation amounts for imports could, in principle, be demanded. However, as pointed out by Sir Joseph Gold (27 (1980) *Staff Papers of the IMF* 622) it is very doubtful whether the Court correctly assessed the facts. It seems that the value of the lira was adjusted to 631.343 lire per US dollar in December 1971 (ie by an amount which did not exceed the permitted margin of 1%). Subsequently, under the Smithsonian Agreement the dollar was depreciated by 7.897%, with the result that the lira had appreciated by 7.48% against the dollar. But this fact should have taken the case outside Art 1(1) of the Regulation, for the Smithsonian Agreement should not have been regarded as "international rules" for that purpose—see the discussion of the Smithsonian Agreement at para 2.10 above.

taken to have referred to an official process of devaluation which no longer exists.

I. The Existence of Distinct Monetary Systems

The existence of a unit of account serves to distinguish it from predecessor units which have been used in the same territory.[96] That unit also serves to identify and to distinguish it in relation to other monetary systems. **2.48**

In most cases, this will be obvious; whatever their historical links may have been, it is impossible to suggest that the modern pound sterling and the modern US dollar share any characteristics which might make them a part of a common monetary system. Nevertheless, and whilst the point will arise only very rarely, it may be necessary to determine whether a country has established a unit of account and has thus created an independent monetary system, or whether it has adopted a currency in use in some other country. **2.49**

It is submitted that a unit of account and, consequently, an independent monetary system exists, if the currency rests upon the country's own and independently exercised law-making powers. There must be evidence that the relevant State has exercised its monetary sovereignty with a view to organising a monetary system. The State theory of money reappears in this context; only the State may define and organise a monetary system and a monetary system only exists if the State has exercised that power. The question whether a distinct monetary system existed arose in two types of case. **2.50**

The Latin Monetary Union between France, Belgium, Italy, Greece, and Switzerland was established in 1865.[97] These countries formed a convention "pour ce qui regarde le titre, le poids, le diamètre et le cours de leurs espèces monnayées d'or et d'argent". The moneys were legal tender as against the Treasuries of each country but not as between nationals of different countries. Legislation passed in the participating States was by no means uniform; matters such as the issue of the inconvertible money, the exactness of coinage and similar matters were all left at the discretion of individual States. It seemed clear therefore that in each participating country there existed a separate monetary system, and this was the result reached by the courts in cases connected with bonds issued by a Belgian company at a denomination of "500 francs" each. After the **2.51**

---

[96] This subject has already been discussed at para 2.34 above.

[97] As will be seen, the arrangements involved an international currency standard, rather than a monetary union in the modern sense of that term. Consequently, the subject is considered here, rather than in Part VI.

First World War, some of the bonds fell due for repayment and the company proposed to effect it by paying 500 francs of the Belgian currency in respect of each bond. A bondholder brought an action in the English courts, arguing that the bonds secured a payment of 500 *gold* francs.[98] In support of this contention, it was argued "that a number of countries had agreed upon the gold standard of the gold franc by various treaties from 1865 onwards, and that it must have been in the contemplation of the parties when the bargain which is contained in the bond was made that there should be repayment in that which he (counsel for the plaintiff) has from time to time lapsed into calling the international franc, but which he says he does not really mean to call the international franc". The court rightly dismissed the bondholder's claim, on the basis that the so-called international franc was nothing but "a standard which the different countries have agreed upon between themselves which their franc shall attain, and on condition that it attains that standard, it shall be freely interchangeable between the treasuries of the high participating parties". If currencies are interchangeable, then it must follow that they are not the same currency; in other words, each participating State retained its own separate national currency.[99]

2.52   Similar problems arose when considering the relationship between the monetary systems of the former colonial powers and their possessions overseas. The problem is now of historical interest,[100] but it remains instructive to consider those cases which have involved an investigation of the Australian monetary system.[101] By section 51(xii) of the Commonwealth of Australia Act 1900, Australia was

---

[98] See *Hopkins v Compagnie Internationale des Wagons-Lits* 26 January 1927. The decision is reproduced in the Fifth Edition of this work, 559.

[99] The same result was reached in similar cases in France and Germany—see Cass Civ 21 December 1932, S 1932 1, 390 and *Clunet* 1933, 1201; Berlin Court of Appeal, 25 September 1928, *JW* 1929, 446. Had there been a dispute as to whether "franc" referred to the Belgian, French or Swiss unit, this would have had to be determined by reference to the principles discussed in Ch 5 below.

[100] By way of examples, an arbitral award of 16 April 1964, Revue de Banque, 1965, 186 concluded that the Belgian franc and the franc issued by the Belgian Congo had to be treated as separate units of account. The Dutch courts likewise generally took the view that the Netherlands Indies guilder was a separate currency which was independent of the Dutch guilder, and that the sums expressed in terms of the Netherlands Indies guilder were converted into the local unit upon independence: Hoge Raad, 14 January 1955 [1957] Int LR 73; Court of Appeal of Amsterdam, 5 December 1951 [1951] Int LR 81; for a different view, see the decision of the Hoge Raad, 19 February 1954 [1954] Int LR 63, where the lower court regarded the Netherlands Indies guilder "as merely a local variant" of the Dutch unit.

[101] Similar cases also arose in South Africa. In 1912, it was held that the pound was the same unit in England, Rhodesia, and South Africa: *Joffe v African Life Assurance Society* (1933) South African LR (Transvaal Division) 187. By 1931, it was possible to hold that the English and South African pounds were distinct units of account: *Aktiebolaget Tratalja v Evelyn Haddon & Co Ltd* 1933 South African LR (Cape Provincial Division) 156. In similar vein, an Australian court was called upon to decide whether Australian notes were legal tender in New Guinea: *Jolly v Mainka* (1933) 7 ALJ 214.

given the power to make laws with regard to currency, coinage, and legal tender. Under the Australian Coinage Act 1909, "Australian coins" were issued on the basis of a standard weight and fineness identical with that laid down in the British Coinage Act of 1870, and were made legal tender side by side with British coins. Under the Australian Notes Act of 1910, the Governor-General was given power to authorise the issue of "Australian notes", which were declared to be legal tender throughout the Commonwealth and to be payable in gold coin at the Commonwealth Treasury.[102] As a result of the outbreak of the First World War, gold coins disappeared from circulation and notes issued under the 1910 Act were the only form of legal tender.[103] On this basis, it is suggested that Australia created an independent monetary system in 1909, when it began to issue its own coins.[104] This view is, however, in conflict with decisions of the House of Lords and the Privy Council which, in turn, differ from each other.

The decision of the House of Lords in *Adelaide Electric Supply Co v Prudential* **2.53** *Assurance Co*[105] involved a company incorporated in England but whose business was wholly conducted from Australia. In 1921, the shareholders passed a resolution to the effect that all dividends should be declared at meetings to be held in Australasia and should be paid in or from Adelaide or elsewhere in Australasia. The holders of certain £1 preference shares claimed that they were entitled to be paid their dividends in pounds sterling for the full nominal amount thereof, and not subject to deductions for Australian exchange. Reversing the courts below and overruling the Court of Appeal's decision in *Broken Hill Proprietary Co v Latham*,[106] the House of Lords held that the company had discharged its obligations by paying in Australian currency that which was in Australia legal tender for the nominal amount of the dividend warrants.[107] The decision was unanimous but the various judgments differ as to whether the Australian pound and the English pound should be treated as distinct monetary

---

[102] Although not stated, it must be implied in this legislation that a debt of "one pound" could henceforth be discharged by payment in Australian notes, ie the "recurrent link" was one-to-one.

[103] Bank of England notes never were legal tender in Australia.

[104] This is at variance with the submission of Dr Mann in the Fifth Edition of this work, 56, where it is suggested that such system came into being in 1900. But a monetary system does not exist merely because a State enjoys the sovereignty which is necessary to create it; it only comes into existence upon an exercise of that sovereignty. This is especially the case in the modern context, where legislation will be required to establish a central bank or other authority responsible for the conduct of monetary policy.

[105] [1934] AC 122. For an Australian decision to the effect that the English and Australian units were distinct, see *Re Tillam Boehme & Tickle Pty Ltd* (1932) Vict LR 146, 148. See also the High Court of Australia in *McDonald & Co v Wells* (1931) 45 CLR 506.

[106] [1933] Ch 373.

[107] This particular aspect of the case, and the decision in *Auckland Corp v Alliance Assurance Co Ltd* [1937] AC 587 is considered at n 110 below.

systems. Lord Atkin and Lord Tomlin expressed the view that the pound was the same unit in both countries in 1921.[108] Lord Warrington and Lord Russell of Killowen expressed the view that the pound was one and the same in both countries.[109] Only Lord Wright arrived at the opposite conclusion; it is thus necessary to review the basis of these differing opinions.[110]

2.54 The pith of Lord Tomlin's opinion lies in his conclusion, based upon a consideration of the Australian legislation, that:

> . . . there has never in fact been either in the United Kingdom or in Australia so far as I am aware any statute or Order in Council . . . expressly separating the money of account of the United Kingdom from the money of account of Australia or creating a distinct Australian unit. The Commonwealth of Australia created in 1900, was given full powers to make laws with respect to currency coinage and legal tender. It has in fact never affected expressly to alter the money of account or to set up a distinct Australian money of account . . . I ask myself, if there has been a change in the money of account, when did it take place and what caused it, and I find no answer . . .

2.55 Lord Tomlin thus did not merely base his conclusion on a factual appreciation of legislation in Australia; he also established and applied a legal test, namely, the "express" exercise of the law-making power for the purpose of setting up an Australian money of account distinct from the English unit.[111] To him, neither the mere existence of a law-making power over currency, nor its implied exercise by the incorporation of the English pound as an exogenous element, nor the conversion of English sterling debts into Australian pound debts impliedly permitted by the Australian Bank Notes Act 1910 was sufficient. As noted earlier, it is submitted that the mere existence of a sovereign power to establish a monetary

---

[108] See 135 (Lord Atkin) and 143 (Lord Tomlin). However, Lord Atkin also expressed the view that sterling and the Australian pound were separate units as at the date of judgment.

[109] This view apparently referred to the position as at the date of judgment—see 138 (Lord Warrington) and 148 (Lord Russell of Killowen).

[110] It may be added that, whichever opinion is to be preferred, the Privy Council was justified in holding that neither of them could in any way affect the meaning of the word "pound", neither of them being inconsistent with the view that "for the purpose of assessing an Australian taxpayer to income tax, under the Australian revenue legislation, it is necessary that his assessable income should be expressed in terms of Australian currency": *Payne v The Deputy Federal Commissioner of Taxation* [1936] AC 497, 509. In *Auckland Corp v Alliance Assurance Co Ltd* [1937] AC 587, the Privy Council refrained from expressing a view on the point considered in the text. A few remarks in Lord Wright's judgment—eg on the one hand, his reference to the "New Zealand currency" and "the sterling currency in England" and, on the other hand, his reference to the pound as the unit of account common to England and New Zealand, do not conclusively point in either direction. See also *De Bueger v Ballantyne & Co Ltd* [1938] AC 452 (PC).

[111] Notwithstanding the present writer's views on Knapp's use of the recurrent link as a means of defining the unit of account (see n 68 above), it must be admitted that Lord Tomlin's formulation implicitly seeks a recurrent link as a means of deciding whether Australia had in fact established an independent monetary system.

system does not equate to the actual creation of such a system and, to that extent, Lord Tomlin's formulation is correct. However, Australia moved to establish its own monetary system by virtue of the Australian Coinage Act of 1909 and the Australian Notes Act of the following year. As has been shown, these two Acts impliedly placed the Australian currency at par with the English unit, ie a recurrent link of one-to-one was established. It is submitted that the establishment of an independent monetary system should have been recognised with effect from 1909 and that, if an express exercise of monetary sovereignty was required, the two Acts of 1909 and 1910 were more than sufficient for that purpose.

On the other hand, Lord Wright traced the history of the Australian pound and **2.56** the development of exchange rates. He concluded that the two systems were distinct on the ground[112] that "this difference is inherent in the difference of the law-making authority at either place, as well as in the different commercial conditions prevailing". It is submitted that Lord Wright's conclusion that the two monetary systems were distinct was a correct one, but that he reached it on incorrect grounds; the mere existence of law-making authority did not suffice to create a separate monetary system but the 1909 and 1910 Acts were in fact sufficient to create such a system.[113]

Nevertheless, and although his reasoning was not shared by the other judges, **2.57** Lord Wright's emphasis upon the significance of the law-making power became the foundation of the opinion of the Privy Council in *Bonython v Common-wealth of Australia*.[114] In 1895, the Government of Queensland had issued debentures expressed in "pounds sterling" and which matured in 1945. The holder was entitled to payment in Brisbane, Sydney, Melbourne, or London, at his option. A holder exercised the London option and demanded payment in (English) sterling. There were various factors which suggested that the debt should be taken to be expressed in Australian currency; for example, the

---

[112] At 150. Similarly, Romer LJ in *Broken Hill Proprietary Co v Latham* [1933] Ch 373, 407, relied on the fact that "Australia had in 1920 its own currency system and every such system must be based on a standard unit of value".

[113] It should be repeated that Dr Mann expressed a different view on this subject—see the Fifth Edition of this work, 58–9. However, especially in the modern context, it would be difficult to argue that a State had created its own, independent monetary system if it had not in fact established a central bank and taken measures for the control of interest rates and related matters. These steps involve an actual exercise of monetary authority in the manner stated in the text. Amidst the confusion caused by the decisions considered in this section, it should be noted that the Australian courts themselves held that an independent monetary system came into existence in Australia in 1909—see *Goldsbrough Mort & Co v Hall* (1949) 78 CLR 1. This conclusion is consistent with the views noted in para 2.55 above. See also Dicey and Morris, *The Conflict of Laws* (13th edn, Sweet & Maxwell, 2001) para 36-037.

[114] [1950] AC 201.

debentures were governed by the laws of Queensland and there is a presumption that a government intends to issue debt in its own currency when it uses terminology which is apt to refer to its own monetary system. As a result it became necessary to consider whether the Australian pound existed as a distinct currency in 1895; the Privy Council held that Queensland did indeed have a separate currency at the time of the issue of the bonds, and that they were thus payable in Australian currency. Although it is not easy to follow the reasoning of Lord Simonds in all its details,[115] it is clear that he saw "the vital distinction between the two monetary systems in that they depend on different law-making powers"[116] and "that which was lawful money in the self-governing Colony of Queensland was lawful money by virtue of the law of Queensland" and "rested on the inherent law-making power of the Queensland legislature".[117] A monetary system was held to be characterised by the mere existence of a currency-making power. It may well be that English currency was lawful money in Queensland by virtue of the laws of Queensland, but, at least in the view of the present writer, that does not mean that Queensland had created an independent monetary system. Further, it must be said that the Privy Council decision in the *Bonython* case is inconsistent with the views of the majority in the *Adelaide* case and it is in any event doubtful whether Queensland could be said to have enjoyed any sufficient degree of monetary sovereignty as early as 1895.[118] Certainly, such monetary powers as Queensland then possessed were not exercisable independently, and it thus lacked the law-making authority which was a requirement even in the context of the less stringent formulation proposed by Lord Wright in *Adelaide*.[119]

2.58 By way of conclusion, it may be appropriate to note that, whilst the *Adelaide* and the *Bonython* cases propounded different tests for the identification of an independent monetary system, both cases nevertheless implicitly approved the State theory of money.

---

[115] For a fuller discussion, see Mann, "On the Meaning of the Pound in Contracts" (1952) 68 LQR 195.

[116] At 218.

[117] At 217.

[118] In *National Bank of Australasia Ltd v Scottish Union and National Insurance Ltd* [1952] AC 493, Lord Cohen observed (at 512) that the views of the majority in the *Adelaide* case were merely "some *obiter dicta* of certain of their Lordships". This view is untenable because the existence or otherwise of a distinct Australian monetary system was the determining factor in that case. On this decision, see Mann (1953) 69 LQR 18 and Morris (1953) 2 ICLQ 300.

[119] That Queensland lacked such power was a consequence of the Coinage Act 1870, read together with the Colonial Laws Validity Act 1865. The point is now of limited interest but it is discussed in the Fifth Edition of this work, 59–60.

PART II

THE PRIVATE LAW OF MONETARY OBLIGATIONS

INTRODUCTION

The present Part will consider a variety of questions which may arise in considering monetary obligations of a private character.[1] It will be obvious that this
involves a wide-ranging inquiry into both domestic and international questions,
and the choice of subject matter will inevitably be selective.[2]

Intro.2.01

Given that domestic and foreign monetary obligations are now in many respects
to be treated on the same footing,[3] it is no longer felt necessary to draw a sharp
distinction between the two forms of obligation.[4] As a result, this Part will
consider the rules which must be applied both in purely domestic contexts and
in those cases in which questions of private international law arise for
consideration.

Intro.2.02

Against that rather general background, Part II will consider:

Intro.2.03

(a) the character of a monetary obligation;
(b) the interpretation of a monetary obligation where there is some initial
uncertainty as to the money of account;
(c) the interpretation of a monetary obligation where the money of account
ceases to exist or is affected by territorial changes;
(d) the performance of a monetary obligation; and
(e) the impact of the commencement of legal proceedings upon monetary
obligations.

---

[1] For the position where monetary obligations arise as between States and are governed by
international law, see Ch 23 below.

[2] It may be added that the principle of nominalism is highly relevant in the field of private
monetary obligations, but it seemed more convenient to deal with that principle separately—see
Part III below.

[3] See the discussion of the Court of Appeal decision in *Camdex International Ltd v Bank of
Zambia (No. 3)* [1997] CLC 714 at para 1.61 above.

[4] This distinction was a feature of the Fifth Edition of this work which did, of course, pre-date
the *Camdex* decision.

3

THE CHARACTER OF MONETARY OBLIGATIONS

A. Introduction	3.01	B. The Character of a Monetary Obligation	3.03

A. Introduction

It has already been observed[1] that one of the most important functions of money is to serve as a general medium of exchange or payment. Money, where it is legal tender, serves as the means of fulfilling many obligations, whether compulsorily imposed or voluntarily contracted. Furthermore, in the context of almost any claim (contractual, tortious, or otherwise) the defendant must ultimately discharge his obligations by means of a *monetary* payment.[2]   **3.01**

With these general considerations in mind, it is necessary to attempt a formulation which defines a monetary obligation or which at least describes those characteristics which distinguish it from other forms of obligation.   **3.02**

B. The Character of a Monetary Obligation

Monetary obligations[3] primarily exist where the debtor is bound to pay a fixed, certain specific, or liquidated sum of money. This definition pre-supposes that   **3.03**

---

[1] See paras 1.35–1.36 and 1.54–1.59

[2] Note the central principle of the law of damages that the injured party is entitled to *restitutio in integrum*. This does not mean that the claimant is to be restored to his original position; it merely means that his loss is to be adequately and fully compensated by a payment of money. For a discussion of this principle in general terms, see McGregor, *Damages* (Sweet & Maxwell, 17th edn, 2003) paras 1-021–1-023.

[3] It should be emphasised that the text is principally concerned with liquidated obligations, including (a) debts in the classical sense (see *Webb v Stanton* (1882–3) 11 QBD 518); and (b)

money is to be paid in the sense of a medium of exchange or in a similar monetary context, for example, where a bank advances a loan to its customer.[4]

3.04 Monetary obligations of the type now under discussion exist principally where:

(a) a party incurs an obligation to pay a stated sum of money, for example, £100. Such an obligation remains a monetary obligation even though the parties may make more detailed provision as to its performance (for example, by requiring that payment be made in £20 notes, or by stipulating payment by way of credit to a particular bank account);[5]

(b) a party incurs an obligation to pay an unascertained—but ascertainable—sum of money, for example, where a party agrees to pay an amount equal to the closing price of a listed security on a specified date. This is a monetary obligation even though its amount is uncertain as at the date on which the obligation is incurred, for the amount will have been ascertained by the date on which the obligation falls due for performance; or

(c) a party incurs an obligation to pay damages as a result of a breach of a non-contractual obligation in a contract, or as a result of a breach of a non-monetary obligation. Damages involve a duty to pay money, and the resulting obligation is therefore a monetary one. The monetary character of the obligation is in no way impaired by the fact that it is unliquidated or unascertained. It is true that the debtor, though bound to pay, cannot be said to be indebted to the creditor until the amount of the compensation is agreed or settled by the court. It is likewise true that, as a result of those characteristics, the debtor cannot tender payment and many rules relating to "debts" cannot be applied.[6] But these distinctions between debt and damages should not be allowed to overshadow the fact that, in both cases, sums of money are to be paid, that in both cases alike, the court has power to award interest for the whole or any part of the period between the date when the cause of action arose and the date of judgment, and that, in any event, the meaning of the word "debt" depends on the context and that there is therefore justification for uniting both under the heading of monetary obligations.

---

executory obligations of a monetary character, such as an obligation to pay the price of goods not yet delivered. The monetary position of unliquidated claims is considered in Ch 10 below.

[4] This is plainly a monetary transaction even though, in such a context, money is being advanced by way of a loan; it is not being used as a medium of exchange. The point was made by Phillips MR in *Camdex International Ltd v Bank of Zambia (No. 3)* [1997] CLC 714.

[5] Where a contract provided that the obligation had to be settled in gold coin, the essential monetary character of the obligation was not affected. See the discussion on these clauses at para 11.05 below.

[6] eg, a "debt" can form the subject matter of a garnishee order, whilst an unliquidated obligation may not.

Obligations of this kind are of a monetary character not only because they **3.05** necessarily involve a payment of money but also because they may be satisfied through any form of money which constitutes legal tender in the currency concerned—there is no obligation on the debtor to tender any specific notes, for money is entirely fungible in this sense. If the pound sterling ceased to exist as a currency, then the theory of the "recurrent link"[7] will practically always provide for the conversion of the promised sum expressed in the extinct currency into a corresponding sum of money in the new currency. These considerations lead to a conclusion which is fundamental to the law of money; so far as English law is concerned[8] a monetary obligation cannot become impossible to perform— whether expressed in sterling or a foreign currency.[9] Circumstances peculiar to the debtor, such as his poverty,[10] his ongoing attempts to negotiate an overall restructuring of his indebtedness,[11] his inability to raise the anticipated financing for the transaction[12] or the inability to access the intended source of funds[13] will not relieve the debtor of his monetary obligation. Likewise, the depreciation

---

[7] On the recurrent link as part of the *lex monetae*, see para 2.34 above.

[8] No doubt the same view would apply under most systems of law. In relation to German law, eg, see Grothe in *Kommentar zum Bürgerlichen Gesetzbuch* Bamberger & Roth (eds) (Munich, 2003) Vol 1, paras 1–610, s 244 BGB para 12.

[9] Of course, specific legislation could render payment unlawful; the present discussion is directed to other types of circumstance which may render performance impossible. It is sometimes said that a monetary obligation cannot be frustrated, but this is not quite an accurate statement, for the doctrine of frustration acts upon the contract as a whole rather than upon individual obligations comprised within it. It would be more correct to say that, in the absence of legislation which renders payment unlawful, changes affecting the monetary obligations under a contract generally provide the source of a frustrating event. That monetary obligations are capable of frustration in this sense was noted in *Libyan Arab Foreign Bank v Bankers Trust Co* [1989] QB 728.

[10] See, eg, *Universal Corp v Five Ways Properties Ltd* [1978] 3 All ER 1131. The New York courts have confirmed that economic hardship does not excuse performance of a financial obligation, even if the debtor is thereby rendered insolvent—*Bank of America NT & SA v Envases Venezolanes* (1990) 740 F Supp 260, affirmed (1990) 923 F 2d 843. One may compare the position of a seller of goods by description; he is obliged to deliver goods of that description, even though (without fault of the seller) his source of supply has disappeared—see *Intertradex SA v Lesieur-Torteaux SARL* [1978] 2 Lloyd's Rep 509 (CA).

[11] That the existence of such negotiations cannot prevent the creditor from obtaining judgment has been emphasised in a series of recent cases decided in New York in cases involving sovereign debtors. See, eg, *Elliott Associates v Republic of Panama* (1995) 975 F Supp 332 (SDNY); *Pravin Banker Associates Ltd v Banco Popular del Peru* (1997) 109 F 3d 850 (2nd Cir), affirming (1995) 895 F Supp 660 (SDNY); *Elliot Associates v Banco de la Nacion and Republic of Peru* (1999) 194 F 3d 363, reversing (1998) 12 F Supp 2d 328 (SDNY). The same principle has been affirmed by the English courts, although the sovereign status of the debtor and its overall debt restructuring efforts have been taken into account in determining the remedies which should be made available to the creditor by way of execution. See *Camdex International Ltd v Bank of Zambia (No. 2)* [1977] 1 All ER 728. These cases are discussed by Proctor, "Sovereign Debt Restructuring and the Courts—Some Recent Developments" (2003) 8 JIBFL 302, (2003) 9 JIBFL 351, and (2003) 10 JIBFL 379.

[12] *British and Commonwealth Holdings plc v Quadrex Holdings Inc* [1989] QB 842 (CA).

[13] *Congimex SARL (Lisbon) v Continental Grain Export Corp (New York)* [1979] 2 Lloyd's Rep 346 (CA) and *Paczy v Haendler & Natermann GmbH* [1987] 1 Lloyd's Rep 302 (CA).

of the market value of the money of account as against other currencies will only in extreme circumstances result in the application of the doctrine of frustration under English law.[14] Changes in the monetary system, such as the emergence of a new currency, the elimination of protective clauses, or the introduction of exchange control do not release the debtor from a monetary obligation governed by English law.

3.06 In other words, the performance of a monetary obligation cannot ever become objectively impossible of performance, for money is always and everywhere in existence and available. Equally, circumstances peculiar to the debtor personally cannot excuse performance, for in law everyone is responsible for his or her own solvency.[15] Even a legally imposed moratorium can only delay payment (rather than render it impossible), for a law purporting to reduce, discharge, or delay the debt can only have effect if that law forms a part of the law applicable to the debt.[16]

3.07 Monetary obligations have other distinct characteristics. For example, interest has been defined as payment by time for the use of money. It follows that interest can only be awarded or calculated once a monetary obligation has come into existence. In similar vein, the principle of nominalism[17] uniquely applies to obligations of a monetary character and can have no relevance in other contexts.

3.08 It follows from this discussion that a monetary obligation is an obligation (a) whose subject matter is the payment of money (whether fixed at the outset or subsequently ascertained prior to the date on which performance is due), (b) which cannot become impossible to perform, (c) which is capable of bearing interest, and (d) to which the principle of nominalism is capable of application.[18] In some respects, it is perhaps unappealing to define a monetary obligation by reference to its *consequences* but this perhaps serves to emphasise the main characteristics of such an obligation; it is difficult to develop an alternative formulation for these purposes.

---

[14] See *Larrinaga & Co Ltd v Société Franco Américaine de Medulla* (1923) 129 LT 65.

[15] In the context of insolvency laws generally, it may be observed that the application of "clawback" and similar provisions is denied in cases where the finality of payments is necessary to avoid systemic risk in the financial markets. The point is not directly relevant to the present work, but on the subject generally, see the Settlement Finality Directive (981/26/EC) as implemented in the UK by the Financial Markets and Insolvency (Settlement Finality) Regulations 1999 SI 1999/ 2979; for a discussion of these rules, see Pitt, "Improving the legal basis for settlement finality" (2003) 9 JIBFL 341.

[16] In the case of a contractual obligation, see Rome Convention, Art 10(1)(a). The subject is considered in Ch 4 below.

[17] On this principle see, generally, Part III below.

[18] The corresponding formulation in the Fifth Edition of this work (p 74) was cited with apparent approval in *Eagle Trust plc v KPMG Peat Marwick McLintock* (23 March 1995).

It should be appreciated that the above reasoning applies only where money is **3.09** being used as a means of exchange or in some other monetary fashion which necessarily imports the fungible character of money. This statement can be tested by considering those very rare occasions on which notes or coins may be delivered as a commodity, rather than as money.[19] Thus, an obligation to deliver a *specific* coin which has acquired a rarity value is not a monetary obligation, for the coin is being purchased as a commodity, and not as money.[20] Consequently, an obligation of this kind could become impossible to perform if the coin were lost or destroyed. Likewise, an obligation to deliver a specific quantity of gold (or any other commodity) having a specific monetary value is not a monetary obligation, because the obligation is one of delivery, not of payment.[21] A failure to perform delivery obligations of this kind would merely confer upon the injured party a right to claim damages representing the cost of acquiring equivalent items (or commodities) from a third party; but the failure would not give rise to a liquidated claim.

Thus far, the discussion has focused on the hallmarks of an obligation to pay **3.10** money. But it is appropriate to note that a monetary obligation—although in some respects distinctive—shares the attributes of many other types of obligation. For example, it must be interpreted and performed; the subject matter (including the currency in which it is expressed) must be identified; the obligation may be discharged in certain cases; and the creditor must be entitled to recompense in the event of late performance. It thus becomes necessary to ask which system of law governs all of these questions? In a purely domestic context involving local parties, an obligation governed by local law and an obligation expressed and payable in the national currency, it is plain that a single system of law will usually govern all of the issues just outlined. But in a cross-border situation involving one or more overseas parties, a contract governed by a

---

[19] That money will only now very rarely be held to be delivered as a commodity follows from the decision in *Camdex International Ltd v Bank of Zambia (No 3)* [1997] CLC 714. This point has already been discussed at para 1.43 above.

[20] See the discussion of *Moss v Hancock* [1899] 2 QB 111, at para 1.10 above.

[21] A quantity of gold would not generally be "money" for a number of reasons, eg because it is not denominated by reference to a unit of account established by the State. However, the US Supreme Court, held to the contrary in *Holyoke Water Power Co v American Writing Co* (1936) 300 US 324. The result was that an obligation to deliver gold was found to be "an obligation payable in money of the United States", and the obligation was thus avoided by the Joint Resolution of Congress of 5 June 1933, on which see para 12.16 below. Given the quoted wording of the Resolution, its terms should apply where gold was to be used for the purpose of stabilising the value of the dollar, but not where gold was acquired for manufacture or for artistic or other (non-monetary) purposes; on this point, see *Emery Bird Thayer Dry Goods Co v Williams* (1939) 107 F 2d 965.

foreign system of law or a contract involving a foreign currency, matters clearly become more complex; different systems of law may govern different aspects of the contract or its performance. All these subjects will be considered in the ensuing chapters of this Part.[22]

---

[22] Conflict of law questions are discussed specifically in Ch 4 below, whilst the following chapters will draw upon the principles there established.

4

MONETARY OBLIGATIONS AND THE CONFLICT OF LAWS

A. Introduction

Before moving to a detailed consideration of the interpretation and performance **4.01** of monetary obligations, it is appropriate to reflect upon the system of law which will govern the solution to the various problems and difficulties which may arise in this area.

It should be said at the outset that this text is not intended to provide a detailed **4.02** review of questions of private international law; apart from other considerations, there are many other texts which already fulfil that function. Nevertheless, countless cross-border financial transactions occur on a daily basis, and a brief discussion of the essential private international law framework is thus felt to be necessary.

It should be appreciated that a system of private international law exists in order **4.03** to resolve the difficulties which may arise where different systems of law may have a bearing upon the same issue.[1] Consequently, the points noted in the

---

[1] The point is explicitly made in Art 1(1) of the Rome Convention on the Law Applicable to Contractual Obligations. In a contractual context, such a system is also designed to ensure that the original intentions of the parties are respected, subject to the mandatory rules and public policy of the jurisdiction in which the proceedings occur. This point will become apparent as the present discussion is developed.

present chapter would have no application in the context of monetary obligations of a purely domestic character—for example, where a British bank, acting through its London branch, agrees to make a sterling loan available to a company incorporated in England. Such an arrangement involves only one system of law, and no question of a conflict will thus arise; English domestic law will be applied as a matter of course. Inevitably, however, matters become more complex when a transaction involves the laws of two or more jurisdictions.

4.04 Against that brief introductory background, it is proposed to examine the impact which the laws of various jurisdictions may have upon a monetary obligation. In particular, it will be necessary to consider the following:

(a) the law applicable to the contract;
(b) the law of the place of performance;
(c) the law of the countries in which the parties are established;
(d) the law of the State in which legal proceedings arise with respect to that monetary obligation; and
(e) the law of third countries with which the monetary obligation may have some connection.

4.05 It may be noted that every State is entitled to establish its own system of private international law for the purpose of resolving conflict questions; public international law does not generally appear to prescribe any particular standards or rules with which such a system must comply. Yet, in spite of this apparent flexibility, there is a considerable degree of uniformity amongst the systems which have emerged. Common law jurisdictions naturally tended to evolve similar rules in this area. The Member States of the European Community adopted a uniform code on the conflict rules applicable in a contractual context, and that code in turn reflects principles which had been developed in England and in civil law countries. For convenience, it is proposed to work by reference to the Rome Convention on the Law Applicable to Contractual Obligations (hereafter, the Rome Convention), but it should not be thought that these general principles are confined to a European context. The Rome Convention has had effect in the United Kingdom since 1 April 1991[2] and—apart from the

---

[2] By virtue of the Contracts (Applicable Law) Act 1990 (Commencement No. 1) Order 1991, SI 1991/707. For the background on the Convention see Plender and Wilderspin, *The European Contracts Convention* (Sweet & Maxwell, 2nd edn, 2001) ch 1. In passing, it may be added that the Rome Convention came into effect in the year in which the Fifth Edition of this book was published, and it is thus unsurprising that Dr Mann did not refer to it in detail. His views on the Convention are tolerably clear from remarks contained in the (1983) 32 ICLQ 265, where he describes it as "one of the most unnecessary, useless and indeed unfortunate attempts at unification or harmonisation of the law that has ever been undertaken". He was by no means alone in this view (although few expressed it with such clarity), but the Convention is now well established in English law, and the passage of time renders it unnecessary to pursue that particular debate.

very occasional dispute which may still arise under contracts entered into before that date—the Convention will thus now apply to all contractual conflict cases which fall within its scope.[3] Reference will also be made to the Giuliano-Largarde Report on the Convention, which contains a detailed commentary on the terms of the Convention and its background. The Report may be taken into account by an English court when seeking to interpret the Convention.[4]

B. The Applicable Law

It has been observed that no contract can exist in a vacuum; it must subsist against the background of a legal system which clothes the arrangement with some meaning and effect.[5] It is necessary to ask at the outset how the relevant legal system is to be identified. The problem can only arise in cases involving a cross-border element,[6] but when it does arise, the question can be one of some difficulty. How is it to be resolved?   **4.06**

In the first instance, Article 3(1) of the Rome Convention reflects the principle of party autonomy and allows the parties the freedom to select the system of law which is to govern their agreement. It provides that: **4.07**

> A contract shall be governed by the law chosen by the parties. The choice must be express or demonstrated with reasonable certainty by the terms of the contract or by the circumstances of the case. By their choice, the parties can select the law applicable to the whole or a part only of the contract.

This provision is clear and it is not proposed to discuss it in depth, although it will be necessary to return to the concept of a "split" governing the law in the   **4.08**

---

[3] In this context, it should be mentioned that a number of issues are excluded from the scope of the Rome Convention. In relation to monetary obligations, it should be noted that questions arising under bills of exchange and promissory notes are excluded from the Convention, to the extent to which those questions arise from the negotiable character of such instruments—see Art 1(2)(c) of the Convention. Other conflict of laws issues relating to such instruments would continue to be governed by the Bills of Exchange Act 1882, s 72. It may be noted in passing that the EC Commission has proposed that the Convention should be replaced by a Regulation—see COM (2002) 654 (final), 14 January 2003. On the general subject, see Max Planck Institute for Foreign and Private International Law: *Comments of the European Commission's Green Paper on the Conversion of the Rome Convention of 1980 on the law applicable to contractual obligations into a Community instrument and its modernisation* (*RabelZ*, 2004) 1–118.

[4] Contracts (Applicable Law) Act 1990, s 3(3)(a). The Report is printed in [1980] OJ C282/1, and is reproduced in Plender and Wilderspin (n 2 above) 302.

[5] See *Amin Rasheed Shipping Corp v Kuwait Insurance Co* [1984] AC 50 (HL).

[6] The point is acknowledged by Art 1 of the Rome Convention, which states that it is to apply "to contractual obligations in any situation involving a choice between the laws of different countries".

context of the *lex monetae* principle.[7] For present purposes, it is sufficient to note that the first sentence of Article 3(1) is expressed in mandatory terms. Consequently, the parties' choice of law must be respected even if it has no connection with the contractual situation as a whole.[8]

4.09 Matters become rather complex where the applicable law cannot be identified in accordance with Article 3 of the Convention. In such event, Article 4 begins with the simple formulation that "the contract shall be governed by the law of the country with which it is most closely connected";[9] once again, by way of exception, the Article allows that "a severable part of the contract which has a closer connection with another country may by way of exception be governed by the law of that other country". The remainder of Article 4 then sets out a series of presumptions and other provisions which are designed to assist the court in applying the "closest connection" test, as follows:

(1) Article 4(2) creates a rebuttable presumption to the effect that:

> . . . the contract is mostly connected with the country where the party who is to effect the performance which is characteristic of the contract has, at the time of conclusion of the contract, his habitual residence or, in the case of a body corporate or unincorporate, its central administration. However, if the contract is entered into in the course of that party's trade or profession, that country shall be the country in which the principal place of business is situate or, where under the terms of the contract the performance is to be effected through a place of business other than the principal place of business, the country in which that other place of business is situated . . .

(2) Article 4(5) confirms the rebuttable nature of the presumption by stating that it will not apply if the "characteristic performance" cannot be ascertained or if it appears from the circumstances as a whole that the contract is more closely connected with another country.[10]

---

[7] For general discussions of Art 3, see Dicey and Morris, *The Conflict of Laws* (Sweet & Maxwell, 13th edn, 2000) para 32R-059; Plender and Wilderspin, *The European Contracts Convention* (Sweet & Maxwell, 2nd edn, 2001) ch 5. For a consideration of some of the difficulties which may arise when the parties agree to apply different systems of law to different aspects of the contract, see McLachlan, "Splitting the Proper Law in Private International Law" [1990] BYIL 311.

[8] See *Vita Food Products Inc v Unus Shipping Ltd* [1939] AC 277; Dicey and Morris, (n 7 above) para 32-063. See also the ICSID Award (para 94) in *Aucoveri v Venezuela* (Arb 00/5 Award dated 23 September 2003).

[9] Article 4(1) of the Convention. That Article continues the theme of the "split" proper law, by stating that "a severable part of the contract which has a closer connection with another country may by way of exception be governed by the law of that other country". Article 4(1) is considered by Dicey and Morris (n 7 above) para 32R-105. For a discussion of alternative approaches to the application of Art 4, see Atrill, "Choice of Law in Contract: The Missing Pieces to the Article 4 Jigsaw?" (2003) 53 ICLQ 549.

[10] It may be added that Art 4(3) and (4) create additional presumptions dealing specifically with contracts relating to real estate and the carriage of goods. It is not necessary to deal with those presumptions in the present context.

In the light of these provisions, it is necessary to ask—what is the role of money   **4.10**
or monetary obligations in helping to identify the law which is to govern a
contract? In the application of the presumption created by Article 4(2), can the
obligation to pay money constitute the "characteristic performance" of a contract? A moment's reflection will reveal that this cannot generally be so. Nearly
every contract will involve a monetary obligation of some kind, and an obligation which is common to all contracts can scarcely be said to "characterise"
individual contracts, or to provide them with their distinctive quality.[11] It
follows that it will usually be the party which is to provide goods or services
whose obligations will be "characteristic" of the contract. To this extent, it may
be said that monetary obligations will generally play a limited role in the identification of the law applicable to the contract as a whole. The obligations of the
creditor may characterise the contract, but those of the *debtor* will not. For the
same reasons, the currency in which a monetary obligation is expressed will not
generally lead to the conclusion that the contract as a whole is governed by the
law of the country which issues that currency.[12]

It is necessary to enter one important reservation to the points which have been   **4.11**
noted above. The first sentence of Article 3(1) of the Convention provides that
"by their choice the parties can select the law applicable to the whole or a part
only of the contract". In accordance with the earlier provisions of that Article,
such choice "must be express or demonstrated with reasonable certainty by the
terms of the contract or the circumstances of the case". Article 4(1) likewise
allows that "a severable part of the contract which has a closer connection with
another country may by way of exception be governed by the law of that
country". Thus, a contract governed by English law may select "dollars" as the
medium of payment. English law must therefore determine whether the parties
intended to refer to US dollars, Canadian dollars, Australian dollars or some
other unit of that name, for questions of interpretation will be governed by the

---

[11] This position is confirmed by the Giuliano-Lagarde Report In its commentary on
Article 4(2), the Report notes that a monetary obligation "is not, of course, the characteristic
performance of the contract. It is the performance for which the payment is due, *i.e.* depending
on the type of contract, the delivery of goods, the granting of the right to make use of an item of
property, the provision of a service, transport, insurance, banking operations, security etc which
usually constitutes the centre of gravity and the socio-economic function of the contractual
transaction."

[12] Thus, where a German publisher entered into a contract with a foreign author, the contract
was found to be governed by German law even though the author's fees were payable in a foreign
currency—BGH, 22 November 1955, 19 *BGHZ* 110. In the pre-Rome Convention era, the
money of account in which an obligation was expressed might occasionally lead to the conclusion
that, in the absence of an express choice of law, the parties intended their contract to be governed
by the law of the issuing country—see, eg, *The Assunzione* [1952] P 150 (CA); *Rossano v
Manufacturers Life Insurance Co* [1963] 2 QB 352. These authorities can no longer stand in the
light of the express provisions of Art 4 of the Rome Convention.

law applicable to the contract as a whole.[13] But if it is found that the parties intended to refer to US dollars, how can the court proceed from there? English law does not itself define the US dollar or any other foreign currency. Instead, the reference must be made to the federal law of the United States for that purpose. This is the foundation of the *lex monetae* principle, the consequences of which will be discussed in more detail elsewhere.[14] For present purposes, it is sufficient to note that the application of the *lex monetae* principle within a contractual matrix must now be taken to rest upon the application of the "exception" language in Article 3(1) or Article 4(1) (as the case requires) of the Rome Convention. This may be regarded as an illustration of *depécage*, or the entitlement of contracting parties to select the law applicable to their entire contract, or to different parts of it.[15] The point will only rarely arise in a practical context, if only because it will rarely be disputed; yet it must be noted, for it is suggested that the long-established rules of monetary law must now be applied in a manner which is consistent with the terms of the Rome Convention.

4.12   For the present, it is necessary to leave aside specific questions touching the identification of the applicable law[16] and to proceed on the basis that the governing law has been identified. The law applicable to a contract governs a broad spectrum of contractual issues, including the following:

(a)   the material validity of the contract;[17]

(b)   the formal validity of the contract;[18]

(c)   the interpretation of the contract;[19]

---

[13] On the type of problem identified in the text, see the discussion on "initial uncertainty" in Ch 5 below.

[14] See in particular, Ch 13 below.

[15] See Plender and Wilderspin, *The European Contracts Convention* (Sweet & Maxwell, 2nd edn, 2001) paras 5-1 and 11-07, where it is rightly stated that it would be "wholly unreasonable to take the view that Article 10(1)(a) compels recourse to the applicable law, to the exclusion of the law of the money of account".

[16] There is, inevitably, a growing body of case law on this subject—see Dicey and Morris, *The Conflict of Laws* (Sweet & Maxwell, 13th edn, 2000) paras 32R-059–32-101; Plender and Wilderspin, (n 15 above) chs 5 and 6.

[17] Article 8(1), Rome Convention. The term "material validity" includes the very existence of a contract, whether it is void for mistake or illegality, whether it is voidable on the grounds of misrepresentation and similar matters. On these subjects, see Dicey and Morris (n 16 above) paras 32-151–32-170; and Plender and Wilderspin (n 15 above) paras 10-01–10-08.

[18] Article 9(1), Rome Convention. Requirements as to formal validity may include any rule that particular contracts must be reduced to writing. It must be said that the applicable law is a basis, but not the sole basis, upon which formal validity may be judged. On these points, see Dicey and Morris (n 16 above) paras 32-173–32-183 and Plender and Wilderspin (n 15 above) paras 10-09–10-12.

[19] Article 10(1)(a), Rome Convention. Questions concerning the interpretation of monetary obligations will be discussed in detail in Ch 5 below.

(d) the performance of the contract, save that the law of the place of performance may be taken into account in the context of the mode of performance and the steps to be taken in the event of defective performance;[20]

(e) the consequences of a breach of contract, including the assessment of damages, in so far as this process is governed by rules of law;[21]

(f) the various ways of extinguishing obligations and prescription and limitation of actions;[22] and

(g) the consequences of the nullity of the contract.[23]

In broad terms, it is entirely appropriate that the applicable law should govern the matters just described. If the parties have chosen to contract by reference to the law of a particular country, then it is natural that those laws should govern the essential validity and meaning of their bargain, and prescribe the general consequences of non-performance.[24] Thus, if a contract governed by English law requires the payment of an amount in US dollars in London, the federal law of the United States will define the currency in which the obligation is expressed and is to be performed, but that will be the limit of such laws in the context of the dispute; all other substantive questions will fall to be governed by English law.[25] Consequently, whilst the *lex monetae* will be a frequently recurring topic of discussion in this book, it is necessary to retain a sense of proportion; the *lex*

4.13

---

[20] Article 10(1)(b), read together with 10(2), Rome Convention. Once again, questions touching the performance of monetary obligations will be considered in Ch 7 below. For present purposes, it may be sufficient to note that the laws of one country cannot generally discharge monetary obligations arising under a different system of law. The House of Lords has recently had occasion to remark that an English court order cannot discharge a debt governed by Hong Kong law—see *Société Eram Shipping Co Ltd v Hong Kong and Shanghai Banking Corp Ltd* [2003] UKHL 30. For earlier cases and discussion of the subject generally see Dicey and Morris, *The Conflict of Laws* (Sweet & Maxwell, 13th edn, 2000) paras 32-191–32-197.

[21] Article 10(1)(c), Rome Convention. The qualification at the end of Art 10(1)(c) means that questions touching the recoverable heads of damage and remoteness are governed by the applicable law, whilst the qualifications of those damages is governed by the procedural rules of the forum court—see *J D'Almeida Araujo Ltd v Sir F Becker & Co* [1953] 2 All ER 288. It seems that the Private International Law (Miscellaneous Provisions) Act 1995 adopts a similar rule in the context of the law of tort—see *Edmunds v Simmons* [2001] 1 WLR 1003.

[22] Article 10(1)(d), Rome Convention. Whether or not a debt has been discharged by some means other than payment must therefore likewise be determined by the governing law and generally speaking, no other system of law can have any influence upon the question. The Privy Council recently had occasion to consider this point in the context of a contract governed by the laws of Bangladesh—see *Wright v Eckhardt Marine GmbH* 14 May 2003 (Appeal 13 of 2002). For earlier cases, and a general discussion on the subject, see Dicey and Morris, *The Conflict of Laws* (Sweet & Maxwell, 13th edn, 2000) paras 32-201–32-206.

[23] Article 10(1)(e), Rome Convention. This provision deals with claims of a restitutionary or quasi-contractual character. The provision is mentioned for completeness but it does not apply to the UK—Art 22, Rome Convention and the Contracts (Applicable Law) Act 1990, s 2(2).

[24] See the remarks of Lord Wilberforce in the *Amin Rasheed* case, n 5 above.

[25] This is one of the consequences of the decision in *Libyan Arab Foreign Bank v Bankers Trust Co* [1989] QB 728, which will be considered in more detail in Ch 7 below.

monetae defines the monetary unit in which an obligation is expressed or is to be performed, but the applicable law will generally define the amount of the obligation, the date on which it is to be performed and the consequences of non-performance. The scope of the *lex monetae* is thus limited to that extent.[26]

C. The Law of the Place of Performance

4.14   In the previous section, it was noted that questions touching the substantive performance of monetary obligations will be governed by the law applicable to the contract as a whole. However, Article 10(2) of the Rome Convention provides: "In relation to the manner of performance and the steps to be taken in the event of defective performance regard shall be had to the law of the country in which performance takes place . . .".

4.15   In the context of a monetary obligation, this provision detracts from the all-embracing dominance of the applicable law; inevitably, there will be marginal areas in which the applicable law and the law of the place of performance will compete and conflict with each other. The point may be of some importance, especially where a monetary obligation is required to be performed in a country other than its State of issue. How are such difficulties to be resolved? A series of points may be made in this context:

(1)   The applicable law remains the primary determinant of questions which arise in the field of performance. This point is emphasised by the language of Article 10(1) which stipulates that the law applicable to a contract "*shall govern . . . performance*".

(2)   In contrast, Article 10(2) provides a role for the law of the place of performance, but—at least in the context of a monetary obligation—the role appears to be a very limited one. First of all, the law of that place only has a role in the context of the *manner* of performance—an expression which itself tends to reaffirm the dominance of the applicable law in the context of matters of performance. Even then, Article 10(2) does not require that such law *must* be applied in relation to the mode of performance—it merely requires that "regard shall be had" to that law. As the Guiliano-Lagarde Report states in its commentary on Article 10(2), this means that "the court may consider whether such law has any relevance to the manner

---

[26]   There is an argument to the effect that Art 7(1) of the Rome Convention may have extended the sphere of influence of the *lex monetae* in certain respects, although it should be appreciated that this particular provision does not apply in England. The point is considered at para 4.24 below. The recent introduction of the euro led some commentators to suggest that the *lex monetae* principle should be interpreted more broadly than was previously the case. The point is discussed at para 4.25 below.

in which the contract should be performed and has a discretion whether to apply it in whole or in part so as to do justice between the parties". It is suggested that this analysis is plainly right, and serves as further confirmation of the limited role of the law of the place of performance. That law may be entirely disregarded if its application is unnecessary to achieve justice between the parties.

(3) The scope of Article 10(2) is yet further limited by the Guiliano-Lagarde Report, which suggests that the term "manner of performance" should be construed according to the laws of the country in which the proceedings take place,[27] but should in particular be taken to refer to matters such as the rules governing public holidays. This point may be relevant in the context of monetary obligations,[28] but again this tends to emphasise the limited relevance of the law of the place of performance in the present context.

The diminished relevance of the law of the place of performance in the context **4.16** of monetary obligations will be something of a recurrent theme—it will receive particular attention in the context of exchange controls.[29]

D. The Law of the Countries in which the Parties are Established

The preceding sections have explained the essential dominance of the applicable **4.17** law in the field of monetary obligations. But, in a conflict of laws situation, multiple jurisdictions are necessarily involved, and it is necessary to consider whether the laws of any of those other jurisdictions may have any impact upon monetary obligations.

In a sense, the dominance of the applicable law almost answers this question by **4.18** itself. It is thus unsurprising that the law of the place of the parties' residence or establishment is of limited consequence.

---

[27] This seems to be at odds with the notion that, as a harmonising measure, the Convention should be uniformly interpreted throughout all Member States—see Dicey and Morris, *The Conflict of Laws* (Sweet & Maxwell, 13th edn, 2000) para 32-194. For a different view, see Plender and Wilderspin, *The European Contracts Convention* (Sweet & Maxwell, 2nd edn, 2001) para 11-10.

[28] eg in determining whether a payment due to be made on a bank holiday should instead be made on the day before or the day after such holiday. If, however, the point is dealt with in the contract itself, then this would prevail over the law of the place of performance.

[29] See Ch 16 below. It may be added that regardless of Art 10(2), English contract law itself assigns a particular status and significance to the law of the place of performance. This arises principally from the Court of Appeal decision in *Ralli Bros v Compania Naviera Sota y Aznar* [1970] 2 KB 287. This topic is discussed at para 16.38 below, where it is suggested that a fresh approach is required.

4.19   It is true that the capacity of an individual to enter into a contract may be determined by the law of his country of domicile[30] and the corporate capacity of a legal entity will generally be governed by the law of the place of incorporation.[31] Questions of this kind may be of importance in determining whether a monetary obligation has been validly incurred in the first instance but will not subsequently have any impact upon the character or scope of such an obligation.[32] Thus, for example, a breach of exchange control regulations in a borrower's home jurisdiction will not usually afford a defence to an action in England under a loan contract governed by English law, for exchange control regulations do not affect individual or corporate capacity.[33]

E. The Law of the Forum State

4.20   It has already been noted that the law applicable to a contract will govern the majority of the key areas of dispute which may arise, for example, as to the proper meaning of the contract, its performance, and the measure of damages in the event of a breach. This approach is designed to give effect to the contractual intentions of the parties and, in principle, it should therefore prevail regardless of the forum in which the relevant proceedings happen to take place. Thus, so far as the English courts are concerned, a contract which is binding under its applicable law should be enforced in this country, even though a corresponding arrangement governed by English law would be unenforceable for some reason.[34]

4.21   There must, however, plainly be some limit to this approach. Respect for the intentions of the contracting parties must be balanced by a degree of respect for the fundamental laws and principles of the State in which the proceedings are

---

[30] The point is not entirely clear—see Dicey and Morris, *The Conflict of Laws* (Sweet & Maxwell, 13th edn, 2000) para 32-215. Questions of the contractual capacity of individuals are generally, although not entirely, outside the scope of the Rome Convention—see Art 1(2)(a) read together with Art 11 of the Convention.

[31] See Dicey and Morris (n 30 above) para 30R-020. Questions concerning corporate capacity are outside the scope of the Rome Convention—see Art 1(2)(e) and (f) of the Convention.

[32] Even this limited statement must be treated with some care. If a transaction is beyond the capacity of a corporation or has not been properly authorised under the laws of the home State, it may nevertheless be binding upon it if the relevant officials of the corporations had ostensible authority to enter into the contract under the laws which governed it. Questions of this kind are beyond the scope of the present work, but for discussion, see Plender and Wilderspin, *The European Contracts Convention* (Sweet & Maxwell, 2nd edn, 2001) paras 4-36–4-39 and Dicey and Morris (n 30 above) paras 30-025 and 130-028. The point was recently considered by the New York Court of Appeals in *Indosuez International Finance v National Reserve Bank* (2002) NY Int 55.

[33] *Kleinwort Sons & Co v Ungarische Baumwolle Industrie AG* [1939] 2 KB 678. Exchange control questions pose particular difficulty, and will receive detailed consideration in Part IV below.

[34] For an example, see *Re Bonacina* [1912] 2 Ch 394.

taking place. The balancing of these potentially competing interests finds expression in two core provisions of the Rome Convention. First of all, Article 7(2) of the Rome Convention provides that: "Nothing in this Convention shall restrict the application of the rules of the law of the forum in a situation where they are mandatory irrespective of the law otherwise applicable to the contract." Thus, for example, rules governing cartels, competition, restrictive practices, and consumer protection must be applied by the English courts even if the contracts and monetary obligations at hand are governed by a foreign system of law.[35] Equally, laws designed for the protection of policyholders resident in this country may be of mandatory application even though the policy concerned is subject to the laws of a different country.[36] Article 7(2) may apply to a wide variety of domestic rules of the forum.[37] In the present context, it is sufficient to note by way of example that Article 7(2) provides the basis upon which the English courts may give effect to Article VIII(2)(b) of the Articles of Agreement of the International Monetary Fund, even in relation to obligations governed by a foreign system of law.[38]

Secondly, Article 16 of the Rome Convention provides that: "The application of a rule of law of any country specified by the Convention may be refused only if such application is manifestly incompatible with the public policy (*ordre public*) of the forum." This again is a complex subject.[39] For present purposes, it must suffice to note that in England, public policy may prohibit the enforcement of foreign law contracts whose performance would be unlawful in England,[40] or which created monetary obligations involving the improper use of influence or corruption.[41] Likewise, the English courts may refuse to enforce foreign laws which are discriminatory[42] or which are inconsistent with the relevant country's treaty obligations to the United Kingdom.[43]

4.22

---

[35] These are the examples given by the Giuliano-Lagarde Report in its commentary on Art 7(2).

[36] *DR Insurance Co v Central National Insurance Co* [1996] 1 Lloyds Rep 74.

[37] On the subject generally see Dicey and Morris, *The Conflict of Laws* (Sweet & Maxwell, 13th edn, 2000) paras 32R-128–32-140; Plender and Wilderspin, *The European Contracts Convention* (Sweet & Maxwell, 2nd edn, 2001) paras 9-01–9-022. It may be added that the Convention makes further reference to rules of a mandatory character in a variety of specific contexts—see in particular Arts 3(3), 5(2), 6(1), and 9(6). It is not necessary to examine these provisions for present purposes.

[38] On this general subject, see Ch 16 below.

[39] In relation to public policy and contractual obligations, see Dicey and Morris (n 37 above) paras 32-227–32-238; Plender and Wilderspin (n 37 above) paras 9-023/9-026.

[40] In the context of a contract which infringed exchange control regulations in the UK, see *Boissevain v Weil* [1950] AC 327.

[41] *Hope v Hope* (1857) 8 DeG M & G, 731; *Lemenda Trading Co Ltd v African Middle East Petroleum Co Ltd* [1988] QB 448.

[42] *Holzer v Deutsche Reichsbahn Gesellschaft* (1938) 277 NY 473; *Oppenheimer v Cattermole* [1976] AC 249 (HL) and *Re Helbert Wagg & Co Ltd's Claim* [1956] Ch 323.

[43] *Royal Hellenic Government v Vergottis* (1945) 78 Ll LR 292.

F. The Law of Connected Third Countries

4.23 It is finally necessary to consider whether the law of some third country may have consequences for a monetary obligation, where there is some link between that obligation and the country concerned.

4.24 Those who seek the greatest possible degree of certainty in contractual relationships may find it difficult to support such an apparently vague principle. Nevertheless, the concept finds its voice in Article 7(1) of the Rome Convention:

> When applying under this Convention the law of a country, effect may be given to the mandatory rules of the law of another country with which the situation has a close connection, if and in so far as, under the law of the latter country, those rules must be applied whatever the law applicable to the contract. In considering whether to give effect to those mandatory rules, regard shall be had to their nature and purpose and to the consequences of their application or non-application.

4.25 The difficulty with this provision is its inherent vagueness; when does a country have a sufficiently "close connection" with a contract such that its mandatory laws are entitled to be taken into account? It may be, for example, that the provision could be invoked to upgrade the influence of the law of the place of performance in certain cases.[44] Article 7(1) could also be used to enlarge the scope of the *lex monetae* in some cases, for example, where the issuing State effects a general revalorisation of debts expressed in its currency.[45] The provision appears to acknowledge that there may be cases in which a State has an overriding interest in the enforcement of certain of its mandatory laws, and that foreign courts should thus consider whether those rules should be applied in particular cases.[46] The Article could, for example, justify the application of an embargo applied by another State with which the forum State is on cordial terms.[47]

---

[44] The limited scope of the law of the place of performance has been discussed earlier in this chapter. The language of Art 7(1) does not expressly exclude the possibility of enhancing the role of the law of that place in this way but it is submitted that a court should proceed with caution in this area; Art 7(1) should not generally be used to broaden the influence of the law of the place of performance when the Convention itself has placed limits upon its sphere of influence.

[45] As will be shown, revalorisation laws often only have effect if they form a part of the law which governs the contract as a whole; they will not be applied merely because they form a part of the *lex monetae*. Further, whilst n 44 above argued that Art 7(1) could not be used to magnify the limited influence of the law of the place of performance, that line of argument cannot be used in relation to the *lex monetae* because the Convention does not, in terms, deal with the scope or influence of that system of law at all.

[46] See the commentary in the Giuliano-Lagarde Report on Art 7(1), which frankly acknowledges some of the difficulties noted in the text.

[47] This, essentially, was the position which arose in *Regazzoni v KC Sethia (1944) Ltd* [1958] AC 301 (CA), although such a case can equally be decided on public policy grounds in reliance on Art 16 of the Rome Convention.

However, it is submitted that the Article could not be invoked in order to enforce the public laws of a foreign State, in defiance of a long line of authority which forbids such enforcement;[48] nor should it be invoked in order to give effect to exchange controls which have a connection with the contract solely because the debtor is resident in the State which imposes such controls.[49]

The English lawyer may be grateful that he does not have to wrestle with this particular provision, for the decision was made that it should not apply in this country.[50] The United Kingdom was not alone in this position; Germany, Ireland, and Luxembourg likewise entered reservations to Article 7(1).[51] Nevertheless, it is not appropriate simply to disregard this provision. Article 7(1) obviously applies in those Member States which elected not to enter a reservation; and a similar rule of private international law may be found to exist in countries which are not even party to the Rome Convention. It will be apparent from the points made in the last paragraph that Article 7(1) may be relevant to the application of revalorisation laws and of foreign exchange controls. It will therefore be necessary to return to the provision in those contexts.[52]

4.26

This brief review of the relevant rules of private international law provides the basis upon which the ensuing chapters will review the rules applicable to the interpretation and performance of monetary obligations.

4.27

---

[48] See, eg, the discussion at para 16.10 below.

[49] See the discussion at para 4.19 above.

[50] In view of the difficulties to which reference has been made, Member States reserved the right not to give effect to Art 7(1)—see Art 22(1)(a) of the Convention. The UK has exercised that right—see Contracts (Applicable Law) Act 1990, s 2(2).

[51] See *Internationales Privat-und Verfahrensrecht*, Jayme and Hausmann (eds) (Beck Juristische Verlag, 11th edn, 2002) 179, note 12 to Art 22 of the Rome Convention.

[52] In relation to revalorisation laws, see para 13.13 below; in relation to exchange controls, see para 16.31 below.

5

THE INTERPRETATION OF MONETARY OBLIGATIONS—INITIAL UNCERTAINTY

A. Introduction

The interpretation of a monetary obligation involves two key elements namely **5.01**
(1) the identification of the currency in which the obligation is expressed (usually referred to as the "money of account"); and (2) the ascertainment of the
amount required to be paid by reference to the currency so identified.[1]

This may appear to be a statement of the obvious, and (in most cases) so it will **5.02**
be. But the identification of the currency in which an obligation is expressed
will, in occasional cases, cause extreme difficulty. For present purposes, it is
proposed to examine two types of situation.

First of all, uncertainty may arise from the fact that the parties have contracted **5.03**
in terms of a currency, the name of which is common to two or more currency
systems, without stipulating the particular system to which they intended to
refer. Equally, if an international supply contract stipulates (expressly or implicitly) for a reasonable price to be paid for goods dispatched to a buyer then it
will be necessary to determine whether the parties intended the price to be paid

---

[1] The term "money of account" was used by Lord Tomlin in *Adelaide Electric Supply Co v
Prudential Assurance Co* [1934] AC 122, 146. The expression must be carefully distinguished
from "money of payment", which refers to the currency which can be tendered in the performance of an obligation. In view of that role, the money of payment is considered in Ch 7
below. For a case in which both the money of account and the money of payment were uncertain,
see para 20.17, note 34 below.

in the currency of the seller's country, the buyer's country, or some third currency. A contract may also refer to several distinct currencies without making it clear which one of them is intended to be the money of account. Such difficulties are inherent in the contract from the date at which it is made, and may thus be referred to as cases involving an "initial uncertainty".

5.04 Secondly, the parties may have clearly contracted with reference to a single monetary system, but that system may subsequently be split into two or more separate systems.[2] In such a case, the money of account was initially certain, but subsequently became uncertain as a result of political developments affecting the State which issued the money of account. These may therefore be referred to as cases of "subsequent uncertainty".[3]

Initial uncertainty and subsequent uncertainty clearly raise different types of problems and arise from different types of circumstances. They will therefore be considered separately; the present chapter deals with the problems posed by initial uncertainty, whilst the next chapter will deal with subsequent uncertainty.

B. The Money of Account—Initial Uncertainty

5.05 As noted above, initial uncertainty may arise where the parties refer (say) to "dollars", without specifying whether this refers to US dollars, Canadian dollars, Australian dollars, or indeed many others. Even worse, the parties may have simply referred to payment of "1,000", without specifying any currency unit at all. In such a case, the court may have to choose between dollars, sterling, and many other currencies. Separately, initial uncertainty may occur where it was not possible for the parties to stipulate the relevant monetary system at the outset, for example, where one party agrees to indemnify another against loss, and the currency in which that loss may ultimately be suffered will depend upon a variety of circumstances. In each of these cases, an essentially similar problem arises; there plainly exists an obligation and that obligation has a monetary character, but there is some doubt as to the currency in which such obligation

---

[2] For a recent example, Czechoslovakia divided into the Czech Republic and the Slovak Republic, forming two new States with effect from 1 January 1993. The States adopted the Czech Crown and the Slovak Crown respectively. The position in relation to Czechoslovakia is discussed at para 6.15 below.

[3] It will be noted that "subsequent uncertainty" as here defined refers to the *division* of a monetary system. The *unification* of previously separate monetary systems does not give rise to the same measure of difficulty, for the obligations expressed in the two extinct currencies would be converted into the single currency by reference to the recurrent link; there is no choice in identifying the supervening money of account. On the recurrent link, see para 2.34 above, and, for a recent example of such a unification of monetary systems, see generally the discussion of monetary union in Europe in Part VI below.

should be expressed. Issues of an essentially similar kind may arise in the context of a claim for unliquidated damages.

The present chapter seeks, in each of these cases, to answer the question—which system of law is to determine the money of account and to determine the amount of the obligation? In other words, which legal system is to determine the substance and measure of the obligation in question? It should be mentioned again that the *measure* of the obligation (the money of account) may differ from the *mode of performance* of that obligation (ie the money of payment, in which the obligation is required to be discharged). The quite separate questions touching the money of payment are discussed elsewhere.[4]

5.06

It is necessary to emphasise the distinction between (a) the *identification* of the system of law which governs the determination of the money of account and (b) the *identity* of the currency found to constitute the money of account by application of the legal system so determined. In other words, a clear line of demarcation must be drawn between issues of private international law and questions of municipal or domestic law.[5] To express matters in another way, one must first of all determine the system of law which governs an obligation;[6] thereafter, one must apply that system of law in order to ascertain the money of account. As Lord Denning MR put it, "we must apply the proper law of the contract and then, as a matter of construction, decide what was the currency of account".[7] Thus, if it is found that a contract is governed by English law, then references to "pounds" will usually mean pounds sterling, but this is not necessarily so; the court must interpret the contract according to its terms and by reference to the surrounding circumstances in order to ascertain the identity of the money of account.[8] Furthermore, if an English law contract refers to "dollars", then it plainly cannot refer to the domestic unit of account; but English law principles of construction must be applied in order to determine

5.07

---

[4] See Ch 7 below.

[5] The failure to make this distinction clear is responsible for the confusion caused by the *Adelaide* and *Auckland* cases—see para 5.18 below.

[6] Of course, in the context of a purely domestic contract, the determination of the governing law will readily be ascertained—in practice, it will usually be taken for granted. For a general discussion of conflict of law issues in the monetary arena, see Ch 4 above.

[7] *W.J. Alan v El Nasr Export and Import Co* [1972] 2 QB 189, 206. See also *The Alexandra I* [1971] 2 Ll LR 469, 474.

[8] In this sense, see *National Mutual Life Association v A-G for New Zealand* [1956] AC 369, 387; *Broken Hill Proprietary Co v Latham* [1933] Ch 373, 409; *Joffe v African Life Assurance Society* (1933) South African LR (Transvaal Division) 189; *National Bank of Australasia Ltd v Scottish Union National Insurance* (1951) 84 CLR 177, 208. But see also *Ivor An Christensen v Furness Withy & Co* (1922) 12 Ll LR 288; *Westralian Farmers v King Line* (1932) 43 Ll LR 378, 382; *Adelaide Electric Supply Co v Prudential Assurance Co* [1934] AC 122, 145.

whether the parties intended to refer to US dollars or some other currency under that name.[9]

5.08 In closing these introductory remarks, it is perhaps appropriate to re-emphasise that the identity of the money of account will usually be of crucial importance to the contracting parties, for it defines both the quantum and the substance of the obligation. In contrast, the money of payment will usually be of lesser significance, for it determines only the mode or method of payment, and should thus have limited bearing on the "value" paid or received.[10]

C. Liquidated Sums

The current position

5.09 It must be stated at the outset that the determination of the money of account is a question of interpretation of the contract in question, and is so treated in all legal systems;[11] the question is therefore to be determined by reference to the law applicable to the contract as a whole. In any case involving difficulties of contractual interpretation (whether affecting the money of account or any other matter), it is necessary to have regard to all of the circumstances of the case and thereby attempt to deduce the intention of the parties. The nature of the transaction; the nationality, residence, and domicile of the parties; the valuation of the respective currencies at the time when the contract was made; the place where the contract was made and where it was to be performed—all these and similar facts will have to be examined and evaluated.[12] It follows that the money of account must be determined with reference to the circumstances prevailing as at the contract date.[13]

---

[9] The same point is emphasised by van Hecke, *International Encyclopaedia of Comparative Law*, Vol III (Brill, 1972) ch 36.

[10] The statement in the text perhaps represents a fairly traditional view of the nature, role, and status of the money of payment. In a modern context, it is suggested that the identity of the money of payment is of far greater significance. The point is discussed at para 7.42 below.

[11] Certainly, the determination of the money of account is a matter of contractual interpretation in all EU Member States—see the Rome Convention, Art 10(1)(a). That the identification of the money of account is to be decided by reference to the law which governs the contract as a whole has been clear since the decision in *Bonython v Commonwealth of Australia* [1950] AC 201. The French court proceeded likewise in deciding whether a contractual reference to "francs" meant French francs or CFA francs—Cass Civ 24 April 1952; *Clunet* 1952, 1326. The matter has not always been so clear—see the discussion of the *Adelaide* and *Auckland* decisions at para 5.18 below.

[12] In England, the facts as they stand as at the date of the contract are exclusively relevant, and the subsequent conduct of the parties cannot be taken into account as a means of interpreting the contract—see *Noel v Rochford* (1836) 4 Cl & Fin, 158, 201 and *FL Schuler AG v Wickman Machine Tool Sales Ltd* [1974] AC 235.

[13] *Noel v Rochford* (1836) 4 Cl & Fin 158, 201 and *Auckland Corp v Alliance Assurance Co* [1937] AC 587, 603 (PC). Consistently with the point made in n 12 above, subsequent conduct

Against this background, it is appropriate to consider some of the cases where **5.10** the money of account was not entirely clear when the contract was originally made or the relevant obligation was incurred, and to examine the reasoning and solutions adopted by the courts in question:

(a) Where the capital sum payable on a life insurance policy issued by a Canadian insurer in the United States was expressed to be payable in "dollars", this was found to refer to Canadian dollars, largely because the premiums had been expressed to be payable in that currency.[14] The regulatory framework applicable to Canadian insurance companies reinforced the view that the money of account was Canadian dollars, even though amounts actually payable under the policy were required to be paid in the United States.[15]

(b) Where a percentage commission is payable to a broker or agent but the money of account is not specified, it may be inferred that the broker is entitled to his percentage based upon the money of account agreed between the buyer and seller in the contract arranged by the broker.[16]

(c) The government of a self-governing country is (rebuttably) presumed both to make contracts[17] and to legislate[18] in terms of its own monetary system,

---

could not be taken into consideration for the purpose of determining the money of account— *National Bank of Australasia v Scottish Union and National Insurance Co* [1952] AC 493 (PC), on which see Mann (1953) 63 LQR 18. See also *Liebeskind v Mexican Light & Power Co Ltd* (1941) 116 F 2d 971. In practical terms, however, the court's view of the matter may plainly be influenced by the conduct of the parties where all previous payments under a contract had been made in a particular currency—see *Groner v Lake Ontario Portland Cement Co Ltd* (1960) 23 DLR (2d) 602 (Court of Appeal, Ontario) and it is of course possible for the parties to revise the terms of their contract (expressly or by implication from their conduct) such that the money of account is varied: *WJ Alan v El Nasr Export and Import Co* [1972] 2 QB 189.

[14] See the decision of the Supreme Court of Canada in *Weiss v State Life Insurance Co* (1935) SCR 461; *Groner v Lake Ontario Portland Cement Co Ltd* (1960) 23 DLR (2d) 602. This appears to be a legitimate approach to interpretation; if Canadian dollars were paid for life cover, it is reasonable to infer that the cover was provided in the same currency.

[15] See *Weiss v State Life Insurance Co* (n 14 above).

[16] *Westralian Farmers v King Line* (1932) 43 Ll LR 378 (HL) 383, and the decision of the German Supreme Court 7 December 1921, *JW* 1922, 711. The point made in the text is well illustrated by the decision in *Myers v Union Natural Gas Co* (1922) 53 Ontario LR 88 where a US lessor agreed to take by way of rent 1.5 cents for each 1,000 cubic feet of gas produced on the premises. Since all parties knew that the gas was produced and sold in Canada and paid for in Canadian currency, the money of account was held to be Canadian (rather than US) dollars.

[17] *Bonython v Commonwealth of Australia* [1950] AC 201, 222 (PC) and see also (1952) 68 LQR 195, 202.

[18] *Bonython v Commonwealth of Australia* (n 17 above); *Payne v The Deputy Federal Commissioner of Taxation* [1936] AC 497. In Commonwealth jurisdictions, references (possibly erroneous) to "pounds sterling" have been construed as references to the local monetary unit—see *Roberts v Victorian Railway Commissioners* (1953) VLR 383; *Jones v Shelton* 79 WN NSW 249, affirmed by the Privy Council, [1962] 1 WLR 840; and see cases cited by Cowen (1962) 78 LQR 533. As a general rule, however, references to "sterling" will imply a reference to English currency—see *De Buerger v J Ballantyne & Co Ltd* [1938] AC 452 and Currency Act 1982, s 1(2). In a different era,

even if the words used are apt to refer also to other systems. In the case of a contractual obligation undertaken by a government, the presumption just stated will usually be superseded by the presumption founded upon the law of the place of payment.[19]

(d) Various presumptions or inferences may arise in other, different types of commercial cases. For example, contracts involving shares listed on a particular stock exchange will generally have to be settled in the currency which is local to the stock exchange concerned.[20] A court may be presumed to give judgment in terms of its own currency,[21] and lawyers fees are presumptively expressed in the currency of the country in which they practise.[22]

(e) The past course of dealings between the parties or the subject matter of the contract may provide an indication as to the intended money of account. For example, where the contract is one for a loan, it may be presumed that in relation to the borrower's repayment obligations, the money of account should correspond to that in which the loan was originally made.[23] Transactions involving real property will usually be intended to be expressed in the currency of the country where the property is situate.[24] Equally, the US dollar is well known to be the currency of the international oil industry,

---

legislation enacted by an Imperial power would generally refer to the monetary system of that power, even when the legislation fell to be applied by courts sitting in the overseas territories to which it applied—see *The Commonwealth v Asiatic Steam Navigation Co Ltd* (1956) 1 Ll LR 658 (High Court of Australia). Cases of this type are, of course, now of limited interest.

[19] On the latter presumption, see para 7.56 below. It should be said that neither of the presumptions noted in this paragraph can be regarded as compelling in a modern context.

[20] German Supreme Court, 15 December 1920, *RGZ* 101, 122; 11 July 1923, *RGZ* 108, 191; but see 24 October 1925, *RGZ* 112, 27.

[21] German Federal Supreme Court 29 September 1961, *Juristenzeitung* 1962, 678. This general (and rebuttable) presumption does not in any way affect the powers of an English court expressly to award a judgment denominated in a specified foreign currency—on this subject, see Ch 8 below.

[22] See, eg, the approach adopted by the ECJ in *European Ballage Corp v EEC Commission* [1976] 1 CMLR 587.

[23] See *National Mutual Life Association of Australasia Ltd v A-G for New Zealand* (1954) NZLR 754, affirmed by the Privy Council [1956] AC 369.

[24] Thus, a loan expressed in "francs" and payable in Switzerland was nevertheless held to be expressed in French francs, because the loan was secured on property situate in France—see Cass Civ 19 July 1937. Nevertheless, the presumption noted in the text should not be overstated—see, eg, *Landsowne v Landsowne* (1820) 2 Bl 60 (where there was, however, an express contractual reference to the "lawful money of England"), followed by the Irish Supreme Court in *Northern Bank v Edwards* [1985] IR 284. Likewise, where rent for premises in Southern Rhodesia was payable in South Africa, the law of the place of payment was applied, with the result that the money of account was South African pounds (rather than Rhodesian pounds)—*Mundell v Radcliffe* (1933) 50 South African LJ 402. In another case, the property concerned was in Canada and payment was required to be made there, but nevertheless US dollars were held to be the money of account because (amongst other factors) both contracting parties were resident in the US—see *Ehmka v Border Cities Improvement Co* (1922) 52 Ontario LR 193. Each of these cases initially turns upon an assessment and balancing of those features which suggest a connection with the

and contracts made within the framework of that industry are thus presumed to be expressed in US dollars.[25]

(f) Where a contract governed by English law refers to "sterling", this will almost invariably lead to the conclusion that the parties contemplated English currency as the money of account.[26] But in the final analysis this will always be a question of interpretation and it can by no means be assumed that the general rule just stated would apply with equal force to contracts or obligations governed by a foreign system of law.[27] Thus, where a seller based in Kenya fixed the price of goods at "shs 262/-", the money of account was Kenyan currency rather than sterling, because it was, at the time, customary to express sterling amounts in pounds and shillings.[28] But in Israel, the sign "£" was taken to refer to English currency, because the local unit was invariably referred to as "£P" or "£I".[29]

(g) There may be occasions in which the contract confusingly refers to two currencies, and it is necessary to determine which of them supplies the money of account in respect of the obligation concerned. In one case, charterers of a Norwegian vessel had undertaken to procure a policy against war risks "on Norwegian terms for 2,000,000 kroners . . . towards the cost of which the owner agrees to contribute a premium at the rate of £4½ per cent". The House of Lords decided that this was an agreement to provide a sterling policy, the reference to kroners being merely "to value and not to currency".[30]

(h) A similar difficulty may arise where parties stipulate for an equivalence between two different currencies. The Ontario Supreme Court was confronted with a loan for "3,500,000 pounds = 88,060,000 francs", and

---

currency of one country or another. It may be that the problem is not solved by provisions such as Art 4(3) of the Rome Convention (contracts relating to immoveable property presumed to be the most closely connected with the country in which it is situate), for that provision deals with the identification of the law applicable to the contract and not with the interpretation of its terms or the identification of the money of account.

[25] *BP Exploration Co (Libya) Ltd v Hunt* [1979] 1 WLR 783, 843, affirmed by the Court of Appeal [1981] 1 WLR 232. The same observation would apply equally to gold and other commodities. A similar solution is adopted by the Uniform Foreign-Money Claims Act; in the absence of an express selection of the currency of account by the parties, the currency of account with respect to the claim will be that previously used in dealings between the parties or (failing that) the currency used in the particular international market for the commodities concerned—see s 4 of the Act.

[26] *Broken Hill Proprietary Co v Latham* [1933] CR 373, 409 (CA); *De Buerger v J Ballantyne & Co Ltd* [1938] AC 452; Currency Act 1982, s 1(2).

[27] A point illustrated by the decision in *Bonython v Commonwealth of Australia* [1950] AC 201 (PC), on which see (1952) 68 LQR 195, 206. Ultimately, a question of construction is involved which must be determined by reference to the circumstances prevailing at the time of the contract.

[28] *WJ Alan & Co v El Nasr Export & Import Co* [1972] 2 QB 189.

[29] Israel Supreme Court in *Rivlin v Wallis* Jerusalem Post (Law Reports) 2 February 1958.

[30] See *Larsen v Anglo-American Oil Co Ltd* (1924) 20 Ll LR 67, 69; cf *Ivor An Christensen v Furness Withy & Co* (1922) 12 Ll LR 288.

held that the loan was denominated in francs only because the main text of the bonds and coupons referred exclusively to that currency.[31]

(i) In the context of a will, it may be presumed that legacies were intended to be paid in the currency of the country in which the testator was domiciled[32] although the presumption could be rebutted if, for example, the testator had stipulated that the legacies should be paid in a foreign country free of exchange (thereby implying that the beneficiary was not to be put to the inconvenience or expense of an exchange transaction).[33]

5.11 It may be noted that the above examples—whilst providing a helpful guide—depend on their own specific circumstances. They provide indicators of the attitude which the court should adopt in particular cases; but they do not lay down any general principles. All depends upon the interpretation of the contract against the background of the circumstances subsisting when the agreement was made.[34]

5.12 If all other attempts to identify the money of account have failed, then it is submitted that English law[35] will presume that the parties intended to contract by reference to the currency of the country with which the monetary obligation itself is most closely connected.[36] This, in turn, will frequently lead to the

---

[31] *Derwa v Rio de Janerio Tramway Light & Power Co* (1928) 4 DLR 542.

[32] *Permanent Trustee Co of New South Wales v Pym* (1939) 39 SR NSW 1.

[33] *Thompson v Wylie* (1938) 38 SRNSW 328.

[34] It might be thought that the scope for this kind of difficulty in the context of currencies labelled "franc" will have been reduced as a result of monetary union in Europe and the substitution of the euro for those currencies. For the future, that is plainly true but the question may yet arise for a considerable period. In a contract executed immediately prior to the creation of the single currency, it would still be necessary to ascertain whether "franc" referred to the French or the Belgian unit, for different euro substitution rates applied in each case. In any event, the general subject continues to be of importance in relation to the numerous national currencies labelled "dollar".

[35] The rule about to be stated is a rule of English domestic law, rather than a rule of private international law. Consequently, if the contract is governed by a foreign system of law, the search for the money of account must be conducted by reference to any relevant canons of interpretation provided by that system of law.

[36] It should be emphasised that this formulation looks to the country with which the *monetary obligation* is most closely connected. Dicey and Morris, *The Conflict of Laws* (Sweet & Maxwell, 13th edn, 2000) in the same context refer to the currency of the country with which the *contract* is most closely connected—see Rule 209. In most cases, no doubt, this difference of emphasis would have no material impact on the outcome. But if it is necessary to have resort to the "closest connection" test in order to ascertain the money of account, then the investigation should focus specifically on such contractual provisions as may seek to address the payment obligations themselves, such as the place of payment and the currency in which the seller is known to conduct his business. The comments about to be made in the text preserve Dr Mann's submission that the place of payment gives rise to a *presumption* as to the money of account. As noted in the text, however, the presumption only arises when all other attempts to ascertain the money of account have failed. It is, therefore, only the weakest of presumptions—see the discussion in Dicey and Morris, para 36-035, citing *Goldsborough Mort & Co Ltd v Hall* (1949) 78 CLR 1.

conclusion that the money of account is the currency of the place in which payment is ultimately required to be made. There is significant authority for this proposition both in England[37] and elsewhere.[38]

The presumption that, in the absence of countervailing circumstances, it is the money of the place of payment which constitutes the money of account deserves approval.[39] Since the money of the place of payment will frequently be the money of payment,[40] the presumption leads to a convenient identity of both the money of account and the payment of money. This, in turn, leads to the avoidance of a foreign exchange operation and the risks inherent in it—risks which, in the modern commercial context, the parties may probably have intended to avoid.[41] In similar vein, the presumption will lead to the conclusion

5.13

---

[37] See, eg, *Gilbert v Brett* (1604) 18 Davies Rep (Ireland) 28. In *Taylor v Booth* (1824) 1 C & P 286, a bill drawn in Ireland for £256 18s Irish currency was expressed to be payable in England, where the equivalent was £232 4s. During the course of argument, the Court observed (at 287) that "if a man draws a bill in Ireland upon England and states that it is for sterling money, it must be taken to mean sterling in that part of the United Kingdom where it is payable; common sense will tell us this". The case turned upon a point of pleading, as did *Kearney v King* (1819) 2 Barn & Ald 301, and *Sprawle v Legg* (1822) 1 Barn & Cres 16. In each case, the court had to decide whether the declaration and the proof were consistent. More recent authorities to like effect decided by the English courts or by the Privy Council include *Macrae v Goodman* (1856) 5 Moo PC 315; *Adelaide Electrical Supply Co v Prudential Assurance Co Ltd* [1934] AC 122 (HL); *Auckland Corp v Alliance Assurance Co* [1937] AC 587 (PC); *De Bueger v J. Ballantyne & Co Ltd* [1938] AC 452 (PC). In *National Mutual Life Association of Australasia Ltd v A-G for New Zealand* [1956] AC 369, 387, it was stated that "if there is only one place of payment, this is an important but not a decisive factor" in ascertaining the money of account. In that case, the contract provided that payment was to be made 'free of exchange' which reinforced the view that payment was required to be made in the currency of the place of performance.

[38] US: *Liebeskind v Mexican Light & Power Co Ltd* (1941) 116 F 2d 971 (CCA 2d) at 974; Canada: *Simms v Cherenkoff* (1921) 62 DLR 703 (Saskatchewan King's Bench); *Weiss v State Life Assurance* (1935) SCR 461. South Africa: *Fisher, Simmons & Rodway (Ppty) Ltd v Munesari* [1932] NLR 77; *Joffe v African Life Assurance Society* (1933) South African LR (Transvaal Division) 189; Brazil, Supreme Court, 22 May 1918, *Clunet* 1921, 993; Victoria, *Re Tillam, Boehme & Tickle Pty Ltd* (1932) Vict LR 146, 149, 150. See also Uniform Law on Bills and Notes, art 41(4), and Uniform Law on Cheques, art 36: "If the amount of the bill of exchange (cheque) is specified in a currency having the same denomination, but a different value in the country of issue and the country of payment, reference is deemed to be made to the currency of the place of payment." The same solution is adopted by Art 75(2) of the Convention on International Bills of Exchange and International Promissory Notes; (1989) *International Legal Materials* 206.

[39] The Canadian decision in *Saskatoon City v London & Western Trusts Co Ltd* [1934] 1 DLR 103 seems to contradict this proposition, but the decision appears to turn upon the interpretation of the legislation which authorised provincial cities to issue securities. The proposition does, however, draw some support from another Canadian decision: *Simms v Cherenkoff* (1921) 62 DLR 703.

[40] The money of payment is the money in which the debtor is obliged to discharge his obligation. On the money of payment, see generally Ch 7 below.

[41] See the observations made in *Adelaide Electric Supply Co v Prudential Assurance Co* [1934] AC 122, 156. Quite apart from the risks involved, a foreign exchange transaction also involves a cost to one of the parties. Although the presumption in favour of the place of payment is a weak one, the cost factor may in some respects reinforce it. In a competitive world, it may be assumed that the parties did not intend unnecessarily to add to the cost of their transaction.

that the money of account corresponds to the currency which can most conveniently be paid and cleared in the place of performance. But the scope of application and value of this presumption must not be overstated. First of all, it must be remembered that the presumption can only enter the arena if the contract contains no material indicators as to the money of account originally intended by the parties.[42] Secondly, there will be many cases in which the place of payment itself has not been expressly agreed and can only be ascertained by the application of a further presumption[43] and the resultant "doubling" of presumptions may operate to falsify the real intentions of the contracting parties.[44] Consequently, the presumption now under discussion may more readily be applied when the place of payment has been expressly agreed; it is less easy to apply where the place of payment has to be inferred from the other terms of the contract. Thirdly, the presumption will plainly not assist where the parties have merely referred to "dollars", but the place of payment is London or Paris.[45] Finally, the presumption is based upon the premise that there is only one place of payment which is expressly or impliedly allowed by the contract. It must be remembered that an option to make or to receive payment in different places is only an "option of place"; it does not affect the fact that the underlying obligation must be expressed in a single money of account.[46] In any event, it is plain

---

[42] For a similar view, see van Hecke, *International Encyclopedia of Comparative Law*, Vol III (Brill, 1972) ch 36.

[43] On the identification of the place of payment, see para 7.84 below.

[44] Although, on the other hand, it must be said that the use of presumptions has in the first place only become necessary because the parties failed to make their intentions clear.

[45] It may be noted in passing that the number of cases in which this type of difficulty may arise has been reduced by the advent of monetary union in Europe. If, in 1996, a Swiss company undertook to pay "francs" to a French company by way of credit to an account in Brussels, the money of account could have been French francs, Swiss francs, or Belgian francs; the application of the presumption mentioned in the text would point to Belgian francs. A similar contract entered into today would raise no such difficulties; neither France nor Belgium now has a currency called the "franc", and it must follow that Swiss francs would be the money of account in the example just given. The problem would, however, continue to subsist with respect to contracts which were made in the pre-monetary union period.

[46] Of course, the contract may explicitly confer on one party a right to pay (or to receive payment) in different currency—an option of currency—see *Bonython v Commonwealth of Australia* [1950] AC 201, 221. The French Cour de Cassation noted that a promise to pay francs in France or Switzerland merely implied a choice as to the *place* of payment and not as to the *currency* of payment, which remained to be ascertained under the terms of the contract—Cass Civ 21 December 1932, *Clunet* 1933, 1201 *re Chemin de fer de Rosario à Puerto-Belgrano*; Cass Req 6 December 1933, *Clunet* 1934, 946 and *DH* 1934, 34, *re Société Internationale des Wagon-Lits*; Cass Civ 5 June 1934, *Clunet* 1935, 90 *re Est Lumière*; Cass Civ 21 July 1936, *DH* 1936, 473, *re Papeteries de France*. The distinction between an "option of place" and an "option of currency" is clearly illustrated by a decision of the Appellate Division of the New York Supreme Court in *Levy v Cleveland CC & St LRR Co* (210 App Div 422, 206 NY Supp 261, 1 December 1924). In 1910, the defendant railway company had issued bonds for a sum of "500 francs" each, payable in France or (at the holder's option) in Belgium or Switzerland. A holder demanded payment in Switzerland in Swiss francs, but (as the Court found) the issuer had fully discharged its obligations

that the "place of payment" presumption is of very little assistance in identifying the money of account where the contract allows for alternative places of payment.[47]

It must therefore be appreciated that the present presumption whilst useful, is **5.14** both a last resort and easily rebuttable—it can be displaced by even relatively minor indications in the contract as to the intended money of account.[48] The presumption is, perhaps, further weakened when it is remembered that, where sterling is to be paid, it does not necessarily follow that payment must be made in Britain. Conversely, a requirement for payment in a foreign currency does not necessarily exclude a place of payment in Britain.

It must not be overlooked that the creation of monetary obligations is not **5.15** limited to contracts, and that the identification of the money of account can cause difficulties in other contexts. Thus, in the context of a will, a pecuniary legacy expressed in "dollars" can give rise to exactly the type of difficulty discussed earlier in this section. But once again, the identification of the money of account will be a question of interpretation or construction of the will, and is

---

by payment in depreciated French francs. The court noted that the primary obligation to pay francs in Paris connoted that the obligation was expressed in French francs, ie it applied the "place of payment" presumption noted in the text. The option to receive payment elsewhere could not be read as an option to receive payment in a different currency, especially since the bonds did not refer to Swiss or Belgian francs. In the course of its decision, the court referred to judgments of the Brussels Court of Appeal, 11 March 1921 BIJI 6 (1922) No 1260, and *Pasicrisie Belge* 1921 ii 70 (*Société d'Éclairage v Magerman*). It may be observed that in all of these cases (and in *Oppenheimer v The Public Trustee*, reproduced in Appendix 3 to the Fifth Edition of this work) difficulties only arose when the Latin Monetary Union was dissolved and greater fluctuations occurred in the relative values of the (formerly) participating currencies.

[47] *Bonython v Commonwealth of Australia* [1950] AC 201 (PC). The principle of this case was followed in *National Bank of Australasia Ltd v Scottish Union and National Insurance Co Ltd* [1952] AC 493, on which see Mann (1953) 69 LQR 18. Loan stock had been issued in substitution for debts payable in London, Sydney, and Brisbane; the stock was registered in each of these locations and could be transferred from one register to another. The uniform nature of the stock led to the conclusions that the money of account was (a) identical everywhere and (b) the money of Queensland.

[48] As the French Cour de Cassation has noted, "en cas de doute sur la monnaie que les parties ont eue en vue lors de la convention, l'indication dans le contrat d'un lieu de paiement ne constitue à cet égaard qu'une présomption de leur intention susceptible d'être combattue par toutes dispositions" Cass Req 13 June 1928, *Clunet* 1929, 112 (*La Bâloise*); Cass Req 28 Nov, 1932, *Clunet* 1934, 133 (*La Bâloise*); Cass Req 21 March 1933, *Clunet* 1934, 373 (*Société Suisse d'Assurance Générale*); Cass Civ 17 July 1935, *Clunet* 1936, 880 (*Brasseries Sochaux*). Despite this general warning, however, lower courts have sometimes been more robust in applying the place of payment presumption. See, eg, Cour de Paris 29 January 1923 *DP* 1923, 2, 129 (*Schwab v S Montagu & Co*). The defendants sold gold bars owned by Schwab, and received the proceeds in sterling. However, the defendants converted those proceeds into French francs before remitting them to Schwab in Paris. Schwab claimed that the proceeds should have been paid to him in sterling, but failed on the grounds that (in view of correspondence between the parties) Paris was the place of payment.

accordingly to be determined by reference to the system of law which is the "source" of the obligation, ie the law which governs the will itself. There is a rebuttable presumption that the testator intended the law of his domicile to govern the will.[49] If a testator dies domiciled in Australia, then it must follow that pecuniary legacies expressed in "dollars" must be presumed to refer to Australian dollars. But once again—and for reasons essentially similar to those discussed in a contractual context—it is impossible to lay down hard and fast rules in this area. If, for example, the testator was domiciled in Australia but, as at the date of the will, most of his personal assets were located in the United States, then a reference to US dollars may be inferred.

5.16   The present discussion has in some respects been unhelpful in the sense that the decided cases merely provide guidelines and examples rather than firm rules. This is perhaps inevitable, given that it is the duty of the court to respect the intentions of the parties in individual cases. Nevertheless, it is suggested that the following general points should be borne in mind in seeking to determine the money of account:

(1)   A clear distinction must be drawn between the substance of the obligation (determined by reference to the money of account) and the instrument or means of performance (ie the money of payment).

(2)   The determination of the money of account is a question of construction. It is thus to be determined solely by reference to the law applicable to the contract, rather than the law of the place of payment.

(3)   In the absence of countervailing circumstances, there is a presumption (admittedly weak) that the parties intended to select the currency of the place of payment as the money of account.

The older cases

5.17   It has been established that the identification of the money of account is a question of construction to be determined by reference to the law applicable to the contract. This statement of the relevant principle of private international law no longer appears exceptional. It is now confirmed by the Rome Convention[50] and was confirmed by the Privy Council more than fifty years ago. In *Bonython v Commonwealth of Australia*,[51] the court was confronted with bonds payable in "pounds sterling" in Brisbane, Sydney, Melbourne, or London; it was argued that if payment was made in London, then English law—as the law of the place of performance—governed the contract and determined the measure

---

[49] On this point, see Dicey and Morris, *The Conflict of Laws* (Sweet & Maxwell, 13th edn, 2000) para 27R-054, and the cases there noted.

[50] See the discussion of the role of the applicable law under the Rome Convention in Ch 4 above.

[51] [1950] AC 201.

of the obligation. Viscount Simonds rejected this contention,[52] noting that: "The mode of performance of the obligation may, and probably will be determined by English law; the substance of the obligation must be determined by the proper law of the contract." Although a decision of the Privy Council, this case effectively settled the position so far as the English courts are concerned; indeed even without the benefit of direct authority, the point might be regarded as self-evident. Yet the position has not always been so clear and it is necessary to describe earlier decisions which adopted a different view.

Adelaide Electricity Supply Co v Prudential Assurance Co[53] involved a company   **5.18** incorporated in England but whose business was conducted in Australia. All dividends had previously been paid in England, but, in 1921, the shareholders passed a resolution altering the articles to provide that dividends should henceforth be declared at meetings to be held within Australasia and should be paid from a place within that territory. The respondents claimed that the holders of certain preference shares issued before the 1921 resolution were entitled to be paid their dividends in sterling in English legal tender for the full nominal amount thereof without deduction for Australian exchange. Reversing the order of the courts below and overruling the decision of the Court of Appeal in *Broken Hill Proprietary v Latham*,[54] the House of Lords held that the company had discharged its obligations by paying in Australian currency what was in Australia legal tender for the nominal amount of the dividend warrants.

Whether English or Australian pounds were owed was a question of interpreta-   **5.19** tion.[55] That question of interpretation clearly fell to be determined by English law, because the contract which applies as between a company and its shareholders arises under the terms of companies' legislation in this country.[56] On this basis, one might have expected the court to adopt reasoning along the following lines:

(a) The articles of association in their original form contemplated English pounds as the money of account. If the English and Australian pounds are found to have been different units in 1921,[57] then it is a question of construction whether the 1921 resolution was intended to substitute the Australian pound for the English unit as the money of account. If the answer was in the positive, then the Australian unit would define the

---

[52] At 219. As noted elsewhere, the role of the place of performance has now been downgraded even further by virtue of Art 10(2), Rome Convention.

[53] [1934] AC 122 (HL).   [54] [1933] Ch 373.

[55] The point was emphasised by Lords Warrington and Tomlin at 136 and 145.

[56] For the current version of the statutory contract, see the Companies Act 1985, s 14. The same point is made in the judgments in the *Adelaide* case itself.

[57] Whether or not Australian and English pounds were different or the same currency at that time is a difficult question; it has already been discussed at para 2.52 above.

company's obligation to pay dividends and the claim of the preference shareholders would have to fail. If, on the other hand, the answer was in the negative, then English currency would be the money of account. It would therefore be necessary to consider the means by which the company could discharge its obligations. It could probably discharge them either by payment in pounds sterling or by payment in Australian pounds of the amount necessary to produce the required amount of sterling in the London foreign exchange market.[58]

(b) If, however, the English and Australian currencies were the same at the time of the 1921 resolution, then plainly the alteration in the articles of association could not have changed the money of account, and only questions touching the money of payment would remain to be resolved.[59]

5.20 The House of Lords arrived at the latter result, albeit via a different route. The decision was unanimous, although the individual judgments display a considerable variance in their reasoning. Lords Warrington, Tomlin, and Russell started from the view that both countries had a common unit of account although there was a "difference in the . . . means whereby an obligation to pay so many of such units is to be discharged".[60] It necessarily followed that performance of the dividend obligation could be completed by payment in Australian legal tender; since the Australian and English pounds were in legal terms identical, no additional payment could be required in respect of the superior exchange value of the English money of account. On this basis, it appears that the opinions of the majority are not directly relevant to the determination of the money of account. They merely relate to the money of payment and establish a fairly obvious proposition.[61]

5.21 The opinion of Lord Wright (with whom Lord Atkin broadly agreed) is more difficult to follow. He started from the proposition that: "Whatever is the proper law of the contract regarded as a whole, the law of the place of performance should be applied in respect of any particular obligation which is performable in a particular country other than the country of the proper law of the contract."[62] This statement is far too widely drawn, although perhaps Lord Wright intended to refer only to questions touching the *manner* of performance. He then stated his

---

[58] See the remarks of Lord Tomlin at 146.

[59] There was in fact a difference in the commercial value of the pound in England and the pound in Australia, but considerations of this kind must be denied any legal relevance if the two units were in fact part of a single and unified monetary system. This is the only view which would be consistent with the principle of nominalism, considered in Part III below.

[60] Lord Warrington, at 138.

[61] That proposition must, however, now be read in the light of Art 10(2) of the Rome Convention; see the discussion at para 7.56 below.

[62] At 151.

reasons for regarding the English and Australian pounds as separate currencies.[63] He then states[64] that "in determining what currency is intended, the general rule *prima facie* applies that the law of the place of performance is to govern". Lord Wright thus leaves the identification of the money of account—plainly a question of substance—to the law of the place of performance.[65] It is unfortunate that his judgment is confusing in this area because, working from his premise that the English and Australian currencies were separate, it was important for him to distinguish carefully between the money of account and the money of payment. The impression that he failed to make this distinction is reinforced by his remarks in later cases, where he noted that the *Adelaide* case involved questions touching performance, rather than matters of substance[66] and that the case was concerned with "the 'means' of discharging the obligation".[67]

Lord Wright again returned to this general theme when he delivered the opinion of the Privy Council in *Auckland Corporation v Alliance Assurance Co.*[68] In 1920, the City of Auckland issued bonds providing for a sum of "pounds" payable in London or Auckland at the holder's option. On the basis that the London option had been validly exercised, the question arose whether the holder was entitled to demand payment of the stipulated sum of New Zealand money converted into pounds sterling at the rate of exchange of the day. Lord Wright apparently accepted that the bonds were governed by New Zealand law, and made it clear that the case involved a question of construction. He then stated the effect of the *Adelaide* case twice, but in different terms. He first stated that: "it was held that, in the absence of express terms to the contrary, or of matters in the contract raising an inference to the contrary, the currency of the country in which it was stipulated that payment was to be made was the currency meant". But later, he said[69] that the principle of the *Adelaide* case was that: "the House of Lords held that the true meaning of the word 'pounds' must be determined on the basis of a rule depending on a well known principle of the conflict of laws—namely that the mode of performance of a contract is to be governed by the law of the place of performance . . .". **5.22**

---

[63] At 155. This aspect of Lord Wright's opinion has already been discussed at para 2.56 above.

[64] At 156.

[65] The confusion caused by this formulation is reflected in the Manitoba decision in *Johnson v Pratt* [1934] 2 DLR 802 where it is stated erroneously that the money of account, being a matter related to the mode of performance, is to be governed by the law of the place of performance. See also the remarks of Scott LJ in *Radio Pictures Ltd v IRC* (1938) 22 TC 106, 132.

[66] *Mount Albert BC v Australasian Temperance & General Mutual Life Assurance Society Ltd* [1938] AC 224, 241. Yet, on the view which Lord Wright adopted in relation to the distinct monetary systems, a question of performance plainly did arise.

[67] *De Buerger v J. Ballantyne & Co Ltd* [1938] AC 452, 459.   [68] [1937] AC 587.

[69] At 606. In *Bonython v Commonwealth of Australia* [1950] AC 201, at 220 Lord Simonds referred to this passage and distinguished it on grounds which appear tenuous—see Mann (1951) 68 LQR 195, 205.

5.23   Undoubtedly, it was the former principle which was laid down in the *Adelaide* case as a principle of English domestic law;[70] it is consistent with the "place of payment" presumption discussed earlier in this chapter and which forms a part of English domestic law. The latter principle, however, touches questions of private international law and references to it are to be found only in the judgment of Lord Wright himself in *Adelaide*. Nevertheless, in the *Auckland* case, both of these principles allowed Lord Wright to arrive at the result that the obligation was discharged by the payment of the stipulated amount of "pounds" in English currency.

5.24   It is submitted that the decision in the *Auckland* case proceeds on the footing that "as in the *Adelaide* case, the pound is the common unit of account".[71] If this is correct, then the decision is merely an application of the principles in the *Adelaide* case, except that it takes them one step further; as the holder was held to be entitled to one (English) pound for one (New Zealand) pound, both being "the same", the decision in effect substituted an option of currency not stipulated by the parties for a mere option of place. This result regrettably has the effect of altering the originally contracted terms,[72] but this result was probably unavoidable in the light of the *Adelaide* case.

5.25   It has been necessary to review the older cases to demonstrate that the identification of the money of account has often been a source of considerable difficulty and to examine the approaches which the courts have adopted in dealing with this problem. But the difficulties posed by these decisions should now be a matter of history, especially in the light of the clarity brought to some of the relevant rules of private international law issues by the Rome Convention.[73]

D. Unliquidated Claims

5.26   Thus far, the discussion has been confined to those cases in which the parties clearly intended to create a monetary obligation, but the currency in which that obligation was intended to be expressed was, for some reason, not entirely clear. Nevertheless, the parties plainly intended to create an obligation of a monetary character, and this very fact facilitates the search for the money of account for

---

[70] This was necessarily the case, for the *Adelaide* decision was concerned with a contract which was itself governed by English law.

[71] [1937] AC 587, 606, and see 599.

[72] See the discussion of the decision in *National Bank of Australasia Ltd v Scottish Union and National Insurance Co Ltd* [1952] AC 493, in n 47 above.

[73] Rome Convention, Art 10(2) clearly "downgrades" the rule of the law of the place of performance—see the discussion at para 4.14 above. The emphasis which Lord Wright placed on the place of performance in identifying the money of account can thus no longer be supported.

there is at least a contract in existence. In other words, the background and terms of the contract will provide some clues in the search for the money of account.

It is now necessary to consider the money of account in cases where the liability **5.27** concerned is *not* foreseen by the parties.[74] It may be inferred that such cases will pose even greater difficulty, for the parties themselves will usually not have provided even the faintest clues as to the money of account; they never intended to create the particular monetary obligation in the first place.[75] As a result, the law in this area can be obscure.[76]

It is suggested that a two-stage approach will generally be necessary in order to **5.28** identify the money of account in the context of an unliquidated claim, as follows:

(a) it is necessary to ascertain which domestic system of law is to govern the identification of the money of account; and

(b) it is necessary to apply the rules of that system of law in order to determine the money of account.[77]

As in the case of liquidated claims, it thus remains necessary in the present context carefully to distinguish between the first question which is governed by private international law, and the second question which is determined by the domestic system of law thereby identified. It is appropriate to consider each of these steps separately.

Governing law

Which system of law must be applied in order to ascertain the money of account **5.29** in the context of an unliquidated claim?

Where the unliquidated amount represents a claim by way of damages for **5.30** breach of a contract, then "within the limits of the powers conferred on the court by its procedural law, the consequences of breach, including the assessment of damages, in so far as it is governed by rules of law" are to be determined

---

[74] eg because the liability arises by way of damages for a breach of contract, or the claim arises in tort.

[75] This comment will apply equally to claims for breach of contract as it does to claims in tort.

[76] See the Law Commission's Report on Foreign Money Liabilities (Cmnd 9064, 1983).

[77] The distinction between the two points noted in (a) and (b) is clearly drawn by Lord Wilberforce in *The Despina R* [1979] AC 685, 700. This process may be complicated where the claim has to be assessed in a foreign currency, the identity of which may be uncertain. Where, eg, damages are claimed following a collision between ships, it may make a difference whether that which is converted is a sum of euros spent by the shipowner to carry out the repairs, or a sum of US dollars, with which he may have bought the euros required for that purpose.

by reference to the law applicable to the contract concerned.[78] It may be inferred from this language that the money of account in respect of the damages claim is determined by reference to the law applicable to the contract as a whole. Like-wise, a restitutionary claim which arises in connection with a contract will generally be governed by the law applicable to the contract itself.[79]

5.31 By analogy, it is suggested that the identification of the money of account in tort claims must likewise be governed by the proper law of the obligation itself, ie the system of law which governs the substance of the claim, rather than the law of the country in which proceedings are taken.[80] In general terms, the law applic-able to a tort will be the law of the country in which the events constituting the tort take place, although it should be appreciated that this rule is by no means unqualified.[81] Thus, if a British serviceman stationed in Malta is injured in consequence of the negligent driving of one of his colleagues, the law of Malta must usually be applied in deciding whether the money of account is the local currency, pounds sterling, or some other currency.[82]

5.32 The preliminary question has been answered: in the context of a claim for damages whether in contract or in tort, the identification of the money of account is determined by the system of law which governs the substance of the obligation as a whole.[83]

---

[78] Rome Convention, Art 10(1)(c). On the Rome Convention generally, see Ch 4 above.

[79] In this context, see Dicey and Morris, *The Conflict of Laws* (Sweet & Maxwell, 13th edn, 2000) para 34R-001. Note that the law applicable to such claims is not (in the UK) governed by Art 10(1)(e) of the Rome Convention, because that provision is excluded by the Contracts (Applicable Law) Act 1990, s 2(e).

[80] *Jean Kraut AG v Albany Fabrics Ltd* [1977] QB 182; *The Folias* [1979] AC 685.

[81] Private International Law (Miscellaneous Provision) Act 1995, s 11(1). On this rule, and the various exceptions and qualifications to it, see Dicey and Morris, *The Conflict of Laws* (Sweet & Maxwell, 13th edn, 2000) para 35R-078. In the US, a slightly different approach is adopted. The rights and liabilities of the parties are determined by the local law of the State which has the most significant relationship with the occurrence and the parties—see Restatement, Second on the Conflict of Laws, s 145 and *Babcock v Jackson* (1963)12 NY 2d 473, 191 NE 2d 279.

[82] cf *Boys v Chaplin* [1971] AC 356. This illustration serves to emphasise, if further emphasis is needed, that the initial question of private international law and the subsequent question of domestic law must be carefully distinguished.

[83] This position is consistent with the general rule that the identification of the money of account is to be regarded as a matter of substance. Whilst the point goes beyond the scope of this work, it should be noted that questions touching the award of damages can raise quite different questions in the arena of private international law. It seems that the available "heads" of damage, the existence of an obligation on the claimant to mitigate his loss, and questions of remoteness are all questions of substance, which are thus subjected to the proper law of the obligation. On the other hand, the quantification of damages is regarded as a matter of procedure and is thus governed by the law of the forum. In the case of actions for breach of contract, this rule is to be found in the Rome Convention, Art 10(1)(c). In the context of tort claims, an essentially similar rule results from the provisions of the Private International (Miscellaneous Provisions) Act 1995, s 14(3)(b). That the law of damages in tort claims remains partly substantive and partly procedural in the sense just described was confirmed in *Edmunds v Simmonds* [2001] 1 WLR 1003.

Determination of the money of account

It must now be supposed that English law governs the obligation and thus **5.33** determines the money of account. Once again, let it be repeated that this does *not* mean that sterling is the money of account; it merely means that the rules of English law are to be applied in identifying the money of account.[84] What then, is the nature of the English rules which are to be applied in this context? It must be accepted that no hard and fast rules can be laid down, for they cannot possibly cater for the many and varied contexts in which the question may arise. Thus, it cannot be said that the money of account must necessarily be that of the country whose law governs the obligation or that of the country in which the breach of contract or the tort occurs, for it is a fact of frequent occurrence that liability arises in a different currency. It is suggested that no single solution is possible; rather it is necessary to evolve and recognise a number of different rules conforming to the legal nature of, and the demands of justice in, a variety of cases which have to be distinguished. Recognising that this open-textured formulation may be of limited practical assistance, it is necessary to examine various cases which have arisen in this area.

(a) Where the liability for damages is derived from a contractual relationship, it may be possible to find in the contract some indication of the money by which the liability should be measured. It may be apparent that the parties intended to adopt a particular currency as the money of account for *all* transactions and liabilities arising in respect of the contract and, in such a case, damages should be measured by reference to that currency.[85] A number of cases may be cited where this line of reasoning has been adopted. The wrongful dismissal of an employee salaried in a foreign currency seems to involve the liability of the employer to pay damages in terms of the same foreign money.[86] Likewise, a Greek seaman who was paid in Greek currency and suffered injury whilst working on board a Greek-registered vessel was held to be entitled to damages in terms of Greek currency.[87] Where goods in New York are sold fob New York at a price expressed in Canadian dollars and the buyer fails to accept delivery, the seller is entitled to damages in Canadian dollars.[88] Similarly, a South African seller liable to pay damages

---

[84] There will be many cases involving contracts governed by English law which will have no connection either with this country or its currency. Maritime cases such as *The Folias* [1979] AC 685 provide obvious examples.

[85] *The Despina R* [1979] AC 685, 700.

[86] *Ottoman Bank v Chakarian* [1930] AC 277, 284, as explained in *Ottoman Bank v Dascalopoulos* [1934] AC 354, 364.

[87] *Vlachos v The Roso* [1986] AMC 2928.

[88] *Bain v Field* [1920] 5 Ll LR 16 (CA); *Compania Engraw Commercial E Industrial SA v Schenley Distillers Corp* (1950) 161 F 2d 876.

for non-delivery to an Austrian buyer was required to pay damages expressed in US dollars, because the contract price was agreed to be paid in that currency.[89] Even where a contract involves calculations in several different currencies, it may be possible to infer from the contract which of those currencies is intended to serve as the medium for the computation of damages.[90]

(b) Similarly, where the claim is of a restitutionary or quasi-contractual nature, it will often be possible to determine the money of account by reference to the terms of the original contract or arrangement. Thus, if US dollars were paid as the price of goods, a total failure of consideration will make the seller liable to repay US dollars, even if sterling was paid and accepted on account or in discharge of the US dollar liability.[91] Moreover, if the court has to value the benefit of services rendered under a contract which has been frustrated, it will have regard to the currency of account for measuring the contractual indebtedness as well as the currency of the expenditure incurred in making the services available.[92]

(c) In another group of cases, an indication as to the proper money of account may be derived from the fact that, under the law applicable to the case, the defendant is under a duty to restore to the claimant the value of an article or interest. In such cases, it seems that the liability is expressed in the currency in which the value is ascertained and in the place in which the property ought to be restored to the claimant. Thus, if the value of a particular item of property is customarily expressed in US dollars and ought to be (or ought to have been) restored to the claimant in England, then it is suggested that US dollars should be the money of account of the restitutionary claim, whilst the amount of the claim would be the amount of US dollars that would have to be paid in London for that property or commodity. If, however, the relevant property is not customarily expressed by reference to a particular currency, then sterling would be the money of account.[93]

---

[89] *Voest Alpine Intertrading GmbH v Burwill & Co SA (Pty) Ltd* (1985) 2 SALR 149.

[90] For an example which arose in the credit derivatives market, see *Nomura International plc v Credit Suisse First Boston* [2002] EWHC 160 (Comm), where it was held that an award in US dollars would most closely reflect the claimant's loss.

[91] cf Law Reform (Frustrated Contracts) Act 1943, ss 1 and 2(3).

[92] *BP Exploration Co (Libya) Ltd v Hunt* [1979] 1 WLR 783, 843, affirmed by the Court of Appeal [1980] 1 WLR 232.

[93] That the market value is ascertained by reference to the law of the place in which delivery is required is supported by decisions such as *Rodocanachi v Milburn* (1886) 18 QBD 67, 78, 80; *Stroms Bruks AB v Hutchinson* [1905] AC 515; *The Arpad* [1934] P 189, 222. That the money of account would usually be the currency of the place of delivery is supported by the decision in *Di Ferdinando v Simon Smits & Co* [1920] 3 KB 409, 414 even though, in a broader sense, the authority of that decision is in most respects doubtful—see *The Folias* [1979] AC 685, 700.

(d) The relationship of principal and agent may create a different set of questions in the context of the money of account. The very nature of the relationship suggests that, where an agent has received US dollars from or for the account of his principal, the agent's obligation to return or pay that money must likewise be expressed in US dollars,[94] for the obligation is to pay over that which has been received.[95] Likewise, where an agent based in the United Kingdom is entitled to an indemnity against overseas travelling or hotel expenses paid out in a number of different currencies, the money of account of his indemnity claim should be sterling, because the agent will usually have used his domestic funds to purchase the necessary foreign currencies. In such cases, it may readily be stated that the principal must indemnify the agent against expenses paid or incurred in the course of his agency; but the identification of the money of account in respect of the indemnity claim may require further investigation into the relationship between the parties.

(e) Having dealt with claims for damages arising from contractual and commercial cases, it is now necessary to consider claims in tort. In cases involving the destruction or loss of property, the money of account of the claim will usually be the currency of the country in which the loss or destruction occurred, for it is in that country that the claimant needs to purchase replacement goods or property.[96] Thus, if a defendant in England is sued for his negligent destruction of property in France, then the money of account will be the euro (and not sterling). Likewise, if an American traveller in London loses his baggage through the negligence of his hotel, his claim will be measured in sterling, because replacement items would have to be purchased in this country—in other words, it is the value at the place of the loss which must be made good.[97]

(f) In a final and most comprehensive group of cases, the money of account in respect of the claim will be expressed in the currency of the place where the

---

[94] To the extent to which the decision in *Ottoman Bank v Jebara* [1928] AC 269 suggests a different rule, it appears that the decision rests on its special facts and the course of business between the parties.

[95] German Federal Supreme Court, 30 September 1968, *IPRspr* 1968/1969, No. 175. For the same reason, the German Supreme Court decided that (in the absence of special terms) a bank which collects a cheque expressed in a foreign currency must account to the customer in that currency, and has no general right to convert the proceeds into the domestic currency: 10 January 1925, *RGZ* 110, 47; 20 March 1927, *RGZ* 116, 330.

[96] This principle was accepted by the Arbitral Tribunal on Property, Rights and Interests in Germany in *Italy v Federal Republic of Germany* (Decisions, vii 213).

[97] For an English decision to this effect, see *Metaalhandel JA Magnus v Ardfields Transport Ltd* [1988] 1 Lloyd's Rep 197. Under German law, it appears that the owner of goods must be compensated on the basis that (had there been no wrongful act) the goods would have continued to serve the purposes of the owner; in the example given in the text, this would point to an award in US dollars: Federal Tribunal, 14 February 1952, *BGHZ* 5, 138; 14 January 1953, *BGHZ* 8, 297.

victim resides or carries on business, and where, for this reason, his financial resources are most likely to be affected. The money of account thus identified will most closely reflect the loss actually suffered by the victim.[98] This will frequently mean that the claimant should be entitled, not to the currency actually and directly used to cover his losses,[99] but to the currency ultimately employed by him for the purpose of obtaining the currency so used. In other words, as a rule the claimant is likely to be able to claim—and may be required to claim—his own currency in the sense of the currency in which the loss was effectively felt or borne by him, rather than the currency in which his expense or loss was ultimately sustained. This is the principle which was laid down by the House of Lords, both in relation to claims for damages in tort[100] as well as breach of contract.[101] In the context of tort claims, the House was concerned with maritime collision damage. Repairs were carried out in China, Japan, England, and the United States and were in each case paid for in the relevant local currency. The owner was a Liberian company with its head office in Greece and its managing agent in New York. The money of account of the claim was found to be US dollars, because that was the currency in which the owner normally conducted its trading operations.[102] In the context of another claim for damages for breach of contract, a French charterer had been required to pay damages to cargo receivers in Brazilian cruzeiros, which the charterer had acquired by using French francs. The owner of the ship was required to indemnify the charterer in French francs, because the charterers had

---

[98] This solution has the support of the Permanent Court of International Justice—*The Wimbledon* (1923) PCIJ Series A, No. 1. See also the decision of the Court of Appeal, Berlin West 12 March 1951, *NJW* 1951, 486: the wrongdoer has to pay damages in the currency circulating at the place of the victim's ordinary residence.

[99] For discussions of this problem area, see Remien, *RabelsZ* 1989, 245. Professor von Hoffmann in *Festschrift fur Karl Firsching* (1985) 125 suggests an unqualified principle according to which claims for damages are expressed in the currency of the creditor's place of business or ordinary residence. German judicial practice provides for damages to be awarded in the domestic currency, with foreign currency losses forming an item within the calculation: German Supreme Court, 4 June 1919, *RGZ* 96, 121; Federal Supreme Court, 11 February 1958, *Izkspr* 1958–9, No. 111, at 304; 10 July 1954, *BGHZ* 14, 212, 217 or *NJW* 1954, 1441; 9 February 1977 WM 1977, 478 *IPRspr* 1977 No 11; 20 November 1990, *NJW* 1991 634 (637). See Karsten Schmidt, *Geldrecht* (Berlin, 1983) para 244.

[100] *The Despina R* [1979] AC 685, 695, followed in *The Agenor* [1985] 1 Lloyd's Rep 155; *The Lash Atlantico* [1987] 2 Lloyd's Rep 114 (CA); and *The Transoceania Francesca* [1987] 2 Lloyd's Rep 155.

[101] *The Folias* [1979] AC 685, 699, followed in *The Federal Huron* [1985] 3 All ER 378; *The Texaco Melbourne* [1994] 1 Lloyd's Rep 473. A similar rule may be applied by virtue of s 4(b) of the US Uniform Foreign-Money Claims Act. If the parties have not agreed the money of account in respect of any claims which may arise, then this will be either (a) the currency of their previous dealings, (b) the currency used to settle international trades in the commodity concerned, or (c) the currency in which the loss is felt.

[102] *The Despina R* [1979] AC 685, 698.

discharged the cargo receiver's claim by providing francs and—until those francs were provided—the charterer had suffered no loss.[103] The fact that US dollars constituted the money of account for the purposes of the charterhire payments did not necessarily lead to the conclusion that damages for breach should be paid in the same currency.[104] Likewise, in *The Lash Atlantico*,[105] a ship's agent paid for repairs to a vessel in several different currencies. However, the agent was based in Greece and operated in Greek drachmas; the invoice which the agents presented to the owners was thus expressed in drachmas. The owner received an award in that currency because that was the currency in which the owner had suffered the loss.[106] The general point is reinforced by the more recent decision of the House of Lords in *The Texaco Melbourne*.[107] In that case, the Ministry of Fuel and Energy in Ghana was the owner of fuel oil which was loaded onto the *Texaco Melbourne* for a coastal trip to another part of Ghana. The oil was not delivered and the Ministry claimed damages against the carrier. Had the Ministry purchased a substitute cargo, it would have had to pay US dollars to the seller. However, the claimant maintained its books and accounts in Ghanaian cedis and, in view of the stringent exchange control system applied in Ghana, the Ministry could only have obtained dollars through the Central Bank, by paying the countervalue in Ghanaian cedis. It followed that the loss was "felt" in the local currency, and the cedi was the money of account for the purposes of the claim.[108] As a result, damages had to be assessed in that currency, and the claimant was left to bear losses flowing from the depreciation of the cedi (as against the US dollar) between the date of breach and the date of judgment.[109] In other words, the money

---

[103] *The Folias* [1979] AC 685, 698, 702.

[104] ibid, 701. Compare the points noted in the current text (para 5.33) at point (a). The issues under discussion seem to have arisen principally in shipping cases. However, these principles also found voice in a claim under the Fatal Accidents Act 1976 on behalf of a child, whose mother had died in childbirth. Since the child's extended family lived in Italy and he would therefore have to be brought up there, the major part of the award was made in Italian lire: *Bordin v St Mary's NHS Trust* [2000] Lloyd's Rep Med 287.

[105] [1985] 2 Lloyd's Rep 464.

[106] Consistently with the decision in *The Texaco Melbourne*, which is about to be discussed, it was perhaps insufficient merely to identify the currency in which the owner had made payment to its own agent. The question was—which currency had the owner used in order to acquire the necessary Greek currency?

[107] [1994] 1 Lloyd's Rep 473. For an earlier decision which preceded on the same footing, see *The Federal Huron* [1985] 3 All ER 378 (French cargo owners who conducted their business in US dollars entitled to damages calculated by reference to that currency).

[108] This is also a possible explanation of the decision in *Ozalid Group (Export) Ltd v African Continental Bank Ltd* [1979] 2 Lloyd's Rep 231, on which see Gold, *Legal Effects of Fluctuating Exchange Rates* (IMF, 1990) 261.

[109] At any rate, this was one of the arguments put forward by the claimant. Once the money of account had been determined to be the cedi, its value against the US dollar ceased to be a relevant

of account in respect of the claim had to be ascertained by reference to the circumstances subsisting as at the date of breach, and subsequent fluctuations in the external value of that money cannot be taken into account.[110] The factual matrix in *The Mosconici*[111] justified a different conclusion. Cargo belonging to the Italian claimant had been lost overboard; the necessary replacements had been purchased with Italian currency. Despite these connections with Italy, the award was made in US dollars because the claimant was part of a US-based group of companies and it had contracted to sell the goods for a consideration in US dollars. A more difficult case arose from the collapse of Barings Futures Singapore; the company collapsed following unauthorised trading which was funded out of the proceeds of Japanese yen facilities provided by banks within Singapore. It was held that the damages to be awarded against negligent auditors should be expressed in yen, even though the company was in liquidation in Singapore and the currency of that liquidation was the Singapore dollar.[112] But whatever the difficulties, the approach described above is perhaps reflective of the principle of nominalism[113] and is also consistent with the principle of *restitutio in integrum*, for the claimant receives the currency which represents his actual loss.[114]

(g) These rules govern many different types of cases which may come before the English courts. Thus, if a foreigner, temporarily in England on holiday is injured or killed here, damages for loss of earnings can only be assessed by reference to the amount which that person would have earned in his "home" currency.[115] That currency will thus be the money of account in

---

consideration. There can only be one money of account in respect of a particular claim, and the comparative value of that money as against other currencies is not in point. Perhaps to this limited extent, it may be said that the principle of nominalism applies to unliquidated claims. On the principle generally, see Part III below.

[110] The point is specifically made by Lord Goff ([1994] 1 Lloyd's Rep 473) at 476.

[111] [2002] 2 Lloyd's Rep 313.

[112] *Barings plc (in liquidation) v Coopers & Lybrand* [2003] EWHC 2371. The result in this case appears to have been influenced by the absence of any evidence to demonstrate that the loss was, in fact suffered in Singapore dollars. As the court pointed out, the fact that the company was in liquidation could not affect the currency in which the loss was felt.

[113] ie to the limited extent to which unliquidated claims can be said to be subject to that principle. On this point, see para 9.23 below.

[114] For amplification of these points, see *The Federal Huron* [1985] 3 All ER 378. It may be noted that, in one case, the obvious candidate currency for the award was the Spanish peseta, but the Court of Appeal made its award in US dollars because, on the facts, both parties must have been aware that the seller would hedge the contract in that currency—see *Virani Ltd v Manuel Revert y Cia SA* (18 July 2003).

[115] It was formerly held that damages in tort must be assessed in the currency of the place in which the loss was suffered: *The Canadian Transport* (1932) 43 Ll LR 409 (CA). This rule can no longer be applied rigidly.

respect of that aspect of the claim.[116] Similarly, if a British seller fails to deliver goods to a German buyer and the buyer spends euros in order to obtain substitute goods, the English court should generally find that the euro is the money of account in respect of the breach of contract claim, even though the original contract price may have been expressed in sterling.[117] Difficulties may arise in applying the present rules where the claimant is a multinational company which maintains accounts in numerous currencies. In such cases, a factual enquiry will be necessary to determine whether the loss was in the ordinary course of business incurred in the claimant's "home" currency, or in some other currency in which it conducts its activities.[118]

There is not much to be gained by multiplying examples. It may, however, be noted that, as a result of the reasoning adopted in *The Despina R*,[119] the identification of the money of account in the context of unliquidated claims should be approached in a flexible and non-technical manner; the court should adopt a **5.34**

---

[116] Although it should be noted that general damages in respect of pain and suffering would be assessed in sterling—see *Hoffman v Sofaer* [1982] 1 WLR 1350; *The Swynfleet* [1948] Ll LR 16. The Court of Appeal in Cologne adopted a different approach in a case concerning an Israeli resident, who was involved in a motor accident in France, and incurred hospital/medical expenses in French francs. She was awarded French francs, rather than the Israeli currency which she had presumably used to acquire those francs: 18 December 1986, *IPRspr* 1986 No 37A, discussed by Alberts, *NJW* 1989, 609.

[117] See *Re British American and Continental Bank, Re Lisser and Rosenkranz's claim* [1923] 1 Ch 276, 285 and 291. The actual decision in that case is no longer good law—see *Camdex International Ltd v Bank of Zambia (No 3)* [1997] CLC 714.

[118] Two cases discussed above illustrate the dilemma. In *The Texaco Melbourne*, the court opted for the claimant's "home" currency, whilst the loss was found to have been felt in a different currency in *The Mosconici*. Further questions may arise in specific contexts, eg in the context of a "both to blame" maritime collision, where the decision in *The Khedive* (1882) 7 App Cas 795 requires a single judgment for the difference between the two liabilities after set-off against the ship subjected to the greater liability. The first instance decision in *The Despina R* [1977] 3 All ER 829 suggests that, for these purposes, the lesser liability must be converted into the currency of the greater liability, so that the set-off can be effected and judgment given in terms of the currency of the greater liability. If a single, "net" judgment is required, then this approach appears appropriate: *The Transoceanica Francesca* [1987] 2 Lloyd's Rep 155; *Smit Tak International Zeesleepen Bergingsbedrift v Selco Salvage Ltd* [1988] 2 Lloyd's Rep 398. Any applicable interest should be added to the respective claims before they are converted for the purpose of ascertaining the net sum: *The Botany Triad and the Lu Shan* [1993] 2 Lloyd's Rep 259. It may be added that the money of account in respect of a claim for interest will usually "follow" the money of account of the principal sum. However, it will not necessarily follow that the rate of interest to be awarded should reflect the cost of borrowings made in that currency: see *Helmsing Schiffahrts GmbH v Malta Drydock Corp* [1977] 2 Lloyd's Rep 444 and *Westpac Banking Corp v "Stone Gemini"* [1999] FCA 917.

[119] [1979] AC 685. Following this case, it seems that decisions such as *The Volturno* [1921] 2 AC 544; *Di Ferdinando v Simon Smits & Co Ltd* [1920] 3 KB 409; and *The Canadian Transport* (1932) 43 Ll LR 409 can no longer be regarded as good law. On the other hand, the decisions in *Jugoslavenska Oceanska Plovidba v Castle Investment Co Inc* [1974] QB 292; and *Jean Kraut AG v Albany Fabrics Ltd* [1977] QB 182 were expressly approved.

broad approach which seeks to meet the justice of the case. In each case, it must be remembered that an award of damages is designed to achieve *restitutio in integrum* for the claimant. The ascertainment of the proper money of account should thus be regarded as a part of the process which is designed to achieve that end. This overriding principle may perhaps be regarded as a satisfactory, if broad, principle underlying the cases which have been discussed above.[120]

---

[120] It should be appreciated that the present chapter has considered the difficulties surrounding the identification of the money of account, ie the currency in which an account is owing or in which damages should be calculated. Whether or not an English court can or should give judgment expressed in a foreign currency is an entirely separate issue—see, generally, Ch 8 below.

6

THE INTERPRETATION OF MONETARY OBLIGATIONS—SUBSEQUENT UNCERTAINTY

A. Introduction

The money of account, though originally clearly defined, may become **6.01** uncertain during the life of the legal relationship. This may occur in three categories of cases, namely:

(1) where a system of law having some impact on the obligation or the parties to it purports to alter the money of account;
(2) where a new monetary system emerges as a result of changes in territorial sovereignty, but the old monetary system continues to exist; and
(3) where a monetary system becomes extinct.

Each of these possibilities must be considered in turn.[1]

---

[1] It may be legitimate to add a fourth category, ie where a State joins a monetary union and thus gives up its own national currency. However, that aspect is left out of account for present purposes, since the whole subject is considered in detail in Part VI below.

B. Changes in Law

6.02   A State may seek to legislate in a manner which affects subsisting monetary obligations. For example, a State encountering serious economic problems may provide that foreign money obligations are henceforth to be settled by payment to a State agency in the domestic currency;[2] similar action might be taken by a State which wishes to inconvenience creditors in a State which it perceives to be hostile.[3] Such a law would deal with questions touching the identification, substance, and performance of monetary obligations and, in principle, would thus apply only where the contract or obligation concerned was governed by the law of the legislating State.[4] A law of this kind will usually further some governmental objective of high policy; it will usually be written in terms which are both clear and mandatory.[5] Why, then, should such laws require consideration in a chapter dealing with uncertainty of the money of account? It is probably true that, in a purely domestic context, no question of uncertainty will arise; a national court sitting within the State concerned will simply give effect to the law in accordance with its terms, regardless of the law applicable to the contract or any other matter.

6.03   Uncertainties may, however, arise where the monetary obligations at issue subsist within an international framework and fall for consideration by a court sitting outside the legislating State. Should a court give effect to the law in question? Subject to two points noted below, it is suggested that the question falls to be determined entirely by reference to the law which governs the contract or obligation at hand.[6]

6.04   The principle is neatly illustrated by two cases. In *Confederation Life Association*

---

[2] This was the position in *Re Helbert Wagg & Co Ltd's Claim* [1956] Ch 323. It is necessary to emphasise the language employed in the text. The present section is concerned with cases in which legislation seeks to substitute one form of money (usually, the local currency) for another (usually a foreign currency). The points about to be discussed do not apply to a mere substitution of the internal monetary system; the recognition of such an arrangement would be determined by the *lex monetae* principle, which is considered in Ch 13 below.

[3] Some of the Cuban legislation described later in this chapter would fall into this category.

[4] This follows from the rule that such questions are to be determined by reference to the governing law—see the discussion of Art 10 of the Rome Convention in Ch 4 above. The German law at issue in *Re Helbert Wagg & Co Ltd's Claim* was applied by the English courts because the contract was governed by German law. This observation made in the text must, however, be read subject to the discussion (in para 6.04 below) on Art 7(1) of that Convention.

[5] A prime example is offered by the Cuban monetary laws about to be discussed.

[6] This view is consistent with the principle of private international law which has been maintained throughout, namely that the identity of the money of account is a matter of substance and is accordingly to be determined by reference to the law which governs the contract as a whole.

v Ugalde,[7] the court was confronted with an insurance policy governed by Cuban law and which was expressed to be payable in US dollars in Cuba. While the policy was in force, Cuba introduced a new law to the effect that "all obligations contracted or payable in Cuba" in the US dollar would be substituted by an obligation to pay in Cuban pesos on a one-for-one basis. The Court gave effect to the substitution on the ground that the policy was governed by Cuban law. In contrast, when considering a similar policy, the Ontario High Court in *Serpa v Confederation Life Association*[8] held that the policy was governed by the law of Ontario, with the logical and inevitable result that the new Cuban law had to be disregarded when seeking to identify the money of account. On the footing that the law applicable to the policy was correctly identified in each case, the ultimate decisions are unimpeachable. The clear logic of these judgments must not, however, be allowed to obscure two points:

(1) A law which implements a currency substitution of this kind may be disregarded on public policy grounds, even though it forms a part of the law applicable to the obligation at issue. A court may thus decide not to give effect to such a law on the grounds that it is expropriatory, discriminatory, or is otherwise objectionable.[9]

(2) In countries whose system of private international law incorporates rules of the kind exemplified by Article 7(1) of the Rome Convention,[10] effect may be given to the mandatory rules of the law of a country which does *not* constitute the governing law of the contract but with which the situation has a close connection. In deciding whether or not to give effect to such mandatory rules, the court must have regard to their nature and purpose and to the consequences of their application or non-application. Plainly, in a case similar to *Serpa*, a provision of this kind would allow the court to give effect to the Cuban monetary legislation,[11] even though it does not form a part of the governing law. But, if the court *may* give effect to such laws, then under what circumstances *should* it do so? It is naturally very difficult to state general principles, for so much will depend on the facts of individual

---

[7] (1964) 164 So 2d 1, affirming (1963) 151 So 2d 315. For similar cases, see *Johnson v Confederation Life Association* (1971) 447 F 2d 175; *Santovenia v Confederation Life Association* (1972) 460 F 2d 805.

[8] (1974) 43 DLR (3d) 324.

[9] No such grounds were found to exist in the *Ugalde* case. Since this point touches upon the monetary sovereignty of the legislating State and the extent of any limitations on it, the subject is discussed in more detail in Ch 19 below.

[10] Happily, this provision does not apply in the UK. The point has been discussed in Ch 4 above.

[11] Monetary legislation of the kind now under discussion will invariably be of a mandatory nature. In addition, the obligor will usually be carrying on business within the country in which the new legislation is introduced, with the result that the situation has a close connection with that country. In principle, therefore, a case of this kind will fall within the scope of Art 7(1).

cases. But there may be significant arguments in favour of giving effect to the foreign monetary legislation in such a case. It is not necessarily unfair to the beneficiary of the obligation that this should be so; in choosing to deal with a counterparty in that country, the creditor has in some respects agreed to accept the sovereign, legislative, and other risks inherent in dealing with parties in that jurisdiction.[12] Further, it may be said that the court should respect the monetary sovereignty of the legislating State, given its close connection to the contract. However, such generalised arguments should not prevail; in the cases under discussion, the legislating State has unilaterally *imposed* its own monetary system upon an obligation previously expressed in the currency of another country and governed by a foreign system of law. There is no consideration of international law which requires foreign courts to respect such drastic action. Despite the possibilities which have been discussed, it is suggested that Article 7(1) of the Rome Convention should not be invoked in order to give effect to a foreign monetary law of this kind which does not form a part of the law applicable to the contract as a whole.[13] The case for an application of foreign monetary legislation in reliance on this provision may become more compelling where the issuing State has found it necessary to revalorise debts expressed in its national currency following a major collapse in its value. There may be a certain justice between the parties if the court gives effect to such revalorisation, even though the relevant law does not form a part of the law applicable to the contract. Further, the court would thereby respect the policy objectives of the issuing State.[14] Of course, it will be appreciated that a revalorisation is favourable to the creditor whilst the other forms of legislation are intended to operate to his detriment.

C. Changes in Territorial Sovereignty

6.05 For obvious reasons, a change in territorial sovereignty or the curtailment of a monetary system may have an impact on those obligations whose money of

---

[12] Although in favour of the creditor, it may be argued that he selected a different governing law as a means of insulating himself from legislative changes in that country, and there is no reason to overturn any prudent steps which the creditor may have taken for his own protection. This argument is reinforced by the fact that the Rome Convention largely preserves the parties' freedom to select the law applicable to their contract.

[13] It may be repeated that the text is concerned with the mandatory substitution of one currency for another as the contractual money of account, and not with changes to an internal monetary system to which the *lex monetae* principle would apply.

[14] As noted in Ch 13 below, the English courts will refuse to give effect to legislation which revalorises a debt, unless it also happens to form part of the law which governs the contract as a whole.

account was expressed in the currency of the territory affected by the change.[15] The problem may have to be considered in a purely domestic context, where the obligation at issue was contracted by persons within the territory concerned and falls for consideration by a local court. Alternatively, the money of account may have been used in a cross-border contract and the subject may fall for consideration by a foreign court. It is proposed to consider these two types of cases separately.

Domestic cases

Changes in territorial sovereignty[16] may impact upon a monetary system in a variety of ways. If one State acquires *part* of the territory formerly belonging to another State (for example, as a result of negotiations leading to the settlement of a boundary dispute or by way of cession), then the money of the acquiring State may become the currency of the territory so acquired, or a new currency may be introduced in that area. But the former sovereign continues to exist separately as a State; its monetary system continues to function, and its banknotes and coins may circulate thenceforth as *foreign* currency within the territory affected by the change in sovereignty.

6.06

Now, when the new currency is introduced into the area affected by the change in territorial sovereignty, the relevant law will no doubt include a recurrent link[17] establishing the rate of conversion between the old and the new currency. At this point, a difficulty becomes apparent; both the old *and* the new currency

6.07

---

[15] It is necessary to emphasise the last part of this formulation in the light of a decision of the German courts which arose from the break-up of Yugoslavia: Court of Appeal of Frankfurt am Main, 27 September 1995, *NJW-RR* 1996, 186 or *IPRspr* 1995, No. 153, vacated by the German Federal Supreme Court, 22 October 1996, *NJW* 1997, 324 or *IPRspr* 1996, No. 158. A Croatian who lived and worked in Frankfurt had established a foreign currency account with a Slovenian bank in 1978; the account was to be managed by the Croatian branch of the Bank in Zagreb. Both Slovenia and Croatia were part of a single State when the account was established but, of course, they were separate and independent countries by the time of the proceedings. The Court of Appeal of Frankfurt declined jurisdiction on the basis that foreign currency reserves of Slovenian and Croatian banks formerly had to be deposited with the Yugoslav central bank in Belgrade, and no agreement had yet been reached as to the fate of these funds; it was accordingly not possible for the German courts to adjudicate upon the claim because it would require a consideration of intricate international issues which had not been resolved. This, however, overlooks the fact that the depositor's claim was in debt and was thus a matter of private law. The fact that the Slovenian bank may have difficulty in repaying the deposit because its own foreign currency funds were blocked in Belgrade was an entirely irrelevant consideration and the question of an international settlement between Yugoslavia, Croatia, and Slovenia was simply not germane to the issue. The decision was thus rightly vacated by the Federal Supreme Court. Since the deposit obligation was expressed in a foreign currency, the break-up of Yugoslavia had no consequences whatsoever in the context of the identification of the money of account.

[16] The present section assumes that the State which has ceded territory continues to exist and enjoys sovereignty over other territory. Where it does not, see para 6.24 below.

[17] On the recurrent link, see para 2.34 above.

continue to exist. It is therefore necessary to decide (a) which debts are converted into the new currency and (b) which debts are unaffected by the substitution, and thus remain denominated in the old currency? Under such circumstances it is necessary that the legislation creating the new monetary system(s) must not only provide a recurrent link, but must also define the scope of its application, ie to which class or category of debts does the substitution apply?

6.08 History supplies many examples of cases in which the territorial ambit of a monetary system has been curtailed, or in which two or more monetary systems have been created in substitution for a former single currency.[18] This happened in Australia, which originally shared the United Kingdom's currency but subsequently developed its own monetary system.[19] In June 1948, both the Federal Republic of Germany and what became the German Democratic Republic discontinued the use of the reichsmark as the unit of account, and both introduced separate currencies known as the Deutsche mark. More recently, the former republics of the Soviet Union attained independence and created new national currencies, whilst Russia retained the former rouble as its own unit of account.[20] The disintegration of the Federal Republic of Yugoslavia also led to the creation of a number of newly independent States each of which needed to adopt a new monetary system. Likewise, with effect from January 1993, Czechoslovakia divided into two separate States; the Czech Republic and the Slovak Republic adopted the Czech crown and the Slovak crown respectively.[21]

---

[18] It should be appreciated that a different set of problems may arise where a new monetary system is created by an insurgent government in the course of an unsuccessful revolution, when legally a single independent monetary system exists in the country concerned, but the parties believe that there are two such systems. Of course, these problems arise in a particularly acute form if both units of account bear the same name. Thus, during the Civil War in the US, the Confederate dollar came into use. If two persons within the territory of the Confederation contracted in terms of "dollars" it became, after the termination of the Civil War, a matter of construction in what sense the word "dollar" had been used in the contract: *Thorington v Smith* (1869) 75 USA 1, 13,14.

[19] See the discussion of this subject in Ch 2 above.

[20] Russia is generally regarded as the successor of the former Soviet Union for the purposes of international law—see *Coreck Maritime GmbH v Sevrybokholodflot* (1994) SLT 893 (Court of Session).

[21] The whole episode, including the economic and monetary background to the currency separation is very clearly described in Dedek, *The Break-up of Czechoslovakia: An In-depth Economic Analysis* (Avebury, 1996) 117–42. The two countries began their separate existence by continuing with the former single currency under the terms of a monetary agreement concluded in October 1992. This arrangement was always intended to be temporary, but that openly declared intention proved to be the cause of significant economic instability. In the event, the arrangement lasted for a mere 38 days; both Republics introduced their new currencies on 8 February 1993. The logistical task involved in managing the currency separation process and in stamping existing banknotes so as to differentiate between those which were to form a part of each of the separate currencies, and the need to prohibit cross-border cash flows in order to avoid speculative activity, are described by Dedek at pp 130–5. The process was managed under the

Where the territorial ambit of a monetary system is reduced,[22] the legislator has, **6.09** theoretically, a choice between a number of tests for delimiting the new from the old currency. These include, the nationality, domicile, or residence of either creditor or debtor; the place of payment; the law applicable to the debt; or the economic connection of the particular transaction with the one or the other territory. The test selected by the legislator may be made compulsory or optional.[23] He may also delimit "old" currency obligations from "new" currency obligations by express legislative provisions; or he may say nothing of such delimitation, and the intention will have to be inferred.

There does not appear to be any universally agreed approach to this problem. **6.10** Certain tests can be dismissed on the grounds that these would produce results which are effectively arbitrary because they have little connection with the monetary character of the obligation. Tests such as the nationality or domicile of the parties, and the system of law applicable to the obligation, may all be dismissed on this ground. In practical terms, legislation of this kind has tended to adopt the residence of the debtor or the place of payment as the applicable test.[24] In other words, the new currency will be substituted as the money of account if that is the effect of the law of the place in which the debtor is resident or in the place of payment (as the case may be); otherwise, the money of account of the obligation remains that of the old currency.

It may be instructive to note a few cases in which courts have been confronted **6.11** with cases involving a delimitation of this kind and to describe some of the more recent legislative provisions which have been introduced in this context:

(a) Australian monetary law offers an example of implied delimitation. Australia had power to make its own rules with respect to currency, coinage, and legal tender, ie it could establish its own independent monetary system.[25] Until these powers were exercised, the pound sterling was also the lawful

---

terms of an Act on Currency Separation and was supervised by a Currency Separation Central Management Committee. The arrangements apparently met with the approval of the IMF and were recommended to the other republics which had formerly been a part of the Soviet Union and needed to establish independent monetary systems (Dedek, p 142).

[22] The discussion on this subject is in some respects based upon Dr Mann's paper published in (1952) LQR 195.

[23] Of course, monetary laws of this kind will usually be of mandatory application in the context of those obligations which fall within their scope.

[24] Note, however, that when Algeria became independent of France in 1962 and, in 1964, introduced the dinar currency, it was provided that debts "sont réputées libellées dans la monnaie du domicil du contrat . . ."—see Art 20 of the Evian Agreements UNTS 507, 25. It might be thought that this expression refers to the jurisdiction with which the contract is most closely connected. However, the translation given by the UNTS 507, 25 refers to the "place where the contract was concluded".

[25] Commonwealth of Australia Act 1900, s 51 (xii).

currency of Australia. In 1909, "Australian coins" were issued on the basis of a standard of weight and fineness identical with that applicable to British coins under the Coinage Act 1870.[26] Subsequently, the issue of Australian notes was authorised, which were declared to be "legal tender throughout the Commonwealth and throughout all territories under the control of the Commonwealth" and to be "payable in gold coin at the Commonwealth Treasury at the Seat of Government".[27] Several points may be inferred from these provisions. First of all, Australia effectively provided that debts expressed in "pounds" (which, up to that point, necessarily referred to English pounds) could be discharged by payment in the new, Australian pound. Secondly, in the absence of explicit provision, it must be inferred that the recurrent link was established to be one Australian pound for one English pound. Thirdly, it necessarily follows that Australia had created a new monetary system which was substituted for the English currency, but had delimited the application of that system to Australia itself and its territories. This was apparent both from the legal tender provisions included in the new legislation,[28] and from the accepted fact that Australian law could not affect obligations expressed in pounds sterling and payable outside Australia. In accordance with the principles discussed in the introduction to this section, Australian law thus had to delimit the scope of its new monetary legislation, and it impliedly selected the "place of payment" test. The legislation thus did not apply to debts which were expressed to be payable outside Australia.

(b) Following the First World War, certain German provinces came under Polish sovereignty. Poland introduced the zloty currency and provision was made for the conversion of mark debts into zloty debts. German courts held that the Polish legislation only applied to mark debts which were payable in areas under Polish sovereignty. In other words, the place of payment was the delimiting factor which had to be used to identify those mark debts which were converted into zloty.[29]

(c) Following its independence from the Austro-Hungarian monarchy, Czechoslovakia introduced a new monetary system. Under the terms of the

---

[26] See the Australian Coinage Act 1909, ss 2 and 4. By s 5 of that Act, both British and Australian coins were legal tender.

[27] On these points, see the Australian Notes Act 1910, ss 5 and 6. Gold coins virtually disappeared from circulation as a consequence of the outbreak of the First World War.

[28] See the language (reproduced above) of Australian Notes Act 1910, s 5.

[29] German Supreme Court, 11 March 1922, *JW* 1923, 123; 28 November 1922, *JW* 1922, 1122; 22 March 1928, *JW* 1928, 3108; 27 June 1928, *RGZ* 121, 337, 344; Berlin Court of Appeal, 9 March 1922, *JW* 1922, 1135. For French decisions relating to the ambit of the rate of exchange introduced in Alsace-Lorraine, see Cass Cir, 26 May 1930, *Clunet* 1931, 169; 8 February 1932, *Clunet* 1932, 1015; 29 November 1932, *Clunet* 1933, 686; Cas Rec, 25 October 1932, *Clunet* 1933, 689.

relevant law dated 10 April 1919, debts expressed in Austro-Hungarian crowns and payable within Czechoslovakia were to be paid in Czechoslovak crowns, on the basis of a one-to-one substitution rate. Once again, therefore, the new monetary law adopted the place of payment as the delimiting factor.[30] Before the separation, a railway company whose undertaking was mainly situate on Czechoslovak territory had issued bonds denominated in "crowns"; they were stated to be payable in Austria, where the company had its head office. Now, in view of the delimiting factor adopted by the Czech monetary law, it might have been thought that payment in the Austrian currency would be the necessary consequence. But in fact, both the Czechoslovak Supreme Court and the Austrian Supreme Court[31] disregarded the statutory rule and searched for the "economic home" of the obligation.[32] This was found to be in Czechoslovakia and payment was thus required to be made in Czechoslovak crowns, even though the place of payment was in Austria. This result—at first sight, confusing—is in fact entirely logical. Whilst the Czech monetary law could plainly require that local crowns must be paid where the place of payment was within Czechoslovakia, it could not prevent the use of its currency as a means of payment in another jurisdiction.

(d) As noted previously, the Czech Republic and the Slovak Republic (Slovakia) came into being in January 1993, upon the dissolution of Czechoslovakia. In the Czech Republic, the monetary consequences of the separation were addressed by an Act on Currency Separation.[33] The legislation provides a recurrent link between the former Czechoslovak crown and the new Czechoslovak crown, stipulating that "the nominal value of payables and receivables expressed in Czechoslovak crowns shall be converted on the day of currency separation to Czech crowns at parity".[34] This provision does not deal with the question of delimitation and, of course, many debts expressed in Czechoslovak crowns would in fact be converted into Slovak crowns instead. How was the line to be drawn? Whilst the point is not clear, it seems that the Act impliedly adopts the rule that debts were to be converted into the new Czech crown if the debtor was resident in the Czech

---

[30] As will be seen, the point was less clearly addressed when the Czech Republic and the Slovak Republic were respectively established in 1992.

[31] Czechoslovak Supreme Court, 4 June 1925, Austrian Supreme Court, 14 July 1926—*Zeitschrift für Ostrecht* (1927) 119,142.

[32] Similar language is employed by Dicey and Morris, *The Conflict of Laws* (Sweet & Maxwell, 13th edn, 2000), para 36-037. Where "an ambiguity develops between the making of the contract and its performance, it seems that, according to the better view, the debt must be calculated in the currency of the country in which the contract had its financial environment".

[33] Act No. 60/1993 of 2 February 1993. The description of the legislation is based upon a translation made available to the present writer.

[34] Act on Currency Separation, s 1(4).

Republic. This view is derived from the provisions of the Act which deal with the exchange of banknotes; natural persons and companies resident within the Czech Republic could exchange their old currency with relative ease, whilst restrictions were placed upon exchanges for foreign individuals and enterprises.[35]

(e) In contrast, upon its secession from the Federal Republic of Yugoslavia, Slovenia appears to have dealt with the question of delimitation in slightly more clear terms. The Monetary Unit of the Republic of Slovenia Act 1991[36] provided for a substitution rate of one Slovenian tolar for one Yugoslavian dinar. Once again, some debts would clearly remain outstanding in the Yugoslav unit, which continued to exist, whilst others would be converted into the currencies established by other, new States which emerged from the former Federal Republic. Whilst the Act does not deal with the question of delimitation in express terms, it does provide[37] that "banknotes and coins, designated as the monetary unit of the Republic of Slovenia, are *the only legal means of payment on the territory of the Republic of Slovenia* . . . the name of the monetary unit of the Republic of Slovenia is used for all cash and cashless payments, as well as for indicating all monetary values and amounts". It may be inferred from the language employed that the place of payment was intended to be the delimiting factor. If a debt expressed in dinars was payable within Slovenia, then it would be converted into the local tolar on a one-for-one basis. If, however, a national or resident of Slovenia owed a dinar debt which was payable outside Slovenia, then it would not be caught by Slovenia's monetary legislation and would thus remain outstanding in dinars.[38]

6.12 Where the legislator has not (expressly or impliedly) dealt with the question of delimitation, then the determination of the money of account becomes a

---

[35] Act on Currency Separation, ss 2(1), 3, and 4. It must, however, be said that such indications as the Act provides are equally consistent with the view that payables and receivables were only to be converted into the new Czech crown if they were payable within the territory of the Czech Republic. In view of the uncertainty which surrounds these provisions, a court might even be compelled to conclude that the legislation does not deal with the question of determination at all, and would then have to proceed in the manner described below.

[36] Again, the discussion is based upon a translation made available to the present writer.

[37] Monetary Unit of the Republic of Slovenia Act, art 2.

[38] It is instructive to compare the legislation passed in the Czech Republic and Slovenia. The Czech Act on Currency Separation places some emphasis on the rights of citizens and residents to acquire the new currency, thus suggesting a "personal" form of delimitation; debts expressed in Czechoslovak crowns are converted into new Czech crowns if the debtor is resident in the Czech Republic. In contrast, the Slovenian legislation refers to the tolar as the only legal means of payment *on the territory of the Republic of Slovenia*, thus establishing a "territorial" form of delimitation; debts expressed in Yugoslav dinars are thus converted into tolars if they are payable within Slovenia itself.

question of construction.[39] In the case of an initial ambiguity, it is necessary to enquire which currency the parties contemplated when they made their contract;[40] likewise, in the case of a subsequent ambiguity, one must ask which currency the parties would have contemplated if they had foreseen the territorial and concomitant monetary changes which affect the obligation concerned.[41] This, of course, involves a significant degree of artificiality, for the court will almost invariably have to impute to the parties an intention which they never formed, in relation to circumstances which they did not contemplate.[42] All the circumstances of the case will have to be reviewed and weighed, and to this extent it is legitimate to try to ascertain the country in which the contract has its "economic home", or to which it may be said to "belong".[43] As in the case of initial ambiguity of the money of account, it may well be that, as a matter of last resort, it is the currency of the place of payment that is, or rather becomes, the money of account.[44] It should, however, only be necessary to apply this rule in the rarest of cases, where strenuous attempts to interpret both the relevant

---

[39] This must necessarily be so; as has been noted on a number of occasions, the identification of the money of account is a question of contractual interpretation.

[40] See the discussion at para 5.10 above.

[41] When the German courts were confronted with this problem following the division of Germany, they tended to the view that the currency in circulation in the debtor's place of residence should be treated as the money of account: BGH 26 Jan 1951, *BGHZ* 1, 109, although, see also *BGH* 18 February 1965, *BGHZ* 43, 162 and BGH 19 February 1959, *BGHZ* 29, 320. However, in view of the principle stated in the text, it is submitted that the debtor's residence is merely one of the factors to be taken into account in determining the intention of the parties.

[42] The task is not an easy one, but it is one with which lawyers are familiar; the court must imply the intention which the parties (as just and reasonable persons) would have formed if they had thought of the question when the contract was made—see comments to this effect in *Mount Albert Borough Council v Australasian Temperance and General Mutual Life Assurance Society* [1938] AC 224, 240 where Lord Wright remarked that "the parties may not have thought of the matter at all. Then the court has to impute an intention, or to determine for the parties what is the proper law which, as just and reasonable persons, they ought or would have intended if they thought about the question when they made the contract." In *Goldsbrough Mort & Co Ltd v Hall* [1949] CLR 1, 35, 36, Dixon J said, "it may be more difficult to resolve such a case by means of presumed contractual intention. But I cannot see what other test there can be."

[43] These tests were respectively formulated in the Czechoslovak decision mentioned at n 31 above and in the *Goldsbrough Mort* case mentioned in the preceding footnote. See also Brussels Court of Appeal, 24 May 1933, *Clunet* 1933, 169 and AD 1933–4, No 41. The factual background to the decision of the Romanian Supreme Court (20 February 1931, AD 1931–2, No. 37) illustrates some of these difficulties in a particularly acute form. A buyer in Cernautzi (then part of Austria) agreed to purchase goods from a seller in Teschen (then also part of Austria) for a price expressed in Austrian Crowns. Later, Cernautzi became part of Romania, whilst Teschen became part of Czechoslovakia. The seller claimed payment in Czechoslovakian crowns, whilst the buyer sought to discharge his debt in Romanian lei at the official exchange rate for Austrian crowns. The buyer succeeded, mainly on the grounds that doubts had to be resolved in favour of the debtor; for this reason, the actual decision is of only limited interest.

[44] On this point, see para 5.12 above.

monetary legislation and the terms of the obligation itself have failed to produce a solution.

6.13 In summary, therefore, a court sitting within a State affected by a monetary delimitation will not normally be required to consider questions of private international law. Instead it will be confronted with domestic legislation which will be expressed in mandatory terms. But even then, a difficult question of statutory interpretation will be involved; the new monetary law will be mandatory in its application *to those debts to which it is expressed to apply*—for example, to debts payable within the jurisdiction or payable by persons resident within the jurisdiction. Thus, if the debt is payable abroad or the debtor is resident outside the jurisdiction, the monetary law will be inapplicable and the court must apply such general rules as may be relevant.

International cases

6.14 When considering obligations having international aspects, the position inevitably becomes more complex and the potential for conflict between the decisions of courts in different jurisdictions becomes correspondingly greater.

6.15 The complexities may perhaps best be illustrated by an example. Prior to the division of the country in 1993, the currency of Czechoslovakia was the crown. As noted above, following the establishment of the Czech Republic and Slovakia as separate States, the Czech Republic adopted the Czech crown as its unit of account, whilst Slovakia adopted the Slovak crown. The new Czech monetary law provided that all debts payable by debtors resident in the territory of the Czech Republic and expressed in the old Czechoslovakian crown should be converted into Czech crowns on the basis of a one-to-one substitution rate. Once it has been established that the debtor is indeed resident within the territory of the Czech Republic,[45] then the statutory rule is plainly mandatory in its application. So far as the Czech courts are concerned, the debt has been re-expressed in Czech crowns on the basis of the conversion rate just noted, and the court must proceed accordingly, regardless of the law applicable to the contract, the place of residence of the creditor, the place of payment, or any other factor which might ordinarily be material. As noted above, a court sitting within a country affected by the division of the monetary system may be confronted with difficult issues of domestic law but it will not normally be concerned with questions of private international law.

6.16 The position is plainly different where the same question arises before a court

---

[45] For the purposes of the present illustration, it has been assumed that the residence of the debtor is the delimiting factor for the purposes of the Czech Act on Currency Separation. The difficulties involved in this approach have already been recorded in n 35 above.

sitting outside the countries directly affected by the change to the monetary system concerned. There will usually be no direct and positive rule of (say) English law which will point the court towards a decision that the Czech or Slovak crown should now be regarded as the money of account. Furthermore, the *lex monetae* principle[46] does not assist; that principle deals largely with the substitution of *one* monetary system for another, but in the present case, the very question is—which of the *two* competing monetary laws is to prevail?

Under these circumstances, the English court must begin its enquiry with the principles of private international law. It is thus necessary to ask which system of law has the power to recognise, sanction, and enforce a change in the money of account? Since this involves a change to the *substance* of the monetary obligation, it must follow that only the law applicable to the obligation can fulfil this role.[47] At this point, it may be helpful to consider some of the cases which might arise in practice:

    6.17

(a)   Where the system of law applicable to an obligation is that of the country whose currency was originally stipulated to be the money of account and that currency continues to exist (albeit subjected to the type of territorial delimitation discussed above), then the money of account will usually remain the originally agreed currency as stipulated in the contract concerned. A country which has foregone a part of its own territory is unlikely to legislate for the conversion of debts expressed in its own currency into the unit created by the new sovereign in respect of the territory concerned. Likewise, third States not involved in the changes in territorial sovereignty or delimitation of a monetary area are unlikely to amend their domestic laws to cater for changes in obligations expressed in the old money of account. Again, therefore, where the contract is governed by English law (or some other "external" law), it is likely that the law applicable to the obligation will not contain any rules which might operate to replace the money of account under circumstances of this type. Consequently, the originally agreed money of account continues to form the substance of the obligation. It is suggested that this position should be adopted both in the State concerned and in third States (for example, in the event of proceedings before the English courts) because this result is dictated by the system of law which governs the substance of the obligation in question. Of

---

[46] The *lex monetae* principle is discussed in detail in Ch 13 below.

[47] In the case of a contractual obligation, see Rome Convention, Art 10(1). It should be appreciated that the law of the place of payment does not, as such, have any relevance in the present context. Article 10(2) of the Convention allows to that law some influence in the context of the *method* or *manner* of performance, but not in relation to the substance of the obligation itself. The general point has been discussed in Ch 4 above.

course, as noted above, courts sitting in the territory affected by the change of sovereignty may have to adopt a different attitude, because domestic monetary laws will be binding upon them, regardless of the system of law applicable to the obligation.

(b) It may be helpful to illustrate these abstract statements by means of a separate example. At a time when England and Australia shared a common monetary system, a contract expressed in "pounds" necessarily referred to the English unit. If the obligation was governed by English law, then the money of account would remain English pounds, even though Australia subsequently created its own independent currency. As noted previously, English law governs the substance of the obligation and thus the identification of the money of account; and there would be no provision of English law which would authorise or sanction the substitution of the Australian unit for these purposes. The same result ought to follow in any court outside Australia, for it should give effect to English law as the governing law of the contract. In the event of proceedings in Australia itself, there may again be many cases in which the court is bound to apply the country's monetary law, regardless of the law governing the relevant obligation. But even there, much would depend upon the scope of the monetary law. If it was not of mandatory application in cases where, for example, the place of payment is outside Australia, then an Australian court should have likewise applied English law in order to determine the substance of the obligation and, thus, the money of account.

(c) It is suggested that the conclusions reached thus far flow logically from the dominance of the governing law in ascertaining the substance of an obligation, subject to the obligation of local courts to apply the domestic laws of their own jurisdiction, where they are of mandatory application and under circumstances in which those laws, on a proper construction, are indeed applicable. The points discussed thus far do, however, assume that the applicable law remains static throughout. Clearly, if the law applicable to the obligation were changed, and became that system of law which applies in the area which has just created the new currency, then the analysis may likewise change. In particular, the new currency law would form a part of the law applicable to the contract. That law—including its provisions for the substitution of the new currency for the former unit—should in principle be applied by all courts, wherever they may sit. In the context of proceedings in foreign courts, this would lead to a conclusion directly opposite to that described in paragraphs (a) and (b) above. But when can the system of law applicable to a contract change in this way? In the previous edition of this work, it was noted that the governing law can change when both parties are subject to the new sovereign of the territory concerned, either because they are resident there or subsequently submit themselves to that sovereign.[48] It is, however, now difficult to see how a court sitting in an EU Member State could apply this principle in the light of the provisions of the Rome Convention. The scheme of the Convention requires that the applicable law must be ascertained with reference to the circumstances subsisting as at the time the contract was made.[49] Whilst the Convention contemplates that the governing law may change at a later date, this can only happen by explicit consent of the parties, and not as a result of external changes such as a change in sovereignty.[50] On this basis, a French decision dating from 1935 may well represent the modern law, but the position can perhaps best be described as obscure.[51]

(d) If the law applicable to the contract was (from the outset) the legal system of the country which has introduced the new currency, then the substitution rules contained in the relevant legislation form a part of the law which governs the substance of the obligation, and should thus be applied by courts everywhere. As a result, the new currency would become the money of account for the purposes of the obligation concerned.[52]

---

[48] See the Fifth Edition of this work, 262, citing decisions of the German Supreme Court in this context—22 March 1928, *JW* 1928, 1447; 27 June 1928, *RGZ* 121, 337, 344; 25 October 1928, *JW* 1928, 3108; 16 January 1929, *RGZ* 123, 130; 5 December 1932, *RGZ* 139, 76, 81.

[49] See generally Arts 3 and 4 of the Convention.

[50] Article 3(2) of the Convention allows the parties to "*agree* to subject the contract to a law other than that which previously governed it". It may be that the necessary consent could be implied from the conduct of the parties, eg where they continue to perform their obligations under the changed circumstances following the transfer of sovereignty. Of course, if the parties had originally selected the law of a State which has entirely ceased to exist, then a solution of the type described in the text would necessarily have to be adopted.

[51] See Cass Civ 15 May 1935, *Clunet* 1936, 601 and S 1935, I, 244. In 1914, a firm in Alsace-Lorraine (then subject to German sovereignty) sold goods to a Paris firm under a contract governed by German law. At the time of the proceedings, both parties were subject to French sovereignty and the litigation had acquired an essentially domestic character. Nevertheless, the court took the view that German law continued to govern the substance of the contract.

[52] For the reasons developed in the text, one must feel grave doubts about the interesting decision Cass Civ, 24 April 1952, *Rev Crit* 1952, 504 with note by Motulsky, *Clunet* 1952, 1234 and S 1952, I 185 with note by Batiffol, affirming Court of Appeal at Aix, 13 July 1948, *Rev Crit* 1949, 332 with approving note by Dehove and Batiffol; see also the latter's remarks in *Lectures on the Conflict of Laws and International Contracts* (University of Michigan Law School, 1951) 77, 78. A company in Paris sold to a company in Marseilles land situate in French West Africa for 5,500,000 francs. Completion took place in French West Africa on 18 December 1945. On 26 December 1945, the French West African franc was established at a rate of 100 West African francs for 170 Metropolitan francs. Article 2 of the decree exempted from conversion debts due from a resident in one "zone" to a resident of another "zone", but made no provision for the case in which both parties resided in the same "zone". It was held that the contract was localised in French West Africa and that the debt was reduced to about 3,235,000 West African francs. If the contract was subject to West African laws, the sole question was whether the decree applied to a case such as this (which seems doubtful, because payment was due before the date of the decree and because art 2 seems to supply an *a fortiori* argument in the case of both parties residing in Metropolitan France). If the contract was subject to the law of Metropolitan France, there was no warrant for changing the money of account agreed by the parties. On the other hand, two

6.18   The propositions just stated are, it is suggested, consistent with principle and are also consistent with a series of older decisions of the German courts.[53] It is, however, possible to conceive of a further variation on this theme which will introduce further layers of complexity—for example, where the obligation of the debtor is the subject of an option as to place of payment; at the time of the contract, the two places are within the same monetary area, but they fall into different countries or currency zones by the time the date of payment arrives. This state of affairs may appear contrived, but history affords numerous examples of territorial changes of this kind.[54] The issues may, however, be illustrated by a hypothetical (if perhaps controversial) example.

6.19   Suppose that a firm established in Scotland borrows £100 in 2005. Repayment is required in 2015, and the borrower has the option to pay by way of funds transfer to the creditor's account in London or Edinburgh. Suppose further that, in 2010, Scotland introduces its own independent monetary system; the relevant Scottish legislation converts into Scottish pounds (on a one-for-one basis) any debts expressed in terms of the "common" pound and which are

decisions relating to Algeria correctly recognised the substitution of dinars for francs on the ground that the contract was governed by Algerian law; Cass Civ 15 February 1972, *Rev Crit* 1973 with note by Batiffol; 14 November 1972, Bull Civ 1972, 1, No. 238. The former decision gives rise to doubts, because the contract was made before Algeria became independent (1 July 1962) and was, therefore, unlikely to be subject to Algerian law. The decision of the Paris Court of Appeal, 24 March 1973, *Rev Crit* 1976, 73 with note by Malaurie is founded on reasoning which in many respects would seem to lack persuasiveness.

[53]   The court held that a debt expressed in Austro-Hungarian crowns, which was contracted by a German with the Prague office of a Vienna bank and which was subject to German or Austrian law, was in the absence of a contractual or actual submission to Czechoslovakian law expressed in the old currency or in what had replaced it by Austrian law, because neither German nor Austrian law provided for conversion into Czechoslovakian crowns. 13 July 1929, *IPRspr* 1930, No. 30; 14 January 1931, *IPRspr* 1931, No 30; 30 April 1931, *IPRspr* 1931, No. 31; 16 December 1931, *IPRspr* 1932, No. 113. Similarly, the court held that mark debts contracted under German law in German South-West Africa were not affected by the Debts Settlement Proclamation of 15 December 1920 providing for the conversion of mark debts into pounds sterling at the rate of 20 marks to 1 pound sterling; 8 December 1930, *RGZ* 131, 41; 31 July 1936, *RGZ* 152, 53 and AD 1935–7 No. 76. On the fate of rupee debts see Czechoslovakian-German Mixed Arbitral Tribunal, *Rec* v, 551, 575 et seq; Greek-German Mixed Arbitral Tribunal, *Rec* vii, 14; and French-German Mixed Arbitral Tribunal, *Rec* vii, 604. Where liabilities arose from relationships which, as a result of Austria's secession from Germany in 1945, acquired an international character, Austrian courts seem to have held the liability to be expressed in the currency of the place of performance; if this was in Austria, the reichsmark debt was converted into schillings at the rate of 1:1 (Austrian Supreme Court, 18 January 1951, *SZ* xxiv, No. 190; 16 January 1952, *SZ* xxv, No. 11; 17 February 1954, *SZ* xxvii, No. 33), but where it was in Germany, the debt remained expressed in reichsmarks and was in 1948 converted into Deutsche marks (Austrian Supreme Court, 30 April 1953, *SZ* xxvi, No. 117, also *Clunet* 1957, 1014). But Stanzl in Klang's Commentaries, iv, 744, suggests that the courts in the first place ascertain the proper law of the contract and if this is not Austrian, then the currency cannot have been changed from reichsmarks into schillings even though the place of performance is in Austria. This would be in line with the approach suggested in the text.

[54]   The decision of the Romanian Supreme Court (20 February 1931, AD 1931–2, No. 37) provides an example of this type of case.

payable in Scotland.[55] In such a case, when payment falls due in 2015, the following analysis is suggested:

(a) So far as the courts of Scotland are concerned, the debtor may discharge his obligation by payment in Scottish pounds in Edinburgh. This result will apply regardless of the law applicable to the contract concerned, because the application of the new monetary law will be mandatory in the circumstances just described. However, the debtor may also elect to meet his obligation by payment in London. On the assumption that such option has been validly exercised, a Scottish court should hold that the debt is payable in English pounds. The new Scottish monetary law does not apply to debts payable outside Scotland, and there is thus no basis for altering the money of account as originally agreed between the parties.

(b) So far as the English courts are concerned, the application of the new Scottish monetary law will not be mandatory. As a result, it is necessary to refer to the law applicable to the obligation in order to determine whether English or Scottish pounds should be regarded as the money of account. If the loan contract is governed by English law then it appears that the English pound must remain the money of account, regardless of the place of payment selected by the debtor. Even if the debtor selects Edinburgh as the place of payment, there is no basis for applying Scottish law to vary the money of account, for English law continues to govern the substance of the obligation.[56] If, however, the contract is governed by the laws of Scotland then (1) if Edinburgh is selected as the place of payment, the English court should apply the new monetary law as a part of the governing law, with the result that the Scottish pound becomes the money of account[57] and (2) if London is the selected place of payment, then the new Scottish monetary law does not apply to the circumstances which have arisen, with the result that the English pound remains the money of account.

Under these admittedly unusual circumstances, it may be said that a contractual option of place may in fact amount to an option of currency by the time the date for payment arrives.[58]

---

[55] For the purposes of this hypothetical example, let it be assumed that Scotland has power to take such a step.

[56] In this context, contrast the provisions of Art 10(1)(a) and 10(2) of the Rome Convention.

[57] For the rare cases in which an English court should refuse to apply a foreign monetary law, see Ch 19 below.

[58] It may be added that this situation is wholly different from that which was assumed to exist in *Auckland Corporation v Alliance Assurance Co* [1937] AC 587, discussed at para 2.53 above. That case proceeded on the assumption that, at the material times, England and New Zealand had the same monetary system. The text deals with the case where a new monetary system is created in part of a formerly unitary monetary area and where, therefore, the effect of the new sovereign's supervening legislation upon existing obligations falls to be considered.

6.20 Against this general background, it becomes appropriate to consider some of the cases in which the court has had to consider the consequences of a division of a single monetary system, and the applicable money of account following that division. In doing so, it is suggested that certain key points must be carefully kept in mind and (even at the risk of repetition) these should be set out:

(1) A court sitting in the territory which has introduced the new currency will be obliged to apply the new monetary law in accordance with its terms, regardless of the law applicable to the obligation concerned.

(2) Subject thereto, the determination of the money of account is a matter governed by the law applicable to the contract concerned. This, in turn, involves two questions namely (a) what is the identity of the law applicable to the contract (ie a question of private international law) and (b) what rules will that law apply in order to determine the money of account (ie is it a question of municipal or domestic law)?

6.21 With these points in mind, it is necessary to turn to the Australian decision in *Goldsbrough Mort & Co Ltd v Hall.*[59] The case proceeded on the assumption that England and Australia had a common monetary system until 1909, at which point the Australian monetary system became separate and independent.[60]

6.22 In 1895, a company incorporated in Victoria issued debenture stock expressed in "pounds" which, at the time, necessarily referred to the single and common unit of account of England and Australia. Registers of stockholders were maintained both in Melbourne and in London, but the trustees were resident in England. The 1895 debenture stock trust deed was subsequently amended on a number of occasions, but it does not appear to have been suggested that any of these revisions resulted in an alteration in the money of account. When the loan stock fell due for redemption in 1948, it became necessary to decide whether English or Australian pounds should now be treated as the money of account. By a bare majority, the High Court of Australia decided that English pounds remained the money of account, and redemption of the loan stock had to be effected accordingly.

6.23 The case is complicated by the different approaches adopted by the five judges involved. Nevertheless, a few general points may be made. First of all, two judges[61]

---

[59] (1949) 78 CLR 1; see also the first instance decision reported at (1948) VLR 145.

[60] The *Goldsbrough* decision preceded the decision in *Bonython v Commonwealth of Australia* [1950] AC 201 (PC) where it was held that Queensland had its own currency in 1895. In *Adelaide Electric Supply Co Ltd v Prudential Assurance Co Ltd* [1934] AC 122 (HL), the majority of the House of Lords believed that the pound remained the same unit in both England and Australia. The confusion is unfortunate but it does not affect the general principles.

[61] Latham CJ and Rich J.

sought to interpret the contract without first identifying the governing law. Various tests were proposed to determine whether English or Australian pounds should be regarded as the money of account—for example, where was the commercial "setting" of the contract, where did the obligation "belong" and[62] what would the parties, as fair and reasonable men, have agreed upon under the circumstances which had now arisen? It is submitted that this approach was flawed, and it is perhaps instructive that the two judges reached opposite conclusions. In any case involving cross-border obligations (and subject in appropriate cases, to the mandatory laws of the forum) one must invariably begin by ascertaining the law applicable to the contract in question,[63] for that is the system of law which governs the substance of the obligation (including the identification of the money of account). Applying these tests, the High Court of Australia should have posed the following questions:

(a) Did Australian monetary law require the court to substitute Australian pounds for English pounds in the circumstances of the case? If this question was answered in the positive, then this would dispose of the issue before the court, for a mandatory law of this kind must be applied irrespective of the law applicable to the contract.

(b) Subject thereto, it was necessary to ascertain the law applicable to the trust deed and the loan stock issued under it. Once this had been done, it would be necessary to apply that system of law in order to determine the money of account.

(c) If the loan stock were found to be governed by English law, then the money of account—indisputably English pounds at the outset—would remain English pounds. Australian law cannot vary the terms of an obligation created and governed by English law. Under these circumstances, no further question of contractual interpretation would arise, and it would be unnecessary to consider the "setting" of the contract or other matters going to the parties' presumed intentions.[64] They had contracted by reference to English pounds and that "setting" had not changed.

(d) If the loan stock were found to be governed by Australian law then, in the absence of mandatory, domestic rules of the type described in (a) above, it would be necessary to construe the contract in order to determine whether the parties would have intended to refer to the Australian or the English currency. At this point, consideration of the economic "setting" of the

---

[62] Following *Dahl v Nelson* (1881) 6 App Cas 38.

[63] A point emphasised both in the *Bonython* case, in *Amin Rasheed Shipping Corp v Kuwait Insurance Co* [1984] AC 50, and by the Rome Convention, Art 1(1).

[64] After some discussion of other matters, this appears to be the approach adopted by Dixon J.

transaction, and other tests, would have been prayed in aid.[65] This analysis would also lead to the conclusion that the English pound remained the currency of account, for Dixon J arrived at the "reasonably plain deduction that the parties to the contract embodied in the trust deed and the stock certificates, treated the legal and financial system of England as the foundation of the transaction. It was the country with which they instinctively contrived to connect their contract most closely."[66]

D. Extinction and Replacement of a Monetary System

6.24 An independent monetary system may become extinct as a result of the fact that the whole of the territory to which it applied passes to one or more new sovereigns, none of whom continues the old standard of currency. As noted previously, German monetary history affords examples of this type of change. In June 1948, both the Federal Republic of Germany and what became the German Democratic Republic discontinued the use of the reichsmark and adopted separate currencies—both of which, confusingly, were called the Deutsche mark.

6.25 How is the money of account of an obligation to be ascertained if that obligation is expressed in a currency which has ceased to exist prior to payment? In this context, it is necessary to examine two distinct types of situations namely (a) those where a single monetary system is substituted for the outgoing currency and (b) those in which the extinct currency is replaced by two or more monetary systems.

6.26 It is, however, necessary to make a few preliminary observations about the obligations of States which may find themselves in this position. First of all, the successor State has a discretion as to whether the currency of the predecessor State will remain in circulation, or whether it will introduce its own currency in substitution therefor. But it must take one course or the other.[67] It should therefore be remembered that the obligation to pay which is expressly or impliedly acknowledged by a banknote amounts to a proprietary right so far as the holder is concerned; it follows that—at least so far as foreign holders of that currency are concerned—the simple cancellation of the former currency would

---

[65] To put matters in another way, discussion of the economic setting and other tests outlined in the case are important when a question of interpretation does arise. However, given that the loan stock was rightly found to be governed by English law, no such question should have arisen in the *Goldsbrough* case itself.

[66] At p 45.

[67] There may be cases in which a new currency would be introduced covering only the acquired territory, but this would be unusual and does not, in any event, affect the general principles about to be noted.

amount to confiscation, which would attract the international responsibility of the incoming State.[68]

Substitution of a Single Monetary System

The extinction of a currency involves no legal difficulty if a new, single currency system is substituted for it as a whole. The same remark applies where two or more currencies are replaced by a single currency.

6.27

Usually, this occurs where a State adopts a new monetary system—for example, when Germany, in 1924, replaced the then mark currency by the reichsmark; and when Hungary, in 1946, introduced the forint in substitution for the pengö currency. The outstanding recent example of this type of arrangement is offered by monetary union in Europe where the euro was substituted for the national currencies of the participating Member States.[69] In such cases, debts expressed in the old currency or currencies are uniformly and inevitably converted into the new currency at the rate of conversion (recurrent link) laid down by the legislator.[70] This follows from the principle of nominalism, which will be discussed at a later stage.[71]

6.28

The legal position is in no way different if an independent monetary system comes to an end as a result of the territory to which it applies passing to a new sovereign who introduces a new monetary system in that area, or imposes his existing currency system within the acquired territory. Again, the principle of nominalism applies; the old currency has ceased to exist and accordingly, the *lex monetae* and the recurrent link must be applied by all courts, regardless of the country in which they sit and irrespective of the governing law of the obligation concerned.[72] A relatively recent example is provided by the reunification of Germany. On 1 July 1990, the former mark of the German Democratic Republic

6.29

---

[68] See O'Connell, *Succession of States*, (Cambridge University Press, 1955) 192. For the position where a monetary system ceases to exist as a result of the actions of a belligerent occupant, see Ch 20 below, which discusses the obligations of such an occupant towards the monetary system of the vanquished State.

[69] This subject is considered in Part VI below.

[70] When multiple currencies are replaced by a single currency, it will be necessary to provide a different recurrent link in relation to each defunct currency, but this does not affect the general principle stated in the text. On the recurrent link, see para 2.34 above.

[71] See the discussion of the principle of nominalism, in Part III below.

[72] Thus, in *Trinh v Citibank NA* (1985) 623 F Supp 1526 affirmed (1988) 850 F 2d 1164 the District Court did not hesitate to follow the fate of the Vietnamese piaster, which in 1975 became South Vietnamese dongs and in 1978 Vietnamese dongs. The court did not even discuss the recurrent link or the principle of nominalism. For cases involving the 1948 substitution of the Israeli pound for the Palestinian pound on a one-for-one basis, see the decision of the Federal Supreme Court, 28 October 1959, *RzW* 1960, 172 (with note by Dr Mann) affirming Court of Appeal of Karlsruhe *RzW* 1959, 399. For a discussion of a decision of the Israeli courts (*Braunde v Palestine Corporation Ltd*), see Mann (1955) 4 AJCL 241.

was replaced by the Deutsche mark previously and continuously in circulation in the Federal Republic of Germany; two units of the East German currency were replaced by one Deutsche mark.[73] The reunification of Germany and the disappearance of the East German currency has given rise to a very doubtful decision of the Court of Appeal at Hamm. In that case, a court sitting in Czechoslovakia had, in 1986, handed down a judgment expressed in the East German unit. As a general rule, foreign judgments given in a foreign currency can be enforced in Germany without conversion into the local currency. The Court of Appeal had to decide whether the Czechoslovakian judgment should be enforced locally. One might have thought that this would be a relatively straightforward process. The judgment expressed in the East German unit would be converted into Deutsche marks based upon the substitution arrangements established by the treaty on currency union of 1990; the resultant amount would then be converted into euros by reference to the conversion rates established with effect from 1 January 1999. However, the Court of Appeal declined to take the first step, because (a) the claimant was a Czech citizen and (b) the one-to-one conversion rate laid down by the 1990 Treaty applied only to GDR citizens. The court concluded that there was no applicable conversion rate which could be applied in this case, and that it would be contrary to German public policy to enforce a foreign order where the amount payable by the debtor was uncertain. The court's decision is an unhappy one. It is true that the 1990 treaty established differential substitution rates, largely for the purpose of deterring speculation. Nevertheless, the 1990 treaty did establish a recurrent link between the East German currency and the Deutsche mark and the court ought to have applied it. The result was to disallow a daughter's claim for maintenance on public policy grounds; yet it is difficult to see how an otherwise perfectly acceptable foreign judgment can become objectionable under the principles of private international law when the only obstacle to its enforcement is some doubt or difficulty over the interpretation of a domestic law within Germany itself.[74]

---

[73] Annexe 1 to the State Treaty of 18 May 1990. The recurrent link is clearly two-to-one, although a rate of one-to-one applied in limited cases. These arrangements were frequently referred to as "German monetary union". In a loose sense, that is no doubt an adequate description but it was not a monetary union in the strict legal sense for such a union presupposes the continued existence of two or more independent States within the currency zone—see the definition discussed in Ch 24 below. At the time of German reunification, the economic and monetary arrangements were a key concern, especially given the different levels of economic development of West and East Germany. Economists tended to the view that the ostmark should continue to be used as a separate currency so that it could help to balance the economies of East and West as the ostmark found an appropriate value on the free market; others favoured a fixed but adjustable peg between the two currencies, of the kind considered in Ch 33 below. Ultimately, it was decided that the Deutsche mark should be the single currency for the entire country. This was perhaps primarily a political decision.

[74] Court of Appeal of Hamm, 25 July 2003, *Zeitschrift für das Gesamte Familienrecht* 2004 with note by Grothe which mentions the criticisms outlined in the text.

In a slightly different context, it is noted elsewhere that an insurgent government **6.30** which enjoys *de facto* control over a particular area may create a monetary system which ought to be recognised as such in law.[75] Thus, the Confederate dollar was issued during the course of the American Civil War, and at the end of that war, it was effectively replaced by the US dollar. However, no US legislation provided for any substitution rate for debts contracted in terms of the Confederate dollar; consequently, there was no recurrent link which the courts could apply for these purposes. The Supreme Court held that it was a constitutional requirement to assess the value of the Confederate currency in terms of the US dollar, and that the actual value of goods purchased with the Confederate dollar was immaterial. The creditor could therefore recover the "actual value [of the Confederate dollars] at the time and place of the contract in the lawful money of the United States".[76]

Replacement by two or more monetary systems

The extinction of a currency leads to far more serious complications if it is **6.31** incidental to the partition of a State and the consequent dissolution of a unitary currency system into two (or more) new, independent systems. At the international level, the two States concerned must apportion the obligations represented by the (former) currency between themselves in a manner which is proportionate to the amount of the treasury which they have respectively acquired. In other words, the debt represented by the (former) currency must follow the underlying assets, so far as it is possible to achieve such a division.[77] It is, however, unnecessary to pursue this point, for the present discussion is concerned with private monetary obligations.

One of the leading modern examples of this type of problem is provided by the **6.32** Federal Republic of Germany and the German Democratic Republic[78] which,

---

[75] On this point, see para 1.23 above.

[76] *Thorington v Smith* (1869) 75 US 1; *Wilmington and Welden RR Co v King* (1875) 91 US 3; *Effinger v Kenney* (1885) 115 US 566. If, therefore, a cord of wood was bought for one Confederate dollar and this had a value of 5 cents in terms of the US dollar, then the purchaser would have to pay the latter sum. The value of the wood had thus to be disregarded when the court was seeking to establish the appropriate substitution rate for these purposes; in other words, the required comparative valuation had to be achieved as between the two *means* of exchange and the *object* of exchange had to be left out of consideration.

[77] For the procedures adopted upon the dissolution of the Austrian-Hungarian Empire and upon the partition of India and Pakistan, see O'Connell, *Succession of States* (Cambridge University Press, 1955) 192. On the division of Federal assets to the successor republics following the dissolution of Czechoslovakia, see Dedek, *The Break-up of Czechoslovakia: An In-depth Economic Analysis* (Avebury, 1996) 99–116.

[78] It may be added that the UK did not recognise the German Democratic Republic until 1969. Issues of this kind perhaps assume an importance which must now be regarded as historical, but the point about to be discussed in the text requires discussion from the point of view of legal principle.

in June 1948, simultaneously abandoned the old monetary system represented by the reichsmark and each introduced new, separate currencies. Both currencies were, confusingly, labelled the "Deutsche Mark". Under these circumstances, how was a court to determine whether a pre-existing obligation expressed in "reichsmarks" should subsequently be regarded as an obligation expressed in the Deutsche mark of the Federal Republic of Germany or the Deutsche mark of the German Democratic Republic? One needs only to state this question to realise that it will not be susceptible of a straightforward answer. Nevertheless, it is suggested that the following points may helpfully be borne in mind:

(1) It is essential to obtain a clear picture of the nature of the problem at hand. In the absence of applicable statutory provisions, the problem cannot be solved by the law of either of the new currencies concerned, for neither has any legal claim to precedence over the other.

(2) It must be remembered that the current process is designed to identify the money of account in relation to the obligation concerned. Consequently, the real question is—which of the two distinct monetary systems defines the *substance* of the obligation?[79] As noted earlier, it is the contract alone which can supply the answer to this question. There is no difference in principle between the case in which the parties have at the outset failed to make an unequivocal choice of the money of account, and the case in which the money of account becomes uncertain during the life of the contract, whatever the reason for such supervening uncertainty may be. As a result, the identification of the (substituted) money of account in such cases will depend upon the proper construction of the contract and, in cases of this kind, the process of construction will inevitably depend upon the implied or presumed intention of the parties. As has been noted previously, this type of exercise will be a difficult and delicate task and it is inevitably tainted by a very high degree of artificiality; but it is not in essence very different from other cases in which the judge is compelled to fill a contractual gap created or made apparent by an unexpected turn of events.[80]

(3) Thus, if an English court is confronted with a situation of this kind involving obligations expressed in a foreign currency which has been completely replaced by two or more currency systems, then its first task is to ascertain the law applicable to the obligation concerned. If the contract is found to be governed by English law, then the court would seek to establish the economic "setting" with reference to which the contract was made, and this would in turn point towards the appropriate monetary system.[81] If the

---

[79] See para 5.07 above.

[80] See, eg, *Dahl v Nelson* (1881) 6 App Cas 38.

[81] On the test just described, see the discussion of the Australian decision in *Goldsbrough Mort & Co Ltd v Hall* (1949) 78 CLR 1 at para 6.21 above.

contract were governed by a foreign system of law, then the English court would have to attempt to apply the appropriate rules of contractual interpretation provided by that system.

(4) Issues of particular difficulty may arise if one of the States involved in the creation of the new monetary systems is not recognised by the United Kingdom—as was the case (until 1969) with the German Democratic Republic.[82] In principle, the English courts should not give effect to the monetary legislation of an unrecognised State. In the light of the State theory of money, which views money as the creation of a legal system, it is difficult to see how an English court could recognise the existence of a monetary system if the United Kingdom itself does not recognise the issuing State or its independent legislative capacity. It is true that even in such a case, recognition may be extended to those laws which deal with private or commercial rights,[83] but it is by no means clear that this principle could be extended to the monetary system as a whole. The creation of such a system implies the possession of national monetary sovereignty, the very point which is denied by non-recognition.

(5) As is invariably the case, a different approach will be involved when a question of this kind arises before a court sitting in one of the countries which has introduced one of the new currencies concerned. At the outset, the judge will turn to his legislator for guidance. The local law may have adopted one of the traditional tests[84] for these purposes and, if the rule is of a mandatory character, then the local court must necessarily apply it. But if there is no such rule, or if (by its terms) the application of that law is not mandatory in the particular circumstances, then even the domestic court must take a circuitous route. It must first of all determine the law applicable to the obligation concerned. This involves an application of the local conflict of law rules and may involve peculiar difficulty (and sensitivity) in this type of case. For example, if a contract were made in 1935 and expressed to be governed by "German law", would this term, in 1960, have been interpreted to refer to the law of the Federal Republic of Germany, or the law of the German Democratic Republic? Having answered this preliminary question and identified the governing law, the court would again have to apply such rules of interpretation as may be supplied by that system of law in order to resolve ambiguities in the money of account.[85]

---

[82] For a description of some of the legal problems which may flow from non-recognition, see the decision in *Carl Zeiss Stiftung v Rayner & Keeler Ltd* [1967] AC 853 (HL).

[83] See Mann, *Foreign Affairs in the English Courts* (Oxford University Press, 1988) 43.

[84] eg the residence of the debtor or the place of payment—see the discussion at para 6.10 above.

[85] It should be added that, in the period following the Second World War, some West German courts adopted a different approach and held that a reichsmark debt became expressed in the currency of the successor country in which the debtor had his ordinary residence—Supreme

6.33   It remains to note that many of the points here discussed will also be relevant in discussing a possible withdrawal from a monetary union; indeed, many of these points will arise in a particularly acute form in that context.[86]

Court for the British Zone 13 April 1950, *NJW* 1950, 644 with critical note by Mann, p 906; Federal Tribunal, 26 January 1951, *BGHZ* 1, 109 and *Clunet*, 1954, 916; 31 January 1952, *NJW* 1952, 871; 3 April 1952, *BGHZ* 5, 303, 309 and *Clunet* 1954, 900. However, this test is much too arbitrary (although no doubt convenient for that reason), because it does no justice to the complexity of the subject. For example, the debt (or the transaction from which it arises) may have its closest connection with some other jurisdiction; or the debtor may not reside in either of the countries affected by the currency substitution; or there may be joint debtors who are resident in different jurisdictions. The subject is discussed at length by Mann, *NJW* 1953, 643. The Federal Supreme Court (24 March 1960, *WM* 1960, 940) stated that the "debtor's residence" test only applied where the transaction involved points of contact with the Soviet Zone, and thus applied the conversion rules provided by West German currency law in a case involving parties resident in France and England. This decision appears correct, but it was overruled by a later decision of the same court (18 February 1965, *BGHZ* 43, 162 or *JZ* 1965, 448, with note by Mann).

[86] The consequences of one or more withdrawals from a monetary union are discussed in Ch 32 below.

7

THE PERFORMANCE OF
MONETARY OBLIGATIONS

A. Introduction

Chapters 5 and 6 dealt with the interpretation of monetary obligations, and **7.01** the difficulties which could arise if the money of account was uncertain at the time of the contract or became uncertain as a result of subsequent events. In some respects, those chapters were coloured by the application of Article 10(1)(a) of the Rome Convention, at least in so far as obligations of a cross-border character were concerned. At the same time, those chapters considered such rules of municipal law as fell to be applied following the identification of the governing law.

In contrast, the present chapter is more directly concerned with Article **7.02** 10(1)(b), read together with Article 10(2), of the Rome Convention, although once again the relevant rules of domestic law will also be considered. The analysis in the previous chapters has explained whether or not a monetary obligation has actually come into existence, and has explained both the nature and scope of such an obligation and the identification of the currency in which it is expressed. The present chapter assumes that a valid and enforceable monetary obligation does indeed exist; it therefore seeks to determine whether the steps taken by the debtor have been sufficient to discharge that obligation.[1] In other words, has the debtor satisfied his monetary obligation, or is he in breach of it?

7.03   In order to answer this general question, it is proposed to consider the following matters:

(1)   the concept of payment and the performance of monetary obligations;
(2)   the money of payment;
(3)   payment in the context of private international law; and
(4)   the performance of monetary obligations abroad.

B. The Concept of Payment

7.04   The concept of payment is, of course, a fundamental aspect of the law of money.[2] Payment in the legal sense must connote any act offered and accepted[3] in performance of a monetary obligation without changing the essential nature of the original obligation.[4] This approach is in some respects supported by remarks

---

[1] On the subject of payment generally, see Goode, *Payment Obligations in Commercial and Financial Transactions* (Sweet & Maxwell, 1983); Goode, *Commercial Law* (Penguin, 2nd edn, 1995) 500–17 and 1130–4; Brindle and Cox (eds) *Law of Bank Payments* (Sweet & Maxwell, 3rd edn, 2004) chs 1 and 3. For detailed discussion of payments through the banking system, see Geva, *The Law of Electronic Funds Transfers* (M. Bender, 1992).

[2] Indeed, as noted in Ch 1 above, the concept of payment is in many respects more important than the definition of money itself. It should not be overlooked that the expression "payment"—like "money"—may have different meanings in different contexts—see, eg, *Kingsby v Sterling Industrial Securities Ltd* [1966] 2 All ER 414 (CA), where the court had to consider the meaning of "actual payment" where it appeared in a statutory instrument. Likewise in *Hillsdown Holdings plc v IRC* [1999] STC 561 it was held that a "payment" connotes a transfer of funds which has some real and effective value to the recipient, although that decision again depended on a specific, statutory context. The expression "payment" does, however, necessarily connote the discharge of a monetary obligation: *White v Elmdene Estates Ltd* [1960] 1 QB 1. The same theme was taken up by the House of Lords in *MacNiven (Inspector of Taxes) v Westmoreland Investments Ltd* [2001] UKHL 6. In that case, a taxpayer had made a payment of interest out of funds loaned to it by the original lender. The Crown claimed that this was a device to avoid tax, and that for the purpose of the relevant statutory provisions, the payment should accordingly be disregarded on the basis of the approach adopted in *W T Ramsay Ltd v IRC* [1980] AC 300. However, the House of Lords held that "payment" "means an act, such as the transfer of money, which discharges the debt" (*per* Lord Hoffman, at para 67). The words "paid" and "payment" were to be given their ordinary commercial meaning and it was not possible to adopt a different approach to that point merely because the question arose in the context of a taxing statute.

[3] This language is employed by Goode, *Commercial Law* (Penguin, 2nd edn, 1995) 501, and is quoted with apparent approval by Brindle and Cox (eds) *The Law of Bank Payments* (Sweet & Maxwell, 3rd edn, 2004) para 1.1. It appears to be generally accepted that "payment" requires some act of acceptance on the part of the creditor, whilst a valid tender is a unilateral act on the part of the debtor—the point is discussed below.

[4] Thus, if the parties agree that the debtor shall hand over his car in discharge of a debt of £10,000, the car does not thereby become "money" nor does the act of delivery amount to "payment", for the parties have varied the original contract by discharging the monetary

made in the *Libyan Arab Bank* case,[5] where Staughton J stated, "in my view, every obligation in monetary terms is to be fulfilled, either by the delivery of cash or by some other operation which the creditor demands and which the debtor is either obliged to, or is content to perform".[6]

Of course, in practice, the lawyer is less likely to be concerned with purely conceptual issues. He is more likely to confront problems of a more direct nature, for example, whether the steps offered by a debtor amounted to an adequate tender of payment in compliance with the contract at issue. The subject therefore requires discussion in some depth. For convenience, it is proposed to consider sterling and foreign currency obligations separately for these purposes. This treatment merely reflects the fact that, in the case of a foreign money obligation, a right of conversion into sterling may arise where the debt is payable in England; it does not detract from the general view that no material distinction should now be drawn between domestic and foreign money obligations.[7] As will be seen, most of the relevant principles are applicable to both forms of obligations. **7.05**

Sterling obligations

How is a debtor to perform an obligation payable in sterling and to be performed in England? It is necessary to explain at the outset that the present discussion is concerned with the performance of liquidated debts or obligations.[8] In England, it is well established that a claim for an unliquidated sum cannot be discharged by payment alone—for how can one pay a sum of an indeterminate amount? An unliquidated obligation can only be discharged by accord and satisfaction—that is to say, (a) a contract between the parties which settles the amount to be paid (thus discharging the unliquidated obligation) and (b) the payment of the consideration which makes the contract operative.[9] In **7.06**

---

obligation *without* payment. But a monetary obligation retains its original character even though it is subsequently discharged by the tender and acceptance of cash, cheque, by means of a bank transfer, by means of set-off, or by any other means which might ordinarily be described as "payment": see *Charter Reinsurance Co Ltd v Fagan* [1997] AC 313, 384 (noted by Brindle and Cox (n 3 above) para 1.1).

[5] See *Libyan Arab Foreign Bank v Bankers Trust Co* [1989] QB 728, 764.

[6] Of course, it must not be overlooked that in any particular case, the concept of payment must be defined by reference to the law applicable to the obligation at issue, for questions of performance are ascribed to that system of law by Art 10(1)(b) of the Rome Convention. See the discussion at para 4.12 above.

[7] See the discussion of *Camdex International Ltd v Bank of Zambia (No. 3)* [1997] CLC 714 at para 1.61 above.

[8] The distinction between liquidated and unliquidated sums will be discussed in more detail in the context of the nominalistic principle—see Chs 9 and 10 below.

[9] On this point, see *Chitty on Contracts* (Sweet & Maxwell, 29th edn, 2004) para 22-012; *British Russian Gazette and Trade Outlook Ltd v Associated Newspapers Ltd* [1933] 2 KB 616, 643.

other words, a contract between the parties is required effectively to convert the unliquidated obligation into a liquidated debt, so that it can be discharged in accordance with the rules about to be discussed.

7.07 In contrast, the payment of a liquidated obligation pre-supposes the existence of a contract between the parties.[10] No further agreement is therefore required either to fix or to discharge the obligation. However, when notes and coins are handed over to the creditor, or money is transferred in any other way, it seems that the purpose of the transfer must either be made clear to the creditor or it must otherwise be apparent from the circumstances. The debtor must intend to discharge his obligation by the payment in question. The point may seem obvious but difficulties can arise in particular cases. For example, if a company owes a series of ten debts of £1,000 each, which of those debts is discharged if it pays £2,000 to its creditor? The point may be important, especially where each debt carries a different rate of interest.[11] Likewise, suppose that a father owes a debt of £1,000 to his son. Shortly before his death, the father hands £1,000 (or a larger sum) to his son in cash. Did the father intend to repay his debt, or did he intend to make a gift to his son in anticipation of the father's death? In the latter case, the debt could be recovered from the father's estate, whilst in the former case it plainly could not. Applying the rules discussed above it seems that (in the absence of any intimation that the father intended to discharge his debt) the payment would fall to be treated as a gift.

7.08 If the intention of the debtor is important, then one is naturally driven to enquire as to the relevance of the intention of the creditor. The debtor will have undertaken to pay the creditor under the terms of the contract and (by necessary implication) the creditor must have agreed to accept it. Why, otherwise, has he entered into the contract at all? But in spite of this reasoning, it seems clear that no creditor is under any positive, legal duty to accept payment, nor can the debtor effectively force payment upon the creditor. If payment is to be made in a legal sense, then the consent of the creditor is necessarily required.[12] If the creditor declines to accept the proffered funds—even though tendered in strict conformity with the terms of the contract—then payment does not occur in the

---

[10] An obligation to pay a liquidated amount may also arise in other ways, eg pursuant to statute, but for present purposes the discussion is limited to contractual claims.

[11] Under English law, the debtor has the right of appropriation. But if he fails to communicate that appropriation to the creditor at the time of payment, then the creditor may instead exercise the right of appropriation—see *Chitty on Contracts* (n 9 above) paras 21-059 and 21-061. The debtor's intention was important in *The Turiddu* (CA, 29 June 1999).

[12] For another formulation, see Goode, *Payment Obligations in Commercial and Financial Transactions* (Sweet & Maxwell, 1983) 4. The point made in the text would also follow from the definition of "payment" given above, which refers to an act offered *and accepted* in discharge of a monetary obligation. The same point is emphasised in Brindle and Cox (eds) *Law of Bank Payments* (Sweet & Maxwell, 3rd edn, 2004) para 1.1.

legal sense, even thought the creditor's refusal is apparently at odds with the terms of the contract. All the debtor can do is to *tender* payment, ie he may make an unconditional offer to pay in the agreed manner. In the event of non-acceptance, this places the creditor in default because he is responsible for the delay in performance.[13] If the tender complies with the terms of the contract and the debtor thereafter remains ready and willing to pay in that manner, then any action brought against him will be dismissed with costs, provided that the money is paid into court immediately after service of the proceedings.[14] Under English law, therefore, it is necessary to re-emphasise the distinction between tender and payment in accordance with the terms of the contract. Tender is a unilateral act of the debtor, whereby he takes all of the steps which are open to him, acting alone, to complete the payment in accordance with the terms of the contract. On the other hand, payment is a bilateral act requiring the consent both of the debtor and creditor.[15]

In English law, therefore, the question of law is not how payment is to be made, **7.09** for it may be made by any means agreed between the parties or which the creditor may otherwise choose to accept. Anything so agreed and accepted constitutes a payment provided that the creditor is put in a position freely to dispose of the money transferred to him, to the extent required by the terms of the contract.[16] The correct question is—how is a valid and effective tender to be made, such that it will produce the legal consequences described above? In principle, the answer is that a valid tender is made by unconditionally[17] proffering

---

[13] cf Code Civil, art 1257 and German Civil Code, ss 293 and 294. Under the latter provisions, the debtor must tender payment in accordance with the terms of the contract, and the creditor who refuses to accept such performance is in default of his contract. So far as English law is concerned, the creditor's refusal to accept payment does not of itself appear to constitute a breach of contract, with the result that the debtor would not thereby become entitled to damages in respect of the non-acceptance. Even if it did constitute a breach, the debtor would usually find it difficult to show that he had suffered any loss as a result of the non-acceptance.

[14] Civil Procedure Rules 1998, r 37.3. Any claim for damages or interest will generally also be dismissed—*Rourke v Robinson* [1911] 1 Ch 480. However, an award of interest may be made if the debtor continues to make use of the money following the tender—*Barratt v Gough-Thomas* [1951] 2 All ER 48. The formulation of these rules in the Fifth Edition of this work, 75 was cited with approval in *TSB Bank of Scotland v Welwyn & Hatfield DC* [1993] 2 Bank LR 267 and in *Commissionsers of Customs and Excise v National Westminster Bank plc* [2002] EWHC 2204. On the procedural issues, see *Greening v Williams* The Times, 10 December 1999.

[15] See *Chitty on Contracts* (Sweet & Maxwell, 29th edn, 2004) para 21-039; Goode (n 12 above) 14.

[16] See *Seligman Bros v Brown Shipley & Co* (1916) 32 TLR 549; *The Chikuma* [1981] 1 All ER 652 (HL). In the same sense, see *China Mutual Trading Co Ltd v Banque Belge pour l'Etranger* (1954) Hong Kong LR 144, 152—"payment by a debtor into a blocked account cannot be a good discharge of a debt".

[17] A conditional tender will not usually suffice—see *Re Steam Stoker Co* (1875) LR Eq 416. However, where there is some doubt about the creditor's contractual entitlement to the payment, the debtor may elect to make payment "under reserve", which creates a right to reimbursement if the creditor's claim is ultimately held to be ill-founded—see *Banque de I' Indochine et de Suez v JH Rayner (Mincing Lane) Ltd* [1983] 1 All ER 468.

to the creditor the amount due in legal tender,[18] or otherwise in compliance with the terms of the contract. This rule enjoys general recognition[19] and is firmly established in England. In so far as the rule relates to cash, there exists a long line of decisions of the Court of Appeal which have expressed it in the clearest terms and occasionally in remarkable circumstances. At the end of the nineteenth century, the Court of Appeal held that £463—then a substantial amount—had to be proffered in legal tender. As a result, a solicitor had no authority on behalf of his client to accept another solicitor's cheque, and accordingly such a cheque could not constitute a valid tender.[20] A year later, the Court of Appeal likewise held that an auctioneer was entitled to insist upon a deposit being paid "in cash", ie in legal tender rather than by cheque; and the rule was held still to be "strictly" applicable even as late as 1974.[21] The rule is, however, in all respects subordinate to the terms of the contract and (in the light of modern commercial practice) the courts will be very astute to find that the obligation to pay in cash has been varied or waived.[22]

7.10   Where large amounts are involved, payment by legal tender is frequently unthinkable and cannot possibly be within the contemplation of the parties. Accordingly, whilst a contractual requirement for payment "in cash" may in some cases connote a requirement to pay by means of legal tender,[23] terms of this kind must always be interpreted against the background of modern commercial practice. Consequently a contractual requirement for "payment in cash" was interpreted to indicate "any commercially recognised method of transferring the funds the result of which is to give the transferee the unconditional right to the use of the funds transferred".[24] The robust process of interpretation

---

[18] On the notes and coins which constitute legal tender in the UK, see Currency and Banking Notes Act 1954, s 1 and Coinage Act 1971, s 2 as amended by Currency Act 1983, s 1(3).

[19] See, eg, the decision of the German Federal Supreme Court, 25 March 1983, *BGHZ* 87, 162.

[20] *Blumberg v Life Interests and Reversionary Securities Corp* [1897] 1 Ch 171, affirmed [1898] 1 Ch 27.

[21] *Pollway Ltd v Abdullah* [1974] 1 WLR 493, dealing with a sum of £555 and where (on the particular facts) the Court was justified in concluding that a requirement for payment "in cash" involved an obligation to pay with legal tender.

[22] Thus, if a creditor objects to the amount of a tender but does not complain about its mode or form, then he will be taken to have waived any objection to the tender on the latter ground. The whole subject of tender is considered in *Chitty on Contracts* (Sweet & Maxwell, 29th edn, 2004) paras 21-083–21-096. In so far as those principles deal with a tender in physical cash, it will be noted that the English authorities there cited are of some antiquity; this perhaps reflects the realisation that the courts cannot now be expected to lend their assistance to a vexatious creditor who refuses to accept a reasonable means of payment. To the collection of English cases cited by Chitty, there may be added the American decisions in *Atlanta Street Railway Co v Keeny* (1896) 25 SE 629; *Jersey City and Bergen Railroad v Morgan* (1895) 160 US 288 and *US v Lissner* (1882) 12 Fed Rep 840. Once again, these cases are largely of historical interest.

[23] eg as in *Pollway Ltd v Abdullah* [1974] 1 WLR 493.

[24] *The Brimnes* [1973] 1 WLR 386, 400. This definition was approved by the Court of Appeal in the same case, [1975] QB 929, 948, 963 and 968. It was also approved by the Court of

just described can only be further accelerated by the current (and strenuous) governmental efforts to prevent money laundering and to trace the proceeds of crime, and which thus render problematical the acceptance of physical cash in many cases.[25] But the existence of such an implied term (or the existence of the creditor's consent) was perhaps surprisingly denied in a case involving the repayment of some US$292 million, with the result that the debtor would have been required to pay that sum in cash.[26]

If it follows from the above discussion that a creditor may often be compelled to accept a payment in the "commercial equivalent" of cash (or, perhaps more accurately, the debtor may be entitled to make his tender by proffering such an equivalent), then it naturally becomes necessary to identify that which will amount to a commercial equivalent. Plainly, it would not include a cheque, for in the absence of his express or implied consent, the creditor cannot reasonably be expected to take the risks of countermand or dishonour; further, pending clearance, the effect of payment by cheque is to allow the debtor a few days continued use of the money.[27] But if the creditor refuses to accept a banker's draft issued by a reputable institution and insists on legal tender, then the Court should treat the creditor's attitude as vexatious and uphold the validity of the tender. It may pray in aid the judgment of the US Supreme Court in support of its approach.[28] Thus, an obligation to pay "in cash" to the credit of

7.11

Appeal in *Mardorf Peach & Co Ltd v Attica Sea Carriers Corp of Liberia* [1976] QB 835, 849–54. The Court of Appeal's comments remain valid even though its decision was reversed by the House of Lords, [1977] 3 All ER 124. For a good example of the Court's attitude, see *Farquharson v Pearl Assurance* [1937] 3 All ER 124. Where the debtor has, with the creditor's approval, established a direct debit with his bank for payments to be made over an extended period, it may be that the existence of the direct debit mandate constitutes a sufficient tender in respect of each instalment, even though the creditor omits to collect the funds: *Weldon v SRE Linked Life Assurance* [2000] 2 All ER 914 (Comm).

[25] In relation to the UK, it is an offence to be concerned in arrangements which assist in the retention or concealment of "criminal property", a term which includes the monetary fruits of crime—see Proceeds of Crime Act 2002, Pt 7; some of the difficulties which can arise in this context are discussed and considered in *P v P (Ancillary Relief: Proceeds of Crime)* [2003] EWHC Fam 2260. In the context of terrorist funds, see Anti-Terrorism, Crime and Security Act 2001, Pts 1 and 2. These UK measures reflect international trends in the same area.

[26] *Libyan Arab Foreign Bank v Bankers Trust Co* [1989] QB 728. It will be necessary to return to this case in the context of the performance of foreign money obligations and the debtor's option to pay in sterling—see para 7.23 below.

[27] That the offer of a cheque does not constitute a valid tender was decided in *Re Steam Stoker Co* (1875) LR 19 Eq 416 and in *Johnson v Boyes* [1899] 2 Ch 73; more recent authority to the same effect may be found in *OK Bakery Co v Morten Milling Co* (1940) 141 SW (Texas) 436. In many cases, the contract may stipulate for payment by cheque or the creditor may elect to accept it anyway, but that does not in any sense affect the statement in the text.

[28] *Simmons v Swan* (1927) US 113, where the creditor had rejected an instrument in the nature of a banker's draft. Mr Justice Holmes said: "If without previous notice he insisted upon currency that was strictly legal tender instead of what usually passes as money, we think that at least the plaintiff was entitled to a reasonable opportunity to get legal tender notes and as it was too late to get them that day might have tendered them on the next."

an account at a particular bank may be performed by means of a bank transfer, for the net result for the creditor is the same in either case.[29] Likewise, in some cases, it will be possible to infer from previous dealings that the creditor is prepared to accept payment in a particular manner, or a similar inference may be drawn from the conduct of the parties or the surrounding circumstances.[30] If a creditor has agreed to accept payment by cheque, then the delivery of the cheque constitutes a valid tender, but the debt is still only discharged when the creditor accepts the cheque.[31]

7.12 It should not be overlooked that this process of interpretation is necessary in order to conclude that the creditor—whether expressly or impliedly—has waived his right to receive payment in cash.[32] For the reasons just given, this type of interpretation will usually be reached with ease, but it must nevertheless be emphasised that the validity of any payment or tender otherwise than by legal tender does depend upon the express or implied consent of the creditor; whilst this may easily be inferred it is not possible to dispense with it.[33] Furthermore, it may be necessary in particular cases to consider the nature and extent of the consent which the creditor has given. For example, the debtor may happen to know that the creditor has several bank accounts; has the creditor consented to payment to any of these accounts, or merely to selected accounts? The point may be important if the recipient bank fails shortly following receipt of the payment and before the creditor has been notified of the funds transfer. If the payment was so made without the creditor's (express or implied) consent, then it is difficult to see why the creditor should be saddled with the loss under such circumstances; if such a payment were treated as a valid discharge of the obligation, then the creditor would necessarily also lose the benefit of any guarantee or security which he might hold. So far as English law is concerned, it is now clear that payment to the account of the creditor with a particular bank will not discharge the obligation—nor will it even constitute a valid tender—in the absence of the creditor's consent; the same principle appears to have been

---

[29] See *Mardorf Peach & Co Ltd v Attica Sea Carrier Corp of Liberia* [1977] AC 850. The very fact that the contract includes details of the creditor's bank account must surely imply that payment by means of a funds transfer is to be accepted in lieu of cash.

[30] Thus where the creditor includes details of his bank account on notepaper or invoices, he must be taken to have consented to payment by way of transfer to that account: German Federal Supreme Court, 13 May 1953, *NJW* 1953, 897; contrast the decision in *Commissioners of Customs & Excise v National Westminster Bank plc* [2002] EWHC 2204.

[31] *Official Solicitor to the Supreme Court v Thomas* The Times, 21 February 1988, and noted in *Butterworth's Encyclopaedia of Banking Law* (Looseleaf, 1996) para D1.

[32] The waiver may be an express or implied term of the contract or it might be derived from the subsequent conduct of the creditor.

[33] For a telling example, see the decision of the Court of Appeal at Frankfurt, 22 September 1986, *JZ* 1986, 1072: a taxi driver may insist on payment in cash and refuse a euro-cheque.

applied elsewhere.[34] In other words, whilst "bank money" may in general practice be accepted by creditors as a means of payment, it does not follow that they are legally bound to do so. Bank money and other non-cash forms of money can thus only function as money with the creditor's consent but, as noted elsewhere,[35] this does not in any sense disentitle them to their label as "money".

It has been shown that a monetary obligation can be discharged by any means   **7.13**
agreed between the parties or to which the creditor is prepared to consent. In most cases, of course, the creditor will be very willing to accept any reasonable form of payment tendered to him, even if it does not strictly conform to the express or implied terms of the original agreement. Creditors will accept payment by means of cheque, letter of credit, or other instruments. Instruments of this kind are regarded by the courts as "equivalent to cash", so that, following dishonour, judgment for the face amount of the instrument will generally follow as a matter of course.[36] The drawer of the cheque cannot raise defences or counterclaims arising under the underlying commercial contract, at any rate in the absence of fraud.[37] Of course, the mere acceptance of the cheque or other instrument by the creditor does not of itself constitute "payment", for it does not have the immediate effect of making funds available to the creditor;[38] such instruments only constitute payment if they are subsequently honoured, but if this happens then the date of payment is deemed to be the date on which the cheque, letter of credit, or other instrument is given.[39] If the creditor has authorised the debtor to pay by cheque and send it through the post, then the creditor

---

[34] In England, see *Commissioners of Customs & Excise v National Westminster Bank plc* [2002] EWHC 2204; see also the decisions of the German Supreme Court, 25 March 1983, *BGHZ* 87, 163; 5 May 1986, *BGHZ* 98, 24, 29, 30. In relation to France, see Cass Civ, 12 February 1960, S 1960, 131; Cass Com, 19 July 1954, D 1954, 629, Cass Civ, 12 January 1985, D 1989, 80.

[35] See para 1.51 above.

[36] Such instruments are "equivalent to cash" in the sense that, in the absence of fraud, judgment must usually be given for the full face amount of the instrument, disregarding any counterclaims of the drawer. As noted previously, however, the creditor cannot be compelled to accept a cheque in the absence of a contractual obligation to do so, for he cannot be required to run the risk of dishonour. Consequently, a cheque is not "equivalent to cash" in this latter sense. In *Stirling Properties Ltd v Yerba Pty Ltd* [1987] 73 ACTR 1, an Australian court noted that under modern commercial conditions, the parties may expect to make and receive payment by cheque, but that the entitlement to pay by cheque is not absolute and depends upon the acceptance of the tender by the creditor.

[37] See, eg, *Nova (Jersey) Knit v Kammgarn Spinnerei GmbH* [1977] 2 All ER 463, HL. In the context of documentary credits, this rule is frequently referred to as the "autonomy" principle. It now appears that similar treatment is to be accorded to a direct debit, on the footing that it is an assurance of payment which is separate from the commercial contract—see *Esso Petroleum Ltd v Milton* [1997] 1 WLR 938, CA.

[38] This is especially the case in the context of bills of exchange and documentary credits, which may have maturity periods of several months or even longer.

[39] See *Chitty on Contracts* (Sweet & Maxwell, 29th edn, 2004) paras 21-073 and 21-084. English decisions on the subject include *Re Hone* [1951] Ch 85; *ED & F Man Ltd v Nigerian Sweets and Confectionary Co Ltd* [1977] 2 Lloyds Rep 50. The same point arose for decision in

runs the risk that the cheque will be stolen and paid to a third party.[40] By contrast, payment by means of a credit card will usually involve the unconditional and absolute discharge of the debtor, for the supplier of goods or services accepts the issuing company's payment obligation in place of the customer's liability. The customer thereupon assumes an obligation to make a corresponding payment to the card issuer.[41]

7.14 Important though the foregoing means of payment may be in daily life, it must be said that the most difficult types of dispute which may have arisen in recent years have centred on payment by means of bank transfers.[42] No doubt this is because transfers of this kind are now viewed as both a secure and more rapid means of transferring funds, and because the higher values which may be involved create a greater incentive to litigation in the very few cases in which some difficulty occurs.[43] In practical terms, most disputes have centred on the

---

WJ Alan & Co Ltd v El Nasr Export & Import Co [1972] 2 All ER 127 (CA), a case which has broader monetary law implications and will thus be referred to in other contexts. More recent confirmation of the same rule is provided by *Day v Coltrane* The Times, 14 April 2003. The position in the US is similar: *Ornstein v Hickerson* (1941) 40 F Supp 305. See also the remarkable decision of the Appellate Division of South Africa in *Eriksen Motors (Wellcom) Ltd v Protea Motors, Warrenton and others* (1973) 3 South African LR 685, 693. Since the payment "relates back" to the date on which the instrument was given, it follows that any contractual right to interest cannot accrue from that date, even though the creditor may be out of funds for a few days pending presentation and clearance of the cheque. The French courts have likewise held that payment occurs on the receipt of the cheque, subject to clearance—Cour de Cassation, Ch Soc 17 May 1972, D 1973, 129, whilst the German courts seem to look to the date of the dispatch (not receipt) of the cheque—Federal Supreme Court, 7 October 1965, *NJW* 1966, 47 and 29 January 1969, *NJW* 1969, 875.

[40] This was so decided by the Court of Appeal in *Norman v Ricketts* (1886) 3 TLR 182. It appears that the authorisation to post the cheque must be explicit and cannot be derived from a previous course of dealing—*Pennington v Crossley* (1897) 77 LT 43. Both of these decisions merit reconsideration, but they were followed in *Thairwall v Great Northern Railway Co* [1910] 2 KB 509. As noted in the text, a cheque is treated as a payment, on condition that it is subsequently honoured; this must mean that the cheque must be paid when presented for payment by or on behalf of the creditor himself. Of course, if the paying bank becomes insolvent at this point, then the cheque will not be met and the creditor must pursue the drawer of the cheque, who will not have been discharged. For the position where the collecting bank becomes insolvent, see *Re Farrow's Bank Ltd* [1923] 1 Ch 41 and the discussion in Goode, *Commercial Law* (Penguin, 2nd edn, 1995) 588.

[41] For an analysis of the obligations of the debtor, creditor and card issuer, see *Re Charge Card Services Ltd* [1989] Ch 497.

[42] The means by which banks effect such transfers and the systems established for that purpose are beyond the scope of this book. For a discussion, see Goode, *Commercial Law* (Penguin, 2nd edn, 1995) 505–17; Brindle and Cox (eds) *The Law of Bank Payments* (Sweet & Maxwell, 3rd edn, 2004) ch 3. For present purposes, it must, however, be noted that a payment by means of funds transfer will generally (although not invariably) involve the use of the payment and clearing systems in the country which issues the currency concerned—see the discussion of this difficult subject in Brindle and Cox (above) paras 3-24–3-293.

[43] The expression "bank transfers" is well understood in practice; the processes involved are well described in the note to art 4A of the Uniform Commercial Code—the text is reproduced by Goode (n 42 above) 507. Nevertheless, the term is liable to obscure the subject, for in fact nothing

precise time and the date at which payment has been received. If payment was tendered later than the contractual date and time, then a number of consequences may ensue. First of all, the creditor may become entitled to interest or other damages in respect of the late payment. Alternatively, the creditor may be contractually entitled to reject the tender, to terminate the arrangements and, in a rising market, employ his assets more profitably elsewhere.[44]

Whether or not a payment or tender by means of a bank transfer has complied **7.15** with the terms of the contract between the creditor and the debtor inevitably involves (a) an analysis of the contract in order to ascertain what he was obliged to do and (b) an analysis of the steps taken by him in the intended performance obligation. This statement of the obvious means that one must separately consider the *contractual* time of payment and the *actual* time of payment.

As to the first point, the time at which payment should be made (or, more **7.16** accurately, tendered) is once again a matter of substance which must be ascertained by reference to the law applicable to the contract.[45] Each case will thus depend upon the terms of the contract at issue. A few general points may however be noted in an English law context:

(1) If no time for payment is expressly stipulated, then it must be inferred from the terms of the contract. Where the contract involves the provision of services, payment will often be due once the work has been completed and

---

is "transferred" at all. There is no transfer of "property"; there is merely the extinction of the debt owing by the debtor's bank to the debtor and the creation of a new debt owing by the creditor's bank to the creditor. This led to the conclusion that a defendant could not be convicted of the offence of obtaining property "belonging to another" by deception when he had dishonestly procured the proceeds by a bank transfer, because the property thereby obtained (ie the benefit of the debt owing by the bank to the defendant) had never "belonged" to anyone else—see *R v Preddy* [1996] AC 815 (HL) and contrast *R v Hilton* The Times, 18 April 1997, CA. The decision in *R v Preddy* was reversed by the Theft (Amendment) Act 1996. The court in *R v King* [1991] 3 All ER 705 suggested that a payment order through the Clearing House Automated Payments System (CHAPS) operated to transfer a proprietary right in the chose in action represented by the bank credit. For the reasons just given, no assignment of the credit is involved, and the decision must be regarded as incorrect to that extent; this aspect of the decision does, in any event, seem to be nullified by the House of Lords' analysis of bank transfers in the *Preddy* case—see the discussion in Brindle and Cox, (eds) *The Law of Bank Payments* (Sweet & Maxwell, 3rd edn, 2004) para 1-005. That the use of the word "transfer" may lead to confusion in this area was also noted by Staughton J in *Libyan Arab Foreign Bank v Bankers Trust Co* [1989] QB 728, 750.

[44] It is no accident that a number of the cases which dealt with the precise time of payment involved shipowners who wished to terminate charterparties in order to obtain the higher returns then available in the market. Had the market been moving in the opposite direction, the owners would no doubt have contented themselves with payments which had been tendered, even though technically out of time.

[45] Rome Convention, Art 10 (1)(a).

the debtor has had an opportunity to confirm its completion to a proper standard.[46]

(2) The time of payment is not usually of the essence of the contract[47] unless the express terms or the nature of the contract require a contrary conclusion or, following notice to perform given by the creditor, the debtor's continuing delay becomes a matter which goes to the root of the contract breach.[48]

(3) The mere stipulation of a date for payment will not usually indicate that time is of the essence of the contract. But where time has been expressed to be of the essence, then the courts will be slow to find a waiver of that term. Thus, where a contract provides for "punctual" payment on a Sunday, payment on Monday is too late.[49] Where payment has to be made "on demand", the debtor has to have it ready at a convenient place where he can get it within a reasonable time and without having to make time-consuming arrangements.[50]

Whilst the identification of the date on which payment is contractually due may occasionally be obscure, the time at which payment is in fact made can usually be determined without difficulty.[51]

7.17 Where the creditor is to accept payment by means of a transfer of funds to his bank account, it is suggested that payment occurs only when the account has been unconditionally credited with the requisite amount. It is sufficient if the amount was credited intentionally and in good faith, and not as a result of error or fraud, and under circumstances that the credit is unconditional and cannot properly be reversed. Payment is deemed to be made at that point, because the bank has unconditionally recognised that the recipient has become a creditor of the bank to the extent of the amount so transferred.[52] Notification to the

---

[46] For examples, see *Hughes v Lenny* (1839) 5 M & W 183; *The Tergeste* [1903] P 26.

[47] See, eg, Law of Property Act 1925, s 41 and Sale of Goods Act 1979, s 10(1).

[48] For the relevant rules in this area, see *Chitty on Contracts* (Sweet & Maxwell, 29th edn, 2004) paras 21-011 and 21-026. Time may also be of the essence in certain contracts of a financial nature where the only material obligations of both parties are of a monetary character, eg interest rate swaps, currency swaps, or similar transactions. The point will invariably be academic, since such contracts will usually contain express provisions dealing with the consequences of a payment default.

[49] *Mardorf Peach & Co Ltd v Attica Sea Carriers Corp of Liberia* [1977] AC 850. This would remain the case even if the law of the place of payment allowed for later payment as a result of the holiday, for the law applicable to the contract should be given effect where the contract stipulates for a specific date and makes it clear that nothing later will suffice. In each case, the express terms of the contract would appear to override the court's discretion to "have regard" to the law of the place of payment: see Art 10(2) of the Rome Convention.

[50] *RA Cripps v Wickenden & Son Ltd* [1973] 1 WLR 944, 955.

[51] See generally the Report and the proposed rules submitted by the Monetary Law Committee of the International Law Association, Warsaw Conference (1988).

[52] On this formulation, see Goode, *Commercial Law* (Penguin, 2nd edn, 1995) 513.

creditor is not required in order to perfect or complete the payment, or to render it effective;[53] nor is it even necessary that the creditor's bank has actually received a corresponding payment from the debtor's bank.[54] It must be re-emphasised that the creditor must have complete, unconditional, and immediate access to the full amount of the funds concerned. Thus, if payment is due on 22 January and is credited to the creditor's account on that date, but subject to the proviso that the "value date" is 26 January, then payment is only deemed to be made on 26 January, for the creditor only has full access to the required funds on the latter date. This remains the case even though the creditor could access the funds on 22 January subject to minor interest or other charges, for the requirement for such deductions derogates from the full and complete unconditionality which is an essential feature of this form of payment.[55]

It may be argued that (as between the parties) payment should be treated as **7.18** made when the requisite funds are received by the creditor's bank, ie before they will actually have been allocated to the creditor's own account. There is something to be said for this view, in that the debtor has done everything in his power to ensure payment and he should not be prejudiced by errors or delays within the creditor's bank in ensuring proper allocation—the creditor must take all the risks associated with his own choice of bank. This appears to be the justification for the first instance decision in *The Afovos*,[56] where payment was held to be complete at the point at which the receiving bank had received and tested the incoming telex from the paying bank. However, the decision was reversed and no firm views were expressed on the point in the

---

[53] On these points, see *Momm v Barclays Bank International Ltd* [1977] QB 790. This case is of particular interest because both the creditor and the debtor had accounts at the same bank, and the transfer was thus to be achieved through actions to be effected entirely "in-house".

[54] This point, which might otherwise easily be overlooked, is made by Professor Goode, *Commercial Law* (Penguin, 2nd edn, 1995) 109. In many cases, the creditor's bank may not even expect to receive a directly corresponding and immediate payment from the debtor's bank. It may simply debit an account which the debtor's bank has with the creditor's bank and this may well happen *after* the creditor's own account has been credited.

[55] This is the effect of the House of Lords decision in *The Chikuma* [1981] 1 WLR 314. The decision itself may be criticised on the facts, because the "value date" condition was stipulated as between the transferring and the receiving institutions, but does not appear to have been reflected as a condition of the credit to the creditor's own account. For criticism, see in particular Mann (1981) 97 LQR 379. Despite these criticisms, the decision does make it clear that in the context of a monetary obligation, performance must be *complete*, and not merely *substantially* complete. There is thus no room for the argument that payment of £999,990 constitutes substantial performance of an obligation to pay £1 million. This may be contrasted with other forms of obligation where, eg, a duty to deliver 12,600 tons of maize may be adequately performed by the delivery of 12,588 tons, if that would reflect the intention of the parties—see *Margaronis Navigation Agency Ltd v Henry W Peabody & Co of London Ltd* [1965] 1 QB 300.

[56] [1980] 2 Lloyd's Rep 479. The decision in this case would seem to be inconsistent with the earlier decision in *The Effy* [1972] 1 Lloyd's Rep 18—see n 60 below.

House of Lords.[57] In the United States, it has been held that payment is treated as made once the electronic transfer instructions to the receiver bank have become incapable of alteration or revocation—an actual credit to the creditor's account was not a necessary part of the payment process.[58] But in spite of these decisions, it is suggested that payment can only be deemed to be made when the necessary credit entry has been made to the creditor's account, for it is only at that point that the creditor will acquire the immediate and unconditional use of his money which, as has been shown, is an essential ingredient of payment. Thus in *The Brimnes*[59] the Court of Appeal noted that "the credit of the owner's account so as to give them the unconditional right to the immediate use of the funds transferred was good payment" and " 'payment' is not achieved until the process has reached the stage at which the creditor has received cash or that which he is prepared to treat as the equivalent of cash or has a credit available on which, in the normal course of banking practice, he can draw, if he wishes, in the form of cash". It is submitted that these statements are entitled to approval,[60] and that accordingly, nothing short of a credit entry is sufficient to achieve payment under these circumstances.[61]

7.19   The foregoing discussion has naturally focused on the *monetary* questions which

---

[57]   [1983] WLR 195. It was suggested (at 204) that the practice of bankers should be regarded a decisive in this area, but this statement must be treated with some care given that it is the rights and obligations of non-bank parties which are at issue.

[58]   *Delbreuck & Co v Manufacturers Hanover Trust Co* (1979) 609 F 2d 1047. It should be said that this case involved an attempt by a debtor to revoke payment instructions given to its own bank; and it is fair to observe that (under the rules of systems which effect this type of payment) revocation of the instructions may become impossible some time before the funds are actually allocated to the creditor's account, ie revocation may become impossible whilst the payment is going through the system. Whilst the decision is an important one, it may not necessarily be of direct relevance in the context of payment as between the debtor and creditor themselves.

[59]   [1975] QB 929, 948 and 963.

[60]   In *The Brimnes* [1973] 1 WLR 386 the charterer's bank asked the owner's bank to make an internal transfer of the amount due in respect of hire to the owner's account. The telex which made this request arrived before the owners gave notice to terminate the charter, but that notice was given before the recipient bank had made the decision to allocate funds to the owner's account. The despatch of the telex could not be regarded as "payment" because it did not create a source of immediately available funds so far as the owner was concerned. The decision in *The Effy* [1972] 1 Lloyd's Rep 18 was perhaps a little harsher from the perspective of the charterer, although it is entirely consistent with the principles just described. In that case, the necessary funds arrived at the owner's bank on the due date (5 October 1970) but owing to the incompleteness of instructions given to one of the correspondent banks involved in the process, the payment was not actually credited to the owner until he had been given notice to terminate the charter. Once again, the notice was found to have been validly given, because the owner did not have unconditional access to the necessary funds on the due date.

[61]   This point has been decided by the German Federal Supreme Court, 25 January 1988, *BGHZ* 103, 143, which also confirms that notification to the creditor is unnecessary to complete the payment. The International Law Association (Warsaw 1988, Report of 63rd Conference) also regards an unconditional credit as both necessary in order to achieve payment, and sufficient for that purpose.

arise for consideration in relation to the performance of a financial obligation. It is, however, necessary to add a few comments about the *personal* aspects of such an obligation. In particular:

(a) Reference has been made to the "debtor" and the "creditor" with respect to a monetary obligation. Whilst the point will only arise infrequently, it should be remembered that the identity of either of these parties may be in dispute.[62] The point is plainly important in those few cases in which it does arise. The obligations of a debtor can only be imposed upon a party which has agreed to perform them, and the debtor cannot usually obtain a good discharge by payment to a person other than the creditor.

(b) Difficult problems may also arise where agents or intermediaries become involved in the payment process. Where a third party purports to make payment on behalf of the debtor, the debtor's obligation will only be discharged if the third party purported to act as the debtor's agent and the debtor had approved or subsequently ratified that arrangement.[63] Equally a payment made by the debtor to a third party will only result in an effective discharge of the obligation if the creditor has authorised him to receive payment, or has held him out as having such authority.[64]

(c) Payment to a bank or other intermediary does not discharge the obligation if it is made subject to a condition which is not permitted under the terms of the contract, for generally the funds must be at the full disposal of the creditor to deal with as he thinks fit.[65]

(d) Further, payment by transfer to the creditor's bank account will not of itself normally operate to discharge the debtor's obligation. It has been shown that payment can only be achieved with the consent of the creditor and, whilst his bank may have authority to *receive* payment, it will not normally have authority to *accept* it on behalf of the creditor in the contractual sense just described. The tender is only accepted when the creditor treats the funds as his own[66] or where he fails to take steps to reject the funds within a

---

[62] eg see *Stag Line Ltd v Tyne Shiprepair Group Ltd* [1984] 2 Lloyd's Rep 211; *Empresa Lineas Maritimas Argentinas v Oceanus Mutual Underwriting Association (Bermuda) Ltd* [1984] 2 Lloyd's Rep 517.

[63] *Keighley Maxted & Co v Durant* [1901] AC 240, (HL); *Owen v Tate* [1976] QB 402; Goode, *Commercial Law* (Penguin, 2nd edn, 1995) 503–4.

[64] For cases in which this type of issue has arisen, see *A-G for Ceylon v Silva* [1953] AC 461 (PC); See *Mardorf Peach & Co Ltd v Attica Sea Carrier Corp of Liberia* [1977] AC 850; *Cleveland Manufacturing Co Ltd v Muslim Commercial Bank Ltd* [1981] 2 Lloyd's Rep 646; *Armagas Ltd v Mundogas SA* [1986] AC 717 (HL); *First Energy (UK) Ltd v Hungarian International Bank Ltd* [1993] 2 Lloyd's Rep 194 (CA).

[65] *Re Steam Stoker Co* (1875) LR 19 Eq 416; *Seligman Bros v Brown Shipley & Co* (1916) 32 TLR 549; *The Chikuma* [1981] 1 WLR 314 (HL).

[66] *TSB Bank of Scotland plc v Welwyn Hatfield DC and Brent LBC* [1993] 2 Bank LR 267.

reasonable time of becoming aware of the credit.[67] On the other hand, having received the funds transferred, it was not open to the creditor's bank to reject the transfer and return the funds to the debtor's bank, unless it has authority from the creditor for that purpose. To express matters in a different way, the bank becomes indebted to the customer when it receives the funds for credit to his account, and there is no implied term of the contract which entitles the bank unilaterally to cancel that debt. This may seem to be a curious statement, yet it became the practice of some banks to reject or to return funds transfers if there were grounds for suspecting that they were the proceeds of criminal activity. It has now been decided that a bank could not commit a money laundering offence merely on the grounds that it received and retained funds under these circumstances, although the bank would have to comply with the reporting requirements laid down by the Proceeds of Crime Act 2002. Where a bank returned the funds to the remitting bank in such a case, it did so without lawful authority and thus remained indebted to the customer for the amounts which had temporarily been credited to his account.[68]

Foreign currency obligations in England

7.20 How, in principle, is a foreign money obligation to be paid in England?[69] Many of the issues of a purely monetary law character have been discussed above in the context of sterling obligations. The starting point must therefore be that a foreign currency obligation governed by English law must be discharged by the payment of legal tender prescribed by the *lex monetae*. As discussed earlier, however, this *prima facie* rule may be displaced by the express or implied consent of the creditor, whether expressed in the contract itself or at the point of payment.

7.21 The obligation to pay in the legal tender of the *lex monetae* is inherent in the nominalistic principle as understood in England.[70] It defines not only the quantum of the obligation, but also the form of payment. Thus, it was held that the obligation to repay in Gibraltar a loan of pesetas involved the duty "to pay in whatever at the date of repayment was legal tender and legal currency in the country whose money was lent".[71] In strict terms, this remains the case if the

---

[67] *Mardorf Peach & Co Ltd v Attica Sea Carriers Corp of Liberia* [1977] AC 850 (HL); *HMV Fields Properties Ltd v Bracken Self Selection Fabrics Ltd* [1991] SLT 31.

[68] See *Tayeb v HSBC Bank plc* [2004] EWHC 1529 (Comm) The case contains a useful description of the Clearing House Automated Payments System (CHAPS) and an analysis of the bank's potential liability as a constructive trustee if it is found that a customer was not the true owner of the funds passed through his account.

[69] The present section works on the basis that England is the place of payment.

[70] The nominalistic principle is considered generally in Part III below.

[71] *Pyrmont Ltd v Schott* [1939] AC 145, 153 (PC).

original loan was made by means of a cheque or bank transfer in favour of the borrower.[72] Yet it must be repeated that, at least in commercial cases, the requirement for payment in legal tender has both a dated and unrealistic flavour; consequently, the requirement for payment in this form should readily be set aside in modern business conditions, especially where large sums are involved.[73]

As has been noted on a number of occasions, English law now strives, so far as **7.22** possible, to treat sterling and foreign money obligations on an essentially similar footing. Both types of obligations are classified as "debts" and the legal framework applicable to their enforcement in England will be the same in each case. Yet it is clear that this assimilation of domestic and foreign money obligations cannot be regarded as entirely complete. The very fact that an English law contract is expressed in a foreign currency raises private international law questions which would not arise in the context of a sterling obligation arising between the parties in England. Furthermore, where payment is to be made by means of an inter-bank funds transfer, it will frequently be necessary to record and give effect to that transfer through the payments or clearing system operated in the country which issues the currency concerned. If the contractual place of payment is *outside* that country, then it is plain that further conflict of law issues can arise.

Such questions arose in a particularly acute form in English litigation concerning **7.23** US sanctions against Libya. In the leading case on the subject, *Libyan Arab Foreign Bank v Bankers Trust Co,*[74] a Libyan entity maintained accounts with both the London and New York branches of the defendant American bank. In January 1986, the US President imposed sanctions against Libya by blocking Libyan property held by US persons, both within and outside the United States. The Presidential Order thus prohibited repayment of the London deposits by Bankers Trust. The case is one of some complexity, but for present purposes it is sufficient to note that: (1) the London account was found to be governed by English law;[75] and (2) following demand, amounts owing to the depositor were repayable in London. It followed that the Libyan depositor was entitled to judgment because:

---

[72] If England is the place of payment, the debtor may have the option to pay in sterling in accordance with the principles outlined at para 7.30 below.

[73] It must, however, be acknowledged that this statement is in some respects at odds with the decision in *Libyan Arab Foreign Bank v Bankers Trust Co* [1989] QB 728.

[74] [1989] QB 728.

[75] This point would now flow from the application of Art 4(2) of the Rome Convention, but it is also consistent with the pre-existing rules of private international law.

(a) the US Presidential Order plainly could not vary, suspend or discharge an obligation governed by English law;[76] and

(b) although the English courts will not enforce a contract where the steps necessary for performance are illegal in the place of performance,[77] the rule did not apply in this case. The place of performance was London, where the depositor was entitled to receive his money. The fact that funds would have had to be cleared through New York in order to achieve that payment did not mean that New York thereby became the place of payment.

7.24   In the result, the Court held that the Libyan depositor was entitled to the repayment of some US$292 million in cash, because the right to receive payment in that form was not affected by market practice or by the previous course of dealings between the parties. This decision was made in the face of cogent expert evidence to the effect that eurodollar deposits of this kind and amount are never repaid in cash. In other words, it was not possible to imply into the contract a term which required that payment should only be made through the clearing system operated in New York. Nor could it now be argued that the obligation was to procure a credit to an account in New York, so that such obligation ceased to have a purely monetary character and could thus become impossible to perform;[78] such an argument in any event becomes more difficult to maintain in the light of the definition of "payment" which was adopted earlier in this chapter. Whilst this result understandably caused some consternation in international banking circles, it may be seen as satisfactory from the purely monetary law perspective. It would be unfortunate if a debtor acquired additional defences to a monetary obligation merely because he has to pay by means of bank transfer rather than in cash or, to put matters another way, the intended *mode* of performance should not have an impact on the broad *substance* or *enforceability* of the obligation; such a state of affairs would subvert the dominance of the applicable law of the contract over the law of the place of performance.[79] Further, a single monetary obligation must have a single place of performance; this is sound both from a logical perspective and also because it

---

[76] However, had the deposit contract been governed by New York law, then the Presidential Order would have formed a part of the law applicable to the contract. In the absence of some countervailing consideration of public policy, the English courts would then have to give effect to the blocking arrangements—see *Libyan Arab Foreign Bank v Manufacturers Hanover Trust Co (No. 2)* [1989] 1 Lloyd's Rep 608.

[77] This is the rule in *Ralli Bros v Compania Naviera Sota y Aznar* [1970] 2 KB 287. For a criticism of this rule, see para 16.38 below.

[78] The suggestion was made in the Fourth Edition of this work, 193. It could be argued that this view derived some support from the decision in *Re Banca Commerciale Italiana* [1942] 2 All ER 208, but the point is not convincing.

[79] The relative priority of the applicable law in this area is established by Art 10(1)(b) of the Rome Convention, read together with 10(2).

ensures that the unfortunate rule in the *Ralli Bros* case is confined within proper limits.[80]

It was for some time thought that a distinction ought to be drawn between, on the one hand, an ordinary foreign currency obligation and, on the other, an obligation to repay a eurocurrency deposit.[81] The distinction between the two types of obligation is one of fact. For example, an individual may hold a foreign currency account with a London bank. Funds may periodically be paid into or out of the account; cheques may be drawn upon it. This ordinary type of account must be distinguished from a eurocurrency deposit, which will usually involve a single deposit of a very significant sum of money for a fixed term and at a pre-agreed interest rate; the transaction consists solely of the initial deposit and its subsequent repayment with interest. Deposits of this kind are normally placed and repaid by means of bank transfers. It was suggested that the latter type of deposit was only repayable via CHIPS or the corresponding payment system in the country of issue. It was therefore argued that eurodollar deposits should in this respect be treated differently from ordinary foreign currency accounts, and the suggestion met with some academic support.[82] However, since the existence of the implied term was rejected in the *Libyan Arab Bank* case, it seems likely that there are no legally relevant distinctions to be made between the two types of account.[83]

7.25

Leaving aside these special difficulties, it becomes necessary to ask the more general question—how is a foreign money obligation required to be performed in England?[84] The essential question may be briefly stated: how (*quomodo*)

7.26

---

[80] For a discussion of the *Libyan Arab Bank* case, see Smedresman and Lowenfeld, "Eurodollars, Multinational Banks and National Laws" (1989) 64 New York University LR 733. The authors are critical of the court's reasoning, on the ground that eurodollar deposits were always repaid via CHIPS, and never in cash (p 761), although they approve the result (p 801) on the basis that the law of the place where the deposit is maintained should govern. But the case was decided on the basis that English law alone was applicable to the London deposit. The issue was whether the English contract included an implied term that payment would not be made in cash. Since the authors believe that such a term ought to have been implied, the decision would not "have come out as it did" (p 801).

[81] The US Supreme Court has defined eurodollars as "United States dollars that have been deposited with a banking institution outside the US with a corresponding obligation on the part of the banking institution to repay the deposit in US dollars" *Citibank NA v Wells Fargo Asia* (1990) 495 US 660. The legal nature of eurodollars has been considered at para 1.67 above.

[82] See, eg, Goode, *Commercial Law* (Penguin, 2nd edn, 1995) 118–20.

[83] In the Fifth Edition of this work, 200, it was suggested that the debtor's option to pay in sterling might be excluded in the case of a eurodollar deposit. However, this argument would likewise appear to be unavailable following the decision in the *Libyan Arab Bank* case; the court saw no objection to ordering payment in sterling if payment in US dollars proved to be impossible.

[84] In cases in which there is no doubt that an obligation expressed in foreign money is required to be settled in that money, there will usually be no difficulty. If the debtor is to pay in cash, he must proffer whatever constitutes legal tender for the requisite amount in accordance with the

should the debtor discharge his obligation to pay a sum of foreign money which he owes and the identity (*quid*) and extent (*quantum*) of which is defined? If a debtor has incurred an obligation of US$1,000 payable in London, is he obliged to tender that sum in US dollars, or is he entitled or even obliged to tender the equivalent sum in sterling? In other words, can or should the money of the place of payment be substituted for the agreed money of account where there is a lack of identity between them, so that the mode of payment differs from what appears to be the substance of the obligation?[85]

7.27   It is, of course, true that in most cases, the debtor who owes US$1,000 payable in London will simply tender that amount in US dollars, whether in cash or in some other convenient form acceptable to the creditor. It will probably not occur to either party even to consider adopting a different course of action. Furthermore, payment should be effected in such a manner as to ensure that the creditor or the debtor does not receive or pay any more or any less than he contracted for; the best way to achieve this result is to require payment of the stipulated sum *in natura*. If there is a promise to pay US$1,000 in London, and if it is performed by the payment of US$1,000, neither party has any ground of complaint.[86] That the international value of US$1,000 may have risen or fallen between the date of the contract and the stipulated maturity date is an entirely irrelevant consideration, for only the US dollar is at issue.[87] In such a case, it is clear that the mode of payment is in accordance with what is determined by the substance of the debt, because the money of account and the money of payment are identical; the money of the place of payment does not even fall for consideration.

7.28   On the other hand, there may be many cases where no prejudice to either the creditor or the debtor would be involved if, for the purpose of performing the contract, the money of account is converted into a different money of payment. This would generally be so in times of relative monetary stability and may even be so when monetary values are fluctuating, at least if payment is made on the stipulated maturity date. Furthermore, if the creditor generally carries on business in sterling, he would in all probability convert the dollar proceeds into

---

lex monetae—see *Marrache v Ashton* [1943] AC 311 and the discussion at para 7.09 above. If he is to transfer funds to the creditor's bank account, then the principles described at para 7.17 above (in relation to sterling payments) will apply equally in this context.

[85] It will be apparent that this type of problem arises only where the money of account differs from that of the place of payment.

[86] This self-evident proposition finds judicial support in *Société des Hôtels Le Touquet v Cummings* [1923] 1 KB 451 (CA).

[87] The statement in the text reflects the principle of nominalism.

sterling upon receipt. It may well be that nothing is lost by such an arrangement, and the creditor will have no objection at all.[88]

Under these circumstances, it becomes necessary to consider whether such a right of conversion exists, who is entitled to exercise any such right and what rate of exchange is to be used; it must also be asked whether the right of conversion can be excluded, and whether the right continues to apply when the debt is overdue. Each of these questions requires separate consideration. **7.29**

The right of conversion

There seems to be no doubt that a general right of conversion exists where foreign money is to be paid in England.[89] The origins of this right lie in the law merchant of the Middle Ages. In connection with bills of exchange, it was conceived at an early date that, from the point of view of both parties and the State, it was convenient and advisable to avoid the recurrent remittance of a domestic currency to a foreign place of payment. This objective could be achieved by requiring the creditor to accept local money at the place of payment. **7.30**

Against that background, it is perhaps unsurprising that the right of conversion became recognised in most countries.[90] The general right of conversion is recognised in the United States[91] and is perhaps most firmly established in relation to bills of exchange.[92] Whilst there exists widespread agreement on the principle **7.31**

---

[88] This line of reasoning does, however, have its limitations—eg an international bank makes and receives countless payments on every business day. It would be very inconvenient if its borrowers or counterparties could all elect to meet their obligations in sterling instead of the stipulated currency. In practical terms, however, the point will arise only rarely; London will not usually be the place of payment for financial obligations expressed in US dollars (although, see the discussion of the *Libyan Arab Bank* litigation, at para 7.23 above).

[89] This statement must, however, now be read subject to the provisions of Art 10(2) of the Rome Convention. The relevance of this provision in the present context is discussed later in this section.

[90] For an illuminating comparative survey, see Dach (1954) 3 AJCL 155.

[91] Section 3-107 of the Uniform Commercial Code reads:

A promise or order to pay a sum stated in a foreign currency is for a sum certain in money and, unless a different medium of payment is specified in the instrument, may be satisfied by payment of that number of dollars which the stated foreign currency will purchase at the buying sight rate for that currency on the day on which the instrument is payable or, if payable on demand, on the day of demand. If such an instrument specified a foreign currency as the medium of payment, the payment is payable in that currency.

For a South African case which recognises the right of conversion, see *Barry Colne & Co (Transvaal) Ltd v Jacksons Ltd* (1922) South African LR, Cape Prov Div 372.

[92] Article 14 of the Uniform Law on Bills of Exchange and Notes (League of Nations Official Journal, xi (1930), 933) reads as follows:

When a bill of exchange is drawn payable in a currency which is not that of the place of payment, the sum payable may be paid in the currency of the country, according to its value on the date of maturity. If the debtor is in default, the holder may at his option demand that the amount of the bill be paid in the currency of the country according to the rate of the day of maturity or the day of payment.

of conversion into the money of the place of payment, different answers have been given to some of the detailed questions—for example, whether the debtor may or must convert, the rate of exchange to be used and similar matters.[93] It is obvious that these questions of detail may have significant consequences for the parties. For example, the rate of exchange as at the date of payment is plainly acceptable if the debtor meets his obligations on the maturity date, for the creditor receives full value for the amount owing. But what rate should be adopted if the debtor is in default? The rate of exchange as at the maturity date may differ from that which prevails as at the date of payment; whether this position favours or disadvantages the debtor or the creditor will of course depend upon exchange rate movements in the intervening period. Neither the selection of the rate of exchange as at the due date or that applicable as at the date of payment can be guaranteed to produce a fair result in every case. In truth, the crux of the matter lies in the fact that the selection of either date cannot eliminate the need for the creditor to be able to claim damages for monetary depreciation during the period of the debtor's default.[94] Where no such claim can be entertained, the creditor must effectively take his risk on monetary depreciation.

7.32 Under these circumstances, perhaps the best solution is that to be found in the Uniform Law on Bills of Exchange and Notes.[95] The debtor may elect to pay in the currency of the place of payment provided that payment is made on the maturity date.[96] But if payment is made *after* the maturity date, the creditor may select either the rate of exchange which prevailed at the maturity date or that

---

The usages of the place of payment determine the value of foreign currency. Nevertheless the drawer may stipulate that the sum payable shall be calculated according to a rate expressed in the bill.

The foregoing rules shall not apply to the case in which the drawer has stipulated that payment must be made in a certain specified currency (stipulation for effective payment in foreign currency).

In so far as it relates to foreign currency obligations payable in Germany, a similar rule is to be found in art 244 of the German Civil Code. Article 244 was amended with a view to the introduction of the euro. It is thought that art 244 should be applied by the German courts regardless of the law which governs the contract at hand, because the article would form a part of the law of the place of performance for the purposes of Art 10(2) of the Rome Convention, although see the discussion in n 110 below.

[93] This state of affairs prompted the International Law Association to take up the subject and, in 1956, it accepted the "Dubrovnik Rules" prepared by its Monetary Law Committee—*Report of the 47th Conference* (1956) 294. These rules were considered by the Council of Europe which, in 1967, opened for signature the European Convention on Foreign Money Liabilities (European Treaty Series No 60). However, the Law Commission rejected the Convention and the Government accordingly declined to sign it. The text is reproduced in Appendix IV to the Fourth Edition of this work.

[94] As to the circumstances in which a claim for such damages may be made, see paras 9.36–9.45 below.

[95] See Article 14, reproduced in n 92 above.

[96] As mentioned above, in the absence of some contrary stipulation, the creditor should have no objection to this arrangement, for he receives the value to which he is entitled.

which prevails as at the date of payment. Thus, in the event of delayed payment, the creditor will receive the full value reflected by the substance of the debt, and the debtor cannot profit from his delay.

Where this happy solution does not apply, some countries have adopted a rule **7.33** requiring conversion at the maturity date, whilst others have adopted the rate as at the date of payment.[97] For reasons given earlier, neither solution will be satisfactory in every case. In the United States, however, the legal effect of the debtor's default has at least found a more secure solution. It was stated by Mr Justice Holmes, giving the judgment of the Supreme Court in *Hicks v Guinness*.[98]

On 31 December 1916, a German debtor owed to an American creditor **7.34** a sum of 1, 079.35 marks on an account stated; the creditor brought an action claiming the dollar equivalent on 31 December 1916. Mr Justice Holmes said:[99]

> We are of the opinion that the Courts below were right in holding that the plaintiffs were entitled to recover the value in dollars that the mark had when the account was stated. The debt was due to an American creditor *and was to be paid in the United States.* When the contract was broken by a failure to pay, the American firm had a claim here, *not for the debt, but, at its option, for damages in dollars. It no longer could be compelled to accept marks.* It had a right to say to the debtor, you are too late to perform what you have promised and we want the dollars to which we have the right by law here in force . . . The event has come to a pass upon which your liability becomes absolute as fixed by law . . .

As was made clear in a later case,[100] these remarks were based on the assumption **7.35** that the obligation was subject to the law of the United States. Thus, under the rules laid down in *Hicks v Guinness*, a debtor is entitled to meet his obligation on the stated maturity date by payment of the requisite amount of foreign currency stipulated in the contract. However, in the event of late payment, the creditor acquires an optional right to payment in US dollars calculated at the rate of exchange prevailing on the maturity date. These rules apply if the obligation is subject to the laws of the United States and the obligation is payable within that country.[101]

What, then, is the solution so far as English law is concerned? There is no **7.36**

---

[97] For comparative materials, see the Fifth Edition of this work, 316–19.
[98] (1925) 269 US 71.
[99] At 80, emphasis added.
[100] *Deutsche Bank Filiale Nürnberg v Humphreys* (1926) 272 US 517, 519. See also *Sutherland v Mayer* (1926) 271 US 272. These cases are noted in more detail at para 8.12 below.
[101] For a more recent application of the rule, see *Jamaica Nutrition Holdings v United Shipping* (1981) 643 F 2d 376, although it is difficult to understand why the plaintiffs did not sue for the sum of US dollars with which they procured the Jamaican dollars.

statutory provision which deals with the matter.[102] The problem admits of three possible solutions:

(a) the debtor who has to meet a foreign currency debt in England has an obligation to tender that foreign money only;

(b) the debtor may be required to tender sterling only; or

(c) the debtor may have the option of tendering the stipulated foreign currency or sterling.[103]

7.37 As to the first alternative, it can only be said that this does not prevail; it would be curious if the creditor could reject a tender in his own currency and which provides to him the monetary value for which he contracted.[104] The second alternative is unattractive for it is difficult to see why English law should prevent the debtor from tendering that which he has undertaken to pay; and if as a result of some express stipulation there may be a positive duty to tender foreign currency, the absence of such a term cannot very well have the effect of excluding the mere right to do so.[105] Further, if the debtor were positively *prevented* from making payment in the contractual currency, then this position would seem to be irreconcilable with the principle of nominalism, which is a fundamental tenet of monetary law. Thus there remains the third alternative, which allows the debtor the option of paying in the stipulated currency or in sterling.[106] This is, in fact, the prevailing rule in England:

---

[102] Bills of Exchange Act 1882, s 72(4) formerly allowed for payment in the currency of the place of performance, but this provision was repealed by Administration of Justice Act 1977, s 4. Cases on s 72(4) include *Syndic in Bankruptcy v Khayat* [1943] AC 507 and *Barclays International Ltd v Levin Bros* [1977] QB 270.

[103] In some countries, of course, the ability to tender foreign currency may be limited by exchange controls of the kind described in Ch 14 below, but this aspect has to be left out of account for the purposes of the present discussion.

[104] As will be seen, however, the debtor may assume a contractual obligation to tender *only* the foreign currency in question—see para 7.43 below. It would be wrong to attach any weight to the mere assumption in *Marrache v Ashton* [1943] AC 311, 317 that a debtor who tenders Spanish pesetas in Gibraltar would specifically perform his obligation to deliver a commodity, and that a breach of this duty involves a liability to pay damages. The notion of foreign currencies as "commodities" must be regarded as suspect following the decision in *Camdex International Ltd v Bank of Zambia (No. 3)* [1997] CLC 714.

[105] Again, not too much should be read into Lord Reid's observation that "all payments which had to be made in Melbourne must be made in Australian currency": *National Mutual Life Association of Australasia v A-G for New Zealand* [1956] AC 369, 389.

[106] A further alternative might allow the creditor the option to require payment either in the foreign currency or in sterling. Whether or not the creditor enjoyed the right to demand payment in sterling in lieu of the stipulated foreign currency was left open by the court in *Libyan Arab Foreign Bank v Bankers Trust Co* [1989] QB 728, but it is suggested that this solution would be impracticable. It would, eg, be necessary to stipulate for the creditor to give a period of notice prior to the maturity date, so that the debtor would know what was expected of him and he would have adequate time to make the necessary arrangements. It must be said that the statement departs from the old decision in *Willshalge v Davidge* (1586) 1 Leon 41: the creditor was entitled to a payment in "ducats" and "portugues" and it was held that it was "in his election" to demand

I think it is clear that when someone is under an obligation to pay another a sum of money expressed in a foreign currency but to pay it in this country, the person under the obligation has an option, if he is to fulfil his obligation at the date the money is payable, either to produce the appropriate amount in the foreign currency in question or to pay the equivalent in sterling at the rate of exchange prevailing at the due date. This proposition seems to me to be elementary and a matter of common sense.[107]

7.38 Earlier authorities are less explicit but clearly operate on the basis of the same proposition by accepting that the debtor can pay in the money of the place of performance.[108] Thus in one case, Bankes LJ remarked:[109]

In my experience, I have never heard the proposition challenged that in an ordinary commercial contract where a person has entered into a contract which is to be governed by English law and has undertaken an obligation to pay in foreign currency a certain sum in this country the true construction of the contract is that when the time comes for payment the amount having to be paid in this country will be paid in sterling, but at the rate of exchange of the day when payment is due, applicable to the particular currency to which the contract refers.

7.39 This language suggests that the debtor's option to pay in sterling can only arise where the contract is governed by English law, for a matter of construction is involved. Yet it is submitted that this is not the correct approach to the debtor's option. If the obligation is expressed in a foreign currency, then a right to discharge it by payment in sterling must be regarded as a rule which deals with

---

payment either in the proper coin of the contract or in sterling. For the reasons just given, this solution is not practicable. As noted earlier, art 244 of the German Civil Code allows a debtor to settle a foreign currency debt in Germany by payment in the domestic currency. It has been expressly decided that the option is that of the debtor, and the creditor has no right to demand that such a debt be paid in the domestic currency: German Federal Supreme Court, 7 April 1992, *IPRax* 1994, 336, with note by Grothe (at 346).

[107] *Barclays International Ltd v Levin Bros* [1977] QB 270, 277. The reference to the rate of exchange at the due date is correct if payment is made on that date, and the court rightly emphasised the requirement for punctual payment. That the debtor enjoys this option is confirmed by some of the older cases, eg *Adelaide Electric Supply Co Ltd v Prudential Assurance Co Ltd* [1934] AC 111. The same rule has more recently been confirmed in *Libyan Arab Foreign Bank v Bankers Trust Co* [1989] QB 728. If payment is delayed, see *George Veflings Rederi A/S v President of India* [1979] 1 WLR 59, considered below.

[108] *Ralli Bros v Compania Naviera Sota y Aznar* [1920] 2 KB 287, 291, 294 and 299; *Rhokana Corp Ltd v IRC* [1937] 1 KB 737, 797 (reversed on other grounds, [1938] AC 380); *New Brunswick Railway Co v British & French Trust Corp* [1939] AC 1, 23. If the debtor is for some reason prohibited from tendering the required amount of foreign money in England, then it seems that he must exercise the option to pay in sterling—see *Libyan Arab Foreign Bank v Bankers Trust Co* [1989] QB 728. In other words, the debtor has an option to pay either in sterling or the relevant foreign currency, but he cannot exercise that option in a manner which effectively deprives the creditor of the right to payment.

[109] *Anderson v Equitable Assurance Society of the United States of America* (1926) LT 557, 562. See also the remarks of Warrington LJ at 564: "the payment having been made in London would be a payment in sterling". The decision in this case was followed in *Heisler v Anglo Dal Ltd* [1954] 1 WLR 1273.

the mode of performance rather than its substance, and this remains the case regardless of the identity of the law which is applicable to the contract as a whole. Accordingly, if a foreign money obligation is payable in England, the debtor's option to discharge the debt in sterling forms part of the law of the place of performance and can be taken into account if necessary to do justice between the parties.[110]

7.40 If the option to pay in sterling is exercised, it has already been shown that the date with reference to which the exchange rate is ascertained may have a significant impact. Whilst the creditor should not object to receiving sterling so long as he receives full "value", an exchange arrangement which affects the quantum of his receipt would interfere with the substance of the obligation and is thus plainly unacceptable from that perspective. Fortunately, it is now possible to say that the conversion is to be effected at the rate of exchange on the date of payment, "this is the clear result of the *Miliangos* case".[111] Thus, it is the rate at the date of actual payment (and *not* at the contractual maturity date) which will determine the amount of sterling which the debtor must tender in discharge of his foreign currency obligations.

7.41 It will be necessary to identify a rate of exchange to be applied in the event that the debtor exercises his option to pay in sterling. It is tempting to think that the rate of exchange should be ascertained in accordance with the law of the place of payment (ie English law, in this context) because that is the place in which the creditor will receive his funds. However, since the selected rate may affect the amount which the creditor will receive, it is submitted that the identification of

---

[110] The rule deals with the mode of performance and regard may be had to that rule in accordance with Art 10(2) of the Rome Convention. It is submitted that the provision applies even to foreign currency contracts made between persons in England governed by English law and requiring that payment is made in England. As has been noted in Ch 4 above, a contract expressed in a foreign currency necessarily involves, albeit to very limited extent, the "splitting" of the law applicable to the contract. The agreement thus falls within the scope of Art 1(1) of the Convention, which applies to "contractual obligations in any situation involving a choice between the laws of different countries". Similar questions have arisen in relation to art 244 of the German Civil Code which, upon the introduction of the single currency, was amended to state that foreign currency obligations payable within Germany could be discharged by payment of the corresponding amount in euros, unless the parties have explicitly agreed to the contrary. Although the point remains controversial, it has been suggested that in the light of Art 7(2) of the Rome Convention, art 244 of the Code should be applied regardless of the law which governs the contract as a whole. This view is maintained by Grundmann, *Münchener Kommentar zum Bürgerlichen Gesetzbuch*, Vol 2a (Kruger, 4th edn, 2003) paras 241–432. However, the parties' option to contract out of the provision, coupled with the fact that the provision deals with the mode of settlement of foreign currency obligations in Germany, suggest that it might not qualify for the status of a mandatory law and thus might alternatively be categorised as a part of the ordinary law of the place of performance. For the time being, the point must remain open.

[111] *George Veflings Rederi A/S v President of India* [1979] 1 WLR 59, 63, *per* Lord Denning MR. The full implications of the *Miliangos* case are considered in Ch 8, below. The same point also forms a part of the decision in *Libyan Arab Foreign Bank v Bankers Trust Co* [1989] QB 728.

the rate of exchange should be regarded as a matter of substance and should accordingly be governed by the applicable law.[112]

It is necessary to make one final observation about the debtor's option to **7.42** discharge his foreign currency obligation in sterling. It has been shown that this option is derived from the fact that English law supplies the law of the place of performance. But the influence of the law of the place of performance has in some respects been diluted by Article 10(2) of the Rome Convention. As a result, it is submitted that the option to pay in sterling now rests on a less secure foundation than was hitherto the case. Since the point may be relevant in any case where the location of the place of payment differs from the money of account (ie it is not confined to cases in which payment is to be made in England), the subject will be considered below.[113]

Exclusion of the conversion option

It is clear that the debtor's option to convert a foreign money obligation into the **7.43** money of the place of payment can be excluded by the parties; this is particularly so in the case of bills of exchange.[114] This seems to mean that a problem of construction is involved; certainly this appears to be the approach adopted by English law.[115] Thus, if an intention to exclude the debtor's sterling option can be discerned, then the debtor will be bound to pay in the stipulated foreign currency. Such a different intention may readily be inferred from the terms of the contract and the surrounding circumstances. There is no need for an express

---

[112] Of course, the distinction is of no consequence if the contract is governed by English law. English law will usually apply the rate at the place of payment in any event: see para 18.10 (3) below.

[113] See "The Money of Payment", para 7.52 below.

[114] Since the repeal of s 72(4) of the Bills of Exchange Act 1882, there is no express provision in England. The so-called "effective clause" is, however, commonly seen in bills of exchange and means that payment must be made in the stipulated currency. The addition of such a clause does not deprive the instrument of its character as a bill of exchange; it remains an unconditional order to pay a fixed sum of money at a specified future date for the purposes of s 3 of the 1882 Act. According to Dicey and Morris, *The Conflict of Laws* (Sweet & Maxwell, 13th edn, 2000) para 36-055, the validity of an "effective" clause should be tested by reference to the law of the place of payment. However, since the "effective" clause is intended to reflect the intention of the contracting parties, and may affect the amount which the debtor is required to pay, it is submitted that this question should be decided by the law applicable to the obligation. Certainly, such a clause is valid if governed by English law. Article 244(1) of the German Civil Code provides that in the case of a foreign currency debt payable within Germany, payment may be made in the local currency "unless payment in the foreign currency is expressly stipulated". On the Supreme Court cases dealing with such a stipulation see Karsten Schmidt, *Geldrecht* (Berlin, 1983) para 244, n 38.

[115] See the discussion (para 7.38 above) of the decision in *Anderson v Equitable Assurance Society of the United States of America* (1926) LT 557. The nature of the contractual relationship between the parties may provide the solution. For example, an agent who collects a foreign currency debt for his English principal must pay over the foreign currency proceeds; he may not convert them into sterling. This perhaps flows from the fact that the relationship between the agent and his principal is not comparable with that which subsists between a creditor and his debtor; a duty to account is not necessarily identical to an obligation to pay.

term, for it is the intention of the parties which matters.[116] This may, for example, be influenced by the existence of a system of exchange control in the place of payment; if and so long as the foreign currency in question is not freely obtainable, then it may well defeat the intention of the parties if the debtor is allowed to pay in sterling.[117] It is probably reasonable to suggest that, where the exercise of the debtor's option to pay in the currency of the place of payment would affect not only the mode but also the quantum of the debtor's obligation, then it is likely to be excluded.[118] Further, as between banks dealing in the eurocurrency markets, it is almost certainly intended that repayment should be effected in the currency in which it was originally advanced, and not in sterling.[119]

Overdue debts

7.44 To what extent do the rules described above continue to apply if a debt is not paid on the stipulated maturity date and thus becomes overdue? Consistently with the decision in *Camdex International Ltd v Bank of Zambia (No 3)*[120] debts must be treated on the same footing, whether they are expressed in sterling or denominated in a foreign currency. Thus, any debt remains a debt even after it is overdue and even after the obligation has been repudiated. In consequence, such a debt can still be discharged by payment in the currency in question rather than by accord and satisfaction.[121] The point is by no means academic; a debtor in

---

[116] An example is offered by the Italian Civil Code (trans Beltramo, 2001). Article 1278 provides that, in the case of a debt expressed in foreign money, "the debtor has the power to pay in legal money at the rate of exchange of the day when the sum is due and at the agreed place of payment". Article 1270 then provides that the option to pay in local currency ceases to be available if the reference to foreign money is reinforced by the word "actual" (effective) or other equivalent term. In many respects, English law adopts an essentially similar approach.

[117] See the remarks of Somervell LJ in *Heisler v Anglo Dal Ltd* [1954] 1 WLR 1273. The rationale seems to be that the creditor would be particularly keen to receive the relatively scarce foreign currency under such circumstances. Yet it cannot always be so, for a person who received foreign currency during the era of exchange controls in the UK was legally obliged to surrender it in exchange for the sterling counter-value—see Ch 14 below.

[118] A narrower formulation is adopted by Dicey and Morris, *The Conflict of Laws* (Sweet & Maxwell, 13th edn, 2000) para 36-056.

[119] The point would only occasionally arise in practice, for payment is usually made by credit to an account located in the country of issue. The court in the *Libyan Arab Bank* case held that eurocurrency and other foreign money obligations were to be treated on the same basis.

[120] [1997] CLC 714. The decision has been noted at para 1.61 above.

[121] Accord and satisfaction has been defined as "the purchase of a release from an obligation . . . not being the actual performance of the obligation itself"—*British Russian Gazette and Trade Outlook Ltd v Associated Newspapers Ltd* [1933] 2 KB 616, 643. This is an apt description, for the original obligation has not been crystallised into a specific amount and is thus itself incapable of being discharged by payment. In the present context, the point is that the debt obligation is performed (albeit after its due date), with the result that no "purchase of a release" from the obligation is required. In *New Brunswick Rly Co v British French Trust Corp* [1939] AC 1, the debtor repudiated a gold clause and it was said (at 29) that thereafter the debtor could "only tender damages". But it is not possible to "tender" damages in the formal sense; rather, the debtor could have elected to comply with the gold clause, even if belatedly.

financially straitened circumstances may be unable to pay as at the maturity date, but may come into funds shortly thereafter. Equally, a debtor who has repudiated his obligation may, on reflection, decide that it would be in his best interests to pay. In each case, the debtor retains the right to discharge his or her debt by payment, or at least to secure the procedural advantages flowing from a valid tender.

That an overdue foreign currency debt can still be discharged by payment under these circumstances is apparent from the Court of Appeal decision in *Société des Hôtels Le Touquet v Cummings*.[122] In 1914, the defendant had contracted a debt of 18,035 French francs to the plaintiff, which was repayable before the end of that year.[123] The defendant failed to pay and the plaintiffs commenced proceedings in 1919. The external value of the franc had fallen heavily by this time, and the plaintiffs accordingly claimed the amount of sterling which would have been equivalent to the amount of the French franc loan as at the end of 1914. While the action was pending, the defendant went to France and handed 18,035 francs to the manager of the plaintiffs; the manager knew nothing of the transaction but apparently had authority to accept money on its behalf. At first instance, the Court awarded the plaintiffs the sterling sum which was equivalent to 18,035 francs on 31 December 1914, less the sterling value of the money paid at the rate of exchange on the day of payment.[124] The Court of Appeal reversed the decision, effectively finding that the French franc debt has been fully discharged by payment in that currency, and that fluctuations in the comparative value of the French franc and sterling were entirely irrelevant. **7.45**

Bankes LJ said that, as the manager knew the money was tendered in discharge of a debt due to the company, and as the plaintiffs had kept the money without protest, the payment must be treated as discharging the debt.[125] **7.46**

Scrutton LJ held that the payment could not be treated as an accord and satisfaction. Instead, he held that the tender and acceptance of the money actually handed over to the plaintiff's manager amounted to payment and thus **7.47**

---

[122] [1922] 1 KB 451. See also *Beaumont v Greathead* (1846) 2 CB 494, 499: "If a man being owed £50 receives from his debtor after the due date £50, what other inference can be drawn than that the debt is discharged?" See, however, *New Brunswick Railway Co v British and French Trust Corp* [1939] AC 1, 29.

[123] In the absence of any evidence as to French law, the court was bound to proceed on the footing that the obligation was governed by English law. In *Lloyd Royal Belge v Louis Dreyfus & Co* (1927) 27 Ll LR 288, 293 and in *Re Chesterman's Trust* [1923] 2 Ch 466, 493, the court suggested that the contract was in every sense a French contract and that this was a distinguishing feature of the *Le Touquet* case. In truth, it was treated as an English contract.

[124] [1921] 3 KB 459.

[125] [1922] 1 KB 451, 456.

discharged the debt: "the plaintiffs who were owed 18,035 francs payable in France must be content with 18,035 francs paid in France".[126]

7.48 Atkin LJ also held that there was no accord and satisfaction.[127] He rejected the notion that, once the English writ was issued, the debt was in some way transformed into a sterling debt of an amount calculated at the rate of exchange on 31 December 1914 and payable in England: "It appears to me that she was sued here for a French debt . . . and that by paying the debt in France, she discharged the debt."

7.49 All three members of the Court of Appeal thus held that, accord and satisfaction being unnecessary, the claim for 18,035 French francs had been "paid", and the action therefore had to fail. The French franc debt thus remained a French franc debt, regardless of default, the falling international value of the franc, the commencement of proceedings, or any other matter.

7.50 The judgment in this case attracted some criticism[128] but in truth, it is submitted that the decision is plainly correct. The Court of Appeal reached the only conclusion which would have been consistent with the principle of nominalism. Furthermore, the decision conforms to good sense; it is not at all obvious why a foreign currency debt governed by English law should be transmuted into a sterling debt merely because there is a delay in payment or legal proceedings are commenced.[129] It is true that the implications of the decision have not always been fully recognised and accepted in later cases, although the key elements of the decision were followed in an interesting New York case.[130] It should, however, be appreciated that the *Le Touquet* decision only applies to claims in debt

---

[126] At 461. This, of course, is a clear application of the principle of nominalism.

[127] At 464.

[128] In *Lloyd Royal Belge v Louis Dreyfus & Co* (1927) 27 Ll LR 288, 293, Scrutton LJ noted that "some doubt had been expressed in various quarters" about the correctness of the *Cummings* decision.

[129] There was therefore no basis for the suggestion that, if legal proceedings are instituted with respect to a foreign currency debt, it could "be said with force that an obligation to pay sterling equivalent arises on that date": *Cummings v London Bullion Co Ltd* [1952] 1 KB 327, 335. Apart from other considerations, this would be contrary to the spirit of the *Miliangos* decision, which is considered in Ch 8 below.

[130] See *Transamerica General Corp v Zunino* (1948) 82 NYS 2d 595. However, the decision of the US Court of Appeals for the Second Circuit in *Competex SA (in liquidation) v La Bow* (1986) 783 F 2d 333 suggests a different approach. In that case, a broker had obtained an English judgment against his client for some £187,000 and started proceedings in New York for the enforcement of that judgment. The Court converted the English judgment into US dollars as of the date on which it was given. The Court found that the debt could no longer be discharged by payment of the sterling sum; so far as New York law was concerned, the debt had to be paid in accordance with the American judgment. This decision may be unfortunate but was perhaps inevitable, given that the process of enforcement had gone so far. In contrast, the defendant in the *Le Touquet* case had made payment before the case had been heard. The subject is discussed by Gold, *Legal Effects of Fluctuating Exchange Rates* (IMF, 1990) 348.

where the concept of payment can apply; it is not applicable to claims for unliquidated damages.[131]

Set-off

It is finally necessary to consider whether payment by means of set-off is   **7.51**
possible as between debts which are expressed in different currencies. Although
in England, the law on set-off is in many respects open to doubt and its importance is in some cases diminished by the availability of a counterclaim, there is
no reason of substance which should prevent set-off in such a case.[132] The
method was indicated by Brandon J at first instance in *The Despina R*:[133]
"the currency of the lesser liability should be converted into the currency of the
greater liability, and the set-off then effected, at the date on which the amounts
of the two liabilities are ascertained by agreement or decision". In such a case,
neither party is liable to pay until the balance has been struck and judgment is
given for the amount of the excess. This is an eminently sensible and practical
procedure.[134]

C. The Money of Payment

In their essence, the rules discussed above have been consistent with the prin-   **7.52**
ciple of nominalism. A debt expressed in sterling or a foreign currency can
generally be discharged by payment of the requisite amount in legal tender or,
subject to the express or implied consent of the creditor, other "cash equivalent"
for the currency concerned. By way of exception, a debtor obliged to pay a
foreign currency amount in England may have an option to tender sterling in
discharge of that obligation. But there may also be cases in which an obligation

---

[131] Thus, had the defendant in the *Le Touquet* case tendered 18,035 French francs in purported settlement of a claim for damages, this would not have discharged her obligation because there was no agreement to that effect and, so far as English law is concerned, the notion of "payment" must be confined to debts; it is not possible to discharge a claim for damages merely by payment. See also the discussion in *The Baarn (No. 1)* [1933] P 215, 271.

[132] Similar views are expressed by Wood, *English and International Set-off* (Sweet & Maxwell, 1989) 602.

[133] [1977] 1 Lloyd's Rep 618, 628. The formulation was adopted in *The Transatlantica Francesca* [1987] 2 Lloyd's Rep 155.

[134] The point has, however, given rise to difficulty in Germany and continues to do so; see Karsten Schmidt *Geldrecht* (Berlin, 1983) 244, No 47 and, since then, the decision of the Court of Appeal, Berlin *RIW* 1989, 815. More recently, the Court of Appeal of Koblenz (3 May 1991, *RIW* 1992, 59 or *IPRspr* 1991, No 174) has held that debts expressed respectively in marks and in a foreign currency may be extinguished by way of set-off provided that the latter currency was freely convertible into marks. On the other hand, the Municipal Court of Kerpen has decided that such a set-off is not permitted, because the claims lack the equivalence (*Gleichartigkeit*) which is a necessary requirement under art 387 of the German Civil Code.

is expressed in one currency but is to be performed in another. It is now proposed to consider this separate category of cases.

7.53 Reference has already been made to the distinction between the money of account and the money of payment. It has been shown that the money of account provides the measure of a financial obligation; it has also been shown that the identification of the money of account is a matter of substance, which is thus governed by the law applicable to the obligation at issue.[135]

7.54 In contrast, the money of payment is the currency which must be used as a means of performing the obligation which has been so defined and measured. The distinction between the money of account and the money of payment was explained with great clarity by Lord Denning MR in *Woodhouse AC Israel Cocoa Ltd v Nigerian Produce Marketing Co Ltd*,[136] where he noted that "the money of account is the currency in which an obligation is measured. It tells the debtor how much he has to pay. The money of payment is the currency in which the obligation is to be discharged. It tells the debtor by which means he has to pay." He then proceeded to illustrate the practical problems which might flow from this distinction:

> Suppose an English merchant buys twenty tons of cocoa-beans from a Nigerian supplier for delivery in three months' time at the price of £5 Nigerian a ton payable in pounds sterling in London. Then *the money of account* is Nigerian pounds. But the *money of payment* is sterling. Assume that, at the making of the contract, the exchange rate is £1 Nigerian for £1 sterling—"pound for pound". Then, so long as the exchange rate remains steady, no one worries. The buyer pays £100 sterling in London. It is transferred to Lagos where the seller receives £100 Nigerian. But suppose that, before the time of payment, sterling is devalued by 14 per cent while the Nigerian pound stands firm. The Nigerian seller is entitled to have currency worth £100 Nigerian because the Nigerian pound is the *money of account*. But the *money of payment* is sterling. So the buyer must provide enough sterling to make up £100 Nigerian. To do this, after devaluation, he will have to provide £116 5s in pounds sterling. So the buyer in England, looking at it as he

---

[135] The money of account has been discussed in some depth at Chs 5 and 6 above. The points about to be discussed should not be allowed to obscure the fact that the usual method of discharging a monetary obligation will be by payment to the creditor of the amount stated in the contract in the currency in which the obligation is expressed. In other words, the money of account and the money of payment will coincide in the vast majority of cases.

[136] [1971] 2 QB 23, 54. The decision was affirmed by the House of Lords [1972] AC 741, where the distinction between the money of account and the money of payment was recognised. On the whole subject, see the Law Commission's Working Paper No 80, *Private International Law: Foreign Money Liabilities* and Report (Cmnd 8318, July 1981). As a matter of historical interest, it may be noted that France used to distinguish between the money of account and the money of payment even in a purely domestic context: "L' ancienne France distinguait la monnaie de compte, qui servait à mesurer la dette (ex: la livre) et la monnaie de paiement (ex: l'ecu, le louis d'or) qui servait au paiement; le louis valait 20 livres", Malaurie and Aynes, *Les Obligations* (Cujas Paris, 1994) para 985.

will in sterling, has to pay much more for his twenty tons of cocoa-beans than he had anticipated. He will have to pay £116 5s instead of £100. He will have to pass the increase on to the customers. But the seller in Nigeria, looking at it as he will in Nigerian pounds, will receive the same amount as he had anticipated. He will receive £100 Nigerian just the same; and he will be able to pay his growers accordingly. But now suppose that in the contract for purchase the price had been, not £5 Nigerian, but £5 *sterling* a ton, so that the *money of account* was sterling. After devaluation, the buyer in England would be able to discharge his obligation by paying £100 sterling; but the Nigerian seller would suffer. For, when he transferred the £100 sterling to Nigeria, it would only be worth £86 Nigerian. So, instead of getting £100 Nigerian as he anticipated, he would only get £86; and he would not have enough to pay his growers. So you see how vital it is to decide, in any contract, what the *money of account* is and what the *money of payment* is.

As is apparent from the commercial illustration provided by Lord Denning, the application of the distinction between the money of account and the money of payment can have far-reaching financial consequences. A default in payment may lead to further difficulties if the money of payment further depreciates against the money of account, for the actual amount payable in the latter currency will increase.[137] Thus, both the creditor and debtor should be aware of the risks they are assuming if they contract for "US$1,000, payable in six months' time in pounds sterling" or "£1,000 payable in US dollars in 12 months' time". In the first case, the amount of sterling to be paid in six months' time is unknown, and a degree of risk is borne by the debtor in that regard. The creditor is protected in that he knows that—regardless of exchange rates prevailing on the date of payment—the amount of sterling which he is to receive will be equivalent to US$1,000. Similar risks would arise in relation to the second example.[138] For these reasons, it remains important for the lawyer to distinguish carefully between the money of account and the money of

7.55

---

[137] This is contrary to the suggestion of Robert Goff J in *BP Exploration Co (Libya) v Hunt* [1979] 1 WLR 783, 840, to the effect that on the maturity date, the money of account is converted into the money of payment, such that the debt is "crystallised" into the money of payment on that date. In the event of delayed payment, "the parties will be taking the risk of fluctuation in the currency of payment" rather than the money of account. It is submitted that this approach cannot be supported. Following the decision in *Le Touquet* (n 131 above), a debt expressed in a particular currency does not change its character merely because the maturity date has passed. Furthermore, the suggested formulation elevates the mode of performance over the substance of the monetary obligation itself.

[138] The distinction between the money of account and the money of payment also arises in other contexts, eg where a loan is made in one currency but is expressed to be payable in another. Thus in *Boissevain v Weil* [1950] AC 327, the borrower of 320,000 French francs, undertook to repay £2,000, so that the money of account was expressed in pounds sterling and French francs were the money of payment. For a similar set of facts, see the decision of the Supreme Court of Missouri in *Re De Gheest's Estate* (1951) 243 SW (2d) 83. In *The Damodar General TJ Park* [1986] 2 Lloyd's Rep 68 demurrage was expressed in terms of US dollars but payable "in external sterling in London". It was held that demurrage was payable in sterling, although it is difficult to see why the point mattered, for by this time sterling was freely convertible into US dollars.

payment. Yet it must be observed that the risks just described would flow from the language which the parties had selected to express their rights and obligations and, to that extent, the risks have been voluntarily assumed. But it is now necessary to turn to other cases in which the creditor may be *compelled* to accept payment in a currency which differs from that stipulated in the contract.

7.56 It has been observed elsewhere that there is no necessary connection between the law which governs a contract and the currency in which the monetary obligations arising under it are to be discharged.[139] This was because the mode of performance was to be determined according to the law of the place in which payment was required to be made. The identification of the currency or money tokens which the debtor was required to proffer in settlement of his obligation was thus decided by reference to the law of the place of performance.[140] As has been shown,[141] a debtor who has an obligation to pay US dollars in London may tender either dollars or their sterling equivalent; and the creditor must accept the sterling amount so offered, or at any rate it constitutes an adequate tender in respect of the US dollar obligation.[142] Thus, a creditor who expected to receive payment in US dollars may be compelled to accept a sterling amount instead.

---

[139] Dicey and Morris *The Conflict of Laws* (Sweet & Maxwell, 13th edn, 2000) para 36-052, citing *Re United Railways of Havana and Regla Warehouses Ltd* [1961] AC 1007, 1060; see also the discussion at para 4.13 above. In many respects, this point is now obvious; in the international financial markets, obligations will usually be governed by English or New York law, but will involve many different currencies.

[140] There are numerous cases on this point. See, eg, *Jacobs v Credit Lyonnais* (1884) 12 QBD 859; *Adelaide Electricity Supply Co v Prudential Assurance Co* [1934] AC 122 (HL); *Auckland Corp v Alliance Assurance Co Ltd* [1937] AC 587 (PC); *Mount Albert BC v Australasian Temperance and General Mutual Life Assurance Society Ltd* [1938] AC 224 (PC); and *Bonython v Commonwealth of Australia* [1950] AC 201 (PC). The money of payment may be specifically agreed between the parties, and such an agreement would generally override any relevant provision of the law of the place of performance in this context. Thus, in *Pennsylvania Railway Co v Cameron* (1924) Pa 458, a bill of lading provided for payment in sterling, but then provided that "freight, if payable at destination (Philadelphia), to be at the rate of exchange of $4.866". Since payment was to be made in Philadelphia, it could be inferred from this language that the US dollar was to be the money of payment in that case. For decisions to similar effect, see *Brown v Alberta & Great Waterways Rly Co* (1921) 59 DLR 520; *Royal Trust Co v Oak Bay* (1934) 4 DLR 697. These different cases involved an option of currency but involved wording which is now out of use; for discussion, see the Fifth Edition of this work, 215–17. In some cases, the parties may agree that the debtor has an option to pay in two or more moneys of payment. In the absence of contrary provision in the contract, the debtor may take advantage of such provisions and discharge his obligation by paying in the currency which is most favourable to him: *Ross T Smyth & Co Ltd v WN Lindsay Ltd* [1953] 2 All E R 1064; *Booth & Co v Canadian Government* [1933] AMC 399.

[141] See para 7.30 above.

[142] As has been noted at para 7.31 above, (a) the *amount* of sterling to be so offered is to be determined by reference to a rate of exchange and (b) since the amount to be paid is plainly a matter of substance, the identification of the required rate is a matter for the law applicable to the contract.

It is suggested that rules of this nature should no longer be applied automatically   **7.57**
or as a matter of course:

(1) As already noted, the courts are now no longer positively required to give effect to the law of the place of performance in matters touching the mode of payment, they are merely required to have regard to that law where the justice of the case so requires.

(2) It is difficult to see why—as a matter of justice as between the parties—the creditor should be obliged to accept payment in a currency different from that which was mutually agreed. The creditor may have stipulated for a particular currency because he requires those funds to meet other obligations or simply because he believes it to be a stable currency. There is no reason why the law should deprive him of the benefit of that bargain, or impose upon him the inevitable cost of converting local currency proceeds into his chosen medium of payment.

(3) The notion that the currency of payment touches merely the mode of performance has limited connection with commercial reality, at least in the modern world.[143] Parties agree that payment should be made in (say) US dollars for a variety of reasons but they will usually regard this as a point of some importance. There seems to be no compelling reason why the debtor should be allowed unilaterally to decide upon payment in the local (as opposed to the agreed) currency.

(4) Rates of exchange may vary from day to day. Thus, if a creditor receives US$10,000 in discharge of an obligation of that amount, he will continue to have US$10,000 on the ensuing day. But if he receives £6,000 in discharge of a US$10,000 obligation at a rate fixed by the applicable law, he will have the sterling equivalent of US$10,000 on the date of payment, but the sterling funds may be worth less than US$10,000 on the ensuing day. Furthermore, the creditor will have received a sterling amount at a rate of exchange fixed by the applicable law, but it will not necessarily follow in every case that he can obtain the identical rate in the place of payment. Even if payment is received through the banking system on the due date and at the appropriate rate, it may arrive towards the end of banking hours, with the result that the creditor is unable to secure to himself the benefit of that day's rate.

---

[143] It may be that the rule is derived from periods in which the exchange control was more widespread and financial markets were less international than they are now. At such times, the rule may have been appropriate because of the practical difficulty involved in obtaining the necessary foreign currency in the place of payment. The payment of an equivalent amount in the local currency may well have reflected the parties' expectations at that time. It is, however, perfectly sensible to argue to the contrary; if the relevant currency is difficult to obtain, then it may have been important to the creditor to receive that particular currency—see *Heisler v Anglo Dal Ltd* [1954] 1 WLR 1273.

7.58   For these reasons, rules forming part of the law of the place of payment and which allow the debtor the option to pay in the local currency will only rarely do justice as between the parties. Rather more frequently, they will pervert the parties' intentions and will consequently lead to injustice. The origins of the right of conversion lie in the mercantile practices of the Middle Ages.[144] They have very limited relevance in the modern commercial world. Accordingly, in the absence of any contrary indication in the contract, it should be assumed that the money of payment is identical to the money of account.

7.59   Inevitably, matters will not always be so straightforward and there will be exceptional cases. For example, the application of such a rule may do justice in a case where payment in the agreed foreign currency has become impossible as a result of supervening illegality. In such a case, payment in the local currency at the appropriate rate of exchange is clearly preferable to no payment; and some payment (rather than none) clearly accords with the justice of the case. Article 10(2) of the Rome Convention should accordingly apply the law of the place of performance in such a case.[145] Likewise, where exchange controls in the place of payment render it impossible to obtain the necessary foreign currency, Article 10(2) may lead to the conclusion that payment in the domestic currency may be required in accordance with the law of that place.[146]

7.60   This analysis suggests that the influence of the law of the place of payment should be regulated in individual cases. In particular, it should not be applied where it would unnecessarily subvert the intention of the parties, or create an option of payment which was not contemplated by the parties. But it may be applied in cases where there is a genuine difficulty in making payment in the agreed currency in the agreed place. In other words, the traditional distinction between the money of account and the money of payment[147] should be less sharply drawn; if the parties have contracted by reference to a particular currency, then (at least as a starting point) the courts should assume that payment is likewise to be made in that currency, irrespective of the law of the place of payment.

---

[144] See "The right of conversion", para 7.30 above.

[145] Thus if a US dollar obligation is payable in London but payment in that currency has become impossible, then payment should be made in sterling. This was the result in *Libyan Arab Foreign Bank v Bankers Trust Co* [1989] QB 728. It was noted earlier that the option to pay in sterling instead of the foreign currency ought not to be conferred upon the creditor. The present suggestion is not inconsistent with this view, for the creditor receives local currency only because payment in the money expressed in the contract has become impossible; no true option arises in such a case.

[146] Where, however, the contract at issue is governed by English law and exchange controls are imposed after the contract was made, it is suggested that payment in the contractual currency should be required to be made in another jurisdiction by virtue of an implied contractual term to that effect. The point is considered in the context of supervening exchange controls—see Ch 16 below.

[147] On this distinction, see para 5.06 above.

D. Payment and Private International Law

It is a well-established principle of English private international law that the question whether a certain payment operates as a discharge of an obligation is governed by its applicable law.[148] But, however clear the principle may be, various specific aspects of the rule require discussion.

7.61

Accord and satisfaction

Whether or not a payment can, in particular cases, by itself discharge an obligation or whether some further action or step is required for that purpose is governed by the applicable law. Thus, it is for the law applicable to the obligation to determine whether the discharge is dependent upon a separate agreement, ie whether a doctrine similar to the English concept of "accord and satisfaction" is to be applied.[149] Thus, if the governing law allows for tender and payment to be made in respect of a claim for *unliquidated* damages, then the English court will give effect to that state of affairs. It would be irrelevant that, under English domestic law, the concepts of tender and payment can be applied only to *liquidated* obligations.[150]

7.62

Tender

In a private international law context, the concept of tender gives rise to peculiar difficulty, in that it has two separate meanings.

7.63

In the first instance, it may mean that tender has been made in accordance with the law applicable to the obligation and that this has resulted in the discharge of the monetary obligation or at least in some alteration in its structure. The effect of such tender should be governed by the applicable law.[151] On the other hand, the plea may mean that by offering the amount due to the creditor, the debtor

7.64

---

[148] The point is now beyond dispute in the light of Art 10(1)(b) of the Rome Convention.

[149] This rule has been expressly laid down in *Ralli v Dennistoun* (1851) 6 Ex 483.

[150] The position may be slightly confused by the observation of Maugham LJ in *The Baarn (No. 1)* [1933] P 215, 271, where he noted that "if the defendant is defending on the grounds of accord and satisfaction he must prove accord and satisfaction according to our procedure". It is necessary to emphasise the distinction between (a) the requirement for, and the content of, the accord and satisfaction, which are matters of substance governed by the applicable law and (b) the means of proving that accord and satisfaction has occurred, which are procedural and evidential matters governed by the law of the country in which the proceedings occur. It seems that Maugham LJ was referring to the latter aspect, in which case his statement is consistent with the principle in the text.

[151] In *Re British American Continental Bank, Lisser & Rosenkranz's Claim* [1923] 1 Ch 276, a tender of marks was made at Hamburg. However, the court did not discuss whether the effect of the tender fell to be determined by English or German law.

has procured for himself the advantages of a plea of tender in the English sense which, if followed by payment into court, merely entitles the debtor to the costs of the action and bars a claim for interest.[152] In the light of the procedural nature of this class of tender, the matter would fall to be governed by English law, as the law of the country in which the proceedings take place.

7.65   It was the failure to draw this distinction which lay at the root of a misunderstanding of the Canadian Gold Clauses Act 1937 in *New Brunswick Rly Co v British and French Trust Corp.*[153] In that case, Lord Maugham said: "I am of the opinion that the questions that arise as to the validity or form of a tender, or the advantage of making one in a particular form, are questions of procedure for the *lex fori*. There may well be special rules in different countries."

7.66   It was for this reason that Lord Maugham held that a creditor enforcing a gold clause in England could not be defeated by a Canadian statute according to which "tender of the nominal or face amount of the obligation [governed by Canadian law] in currency which is legal tender for the payment of debts in the country in the money of which the obligation is payable shall be a legal tender and the debtor shall, on making payment in accordance with such tender, be entitled to a discharge of the obligation". The basis of this view was that the operation of the Canadian statute had to be confined to cases "where the action to recover the amount due is brought in Canada". Yet Lord Maugham's approach was mistaken. The Canadian legislator did not seek to interfere with the law of tender in England or elsewhere; he merely intended to provide that a monetary obligation governed by Canadian law could be reduced or discharged in a particular way.[154] Lord Maugham's opinion thus rests upon a failure to distinguish between the substantive and procedural meanings of "tender".

Set-off

7.67   So far as English law is concerned, rights of set-off are usually seen as matters of procedure which are thus governed by the law of the country in which the proceedings take place.[155]

---

[152] This point has been discussed at para 7.08 above.

[153] [1939] AC 1 (HL) 23–4.

[154] That Canada was entitled to legislate in this way in relation to gold clauses governed by Canadian law and that such legislation should have been recognised and applied by the House of Lords seems to be correct as a matter of principle and would also seem to follow from the decision in *R v International Trustee for the Protection of Bondholders AG* [1937] AC 500 (HL).

[155] For a comparative survey, see Max Planck Institute for Foreign and Private International Law: *Comments on the European Commission's Green Paper on the Conversion of the Rome Convention of 1980 on the law applicable to contractual obligations into a Community instrument and its modernisation*, RabelZ 2004, 1, at 81–6. For an explanation of the law of set-off in a number of jurisdictions, see Wood, *English and International Set-off* (Sweet & Maxwell, 1989).

In a contractual context, however, the right to pay a reduced sum in diminution **7.68**
of a larger debt may be treated as a matter of substance,[156] and in such a case
the availability of such a right must be governed by the law applicable to the
contract which is claimed wholly or partly to be discharged by reason of the
set-off.[157]

Deposit in court

The governing law of the obligation should also determine whether the method **7.69**
of paying a debt by depositing the amount due with a court (*consignation*) which
is known to civil law countries, is available in a given case and whether
such deposit amounts to a discharge of the obligation. This appears to be the
reasoning on which the two difficult cases of *The Baarn*[158] were decided.

Both cases arose out of a collision between a Chilean vessel, owned by a com- **7.70**
pany domiciled in Chile, and a Dutch vessel owned by the defendants, a Dutch
firm.[159] The defendants admitted liability; the Chilean plaintiffs therefore issued
proceedings in England and sought a determination of damages for expenses
incurred by them in Chile in Chilean currency for the repair of their vessel.
During the course of the English proceedings, the defendants deposited the
amount of pesos spent by the plaintiffs with the Court in Chile in accordance
with certain provisions of the Chilean Code. The English Court was thus called
upon to determine whether that payment had discharged the defendant's
obligations.

The economic background to the proceedings can only be understood if it is **7.71**
remembered that the Chilean peso was a "frozen currency", that is to say that
money could not be freely transferred out of Chile. As a result, the value of
blocked accounts held within the country was quoted abroad at a discount,
although the official rate of exchange was unaltered and, within Chile, the
money had an undiminished purchasing power.

At first instance, the Court fell into error in that it assumed that Chilean law **7.72**
governed the issue.[160] Having reviewed the evidence of Chilean law, the court

---

[156] See, eg, the buyer's right to set off losses flowing from the delivery of defective goods: Sale of Goods Act 1979, s 53(1).

[157] This is especially the case in the light of Art 10(1)(b) of the Rome Convention. The applicable law must determine whether the set-off amounts to performance of the monetary obligation.

[158] *(No. 1)* [1933] P 251; *(No. 2)* [1934] P 171.

[159] The collision occurred on the high seas, with the result that the substance of the claim would be governed by English law—see the remarks of Scrutton LJ in *The Baarn (No. 2)* [1934] P 171, 176.

[160] Chilean law plainly could not govern the discharge of an obligation which arose under English law.

held that the payment was valid according to Chilean law. This judgment was reversed on appeal, although each judge offered different reasons. Scrutton LJ took the view "that there is no final decision by the Chilean court that the payment in depreciated pesos is sufficient while proceedings are pending in London"—although it is not at all clear how a Chilean judgment would or could have affected the outcome in England. Greer LJ said that it was not clear whether the payment had discharged the debt under Chilean law; consequently, once damages were assessed in England, the court would have to give credit for that payment "by its equivalent value in sterling at the rate of exchange prevailing on the date when the payment was finally approved by the Chilean judge". Romer LJ held that[161] what happened in Chile could have the effect of a payment only where the relationship of the parties was that of debtor and creditor, and no such relationship subsisted in the present case. During further proceedings the question arose whether the order drawn up by the Court of Appeal in *The Baarn (No 1)*[162] actually reflected the judgments given; it was contended that the Court of Appeal had not intended to exclude the possibility of taking the Chilean payment into account *pro tanto*, and to order payment in England. This contention was rejected by the Court of Appeal.[163] Greer LJ dismissed the defendant's appeal on the ground that they were estopped from challenging the order; Scrutton LJ adhered to his view that there had been no payment (apparently according to Chilean law); whilst Maugham LJ emphasised[164] that he was "unable to see that Chilean law has anything to do with the matter before the court".

7.73   The judgments in these two cases thus present something of a confused picture. Nevertheless, the central point appears to be that the claim for damages was governed by English law[165] and English law must thus determine whether the liability has been discharged. English law should likewise determine whether credit should be given for payment made to a foreign court; it should decline to give credit if the payment so made is "blocked" by local legislation.[166]

---

[161] [1933] P 251, 273.
[162] [1933] P 251.
[163] *The Baarn (No. 2)* [1934] P 171, 176.
[164] At 184.
[165] See n 160 above.
[166] For a similar approach to these cases, see Dicey and Morris, *The Conflict of Laws* (Sweet & Maxwell, 13th edn, 2000) para 36-058. The "blocked account" reasoning may, however, be unjust to the defendants. The plaintiffs were a Chilean entity seeking reimbursement of expenses incurred in Chile. Since they were domiciled in Chile, the fact that the peso payment could not be transferred out of the country should not have affected them.

Conversion for adjustment

It has been necessary at an earlier stage to consider in some detail the identifica- **7.74**
tion of the money of account and of the money of payment. It is now necessary
to consider a further set of cases, where both the money of account and the
money of payment have been identified, but where an item expressed in a
foreign currency has to be converted into the money of payment in order finally
to calculate the amount required to be paid. If, for instance, under an insurance
policy providing for an indemnity in sterling, a claim is made in respect of a loss
expressed in a foreign currency, it is clear that a conversion into sterling is
required; for the insurer is only liable to pay in that currency. Similarly, if
security over property in France has been given by way of security for a sterling
loan and, upon enforcement, the property is sold to a French buyer for a price in
euros, it becomes necessary to convert the euro proceeds into sterling so that the
outstanding balance of the loan can be ascertained. The need for conversion is
thus obvious in both instances.

In such cases, conversion should be effected at the rate of exchange on the day **7.75**
on which, according to the contract and the circumstances of the case, there
arose the right to payment or the duty to give credit and, consequently, the
occasion for conversion likewise arose.[167] This rule renders it necessary in the
first instance to turn to the contract to search for an express or implied agreement between the parties. Thus, where a charterparty provided for the revision
of hire payable in dollars in accordance with wages paid to the crew in Deutsche
marks, the latter are to be converted into dollars as at the date on which the
wages are changed.[168] Equally, it is of the essence of an indemnity policy that the
holder is entitled to the value at the time and place of the fire; if the property is
valued in a foreign currency and the policy is expressed in sterling, the value will
have to be converted at the rate of exchange on the day of the fire.

In the case of reinsurance contracts, conversion will take place with reference to **7.76**
the rate of exchange on the date on which the insurer itself pays and the
reinsurer's liability therefore arises. This point is impressively illustrated by the
decision of the Court of Appeal in *Versicherungs & Transport AG Daugava v
Henderson*.[169] The defendant, an English underwriter, had reinsured the plaintiffs, a Latvian insurance company, against their liability on a fire policy relating

---

[167] Such cases should be distinguished from those in which the conversion has been carried out
and produces a surplus, when it becomes necessary to determine which party is entitled to it. Such
cases tend to turn either upon principles such as subrogation—see, eg, *Yorkshire Insurance Co v
Nisbet Shipping Co* [1961] 2 All ER 487 or upon the interpretation of the contract at issue, eg
Lucas Ltd v Export Credits Guarantee Department [1973] 1 WLR 914. Such cases do not involve
principles of a specifically monetary law character.
[168] ie and not as at the date when the hire is payable or paid—*The Brunswode* [1976] 1 Ll LR 501.
[169] (1934) 49 Ll LR 252.

to buildings in Riga. Following a fire in April 1930, the plaintiff's liability to the defendants was ascertained by the Latvian courts in lats and the sum due was paid in January 1932. As between insurer and reinsurer, the question arose whether the sum in lats should be converted into sterling at the rate of exchange as at the date of the fire or as at the date on which the insurer settled his liability. The Court of Appeal adopted the latter date, on the basis that the reinsurer had no liability until the insurer's liability had been quantified and satisfied.[170]

7.77   A case in which credit has to be given according to the rate of exchange on the day when the obligation to give credit comes into existence arises where the victim of a tort or breach of contract is entitled to damages in terms of sterling, but in mitigating his damage has obtained a sum in US dollars for which credit must be given. It is submitted that the US dollars are to be converted into sterling on the date on which the victim receives them, rather than the date when the damage occurred or the wrongdoer makes payment.[171]

7.78   In *Pape Williams & Co v Home Insurance Co*,[172] American owners of cotton lying in Barcelona insured it with an American insurance company in terms of dollars, subject to terms: "Loss if any payable on the basis of the actual market value at time and place of loss, such loss to be payable in New York exchange to bankers." The goods were confiscated in Barcelona at a time when they had a dollar value of US$30,000. The Spanish Government subsequently paid to the owners compensation in pesetas which produced US$18,000. The court upheld the insured's claim for the difference, and rejected the insurer's argument that the loss had been made good by payment of the value of the goods in pesetas. The compensation paid by the Spanish Government was merely an item to be brought into account; for this purpose, it was to be converted into US dollars at the rate prevailing at the time of receipt of the credit.[173]

---

[170] The Court would also have adopted the rate of exchange as at the date of payment in *Noreuro Traders v Hardy & Co* (1923)16 Ll LR 319, except that the rate was to be ascertained in Antwerp; this could not in fact be done at the relevant time in view of the German occupation. In a different context, a Canadian court dealing with the taxation of costs of the successful party held that disbursements incurred in a foreign currency should be converted into Canadian dollars on the date on which the bill of costs was certified by the court: *Dillingham Corp Canada Ltd v The Ship Shiuy Maru* (1980) 101 DLR (3d) 447.

[171] This was the position reached by the German Administrative Court, 13 December 1973, *RzW* 1974, 186. Compare the decision of the German Federal Supreme Court, 12 June 1975, *RzW* 1975, 301; if a claimant is entitled to recover medical expenses incurred in a foreign currency, they were to be converted into the German unit at the rate on the day on which the expenses were incurred.

[172] (1943) 139 F 2d 231 and [1944] AMC 51 (CCA, 2d).

[173] Rules of this kind may cause particular difficulty in the context of the administration of estates, where a significant period may elapse between the date of the death and the final distribution of the estate, thus enlarging the potential for significant exchange rate damages during the period at issue; eg see *Re Heck's Estate* (1952) 116 NYS 2d 255.

A final example is provided by a line of cases which arose in the sphere of taxation, as a consequence of the rule that the domestic currency is an unchanging measure of value, whilst foreign currencies can fluctuate against it. The decision in *Bentley v Pike*[174] arose in the context of capital gains tax. In October 1967, a British taxpayer became entitled to a German property then worth DM132,000. She sold it in July 1973 for DM152,000. The question was whether the taxable gain was (a) DM 20,000 converted into sterling at the rate for July 1973, or (b) the excess of the sterling value of DM152,000 in July 1973 over the sterling value of DM132,000 in October 1967. The court decided in the latter sense, so that the taxpayer largely paid tax "on a gain resulting from the devaluation of the pound in November 1967". It is submitted that the former solution would have been preferable on the basis that no question of converting anything into sterling should have arisen until the disposal in July 1973.[175] In contrast, in *Goodbrand v Loffland Brothers North Sea Inc*,[176] the taxpayer was affected by currency fluctuations which occurred after the disposal of four drilling rigs at a pre-determined price expressed in US dollars. The whole amount of the applicable capital gain was taxable in the year of disposal, but the dollar consideration was to be paid to the seller over a period of nine years. As a result of exchange rate fluctuations over that period, the company had paid more capital gains tax than would have been justified by the overall sterling equivalent of the gain. However, the taxpayer's attempt to adjust the assessment failed, because the consideration for the rigs had been expressed in US dollars, and payment of that sum had been received in full. The conversion of the dollar amount into sterling was a mere valuation exercise for the purpose of computing the tax payable; the taxpayer had never expected to receive payment in sterling and changes in the exchange rate which post-dated the assessment were accordingly irrelevant. Nevertheless, fluctuating rates of exchange cannot be invoked in order to create a taxable profit or gain where none has in fact been made. Thus, in *Pattison v Marine Midland Ltd*,[177] an international bank borrowed US dollars in order to make loans to customers seeking advances in that currency. Upon receipt of US dollar repayments from its customers, the bank made corresponding repayments to its own financier. The sterling value of the dollars originally borrowed was £6 million, whilst the sterling value of the same amount of dollars received on repayment was £8 million. The Inland Revenue claimed that the difference amounted to an income profit, which was liable to corporation tax accordingly. The House of Lords held that the transactions had been

---

[174] [1981] STC 360. See also para 1.64 above.

[175] For conversion questions which arise or used to arise in relation to stamp duty, see Stamp Act 1891, s 6.

[176] [1998] STC 930.

[177] [1984] 1 AC 362, followed in *Capcourt Trading Ltd v Evans* [1993] 2 All ER 125.

effected entirely in US dollars, and no question of exchange gains or losses could therefore arise.[178] Thus, whilst a conversion of currencies may be needed to effect any necessary adjustment, it should be appreciated that this is only required where the context positively demands that a sterling value must be placed on a foreign currency amount.

Performance of monetary obligations abroad

7.80 It has been shown that the determination of the money of account can cause particular problems in cases involving a conflict of laws.[179] The determination of the money of payment raises slightly different, but equally difficult problems. The point may perhaps be illustrated by an example. Suppose that, under English law, a debtor owes a sterling amount which is payable in Paris. Applying the English rules on conversion, the debtor should be entitled to discharge his debt by payment of the corresponding amount in euros. But should not the latter point be decided by French law, as the law of the place of payment? In other words, should the rule[180] of English municipal law that a monetary obligation is discharged by tendering the *money* of the place of payment be extended to a rule of private international law, to the effect that the determination of the money of *payment* falls to be decided by the *law* of the place of payment?

7.81 The situation involves two distinct questions, namely:

(1) which system of law determines whether the debtor has a right or duty to convert the money of account into the local money of payment; and

(2) which legal system governs the mechanics of conversion (for example, the rate of exchange to be employed and the date and place with reference to which such rate is to be ascertained)?

7.82 As to the first question, it has been noted that, at least in a more traditional line of reasoning, the creditor suffers no prejudice from the fact that he receives payment in the currency of the place of payment. In general therefore, and in the absence of indications to the contrary in the contract, it seems that the availability of an option or obligation to settle the debt in the local currency can be treated as one relating to the mode of performance; the court may therefore have regard to the law of the place of payment in this context.

---

[178] For similar cases in the US and Australia, see *National Standard Co v Commissioner of Inland Revenue* (1983) 80 TC 551; *AVCO Financial Services Ltd v Commissioner of Taxation* 56 ALJR 668 and *Federal Commissioner of Taxation v Hunter Douglas Ltd* [1983] 14 ATR 639. The cases are considered by Gold, *SDRs, Currencies and Gold* (IMF, Pamphlet Series No. 44, 1987).

[179] See generally Chs 5 and 6 above.

[180] If a rule it continues to be. It has been submitted at para 7.58 above that the rule requires reconsideration in the light of Art 10(2) of the Rome Convention.

As to the second question, however, a different approach is required. The rate **7.83** of exchange to be employed and the date with reference to which it is to be ascertained will clearly affect the *amount* which the debtor is required to pay, ie they go to the substance of the obligation. As a matter of principle, it must follow that such questions must be governed by the law applicable to the obligation.[181]

The place of payment

So far as English private international law is concerned, the "place of payment" **7.84** is the place in which the debtor is obliged to tender payment; this must, of course, correspond to the place in which the creditor is contractually entitled to receive the payment.[182] Subject to that formulation, the identity of the place of payment will be determined by the law applicable to the contract, by establishing where the creditor is entitled to receive his money in accordance with that law. The place of payment is often fixed by the parties, either expressly or impliedly. But in the absence of such a determination, the general rule—under a contract governed by English law—is that the place of payment is the place where the creditor resides or carries on business[183] at the time of the contract.[184]

The function of the place of payment may vary in different legal systems as well **7.85**

---

[181] A similar line of reasoning applies where a foreign money obligation is to be settled in England—see para 7.30 above. In the same sense see, Dicey and Morris, *The Conflict of Laws* (Sweet & Maxwell, 13th edn, 2000) para 36-055.

[182] Thus, if payment is to be made by means of an international credit transfer, the place of payment is the place in which the bank branch holding the creditor's account is situate. The debtor may have to take preparatory steps to organise the payment from the country in which his own bank is situate, but that country does not thereby become the place of payment: *Libyan Arab Foreign Bank v Bankers Trust Co* [1989] QB 728.

[183] *Chitty on Contracts* (Sweet & Maxwell, 29th edn, 2004), para 21-054 and cases there referred to, in particular *Rein v Stein* [1892] 1 QB 753, 758; *Drexel v Drexel* [1916] 1 Ch 251; and *Bremer Oeltransport GmbH v Drewry* [1933] 1 KB 753, 765. A creditor under an English judgment has only the right to be paid in England, even though he resides abroad: *Re a Debtor* [1912] 1 KB 53. Conversely, an award ordering payment abroad is not to the same effect as a judgment to pay a sum of money here: *Dalmia Coment v National Bank of Pakistan* [1975] QB 9, where it was suggested at 24 that an action claiming payment abroad was an action for damages. In *Pick v Manufacturers Life Insurance Co* (1958) 2 Ll LR 93, the contract required payment to be made to a foreign creditor by means of sterling banker's drafts drawn on a London bank. Somewhat surprisingly, London was held to be the place of payment. Based upon the principle outlined in the text, the place of payment was the creditor's country of residence, where the drafts would have to be tendered to him.

[184] Otherwise, the creditor would unilaterally alter one of the debtor's obligations by moving abroad: *The Eider* [1893] P 119. The seller's (creditor's) place of business is also the place of payment under art 59 of the Uniform Laws on International Sales Act 1967 and art 57 of the Vienna International Sales Law 1980. Under French law, however, art 1247 of the Code Civil provides that the place of payment is the debtor's residence, and it has been held that this refers to the debtor's residence at the time of payment, rather than the date of the contract: Cass Civ, 9 July 1895, D 1896 I 349.

as in different contexts. So far as English law is concerned, the present work examines two particularly important legal characteristics of the law of the place of performance. First of all, it has been shown that English private international law pays regard to the law of the place of payment in questions touching the mode of performance.[185] Secondly, it will be shown that the English courts will not enforce an obligation whose execution would be illegal in the law of the place of performance.[186] But it is also necessary to enquire whether the place of performance and its laws have any wider or deeper consequences than those just described. Although the point does not appear to have been explored directly in decided cases, it seems that (so far as English law is concerned) the character and purpose of the place of payment is determined by (a) the express or implied terms of the contract and (b) the overall rationale and purpose of the contract. Thus, as a matter of construction, the place of payment may be the place at which the debtor is both entitled and bound to pay. Alternatively it may be a place in which the debtor is entitled to pay; payment in that place is not mandatory but is "permissible",[187] or such place may be the "primary" (if not the exclusive) place of payment.[188] A nominated place of payment may be unalterably fixed, or it may be intended that it should be changed under circumstances which are expressly or impliedly defined by the terms of the contract. The mere fact that a contract specifies a place of payment does not necessarily or conclusively mean that there cannot be another one. It may be specified so as to be binding upon both parties or for the benefit of one of them, so as to allow either such party to make or require payment elsewhere. The difficulty which may thereby be caused in identifying the contractual place of performance can cause difficulties in related contexts. For example, in dealing with matters relating to performance of a contractual obligation, the court may have regard to the law of the place of performance. The application of this provision is obviously problematical if the place of payment cannot readily be identified, or if the creditor or debtor have options to require that payment be made in alternative locations.

---

[185] Article 10(2) of the Rome Convention, which has already been noted on a number of occasions.

[186] See the decision in *Ralli Bros v Compania Naviera Sota y Aznar* [1970] 2 KB 287. The rule appears to apply only to contracts governed by English law. It is thus a rule of English domestic law, rather than private international law. Nevertheless, the rule necessarily only applies in cases where the laws of more than one jurisdiction are invoked, and the application of the rule can only be considered once the place of payment has been identified.

[187] See *Rossano v Manufacturers Life Insurance Co* [1963] 2 QB 352.

[188] See *Pick v Manufacturers Life Insurance Co* (1958) 2 Ll LR 93, where (even though the parties were respectively resident in Israel and Canada) London was held to be "the primary place of payment in the strict sense" because payment was to be made by means of drafts on London.

The law of the place of payment may be of particular significance in the context **7.86** of international banking transactions. For example, where under an English law contract a bank deposit is repayable on demand at a foreign branch of an English bank and payment there is unlawful, the head office is not liable.[189] If foreign law governs, it will have to answer questions touching the liability of the head office. The law is less clear in the case of liabilities which are not payable on demand at a specified place. But there is much to be said for the view that if the law of the head office governs the contract and if, therefore, the (different) law of the place of payment cannot encroach upon the existence, nature, or extent of the monetary obligation, then the bank cannot avoid liability by referring the creditor to the place of payment, where payment may be impossible.[190]

---

[189] *Joachimson v Swiss Bank Corp* [1921] 3 KB 110; *Arab Bank Ltd v Barclays Bank DCO* [1954] AC 495. In the US, the head offices of American banks are likewise not responsible for the "blocked" obligations of their overseas branches if "the branch cannot repay the deposit due to (1) an act of war insurrection or civil strife or (2) an action by a foreign government or instrumentality (whether de jure or de facto) in the country in which the branch is located". See US Code, Title 12, s 633, which allows the bank to negate this provision by contract. However, that legislation effectively reversed a line of decisions in which the head office had been held to be so responsible: *Vishipco Line v Chase Manhattan Bank* (1982) 660 F 2d 976; *Trinh v Citibank* (1988) 850 F 2d 1164; *Wells Fargo Asia Ltd v Citibank* (1988) 852 F 2d 657. In the last-mentioned case, the court drew a distinction between the place of repayment ("location where the wire transfers effectuating repayment at maturity were to occur") and the place of collection ("the place or places where plaintiff was entitled to look for satisfaction of its deposits in the event that Citibank should fail to make the required wire transfers at the place of repayment"). For reasons given above, this distinction is of very doubtful value, and the decision of the Supreme Court which sent the case back to the Court of Appeals does not contribute to the clarification of the distinction: *Citibank v Wells Fargo Asia Ltd* (1990) 495 US 660. On remand, the Court of Appeals held that the deposit contract was governed by New York law and that a creditor could collect his debt at the agreed place for repayment. In the absence of any restriction on the *situs* of collection, the depositor could recover its deposit from Citibank in New York: see *Wells Fargo Asia Ltd v Citibank NA* (1991) 926 F 2d 273 (2nd Cir), cert denied (1992) 505 US 1204.

[190] The difficulty with this line of reasoning is that it may be inconsistent with the decision in *Ralli Bros*, on which see para 7.24 above.

8

LEGAL PROCEEDINGS AND THEIR EFFECT UPON MONETARY OBLIGATIONS

A. Introduction

Does the institution of legal proceedings have any impact upon the nature or **8.01** quality of a monetary obligation? At first sight it is tempting to answer this question in the negative. The commencement of legal process is a procedural step which is designed to enforce a pre-existing obligation; such a step should therefore have no effect upon the substance of the obligation at issue. This view can only be reinforced when it is considered in a private international law context, where the substance of the obligation is governed by its applicable law whilst procedural questions are subject to the law of the country in which the proceedings have been instituted.

On the whole, English law now broadly reflects the principle just outlined, **8.02** although inevitably that principle cannot always be applied uniformly; in particular, difficulties may arise where it is necessary to convert one currency into another, for the date of calculation and other matters may tend to distort the substance of the original obligation.[1] The application of the principle will be illustrated by reference to a discussion of English and American law; exceptions to it will be examined in the context of procedural questions which come to the fore in the context of insolvency and the division of trust funds.

---

[1] As will be apparent from this remark, the present chapter is primarily concerned with liquidated obligations which are expressed or payable in a foreign currency.

B. The Position under English Law

8.03   In 1898, Lord Lindley observed[2] that:

> . . . if the defendants were within the jurisdiction of any other civilised State and were sued there, as they might be, the courts of that State would have to deal with precisely the same problem, and to express in the currency of that State the amount payable by the defendants instead of expressing it in Mexican dollars . . .

The assumptions that the English courts could only give judgment in sterling, and that a foreign currency obligation therefore had to be converted into sterling for that purpose, became an accepted feature of English law.[3] It is submitted that this attitude rested upon an unduly narrow view of the court's powers;[4] there is no obvious reason why a court could not express its judgment in a foreign currency where appropriate.[5] Even if that principle were acceptable, one would have thought that a court could give judgment for such sum of sterling as at the date of payment represented the equivalent of the required sum of foreign money; this would have ensured that the procedural requirement for a sterling judgment would not materially interfere with the substance of the obligation. Yet immediately after the First World War, the courts propounded the breach-date rule by insisting that judgment had to be given for a sum of sterling calculated by converting the foreign money at the rate on exchange on the date of the breach or wrong.[6] Since the period between the date of the breach and the date of payment in respect of any eventual judgment could be a lengthy one, the breach-date rule meant that the eventual award would not

---

[2] *Manners v Pearson* [1898] 1 Ch 581, 587.

[3] Following *Manners v Pearson*, the rule was taken for granted or repeated on a number of occasions: *Di Ferdinando v Simon Smits & Co* [1920] 3 KB 409, 415; *The Volturno* [1921] 2 AC 544, 560; *Re Chesterman's Trust* [1923] 2 CH 466, 490; and *Re United Railways of Havana and Regala Warehouses Ltd* [1961] AC 1007, 1052 and 1069.

[4] It also rested, no doubt, upon the role of sterling as the world's main reserve currency. Lord Denning reflected on the point when deciding that a change of practice was required. In *Schorsch Meier GmbH v Hennin* [1975] 1 All ER 152, he said of sterling: "It was a stable currency which had no equal. Things are different now. Sterling floats in the wind. It changes like a weathercock with every gust that blows. So do other currencies."

[5] Although the point cannot be stated with any confidence, it may be that the narrowness of the English approach was influenced by two factors. First of all, the debtor may at times have encountered difficulty in satisfying a foreign currency obligation in the light of the restrictions imposed by the Exchange Control Act 1947. Secondly, the English courts tended to regard a foreign money obligation as an obligation to deliver a commodity, the breach of which gave rise to a claim for damages (as opposed to a claim in debt). The latter notion has been exploded by the decision in *Camdex International Ltd v Bank of Zambia (No. 3)* [1997] CLC 714—see the discussion at para 1.61 above.

[6] In relation to debts expressed in a foreign currency, the rule was stated in *Re British American Continental Bank Ltd* [1922] 2 Ch 575, 587 and was followed in Australia: *McDonald & Co Pty Ltd v Wells* (1932) 45 CLR 506. For full discussion, see in particular in *Re United Railways of Havana and Regla Warehouses Ltd* [1961] AC 1007 and authorities there cited. In relation to

necessarily reflect the actual loss suffered by the claimant. This is objectionable both on the ground that it is inconsistent with the restitutionary nature of a claim in damages and on the ground that a procedural rule may thereby diminish the substance of the claim. It is true that, in the early part of the twentieth century, the breach-date rule would tend to protect the creditor in such cases; indeed, it would often work to his positive benefit, because sterling remained strong and debts expressed in foreign currencies tended to depreciate in relation to it. The difficulty, of course, was that the breach-date rule would penalise the debtor, and the currency conversion process effectively allowed to the creditor liquidated damages in respect of the debtor's breach.[7] Of course, once sterling began to decline, the breach-day rule had the opposite effect and became prejudicial to the creditor.[8] As a matter of logic and legal reasoning, the breach-date rule was untenable but, despite various efforts, the Government declined to intervene with new legislation on the point.[9] Nevertheless, the injustice which could be caused by the breach-date rule and the requirement for judgments to be expressed in sterling was becoming apparent to the courts. Lord Denning MR described the common law rules on the subject as "most unsatisfactory"[10] and eventually, the courts began to make inroads into the rule.

First of all, the Court of Appeal held that an arbitration award could be both made and enforced in terms of a foreign currency.[11] Subsequently, the Court of Appeal refused to apply the breach-date rule on grounds which in strict law were far from convincing, but produced a result that in justice could only be

8.04

---

damages for breach of contract, see, eg, *Ottoman Bank v Chakarian (No. 1)* [1930] AC 277 and, in relation to damages in tort, see *The Volturno* [1921] 2 AC 544.

[7] In *Librairie Hachette SA v Paris Book Centre Inc* (1970) 309 NY Supp 2d 701, 705, the New York Supreme Court openly admitted the point, noting that "in this case, the equities favor application of the 'breach day rule'. If it were not applied, the defendant would be rewarded for defaulting in his obligation to pay for the merchandise."

[8] See, eg, *Madeleine Vionnet & Cie v Wills* [1940] 1 KB 72.

[9] The subject was taken up by the Monetary Law Committee of the International Law Association, which in 1956 produced its "Dubrovnik Rules", the adoption of which would have led to conversion as at the date of payment. In the UK, the rules were referred to the Private International Law Committee which, however, declined to recommend any change in the law—Cmnd 1648. Subsequently, the European Convention on Foreign Money Liabilities was opened for signature, but events were then overtaken by the decisions about to be described.

[10] *The Teh Hu* [1970] P 106, 124. Yet it may be noted that Lord Denning had been a party to the confirmation of those rules in *Re United Railways of Havana and Regla Warehouses Ltd* [1961] AC 1007.

[11] *Jugoslavenska Oceanska Plovidba v Castle Investment Co Inc* [1974] QB 292. The Court of Appeal rightly made the obvious point that the claimants "want an award which will enable them to recover the same amount as that which they ought in the first instance to have received. They do not want that recovery to be exposed, if that can be avoided, to exchange fluctuations between the currency in which they ought to have received the amount initially and the pound sterling, especially since the latter was allowed to float." The power of an arbitrator to express his award in any currency was subsequently confirmed by statute: see Arbitration Act 1996, s 48(4) considered in *Lesotho Highlands Development Authority v Impregilo SpA* [2004] 1 All ER (Comm) 97.

described as compelling.[12] Further in the same case, the Court of Appeal held that judgments could generally be given in foreign currency; again, the reasoning is not at all convincing but the result was commercially satisfactory and even necessary.[13] The point was subsequently confirmed by the House of Lords, which held that the creditor of a foreign currency debt is both entitled and obliged to seek judgment in the currency concerned;[14] only at the point of payment or enforcement will conversion into sterling become necessary, and conversion will be effected at the rate of exchange prevailing at that time.[15] These rules apply whether the claim is for payment of a specific sum contractually due[16] or for damages for breach of contract[17] or tort[18] for just a sum in respect of undue enrichment[19] or for restitution.[20] It has further been decided that the English

---

[12] *Schorsch Meier Gmbh v Hennin* [1975] QB 416. This decision involved a departure from the position adopted by the House of Lords in the *Havana Railways* case.

[13] Lord Denning invoked Art 106 of the EC Treaty which then required each Member State "to authorise, in the currency of the Member State in which the creditor or the beneficiary resides, any payments connected with the movement of goods, services or capital . . . to the extent that the movement of goods, services, capital or persons between Member States has been liberalised pursuant to this treaty". From this, Lord Denning argued that a debtor was obliged to pay the creditor in the currency specified in the contract, and that the English courts would be acting contrary to the spirit of the Treaty if they compelled the creditor to accept a depreciated payment in sterling following the debtor's breach. Whilst these conclusions are entirely acceptable from a commercial perspective, they cannot be justified by reference to Art 106. The point was made by Lord Wilberforce in the *Miliangos* case (below); for further criticism, see White, "Judgments in Foreign Currency and the EEC Treaty" (1976, January) Journal of Business Law 7.

[14] *Miliangos v George Frank (Textiles) Ltd* [1976] AC 443. The creditor is not entitled to convert his foreign currency claim into sterling because the option to pay in sterling rests with the debtor and not with the creditor—see para 7.37 above. See also *Veflings A/S v President of India* [1979] 1 All ER 380. In *Ozalid Group (Export) Ltd v African Continental Bank Ltd* [1979] 2 Lloyd's Rep 231, the court held that the claimant retained the option to claim payment either in sterling or in the relevant foreign currency. For the reasons just stated, this view is not acceptable in so far as it relates to the debt claim itself. It is, however, true that a claim for special damages flowing from the breach of contract can be made in a different currency in which the claimant actually "felt" the consequent loss. On this point, see para 5.33 above.

[15] *Miliangos v George Frank (Textiles) Ltd* [1976] AC 443—see in particular the remarks of Lord Wilberforce (at 463, 468, 469), Lord Cross (at 497–8), and Lord Edmund-Davies (at 501). The requirement for conversion as at the date of payment, rather than any earlier date, ensures that the debtor—as the party in default—bears the risk of currency fluctuations up to the point of actual payment. The rule now seems to be applied as a matter of course: see, eg, *Diary Containers Ltd v Tasman Orient Line CV* (Privy Council Appeal No. 34 of 2003, 20 May 2004), where the Board held that the liability of a carrier was limited to £5,500 and that the claimant was "entitled to an amount in New Zealand dollars which it can exchange for that amount at the date of payment".

[16] As in the *Miliangos* case itself.

[17] *Services Europe Atlantique Sud v Stockholm Rederi Aktiebolag (The Folias)* [1979] AC 699, approving *Jean Kraut AG v Albany Frabrics Ltd* [1977] QB 182.

[18] *The Despina R* [1979] AC 685, on which see Knott, (1980) 43 MLR 18.

[19] *BP Exploration Co (Libya) Ltd v Hunt* [1979] 1 WLR 783, 840–1 affirmed [1981] 1 WLR 232, 245.

[20] Thus in *Re Dawson* [1966] 2 NSWR 211, a trustee who in 1939 wrongfully took £4,700 New Zealand currency was in 1966 liable to restore the then value of that amount in terms of Australian currency. The decision was approved by the House of Lords in the *Miliangos* case, at 468.

courts may give judgment in a foreign currency regardless of the law applicable to the obligation in question.[21] That being the case, it must follow that the creditor's entitlement to judgment in a foreign currency (or to the sterling equivalent as at the date of payment/enforcement) must be regarded as a procedural question which will always be governed by the law of the forum.[22] If it becomes necessary to take execution proceedings in order to enforce a judgment expressed in a foreign currency, then it is the established practice of the courts to specify a sterling exchange rate for that purpose, but failure to do so does not vitiate any order which the court may have made for that purpose.[23]

The rule established in the *Miliangos* case had already been extended into many other areas.[24] An Admiralty Marshall who sells an arrested ship for a US dollar consideration is under no obligation to convert that sum into sterling prior to its distribution;[25] a garnishee order could be made against a foreign currency bank account held with a financial institution in England;[26] a statutory demand under the Insolvency Act 1986 was valid if expressed in a foreign currency and even though it omitted to state the sterling equivalent, the rate of exchange or other matters[27] and a company incorporated in the United

8.05

---

[21] The contract in the *Miliangos* case was governed by Swiss law, but the principle was extended to English law contracts in *Federal Commerce and Navigation Co Ltd v Tradax Export SA* [1997] QB 324, reversed on other grounds by the House of Lords [1978] AC 1. See also *Barclays Bank International Ltd v Levin Brothers (Bradford) Ltd* [1977] QB 270; *The Despina R* [1979] AC 685; *The Texaco Melbourne* [1994] 1 Lloyd's Rep 973 (HL).

[22] See Dicey and Morris, *The Conflict of Laws* (Sweet & Maxwell, 13th edn, 2000) para 36-067. It follows that the question cannot be treated as a part of the rules dealing with the assessment of damages, for that question is assigned to the applicable law of Art 10(1)(c) of the Rome Convention. It must also be observed that the rule requiring that judgments should be given in sterling was unattractive on other grounds. In particular, it allowed the domestic procedural rules to override the contractual rights of the claimant to payment in a different currency. Whilst the rule in *Miliangos* is likewise a procedural rule, its application will be in harmony with the substantive rights created by the terms of the contract itself—the point was noted by Lord Wilberforce in *Miliangos* at 465.

[23] *Carnegie v Giessen* [2004] All ER (D) 171. It may be important to make it clear in the judgment that the foreign currency concerned is intended to be the money of account, so that any rate of exchange required in connection with local enforcement proceedings will be that prevailing as at the date of payment, rather than the date of judgment. This is necessary to ensure that the claimant retains the economic benefit of the judgment, expressed in the foreign currency concerned. For a case in which this type of difficulty arose, see *Trinidad Home Developers Ltd (in voluntary liquidation) v IMH Investments Ltd* [2003] UKPC 85.

[24] It is, of course, no coincidence that these changes in judicial policy occurred after the collapse of the Bretton Woods system of fixed parities and the era of floating currencies had begun. Indeed, the point was openly made by both Lord Denning in the *Schorsch Meier* case (see n 12 above) and the *Jugoslavenska* decision (see n 11 above). An essentially similar remark was made by Lord Wilberforce in the *Miliangos* case (n 14 above, at 467).

[25] *The Halcyon the Great* [1975] 1 WLR 515.

[26] *Choice Investments Ltd v Jeromnimon* [1981] QB 149 (CA).

[27] *Re a Debtor* (No 51–SD 1991) [1992] 1 WLR 1294.

Kingdom may issue shares denominated in a number of different foreign currencies.[28]

8.06 It is thus possible to conclude that, so far as English law is concerned, the institution of legal proceedings does not have the effect of altering the substance of the debt or the debtor's obligations; further, this observation applies equally to obligations expressed in sterling and in foreign currencies, and will apply regardless of the law applicable to the substance of the obligation in question. This conclusion displays a pleasing symmetry with the principle of nominalism, which occupies a central position in the field of monetary law.[29] Any case law on the subject which pre-dates the *Miliangos* case must now be of very doubtful authority.[30] Nevertheless, it remains necessary to emphasise a few final points:

(1) As noted earlier, it will be necessary to convert the foreign currency amount of the judgment into sterling as at the date on which the court authorises enforcement of the judgment. It is necessary to ascertain an equivalent date for procedures which are effected without resort to the courts or which do not involve a judgment given in terms of a foreign currency. Thus, where a company is being wound up by the court, conversion should be effected as at the date of the winding-up order;[31] likewise, where a company goes into voluntary liquidation, the conversion rate is ascertained as at the date of the winding-up resolution.[32]

(2) It has been shown that the rule in the *Miliangos* case is of a *procedural* character—it entitles the creditor to judgment in the currency by reference to which the contract was made. *Miliangos* thus does not affect questions of substance. In particular, it does not in any way affect the question whether compensation for currency depreciation should be allowable as part of a claim for damages flowing from the debtor's breach. That is an entirely

---

[28] *Re Scandinavian Bank Group plc* [1988] Ch 87. It was held to be possible to issue shares with nominal amounts expressed in different currencies notwithstanding Companies Act 1985, s 2(5)(a) which requires the division of share capital "into shares of a fixed amount". The decision is discussed by Instone (1987) 104 LQR 168. The statement by Lord Wright in *Adelaide Electric Supply Co v Prudential Assurance Co* [1934] AC 122, 146, to the effect that the share capital of an English company must be fixed in sterling, must now be regarded as out of date.

[29] On the principle of nominalism generally, see Part III below.

[30] The point was made in *Monrovia Tramp Shipping Co v President of India* [1978] 2 Lloyd's Rep 193, 197, affirmed by the Court of Appeal [1979] 1 WLR 59. On changes brought by the *Miliangos* decision, see Morris, "English judgments in Foreign currency: A Procedural Revolution" (1977) 41 *Law and Contemporary Problems* No. 2.44.

[31] *Re Dynamics Corp of America* [1976] 1 WLR 757, on which see Mann (1976) 92 LQR 165. The point is now regulated by the Insolvency Act 1986, s 322 and r 4.91 of the Insolvency Rules 1986. Rule 4.91 provides that foreign currency debts must be converted into sterling at the official exchange rate on the day the company went into liquidation. The official exchange rate is the middle market rate published by the Bank of England for the day in question or, in the absence of such a rate, the rate determined by the court.

[32] *Re Lines Bros Ltd* [1983] Ch 1 (CA).

separate question which is governed by the law applicable to the obligation at issue.[33]

(3) Although the *Miliangos* decision in large measure eliminates the concern that the sterling value of foreign currency debts may fall over time, it does not entirely eliminate that exposure. A period of time may elapse between the date on which execution is authorised and the date on which funds are ultimately received by the creditor; currency fluctuations may continue to occur during that period. It was suggested in the previous edition of this work[34] that the judgment creditor should be entitled to damages if the relevant foreign currency depreciates in terms of sterling during this period, on the basis that a judgment debt should not be treated differently to any other debt in that respect. This does, however, seem to be doubtful, in that the judgment must bring some finality to the matter and late payment would normally be dealt with by means of an award for interest;[35] in any event, the concept of a cause of action in damages for late payment of damages is unknown in English law.[36] Nevertheless, once the foreign currency judgment has been given, it would seem that the debtor could then discharge the debt thereby created by payment in sterling.[37]

(4) It should be added that the *Miliangos* decision was soon applied in a number of other jurisdictions and has thus gained international acceptance.[38]

---

[33] The availability of damages in this type of case is discussed at para 9.36 below.

[34] See the Fifth Edition, 357, n 90.

[35] It is perhaps for this reason that standard forms of loan agreement in use in the international financial markets contain an explicit and independent indemnity provision which seeks to create a further right of recourse under these circumstances.

[36] The point was made in *President of India v Lips Maritime Corp* [1987] 3 All ER 110.

[37] On the debtor's option to pay in sterling, see para 7.30 above. It would be absurd if the debtor's option to pay a judgment debt in sterling only arose once execution proceedings had started.

[38] In Scotland, see *Commerzbank AG v Large* [1977] SLT 219 (First Division of the Inner House), and in Ireland, see *Northern Bank Ltd v Edwards* (1984) IR 284. Australia: *Maschinenfabrik Augsburg-Nürnberg v Altiker Pty Ltd* (1984) 3 NSWLR 152; *Australian and New Zealand Banking Group Ltd v Cawood* (1987) 1 Qd R 131; *Brown Boveri (Australia) Pty Ltd v Baltic Shipping Co* [1989] 1 Lloyd's Rep 518; *Mazzoni v Boyne Smelters Ltd* [1998] 1 Qd R 76. New Zealand: *American Express Europe Ltd v Bishop* [1988] NZ Recent Law 87. Canada: the Courts of Justice Act 1990, s 121 provides for conversion of the foreign currency judgment into Canadian dollars immediately before the judgment is satisfied. Canadian courts had formerly adopted that rate of exchange as at the date of judgment—see *Batavia Times Publishing Co v Davis* (1978) 88 DLR (3d) 144 affirmed without opinion (1980) 102 DLR (3d) 192; *Clinton v Ford* (1982) 137 DLR (3d) 281; *Williams & Glyn's Bank Ltd v Belkin Packaging Ltd* (1979) 108 DLR (3d) 585, reversed on other grounds (1981) 123 DLR (3d) 612; *Dino Music AG v Quality Dino Entertainment Ltd* [1994] 1 WWR 137; *Ticketnet Corp v Air Canada* (1997 154 DLR (4th Cir) 271 (Ontario Court of Appeal). South Africa: *Murata Machinery Ltd v Capelon Yarns Pty Ltd* (1986) 4 SA 671 (C); *Elgin Brown and Hamer Pty Ltd v Dampskibsselkabet Torm Ltd* (1998) 4 SA 671 (N) and *Mediterranean Shipping Co Ltd v Speedwell Shipping Co Ltd* (1989) (1) SA 164 (D). Zimbabwe: *Makwindi*

(5) It may be added that the now discredited breach-date rule has not been adopted as part of EC law. Where the Community is required to pay damages for breach of contract or in tort under the terms of Article 288 of the EC Treaty, any necessary conversion is to be effected as at the date of the judgment.[39]

C. The Position in the United States

8.07 In the United States, it was provided by statute that "all proceedings in the courts shall be kept and had" in US dollars.[40] This provision was repealed in 1982, but according to federal common law it remained settled practice "that a United States District Court can award judgment only in dollars".[41] In view of developments elsewhere, it is perhaps unsurprising that the courts started to move away from this strict view. They have, for example, enforced a provision in an insurance contract calling for payment in Jamaican currency,[42] a foreign arbitration award expressed partly in US dollars and partly in sterling,[43] and an arbitration award expressed in Japanese yen.[44] The current position is that judgments involving foreign currency claims may be awarded in US dollars if the plaintiff so requests, but there is no positive requirement that judgments be rendered in the local currency.[45] The present discussion will proceed on the basis that judgment is sought in US dollars.

Oil Procurement Ltd v National Oil of Zimbabwe Ltd (1988) (2) SA 690. Cyprus: *Lamaignere v Selene Shipping* (1982) 1 CLR 227. These and other authorities are cited in Dicey and Morris, *The Conflict of Laws* (Sweet & Maxwell, 13th edn, 2000) para 36R-060, and the application of the *Miliangos* case before the courts of other countries is discussed in detail by Gold in *Legal Effects of Fluctuating Exchange Rates* (IMF, 1990) ch 14. On the procedural rules applicable to a claim expressed in a foreign currency, see Civil Procedure Rules 1998, Pt 16, Practice Directions, para 11.

[39] *Dunortier Frères v Council of the European Community* [1982] ECR 1733.

[40] For an argument to the effect that this type of provision does not prevent the entry of judgments expressed in a foreign currency, see Becker, *The Currency of Judgments* 25 AJCL 152.

[41] See, eg, *BV Bureau Wijsmuller v US* (1976) 487 F Supp 156, 176; *Re Good Hope Chemical Corp* (1984) 747 F 2d 806, 809, cert denied (1985) 471 US 1102; *Trinh v Citibank NA* (1985) 623 F Supp 1526, 1536; *Newmont Mines Ltd v Adriatic Insurance Co* (1985) 609 F Supp 295, 126. See also *Fils et Cables d'Acier de lens v Midland Metals* (1984) 584 F Supp 240, 246; *Vishipco Line v Chase Manhattan Bank NA* (1981) 660 F 2d 854, 865. The requirement for conversion into US dollars has also been applied when enforcing a foreign judgment expressed in a currency other than dollars: *Competex SA v LaBow* (1985) 613 F Supp 332 (SDNY) affirmed (1986) 783 F 2d 333 (2nd Cir).

[42] *Barton v National Life Assurance Co of Canada* (1978) 413 NYS 2d 807.

[43] *Waterside Ocean Navigation Co Inc v International Navigation Ltd* (1984) 737 F 2d 150 (2nd Cir).

[44] *Mitsui & Co Ltd v Oceantrawl Corp* (1995) 906 F Supp 202 (SDNY).

[45] See the discussion of *Hicks v Guinness*, below. Section 4 of the Uniform Foreign-Money Claims Act expressly permits the parties to select the currency which is to be used to meet any claims arising out of their transaction. In the absence of such a stipulation, judgments may be

The modern *federal* law on this subject seems to draw a distinction based upon the place in which the breach or wrong occurred. If the wrong occurred within the United States, then the damages are measured in dollars and any necessary conversion is effected by reference to the rate of exchange *as at the date of the breach*. Where, however, the wrong occurred in a foreign country, the damages are measured in the currency of that country; the claimant can then recover the amount in US dollars which is equivalent to that foreign currency *as at the date of judgment.*[46]   **8.08**

The first part of this proposition is supported by the decision in *Hicks v Guinness.*[47] In that case, a German debtor owed a sum in marks to an American creditor which was payable within the United States and was due on 31 December 1916. Following default, the plaintiff acquired an optional right to be paid in US dollars at the rate of exchange prevailing on 31 December 1916, ie the date of the breach.[48] Similarly, where two ships collided in New York harbour and the resultant damages were to be measured in sterling, it was held that the rate of exchange as at the date of the collision was to be applied, since the wrong occurred within the United States.[49]   **8.09**

Authority for the second part of the proposition is provided by the decision in *Deutsche Bank Filiale Nürnberg v Humphreys.*[50] The plaintiff, an American citizen had placed a deposit in German marks with the defendants in Germany; the contract was thus governed by German law and Germany was the place of   **8.10**

---

given in foreign money but the debtor has the option to settle in US dollars by reference to the exchange rate as at the date of payment. According to the introductory note: "The principle of the Act is to restore the aggrieved party to the economic position it would have been in had the wrong not occurred." The Act has, however, won only limited acceptance and, in particular, it has not been adopted in New York.

[46] In some respects, this distinction may be seen as artificial and even absurd—see Rosenn, *Law and Inflation* (University of Pennsylvania, 1982) 282 and literature there cited. It must, however, be said that the distinction continues to find support. The court which heard *Re Good Hope Chemical Corp* (1984) 747 F 2d 806, cert denied (1985) 471 US 1102, expressed the point neatly when it observed (at 811) that "the judgment day rule applies only when the obligation arises entirely under foreign law. If, however, at the time of breach the plaintiff has a cause of action arising in this country under American law, the breach day rule applies." This formulation was quoted with approval in *ReliaStar Life Insurance Co v IOA Re Inc and Swiss Re Life Canada* (Court of Appeals for the 8th Cir, 13 June 2002); since the claim in that case arose within the US, the breach-date rule applied, and the amount of the Canadian dollar obligation at issue in that case accordingly had to be converted into US dollars as at the date of the failure to pay.

[47] (1925) 269 US 71.

[48] That the right to payment in US dollars is an optional right of the claimant has been confirmed by the decision in *ReliaStar Life Insurance Company v IOA Re Inc and Swiss Re Life Canada* (n 46 above), explaining and following *Hicks v Guinness* and concluding that the District Court is not compelled to give judgment in US dollars.

[49] *The Verdi* (1920) 268 Fed 908 (District Court, Southern District of New York).

[50] (1926) 272 US 517. There were earlier decisions to the same effect. In *The Vaughan and Telegraph* 14 Wall 258 (1872), a cargo of barley shipped from Canada had a value of C\$2,436 at the time and place of shipment. The cargo was lost owing to a collision in the Hudson River.

performance. The defendants failed to repay the deposit following a demand made on 12 June 1915. The lower courts held that the marks were to be translated into US dollars as at the date of the breach; since the deposit was repayable on demand, the rate applicable on 12 June 1915 would be used. However, a sharply divided Supreme Court reversed the judgments. Speaking for the majority, Mr Justice Holmes said:[51]

> In this case, unlike *Hicks v. Guinness*, at the date of the demand the German bank owed no duty to the plaintiff under our law. It was not subject to our jurisdiction and the only liability it incurred by its failure to pay was that which the German law might impose. It has incurred no additional or other one since. A suit in this country is based upon an obligation existing under foreign law at the time when the suit is brought, and the obligation is not enlarged by the fact that the creditor happens to be able to catch his debtor here. We may assume that when the bank failed to pay on demand, its liability was fixed at a certain number of marks both by the terms of the contracts and by the German law—but we may also assume that it was fixed in marks only, not at the extrinsic value that those marks then had in commodities or in the currency of another country. On the contrary, we repeat, it was and continued to be a liability in marks alone and was open to satisfaction by payment of that number of marks, at any time, with whatsoever interest may have accrued, however much the mark might have fallen in value as compared with other things: see *Société des Hôtels Le Touquet v. Cummings* [1922] 1 KB 451. An obligation in terms of the currency of a country takes the risk of currency fluctuations and whether creditor or debtor profits by the change the law takes no account of it. Obviously in fact a dollar or a mark may have different values at different times, but to the law that establishes it, it is always the same. If the debt had been due here and the value of dollars had dropped before suit was brought, the plaintiff could recover no more dollars on that account. A foreign debtor should be no worse off.

8.11 Later he added:[52] "Here we are lending our courts to enforce an obligation (as we should put it, to pay damages) arising from German law alone and ought to enforce no greater obligation than exists by that law at the moment when suit is brought."

Since the US and Canadian dollars were then of equal value, the District Court gave judgment for the plaintiffs for US$2,436 and interest. When the case came before the US Court of Appeals, the US currency had so depreciated that C$2,436 was equivalent to US$4,896.36; the Court of Appeals thus gave judgment for the latter sum in US dollars. By the time the case reached the Supreme Court, the US dollar had greatly appreciated so that US$4,896.36 would produce much more than the original Canadian dollar amount. Nevertheless, the Supreme Court (by a majority) upheld the decision of the Court of Appeals on the grounds that the judgment was correct when rendered and any hardship to the debtors was caused by their own delay in payment. In *The Hurona* (1920) 268 Fed 911, the District Court was confronted with a French franc loan repayable in Marseilles; since the contract was due to be performed in France and the breach had occurred there, the rate of exchange prevailing as at the date of judgment was applied. See also the decision in *The Saigon Maru* (1920) 267 Fed 881 (District Court, District of Oregon).

[51] At 519. The judgment relies in part upon the earlier Supreme Court decision in *Chicago, Milwaukee & St Paul Railway Co v McCaull-Dinsmore Co* (1920) 253 US 97.

[52] At 520.

It is generally held that the concluding three words of Mr Justice Holmes are **8.12**
due to an obvious error and that he meant to and did apply the rate of exchange
prevailing at the date of judgment.[53] The distinction between *Hicks v Guinness*
(where the debt was payable in New York and subject to local law) and the
Deutsche Bank case (where the debt was governed by the laws of Germany and
payable within that country) has been emphasised by the Supreme Court on
subsequent occasions.[54]

Although the doctrine thus propounded by the Supreme Court has since been **8.13**
followed in the Federal courts,[55] some details have not yet been established. In

---

[53] *Thornton v National City Bank* (1930) 45 F 2d 127, 130; *Tillman v Russo-Asiatic Bank*
(1931) 51 F 2d 1023, 1025; *Royal Insurance Co v Compania Transatlantic Espanola* (1932) 57 F 2d
288, 292; *The Integritas* [1933] AMC 165 (District Court, District of Maryland, 1933); *The
Macdonough* [1934] AMC 234 (District Court of New York); *Indian Refinery Co v Valvoline Oil
Co* 75 F 2d 797 Court of Appeals, (7th Cir); *The West Arrow* [1936] AMC 165 (US Circuit Court
of Appeal, 2d 1936) and other cases referred to and followed in *Reissner v Rogers* (1960) 276 F 2d
506 where the Court of Appeals, District of Columbia Circuit said (at 511): "The view urged here
that *Deutsche Bank* has been misread and that it really establishes as a conversion date the date on
which the claim was filed has been considered and rejected in several of the cases cited above. We
think that the question is now to be regarded as settled and that we are bound to apply the
judgment date rule in cases like the present." More recent cases include *The Island Territory of
Curaçao v Solitron Devices Inc* (1973) 356 F Supp 1, at 14 and *Gutor International AG v Raymond
Packer Co* (1974) 493 F 2d 938, 943. Despite this line of authority and in spite of an argument
based upon the terms of this footnote, the House of Lords in *Re United Railways of Havana and
Regla Warehouses Ltd* [1961] AC 1007 expressed the view that the Supreme Court had selected the
date on which the suit was brought as the date on which the rate of exchange must be fixed (see in
particular at 1048 and 1052). It is true that Holmes J did not specifically mention the rate as at
the date of judgment, but he was so understood by Mr Justice Sutherland (speaking for the
minority), and by many later judges and commentators. Even if he was misunderstood at the time,
continuous practice over an extended period has produced what must be considered the true
interpretation: see H.L. Jones (1969) iii *The International Lawyer* 277. The point was corrected by
Lord Wilberforce in the *Miliangos* case [1976] AC 443, 469.
[54] See *Zimmerman v Sutherland* (1927) 274 US 253, 255 and 257; see also *Sutherland v Mayer*
(1926) 271 US 272. The distinction was also very sharply drawn in the *ReliaStar* case
(n 46 above).
[55] See the cases mentioned in n 53 above. See also *Paris v Central Chiclera SàRL* (1952) 193 F
2d 950 (CCA 5th Cir) with note in (1952) 61 Yale LJ 758 and the interesting decision in *The
Tamaroa (Shaw Savill Albion & Co v The Friedricksburg)* (1951) 189 F 2d 952 (CCA 2d) also
[1951] AMC 1273: In 1944, a collision occurred between a British and a US ship in British
territorial waters. The British ship was repaired in the US at a cost of US$118,000 which was paid
to the repairers on behalf of the British Government and debited by it to the owners at the sterling
equivalent of £29,000. In 1951, following the devaluation of sterling, the owners were awarded
$82,000, which was by then the dollar equivalent of £29,000. By a majority, the court applied the
judgment-date rule. It is submitted that this decision is open to much doubt. It may be that the
US dollar was the proper money of account for the claim, in which event US$118,000 should
have been awarded and no question of conversion would have arisen; alternatively, the court
should have awarded the damages expressed in sterling in accordance with the approach later
adopted in *The Texaco Melbourne* [1994] 1 Lloyd's Rep 473 (HL). The latter approach would
appear to be more appropriate. The case is discussed by Brandon (1953) ICLQ 313. Another
example is *Conte v Flota Mercante del Estado* (1960) 277 F 2d 664 (CCA, 2d) where the court
applied Argentine law both to the questions of liability and quantum, stating (at 761) that:

Hicks v Guinness the obligation was both subject to American law and payable in America; in *Deutsche Bank Filiale Nürnberg v Humphreys* it was both subject to German law and payable in Germany. The question of how the conversion is to be effected if the place of payment is in another country than that to whose law the contract is subject, which law governs the determination of the place of payment, and how the money of account is to be ascertained have not yet received a complete answer; in the last connection, it is apparently assumed that an obligation which "arises" in a certain country is subject to the laws of that country and is payable within it.[56] On the other hand, it seems to have been assumed in one case that an obligation "arose" in the United States merely because the contract was subject to the laws of Minnesota.[57] It appears that no distinction is made between a claim for damages and a claim for payment of a debt[58] and the judgment-date rule applies in Admiralty and other cases of federal concern.[59]

"conversion is made at the rate prevailing at the date of judgment, but we determine the amount to be converted as would the foreign court". In *Trinh v Citibank NA* (1985) 623 Supp 1526, the court stated that in non-diversity cases federal courts consistently applied the judgment-date rule. That rule was applied in *Black Sea & Baltic General Insurance Co v S/S Hellenic* (1984) AMC 1055 and *Vlactos v M/V Proso* (1986) AMC 269. On the other hand, in *The Gylfe v The Trujillo* (1954) 209 F 2d 386 (CCA 2d), it was held that, where repairs were paid in foreign currency, the rate as at the date of the expenditure (rather than the date of judgment) should be applied. A similar approach was adopted in *Jamaica Nutrition Holdings Ltd v United Shipping Co* (1981) 643 F 2d 376 (CCA, 5th Cir); *Seguros Banvenez SA v S/S Oliver Drescher* (1985) AMC 2168 (CCA, 2nd Cir) and *Nissto Co Ltd v The Stolthorn* (1986) AMC 269.

[56] Such a view becomes plausible if it is remembered that Professor Beale's territorial theory always exercised great influence on Mr Justice Holmes—see, eg, his opinion in *Slater v Mexican National Railway Co* (1904) 194 US 120. In *The Verdi* (1920) 268 Fed 908, it was apparently believed that the mere fact that the tort was committed in New York meant that the damages were payable there. In *The West Arrow* [1936] AMC 165 (US Circuit Court of Appeal, 2d 1936), the court seems to have assumed that, as the breach occurred in Holland and the ensuing obligation was expressed in Dutch guilders, it was performable in Holland. In *Det Forenede Dampskibs Selskab v Insurance Co of North America* (1928) 28 F (2d) 449 (SDNY), affirmed 31 F 2d 658, cert denied (1929) 280 US 571, it was held that the right to contribution in general average "crystallised upon the termination of the voyage, and since the voyage ended in an American port, the owner became then and there entitled to receive contribution in dollars. This indebtedness arose in the United States was payable in its currency and subject to its laws." Therefore the rate of exchange prevailing on the date of the termination of the voyage was applied. See also *Nevillon v Demmer* (1920) 114 Misc 1, 185 NY Supp 443, where francs which were promised in a note and were payable in Paris were converted into dollars at the rate of exchange prevailing at the commencement of the action because the notes "became payable in dollars [sic] upon the plaintiff's demanding of the defendant their payment in this State. The commencement of the action was equivalent to such a demand."

[57] See the *ReliaStar* decision (n 46 above).

[58] *The Integritas* [1933] AMC 165 (District Court of Maryland).

[59] *Compania Engraw Commercial E Industrial SA v Schenley* (1950) 181 F 2d 876. Yet the First Circuit and a New York District Court did not hesitate to apply the judgment-date rule in diversity cases: *Gutor International AG v Raymond Packer Co* (1974) 493 F 2d 938, 943; *The Island Territory of Curaçao v Solitron Devices Inc* (1973) 356 F Supp 1, 14.

In States other than New York,[60] there were a number of cases in which the **8.14** judgment-date rule was applied,[61] but the breach-date rule was dominant.[62] The practice is so obviously unjust that the judgment-date rule may ultimately be expected to prevail.[63] Nevertheless, it must not be overlooked that the judgment-date rule can itself work harshly against the creditor where, for the purpose of giving judgment, the foreign currency claim has to be converted into US dollars.[64]

In New York, section 27(b) of the Judiciary Law was enacted in 1988.[65] It **8.15** provides that where a cause of action "is based upon an obligation denominated in a currency other than the currency of the United States, a court shall render or enter a judgment or decree in a foreign currency of the underlying obligation", the amount of the judgment is to be converted into US dollars "at the date of entry of the judgment or decree". This goes a long way towards solving the problem, although in the light of the English experience it might have been better to provide for conversion on the actual date of payment, thus protecting the judgment creditor against a depreciation of the dollar between judgment and payment.[66] The difficulty is resolved altogether if the court is prepared to enter judgment in the foreign currency concerned.[67]

---

[60] The position in relation to New York is considered below.

[61] See the *Curaçao* case mentioned in n 59 above; *Application of United Shellac Corp* (1950) 97 NY Supp 2d 817; *Bonnell v Schultz* (1950) 95 NY Supp 2d 617; *Sirie v Godfrey* 196 App Div 529, (1921) 188 NY Supp 52; *Metcalf v Mayer* 213 App Div 607, (1925) 211 NY Supp 53; although see *Orlick v Wiener Bankverein* 204 App Div 432, (1923) 198 NY Supp 413.

[62] *Competex SA v LaBow* (1986) 783 F 2d 333 and the numerous cases there referred to; *Vishipco Line v Chase Manhattan Bank NA* (1981) 660 F 2d 854. See also *Trinh v Citibank NA* (1985) 623 Supp 1526 affirmed without reference to the point, 850 F 2d 1164 (6th Cir); *Re Good Hope Chemical Corp* (1984) 747 F 2d 806, 809 (1st Cir).

[63] However, para 823 of the Restatement (Third) of the Foreign Relations Law (1987) should not serve as a guide, for it provides that conversion should "be made at such rate as to make the creditor whole and not to avoid rewarding a debtor who has delayed in carrying out the obligation". Whilst the objective is apparently laudable, this would introduce into a purely procedural rule an element of substantive justice which should properly be determined by reference to the applicable law. It must, however, be said that the provision was cited with approval in *ReliaStar Life Insurance Company v IOA Re Inc and Swiss Re Life Canada* (n 46 above).

[64] In *Paris v Central Chiclera* (1952) 193 F 2d 960, a Mexican supplier sued a US buyer who had defaulted on a contract to purchase a quantity of gum. The contract price was expressed in Mexican pesos. At the time of the breach, US$1 could be purchased with 4.7 pesos; by the time of the judgment, 8.62 pesos were required for that purpose. The US Court of Appeals required the use of the exchange rate as at the date of judgment, which reduced the value of the award by some 40% and effectively allowed the US buyer to benefit from his own breach.

[65] This followed the decision in *Teca-Print AG v Amacoil Machinery Inc* (1988) 525 NYS 2d 535 and a report by a Committee of the New York Bar Association, (1986) 18 *New York University Journal of International Law and Politics* 812.

[66] By the same token, the judgment debtor would benefit from any depreciation of the relevant foreign currency during this period.

[67] See the various foreign currency judgments mentioned in para 8.07 above.

D. Insolvency and Shares in a Fund

8.16 The problems considered above arise in a slightly different form when it becomes necessary to decide upon entitlement to shares in a specific and finite fund, for one is then concerned not merely with the mechanics of conversion but also with equity as between the various participants. Because the fund is finite, it is necessary to ensure equality and uniformity of treatment and to avoid the incidence of mere chance or speculative gain.

8.17 In order to achieve this objective, both the assets of the fund and liabilities which constitute claims upon it must be converted into one currency at a uniform rate. This is achieved by requiring such conversion to be effected by reference to the applicable exchange rate on the date when the fund is constituted.[68] This formulation naturally gives rise to two questions, namely, (a) which currency is to be used as the reference point, and (b) for the purpose of ascertaining the appropriate rate, when is the relevant fund deemed to be constituted?

8.18 As to the first point, it would seem possible to select either the currency of the place in which the proceedings are taking place or the currency identified by the law which governs the trust. It seems appropriate to discard the first option; it could only be justified on grounds of convenience, and would mean that the substantive rights of the beneficiaries may be affected by the happenstance that proceedings take place in one jurisdiction rather than another. The second choice is rather more appealing in the sense that it should lead to a uniformity of treatment and, consistently with principle, allows that substantive rights are exclusively determined by the law which governs them. Thus, when the point falls for decision in relation to a trust fund, the appropriate currency is to be selected in accordance with the law applicable to the trust.[69] It should be emphasised that the governing law of the trust is applied in order to ascertain the appropriate currency; it does not state nor does it invariably follow that sterling should be the reference currency for all trusts governed by English law. The court should perhaps select the currency of the country in which the major trust assets are determined.

---

[68] This contrasts sharply with the rules discussed earlier in this chapter, where the date of judgment or payment may be applied. Such a rule could operate unjustly between competing claimants to a single fund. The rule outlined in the text was pressed by Belgium in the *Case of Barcelona Traction Light & Power Ltd (Belgium v Spain)* [1970] ICJ Rep 3, but the Court did not find it necessary to determine the point.

[69] The law applicable to a trust is that selected in the trust deed or, in the absence of such a selection, the law with which the trust is most closely connected—see the Recognition of Trusts Act 1987 and the discussion of that subject by Dicey and Morris, *The Conflict of Laws* (Sweet & Maxwell, 13th edn, 2000) ch 29.

The identification of the date with reference to which the conversion rate **8.19** should be ascertained is likewise apt to affect the substantive entitlements of the beneficiaries. In principle, therefore, the second question should likewise be submitted to the law which governs the trust.[70]

In insolvency proceedings in England, the relevant fund is deemed to be **8.20** constituted when the winding-up order is made or the necessary resolution is passed, and the necessary rate of exchange is thus to be ascertained by reference to that date. This rule is established in England[71] and in some other jurisdictions,[72] but in the United States the courts have applied the rate of exchange prevailing on the date on which the particular creditor's claim was admitted or allowed.[73]

Where an order is made for the administration of a deceased person, conversion **8.21** is effected as at the date of the order.[74] A striking illustration of the same basic principle is provided by the decision in *Re Chesterman's Trust*.[75] A fund in court represented the sterling proceeds of sale of a property. One of the beneficiaries had mortgaged his interest in the fund to secure an obligation expressed in German marks. The question was, how much of the sterling trust fund should be paid to the mortgagee? It was made clear at first instance and in the Court of Appeal that the court was not dealing with an action to enforce the repayment obligation in the mortgage; rather it was "dividing the funds" and for this purpose had to ascertain what sums were payable to the mortgagees.[76] For that purpose, it was held that the proper date for the conversion was the date of the Master's certificate in the inquiry. This decision was followed in Canada, in a

---

[70] This may be regarded as a question as to the interpretation and effect of a trust, or conceivably as a matter touching the administration of the trust, but in each case, the law applicable to the trust would govern the subject: *Chellaram v Chellaram* [1985] Ch 409 and other cases noted by Dicey and Morris (n 69 above) para 29-012.

[71] *Re Dynamics Corp of America* [1976] 1 WLR 757, reviewing a number of earlier authorities; *Re Lines Bros Ltd* [1983] Ch 1. See now Insolvency Rules 1989, r 4.91, to which reference has already been made in n 31 above. On the problem in general, see Hanisch (1980) *Annuaire Suisse de Droit International* 127 and (1988) *Zeitschrift für Wirtschaftsrecht* 341.

[72] Germany: see Federal Supreme Court, 22 June 1989, *BGHZ* 108, 123; Netherlands: Hoge Raad, 4 February 1977, *NJ* 1978, 66.

[73] *Wyse v Pioneer Cafeteria Feeds Ltd* (1965) 340 F 2d 719, 725. The decision on this point is inadequately reasoned and is open to the objection that different rates of exchange would be applied to different claims.

[74] *Re Hawkins* [1972] 3 WLR 255. Similarly, where a limitation fund was established in a shipping case, the rate was established as at the date of the fund's constitution: *The Abadesa* [1968] P 656; *The Mecca* [1968] P 665.

[75] [1923] Ch 466.

[76] See 474 (Russell J), 479 (Lord Sterndale MR) and 485 (Warrington LJ). It is noteworthy that the amounts owing by the mortgagor were due and payable long before the date of the Master's certificate.

case in which a trustee for bondholders claimed an account for the purpose of ascertaining the principal and interest due to the bondholders out of the proceeds of sale of the mortgaged property. The date of the Master's report was ordered to be the date of conversion, even though the bonds and coupons had fallen due for payment many years earlier.[77]

---

[77] *Montreal Trust Co v Abitibi Power & Paper Co Ltd* (1944) Ontario Reports 515, 523–5.

Part III

THE PRINCIPLE OF NOMINALISM

INTRODUCTION

Part II of this work has considered the nature and extent of monetary obliga- **Intro.3.01**
tions and numerous questions touching the interpretation and performance of
such obligations. It is now necessary to consider the principle of nominalism,
which in many ways supplements the rules discussed in Part II. In its essence,
the principle establishes that obligations expressed in money are to be treated as
independent and self-standing measures of value; they are not liable to adjustment on the basis of factors which are extraneous to the monetary system or the
unit of account.

Chapters 9 and 10 will accordingly consider the application of the principle of **Intro.3.02**
nominalism to liquidated and unliquidated obligations.

Chapters 11 and 12 will examine the attempts which have at times been made **Intro.3.03**
to avoid the application of the principle and the hardship which this may from
time to time cause; they will also examine the response of the courts to these
efforts.

Chapter 13 will review the principle of nominalism in a private international **Intro.3.04**
law context and will examine the very important *lex monetae* principle.

9

MONETARY OBLIGATIONS, LIQUIDATED SUMS, AND THE PRINCIPLE OF NOMINALISM

A. Introduction

It has previously been noted that the debtor of a monetary obligation is under a **9.01** duty to pay money which, amongst other peculiarities, incorporates a reference to a distinct unit of account.[1] It has also been shown that money is not merely a quantity of metal or paper, but an abstract unit of measurement which in this country cannot even be defined by an historical analysis.[2] It has, therefore, been said, with some justification, that "a debt is not incurred in terms of currency, but in terms of units of account",[3] and that "contracts are expressed in terms of the unit of account, but the unit of account is only a denomination connoting the appropriate currency".[4]

---

[1] See the discussion of the unit of account at paras 1.32–1.34 above.
[2] On this point, see para 1.49 above.
[3] *Adelaide Electric Supply Co v Prudential Assurance Co* [1934] AC 122, 148.
[4] *Auckland Corp v Alliance Assurance Co* [1937] AC 587, 605 (PC). In the same sense, see the first instance decision in *Broken Hill Proprietary Co v Latham* [1933] Ch 373, 391, approved in this particular respect in *Adelaide Electric Supply Co v Prudential Assurance Co* [1934] AC 122, 160. The Court of Appeal in the *Broken Hill* case (at 407), clearly explained that a pound is not a coin and that a contract to pay pounds is "a contract to pay so many standard units of value by

9.02 But how many such units of account is the debtor bound to pay? Legal tender legislation does not, of itself, supply an answer to this question; it determines the medium through which performance is to be achieved but it does not determine the amount to be paid. Such legislation merely provides that banknotes must be accepted according to their face or nominal value; it has no bearing upon the question of how many banknotes have to be tendered.[5] It is this question of the value of money or the extent of monetary obligations which has not yet been answered, and which it is now necessary to address. This, in turn, requires a consideration of the principle of nominalism.

9.03 It may be helpful at the outset to state the principle of nominalism in succinct terms, so that the remainder of this Part can proceed by reference to that explanation. The principle has been formulated[6] as follows:

> A debt expressed in the currency of another country involves an obligation to pay the nominal amount of the debt in whatever is the legal tender at the time of payment according to the law of the country in whose currency the debt is expressed (*lex monetae*), irrespective of any fluctuations which may have occurred in the value of that currency in terms of sterling or any other currency, of gold, or of any commodities between the time when the debt was incurred and the time of payment.

9.04 The parties thus contract by reference to a currency and the units of account in which it is expressed. It is implicit in the principle of nominalism that an obligation expressed in money is intended to have a uniform and unvarying value, which is not affected by supervening events which are extraneous to the monetary system itself.

B. The Foundations of Nominalism—Competing Theories

9.05 It has been noted previously that the existence of the general principle of nominalism flows, at least in part, from the State theory of money.[7] Whilst that theory can no longer be accepted in all its aspects, it nevertheless survives to the extent that the State enjoys the right to define the unit of account and to organise the monetary system.[8] In this sense, the remnants of the State theory continue to support the essential feature of nominalism—ie that an obligation

---

tendering coins or notes or other legal tender for the amount". These remarks remain valid even though the *Broken Hill* case was overruled by the decision in *Adelaide Electric*. See also *Re Chesterman's Trusts* [1923] 2 Ch 466 and *Ottoman Bank v Chakarian (No. 2)* [1938] AC 269, 271.

5 See Dawson and Cooper (1935) 33 Mich LR 852, 904.

6 Dicey and Morris, *The Conflict of Laws* (Sweet & Maxwell, 13th edn, 2000) Rule 206.

7 See the discussion of the State theory of money in Ch 1 above.

8 See, in particular the discussion at para 1.50 above.

to pay 100 units of a particular currency can be discharged by payment of 100 units of that currency, regardless of any changes in the purchasing power or external value of that currency between the date of the contract and the date of payment. In other words, the State establishes a currency and its units of account represent their own independent value in terms of the domestic legal system, regardless of any external factors which may have an economic impact upon that currency. The need to revise the State theory of money has thus not in any sense brought into question the continued validity of the nominalistic principle. It nevertheless remains necessary to expand upon those points, and to examine other theories which have been put forward in support of the principle.

The so-called *intrinsic* value of money, ie its substance or parity in terms of gold **9.06** or any other substance, cannot have any bearing upon the value of money or the extent of monetary obligations. Neither the pound sterling nor any other unit of account is identical to a quantity of metal; as a consequence, the obligation to pay pounds (or other money) cannot be equiparated to an obligation to deliver a certain weight of metal.[9] For the same reason, it is impossible to hold that the extent of an obligation to pay pounds is determined by the rate of exchange or by the value of gold or any other metal. If an obligation to pay one pound was incurred in 1930 but payable in 2000, it remained an obligation to pay one pound when the date for performance arrived, even though a pound in 1930 would purchase far more gold than a pound in 2000 could acquire.[10] It should be said at this point that Savigny[11] propounded a rate-of-exchange theory to the opposite effect and which is not very different from metallism in the narrower sense of the word. This theory pre-supposes that all currency systems are necessarily founded on the adoption of a certain precious metal as the standard of value. This primary prerequisite of the theory plainly does not exist, and it is thus unnecessary to consider it further.[12] It does, however, serve to emphasise that the notion of the intrinsic value of money was born in a bygone age when the banknote had not acquired its modern status and function, and when only metallic money circulated which was liable to be debased by the Crown or pared by the clipper, so that there existed "one class which would give money only by tale and another which would take it only by weight".[13]

---

[9] It has rightly been said that nominalism implies a monetary system which dissociates itself from the metallic system—see Nussbaum, *Money in the Law, National and International* (The Press Foundation, 2nd edn, 1950) 17. See also para 2.33 above.

[10] On this point, see para 9.19 below.

[11] *Obligationenrecht* (1851) 432, 454.

[12] Savigny's theory was expressly rejected by the Roumanian-German Mixed Arbitral Tribunal, *Rec VII* 738.

[13] Macaulay, *History of England* (Harper Brothers, 1849) ch xxi, which includes a vivid account of the alarming state of the currency which had resulted from a long period of clipping and which, by 1695, called for urgent reform.

9.07   The extent of monetary obligations is also independent of any *functional* or *exchange* value of money, ie its value in terms of its purchasing power.[14] Economists may be concerned with the exchange value of money and the quantity theory.[15] Economic principles of this kind have led some legal writers—often working at times of severe monetary disruption—to propose a legal theory of *valorism*. The theory[16] relies upon the supposed (or alleged) intention of the parties to secure "economic value" in their contractual relations, and develops a system of valorisation which is to apply whenever money loses its relative stability of value. In other words, the amount of the obligation would, where necessary, be adjusted to reflect the reduction in the purchasing power of money between the date at which the obligation is incurred and the date on which it falls to be performed.

9.08   The theory of valorism has superficial attractions, especially in times of high inflation. But however that may be, it is suggested that monetary law cannot accommodate or pay attention to the functional value of money or any valoristic theory based upon it. There are three reasons for this view, which require explanation:

(1) The law must firmly reject any idea of permitting adjustments on account of changes in the price of goods, for such a risk must clearly be imposed upon the parties themselves. The theory of valorism assumes that the parties intend to maintain the "economic value" of their contract. But frequently, their intention may be the precise opposite. For example, a party may contract to purchase oil at a pre-set price and for delivery over a long period; he will do so because he wishes to avoid the additional costs which might flow from a general increase in the price of oil. Likewise, his seller will agree to sell at the pre-set price in order to insulate himself from a fall in the general price. Plainly, an adjustment to the agreed price would be inappropriate in such a case.[17]

(2) It might perhaps be more feasible to stipulate for a price adjustment if it could be shown that, for example, inflation had been caused by an expansion

---

[14] At least, this is the case in the absence of any explicit contractual provisions designed to deal with changes in the real value of money. On this subject, see Ch 11 below.

[15] See, eg, Andrew Crockett, *Money* (Nelson, 2nd edn, 1979) 48–65; Milton Friedman, *Quantity Theory of Money in Money* (The New Palgrave, 1989) 1.

[16] The theory of valorism was propounded principally by Eckstein, *Geldschuld und Geldwert* (Berlin, 1932), and see also Hubrecht, *La Stabilisation du franc* (Paris, 1928). The theory is reviewed by E. Hirschberg through a number of publications in the 1970s—see *The Nominalistic Principle, A Legal Approach to Inflation, Deflation, Devaluation and Revaluation* (Bar-Ilan University, Israel, 1971) 89–134 and *The Impact of Inflation and Devaluation on Private Law Obligations* (Bar-Ilan University, 1976) 403.

[17] Forward contracts in the foreign exchange markets will frequently be excluded on the same basis; these examples could readily be multiplied.

in the money supply, as opposed to an increase in the price of goods. It could be argued that the diminishing value of money had affected the expectations of the parties, and that the requirement for a price adjustment could thus constitute an implied term of the contract. In reality, however, it is impossible sharply to distinguish between these supposedly different types of inflation,[18] and thus economic theory does not supply reliable means of identifying causes of inflation or other changes in the value of money which could reliably be used in a contractual context. There are thus no legally relevant criteria upon which a provision for an inflation adjustment could be implied into the terms of a contract or an agreement.[19]

(3) The extent of monetary obligations cannot be determined by reference to the functional value of money because there are no legally appropriate means of measuring changes in monetary values for these purposes. The indices which are available are, from a legal point of view, somewhat arbitrary.[20] They measure the price of baskets of goods or services which are necessarily selective and may therefore be wholly inappropriate to the particular case in hand. In other words, the relevant indices tend to be of a generic nature, whereas the court will have to deal with very specific issues. As noted in (1) above, the problem is particularly acute in the context of long-term contracts.[21] For example, it would be inappropriate now to adjust a ground rent agreed in 1914 by reference to a current cost of living index, because the value of land is in general independent of the cost of the goods or services which make up that type of index. The indices of the type now under discussion are thus too arbitrary for legal purposes and, in any event, they cannot distinguish between changes in the value of goods (which are legally irrelevant)[22] and changes in the value of money, which might potentially have some legal relevance.[23]

---

[18] See Desai in *Money* (The New Palgrave, 1989) 146. For legal purposes, the distinction was rejected by the German Supreme Court in 1925–31 March 1925, *RGZ* 110, 371.

[19] In the case of a supply of contract which has no stipulated termination date, the courts may take notice of the fact that the purchasing power of money declines over time, Thus, in *Staffordshire Area Health Authority v South Staffordshire Waterworks* [1978] 1 WLR 1387, the court implied a term to the effect that the agreement could be terminated on reasonable notice. It has to be noted that the court dealt with the manifest injustice caused to the supplier by extending to it a right of termination; no attempt was made to revalorise or adjust the monetary obligations of the buyer.

[20] During and after the great German inflation, the German Supreme Court repeatedly drew attention to the dangers inherent in the selection of the appropriate index: *RGZ* 108, 379; *RGZ* 109,158.

[21] In the nature of things, questions involving the erosion of the value of money are less likely to arise in contracts which are to be wholly performed within a relatively short period of time.

[22] See point (1) above

[23] See point (2) above.

It will appear later that, for these and other reasons, the law has fully adopted the conclusion to which the foregoing discussion inevitably leads—namely, that there is no general legal rule which allows the revision of the quantum of a monetary obligation in response to changes in monetary values.[24]

9.09 In the absence of a general rule allowing for the post-contractual adjustment of an obligation expressed in money, it must follow that the extent of monetary obligations cannot be determined otherwise than by the adoption of *nominalism*. As noted at the beginning of this chapter, the nominalistic principle means that a monetary obligation involves the payment of so many notes and coins, being legal tender at the time of payment and which, if added together according to the nominal values indicated thereon, produce a sum equal to the amount of the debt. In other words, the obligation to pay £10 is discharged if the creditor receives those notes and coins which, at the time of performance, constitute £10, regardless of both their intrinsic and their functional value.[25] It follows that a monetary obligation has no other "value" than the nominal value which it expresses.[26] Nominalism in this sense is a legal principle, but it is empirically derived from a generalisation of the normal factual situation.[27] In the vast majority of cases, the possibility of changes in monetary value does not enter the parties' minds, though they may have a definite idea of the exchange value, or purchasing power, of the stipulated amount of money. If they do have regard to that possibility, then they may safeguard themselves by appropriate

---

[24] It should be said, however, that there are some legal rules which relate to the determination of prices and the influence of price changes. These rules equally apply where it is obvious that it is not the price which increases or falls but money which appreciates or depreciates, these being different aspects of the same phenomenon. It appears that no other solution is workable—see point (2) above and the decision of the German Federal Finance Court, 14 May 1974, *BFHE* 112, 546, 557 or *NJW* 1974, 2330.

[25] The nominalistic principle applies equally if payment is made by other means, such as a cheque or bank transfer.

[26] The opening sentences of this paragraph were quoted with apparent approval by the Federal Court of Australia in *Cusak v Commissioner of Taxation* [2002] FCA 212. In that case, it was argued that Australia had two monetary systems, one consisting of gold coins and the other, consisting of base metal coins and banknotes. The taxpayer asserted that income in gold coins had a value of five times that of legal tender and that since the two currencies had to be interchangeable, an income of A$500 should be taxed as if it were an income of A$100. The court understandably dismissed this argument in a brief judgment. Had the taxpayer actually received payment in gold coin, then he would almost certainly have been taxed on the market (rather than the nominal) value of such coins: see the decision in *Jenkins v Horn* [1979] 2 All ER 1141, noted at para 1.43(4) above.

[27] This sentence (in its German version translated from the Second Edition of this work) was approved by the German Federal Finance Court, 14 May 1974, *BFHE* 112, 546, 556 or *NJW* 1976, 2330. It must, however, be observed that, in non-contractual cases, the court may have power to adjust periodic payments and that any general fall in the purchasing power of money could legitimately be taken into account as part of that process. Payments for maintenance provide an obvious example, where the payment period may be a lengthy one. Nevertheless, specific cases of this kind do not undermine the general principles outlined in the text.

protective clauses;[28] if they fail to do so, then they must be taken to have accepted the risks involved in a possible monetary dislocation during the period of the contract.[29] As a result, in the absence of express clauses to the contrary, parties must be understood to contract (or Parliament must be understood to legislate) with reference to the nominal value of the money concerned, as expressed by whatever is legal tender at the time of payment.[30] Nominalism thus finds its justification in the legally relevant intention.[31] Nominalism may be described as a legal principle, rather than a mere rule of construction, but it is derived from the presumed intention of the parties or the legislator. In the case of a contract, it is thus apt to say that the principle of nominalism operates as an implied term of the contract; in the case of a will, the principle operates by reference to the presumed intention of the testator.[32] The main practical consequence of the application of the nominalistic principle may be briefly stated— the creditor of the sum in question bears the risk that the purchasing power of the contractual currency will have fallen by the time the date of payment arrives, whilst the debtor bears the converse risk.[33] Given that the principle of nominalism touches the substance of the obligation, it follows that the application of the principle will at all times be directed by the governing law of the obligation concerned. Although it is important not to lose sight of the point just made, it

---

[28] This comment reflects the fact that (in a contractual context) the nominalistic principle operates as an implied term of the contract; it must follow that the application of the principle can be varied or avoided by means of an express term. On this subject, see Ch 11 below.

[29] This is particularly so where the risk emanates from the possible actions of the State which issues the currency in question. In this sense, it has been said that monetary obligations are the foremost example of contracts which "have a congenital infirmity": *Norman v Baltimore and Ohio Railroad Co* (1934) 294 US 240, 307.

[30] See, eg, *Electricity Trust (SA) v CA Parsons & Co Ltd* (1978) 18 ALR 223, 225; *Commissioner of Taxation v Energy Resources of Australia Ltd* (1995) 54 FCR 25, 37.

[31] In the same sense, see Dicey and Morris, *The Conflict of Laws* (Sweet & Maxwell, 2000) Rule 206. The leading judicial discussion of the principle is to be found in *Knox v Lee* and *Parker v Davies* (1870) 12 Wall (79) US 457, 548—the relevant extract is reproduced at para 9.21 below. The Swiss Federal Tribunal noted that "Les fluctuations des changes constituent donc un des aléas du contrat". In *Searight v Calbraith* (1796) 4 US 325, the plaintiff sued on a bill of exchange for "150,000 livres tournois" payable in Paris. After the bill was issued assignats were introduced in France, but the plaintiff refused payment in this form. The court said "the decision depends entirely on the intention of the parties . . . If a specie payment was meant, a tender in the assignats was unavailing. But if the current monies of France was in view, the tender in assignats was lawfully made." These cases reinforce the view that the nominalistic principle is ultimately derived from a generalisation of the (presumed) intention of the parties. As a result, it is unsurprising that the German Constitutional Court held that nominalism is not a rule of constitutional law: *WM* 1990, 287.

[32] It may thus seem odd to describe nominalism as a "legal principle", when it rests merely upon the presumed intention of the contracting parties. Nevertheless, the label is justified, for only in the rarest cases will a different intention be found.

[33] The point is graphically illustrated by the decision in *Re Chesterman's Trusts* [1923] 2 Ch 466 (CA); see also *Addison v Brown* [1954] 1 WLR 779, 785.

will hardly ever be of practical relevance because the principle of nominalism enjoys universal acceptance.[34]

C. The Historical Development of Nominalism

9.10 It was noted earlier[35] that the notion of money as a creature of the law, together with the "recurrent link" principle, form integral aspects of the State theory of money. The principle of nominalism is also a necessary part of the State theory, but in fact its early origins enjoy a respectable antiquity. This is perhaps unsurprising, because problems associated with the value of money—and in particular, its depreciation—have existed for centuries. The history of the principle is of some importance and must therefore be described, at least in outline.[36]

9.11 The nominalistic principle is usually said to have been first laid down by Aristotle in his *Nichomachean Ethics* where he said[37] "money has been introduced by convention as a kind of substitute for a need or demand . . . its value is derived

---

[34] See paras 9.27 and 9.28 below. The text will work on the basis that the application of the principle will be derived from the law which governs the obligation; this seems to be consistent both with general principles of private international law and with the decision in *Re Chesterman's Trusts* (n 33 above). There may, however, be cogent arguments for ascribing the application of nominalism to the law of the currency (*lex monetae*) in which the obligation is expressed, rather than to the law which governs the obligation as a whole. This would have significant consequences—in particular, a revalorisation law forming a part of the *lex monetae* would have to be applied by foreign courts which were confronted with an obligation expressed in that currency. Yet this is by no means necessarily an unreasonable or unfair result. On the contrary, if parties had stipulated for payment of (say) 1,000 pesos and the issuing State sees fit to adjust such a debt to 5,000 pesos to compensate the creditor for the effects of inflation, then it is by no means obvious why the creditor should lose this benefit merely because the contract happens to be governed by a different system of law. In other words, if the parties chose to refer to "1,000 pesos", they may have intended to embrace not only a mere reference to the currency but also a reference to the *measure of value* imported by 1,000 units of that currency. It is submitted that arguments of this kind become all the more forceful in the modern world, where currencies are no longer linked to the gold standard and are thus effectively independent of each other. There would be some equity in a rule which ascribed the amount of a debt to the *lex monetae*, so that revaluation legislation passed before the date of payment could be given effect. However desirable such an approach may be thought to be, it would represent a major departure from established thinking. Consequently, the present text proceeds on the basis described above.

[35] See generally Ch 1 above.

[36] Those requiring a more detailed historical discussion are referred to the Fifth Edition of this work, 92–102.

[37] Book 5, ch 5, translation by F.H. Peters (London, 15th edn, 1893) 56. It has, however, been suggested that the reference to "law" should instead be translated from the original Greek as "convention" or "usage" which would clearly change the sense considerably—see Eric Roll, *A History of Economic Thought* (Faber, 4th edn, 1973) 33, quoting Gray, *The Development of Economic Doctrine* (Ams Pr, 1978) 27. A second edition of Gray's book was published by Longman in 1981.

not from nature but from law, and can be altered or abolished at will". This early statement emphasises both that money is a creature of the law and that its value is in a sense an abstract and independent concept, derived from its use as a medium of exchange.

In Rome, a number of depreciations of money occurred,[38] but the principle of nominalism does not appear to have been firmly established at that time. The main authorities draw a distinction between substance and quantity of money and suggest that quantity, rather than substance, is the governing factor. This would suggest an acceptance of the nominalistic principle, although it is difficult to draw entirely firm conclusions.[39] However, when the books of Justinian were studied by the school of glossators, they were interpreted in a manner which supported a metallistic (as opposed to a nominalistic) principle.[40] The post-glossators, adopting the approach of their predecessors, developed the distinction between *bonitas intrinsica* and *bonitas extrinsica*, and it was the former, ie the metallic value of money, which was held to be the subject matter of monetary obligations. However, a decisive reaction in favour of the nominalistic principle set in after the publication, in 1546, of Carolus Molinaeus's (Dumoulin's) *Tractatus contractuum et usurarum*, where early work was interpreted by the words, "*Quantitas, id est valor impositus*".[41] This view was attractive to kings and governments, whose financial interests demanded a theoretical basis for their practice of debasing the coinage. Thus in France, a decree of 1551 compelled the parties to contract by tale (sous, livres, deniers) and not by weight (metal). During the eighteenth century, Pothier affirmed the principle and declared "Notre jurisprudence est fondée sur ce principe, que dans la monnaie on ne considère pas les corps et pièces de monnaie, mais seulement la valeur que le prince y a attachée . . . Il suit de ce principe que ce ne sont point les pièces de monnaie, mais la valeur qu'elles signifient qui fait la matière du prêt ainsi que

9.12

---

[38] eg, the pure silver content of the denarius was about 4.55 grammes around 200 BC, but only 3.41 grammes by the time of Nero (AD 54–68); similarly, a pound of gold cost 1,000 denarii at the time of Augustus (31 BC–AD 14) but had risen to some 3.3 million denarii by AD 419.

[39] The main texts are Papinianus (D 46, 3, *de solut* 94.1) "*sive in pecunia non corpora quis cogitet sed quantitatem*" (in the case of money, it is not the content which matters, but the quantity) and Paulus (D. 18, 1 *de contrah emptione* 1) "*eaque materia forma publica percussa usum dominiumque non tam ex substantia praebet quam ex quantitate*" (the material has been stamped with the authority of the State, and it is thus held out to have value by reference to the number of coins tendered, rather than by reference to their content) and (D 4, 6, 3 *de solut* 99) "*creditorem non esse cogendum in aliam formam nummos accipere si ex ea re damnum aliquid passurus sit*" (a creditor cannot be compelled to accept coins in a different form if he would suffer some loss as a result). (Author's translations.)

[40] The summary of Accursias (1182–1260) reads "*tantum valet unus nummus quantum argenti tantusdem in massa*" (a coin is worth just as much as its silver content). (Author's translation.)

[41] This may be taken to mean that the quantity of money is represented by the value imposed upon it by law.

des autres contracts . . .".[42] So far as France is concerned, the nominalistic principle found expression in Article 1895 of the Code Civil of 1803:

> L'obligation qui resulte d'un prêt d'argent n'est toujours que de la somme numérique énoncée au contrat. S'il y a eu augmentation ou diminution d'espèces avant l'époque du paiement, le débiteur doit rendre la somme numérique prêtée, et ne doit rendre que cette somme dans les espèces ayant cours au moment du paiement.

9.13   It would be difficult to formulate a more accurate or concise statement of the principle and its consequences.[43] Germany also ultimately adopted the nominalistic principle, although as late as 1793 Goethe was able to write that "money is money, not on account of the stamp, but as a result of the intrinsic value".[44] Although periodic attempts have been made to replace nominalism by metallistic or valoristic doctrines, it cannot be doubted that, in continental Europe, the principle is secure and nominalism universally predominates.[45]

9.14   The principle is equally well established in common law jurisdictions. It appears to have been recognised in the Middle Ages that the King had not only the prerogative of issuing coins, but also of determining the denomination or value at which the coin was to pass current.[46] Consequently, the King could debase or enhance the value, a power which was in fact used on repeated occasions.[47] The whole issue (including the nominalistic principle developed in Continental Europe) was very fully discussed in the decision of the Privy Council of Ireland in the *Case de Mixt Moneys (Gilbert v Brett)*.[48] Gilbert of London had sold goods to Brett of Drogheda for "£100 sterling current and lawful money of England"

---

[42] *Traité du prêt de consommation* v 55; *du contrat de vente* iii 173; *du contrat de constitution de rente* iii 473 (edition Bugnet).

[43] Nevertheless, the provision does not assume the character of *ordre public*, with the result that contractual terms to protect the creditor against monetary depreciation are in principle valid: Cass Civ 1, 27 June 1957 (*Guyot v Praguin*).

[44] *Goethes Amtliche Schriften* (Weimar, 1968) II, 379.

[45] Germany's Federal Constitutional Court has said that nominalism is "a basic principle regulating the prevailing monetary order and economic policy", 19 December 1978, *BVerfGE* 50, 57 at 92. It must, however, be remembered that the parties can vary the application of the principle by the terms of their contract. Consequently, nominalism was found not to be a necessary ingredient of the law or a constitutional requirement: Federal Constitutional Court, 15 December 1989, *WM* 1990, 287.

[46] YB 21 Eds II, f.60b, 9 Edw IV f, 49a; Dyer 816–83a; Blackstone 1, 278. See also Breckenridge, *Legal Tender, A Study in English and American Monetary History* (Greenwood Press, New York, 1969) first published in 1903.

[47] For an historical discussion of the debasement of the coinage, see Chown, *A History of Money from AD 800* (Routlegde, 1994) chs 2 and 5. Blackstone (I278) opined that this power was limited, so that the King could not debase or enhance the coinage below or above its sterling metal value in gold or silver, whilst Sir Matthew Hale (1 Hale PC 194) held that there was no such limitation to the King's power.

[48] (1604) Davies 18; 2 State Trials 114. The case was of great importance in the context of the US Supreme Court decision in the Legal Tender Cases, discussed below.

to be paid in Dublin. After the contract was made, but before payment fell due, Queen Elizabeth recalled the existing currency of Ireland and issued a new debased coinage (called mixed money). The new coinage was declared to be the current money of Ireland, and every creditor was bound to accept it according to its denomination or value—a refusal to do so was a punishable offence. Brett tendered payment in the debased coin, and it was thus necessary to decide whether or not this was a good and sufficient tender. The reporter dealt with the necessity of having a certain standard of money in every commonwealth and with the royal prerogative to issue money and to determine its substance, form, and value. The report then draws the distinction between (a) the value of money by reference to its metallic fineness and weight (*bonitas intrinsica*) and (b) the value of money by reference to its denomination and character (*bonitas extrinsica* or *valor impositus*). The latter was held to be the true description of money, for money is essentially an artificial, legal (rather than physical) creation.[49] It necessarily followed that the mixed money, having been proclaimed to be the current and lawful money within Ireland, ought to be taken and accepted for sterling money. The reporter then determined that the mixed money circulating in Ireland could be said to be current and lawful money "of England" for the purposes of the contract. Having reached an affirmative answer, he then proceeds to examine the importance of the fact that "better" money was in circulation at the time the contract was made. This was determined to be an irrelevant consideration, for payment was to be made at a future time, and a monetary obligation must be discharged in legal tender at that time. The case is thus a clear authority for the application of the nominalistic principle in this country;[50] an obligation to pay £100 sterling is to pay what the law denominates as £100 sterling at the time of payment.[51]

Since it became established, the English courts have consistently applied the nominalistic principle.[52] The subsequent history of the principle in England— **9.15**

---

[49] In this respect, the Court cited Aristotle, Ethicorum, lib 5, reproduced at para 9.11 above.

[50] The decision does, of course, also stand as authority for the adoption of the State theory of money as part of English law.

[51] The acceptance of the nominalistic principle in Scotland is apparent from the decision in *Hamilton v Corbet* (1731) M 10142. Without in any sense wishing to detract from the general principle established by *Gilbert v Brett* or the general authority of that case, it should be pointed out that a different approach might have been adopted in a later era, when the courts had more fully developed the modern principles of private international law. Given that "English" sterling continued to exist, the court might have begun by examining the law governing the obligation. If this was English law, then there was no basis upon which the new monetary law in Ireland could have varied the substance of the obligation. In other words, the court should apply the rules which became relevant upon the division of a previously unitary monetary system—see Ch 6 above.

[52] The only possible exception appears to be *Deering v Parker* (1760) 4 Dallas xxiii, a Privy Council decision on appeal from the Chancery Court of New Hampshire. The decision in that case perhaps turns on its own very specific facts but the Privy Council appears to have proceeded

including its extension to banknotes—must nevertheless be recorded in some detail.

9.16 In 1811, the Bullion Committee in their Report[53] had arrived at the conclusion that the rise in prices prevalent at that time was due to an over-issue of Bank of England notes, as a result of which the value of such notes had depreciated. On 6 May 1811, a resolution was introduced in the House of Commons, supporting the Report and affirming the depreciation of money.[54] Although sterling had fallen in value against gold, foreign currencies, and commodities, the resolutions were lost by large majorities. A week later, Vansittart introduced resolutions which rejected the Bullion Report.[55]

9.17 These resolutions were passed with large majorities, and included the memorable statement "that the promissory notes of the said Company [the Bank of England] have hitherto been, and are at this time, held in public estimation to be equivalent to the legal coin of the realm and generally accepted as such in all pecuniary transactions to which such coin is lawfully applicable". However, commercial considerations rapidly overtook the political debate when Lord King announced that, in view of the depreciation of money, he would no longer accept banknotes from his tenants in payment of rent; instead, he would calculate those rents on a gold basis. This provoked strong resentment, on the grounds that a person who contracted to receive a pound should accept whatever was regarded as a pound at the time of payment—a plain statement of the nominalistic principle.[56] As a consequence, Parliament at once passed Lord Stanhope's Act,[57] by which banknotes were effectively made legal tender and which provided that no one should pay or receive more for guineas or less for banknotes than their face value. The Vansittart Resolution and the speed with which Lord King's proposals were defeated should be seen together with the

---

by reference to a metallistic (rather than nominalistic) principle, for the Board valued the amount of the debt in question by reference to the price of silver as at the date on which payment fell due—and not as at the date on which the contract was made. However, the decision does not appear to have been either reported or relied upon in this country. Since the decision is now of considerable antiquity and is plainly out of step with all other English decisions in this area, it is safe to disregard it.

[53] The Report has been described as "one of the most important documents in English currency history"—Feavearyear, *The Pound Sterling* (Clarendon Press, 2nd edn, 1963) 195.

[54] *Hansard*, 6 May 1811, p 831.

[55] *Hansard*, 13 May 1811, p 70.

[56] Lord King's opponents "held to the principle that a man who had contracted to receive a pound must take whatever was by general consent called a pound when payment was made. This was the general principle which had been followed for a thousand years in spite of all the many changes of form and value, some of them very rapid, which the pound had undergone", Feavearyear (n 53 above) 206.

[57] 51 Geo III ch 127. The Act became law on 24 July 1811.

lack of success of all attempts to remedy the serious effects of deflation that followed from the restoration of the gold standard in 1821.[58]

Similarly, 110 years later, the abandonment of the gold standard in 1931 was accepted so quietly and readily and entailed so insignificant a "flight from sterling" that the monetary discipline implied by the nominalistic principle may be said to have become an accepted part of national life. Indeed, it was at that very moment that nominalism was judicially reaffirmed by Scrutton LJ:[59]   **9.18**

> I take it that if a tort had been committed in England before England went off the gold standard, the plaintiff could not say "We insist, after England has gone off the gold standard and the pound has depreciated in purchasing power, on being paid the value of the gold standard pound at the time of the commission of the tort." A pound in England is a pound whatever its international value.

The nominalistic principle continues to hold sway, and is supported by high judicial authority. Thus Viscount Simonds[60] said that "the obligation to pay will be satisfied by payment of whatever currency is by the law of Queensland valid tender for the discharge of the nominal amount of the debt". Lord Denning also made a characteristically clear and emphatic statement of the rule:[61] "A man who stipulates for a pound must take a pound when payment is made, whatever the pound is worth at that time. Sterling is the constant unit of value by which in the eye of the law everything else is measured. Prices of commodities may go up or down, other currencies may go up or down, but sterling remains the same."   **9.19**

The continued adherence to the principle does not, however, lead to the conclusion that the judiciary is blind to the injustice which its strict application can occasionally cause. Such injustices may occur as a result of the devaluation of the currency or during periods of high inflation, or as a result of some other monetary   **9.20**

---

[58] It was at this stage that there appeared in England what was probably the first proposal for something in the nature of an index currency: Joseph Lowe, *The Present State of England* (1822) who discusses the harmful effects of fluctuations in the value of money and proposes (at 279) that "a table exhibiting from year to year the power of money in purchase would give to annuitants and other contracting parties the means of maintaining an agreement, not in its letter only, but in its spirit; of conferring upon a specific sum a uniformity and permanence of value by changing the numerical amount in proportion to the change in its power to purchase".

[59] *The Baarn (No. 1)* [1933] p 251, 265. This was perhaps, the most explicit confirmation of the nominalistic principle since *Gilbert v Brett* (1604), although the substance of the point is also apparent from a number of cases decided during the intervening period—see, eg, *Anderson v Equitable Life Assurance Society of the United States of America* (1926) 134 LT 443; *Re Chesterman's Trusts* [1923] 2 Ch 466 (CA) and *Franklin v Westminster Bank* (1931) reproduced in the Fifth Edition of this work, 561.

[60] *Bonython v Commonwealth of Australia* [1950] AC 201, 222.

[61] *Treseder-Griffin v Co-operative Insurance Society* [1965] 2 QB 127, 144. In the same sense, see his remarks in *Phillips v Ward* [1956] 1 WLR 471, 474 and *Re United Railways of Havana* [1961] AC 1007, 1069.

dislocation which reduces the purchasing power of money.[62] These injustices were to some extent remedied, not by departing from the basic principle of nominalism, but by other means. For example, the courts decided to allow creditors to obtain judgment in the currency in which their debt was expressed, thus avoiding the need to convert the obligation into sterling with all of the exchange risks which that process involved.[63] Similarly, where a long term contract for the sale of water became onerous to the supplier because of the currency's loss of internal purchasing power, the court implied into the contract a provision allowing for its termination on reasonable notice.[64] It is perhaps fair to observe that nominalism was a perfectly satisfactory principle of English law while sterling was a major currency, but flexibility in some related areas has been necessary in the context of the currency's decline. The judiciary in this country has not sought to undermine the principle of nominalism; rather, it has construed contracts in a manner which mitigates the harshness of the principle so far as the creditor is concerned. Thus, where a fundamental change of circumstances, such as a major erosion of monetary values, occurs over a period of time, "the contract ceases to bind at that point—not because the court in its discretion thinks it just and reasonable to qualify the terms of the contract, but because on its true construction it does not apply in that situation".[65]

9.21   It remains to consider the adoption of the principle of nominalism in the United States. The leading authority in this area is the decision of the Supreme Court in the so-called Legal Tender Cases.[66] The factual position in *Knox v Lee* is of some historical interest and must be described. Before the Civil War (or "the rebellion", as it is described in the report), a Mrs Lee owned a flock of sheep in Texas. Mrs Lee left the sheep in the charge of her shepherd when the rebellion

---

[62] In the case of the UK, sterling was devalued in 1949 and 1967; periods of high inflation were recorded throughout the 1970s; and the country inevitably suffered from the collapse of the Bretton Woods system of fixed exchange rates in 1971. The Court of Appeal has, however, declined to increase an award of damages merely on the ground that sterling had declined in value between the date of the damage and the date of the award: *Phillips v Ward* [1956] 1 WLR 471. This aspect of the decision was followed in *Clark v Woor* [1965] 2 All ER 353.

[63] On the subject of judgments expressed in foreign currency, see Ch 8 above.

[64] *Staffordshire Area Health Authority v South Staffordshire Waterworks* [1978] 1 WLR 1387. It may be noted that (at 1397) Lord Denning expressed the view that "times have changed" since the decision in *Treseder-Griffin* and that "the time has come when we may have to revise our views" on the subject of nominalism. In fact, as stated in the text, the essential principle itself has not altered; the courts have merely devised other means of avoiding its strict application under harsh circumstances. It is noteworthy that the *South Staffordshire* case was decided during a period of high inflation in the 1970s.

[65] *British Movietonews Ltd v London and District Cinemas Ltd* [1952] AC 166, 186. The point is thus a question of contractual construction. The principle of nominalism is not, in strict terms, undermined, for the English court will not revalorise the amounts due under the contract; they will merely hold that the contract has come to an end.

[66] *Knox v Lee* and *Parker v Davies* (1870) 12 Wall (79 US) 457.

broke out. Mrs Lee was "a loyal citizen of the United States" and, as a consequence, the Confederate Government regarded her as an alien enemy. In reliance on Confederate legislation designed to deal with the property of such persons, the Confederate Government sold her sheep to Mr Knox, who purchased them for $10.87 each, "confederate money", which was then worth about one-third of the corresponding sum in coin. After the rebellion had been suppressed, Mrs Lee brought an action in conversion against Mr Knox. In valuing the claim, Mrs Lee sought to introduce evidence to demonstrate the difference in value between gold and silver (on the one hand) and the "greenback" (on the other). The Circuit Court for the Western District of Texas refused to admit such evidence, on the ground that the greenback had been made legal tender and it was thus not open to the court to assess the value of the greenback against that of gold and silver currency. The Supreme Court upheld this approach, and observed that:[67]

> ... it was not a duty to pay gold or silver or the kind of money recognised by law at the time the contract was made, nor was it a duty to pay money of equal intrinsic value in the market ... The expectation of the creditor and the anticipation of the debtor may have been that the contract would be discharged by the payment of coined money, but neither the expectation of one party nor the anticipation of the other constitutes the obligation of the contract. There is a well recognised distinction between the expectation of the parties to the contract and the duty imposed by it. Were it not so, the expectation of results would always be equivalent to a binding engagement that they should follow. But the obligation of a contract to pay money is to pay that which the law shall recognise as money when the payment is to be made[68] ... Every contract for the payment of money, simply, is necessarily subject to the constitutional power of the government over the currency, whatever that power may be, and *the obligation of the parties is therefore assumed with reference to that power* ...

Once again, this amounts to a very clear statement of the principle of nominalism and its unmistakable relationship to the State theory of money. The principle

9.22

---

[67] Justice Strong, at 548—emphasis added. Further support for the principle of nominalism may be derived from the Court's observation that legal tender notes "have become the universal measure of values". In this sense, the Supreme Court departed from its earlier decision in *US v Marigold* (1850) 50 US 560, where the court noted that the power to coin money and to regulate its value was delegated to Congress as a means of "creating and preserving the uniformity and parity of such a standard of value", thus suggesting that the Constitution provided only for a metallic system of money. The case, however, was concerned with States counterfeiting, and was thus decided in a rather different context.

[68] The Court then cited *Barrington v Potter* Dyer, 81b, and *Faw v Marsteller* 2 Cranch 29. It followed from the statement in the text that Legal Tender Acts were valid; they could not be impugned on the ground that they applied to pre-existing contractual obligations and were thus retrospective to that extent.

has been restated and reinforced by a number of subsequent decisions of the Supreme Court.[69]

D. The General Nature of Nominalism

9.23 It has been shown earlier that—whilst nominalism is a key feature of monetary law—the principle relies upon, or results from, the presumed intention of the parties or the legislator.[70] The nature and scope of the principle must be determined from this reference point. With this in mind, the following points may be noted:

(a) Nominalism is not derived from the English law of money. Nor is it the product of public law, although here (as elsewhere) it would be open to the legislator to give statutory force to the principle.[71] Neither is the principle a matter of mandatory law or of public policy. As a consequence, the parties to a contract are generally free to avoid its effects by making express provision to that effect.[72]

(b) As nominalism is not a principle of public policy, a judge is both entitled and bound to take notice of inflation,[73] ie of the undoubted fact that

---

[69] See in particular *Juilliard v Greenman* (1883) 110 US 421, 449; *Ettinger v Kenney* (1885) 115 US 556, 575; *Woodruff v State of Mississippi* (1895) 162 US 292, 302; *Ling Su Fan v US* (1910) 218 US 302, where it was said that "public law gives to such coinage a value which does not attach as a mere consequence of intrinsic value. They bear, therefore, the impress of sovereign power which fixes value and authorises their use in exchange" and where it was accordingly concluded that this power includes that of prohibiting the exportation of money. It has also been remarked that "obviously in fact a dollar or a mark may have different values at different times but to the law that establishes it, it is always the same": *Deutsche Bank filiale Nürnberg v Humphreys* (1926) 272 US 517.

[70] This is the position under English law—see para 9.09 above.

[71] Such legislation would not involve a taking of property by the State, or an unwarranted interference with contractual rights—see *Knox v Lee* and *Parker v Davis* (1870) 12 Wall (79 US) 457, 551, noted above.

[72] The means by which the operation of the principle may be avoided are discussed in Ch 11 below. In *Treseder-Griffin v Co-operative Insurance Society* [1956] 2 QB 127, 145, 163 Lord Denning inclined to the view that the nominalistic principle could not be avoided in this way, but Harman J expressed a view consistent with that stated in the text. So far as English law is concerned, the accuracy of the point stated in the text can no longer be open to doubt in the light of the decision in *Multiservice Bookbinding Ltd v Marden* [1979] Ch 84.

[73] The same may be said of deflation, although inflation has been the rather more common problem. Inflation as a term of art has not found its way into legislative or contractual language, partly because it is so difficult to define. Nussbaum described inflation as "a general abundance of available cash, enhancing prices heavily and continuously"—see *Money in the Law, National and International* (The Press Foundation, 2nd edn, 1950) 192 and the further discussion by the same writer in "The Meaning of Inflation" (1943) 48 Pol Sci Q 86. It scarcely needs to be stated that this is an economic definition, for it contains no legally relevant criteria. That the English courts have taken notice of the consequences of inflation is beyond question. The point was illustrated by Lord Denning MR with customary clarity in *Woodhouse AC Israel Cocoa Ltd v Nigerian Produce*

monetary values change—whether suddenly or over a period of time, and whether internally or as against other currencies. There can be little doubt that the diminution in the internal value of sterling was one of the influential factors in the *South Staffordshire* case, which has already been discussed[74] and that the fall in the external value of sterling was one of the factors which influenced the court's reasoning in the *Miliangos* decision.[75] Nor should it be thought that judicial notice of this subject is an entirely modern phenomenon, for the Exchequer Chamber took note of the declining value of money in 1868. In *Bryant v Foot*,[76] the Rector of the Parish of Horton claimed a marriage fee of 13 shillings. It could be shown that the fee had been paid since at least 1808, but the court refused to draw the inference that the right had existed since time immemorial. In view of the difference in value of money in 1189 and 1868—a fact of which the court took special notice—it was impossible to infer that a 13 shilling fee had been paid on every marriage since 1189. A claim to the fee by prescription accordingly failed.

(c) Given that the principle depends upon the implied intentions of the parties or the legislator, nominalism cannot apply to unliquidated sums.[77] It can apply only to liquidated amounts, whether payable pursuant to contracts, declarations of trust, wills, or statutory provisions. In the case of statutory rules or regulations, the principle of nominalism must plainly be applied

---

Marketing Co Ltd [1971] 2 QB 23 (affirmed [1972] AC 741 (HL)). The relevant part of Lord Denning's remarks are reproduced at para 7.54 above.

[74] See para 9.20 above.

[75] The decision in *Miliangos* is considered in Ch 8 above.

[76] (1868) LR 3 QB 497. See also *A-G v Lade* (1746) Park 57 and *Lawrence v Hitch* (1868) LR 3 QB 521. Application to the court in cases such as *Re Lepton's Charity* [1972] Ch 277 (where a charitable trust no longer had sufficient funds to fulfil its purposes) are frequently necessary only because money has lost its value over a period of years.

[77] It should be said that both Dicey and Morris, *The Conflict of Laws* (Sweet & Maxwell, 13th edn, 2000) para 36-013 and *Chitty on Contracts* (Sweet & Maxwell, 29th edn, 2004) para 30-177 both contain statements to the opposite effect; both texts rely on the judgment of Lord Wilberforce in *The Despina R* [1979] AC 685, 689, although it is not entirely clear that those remarks support that proposition. However, the difference between these views and that expounded in the text may not be as great as it seems. Dicey and Morris state that the court must determine the date with reference to which, and the currency in which, damages must be assessed by the court; once that has been done, fluctuations in the external value of the selected currency occurring after the relevant date (usually, the date of the breach of contract or duty) cannot be taken into account. Of course, one can immediately see the parallels between this formulation and the principle of nominalism but it might perhaps be more appropriately seen as a part of the law relating to the assessment of damages, as opposed to a rule of monetary law; it helps to define those categories of damage which the claimant may (or may not) recover. It may be thought that this point is likely to be of limited practical importance and, in the vast majority of cases, that will doubtless be so. It is, however, submitted that the attempt to apply the principle of nominalism to unliquidated claims led the court into error in *Phillips v Ward* [1956] 1 WLR 471 and other cases discussed at para 10.11 below.

unless the legislator has manifested a contrary intention. But in this particular context, it should be observed that nominalism may produce unfortunate or unintended consequences. For example, in 1677, section 17 of the Statute of Frauds required any contract for the sale of any "goods, wares or merchandises" for a price in excess of £10 to be reduced to writing, failing which they would be unenforceable. The provision was only repealed in 1954 when (solely as a result of the decline in the internal value of sterling) a large number of contracts must have fallen within the scope of the section which, it may be inferred, were not within the contemplation of the legislature in 1677.[78]

(d) It is in the field of taxation that nominalism is liable to result in unjust consequences. For example, during periods of inflation, capital gains tax would have been payable on the disposal of chargeable assets by reference to the nominal amount of the gain, even if the rise in the value of the asset was attributable purely to inflationary factors. Attempts by the taxpayers to treat an apparent capital gain as mere compensation for the depreciation of the original investment failed both in the United States[79] and in the United Kingdom.[80] A more determined (but ultimately unsuccessful) attempt to defeat the application of nominalism in the field of taxation was made in Germany. In the first line of cases, the taxpayer alleged that interest at 3.5 per cent on a savings account did not represent taxable income, except in so far as it exceeded the annual average rate of monetary depreciation (approximately 2.5 per cent). The Federal Finance Court rejected this contention[81] which was bound to fail, and the Federal Constitutional Court held the decision to be consistent with constitutional requirements.[82] The Federal Finance Court reached the same result for the years 1969 to 1971[83] and 1973 to 1974.[84] The last decision led to a further review by the Federal Constitutional Court,[85] which rejected the contention that the constitutional prohibitions against discrimination or arbitrariness required the

---

[78] Most of the 1677 Act was repealed by the Law of Property Act 1925, s 207.

[79] *Bates v US* (1939) 108 F 2d 407, cert denied (1940) 309 US 666.

[80] *Secretan v Hart (Inspector of Taxes)* [1969] 3 All ER 1196, where the court proceeded on narrow grounds of statutory interpretation, but was clearly alive to the injustice complained of by the taxpayer. See also the cases noted in para 7.79 above.

[81] 27 July 1967, *BFH* 89, 422. For similar cases, see 10 November 1967, *BFH* 90, 396; 1 December 1967, *BFH* 91, 261; 12 June 1968, *BStBL* 1968 ii 653.

[82] 21 January 1969, *HFR* 1969 347 or *Betrieb* 1969, 1819.

[83] 14 May 1974, *BFHE* 112, 546 or *NJW* 1974, 2330; *BFHE* 112, 567 or *NJW* 1974, 2331.

[84] 30 April 1975, *BFHE* 115, 510; 1 June 1976, *BFHE* 119, 75.

[85] 19 December 1978, *BverfGE* 50,57. A petition against this decision to the European Commission for Human Rights was held to be manifestly ill-founded: Decisions and Reports 20, 226 (6 March 1980). In the same sense as the German decision, see the Italian Constitutional Court, 8 November 1979, Foro Italiano 1979 I 2807.

indexation of taxes or that nominalism had the effect of confiscation in this context.[86] The Austrian Constitutional Court reached a similar conclusion and stated that even if—on account of inflation—income tax had in a commercial sense to be paid out of capital, this did not constitute confiscation.[87]

(e)   The principle of nominalism applies primarily to fluctuations in the value of money which are slow, gradual, moderate, and "creeping". It is this limitation on the principle of nominalism which creates the most difficult problems of law and policy. The principle may not necessarily apply to "hyperinflation", where inflation may be said to be "galloping"—that is to say, a situation in which the currency depreciates in such a sudden, violent, and extreme manner as to lead to a collapse of the monetary system concerned.[88] History demonstrates that, in such situations, nominalism cannot realistically be maintained, and that either the legislator or the judge must find a means of avoiding the application of the principle. Plainly, nominalism would impose unacceptable burdens on the creditor in such a situation.[89] Hyperinflation has not occurred in the United Kingdom, but it may be inferred that the English courts would discard the principle of nominalism under such circumstances, and/or seek an equitable solution to the problem.[90] There is much material dealing with hyperinflation and the consequent collapse of the monetary systems involved but inevitably there is no clear distinction between "creeping" inflation (where the principle of nominalism should be upheld) and "galloping" inflation (where some

---

[86] For a survey of money in the practice of the German Federal Finance Court, see Klein, *WM* 1985, 1189.

[87] 17 March 1976, *EuGRZ* 1976, 384.

[88] The best known example of hyperinflation is to be found in the German history of the 1920s—for a more general discussion, see Widdig, *Culture and Inflation in Weimar Germany* (University of California, 2001). A more recent example is provided by Zimbabwe, where the annual inflation rate was some 270% in 2003, but the instances could be multiplied.

[89] On the German experience during the period 1919–23, its development and its legal consequences, see Nussbaum, *Money in the Law, National and International* (The Press Foundation, 2nd edn, 1950) 199–215; Fischer, "The German Revalorisation Act 1925" (1928) 10 Journal of Comparative Legislation 94; Kahn, "Depreciation of Currency under German Law" (1932) 14 *Journal of Comparative Legislation* 66.

[90] Even against a background of "creeping" inflation, the Court of Appeal has indicated that the nominalistic principle needs to be viewed with some care—see the approach of Lord Denning in *Staffordshire Area Health Authority v South Staffordshire Waterworks* [1978] 1 WLR 1387, where a unilateral right to terminate an open-ended contract was implied, thus allowing a supplier to extricate itself from a long-term contract which had become uneconomic as a consequence of inflation over a period of years. It is suggested that this means of dealing with the matter was only appropriate because the contract had no other explicit termination provisions.

alternative solution must be found). It must be hoped that the English courts will not be called upon to decide questions of this kind.[91]

(f) Despite the comments made in (e) above, it must be said that recent decisions of the European Court of Human Rights have tended to reinforce the principle of nominalism even in the face of rampant inflation. It is true that these cases arose in connection with Article 1 of Protocol 1 to the European Convention on Human Rights and must thus be viewed in their specific context. It is equally true that the principle of nominalism was not expressly mentioned in any of these cases. Nevertheless, it is submitted that the principle lies at the heart of these decisions. In the first case,[92] the claimant's father had opened a special savings account for her with a State savings bank. The account was specifically designed to assist holders in the acquisition of a house or an apartment. As a result, the account attracted a special rate of interest; the holders could become entitled to a special award of compensation to provide a measure of protection against the effects of inflation and the resultant increase in property prices. The State thus guaranteed that monies accumulated in these special savings accounts were to be reassessed so to maintain their purchasing power.[93] These rules were later revised to the disadvantage of the account holder, and she alleged that this amounted to an unlawful deprivation of property.[94] The Court effectively endorsed the nominalistic principle, holding that there was no obligation on States to maintain the purchasing power of moneys deposited with financial institutions. In other words, the sum in Polish zlotys could be repaid by the bank "at par" and this would be sufficient to discharge its obligations in full. The same effective result followed in two cases from Russia[95] and even in a case emanating from Ukraine, where the State had "undertaken to maintain the real value of individual savers' deposits and to pay them compensation"; this entitlement did not amount to a "posses-

---

[91] For materials in English which deal with the consequences of hyperinflation in other jurisdictions, see Rosen, *Law and Inflation* (University of Pennsylvania, 1982); Yoran, *The Effect of Inflation on Civil and Tax Liability* (Kluwer Law International, 1984); Karst and Rosenn, *Law and Development in Latin America* (University of California Press, 1975) deal with inflation and provide English translations of decisions and other materials at pp 421–573; as to China, see S.H. Chou, *The Chinese Inflation 1937–1949* (New York, 1963) and as to earlier inflationary difficulties in Argentina, see Harris, "Texas" (1979) Int LJ 37. See also the decision of the Buenos Aires Court of Appeal, 9 November 1975, *Clunet* (1980) 690.

[92] *Rudzinska v Poland* (1999) ECHR–VI 45223/97.

[93] This was apparently achieved by means of an Ordinance of the President of the National Bank of Poland, dated 24 February 1983.

[94] It may be noted at this point that the Polish Civil Code also provided for monetary obligations to be revalued in order to compensate for inflation, but this provision specifically did *not* apply to bank deposits.

[95] *Appolonov v Russia* (2002) ECHR 67578/01; *Rabykh v Russia* (2003) ECHR 52854.

sion" for the purposes of Article 1 of Protocol 1,[96] and thus did not qualify for the protection of that Article. It appears to follow from these cases that international conventions designed to preserve rights of property in a general sense will not operate to undermine the principle of nominalism, even in cases involving inflation of a very high order.

E. Nominalism in Specific Contexts

Against the background provided above, it is now proposed to consider the effects of the principle of nominalism in seven specific contexts namely:

9.24

(1) in relation to debts governed by English law;
(2) in relation to debts governed by foreign laws;
(3) in relation to claims for interest and damages generally;
(4) in relation to domestic monetary depreciation and a claim for damages following a default in payment;
(5) in relation to foreign monetary depreciation;
(6) in relation to the discharge and termination of contracts; and
(7) in relation to the remedy of specific performance.

English law debts

So far as English law is concerned, the control of the nominalistic principle has never been seriously doubted.[97] In any event, English law lacks any rules which would entitle or enable the court to revise or adjust the substance of a liquidated claim in order to cater for a decline in monetary values.[98] For example, where the price payable by a buyer under a contract is stated in explicit terms, it is not permissible to imply terms which contradict the terms of that agreement,[99] although it may occasionally be possible to imply termination rights which might relieve a supplier from a long-term obligation which becomes uneconomic

9.25

---

[96] *Gayduk v Ukraine* (2002) [2002] ECHR–VI 45526/99.

[97] In so far as they applied to a period of "creeping" inflation, it is suggested that the doubts briefly expressed in the *South Staffordshire case* were without foundation. Possible exceptions in the principle were mentioned in *Gilbert v Brett* (1604) Davies Rep 18, 27, 28; State Trials ii, 130 and are also noted in *Pilkington v Commissioners for Claims of France* (1821) 2 Knapp PC 7, 20. However, these isolated observations have no place in the modern law and do not in any sense detract from the generally accepted principle.

[98] Interpretative devices of the type occasionally invoked by foreign courts are not available to the English courts in the light of cases such as *British Movietonews Ltd v London and District Cinemas Ltd* [1952] AC 166.

[99] See, eg, *Gyllenhammar & Partners International Limited v Sour Brodogradevna Industrija* [1989] 2 Lloyd's Rep 403, 415 and other cases cited in *Chitty on Contracts* (Sweet & Maxwell, 29th edn, 2004) para 13-009, n 42.

as a result of declining monetary values.[100] Where the currency of account (whether sterling or a foreign currency) becomes the subject of hyperinflation or otherwise collapses, English law may be able to relieve undue hardship through the application of the doctrine of frustration. But it should not be forgotten that a contract is only frustrated where a change in circumstances has occurred since the date of the contract which was not foreseen by the parties and which renders performance of the contract radically different from that contemplated by the parties at the outset.[101] Where hyperinflation or monetary collapse set in after the contract was made, then this may be treated as a change in circumstances sufficient to justify the view that the contract has been frustrated.[102] In such a case, the court could order the refund of payments made prior to the discharge of the contract, and could make certain other orders pursuant to the Law Reform (Frustrated Contracts) Act 1943.[103] This may afford a measure of relief in relation to obligations which would otherwise fall to be performed after the date on which the contract was discharged. But the fact remains that initial payments will have been made in "valuable" currency, whilst the refunds subsequently ordered by the court would be made in depreciated currency. This provides a windfall gain to the originally payee, for the 1943 Act does not appear to afford a basis for the court to make an order compensating a party for the resultant loss.[104]

9.26   Apart from the limited examples just mentioned, the English courts are unable to interfere with the application of the nominalistic principle,[105] and have applied it even under circumstances where justice might otherwise have suggested a departure.[106] Legislative action would therefore be required for that

---

[100]   See *Staffordshire Area Health Authority v South Staffordshire Waterworks* [1978] WLR 1387.

[101]   See the tests formulated in *Davis Contractors Ltd v Fareham UDC* [1956] AC 696 and, on the doctrine of frustration generally, see *Chitty on Contracts* (n 99 above) ch 23.

[102]   Whether the doctrine of frustration can be applied would inevitably depend upon the particular circumstances of the case. But the general point remains that a change in monetary values is a factor which *could* lead to the frustration of a contract in an appropriate case.

[103]   See in particular s 1(2) of the 1943 Act. For a recent case on the application of s 1(2), see *Gamerco SA v ICM Fair Warning (Agency) Ltd* [1995] 1 WLR 1226.

[104]   Compare the discussion at para 9.36 below, in relation to damages for monetary depreciation.

[105]   After a survey of a number of cases, Mr T.A. Downer (1985) 101 LQR 98 suggests that the English courts could revalorise the contract, by allowing the buyer either to rescind the contract or to insist that the seller continue to perform against an indemnity against the monetary risks which have arisen. It is submitted that there is no sound legal basis upon which the English courts could adopt such an approach.

[106]   See, in particular, *Treseder-Griffin v Co-operative Insurance Society* [1956] 2 QB 1270 and *Anderson v Equitable Assurance Society of the United States of America* (1926) 134 LT 557.

purpose.[107] It follows that English law has essentially adhered to the nominalistic principle. It remains to consider the experience elsewhere.

Foreign law debts

In the United States, the available case law essentially mirrors the principles **9.27** adopted in England. The nominalistic principle has its roots in the Legal Tender Cases.[108] Courts in that country have also adopted the view that nominalism is based upon an implied term of the contract; by stipulating for payment in a given currency, the parties had impliedly accepted that risk of changes in the external value of that currency.[109] In a relatively recent case, a court of first instance found itself entitled to vary the terms of a contract to accommodate an unexpected increase in prices,[110] but this decision appears to be an isolated one and cannot be supported.[111] The Supreme Court of the State of Iowa has applied the nominalistic principle in a deflationary environment; where monetary deflation had reduced the value of mortgaged land, the Court rejected the argument that the debt secured on that land should be correspondingly scaled back.[112]

Turning now to Continental Europe: **9.28**

(a) In France, the nominalistic principle has held sway even though the French franc depreciated rapidly during the first half of the twentieth century.[113] In a case which bears some factual resemblance to the *South Staffordshire* case[114] but where the ultimate decision was different, the Cour de Cassation had to consider two agreements executed in 1560 and 1567, under which landowners agreed to pay a fixed annual amount for water to be supplied

---

[107] Parliament has, on occasion, passed legislation to mitigate the consequences of nominalism. In particular, it has provided for the indexation of capital gains, with the intention that tax should not be levied on gains attributable to inflation—Taxation of Chargeable Gains Act 1992, s 53.

[108] *Knox v Lee* and *Parker v Davies* (1870) 12 Wall (79 US) 457 (n 66 above), and see also *Dooley v Smith* (1871) 13 Wall (80 US) 604; *Bigler v Waller* (1871) 14 Wall (81 US) 297. For a discussion of the US case law, see Dawson and Cooper (1935) 33 Mich LR 852.

[109] See, in particular, *Deutsche Bank Filiale Nurenberg v Humphrey* (1926) 272 US 517 and *Sternberg v West Coast Life Assurance Co* (1961) 196 Cal App 2d 519.

[110] *Aluminium Co of America v Essex Group Inc* (1980) 499 F Supp 53.

[111] See Rosen, *Law and Inflation* (University of Pennsylvania, 1982) for a summary of many of the relevant problems in this area.

[112] *Federal Land Bank of Omata v Wilmerth* (1934) 252 NW 507. The decision of the Supreme Court in *Willard v Taylor* (1869) 8 Wall (75 US) 557 allowed for the revision of the dollar price payable under an option agreement following the issue of greenbacks. The decision is discussed in another context (see para 9.52 below), but on this particular point, its authority is very doubtful.

[113] See Carbonnier, *Droit Civil*, Tome IV (22nd edn, 2000) Titre II, Chapitre II or Mazeaud, *Leçons de Droit Civil*, Tome II, Chabas (ed) (9th edn, Paris, 1998) para 869, and see in particular Cass Req 25 June 1934, *DH* 1934, 427.

[114] On this case, see n 90 above.

from a particular canal. By 1876, the sum was of negligible real value, but the Court rejected an attempt to increase the stipulated payment. Relying in part on Article 1134 of the Code Civil and on Article 1895 of the Code[115] the Cour de Cassation said that "dans aucun cas il n'appartient aux tribunaux, quelque equitable qui puisse leur paraître leur decision, de prendre en considération le temps et les circonstances pour modifier les conventions des parties et de substituer des clauses nouvelles à celles qui ont été librement acceptées par les contractants".[116]. The difficulties arising in this context are usually discussed in the context of the *theorie d'imprévision*, dealing with the consequences of unforeseeable and supervening events. That theory was principally developed by the Conseil d'Etat in the context of public law contracts. Perhaps because of the nature of its role and the importance of securing the completion of public works contracts, the Conseil d'Etat has taken a less rigid approach to the nominalistic principle; in 1916, the court provided for an increase in the amounts payable to the supplier of gas to the City of Bordeaux, on the grounds that the outbreak of war had resulted in a very significant—and previously unforeseeable—rise in the price of coal, and that this completely destroyed the economic equilibrium of the contract.[117]

(b) In Italy, the principle of nominalism is enshrined in Article 1277 of the Codice Civile, which reads as follows:[118]

> (Debito di somma di danaro).—I debiti pecuniari si estinguono con moneta avente corso legale nello Stato al tempo del pagamento e per il suo valore nominale.
>
> Se la somma dovuta era determinata in una moneta che non ha più corso legale al tempo del pagamento, questo deve farsi in moneta legale ragguagliata per valore alla prima.

---

[115] Article 1895 has already been reproduced at para 9.12 above. Article 1134 reads: "Les conventions légalment formées tiennent lieu de loi à ceux qui les ont faites. Elles ne peuvent être révoquées que de leur consentement mutual, ou pour les causes que la loi autorise. Elles doivent être executées de bonne foi."

[116] ". . . it is not open to the courts, no matter how fair they may think it to be, to take time and circumstances into account in order to modify the agreement between the parties and to substitute new provisions for those which were freely accepted by the parties". See the decision in the *Canal de Craponne* case, 6 March 1876, S 1876, 1–161. As will be seen below, the German courts were compelled to take a different view when confronted with the effects of hyperinflation.

[117] CE 30 March 1916, S 1916.3.17, *Compagnie Générale d'Éclairage de Bordeaux v Ville de Bordeaux*. The case is discussed by Rosen, *Law and Inflation* (University of Pennsylvania, 1982) 85–6.

[118] This may be translated as follows:

Debt of sum of money. Pecuniary debts are to be paid with money which is legal tender in the State at the time of payment, at its face (or nominal) value.

If the sum due was indicated in money which is no longer legal tender at the time of payment, such payment shall be made with legal money equal in value to the former.

(c)   It is clear that, as a general rule,[119] the German courts have also adhered to the principle of nominalism.[120] Thus, in periods of "creeping" inflation, the courts have refused any attempt to revalorise (or increase) contractual or statutory payments.[121] Equally, where deflation caused the purchasing power of money to rise during the 1930s, the debtor was not permitted to devalorise (or reduce) the amount of his payment obligation.[122] It is, however, appropriate to note that, within the relatively short period of twenty-five years, Germany suffered two monetary disasters of great violence.[123] In November 1923, the inflationary development of the mark reached a point at which one pound sterling had a value equivalent to approximately 20 billion marks. If a German national had, in 1914, borrowed 10,000 marks to buy property in Germany and that property had retained its intrinsic value, could the borrower be allowed to discharge his debt by tendering 10,000 marks in 1923, at a time when the cost of a postage stamp was 1,000 million marks? Likewise, in 1924, when the reichsmark was introduced on the basis that 1,000,000,000,000 marks equals one reichsmark, could he have discharged his debt by tendering a tiny fraction of the new unit of account, in reliance on the "recurrent link" principle? Plainly, strict adherence to nominalism is wholly impracticable and unjust under such extreme circumstances, and legislative and judicial measures, encroaching upon the nominalistic principle and allowing a partial or total revalorisation, became inevitable. So far as the judiciary was concerned, the required process of revalorisation was achieved through the requirement that a debtor must perform his obligation according to the requirements of equity

---

[119] The Federal Labour Court, 28 May 1973, *BGHZ* 61, 31 remarked that German law "regards the principle of nominalism (mark equals mark) as one of the fundamental bases of our legal and economic organisation". For some exceptions to this general statement, see point (e) below.

[120] For a brief but useful discussion, see Horn, "Legal Responses to Inflation in the German Law of Contracts, Torts and Unjust Enrichment" in *Deutsche Landesreferate zum Privatrecht und Handelsrecht* (Heidelberg, 1982).

[121] Federal Labour Court, 30 November 1955, *NJW* 1956, 485; 12 March 1965, *NJW* 1965, 1681, both making it clear that the result might be different if payment of the stated sum "no longer constitutes such performance as the contractual purpose requires". This qualification reflects the distinction between "creeping" and "galloping" inflation, to which reference has already been made. In the same sense, Bundesgerichtshof, 14 October 1959, *NJW* 1959, 2203, Federal Supreme Court, 11 January 1968 *WM* 1968, 473 and Federal Administrative Court, 7 June 1962, *NJW* 1962, 1882.

[122] 10 August 1932, *JW* 1932, 3219; 21 January 1933, *JW* 1933, 1276; 24 May 1933, *JW* 1933, 1677.

[123] It is true that other countries have suffered even worse monetary collapses, eg Greece, in 1944, Hungary in 1946, and Romania in 1947. But it is proposed to concentrate on the German experience since this has had the greatest impact on monetary practice and the nominalistic principle.

and good faith, having regard to common practice;[124] the requirement of good faith precluded the debtor from tendering payment of his debt in a currency which had become effectively worthless. The court was thus required to determine the rate and means at and by which a mark debt was to be translated into reichsmarks; in doing so, the court had to take into account all relevant factors, including the financial position of the respective parties and the general diminution in national wealth flowing from the inflation.[125] A few general points may be made in this context. First of all, the court's ability to revalorise obligations was governed exclusively by article 242 of the Civil Code,[126] and not by any broader or general principle.[127] As a result—at least in purely domestic cases—any comparison of the value of the mark by reference to more stable currencies was not permitted as part of the revalorisation process.[128] Secondly, a subsequent fall in the purchas-

---

[124] German Civil Code (BGB, art 242). The German text reads: "Der Schuldner ist verpflichtet, die Leistung so zu bewirken, wie Treu und Glauben mit Rücksicht auf die Verkehrssitte es erfordern." The first major decision in this field was taken by the Reichsgericht, 28 November 1923, 107 *RGZ* 78 (*ST v R*). In that case, a mortgagee had lent money on the security of property in Southwest Africa in 1913; the court upheld his refusal to release his mortgage unless he received a sum equivalent in *real* (as opposed to *nominal*) value to that which he had advanced in 1913. The reasoning employed in this decision—although not the result—is criticised by Rosen, *Law and Inflation* (University of Pennsylvania, 1982) 91–2, who notes that either the foreign exchange rate, the consumer price index, or the wholesale price index was generally used as a yardstick for the revalorisation of monetary obligations.

[125] See in particular the approach adopted by the Supreme Court, 10 January 1933, *JW* 1933, 2449. In this context, it should not be forgotten that the nominalistic principle is derived from the presumed intention of the parties, with the necessary result that revalorisation is only possible in the case of liquidated sums. The approach to revalorisation had to be considered in a variety of contexts. See, eg, Supreme Court 15 December 1927, *JW* 1928, 885; 14 October 1929, *JW* 1929, 3488; 13 June 1929, *JW* 1930, 995 (revalorisation of legacies) and Federal Tribunal 27 February 1952 *BGHZ* 5, 197 (revalorisation of claim where money paid to defendant's use). For cases in which the English courts have applied German revalorisation rules, see *Re Schnapper* [1936] 1 All ER 322; *Kornatzki v Oppenheimer* [1937] 4 All ER 133. However, the application of these rules flowed from the fact that the underlying obligation was governed by German law. The decisions are thus consistent with the rule that the substance of a monetary obligation is determined by the law applicable to it. The German courts could thus apply revalorisation principles based upon art 242 to any contract governed by German law, even though the contract stipulated for payment in a foreign currency which had suffered catastrophic depreciation—Reichsgericht, 27 January 1928, *RGZ* 120, 70.

[126] See the decision of the Reichsgericht, 28 November 1923, *RGZ* 107, 78, where the availability of art 242 as a means of revalorising mortgage debts was specifically noted and discussed.

[127] Article 242 had previously only been invoked to deal with some of the disruption to contractual relations which was caused by the First World War; otherwise the courts had shown a marked reluctance to rely on this provision. The use of art 242 to deal with hyperinflation may thus be regarded as revolutionary. Subsequently, both Germany and Central European countries enacted specific laws dealing with the question of revalorisation—for references, see von Hecke, *International Encyclopaedia of Comparative Law* (Brill, 1972) ch 36, para 36-7. For a very illuminating discussion of art 242 and a summary of some of the leading cases, see Markesinis, Lorenz, and Dannemann, *The German Law of Obligations*, Vol 1 (Clarendon Press, 1997) ch 7.

[128] Assembled Civil Chambers of the Supreme Court, 31 March 1925, *RGZ* 110, 371.

ing power of the reichsmark itself as compared to the mark did not justify an increase in the rate of revalorisation.[129] Thirdly, it was not open to German courts to revalorise debts in a general sense; the principle of good faith had to be applied on a case-by-case basis and, as a result, no general principles of revalorisation emerged from the German case law.[130] Fourthly, if a creditor sought to protect himself by contracting in terms of US dollars, he could not later seek additional payment when the value of the dollar later fell as compared to the reichsmark.[131] Fifthly, certain debts were ultimately revalorised by legislation.[132] Finally, it is appropriate to add that, in the modern context, questions of revalorisation would be governed by article 313 of the German Civil Code which was introduced in 2001.[133]

(d) Again, between 1945 and 1948, the reichsmark became depreciated to such an extent that the Occupation Authorities in the Western Zones were compelled to introduce the Deutsche mark on the basis of a recurrent link of one Deutsche Mark equals one reichsmark, even though most debts were converted on the basis of one Deutsche mark = ten reichsmark.[134]

---

[129] Supreme Court, 21 November 1927, *JW* 1928, 962; 16 June 1930, *RGZ* 129, 208; 28 November 1930, *RGZ* 130, 368, 375.

[130] For a discussion of this subject, see J.F. O'Connor, *Good Faith in English Law* (Dartmouth, 1989) 86–8.

[131] Supreme Court, 30 May 1929, *RGZ* 125, 3. The point would appear to be obvious for the contract was made by reference to the US dollar. No consideration of fairness or good faith would appear to impose upon the debtor an obligation to compensate the creditor for the depreciation of that currency as against the mark or indeed, any other currency.

[132] ie by the *Aufwertungsgesetz* (Revalorisation Act) of 1925. Various types of investments were revalued in different ways. Mortgages and industrial bonds were revalued by 25% and 15% respectively; insurance policies and similar investments were revalued by reference to the available reserves of the issuing company; public debt was only slightly revalued whilst bank accounts were left untouched. It is fair to note that the judiciary's approach to revalorisation was criticised by many, on the grounds that courts were re-writing contractual obligations in accordance with personal notions of equity; equally the judiciary itself reacted to the proposed legislative revaluation with a remarkable public protest. The whole episode is described by Nussbaum, *Money in the Law, National and International* (The Press Foundation, 2nd edn, 1950) 206–15.

[133] Bundesgesetsblatt 2001, Part 1, 3138. On this reform in general, see Zimmerman, "Modernising the German Law of Obligations?" in Birks and Andretto (eds) *Themes in Comparative Law in Honour of Bernard Rudden* (Oxford University Press, 2002) 265. The provision deals with the occurrence of circumstances which affects the foundation of the contract. In such a case, one party may seek an adaptation of the contract; if the other party does not agree then the contract may be avoided or terminated. This special provision would now have to be applied instead of art 242, although it is generally thought that art 313 is merely an express affirmation of the principles which the court had formerly derived from art 242.

[134] The one-to-one recurrent link was accepted by the Federal Supreme Court (14 July 1952, *BGHZ* 7, 134, 140). This view is in no way invalidated by the fact that all debts *except* those specified in s 18 of the Conversion Law were scaled down at the rate of ten-to-one. The point was of importance where the debt was not governed by German law, see Mann, "Die Behandlung von Reichsmarkverbindlichkeit bei ausländischem Schuldstatut" in *Festschrift für Fritz Schulz* (Weiman, 1951) ii 298. Once the legislator had stipulated for debts to be converted in this way, the court had no residual authority to revalorise contractual obligations on the basis of the "good

(e)   In so far as Germany is concerned, it may be noted that the decisions of the courts departing from the nominalistic principle during times of monetary collapse were entirely justified. A strict adherence to the principle of nominalism during such periods would represent an unhappy victory of dogmatism over fairness and pragmatism; and accordingly, as has been noted earlier, the principle is not applicable during such periods.[135] At other times, however, the courts have not always been entirely consistent in their application of the nominalistic principle. In one case, fixed royalty payments had been agreed in return for a right to mine potash. After the contract had been in force for some sixty years, the payee sought an increase in those payments. He failed, on the grounds that German law did not know of an "implied index clause" to protect the creditor against the falling purchasing power of money.[136] Likewise, in 1974 and 1976, the Federal Supreme Court rejected claims to proportionate increases in ground rents under arrangements executed in 1954 and 1957, even though the cost of living index had increased by 30 per cent and residential rentals had increased by some 130 per cent during the intervening period.[137] In these cases, the courts adhered rigidly to the nominalistic principle. Subsequently, however, the Supreme Court allowed a ground rent created in 1959 to be revalorised in 1980, where it appeared that the value of the payment had fallen by 69 per cent.[138] It is suggested that the circumstances of this particular case did not warrant a departure from the principle of nominalism. The courts have also allowed for revalorisation where the payments concerned involved a measure of maintenance or living expenses, and (even in the absence of "galloping" inflation) an increase may be said to be justified so that the payment stream can continue to meet its original objectives. Thus, when prices rose by 40 per cent between 1955 and 1972, it was decided that pensions granted at the beginning of that period should be adjusted

---

faith" provision in art 242 of the Civil Code—a point accepted by the Federal Supreme Court: 14 January 1955, *BGHZ* 16, 153, 158, 17 December 1958, *BGHZ* 29, 107, 112. The debtor could not be said to be acting in bad faith if the inflationary problems had been addressed by national legislation and the debtor had discharged his obligation in accordance with that law.

[135]   See para 9.23(e) above.

[136]   Federal Supreme Court, 14 October 1959, *NJW* 1959, 2203; 21 December 1960, *NJW* 1961, 449; 2 November 1965, *NJW* 1966, 105.

[137]   29 March 1974, *NJW* 1974, 1186; 1 October 1975 *NJW* 1976, 142; 23 January 1976, *NJW* 1977, 846. It is noteworthy that in the face of devastating inflation, Japan (whose legal system has German origins) did not adopt any measure of statutory or judicial revalorisation— Igarashi and Riecki (1967) 42 Washington LR 445, 454.

[138]   23 May 1980, *BGHZ* 77, 188 or *NJW* 1980, 2441. See also another decision of the same date, *BGHZ* 77, 194 or *NJW* 1980, 2443.

accordingly.[139] Finally, the reunification of Germany provided a further opportunity for the Federal Supreme Court to depart from the principle of nominalism and to invoke article 242 as a means of adjusting the monetary obligations arising under a contract and redistributing the balance of risks assumed under it. In that case, the basis of the contract was found to have collapsed because the East German party had anticipated financial support from the State. This had failed to materialise following the collapse of the DDR.[140]

(f) In a more general sense, it should be noted that national legislatures have periodically sought to revalue or to revalorise obligations which have been affected by a serious fall in the value of the currency. This is a notoriously difficult exercise, not least because inflation is not uniform, ie the price of all goods and services does not necessarily rise by a uniform percentage. Legislation of this kind can thus only achieve a very rough form of justice as between debtor and creditor. Once again, German monetary history perhaps offers the best example.[141] It has already been shown that the judiciary adopted an active approach to the need for revalorisation, but the legislature was not to be excluded. As noted above, the Revalorisation Law (*Aufwertungsgesetz*) of 1925 applied differently to various classes of obligations.[142] The percentage rates used in the revalorisation process make it clear that no serious attempt was made to restore the real value of assets or obligations expressed in the depreciated currency; indeed, such relief as was afforded to creditors by the modest revalorisation of their assets was in many ways offset by a six-year moratorium which was granted to debtors to enable them to raise the necessary funds for repayment. The Revalorisation Law should therefore be seen as a political compromise in the face of the directly conflicting interests and demands of creditors and debtors.[143]

Interest and damages

It has been noted previously that a debt can be discharged by the payment of the stipulated amount in lawful currency at the time of payment[144] and that the **9.29**

---

[139] Federal Labour Court, 30 March 1973, *NJW* 1973, 959; see also Federal Supreme Court, 28 May 1973, *BGHZ* 61, 31 and 23 May 1977, *NJW* 1977, 1536. The periodic review of pensions was subsequently placed on a statutory basis.

[140] 14 October 1992, *NJW* 1993, 259. The case is noted by Markesinis, Lorenz and Dannemann, *The German Law of Obligations*, Vol 1 (Clarendon Press, 1997) 609.

[141] Other examples are offered by France, the US, Poland and Austria—these are discussed by Rosen, *Law and Inflation* (University of Pennsylvania, 1982) ch 4.

[142] For a description, see para 9.28(c) above.

[143] Rosen, *Law and Inflation* (n 141 above) 82.

[144] See para 7.45 above and, in particular, the decision of *Société des Hôtels Le Touquet v Cummings* [1922] 1 KB 451.

debt is thereby validly discharged even though payment was made after the due date. This rule flows from a very specific application of the principle of nominalism as set out at the beginning of this chapter.

9.30　The English courts appear to have been conscious of this position from an early stage, and the principle of nominalism may help to explain their reluctance to award *general* damages[145] following the breach of a monetary obligation.[146] Thus in 1893, the House of Lords refused to award interest by way of general damages for late payment on a debt[147] and the House felt unable to depart from that rule in 1984.[148] However, the House of Lords approved the earlier Court of Appeal decision in *Wadsworth v Lydall*,[149] to the effect that interest may be awarded by way of *special* damages.[150]

9.31　If this position represents "an extraordinary quirk in the development of English law",[151] it is nevertheless, perhaps, an acceptable one. If the debtor could not have known that the creditor would have suffered costs or lost the benefit of an interest stream as a result of non-payment, then there is no compelling reason why he should be fixed with liability for such amounts. On the other hand, the debtor will usually be aware that the creditor needs the proceeds to redeem other debt[152] or at least would have the benefit of placing the funds on deposit. Even though these factors may not have been specifically communicated to the debtor, he will frequently be aware of them from the nature of the contract or circumstances under which it is made. Consequently, it is submitted that it

---

[145] ie general damages under the first "limb" of the rule in *Hadley v Baxendale* (1854) 9 Exch 341, which allows the recovery of damages which arise in the ordinary course as a consequence of the breach. On the whole subject, see *Chitty on Contracts* (Sweet & Maxwell, 29th edn, 2004) para 26-044.

[146] *Cook v Fowler* (1874) 7 LR 27 (HL): it was said that a claim for interest after the due date "would be a claim really not for a stipulated sum, but for damages" (*per* Lord Chelmsford, at 35). The House thus upheld an award of 5% interest on the unpaid sum, rather than the higher, contractual rate. This approach can no longer stand in the light of more modern rules about to be discussed.

[147] *London Chatham & Dover Railway Co v South Eastern Railway Co* [1893] AC 429.

[148] *President of India v La Pintada Cia Navegacion SA* [1985] 1 AC 104, on which see Mann (1985) 101 LQR 30. The House of Lords refused to depart from the earlier decision even though it had "left creditors with a legitimate sense of grievance and an obvious injustice without remedy" (*per* Lord Roskill at 106). The High Court of Australia declined to follow this rule, and may thus award interest by way of general damages—see *Hungerford v Walker* (1989) 84 ALR 119.

[149] [1981] 1 WLR 398. This decision is considered at para 9.38(a) below.

[150] That is to say, special damages under the second "limb" of the rule in *Hadley v Baxendale* (1854) 9 Exch 341, which allows for the recovery of damages flowing from the breach under special circumstances pertaining to the contract and which were known to the defendant.

[151] This description was employed by Dr Mann in the Fifth Edition of this work, 71.

[152] This was the position in *Wadsworth v Lydall* [1981] 1 WLR 398, to which reference has already been made.

would frequently be possible to invoke the second "limb" of the rule in *Hadley v Baxendale* in order to recover interest by way of damages.[153]

The effect of the decision in the *London Chatham & Dover Railway* case is **9.32** further restricted by modern practice and statutory developments. First of all, subject to a few statutory provisions to the contrary, an express contractual provision for the payment of interest until discharge of the principal sum is valid and will be enforced by the courts in accordance with its terms. A right to interest may arise from a course of dealing between the parties, or from trade custom.[154] In accordance with the prevalent practice of the financial markets, it has been held that banks are entitled to capitalise interest, and thus to charge compound interest, on sums which are overdue. The right to charge interest in this way continues notwithstanding that the bank has made demand.[155] The same approach has been adopted in Canada where the Supreme Court has held that compound interest was the "norm" in the financial markets. In a compelling judgment, the Supreme Court noted that both simple interest and compound interest measure the time value of the initial principal sum but that simple interest makes an artificial distinction between principal and interest. On the other hand, compound interest treats a dollar as a dollar and thus provides a more accurate measure of the value of possessing money for a period of time.[156]

---

[153] This result appears to have been followed in *Hartle v Laceys* [1999] 1 Lloyd's Rep PN 315 (CA), where a solicitor knew that his client had borrowed funds on a "compound interest" basis and needed to reduce those borrowings by means of a property sale with which the solicitor had been entrusted. When the sale opportunity was missed as a result of the solicitor's negligence, the claimant could recover compound interest under the second "limb" of the rule in *Hadley v Baxendale*, because the loss which the claimant would suffer was clearly known to the defendant solicitor. For a decision to similar effect, see *Bacon v Cooper (Metals) Ltd* [1982] 1 All ER 397, and see also *Araba Afedu Ata-Amonoo v Grant Seifert & Grower* [2001] EWCA Civ 150. Where interest is to be awarded to compensate the claimant for his borrowing costs, the rate should reflect the rate at which he actually had to borrow, even if this was effected abroad and in a different currency: *Helmsing Schiffahrts GmbH v Malta Docks Corp* [1977] 2 Ll LR 444.

[154] On this point, and for case references, see *Chitty on Contracts* (Sweet & Maxwell, 29th edn, 2004) para 38-249.

[155] *National Bank of Greece v Pinios Shipping Co (No 1)* [1990] AC 637, on which see Mann, (1990) 106 LQR 176. The ability of a bank to compound overdue interest in this way has recently been confirmed by the Privy Council in *Financial Institutions Services Ltd v Negril Negril Holdings Ltd* [2004] UKPC 40. Compound interest cannot be awarded in the absence of agreement, custom or fraud: *Westdeutsche Landesbank v Islington LBC* [1996] 2 All ER 961, discussed in *Clef Acquitaine v Laporte Materials Ltd* [2000] 3 All ER 493 and *Black v Davies* [2004] EWHC 1464. Community law may require an award of compound interest—see *Sempra Metals v IRC* [2004] EWHC 2387. On the award of interest by international tribunals, see the ICSID award in *Middle East Cement Co v Egypt* (Arb 99/6, Award dated 12 April 2002).

[156] *Bank of America Canada v Mutual Trust Co* [2002] SCR 601. The case considers both statutory and common law powers to award interest; it also analyses the time value of money and the effectiveness of simple and compound interest in compensating for any loss of that value. The Law Commission has recommended that the English courts should have the power to award compound interest in larger cases; this would "enable the courts to compensate claimants more accurately for being kept out of their money"—see the Law Commission's Report (*Law Com No 287*) on Pre-Judgment Interest on Debts and Damages (Compound Interest), February 2004.

The courts have also adopted a liberal approach to contractual interest provisons, and have tended to uphold them wherever possible. In one case,[157] a contractual provision allowing for compound interest at variable rates was upheld, notwithstanding an argument that such a provision was "unfair" for the purposes of the Unfair Terms in Consumer Contracts Regulations 1994.[158] Further, a provision for a 1 per cent increase in the applicable interest rate following a default was held not to be a penalty, for the additional amount was a fair reflection of the increased risk which a lender bears following the occurrence of a default.[159] Finally, a clear contractual provision which enables the lender unilaterally to vary the interest rate is valid and effective, although it is an implied term that such a power will be exercised reasonably—that is to say, the lender must not seek to apply the clause in a dishonest, capricious, or arbitrary manner.[160] In cases involving the conflict of laws, the right to receive contractual interest will be dependent upon the proper interpretation of the contract, which will in turn be determined by reference to the law applicable to it.[161] Since the right to interest is contractual, the applicable law will also determine the rate at which it is to be charged.

9.33 Quite apart from contractual provisions of the type just discussed, statutory developments have also mitigated the effect of the decision in the *London Chatham & Dover Railway* case. For example, it is now an implied term of a contract for the supply of goods or services that simple interest will accrue on overdue debts at a prescribed rate.[162] The courts also have statutory powers to award interest in appropriate cases.[163] Although these statutory powers are discretionary and thus do not confer any positive rights on the creditor, the discretion should be exercised in his favour where the defendant's breach of contract deprived the claimant of the opportunity to put the subject matter of the claim to work to earn profits or income.[164] A slightly different category of

---

[157] *Director General of Fair Trading v First National Bank plc* [2002] 1 AC 481 (HL).

[158] SI 1994/3159.

[159] *Lordsvale Finance plc v Bank of Zambia* [1996] QB 752; *Citibank v Nyland and the Republic of the Philippines* (1989) 878 F 2d 620 (2nd Cir). These and other cases are noted and discussed by Cranston, *Principles of Banking Law* (Oxford University Press, 2nd edn, 2002) 311.

[160] *Paragon Finance plc v Nash* [2000] 1 WLR 685 (CA) where, however, it was found that the claimant had no serious prospect of establishing a breach of the implied term.

[161] Rome Convention, Art 10(1)(a); *Lesotho Highlands Development Authority v Impregilo SpA* [2002] EWHC 2435 (Comm).

[162] See generally the Late Payment of Commercial Debts (Interest) Act 1998. The Act applies only where both parties are acting in the course of a business.

[163] For the High Court, see Supreme Court Act 1981, s 35A and for the County Court, County Courts Act 1984, s 69. In relation to claims involving bills of exchange, interest may be awarded under the Bills of Exchange Act 1882, s 57.

[164] For this formulation, see *Chitty on Contracts* (Sweet & Maxwell, 29th edn, 2004) para 26-150, where the power is considered in depth. The statutory power conferred on the court

statutory provision is offered by section 44A of the Administration of Justice Act 1970.[165] Where a court awards a judgment in a foreign currency, it may stipulate for interest on that debt at such rate as it thinks fit. The rate will usually reflect the commercial rate at which the creditor could fund the required amounts in the currency in question.[166]

In practice, the courts have also found other means of compensating the claim-   **9.34** ant for losses in monetary value. In the context of a claim for damages following a breach of contract, the general rule is that damages should be assessed as at the date of the breach with the result that monetary depreciation between the date of the breach and the date of the judgment cannot be taken into account.[167] But the courts have mitigated the effect of this rule, and have power to postpone the date of assessment where the application of the general rule would cause injustice.[168] Thus, when assessing damages for failure to complete the sale of a house during the inflationary period of the 1970s, the court worked by refer-ence to the value of the house as at the date of judgment, rather than the date of breach.[169] There seems to be very little direct authority as to whether the rise or fall of a currency may be taken into account in assessing damages. The Privy Council long ago expressed the view that the confiscation by the French

does not apply if the contract provides for interest or if interest is recoverable under some other statutory provision, eg the Late Payment of Commercial Debts (Interest) Act 1998.

[165] The provision was inserted into the 1970 Act by the Private International Law (Miscellaneous Provisions) Act 1995, s 1(1).

[166] There will, however, be exceptional cases. The decision in *Helmsing Schiffahrts GmbH v Malta Docks Corp* [1977] 2 Ll LR 444 concerned a contract expressed in Maltese pounds. Judgment for the principal sum was given in that currency, but interest was awarded by reference to the cost of borrowing in Germany. This reflected the fact that the creditor was based in Germany and would have had to fund the unpaid Maltese pounds by means of borrowings in Germany. The difficulty of applying this type of rule in the context of a multinational bank which functions in a number of different currencies is well illustrated by the decision of the Federal Court of Australia in *Westpac Banking Corp v "Stone Gemini"* [1999] FCA 917. It was argued that, as an Australian bank, the claimant should be entitled to interest at the rates applicable to the Australian dollar. However, the international nature of the bank's operations, the daily use of many different currencies, and the fungibility of money made it impossible to determine in which currency the claimant "felt" the cost of funding the unpaid sums. The court thus fell back on the "usual rule" that an award in US dollars should attract US dollar interest rates. It should, however, be emphasised that the foregoing commentary is concerned with the award of interest as a matter of procedural law, and the relevant provisions confer a measure of discretion on the court. There is no room for the application of these provisions where the substantive law applicable to the contract creates a positive right to interest on overdue sums. In such a case, the creditor is entitled to interest and he cannot be deprived of that right by the exercise of a procedural discretion: see *President of India v La Pintada Cia Navegacion SA* [1985] AC 104, at 131 and *Lesotho Highlands Development Authority v Impreglio SpA* [2004] 1 All ER (Comm) 97.

[167] See *Chitty on Contracts* (Sweet & Maxwell, 29th edn, 2004) para 26-057.

[168] *Johnson v Agnew* [1980] AC 367.

[169] *Wroth v Tyler* [1974] Ch 30. The decision is in part explained by the fact that damages were awarded in lieu of specific performance. The same approach has been adopted in later cases, eg *Malhotra v Choudhury* [1980] Ch 52 (CA); *Johnson v Agnew* [1980] AC 367.

Government of assignats belonging to an English claimant was a wrong which had to be wholly undone, and if the wrongdoer "has received the assignats at the value of 50d., he does not make compensation by returning an assignat worth 20d; he must make up the difference between the value of the assignats at the different dates".[170] The remark may be of some value where damages in tort fall to be assessed by reference to a depreciating foreign currency.

9.35 In each of the instances which have just been considered the creditor does, of course, recover a greater sum than the original principal amount of the debt. However, it is clear that the award of interest does not in any sense revalue or revalorise the debt itself. The nominal amount of the debt remains untouched and, as has been shown, the debt itself can still be discharged by payment of its face amount. The additional amounts which may be awarded to the creditor represent the time value of his money and reflect the delays flowing from the debtor's breach. It may therefore be concluded—it is, perhaps, a very obvious conclusion—that the availability of contractual and statutory rights to interest does not in any sense detract from the principle of nominalism.

Damages for domestic monetary depreciation

9.36 Is a creditor who is not paid by his debtor on the contractual due date entitled to claim damages in respect of the depreciation of the domestic monetary unit between the due date and the actual date of payment? Is the mere reduction in the purchasing power of money an item of damage which, notwithstanding the principle of nominalism, the law recognises as recoverable? Is it possible to recover loss suffered by reason that (had he received his money on the due date) the creditor could have bought some property (or foreign currency) more cheaply than at the time of actual payment? It should be emphasised at the outset that this question deals with the recoverable heads of damage; consequently, the answer to this question will fall to be determined by reference to the law applicable to the contract concerned.[171]

9.37 What, then, will be the position under a contract governed by English law, where the debtor pays after the due date and the currency concerned has depreciated in the meantime? The point appears to have been considered in relatively few cases. But a failure to pay on the due date plainly represents a breach of contract, and, in principle, damages representing a change in the value of money could theoretically be recoverable. Consistently with the discussion in the previous section in relation to interest, it might be thought that the court could not award *general* damages in this context, but that it may be able to award *special* damages for losses which were foreseeable or were in the contemplation of the

---

[170] *Pilkington v Commissioner for Claims on France* (1821) 2 Knapp PC 7, 720.
[171] ie in accordance with Art 10(1)(c) of the Rome Convention—see the discussion at Ch 4 above.

parties at the time the contract was made.[172] Indeed, this very assumption had been made by the lower courts in *President of India v Lips Maritime Co.*[173] In that case, however, the House of Lords held that the decision in the *London Chatham & Dover Railway* case[174] was limited to the recovery of interest as damages for late payment of the debt; the decision thus did not restrict the recovery of damages for exchange losses incurred as a result of the late payment. It follows that losses of this kind may be recovered by way of both general and special damages under the rule in *Hadley v Baxendale*.[175] Thus, it was foreseeable that an English creditor operating in his domestic currency would suffer loss if a dollar debt was not paid on time; the creditor accordingly obtained damages representing the difference between the sterling equivalent on the due date for payment and the sterling equivalent on the actual date of payment.[176] Where the debt has not been paid by the time of the proceedings, it appears that judgment should be given in the currency in which the debt is expressed,[177] whilst an award in respect of the exchange losses should be made in the currency in which the claimant operates or has "felt" his loss.[178]

An award of damages based upon depreciation or a fall in the purchasing power **9.38** of the currency of account is not precluded by the rule that—where an award of damages can be made in respect of the breach of a monetary obligation—the measure of damages for non-payment of a debt should be interest only,[179] for it does not apply where substantial damages are reasonably within the contemplation of the parties.[180] Nor are substantial damages necessarily too remote to be recoverable, for questions of remoteness are essentially questions of fact.[181] It

---

[172] This type of damages should be carefully distinguished from a claim for interest following non-payment. As the House of Lords has pointed out, an award for damages to take into account inflation is designed to preserve the "real" value of money, whilst an award of interest compensates him for the time he has been kept out of that value: *Pickett v British Rail Engineering Ltd* [1980] AC 136, 151, 164, and 173. The US-Iran Claims Tribunal thus erred when it regarded an award of interest as compensation for the effects of inflation—*CMI International v Iran* Reports 4, 263, 270.

[173] [1988] AC 395 (HL). For criticism of some aspects of this decision, see Mann (1988) 104 LQR 3.

[174] See the discussion at para 9.30 above.

[175] There may be cases in which part of the exchange losses arise naturally as a result of the breach, and are thus recoverable under the first limb of the rule, whilst other aspects of the losses may only be recoverable under the second limb if the special circumstances giving rise to them were communicated to the debtor at the time of the contract.

[176] *Ozalid Group (Export) Ltd v African Continental Bank Ltd* [1979] 2 Ll LR 231.

[177] ie consistently with the *Miliangos* principle, discussed in Ch 8 above.

[178] *International Minerals & Chemical Corp v Karl O Helm AG* [1986] 1 Lloyd's Rep 81.

[179] See *Fletcher v Taylor* (1855) 17 CB 21 and *Prehn v Royal Bank of Liverpool* (1870) LR 5 Ex 92, 100. The rule was justifiably criticised in *Wallis v Smith* (1882) 21 Ch D 243, 275.

[180] *Trans Trust SPRL v Danubian Trading Co* [1952] 2 QB 297; *Ozalid Group (Export) Ltd v African Continental Bank Ltd* [1979] 2 Ll LR 231; *Wadsworth v Lydall* [1981] 1 WLR 398; and *President of India v La Pintada Cia Navegacion SA* [1985] 1 AC 104.

[181] See *Mehmet Dogan Bey v Abdeni & Co Ltd* [1951] 2 KB 405—a decision arising from the devaluation of sterling in 1949. In that case, freight expressed in sterling was due to be paid to a

must follow that cases in which damages are sought for the loss in value of a currency must necessarily turn upon their own circumstances.[182] Nevertheless, a few general propositions may be noted:

(a) Where, in an entirely domestic case, an English debtor owes sterling to an English creditor, the creditor will only exceptionally be able to prove that he could and would have protected himself against damage caused by inflation during the period of the debtor's default and that such damage was within the contemplation of the parties. But if the creditor can prove that, as a result of the debtor's default, the creditor was deprived of an opportunity to make a cheaper purchase, then the creditor ought to be able to recover damages for the consequent losses. The position is neatly illustrated by the decision of the Court of Appeal in *Wadsworth v Lydall*,[183] where a vendor of property—anticipating the receipt of sales proceeds —contracted to purchase a new property. The purchaser of his property failed to complete on time, whereupon the claimant had to renegotiate his own purchase, suffering interest and other costs as a result. The Court of Appeal held that these amounts were recoverable because the losses were foreseeable at the time of the contract and were not too remote.[184]

Turkish shipowner on 6 September 1949. In fact, payment was made on 14 September and, after obtaining exchange control approval, the funds were remitted to the owners on 5 October. In the interim period, the British Government had devalued sterling on 18 September, with the result that the owner received fewer Turkish pounds than he would have had payment been made when due. The court did not find that the claim for the loss was inadmissible as a matter of law. Rather, it held that the devaluation was not foreseeable because—despite intense speculation about the Government's policy in this area—the Chancellor of the Exchequer repeatedly denied any intention to devalue sterling. Consequently, the loss flowing from the devaluation was not a foreseeable consequence of the late payment, and the damage thus caused was too remote.

[182] For a very helpful discussion of the whole problem of changes in monetary values in the assessment of damages, see McGregor, *Damages* (Sweet & Maxwell, 17th edn, 2003) paras 16-008–16-053.

[183] [1981] 1 WLR 398. The decision in this case was expressly approved by the House of Lords in *President of India v La Pintada Cia Navegacion SA* [1985] 1 AC 104.

[184] It may be added that the "foreseeability" test may be more readily satisfied in this type of case where the parties are involved in a "chain" of property transactions in the UK at times of rapid increases in house prices. It should be appreciated that it is the rate of inflation applicable to the *particular* asset concerned in any given case, as opposed to the *general* rate of inflation, which would be relevant in this context. In other words, the very nature of the transaction and its position in a sequence of related purchases enables a claim for damages to be made under the second limb of *Hadley v Baxendale*. It should be added that in the US, courts have rejected claims for damages made in similar circumstances—*Meinrath v Singer Co* (1980) 87 FRD. The decision relied on *London v Taxing District* (1881)104 US 771, according to which interest is the only measure of damages for non-payment. Courts in Canada and New Zealand have likewise refused to allow an "inflation factor" by way of damages—see *McGrieg v Reys* (1979) 90 DLR (3d) 13; *Leitch Transport Ltd v Neonex International Ltd* (1980) 27 OR 2d 363; *Caltex Oil (NZ) Ltd v Aquaheat Industries Ltd* [1983] NZLR 120. It should, however, be added that damages on account of losses resulting from late payment and the intervening fall in the value of money were frequently awarded by German courts during the great inflation, see Karsten Schmidt, *Geldrecht* (Berlin, 1983), D335–339.

In this sense, it may be said that the vendor recovered damages for monetary depreciation, because the purchasing power of the money which he received had declined in relation to the asset which, to the knowledge of the purchaser, the vendor had intended to acquire with those proceeds.

(b) It may be easier to establish a claim for damages of this kind where the contract is governed by English law but involves some material cross-border aspect. In such a case, one may not merely be concerned with the loss of the internal purchasing power of (say) sterling, but also with the external value of sterling as compared to the currency in which the creditor runs its business. The scope for loss (and thus a potential claim) is thereby broadened. It is true that the Court of Appeal in *The Teh Hu*[185] refused to award damages reflecting the devaluation of sterling in 1967 and its consequences for a salvage claim. But it is suggested that the true principle was accurately applied by the New Zealand Court of Appeal[186] where sterling fell in value in relation to the New Zealand dollar between the due date and the date of actual payment. The resultant exchange losses could be recovered by the creditor by way of special damages.[187]

(c) If the parties make specific contractual provision with respect to the consequences of inflation or exchange rate movements, then the court will generally respect those provisions and give effect to them.[188]

(d) Where the claim is for damages for breach of contract, as opposed to the recovery of a debt, exchange losses cannot be recovered because damages for breach only become payable when the award or judgment is handed down, and English law does not allow a further cause of action in damages for the

---

[185] [1970] P 106. The difficulty in this case arose because a foreign salvor was then required to formulate its claim in sterling. On the other hand, Lord Denning suggested (in a dissenting judgment in that case) that the award for salvage should be subject to an "uplift" to compensate the foreign salvor for the declining value of sterling. This view relied upon the equitable nature of the claim and was in large measure motivated by the inability of the courts to award judgment in foreign currencies at that time. This imaginative solution was adopted by a District Court in the US, which allowed an uplift in a salvage award to a Dutch salvor, in order to take account of the falling value of the dollar: *BV Bureau Wijsmuller v US* (1976) 487 F Supp 156.

[186] *Isaac Naylor & Sons Ltd v New Zealand Co-operative Wool Marketing Association Ltd* [1981] 1 NZLR 361, on which see Rickett, "Contract damages for exchange losses—a New Zealand development" [1982] LMCLQ 566.

[187] The principle discussed in this paragraph is in some respects linked to the rule that damages should be expressed in the currency in which the claimant has actually suffered (or "felt") the loss flowing from the defendant's breach of contract. This principle has been discussed in Ch 5 above.

[188] This flows from the fact that nominalism reflects the *presumed* intention of the parties; the principle thus cannot stand in the face of an *express* contractual term to the contrary. On this subject, see *Aruna Mills Ltd v Dhanrajmal Gobindram* [1968] 1 QB 655 and the discussion in Ch 11 below.

late payment of damages. Consequently, it was only possible to compensate the creditor by means of an award of interest.[189]

(e) In cases involving conflict of law questions, the right to claim interest by way of damages for breach of contract would appear to be governed by the law applicable to it, for it forms a part of the consequences of breach of the agreement,[190] but the rate of interest to be awarded in such a case would seem to be a matter of procedure and thus to be governed by English law.[191]

9.39 Once again, it should be emphasised that the points discussed above do not in any sense detract from the principle of nominalism; an obligation to pay £10,000 may be discharged by the payment of £10,000, even after the due date. The points noted above merely reflect the fact that—in certain contexts—special damages may be available if the debtor fails to perform his obligation punctually. The availability of damages for breach of contract and a resultant loss of monetary value to the claimant thus does not have the effect of diluting the general nominalistic principle.

Damages for foreign monetary depreciation

9.40 If the international value of a foreign money of account[192] falls between the maturity date and the actual date of payment, it is necessary to ask whether the creditor is entitled to damages for the loss suffered.

9.41 In a number of countries, it has been held that damages for non-payment of debt are not limited to interest. If the creditor would have avoided his loss by converting the moneys which he ought to have received on the due date, then he is in principle entitled to damages reflecting the monetary loss of the value during the period of default. It has been so decided in Germany[193] and in

---

[189] *President of India v Lips Maritime Corp* [1988] AC 395. Whilst there is a certain logic to this formulation, it may be that the House of Lords applied it a little too rigidly in that case. The proceedings involved a claim for demurrage, ie for liquidated damages. It is submitted that the claim for such damages should be treated on the same footing as a claim in debt, and that exchange losses should accordingly have been recoverable in accordance with the principles discussed above.

[190] Rome Convention, Art 10(1)(c). The point seems to be clear although the Court of Appeal declined to express a final view on the point in *Lesotho Highlands Development Authority v Impregilo SpA* [2002] EWHC 2435 (Comm).

[191] On the whole subject, see Dicey and Morris, *The Conflict of Laws* (Sweet & Maxwell, 13th edn, 2000) Rule 196.

[192] Once again, the discussion proceeds on the basis that the relevant obligation is of a contractual or liquidated nature.

[193] See, eg, 25 Feb 1926, *JW* 1926, 1323 (francs); 22 Feb 1928, *RGZ* 120, 193, 197 (francs); 13 May 1935, *RGZ* 147, 377 (dollars). This result is unsurprising, given that the German courts also awarded damages for delayed payments in marks during the great inflation of 1920–3—see the Supreme Court, 29 September 1926, *JW* 1928, 2841 with further references.

Italy.[194] Likewise, courts in Austria[195] and Switzerland[196] awarded damages where the payment of a sterling debt was delayed until after the depreciation of sterling in 1931, because the creditor demonstrated that he would have converted those funds into his domestic currency upon receipt.

Despite a certain amount of confusion in the English case law, it is submitted **9.42** that damages of this kind may also be awarded by the English courts. It is true that Scrutton LJ once remarked:[197]

> It occurred to me it might possibly be true that subsequent variation in the exchange could be included in the damages, in the nature of interest. I have been unable to find that interest by way of damages has ever been allowed to cover alteration in the exchange . . . I think the reason is . . . that those damages are too remote. The variation of exchange is not sufficiently connected with the breach as to be within the contemplation of the parties . . .

This apparently negative statement does in fact make it clear that questions of fact are involved, and that damages may be awarded to cover the exchange variation if the loss arises naturally from the breach or was in the contemplation of the parties when the contract was made.[198]

If the loss was foreseeable and is a natural and probable consequence of the **9.43** breach, then damages for delayed payment of a foreign currency debt should be available to reflect its reduced value as at the date of payment. The loss is likely to be foreseeable if the creditor, on receipt of the foreign currency remittance, was obliged forthwith to surrender that currency for the domestic unit in accordance with the foreign exchange rules applicable in his place of residence. Thus, when exchange controls were in force in England, a creditor in respect of an obligation expressed in US dollars was held entitled to receive damages reflecting the diminution in the sterling value of the US dollar sum during the period of the debtor's default.[199] In similar vein, an American creditor

---

[194] Corte de Cassazione, 30 March 1966, Foro Italiano 1966, I, 1539, also *Clunet* 1968, 377.

[195] Austrian Supreme Court, 18 March 1932, *JW* 1932, 2839 and *Clunet* 1936, 191.

[196] Federal Tribunal 10 October 1934, *BGE* 60 and *Clunet* 1935, 1100. The Swiss Court also allowed a claim for damages in respect of a Swiss franc obligation, when the maturity date and the actual date of payment spanned the devaluation of the Swiss franc in 1936: Federal Tribunal, 31 October 1950, *BGE* 76, ii 371 and *Jahnbuch für schweizerisches Recht* 1952, 265, with note by Gutzwitter.

[197] *Di Fernando v Simon Smits & Co* [1920] 3 KB 409, 416; the decision in that case was overruled by the House of Lords in *The Despina R* [1979] AC 685. See also *Manners v Pearson* [1898 1 Ch 581; *Société des Hôtels Le Touquet v Cummings* [1922] 1 KB 451, 460–1; *SS Cecilia v SS Volturno* [1921] AC 544, 560 and 567.

[198] In other words, the availability of damages for currency variations in the case of late payment is essentially governed by the rule in *Hadley v Baxendale* (1854) 9 Exch 341.

[199] *Ozalid Group (Export) Ltd v African Continental Bank* [1979] 2 Ll LR 231. The reasons for the decision are set out in great detail, but this perhaps reflects the fact that the award was based upon the general principles of the law of damages, to which reference has been made above.

conducting its business in US dollars has recovered damages from a debtor who owed him Swiss francs where the Swiss unit depreciated against the US dollar between the stated maturity date and the date on which payment was finally made.[200] It may be added that, in the event of delayed payment of a foreign currency obligation, the creditor's loss will usually be reasonably foreseeable for the purposes of the first "limb" of the rule in *Hadley v Baxendale*; it will therefore not usually be necessary to have resort to the second "limb" with the resultant need to prove that such losses were specifically within the contemplation of the parties.[201] It may be, however, that this formulation applies to debts but not to contractual claims for liquidated damages. This would appear to be the conclusion drawn from the House of Lord's decision in *President of India v Lips Maritime Corp*,[202] where it was remarked that, for non-payment, "the only remedy which the law affords to the owners is interest on the sum remaining unpaid".[203] Although the point is not clear, it may be that this approach can be justified on the basis that an award of liquidated damages is designed to compensate the creditor for all losses flowing from the breach; there is thus no room for a further award in respect of monetary depreciation.

9.44   The general principles described above apply equally to foreign exchange contracts, where the obligations of both contracting parties involve the payment of money.[204] Indeed, in some respects, those principles apply with even greater force, because the parties are directly concerned with the different values of particular currencies on a specified date. Thus, in *Richard v American Union Bank*,[205] the plaintiff, a New York foreign exchange dealer, contracted with the defendant New York bank to establish a credit of 2,000,000 lei in the plaintiff's favour with a bank in Romania. The plaintiff paid to the defendant US$72,755 for these purposes. The credit was intended to be established in November

---

[200]   *International minerals & Chemical Corp v Karl O Helm AG* [1986] 1 Lloyd's Rep 81. In that case, the claimant were entitled to a payment of 12 million Belgian francs in 1981. By the time of the hearing, that sum had depreciated by some 40% in relation to the US dollar. Since the creditor would have converted the receipt into US dollars, it was awarded the 12 million Belgian francs plus damages in terms of US dollars to reflect the losses resulting from the depreciation of that unit. For a New Zealand case on the same point, see *Issac Naylor & Sons Ltd v New Zealand Co-operative Wool Marketing Association Ltd* [1981] 1 NZLR 361.

[201]   This point is established by the decision in *President of India v Lips Maritime Corp* [1988] AC 395. The subject has already been noted at para 9.37 above.

[202]   [1988] AC 395.

[203]   At 425. See also n 189 above.

[204]   In the Fifth Edition of this work, 295, it was stated that different rules applied in the present context because money constituted the "object" of the commercial transaction. This, in turn, referred to the commodity theory of foreign money. However, this approach can no longer stand in the light of the Court of Appeal decision in *Camdex International Ltd v Bank of Zambia (No. 3)* [1997] CLC 714. This general subject has already been considered at para 1.61 above.

[205]   (1930) 253 NY 166; 170 NE 532. See also the French decision, Cour de Paris, 10 November 1962, S 1963, 147.

1919, but this did not in fact happen until August 1921, by which time the market value of the lei had depreciated to US$24,440. In the ensuing proceedings, the Court held that the plaintiff was entitled to damages reflecting the difference (expressed in US dollars) between the value of the lei at the contractual time of delivery and the actual date of the performance.[206]

Although the point ought to be clear, it may be as well to emphasise that the foregoing discussion can only become relevant where a debtor fails to perform a monetary obligation on its due date, and that any assessment of damages relates only to depreciation occurring between the maturity date and the actual date of payment. No claim for losses due to depreciation of the money of account can be made in respect of the period up to the maturity date, for any such loss is effectively borne by the creditor as a result of the application of the nominalistic principle and his original agreement to accept payment at a specific time. Furthermore, if payment is made on the due date, then no claim could be made in any event, for there would be no breach of the monetary obligation which could give rise to an award of damages.[207]

9.45

Discharge and termination of contracts

Can a change in monetary values and its consequent economic effects result in the termination or discharge of a contract? It must be stated at the outset that this question will always fall to be resolved by reference to the governing law of the contract, for it plainly affects the substance of the parties' obligations.[208] So

9.46

---

[206] It is true that the case proceeded on the footing that the Romanian currency was to be treated as a commodity in New York, and thus damages could be assessed in the manner similar to that to be applied where a seller fails to deliver goods—see the Fifth Edition of this work, 295. The same point is emphasised by Brindle and Cox (eds) *Law of Bank Payments* (Sweet & Maxwell, 3rd edn, 2004) para 2-28, where it is observed that "viewing the Romanian currency as a commodity rendered this reasoning straightforward. If, on similar facts, the obligation to deliver the foreign currency is treated simply as an obligation in the nature of a debt, then the recovery of such damages is much more difficult." There is no doubt that the commodity theory of money had certain attractions, and these are highlighted in the materials just cited. Nevertheless, and despite those comments, it is suggested that damages in respect of exchange depreciation may be claimed even though it would now be necessary to characterise the duty to deliver Romanian lei as a purely monetary obligation.

[207] Although it has been convenient to consider the effect of depreciation separately in relation to domestic and foreign money obligations, it is submitted that, consistently with the decision in *Camdex International Ltd v Bank of Zambia (No. 3)* [1997] CLC 714, they should henceforth be treated on the same footing. Whether or not damages should be recoverable for depreciation of money should be determined by reference to the rule in *Hadley v Baxendale* and the rules on the remoteness of damage. Since an award of damages is intended to compensate for losses actually suffered, there is no reason why the principle of nominalism should stand in the way of such an award, even in purely domestic cases, provided that the loss was foreseeable. The point seems to have arisen in an ICSID arbitration against The Slovak Republic (Art. 9714).

[208] A point reflected in the Rome Convention, Art 10(1)(d). See the general discussion of this subject at para 4.12 above.

far as English law is concerned, the position depends on the general doctrine of frustration as developed since *Taylor v Caldwell*[209] and, perhaps to a lesser extent, upon the theory of an implied term.[210]

9.47 Dealing first with the doctrine of frustration, a contract may be frustrated if an unforeseen change or circumstances renders performance of the contract radically different from that originally contemplated by the parties.[211] Can a change in monetary values trigger the operation of this doctrine? The following points may be noted:

(1) A general rise in the price of goods and services, such as that occasioned by the outbreak of war, does not bring contracts to an end, even though the seller's or supplier's cost of performance will necessarily differ from his original expectations.[212]

(2) The doctrine of frustration does not operate merely because an unexpected turn of events renders performance more onerous for one party.[213] Thus, if an English seller agrees to sell goods to an English buyer for a price expressed in sterling, the contract remains binding on the seller even though he has to import the necessary goods from the United States, and this

---

[209] (1863) 3 B & S 826.

[210] It should be said that a fall in the monetary values would not of itself constitute a repudiation of the contract for the reason that repudiation usually involves a unilateral act by one of the parties, and a collapse in monetary values would not be attributable to one of the contracting parties. Even if it were, eg because one of the parties to the contract were a State involved in the devaluation of its currency, the act would not usually be referable to the contract.

[211] The general doctrine of frustration is considered in the context of the creation of a monetary union and its implications for financial obligations—see Ch 30 below. French law (*théorie de l'imprévision*) and German law (*Wegfall der Geschäftsgrundlage*) have similar doctrines which may enable the court to annul or to revise the terms of a contract in the event of an anticipated change in the economic or other conditions upon which its performance depends. On the German theory, see Markesinis, Lorenz, and Dannemann, *The German Law of Obligations* (Clarendon Press, 1997) ch 7. On the French theory, see Mazeaud (n 213 below).

[212] *Tennants (Lancashire) Ltd v Wilson & Co Ltd* [1917] AC 495; *Bolckow Vaughan & Co v Compania Minera de Sierra Minera* (1916) 33 TLR III (CA); and *Greenway Bros Ltd v Jones & Co* (1916) 32 TLR 184; cf *Blythe & Co v Richard Turpin & Co* (1916) 114 LT 752.

[213] *Davis Contractors Ltd v Fareham UDC* [1956] AC 696. In general terms, it seems that courts in France and Germany have adopted a similar attitude. There has been some conflict of opinion about the scope of the French doctrine of *imprévision*—the conflicting views and other difficulties are discussed by Mazeaud, *Obligations* (Montchrestien, 9th edn, 1998) paras 734–741. Nevertheless, the approach to be adopted in commercial cases has been fairly clear. Thus, "si, en principe, le débiteur ne répond pas de la force majeure, cette règle n'est pas applicable lorsque l'empêchement invoqué a eu seulement pour effect de rendre plus difficile ou plus onéreuse l'exécution des obligations" and "le juge ne saurait faire état des hausses de prix, même homologuées pour soustraire l'un des contractants à l'accomplissement des engagements clairs et précis qu'il a librement assumés"—Cass Com, 18 January 1950, D 1950, 227. See Cass Civ, 17 November 1925 DH 1926, 35; 5 December 1927, DH 1928, 84. Likewise, in Germany, creeping inflation does not constitute a ground upon which a party may be relieved of his contractual obligations—see the decisions of the Federal Supreme Court, 1 October 1975, *NJW* 1976, 142; 8 February 1978, Betrieb 1978, 1267.

exercise has become more expensive on account of the devaluation or depreciation of sterling. It seems that courts in the United States will likewise take the line that increased expense of this kind does not render the performance of the contract impracticable, and the parties are thus likewise held to their bargain.[214] Save in the most exceptional of cases, the depreciation of the money of account will not entitle the creditor to treat the contract as discharged or frustrated. It has been aptly observed that "rarely, if ever, is it a ground for inferring frustration of an adventure that the contract has turned out to be a loss or even a commercial disaster for somebody".[215]

(3) If a contracting party had hoped to discharge his obligations by repatriating foreign currency held abroad and converting it into sterling, he cannot claim to be discharged from his obligations merely because he finds himself unable to access those funds as a result of exchange control restrictions or because exchange rate fluctuations mean that insufficient sterling is yielded on conversion.[216]

(4) It should not, however, be thought that the doctrine of frustration is entirely blind to the consequences of monetary collapse. It may well be that extreme circumstances are required, but it seems that a serious and sudden depreciation of monetary values could disrupt the intended equivalence of performance on either side of the contract; such an occurrence could be found to satisfy the requirements for the application of the doctrine, as outlined above. Thus, whilst an unexpected turn of events, such as a wholly abnormal rise or fall in prices or a sudden depreciation of the currency, would not by themselves lead to the application of the doctrine, the true construction of the contract may show that the parties never intended to be bound in a fundamentally different situation, and the contract thus ceases

---

[214] See, eg, *Neal-Cooper Grain Co v Texas Gulf Sulphur Co* (1974) 508 F 2d 283, 293—"the fact that performance has become economically burdensome or unattractive is not sufficient for performance to be excused". This is in line with the decision of the Supreme Court in *Columbus Railway Power & Light Co v City of Columbus* 249 US 399 (1919) at 414—"equity does not relieve from hard bargains simply because they are such". The Californian court in *City of Vernon v City of Los Angeles* 45 Cal 2d 710, 310 P 2d 841 was more liberal to the burdened party, observing that "a thing is impossible in legal contemplation when it is not practicable; and a thing is impracticable when it can only be done at an excessive and unreasonable cost". See also *Mineral Park Land Co v Howard* (1916) 172 Cal 289, 156 P 458; *Transbay Construction Co v City and County of San Francisco* (1940) 35 F Supp 433; Rosen, *Law and Inflation* (University of Pennsylvania, 1982) 98.

[215] *Larrinaga v Société Franco Américaine de Medulla* (1929) 129 LT 65, 72.

[216] *Universal Corp v Five Ways Properties Ltd* [1978] 3 All ER 1131. The fact that a debtor lacks the means to pay or may be driven into insolvency cannot amount to a defence to the creditor's claim: *R v Hackney LBC, ex p Adebiri* The Times, 5 November 1997; *Bank of America NT & SA v Envases Venezolowes* (1990) 740 F Supp 260 affirmed (1990) 923 F 2d 843. German courts have adopted a similar line—see the decision of the Federal Supreme Court, 14 October 1992, *NJW* 1993, 259.

to be binding at that point.[217] This view may be reinforced by the fact that English law knows of no doctrine of revalorisation which might mitigate the hardship to the creditor.

9.48 Turning now to implied contractual terms, it is fair to observe that—even though adhering to the principle of nominalism—the courts will take judicial notice of inflation and the diminishing purchasing power of money[218] and this may influence the court's attitude even where the economics of the contract have been affected by long-term or "creeping" inflation.[219] The consequences of this approach are naturally most evident in long-term contracts, where the erosion of monetary values is gradual but, ultimately, of a serious nature. Thus, in one case, a water company contracted in 1929 to supply water at 2.9p per 1,000 gallons "at all times hereafter"; by 1979, the ordinary rate was 55p per 1,000 gallons. The Court of Appeal held that the contract could be terminated on reasonable notice, because such a term must have been within the contemplation of the parties when they originally entered into such a long-term contract.[220] It may well be that the implication of a simple, unilateral right to terminate the contract is something of a blunt instrument, but alternative approaches may lead to greater degrees of complexity and uncertainty.[221]

9.49 Whatever the difficulties may be, it is noteworthy that the courts have preferred to intervene on the basis of an implied contractual term, rather than by reference to the doctrine of frustration. If the courts attempted to alleviate the problems of a depreciating currency by reference to the latter doctrine, then this

---

[217] *British Movietonews Ltd v London & District Cinemas Ltd* [1952] AC 166, 185. If the parties have agreed indexation or other similar provisions (as to which see para 11.38 below), then the courts should generally respect and give effect to those provisions, such that doctrines of frustration or impossibility could not be applied. The decision in *Aluminium Co of America v Essex Group Inc* (1980) 499 F Supp 53 is to the contrary, and is unacceptable for that reason.

[218] For a case in which the Supreme Court of Missouri took judicial notice of the falling, *internal* value of the dollar, see *Curotto v Hammack* (1951) 241 SW 2d 897, 26 ALR 2d 1302.

[219] ie as opposed to the sudden and violent depreciation of monetary values contemplated by the *British Movietonews* decision, above.

[220] *Staffordshire Area Health Authority v South Staffordshire Waterworks Co* [1978] 1 WLR 1387. For similar cases, see *Crediton Gas Co v Crediton UDC* [1928] Ch 174, 447; *Winter Garden Theatre (London) Ltd v Millennium Productions Ltd* [1948] AC 173; and *Australian Blue Metal Ltd v Hughes* [1963] AC 74. For a general discussion of this subject and further cases, see *Chitty on Contracts* (Sweet & Maxwell, 29th edn, 2004) para 13-026. The view is there expressed that the existence of a termination provision is a matter of construction, rather than an implied term. This particular point is, however, of limited importance in the present context.

[221] In the Fifth Edition of this work, 118, Dr Mann suggested that it would "be preferable to imply a term to the effect that in the event of the price becoming disproportionately low as a result of inflation (or the rise in the price of the commodity in question) the contract could be terminated on reasonable notice". This suggestion would most closely respect the considerations of monetary depreciation which have motivated the courts in decisions such as the *South Staffordshire* case itself and ought in principle be adopted. As a practical matter, however, such a formulation would necessarily involve difficult value judgments which a court may not be well placed to make.

would inevitably have eroded the principle of nominalism. Since that principle lies at the heart of monetary law and ought to be preserved, it is submitted that the theory of the implied term has rightly been preferred by the courts.

Specific performance

It has been shown that a fall in monetary values or a rise in prices will not generally result in the termination of a contract or otherwise give rise to a right of relief so far as the disadvantaged party is concerned. It now remains to consider the matter from another perspective: can the party (the debtor) who is advantaged by the monetary collapse insist upon performance by the other party to the contract, or is he confined to an action for damages in the event of non-performance? This, in turn, depends upon the court's willingness to grant an order of specific performance against the disadvantaged party.[222] Given that the circumstances now under discussion occur but rarely and that an order of specific performance is at the discretion of the court, it is difficult to state any definitive principles in this area. It is nevertheless possible to draw a few points from the limited authority which does exist in this field.

9.50

In some respects, the question formulated in the last paragraph almost answers itself. If the contract is not discharged as a result of monetary depreciation, then the contract remains enforceable. In that case, the availability (or otherwise) of the discretionary remedy of specific performance should be determined by reference to the general principles which courts have developed in this area;[223] the fact that the value of the monetary consideration has depreciated to the detriment of the creditor should be irrelevant. It is true that in 1721, Lord Macclesfield refused to order specific performance in a case which arose out of the South Sea Bubble, on the grounds that "a Court of Equity ought to take notice under what a general delusion the nation was at the time the contract was made . . . when there was thought to be more money in the nation than there really was, which induced people to put imaginary values on estates".[224] But that case is now distinctly out of favour and can no longer be regarded as authoritative. The leading principle[225] requires that an order of specific performance should be granted in such a case[226] unless the inadequacy of the monetary consideration is such as "shocks the conscience and amounts in itself to conclusive

9.51

---

[222] It should be remembered that a creditor who is entitled to receive set payments over an extended period may be able to obtain an order for specific performance of the monetary obligation—see *Beswick v Beswick* [1968] AC 58, 81 (HL).

[223] The rules formulated by the courts in this area are discussed in *Chitty on Contracts* (Sweet & Maxwell, 29th edn, 2004) ch 27.

[224] *Savile v Savile* (1721) 1 P Wms 745.

[225] As stated by Lord Eldon in *Coles v Trecothick* (1804) 9 Ves 246.

[226] Assuming, of course, that the discretionary criteria referred to in n 223 above are otherwise satisfied.

and decisive evidence of fraud".[227] On this basis, specific performance could not even be refused on the basis of a complete monetary collapse between the date of the contract and the date of performance.[228] That this is the correct solution is conclusively demonstrated by the decision in *British Bank for Foreign Trade v Russian Commercial & Industrial Bank (No 2)*.[229] The claimants had borrowed 750,000 Russian roubles from the defendants, and the loan was secured by a charge over receivables. Before the loan was due for repayment, the rouble collapsed and became effectively valueless. The claimants tendered worthless roubles and sought the redemption of their security. The defendants argued that, in the light of the equitable nature of the redemption action, the claimant was required to act equitably. This line of reasoning was rejected. The claimants were entitled to redeem their security if they had fulfilled their contract; there was no authority which entitled the court to refuse redemption or to vary the terms on which it was effected, merely because the mortgage contract unexpectedly operated harshly in relation to the creditor. The risk of depreciation and the benefit of appreciation rested with the lender. The defendant's request to throw the risk of fluctuation on the debtor could not be accepted, since this "would in effect be changing the loan from a paper rouble to a sterling loan".[230] It must be concluded that monetary depreciation does not of itself afford a ground upon which an order of specific performance should be refused; equitable remedies cannot generally be invoked as a means of alleviating hardship caused by the depreciating value of money.[231] This must be the correct position; if the courts were to decline orders of specific performance on the sole ground that the monetary consideration had fallen in value, then this would again constitute an unfortunate inroad into the principle of nominalism.[232]

---

[227] On hardship as a ground for refusing specific performance, see *Hangkam Kwingtong Woo v Liu Lan Fong* [1951] AC 707, 722; *Patel v Ali* [1984] 1 All ER 978, referring to "hardship amounting to injustice".

[228] In such a case, however, the question of specific performance may not arise; the contract may be held to have been frustrated on the grounds discussed in the previous section.

[229] (1921) 38 TLR 65, 67.

[230] This decision may accordingly be regarded as authority for the proposition that the implications of the nominalistic principle are essentially the same both in the context of domestic currency and foreign currency.

[231] This point constitutes a part of the decision in *Multiservice Bookbinding Ltd v Marden* [1979] Ch 84.

[232] It should be said that Zambia experienced serious fluctuating pressures during the 1990s, and this resulted in a number of cases where the question arose for consideration. In *Zambia Industrial and Mining Corp (In Liquidation) v Lishomwa Muuka* (10 February 1998, unreported), the Zambian Court of Appeal had to consider a contract for the sale of land which had been entered into in 1975. The contract price was 60,000 kwacha. On 5 October 1985, the kwacha was formally devalued and its international value continued to depreciate. When the Court of Appeal was minded to grant specific performance of the contract, it was invited to increase the price by reference to a formula, which had been calculated on the basis of a comparative US dollar

The US Supreme Court appears to have come to a similar conclusion in *Willard*   **9.52**
v Taylor,[233] although the decision is unsatisfactory from a monetary law perspective. In 1854, the plaintiff took a ten-year lease of real property coupled with an option to purchase the property for $22,500, $2,000 of which was payable upon the exercise of the option. Shortly before the lease expired in 1864 when, owing to the issue of greenbacks, the premium of gold was more than 50 per cent, the plaintiff exercised the option and paid the $2,000 in notes; the defendant refused to accept them. The plaintiff applied for specific performance, which was granted on condition that he paid the purchase price in gold. The court, thus on the one hand granted specific performance in spite of the monetary depreciation which had occurred, and yet attached conditions to its order which protected the defendant from the consequences of such depreciation. It is the latter aspect of the decision which is insupportable in monetary law terms,[234] for it overlooks the fact that a contractual obligation to pay one dollar involves an obligation to pay whatever constitutes one dollar on the date due for payment.[235]

---

exchange rate over the period. The Court rejected this approach, noting that "there is in our considered view clearly discernible from the cases ample authority and reason for disallowing attempts in transactions expressed in kwacha to hedge against the depreciation of the internal value of our currency by notionally storing the same in a foreign currency at an earlier and more favourable rate of exchange and then reconverting the foreign sum at today's rates. It is unrealistic to look at our currency in that fashion." Quoting from an earlier, unreported decision of the Court of Appeal in *Apollo Enterprises Ltd v Kavindele* (1998), the Court also observed that "the kwacha in Zambia . . . is the constant unit of value by which we measure everything". The Court of Appeal was thus very conscious of the principle of nominalism and it is submitted that the Court's observations were plainly correct. The defendant was entitled to interest on the unpaid purchase price during the period of delay, but was not entitled to any adjustment on account of monetary depreciation.

[233] (1869) 8 Wall (75 US) 557.

[234] See the various cases discussed at para 9.51 above and the detailed criticism of Dawson and Cooper (1935) 33 Mich LR 852, 865–76.

[235] In other words, the Court entirely disregarded the effect of the principle of nominalism. The Supreme Court thus fell into error when it noted (at 574) that "it strikes one at once as inequitable to compel a transfer of the property for notes, worth when tendered in the market only a little more than one half of the stipulated price. Such a substitution of the notes for coin could not have been in the possible expectation of the parties. Nor is it reasonable to suppose, if it had been, that the covenant would have been inserted in the lease without some provision against the substitution." Once it had been determined that the obligation was expressed in the domestic money of the US, both the expectations of the parties and the "market value" of the currency should have been treated as irrelevant.

10

MONETARY OBLIGATIONS—
UNLIQUIDATED AMOUNTS

A. Introduction

As has been shown in Chapter 9 above, nominalism has developed and operated **10.01** in the context of liquidated sums. The origins of the principle depend upon the presumed intention of the parties—whether that intention is mutually expressed (as in the case of a contract) or unilaterally stated (as in the case of a statutory provision, a judgment or award, or a pecuniary legacy). It must follow that the principle of nominalism can only apply to fixed or stated sums and that the principle cannot apply to obligations involving an unliquidated amount or claim.[1] Instead, the extent of unliquidated amounts depends upon the principles applicable to the relationship at issue; it does not depend upon the law of money. It is the law of damages, breach of trust, restitution, agency, or other legal area which must determine the relevance and impact of variations in monetary value. In all these cases, the claims are unliquidated and require assessment by means of a valuation in terms of money. The extent of these obligations—and the outcome of the valuation process—depends upon the

---

[1] Of course, if an unliquidated claim is to be satisfied or discharged in any way, then it must at some point become a liquidated amount to which the principle of nominalism can be applied. This would generally occur as a result of a contractual settlement or an award made by a judge or arbitrator. In such cases, the presumed intention of the parties or of the tribunal will determine that the principle of nominalism is to apply. This serves to emphasise that the principle of nominalism in its fullest rigour can only apply in the context of a fixed and determined sum. See, however, the discussion in Ch 9, n 77 above.

time and criteria by reference to which such process is carried out. As the German Supreme Court has noted, unliquidated claims contemplate the payment of money, but their extent is determined by relation to non-monetary elements, such as the price of goods at a particular time.[2] In other words, unliquidated claims imply that an amount of money must be ascertained by reference to (or by comparison with) the value of the goods, services, or other items at issue. Whilst a fixed or liquidated sum is constant and unchanging in character, the valuation of a particular item implies that the monetary value attributable to an unliquidated claim can vary from time to time, with the result that the time at which the valuation process is undertaken will itself be one of the key determinants of value.[3]

10.02 This abstract point can perhaps be illustrated by an example. Suppose that a claimant succeeds in proceedings in tort against a defendant and that, at all relevant times, money has been depreciating. In such a case:

(a) If the amount of damages is assessed with reference to the circumstances existing as at the date of *judgment* or *payment*, then the claimant is thereby protected. He will receive a higher, nominal amount in damages reflecting the fact that money has depreciated between the date on which the claim arose and the eventual date of judgment or payment.[4]

(b) If, however, the claim is valued with reference to the date on which the claim arose or the action was brought, then the claimant will necessarily be awarded a lesser amount, for the assessment would inevitably have to leave out of account any monetary depreciation occurring after the valuation date. If this second solution is adopted, then the claimant is disadvantaged and (it may be added) a quasi-nominalistic approach is introduced in the context of unliquidated claims.[5]

10.03 It follows that the date by reference to which the valuation is made may have a significant impact upon the ultimate amount of damages awarded, whether the

---

[2] Federal Supreme Court of Germany, 23 October 1958, *BGHZ* 28, 259, 265.

[3] Essentially the same points are made by Horn, "Legal Responses to Inflation in the German Law of Contracts, Torts and Unjust Enrichment" in *Deutsche Landesreferate zum Privatrecht und Handelsrecht* (Heidelberg, 1982), where he notes that "in tort liability the debtor owes the compensation based upon damage occurring, not a fixed sum of money. Therefore, the principle of nominalism has no direct application. Instead the court must fix the sum of money necessary to make good the damage...Once the sum of compensation has been fixed by a judgment or settlement, this sum is again subject to the principle of nominalism."

[4] This statement does, of course, assume that, as is almost always the case, the value of money in terms of its purchasing power is falling during the period leading up to the eventual judgment.

[5] For reasons given above, the nominalistic principle should not be applied to unliquidated claims; furthermore, since nominalism reflects the *presumed* intention of the parties in particular contexts, there are no considerations of policy which require the principle to be applied to unliquidated claims.

case involves the commission of a tort, a breach of contract, or any other basis of claim. But which valuation date is to be adopted in any particular case? The law of money does not itself supply an answer to this question. Instead, the proper date must usually be identified by reference to the law which governs the substance of the obligation, although the question may very occasionally be influenced by the procedural law of the forum.[6]

If the date of valuation of the claim itself may be of critical importance, then it should not be forgotten that the claim may have to be adjusted by reference to other factors which themselves require valuation. In particular:　　**10.04**

(1) If the claimant is under a duty to mitigate his loss and either (a) incurs expense to that end or (b) fails to comply with that duty, what are to be the consequences for the valuation of his claim?
(2) Is the defendant required to make good any further damage resulting from late payment?

Once again, it is necessary to emphasise that neither of these questions is governed by the law of money. But they do have a monetary consequence, in the sense that the selection of any particular valuation date—be it the date of the breach, the date on which the proceedings are commenced, or the date on which judgment is ultimately given—necessarily involves a decision to *exclude* the consequences of monetary depreciation which occur after the selected date.

Against this general background it is now proposed to consider the approach adopted by the English courts in this area. This will be followed by a review of the position adopted by courts in the United States.[7]　　**10.05**

B. The Assessment of Damages

The English law of damages has become more clearly drawn over the last twenty-five years. Referring to the so-called "breach-date" rule, Lord Wilberforce made two observations. First of all, he noted that "as a general rule in English　　**10.06**

---

[6] Thus, in a claim for damages for breach of contract, the assessment of damages (including, it is submitted, the identification of the relevant valuation date) will generally be governed by the law applicable to the contract itself, although this may in some respects be constrained by the procedural rules of the court in which the claim is being heard—see Rome Convention, Art 10(1)(c). In tort claims arising before the English courts, the recoverable *heads* of damage are governed by the law applicable to the tort, whilst the *quantification* or *assessment* of those damages will be governed by English procedural law—see Private International Law (Miscellaneous Provisions) Act 1995, s 14(3)(b) and Dicey and Morris, *The Conflict of Laws* (Sweet & Maxwell, 13th edn, 2000) para 33-386.

[7] A brief survey of the corresponding position in various European jurisdictions may be found in the Fifth Edition of this work, 123–7.

law, damages for tort or breach of contract are assessed as at the date of breach". But he then continued "it is for the courts, or for arbitrators, to work out a solution in each case best adapted to giving the injured plaintiff that amount in damages which will most fairly compensate him for the wrong which he has suffered".[8]

10.07 It is debateable how far the "general rule" may continue to exist; it is fair to say that a more flexible approach—based upon the restoration of the claimant to his former position[9]—is now likely to be adopted. The application of this approach underlines the court's natural desire to achieve a result which meets the demands of justice on the particular facts of the case. But the detailed position must be considered separately in relation to contract and tort claims.

Breach of contract

10.08 Before 1979, the breach-date rule was rigidly applied in a number of contractual cases.[10] In other cases, however, the court took into account factors occurring after the breach, thus effectively postponing the date of valuation of the claim.[11]

10.09 In 1979, the House of Lords stated:[12]

> The general principle for the assessment of damages is compensatory, *ie* the inno-cent party is to be placed, so far as money can do so, in the same position as if the contract had been performed. Where the contract is one of sale, this principle normally leads to assessment of damages as at the date of the breach—a principle recognised and embodied in s. 51 of the Sale of Goods Act 1893. But this is not an absolute rule: if to follow it would give rise to injustice, the court has power to fix such other date as may be appropriate in the circumstances.

10.10 The general principle of restoration and the overriding intention to ensure justice as between the parties in the assessment of damages cannot seriously be impugned on the grounds of either policy or general merit. Inevitably, however, the application of such an open-textured principle is likely to cause difficulty in individual cases. But if the principles of compensation and justice are kept in

---

[8] *Miliangos v Geo Frank (Textiles) Ltd* [1976] AC 443, 468. On changes in the value of money and the assessment of damages, see McGregor, *Damages* (Sweet & Maxwell, 17th edn, 2003) paras 16-008–16-053. Strict adherence to the breach-date rule by the Permanent Court of International Justice caused Lord Finlay to dissent from the judgment of the Court in *The Chorzow Factory Case* (1928) PCIJ Series A, No. 17.

[9] See *Robinson v Harman* (1848) 1 Exch 850, 855.

[10] *Rice v Baxendale* (1861) 7 HN 96; *O'Hanlon v Great Western Railway Co* 6 B & S 484; *Ströms Bruks Aktie Bolag v Hutchison* [1905] AC 515; *The Arpad* [1934] P 189.

[11] *Harrison v Harrison* (1844) 1 C & P 412; *Owen v Routh & Ogle* (1854) 14 CB 327; *Elliot v Hughes* (1863) 3 F & F 387.

[12] *Johnson v Agnew* [1979] 2 WLR 487, 499; see also *Radford v De Froberville* [1977] 1 WLR 1262.

mind, it becomes possible to formulate the following (non-exhaustive) list of general propositions:

(1) It remains appropriate for the claim to be valued as at the date of the breach where (a) substitute performance is readily available in the market concerned and (b) it is reasonable to expect the claimant to access that market in the appropriate manner.[13] Under such circumstances, it may be unjust to the defendant to value the claim at a later date, for the claimant would have failed in his obligation to mitigate his loss.

(2) If there is no readily available market for the items concerned (or if, under the circumstances, it is not reasonable to expect the claimant to access such market) then damages should be assessed as at the date of judgment. Thus, if the claim relates to the non-delivery of goods, the valuation date should be the date of judgment, such that the claimant could purchase the goods on that date. As a result, increases in the value of the goods concerned must normally be taken into account as consequential loss, for this is in line with the compensatory requirements of the award.[14] This approach may, of course, favour the defendant if the price of the goods concerned has fallen by the time judgment is given, but it is consistent with the overriding principles of compensation and restitution.

(3) It must follow from the points made in (2) above that increases in, say, the cost of living attributable to inflation generally (as opposed to specific factors affecting the price of the particular goods concerned) should not usually be taken into account in contractual cases, simply because they are not relevant to the assessment which the court is required to make. There is thus no general right to have inflation taken into account in this area.[15] Once again, this approach is a necessary ingredient of the compensation principle.

With these points in mind, it is necessary to turn to the Court of Appeal decision in *Philips v Ward*.[16] In that case, the plaintiff purchased a house in 1952. He relied upon a report by the defendant surveyor, who had broken his contract with the plaintiff by failing to report on the need for certain repairs which (in 1952) would have cost £7,000. The Court of Appeal held the defendant liable only for the difference between the price actually paid for the house **10.11**

---

[13] On this point, see McGregor, *Damages* (Sweet & Maxwell, 17th edn, 2003) para 16-002.

[14] As the Court of Appeal has noted, inflation affecting the value of the goods in question should be taken into account as an appropriate element of the award because it was foreseeable "as a reasonable possibility"—see *H Parsons (Livestock) Ltd v Uttley Ingham & Co Ltd* [1978] QB 791.

[15] See *McGrieg v Reys* (1979) 90 DLR (3d) 13; *Leitch Transport Ltd v Neonex International Ltd* (1980) 27 OR 2d 363; and *Caltex Oil (NZ) Ltd v Aquaheat Industries Ltd* [1983] NZLR 120.

[16] [1956] 1 WLR 471.

(£25,000 in 1952) and the actual value of the house without the necessary repairs (£21,000 in 1952). Denning LJ remarked that the fall in value of money since 1952 "does not affect the figure, for the simple reason that sterling is taken to be constant in value".[17] For reasons discussed earlier in this chapter, the nominalistic principle has only limited relevance in the context of unliquidated claims, and the validity of this statement in its particular context is therefore highly questionable.[18] Nevertheless, the decision was followed by a later Court of Appeal.[19] It is, however, submitted that the compensatory principle required (as a minimum) an award reflecting the excess of (a) the value of the house in 1956 had the report been accurate and (b) the actual value of the house in 1956 in its unrepaired state. In other words, the date for the valuation of the liquidated claim should have been the date of the judgment itself—there was no basis for adopting an earlier date. It has also been held by the House of Lords that, where an architect fails to discover building defects and is thus in breach of his contract, the owner is entitled to the cost of reinstatement at or at a reasonable time after the discovery of the defect—in other words, the date of valuation of the unliquidated claim reflects the cost of repairs to the claimant as at the date on which he could reasonably be expected to effect them, and thus pre-dates the date of judgment itself.[20] In such a case, a subsequent fall in the value of money (and a consequent increase in the cost of repairs) should be left out of account in computing damages, for they occur after the valuation date.[21]

10.12   It is difficult to say much by way of firm conclusion from the matters just discussed. It may, however, be observed that the date with reference to which an unliquidated claim is to be assessed can have important consequences in the sense that it may operate to exclude elements which reflect monetary inflation

---

[17] At 474.

[18] As noted elsewhere, Lord Denning himself later moved away from this strict view—see para 9.47 above and the discussion of the decision in *Staffordshire Area Health Authority v South Staffordshire Waterworks* [1978] 1 WLR 1387.

[19] *Perry v Sydney Phillips & Son* [1982] 1 WLR 1297. The Court in that case distinguished *Dodd Properties (Kent) Ltd v Canterbury City Council* [1980] 1 WLR 433, on the grounds that the latter was a tort case. In the present context, it is submitted that this distinction is both unrealistic and unattractive, and is likely to disappear over time; the principles of compensation and restitution would seem to dictate a similar approach in both types of case.

[20] *East Ham Corp v Bernard Sunley & Sons Ltd* [1966] AC 406, on which see Duncan Wallace (1980) 96 LQR 101 and (1982) 98 LQR 406, who also refers to some comparative material. It may be that the principle in the *East Ham* case applies only where it is reasonable to expect the owner to reinstate the property within a reasonable time following discovery of the defects in question.

[21] Whether this rule operates fairly or ought to be applied in particular cases may involve difficult judgements of fact and degree. For example, if the necessary repairs are particularly extensive having regard to the value of the property itself, then it may be that the claimant cannot be expected to carry them out until damages have actually been obtained. In such a case, an assessment of damages as at the date of the judgment may be more appropriate.

occurring after that date. This, in turn, renders it difficult to apply the principle of nominalism in its fullest rigour to claims of unliquidated character.

Damages in tort

The present practice is perhaps more firmly established in relation to damages in tort. It is, however, appropriate to begin with a short historical discussion which will serve to place matters in context. For a long time, a certain type of case was governed by a dictum of Lord Wrenbury,[22] according to which, if the claimant had been damaged by the defendant tortiously depriving him on 1 January of three cows at a value of £150:

10.13

> It would be *nihil ad rem* to say that in July similar cows would have cost in the market £300. The defendant is not bound to supply the plaintiff with cows . . . The defendant is liable to pay damages, that is to say, money to some amount for the loss of the cows: the only question is, how much? The answer is, such sum as represents the market value at the date of the tort of the goods of which the plaintiff was tortiously deprived.

The case in which this passage occurs is now effectively overruled,[23] but in any event, it is submitted that these views cannot be supported. The defendant is not obliged "to supply the plaintiff with cows" on 1 July; rather, he is obliged to pay damages for having deprived the plaintiff of the cows on 1 January. Therefore, he must put the plaintiff in the position on 1 July (or at the date of judgment) in which he can acquire three replacement cows. If, as at the date on which the claim is valued, three cows will cost £300, then the plaintiff should be awarded that sum. Equally, if three cows then cost £75, then the award should reflect that cost. In either case, the award of £150 would be quite inappropriate, since it does not accurately reflect the actual replacement cost; as a result, it cannot satisfy the principles of compensation and restitution which have already been described.[24] Where the cost of three cows has increased as a result of inflation between the date of that tort and the valuation of the claim as at the date of judgment, the defendant can scarcely claim that such inflation was not foreseeable and thus should not be recoverable on the ground that such damage is too remote.

10.14

The law of damages is inevitably not as straightforward as just suggested. For example, if the cost of the cows had increased to £300 by the date of judgment, the plaintiff may not receive the full figure if he was obliged to mitigate his loss but failed to do so.[25] By the same token, if the cost of cows has fallen to £75, the

10.15

[22] *The Volturno* [1921] AC 544, 563.
[23] *The Despina R* [1979] AC 685.
[24] The example given in the text may also be regarded as a further illustration of a general rule stated earlier, namely that the nominalistic principle cannot apply to unliquidated claims.
[25] On the duty to mitigate loss under these circumstances, see para 10.20 below.

plaintiff may be able to recover a larger amount if he can demonstrate that the value had exceeded £75 during the intervening period and that he would have had the benefit of such higher price (for example, by effecting a sale).[26]

10.16   In a rational legal system, the abandonment of Lord Wrenbury's theory is also required for the sake of consistency. For example, it would appear that damages in an action for the destruction of the cows should be assessed on the same basis as an action involving the conversion and non-return of the cows, for the consequences to the claimant are effectively identical. In the latter type of case, it seems clear that damages must be assessed as at the date of judgment;[27] the same rule has been applied in other contexts.[28] It is true that the Court of Appeal decision on which these submissions are based involved an action for detinue and that this particular form of action has been abolished[29] but this does not provide a basis for disregarding that aspect of the decision which deals with the assessment of damages. Yet in a case in which the claimant's property was permanently and irreversibly converted, he was held to be entitled to damages reflecting the value as at the date of conversion[30] and a series of maritime cases suggest that damage to or loss of property is to be assessed with reference to the value as at the date and place of the tort.[31] It is perhaps not altogether clear whether an increase in value between the date of the tort and the date of the judgment was at issue in any of these cases.[32] Nevertheless, if these cases were to re-occur in a more modern era which is more conscious of the consequences of inflation, it is again suggested that the courts should allow for the recovery of the value as at the date of judgment. This would reflect the fundamental rule which requires the restoration of the claimant's financial position to that which would have prevailed had the tort not been committed.[33]

---

[26] English law, however, is unlikely to accommodate a claim of this kind.

[27] *Sachs v Miklos* [1948] 2 KB 23; *Munro v Willmott* [1949] 1 KB 295. The qualification introduced by the former case is merely an application of the rule which requires the claimant to mitigate his damage.

[28] *Joseph D Ltd v Ralph Wood & Co Ltd* (1951) WN 224. See *Wroth v Tyler* [1974] Ch 30 and other contractual cases referred to in n 15 above.

[29] For the Court of Appeal decision, see *Rosenthal v Alderton & Sons Ltd* [1946] KB 374. For the abolition of the action in detinue, see Torts (Interference with Goods) Act 1977, s 2.

[30] *BBMB Finance (Hong Kong) Ltd v Eda Holdings Ltd* [1990] 1 WLR 409 (PC). In this case the value of the shares as at the date of conversion was awarded even though the defendant replaced the shares at a later date, when they had a lower value. The Canadian courts have also assessed damages by reference to the date of conversion: *Canadian Laboratory Supplies Ltd v Engelhard Industries of Canada Ltd* (1975) 68 DLR (3d) 65.

[31] See in particular, *The Columbus* (1849) 3 WM Rob 158; *The Harmonides* [1903] P 1; *The Philadelphia* [1917] P 101; *Liesbosch Dredger v SS Edison* [1933] AC 463, 464.

[32] As will be apparent from the discussion thus far, the case law is by no means consistent and it is thus impossible to state the position with any real confidence.

[33] An interesting illustration of this rule is provided by the decision of the Supreme Court of Canada in *Canadian Forest Products Ltd v Her Majesty in Right of British Columbia* [2004] SCC 38. In that case, the Government of British Columbia claimed compensation for forest fires caused

Having thus addressed the subject in fairly general terms, it is necessary to make a few specific comments in relation to damages for personal injuries.[34] The valuation of such claims is always a matter of particular difficulty. However, especially in serious cases, the *monetary* aspects of that exercise assume a special importance, for the award ought in principle to replace the income which the claimant would otherwise have earned over an extended period of years. The likelihood of future inflation ought therefore to be taken into account as a part of the valuation process, although the difficulties involved in such predictions are obvious.

10.17

With these problems in mind, how is the court to approach the problem in the context of a personal injury case? It has been said that "there is today universal acceptance of the sensible and realistic rule that trial courts must look at the position at the time of their judgment and take account of any changes of circumstances which may have taken place since the injury was inflicted".[35] The essential consequences of this proposition are as follows:

10.18

(1) For the purposes of assessing damage, the court is entitled to have regard to such monetary depreciation as has occurred prior to the date of the damage.[36] It follows that where a conventional scale was adopted as, for instance, for the loss of expectation of life[37] or, in Scotland, for solatium, an award was not excessive merely because it took such depreciation into account and therefore exceeded the conventional sum. Thus, if the conventional award in 1941 was £200, it was appropriate to award £500 in

---

by the defendant. Damages were assessed as at the date of the hearing, and by that time much of the damaged timber had been sold by the Government. The defendants were therefore entitled to credit for the accelerated income which the Government received as a result of these sales.

[34] On the whole subject, see *McGregor on Damages* (Sweet & Maxwell, 17th edn, 2003) ch 37.

[35] McGregor (n 34 above) para 35-002.

[36] This has been described by the High Court of Australia as "accrued depreciation"—see *O'Brian v McKean* (1968) 118 CLR 540. The South African courts have also determined that the decreasing value of money is a factor to be taken into account in the assessment of damages: see the decision of the Appellate Division in *Norton v Ginsberg* (1953) 1 South African LR 537 and the decisions in *May v Parity Insurance Co Ltd* (1967) 1 South African LR 644; *Lutzkie v South African Railways and Harbours* (1974) 4 South African LR 369; *Burger v Union National South British Insurance Co* (1975) 4 South African LR 72; *Matrass v Minister of Police* (1978) 4 South African LR 78. See also the Rhodesian Appellate Division in *Stephenson v General Accident Fire & Life Assurance Corp* (1974) 4 South African LR 503.

[37] *Benham v Gambling* [1941] AC 157. The right to such damages was abolished by the Administration of Justice Act 1982, s 1. See *McGregor on Damages*, (Sweet & Maxwell, 17th edn, 2003) para 16-010. It seems that the *assessment* of a conventional sum must always be regarded as a matter of procedure, and is thus governed by English law as the law of the forum, rather than (eg) the law of the place in which the claimant resides or in which the tort occurred: *Hoffman v Sofaer* [1982] 1 WLR 1350. Yet, if this proposition is correct, it should remain the case that the *availability* of such an award is governed by the law applicable to the tort itself.

1967, because the effective value of the two sums on their respective dates was the same.[38] As Lord Normand observed,[39] "permanent changes in the value of money must be considered in making awards for *solatium*".[40]

(2) The principle means that "in considering damages occasioned by the wrongful act, all those facts which have actually happened down to the date of the actual trial must be taken into account".[41] If, by the time of the trial, "what was uncertainty has been turned into certainty",[42] then it is the judge's duty to have regard to the established facts rather than to speculate, to calculate rather than to guess. This rule has been applied in a number of contexts.[43] Thus, if the claimant has been permanently incapacitated as a result of the defendant's tort and if, by the date of the trial, his earnings would have increased, then the court must take that increase into account in making its assessment. This will be so regardless of the precise cause of the increase, and an increase purely on account of inflation should thus be included in the calculation.[44]

(3) It also follows from the general principle that inflation which might occur after the date of the judgment cannot be taken into account. In 1970, Lord Diplock[45] recognised that "during the last twenty years sterling has been subject to continuous inflation. Its purchasing power has fallen at an average rate of 3 per cent to 3½ per cent per annum and the increase in wage rates has more than kept pace with the fall in the value of money." Notwithstanding this widely understood position, "damages will be paid in currency which has been the value of sterling at the date of the judgment" and "money should be treated as retaining its value at the date of judgment". It followed that the award would only take into account

---

[38] See *Naylor v Yorkshire Electricity Board* [1968] AC 529 (HL), especially at 538. In 1973, the conventional sum had been increased to £750: *McCann v Shepherd* [1973] 1 WLR 540. By June 1979, the figure was £1,250: *Gammell v Wilson* [1980] 2 All ER 557.

[39] *Glasgow Corp v Kelly* (1951) 1 TLR 345, 347 (HL). In the same sense, see *Sands v Devan* (1945) SC 380 and, in England, *Hart v Griffiths-Jones* [1948] 2 All ER 729. See also Dixon J in *Pamment v Pawelski* (1949) CLR 406, 411.

[40] For a recent case which considers conventional sums and explains the court's approach to assessment under the various "heads" of damage, see *Herring v Ministry of Defence* [2003] EWCA Civ 528.

[41] *Carslogie Steamship Co Ltd v Royal Norwegian Government* [1952] AC 292, 300 and 307 (HL).

[42] *Bishop v Cunard White Star Ltd* [1950] P 240, 259 (pension awarded to a widow eight years after the accident causing her husband's death).

[43] For a relatively recent case, see *Jobling v Associated Diaries Ltd* [1981] 3 WLR 155 (HL), and cases there cited.

[44] *The Swynfleet* [1948] 81 Ll LR 116.

[45] On the points about to be made, see *Mallet v McMonagle* [1970] AC 166, 175; the same judge had already expressed a similar opinion in *Fletcher v Autocars & Transporters Ltd* [1968] 2 QB 322, 348. In the same sense, see *Taylor v O'Connor* [1971] AC 115.

inflation occurring up to the date of judgment. Once he had received his money, the claimant had to take steps to protect himself against the effects of future inflation "by prudent investment in buying a home, in growth stocks or in short-term high-interest bearing securities". Whether Lord Diplock's advice would have been especially helpful to a worker who had lost both his health and livelihood as a result of his employer's negligence may be open to doubt, although it certainly respects the "judgment date principle" which has been supported throughout this section. The rule was further confirmed by Lord Diplock in 1979, when he said[46] that "the likelihood of continuing inflation after the date of the trial should not affect the figure . . . inflation is taken care of in a rough and ready way by the higher rates of interest obtainable as one of the consequences of it". The rule so adopted is in line with an earlier decision of the High Court of Australia in a personal injuries case, during the course of which Barwick CJ observed that "the date of verdict is, in my opinion, the proper date as at which to make the assessment" and that, therefore, the assessment will "in general be made in relation to the purchasing power of the currency at the date of the assessment of the damages".[47] As a result, no allowance for future changes in the value of the currency would be made in so far as it affects the claimant's future earning capacity. Future increases in the cost of goods and services (such as medical treatment, nursing, etc) may be recovered on "solid proof" but in general should be ignored since the evidence is likely to be too speculative. It should also be noted that the Supreme Court of Canada has rejected Lord Diplock's approach as "unrealistic" and thus allows consideration to be given to future monetary developments.[48]

10.19 It is possible to conclude that, as a general rule, one may expect judges to be inclined towards the assessment of compensation as at the date of judgment. It may be repeated that this approach appears consistent with the principles

---

[46] *Cookson v Knowles* [1979] AC 556, 571 (HL); *Lim Poh Choo v Camden and Islington Area Health Authority* [1980] AC 174, 193 (HL). These cases were followed in *Hodgson v Trapp* [1989] AC 807. Since the possibility of future inflation cannot be taken into account, actuarial or other evidence on the likely rates of such inflation is inadmissible—see *Auty v National Coal Board* [1985] 1 WLR 784.

[47] *O'Brian v McKean* (1968) 118 CLR 540. The decision to exclude future inflation from the assessment process was followed by the High Court of Australia in *Barrell Insurance Pty Ltd v Pennant Hills Restaurants Pty Ltd* (1981) 34 ALR 102 and in *Todorovic v Waller* (1981)150 CLR 402.

[48] *Andrews v Grand & Toy Alberta Ltd* [1978] 2 SCR 229, 254; *Arnold v Teno* [1978] 2 SCR 287. Two other cases in the same sense are *Thornton v Board of School Trustees* [1978] 2 SCR 267 and *Keizer v Hanna and Buch* [1978] 2 SCR 342. On these cases, see Rea (1980) III, Can Bar Rev 280. These decisions also deal with the rate of discount to be applied to an award of damages in a

of compensation and restitution.[49] In a period of inflation this will inevitably lead to higher awards of damages than those which would have been awarded on the basis of an earlier valuation date (for example, the date on which the tort was committed). But there is no trace of a public policy to the effect "that inflation must be contained and the victim of the tortfeasor should help to contain it by a progressive reduction in the real value of the compensation awarded".[50] On the contrary, inflation neither can be nor should be resisted by means of inflicting harm upon the unfortunate victim of a wrongful act.

Mitigation of damage

10.20   It remains to enquire whether the victim of a breach of contract or of a tort is under a duty to mitigate the damage and, if so, whether he is entitled to recover his expenditure (with interest) or can claim compensation for the loss in purchasing power which repayment of the expenditure in depreciated currency would cause him. To return to Lord Wrenbury's three cows, the claimant elects to purchase three replacement cows at the cost of £150 but, by the time of the trial, three similar cows would cost £300. Does the claimant recover £150 or £300?[51]

10.21   Under English law, the claimant need not risk his money too far but, subject to that qualification, he is required to incur expense in order to mitigate his damage if it is reasonable in all the circumstances for him to do so. However, a claimant is not expected to take steps which are beyond his financial means in order to reduce the damages.[52] In judging reasonableness in individual cases, the court may have regard to the impact of inflation upon any expenditure which is required to be made, and its consequences for the victim.

10.22   If the claimant does in fact mitigate his loss, then the expenditure so incurred has the effect of "crystallising" that aspect of the claim for damages.[53] At this point, the claim becomes liquidated, with the result that the principle of

---

personal injury case (ie the amount to be deducted on the basis that the claimant receives an advance payment in respect of the sums which he would otherwise have earned over an extended period). On that aspect of the cases and for further materials, see Landsea (1982) 28 McGill LJ 102.

[49] As the House of Lords has pointed out, "the word 'compensation' would be a mockery if what was paid was something that did not compensate". It thus disapproved the use of an "out-of-date valuation" for the purpose of assessing damages—see *Ascot Midlands Baptist (Trust) Association v Birmingham Corp* [1970] AC 874, 904.

[50] *Walter v John McLean & Sons Ltd* [1979] 1 WLR 760, 766 (CA).

[51] See generally, Feldman and Libling (1979) 95 LQR 270; Waddams, (1981) 1 OJLS 134.

[52] *Dodd Properties (Kent) Ltd v Canterbury City Council* [1980] 1 WLR 4333.

[53] See the remarks of Hodson J in *Bishop v Cunard White Star Lines Ltd* [1950] P 240, 246.

nominalism applies to it and the claimant is restricted to the amount actually expended.[54]

Experience in the United States

In view of its experience during the greenback period (1861–79), when gold coins and treasury notes were both legal tender and, at one point, the premium on the former was more than 100 per cent in terms of the latter, courts in the United States were confronted with acute difficulties in this area of monetary law. To what extent could the real purchasing power of notes be taken into account in the assessment of damages? The problem became pressing once the Supreme Court had given judicial recognition to the depreciation of legal tender notes.[55] However, it must be said that the developments of that time—whilst interesting from a historical perspective—appear to have limited impact on modern judicial practice.   **10.23**

In terms of the assessment of damages, it has frequently been stated that damages were to be assessed as at the date of the breach of contract or the commission of the tort.[56] It followed from this rule that inflation occurring between the date of the breach and the date of the judgment could not be taken into account.[57] Yet, as has happened in England, the breach-date rule has been qualified to a very significant extent—no doubt with a view of mitigating the injustice which that rule may otherwise cause. The Restatement (Second) seems to be correct in stating[58] that "any event occurring prior to the trial that increases the harmful consequences of the defendant's tortious conduct . . . increases the damages recoverable to the same extent, whether the event has   **10.24**

---

[54] *Dodd Properties (Kent) Ltd v Canterbury City Council* [1980] 1 WLR 433. The claimant may be entitled to interest on the sum expended, but he cannot claim any further amount by way of damages.

[55] See *Bronson v Rhodes* (1868) 7 Wall (74 US) 229. On this basis, it was held to have been appropriate for a California court to hold that the identical services could be valued at $1,000 in notes or $500 in gold coin because the question was "not whether a dollar in greenbacks is worth less than a dollar in gold, but what are the goods and services worth"—see *Spencer v Prindle* (1865) 28 Cal 276. This formulation did, however, have the effect of side-stepping the monetary law question (ie the equivalence of gold coin and notes) which was actually raised by the case. For an illuminating account of the subject, see Dawson and Cooper, (1935) 33 Mich LR 852.

[56] In relation to a contract for the sale of goods, this principle was affirmed by the Supreme Court in *Ansaldo San Giorgio v Rheinström Bros* (1934) 294 US 494. See also *Kunianly v Overmyer Warehouse Co* (1968) 406 F 2d 818.

[57] *HK Parker Co Inc v Goodyear Tire & Rubber Co* (1976) 536 F 2d 1115. This approach was stated to be justified because "there is no guarantee that, had Parker received the money in 1962–71, it would have been able to protect the value of that money from the effects of inflation other than by use of the money as investment capital" (at 1124). This line of reasoning overlooks the fact that the successful claimant never had the opportunity to take such steps, because the defendant had denied him recompense between the date of the wrong and the date of the judgment.

[58] (1979) para 910, Comment (b).

occurred before the suit is brought or after the suit". Thus, in personal injury cases, an award of damages will not be deemed excessive merely on the grounds that it is based on the value of the dollar as at the date of the judgment, rather than the date of the wrong.[59] Indeed, it has even been said that "it is plain common sense and simple honesty for a court or jury in appraising the damages suffered by reason of any tortious act of the defendant to compute the amount of damages according to the current value of the dollar".[60]

10.25 The question whether *future* inflation may be taken into account in the assessment of damages is a more difficult one.[61] Some courts in the United States essentially follow the English approach, and leave such inflation out of account on the basis that it is too speculative.[62] Some courts allow for an element in respect of future inflation provided that the claim is supported by expert evidence from trained economists,[63] whilst others will simply place reliance on common sense.[64] The US Supreme Court has also laid down a series of rules for

---

[59] In *Hurst v Chicago BQR Co* (1920) 280 Mo 556, 219 SW 566, the Supreme Court of Missouri said "the value of money lies not in what it is, but in what it will buy. It follows that if "$10,000 was a fair compensation in value for such injuries . . . as are here involved 10 years ago, when money was dear and its purchasing power was great, a larger sum will now be required when money is cheap and its purchasing power is small". On this basis an award of US$15,000 was held not to be excessive. The court cited numerous authorities and emphasised that "ordinary variations" should not give rise to any increase or reduction in an award, but "when radical, material and apparently permanent changes in social and economic conditions confronts mankind, courts must take cognisance of them". For a further decision of the Supreme Court of Missouri to similar effect, see *Talbert v Chicago RI & P Rly Co* (1929)15 SW 2d 762. In *Halloran v New England Tel & Tel Co* (1920) 95 Vt 273, 115A, 143, it was held appropriate to take account of the declining value of the dollar in assessing damages; on this case, see (1922) 35 Harv LR 616. Further cases are listed in the Note on Fluctuating Dollars and Tort Damage Verdicts (1948) 48 Col LR 264. The subject is further explored in *Willard v Hudson* (1963) 378 P 2d 966, a decision of the Supreme Court of Oregon which provides a long list of earlier authorities.

[60] *Gist v French* (1955) 288 P 2d 1003, 1020 (Californian District Court of Appeal).

[61] As noted above, English law appears to disregard that possibility in carrying out the necessary computation.

[62] *Williams v US* (1970) 435 F 2d 804; *Magill v Westinghouse Electric Corp* (1972) 464 F 2d 294; *Hoffman v Sterling Drug Inc* (1974) 485 F 2d 726; and *Huddel v Levin* (1974) 537 F 2d 726.

[63] *Feldman v Allegheny Airlines Inc* (1975) 524 F 2d 384; *US v English* (1975) 521 F 2d; *Vesey v US* (1980) 626 F 2d 627; *Burlington Northern Inc v Boxberger* (1975) 529 F 2d 284; *Sauers v Alaska Barge* (1979) 600 F 2d 238; *Steckler v US* 549 F 2d 1372; and *Doca v Marina Mercante Nicarguense* (1980) 634 F 2d 30.

[64] See *Bach v Penn Central Transportation Co* (1974) 502 F 2d 1117; *Johnson v Serra* (1975) 521 F 2d 1289; *Riha v Jasper Blackburn Corp* (1975) F 2d 840; and *Hysell v Iowa Public Service Co* (1977) 559 F 2d 468. In the same sense, see the decisions of the Supreme Courts in Wisconsin and Oregon in *Dabareiser v Weistlog* (1948) 253 Wis 23, 33 NW 2d 220 and *Willard v Husdon* (1963) 378 P 2d 966 respectively. On the effect of anticipated inflation on damages for future losses, see Rosenhouse, 21 ALR 4th 21; Depperschmidt, (1986) 18 Memphis State University LR 51; Fleming (1982) AJCL (Supplement) 97. The question whether past earnings could be increased to take account of inflation when considering the computation of damages answered in the affirmative was in *Steckler v US* 549 F 2d 1372, but in the negative in *Payne v Panama Canal Co* (1979) 607 F 2d 155. That future inflation occurring after the award may be taken into

the calculation of damages in personal injury cases.[65] and the courts have attempted to develop methods by which the likelihood of future inflation can be taken into account.[66]

Where the claimant has mitigated his loss, it would seem that he may be **10.26** compensated for the falling value of money between the date of the breach and the date of the judgment, although there seems to be no direct decision on the point.[67] The Supreme Court of Canada laid down a flexible rule in this area,[68] and it is suggested that this broad approach is desirable to ensure that a fair assessment of damages can be made in individual cases.

C. Other Valuation Questions

The process of valuation of unliquidated amounts is, of course, by no means **10.27** confined to actions for a breach of contract or the commission of a tort. It is not proposed to discuss in detail the numerous specialised areas in which such questions may arise, but two examples may help to provide a broad understanding of the issues.

The first example is provided by the expropriation of land by a State or a local **10.28** authority, where a sum by way of compensation becomes payable. The problems which may occur in such a case are very similar to those which have just been discussed in the context of unliquidated damages. The right to compensation may arise when official notice of the acquisition is given, but there is frequently a significant time lag before compensation is actually paid. The effects of

---

account seems to have been firmly settled by the decision of the Fifth Circuit to that effect in *Cutler v Slater Boat Co* (1982) 688 F 2d 280, overuling *Johnson v Penrod Drilling Co* (1975) 510 F 2d 234.

[65] It is not proposed to review those decisions but they are: *Norfolf & Western Rly Co v Liepelt* (1980) 444 US 490; *St Louis Southwestern Rly Co v Dickson* (1985) 470 US 409; *Jones & Laughlin Steel Corporation v Pfiefer* (1983) 462 US 523; *Beaulieu v Elliot* (1967) 434 P 2d 665; *Monessen South Western Rly v Morgan* (1988) 486 US 330.

[66] See *Feldman v Allegheny Airlines Inc* (1975) F 2d 384; the Supreme Court of Alaska sought to achieve this end by refusing to discount lump sum damages to present day value, on the basis that this would diminish the income earning capacity—see *Beaulieu v Elliott* (1967) 434 P 2d 665. For similar efforts on the part of the Canadian courts, see *Andrews v Grand & Toy Alberta Ltd* [1978] 2 SCR 229; *Thornton v Board of School Trustees of School District No. 57* [1978] SCR; *Arnold v Teno* [1978] 2 SCR 287; *Keizer v Hanna* [1978] 2 SCR 342.

[67] The most comparable case appears to be the decision of the US Supreme Court in *Galigher v Jones* (1889) 129 US 193. Of course, if the tort involves damage to property and the claimant effects the repairs, he is not entitled to recover any part of those costs which are attributable to the improvement of the property—see *Freeport Sulphur v SS Hermosa* (1977) 526 F 2d 300.

[68] See *Re Asamera Oil Corp* (1978) 89 DLR 3d 1 and note the comparative survey undertaken by the court.

monetary depreciation during the intervening period may be substantial—should they be borne by the owner, or by the expropriating authority? Questions of this kind may be explicitly settled by the relevant legislation, although questions of statutory interpretation may naturally arise in some cases. In England, it was long thought that the value as at the date of the official notice to treat was decisive, but in 1969 the House of Lords held that where the owner is entitled to reinstatement, the assessment has to be made with reference to the date on which reinstatement becomes reasonably practicable.[69] In the United States, notwithstanding the constitutional requirements of just compensation for expropriated property, courts have tended to hold that the assessment must be made with reference to the value as at the date of the acquisition, with the necessary result that monetary depreciation occurring after that date cannot be taken into account.[70]

10.29   The second example involves the valuation of property for the purpose of calculating a share in a fund. A common example is provided by a beneficiary who is required to bring advances into hotchpot. What is the value to be placed on advances made by the deceased many years prior to his death? In England, advances are required to be valued and brought into hotchpot at the date of death[71]—in principle, on an equal footing, because all assets to be brought into account will be valued by reference to the same date. But it is in this context that the principle of nominalism may operate unjustly; consistently with that principle, £20,000 given to a beneficiary twenty years before the date of death must continue to be taken into account as £20,000, regardless of the effect of monetary depreciation which has occurred during the intervening period.[72] As a result, the recipient of a gift in sterling may be advantaged as compared to the beneficiary

---

[69] *West Midland Baptist (Trust) Association v Birmingham Corp* [1970] AC 874. The House of Lords also indicated that where the owner is entitled to compensation for the value of the land, then the relevant date is the date on which the valuation is assessed or (if earlier) the date on which possession is taken. This aspect of the decision is doubtful; on this point and the case generally, see Mann (1968) 85 LQR 516.

[70] This is the conclusion reached in Mr G.B. Crook's Annotation in (1963) 92 Amer LR 2d 772. For the case law in this area, see *US v Dow* 3 (1958) 57 US 17; *US v 158.76 Acres of land* (1962) 298 F 2d 559; *US v Clark* (1980) 63 L Ed 2d 373. Further comparative commentary will be found in the Fifth Edition of this work, 139–40.

[71] See *Re Hillas-Drake* [1944] Ch 235.

[72] The Intestates' Estates Act 1952 requires that "*any money* or property . . . shall be brought into account at a valuation". It is submitted that this language does not allow for a sterling sum to be "revalued" as at the date of death, for this would fly in the face of the nominalistic principle; a pound remains a pound in terms of its value—see *Treseder-Griffin v Co-operative Insurance Society* [1956] 2 QB 1276 and the discussion at para 9.19 above. This view is reinforced by the fact that the estate would ultimately have to be valued in sterling in any event.

who received some other form of gift which has appreciated and which falls to be revalued for hotchpot purposes. As noted above, the principle of nominalism may operate unjustly in this type of case, but the principle is so fundamental that it is difficult to remedy the position by means of any purely monetary law proposition.

11

EXCLUDING THE EFFECTS OF NOMINALISM

A. Introduction

It has been shown that, in the context of liquidated claims arising under long-term contracts, the creditor is exposed to the erosion of his claim as a consequence of "creeping" inflation.[1] The general principles of private law do not afford to the creditor any protection against this erosion in value, since nominalism is *presumed* to reflect the intention of the parties. If contracting parties wish to displace the principle of nominalism, then this can only be done by means of an express contractual term to that effect.

11.01

Given that parties are free to contract out of the principle of nominalism, it is perhaps not surprising that they occasionally seek to exercise that right when entering into long-term commitments. Various techniques have been evolved which seek to preserve the effective value of a payment stream over a period, even though (in strict terms) such techniques do not directly affect the nominalistic principle. For example:

11.02

(a) In contracts with an international dimension, the creditor may stipulate for payment in a currency (for example, the US dollar) which he believes is

---

[1] See the discussion at para 9.23(e) above.

most likely to maintain its international value over the period. However, the obligations concerned would continue to be discharged on a dollar-for-dollar basis, with the result that (regardless of the perceived "value" of the stipulated currency) the nominalistic principle will continue to apply in the usual way.[2]

(b) Alternatively, parties may elect to contract in terms of barter, so that counter-performance involves the delivery of a set quantity of wheat, gold, or other commodity. Plainly, the application of nominalism is avoided in cases not involving a monetary obligation but (equally plainly) contracting parties would only very occasionally go to these lengths purely in order to avoid the impact of nominalism.

11.03 In other cases, it may be felt necessary to vary the principle of nominalism more directly, such that the nominal amount of the monetary obligation is increased as the value of money declines. Purely by way of example, it may be noted that a long-term contract for the supply of a particular commodity should include a provision for periodic price reviews.[3]

11.04 These introductory remarks have served to highlight the difficulties which may be posed by the principle of nominalism in relatively common commercial situations. It is now proposed to consider the types of contractual provisions which have at various times been developed to counteract the principle. It should, however, be clearly understood that the purpose of any protective clause is invariably to protect the creditor against a reduction in the value of the currency to which the clause is attached. In domestic contracts, protection is usually required against the consequences of (internal) inflation; in international contracts, the creditor is generally seeking protection against adverse exchange rate movements. Where the protected currency is formally depreciated or is allowed to "float" downwards, the protective clause is likely to come into operation. Where another currency is revalued or appreciates, the protected currency remains stable in terms of all other currencies, save the one in relation to which its value is necessarily reduced or depreciated. Whether a protective clause applies in such a case will naturally be a question of construction; the clause is likely to apply in such a case if it is not merely designed to protect against the depreciation of the currency concerned, but is designed to ensure

---

[2] In other words, this technique does not avoid the principle of nominalism at all; it merely shifts the risk which is inherent in that principle to another currency which the creditor hopes or believes to be more reliable.

[3] A lesson learnt from the contract at issue in *South Staffordshire Area Health Authority v South Staffordshire Waterworks* [1978] WLR 1387. Long-term office leases or residential leases may be agreed at rents which become unrealistic over an extended period, and provision must be made for an increase at appropriate intervals.

effective equivalence between the two currencies and to guard against the disturbance of any intended pattern of uniformity.[4]

B. Gold Clauses

So long as there existed a gold standard in any of its various emanations,[5] that is to say, until 15 August 1971, gold was the most stable standard of value and dominated the world of money. Since gold was "demonetised" in the 1970s, no fixed and stable standard of value exists. It is very necessary to emphasise and ponder this fact of singular starkness. Gold was fixed in terms of the US dollar for the entire period between 1934 and 1971, at a rate of US $35 per ounce. Since that date, the price has been free to fluctuate and has frequently done so. Gold is now merely a commodity, just as silver, copper, or wheat are commodities; it no longer holds a special place in national monetary systems.[6]

11.05

Gold clauses are now a matter of history.[7] Whilst the use of the word "never" is always dangerous, it is now very difficult to envisage any circumstances under which any form of gold standard could be reintroduced in any meaningful way.[8] It should, however, be acknowledged that the law relating to protective clauses generally has largely developed within the framework of the gold clause; as a result, the general principles derived from the gold clause are relevant both to index clauses and to other types of protective provisions which may be developed at a future date. In addition, cases have occasionally come before the courts in relatively recent times which have involved silver or similar commodity provisions.[9] There has also been a recent lines of cases which have considered gold clauses which remain effective in international conventions. For these

11.06

---

[4] In this sense, see the *Young Loan Case* (1950) 59 Int LR 494, and in particular, para 24 of the majority opinion. The case has already been discussed at para 2.46 above.

[5] See the discussion at paras 2.06–2.10 above.

[6] The point was further emphasised by the significant disposals of gold by a number of central banks in the late 1990s.

[7] At least this is so in a contractual context. As will be seen, gold clauses fall for consideration in the context of certain international conventions.

[8] Even now, however, some organisations continue to support the use of gold as a basis of monetary value. The gold dinar was in use among Muslim countries until the collapse of the Ottoman calliphate in 1924. A proposal led by the Government of Malaysia would see the reintroduction of the gold dinar as a means of settling bilateral payments between countries in the Islamic world; the unit would thus not exist in physical form but would constitute an official measure of value. The proposal was considered at two conferences held in Kuala Lumpur—*The Gold Dinar in Multinational Trade* (October, 2002) and *Gold in International Trade—Strategic Positioning in the Global Monetary System* (October, 2002). On the whole subject, see Umar Ibrahim Vadillo, *The Return of the Gold Dinar* (Madinah Press, 2001).

[9] See in particular the decisions in *Sternberg v West Coast Life Insurance Co* (1961) 16 Cal Rep 546 and *Judah v Delaware Trust Co* (1977) 378 A 2d 624 which are discussed at para 11.12 below.

reasons, it is necessary to consider both the gold clause itself and some of the litigation to which it gave rise.[10]

The existence of a gold clause

11.07   At the outset, it is necessary to ask—what was a gold clause and how did it come into existence? A gold clause was a contractual provision which in some way referred to gold in connection with the monetary obligations created by the contract. As will be seen below, the reference to gold may have a variety of meanings, depending upon the manner in which the expression is employed.

11.08   It is implicit in this definition that a gold clause could only come into being as a result of an agreement between the parties. So far as English law is concerned, such a clause could thus be expressly stated or (in appropriate but very rare cases) could constitute an implied term of the contract.

11.09   There can be no doubt that a gold clause should be treated as valid and binding under English law. It is apparent that such a clause runs directly contrary to the principle of nominalism but, as shown earlier, the application of that principle under English law depends upon the presumed intention of the parties; it can thus be excluded by express or implied terms of the type just described.[11] It is necessary to consider the two possibilities separately.

Express terms

11.10   If a reference to "gold" was attached to a monetary obligation, then the relevant provision had to be construed in accordance with the law applicable to the contract concerned.[12] One immediate difficulty which arose in this context was the purpose underlying the use of the word "gold". Was it intended to define the extent of the debtor's obligation, so as to create an enforceable gold clause? Or did expressions such as "gold franc" connote the lawful currency of France, with "gold" merely being descriptive of the fact that, at the time the obligation was incurred, France was on the gold standard? In the former case, the debtor's obligation to pay would vary in amount according to the price of gold; in the latter case, the nominalistic principle would continue to apply. Where the

---

[10] Nevertheless, it must be acknowledged that time has in some respects diminished the value of the learning which surrounds the gold clause. For that reason, the current discussion will be confined to a review of the general principles. For a fuller discussion and further references, see the Fifth Edition of this work, 147–64; see also Nussbaum, *Money in the Law, National and International* (The Press Foundation, 2nd edn, 1950) sections 15 and 16.

[11] The principle of nominalism is not a matter of public interest and attempts to avoid the principle cannot be struck down on public policy grounds. No statute was ever passed in this country to prohibit the use of gold clauses—see generally, Ch 12 below.

[12] Whether or not the reference to "gold" was intended to be attached to the monetary obligation itself will likewise be a question of interpretation.

contract is governed by English law, then the court must ascertain the parties' intention from the words which have been employed. This is fully in accord with the principle formulated by the Permanent Court of International Justice in the *Case of Brazilian Loans*:[13]

> One argument against the efficacy of the provision for payments in gold is that it is simply a "style" or a routine form of expression. This, in substance, would eliminate the word gold from the bonds. The contract of the parties cannot be treated in such a manner. When the Brazilian Government promised to pay "gold francs", the reference to a well known standard of value cannot be considered as inserted merely for literary effect or as a routine expression without significance. The Court is called upon to construe the promise, not to ignore it.

It must be said, however, that the judicial approach to gold clauses was not always in line with this approach, and other cases demonstrate a distinct tendency to treat references to "gold" as merely descriptive, or merely as a synonym for the currency in question and referring to its statutory quality as a currency based on a gold standard, ie without contractual content and thus not affecting the application of nominalism. This view was even taken[14] in the context of a very elaborately drafted promise to pay "pesos of 183.057 millionths of a gramme of fine gold", although a different view was subsequently adopted by the Supreme Court of Chile.[15]   **11.11**

A number of other cases have adopted a purely descriptive (or non-substantive) approach to contractual references to "gold" in the context of monetary obligations,[16] and it must be said that courts in both England and the United States have likewise tended to adopt the "descriptive" approach.[17] More recent cases   **11.12**

---

[13] PCIJ Series A, No. 21 (1928–30) 115, 116.

[14] *St Pierre v South American Stores Ltd* [1937] 1 All ER 206, affirmed by the Court of Appeal [1937] 3 All ER 349. For a case in which a Singapore court seems to have held that a reference to "dollars (gold)" was not a gold clause but merely a reference to the US currency, see *Nanyo Printing Office v Linotype & Machinery Ltd* [1933] MLJ 186.

[15] 1 January 1938, BIJI 39 (1930) 349.

[16] eg, the Austrian Supreme Court (12 March 1930, *JW* 1930, 2480) held that a clause requiring "effective payment in the gold currency of Germany" merely meant that payment must be made in accordance with German monetary laws. In Belgium (Cass 19 June 1930, *Rev dr banc* 1931, 266) the clause "au cours de l'or" was held to be a mere "clause de style" which did not affect the substance of the obligation. In Sweden (Supreme Court, 10 June 1938, BIJI 39 (1938), 108), the words "in Gold" were held merely to refer to the monetary laws in effect at the time.

[17] See, eg, the decision in *Campos v Kentucky & Indiana Terminal Railroad Co* [1962] 2 Ll LR 459, where a reference to payment "in gold coin" was held to be merely descriptive of an obligation to pay in legal tender; the decision is criticised by Mann (1963) 12 ICLQ 1005. A similar result, open to the same criticism, had previously been reached in *Lemaire v Kentucky & Indiana Railroad Co* (1957) 242 F 2d 884. It has been shown elsewhere that the decision in *Treseder-Griffin v Co-operative Insurance Society* [1956] 2 QB 127 is a useful illustration of the nominalistic principle in general terms. Nevertheless, the case referred to gold sterling and (as Harman J's powerful dissenting judgment points out) the decision effectively disregards some of the express terms of a written contract.

which have arisen in the United States have confirmed this general trend. Thus, a reference to the "Chinese silver dollar" which was contractually defined as a unit of currency containing a certain amount of silver, was found by the Supreme Court of Delaware to be merely an effort to describe the currency in question which did not create a protective clause of any kind.[18] In similar vein, an obligation expressed to be payable in "taels, Shanghai Sycee currency of the present weight and fineness" created an obligation of a purely monetary character which was not protected by reference to the value of silver.[19]

11.13 Despite this generally negative judicial approach, it nevertheless remains clear that a provision for payment in gold constitutes a valid contractual provision. So long as it is clear that the reference to gold was intended to govern the substance of the obligation, then a court should give effect to it in accordance with its terms. It remains to add that in cases involving a conflict of laws, the validity, substance, and effect of a gold clause falls to be determined by reference to the law applicable to the contract concerned, and not by reference to the *lex monetae*.[20]

Implied terms

11.14 It is now necessary to consider whether a gold clause could be implied into a contract which contains no express reference to gold. If it is remembered that the nominalistic principle applies in consequence of the presumed intention of the parties, then the notion that a *presumed* intention can be displaced by an *implied* term is inherently unattractive. It should follow that the circumstances under which a gold clause could be implied into an English law contract should, in principle, arise only on the rarest of occasions. To express matters in a different way, to imply a gold clause into a contract would usually fly in the face of the nominalistic principle. As a result, the evidence upon which a gold clause could be implied into the contract must be derived from the terms of the contract itself or the circumstances surrounding its conclusion; it could not in any sense be inferred from the presumed intention of the parties.[21] It must be emphasised again that, if there exists a mere promise to pay a certain sum of money of a certain currency, payment must be made in whatever is the money of that currency system at the time of maturity;[22] the fact that the stipulated currency

---

[18] *Judah v Delaware Trust Co* (1977) 378 A 2d 624. It may thus be said that, in this particular area, the courts tended to favour the position of the debtor over that of the creditor.

[19] *Sternberg v West Coast Life Insurance Co* (1961) 6 Cal Rep 546.

[20] Rome Convention, Arts 8 and 10(1)(a). The legal analysis is essentially the same in the context of revalorisation provisions which are considered at para 13.09 below.

[21] See the remarks to this effect in *State of Maryland v Baltimore & Ohio Railroad* (1874) 89 US 105, 111. See also *Ottoman Bank v Chakarian (No 2)* [1938] AC 260, 272. The presumption as to the intention of the parties is, of course, to the opposite effect.

[22] This fundamental point has been discussed at para 9.03 above.

was on a gold standard at the time the contract was made did not alter this essential rule or the manner of its application. It follows that a mere promise to pay an amount in foreign currency—even if linked to gold at the time of the contract—could not be treated as a promise to pay that currency at its gold value.[23] Similarly, a bare promise to pay "francs" did not at any time imply a promise to pay gold francs. Something more than a mere reference to the currency was therefore necessary to lead to any implication of a gold clause. There had to be further evidence leading to a gold clause; an explicit reference to gold would therefore almost invariably be required,[24] for as the French courts have noted, "la stipulation d'un paiement international à effectuer en francs—or ne peut résulter que de la convention des parties".[25]

As has been shown, a gold clause could not be implied to give effect to any **11.15** presumed intention of the parties. It could thus only be implied *either* from the terms of the contractual documents or from the circumstances prevailing at the time the contract was made.[26] It is necessary to consider these two categories separately.

---

[23] *Ottoman Bank v Chakarian (No 2)* [1938] AC 260, 272; German Supreme Court, 20 April 1940, *RGZ* 163, 324; 28 May 1937, *RGZ* 155, 133 with references to earlier decisions. A reference to a monetary system as at a particular date may imply a gold clause. Thus, the Court of Appeal at Liège held that an obligation to pay "en monnaie Suisse de 1930" was a gold clause: 10 February 1939, *BIJI* 40 (1939) 283.

[24] *New Brunswick Railway Co v British and French Trust Corp* [1939] AC 1, 18–19.

[25] Cass Civ, 23 January 1924, *Clunet* 1925, 169; Cass Civ, 21 December 1932, *Clunet* 1933, 1201 and S 1932, I 390 Cass Req, 6 December 1933, *Clunet* 1934, 946 and DH 1934, 34; Cass Civ, 24 January 1934, DP 1934, I 78; 14 February 1934, Cass Req, 5 November 1934, S 1935, I 34; cf Cass Civ, 23 January 1924, S 1925, I 257. In view of the international character of the French franc and its importance in a number of countries, it is perhaps unsurprising to find that a different approach was occasionally adopted. Thus, in Egypt, the Court of Appeal of the Mixed Tribunal in Alexandria held that the Suez Canal Company had to repay their bonds—denominated in "francs"—at the gold value, on the basis that the franc referred to in the bonds was "ni le franc dit française, ni le franc dit egyptien, mais que ce franc était plus exactement le franc tout court, le franc universel d'un étalon monétaire commun à plusieurs pays, ayant une valeur fixe et determinée en Egypte où le louis d'or avait alors cours légal en vertu des dispositions legislatives de 1834" (4 June 1925, *Clunet* 1925, 1080; see also Paris Court of Appeal, 25 February 1924, *Clunet* 1924, 688). Subsequently, however, the Court of Appeal departed from this view, holding that the franc was not "une monnaie internationale", but that it was legal tender in Egypt at a tariff fixed in 1834, "non pas comme une monnaie étrangère, mais comme une monnaie nationalisée ou adoptee": See the three judgments of 18 February 1936 in *Gazette des Tribunaux Mixtes* xxvi 147, No 127 (*Re Crédit Foncier Egyptien and Land Bank of Egypt*). For decisions of the French courts in the same context, see Trib Civ De la Seine, 31 May 1933 and Cour de Paris, 3 April 1936, D 1936, 2, 88. The Syrian Cour de Cassation took the view that references to the franc could be treated as a measure of gold value, rather than simply as a reference to the lawful currency of France (20 June 1928, S 1929, 4.1 where the court said "le mot franc signifie non pas la monnaie ayant cours libératoire dans tel ou tel pays, mais un certain poids d'or relié par un rapport fixe avec le poids de metal fin contenu dans le livre turque").

[26] For the general rules on implied terms, see *Chitty On Contracts* (Sweet & Maxwell, 29th edn, 2004) ch 13.

11.16   The process of implying terms into the contract from the provisions of the agreement itself is a difficult one. The decided cases are not entirely consistent but they do, in any event, depend upon the precise terms of the documents before the court in individual instances. The question has arisen mainly in the context of international bond issues. For example, the House of Lords held that a gold clause included in the terms and conditions of a bond issue was not negated by the fact that the face of the bonds omitted any reference to gold;[27] but in a converse case, the Supreme Court of Ontario refused to infer a gold clause from the use of the term "Gold Bond" on the face of the instrument.[28] The House of Lords also held that a gold clause could not be implied into interest coupons even though the bonds themselves were expressly subject to such a provision[29] although this seems to disregard the relationship between principal and interest, and is inconsistent with conclusions reached elsewhere.[30] Where interest had been paid over a period of years on a gold basis, the Privy Council held that the principal sum had likewise to be paid in gold, even in the absence of an appropriate clause in the contract itself.[31]

11.17   If the relevant contract provided for payment in one of several currencies at the option of the creditor and a gold clause was attached to one currency only, then it will not extend to the other currencies.[32] Where bonds were issued without any reference to gold, but the relevant prospectus included a description of a gold clause, it was unclear whether the gold clause should be imputed to the bonds themselves.[33]

11.18   If the terms of the documents themselves were not sufficient to give rise to an implied term, in what type of case could a gold clause be implied from the situation prevailing at the time of the contract and the surrounding circumstances? As a general rule, the conduct of the parties in relation to the contract can only be taken into account if it indicates that a gold clause was intended to operate from the outset, or if leads to the conclusion that the parties agreed to

---

[27] *Feist v Société International Belge d'Electricité* [1934] AC 161, 168.

[28] *Derwa v Rio de Janeiro Light & Power Co* [1928] 4 DLR 542, 553.

[29] *New Brunswick Railway Co v British and French Trust Corp* [1939] AC 1.

[30] See in particular *Case of Brazilian Loans* PCIJ Series A No 2 (1928–30) 110. The German Supreme Court has held that a gold clause applicable to the capital sum should extend equally to the corresponding interest obligation (11 April 1931, DJZ 1931, 1201). This seems to be a preferable approach.

[31] *Apostolic Throne of St Jacob v Said* [1940] 1 All ER 54.

[32] *International Trustee for the Protection of Bondholders AG v The King* [1936] 3 All GR 407, 431 (CA).

[33] The gold clause was read into the bonds in such a case by the Permanent Court of International Justice in the *Case of Brazilian Loans* (above) at 113. The position was less clear in England—see *International Trustee for the Protection of Bondholders AG v The King* [1937] AC 500 and the comments by Mann [1959] *British Year Book of International Law* 42.

vary their contract at a later date so as to incorporate such a provision. Such cases will invariably depend upon their own peculiar facts—a point graphically illustrated by the Privy Council, when it reached opposite conclusions in two cases with an almost identical factual background.[34]

C. Gold Coin or Gold Value

The text has thus far dealt with the gold clause in rather general terms. But once it had been established that a gold clause constituted an express or implied term of the contract, then it was necessary to interpret that clause and to clothe it with some legal effect.[35] In practice, such a clause could require either:

11.19

(a) that the debtor had to deliver the quantity of gold coin[36] to which the contract referred; or

(b) that the debtor had to pay an amount in *money*, but that the amount of the obligation was to pay the amount of the relevant currency required to purchase the set amount of gold as at the date on which payment fell due.[37]

The first type of provision deals with the mode of payment (a *modality clause*) whilst the second fixes the substance or amount of the debt (a *value clause*).

---

[34] See *Ottoman Bank of Nicosia v Dascalopoulos* [1934] AC 354 and *Ottoman Bank v Chakarian (No. 2)* [1936] AC 260. A gold clause was implied into the pension arrangements in the former case, but not in the latter. The pension obligations of the Ottoman Bank gave rise to a number of cases in different jurisdictions, and inevitably the results were not always consistent. For further cases, see *Sforza v Ottoman Bank* [1938] AC 282; *Ottoman Bank v Menni* [1939] 4 All ER 9; *Krocorian v Ottoman Bank* (1932) 48 TLR 247; decision of the Court of Appeal of the Mixed Tribunal at Alexandria, 18 June 1934, *Gazette des Tribunaux Mixtes* xxiv 349, No. 412 (*Hanna v Ottoman Bank*); 13 April 1935 *Gazette des Tribunaux Mixtes* xxv 326, No. 362 (*Mazass v Ottoman Bank*).

[35] Plainly, this process is much more difficult when dealing with an *implied* gold clause.

[36] An obligation to pay a gold coin nevertheless remained a *monetary* obligation—see the observations of Lawrence LJ in *Feist v Société Intercommunale d'Electricité Belge* [1933] Ch 684, 702 and in *British and French Trustee Corp v The New Brunswick Railway Co* [1936] 1 All ER 13, whose remarks on this subject remain valid notwithstanding the decision of the House of Lords in the same case [1939] AC 1. The German Supreme Court took a similar view: 22 January 1902, *RGZ* 50, 145,148; 16 January 1924, *RGZ* 107, 402 and 3 December 1924, *JW* 1925, 1183. In the US it was at one time thought that "a contract to pay a certain sum in gold and silver coin is in legal effect a contract to deliver a certain weight in gold and silver by fineness to be ascertained by the court"—see, eg, *Bronson v Rhodes* (1868) 7 Wall (74 US) 229 and *Butler v Horowitz* (1868) 7 Wall (74 US) 258. This "commodity theory" was expressly rejected by the Supreme Court in *Norman v Baltimore & Ohio Railway Co* (1934) 294 US 240, 302 and in *Nortz v US* (1934) 294 US 317.

[37] For a third approach to the interpretation of this type of clause (albeit not involving gold) see *Meseroe v Ammidon* (1872) 109 Mass 415 and *Moore v Clines* (1933) 247 Ky 605, 57 SW (2d) 509.

11.20 In periods of relative monetary stability, the distinction between these two types of clause would be of limited practical importance; it mattered little to the creditor whether he received gold or the amount of money necessary to purchase that gold at the time of performance. The distinction became important in times of monetary disturbance, for States would often resort to the remedy of permitting monetary obligations to be discharged by the payment of notes according to their nominal value. Under circumstances of this kind, the distinction between the two types of clause became important, because:

(1) a value clause determined the *substance* of the obligation, ie the amount which the creditor was entitled to receive[38]—this objective was achieved by stipulating that the monetary amount to be paid was to be calculated by reference to the value of gold as at the due date; but

(2) a modality clause merely defined the instrument of payment, with the result that following official action of this kind the creditor would only be entitled to receive so many notes as correspond to the nominal amount of the obligation.[39]

In the first case, the *lex monetae* can have no impact, for the substance of the obligation is governed solely by the law applicable to the obligation. In the second case, however, the clause merely refers to the law of the issuing State, with the result that the *lex monetae* is to be applied and the obligation could be discharged by payment in notes.

11.21 By way of illustration:

(a) A gold *value* clause may have read "The debtor undertakes to pay such sum of sterling which as at the date of payment represents the value of the quantity of gold referred to at the time of this contract." Such a clause clearly constitutes the measure or substance of the obligation, for it determines the

---

[38] The essence of a gold value clause has been clearly described as "a measuring rod or measure of liability" (*International Trustee for the Protection of Bondholders AG v The King* [1936] 3 All ER 407, 419 (CA)) or as a "measuring point or yardstick" (*New Brunswick Railway Co v British and French Trust Corp* [1939] AC 1, 30). Given that the gold value clause might necessarily involve a fluctuating or variable monetary obligation, one might have thought that such an obligation would not amount to a "sum certain" for the purposes of the Bills of Exchange Act 1882, s 3 and yet this was the result reached (admittedly without full argument or investigation) in *Syndic in Bankruptcy v Khayat* [1943] AC 507, on which see Mann (1943) 59 LQR 303. The ultimate outcome of the case is, however, probably satisfactory and is in conformity with the law of the US—*Chrysler v Renois* (1870) 43 NW 209.

[39] A requirement for payment to be made in gold coin did not affect the monetary character of the obligation—see *Feist v Société Intercommunale d'Electricité Belge* [1933] Ch 684, 702 and in *British and French Trustee Corp v The New Brunswick Railway Co* [1936] 1 All ER 13; these points remain valid notwithstanding the later decision of the House of Lords in the latter case.

extent of the debtor's obligation;[40] In such a case, the abrogation of the gold clause by the *lex monetae* has no impact upon the extent of the debtor's monetary obligation.

(b) In contrast, a gold *modality* clause might have created an obligation "to pay 100 francs in gold coin". In such a case, one would have to refer to French law as the *lex monetae*, and would find that the delivery of notes would constitute sufficient performance of the obligation.

It may be added that the distinction between the substance of an obligation and the mode of its performance is well recognised in the conflict of laws,[41] and has been applied by the Permanent Court of International Justice in a specifically monetary context.[42]

Whilst questions of contractual interpretation would necessarily arise in indi- **11.22** vidual cases, express contractual references to gold (and in particular, to the unit price of gold) would usually be treated as gold value clauses, thus defining the substance of the debtor's obligation, and protecting the creditor against the declining value of money between the date of the contract and its maturity date.[43] Thus, the Permanent Court of International Justice, with reference to a promise to pay "gold francs" said that "The treatment of the gold clause as indicating a mere modality of payment without reference to a gold standard of value, would be, not to construe, but to destroy it."[44] Under the influence of this decision, gold value clauses were found to exist where the obligation involved payment of "£100 in sterling in gold coin of the United Kingdom of or equal to the standard of fineness existing on September 1, 1928" or "£100 sterling gold coin of Great Britain of the present standard of weight or fineness".[45]

So far as the US dollar is concerned, it was at one time customary to state that **11.23** payment was to be made "in gold coin of the United States of America of or

---

[40] The specimen clause is derived from the decision in the *Case of Brazilian Loans* PCIJ Series A, No. 21 (1929) 110.

[41] See, eg, Rome Convention, Art 10(1) and (2).

[42] *Case of Serbian Loans* PCIJ Series A, No. 14 (1928–30) 32, 41.

[43] From the point just made and the issues noted in para 11.12 above, it may be said that the courts were generally slow to hold that any form of effective gold clause formed a part of a contract, but once such a clause was found to exist, then it would generally be treated as a gold value provision (as opposed to a mere modality clause).

[44] *Case of Serbian Loans* PCIJ Series A, No. 14 (1928–30) 32.

[45] See, respectively, *Feist v Société Intercommunale Belge d'Electricité* [1934] AC 161 and *The King v International Trustee for the Protection of Bondholders AG* [1937] AC 500. See also *New Brunswick Railway Co v British and French Trust Corp* [1939] AC I. It may be added that the mere words "gold Turkish pounds" were found to imply a gold value clause in *Syndic in Bankruptcy v Khayat* [1943] AC 507. This Privy Council decision on the laws of Palestine was out of step with the approach adopted by the English courts, which would have held such language to be merely descriptive, with the result that neither a gold value nor a modality clause would have been found to exist—see, eg, *Campos v Kentucky & Indiana Terminal Railway Co* [1962] 2 Ll L R 439.

equal to the standard of weight and fineness existing on . . .". The Supreme Court held this language to be a gold value clause (as opposed to a mere modality provision).[46] This view was accepted in England[47] and in many other countries.[48]

11.24 At this point, it may be of some interest to note that the English courts have been confronted with gold value clauses in relatively recent times and appear to have no difficulty with their application. In *The Rosa S,*[49] the court had to consider bills of lading which incorporated the Hague Rules of 1924; those rules provided for the liability of the carrier to be limited by reference to the gold value of the pound sterling. Since gold coins were still legal tender in this country, it remained possible to determine the gold content of one pound. Further, the relevant provisions prescribed a standard of value, as opposed to a means of payment. The limitation of liability was thus to be determined by reference to the gold (rather than the nominal) value of sterling, and the court held that one pound sterling was equivalent to £66.30. Courts in Australia and New Zealand have also had to apply gold value clauses derived from international conventions. In a cargo case, the New South Wales Court of Appeal was concerned with Articles IV and IX of the Hague Rules, which limited the carrier's liability to a sum "in pounds sterling" and that monetary unit was "to be taken to be gold value". The Court held this to be an effective gold clause, and awarded damages in Australian dollars, calculated by reference to the then prevailing price of gold, expressed in sterling.[50] Two years later, the same Court was confronted by a claim involving carriage by air, so that the limitation of liability for the benefit of the carrier fell to be determined by Article 22 of the Warsaw Convention. That Article provided that "the liability of the carrier is limited to a sum of two hundred and fifty francs per kilogramme . . . the sums referred to in this Article shall be deemed to refer to a currency unit consisting of sixty five and a half milligrammes of gold of millesimal fineness nine hundred . . . Conversions of the sums into national currency other than gold shall in the case of judicial proceedings be made according to the gold value of such currencies as at the date of judgment." The Court thus had little difficulty in

---

[46] *Norman v Baltimore & Ohio Railway Co* (1934) 294 US 240, 302; *Perry v US* (1934) 294 US 330, 336, 338.

[47] The Court of Appeal accepted this general view in *The King v International Trustee for the Protection of Bondholders AG* [1936] 3 All ER 407. The actual decision was reversed on appeal ([1937] AC 500) on the grounds that the contract was governed by US law under which gold clauses had, by this time, become unlawful.

[48] It may be observed here that the existence and effect of a gold clause is governed by the law applicable to the obligation (ie not by the *lex monetae*). The fact that the US Supreme Court treated such provisions as gold value clauses in relation to the US dollar did not impel the courts of other countries to do so, at least where the contract was not governed by US law.

[49] [1989] 1 All ER 489.

[50] *Brown Boveri (Australia) Pty Ltd v Baltic Shipping Co* [1989] 1 Lloyd's Rep 518.

applying the market value of gold as at the date of an "official" price quotation.[51] The New Zealand Court of Appeal likewise seems to have thought that Articles IV and IX of the Hague Rules created a gold value clause; however, the terms of those Articles were held to be overridden by the terms of the contract between the parties.[52] When the same case came before the Privy Council,[53] the Board cited *The Rosa S* with approval, noting that "the effect of Article IX is to make plain that what Article IV refers to is the gold value of the pound sterling and not its nominal or paper value".[54] Thus, in each case, the references to gold were held to be substantive and defined the quantum of the debtor's obligation.

D. Operation of Gold Value Clauses

As is apparent from some of the examples noted above, some gold value clauses were drafted in a fairly elaborate manner, dealing with weight, fineness, and other details.   **11.25**

In other cases, gold value clauses may have been held to exist but may have lacked the sophistication just described. In such cases, it would be necessary to ascertain the parties' intentions by reference to the circumstances prevailing at the time of the contract. Those circumstances would plainly include the status of gold within the relevant monetary system at that time. Thus a gold value clause contained in a contract entered into while this country was on the gold standard must generally be taken to refer to the "classical" definition of a gold pound as contained in the Coinage Act 1870.[55] It is difficult to imagine that the parties could have had any other standard in mind. If a gold value clause had been contracted long after the gold standard had been abandoned in this country, then it may be that the parties had in mind the gold pound of par value as declared to the International Monetary Fund.[56] It would be much more difficult   **11.26**

---

[51] *SS Pharmaceutical Co Ltd v Quantas Airways Ltd* [1991] 1 Lloyd's Rep 319.

[52] *The Tasman Discoverer* [2002] 2 Lloyd's Rep 528.

[53] *Dairy Containers Ltd v Tasman Orient Line CV* (Privy Council Appeal No. 34 of 2003, 20 May 2004).

[54] The Board also rightly observed that the Hague Regulations had been adopted in 1924 and that, given the depreciation of sterling during the intervening period, "the practical effect of Article IX has become increasingly great". In the result, however, the Board agreed that the gold value provisions could not be applied in the face of the terms expressly agreed between the parties; accordingly "the carrier's liability is limited to £5,500 sterling in ordinary or paper currency".

[55] It is believed that this is the solution which should have been reached in *Campos v Kentucky & Indiana Railroad Co* (1962) 2 Ll LR 439 and in *Lemaire v Kentucky & Indiana Railroad Co* (1957) 242 F 2d 884 on which see Mann (1963) 12 ICLQ 1005.

[56] ie under Art IV, s 1 of the original Articles of Agreement of the Fund.

to discern the parties' intentions if such a clause were contracted following the collapse of the Bretton Woods system of parities in 1971.[57] But in any event, it should be clear that the standard of value at the time of the contract will have to be given effect, for this is the reference point for ascertainment of the parties' intentions. The Permanent Court of International Justice has confirmed this rule, noting that "The engagement would be meaningless, if it referred to an unknown standard of a future day . . .".[58] It may be added that a similar problem used to arise in a legislative context, especially where legislation sought to implement international treaties referring to monetary units in gold value. Again, it was necessary to ascertain the intention of the legislation or convention by reference to the circumstances prevailing as at the date on which it was made.[59]

E. The Price of Gold

11.27   In the context of a gold value clause, a further set of difficulties could arise if, as at the date of payment, no price for gold was available or (alternatively) a number of different quotations were available.[60]

11.28   The latter state of affairs occurred between 17 March 1968 and 15 August 1971, when there existed a "two-tier" market for gold, ie a market for gold as a commodity and a market for monetary gold based on the convertibility of the US dollar at the price of $35 per ounce. In such a case, which rate should be applied in determining the amount of money payable by a debtor under the terms of a gold value clause? It appears that no English court had to address this particular point, but in the Netherlands, the Hoge Raad decided that the official rate for monetary gold should be applied, since this would ensure certainty and uniformity whenever the question arose. The opposite solution would give rise to uncertainty as to the extent of the debtor's obligation, for the price of gold *as a commodity* varied both from day to day and from place to place.[61]

---

[57] This subject has been discussed at paras 2.06–2.10 above.

[58] *Case of Brazilian Loans* PCIJ Series A (1928–30) 116.

[59] See in particular *The Rosa S* [1989] 2 WLR 162 and the decision of the Court of Appeal of New South Wales in *Brown Boveri (Australia) Pty Ltd v Baltic Shipping Co* [1989] 1 Lloyd's Rep 518. Both decisions refer to other judgments rendered in Canada, France, Italy, India, and Bangladesh.

[60] See Martha, (1985) Netherlands International LR 48, with many references to earlier articles.

[61] 14 April 1972 NJ 1972, 728; in English, 70 Int LR 445. It is believed that the decision of the Netherlands court is correct but it should be noted that other courts have (in similar contexts) adopted the commodity price of gold as the governing factor—see the decisions of the Court of Appeal in Athens, 10 January 1974, as reported by Larsen, (1975) 63 Georgetown LJ 817, 824,

Matters naturally became even more complicated with effect from 15 August **11.29** 1971 when, in consequence of the demonetisation of gold caused by the decision of the United States rendering foreign official holdings of dollars inconvertible into gold, there existed no official price for gold. The par value system created by the Bretton Woods arrangements accordingly collapsed, and from that time, gold could only be priced by reference to its value as a commodity. This, in turn, created difficulty in the context of international transport conventions, which sought to limit the carrier's liability by reference to an amount expressed (for example) in "gold francs". In some cases, domestic legislation was introduced in order to fill this gap by providing a statutory conversion rate.[62] Where, however, the municipal legislator had failed to intervene, it still remained necessary to apply any treaty or statutory provision referring to "gold francs". In such a situation, a process of construction was necessary, involving an assessment of the "official" value of gold according to the practice of the central bank in the place of payment; and in the absence of any official practice, it would be necessary to refer to the market value of gold in the place concerned. Thus, the Hamburg Court of Appeal applied the "central rate" established for a time and practised extra-legally under the Smithsonian Agreement of 18 December 1971; in other words, it sought to identify and apply an "official" rate.[63] The official rate had to be applied wherever available.[64] However, in the absence of an official rate, the gold clause can best fulfil its functions if a market rate is used.[65]

---

the Tribunal of Genoa, 6 September 1978 (*Il diritto marittimo* 1979, 91) and the Tribunal of Milan, 25 October 1976 (*Il diritto marittimo* 1978, 83). A different approach was adopted in France, where the Cour de Cassation determined that (in the absence of a legal basis for conversion) courts should obtain and apply a governmental certificate on the subject—7 March 1983, *Rev Crit* 1984, 310. It has occasionally been asserted that treaties involving monetary obligations expressed in gold currencies would come to an end once gold ceased to form the basis of these currencies, eg by virtue of Art 62 of the Vienna Convention on the Law of Treaties. However, this view is not sustainable in view of the requirement for the contracting States to perform their obligations in good faith and the decision in the *Franklin Mint* case, below.

[62] See, eg, The Carriage by Air (Sterling Equivalents) Order 1977, SI 1977/1, which is no longer in force, but which fixed the value of special drawing rights by reference to the gold content of the US dollar prior to the collapse of the Bretton Woods arrangements in 1971. In the US, the Civil Aeronautics Board issued orders to convert into dollars the gold franc amounts referred to in the Warsaw Convention on International Carriage by Air. The Supreme Court upheld this approach, on the basis that the objective of the Convention was to set down clearly defined monetary limits on the liability of a carrier; that objective would be defeated if the maximum level could fluctuate on a daily basis by reference to the changing market value of gold—see *Trans World Airlines v Franklin Mint Corp* 486 US 243 (1984), also (1984) 2 Lloyd's Rep 432. A similar approach was adopted by the Federal Supreme Court of Germany, 9 April 1987, *BGHZ* 100, 340.

[63] 2 July 1974, Versicherungsrecht 1971 933, also (1974) 9 European Transport Law 701 and Uniform LR 1975, 240. On the Smithsonian Agreement, see para 2.10 above.

[64] *Trans World Airlines v Franklin Mint Corp* 486 US 243 (1984) also [1984] 2 Lloyd's Rep 432.

[65] *SS Pharmaceutical Co Ltd v Quantas Airways Ltd* [1991] 1 Lloyd's Rep 288. See also para 11.24 above.

11.30   Whilst these issues are mainly of historical interest, the difficulties encountered during the period 1968–1978 should be noted as an instructive precedent in the context of future monetary dislocations.

F. The Place of Valuation

11.31   Finally, it is necessary briefly to discuss the spatial operation of protective clauses. Gold clauses tended not to indicate the place with reference to which the money value of the defined quantity of gold was to be ascertained. The point would clearly remain important whilst the market price of gold could fluctuate from place to place, and this gap would inevitably have to be filled by a process of contractual construction. In practical terms, the choice would lie between:

(a)   the market value of gold in the contractual place of payment;
(b)   the market value of gold in the country which issued the currency in which the obligation was expressed; and
(c)   the market value of gold in London as the principal centre for gold trading.

11.32   It would, however, be inappropriate to have regard to a "black market" rate in any particular country, for such a market exists in disregard of that country's exchange control or other restrictions;[66] as a general principle, an English court should not give extraterritorial recognition to a market whose existence is unlawful in its home country.

G. Unit of Account Clauses

11.33   With the demise of the gold clause, financial markets inevitably sought alternative means of protecting the creditor from the falling domestic purchasing power or international value of a particular currency.[67] One of the solutions—albeit adopted only in specialised fields—was the unit of account clause. The common feature of these clauses is that they are based on the notion of a "basket"; the unit is derived from averaging the value of the various constituent

---

[66] Supreme Court of Israel in *Marrache v Masri*, Gorney, *International Lawyers Convention in Israel* (Jerusalem, 1959) 309, 310.

[67] Such questions were naturally of great importance during periods of high inflation which, at the time of writing, has become less of a general concern in the developed world. The problem of the fluctuating comparative value of currencies has naturally become an enduring one since the collapse of the Bretton Woods arrangements. In a European context, the scope of such risks has been reduced by the introduction of a common currency for the eurozone Member States; in other contexts, such risks may to some extent be reduced by forward exchanges or hedging contracts.

currencies.[68] Most units of account were derived from some official method of accounting but some were privately devised. Such legal problems as might arise would generally relate to the construction of the relevant clauses, which were frequently of some complexity.

Various examples may be cited. The first unit of account used in a European Community context was the European Unit of Account (EUA). The EUA was established in 1950 in the context of the European Payments Union and its value was equated to the gold value of one US dollar (0.88867088 grammes of fine gold).[69] For a period of about ten years commencing in the early 1950s, a significant number of bond issues expressed in the EUA were sponsored by financial institutions in Europe—especially by Kredietbank in Belgium.[70] However, on 21 April 1975, the EUA was re-based by reference to a basket of currencies. On 13 March 1979, the EUA was replaced by the European Currency Unit (ECU), although this was effectively only a re-naming exercise, for the arrangements for the calculation of the ECU "basket" mirrored those which were then applicable to the EUA. All other units of account in use within the Community were subsequently abolished, and the ECU became its sole unit of account.

11.34

In subsequent years the Special Drawing Right (SDR) of the International Monetary Fund and the ECU gained popularity, in that they were based on recognised formulae enjoying broadly-based official backing, and had a value in terms of individual currencies which could be readily ascertained from published sources.[71] Although the ECU was based solely on European currencies and thus excluded the US dollar, it nevertheless proved popular for a number of debt issuers. The composition of the SDR latterly comprised only the US dollar, the French franc, the Deutsche mark, the Japanese yen and the pound sterling. In view of impending monetary union in Europe, this composition was altered, with the euro replacing the franc and the mark. Some care is necessary when

11.35

---

[68] As a result, it will be apparent that unit of account clauses are principally of value where the creditor is concerned with the comparative value of different currencies; they are less appropriate where the creditor is concerned with the *internal* purchasing power of money. This may be contrasted with index clauses, below.

[69] In its original form, the EUA thus gave rise to the question whether it involved a gold clause. The answer was probably in the affirmative, for, as noted in the text, the value of the unit was based upon the then gold value of one US dollar. The extent of the obligation was measured in gold—see note in (1962) 71 Yale LJ 1294 and Mehnert, *User's Guide to the ECU*, (Graham & Trotman, 1992) 40. The existence of a gold clause was denied by the author of the scheme, Fernand Colin (eg in *Formation of a European Capital Market*, 25) and by Blondeel (1964) 64 Col LR 995, 1005.

[70] It may be added that a number of other units of account were created within the EC framework, including the "Unit of Account" established in 1962; the "European Monetary Unit of Account" and the "European Composite Unit of Account".

[71] The ECU, of course, no longer exists—see the discussion in Ch 25 below.

contracting in terms of a unit of account of this kind; in the absence of further words of elaboration, an obligation to pay an SDR or an ECU in two years' time will involve an obligation to pay an SDR or an ECU as it exists at the time of payment.[72] In other words, the parties assume the risk that the composition of the relevant unit might change between the date on which the obligation is incurred and the date on which it falls due for performance. It is also necessary to stipulate a "fallback" position in the event that the relevant unit is abolished.[73]

11.36 Unit of account or "basket" clauses do not guarantee the absolute maintenance of values; they merely provide such relative stability as the averaging process permits, for the depreciation of any of the constituent currencies reduces the value of the total. For the investor who was reluctant to entrust his money to the possible gyrations of one currency, the unit of account perhaps offers at least a degree of protection and at least the prospect of maintaining value although—for the reasons just given—it is by no means a complete solution.

11.37 It remains briefly to note that, as a result of a number of international confe-rences, particularly those concerned with transport by sea and air, the SDR has in some cases been substituted for gold francs as a measure for valuing or limiting liability[74] although developments have by no means been uniform and, as has been seen, the gold clause continues to occupy the courts at periodic interval.[75] As far as the law of England is concerned, the law is now complicated in that no uniform legislation on this point has been enacted[76] and, characteristically, the subject has been dealt with in a somewhat piecemeal fashion. The figures may change from time to time and the point is of limited general interest; consequently, a few details may suffice to describe the posi-tion.[77] As a result, the amounts of limitation are liable to differ from the

---

[72] Although it might strictly be argued that an obligation to "pay" SDRs is not strictly a monetary obligation, the parties will in practice treat it as such, with the result that the principle stated in the text should apply.

[73] That the parties did indeed accept that performance was due in the SDR/ECU *as at the time of payment* is apparent from the terms of bond documentation in use at the time. The parties also dealt with the problems which could arise if the ECU ceased to be used as a unit of account. For an example, see the prospectus for an ECU 150,000,000 bond issue by Belgium, reproduced by Mehnert, *User's Guide to the ECU* (Graham of Trotman, 1992) 314.

[74] For discussions, see Bristow (1978) 31 LMCLQ 918 and Costabel (1979) LMCLQ 755.

[75] See the English, Australian, and New Zealand cases noted at para 11.28 above.

[76] Contrast the German Gold Conversion Act of 9 June 1980, *Official Gazette* 1980 II 721.

[77] The gold francs referred to in the Carriage by Air Act 1961 and the Warsaw Convention scheduled thereto were intended to be converted into SDRs by virtue of the Carriage by Air and Road Act 1979, s 4(1); however, s 4(1) was never brought into force and sterling was substituted for gold francs by Orders made under s 4(4) of the 1961 Act, the Order currently in force being SI 1986/1778. As regards the Carriage of Goods by Road Act 1965, s 4(2) of the 1979 Act (put into force by SI 1980/1966) substitutes SDRs for gold francs. The Carriage of Passengers by Road Act

figures adopted in other countries, and will only apply if English law governs the case in point.[78]

H. Index Clauses

It has been shown that unit of account provisions or "basket" currencies may afford some degree of protection to the creditor, but that the value and extent of that protection is by no means certain; the creditor remains exposed to the depreciation of currencies comprised in the basket. Furthermore the domestic investor may be more concerned to protect the value of his investment in terms of its *internal* purchasing power rather than its *external* value in terms of other currencies. It was therefore necessary to develop other approaches to the problem.

11.38

One solution[79] was identified in the form of the index (or cost of living) clause, which linked the amount payable to the creditor to price or other indices. As noted above, this type of provision is mainly applicable to domestic transactions because it seeks to protect the creditor against the internal depreciation of the domestic currency's purchasing power as a result of inflation. The use of clauses linking remuneration to a cost of living index was at one time popular in the context of collective wage bargaining, although they are now less frequently seen in that context.[80]

11.39

Index clauses found their way into various aspects of financial and commercial life. For example, in the United Kingdom, the Government, in March 1981, issued £1 billion of 2 per cent index-linked Treasury Stock 1996. The value of the principal on repayment was linked to the movement of the UK General Index of Retail Prices during the life of the stock. Likewise, interest payments

11.40

1974 was intended to be similarly amended by s 4(3) of the 1979 Act, but this has not yet been brought into force. The Hague Rules as amended in 1968 and scheduled to the Carriage of Goods by Sea Act 1971 and similar provisions were amended by the Merchant Shipping Act 1981, which substituted SDRs for gold; the relevant statutory instrument is SI 1983/1906.

[78] See Mann (1983) 99 LQR 376 or *Further Studies in International Law* (Oxford University Press, 1990) 270.

[79] An elaborate scheme, in some ways the forerunner of the index clause, was put forward by Alfred Marshall—Remedies for Fluctuation of General Prices, *Contemporary Review* li (1887) 355, where it is suggested that contracts could be expressed optionally in currency or in terms of a defined standard unit of purchasing power.

[80] For a judicial consideration of this type of provision in Australia, see *Australian Workers Union v Commonwealth Railway Commissions* (1933) 49 CLR 589. For a discussion of index clauses under French law, see Bayer, *A propos des clauses d'indexation: du nominalisme monétaire à la justice contractuelle* (1978) and for a more general discussion, see Rosen, *Law and Inflation* (University of Pennsylvania, 1982) ch 10.

were multiplied by the Index ratio for the month in which payment fell due.[81] In the United States, index-linking techniques were also developed in the context of annuities and the cost of fuel;[82] the English courts have recently had occasion to review a complex price adjustment provision in the context of a long-term contract for the supply of natural gas.[83]

11.41 Index clauses should in principle be valid and enforceable, unless the local legislator has restricted their application.[84] Their attraction lies in the ability of the parties to index their claim by reference to the most appropriate indicator; for example, a utility which agrees to supply electricity over a long period could link its charges to underlying increases in the cost of coal or other fuel, by reference to an appropriate set of published figures. This would provide a fairly accurate reflection of the increase in the supplier's underlying costs, thus helping to ensure that the clause meets its purpose.[85]

11.42 In practice the adoption of an index clause pre-supposes the existence and identification of a suitable index or scale, but if this is adequately defined in the contract then there should be no difficulty in applying and enforcing the provision. The enforcement of such provisions would be a matter of construction of the contract, and few issues of monetary law are likely to arise in this context; few cases appear to have arisen in practice.[86] Difficulties may arise where the parties have referred to an index which ceases to exist during the life of the contract. If the parties have failed to address that circumstance, then the court should generally imply a contractual term which refers to such successor index as most closely corresponds to the discontinued index.[87]

---

[81] A corporate loan stock with a cost of living clause was issued in 1965: *The Times Book of New Issues of Public Companies*, Vol 137 (1965) 30.

[82] On these points, see (1965) 19 Rutgers LR 345 (note) and Trigg (1958) 106 University of Pennsylvania LR 964, and see, generally, Rosen (n 80 above), 139. See also the 1973 OECD publication *Indexation of Fixed Interest Securities*, which contains materials on Finland, Germany, and Switzerland.

[83] *Esso Exploration & Production UK Ltd v Electricity Supply Board* [2004] EWHC 723 (Comm).

[84] Possible limitations on the validity and enforceability of clauses which avoid the application of the nominalistic principle are considered in Ch 12 below.

[85] In other words, there is no need to refer to a general cost of living index; it is possible to refer to an index which is referable to the specific ingredients of the contract.

[86] See *Stanwell Park Hotel Co Ltd v Leslie* (1952) 85 CLR 189. In Australia, so-called "Rise and fall clauses" were used in building contracts and gave rise to difficult questions of interpretation— see *TC Whittle Pty Ltd v T & G Mutual Life Society* (1977) 16 ALR 431 (High Court of Australia) and *Max Cooper & Sons Pty Ltd v Sydney City Council* (1980) 29 ALR 77 (Privy Council).

[87] In a slightly different context, see *Re Z* (1977) 2 NZLR 444, where the court increased an annuity payable under a will on the basis that the testator had been in breach of a moral duty by failing to foresee that the annuity might become inadequate; to deal with that point for the future, the court also imposed a cost of living clause. The decision relies upon the provisions of the New Zealand Family Protection Act 1933. For a further discussion of the general subject, see Rosen, *Law and Inflation* (University of Pennsylvania, 1982) 140–54.

I. Escalation Clauses

It is finally necessary to consider escalation clauses. As has been shown, an index **11.43**
clause involves the linking of the monetary obligation to some independent
measure of the cost of living or some other identifiable cost or commodity.
Escalation clauses are different, in the sense that they do not depend upon any
form of independent index. Instead, provision is made for the value of a
particular asset—such as the right to occupy property—to be revalued at periodic intervals by reference to prevailing market values. Escalation provisions
can be relatively complex and may provide for arbitration or expert determination in the absence of agreement between the parties. But the underlying
principles are clear and it will suffice to provide a general example of frequent
occurrence and a specific example which fell for consideration by the Privy
Council.

In the UK residential property market where long-term leasehold interests of **11.44**
ninety-nine years or more are a particular feature, ground rents have tended to
lose much of their value over the period of the lease.[88] In recent times, new leases
have therefore tended to stipulate for substantial escalations in ground rent by
way of increases of fixed amounts at periodic intervals. Such provisions do not
strike at the heart of the principle of nominalism, for the rent will still be
discharged on a pound-for-pound basis in accordance with the requirements of
the lease. Whether the figures stated in such leases will ultimately compensate
for the declining value of money is entirely a matter of speculation. Leases of
offices or other commercial premises will frequently include provision for a
periodic rent review by an appropriate expert. The purpose of such reviews is to
ensure that the level of the rent remains in line with the market. As a result, such
a review may in practical terms take account of the effects of monetary depreciation, although the point will usually not be explicitly stated. The interpretation, validity, and effect of such escalation clauses[89] are governed by the law
applicable to the contract itself; they do not in themselves involve any specific
principle of monetary law. So far as English contract law is concerned, there
should be no real obstacle to the enforcement of escalation clauses, provided

---

[88] See, eg, the position which arose in *Treseder-Griffin v Co-operative Insurance Society* [1956] 2
QB 127.
[89] For another example of this type of clause and of the judicial use of the term, see *Finland
Steamship Co Ltd v United Baltic Corp Ltd* [1980] 2 Lloyd's Rep 287. In the context of real
property, the clauses will usually be governed by the law of the country in which the premises are
situate.

that they are drafted with sufficient clarity and the intention of the parties is thereby made sufficiently clear.[90]

11.45   Yet in the absence of elaborate escalation clauses of the type which are so frequently drafted and negotiated with painstaking care, the courts will strive to enforce a long-term commercial contract in accordance with the apparent intention of the parties. The point is well illustrated by the Privy Council decision in *The Queensland Electricity Generating Board v New Hope Colleries Pty Ltd.*[91] In that case, a long-term supply contract stipulated that price variations "shall be agreed by the parties", but there was no express mechanism which dealt with the failure to agree the necessary revisions. Against the background of a long-term and elaborately prepared agreement, the Privy Council, in a judgment delivered by Sir Robin Cooke, found it unattractive to hold the agreement to be void for certainty. Rather, the parties were taken to have accepted:

> . . . implied primary obligations to make reasonable endeavours to agree on the terms of supply beyond the initial five year period and, failing agreement, and upon proper notice, to do everything reasonably necessary to procure the appointment of an arbitrator. Further, it is implicit in a commercial agreement of this kind that the terms of the new price structure are to be fair and reasonable as between the parties . . .

11.46   As the Privy Council pointed out, this had already been the position in Canada, New Zealand, and Australia for many years.[92] From the monetary law perspective, however, the importance of this case rests in the implicit recognition of monetary depreciation in relation to long-term contracts, and the corresponding need to imply a term which enables the problem to be addressed in a manner which is fair to the supplier. Furthermore, it has been noted that the

---

[90] It will be necessary to make clear both (a) the precise circumstances under which the payment provisions can be revised and (b) the manner in which the amount of the revision is to be ascertained, especially where the parties are unable to agree the required revision through negotiation. The absence of an express escalation clause was at the root of the difficulties which arose in *Staffordshire Area Health Authority v South Staffordshire Waterworks* [1978] WLR 1387. An example of a relatively simplistic escalation clause which was enforced by the Court of Appeal is offered by the decision in *Greater London Council v Connolly* [1970] 1 All ER 870. In that case, the terms of a tenancy agreement for a council house provided that "The weekly rent and other sums . . . are liable to be increased or decreased on notice being given." The court found that the condition was not void for uncertainty because it was possible to calculate the rent at any given time, even though the increase was dependent upon the whim of the landlord.

[91] [1989] 1 Lloyd's Rep 205. The decision was rendered in 1984, but was not reported in England until 1989.

[92] *Calvan v Consolidated Oil and Gas Co Ltd v Manning* [1959] SCR 253; *A-G v Barker Bros Ltd* [1976] 2 NZLR 495; *Booker Industries Pty Ltd v Wilson Parking (Qld) Pty Ltd* (1982) 56 ALJR 825. It is, however, fair to observe that the English courts have also been reluctant to hold contracts to be void on the ground of uncertainty—see *Hillas & Co Ltd v Arcos Ltd* (1932) 147 LT 503.

principle of nominalism reflects the *presumed* intention of the parties and that it can thus be set aside by means of an *express* term of the contract; the *Queensland Electricity* case demonstrates that, in an appropriate case, nominalism can also be displaced by means of an *implied* term of the contract.[93] There is a degree of theoretical difficulty with this result, for it is not easy to see how an implied term can set aside an intention which the parties are presumed to have had.[94] Nevertheless, it is difficult to deny the justice of the ultimate decision.

---

[93] It may well be that the formulation of the implied term adopted in this case would also have offered a fair solution to the difficulties which arose in the *South Staffordshire* case (n 90 above). In that case, the agreement was to apply "at all times hereafter", and the Court of Appeal's decision to imply a right of termination on reasonable notice thus sits uncomfortably with the express terms of the contract; an implied right to arbitration over the future price would not have been open to this objection.

[94] Perhaps the answer lies in the fact that the principle of nominalism reflects the presumed intention of the parties in a very *general* sense, whilst an implied term must be derived from circumstances peculiar to the *specific* contract. The latter is thus perhaps entitled to precedence over the former. Compare the discussion in paragraph 11.14 above.

12

NOMINALISM, LEGISLATION, AND PUBLIC POLICY

A. Introduction

Chapter 11 considered various means by which the application of the **12.01** nominalistic principle may be avoided or modified. It has been implicit in that discussion that there was no general consideration which might vitiate any such arrangement. But it is now appropriate to consider the matter explicitly. Is the principle of nominalism such an entrenched part of monetary law that attempts to disregard it should be viewed with suspicion and struck down by the courts? The remaining sections of this chapter will consider the possible areas of objection to clauses which seek to avoid the application of the principle.

B. The Nominalistic Principle

It appears to be accepted that the nominalistic principle as such does not of itself **12.02** invalidate gold, index, or similar protective clauses. Although the point is not directly discussed in any English decision, it is nevertheless plain that English law treats such clauses as valid.[1] This conclusion is certainly logical if it is borne

---

[1] In so far as this point relates to a gold clause, the point is implicit in the decision in *Feist v Société Intercommunale Belge d'Electricité* [1934] AC 161 (HL), where judgment was given in a manner which reflected the terms of the gold clause at issue and thus presupposed its essential validity. The decision in *Multiservice Bookbinding Ltd v Marden* [1979] Ch 84 dealt with the

in mind that—under English law—the principle of nominalism reflects the *presumed* intention of the parties; if they have clearly expressed an *actual* intention to the contrary, then the latter should clearly prevail. It may seem curious that the principle of nominalism, which lies at the heart of monetary law, can be so lightly set aside by the contracting parties in any individual case but the English law approach to the principle permits of no other conclusion.[2] In other words, there is no room for the argument that the principle of nominalism constitutes a mandatory rule of English law which can override the wishes of the parties.

12.03 The same position would appear to apply in other countries, even where nominalism has been placed on a statutory basis. Thus, in France, where the principle is enshrined in Article 1895 of the Code Civil, the application of nominalism is *not* mandatory law but will give way to a contrary intention of the parties.[3] As a result, gold and similar clauses were generally upheld by the French courts.

12.04 It follows from this analysis that the nominalistic principle does not have the quality of mandatory law which can override the expressed intentions of the creditor and the debtor.

C. Legal Tender Legislation

12.05 The fact that legal tender legislation provided for payment in *convertible* money[4]—in the sense that it was convertible into gold—did not vitiate protective clauses of the type here under discussion.[5] There is no need to dwell on this subject, given that in modern times all legal tender is inconvertible in the sense just described. It is thus possible immediately to move on to a consideration of this subject in the context of more modern legal tender legislation.

---

subject from the viewpoint of public policy rather than the nominalistic principle. The case is therefore discussed at para 12.13 below.

[2] The ability of the parties to contract out of the principle has occasionally been said to undermine the soundness of nominalism generally—see Eckstein in Bernd von Maydell (ed) *Geldschuld und Geldwert* (Beck, 1974) 60–74.

[3] The main decision is Cass Civ, 27 June 1957, D 1957, 649, see also 4 December 1962, *Clunet* 1963, Bull 1963: No 516. Article 1895 is reproduced at para 9.12 above.

[4] ie paper money subjected to the gold standard.

[5] See the concluding remarks of Lord Russell in *Feist v Société Intercommunale Belge d'Electricité* [1934] AC 161, 174. It may be added that the statement in the text was formerly clouded by provisions such as the Coinage Act 1870, s 6 and the Exchange Control Act 1947, s 2; the latter provision might have prohibited the enforcement of gold coin (or modality) clauses, although it should not have affected the enforcement of gold value provisions. But both of these sections have now been repealed, and it is thus unnecessary to pursue this aspect. The point is fully considered in the First, Second, and Third Editions of this work.

The question whether protective clauses are invalidated by the issue of **12.06**
incovertible paper money, ie the introduction of fiat money or compulsory
tender, has caused rather more difficulty. So far as English law is concerned,
it cannot be doubted that gold value clauses remained valid and enforceable
notwithstanding the issue of incovertible paper money initiated by the Gold
Standard (Amendment) Act 1931—this point is apparent from the House of
Lords' decision in *Feist v Société Intercommunale Belge d'Électricité*.[6] It has been
pointed out that the gold value clause in that case was upheld notwithstanding
the provisions of the Currency and Bank Notes Act 1928.[7] But there is nothing
in the 1928 Act which can be said to invalidate a gold or other protective clause,
either expressly or by necessary implication.

In the United States, a number of State courts had held gold and silver value **12.07**
clauses to be invalid by implication, in that the legislation of Congress had made
inconvertible greenbacks legal tender; contractual provisions undermining the
legal tender legislation had necessarily to be invalid.[8] This stance was, however,
reversed by the Supreme Court decisions in *Bronson v Rodes* and *Butler v Horwitz*[9]
upholding contractual provisions of this kind, but only on the basis that they
constituted an obligation to deliver a certain weight of gold.[10]

Shortly after the two Supreme Court decisions, the French Cour de Cassation **12.08**
decided to follow the first line of authority, holding that legal tender legislation introduced in August 1870 invalidated all protective clauses (whether referring to gold, foreign exchange, or otherwise). The monetary laws in question
were "d'ordre public" and, thus, mandatory in their application before the
French courts. As a result, a creditor could not refuse payment in paper money
in the amount which the law deemed to be equivalent to the nominal value of
the debt.[11] The same principle operated to strike down index or commodity
linked clauses if they were intended to protect the creditor against the depreciation in the value of money—thus defeating the application of legal tender rules
and the nominalistic principle—but not if there was some other, genuine

---

[6] [1934] AC 161. The 1931 Act was repealed by the Statute Law (Repeals) Act 1986, but the
principle of inconvertibility does, of course, remain.
[7] See Gutteridge (1935) 51 LQR 115.
[8] See the references in Dawson, "Gold Clause Decisions" (1935) 33 Mich LR 647, 674.
[9] (1868) 7 Wall (74 US) 229 and 258.
[10] These decisions were rejected on the basis that the gold clause did not affect the monetary
character of the obligation—see *Nortz v US* (1934) 294 US 317 and *Norman v Baltimore & Ohio
Railway Co* (1934) 294 US 240 302. Nevertheless, the early decisions were important in that they
established the essential validity of the gold clause.
[11] Cass Civ, 11 February 1873, S 1873, 1, 97—"le créancier ne peut légalement se refuser à
recevoir en paiement un papier de crédit auquel la loi a attribué une valeur obligatoirement
équivalent à celle des espèces métalliques".

economic reason for including the clause.[12] However, this reasoning was founded purely upon domestic considerations, with the result that the mandatory rule applied only to domestic payments made between French nationals within France; it did not apply to cross-border payments.[13]

12.09   However that may be, all of these decisions were swept away by a revolutionary decision of the Cour de Cassation in 1957.[14] In a case concerned with a loan of French francs granted by a corn merchant to a farmer and repayable by amounts based on the price of wheat, the court held that:

(a)   the relevant contractual provisions could not be struck down on ground of "ordre public".[15] It was quite legitimate for the parties to agree provisions which protected the overall purchasing power of the lender's money by reference to the price of a particular commodity—in other words, indexation clauses were in principle valid under French law;

(b)   protective clauses could not be held to be a danger to the stability of monetary values, because their likely effect in this area was too uncertain;[16]

(c)   the invalidity of protective clauses could not be derived from legal tender legislation, since this had nothing to do with the intrinsic purchasing power of money.

12.10   Against that background, gold value clauses and foreign currency obligations have subsequently been held to be valid and enforceable, both in an international and in an entirely domestic context.[17] The position is now governed by legislation, rather than judicial decision.

---

[12] In other words, the clause was only struck down if the parties had an "intention monétaire" as opposed to an "intention économique". The distinction is neatly made in Cass Civ, 24 July 1939, *GdT* 3 February 1940; 22 November 1951, *Gaz Pal* 1951, 2 395, on which see note at (1952) 65 Harv LR 1459. In a clause requiring the payment of a set minimum sum with indexing provisions designed only to increase (and never to decrease), that sum would offend the rule—Cass Civ, 15 November 1950, S 1951, 1, 131. On the whole subject, see Vasseur (1955) 4 ICLQ. 315; (1955) 20 Tulane LR 75, and Levy (1966) 16 Amer Univ LR 35. The approach adopted by the French courts in this area was apparently mirrored in Greek judicial practice—see Ligeropoulos (1955) 8 *Revue Hellénique de droit international* 20, 22.

[13] Cass Req, 7 June 1920, S 1920, I, 193 (*Compagnie d'Assurance La New York v Deschamps*).

[14] Cass Civ, 27 June 1957 (*Guyot v Praquin*).

[15] It will be apparent that there is an unavoidable overlap between the material discussed in the present section and under "Public Policy", para 12.12 below.

[16] The Supreme Court of Israel likewise took the view that protective clauses could not be invalidated on this ground, because the expert evidence as to the inflationary or prejudicial effect on the economy was uncertain and conflicting—see *Rosenbaum v Asher, Selected Judgments of the Supreme Court of Israel*, Vol ii (1954–8), 10 and *Becher v Biderman* Jerusalem Post, 30 June 1963.

[17] Gold clauses: Cass Civ, 4 December 1986, *Clunet* 1963, 751 with note by Goldman, 26 November 1963, Sem Jur, 1964 13, 652 or Bull 1963, I No. 516 (*Rolland v Fournet*). Foreign currency liabilities: Cass Civ, 10 May 1966, *Clunet* 1967, 90 with note by Goldman; 17 January 1961, Bull Cass Civ 1961, I, 32.

Although they occurred in different periods, it may be observed that the **12.11**
American and the French experiences in this context were somewhat similar; an
early determination that protective clauses were inconsistent with legal tender
legislation, coupled with a later (and dramatic) reversal of that view. In this
context, the English courts have not considered the point in a direct manner,
but such authority as exists appears to confirm that protective clauses cannot be
regarded as inconsistent with domestic legal tender legislation. An Australian
court, however, has declined to enforce a gold clause on the grounds that the
debt could be discharged by payment in notes pursuant to the provisions of the
Commonwealth Bank Act—thus impliedly disregarding the gold clause because
of its inconsistency with legal tender legislation.[18]

D. Public Policy

If domestic legal tender legislation will not generally operate to invalidate **12.12**
protective clauses, then are they liable to be struck down on more general public
policy grounds? So far as English law is concerned, questions of public policy
were not explicitly raised in the *Feist* case,[19] but the award of judgment in favour
of the creditor necessarily implies that there was no public policy impediment to
their enforcement. The point was more explicitly addressed by the High Court
of Australia in a domestic case decided in 1952,[20] when the Court noted that the
index clause involved a measure of the substantive liability of the debtor, as
opposed to the mode of performance. In other words, one had to ascertain the
measure of the liability before one became concerned with issues touching legal
tender legislation and the mode of discharge. The Court observed that there was
"no principle of law preventing parties adopting a fixed figure as the primary
monetary expression of a liability and their proceeding to effect a substantive
variation of the liability by providing that more or less money must be actually
paid according as index numbers evidence a variation of price levels. That is
only a method of measuring the actual liability contracted for." It is submitted
that this analysis is plainly right, in the sense that no public policy issue can arise
in construing the contract and seeking to ascertain the quantum of the liability
in accordance with its terms.[21]

---

[18] *Jolly v Mainka* (1934) 49 CLR 242.
[19] *Feist v Société Intercommunale Belge d'Electricité* [1934] AC 161 (HL).
[20] *Stanwell Park Hotel Co Ltd v Leslie* [1952] 85 CLR 189, 200.
[21] The views of Lord Denning MR in *Treseder-Griffin v Co-operative Insurance Society* [1956] 2
QB 127 must be noted. At least in a domestic context, he was strongly inclined to the view that
gold clauses were contrary to public policy, since these might undermine the credibility and
standing of sterling and might thus have inflationary consequences. It is submitted that this view
cannot be supported, on the grounds that issues affecting the money supply, inflation, and related

12.13   With these points in mind, it is satisfactory to note that in *Multiservice Bookbinding v Marden*,[22] Browne-Wilkinson J (as he then was) rejected the submission that "an index-linked money obligation is contrary to public policy". In that case, an English mortgage included the clause that "moneys hereby secured shall be increased or decreased proportionately . . . if the rate of exchange between the Swiss Franc and the pound sterling shall vary by more than 3 per cent from the rate of 12–07 francs to £1". Whilst a mortgage could be unenforceable to the extent to which its terms were unfair and unconscionable, the mere addition of an index clause did not by itself have this effect.[23] The judge's unqualified rejection of the public policy argument is to be welcomed under these circumstances;[24] the court also held that it had no jurisdiction to afford equitable relief merely because sterling has depreciated and the debtors would suffer hardship as a result. This line of reasoning was subsequently adopted by Peter Gibson J, who held that building societies could grant mortgages which carried a rate of interest which varied by reference to the retail price index.[25]

12.14   It may be added that index clauses have received a mixed reception in other jurisdictions. The British Columbia Court of Appeal has decided that an index clause in a mortgage did not constitute an unfair or unconscionable bargain or a clog on the equity of redemption.[26] In the United States, courts have refused to apply index clauses where these were seen to inflate the amounts payable under the agreement and thus to contravene local usury laws which limit the absolute

---

matters are political issues which thus fall outside the scope of the judicial function—in this context, see Goodhart [1956] 72 LQR 311; Mann [1957] 73 LQR 181; Unger [1957] 20 MLR 260; Yale (1956) CLJ 169; Hirschberg [1970] Israel LR 155.

[22] [1979] Ch 84.

[23] As the judge pointed out, it would have been difficult to reject the concept of index-linking, given that the Government had issued index-linked savings bonds and certain legislation also made provision for indexation—see, eg, Taxation of Chargeable Gains Tax Act 1992, s 53, which provides for indexation of base values for CGT purposes.

[24] A similar approach is adopted by the US Uniform Foreign-Money Claims Act, s 4(c) which specifically sanctions index clauses by reference to foreign currencies. It provides that a monetary claim "is neither usurious nor unconscionable because the agreement on which it is based provides that the amount of the debtor's obligation to be paid in the debtor's money, when received by the creditor, must equal a specified amount of the foreign money of the country of the creditor". It will, however, be apparent that the provision only explicitly allows for an index clause which enables the creditor to protect himself by reference to the value of his "home" currency. In France, contracts denominated in a foreign currency but concluded in a purely domestic context have been held to contribute a form of indexation which contravened ordinances passed in the 1950s—see Gold, *Legal Effects of Fluctuating Exchange Rates* (IMF, 1990) 379, discussing the decision in *de Brancovan v Mme Galitzine* Rec Dalloz Sirey No 8.

[25] *Nationwide Building Society v Registry of Friendly Societies* [1983] 3 All ER 926.

[26] *Commonwealth Savings Plan Ltd v Triangle "C" Cattle Co Ltd* British Columbia, Court of Appeal.

rate of interest payable.[27] The French Cour de Cassation has upheld indexation clauses on the basis that they are not inconsistent with the principle of nominalism.[28]

E. Special Legislation

There thus remains only one possibility of invalidating gold and other protect- **12.15**
ive clauses, namely by means of express legislation passed for that purpose. This method has been resorted to in this country when, for whatever reason, it was desired to ensure the strictest observation of the nominalistic principle. The absence of such legislation at the present time is further proof, if such be needed, that protective clauses are currently to be regarded as valid under English law.

But statutory attempts to reinforce nominalism have been made from time to **12.16**
time and enjoy a respectable antiquity. As early as 1352[29] it was made an offence to give or to receive any coined gold or silver money for a value in excess of its current or nominal value. During the Bank Restriction Period, this legislation prevented traders from quoting openly two prices for commodities, one for payment in guineas and the other for payment in paper; however, the practice existed in secret and it was usual to buy guineas for paper at more than face value. Two obscure men were prosecuted for this offence, but were ultimately acquitted.[30] The effect of this decision was, however, promptly reversed by Parliament, which prohibited any "device, shift or contrivance" involving the payment or receipt of gold coin for a value in excess of its legal tender or face value.[31] These enactments, whilst of some historical interest, have long since been repealed[32] and have not subsequently re-appeared in this country. But

---

[27] See, eg, the Pennsylvanian decision in *Olwine v Torrens* (1975) 344 A 2d 665 and the decision of the Supreme Court of Tennessee in *Aztec Properties Inc v Union Planters National Bank of Memphis* (1975) 530 SW 2d 756. These decisions are difficult to defend in so far as they relate to the principal (rather than the interest) element of the loans concerned, for it necessarily means that the court has to regard the indexation clause as a disguised form of interest—a tenuous construction. In the latter case, the court emphasised that there was no objection to indexation clauses in the context of non-interest bearing obligations, such as wages, salaries, and rental obligations, where they formed a part of normal business practice. For a general discussion on the law in the US, see 90 ALR 3d 763.

[28] Cass Civ 1, 27 June 1957.

[29] Statute 25 Edn III Ch 12, re-enacted by the Statute 5 & 6 Edw VI, ch 19.

[30] *De Yonge's Case* (1811) 14 East 403. The case gave rise to debates in the House of Commons on 5 April and 9 July 1811, *Hansard* xix 723 and xx 881.

[31] 51 Geo III ch 127 (24 July 1811); 52 Geo III, ch 50 and 56 Geo III, ch 68 (Lord Liverpool's Act of 1816).

[32] By 2 & 3 Will IV ch 34, s 1; Coinage Act 1870, s 20; and Statute Law Revision Act 1873.

many countries[33] felt impelled by monetary disturbances to invalidate gold and other protective clauses by legislation. Most notably, the United States nullified gold clauses through the Joint Resolution of Congress dated 5 June 1933, which applied to all obligations requiring payment of US dollars "in gold or a particular kind of coin or currency".[34] The Joint Resolution required that the discharge of obligations in the United States had to be effected in US dollars, and this was construed so as to render unenforceable any obligation or option to pay in a foreign currency which accompanied a gold clause.[35] More than forty years later, following the demonetisation of gold, the Resolution was repealed in respect of future obligations by an Act of 28 October 1977,[36] thus bringing to an end a period during which the condemnation of gold and similar clauses seemed to be almost an article of faith in the United States.[37]

12.17   German law has also long prohibited value maintenance provisions which have the effect of denying the principle of nominalism. Section 3 of the Currency Act (*Währungsgesetz*) provided that:

> Monetary obligations denominated in a currency other than Deutsche mark require the permission of the competent authority. This also applies to monetary obligations whose amount in Deutsche mark is to be determined by the exchange rate of another currency or by the price of an amount of fine gold or by other goods and services.

12.18   This statutory defence of the niminialistic principle applied only to domestic contracts and it was in any event repealed upon the introduction of the euro.[38] However, Germany continued its defence of nominalism by introducing an Act on the Rules for Prices. Section 2 provides that:

---

[33] For a survey of the law in 13 countries in the 1950s, see the material collected by Norway in the *Case of Certain Norwegian Loans (France v Norway)* in the International Court of Justice: *Pleadings* I, 491.

[34] The terms of the Joint Resolution plainly applied only to gold clauses affecting obligations in US dollars, yet the Supreme Court of Tennessee applied the Resolution in the context of an index clause—see *Aztec Properties Inc v Union Planters National Bank of Memphis* (1975) 530 5F 2d 756. The decision is unacceptable.

[35] For the decisions of the US Supreme Court in this area, see *John M Perry v US* (1935) 294 US 330; *F Eugene Nortz v US* (1935) 294 US 317; *Norman v Baltimore & Ohio Railway Co* (1934) 294 US 240; *Guaranty Trust Company of New York v Berryman Henwood* (1939) 307 US 247; and *Bethleham Steel Co v Zurich General Accident Insurance Co Ltd* (1939) 307 US 265.

[36] Public Law 95-147, s 3(c).

[37] A law of 31 December 1974 had lifted the prohibition (created by the Gold Reserve Act of 1934) on dealings in gold. However, that legislation did *not* have the effect of an implied repeal of the Joint Resolution—*The Equitable Life Assurance v Grosvenor* 582 F 2d 1279 (1978), affirming without opinion (1976) 426 F Supp 2d 67. For decisions of State courts to similar effect, see *Southern Capital Corp v Southern Pacific Co* 568 F 2d 590 (1978); *Feldman v Great Northern Railway* (1977) 428 F Supp 979; *Henderson v Mann Theaters Corp* (1977) 135 Cal Rep 266.

[38] See Gesetz zur Einführung des Euro, 9 June 1998, Bundesgesetzblatt 1998, Pt I, p 1242 (Articles 9 and 13).

The amount of monetary obligations must not be defined immediately and automatically by the price or the value of other goods or services that are not comparable with the goods or services that are the subject of the contract. The Federal Ministry of Economics may on request grant exemptions if payments have to be made on a long-term basis if specific reasons of competition justify a value maintenance provision . . . Financial and capital market transactions . . . remain exempt from the prohibition of indexation. Likewise, contracts between merchants residing in Germany with parties residing abroad remain exempt from the prohibition.

The provision would appear to represent a matter of national policy and would therefore have to be applied even if the contract at hand were governed by a foreign system of law.[39] It must, however, be very doubtful whether Germany retained the national legislative competence to introduce a rule of this kind. Questions touching the principle of nominalism are an integral part of the monetary or currency law, and sovereignty in such matters was ceded to the Community upon the creation of the single currency.[40] The validity of this rule is therefore highly questionable,[41] but as yet, there is no case law on the subject.

It is not now necessary to embark upon a detailed consideration of the different types of legislation which were directed at gold and other protective clauses,[42] but it is appropriate to consider three points of a general character which might well recur and are in any event of broader interest. In particular: (a) what is the effect of the abrogating legislation in point of time; (b) what is the territorial extent of such legislation; and (c) to what extent are courts sitting in other States obliged or entitled to give effect to that legislation?

Effect in point of time

What are the consequences of the abrogating legislation in point of time? Are protective clauses prohibited for the future only? Or are they invalidated even if the relevant contract pre-dates the legislation? Questions of this kind plainly depend upon the terms of the legislation in question. It is therefore difficult to lay down any general rule, but in some jurisdictions there may be a presumption against retrospective legislation and this is reflected in one of the leading cases on gold clauses.[43] If gold clauses were abrogated with retrospective effect, then it

12.19

12.20

12.21

---

[39] ie its application would be mandatory for the purposes of Art 7(2) of the Rome Convention.
[40] On the general subject of sovereignty and the euro, see Ch 31 below.
[41] See Grundmann, *Münchener Kommentar zum Burgerlichen Gesetzbuch*, Vol 2a, para 70.
[42] For a fuller discussion, see the Fifth Edition of this work, 176–8. The legislation passed in various continental jurisdictions is considered by von Hecke, *International Encyclopaedia of Comparative Law* (Brill, 1972) ch 36, para 36-9.
[43] *New Brunswick Railway Co v British & French Trust Corp* [1939] AC 1. The House of Lords apparently decided the case on the basis that a 1937 Canadian Statute dealing with Gold Clauses

was suggested in the same case[44] that the creditor might thereby become entitled to take immediate action for money had and received; it must respectfully be stated that this suggestion is entirely without foundation. However, even if there existed any legal basis for such actions, they could not lead to an indirect enforcement of the gold clause but, in accordance with the principle of nominalism, would merely secure to the creditor the repayment of the sum of money paid by him, ie they would give him what he was entitled to under the contract from which the gold clause had been abrogated.

Territorial extent

12.22 Courts sitting in the country in which abrogating legislation has been passed will invariably have to give effect to that legislation, for it will be of mandatory application, regardless of the system of law which governs the gold or other protective clause in question.[45] But it remains necessary to determine certain matters relating to the territorial scope of the legislation, for example, (a) does it apply solely to obligations in the domestic currency, or does it extend to foreign money obligations; and (b) does it apply to obligations which are to be paid or collected anywhere, or only to those payable within the country concerned?

12.23 Once again, these issues will turn upon the terms of the legislation itself. However, given that statutory rules abolishing protective clauses were generally introduced with a view to safeguarding the national economy and currency, it could usually be assumed that such statutory provisions did not apply to foreign money obligations.[46] Equally, given that the abolition of protective clauses was designed to protect the currency, it could not be assumed that the relevant statutory provisions were intended only to apply to domestic transactions. These two propositions are borne out by the Joint Resolution of Congress, which made it clear that it applied only to obligations in US dollars; however, it was also made clear that it applied regardless of the nationality of the parties, and whether or not payment was to be made within the United States.[47]

---

did not have retrospective effect—see in particular pp 26, 29, and 34. The House of Lords placed such a narrow interpretation on the Statute of 1937 that the Canadian Parliament passed the Gold Clauses Act 1938, which largely nullified the effect of the decision.

[44] At 24.

[45] cf Article 7(2) of the Rome Convention which has been discussed at para 4.21.

[46] See, eg, Supreme Court of Romania, 29 September 1925, *Zeitschrift für Ostrecht*, 1925, 600.

[47] *Compania de Inversiones v Industrial Mortgage Bank of Finland* (1935) 269 NY 22, 198 NE 617, cert denied (1936) 1297 US 705. It was suggested in this case that courts in the US would have to give effect to the Joint Resolution even though the relevant dollar obligation was governed by a foreign system of law. In view of the essential public policy imperatives which underlie legislation of this kind, it is submitted that this view is plainly correct, although it was criticised by Nussbaum, *Money in the Law, National and International* (The Press Foundation, 2nd edn, 1950)

External courts

Should an external court give effect to abrogating legislation in another State? **12.24** This type of question can give rise to very difficult conflict of law issues, both in the present, very specific context and in much broader fields.[48] But it will generally be necessary for the external court to consider three questions for this purpose, namely:

(1) As a conflict of laws question, is the foreign law applicable at all? If the contractual obligation is governed by the laws of the country in which the abrogating legislation was passed, then it should in principle be applied by the external court.[49] However, if the obligation is governed by the laws of any other jurisdiction, then the abrogating legislation should be disregarded, since it does not form a part of the law which governs the substance of the obligation.[50] In this context it must be remembered that legislation of this type cannot be applied by a foreign court merely on the grounds that it forms a part of the *lex monetae*.[51]

(2) If the abrogating legislation does form a part of the law which governs the obligation, then it must be asked whether the abrogating legislation applied to the particular case in hand. In other words, does it purport to have extra-territorial effect in the circumstances which the external court has to consider?[52]

(3) If the tests stated at (1) and (2) above are met, then the external court should give effect to the abrogating provision *unless* the private international law of the forum refuses to recognise them. It is submitted that conflict of law rules would not generally provide a basis for refusing to recognise the abrogating legislation.[53] On the contrary, policy considerations

---

436. In similar vein, the American legislation restricting dealings in gold was enforced even as against foreigners holding gold outside the US—*Übersee Finanz Corp v Rosen* 83 F 2d 225 (CCA 2d 1936), cert denied (1936) 298 US 679.

[48] On the general problem, see Mann, "Statutes and the Conflict of Laws" (1972–1973) 46 BYIL 117.

[49] Thus, where an issue of bonds was governed by New York law, the English courts were required to give effect to the American legislation which abrogated the gold clause: *R v International Trustee for the Protection of Bondholders AG* [1937] AC 500.

[50] Article 10(1)(a) of the Rome Convention. In *Mount Albert Borough Council v Australian Temperance and General Mutual Life Assurance Society Ltd* [1938] AC 224, the Privy Council was concerned with bonds governed by the laws of New Zealand, although the place of payment was Victoria. On this basis alone, the Privy Council should have held that the Victorian Financial Emergency Acts (reducing the amount of interest payable on certain obligations) could not affect the bonds, for they did not form a part of the system of law which governed the obligation.

[51] On the scope of the *lex monetae* principle, see Ch 13 below.

[52] This was the basis upon which the Privy Council in fact decided the *Mount Albert* case mentioned in n 50 above—as a matter of statutory interpretation, the Victorian legislation was not intended to apply for the protection of borrowers established outside Victoria itself.

[53] On this point, see para 13.16 below.

would generally lead to the conclusion that effect should be given to the abrogating provision, consistently with the duty to recognise the monetary sovereignty of the legislating State.[54]

F. Legislative Policy

12.25   It remains to mention a few points of legislative policy surrounding protective clauses. Whilst contractual gold clauses are now effectively extinct, the experience of them remains very instructive in this area. It has been seen that they were normally adopted in an effort to preserve the real value of the creditor's claim. Clauses of this type were broadly left intact during periods of monetary stability, when it was unnecessary to invoke them in any material way; they would then be abrogated at precisely the point in time at which they might otherwise have begun to serve their purpose.

12.26   This state of affairs is no doubt unfair to the creditor, who is deprived of a means of protection which he had negotiated for himself. Equally, however, the widespread use of indexation or similar protective clauses would no doubt lead to undesirable social disparities.[55] Furthermore, although economists may not be unanimous on the point, there exists much support for the view that index clauses are liable to promote inflationary tendencies.[56] It seems to follow that there is a choice to be made between (on the one hand) the protection of the creditor and the validity of the bargain which he has made and (on the other) the avoidance of social disharmony which might flow from the continued enforcement of protective clauses. Since these matters fall to be considered at times of monetary dislocation or disturbance, it is perhaps unsurprising that the legislator prefers the (perceived) general good over the need to respect private rights.

---

[54] It was periodically suggested that legislation of this type should not be given effect by foreign courts in the light of its public (or political) character. However, this overlooks the fundamental point that the courts must recognise the effect of foreign public laws, even if they will not positively enforce them. Further, courts in Germany and Belgium have specifically rejected this particular line of argument: OLG Düsseldorf, 26 September 1934, *IPRspr* 1934 No 936; Cour de Bruxelles, 4 February 1936, Pas 1936 II 52.

[55] This was emphasised by the Supreme Court in *Norman v Baltimore & Ohio Railroad Co* (1934) 294 US 240, 315 where, with reference to the constitutional validity of the 1933 Joint Resolution, the Court noted that "it requires no acute analysis or profound economic inquiry to disclose the dislocation of the domestic economy which would be caused by such a disparity of conditions in which, it is insisted, those debtors under gold clauses should be required to pay $1.69 in currency, while respectively receiving their taxes, rates, charges and prices on the basis of $1 of that currency".

[56] The disagreement between economists as to the effect of indexing was one of the reasons which led the court in *Multiservice Bookbinding Ltd v Marden* [1979] Ch 84, 104 to refuse to hold index clauses to be contrary to public policy. Parliament has not felt it necessary to prohibit such clauses, no doubt because their use has not taken root in this country.

Yet it is a curious fact that no legislator can hope to eliminate protective clauses **12.27** altogether. The 1933 Joint Resolution of Congress may have abrogated gold clauses, but it did not prevent parties from protecting themselves against monetary depreciation in other ways (for example, through the use of index clauses, or by contracting in terms of a foreign currency or even in terms of some commodity which was not caught by the prohibition).

Does it follow that legislators should abandon attempts to prohibit protective **12.28** clauses, given that any legislation cannot be comprehensive and may merely drive contracting parties to revise their arrangements in a manner falling outside the new rules? This is not an easy question, and under current conditions it is perhaps not urgent to find an answer. But if indexation provisions should again become common, then it is suggested that the legislator should not interfere with them. Savings and investments are generally felt to serve the national interest; it would be disreputable for a government to encourage investment, only to strike down one of the key terms at the point at which the investor requires the protection afforded by it. Likewise, it must be recognised that inflationary tendencies cannot be resisted by a purely legal armoury and, indeed, the law may well be a quite ineffectual weapon for these purposes.

In conclusion, it is submitted that the legislator should arrive at a deliberate **12.29** policy decision about protective clauses in times of economic stability and should abide by that decision in times of crisis. Given that many arguments about the merits of index clauses are of an economic (rather than a legal) character, it is inappropriate for the judiciary to usurp the role of the legislator in this field; consequently, they should generally uphold the terms of the agreed bargain.

13

NOMINALISM, PRIVATE INTERNATIONAL LAW, AND THE *LEX MONETAE* PRINCIPLE

A. Introduction

It has been noted elsewhere[1] that, so far as English law is concerned, obligations expressed in sterling or in a foreign currency are now to be treated on broadly the same footing. This, however, should not be taken to imply that private international law has no role to play in the field of monetary obligations.[2] This point, should, in many ways, be obvious. For instance, many contracts governed by English law will include obligations expressed in currencies other than sterling, and a description of a foreign currency obligation inevitably rests to some extent upon the law of the issuing country which defines the monetary system. In such cases, it will invariably be necessary to distinguish between the scope and functions of the law applicable to the contract (on the one hand) and the *lex monetae* (on the other). Equally, contracts involving sterling obligations may be governed by a foreign legal system, in which event a converse set of questions will arise.

13.01

The present chapter will accordingly consider the role of the law of the currency and a number of private international law questions.

13.02

---

[1] See para 1.61 above. For a very clear analysis of the *lex monetae* principle from a New York law perspective, see Gruson, "The Scope of the Lex Monetae in International Transactions: A United States Perspective" in Giovanoli (ed) *International Monetary Law: Issues for the New Millennium* (Oxford University Press, 2000).

[2] Ample evidence of this statement has already been provided in Ch 4 above.

B. The *Lex Monetae* Principle

13.03   When on the strength of the principles considered earlier in this work[3] the money of a particular currency system has been found to be due by the debtor, the substance of the obligation is in general clearly fixed and no further comment is required. If, for instance, it appears that an English seller has contracted with a French buyer by reference to a price expressed in euros, the contract price is not affected at all by the fact that the comparative values of sterling and the euro have fluctuated against each other between the date of the contract and the date on which payment falls due; in the absence of an express provision dealing with the point, the external value of the euro is simply not relevant to the obligations of the parties.

13.04   In view of the universal recognition of nominalism in all its aspects,[4] the proposition just stated cannot be open to any serious doubt. The units of account referred to in a monetary obligation are defined by the law of the issuing State and—where there has been a change in the domestic unit of account—by the "recurrent link" rule adopted by that State. Money, being a creature of the law, is regulated by the State; in particular, it is the State which decides which notes and coins are to constitute legal tender for debts expressed in its currency, and the nominal value which is to be ascribed to them. As each State exercises these sovereign powers over its own currency[5] it must be law of the currency (*lex monetae*) which determines whether particular notes or coins have the character of "money" and, if so, the nominal value to be attributed to them.[6] What constitutes 10,000 Swiss francs must be exclusively determined by Swiss law; there is no other law in the world which would explain the meaning of that denomination and which would lay down whether and for what nominal amount certain notes and coins are legal tender for obligations payable in Swiss francs. One therefore arrives at the rule that the law of the currency determines which chattels are legal tender of the currency referred to, to what extent they are legal tender and how, in the case of a currency alteration, sums expressed in

---

[3] See Chs 5 and 6 above, dealing with the interpretation of monetary obligations.

[4] See generally the discussion in Ch 9 above.

[5] In the context of a monetary union, this sovereign power is necessarily delegated by means of a treaty to a common institution or body. However, the currency continues to derive its ultimate legitimacy from an exercise of monetary sovereignty by the constituent States. Consequently, the existence of a monetary union may affect the practicalities of the matters about to be discussed, but it does not detract from the general theory.

[6] Economists have likewise noted that in the absence of some complete catastrophe, a monetary system must be continuous and that in the event of a substitution, there must be a clear numerical relationship between the former and the new unit—see J.M. Keynes, *A Treatise on Money*, Vol I (Macmillian, 1930) 5.

the former currency are to be converted into the new one.[7] It also thus becomes both possible and necessary to distinguish between the role of the governing law of the obligation and the role of the *lex monetae*. The law which governs the obligation must determine to which currency the parties intended to refer;[8] but once that process has been completed, the law of the issuing State thus identified must be applied in order to define the currency itself and the monetary system of which it forms a part.[9] Of course, a distinction of this type is relatively easy to state but it is much harder to define the precise boundary lines. In particular, it must not be overlooked that, at least so far as English law is concerned, the nominalistic principle owes its existence to the law which governs the obligation,[10] rather than to the *lex monetae*.

But whatever the difficulties may be, it is submitted that the *lex monetae*   **13.05** principle described above enjoys almost universal support; it is also consistent with customary international law.[11] It is true that some dissentient views have occasionally been expressed; in particular, it has been suggested that legal tender legislation has a purely territorial scope and thus cannot be applied by foreign courts;[12] alternatively, it has been suggested that foreign monetary laws are of a public character which are thus incapable of recognition by a domestic tribunal.[13] If such views were accepted, then alterations affecting a domestic monetary

---

[7] This statement is consistent with the principle of nominalism which was set out at para 9.03 above. In the light of the nominalistic principle, it may be added that the comparative metallic or functional value of the old and the new money are quite immaterial for these purposes.

[8] eg if the parties have referred to "dollars" the contract must be interpreted in accordance with the rules of construction provided by the governing law in order to decide whether this means US dollars, Canadian dollars, Australian dollars, etc. The point has been considered in Ch 5 above.

[9] For the reasons discussed in Ch 4 above, it is suggested that the reference to a particular currency involves a choice of the law of the issuing State to govern purely monetary questions.

[10] ie because the principle reflects the presumed intention of the parties—see the discussion at para 9.09 above.

[11] The public international law aspects of this principle are considered in Ch 19 below.

[12] There are various writings and decisions to the effect. In Egypt, the Court of Appeal of the Mixed Tribunal, 19 May 1927, *Clunet* 1928, 765, noted that French legal tender legislation "n'est pas applicable en dehors des frontières de l'État francais", whilst the Supreme Court of Syria, 30 December 1931 AD 1931–2, No. 151 held that Turkish legal tender legislation introducing paper currency only applied within Turkey and thus could not affect a contract between the Municipality of Damascus and an Egyptian contractor.

[13] See the decision of the German Federal Supreme Court, 18 Feb 1965, *BGHZ* 43, 162 also *JZ* 1965, 448 with note by Mann. Monetary laws are, of course, inevitably of a public character. However, there is no public policy or other consideration which prevents the *recognition* (as opposed to the *enforcement*) of public laws. The distinction between recognition and enforcement of such laws is also relevant in the context of exchange controls, and is thus considered in Ch 16 below. The views expressed by the German Federal Supreme Court, *WM* 1960, 940, are in harmony with this approach. It is possible that notions of public policy influence the earlier attempts to deny extraterritorial effect to monetary laws. However, views of this kind are now out of favour.

system would be incapable of international recognition. One only needs to state this consequence in order to recognise its absurdity in the modern world. Moreover, a contention of this kind was explicitly rejected by the Privy Council, in *Ottoman Bank v Chakarian (No 2)*,[14] where it said:

> A further point put forward ... was based on the construction of the Turkish statute which authorised the issue of currency notes and made then legal tender. These statutes were in terms limited to Turkish currency in Turkey. Sir William Jowett has contended that outside Turkey pre-war currency law remained in effect, so that the legal tender outside Turkey remained the Turkish gold pound. Their Lordships were unable to accept this contention. The currency in any particular country must be determined by the law of that country, and that law is naturally in terms limited to defining what is legal tender in that country. But when that is fixed by the local law, it determines what is legal tender of that country for purposes of transactions in any other country, so that a foreign court will, when such questions come before it, give effect to the proper law of legal tender so determined. There is no foundation in their Lordships' judgment for the argument that Turkish paper is only legal tender as equivalent to gold *sub modo*, that is within the territorial limits of Turkish jurisdiction.

13.06   It is submitted that this statement provides a clear and practical guide to the *lex monetae* principle, and should always be referred to in cases of difficulty.[15] The existence of the *lex monetae* principle is thus beyond doubt, but the precise scope of that principle requires further discussion and definition.

13.07   A brief comparative survey will help to demonstrate the general application of this principle:

(a)   In relatively modern times, the *lex monetae* principle gained prominence in Germany in the "Coupons Actions". Austrian railway companies had issued bonds payable either in Austrian (silver) guilders or in thalers which were circulating in Germany when the bonds were issued. Following the establishment of the German Reich in 1871, a uniform mark currency based on gold was adopted, and the German Legal Tender Act provided that debts expressed in thaler were to be converted into mark debts at the rate of 1 mark to ⅓ thaler. Since Germany had adopted the gold standard, silver (and with it, the Austrian silver currency) had depreciated by a very substantial margin; the debtor companies therefore denied that they were

---

[14] [1938] AC 260, 278.

[15] It should be added that in *Ottoman Bank v Dascalopoulos* [1934] AC 354, 362, the Privy Council had regarded it as questionable whether the Turkish currency notes "were ever made legal tender for any payment under the Turkish contract which by that contract had to be made outside of Turkey". It is true that there were some doubts as to the precise effect of the Turkish legal tender legislation. However, in cases of doubt, the robust approach adopted in the *Chakarian* case is to be preferred.

liable in the new mark based on gold. But in Germany, the Supreme Court held that, if the thaler option were exercised, the companies had to pay the bonds and the coupons in marks at the conversion rate established by German law; this was so even though the bonds themselves—and thus the substance of the obligations thereby created—were governed by Austrian law.[16]

(b) French courts have likewise adopted the *lex monetae* principle in cases involving the German mark[17] and the Russian rouble.[18] A further French decision illustrates the frequently forgotten fact that nominalism does not invariably operate in favour of the debtor.[19] The case involved piàstres which circulated in French Indo-China and which appreciated in value as a result of the adoption of the gold standard in 1930. The application of the *lex monetae* principle inevitably led to the conclusion that an obligation formerly contracted with reference to the "paper" currency had inevitably to be settled in gold piàstres.[20]

(c) In Switzerland, the Federal Tribunal decided that (in the absence of a gold clause) a reference to French francs could only refer to money in circulation in France at the relevant time. This remained the case even where the case had international aspects, for only French law could identify its own national currency.[21]

(d) Courts in the United States have applied the *lex monetae* principle in relation

---

[16] Reichsoberhandelsgericht, 19 February 1878 *ROHG* 23, 205; 8 April 1879 *ROHG* 25, 41; Supreme Court, 12 December 1879, *RGZ* 1, 23; 1 March 1882, *RGZ* 6, 126; 9 February 1887, *RGZ* 19, 48. The subject was discussed by E.J. Bekker in *Couponprozesse* (1881). The principle noted in the text has been upheld by the Supreme Court on many occasions. For discussion, see Roth, *Berichte der Deutschen Gesellschaft für Völkerrecht* 20 (1979) 87; Hahn, *Währungsrecht* (1990).

[17] Cass Civ, 23 January 1924 S 1925, 1, 257.

[18] Cass Civ, 25 February 1929, *Clunet* 1929, 1309; Cour de Paris, 23 May 1931, *Clunet* 1932, 44, Trib Civ Seine, 28 October 1925; Cour de Paris, 18 February 1926, *Clunet* 1927, 1061, Trib Civ Seine 23 February 1931, *Clunet* 1931, 396.

[19] Cass Req, 4 April 1938, S 1938, 1, 188 (*Pham-Thi-Hieu v Banque de l'Indochine*).

[20] As the court noted "le prêt d'une somme numérique de piàstres contracté sous l'empire du décret du 8 juillet 1895 devait sous celui de 31 Mai 1930 être remboursé par une somme numériquement égale de piàstres, sans avoir égard à l'augmentation ou à la diminution de la valueur des espéces stipulées".

[21] See the Federal Tribunal's decision in *Re Credit Foncier Franco-Canadien* 23 May 1938, *BGE* 54 ii 275, also *Clunet* 1929, 479, 506, 507—"On ne saurait entrendre par francs français autre chose que la monnaie effective qui a cours en France d'après la loi française et qui est la seule que l'on puisse se procurer tant en France qu' à l'étranger."

to German marks,[22] Russian roubles,[23] cruzeiros,[24] and an old Chinese currency.[25]

(e) The *lex monetae* principle is firmly established in England. It is true that the decision in *Du Costa v Cole*[26] was founded on a different view of the subject. The case concerned an action on a bill of exchange drawn in London on 6 August for 1,000 Mille Rees, payable in Portugal thirty days after sight; on 14 August, the King of Portugal reduced the value of the "Mille Rees" by 20 per cent. Holt CJ declined to recognise this monetary change, but held that: "The bill ought to be paid according to the ancient value, for the King of Portugal may not alter the property of a subject of England." The decision in *Gilbert v Brett*[27] was distinguished on the ground that it involved British money which was changed by the King's authority. The decision in *Du Costa's Case* does not appear to have been expressly overruled, but it has plainly been set aside by a number of modern cases. These decisions lay down the rule that the subject matter of a monetary obligation is whatever the law of the currency designates as legal tender for the nominal amount of the obligation and that obligation, accordingly, will be satisfied by the payment of whatever currency is by the *lex monetae* valid tender for the discharge of the nominal amount of the debt. Further, this rule applies regardless of the law applicable to the obligation at hand.[28]

---

[22] *Deutsche Bank Filiale Nürnberg v Humphreys* (1926) 272 US 517. See also *Matter of Illfelder* (1931)136 Misc 430, 240 NY Supp 413, affirmed 249 NY Supp 903 and also the surprising decision of the New York Court of Appeals in *Matter of Lendle* (1929) 250 NY 502, 166 NE 182.

[23] *Dougherty v Equitable Life Assurance Society* (1934), 266 NY 71, 193 NE 897; *Tillman v Russo-Asiatic Bank* 51 Fed 2d 1023 (Circuit Court of Appeals 2d 1931); *Klocklow v Petrogradski* 268 NY Supp 433 (Supreme Court of New York App Div, 1st Dept 1934); *Matter of People* (1931) 255 NY 428, 175 NE 118 (a case proceeding on incorrect evidence); *Parker v Hoppe* (1931) 257 NY 333; *Richard v National City Bank of New York* (1931) 231 App Div 559, 248 NY Supp 113; and *Tillman v National City Bank of New York* (1941) 118 F 2d 631.

[24] *Tramontana v Varig Airlines* (1965) 350 F 2d 467.

[25] "Taels, Shanghai Sycee"—see *Sternberg v West Coast Life Insurance Co* (1961) 16 Cal Rep 546, (1961) 196 Cal App 2d 519; and *Judah v Delaware Trust Co* (1977) 378 A 2d 624.

[26] (1688) Skin 272.

[27] (1604) Davies Rep (Ireland) 18.

[28] These principles became established in England as a result of numerous foreign monetary depreciations and other events in the first half of the 20th century. For cases involving the Russian rouble, see *Lindsay Gracie & Co v Russian Bank for Foreign Trade* (1918) 34 TLR 443; *British Bank for Foreign Trade v Russian Commercial & Industrial Bank (No. 2)* (1921) 38 TLR 65; *Buerger v New York Life Assurance* (1927) 43 TLR 601 (CA); and *Perry v Equitable Life Assurance Society of the United States of America* (1929) 45 TLR 468. For cases dealing with the German mark, see *Re Chesterman's Trusts* [1923] 2 Ch 466 (CA); *Anderson v Equitable Life Asssurance Society of the United States of America* (1926) 134 LT 557 (CA); and *Franklin v Westminster Bank* (reproduced in the Fifth Edition of this work, p 561). For cases involving the franc, see *Hopkins v Compagnie Internationale des Wagons-Lits* (reproduced in the Fifth Edition of this work, 561); and *Société des Hôtels Le Touquet v Cummings* [1922] 1 KB 451, 461 *per* Scrutton LJ. The pension obligations of the Ottoman Bank led to a series of cases involving piàstres, including *Krocorian v Ottoman*

(f) The principle of nominalism has rightly been described as fundamental to the treatment of foreign money obligations,[29] although it should not be overlooked that the principle is equally applicable where the court is concerned with obligations expressed in the domestic currency.[30] The principle is particularly well illustrated by two Privy Council decisions which arose out of Spanish peseta loans made in Gibraltar. In *Pyrmont Ltd v Schott*,[31] it was held that the borrower was required to repay his loan in what was legal tender in Spain as at the date of repayment. It followed that he could not repay by means of Bank of Spain notes which were not legal tender in Spain at that time, although for certain purposes they had to be, and in practice were, accepted in ordinary transactions.[32] As Lord Porter said,[33] the form in which a payment in pesetas is to be made "must be regulated by the municipal law of the country whose unit of account is in question, and what would or would not be a legal tender must depend upon the law on that subject in force at the time when the legal tender should have been made".[34] In *Marrache v Ashton*,[35] it was held that a loan of pesetas made in 1931 and repayable in 1936 could in May 1939 be repaid in peseta notes, because in January 1939 they had become legal tender

---

Bank (1932) 48 TLR 247; *Ottoman Bank v Chakarian (No. 2)* [1938] AC 260 (PC); and *Storza v Ottoman Bank* [1938] AC 282 (PC). For other cases involving pesetas, see *Pyrmont v Schott* [1938] AC 145 and *Marrache v Ashton* [1943] AC 311. For a case involving the Queensland pound, see *Bonython v Commonwealth of Australia* [1950] AC 201, 222. It may be that a somewhat different principle applies in the context of a claim for unliquidated damages—see *Pilkington v Commissioners for Claims on France* (1821) 2 Knapp PC 7, 20 and the decision in *Société des Hôtels Le Touquet v Cummings* [1922] 1 KB 451, 461 which has been discussed in more detail at 7.45 above. See also *Agenor Shipping Co v Société des Pétroles Miroline* [1968] 2 Lloyd's Rep 359 and, for a decision relating to the pound sterling itself, see *Treseder-Griffin v Co-operative Insurance Ltd* [1956] 2 QB 127 (CA), which has already been considered at para 9.19 above.

[29] Dicey and Morris, *The Conflict of Laws* (Sweet & Maxwell, 13th edn, 2000) para 36-002.

[30] *Gilbert v Brett* (1604) Davies (Ireland) 18 and the Court of Appeal decision in *Treseder-Griffin v Co-operative Insurance Ltd* [1956] 2 QB 127 both involved the domestic currency.

[31] [1939] AC 145.

[32] This, therefore, was a case in which the banknotes were *money*, but were not *legal tender*. The case is authority for the proposition that the *lex monetae* has regard to the foreign legal legislation in its strict sense, and not to foreign monetary legislation in a broader sense. For the purposes of the Privy Council proceedings, it had been conceded that the notes in question did not amount to legal tender in Spain although it is not clear that the point had been adequately proved by expert evidence as to Spanish law. The point was considered on a number of occasions by courts in Tangier, and they accepted the legal tender quality of the notes—see Mixed Tribunal of Tangier, 4 March 1938, 4.31 and Menard, *Rev Crit* 1939, 294.

[33] At 158.

[34] The case really had nothing to do with the system of "guias" which is described in the judgment. All that mattered was that the Bank of Spain notes, with or without "guias" were not legal tender in Spain—see *Marrache v Ashton* [1943] AC 311, 317.

[35] [1943] AC 311, 317.

in Spain;[36] the borrower, according to Lord Macmillan "would have specifically performed his covenants, if he had tendered . . . the appropriate amount of Bank of Spain notes".

(g) The principle of nominalism has also been recognised by international tribunals. For example, the Tripartite Claims Commission between the United States, Austria, and Hungary was confronted by the question whether a US citizen who was entitled to be paid in Austro-Hungarian krone could demand payment in US dollars at the pre-War rate of exchange. In accordance with the nominalistic principle, the question had to be answered in the negative for the krone obligation "is unaffected either by the purchasing power of the krone in Austria or by the exchange value of krone as measured in other currencies".[37]

13.08 This survey of the principle of nominalism serves to demonstrate the general acceptance of that principle. However, a number of points deserve further discussion and elaboration:

(1) A mere change in the value of a foreign unit of account however serious it may be, is irrelevant to the monetary rights and obligations of the parties. In other words, nominalism places the risk of depreciation on the creditor and the risk of appreciation on the debtor; neither party can be heard to complain about any unexpected losses which may flow from such occurrences.[38] The creditor who abstains from requiring an indexation or similar protective clause must suffer the loss resulting from the depreciation of the money of account.[39] Thus, when the US dollar was devalued in 1972, it was not possible to imply a term which would, in effect, create a protective clause in defiance of the nominalistic principle; this was so even though the US dollar had been seen as a stable measure of value for some twenty-five

---

[36] At 313, where it is also explained that the parties had agreed that the date of the issue of the writ was the date with reference to which the debtor's liability was to be ascertained. This agreement was contrary to the principle which then prevailed, namely that it was the date of maturity (1936) which mattered.

[37] *Reports of the International Arbitral Awards* vi 212, 223.

[38] See, eg, *Bonython v Commonwealth of Australia* [1950] AC 201, 222. For further illustration see *Lindsay Gracie & Co v Russian Bank for Foreign Trade* (1918) 34 TLR 443 and the other cases mentioned in n 28 above. Two further points should be noted. First, the principle in the text is subject to the rules governing "galloping inflation", which have been considered at para 9.23(e) above. Secondly, although the text focuses specifically on foreign currencies, the point is equally applicable to obligations expressed in sterling—see *Treseder-Griffin v Co-operative Insurance Ltd* [1956] 2 QB 127.

[39] This point was decided in *British Bank for Foreign Trade v Russian Commercial & Industrial Bank (No. 2)* (1921) 38 TLR 65; *Re Chesterman's Trust* [1923] 2 Ch 466; *Ottoman Bank v Chakarian (No. 2)* [1938] AC 260 (PC). See also the decisions of the German Supreme Court, 15 March 1937, *RGZ* 154, 187; 28 May 1937, *RGZ* 155, 133; 7 February 1938, *JW* 1938, 1109; 20 April 1940, *RGZ* 163, 324.

years and was virtually used as a money of account by way of substitution for a gold clause. It is fundamental that contracting in terms of a particular currency—whether domestic or foreign—involves an element of speculation, and it is of the essence of nominalism, which is empirically derived from the intentions of the parties,[40] that neither party can complain about the outcome of a speculation which has miscarried.

(2) As pointed out earlier in this chapter[41] there is no room whatever for avoiding the effects of nominalism by discarding the *lex monetae* on the grounds that currency laws undoubtedly have the character of public law the application of which is said to be territorially restricted,[42] for attributing a confiscatory character to the creditor's loss[43] or for invoking public policy against a debtor who relies on the depreciation of a currency or a creditor who relies on its appreciation.[44] If, therefore, in 1960 a creditor became entitled to 100,000 Brazilian cruzeiros which by 1965, have depreciated by more than 600 per cent as a result of Brazilian inflation, public policy does not require or permit any deviation from the result which would be reached "had the value of the cruzeiro in terms of the dollar remained unchanged". On the contrary, "an unpredictable and virtually immeasurable factor would be imported into the decision of international conflict of law cases if the otherwise applicable law were subject to being displaced because of the recent history of the relative value of the currencies involved".[45]

(3) The principle of nominalism ordinarily precludes the argument that payment of a monetary obligation has become impossible. Monetary obligations are "indestructible". If a currency system becomes extinct, the amount payable by the debtor will be ascertained by reference to the

---

[40] As already noted on a number of occasions, the principle of nominalism is derived from the presumed intention of the parties.

[41] See para 13.05 above.

[42] The erroneous argument mentioned in the text rests on the failure to distinguish between the positive *enforcement* of a foreign public law (which is, of course, prohibited) and the *recognition* of a foreign law in accordance with a conflict rule such as the *lex monetae* principle—see Mann, *Rec* 132 (1971, i) 182. A similar problem arises in the context of foreign exchange control laws—see Ch 16 below.

[43] In the same sense see the decision of the International Claims Commission of the US in *Claim of Tabar* [1953] Int LR 211; Bindschedter, *Rec* 60 (1956) 179, 224. Confiscation is further discussed in the context of monetary sovereignty—see Ch 19 below.

[44] This was expressly decided by the Belgian Cour de Cassation, 28 January 1967, *Pasionie* 1967 I, 648. Exceptionally, however, a rate of conversion established in Poland for the purpose of converting mark debts incurred before the separation of certain eastern provinces from Germany was held by the German courts to be irreconcilable with German public policy, on the ground that the Polish statute was directly intended to injure German citizens: Berlin Court of Appeal, 25 February 1922, 28 October 1922, 2 November 1928, *JW* 1922, 398; 1923, 128; 1928, 1642.

[45] *Tramontana v Varig Airlines* (1965) 350 F 2d 467, 477 (Court of Appeals, District of Columbia Circuit).

recurrent link.[46] The same principle applied to the substitution of the euro for the national currencies of those EC Member States which adopted that new currency on 1 January 1999.[47] Nor should the debtor be allowed to avoid payment by invoking the legal impossibility of making payment at a particular place.[48]

(4) It should be appreciated that the *lex monetae* will be applied regardless of the law applicable to the contract as a whole and regardless of the place of payment. In particular "the locus of payment cannot change the selected monetary media of payment".[49]

(5) Finally, anything which is legal tender according to the *lex monetae* retains that status until formal demonetisation[50] irrespective of restrictions upon its use, such as prohibitions on the export of notes from the country of issue.[51] A pound is thus a pound, wherever the point arises for decision. It is the character of the money which is always and everywhere subject to the law of the currency concerned. The use which can or cannot be made of that money is an entirely different (and usually, irrelevant) question.[52]

C. Revalorisation

13.09 It has been shown that a country's legal tender legislation determines the composition, denomination, and nominal value of the currency concerned; it has also been shown that such laws must be recognised everywhere. Equally, however, it has been shown that questions touching the substance of a monetary

---

[46] The point is clearly illustrated by the decision in *Franklin v Westminster Bank* (1931) reproduced in Appendix II to the Fifth Edition of this work. The plaintiff was the holder of a note for 9,000,000,000 marks drawn in 1923. Before the note was presented for payment, Germany introduced, on 11 October 1924, a new monetary law which substituted one new reischsmark in substitution for one billion "old" marks. The result was that the holder of the note became entitled to 9/1000 of the new unit—a worthless obligation. The court thus very clearly gave effect to the German *lex monetae* in that case.

[47] The whole subject is discussed at Ch 30 below.

[48] This formulation is regrettably not supported by the English authorities—see in particular *Ralli Bros v Compania Naviera Sota y Aznar* [1920] 2 KB 287 (CA). Since the question arises with particular difficulty in the context of exchange controls, the point is discussed at para 16.38 below.

[49] *Sternberg v West Coast Life Insurance Co* (1961) 16 Cal Rep 546, 550.

[50] See the discussion at para 1.25 above.

[51] This point is established by *Marrache v Ashton* [1943] AC 311 (PC).

[52] The *lex monetae* will usually be readily identifiable. Difficulties may arise where the currency in question has been issued by a State which is not recognised by the UK. However, it is submitted that the lack of formal recognition is irrelevant; the *lex monetae* will be the law which is from time to time enforced by the *de facto* supreme authority in control of the currency. This approach is perhaps most unlikely to reflect the presumed intention of the parties which, as has been noted, forms the basis of the nominalistic principle.

obligation will generally be governed by the law applicable to it.[53] Two systems of law may therefore operate upon a single monetary obligation, and a clear demarcation between their respective spheres of application is necessary if confusion is to be avoided. Where does the line of demarcation lie?

It has been noted elsewhere[54] that any qualification of the nominalistic principle **13.10** cannot result from legal tender legislation. On the contrary, legal tender laws define money and its nominal value, and if anything thus tend to reinforce the principle of nominalism. It is thus outside the range of such legislation to decide whether and under what circumstances redress against its adverse effects may be obtained. Whether or not a creditor should be entitled to an additional payment or compensation on account of the devaluation of money must therefore be regarded as a question of substance which falls outside the province of the *lex monetae*. Rather, it is governed by the law applicable to the obligation concerned. It is in this sense that the line of demarcation should be drawn; the *lex monetae* defines the currency in which the obligation is expressed, but other questions of substance are subjected to the applicable law. Thus, for example, the right to claim damages for depreciation of money between the due date and the date of actual payment is a matter of substance governed by the applicable law, rather than the *lex monetae*.[55] The availability of a right to rescind an executory contract as a result of a monetary collapse would likewise be subjected to the governing law; the *lex monetae* would be inapplicable in that area.

In practical terms, the point arises where a country introduces legislation **13.11** designed to revalorise debts, the value of which has been seriously reduced as a result of a domestic monetary collapse.[56] The difficulties can perhaps be illustrated by reference to a well-known example. Suppose that a debtor had borrowed 10,000 marks in 1914 under a contract governed by English law; by the time repayment fell due in 1925, the German mark had collapsed and had been replaced at a rate of one billion marks to one reichsmark. Suppose also that German law, on the strength of the Revalorisation Act or domestic principles of contract law would revalorise the debt to 2,500 reichsmarks. Would an English court give effect to such revalorisation? In accordance with the principles outlined above, the English courts could only adopt that approach if the process of revalorisation is governed by the *lex monetae*. If revalorisation questions are to be

---

[53] See generally Ch 4 above.

[54] See para 12.05 above.

[55] This point was made by Scrutton LJ in *Société des Hôtels Le Touquet v Cummings* [1922] 1 KB 451, 461.

[56] Revalorisation is thus intended for the protection of the creditor. However, the general rules about to be discussed would apply equally in the case of "devalorisation", ie where the law provides for the reduction of the nominal amount of debts as a result of deflation. Laws of the latter kind would, of course, be introduced for the protection of the debtor.

submitted to the applicable law, then the debt plainly cannot be revalorised since it is governed by English law.[57] This is a typical problem of classification or characterisation; since it affects the quantum or substance of the monetary obligation, the question must be resolved in favour of the law which governs the obligation at issue (ie not the *lex monetae*). This is the solution adopted by most writers[58] and by most (although not all) of the available case law in Germany,[59] Austria,[60] and Switzerland.[61] That this is also the solution adopted by the English courts is clearly demonstrated by the decision in *Anderson v Equitable Assurance Society of the United States*.[62] In 1887, a husband had taken out a life policy expressed in German marks but governed by English law. He died in 1922 and his wife claimed payment under the policy but, of course, the mark had drastically depreciated by this time. In an effort to avoid the inevitable consequences of the nominalistic principle as expressed in earlier cases,[63] she sought to rely on German decisions which allowed revalorisation. The Court of Appeal held such cases to be irrelevant, on the grounds that revalorisation had resulted from the German law of obligations (ie as opposed to German monetary law in the strictest sense), whilst, in the instant case, the court was concerned with a contract governed by English law. The point is emphasised in the judgment of Atkin LJ:[64]

> It seems to me impossible to suppose and I think it is not proved that the law in any way affected the currency value of the mark, or indeed affected what we know as legal tender. It seems to me to be obvious that that is a law not affecting the currency, but affecting the particular contracts which come within the scope

---

[57] Of course, were the contract governed by German law, then the English courts would give effect to the German revalorisation law in accordance with ordinary conflict of law principles.

[58] See Dicey and Morris, *The Conflict of Laws* (Sweet & Maxwell, 13th edn, 2000) para 36R-001. For different views, see Nussbaum, "Internationales Privatrecht" p 254 (advocating the application of the law of the currency) and G.H. Roth, *Fragen des Rechts der Auf und Abwertung* (Müller Juristiche Verlag, 1979), suggesting the application of the legal system which is most favourable to the creditor.

[59] The law of the obligation was applied in numerous cases, including 16 December 1931, *JW* 1932, 1049 and 28 June 1934, *RGZ* 145, 51, 55, but some applied the law of the currency: 9 February 1931, *JW* 1932, 583.

[60] 24 April 1927, *JW* 1927, 1899 (revalorisation of mark debts governed by German law).

[61] See generally, Lalive, "Dépréciation monétaire et contrats en droit international privé" (1971) 35 *Mémoires publiés par la Faculté de Droit de Genéve*. The Swiss Federal Tribunal allowed for the revalorisation of German mark debts contracted under German law, as the governing law of the contract. The Tribunal also found that the application of the German revalorisation laws was not contrary to Swiss public policy, even if those laws had retrospective application: 28 February 1930, *JW* 1930, 1900; 26 February 1932, *JW* 1932, 1163. German mark debts were also revalorised according to the general principles of Swiss contract law: 26 March 1931, *Clunet* 1932, 227; 13 November 1931, *JW* 1932, 2337.

[62] (1926) 134 LT 557 (CA).

[63] See in particular *Re Chesterman's Trusts* [1923] 2 Ch 466 (CA).

[64] At 566.

of it . . . In other words, it is the debt that is valorised and not the currency; and if that is so, it is obvious that the German law cannot affect the operation of the rule of English law which is laid down in *In re Chesterman's Trusts*.

The Court of Appeal thus clearly adopted the theory that the law of the obligation governed; had the view been taken that the question of revalorisation was governed by the law of the currency, then the result would necessarily have been different.[65]

Although the point did not fall for decision in the *Anderson* case, it must necessarily follow that—had the policy been governed by German law—the German revalorisation laws would have been applied by the English courts,[66] at any rate so long as those rules were not manifestly contrary to English public policy.[67] That revalorisation laws forming a part of the governing law of the obligation must be given effect by the English courts is in some respects confirmed by the decision in *Re Schnapper* (another case involving depreciated German marks), although the judgment is unsatisfactory in some respects.[68] The point is, however, further reinforced by the decision in *Kornatzki v Oppenheimer*.[69] In 1905, the defendant had promised to pay the plaintiff an annual sum of 8,000 marks for life. The agreement was made in order to settle an action in the German courts, and was thus governed by German law. How was this obligation to be fulfilled after the mark currency had been replaced by the reichsmark? The court decided that it should apply the German revalorisation practice, and stipulated for an annual payment of £500 in substitution for the former obligation in marks.[70] There is no doubt that the court applied the

13.12

---

[65] It may be noted that the question whether the German rules were part of the law of the currency or of the law of obligations was answered on the basis of German conceptions. This is at odds with the general rule that questions of characterisation are governed by the law of the country in which the court is sitting—see generally, Dicey and Morris, *The Conflict of Laws* (Sweet & Maxwell, 13th edn, 2000) ch 12.

[66] Such revalorisation laws would have formed a part of the law to be applied in accordance with the principle now found in Art 15 of the Rome Convention.

[67] Provided that a revalorisation has been effected for economic purposes and is not discriminatory, it is difficult to see how public policy could provide a valid objection to such arrangements.

[68] [1938] 1 All ER 322. The decision is unsatisfactory because it is not clear that the obligation was governed by German law. The original monetary obligation had been contracted under German law, under which it was void. The obligation was later reconfirmed under the terms of an English will. Perhaps the best explanation is that the English will "clothed" the earlier obligation with a validity which it would not otherwise have enjoyed, but that German law was intended to remain the essential source of the obligations.

[69] [1937] 4 All ER 133.

[70] The court fell into error in making a declaration that payment should henceforth be made in sterling. Under the contract, the money of account and money of payment was the mark which, in accordance with the *lex monetae* principle, had been substituted by the reichsmark. The only question was, how much in reichsmark should be paid and could the contractually stated amount be increased?

German general law of obligations, rather than its monetary law[71] and the case thus stands as clear authority for the principle explained above.

13.13   If questions of this type should arise again in England, then it is submitted that they should be decided in the same way. However, there may be scope for a different result in countries whose system of private international law incorporates Article 7(1) of the Rome Convention or a rule similar to it. As noted previously, that provision allows a court to give effect "to the mandatory rules of the law of another country with which the situation has a close connection, if and in so far as, under the law of the latter country, those rules must be applied whatever the law applicable to the contract". The court has a discretion to give effect to those rules, taking into account their nature and purpose and the consequences of their application. It is submitted that a contract does not have a "close connection" with the laws of a particular country merely because the monetary obligations arising under it are expressed in the currency of that country. However, if other connecting factors are present, it may be open to the court to apply a revalorisation law which is of mandatory application under the law of the issuing country. In taking into account the consequences of the application of such a law, the court could refer to the simple fact that the revalorisation would do justice as between the parties. On the other hand, the court must proceed with caution in this area, for such an approach would greatly broaden the scope of the *lex monetae* and would very significantly detract from the dominance of the applicable law over matters touching the substance of the obligation.

D. Revalorisation in Foreign Courts

13.14   The discussion up to this point has established that, under the relevant rules of private international law:

(a)   the law of the currency applies to the definition of the unit of account;[72] but

(b)   all questions touching the substance and quantum of a foreign money obligation are governed by the law of the obligation.[73]

It is now necessary to expand on the proposition set out in (b) above and to consider its consequences in the context of revalorisation and the conflict of

---

[71] [1937] 4 All ER 133, at 137, G: "There is no doubt whatever that the experts on both sides agree and the parties are agreed, that this is a matter wholly of German law, and ought to be decided according to the law of Germany."

[72] See para 13.11 above.

[73] See "Revalorisation", para 13.09 above.

laws. In this context, it has to be remembered that private international law does not itself provide an answer to particular legal problems; it merely identifies the relevant domestic system of law which must be applied in seeking the solution to those problems. The formulation in (b) above thus leads to the question—to what extent do the substantive rules of domestic legal systems deal with disarrangements of the intrinsic value of money and provide a remedy for the party (usually the creditor) who has been adversely affected by such events?

The rules governing depreciation of foreign currencies are essentially identical to those which would apply where the domestic unit is affected by depreciation. It has been shown that in accordance with the nominalistic principle, an obligation can always be discharged pound-for-pound, dollar-for-dollar and so forth. It has been shown that fluctuations in the value of the *domestic* currency cannot even be taken into account as a mere fact for the purposes of measuring damages, seeking recission, or any other matter. Against that background, it is possible to state the following propositions: **13.15**

(1) As regards the quantum of simple debts expressed in foreign money, there is no rule of English law which enables a party to claim a reduction or increase in the amounts payable on the ground of a rise or fall in the international value of that money. If, under a contract governed by English law, 1,000 euros are owing, the depreciation of that currency does not of itself enable the creditor to claim compensation. Even if the money of account referred to in an English law contract has become worthless, there is no principle of English law which can assist the creditor by revalorising the debt.[74]

(2) Courts in other jurisdictions have frequently adopted a more liberal approach. As noted earlier,[75] the Swiss courts allowed for the revalorisation of German mark debts even where the obligation was governed by Swiss law. This allows a greater play to the *lex monetae* than that which would be allowed as a matter of general principle, but the obligation to perform a contract in good faith may on occasion allow the court to disregard the principle of nominalism where the money of account has suffered a total collapse.[76] In France, likewise, the principle of nominalism was generally observed although on exceptional occasions the court provided for

---

[74] *British Bank for Foreign Trade v Russian Commercial & Industrial Bank (No. 2)* (1921) 38 TLR 65. It should be emphasised that the remark in the text is directed towards the revalorisation of the debt itself, ie an increase in its nominal value. An award of damages or interest may be appropriate in the event of late payment, but the point obviously only becomes relevant in the event of the debtor's breach. English law on that subject has been discussed in detail at para 9.29 above.

[75] See n 61 above.

[76] See the decisions of the Swiss Federal Tribunal mentioned at the end of n 61 above.

revalorisation of foreign money obligations where a different approach would have caused particular hardship for the creditor. The first case[77] involved an obligation to pay a pension expressed in Russian roubles which had subsequently collapsed; in fairness to the creditor, who expected a living pension for the remainder of his life, the court assessed the "value" represented by the rouble obligation when it was originally contracted, and awarded an appropriate sum in francs in substitution therefor. In the second case,[78] a legatee was left 60,000 German marks, which had become worthless. The Court solved this difficulty by holding that (on the facts) the underlying intention of the testator was to divide his estate among the beneficiaries in equal shares. The legacy of 60,000 marks was accordingly revalorised in order to reflect that state of affairs. Whatever the technical merits of these cases, the reason for the court's intervention is clear.

(3) Similar issues fell for consideration by courts in the United States. The decision of the New York Court of Appeals in *Matter of Lendle*[79] involved a testator domiciled in the United States who made his will in 1920 (ie prior to the collapse of the German mark) and who left various "mark" legacies to beneficiaries in Germany. When the testator died in 1927 it fell to be decided how these "mark" legacies were to be paid. It was held that the testamentary reference to the "marks" meant "marks" as at the time the legacies were paid. Consequently, the beneficiaries received 400,000 "reichsmarks" rather than the depreciated "marks". This decision can only be defended if, as a matter of construction, the testator intended to refer to "marks" in circulation at the time of his death, rather than as at the date of his will. For obvious reasons, this is a very doubtful approach, and there is no other principled basis upon which the decision can be defended. The will was governed by the law of the testator's domicile, which accepts the principle of nominalism and thus knows no general theory of revalorisation.[80] Further, the *lex monetae* did not provide a recurrent link between the old and the new unit on a one-for-one basis. It may well be that the court achieved a just result but it seems to have applied neither the law which governed the obligation nor the *lex monetae*. In a later case, where the mark legacies had already been satisfied by payment of the nominal amount of

---

[77] Cour de Paris, 28 November 1927, *Clunet* 1928, 119.

[78] Cass Civ, 19 November 1930, *Clunet* 1931, 691.

[79] (1929) 250 NY 502, 166 NE 182.

[80] See para 9.21 above. It has been suggested that, where the obligation is governed by the law of one of the States of the Union, that law will provide relief in the event of a complete collapse of a foreign currency, either on public policy grounds or on the ground that the collapse would amount to confiscation of property: see Rashba, "Debts in Collapsed Foreign Currencies"(1944) 34 Yale LJ 1. This line of reasoning seems unconvincing.

marks, the court declined to re-open the matter on the basis of the decision in the *Lendle* case.[81]

(4) In view of the inflation which Germany endured in the early 1920s it is perhaps unsurprising that German law developed an elaborate body of revalorisation rules after 1923. In view of the theory that questions of revalorisation are governed by the law applicable to the obligation, it is equally unsurprising that the theory could be applied both to obligations in marks and to foreign currency obligations. As a result, the main question related to the conditions under which foreign money could be regarded as so greatly depreciated that revalorisation was appropriate. The Supreme Court established that a "catastrophic depreciation" was required. On this ground, debts expressed in Russian roubles or in Austrian kronen were revalorised[82] but obligations expressed in other currencies were not.[83] Further, even in cases not involving a catastrophic depreciation of a foreign currency, it was occasionally possible to adjust monetary obligations to reflect a significant depreciation in value on the basis that the change in circumstances had disturbed the equilibrium between the respective obligations of the contracting parties.[84] This principle had to be treated with care and could not be applied in the case of a loan,[85] where the parties had performed their obligations and the consideration had depreciated in the hands of the creditor[86] or where the parties had contemplated a monetary depreciation.[87]

E. Private International Law and Protective Clauses

It has been shown earlier that various techniques have been adopted with a view to avoiding the nominalistic principle in various cases.[88] Most of the relevant

13.16

---

[81] *Matter of Illfelder* (1931) 136 Misc 430, 240 NY Supp 413, affirmed 249 NY Supp 903.

[82] 27 January 1928, *RZG* 120, 70, 76 and 16 December 1931, *JW* 1932, 1048 (Austrian crowns) and *Leipziger Zeitschrift* 1931, 38 (Russian roubles).

[83] 22 February 1928, *RGZ* 120, 193, 197 (French francs); 3 March 1925, Rechtsprechung 1925 No. 134 (Dutch florins); 28 June 1934, *RGZ* 145, 51, 55 (pounds sterling); 20 April 1940, *RGZ* 163, 324, 333 (US dollars).

[84] On this principle, see 15 January 1931, *RGZ* 131, 158, 1 777.

[85] Supreme Court, 28 June 1934, *RGZ* 145, 51, 56.

[86] Supreme Court, 13 October 1933, *RGZ* 142, 23, 34, 35.

[87] Supreme Court, 9 July 1935, *RGZ* 148, 33, 41, 42. The depreciation of the rouble has led to a dispute between Russia and the US, which is recorded in The Times, 27 April 2004 ("All this and more for $2.50 a year"). In 1985, the US had signed a tenancy agreement for its ambassador's residence in Moscow. The rental of 72,500 roubles was agreed, and this represented a substantial sum at the time. However, spiralling inflation reduced this figure to the equivalent of $2.50 per annum. Russia has demanded a revision of the rent to reflect prevailing market values. If the tenancy agreement is governed by Russian law, then the right to a revalorisation of the debt would have to be determined by reference to that law. The dispute is unresolved at the time of writing.

[88] See Ch 11 above.

case law involves the gold clause, the substance of which has been considered elsewhere.[89] The gold clause itself is now obsolete, although the cases on the subject do shed some light on the other forms of protection which a creditor might seek to adopt. In view of these considerations, it is proposed to confine the present aspect of the discussion to a few principles of a general nature:

(a)   Whether or not a contract contains a gold clause is plainly a question of construction and thus falls to be determined by the law applicable to the contract as a whole. That this question is governed exclusively by the applicable law is apparent both from the terms of the Rome Convention[90] and from the Court of Appeal decision in *St Pierre v South American Stores (Gath & Chaves) Ltd.*[91] In that case, a contract governed by Chilean law stipulated for a rent of "93,500 pesos of 183,057 millionths of a gramme of fine gold monthly which shall be paid at the option of the owner either in Santiago de Chile . . . or remitted to Europe according to the instructions which the owner may give". The question arose whether this was a gold clause or whether it was merely a transcription of the relevant article of the Chilean monetary statute. The latter view was adopted because that was the view which Chilean law would have adopted as the governing law of the contract. Chilean law plainly applied to questions of construction and had to be applied in determining the substance of the obligation. The creditor's decision to require that payment be made in London affected the place in which performance had to take place, but this did not lead to the conclusion that English law could have any impact upon the fundamental import of the obligation.[92]

(b)   Whether a particular gold clause was to be construed as a gold coin or a gold value clause[93] must be a question of interpretation which is governed by the law applicable to the contract. This rule was confirmed by the decision of the Court of Appeal in *International Trustee for the Protection of Bondholders AG v R,*[94] where it was held that the contract was governed by English law and where, by applying what had become known as the *Feist*

---

[89]   See paras 11.05–11.32 above.

[90]   See Art 10(1)(a) of that Convention, which has been considered at para 4.12 above.

[91]   [1937] 3 All ER 349; see also remarks in *Re Chesterman's Trusts* [1923] 2 Ch 466 (CA) at 487, 488.

[92]   See the remarks of Greer LJ (at 352) and Slesser LJ (at 354). The plaintiff had unsuccessfully argued to the contrary, in reliance on remarks made in *R v International Trustee for the Protection of Bondholders AG* [1937] AC 500, 574. The plaintiff might more profitably have relied on the views of Lord Wright in *Adelaide Electric Supply Co v Prudential Assurance Co* [1934] AC 122, 151. But the Court of Appeal came to the correct conclusion on the point in the *St Pierre* case.

[93]   The distinction between these two types of provision has been discussed at para 11.19 above.

[94]   [1936] 3 All ER 407.

construction,[95] the court concluded that a gold value clause was intended. Other decisions are less satisfactory, in that they also adopt the *Feist* construction, even though the contract has been found to be governed by a foreign system of law[96] and even though the court has not identified the governing law.[97] It is submitted that the approach in the latter cases is flawed; the process of interpreting a gold or other protective clause should not be attempted until the law applicable to the contract has been identified, and there is no scope for purely English rules of construction where the contract is governed by a foreign law.

(c) The law applicable to the contract also determines its material validity.[98] That law thus determines whether the parties have validly consented to and stipulated for a gold clause and, if so, whether that clause has been discharged or invalidated by later legislation. It is true that enactments which abrogated the gold clause were usually introduced as a matter of monetary policy, but the court cannot apply the law of the currency merely on that ground, for the substance of the parties' obligations is governed by the applicable law.[99] This rule, which is reinforced by the terms of the Rome Convention, has been accepted by courts in England and elsewhere and would thus apply equally to index and other protective clauses.[100] For the same reasons and subject to a possible exception about to be noted, the same principle would exclude from consideration any legislation passed in the law of the place of payment and which was designed to abrogate the gold or other protective clause. The law of the place of performance may affect the method or mode of performance of a monetary obligation[101] but it cannot affect its interpretation or substance. This general rule is, so far as English law is concerned, somewhat obscured by the decision of the Court of Appeal in *Ralli Bros v Compania Naviera Sota y Aznar*,[102] which determines that a contract governed by English law will not be enforced if the

---

[95] ie the interpretative approach to gold clauses adopted in *Feist v Société Intercommunale Belge d' Electricité* [1934] AC 161. This case has been considered at para 11.16 above.

[96] This applies to the House of Lords decision in *R v International Trustee for the Protection of Bondholders AG* [1937] AC 500, 556.

[97] All the members of the House of Lords expressly left open the identity of the governing law in *New Brunswick Railway v British and French Trust Corp* [1939] AC 1.

[98] For further discussion of this point, see para 4.13 above.

[99] For a clear statement that the abrogation of the gold clause is not subject to the *lex monetae*, see the Swiss Federal Tribunal, 1 February 1938, *BGE* 64, ii, 88, AD 1938–40, No 57.

[100] See *R v International Trustee for the Protection of Bondholders AG* [1937] AC 500—see the discussion by Mann [1959] BYIL 42. For a decision of the Ontario Supreme Court to similar effect, see *Derwa v Rio de Janerio Framay Light & Power Co* (1928) 4 DLR 542. The same general principle appears to be accepted by the New York courts although the case was decided in a slightly different context—see *De Sayve v De la Valdene* (1953) 124 NYS 2d 143, 153.

[101] Article 10(2) of the Rome Convention.

[102] [1920] 2 KB 287.

necessary action required to perform the contract would be unlawful in the place in which performance is required to occur. The decision in this case is unconvincing, at least in so far as it relates to monetary obligations,[103] but so long as the decision stands, it may prevent the enforcement of payment obligations arising under a gold, index, or similar protective clause which has been rendered unlawful in the place of payment.[104] Subject only to that qualification, it might be thought obvious that the validity of a protective clause is governed by its applicable law. It is, however, necessary to record that the point arose for decision in the unsatisfactory case of *British and French Trust Corp v New Brunswick Railway*.[105] The defendants, a Canadian railway company, had issued bonds which were governed by Canadian law and promised to repay the bearer "£100 sterling gold coin of the present standard weight and fineness at its agency in London . . . or at the option of the holder, at the office of the company in New Brunswick". The bonds fell due for payment in 1934 and the plaintiffs demanded payment in England on the basis of a gold value clause. The action was dismissed at first instance in 1936. Subsequently, the Canadian Gold Clauses Act 1937 abrogated gold clauses, and the main question on appeal was whether the 1937 Act prevented the plaintiffs from succeeding in their action; both the Court of Appeal and the House of Lords held that it did not. In the House of Lords, the decision was based on a narrow point of statutory interpretation; in substance, the House held that the 1937 Act did not retrospectively apply to bonds which had already matured before the Act was passed. The Court of Appeal, however, proceeded on different lines. In essence, the Court held that the "mode and measure" of performance was governed by English law as the contractual place of payment; since the 1937 Act obviously did not form a part of English law, it could not be applied, with the result that the

---

[103] Since the point is most likely to arise in the context of exchange controls in the place of payment, the general subject is discussed at para 16.38 below. Criticism of this case must, however, in some respects be treated with care, for a similar result would quite probably flow from the application of Art 7(1) of the Rome Convention. Whilst that provision does not apply in this country, it does form a part of the private international law of several other Convention countries.

[104] It should, however, be emphasised that the *Ralli* decision only applies where the required steps would be *unlawful* in the country in which they are to be taken. The Joint Resolution of Congress of 5 June 1933 which abrogated the gold clause rendered them void and unenforceable—it did not render their voluntary performance illegal—see *International Trustee for the Protection of Bondholders AG v R* [1936] 3 All ER 407(CA). Consequently, an English law contract containing a gold clause and requiring payment to be made in New York would remain enforceable despite the *Ralli* principle.

[105] [1936] 1 All ER 13 (High Court); [1937] 4 All ER 516 (CA); [1939] AC 1 (HL).

plaintiffs could succeed on the basis of a gold clause.[106] These conclusions are unconvincing for two main reasons. First of all, to assert that the effect of the abrogation of the gold clause upon a monetary obligation is a matter falling under the head of the mode of performance strains the meaning of that conception; the abrogation of a gold clause should plainly be a matter which goes to the substance of the obligation—namely, the quantum of the debt. Secondly, the bonds contained an option of place between Canada and England; as a result of the Court of Appeal's reasoning, the amount payable in respect of the identical obligation may differ according to the place of payment. It hardly needs to be stated that this is an unattractive result. But, however that may be, it is clear that the law of the place of performance would not enjoy this degree of influence under the modern law.[107]

(d) If a gold or other protective clause is governed by English law, then an English court will enforce such a provision for there is no rule of English law which renders such clauses invalid. This will remain the position even if the relevant clause is unlawful under the laws of the country in which the debtor resides. However, if payment in respect of the clause falls to be made in a jurisdiction in which payment is prohibited, then the implications of the rule in the *Ralli* case has to be considered.[108] If an English law clause of this kind fell for consideration by a foreign court, then it should apply English law as the governing law of the obligation; the English rules should only be disregarded if they are contrary to the public policy of the forum or conflict with rules of mandatory application in the forum.[109] Thus, if a court in the United States had to consider an English law gold clause during the period when the Joint Resolution of Congress was in force, it should have enforced such a clause, for it is difficult to see how the vital interests of the forum should have demanded that the governing law be displaced.[110]

(e) If the contract at hand is governed by the legal system which abrogated the gold or other protective clause, then that law governs all further questions in that regard. Thus, it determines its own territorial ambit, and

---

[106] In reaching this conclusion, the Court of Appeal relied upon an excessively broad formulation of Lord Wright in *Adelaide Electric Supply Co v Prudential Assurance Co* [1934] AC 122, 151, where he said "whatever is the proper law of a contract regarded as a whole, the law of the place of performance should be applied in respect of any particular obligation which is performable in a particular country other than the country of the proper law of the contract".

[107] See in particular Art 10(2) of the Rome Convention.

[108] See the discussion at para 13.16(c) above.

[109] On these general principles, see paras 4.20–4.22 above.

[110] This point arose, but was avoided, in *Lemaire v Kentucky & Indiana Terminal Railway Co* (1957) F 2d 884. As noted previously, the Joint Resolution of Congress rendered such clauses void and unenforceable, but it did not render them illegal.

it determines whether the gold clause has become merely void or positively illegal. Consequently, where the English courts found a gold clause to be subject to American law, this immediately led to the conclusion that the gold clause was unenforceable, for it was in conflict with the Joint Resolution of Congress.[111] As has been shown elsewhere,[112] an obligation is governed by its applicable law *as in force from time to time*, and there is thus no room for excluding the application of the abrogating legislation on the grounds that it could not be foreseen by the parties. Moreover, there is no basis upon which the abrogation of a gold clause by another country can be disregarded on public policy grounds, on the basis that it constitutes an interference with creditors' rights. Any such abrogation would be a matter of monetary or economic policy and is similar to devaluation or other expedients to which nearly every country has from time to time had to resort.

(f) It has occasionally been suggested that laws abrogating the gold clause must be regarded as strictly territorial, and cannot be recognised abroad on the basis of their public law nature. The French courts have applied this doctrine as a means of avoiding the application of such legislation, although it was rejected by courts in Belgium and Germany. Even the Supreme Court of Delaware thought it possible that the abolition of a silver clause by the law of China in 1935 could be a "revenue law" without extraterritorial effect.[113] For reasons which have been given elsewhere, the doctrine that monetary laws are of a purely territorial character cannot be accepted.[114]

(g) The abrogation of gold clauses clearly caused significant losses to many creditors, but the relevant legislation could not be said to be confiscatory; a domestic court was thus unable to invoke that line of reasoning as a means of disregarding that legislation on public policy grounds. This is apparent from the decision of the US Supreme Court in the Legal Tender Cases,[115] where it was noted that the constitutional prohibition against the taking of property without compensation:

> . . . has always been understood as referring only to a direct appropriation, and not to consequential injuries resulting from the exercise of lawful powers. It has never been supposed to have any bearing upon or to inhibit laws that indirectly work harm and loss to individuals. A new tariff, an embargo, a draft or a war may inevitably bring upon individuals great losses, may indeed

---

[111] *International Trustee for the Protection of Bondholders AG v R* [1937] AC 505.

[112] See para 6.02 above.

[113] *Judah v Delaware Trust Co* (1977) 378 A 2d 624. The court did not, however, ultimately decide the point.

[114] See para 13.05 above.

[115] *Knox v Lee* and *Parker v Davis* (1870) 12 Wall (79) US 457, 551. In the same sense, see *Norman v Baltimore & Ohio Railroad Co* (1935) 294 US 240, 306.

render valuable property almost valueless. They may destroy the worth of contracts . . . But was it ever imagined that this was taking private property without compensation or without due process of law?

It thus seems that public policy could only be invoked as a means of disregarding legislation of this kind if it were of an arbitrary or discriminatory nature—for instance, where it was designed exclusively to damage the interests of foreign creditors. Such cases will necessarily be rare.[116]

---

[116] eg, see the decision of the Swiss Federal Tribunal, 1 February 1938 *BGE* 64, ii 88 which rejected the application of German legislation on gold clauses for this reason.

Part IV

EXCHANGE CONTROLS, EXCHANGE RATES, AND SANCTIONS

INTRODUCTION

Exchange control may be described as a system of open restrictions on payments **Intro.4.01**
or transfers to or for the benefit of persons resident in another country, which is
imposed to protect the financial resources of the country and which is thus
primarily concerned with the outward movement of payments or transfers.[1] A
precise definition of exchange control does, however, only assume importance in
specific contexts,[2] although it may be said that a genuine system of exchange
controls is designed for the protection of the economy of the State concerned. In
contrast, a regime of sanctions is usually imposed against a particular State with
a view to persuading it to adopt a particular course of action.[3] Exchange controls
are thus protective whilst sanctions are punitive.[4]

For the lawyer concerned with transactions involving both his domestic cur- **Intro.4.02**
rency and a foreign currency and/or a payment to a foreign resident, there are
three essential questions which have to be addressed, namely:

(1) At what rate will any necessary exchange be effected?
(2) Is the required exchange lawful and/or are any official permissions required
     for that purpose?
(3) Is the payment to the foreign resident lawful under English law?

---

[1] Throughout this book, the term "exchange control" is used in the sense just described,
although it will be necessary to expand upon this definition when considering Art VIII(2)(b) of
the Articles of Agreement of the International Monetary Fund. In some countries, a covert system
of exchange control may exist, eg where financial institutions may be required to hold or invest
funds in the domestic currency. Restrictions of the latter kind are outside the scope of this book.
On occasion, States may have found it necessary to impose exchange controls in an opposite sense,
usually in an effort to restrain excessive inflows of capital which might have inflationary and other
adverse consequences. For example, Switzerland adopted limitations on the acquisition of Swiss
securities by, and the payment of interest to, foreigners and imposed special taxes to restrict
inward movements of capital. Again, however, it is not proposed to consider arrangements of this
kind.
[2] See in particular the discussion of Article VIII(2)(b) of the IMF Agreement in Ch 15 below.
[3] A more detailed definition is attempted in Ch 17 below.
[4] As will be seen, a regime of sanctions is frequently seen as a special form of exchange control.
In view of the distinction drawn in the text, it will be apparent that the present writer does not
subscribe to this view.

The present Part will seek to answer these questions in so far as they may be affected by exchange controls or blocking legislation.

Intro.4.03 Not without some hesitation, it has been decided to reintroduce into the main text a brief chapter on UK exchange control,[5] and it is necessary to explain the reason for this decision. First of all, in their kernel, the exchange control regulations still in use in various parts of the world are essentially similar both in their purpose and in their effect, although there are naturally differences of detail. It was therefore felt that a description of the UK system would serve as a broad introduction to the subject and the manner in which an exchange control system is operated. It was believed that such a description might be valuable; the general dismantling of these types of restrictions over recent years means that there must now be many practising and academic lawyers who have very limited direct experience of any form of exchange control. Furthermore, there remain a number of Commonwealth countries which retain a system of exchange control originally based on the UK model;[6] finally, it will be necessary at a later stage to consider various Court of Appeal decisions relating to the system of exchange control formerly administered by the Bank of Zambia, and the legislation at issue draws heavily upon the British model.[7]

Intro.4.04 With these points in mind, Part IV will consider the following matters:

(a) exchange control in the United Kingdom;
(b) exchange control under the International Monetary Fund Agreement;
(c) the private international law of exchange control;
(d) sanctions and monetary obligations; and
(e) exchange rates.

---

[5] The relevant chapter had been produced as Appendix IV to the Fifth Edition of this work, on the basis that exchange control legislation had finally been repealed in the UK. Ch 14 below is therefore an abbreviated and revised version of Dr Mann's earlier work in this area.

[6] There are numerous examples of exchange control legislation which, in their essence, if not their precise terminology, are similar to the Exchange Control Act 1947. Asian examples include the Indian Foreign Exchange Management Act 1999 and the Malaysian Exchange Control Act of 1953 (Act 17); African examples include the Nigerian Exchange Control Act 1962 and the South African Currency and Exchanges Act 1933, together with the regulations made under it.

[7] See the Zambian Exchange Control Act 1965 (now repealed).

14

EXCHANGE CONTROL—THE UK MODEL

A. Exchange Control up to the Exchange Control Act 1947

The Exchange Control Act 1947 created the statutory regime for the **14.01** administration of exchange control which remained in place for some thirty-two years,[1] until the system was suspended by the Conservative Government in 1979 and, ultimately, repealed in its entirety.[2] As matters stand at present, it would now be virtually impossible for the United Kingdom to reintroduce general and wide-ranging measures of this kind; the United Kingdom cannot now introduce restrictions on the free movement of capital or payments, for this would be inconsistent with its treaty obligations as a member of the European Union.[3]

---

[1] For a recent discussion of UK exchange controls and the events leading up to their abolition, see Kynaston, "The Long Life and Slow Death of Exchange Controls" [2000] JIFM 37.

[2] The suspension of the exchange control system was achieved by means of a general consent given under s 37 of the 1947 Act. The Act itself was finally repealed by the Finance Act 1987 (s 72(7) and Sch 16, Pt XI). It may be added in passing that a system of exchange control should be applied generally and for the purpose of protecting the country's monetary resources. Viewed in that light the use of the Exchange Control Act 1947 to regulate commerce with Rhodesia in the period following its Unilateral Declaration of Independence may be open to objection—see App (Southern Rhodesia) to *Exports from the United Kingdom* (Bank of England Notice to Exporter, 8 September 1970). However, this merely formed a small part of a broader set of sanctions against that country and the point is no longer of practical concern. In the view of the present writer, sanctions should not be seen as a form of exchange control—see para 17.02 below.

[3] The provisions of the EC Treaty dealing with free movement of capital and payments are considered in Ch 25, below, in the context of economic and monetary union.

14.02   Although the present Chapter will focus primarily on the provisions of the 1947 Act, it should not be thought that exchange control was an innovation at that point. On the contrary, this country had sought to legislate against the export of gold and silver for a number of centuries—the development of exchange control can be traced back to the beginning of the thirteenth century, and a detailed scheme was put in place in 1576. The whole matter was again addressed in two later Acts.[4] This legislation remained in force until the end of the Bank Restriction Period when Parliament repealed[5] the long list of statutes prohibiting the export of precious metals and, after more than 500 years, finally established complete freedom of trade. During the First World War, there was no specific prohibition of the export of gold (nor any exchange control in general) but such exports were in fact prevented through purely administrative measures. After that war, the prohibition against the export of gold was placed on a statutory footing,[6] until complete freedom of trade was restored in 1925 and remained intact until the outbreak of the Second World War. At that point, exchange control was reintroduced through the Defence (Finance) Regulations 1939.[7] Subsequently, however, exchange control in this country rested principally upon the Exchange Control Act 1947 and upon numerous statutory instruments and Notices to Banks.[8] The remainder of this chapter will thus consider the 1947 Act, although some of the cases to which reference will be made have been decided on the basis of the corresponding provisions contained in earlier regulations.

B. The General Scheme of the 1947 Act

14.03   The Exchange Control Act 1947 adopted a "streamlined" pattern; it took very broad powers for the prohibition and control of monetary and financial transactions. The ambit of the legislation was then made workable by statutory

---

[4] Respectively, 15 Chas II, ch 7, s 12 and 7 and 8 Will III, ch 19.

[5] By 59 Geo III, ch 49, ss 10–12; 1 & 2 Geo IV, ch 26, s 4.

[6] See in particular the Gold and Silver (Export Control) Act 1920.

[7] SR & O 1939, No. 950. The Order in Council was made on 25 August 1939, pursuant to powers conferred by the Emergency Powers (Defence) Act 1939, s 1. The Defence (Finance) Regulations Amendment Order 1939 (SR & O 1939, No 1620) was made on 23 November 1939 and formed the basis of UK exchange control for a number of years. For a survey of these regulations, see Mann, "Exchange Control in England" (1939–1940) 3 Mod LR 202.

[8] Notices to Banks did not have legal force, but explained the policy of the authorities from time to time and indicated those types of case in which permission might (or might not) be expected to be forthcoming. Consent might sometimes be given subject to conditions, eg a premium rate of exchange would generally be applied if the applicant wished to purchase foreign securities or make capital investments overseas. The general subject was covered in Exchange Control Notices EC 7 and 18. The so-called "dollar premium" was briefly noted in *Shelly v Paddock* [1978] 3 All ER 129.

instruments and Notices to Banks, which permitted numerous transactions which would otherwise have fallen within the scope of the broad prohibitions in the Act itself.

The 1947 Act consists of six Parts, namely: I gold and foreign currency; II payments; III securities; IV import and export; V miscellaneous; and VI supplemental provisions. There are also six Schedules to the Act. Many provisions of the Act are not concerned with money in the narrow sense of the term, but with monetary resources. Thus, Part III relates exclusively to securities, their issue, transfer, and deposit, while section 30 deals with the restrictions which could be imposed upon foreign companies by reason of the fact that their controllers were resident in the United Kingdom. **14.04**

Most of the provisions of the Act are prohibitive; these prohibitions are not absolute, but are relative in the sense that they cease to apply if the consent of the Treasury had been given.[9] Consents could be given specially, in response to a specific application by the party concerned, or generally, that is to say, authorising any transaction which satisfied the criteria set out in the permission concerned. Any such permission could be granted unconditionally or subject to conditions; but (except in certain cases specifically provided by the Act) permissions could not have retrospective effect, or "validate" transactions which had previously been effected in contravention of the Act.[10] **14.05**

The contractual consequences of a contravention of the 1947 Act are considered later.[11] So far as criminal liability is concerned, an offence was committed[12] by "any person in or resident in the United Kingdom" who contravened the prohibitions contained in the 1947 Act, and by "any such person who conspires or attempts or aids, abets, counsels or procures any other person" to contravene those prohibitions. Ignorance of the 1947 Act or its legal effect would plainly **14.06**

---

[9] The official administration of exchange control was in fact delegated by the Treasury to the Bank of England. The Bank, in turn, delegated a number of responsibilities to commercial banks, which were "authorised dealers" for the purpose of the Act. At least in so far as discretions were conferred upon the Treasury of the Bank of England, the exercise of such discretions might be amenable to judicial review if irrelevant factors had been taken into account in reaching a decision. For a New Zealand case which illustrates this point in the context of exchange control, see *Rowling v Takaro Properties Ltd* [1975] 2 NZLR 62.

[10] Thus, if a loan had been made in contravention of s 1 of the Act, then the lender could not recover the amounts owing to him even though permission were obtained subsequently. The injustices to which these provisions could give rise are plainly illustrated by *Boissevain v Weil* [1950] AC 327 (CA) and by the County Court decision in *Mortarana v Morley* (1958) 108 LJ 204. In each case, the debtor was able to avoid his repayment obligations by relying on exchange control regulations but the objective merits of the defence are by no means obvious.

[11] See para 14.20 below.

[12] See Pt II, Sch 5, para 1.

have afforded no defence in criminal proceedings.[13] Given that the 1947 Act was designed to protect the (then precarious) position of the national currency, the courts had to work on the assumption that rigorous enforcement was appropriate.[14] Nevertheless, whilst regulating the ability to make payments to or for the benefit of non-residents, the 1947 Act was not intended to provide a moratorium for debtors.[15]

14.07   It is necessary to emphasise one of the key structural features of the 1947 Act, namely that a sharp distinction was drawn between authorised dealers and other persons. Authorised dealers were banks named as such by the Treasury, and they were entitled to buy and sell and to borrow and lend gold and foreign currency, and to retain specified currency.[16] As a result, British banks could deal in gold and foreign currencies—both with other British banks and with foreign institutions—without any requirement for Treasury permission. The City of London was thus able to develop its role as an international financial centre, notwithstanding the existence of a rigid (domestic) system of exchange control which applied in other contexts.

C. The Offences Created by the 1947 Act

14.08   It is not necessary to undertake a detailed analysis of the offences created by the Exchange Control Act 1947. Instead, it is proposed to undertake an admittedly selective examination of some of the core sections which lie at the heart of an exchange control system and thus provide an outline to those unfamiliar with such a system.

14.09   Section 1(1) of the 1947 Act provided that:

> Except with the permission of the Treasury, no person, other than an authorised dealer, shall in the United Kingdom, and no other person resident in the United Kingdom, other than an authorised dealer, shall outside the United Kingdom, buy or borrow any gold or foreign currency from, or sell or lend any gold or foreign currency to, any person other than an authorised dealer.

---

[13] Ignorance of particular types of directions given by the Bank of England could, in limited cases, constitute a defence under s 37(3) of the Act, but this only marginally detracts from the general statement in the text.

[14] *Pickett v Fesq* [1949] 2 AII ER 705. In spite of this view, it should be emphasised that there are relatively few decisions relating to the 1947 Act. Given the scope of the prohibitions created by the 1947 Act, the absence of a significant body of case law is remarkable.

[15] A point emphasised in *Contract & Trading Co (Southern) Ltd v Barbey* [1960] AC 244.

[16] See ss 1 and 2 of the 1947 Act. The list of authorised dealers was published pursuant to s 42 of the Act. Authorised dealers and certain others were required to comply with directions given by the Treasury and were thus charged with an administrative role in ensuring compliance with the provisions of the Act—see s 34.

Transactions involving foreign currency or gold[17] were thus prohibited if they involved a person resident in the United Kingdom, even though he was abroad at the time of the transaction. Likewise, such a transaction was prohibited if it took place in the United Kingdom, even though both parties were resident abroad. The privileged position of authorised dealers is also highlighted by section 1 and will be further emphasised in other sections of the Act.

Section 2 of the Act provided that: **14.10**

> Every person in or resident in the United Kingdom who is entitled to sell, or to procure the sale of, any gold, or any foreign currency to which this section applies and is not an authorised dealer, shall offer it, or cause it to be offered, for sale to an authorised dealer, unless the Treasury consent to his retention and use thereof or he disposes thereof to any other person with the permission of the Treasury.

Sections 5 and 6 of the 1947 Act dealt with payments made to persons outside   **14.11** the United Kingdom.[18] In the absence of permission from the Treasury "no person resident in the United Kingdom shall . . . in the United Kingdom . . . make any payment to or for the credit of a person resident outside [the United Kingdom]".[19]

Section 1 of the 1947 Act thus prohibited dealings in gold and foreign currencies,   **14.12** whilst section 2 prohibited the holding of foreign currencies by creating an obligation to surrender any such holdings by means of offering them for sale to an authorised dealer. Sections 5 and 6 of the Act prohibited the making of payments—whether in sterling or in foreign currencies—to persons outside the United Kingdom.[20] Without attempting a sophisticated analysis, it is now possible to discern the main elements of the UK system of exchange control. No one could use their sterling funds or assets to acquire gold or foreign currency unless he did so through a bank (authorised dealer) which acted within the

---

[17] "Gold" referred to gold coin and gold bullion—see s 42 of the 1947 Act. The Act was thus directed to gold which had a monetary value as a currency or means of exchange; it did not apply to gold merely on account of its market value. On this point, see *Freed v DPP* [1969] 2 QB 115, (DC).

[18] For ease of illustration, the discussion will proceed on this basis. However, it should be appreciated that payments could generally be made to residents of other countries within the sterling area—referred to as the "scheduled territories" in the 1947 Act. The sterling area is discussed in Ch 33 below.

[19] 1947 Act, s 6(1). Consent was generally given for payments of a current nature, thus securing compliance with this country's obligations in that respect under the terms of the Articles of Agreement of the International Fund—see paras 22.29–22.41 below. Where, however, payment was to be made to acquire an overseas investment, approval from the Bank of England was almost invariably required, and the rate of exchange used to acquire the necessary foreign currency would involve an "investment premium"—see generally, *A Guide to United Kingdom Exchange Control* (Bank of England, July 1973).

[20] These provisions were to some extent supplemented by ss 21 and 22 of the 1947 Act which prohibited both the import and export of banknotes.

scope of the framework operated by the Bank of England. Similarly, in the absence of the necessary permission, it was unlawful to make a payment to a person outside the United Kingdom. These provisions were thus designed to control and preserve the use and availability of financial resources within this country. It necessarily followed from these rules that foreign holdings of sterling were restricted.[21]

14.13 Yet matters cannot end there, for gold, sterling, and foreign currency were by no means the only forms of monetary resources. This point is acknowledged by Part III of the Act, and in particular by sections 8 and 9. In essence, these sections prohibited both the original issue of debt and equity securities to a person outside the United Kingdom *and* the subsequent transfer of any securities to such a person. In the absence of permission, persons outside this country were not permitted to hold securities issued by entities within the United Kingdom, for they would thereby acquire claims upon monetary resources within this country. These provisions thus illustrate that a system of exchange control is not merely aimed at protecting the domestic currency but also serves to protect monetary resources in a much wider sense of that term.[22]

14.14 A person convicted of an offence under the Act was liable both to a fine and a period of imprisonment of up to two years.[23]

D. Personal and Territorial Ambit

14.15 Since the purpose of exchange control was to protect both sterling and other monetary assets by restricting outward transfers, it is perhaps unsurprising that, in a number of respects, the 1947 Act applied to transactions which were effected abroad and which had the effect of transferring such assets to foreigners. Indeed, the Act was expressed to apply to all persons, whether or not they were within the United Kingdom at the relevant time and whether or not they were

---

[21] Thus, whilst the *import* of both sterling and foreign currency banknotes was unrestricted, any foreign currency held by a person resident in the UK had to be offered for sale to an authorised dealer. The *export* of such notes was subject to a requirement for consent under the 1947 Act. In practice, however, a number of exceptions applied—see *A Guide to United Kingdom Exchange Control* (Bank of England, July 1973) 19; Bank of England Notice EC2 to Authorised Banks *Import and Export of Notes, Assurance Policies, Bills of Exchange etc* (29 November 1972).

[22] This point is further considered in the context of Art VIII(2)(b) of the IMF Agreement—see Ch 22 below. It will be apparent that the wide-ranging statutory prohibitions which have just been outlined would, of themselves, render impossible almost any form of international commerce. It is thus necessary to repeat that the provisions were made workable by means of numerous concessions created by means of statutory instruments and Notices to Banks. However, the text is concerned with the broad framework, rather than the detailed exceptions.

[23] For the details, see Sch 5 to the 1974 Act.

British subjects;[24] absence from the United Kingdom and foreign nationality did not necessarily exempt a person from the obligations imposed by the 1947 Act. In practice, however, individual sections tended to deal with the territoriality question in different ways, and invariably restricted the scope of the Act as a result. This particular point is apparent from the statutory language employed in sections 1, 2, 5, and 6 of the 1947 Act which were considered in the preceding section. It followed that a payment or other transaction could infringe the Act if (a) the person responsible for it acted within the United Kingdom, even though he was a foreign national resident abroad and (b) the responsible person acted outside the United Kingdom but was resident in this country.[25] Thus, UK residents were subjected to the provisions of the 1947 Act at all times, whether in or outside the country; foreign nationals were subjected to the Act only whilst they were present physically in, or were acting through, the United Kingdom. That this was intended to be the general rule may be derived from a number of the provisions of the Act,[26] but certain restrictions applied only to persons resident in the United Kingdom.[27] Other provisions applied only to persons "in the United Kingdom",[28] whilst in other cases a person was prohibited from taking certain steps in the United Kingdom, even if not physically here at the relevant time.[29] The scope of the criminal provisions may thus in some cases have exceeded the jurisdiction which international law allows a State to exercise[30] although it is plainly no longer necessary to consider the matter.

E. Exchange Control and Monetary Obligations

Having examined the 1947 Act in terms of its legal effect and territorial scope, it is necessary to examine the terms of the Act in so far as it affected monetary **14.16**

---

[24] See s 42(5) of the 1947 Act.

[25] The concept of "residence" can be an elusive one, but the Treasury had power to determine whether or not a particular person was resident in the UK for these purposes—see s 41(2) of the 1947 Act.

[26] See in particular ss 1, 2, 7, and 10.

[27] See, eg, ss 6, 24, 28, 29, and 30.

[28] See, eg, s 3.

[29] See, eg, s 5—"no person shall do any of the following things in the United Kingdom". The UK refers to the place in which the act is done, not the place in which the relevant person was to be found at the time.

[30] International law would not generally permit the UK to claim criminal jurisdiction over the actions of foreigners abroad—see *Oppenheim's International Law* (Longman, 9th edn, 1991) para 137, discussing *The Lotus Case* (1927) PCIJ Series A, No. 10 and Brownlie, *Principles of Public International Law* (Oxford University Press, 6th edn, 2003) 299–305.

obligations.[31] At the risk of oversimplification, it may be said that the existence of an exchange control regime could affect contractual obligations in three possible ways. First of all, it could affect the very *existence* of the contract itself. Secondly, it could have consequences for the *terms* of contracts which created monetary obligations; finally, it could have an impact upon the *enforceability* of such contracts. These three points must be considered separately.

14.17　The first point rests upon fundamental principles of contract law. Specifically, the parties will not be legally bound to any arrangements which they may have discussed unless it can be shown that they intended to enter into arrangements of a legally binding nature.[32] In a commercial context one may refer to "letters of comfort", where a party provides assurances as to its future conduct but which are framed in a manner which may be intended as a statement of policy or goodwill, as opposed to a binding commitment. The (non-)contractual character of such documents will be a question touching the material validity of the bargain between the parties, and will thus be governed by the putative applicable law in accordance with Article 8 of the Rome Convention.[33] Thus when a bank advanced money to the English subsidiary of a Malaysian parent company, it obtained from the parent a letter confirming that it was its policy to ensure that its subsidiaries were able to meet their respective liabilities as they arose. The Court of Appeal understandably held that this was merely a statement of current policy and it could not be construed as a contractual undertaking to ensure the continued solvency of the subsidiary concerned, or as a guarantee of the underlying loan. In reaching that conclusion, however, the Court was influenced by the fact that the issue of a guarantee by the parent company would have required exchange control in Malaysia, because of the external monetary obligations which such a course would have involved. The existence of the Malaysian Exchange Control Act—coupled with the absence of any intention to apply for approval—justified the inference that the document was not intended to create a binding contractual obligation.[34]

14.18　Turning now to the *terms* of the contract concerned, section 33(1) of the 1947 Act reads[35] as follows:

---

[31] The present discussion again proceeds by reference to the provisions of the 1947 Act. Nevertheless it is suggested that the broad contractual issues which are about to be discussed would apply equally in any country which continues to operate a system of exchange control.

[32] For a discussion of this principle under English law, see *Chitty on Contracts* (Sweet & Maxwell, 29th edn, 2004) paras 2-153–2-179.

[33] On this subject generally, see Ch 4 above.

[34] *Kleinwort Benson Ltd v Malaysia Mining Corporation Bhd* [1989] 1 All ER 785 (CA). It seems to have been accepted that English law governed the question of material validity.

[35] A similar provision remains in effect in several Commonwealth countries, eg see s 36 of the Malaysian Exchange Control Act.

It shall be an implied condition in any contract that where, by virtue of this Act, the permission or consent of the Treasury is at the time of the contract required for the performance of any term thereof that term shall not be performed except in so far as the permission or consent is given or not required: Provided that this subsection shall not apply in so far as it is shown to be inconsistent with the intention of the parties that it should apply, whether by reason of their having contemplated the performance of that term in spite of the provisions of this Act or for any other reason.

According to the House of Lords, it was not clear why section 33(1) was thought **14.19** to be necessary.[36] In the view of the present writer, the subsection was designed to preserve the contractual bargain where (as in the vast majority of cases) the parties would have intended to seek exchange control approval before any relevant payments were made, and to defeat any unmeritorious claim to the effect that the 1947 Act rendered the contract unlawful from the outset; yet the point remains obscure, for judgment on a debt could be obtained even though the requisite approval had not been given.[37] The following points may be noted in this regard:

(a) It is clear that the 1947 Act did not prohibit a person from agreeing to lend foreign currency although, as we have seen, the actual advance of the money would be unlawful until the necessary permission had been obtained under section 1 of the Act. Section 33(1) seems to be consistent with that analysis, and implied an appropriate term into the contract to ensure its validity;

(b) If an exchange control consent was required and the parties included an express condition that the necessary permissions must be obtained, then they would thereby create a valid and binding contract, but neither party would be obliged to perform his obligations unless and until the necessary permission had been given.[38] If the parties had included no express provision on this point but had nevertheless intended to perform their contract lawfully, then the necessary term would be implied by virtue of section 33(1). In either case, the legal position is essentially the same. Generally speaking, the obligation to apply for the necessary permission would fall upon the party who is subject to the relevant prohibitions under the 1947 Act, for it is he who required the consent and he would usually possess the information required in order to obtain it.[39] If the party required to apply for the permission failed to use reasonable diligence to obtain it, then

---

[36] See remarks made in *Contract and Trading Co (Southern) Ltd v Barbey* [1960] AC 244, 245. In accordance with general principles of statutory interpretation, the section could only apply to contracts governed by English law.

[37] See the 1947 Act, Sch 4, para 4.

[38] *Windschuegl Ltd v Alexander Pickering Ltd* (1950) 84 Ll LR 89.

[39] *AV Pound & Co Ltd v MW Hardy & Co Inc* [1956] AC 588.

he would be unable to rely on the condition and may also be liable for damages in respect of his breach.[40]

14.20 Turning now to the *enforceability* of contracts affected by the exchange control regime:

(a) If the evidence demonstrated that the parties intended to disregard their obligations under the 1947 Act, then it was impossible for the court to imply a term requiring that consent be obtained as a condition precedent to performance.[41]

(b) Under these circumstances, non-compliance with the 1947 Act usually rendered the transaction illegal and void. In view of the policy considerations which formed the basis of the UK exchange control system, a payment made in contravention of the 1947 Act could not be recovered by means of an action for money had and received; thus where a British national involuntarily resident in Monaco during the Second World War was forced to borrow money to save her family, it was held that this constituted a breach of the Defence (Finance) Regulations 1939, and the loan contract was thus unenforceable in England whatever its governing law.[42] By way of exception, a plaintiff who had been fraudulently induced to make the illegal payment might be able to recover his money on this basis, because the court would be reluctant to allow the defendant to benefit from his fraud.[43]

(c) Where a contract had been partly performed, this would generally lead to the conclusion that the parties had not intended to obtain the required approval for the payment obligations arising under it. The implied term contemplated by section 33(1) of the 1947 Act could not apply and the contract would thus be unenforceable on the grounds of illegality.[44]

(d) The position should not, however, be overstated. Where a transaction involved a series of contracts, some of those contracts might remain

---

[40] *Brauer & Co (Great Britain) Ltd v James Clark (Brush Materials) Ltd* [1952] 2 All ER 497.

[41] This is apparent from the proviso to s 33(1), which has been reproduced in para 14.18 above.

[42] *Boissevain v Weil* [1950] AC 327, 341. This case illustrates in the clearest terms the injustice which exchange control regulations could cause in certain cases; for criticism, see Mann, *Rec* 111 (1964, i) 124. In *Swiss Bank Corp v Lloyds Bank Ltd* [1982] AC 684, the Court of Appeal noted that actions taken in breach of the 1947 Act were not devoid of legal effect as between the parties, and that they merely exposed the wrongdoer to criminal sanctions. The Court was concerned with s 16(2) of the Act (which dealt with the holding of certificates for securities by authorised depositories) and the comment may be justifiable in that specific context. However, it is plainly not acceptable as a statement of general principle.

[43] *Shelly v Paddock* [1980] 2 WLR 647, distinguishing *JM Allen (Merchandising) Ltd v Clarke* [1963] 2 QB 340.

[44] See, eg, *Boissevain v Weil* [1950] AC 327 (HL); *Bigos v Boustead* [1951] 1 All ER 92; *Re HPC Productions Ltd* [1962] Ch 466; and *Shaw v Shaw* [1965] 638 (CA).

enforceable even though associated contracts contravened the 1947 Act. Thus the ultimate holder of a bill of exchange could enforce the payment obligations of the acceptor, even though the holder derived his title through an intermediate endorsement made in contravention of the 1947 Act.[45]

(e) If a valid debt or monetary obligation had been incurred under the terms of an enforceable contract and under circumstances where an approval was required under the 1947 Act for the payment of that debt, then judgment could be obtained for the payment of that debt even though the latter could only be discharged with a Treasury consent which had not been forthcoming. The result was that judgment could be given against a debtor even though it was unlawful to pay the creditor—payment could be made into court. This point is explicitly made in the 1947 Act, which provided[46] that "a claim for the recovery of any debt shall not be defeated by reason only of the debt not being payable without the permission of the Treasury and of that permission not having been given or having been revoked". Thus, in a case involving a bill of exchange accepted by a person resident in the United Kingdom, the holder of the bill was able to obtain judgment even though the consent required under section 5 of the Act had not been granted; the debt could not be paid without permission but it nevertheless remained a debt obligation in respect of which the creditor was entitled to judgment.[47]

It follows that both the 1947 Act and the courts which were called upon to apply it demonstrated some sensitivity to the conflicting requirements of national financial interest and the need to preserve the sanctity of the contractual bargain. The relative lack of case law on the subject suggests that the successful application of the Act relied heavily on administrative practice and pragmatism.

14.21

---

[45] *Bank für Gemeinwirtschaft v City of London Garages Ltd* [1971] 1 All ER 541(CA). The decision in part reflects s 33(2) of the 1947 Act, which preserved the validity of a bill of exchange notwithstanding any requirement for permission under the Act.

[46] See the 1947 Act, Sch 4, para 4.

[47] *Contract and Trading Co (Southern) Ltd v Barbey* [1960] AC 244, and see also *Credit Lyonnais v PT Barnard & Associates Ltd* (1976) 1 Ll LR 557. In *Shaw v Shaw* [1965] 1 All ER 638, the Court of Appeal had to consider a claim for a refund of a payment made in connection with the purchase of a property in Spain. The Court of Appeal struck out the claim, on the basis that the plaintiff based himself on nothing but the illegal payment. Yet this was not so, for the plaintiff was suing for the return of money paid for a consideration which had wholly failed (see 639). Regrettably, the Court did not consider the Fourth Schedule provisions reproduced above, although it seems unlikely that they would have assisted the plaintiff—they apply only to "debts" and recovery seems precluded by the decision in *Boissevain v Weil* [1950] AC 327.

15

EXCHANGE CONTROL UNDER THE INTERNATIONAL MONETARY FUND AGREEMENT

A. Introduction

As between the 184 or so members of the International Monetary Fund (IMF), **15.01** the law of exchange control differs from the general rules applicable to exchange control.[1] In those member States, the rule of positive law laid down in Article VIII(2) of the Articles of Agreement of the IMF applies. Article VIII(2)(a) provides the background to the present discussion, and requires that: "No member of the Fund shall without the approval of the Fund, impose restrictions on the making of payments and transfers for current international transactions." Article VIII(2)(b) then seeks to provide a measure of international protection for member countries which impose systems of exchange control which conform to the terms of the Fund Agreement. So far as relevant in the present context, that provision reads as follows: "Exchange contracts which involve the currency of any member and which are contrary to the exchange control regulations of

---

[1] On the membership of the Fund and the differing types of exchange rate arrangements, see the Fund's *2002 Annual Report on Exchange Arrangements and Exchange Restrictions*, p 1070.

that member maintained or imposed consistently with this Agreement shall be unenforceable in the territories of any member."

15.02 According to Article XX(1) of the Agreement, every member of the Fund has deposited "with the Government of the United States of America an instrument setting forth that it has accepted this Agreement in accordance with its law and has taken all (steps) necessary to enable it to carry out all of its obligations under this Agreement". It should therefore be possible to infer that all members of the Fund have incorporated Article VIII(2)(b) into their domestic law in such manner as may be required to ensure that their courts give effect to that provision in any relevant proceedings.[2] In the United Kingdom, this obligation was fulfilled by the Bretton Woods Agreement Order.[3] It is understood that the rule has not in fact been incorporated into, or has been removed from, the domestic law of certain member States.[4] It may be that those latter countries are thus technically in breach of the Fund Agreement, but it is not necessary to pursue that point in the present context.

15.03 Article VIII (2)(b)—as incorporated into domestic legal systems—provides a defence to contractual claims if the relevant factual elements can be proved. A reading of the Article immediately suggests that a number of difficult issues of interpretation will arise, and it will be necessary to turn to those at a later stage.[5] At the outset, however, it is necessary to observe that—as has been seen to be the case in other areas touching exchange control regulation[6]—the application of this provision may on occasion cause injustice, and the courts have thus shown marked astuteness in seeking to neutralise its effects.[7]

---

[2] The method by which this is achieved must be a question of the domestic constitutional law of the State concerned.

[3] SR & O 1946, No. 36, which continues in force by virtue of s 6(2) of the International Monetary Fund Act 1979.

[4] According to Dr Mann, a number of States have elected to eliminate this provision from their domestic law—see his preface to the Fifth Edition of this work.

[5] The literature on the subject is vast although much of it has become dated. The most valuable contributions are those of Sir Joseph Gold; and many are collected in four volumes, *The Fund Agreement in the Courts* (1962, 1976, 1986, 1989). Other contributions appeared in the IMF pamphlet series; see in particular, *The International Monetary Fund and Private Business Transactions* (1969) and *The Cuban Insurance Cases and the Articles of the Fund* (1966). Sir Joseph Gold was for many years General Counsel to the Fund, and argued for a much broader interpretation of Art VIII(2)(b) than is advocated in the present work.

[6] See in particular, the decision in *Boissevain v Weil* [1950] AC 327, noted in Ch 14 above.

[7] It may be said that the decision of the English courts to adopt a narrow approach to the meaning of "exchange contracts" is a part of this trend—see below. It is also apparent from the decision Cass Civ 16 October 1967, *Rev Crit* 1968 661, also 48 Int LR 229; in 1948, Janda, a Czechoslovakian, entrusted in Prague US$30,000 to Kosek, a naturalised US citizen who was about to leave Czechoslovakia, to transfer that money to the US. Janda followed later and in 1951 obtained an acknowledgement of the debt from Kosek. The latter's defence, based on Art VIII(2)(b) failed because the Court of Appeal held that Czechoslovakia had not become a member of the IMF and the Cour de Cassation felt unable to interfere with that finding. In truth,

B. Legal Character of Article VIII(2)(b)

At the outset it is necessary to consider the legal nature of the provision set out **15.04**
in Article VIII(2)(b).[8] It may potentially adopt three forms. First of all, it may be
treated as part of the *domestic contract law* of the State which has incorporated
Article VIII(2)(b) into its domestic law; in that event, Article VIII(2)(b) would
be applied only in relation to contracts governed by that system of law.[9] Alternatively, it may be seen as part of the system of a member State's *private international law*.[10] Finally, the Article (as incorporated into national law) may be
regarded as a mandatory rule, the application of which overrides both the law
applicable to the contract and the private international law of the forum.[11]

The difference between these versions may be considerable. For example if Art- **15.05**
icle VIII(2)(b) is to be applied as part of the law applicable to the contract, then
an English court must apply Article VIII(2)(b) as interpreted by the courts of the

---

Czechoslovakia was a member of the Fund at that time and was only compelled to withdraw in
1955; this was, of course, a matter of public record and could be ascertained from the Fund's
annual reports and other publications. The legal aspects of the withdrawal are discussed by Mann
(1968–9) *British Yearbook of International Law*, 7. But the French courts can scarcely be criticised
for seeking to assist the plaintiff; the defence was entirely without merit. A similar case in which a
fair decision was reached by legal reasoning of doubtful merit is *Barton v National Life Assurance
Co of Canada* (1977) 398 NY Supp 2d 941 where the court held that payments under a life
insurance policy issued in Jamaica had to be made in New York on the ground that Art 11 of the
Treaty between Britain and the United States of 1899 guaranteed to US citizens the right to take
possession and dispose of personal property. Although the attitude of the US is uncertain, it is
probable that the IMF Articles of Agreement suspended the operation of the 1899 Treaty in so far
as it related to exchange control.

[8] On this and related issues, see Gianviti, "Reflexions sur l'Article VIII section 2(b) des statuts
de Fonds Monétaire International" (1973) 62 Rev Critique de Droit International Privé 471;
Gianviti, "The Fund Agreement in the Courts", in *Current Legal Issues Affecting Central* Banks,
Vol 1 (1992) 1; Silard, "Money and Foreign Exchange" *International Encyclopaedia of Comparative
Law*, Vol 17 (1975) ch 20, sections 86–93; R.W. Edwards Jr; *International Monetary Collaboration*
(1985) 481–2. For more recent discussions of the legal character of Art VIII(2)(b), see, Lowenfeld,
International Economic Law (Oxford University Press, 2002) 665–70; Dicey and Morris, *The
Conflict of Laws* (Sweet & Maxwell, 13th edn, 2000) paras 36-088–36-097.

[9] This was the view adopted in the unreported case of *American Express International Banking
Corp v Irvani* (23 July 1980), where the Court declined to apply the English approach to Article
VIII(2)(b), on the grounds that the contract was governed by New York law. This approach
overlooks the point that the UK and its courts are under an obligation to implement Article
VIII(2)(b), and that obligation cannot in any sense be diluted by the law applicable to the
contract—see below.

[10] This view was adopted in *Sharif v Azad* [1967] 1 QB 605, 617.

[11] The application of rules of this kind is specifically contemplated by the Rome Convention,
Art 7(2). On the law which governs a monetary obligation, mandatory rules of the forum and
related matters, see Ch 4 above. The provisions of Art 21 of the Rome Convention should also be
noted, for they specifically confirm the continued application of international rules such as Art
VIII(2)(b).

country whose system of law governs the contract.[12] If, by contrast, the English court applies the Article as part of its private international law or as a mandatory rule of domestic law, then English conceptions of the Article will have to be applied. This may make a difference because, as will be seen, the provision has been given different meanings in different member States.[13] Given that the provision is derived from a multilateral treaty, the characterisation of the provision cannot be resolved purely by reference to English canons of interpretation.[14] It is instead necessary to ascertain the meaning of the Article by a broad approach, taking into account its objectives and purpose. In this context, the core provision of the Article reads "Exchange contracts . . . shall be unenforceable in the territories of any member." This language does not make or suggest any reference either to the law applicable to the contract concerned or to the private international law of the forum; nor does the context suggest that the governing law has any relevance to the matter. The broad objective of the Article is to ensure that contracts infringing the exchange controls of member States will not be enforced either in that or in any other member State. Consistently with the United Kingdom's obligations under the IMF's Articles of Association, the rule must have mandatory application, regardless of the governing law of the contract, the residence or nationality of the parties, or any other matter.[15] This approach is also consistent with the Interpretation of the provision published by the Executive Directors of the IMF in 1949,[16] which notes that contracts contravening Article VIII(2)(b) "will be treated as unenforceable notwithstanding that under the private international law of the forum, the law under which the

---

[12] See the Rome Convention, Art 10(1)(a). This point would have no practical importance if (as ought to be the case) the provision had been given a uniform interpretation in the courts of different countries, but in fact this has not been the case—see, eg, Gianviti (n 8 above).

[13] This state of affairs is, of course, to be regretted because a uniform law should have uniform application. On uniform laws generally, see Mann (1983) 99 LQR 376, reprinted in (1990) *Further Studies in International Law* 270. It may be added that the German Supreme Court has adopted a fourth approach, namely that Article VIII(2)(b) (as incorporated into German law) constitutes a rule of procedure. This is considered in more depth at n 148 below.

[14] On the reasons for this statement and a discussion of relevant cases, see Mann, *Foreign Affairs in English Courts* (Oxford University Press, 1986) 107. The principles which should govern the interpretation of "uniform statutes" were laid down in *Fothergill v Monarch Airlines* [1981] AC 251. The Court of Appeal in *Sharif v Azad* [1967] 1 QB 605 suggested a liberal interpretation of Article VIII(2)(b) (see 618), but on the whole, the English courts have tended to adopt a relatively narrow approach to the provision.

[15] ie the application of Art VIII(2)(b) must be regarded as mandatory for the purposes of Art 7(2) of the Rome Convention. This approach appears to reflect by the House of Lords decision in *United City Merchants (Investments) Ltd v Royal Bank of Canada* [1983] 1 AC 168, which confirms the mandatory nature of the rule and the necessary consequence that the parties cannot exclude Art VIII(2)(b) by the terms of their contract. For a similar view, see Lowenfeld, *International Economic Law* (Oxford University Press, 2002) 667.

[16] The Interpretation was published in the IMF *Annual Report* 1949, p 82, and is reproduced in (1954) ICLQ 262 and in Dicey and Morris, *The Conflict of Laws* (Sweet & Maxwell, 13th edn, 2000) para 36-089.

foreign exchange control regulations are maintained or imposed is not the law which governs the exchange contract or its performance".

It is believed that Article VIII(2)(b) would normally present itself to the English **15.06** courts in the manner just described, ie as a rule which must be applied regardless of the governing law of the contract at hand.[17] But this should not entirely exclude consideration of other private international law matters.

In this context, it must be remembered—in view of the breadth of the Fund's **15.07** membership—that Article VIII(2)(b) will usually also form a part of the law applicable to the contract.[18] In such an event, the English court would also have to take that provision into account as part of the law which governs the contract, with the following results:

(a) If the evidence demonstrates that the applicable law takes a broader or different approach to the interpretation of Article VIII(2)(b),[19] then the English court should apply this in the usual way, in compliance with Article 10 of the Rome Convention. There would appear to be no consideration of public policy which should prevent the English court from applying such broader interpretation. In accordance with established conflict of law principles, the mere fact that rules of foreign law differ from the corresponding rules of English law does not of itself entitle the English court to disregard them.[20]

(b) If, in any respect, the foreign law adopts a narrower view of Article VIII(2)(b), then the English court must apply the standards determined by English case law because (as shown) the application of the rule is mandatory before the English courts.

In other words, so far as the English courts are concerned, the English approach **15.08** to the interpretation of Article VIII(2)(b) sets a minimum standard, which must

---

[17] Since the provision forms a part of English domestic law by virtue of the materials mentioned in note 3 above, the application of this provision cannot cause any special difficulty in the context of the conflicts framework created by the Rome Convention. In any event, Art 21 of the Rome Convention confirms that such Convention does not prejudice the application of other conventions binding on the contracting States. Further, in one case, a German court held that it did not need to examine a defence based on Art VIII(2)(b) and an alleged contravention of Austrian exchange controls, on the basis that the contract was governed by German law. This decision was plainly erroneous in the light of the points just discussed, and the decision was reversed by the Supreme Court: *A v B Co*, 9 April 1962. The decision was apparently unreported but is partly reproduced by Lowenfeld, *The International Monetary System* (Matthew Bender, 2nd edn, 1984) 334.

[18] In other words, it will form a part of the body of rules which govern the validity and interpretation of the contract at hand—see Art 15 of the Rome Convention.

[19] ie different to that which the English courts would otherwise adopt. As will be seen (below), the approach to the interpretation of the Article is by no means uniform.

[20] For the approach adopted in this area, see *Loucks v Standard Oil Co* (1918) 224 NY 99; 120 NE 198, 202; *Vervaeke v Smith* [1983] 1 AC 145.

be applied in any event. But Article VIII(2)(b) may render unenforceable a broader range of contracts, if that is the position required under the law applicable to the contract. As noted above, this unsatisfactory position flows from the fact that Article VIII(2)(b) has not benefited from an internationally uniform approach to its interpretation and application. Against that background, however, the approach just suggested is consistent with the conflict of law principles laid down by the Rome Convention.[21]

C. Public Policy under the IMF Agreement

15.09 As is well known, an English court will disregard rules forming part of a foreign system of law if, under the circumstances of the case, the application of that rule would be manifestly contrary to public policy.[22] In the context of foreign exchange control regulations, there can be no doubt that Article VIII(2)(b) demands respect for exchange controls introduced by other member States and which are maintained consistently with the IMF Agreement; it must necessarily follow that the ability of the English courts to disregard such foreign exchange control regulations on public policy grounds is thereby severely circumscribed. Indeed, it is difficult to envisage any circumstances under which regulations which are consistent with Article VIII(2)(b) could be ignored on policy grounds.[23] This view is reinforced when it is remembered that Article VIII(2)(b) is intended to override any contrary municipal law of the member States.[24]

---

[21] It may be observed that, despite the differing approaches to Art VIII(2)(b) which had by then become apparent, no attempt was made to clarify the provision when the Articles of Agreement were amended in 1976—the point is made by Lowenfeld, *International Economic Law* (Oxford University Press, 2002) 667. Whilst it is often hazardous to draw inferences from mere inaction, this may reflect the fact that Art VIII(2)(b)—however interpreted—was not felt to have made a major contribution to the overall objectives of the Fund. The Fund itself has recently noted that exchange control regulations will be effective in the territory of the State which imposes them, but that Art VIII(2)(b) has not always been effective in extending that protection to other jurisdictions—see Anne O Kruger, "A New Approach to Sovereign Debt Restructuring" (2002) International Monetary Fund, 37.

[22] See, in particular, the provisions of Art 16 of the Rome Convention.

[23] This point is made in *Perutz v Bohemian Discount Bank* (1953) 304 NY 533 also [1955] Int LR 715. Similarly *Banco Frances e Brasileira SA v John Doe No. 1* (1975) 36 NY 2d 592, 331 NE 2d 502, where the Court said "United States membership of the IMF makes it impossible to conclude that the currency control laws of other member States are offensive to this State's policy so as to preclude suit in tort by a private party". See also Dicey and Morris, *The Conflict of Laws* (Sweet & Maxwell, 13th edn, 2000) para 36-097. It is necessary to emphasise that the statement in the text will not apply where the system of control is discriminatory or is otherwise inconsistent with Art VIII(2)(b). This general subject is considered in Ch 19 below.

[24] A point made in the 1949 Interpretation of Art VIII(2)(b) issued by the Executive Directors of the Fund and to which reference has already been made. It has been suggested that Article VIII(2)(b) in some respects reversed the long-established rule that the courts will not enforce the revenue laws of another State; these views are noted by Lowenfeld, *International Economic Law*

Other provisions of the IMF Agreement also tend to support the view just **15.10**
expressed. Member States grant to each other the right to "exercise such controls
as are necessary to regulate international capital movements" and the right, with
the consent of the Fund, to "impose restrictions on the making of payments and
transfers for current international payments".[25] Having obtained these rights for
themselves and granted them to other member States by treaty, it is not open to
national courts to reject as contrary to public policy that which those States have
expressly allowed each other to do. On the contrary, policy considerations
demand the recognition of exchange control regulations which are consistent
with the IMF Agreement. Thus, where in accordance with the permission given
by the Agreement, members agree to "cooperate in measures for the purpose of
making the exchange control regulations of either member more effective",[26]
and with this object in view enter into a bilateral treaty, compliance with its
provisions may have to be treated by the judge as a matter of public policy, even
though they are not incorporated into the municipal system.[27]

Yet it would seem that, although exchange control regulations as a whole may **15.11**
be maintained consistently with the Fund Agreement, certain of their specific
effects may be such as to require or permit the refusal to apply them in a given
case on the ground of public policy. This may occur when their application
would be discriminatory or penal in character or otherwise obnoxious. There
is nothing in the Fund Agreement that compels the courts in a given case
to reach decisions which are offensive to their sense of justice; they are precluded
only from ignoring a member State's exchange controls as a matter of
principle or of *a priori* reasoning.[28] It seems that this is the rationale underlying
a decision of the Dutch Hoge Raad, which rejected Indonesian exchange

---

(Oxford University Press, 2002) 667. However, exchange control systems serve a different purpose
and thus should not be placed in the same category as revenue laws generally. Moreover, Article
VIII(2)(b) does not require positive enforcement of foreign exchange controls, for the English
courts would not enforce a duty to surrender foreign exchange to the government concerned—see
Camdex International Ltd v Bank of Zambia (No. 3) [1997] CLC 714.

[25] See Arts VI(3) and VIII(2)(a) of the Agreement.

[26] Article VIII(2)(b), second sentence.

[27] At least in England, it was formerly doubtful whether the English courts would look at an
unincorporated treaty, especially where made between foreign States—see Mann (1991) 107
LQR. It is however, now clear that the English courts can examine the terms of treaties (whether
the UK is a party to them or not) where they form part of the relevant factual background to the
case—eg, see *JH Rayner (Mincing Lane) Ltd v Department of Trade and Industry* [1990] 2 AC 418;
Arab Monetary Fund v Hashim (No. 3) [1991] 2 AC 114; and *Westland Helicopters Ltd v Arab
Organisation for Industrialisation* [1995] QB 282.

[28] This sentence was approved by Judge Holtzman in his dissenting judgment in *Dallal v Bank
Mellat* (1981) 75 Int LR 126, 149. The majority decision was subsequently questioned by
Hobhouse J—see *Dallal v Bank Mellat* [1986] 1 All ER 239, 250.

control regulations.[29] Public policy ought to have been (and perhaps was) one of the reasons why the New York Court of Appeals in *J Zeevi & Sons Ltd v Grindlays Bank (Uganda) Ltd*[30] disregarded Ugandan exchange control restrictions: "As typified by strong anti-Israeli and anti-semitic suggestions made by Uganda's President to the Secretary General of the United Nations", the Bank of Uganda purported to cancel all payments to Israeli companies (including the plaintiff) and the defendant relied on these cancellations to avoid liability under a letter of credit opened prior to such official cancellations. The Court described the cancellations as "confiscatory and discriminatory acts of the Ugandan Government"; under these circumstances it would surely have been contrary to public policy for the New York Court to give effect to the cancellations, and the defendant bank thus could not avoid liability on this basis.[31]

D. The Scope and Interpretation of Article VIII(2)(b)

15.12 It should be appreciated that the scope of Article VIII(2)(b) is relatively limited. It by no means requires the universal recognition and enforcement of exchange control legislation among member States; it merely requires that certain types of contract be treated as unenforceable if they infringe such regulations and certain other conditions are met.

15.13 It should also be appreciated that Article VIII(2)(b) supplements the internal law of the member States. Thus if, Article VIII(2)(b) is inapplicable for some reason, it does not necessarily follow that the contract will be valid and enforceable. On the contrary, it may be unenforceable on other grounds—for example, where the contract forms part of a wider scheme which involves the deliberate commission of actions designed to infringe the laws of a friendly foreign State[32] or because it forms part of a wider scheme involving the commission of illegal

---

[29] (1970) 40 Int LR 7, where the Court said that Art VIII(2)(b) was no obstacle to an assignment in contravention of Indonesian exchange regulations, because the IMF Agreement was "intended solely for the regular financial relations between States".

[30] (1975) 37 NY 2d 220, 333, NE 2d 168.

[31] It may well be that the plaintiff in *Mansouri v Singh* [1986] 1 WLR 1393 could likewise have invoked public policy. Although member States have granted to each other the right to impose exchange controls, it is incumbent on States to perform their treaties in good faith. Thus, if a State imposes exchange control for an improper purpose, other States are absolved from their obligations to respect those regulations. In terms of Art VIII(2)(b), it is likely that such contracts would not have been imposed consistently with the terms of the IMF Agreement—thus providing another ground on which recognition could be refused.

[32] See *Regazzoni v KC Sethia (1944) Ltd* [1958] AC 301. The existence of this principle was recently reaffirmed in *Mahonia Ltd v West LB* [2004] EWHC 1938 (Comm).

acts.[33] Equally, if the contract at hand is governed by the law of the country which imposes the exchange control regulations, the English courts would give effect to any provisions which invalidate the contract by reason of the breach, because those provisions form a part of the law applicable to the contract.[34]

It is to be appreciated that Article VIII(2)(b) is only concerned with the enforce-ability (or otherwise) of certain *contracts*. Thus, there is no room for the appli-cation of the provision in the context of actions *in rem*,[35] restitution, tort,[36] unjust enrichment,[37] or for the enforcement of a foreign judgment,[38] which are governed exclusively by general rules—Article VIII(2)(b) cannot apply in such cases. Some support for these views may be derived from the decision of the

15.14

---

[33] The corresponding commentary in the Fifth Edition of this work (p 372) was specifically approved by the Court of Appeal in *Ispahani v Bank Melli Iran* [1998] 1 Lloyds Bank Rep 133.

[34] See Art 10(1) of the Rome Convention discussed in Ch 14 above. The text differs from remarks which were made in the Court of Appeal in *United City Merchants (Investments) Ltd v Royal Bank of Canada* [1981] 1 WLR 242, where it was suggested that Art VIII(2)(b) displaced the common law principle in the *Regazzoni* case, at least in so far as that principle applied to foreign exchange controls. This view was, in turn, derived from remarks made in *Sharif v Azad* [1967] 1 QB 605, 617. It is, however, suggested that Art VIII(2)(b) does not override a central principle of public policy, which condemns violations of foreign mandatory law by acts done within that foreign country. The German Federal Supreme Court also said that the legal conse-quences of the violation of a member State's exchange control regulations were "conclusively governed by Article VIII (2)(b)"—*BGHZ* 55, 334, 339. In the light of the points made in the text, these observations are too broad.

[35] The Court of Appeal of Hamburg, overturning a decision of the District Court, refused to apply Art VIII(2)(b) in adjudicating upon title to a consignment of charcoal, even though the contract under which title was acquired offended Brazilian exchange control laws—District Court of Hamburg, 9 January 1991, *IPRspr* 1992, No. 71a; Court of Appeal of Hamburg, 4 September 1992, *IPRspr* 1992, No. 71b.

[36] For a different view, see District Court of Hamburg, 24 February 1978, *IPRspr* 1978, No. 126; under an unenforceable exchange contract, the defendant had received a large sum of money for the plaintiff's account. The court declined to treat the refusal to pay as embezzlement giving rise to tortious liability, on the ground that this would amount to indirect enforcement of an unenforceable exchange contract. This unhappy result should have been avoided because by its terms, Art VIII(2)(b) applies only to contracts. For a decision on similar facts, see Court of Appeal, Berlin, 8 July 1974, *IPRspr* 1974, No. 138.

[37] It may be noted that the Austrian Supreme Court has expressly declined to apply Art VIII(2)(b) in the context of a claim for unjust enrichment—30 September 1992, *Zeitschrift für Rechtsvergleichung* 1993, 124.

[38] This was clearly so held by the Court of Appeals (1st Cir) in *John Sanderson & Co Wool Pty Ltd v Ludlow Jute Co Ltd* (1978) 569 F 2d 696, which involved an action on an Australian judgment: Bretton Woods might possibly have been a defence in the Australian action, "but because it was not, such defence is now foreclosed". In the same sense, the German Federal Supreme Court, 11 October 1956, *BGHZ* 22, 24, 31. Further confirmation of this position is offered by a decision of the German Federal Supreme Court: 3 December 1992, *BGHZ* 120, 334, 348 or *IPRspr* 1992, No. 229 (at 570). The claimant sought to enforce a Brazilian judgment in Germany; the defendants invoked Art VIII(2)(b) on the grounds that the judgement infringed Brazilian exchange control laws. The Federal Supreme Court dismissed this argument; it was plainly not open to a German court to find that enforcement would contravene Brazilian exchange controls, when a Brazilian court itself found no such objection when giving the original judgment.

New York Court of Appeals in *Banco do Brasil v Israel Commodity Co Inc*,[39] although it is not easy to see the relevance of Article VIII(2)(b) to the case. The plaintiff, an instrumentality of the Government of Brazil, claimed damages for conspiracy alleged to have been committed by the defendant and a Brazilian coffee exporter with a view to depriving the plaintiff of US dollar funds to which it was entitled under Brazilian exchange control laws. The plaintiff argued that the defendant's participation in a scheme to evade Brazilian exchange control laws afforded a ground of recovery under Article VIII(2)(b). The argument was bound to fail, for, as the Court said, the unenforceability of a contract "is far from implying that one who so agrees commits a tort in New York".[40]

15.15 Furthermore, it is submitted that Article VIII(2)(b) had no bearing upon the type of situation with which the House of Lords was faced in two cases.[41] There, the owner of securities was resident in Czechoslovakia. He entered into a contract of bailment with a local bank whereby the latter undertook to hold securities with a sub-bailee in England. Article VIII(2)(b) does not preclude the owner from claiming the securities by means of a direct action in detinue against the sub-bailee—a point ultimately admitted by the defendants before the House of Lords.[42]

15.16 If a contract does prove to be unenforceable by virtue of Article VIII(2)(b), this does not preclude one party from claiming damages for a failure by the other party to seek and to endeavour to obtain the necessary authorisation, where the latter party was required to do so by the terms of the contract.[43]

15.17 It is thought that Article VIII(2)(b) should not be applied in a purely domestic context, ie where the creditor in country X claims payment in country X from a debtor in country X. In other words, Article VIII(2)(b) presupposes a contract or at least a payment across national frontiers. Thus, in *J Zeevi & Sons v Grindlays Bank (Uganda) Ltd*,[44] the New York Court of Appeals decided that an irrevocable

---

[39] (1963) 12 NY 2d 371. See also *J Zeevi & Sons v Grindlays Bank (Uganda) Ltd* (1975) 37 NY 2d 220, 333 NE 2d 168 which rightly decided that if a private tort is committed in connection with the fraudulent operation of an exchange control system, an action in tort is not barred by virtue of the rule against the enforcement of foreign revenue or public laws.

[40] At 376.

[41] *Kahler v Midland Bank* [1950] AC 24 and *Zivnovstenska Bank v Frankman* [1950] AC 57. Nor does the provision apply where the facts are similar to those in *Ellinger v Guinness Mahon & Co* [1939] 4 All ER 16.

[42] *Kahler v Midland Bank* [1950] AC 24, 43.

[43] On this point, see the discussion in the context of the Exchange Control Act 1947, in Ch 14 above.

[44] (1975) 37 NY 2d 220, 333 NE 2d 168. The same point was made in *Theye v Pan-American Life Insurance Co* (1964) 161 So 2d 70; *Pan-American Life Insurance Co v Blanco* (1966) 362 F 2d 167 and *Libra Bank Ltd v Banco Nacional de Costa Rica* (1983) 570 F Supp 870.

letter of credit for a sum in US dollars established by the defendant in New York in favour of the American plaintiffs could be enforced in New York notwithstanding an order by the Ugandan Government instructing the defendant to cancel it on the grounds that the necessary exchange control approval had been revoked.[45] In such a case, there is no cross-border element of a kind which is sufficient to bring Article VIII(2)(b) into operation. It is for this reason, amongst others, that it is difficult to support the decision of the House of Lords in *United City Merchants (Investments) Ltd v Royal Bank of Canada*.[46] Peruvian buyers had agreed to buy goods from English sellers for approximately US$662,000. Payment was to be made by the defendants in London by confirmed irrevocable transferable letter of credit. It was arranged between the buyers and the sellers that one half of the purchase price, when paid under the letter of credit, would be remitted by the sellers to an account in the United States for the benefit of the buyers. Without direct reference to the evidence, the House of Lords held that it was contrary to the exchange control regulations of Peru to make the US$331,000 available to the buyers in the United States. Payment of this sum was thus held to be contrary to Article VIII(2)(b), but the issuing bank was ordered to pay the balance, which represented the legitimate purchase price of the goods. In other words, the payment by a London bank of money owing to an English creditor and payable in England was held to be unenforceable because it "mirrored" an unlawful payment in a separate contract to which the bank was not a party. This decision is irreconcilable with the autonomous nature of a letter of credit which is so strongly emphasised in the

---

[45] The same view was taken by the German Federal Supreme Court, 30 January 1986 *WM* 1986, 600 or *IPRspr* 1986, No. 118; 8 March 1970, *NJW* 1980, 520. Two German nationals were working in Nigeria, and one of them made a loan to the other in Nigerian currency but to be repaid in Germany by reference to a pre-agreed rate of exchange. The court found that the claim at issue had to be discharged in Germany in German currency, with the result that Art VIII(2)(b) could not apply. The Court of Appeal of Cologne, 10 April 1992, *RIW* 1993, 938 or *IPRspr* 1992, No. 173, has also reaffirmed this principle in an interesting case. The German claimant was owed some 40 million CFA francs by a customer resident in Burkina Faso. The claimant arranged for an employee to collect the money from the customer in cash, and to return to Germany with the money in a suitcase. Flights for this purpose were booked with the defendant airline, which was also a German entity. The return flight to Germany involved a brief stop in Paris, and the defendant agreed to ensure that the suitcase would be transferred directly to the connecting flight to Germany. Due to a misunderstanding, however, an airline employee took the suitcase into the French customs area, where the money was seized and subsequently confiscated. The claimant thereupon sued the defendant airline for damages; and the airline sought to rely on Art VIII(2)(b), on the basis that the export of such a large sum of cash was inconsistent with exchange control arrangements in Burkina Faso. The court rightly rejected the argument, on the basis that the proceedings involved a dispute between two domestic parties involving a contract of carriage. This contract could not have any impact upon Burkina Faso's balance of payments, and the contract had to be viewed entirely separately from the arrangements between the German claimant and his customer in Burkina Faso.

[46] [1983] 1 AC 168, on which see Collier [1983] Cambridge LJ 49 and Mann (1982) 98 LQR 526.

judgment.[47] The decision is perhaps explicable by the fact that the proceedings were brought by a transferee of the credit, who had no interest in ensuring that the Peruvian buyers received their anticipated US dollar payment. But whatever may be said about the contract between the buyers and the sellers, the defendant's obligations under the letter of credit issued by a London bank for the benefit of English sellers were, it is submitted, entirely outside the scope of Article VIII(2)(b).

15.18   It should be appreciated that Article VIII(2)(b) does not impose a broad, general obligation on member countries to have regard to the exchange control laws of their fellow members, and to give effect to them where appropriate.[48] On the contrary, according to the true meaning of the Article, "the Member States were contractually bound to have regard to their exchange control regulations *within the framework envisaged by the treaty*".[49]

15.19   It has, on occasion, been suggested that Article VIII(2)(b) does not apply to transactions of a capital nature, partly because the heading to Article VIII(2)(b) refers specifically to "current transactions", and partly because the scheme of the Agreement distinguishes between current and capital payments; the control of capital transactions is separately permitted by Article VI(3). As a matter of logic, it may be said that capital transfers fall entirely outside the scope of Article VIII(2)(b). Yet it may be argued that it would be a curious position if contracts in the course of trade might be caught by Article VIII(2)(b), whilst gifts, investments, and the purchase of foreign property were not, for it is the latter category of transactions which could pose a greater threat to a member country's exchange resources.[50] Given that the court must strive to achieve a purposive (rather than a merely formal) interpretation, it is thus tempting to suggest that the Article must be taken to apply both to capital and to current transactions; if Article VI(3) allows a country to restrict capital outflows, then exchange control regulations which seek to exercise that right should enjoy the limited degree

---

[47] See in particular, at p 185. The autonomy of the credit should only be undermined in cases of fraud or where the beneficiary is involved in a conspiracy to breach the laws of a foreign State—*Mahonia Ltd v West LB* [2004] EWHC 1938 (Comm).

[48] The suggestion that Art VIII(2)(b) created such an obligation was made by the German Supreme Court—19 April 1962, *IPRspr* 1962 and 1963, No. 163; it is unacceptable for the reasons given in the text.

[49] Emphasis added. See the remarks of the German Federal Supreme Court, 21 December 1976, *WM* 1977, 322 or *IPRspr* 1976, No. 118.

[50] It was for this reason that Dr Mann supported the application of Art VIII(2)(b) to capital controls—see the Fifth Edition of this work, 376. It is submitted that his arguments carried much force, but they can no longer be accepted in the light of the more recent authorities considered below. That Art VIII(2)(b) is not applicable under these circumstances seems to be accepted by Elizalde, "The International Monetary Fund and Current Account Convertibility" (IMF, 4 June 2004).

of protection afforded by Article VIII(2)(b).[51] Yet, attractive though this formulation may be, it cannot be accepted.

The IMF itself instituted discussions in 1997 with a view to extending its **15.20** powers to cover movements of capital, and the Fund thus appears to accept that its writ does not run in this area.[52] Further, a decision of the German Federal Supreme Court affirms the view that Article VIII(2)(b) applies only to transactions of a current nature.[53] In that case a Bulgarian bank was a member of a limited partnership established in Germany. The partnership ran into financial difficulty and the Bulgarian bank agreed to subscribe further funds of DM6.8 million by way of an increase in its interest in the partnership capital. Such a transfer required exchange control approval in Bulgaria, which had not been obtained. The partnership later became insolvent, and the trustee in bankruptcy demanded payment of the outstanding balance; the bank resisted the demand, on the grounds that its undertaking to provide further capital infringed Bulgarian exchange controls and was thus unenforceable by virtue of Article VIII(2)(b). The decision relied partly on the language of the IMF Agreement[54] and partly on an historical analysis—member countries had agreed to surrender some of their sovereignty in relation to current transfers, on the basis that their own, lawfully imposed restrictions would be recognised by other members. However, since sovereignty in the field of capital transfers had not been ceded, there was no basis for applying Article VIII(2)(b) to transfers of that kind.[55]

In a further case before the Federal Supreme Court, a German bank sued an **15.21** Austrian national for payment of a bill of exchange which represented a loan

---

[51] But for the decisions about to be discussed, the present writer would have to adhere to the views expressed by Dr Mann. If exchange regulations should be respected under Art VIII(2)(b), provided they are not imposed inconsistently with the Fund Agreement, there seems to be no reason to refuse that treatment to capital controls.

[52] The proposal for this Fourth Amendment to the Articles of Agreement is discussed by Carreau and Juillard, *Droit international économique* (Dalloz, 2003) 542–3 and by Treves, "Monetary Sovereignty Today" in Giovanoli (ed) *International Monetary Law: Issues for the New Millenium* (Oxford University Press, 2000) 115.

[53] German Federal Supreme Court, 8 November 1993, *NJW* 1994, 390 or *IPRspr* 1993, No. 127. The summary in the text relies upon Ebke, *Article VIII, Section (2)(b) of the IMF Articles of Agreement and International Capital Transfers* at p 762. See also the decisions of February 1994, *NJW* 1994, 1868 or *IPRspr* 1994, No. 129; 28 January 1997, *NJW–RR* 1997, 686 or *IPRspr* 1997, No. 27; District Court of Frankfurt am Main, 14 March 2003 1010, with note by Rheinisch.

[54] eg the fact that the provision appears under the heading "Avoidance of restrictions on current payments".

[55] Without in any sense detracting from the reasoning of the Federal Supreme Court, there may have been a desire to restrict the ambit of Art VIII(2)(b) in the light of the diminishing importance of exchange controls and the emphasis on the movement of capital within the European Union. To this extent, it may be said that the German decision perhaps mirrors earlier English cases which sought—albeit in a rather different way—to restrict the scope of the Article—see para 15.28 below.

granted by the bank. The Austrian defendant pleaded that the loan contravened the Austrian Exchange Control Act (*Devisenrecht*), that the loan should accordingly be characterised as an "exchange contract" and should thus be unenforceable under Article VIII(2)(b). The Court[56] rejected this argument, on the basis that the loan was a transaction of a capital nature which fell outside Article VIII(2)(b).[57]

15.22 In further cases, the District Court of Frankfurt am Main had to consider actions brought by German bondholders against Argentina, which had issued bonds denominated in German marks.[58] In February 2002, in the midst of an economic and financial crisis, Argentina introduced regulations which suspended the payment of its external debts; it pleaded that the bonds should not be enforced because they were "exchange contracts" for the purposes of Article VIII(2)(b). The Court could have contented itself with the observation that the bonds were issued *before* the relevant controls were brought into effect, and this would have been sufficient to dispose of Argentina's contention;[59] instead it held that the bonds represented capital transactions and Article VIII(2)(b) thus had no application.[60]

15.23 Finally, it must be said that Malaysia introduced capital controls in September 1998 which, in their essence, prevented the repatriation of capital investments in Malaysia for a mininum period of twelve months following their realisation. These restrictions attracted some criticism at the time, although this was based on economic, rather than legal, grounds.[61]

15.24 In conclusion, Article VIII(2)(b) is now likely to apply for and against all member countries, whether or not they have invoked the privilege of the transitional period under Article XIV or accepted obligations under Article VIII(1), (2), and (3). Whilst there are arguments to the opposite effect, the point is foreclosed by an interpretative decision of the Fund's Executive Directors in 1949 to the effect

---

[56] German Federal Supreme Court, 22 February 1994, *NJW* 1994, 1868 or *IPRspr* 1994, No. 129.

[57] The Court does, however, appear to have been conscious of the difficulty in distinguishing an earlier decision of 14 November 1991 (German Federal Supreme Court, 14 November 1991, *BGHZ* 116, 77 or *IPRspr* 1991, No. 181) where it was held that a loan from a German bank to a Greek borrower should be characterised as an exchange contract for these purposes.

[58] 14 March 2003, *JZ* 2003, 1010, with note by Rheinisch.

[59] On this "timing" question, see para 15.28(a) below.

[60] It may be noted that the German Federal Constitutional Court declined to intervene on behalf of Argentina—13 February 2003, *DVBl* 2003, 661.

[61] It is also fair to note that the introduction of capital controls in Malaysia ultimately proved to be far more successful than many critics anticipated. For a description of the capital controls imposed by that country, see the IMF's 1999 *Annual Report on Exchange Arrangements and Exchange Restrictions* and for a more general discussion, see *Capital Controls: Country Experiences with their Use and Liberalisation*, IMF Occasional Paper 190 (2000). Appendix III (by Inci Ötker-Robe) deals specifically with Malaysia.

that Article VIII(2)(b) applies "to all members, whether or not they have availed themselves of the transitional arrangements of Article XIV, s. 2 . . .".[62]

Leaving aside these general observations, the precise scope of the Article can perhaps best be ascertained by examining the proper approach to its interpretation. It will be noted that there are six main points which must be proved if Article VIII(2)(b) is to be invoked successfully. Specifically the party asserting the unenforceability of the contract in reliance upon this article must demonstrate that (a) the matter at issue in the proceedings is a contract; (b) the contract at hand is an "exchange contract"; (c) the contract involves "the currency of . . . another country"; (d) that country must be a member of the IMF; (e) the contract must be "contrary to the exchange control regulations" of that member; and (f) those exchange control regulations must be "maintained or imposed consistently with" the IMF Agreement. If all of these conditions are met, then the relevant contract "shall be unenforceable" before the courts of other member States. It is thus necessary to consider each of these aspects of Article VIII(2)(b) in turn.[63]

15.25

In seeking to interpret these provisions, it is submitted that the court should in large measure be guided by the paramount purposes of the Fund, which are "to promote international monetary co-operation" and "to promote exchange stability, to maintain orderly exchange arrangements among members, and to avoid competitive exchange depreciation".[64] The language should not therefore be approached as if it were found in a piece of domestic legislation. Rather, the provisions must be construed as a part of a multilateral treaty and thus interpreted in accordance with principles of interpretation developed by public international law.[65] It is necessary to adhere to these general principles even though, as already noted, a uniformity of approach to Article VIII(2)(b) has not in fact been achieved.

15.26

"Contracts"

Consistently with the points just made, it is necessary to attribute a broad meaning to the expression "contracts" as used in Article VIII(2)(b). It is suggested that the term should embrace any form of consensual transaction,

15.27

---

[62] *Selected Decisions of the Executive Directors* (13th edn, 1987) 290.

[63] It may be added that there was early judicial reluctance to attempt an interpretation of Art VIII(2)(b)—see *Kahler v Midland Bank* [1948] 1 All ER 811; *Cermak v Bata Akciova Spolecnost* (1948) 80 NYS 2d 782. However, it is clear that the courts have an obligation to interpret and apply the provision where appropriate and (in more recent years) they have approached the subject directly—see in particular *Sharif v Azad* [1967] 1 QB 605 and *Wilson Smithett & Cope Ltd v Terruzzi* [1976] 1 QB 638.

[64] Article 1(i) and (iii). A series of other objectives is also listed in Art 1.

[65] On this point, see n 14 above.

such as a conveyance, transfer, assignment, or declaration of trust;[66] as noted earlier, the Article should not apply to claims in tort or other claims arising against the background of a non-consensual factual matrix.[67]

"Exchange contracts"

15.28 It has been noted that Article VIII(2)(b) renders unenforceable "exchange contracts" which contravene the terms of the Article—not *all* contracts, however defined,—but only *exchange* contracts. The meaning of this term must both qualify and restrict the scope and interpretation of the provision; it is thus to be regretted that the meaning of "exchange contract" is obscure and has generated much disagreement. A few general points may be made:

(a) By its terms, Article VIII(2)(b) is concerned with the effectiveness of contracts, ie with their initial validity, as opposed to their legality or the possibility of their performance. Accordingly, if a contract is consistent with relevant exchange control laws at the time of its conclusion, for example, because no authorisation was required at that time, or any necessary authorisation was given, then it cannot *subsequently* become an exchange contract which offends Article VIII(2)(b), for instance, as a result of the introduction of new exchange control legislation or the revocation of any authorisation which had been obtained.[68] Thus, an entirely domestic contract made between two Indian residents and involving the domestic currency may be enforced in England[69] even though (1) one of the parties thereto subsequently becomes resident in the United Kingdom and (2) as a consequence, a requirement for exchange control approval arises under Indian law before payment can be made.[70] Similarly, where the payments

---

[66] The Paris Court of Appeal has held that a transfer of shares in a French entity could be an "exchange contract" for these purposes—see (1964) 47 Int LR 46.

[67] See para 15.14 above.

[68] If, however, the original authorisation had been obtained by fraud on the part of the parties and was consequently revoked with retrospective effect, then it may be that—notwithstanding the general statement in the text—the contract concerned should be treated as an "exchange contract" from the outset. It should be added that the principle discussed in the text leads to the conclusion that "blocking" or "sanctions" legislation cannot be entitled to the protection of Art VIII(2)(b) in so far as that legislation seeks to prohibit payment under contracts which were lawful at the time of their conclusion. The point is discussed later—see para 17.02 below.

[69] Assuming, of course, that the English courts can otherwise claim jurisdiction over the defendant.

[70] For this reason, it is necessary to question two decisions of a court of first instance in Paris (8 and 12 March 1985, D (1985) IR 346). The plaintiffs were residents of Vietnam and had accounts with the local branch of a French bank. The plaintiffs subsequently moved to France, and claimed payment from the head office of the bank. In so far as they failed as a result of the application of Art VIII(2)(b), the decision is unconvincing because the deposit arrangement was plainly not an exchange contract when it was originally made. The reference to Cass Civ, 7 May 1974 Bull Civ I, No. 128 is mistaken, for that decision rests upon express contractual terms.

required to be made under a contract between persons in different countries have been sanctioned by the exchange control authorities in the debtor's country, then the subsequent revocation of the approval does not "convert" the contract into an exchange contract; it thus remains enforceable in England, if the courts otherwise have jurisdiction.[71] In short, Article VIII(2)(b) gives international recognition to the original ineffectiveness of an exchange contract, but it does not affect a contract which, at some subsequent time, becomes contrary to exchange control regulations.[72] In view of this approach to the meaning of "exchange contract", it follows that the application of Article VIII(2)(b) is limited to the initial validity of the contract and the conformity of the contract to Article VIII(2)(b) must thus be judged only with reference to the relevant exchange control position prevailing at the time the contract was made.

(b) The preceding submission finds some support both in the case law[73] and in the legislative history. An early draft of the Article referred to "exchange transactions . . . which evade or avoid the exchange restrictions prescribed". Evasion and avoidance involve an intention on the part of the parties which must necessarily be formed at the time when the contract is made. There is no evidence that the legislator's intention changed.[74] A stronger argument

---

[71] This is one of the lines of reasoning which supports the decision reached by the New York Court of Appeals in *J Zeevi & Sons Ltd v Grindlays Bank (Uganda) Ltd* (1975) 37 NY 2d 220; 333 NE 2d 168. As noted earlier, the position may be different if the approval is revoked on the grounds that it was originally obtained by fraud.

[72] For a different view of this aspect of Art VIII(2)(b), see Francotte, *Current Legal Issues Affecting Central Banks* (Effros (ed) IMF, 1992) 22.

[73] The above submission was expressly approved in *Libra Bank Ltd v Banco Nacional de Costa Rica* (1983) 570 F Supp 870, 900 and by the Federal Supreme Court of Germany, 21 December 1976, *WM* 1977, 322 or *IPRspr* 1976, No 118, which formulated the matter as follows: "Article VIII (2)(b) concerns the effectiveness of exchange contracts, ie not the permissibility of their performance, but their validity, whether initial or subsequently procured as a result of a licence". See also the Supreme Court of Louisiana in *Theye v Pan-American Life Insurance Co* (1964) 161, So 2d 70, 74, approved and followed in *Pan-American Life Insurance Co v Blanco* (1966) 362 F 2d 167, 170, also 42 Int LR 149.

[74] Such material as exists is to be found in *Proceedings and Documents of United Nations Monetary and Financial Conference*, Vol I (Washington, 1948). The Report of Committee 1 of Commission 1 of 13 July 1944 lists three proposals, the first being the Drafting Committee's proposal dealing only with transactions "outside the prescribed variations", the second relating to contracts which "evade or avoid", the third making such transactions an offence. All three suggestions were referred to Commission I (p 576). The latter considered them on the same day and referred them to a new Special Committee (p 599). On the following day this asked the Drafting Committee "to reconcile the differences between" the language of the first and that of the second proposal (p 605). Also on 14 July 1944 the Special Committee's Report was considered, not by the Drafting Committee, but by Commission I itself (p 604) and Art VIII "was adopted as presented by the Drafting Committee, with the inclusion of Section 2 . . . as reworded" (p 628). Finally, the Second Report of the Drafting Committee of Commission I stated (p 808): "All the material contained in this report has been approved in principle by the Commission at previous sessions. The present report contains, however, a new formulation of certain provisions." There

is derived from the text of the provision which speaks of "exchange contracts . . . which are contrary" to exchange regulations. The use of this language is apt to include contracts which are contrary to exchange control regulations at their inception, but is less apt to comprise contracts which subsequently became subject to an exchange control regime or the performance of which becomes impossible in the absence of (or as the result of the revocation of) a licence. "Exchange contracts" connotes a characterisation or classification of contracts which ought not to vary after the contract has been made. The suggested interpretation is also in line with the purpose of the provision, as defined by the heading of section 2, which refers to the "avoidance" of restrictions on current payments[75] thus again suggesting that the contract *at its inception* must have been designed to evade the relevant exchange control regime. It must be remembered that international payments are dealt with separately in Articles VI(3) and VIII(2)(a); therefore, questions relating to the performance of a valid and enforceable contract, whether by payment or otherwise, are unlikely to fall within the scope of Article VIII(2)(b). Finally, restrictions would be intensified rather than avoided if assistance were given to a State's policy to defeat the performance of contracts which were validly concluded at the outset, for such a policy lends itself to abuse. International commerce could be gravely prejudiced if, regardless of the law applicable to a contract, States were obliged to recognise so serious an inroad into contractual duties as the subsequent imposition of unenforceability—an imposition which may even have been preceded by partial or even complete performance by the creditor.

(c) Although Article VIII(2)(b) is principally concerned with exchange contracts at the time of their conclusion, it should be appreciated that an exchange contract which is initially unenforceable may become enforceable if the relevant exchange restrictions are lifted before performance is required. The lifting of restrictions is tantamount to the grant of authorisation,[76] and there is no policy reason for refusing enforcement of the contract under these circumstances. In other words, when Article VIII(2)(b) speaks of contracts which "are contrary" to the member State's exchange control regulations, it should be understood as meaning "are *and remain*" so contrary at the time of the relevant proceedings.

---

follows the final text of Art VIII(2)(b). Although there is an important distinction between the first and the second proposal and although the final text differs from both proposals, it is clear that the members of the Conference thought that the differences related to wording and formulation. There is no evidence that they had any object other than that of the prevention of evasion and avoidance in mind.

[75] On capital payments, see para 15.19 above.

[76] A point well illustrated by the UK's effective suspension of its exchange control legislation in 1979, see Ch 14 above.

(d) The term "exchange" thus leads to the general conclusion that a contract can only be an exchange contract at the point of time at which it is made; it cannot become an exchange contract at a later stage. But this cannot exhaust the consequences of the word "exchange" for, as noted earlier, it must qualify and limit the "contracts" to which Article VIII(2)(b) applies. But, precisely, what is the nature of the limitation? It must be noted that two different answers to this difficult question have each achieved a measure of support.

(e) It has been suggested that Article VIII(2)(b) contemplated contracts to exchange the currency of one country for that of another, as well as contracts which are monetary contracts in disguise.[77] This definition conforms to the ordinary meaning of the words[78] and has the advantage that it confines an unattractive legislative provision to the narrowest possible limits, for most substantive contracts involving the exchange of currencies are effected between banks which are usually outside the scope of the main exchange control regime.[79] The difficulty with this approach is that it effectively equates "exchange contracts" with the term "exchange transactions between [a member's] currency and the currency of other members" in Article IV(3) and (4)(b) of the Fund Agreement; it might be thought that the use of different terminology was intended to demonstrate that the two terms were intended to have different meanings. Despite this difficulty, the narrow approach to the definition of "exchange contracts" was adopted by the Court of Appeal in the *Teruzzi* case[80] in 1976. In that case, the plaintiffs were brokers on the London Metal Exchange. Terruzzi instructed them to execute various transactions on his behalf, but subsequently refused to pay, relying on the fact that the contracts contravened Italian exchange control and thus should not be enforced in England by virtue of Article VIII(2)(b). The defence failed, on the bases that (1) Article VIII(2)(b) was not intended to impede legitimate international trading

---

[77] Nussbaum, *Money in the Law, National and International* (The Press Foundation, 2nd edn, 1950) 542–3; see also (1949) 49 Yale LJ 426.

[78] See, for instance, in a wholly different context the remarks made in *Re United Railways of Havana and Regla Warehouses Ltd* [1961] AC 1007, 1059.

[79] In relation to banks as "authorised dealers" under the former UK exchange control rules, see Ch 14 above.

[80] *Wilson Smithett & Cope Ltd v Terruzzi* [1976] 1 QB 683. See critical comments by Lipstein (1976) Cambridge LJ 203 and Sir Joseph Gold, (1984) ICLQ 777, reprinted in a slightly different version in *The Fund Agreement in the Courts III*. On p 62 of the same volume, it is suggested that the reasoning in the *Terruzzi* case "piles fallacy upon fallacy". The decision of the Court of Appeal in *Batra v Ibrahim* [1982] 2 Lloyd's Rep 11, involved a contract which (on any view of the definition) was an exchange contract; the plaintiff had paid to the defendant an amount in sterling in consideration of payments to be made in India in rupees.

and (2) the arrangements did not involve the exchange of one currency for another, and were thus not "exchange contracts" for the purposes of the Article.[81] The narrow approach to the interpretation of Article VIII(2)(b) must now be regarded as the accepted position so far as the English courts are concerned, following the House of Lords decision in *United City Merchants (Investment) Ltd v Royal Bank of Canada*,[82] although it is to be regretted that the House merely adopted the approach taken in the *Terruzzi* case without further independent reasoning and (apparently) without any significant argument on the point by either of the parties. The House also compounded the difficulties in this area by accepting and applying the concept of the "exchange contract in disguise".[83] This led to a result which can only be described as "remarkable".[84] In the result, a letter of credit for US$662,000 issued by a London bank to an English seller and negotiated by the latter to a London finance house was held to be an exchange contract in disguise. It could only be enforced as to US$331,000, which was the legitimate purchase price of the goods; it could not be enforced as to the balance, because the underlying commercial contract required the seller to refund the remainder of the purchase price to the buyer's US dollar account in Florida—an arrangement which infringed Peruvian exchange control. On the assumption that the issuing bank was unaware of the arrangement just described, this decision must be questionable on various grounds. First of all, it was the underlying commercial contract which was the "exchange contract", and not the letter of credit itself.[85] Secondly, it has been noted earlier that an "exchange contract" connotes an intention to avoid or evade exchange control rules, but in the present case one of the parties to the letter of credit (the issuing bank) had no such intention, nor even knew of the refund arrangements. Despite these difficulties,[86] the "exchange contract in disguise" theory was subsequently applied by the Court of Appeal

---

[81] Since Italian exchange control approval had not been obtained, it is perhaps unsurprising that the Italian court refused to enforce the English judgment—Court of Appeal at Milan, 27 September 1977, *Revista di diritto internazionale privato e processuale* (1979) 271, affirmed by the Corte di Cassazione, 21 July 1982, *Revista di diritto internazionale private e processuale* (1982) 107. Exchange control laws will always be mandatory in their application in proceedings occurring within the territory of the State which imposes them.

[82] [1983] 1 AC 168.

[83] As noted above, this general idea had originally been voiced by Nussbaum, but it was approved by Lord Denning in the *Terruzzi* case, at 714.

[84] The description used by Mocatta J in regard to the submission ultimately accepted by the House of Lords—see 189.

[85] Letters of credit are to be regarded as autonomous contracts in their own right; they are separate and distinct from the underlying contract. Indeed, the point was emphasised by the House of Lords in the *United City Merchants* case.

[86] For further discussion of the points just made, see Collier (1983) Cambridge LJ 49 and Mann (1982) LQR 526.

in *Mansouri v Singh*[87] where there were, in substance, two transactions. First, the plaintiff's husband in Iran purchased air tickets from a travel agent within that country, using the local currency, and arranged for the tickets to be delivered to the defendant in London. Secondly, the plaintiff sold those tickets to the defendant at a favourable rate of exchange; however, the defendant's sterling cheque was dishonoured upon presentation and the plaintiff brought proceedings. The cheque was drawn by a person resident in England and was payable to a person who was also so resident; it was drawn upon a bank carrying on business in the United Kingdom. Of itself, this arrangement could not constitute an exchange contract and judgment on such an instrument would normally follow as a matter of course.[88] However, the Court of Appeal refused to enforce payment on the cheque because it disguised a monetary transaction which was inconsistent with the exchange control rules of Iran, ie "the parties had adopted some stratagem . . . in order to make sterling available to the plaintiff in London in exchange for rials paid to the defendant in Tehran".[89] In each of these cases, the Court appears to have missed the point. In the *United City Merchants* case, the House of Lords took the view that autonomous obligations arising under a letter of credit should not be enforced because a separate contract amongst different parties could not be enforced. Likewise, in the *Mansouri* case, the Court might not have enforced the underlying commercial obligations, but the cheque was not itself an exchange contract. The plaintiff should have obtained judgment on that basis.

(f) The recent English practice described in the preceding paragraph must be contrasted with the alternative test put forward by Dr Mann in earlier editions of this book[90] and at one time accepted by Lord Denning,[91] according to which "exchange contracts" are contracts which in any way affect a country's exchange resources in a manner likely to reduce them. The Fund itself now defines an exchange contract as "any contract that provides for payment between a resident and a non-resident of the country

---

[87] [1986] 1 WLR 1393.

[88] ie because a cheque (like a letter of credit) is usually viewed independently of the underlying contract to which it relates.

[89] At 1401. There may be further difficulties with the application of Art VIII(2)(b) in this context, because it is doubtful whether the Iranian regulations were imposed in a manner consistent with the Fund Agreement—see n 143 below.

[90] In *The Fund Agreement in The Courts* (1977) IMF Staff Papers xxiv 219, Sir Joseph Gold suggests that Art VIII(2)(b) refers to "contracts requiring international payments or transfers in foreign or domestic currency".

[91] *Sharif v Azad* [1967] 1 QB 605, 613, 614.

imposing the control".[92] The difficulty with both of these interpretations is that they render the word "exchange" redundant. If these definitions represented the legislative intent, then the word "exchange" could simply have been omitted; it would have been sufficient merely to refer to "contracts which involve the currency of any member". To disregard the opening word of the Article runs counter to established principles of interpretation, especially when that word would appear to have a qualifying purpose which narrows the scope of the Article as a whole. Yet this approach would be in better harmony with the purpose of the Fund Agreement; and, in the context of a treaty, the process of interpretation should be directed towards the achievement of the overriding objectives of the document.[93] It is perhaps unsurprising that this broader approach to the interpretation of Article VIII(2)(b) found favour with courts in civil law countries.[94] Thus, the Court of Appeal in Paris refused to enforce a contract whereby—in contravention of Dutch exchange control—a Dutch resident sold shares to a German resident, for a consideration in French francs,[95] or a contract between a Japanese company and a Frenchman who was appointed the former's European representative at a fixed monthly remuneration and certain commissions payable in respect of films imported into Japan.[96] The German Federal Supreme Court treated as an exchange contract a guarantee given by a Dutch company to a German seller to secure payment of a

---

[92] See Francotte, "The Fund Agreement in the Courts": Comment in *Current Legal Issues Affecting Central Banks* (1992) 15, 19, noted in Lowenfeld, *International Economic Law* (Oxford University Press, 2002) 668, where it is also stated that the "exchange resources" approach represents a better view. The term "exchange contract" is also said to comprise any contract involving any monetary asset used for international payments and transfer—see Francotte, "The Role of the International Financial Institutions" (1994, August) IFLR.

[93] On this point, see Art 31 of the Vienna Convention on the Law of Treaties, and *Fothergill v Monarch Airlines Ltd* [1981] AC 251 (HL), to which reference has already been made.

[94] Those of a cynical mindset may feel that courts in England and in New York had good reason for adopting a narrower approach to the term. A broader approach might have provided grounds for a challenge to the validity of some of the financial contracts which are made and traded in the London and New York markets.

[95] *Moojen v von Reichert* 20 June 1961, 47 Int LR 46. Adopting the interpretative approach just suggested in the text, the Court noted that the Fund Agreement was designed to promote international monetary co-operation (see Art 1). In order to give effect to that co-operative objective, it was necessary for the Court to examine whether the contract could have an adverse effect on the financial situation of the relevant member State, or if it could in any way affect the exchange resources of that country. If these questions were answered in the positive, then enforcement of the contract should be refused.

[96] *Daiei Motion Picture v Zavicha*, 14 May 1970, (1974) *Rev Crit* 486, affirmed by the Cour de Cassation, 7 March 1972, *Rev Crit* 1974, 486. According to this case, Art VIII(2)(b) applies to any contract which involves the currency of a member State and which affects the monetary resources of that State.

purchase price due from a German buyer.[97] A Deutsche mark bill of exchange accepted by the defendant Dutch company to secure credit granted to a German debtor was similarly unenforceable.[98] A contract between a French buyer and a German seller under which the buyer was entitled to retain 4 per cent of the purchase price was likewise held to be an exchange contract,[99] although in general terms a cross-border agreement for the sale of goods should not have been held to be unenforceable as a result of Article VIII(2)(b).[100] Nevertheless, the Court of Appeal at Bamberg treated a patent licensing agreement as an exchange contract, holding that the term embraced all contractual obligations, including those arising from trade in goods and services, which are calculated to have an impact upon the member State's balance of payments.[101] Some of the German cases may, at first sight, appear to give rise to injustice, but the courts have invariably held that, in construing the term "exchange contract", it was necessary to have regard to the purposes of Article VIII(2)(b) in safeguarding the currency resources of member States and in avoiding any adverse impact upon their balances of payments. As the Berlin Court of Appeal expressed the matter:[102] "the notion of an exchange contract is not confined to currency

---

[97] 11 March 1970, *JZ* 1970, 727; in the same sense the Court of Appeal, Munich, 17 October 1986, *RIW* 1986, 998. In these cases, the guarantee had cross-border characteristics. The Court of Appeal, Düsseldorf, 16 February 1983, *WM* 1983, 1366 held that a guarantee given by a domestic guarantor to secure the unenforceable obligations of a foreigner under an exchange contract was itself likewise unenforceable.

[98] 27 April 1970, *JZ* 1970, 728. The Court noted that bills of exchange may have a particular effect on a member State's balance of payments; in appropriate cases, they had to be treated as exchange contracts for, otherwise, an effective limitation of exchange transactions would hardly be possible.

[99] 24 June 1970, *IPRspr* 1970, No. 102.

[100] Decision of the Federal Supreme Court, 28 April 1988, *NJW* 1988, 3095.

[101] 5 July 1978, *IPRspr* 1978, No. 127. There are a number of other German cases where the contracts at issue have been held to be exchange contracts. See, eg, (a) 17 February 1971, *BGHZ* 55, 334 (arrangements involving a rebate of a purchase price under an agreement between a German and a French firm), (b) 19 April 1962, *IPRspr* 1962 and 1963, No. 163 (an arrangement for the payment of commission between an Austrian manufacturer and its German sales agent), (c) 1 April 1954, *IPRspr* 1954, No. 163; [1955] Int LR 725 (a loan in US dollars was an exchange contract although made between two Austrian residents), (d) 28 December 1954, *IPRspr* 1954 and 1955, No. 164 or 122 [1955] Int LR 730 (a sale by a Hamburg merchant to a Belgian firm for a consideration in US dollars was an exchange contract) and (e) 8 July 1974, *IPRspr* 1974, No. 138 (a right granted by the plaintiff, a resident of Israel to the defendant's predecessor in title to collect and keep for the plaintiff certain Deutsche mark income in Berlin was held to be an exchange contract). The Tribunal Luxembourg said obiter that an exchange contract existed where a French firm sold goods to a resident of Luxembourg and, in violation of French exchange control regulations, a third party made payment to the seller; the actual decision was to the effect that a French judgment ordering the defendant itself to pay could not, as amongst the members of the Bretton Woods Agreement, be treated as contrary to *ordre public*: [1953] Int LR 22, 722.

[102] 8 July 1974, *IPRspr* 1974, No. 138. See also the decisions of the Federal Supreme Court, 21 December 1976, *WM* 1977, 332 and 8 March 1979, *NJW* 1980, 520.

exchange transactions in the narrow sense. Only a wide interpretation takes account of the economic purpose of the treaty. Currency interests are always affected where the currency reserves of a country are involved."[103] More recent German case law has adhered consistently to this line[104] and has held that contracts involving loans, bills of exchange, and the subscription or acquisition of securities can all be characterised as "exchange contracts" in appropriate cases.[105] It must be added that the broader approach to the interpretation of Article VIII(2)(b)—as advocated by Dr Mann—has also found support in the literature on the subject.[106]

(g) Nevertheless the views noted in the preceding paragraph were subjected to withering criticism by the Court of Appeal in the *Terruzzi* case,[107] and as has been noted earlier, the decision in *Terruzzi* was subsequently accepted by the House of Lords in *United City Merchants (Investments) Ltd v Royal Bank of Canada*.[108] The narrow view of the term "exchange contracts" has also been adopted by courts in the United States on the grounds that a wide construction of Article VIII(2)(b) was "doing considerable violence to the text".[109] Likewise those courts have "frowned on an interpretation . . . which sweeps in all contracts affecting any member's exchange resources".[110] Absent a change of mind in the highest courts, the matter would seem to be conclusively settled in favour of the narrow view, at any rate so far as the two countries are concerned. But it remains legitimate to

---

[103] The German Courts have also had to deal with more obvious cases. Thus, eg, where a person resident in Egypt receives local currency and tenders in return a Deutsche mark cheque drawn on a German bank, this must be an "exchange contract" by any definition of that term—Court of Appeal, Düsseldorf, 1989, *NJW* 1990, 1424.

[104] See the German Federal Supreme Court, 14 November 1991, *BGHZ* 116, 77, 83 or *IPRspr* 1991, No. 181 at 374.

[105] German Federal Supreme Court, 8 November 1993, *NJW* 1994, 390 or *IPRspr* 1993, No. 127 at 284. The case is reproduced in English by Ebke, *Article VIII, Section (2)(b) of the IMF Articles of Agreement and International Capital Transfers*. For another decision of the Federal Supreme Court in which a debtor unsuccessfully raised Art VIII(2)(b) by way of a defence to an action on a bill of exchange, see German Federal Supreme Court, 24 November 1992, *IPRspr* 1992, No. 174.

[106] See in particular, the views expressed by Sir Joseph Gold as expressed in his earlier writings—see, for instance, *The International Monetary Fund and Private Business Transactions* (1965) 25; (1984) 33 ICLQ 777.

[107] [1976] 1 QB 683 at 719, 722, 724 and 724, where those views were described as "a tortuous and erroneous construction", as "inconsistent with ordinary intelligence", as involving "obfuscation" and "intemperate logic" and as constituting "not interpretation, but mutilation".

[108] [1983] 1 AC 168.

[109] See in particular *Banco do Brasil v AC Israel Commodity Co* (1963) 12 NY 2d 371, 375–6, 190 NE 2d 235 cert denied (1964) 376 US 906 also 30 Int LR 371.

[110] *J Zeevi & Sons v Grindlays Bank (Uganda) Ltd* (1975) 37 NY 2d 220, 333, NE 2d 168. Against this dictum, see Williams, 9 Cornell International LJ 239, 246. But the decision, which concerned a letter of credit, appears to be correct. Unfortunately, it was not cited to the House of Lords in the *United City Merchants* case.

discuss the merits of this position and the methods of interpretation which led to it. The judgments in the *Terruzzi* case place much emphasis on the fact that, according to Article 1 of the IMF Articles of Agreement, their purpose is not only "to promote international monetary cooperation" but also "to facilitate the expansion and balanced growth of international trade"; amongst other purposes which include the promotion of exchange rate stability, the establishment of a multilateral system of payments and the elimination of exchange restrictions. Lord Denning, in particular, said that "it is in the interest of international trade that there should be no restriction on contracts for the sale and purchase of merchandise and commodities, and that they should be enforceable in the territories of the members".[111] And yet elsewhere, he touches on the difficulty with this line of reasoning; he notes that the defendant "was a gambler in differences. He speculates on the rise or fall of the price of zinc, copper and so forth. He speculated in 1973 on the London Metal Exchange."[112] In other words, there was no genuine trade involved—certainly not trade of the kind which might be within the contemplation of Article 1 of the Fund Agreement. Indeed, speculation of this kind can be damaging to international trade because it may tend to accentuate market volatility. It is therefore legitimate for a State to formulate official policies designed to discourage such activities, and to give effect to those policies through its system of exchange control. It is true that Article 1 refers to international trade but it also specifically refers to "balanced growth" as a desirable objective, and perhaps one which is not served by speculative activities. Furthermore, a general desire to expand international trade did not deprive States of their individual right to determine the type of trade in which they would wish to engage—for example, in essentials or luxuries, in raw materials or manufactured articles. This type of decision must necessarily rest with the individual State, for it depends upon local economic and other conditions. The required degree of regulation can be achieved through customs duties, financial charges, or by means of exchange control.[113] It should not be overlooked that Article VIII(2)(b) is not itself aimed at the promotion of trade without qualification, but is intended to ensure a measure of respect for the right of a member State to control its own financial affairs; nor should it be forgotten that—at the time of *Terruzzi* decision—the United

---

[111] [1976] 1 QB 683, 713.

[112] At 709.

[113] Trade can equally be controlled either by restrictions on the supply of goods or by restrictions on the means of payment. Trade and money are inseparable. Restrictions on trade and exchange controls may therefore have the same economic effects, even though different legislative frameworks are required in each case. See, however, the discussion at para 15.31 below.

Kingdom itself was exercising this type of control through the Exchange Control Act 1947 and, as has been shown,[114] the Act was extremely broad in its scope. In short, respect for a member State's currency resources and balance of payments is by no means alien to the letter or spirit of the Fund Agreement. The restrictive reading of "exchange contracts" in Article VIII(2)(b) places outside its scope a number of arrangements which member States might legitimately wish to regulate or to prohibit in defence of their monetary resources. But in spite of these points, it must not be overlooked that—as between the parties in particular cases—the narrow approach to "exchange contracts" may well lead to a just result in particular cases. It is not reasonable to expect a seller to investigate the exchange control regulations in effect in his buyer's country and an unscrupulous buyer may invoke Article VIII(2)(b) as a means of avoiding payment in circumstances where the defence is entirely without merit.[115]

(h) Whether or not a contract is an "exchange contract" should generally be determined in relation to the individual contract at issue. In other words, the existence of an exchange contract cannot be inferred from a variety of different contracts; if two contracts have some nexus or relationship as part of a single transaction, they should nevertheless be examined separately to determine whether each of them is an exchange contract. This view is only reinforced where the contracts relate to a single transaction but are entered into by separate parties. In effect the New York Court of Appeals so decided in 1959;[116] a debt in dollars due from a New York bank to a New York corporation is not an exchange contract, even though the dollars held by the bank as well as the assignment to the corporation of title to that debt were derived from a transaction between other parties involving Italian lire and in contravention of Italian exchange control.[117] It must, however, be

---

[114] See generally, Ch 14 above.

[115] This point has been made by Dicey and Morris, *The Conflict of Laws* (Sweet & Maxwell, 13th edn, 2000) para 36-092. It must also be said (eg) that the defence in the *Terruzzi* case appears to have been entirely without merit, and had his defence under Art VIII(2)(b) been upheld, then this would have resulted in injustice to the plaintiff. Whether or not such individual injustices are an appropriate price for giving unqualified force to the international objectives of the IMF Agreement is, of course, a debatable matter.

[116] *Southwestern Shipping Corp v National City Bank* (1959) 6 NY 2d 454, 160 NE 2d 836 also (1963) 28 Int LR 539.

[117] Although the point was not directly addressed by the Court of Appeals, it is submitted that this proposition derives some support from the decision in *Ispahani v Bank Melli Iran* [1998] 1 Lloyds Bank Rep 133. In that case, the claimant was resident in Bangladesh, but he held sterling accounts with the London branch of the defendants. Those accounts were opened and maintained by the claimant in admitted breach of the Foreign Exchange Regulations Act 1947 of Bangladesh. Since the claimant's business interests were apparently located entirely within Bangladesh, it seems that the sterling funds must necessarily have been obtained by means of an "exchange contract", even within the narrow meaning of that term. Nevertheless, the defendants do not seem to have alleged that the banker-customer contract represented by the London

said that the position just described is not representative of current English law on the subject, for the House of Lords has taken a different line in the *United City Merchants* case.[118] The House sanctioned the notion that the term "exchange contracts" includes "exchange contracts in disguise". It is submitted that it is not a legitimate interpretation of a treaty to add something to the text which is not included in it or required to achieve its purpose. The mere result achieved by a variety of contracts not all of which are or may be exchange contracts is outside the scope of Article VIII(2)(b). Quite apart from these objections, the contract—a letter of credit—before the House of Lords was not an exchange contract, "whether in disguise or out of it" as a learned writer put it.[119] On the other hand, the contract of sale clearly was an exchange contract, whether one has regard to the whole or only to half of the purchase price. The notion of exchange contracts in disguise caused considerable difficulty in that case, for (on the one hand) the House of Lords wished to preserve the autonomy of the letter of credit,[120] and yet (on the other) struck down the obligations arising under the letter of credit, even though it represented a purely domestic transaction and even though the issuer of the credit may have been unaware of the objectionable nature of the underlying commercial contract. In contrast, the New York Court of Appeals maintained that Article VIII(2)(b) did not interfere with the obligations of banks under documentary credits.[121]

(i) Finally, it may be noted that the Fund could issue an authoritative

---

account was itself an "exchange contract" for Art VIII(2)(b) purposes, no doubt because the acquisition of sterling had been achieved through arrangements involving someone other than the bank itself. But it remains the case that the London bank account could itself come into existence only as a result of the claimant's breach of Bangladeshi exchange controls, and it might have been expected that the account relationship could itself have been impugned in accordance with the *United City Merchants* decision, which is about to be discussed. It is submitted that, had the issue been explicitly raised, the court should have found that there was no legally relevant nexus between the contract for the exchange of Bangladesh currency and the London bank account. It should be added that the *Ispahani* decision must be treated with some care, in that the judgment of the Court of Appeal relates only to an interlocutory issue. The analysis just given would also seem to be inconsistent with the views expressed in the *United City Merchants* case, considered below.

[118] See n 82 above. In this particular sense, the present work would argue for a narrower approach to Art VIII(2)(b). Of course, this approach can only apply where the series of contracts at hand involve separate parties.

[119] Collier (1983) Cambridge LJ 49.

[120] See 185, at E.

[121] *J Zeevi & Sons Ltd v Grindlays Bank (Uganda) Ltd* (1975) 37 NY 2d 220; 222 NE 2d 168. For the same reason, a guarantee should not itself be regarded as an exchange contract merely because the guaranteed debt itself arises under an exchange contract; the guarantee should only be treated as unenforceable if it is an exchange contract in its own right. On the same analysis, a cheque or bill of exchange should not be an exchange contract at least where they come into the hands of a purchaser for value. In this respect, the case of *Sharif v Azad* [1967] 1 QB 605 (on which see Mann [1967] ICLQ 539), must be of doubtful authority.

interpretation of the term "exchange contracts" but has thus far refrained from doing so.[122] It has been pointed out that countries which adopt a broader view of the provision are in effect shouldering a disproportionate burden in enforcing Article VIII(2)(b).[123]

"Involve the currency"

15.29 An exchange contract must "involve the currency" of a member State. Once again, this rather general phrase does not lend itself to straightforward interpretation, but the following points may be noted in this regard:

(a) The phrase "which involve the currency" contemplates, it is submitted, not the *denomination* of a contract in a particular currency, but the *financial area* in which the transaction has economic effects. "Currency" should thus be construed in a broad economic (as opposed to strictly legal) sense. The term may include foreign currency, gold, securities of whatever denomination, even land, moveables or intangibles, for the transfer of such property may "involve the currency" of a member State. A significant example is supplied by the decision of the Court of Appeal in Paris;[124] a resident of the Netherlands sold participations in a French company for French francs to a resident of Germany. This was an exchange contract involving the currency of the Netherlands because it affected the exchange resources of that country, even though neither the participations nor the price were expressed in Dutch currency.[125] This approach to the term is also consistent with the view that Article VIII(2)(b) is, in general terms, directed to the protection of the exchange resources of a country.[126]

(b) Whether or not the currency of a member State is "involved" is independent of the adequacy of the consideration. The term "involve" is neutral, with the result that the court does not have to determine whether the exchange contract is prejudicial or advantageous to the member's currency resources; it would, in any event, be very difficult for a domestic court to determine such a point.[127] It should be added that, according to the Fund

---

[122] On the power to issue this type of interpretation, see Art XXIX(a) of the Fund Agreement. The Fund's failure to adopt this route in the face of conflicting national interpretations serves only to reinforce the impression that Art VIII(2)(b) provides an interesting topic of debate for lawyers, but that it has been ineffective in supporting the exchange control systems of member countries.

[123] See, Francotte, "Legal Issues Affecting Central Banks" (Effros (ed) IMF, 1992) 16.

[124] *Moojen v von Reichert* (1961) 47 Int LR 46.

[125] For a decision of the Austrian Supreme Court (2 July 1958) which appears to reach the correct result on less secure reasoning, see (1958, ii) 26 Int LR 232.

[126] See the discussion under "Exchange contracts", para 15.28 above.

[127] It has been held that contracts for the sale of goods and other normal trading transactions fall outside the scope of Article VIII(2)(b), (1958, ii) 26 Int LR 232—Court of Appeal at Hamburg, 7 July 1959, *IZRspr* 1958–9, No 135a. However, this view must be rejected, for Art

itself, a contract "involves" the currency if either (1) one of the parties to the contract is a resident of the issuing country or (2) the contract is to be performed with assets located within the territory of the issuing country.[128] This formulation again serves to emphasise that the Article is concerned with the *monetary resources* (as opposed to the *domestic currency*) of the State concerned.

(c) The "involvement" of the currency must, however, be referable to the particular exchange contract in issue. Thus, if an English company purchases timber from a Swedish firm, such an arrangement cannot constitute an "exchange contract", because the United Kingdom no longer enforces an exchange control regime. Nor does the contract become an exchange contract merely because the Swedish firm sources the necessary timber from Russia, and the latter arrangement infringes Russian exchange control rules; the contract between the English buyer and the Swedish seller does not thereby "involve" the currency or the exchange resources of Russia.[129]

(d) In a rather obscure decision, the New York Court of Appeals seems to have held that Article VIII(2)(b) does not apply to a Swiss Franc loan made by a Panamanian company to a Turkish bank where subsequent Turkish exchange controls interfere with repayment, because "currency" refers to Swiss francs rather than Turkish currency. This line of reasoning is unconvincing, bearing in mind that "currency" must be understood in a broad, economic sense.[130]

"Of any member"

An exchange contract will only infringe Article VIII(2)(b) if it involves the currency "of any member". Even this deceptively simple part of the Article has given rise to questions of interpretation. The following points may be made in this context:

15.30

(a) as has been noted earlier, Article VIII(2)(b) looks to the initial effectiveness or validity of exchange contracts;[131]

VIII(2)(b) contains no warrant for it. Of course, if one adopts the English approach to the interpretation of "exchange contracts", then a contract for the sale of goods could not fall within the Article, unless it could be characterised as an exchange contract "in disguise"—see para 15.28(h) above.

[128] Francotte, "Legal Issues Affecting Central Banks" (Effros (ed) IMF, 1992) 22.

[129] The view has earlier been expressed that separate contracts must be viewed in isolation for the purposes of an Art VIII(2)(b) analysis, although it is doubtful whether the English courts would adopt this approach—see para 15.28(h) above.

[130] *Weston v Turkiye Garanti Bankasi* (1952) 57 NY 2d 315, 442 NE 2d 1195. The result was, however, correct because the Turkish regulations were only introduced after the date of the contract and, as has been shown, the compatibility of a contract with Art VIII(2)(b) must be judged with reference to the time at which the contract was made.

[131] See para 15.28(a) above.

(b) as a result Article VIII (2)(b) has no impact unless the State concerned was a member as at the date on which the contract was made;

(c) equally, however, it appears that the relevant State must remain a member as at the date on which the Court gives its judgment, for there is no basis to extend the benefit of a treaty provision to a State which no longer subscribes to it.[132]

"And which are contrary to the exchange control regulations"

15.31 Article VIII(2)(b) can only render an exchange contract unenforceable if it is "contrary to the exchange control regulations" of any member. This phrase raises a number of issues touching the expression "exchange control regulations".

(a) It is suggested that the expression "exchange control regulations" refers to enactments which control the outward movement of the currency, property, or services for the purpose of protecting the financial resources of a country.[133]

(b) It follows that tariffs, trade restrictions (such as an embargo), price controls, and prohibitions against trading with the enemy are not "exchange control

---

[132] See *Stephen v Zivnovstenska Banka* (1955) 140 NYS 2d 323 also [1955] Int LR 719. The requirement that the relevant State should remain a member at the time of judgment was the main reason why Art VIII(2)(b) was held to be inapplicable after Cuba's withdrawal from the Fund in 1964: *Pan-American Life Insurance Co v Blanco* (1966) 362 F 2d 167; *Confederation Life Association v Vega y Arminan* (1968), 207 S0 2d, 39, affirmed (1968) 211 S0 2d 169 (Supreme Court of Florida). Prior to Cuba's withdrawal, Art VIII(2)(b) was held to be applicable in *Confederation Life Assocation v Ugalde* (1964) 164 S0 2d 1, also 38 Int LR 138. To that extent the decision is correct but in fact the insurance contracts at issue were not "exchange contracts" as at the date on which they were made. For that reason, the Article should not have been applied.

[133] This definition was first put forward by Dr Mann in the Second Edition of this book. It is rather broader than the definition ("a law passed with the genuine intention of protecting [the country's] economy . . . and for that purpose regulating . . . the rights of foreign creditors") adopted in *Re Helbert Wagg & Co Ltd* [1956] Ch 323, 351. The IMF formerly adopted a much broader definition (a measure "which involves a direct governmental limitation on the availability or use of exchange as such")—Decision 1034 of 1 June 1960 *Selected Decisions* (1987) 298, see also Decision No. 144 at 292; The Fund has also affirmed its view that exchange controls imposed for security reasons are nevertheless within the scope of Art VIII(2)(b) on the ground that it is the effect (rather than the motive) of an exchange control system which is relevant for these purposes—Francotte, "Legal Issues Affecting Central Banks" (Effros (ed) IMF, 1992) 17. This definition is supported by Edwards (1981) AJIL 881 and Gold, *The Fund Agreement in the Courts III*, 475. More recently, the Fund has reformulated the definition as "regulations pertaining to the acquisition, holding or use of foreign exchange as such, or to the use of domestic or foreign currency in international payments or transfers as such", Francotte (see above) 16. It is submitted that this approach is too broad, partly because it lacks a focus on the preservation of national monetary resources and partly because it is doubtful that the Fund Agreement can deprive member countries of their sovereignty in the more general fields of national security and foreign policy. On the general problem of a definition, see Shuster, *The Public International Law of Money* (Clarendon Press, 1973) 31, 73, 229.

regulations" for present purposes. Likewise and although matters of definition will not always be free from doubt, it ought to be clear that "freezing" or "blocking" legislation designed to impose sanctions against a particular State cannot be treated as forms of exchange control regulation for the purposes of Article VIII(2)(b), for such legislation is not aimed at the protection of the national currency.[134] Thus, when President Carter blocked Iranian assets in response to the taking of US citizens as hostages,[135] there was no basis for the argument that foreign courts should regard these as a form of exchange control to which Article VIII(2)(b) could apply.[136]

(c) Legal tender legislation (in the generally accepted sense of that term) cannot be described as a form of exchange control regulation for Article VIII(2)(b) purposes.[137]

(d) As has been noted earlier[138] the relevant exchange control rules must have been in place at the time the contract was made and must continue to apply as at the date of the judgment. If either of these conditions is not met, then Article VIII(2)(b) cannot apply.

(e) Finally, it will be necessary to determine whether the contract does in fact contravene the exchange control rules in question. This can only be proved by appropriate expert evidence as to the laws of the jurisdiction concerned, ie so far as the English courts are concerned, the question will be regarded

---

[134] This is one of many reasons why the English courts were not concerned with Art VIII(2)(b) when considering US sanctions against Libya—see *Libyan Arab Foreign Bank v Bankers Trust Co* [1989] QB 728; *Libyan Arab Foreign Bank v Manufacturers Hanover Trust Co (No. 2)* [1989] 1 Lloyd's Rep 608. For a consideration of "blocking" legislation by a US court, see *Nielsen v Secretary of Treasury* (1970) 424 F 2d 833.

[135] Executive Order of 14 November 1979.

[136] It may be noted that, likewise, the UK may impose sanctions against other States, eg pursuant to s 2 of the Emergency Laws (Re-enactments and Repeals) Act 1964. Under that section, measures may be introduced against a foreign State which is taking steps detrimental to the economic position of the UK. Again, it is suggested that measures of this kind should not be regarded as exchange control regulations for Art VIII(2)(b) purposes, because they are directed at a particular target and are not intended for the protection of the economy in general terms. It should be added that their views expressed in the text are by no means settled and would be vigorously disputed by some writers. The point is discussed further in the context of sanctions and blocking legislation—see para 17.02 below.

[137] Suggestions to the opposite effect which were made in the US were rightly rejected by Gold, *The Cuban Insurance Cases and the Articles of the Fund* (1966) 36. It may be added that a governmental decision to default on its external debt is not a form of exchange control regulation —see Francotte, "Legal Issues Affecting Central Banks" (Effros (ed) IMF, 1992) 18. Even though such a decision may be motivated by the desire to preserve the exchange resources of a country, a contractual default by a sovereign debtor cannot properly be classified as a form of "regulation" for these purposes. Whilst the point does not appear to have been explicitly decided, it may be noted that, in a series of cases, sovereign debtors involved in difficult proceedings have not attempted to raise Art VIII(2)(b) as a defence. Recent cases include *Camdex International Ltd v Bank of Zambia (No. 2)* [1997] 1 WLR 632; *Elliott Associates v Banco de la Nacion and Republic of Peru* (1999) 194 F 3d 363 (2nd Cir).

[138] See para 15.28 above.

as an issue of fact. Difficulties may arise in some cases. For example, is a contract contrary to the exchange control regulations of a member State if (according to its express or implied terms) it is to take effect only upon the grant of the requisite official licence? The answer to this question must be determined principally by reference to the exchange control regulations in question, and is thus governed by the domestic law of the member State concerned. As a part of this analysis, however, it is equally important to determine precisely what steps the parties have agreed to take in order to apply the exchange control regulations to that contract. A determination as to the parties' obligations under the contract must necessarily be achieved by reference to the law applicable to it.[139] Where the contract is conditional on exchange control approval and one party agrees to use reasonable endeavours to obtain the necessary approval, then there should be no objection to proceedings to enforce that particular obligation, for the parties contemplated compliance with (rather than contravention of) the exchange control regime.[140] The position would, of course, be different if the approval was not forthcoming and the parties began to perform their obligations in spite of that fact.

"Of that member"

15.32   The meaning of the words "of that member" is, in substance, determined by the earlier phrase "which involve the currency of any member". In this context:

(a)   If, as has been submitted earlier, the provision contemplates a member's currency, not merely in the legal sense, but in the sense of the member's economic resources which are affected by the exchange contract, then the exchange controls infringed by the exchange contract are those of the country whose resources are so affected. The monetary resources and the exchange control regulations which are infringed must thus belong to the same country, but it is not necessary that the contract should be expressed in the currency of that country.

(b)   Although the provision is expressed in the singular, it should be appreciated that a single contract could affect the monetary resources of more than one country, for example, where payments in a number of currencies from different sources are involved. In such a case, the exchange control regulations of two or more members may have to be considered.

---

[139]   Rome Convention, Art 10(1)(a).

[140]   The former, exchange control legislation in the UK sought to deal with this point by means of an implied contractual term—see s 33 of the Exchange Control Act 1947 and the discussion at para 14.18 above.

"Maintained or imposed consistently with this agreement"

The phrase "maintained or imposed consistently with this Agreement" gives rise **15.33** to a number of difficulties. The following points may be made in relation to this particular aspect of Article VIII(2)(b):

(a) First of all, the word "maintained" refers to exchange control regulations which were in force when the Articles of Agreement took effect, ie on 27 December 1945.[141] In this sense the provision had retrospective effect.

(b) The requirement that the relevant exchange control regulations must be maintained consistently with the Fund Agreement does not imply that each and every provision must in every detailed respect conform to the Agreement. Rather, it is the existence and general character of the regulations which must meet the express or implied requirements of the Agreement. The Fund itself may provide guidance on this point, but ultimately the consistency of the regulations with the Agreement must be determined by the Court. This, in turn, depends upon an analysis of the features which the Fund Agreement regards as fundamental in this area. It is necessary to identify those features.

(c) It appears that the country whose exchange control regulations are at issue must have given effect to Article VIII(2)(b) under its own domestic law. This follows from the specific reference to a measure of reciprocity in Article VIII(1). If a country wishes to have the protection of Article VIII(2)(b), then it must itself extend the corresponding protection to other member countries.

(d) In so far as member States no longer rely on the transitional provisions of Article XIV, but have accepted the obligations of Article VIII(2), (3), and (4) (at present this applies to 156 member States), exchange control regulations cannot ordinarily be consistent with the Agreement if they are imposed so as to restrict payments and transfers for current international transactions. There thus exists the possibility that a municipal judge will have to decide the extremely difficult question of the meaning to be attached to the expression "current transactions", which is only very briefly defined by Article XIX(1). It must suffice to point out, by way of example, the difficulties raised by the question whether the various types of payments made in respect of life insurance contracts can be classified as current rather than capital transactions.[142]

---

[141] See Gold, *The Fund Agreement in the Courts* (1997) IMF Staff Papers xxiv 219, p 65.

[142] On this point, see Gold, *The Cuban Insurance Cases and the Articles of the Fund* (1966) 39. The distinction also arises for a discussion in a European Community context—see para 25.33 below.

(e) The introduction of new exchange control regulations without the approval of the IMF would be inconsistent with the Articles of Agreement. This point assumed some importance when Iran abolished exchange control in 1974, but subsequently reintroduced it in 1978 and 1979. Although the Fund itself does not seem to have gone beyond a mere statement that its approval had not been sought, it seems necessary to conclude that the Iranian measures were inconsistent with the Agreement.[143]

(f) If an exchange control regime is found to be maintained or imposed consistently with the Fund Agreement, then this probably has wider consequences under English law. For example, given the obligation of reciprocity which flows from mutual membership of the Fund, it must be doubtful whether the regulations could be held to be contrary to public policy in England—at any rate unless they were administered in an arbitrary, oppressive, or discriminatory manner.[144] Yet there may remain a residue of cases where exchange control regulations are so plainly contrary to international law that they ought not to be recognised. Thus, in one case, the Supreme Court of Louisiana refused to apply Article VIII(2)(b) to a contract which infringed Cuban exchange control regulations, because the

---

[143] In this sense, for instance, the opinion of Mr Mosk in *Schering Corp v Iran*, Iran-US Claims Tribunal Reports 5, 361, 381. In the same sense, Gold, *The Fund Agreement in the Courts III*, 301. The point noted in the text does not seem to have been raised before the Court of Appeal in *Mansouri v Singh* [1986] 1 WLR 1393, and might have affected the outcome. Likewise, in *American Express International Banking Corp v Irvani* (23 July 1980), the defendant was allowed to continue to resist the proceedings on the grounds that his guarantee might have been an exchange contract which infringed Art VIII(2)(b). This may have been partly through a lack of evidence before the court at that stage of the proceedings, and the bank appears not to have taken the point that—in the absence of Fund approval—any new regulations were not entitled to the protection of Art VIII(2)(b). On the whole problem of monetary questions before the Iran–US Tribunal, see Mouri, "Treatment of the Rules of the International Law of Money by the Iran–US Claims Tribunal," (1993) 3 *Asian Yearbook of International Law* 71; Carten-Daems-Robert, (1988) XXI *Reveue Belge de droit international* 142, particularly at 145–55. In *Cajelo v Bancomer SA* (1985) 764 F 2d 1101, the Fifth Circuit Court of Appeals relied heavily on a letter from the Fund to the effect that certain Mexican regulations were not inconsistent with the Agreement. Whilst this letter was no doubt a very valuable piece of evidence, it could not relieve the Court of its duty to review the point itself. For further discussion of this point, see Lowenfeld, *International Economic Law* (Oxford University Press, 2002) 669–70.

[144] Dicey and Morris, *The Conflict of Laws* (Sweet & Maxwell, 13th edn, 2000) para 36-097, citing *Perutz v Bohemian Discount Bank* (1953) 304 NY 533, 110 NE 2d 6, *Banco Frances e Brasiliero SA v John Doe No 1* (1975) 36 NY 2d 592, 598, 331 NE 2d 502, 506 cert denied (1975) 423 US 867. The operation of the Ugandan exchange control system at issue in *J Zeevi & Sons v Grindlays Bank (Uganda) Ltd* (1975) 37 NY 2d 220, 333 NE 2d 168 was likewise inconsistent with the Fund Agreement, because it was administered to the specific disadvantage of Israeli claimants. The general point has already been noted in the context of public policy and the Fund Agreement—see para 15.09 above.

plaintiff was a Cuban refugee in the United States and thus Cuba lacked any *in personam* jurisdiction over him.[145]

"Shall be unenforceable"

The last words requiring explanation are "shall be unenforceable". In this context: **15.34**

(a) In many countries, the word "unenforceable" or its equivalent has a technical meaning. It generally refers to agreements which are valid, but in respect of which it is open to a party to plead that the contract is not binding upon it. Article VIII(2)(b) is in some respects analogous, but it should be remembered that this provision creates an international obligation of the United Kingdom, the observance of which has an importance going beyond the interests of the parties in the particular case. The point thus cannot be left to the decisions made by the parties in the preparation or pleading of their cases. The court must therefore raise the point on its own initiative; it is its duty to do so, a point now made clear by the Court of Appeal decision in *Batra v Ibrahim*.[146] The same point has been acknowledged by the German Federal Supreme Court, although the court is not obliged independently to investigate the exchange control systems of foreign countries.[147]

(b) The term "unenforceable" connotes the ineffectiveness or nullity of a contract which does not prevent the restitution of any payment already made under contract. As Lord Denning put it in *Batra v Ibrahim*, (above) if money has been paid under the contract "—and the consideration has failed—then the money can probably be recovered back". This result may indeed often be necessary in the interests of the very economy which Article VIII(2)(b) seeks to protect.[148] The approach suggested by *Batra v*

---

[145] *Theye y Arjuria v Pan-American Life Insurance Co* (1964) 161 50 2d 70, 74, also 38 Int LR 456 and cf *Rodriguez v Pan-American Life Insurance Co* (1962) 311 F 2d 429. The argument suggested in the text may also be at the root of the decision in *Re Silk's Estate* 129 NYS 2d 134, also [1955] Int LR 721.

[146] Decided on 2 May 1977 but reported only in [1982] 2 Lloyd's Rep 11, and subsequently followed by the House of Lords in *United City Merchants (Investments) Ltd v Royal Bank of Canada* [1983] 1 AC 168. It may be noted that the courts have taken the view that it must raise certain matters of its own motion where they affect the international obligations of the UK. In the context of State immunity, see the attitude adopted by the Court in *A Co Ltd v Republic of X* [1990] 2 Lloyd's Rep 520.

[147] German Federal Supreme Court, 31 January 1991, *NJW* 1991, 3095 or *IPRspr* 1993, No. 170.

[148] It is for this reason that one cannot accept the view adopted by the German Federal Supreme Court to the effect that Art VIII(2)(b) merely imposes a procedural obstacle but does not affect the validity of the contract itself—see 27 April 1970, 728; 17 February 1971, *BGHZ* 55, 334; 21 December 1976, *WM* 1977 332; 8 March 1979, *NJW* 1980, 520. Nevertheless, the German courts have continued to adhere to this view in more recent years; see German Federal Supreme Court, 301 January 1991, *NJW* 1991, 3095 or *IPRspr* 1993, No. 170; 24 November 1992, *WM* 1993, 99 or *IPRspr* 1992, No. 174; Court of Appeal of Hamburg, 4 September 1992,

Ibrahim to the meaning of "unenforceable" is mirrored by decisions of the French Cour de Cassation, which refer to "*l'inefficacité*" of the contract.[149] It is suggested that this approach is likely to lead to a just result in most cases, and is also consistent with the legislative purpose of Article VIII(2)(b), which renders exchange contracts unenforceable but does not add the stigma (or the consequences) of illegality.[150] It should be appreciated that the duty imposed on the court by Article VIII(2)(b) is in fact of a negative, and thus limited, nature. The provision merely requires that an exchange contract which breaches its terms shall be unenforceable before the domestic courts.[151] It does not require the court to ensure the observance of exchange controls operated by another country, or to take any other positive action with respect thereto. This position is compatible with the rule which prevents an English court from enforcing foreign public laws, on the grounds that this would infringe the sovereignty of the United Kingdom.[152] It does, however, follow that a contract which has been fully performed cannot attract any action by the court as a result of Article VIII(2)(b), for the Article merely prevents parties from seeking the assistance of the court in relation to the obligations which remain unperformed.[153]

(c) Where an exchange contract is unenforceable in the sense described above, then the whole of it is unenforceable. It should not be split into enforceable and unenforceable parts. Whilst the House of Lords decided in the opposite sense in *United City Merchants (Investments) Ltd v Royal Bank of Canada*,[154] it is submitted that the proposition just outlined reflects a plain reading of

---

IPRspr 1992, No. 1716; 6 May 1993, *RIW* 1994, 686, with a note by Mankowski or *IPRspr* 1993, No. 32; Court of Appeal of Cologne, 10 April 1992, *RIW* 1993, 938 or *IPRspr* 1992, No. 173. See also Austrian Supreme Court, 27 March 2001, *Zeitschrift für Rechtsvergleichung* 2001, 229.

[149] 7 March 1972, *Rev Crit* 1974, 486, 491, and a 1969 decision which allowed the repayment of a sum paid in contravention of Art VIII(2)(b)—18 June 1969, *Rev Crit* 1970, 465 or 52 Int LR 10.

[150] A different view was expressed by Gold—see, eg, *The International Monetary Fund and Private Business Transactions* (1965) 23. It is true that the Fund's 1949 Interpretation of Art VIII(2)(b) stated that the obligations arising under exchange contracts "will not be implemented by the judicial or administrative authorities of member countries, for example by decreeing performance of the contracts or by awarding damages for their non-performance". But this does not affect the point made in the text.

[151] On this point, see Qureshi, *International Economic Law* (Sweet & Maxwell, 1996) 153.

[152] The most well-known case which illustrates this principle is *Government of India v Taylor* [1955] AC 491.

[153] See Qureshi, (n 151 above) 155.

[154] [1983] 1 AC 168, 189. It must also be said that, contrary to the submission in the text, the German Federal Court has likewise enforced part of the contract which infringed Art VIII(2)(b)—14 November 1991, No. 181 (at 375). In that case, a loan had been made at an interest rate which exceeded the maximum allowed under Greek exchange control laws. The court allowed the creditor to enforce the contract up to the maximum permitted rate and only the excess balance remained unenforceable. There is an obvious justice to this approach as between the parties, but it may not help to further the overall policy objectives of Art VIII(2)(b).

Article VIII(2)(b), and a different approach both does considerable violence to the text of the Article and is likely to defeat its objectives.

(d) Finally, it should be made clear that Article VIII(2)(b) does not provide the sole ground upon which a contract can be found to be unenforceable by reason of an infringement of exchange control regulations. For example, if an English court is confronted by a contract involving a South African entity and governed by South African law, it must decline to enforce that contract if it infringes local exchange control rules and South African law voids the contract under those circumstances.[155]

It remains only to repeat the view expressed by Dr Mann in earlier editions of this book, namely that the single sentence comprised within Article VIII(2)(b) has always posed disproportionate difficulty in the context of international legal practice; and it is not at all clear that the provision has brought any real benefit to the economies which it was designed to protect. It must be doubtful whether the provision continues to remain relevant in a world in which exchange control regulation generally is in retreat, and it is apparent that its application may disrupt contractual relationships in a manner which seems to be unjustified. Viewed in this light, and for as long as the provision remains a part of English law, it may well be that the narrow approach to the meaning of the term "exchange contracts"[156] can be justified on pragmatic grounds, even if it is otherwise unattractive in certain respects. **15.35**

---

[155] This is the effect of the Rome Convention, Art 10(1).
[156] ie as adopted by the House of Lords in the *United City Merchants* case.

16

THE PRIVATE INTERNATIONAL LAW
OF EXCHANGE CONTROL

A. Introduction

Chapter 15 considered the special consequences of Article VIII(2)(b) of the Articles of Agreement of the International Monetary Fund (IMF) in proceedings before domestic courts. That single provision is at once both very important and yet in many respects relatively insignificant. Important, because the application of that provision constitutes an international obligation of the member States of the Fund; relatively insignificant because—however one chooses to interpret the provision—it is of an essentially limited scope. **16.01**

The difficulties which surround Article VIII(2)(b) are unfortunately apt to obscure the fact that exchange controls may be relevant in many cases in which, for one reason or another, Article VIII(2)(b) has no application. The creation of a system of exchange control represents an exercise of sovereign and legislative power by the State which chooses to impose them. If a contract is governed by **16.02** the laws of that State, then its exchange control laws will form part of the *corpus* of law which should be applied by a foreign court in determining the validity, meaning, and effect of that contract.[1] This conclusion has nothing to do with Article VIII(2)(b); it flows from an application of the ordinary principles of private international law. The line of reasoning just suggested could apply in relation to exchange controls operated by States which are not even members of the IMF.[2] This brief analysis suggests that private international law may offer significant scope for the application of foreign exchange control laws before the English courts; yet it must not be forgotten that a system of exchange control is of an essentially *public* character, and the English courts have traditionally been reluctant to enforce foreign laws of this kind.[3] How are these two conflicting principles to be reconciled in an exchange control context?

16.03   Questions of this kind will be addressed in the opening section of this chapter. Thereafter, the text will consider the impact of foreign exchange control regulations in the context of contractual and proprietary rights.

B. The Status and Application of Foreign Exchange Control Regulations

16.04   It is proposed to consider three questions under this heading. First of all, what is the general *status* of foreign exchange control laws before the English courts? Secondly, to what extent are the statutory rights and obligations arising under such laws capable of enforcement in England? Thirdly, if they are not capable of active *enforcement* by the English courts, to what extent are such exchange control laws capable of *recognition* by the English courts?

Status of foreign exchange control laws

16.05   It has occasionally been asserted that the private international law of exchange control should be dominated by the principle that exchange control regulations are incapable of international recognition.[4] This view has occasionally rested on

---

[1] See Art 15 of the Rome Convention on the law applicable to contractual obligations, read together with Arts 8 and 10.

[2] Even where Art VIII(2)(b) does not apply, it must not be forgotten that the Fund Agreement is expressive of widely accepted norms of conduct in the monetary field. Consequently, the terms of the Agreement may assist the court in formulating relevant rules of public policy in this area.

[3] It scarcely needs to be stated that a court will invariably give effect to domestic exchange controls in force within its own jurisdiction, for they will be mandatory in their application. The present chapter is thus only concerned with cases in which a court has to consider the implications of a foreign system of exchange control.

[4] For discussion of this approach, see Gianviti (1980) *Rev Crit* 479 and 465.

the premise that exchange controls are of a "public law" character, and are thus incapable of recognition by the courts in other countries. This line of argument is misconceived. Whilst foreign public laws require a certain delicacy of treatment in the English courts, they are by no means simply ignored.[5] Sometimes, the courts took the view that monetary laws were of a strictly territorial nature, and thus could not be applied elsewhere. With reference to the exchange control laws of Czechoslovakia, the French Cour de Cassation opined "que les effets de la réglementation des changes de cet État ne pouvaient être reconnus en France".[6] Similarly, in another earlier decision, the Cour de Paris was prepared to enforce a contract made in Russia between nationals and governed by Russian law, even though the contract infringed Russian exchange control regulations as in force at the time of the contract. In relation to those regulations the court noted "que ces lois . . . constituent des textes d'une portée politique dont l'application ne peut par suite qu'être territoriale; que n'ayant d'autre objet que de protéger la monnaie nationale, elles demeurent sans effet devant une juridiction française même en cas de contestation entre ressortisants russes".[7] Similar decisions may be found in the jurisprudence of other civil law countries. Whatever the merits of these individual decisions, it is suggested that they cannot stand in the face of the Articles of Agreement of the IMF. The member countries have acknowledged the right of other members to create and impose a system of exchange control regulations; it is thus not open to domestic courts within those member countries simply to disregard those regulations.

It has also been said that considerations of public policy deprive exchange **16.06** control regulations of any right to international recognition.[8] Thus, in one case, a German debtor owed money to a Swiss creditor, which had in turn assigned it to the plaintiff. The German debtor contended that the assignment was invalid because the necessary consent from the German Foreign Exchange Board had not been obtained; payment was only possible if made to a blocked account within Germany. Although both the original debt and the subsequent assignment were governed by German law, the Swiss Federal Tribunal refused to give effect to the German currency regulations; it held those regulations to be contrary to Swiss public order, because they violated the vested rights of the creditor and constituted a "spoliatory encroachment" upon them.[9]

Even apart from the constraints which are, or ought to be imposed by the **16.07**

---

[5] This point will be developed in the ensuing parts of this section.
[6] 16 October 1967, Bull Civ 1967, i, No. 296 or *Rev Crit* 1968, 661.
[7] Cour de Paris, 30 June 1933, 1963.
[8] In this sense, see Rashba (1943) 41 Mich LR 777, 1098; Rabel, *Conflict of Laws,* III (1950) 49.
[9] 8 October 1935, *BGE* 61, ii, 242. Article 13 of the Swiss Statute on Private International Law now provides that the application of a foreign rule of law is not to be excluded merely on the grounds of its public character.

existence of the IMF Agreement, it is impossible to justify such a wide-ranging principle, especially in those cases in which exchange control is not a supervenient event but is in force at the time the contract is made. Exchange control regulations usually originate from an economic emergency and are applied everywhere for the legitimate purpose of protecting a State's currency resources, just as customs duties are enforced for the purpose of protecting a country's industry. It is true that exchange controls may seriously prejudice foreign creditors, and the Swiss Federal Tribunal may have been right in comparing some of the effects of exchange control to spoliation. Yet this cannot be said to render those regulations inconsistent with public policy. Many countries have from time to time been compelled to adopt systems of exchange control, and domestic courts should not condemn arrangements which their own country may itself have adopted at some point. Furthermore, exchange control is merely an aspect of a broader system of physical control to which the world has become accustomed, and to which it applies general principles of law. Export and import restrictions operate to restrict the sale and purchase of goods, whilst exchange control regulations restrict the making of payments for those goods. These are effectively two sides of the same coin; if the courts will respect the trading arrangements of other countries,[10] then exchange control arrangements should be respected on a similar basis. Courts in the Anglo-American world have thus generally accepted that, in the absence of some aggravating factor, the existence of a foreign system of exchange control does not offend domestic public policy.[11] Likewise the Federal Supreme Court of Germany refused to hold that the then existing German Democratic Republic's exchange control system was contrary to public policy in West Germany.[12] Against this background, it must be concluded that there are no overarching considerations of public policy which would justify a blanket disregard of foreign exchange regulations irrespective of their context or terms.

---

[10] For a case in which such arrangements were respected, see *Regazzoni v KC Sethia (1944) Ltd* [1958] AC 301 (HL).

[11] In England, see *Re Helbert Wagg & Co Ltd's Claim* [1956] Ch 323. The same position has been adopted in the US; in *Egyes v Magyar Nemzeti Bank* 115 F 2d 539, 541 (CCA 2nd 1948), the court remarked that "in view of all that has happened in the world, it seems profitless to characterise the currency manoeuvres of foreign governments as unconscionable". In a number of cases which came before the New York courts during the Second World War, Jewish immigrants claimed the refund of moneys paid in Germany for passage on German ships which, on account of the war, failed to sail. In most cases, the action failed on the grounds that German exchange control laws precluded the payment of a refund in New York and the application of those laws did not offend public policy—see, eg, *Steinfink v North German Lloyd Steamship Co* [1941] AMC 773 (New York Supreme Court). These cases are discussed by Moore (1942) 27 Corn LR 267. Likewise, the Court of Appeals of New York, citing the Second Edition of this work, held that exchange control practices are "recognised as a normal measure of government"—see *French v Banco Nacional de Cuba* (1968) 23 NY 2d 46, 63, 88. The Court of Appeals was unanimous as to the principle but divided as to its application on the facts of the particular case.

[12] 18 December 1979, *FamRZ* 1981, 200.

It would however, be equally wrong to move to the other extreme and to assert   **16.08**
that public policy has no role whatsoever to play in the consideration of foreign
exchange controls. Nor should it be forgotten that the treatment of such controls in a contractual context must be consistent with the general principles of
private international law in this field, as illustrated by the terms of the Rome
Convention. How do foreign exchange controls fit into the framework created
by that Convention? Five points should be noted in this regard:

(1) Amidst the debates and complexities to which foreign exchange controls
    will often give rise, it must not be overlooked that they will, in many cases,
    be irrelevant to the substance of the dispute, even though that position may
    give rise to considerable hardship for the debtor.[13] This is so because—
    subject to the minor exceptions considered below—foreign exchange con-
    trols will only form part of the body of law to be taken into account if the
    contract happens to be governed by the laws of the country which also
    imposes the exchange controls at issue. This necessarily follows from the
    fact that matters touching the interpretation and performance of contracts
    are governed by the law applicable to them.[14] Exchange controls forming
    part of a different system of law will thus generally have no bearing upon
    the substance of such a dispute. No question of public policy is involved—
    the regulations will simply not apply.[15]

(2) Where the contract is governed by English law, payment may not be
    enforced if it is rendered unlawful by exchange control regulations in force
    in the place of performance. This difficult and uncertain point will be
    considered at a later stage.[16]

(3) Where the exchange control regulations form a part of the law of the
    country in which the proceedings take place, then the application of those
    regulations will generally be mandatory, regardless of the law which governs
    the contract as a whole.[17]

---

[13] It may be appropriate at this point to re-emphasise that the present chapter does not deal
with the potential application of Art VIII(2)(b) of the IMF Agreement. That subject is considered
in Ch 15 above.

[14] Article 10 of the Rome Convention, discussed at para 4.12 above.

[15] The point is well illustrated by the decision in *Kleinwort Sons & Co v Ungarische Baumwolle
Industrie AG* [1939] 2 KB 678—a Hungarian debtor pleaded that it could not be compelled to
make a payment because this was prohibited by Hungarian exchange control regulations. This
defence had to fail because the contract was governed by English law. The Hungarian regulations
were thus not relevant to an analysis of the debtor's obligations.

[16] See para 16.34 below.

[17] This statement reflects the provisions of Art 7(2) of the Rome Convention. The point is now
highly unlikely to arise in a Community context for Member States can no longer impose restrictions on the movement of capital and payments—see para 31.45 below. The point is mentioned
for the sake of completeness although it is of no direct relevance to the present chapter, which
considers the application by a court of the exchange control regulations of a foreign State.

(4) In some countries, foreign exchange control laws can be applied if they constitute "the mandatory rules of the law of another country with which the situation has a close connection".[18] In deciding whether or not to give effect to such rules, "regard shall be had to their nature and purpose and to the consequences of their application or non-application". This provision could have material consequences in the context of foreign exchange controls, for it allows for their application even where the contract is governed by a different system of law. For example, a foreign debtor may be precluded from making payment as a result of exchange control laws in his home jurisdiction. Such laws would clearly be of mandatory application, and the situation clearly has a "close connection" with the country imposing them, for the debtor is resident there. It may well be legitimate for the court to exercise its own discretion in favour of the application of such rules, for the "nature and purpose" of the regulations will be the preservation of monetary resources and "the consequences of their . . . non-application" might be a diminution in those resources and a criminal prosecution of the debtor in his home State. This particular provision may thus afford significant arguments in favour of the application of the exchange control rules of the country in which the debtor is resident,[19] although it is submitted that, in most cases which are likely to arise in practice, Article 7(1) should not be used in this way.[20] A provision of this kind introduces a degree of uncertainty and would be contrary to the Anglo–American insistence upon the certainty and enforceability of debt obligations.[21] It is thus perhaps fortunate that this particular provision does not apply to proceedings in the United Kingdom.

(5) It was noted earlier that public policy could not be entirely disregarded in the context of foreign exchange controls. It is now necessary to return to that subject, but this must be done strictly within the confines of the Rome Convention. Bearing in mind the general points noted in paragraph (1) above, let it be supposed that foreign exchange control regulations do form

---

[18] The language is taken from Art 7(1) of the Rome Convention. The provision has already been discussed in general terms—see para 4.24 above. It will be recalled that the provision does not apply in the UK.

[19] The application of Art 7(1) in this fashion could have far-reaching effects—eg, the *Kleinwort* case mentioned in n 15 above could well be decided in the opposite sense. It would, however, be consistent with the view expressed by some Continental scholars to the effect that exchange control regulations, like other regulatory legislation, should be submitted to the law of a special point of contract, such as the law of the country whose economic resources are affected. For an example of this approach, see Vischer, *Beiträge zum schweizerischen Bankrecht* (1987) 440.

[20] See the discussion at para 16.31 below, in relation to the private international law of the forum.

[21] See, eg, *Camdex International Ltd v Bank of Zambia (No. 2)* [1977] 1 All ER 728 (CA); *Elliott Associates v Banco de la Nacion and Republic of Peru* (1999) 194 F 3d 363 (2nd Cir).

a part of the law applicable to a contract. In general terms, an English court must therefore give effect to those regulations in determining the dispute before it. However, this will not always be so, for any laws—including exchange control regulations—may be disregarded if their application would be manifestly contrary to public policy.[22] Thus, if foreign exchange controls are oppressive or discriminatory in their character or application[23] or so inconsistent with treaty obligations[24] or otherwise so contrary to English public policy, they may have to be denied recognition in this country. Thus, whilst the English courts will recognise the right of other countries to protect their economies by means of foreign exchange control and by altering the value of their currencies, the court must satisfy itself that the exchange controls are genuine in the sense that they were passed in order to protect the economy in times of national stress. Foreign laws which ostensibly have the character of exchange control regulations but which were in fact introduced for some ulterior motive may be rejected on public policy grounds, especially where those laws are inconsistent with inter-national law.[25] Public policy may also lead to the conclusion that exchange controls which were originally unobjectionable should be disregarded on the grounds that they have subsequently become an instrument of oppression or discrimination.[26]

---

[22] Article 16 of the Rome Convention, discussed at para 4.22 above.

[23] See the remarks made in *Re Lord Cable deceased* [1976] 3 All ER 417, 435. The term "discriminatory" must be treated with care in this context; it is in the very nature of things that exchange control discriminates between residents and non-residents. In the present context, "dis-crimination" connotes a differentiation between non-residents of different nationalities, or between residents of different racial, religious, or other identifiable groups. An example of the latter occurred in Nazi Germany, where the wholly unobjectionable exchange control regime introduced in 1931 was subsequently used as an instrument of discrimination against the Jews. This was so decided on a number of occasions after the War—see in particular the decisions of the German Federal Supreme Court, 25 October 1961, *RzW* 1961, 118 and of the Supreme Court of Israel in *Deklo v Levi* 26 (1958, ii) Int LR 56. The Dutch Hoge Raad rejected measures which were specifically directed against Dutch nationals, [1970] Int LR 40, 7. Likewise, the German Federal Constitutional Court, 3 November 1982, *BverfGE* 62, 169 held that foreign exchange controls should not be given effect if they are used as a means of compelling the authorities in the country of the creditor's residence to adopt a particular policy (ie and not as a means of protecting monetary resources).

[24] Thus, if a member country of the IMF introduces or administers exchange controls in a manner inconsistent with the terms of the IMF Agreement, public policy may prevent the application of those controls by a foreign court.

[25] These points were made in *Re Claim by Helbert Wagg & Co Ltd* [1956] Ch 323, dealing with the status of German exchange control regulations in the 1930s. The case is discussed by Dr Mann in (1956) 19 MLR 301, and also by Michael Mann, (1956) 5 ICLQ 295; E. Lauterpacht (1956) 5 ICLQ 301.

[26] This very realistic point was again made in *Re Claim by Helbert Wagg & Co Ltd* (n 25 above). In view of the broad discretions which a system of exchange control must confer upon the authorities, such a system is plainly open to abuse in the manner described in the text. It is also necessary to mention that courts in the US have occasionally adopted a different approach. In the

Enforcement of foreign exchange control laws

16.09   To what extent will the English courts actively assist in the enforcement of a system of exchange control imposed by another country? It is only necessary to state this rule in order to realise that such enforcement would be deeply unattractive. The imposition and administration of such a system are highly political acts on the part of the government concerned; the English court should thus have no part in the interpretation or enforcement of such laws, nor should the English courts provide a forum for the enforcement of foreign sovereign authority.

16.10   This reaction finds voice in the rule that the English courts "have no jurisdiction to entertain an action . . . for the enforcement, either directly or indirectly, of a penal, revenue or other public law of a foreign State".[27] It is true that there is some doubt as to the precise meaning of the term "public laws" and the extent to which such laws may be enforced in this country.[28] In particular, there is some authority to the effect that moneys paid out by the State to repair damage caused by the act of the defendant may be recovered in a foreign court, even though the source of the reimbursement obligation is to be found in a statute conferring the corresponding rights on the government concerned.[29] But whatever the scope of these exceptions may be, it must be acknowledged that

---

two cases of *Allied Bank International v Banco Credito Agricola de Cartago* (1984) 23 Int LM 742 and (1985) 757 F 2d 516, the court in determining the effect to be given to foreign exchange controls, decided that it should give effect to the foreign policy of the US. In the second *Allied Bank International* case and in subsequent cases, the courts had resort to the Act of State doctrine, which led them to submit the effect of such regulations to the law of the country in which the debt was situate. On these cases, see Mann, New York (1988/89) Int LR 10, reprinted in *Further Studies in International Law* (1990) 355. This type of reasoning should disappear in the light of the reasoning of the US Supreme Court in *WS Kirkpatrick & Co v Environmental Tectonics Corp* (1990) 493 US 400, where it was held that the Act of State doctrine does not prevent the court from inquiring into the activities or motives of foreign government officials. The decision has been followed on a number of occasions—see, eg, *Riggs National Corp v Commissioner of Internal Revenue Service* (US Court of Appeals, 12 January 1999).

[27]   Dicey and Morris, *The Conflict of Laws* (Sweet & Maxwell, 13th edn, 2000) para 5R-018 and the ensuing commentary. The principle is often said to rely on the decision of the House of Lords in *Government of India v Taylor* [1955] AC 491 but it has also been applied in many other cases. It has occasionally been suggested that exchange controls are "revenue laws" for the purposes of this formulation. This cannot be so, for exchange controls are aimed at the preservation of monetary resources within the economy; they lack any tax-raising or similar revenue features. However, the point is of no practical importance, for the rule here discussed prevents the enforcement of foreign public laws in general, and revenue and penal laws are merely specific illustrations of that wider principle—see Dicey and Morris, paras 5-030–5-037.

[28]   See the reference in n 27 above.

[29]   For a Canadian authority, see the decision of the Ontario Court of Appeal in *US v Ivey* (1995) 130 DLR (4th) 674, affirmed (1996) 139 DLR (4th) 570. Further support for this view may be inferred from the decision of the Court of Justice in Case C-271/100, *Gemeente Steenbergen v Baten* [2003] IL Pr 9. The case turned upon the meaning of the term "civil and commercial matter" for the purposes of the Brussels Convention on Jurisdiction and the Enforcement of

exchange controls are intended for the protection of a country and its economy as a whole. Exchange controls thus cannot be assimilated with quasi-private rights of the type just mentioned. It is apparent from the cases about to be discussed that the term "public laws", in the sense of foreign public laws which cannot be enforced in the United Kingdom, is apt to embrace a system of exchange control.

Two cases have served to emphasise that the English courts will not enforce exchange control regulations imposed by another country. In *Re Lord Cable deceased*,[30] trustees of a will wished to remit funds to India in compliance with that country's exchange control regulations. The beneficiaries applied for an injunction to prevent them from doing so; the Government of India sought to join in the proceedings in order to support the position of the trustees. The court refused to join the Indian Government into the proceedings partly on the basis that the English courts could not entertain proceedings by a foreign government whose sole objective was to enforce compliance with its own exchange control regulations.[31]

16.11

The enforcement of foreign exchange controls received more recent attention from the Court of Appeal in *Camdex International Ltd v Bank of Zambia (No 3)*.[32] In that case, Camdex had obtained money judgments against the Bank of Zambia, which remained unsatisfied. The Bank of Zambia was responsible for the administration of that country's system of exchange control. Zambian Consolidated Copper Mines Ltd (ZCCM) was the country's major copper exporter and was under a statutory obligation to surrender its foreign currency earnings to the Bank of Zambia in return for payment in the local unit (the kwacha) at the official rate.[33] Since some of ZCCM's foreign currency earnings would pass through accounts in London, Camdex sought garnishee orders against ZCCM, requiring that the moneys so owing to the Bank of Zambia should instead be paid to Camdex in reduction of the judgment debt. This attempt failed, principally on the basis that the Zambian exchange control legislation relied on criminal penalties as a means of enforcement; as a result the obligation of

16.12

Judgments in Civil and Commercial matters. The Court found that a governmental right to reimbursement of family maintenance payments could be a "civil matter" for these purposes, even though the right to reimbursement arose under local social security legislation. In fact, the decision is more complex than this brief summary allows. Nevertheless, the court clearly drew a distinction between the "civil" aspects of the legislation which could fall within the scope of the Brussels Convention, and the "public aspects" which fell outside the Convention: see in particular para 37 of the judgment.

[30] [1977] 1 WLR 7.

[31] For further discussion of this decision, see para 16.53 below.

[32] [1997] CLC 714.

[33] This obligation is, in substance, similar to that which was formerly imposed by the UK's Exchange Control Act 1947, s 2—see Ch 14 above.

ZCCM to the Bank of Zambia did not amount to a "debt" which was enforceable by civil action. However, the Court of Appeal also considered whether enforcement of ZCCM's obligation to pay over foreign exchange earnings should be viewed as an obligation arising under a foreign public law and which ought not to be enforced in this country for that reason. On this subject, Simon Brown LJ noted the exchange control regulations "are part of the public law of Zambia enforceable by right of the authority of the Zambian State rather than by way of a private law right in BoZ". He also noted that "the same objectives which arise with regard to the enforcement of foreign revenue and penal laws ... apply, equally to many other public laws, including particularly, exchange control, the enforcement of which is of no less political character".

16.13   It is submitted that these observations are plainly right. Foreign exchange regulations cannot be characterised as revenue or penal laws[34] but they nevertheless represent an exercise of sovereign or political will which, in compliance with the general principle discussed earlier[35] cannot be enforced here. It is thus clear that there is no scope for the positive enforcement of foreign exchange control laws before courts in this country. The fact that both the United Kingdom and the other country concerned are members of the IMF does not give rise to policy considerations in favour of the enforced of foreign exchange controls which are of sufficient weight to displace the general principle which has been discussed.[36] The necessary consequence of this position is that a State which imposes a system of exchange control is unable to enforce it on an extraterritorial basis.[37]

Recognition of exchange control laws

16.14   It was noted in an earlier chapter that one of the key provisions of an exchange control system will be the duty to surrender foreign currency in return for the local unit at an officially prescribed rate.[38] It has also been demonstrated that a foreign law obligation of this kind will not be enforced by the English courts.[39] But if foreign exchange control regulations cannot be *enforced* here, it is plain that the existence and application of those regulations will be *recognised* by the English courts, and effect may thus be given to them where such recognition

---

[34] This point would appear to be borne out by the decision in *Kahler v Midland Bank* [1950] AC 24; see also *Regazzoni v KC Sethia Ltd* [1958] AC 301, 324.

[35] See the *Government of India* case at n 27 above.

[36] See the *Camdex* case discussed in para 16.12 above.

[37] See, further, "Foreign Exchange Control as an Unenforceable Prerogative Right", para 16.50 below.

[38] See Exchange Control Act 1948, s 2 discussed in Ch 14 above.

[39] See *Re Lord Cable deceased* [1977] 1 WLR 7 and *Camdex International Ltd v Bank of Zambia (No. 3)* [1997] CLC 714, discussed in para 16.12 above.

does not amount to the direct or indirect enforcement of those laws to the financial benefit of the State concerned. That foreign public laws of this kind can be recognised, but cannot be enforced, in England seems to be well established and accepted.[40] The result appears to be that foreign exchange legislation cannot be used offensively, in the sense that it may be invoked as a cause of action before the English courts; but it may be used defensively, in the sense that it may render the performance of an agreement illegal, or it may have other contractual consequences. To borrow an expression from a different field, foreign exchange control laws may provide a shield, but not a sword.

The English courts will thus recognise the reality that contractual and proprietary rights arise within spheres of economic activity which may be affected by a system of exchange control regulation. Having arrived at this point, it is now necessary to consider the impact which such regulations may have on particular aspects of contractual and proprietary rights. **16.15**

C. Contractual Consequences of Exchange Control

Preliminary matters

The complexities and unfamiliarity of exchange control should not obscure or lead one to ignore the legal analysis to which such controls must be subjected in a contractual and conflict of laws context. The general principles which apply in this area have already been outlined,[41] but it may be helpful to briefly re-state the core rules, as follows: **16.16**

(1) matters touching the material validity, interpretation, and performance of a contract are generally governed by the applicable law;[42]

(2) the law of the place of payment may usually be taken into account in relation to the manner or method of performance;[43]

(3) the laws of the forum State must be applied where the application of those laws is mandatory irrespective of the system of law which governs the contract;[44] and

(4) a rule forming part of a foreign system of law will not be given effect if its

---

[40] See, eg, Dicey and Morris, *The Conflict of Laws* (Sweet & Maxwell, 13th edn, 2000) paras 5-019–5-021 and authorities there noted. The point was recently reaffirmed in *Camdex International Ltd v Bank of Zambia (No. 3)* [1997] CLC 714, 723.

[41] See Ch 4 above.

[42] These general principles are reflected in the Rome Convention, Arts 8 and 10(1)(a) and (b).

[43] ibid, Art 10(2)

[44] ibid, Art 7(2)

application would be manifestly contrary to the public policy of the forum State.[45]

16.17 With these broad principles in mind, it is proposed to consider the following subjects:

(a)   the impact of foreign exchange controls on the material validity of a contract;

(b)   the position where exchange controls form a part of the law applicable to the contract;

(c)   the consequences of exchange controls which do not form a part of the governing law;

(d)   the impact of the private international law of the forum;

(e)   the impact of exchange controls in the place of payment; and

(f)   the impact of exchange controls on the mode of performance of a monetary obligation.

Material validity

16.18 The issues surrounding the material validity of a contract will fall into two categories namely (1) those in which the relevant exchange control restrictions form a part of the applicable law and (2) those in which the applicable law differs from the system which imposed the exchange control regime in question. It is necessary to consider these two categories separately.

16.19 If, on their proper construction and application, the exchange control regulations of a foreign country render a particular contract invalid *and* the contract is governed by the laws of that country, then—in the absence of any countervailing consideration of English public policy—the contract will likewise be treated as invalid before the English courts. This position reflects the general rule of conflict of laws and is by no means limited to exchange control regulations. This statement of general principle may appear to be unobjectionable but it is necessary to record that its application has led to injustice in cases involving persecution and refugees. It is hardly necessary to relate that many cases of this kind arose in the first half of the twentieth century; regrettably, more modern circumstances have not entirely eliminated the possibility of their recurrence. What is to be the position if A and B both plan to flee a particular country, with A funding the escape against a promise from B to refund him on arrival at their destination; would this arrangement be enforced against B, notwithstanding that it contravened exchange control regulations in the first country?

16.20 In a case of this type—where the arrangement is made between two nationals of the country concerned prior to their attempted flight—there can be little doubt

---

[45]   ibid, Art 16.

that the contract will generally be governed by the law of the oppressor country. If the contract is invalid under the exchange control regulations of that country, then it would follow that the English court would likewise refuse to enforce the creditor's claim in accordance with the principle described earlier. Courts sitting in common law jurisdictions have accepted this result and allowed the debtor to avoid his obligations under circumstances which can only be described as manifestly unjust.[46] If, however, the contract is governed by the law of the forum State, then the exchange control rules of the relevant foreign State cannot be invoked as a defence to a claim for payment.[47] The same general principle was applied by the Austrian Supreme Court although, in order to do so, it had to take the view that the parties had, by virtue of their emigration, impliedly agreed to vary the governing law of their contract.[48] A similar view was taken by the German Supreme Court, where the lender's claim was enforced because the contract was found to be governed by German law.[49] On the basis that the contracts in these cases were respectively governed by Austrian and German law, these decisions are plainly correct, for a foreign system of law cannot vary or affect the substance of the obligations concerned; whether the courts concerned correctly identified the governing law in these cases is an entirely separate matter. But consistently with the general principle, the lender's claim failed where the contract was governed by the system of law which imposed the exchange control system concerned.[50] Adopting a rather different approach, the French Cour de Cassation[51] and the Swiss Federal Tribunal[52] both enforced the lender's claim even though the contracts were governed by the system of law which created the exchange control regime, largely on the basis that domestic courts should simply refuse to give effect to foreign exchange laws. It is suggested that this outright rejection of exchange control rules was inappropriate, bearing in mind that the right to impose exchange controls was and remains acknowledged by international law.

---

[46] The decision in *Boissevain v Weil* [1950] AC 327 (HL) must be regarded as one of the most obvious cases of injustice. See also the respective decisions of the English High Court, the Ontario Court of Appeal and (under slightly different circumstances) of the New York Court of Appeal in *Re Banque des Marchands de Moscou* [1954] 1 WLR 1108, *Etler v Kertesz* (1961) 26 DLR (2d) 209 or (1960) OR 672, and *Industrial Export and Import Corp v Hong Kong and Shanghai Banking Corp* (1951) 302 NY 342, 98 NE 2d 466. In the last case the plaintiffs deposited Chinese dollars in China to obtain US dollars for the purchase of US goods. When the purchase fell through, the plaintiffs claimed US dollars in New York. It was held that Chinese law applied and the plaintiffs were thus entitled to Chinese dollars in China.

[47] *Kleinwort Sons & Co v Ungarische Baumwolle Industrie AG* [1939] 2 KB 678 (CA); *Re Silk's Estate* (1955) 129 NYS 2d 134 or [1955] Int LR 721.

[48] 12 August 1953, *SZ* XXVI, No. 205, *Clunet* 1957, 1020.

[49] ie the country in which the parties intended to settle following their emigration—3 October 1923, *RGZ* 108, 241.

[50] 1 July 1930, *IPRspr* 1930, No. 15.

[51] 16 October 1967, *Rev Crit* 1968, 661.

[52] 28 February 1950, *BGE* 76, ii, 33.

16.21 Although the point can no longer arise, it is necessary to note that the English courts would not enforce a foreign law contract which—by virtue of the residence of the parties concerned, the place of performance, or other connecting factor—infringed the system of exchange control formerly imposed by the United Kingdom.[53]

16.22 What is the position where the system of law which creates a system of exchange control differs from the law applicable to the contract? In accordance with the principles discussed earlier, the material validity of a contract is determined by reference to the system of law which governs it. It necessarily follows that exchange control rules imposed by some other legal system cannot detract from or affect the material validity of such a contract. Thus, so far as English law is concerned, it will usually not matter that the contract infringes the exchange control regulations of a foreign country in which the contract was made[54] or with which the contract has some other connection by virtue of the residence of the parties or some other feature.[55] The law in this field has been stated with particular clarity and force by the New York courts. In one case[56] a Greek national and resident had executed guarantees governed by New York law, to cover debts owed by his companies. He resisted a call under the guarantees, on the basis that the requisite exchange control licence had not been obtained from the Greek authorities, and that the guarantees were therefore null and void under Greek law. The court held that Greek law was irrelevant to the claim and gave summary judgment for the bank. As the court noted, to hold otherwise "would impede international financial transactions of precisely the sort present here. Traditionally, in the absence of treaty provisions to the contrary, our courts have not enforced the foreign exchange controls of other nations, because these controls are contrary to our professed faith in the free enterprise system." This ringing endorsement of the capitalist system could perhaps have been replaced with the more mundane observation that Greek law cannot vary or discharge an obligation governed by New York law.

16.23 The general principle just described does not seem open to doubt. But it should

---

[53] On this point, see *Boissevain v Weil* [1950] AC 327 (HL).

[54] Thus a contract made in Algeria between two Frenchmen and governed by French law was valid, even though it infringed Algerian exchange control laws—Court of Appeal at Reims, 25 October 1976, *Clunet* 1978.

[55] In this sense, see *Kleinwort Sons & Co v Ungarische Baumwolle Industrie AG* [1939] 2 KB 678 (CA); *Cargo Motor Corp v Tofalos Transport Ltd* [1972] 1 South African LR 186, 195–7, and the Dutch Hoge Raad, 12 January 1979, *Rev Crit* 1980, 68. For reasons noted at para 16.08(4) above, the position may be different in those EC Member States which give effect to Art 7(1) of the Rome Convention.

[56] *Irving Trust Co v Mamidakis*, decided on 18 October 1978 but unfortunately unreported. The case was, however, discussed and relied upon in *Bank Leumi Trust Co v Wulkan* (1990) 735 F Supp 72, and is considered in some detail by Gold, *The Fund Agreement in the Courts II* (1982) 277. See also *J Zeevi and Sons v Grindlays Bank (Uganda)* (1975) 37 NY 2d 220.

not be forgotten that the English courts may decline to enforce any contracts governed by English law and which are contrary to public policy,[57] and that it may be against public policy to enforce a contract (regardless of its governing law) "if the real object and intention of the parties necessitates them joining in an endeavour to perform in a foreign and friendly country some act which is illegal by the laws of such country".[58] The principle has a sound moral basis and—in the context of the international relations of the United Kingdom—it would plainly be unhelpful if the English courts were seen to enforce contracts which amounted to a conspiracy to infringe foreign laws. There is no reason to doubt that the principle applies equally to contracts made in defiance of foreign exchange controls,[59] but it should not be applied where the exchange control system at issue was created or administered for purposes which included oppression, discrimination, or persecution.[60] The English courts would be

---

[57] On the application of public policy in this context, see *Chitty on Contracts* (Sweet & Maxwell, 29th edn, 2004) ch 16. It should be appreciated that the public policy which may be applied in a domestic context is broader than that which may be applied under Art 16 of the Rome Convention in a case involving a conflict of laws—see Dicey and Morris, *The Conflict of Laws* (Sweet & Maxwell, 13th edn, 2000) paras 32-227–32-238.

[58] *De Wütz v Hendricks* (1824) 2 Bing 314; *Foster v Driscoll* [1929] 1 KB 470 521; *Mahonia Ltd v West LB* [2004] EWHC 1938 (Comm); see also the Ontario Court of Appeal in *Frischke v Royal Bank* (1977) 80 DLR (3d) 393. The Belgian courts have likewise declined to enforce a contract the purpose of which was to commit a deliberate infringement of exchange controls in Zaire: 24 March 1987, JT 1987, 343. In the Fifth Edition of this work, 406, it was suggested that public policy could likewise defeat the claimant where the main purpose of the contract was to derive an advantage from an act which, in a purely objective sense was contrary to the laws of a foreign country. This extension of the principle was derived from *Regazzoni v KC Sethia Ltd* [1958] AC 301 (HL), criticised by Dr Mann (1958) 21 MLR 130. However, it seems that the principle should not be extended in this way; it applies only where there is a "wicked intention" to infringe the foreign laws concerned. On this point, see Dicey and Morris, *The Conflict of Laws* (Sweet & Maxwell, 13th edn, 2000) para 32-237 and additional cases there noted. This view would appear to be confirmed by the *Mahonia* decision (above). It seems that the principle may be further limited, in the sense that it can only apply where the parties intended to commit or procure the commission of illegal acts *within the territory of the foreign State concerned*—see *Ispahani v Bank Melli Iran* [1998] 1 Lloyds Bank Rep 133 and the *Mahonia* case above. This particular qualification flows from the fact that a court should not give extraterritorial effect to foreign legislation. Nevertheless, since exchange control regulations impose obligations and sanctions on persons who are resident within the imposing State, this particular requirement would almost certainly be met in many cases involving foreign exchange controls.

[59] The principle explained in *Foster v Driscoll* has been applied in this particular context—see *Hesslein v Matzner* (1940) 19 NYS 2d 462; *Southwestern Shipping Corp v National City Bank of New York* (1959) 6 NY 2d 454, 160 NE 2d 836, also 28 Int LR 539. The principle has also been applied by the Dutch Hoge Raad, 16 November 1956, *NJ* 1957, No 1. It would seem to follow from these cases that, as a factual matter, it would be necessary to distinguish between (a) those cases in which the parties deliberately set out to frustrate the application of foreign exchange controls (in which event their contract will not be enforced in England) and (b) those cases in which the breach of exchange control laws is merely incidental to the contract (in which event, the contract will remain enforceable).

[60] The point is suggested in *Regazzoni v KC Sethia Ltd* [1958] AC 301 at 320, 325 and 330. This was the attitude adopted by the Israeli courts in relation to contracts made between Jews

obliged to disregard such laws on public policy grounds; it thus cannot be contrary to public policy to attempt to infringe or to circumvent such laws.

Exchange controls as part of the applicable law

16.24 Where the law of the restricting State and the law applicable to the contract are identical, then the exchange control restrictions form a part of the law to be applied by the English court in determining substantive questions of performance.[61] Consequently, the English court will give effect to such of the restricting State's provisions as relate to payment, to suspension, or to impossibility of performance,[62] and to similar aspects of exchange control.[63] The rationale for this position has been neatly stated; if the law applicable to the contract is identical to the law of the restricting State, then "that law not merely sustains but because it sustains, may also modify or dissolve the contractual bond. The currency law is not part of the contract, but the rights and obligations under the contract are part of the legal system to which the currency belongs."[64]

16.25 Under these circumstances, if the law of the restricting State provides for the conversion of a foreign currency debt into a local currency obligation or for the discharge of the debt by payment into a blocked account,[65] or renders it illegal

---

resident abroad but with a view to escaping persecution—see *Mazur v Kirschbaum, Clunet,* 1964, 162; *Deklo v Levi* (1958) 2 Int LR 26, 56. It has already been noted that exchange control regulations can be disregarded if they are discriminatory or otherwise objectionable.

[61] Rome Convention, Art 10(1)(b), read together with Art 15.

[62] This is not inconsistent with the submission made elsewhere in this book, to the effect that the performance of monetary obligations cannot become impossible. What becomes impossible as a result of exchange control is not the payment of the debt, but the transfer of funds to the creditor. The point is illustrated by the decision in *Universal Corp v Five Ways Properties Ltd* [1978] 3 All ER 1131 and the decision of the Cour de Cassation, 18 June 1958, Cass Civ, iii, No. 257. In both cases, debtors pleaded their inability to pay because of the impossibility of transferring their funds from Nigeria and Vietnam respectively. In both cases, the court rejected this argument on the basis that payment of the price should be effected from other sources.

[63] The nature, scope, and effect of the relevant exchange control regulations—and the consequences of failure to obtain any required licence—will have to be decided on the basis of appropriate expert evidence. For a New York case in which the court appears to have misunderstood the relevant evidence, see *Perutz v Bohemian Discount Bank* 279 App Div 386, (1952) 110 NYS 2d 446, reversed (1953) 304 NY 533.

[64] *Kahler v Midland Bank* [1950] AC 24, 56.

[65] That the courts would acknowledge that performance occurs in accordance with such a law has been explicitly recognised by the New York courts see *Konstantinidis v Tarsus* (1965) 248 F Supp 280, 287; the English decision which would most obviously reflect the same approach is *Re Helbert Wagg & Co Ltd* [1956] Ch 323, considered below. The same point is implicit in Art 10(1)(b) of the Rome Convention, and the English cases about to be discussed. The German Federal Supreme Court, however, reached an opposite conclusion, largely on the basis that it would not apply foreign exchange control rules because of their alleged territoriality: 28 January 1965, *IPRspr* 1964–5, No. 68. It has already been shown that the notions of the territoriality of monetary law are neither helpful nor accurate in this conflict—see para 13.05 above.

or subject to a condition precedent such as a consent, this state of affairs will be recognised by the English courts. Thus:

(a) In *De Beéche v South American Stores (Gath & Chaves) Ltd,*[66] a tenant (incorporated in England but carrying on business in Chile) had agreed to pay rental for the use of premises in Santiago. The leases stipulated that "payment shall be effected monthly in advance in Santiago . . . by first class bills on London". The rent was expressed to be payable in sterling. The tenant alleged that Chilean foreign currency regulations rendered it illegal to acquire the necessary foreign exchange or to pay the rent by drafts on London. Accordingly, the tenant deposited in court in Chile the amount of the rent in Chilean pesos at the current rate of exchange, subject to a 20 per cent deduction directed by Chilean law. The landlord refused this payment and sued for the agreed sum in sterling. The case appears to have proceeded on the footing that the leases were governed by Chilean law.[67] On that basis, it had to follow that performance of the obligation to pay rent would be deemed to have occurred if payment had been made in compliance with the Chilean currency regulations. At least, this is the clear implication of the House of Lords' decision in this case.[68]

(b) The decision in *St Pierre v South American Stores (Gath & Chaves) Ltd*[69] is more straightforward, in that the Court of Appeal explicitly proceeded on the basis that Chilean law governed the leases. In this case, the leases provided for payment in Chile or (at the landlord's option) by remittance of the necessary funds to Europe. The Chilean currency law prohibited payment in Europe, with the result that the latter option could not be exercised. Since the leases were governed by the law of Chile, this position had to be respected and the landlord was thus only entitled to receive payment in Chile.

(c) In *Re Helbert Wagg & Co Ltd*[70] a loan contract between an English bank and a German debtor was found to be subject to German law, which accordingly governed all questions of performance in relation to the monetary obligations arising thereunder. As a result, payment in German marks to a Conversion Office in Germany in accordance with exchange

---

[66] [1935] AC 148 (HL).

[67] Under the modern law and in the absence of an express choice of law, there would be a rebuttable presumption that the leases are governed by the law of the country in which the relevant real property is situate—see the Rome Convention, Art 4(3).

[68] Given that the Chilean law provided for payment of rent under deduction of 20% of the amount due and thus dispossessed the creditor to that extent, it is perhaps surprising that the landlords did not challenge the application of the Chilean regulations, on the basis that they had the effect of expropriating part of their claim and their application would thus be contrary to public policy in England.

[69] [1937] 3 All ER 349.

[70] [1956] Ch 323.

control rules subsequently introduced in Germany had the effect of discharging the obligation, notwithstanding that sterling was the money of account and England was the place of payment.[71] It should be added that the court considered carefully whether the German exchange rules should be disregarded on public policy grounds but, on the facts, it found no basis on which to invoke this principle.

(d) A series of American cases arose in the early 1960s, where US insurance companies had written life policies through branches in Cuba and which were usually expressed to be payable in that country. Cuban legislation passed in 1951 provided for the conversion of US dollar obligations into the local peso on a one-to-one basis. In 1959, Cuba enacted Law No 568 which allegedly prohibited payments in US dollars by American assurance companies to the Cuban policyholders even though, by that time, the policyholder was resident in the United States and payment was to be made there. In view of the points made earlier, one might have expected that the identification of the applicable law might have been the most pressing task; if the policies were governed by the law of a State of the Union, then Cuban exchange control regulations would have to be disregarded. Nevertheless, the point was not always clearly addressed. Where the contract was found to be governed by the law of the State of the Union, then the insurer would not be able to raise the Cuban exchange controls by way of defence.[72] In those cases in which the policy was held to be governed by Cuban law, it necessarily followed that the Cuban monetary legislation formed a part of the law applicable to the contract; accordingly, these policies were payable in Cuban pesos, rather than dollars.[73] Where the policies were exclusively payable in Cuba and the insurer offered payment there in accordance with the Cuban monetary regulations, the courts initially (and rightly) held that no claim could be brought in the United States because the insurer was not in breach of his contract, ie he had tendered payment in accordance with the (Cuban law) terms of the policy.[74] It is necessary to add that, where the

---

[71] For the application of similar principles by the English court in the context of policies issued by a Canadian issuer, see *Pick v Manufacturers Life Insurance Co* (1958) 2 Ll LR 93 and *Rossano v Manufacturers Life Insurance Co* [1963] 2 QB 352. The Canadian Supreme Court adopted the same approach in *Imperial Life Assurance Co of Canada v Colemenares* (1967) 62 DLR (2d) 138.

[72] See, eg, *Theye y Ajuria v Pan-American Life Insurance* (1964) 161 So 2d 70; also 38 Int LR 456, where the contract was found to be subject to the laws of Louisiana. In the same sense, see *Banco v Pan-American Life Insurance* (1963) 221 F Supp 219, apparently affirmed on the same ground by the Court of Appeals, (1966) 5th Cir, 362 F 2d 167.

[73] See the decision of the Supreme Court of Florida in *Confederation Life Association v Ugalde* (1964) 164 So 2d 1 or 38 Int LR 138. This decision was followed in a number of other cases, including *Present v United States Life Insurance Co* (1968) 241 A 2d 237 affirming without opinion (1967) 232 A 2d 132, *Johansen v Confederation Life Association* (1971) 447 F 2d 175 and *Santovenia v Confederation Life Association* (1971) 460 F 2d 805.

[74] *Confederation Life Association v Ugalde* (n 73 above). In another case, however, the District

contract was governed by Cuban law but there was no stipulated place of payment, the court felt able to give judgment in dollars[75] and, where the contract stipulated only for payment in pesos, judgment in dollars was awarded by reference to the current rate of exchange.[76]

The results in these cases appear to be consistent with the general principles **16.26** outlined at the beginning of this section. It is, however, to be noted that the debtor was allowed by the relevant exchange control laws to make payment in accordance with the rules laid down by such laws; in each of those cases, the debtor had made (or was prepared to make) payment in that manner. What is to be the position if the debtor has not made *any* form of payment, on the basis that the exchange regulations comprised within the applicable law suspend performance or prohibit any payment, and thus render payment illegal—even payment in England out of English assets? In other words—and in contrast to the cases discussed earlier—what is the position if the exchange control regulations do not merely mandate a different currency or mode of payment, but prohibit payment outright? In such a case, it is submitted that the debtor, in seeking to rely upon the exchange control regulations forming a part of the applicable law, is effectively seeking to assert the sovereign rights of the restricting State to ensure the implementation of the latter's policy outside the territorial limits of its jurisdiction. This the debtor cannot do any more than the restricting State itself,[77] with the result that the exchange regulations ought not to be applied by an English court in such a case. A further point may be added in this type of case, where the applicable law upholds the substantive obligation but deprives the debtor of the means of performance.[78] Where the applicable law creates a right, the available remedies and enforcement mechanisms are matters of procedure which are governed exclusively by English law, where the proceedings take place here. Once the debt has been established and shown to be outstanding, the English courts may give judgment and order execution against the debtor's property in England. Plainly, the terms of the foreign law applicable to the contract cannot prevent the English courts from exercising these procedural powers. Likewise, the English court is not prevented from

---

Court of Appeal of Florida decided in the opposite sense, on the ground that the policyholder was a refugee who would be unable to return to Cuba to collect payment, and "equitable considerations" therefore required the insurer to make payment in Florida: *Confederation Life Association v Conte* (1971) 254 So 2d 45.

[75] *Menendez v Saks & Co* (1973) 485 F 2d 1355.

[76] *Pan-American Life Insurance Co v Blanco* (1969) 362 F 2d 167, followed in *Oliva v Pan-American Life Insurance Co* (1971) 448 F 2d.

[77] This particular subject is discussed in more detail at para 16.50 below.

[78] Where the applicable law goes further than this and nullifies an obligation which had been validly incurred, then different considerations will apply. The legislation would be confiscatory and should thus be disregarded on public policy grounds—see, eg, *French v Banco Nacional de Cuba* (1968) 23 NY 2d 46. This point is discussed in more depth at para 16.43 below.

giving judgment merely on the grounds that this may compel the debtor to make a payment in England which is prohibited by the laws of the restricting State.[79]

16.27   A further set of problems may arise where the debt affected by the exchange controls comprised within the applicable law has been secured by a guarantee.[80] Can the guarantor who, as a rule, may avail himself of such defences as are open to the principle debtor, invoke the suspension, illegality, or discharge (as the case may be) which is mandated by the exchange regulations concerned? A variety of factors may affect the position. For example, the guarantee may (or may not) be governed by the same legal system as the principal obligation; the relevant exchange regulations may (or may not) form a part of the law applicable to the guarantee; or the guarantee may have been given before (or after) the primary debtor became subject to the exchange regulations concerned. It is not proposed to examine all of the possible variations on this theme, but a leading case is provided by a decision of the French Cour de Cassation.[81] In 1977, the French defendant guaranteed (apparently under French law) a US dollar loan granted by the plaintiff bank to a Brazilian company; the loan was repayable in dollars in New York. In 1983 Brazil introduced exchange controls as a result of which the principal debtor could not pay dollars in New York but could and did deposit the amount due in Brazilian currency within Brazil. Could the guarantee be called under these circumstances? Under Article 2011 of the Code Civil, the guarantor was obliged to satisfy the principal debt "if the debtor does not satisfy it himself". The principal debtor had not remitted dollars to New York, and this was sufficient to compel the French defendant to pay the requisite US dollar sum under the terms of his guarantee. It was thus not necessary to consider the consequences of the payment made in Brazil. Had the guarantee been governed by the laws of Brazil, then the result might have been different but, subject only to that point, it is suggested that this robust approach is appropriate and in accordance with the general principles noted earlier in this chapter.

16.28   In principle, the outcome should be the same where exchange control is already in force in the debtor's country when the guarantee is given, provided that the guarantor acts in good faith and there is no deliberate intention to facilitate a breach of the exchange control regime in question. Even under these circum-

---

[79] See, eg, *Kleinwort Sons & Co v Ungarische Baumwolle Industrie AG* [1939] 2 KB 678, followed in *Toprak Mahsulleri Ofisi v Finagrain Cie Commerciale Agricole et Financière SA* [1979] 2 Lloyd's Rep 98.

[80] The present section contemplates a guarantee in the strict sense of the term. It must be said that guarantees governed by English law now frequently contain indemnity language of a kind which would usually dispense with some of the issues about to be discussed. But these points may continue to arise under foreign law guarantees, and the discussion is instructive in any event.

[81] Cas Com, 18 April 1989, Bull 1989, iv, No. 116.

stances, the guarantee is given for the purpose of securing to the creditor the agreed payment, in the agreed currency, and in the agreed place. Any defect in the contractual obligation of the debtor should not be allowed to frustrate that purpose.[82]

Exchange controls not forming part of the applicable law

If the contract or obligation in question is governed by the law of a country **16.29** other than the restricting country, no effect can generally be attributed to the exchange control regulations of the restricting country which interfere with the performance of the contract as contemplated by the parties. In other words, when considering matters germane to the substantive performance of an English law contract, the existence of exchange restrictions in a foreign country need not, in principle, be considered.[83] Inevitably, matters are not as straightforward as this statement would suggest, and it will be necessary to consider the effect of any exchange controls in force in the place of payment. Nevertheless, it is submitted that this broad statement of principle does provide an appropriate starting point. Especially where the relevant exchange control restrictions are introduced after the date of the contract, and the place of payment is outside the restricting State, the point just noted will usually be determinative of any dispute which may arise. The position is most clearly illustrated where payment is due in England under an English law contract, but the debtor resides in a restricting State which makes it impossible for him to discharge his obligations. The local restrictions affecting the debtor are wholly immaterial, because they are extraneous to a contract governed by English law and performable in England. This point is clearly established in this country.[84] The rule is justified because, otherwise, rules forming part of a foreign legal system could be used to defeat a claim before the English courts based upon an English law obligation. This

---

[82] A different view was adopted by the Court of Appeal, Düsseldorf, 16 February 1983, *WM* 1983, 1366 with critical note by Rutke. The case is discussed in more supportive terms by Gold, *The Fund Agreement in the Courts III*, 276 and 460.

[83] As a result, when an English law contract refers to "payment", it will usually mean payment in such manner as will enable the creditor himself to use and dispose of the funds immediately following their receipt—see *Seligman Bros v Brown Shipley & Co* (1916) 32 TLR 549; *The Brimnes* [1973] 1 WLR 386; *The Chikuma* [1981] All ER 652 (HL). Thus, payment into a blocked account will not discharge the obligation, even if "payment" in that manner is required under the laws of the restricting State.

[84] That matters touching the substance of a payment obligation and its performance are subjected to the governing law of the contract is now confirmed by the Rome Convention, Art 10(1)(b)—see the discussion in Ch 4 above. For cases which illustrate this principle with great clarity, see *Kleinwort Sons & Co v Ungarische Baumwolle Industrie AG* [1939] 2 KB 678 and *Toprak Mahsulleri Ofisi v Finagrain Compagnie Commerciale* (1979) 2 Lloyd's Rep 98. In a related context, it has been stated that the performance of an English law contract in England is not excused merely because the obligor would thereby become liable to some penal sanction in his own country—*Kahler v Midland Bank* [1950] AC 24, 51 (HL); see also *Dalmia v National Bank* (1978) 2 Ll LR 223, 267.

would seem to be unacceptable for a variety of reasons; for example, the creditor may not be aware of the law of the debtor's country of residence, and there is no good reason to put him on inquiry in that regard. A similar rule is accepted in a number of other jurisdictions.[85]

16.30   In principle, it is suggested that exchange controls which do not form part of the applicable law may be taken into account in three main types of cases, namely:

(1)   where the private international law of the forum allows some scope for the application of such controls;

(2)   where, as in the case of English law, the substantive law applicable to the contract itself takes account of exchange controls in effect under the laws of the place of payment; and

(3)   where the obligation is to be settled in cash and the exchange control regulations at issue render it difficult for the debtor to obtain the currency concerned.[86]

The remaining parts of this section will consider issues of this kind.

Private international law of the forum

16.31   It has been noted previously[87] that Article 7(1) of the Rome Convention is inapplicable in the United Kingdom. Nevertheless, the application of the provision in other member States could have material consequences for contracts which are affected by exchange control considerations. It is thus necessary to review its potential application in the present context.[88] Article 7(1) reads as follows:

> When applying under this Convention the law of a country, effect may be given to the mandatory rules of the law of another country with which the situation has a

---

[85] See, eg, *Bank of America National Trust v Envases Venezolanos* (1990) 740 F Supp 260, although this was decided without reference to the New York cases about to be mentioned, and relied mainly on the absence of frustration. Relevant New York decisions include *Central Hanover Bank & Trust Co v Siemens & Halske AG* (1939) 15 F Supp 927, affirmed 84 F 993 (CCA 2d, 1936), cert denied 299 US 585 and *Pan-American Securities Corp v Friedr Krupp AG* (1939) 256 App Div 955, 10 NYS (2d), but there are also other decisions to like effect. As noted earlier, however, these cases must be treated with some caution in an English context, because the New York courts tend to ascribe questions of payment to the law of the place of performance (rather than to the law applicable to the contract). For other decisions, see the South African decision in *Cargo Motor Corp v Tofalos Transport Ltd* [1972] 1 South Africa LR 186, 195–7, and the Zambian decision in *Commonwealth Development Corp v Central African Power Corp* (1968) 3 African LR (Commercial Series) 416.

[86] It may be admitted that this last example is of decreasing importance, but is considered for the sake of completeness.

[87] See Ch 4 above.

[88] For more detailed consideration of Art 7(1) and related provisions of the Rome Convention, see Plender and Wilderspin, *The European Contracts Convention* (Sweet & Maxwell, 2nd edn, 2001) ch 9.

close connection, if and so far as, under the law of the latter country, those rules must be applied whatever the law applicable to the contract. In considering whether to give effect to those mandatory rules, regard shall be had to their nature and purpose and to the consequences of their application or non-application.

The expression "mandatory rules" connotes rules from which parties cannot derogate by means of any contractual term.[89] It is not necessary to go into matters of refined definition, for it is immediately obvious that foreign exchange laws of mandatory application apply in the State which imposes them. Given the role which exchange control laws are intended to play in supporting and protecting the domestic economy, no other conclusion is possible.

It would then become necessary to determine whether the foreign exchange rules have a "close connection" with the "situation" for the purposes of Article 7(1). It would seem that the law of the place of performance has a "close connection" with a contractual situation for these purposes.[90] Consequently, the court would have a discretion to give effect to foreign exchange laws which affected the ability to pay or the means of payment in the law of the place of performance. It would, however, be equally open to the court to hold that the law of the place of residence of the debtor has a "close connection" with the "situation", and thus to give effect to the exchange controls of that country.

16.32

It is, however, submitted that tribunals should exercise extreme caution in the use of Article 7(1) in the present context. Where the contract exhibits genuinely international elements and the contract is legitimately governed by a system of law other than that which creates the exchange control regime, then the application of such rules would detract from the enforceability of contracts and would frequently afford to the debtor a defence which would be entirely lacking in merit. Apart from other considerations, the duty of obtaining any necessary exchange control approvals would have been imposed upon the debtor, and it is unreasonable that his failure to discharge that duty should also constitute a defence to the performance of contractual obligations which are otherwise legitimate.[91]

16.33

Exchange controls as part of the law of the place of payment

It is now necessary to turn to the position where a contract is governed by English law but payment is required to be made within the territory of the

16.34

---

[89] See Plender and Wilderspin (n 88 above) para 9-07. For further discussion on the subject, see Mann, "Effect of mandatory Rules" in K. Lipstein (ed) *Harmonisation of Private International Law by the EEC* (Institute of Advanced Legal Studies, 1978) 31.

[90] Plender and Wilderspin (n 88 above) para 9-09. See also para 16.05(4) above.

[91] Of course, different considerations may apply where the creditor was, in some active way, a party to the debtor's breach of the regulations concerned.

restricting State.[92] Before moving on to the details, however, it is necessary to emphasise that—so far as English private international law is concerned—the "place of payment" is the place in which the creditor is entitled to receive his money, and *not* the place from which the debtor is obliged to remit it.[93] Once again, this has the effect of denying any legal effect to the laws of the country in which the debtor happens to be resident, in which he carries on business, or of which he is a national.[94] It may be that the debtor has to initiate the payment in his home jurisdiction, by instructing his bank to make the necessary transfer to an overseas account of the creditor; and it may well be that such a transfer cannot lawfully be made in the absence of an exchange control approval in the debtor's country of residence. But, for reasons given earlier in this chapter, none of these considerations would constitute a defence in English proceedings arising out of a contract governed by English law.

16.35   What, then, is to be the position once the place of payment has been properly identified in accordance with the principles just noted, and it has been established that payment is unlawful under exchange restrictions which form a part of the law of that place? It is necessary to consider two alternative possibilities.

16.36   First of all, where the exchange restrictions were in effect at the time when the contract was made and the effect of the exchange restrictions is to uphold the obligation and yet deprive the debtor of the means of performance, then the English courts should disregard the restrictions concerned. If there is a valid debt in accordance with the law applicable to it, then the law of the place of performance cannot deprive the creditor of the remedies and procedures which English law may afford to him. Aside from this particular principle of private international law, however, it should not be forgotten that the existence of controls in the restricting State may be relevant to the interpretation of the contract under English law, since (in construing the contract) the court may take into account all of the surrounding circumstances at the time of its conclusion.[95] The contract may contain express terms dealing with the need to obtain

---

[92] The present discussion does, of course, assume that the law of the place of payment does not coincide with the applicable law of the contract.

[93] See in particular, *Libyan Arab Foreign Bank v Bankers Trust Co* [1989] 1 QB 728. This point has already been discussed in another context—see para 7.84 above. Since the formulation stated in the text is a part of English conflict of laws, it will be applied in determining the place of payment, irrespective of any contrary position adopted by the law applicable to the obligation.

[94] *Euro-Diam Ltd v Bathurst* [1980] QB 30 (CA); *Bangladesh Export Import Co v Sucden Kerry SA* [1995] 2 Lloyd's Rep 1; *Jones v Chatfield* [1993] 1 NZLR 617; *Society of Lloyd's v Fraser* [1998] CLC 1630 (CA); *Fox v Henderson Investment Fund Ltd* [1992] 2 Lloyd's Rep 303 and other cases cited in Dicey and Morris, *The Conflict of Laws* (Sweet & Maxwell, 13th edn, 2000) para 13-142.

[95] On the general principle just stated, see *Chitty on Contracts* (Sweet & Maxwell, 29th edn, 2004) ch 12; *Investors Compensation Scheme v West Bromwich Building Society* [1998] 1 WLR 896. As has been noted previously, the interpretation of a contract is determined by reference to the law applicable to it.

local foreign exchange approvals as a condition precedent to the performance of obligations arising under the agreement.[96] Alternatively, it may on occasion be appropriate to imply terms into the contract which address the fact that exchange controls subsist in the place of payment. In some cases, it will be an implied term that exchange control approval will be obtained and that one of the parties will endeavour to obtain it.[97] In other cases, it may be an implied term that funds will be remitted in payment in a manner which allows the creditor to accept and retain the monies so despatched; in other words, the debtor must take steps to ensure that he arranges payment in accordance with the laws of the restricting State.[98] But in each of these cases, the law of the place of payment is not directly applicable to the contract; it only comes into the reckoning because the exchange restrictions are one of the circumstances which surrounded the conclusion of the contract. In other words, the law of the place of payment (including the exchange restrictions there imposed) has only such influence as the governing law of the contract may allow to it as a part of the interpretative process.

The position is less clear in the case of supervening exchange controls, ie where   **16.37** the parties have entered into an English law contract stipulating for payment in a particular place and—between the date of the contract and the due date for payment—the country in which payment is to occur imposes exchange restrictions rendering payment impossible in that place.

The starting point for this discussion must be the decision of the Court of   **16.38** Appeal in *Ralli Bros v Compania Naviera Sota y Aznar*.[99] A contract which was found to be governed by English law provided that freight should be paid in Barcelona; however, by the contractual payment date, a new Spanish law had

---

[96] This type of provision is very common in cross-border banking documentation. As a practical matter—and notwithstanding the points made in the text—the lender will usually be keen to ensure that the agreement is enforceable in the borrower's jurisdiction of residence, since the majority of his assets are likely to be situate there and must be available for the purposes of execution following any judgment which may be obtained.

[97] In the context of the former system of UK exchange control, see Exchange Control Act 1947, s 33(1) and the discussion on this subject in Ch 14 above.

[98] And if payment is not made in compliance with the implied term, then the purported payment will not discharge the obligation concerned. For a series of French cases which illustrate this point in the context of German exchange control, see Cour de Paris, 26 March 1936, *Clunet* 1936, 931; 8 December 1936, *Chronique Hebdomadaire du Receuil Sirey* 1937, No 2; Cour de Colmar, 11 March 1938, *Clunet*, 1938, 812; 9 December 1938, 41 (1939) BIJI No. 10785, 59. In each case, the debtors had made payment in a manner inconsistent with German exchange control regulations, with the result that they had failed to make effective payment in accordance with the terms of the contract.

[99] [1920] 2 KB 287. The decision is not particularly satisfactory, for some of the reasons about to be discussed. For other analyses, see Dicey and Morris, *The Conflict of Laws* (Sweet & Maxwell, 13th edn, 2000) para 32-141; Plender and Wilderspin, *The European Contracts Convention* (Sweet & Maxwell, 2nd edn, 2001) para 9-05.

made it illegal both[100] to pay and to receive more than a maximum freight of 875 pesetas per tonne, ie very much less than had been agreed. The action for the recovery for the amount due under the terms of the contract was dismissed because: "Where a contract requires an act to be done in a foreign country, it is in the absence of very special circumstances, an implied term of the continuing validity of such a provision that the act to be done in the foreign country shall not be illegal by the law of the State."[101] It has to be recorded that this case gives rise to no small difficulty, especially in the context of a monetary obligation governed by English law.[102] In particular:

(a) The quoted statement suggests that the entire payment obligation was discharged, ie the defendant was not obliged to pay anything. It is not clear from the judgment whether the obligation remained valid as to the smaller amount (875 pesetas) which could still lawfully be paid in Spain. The judgments are unclear as to the ultimate fate of the contract.

(b) It is difficult to support the supposed implied term by reference to considerations of business efficacy or the intention of the parties. If a seller or supplier of goods or services has fulfilled his side of the bargain, then both parties would expect him to be paid both the amount and the currency stipulated in the contract.[103] For this reason, it is suggested that it would nearly always be possible to imply a term into the contract which deals with the situation which arose in that case and which preserves the substance of the commercial bargain. In essence, if payment becomes unlawful in the contractual place of performance, then the term would require that payment instead be made to the creditor in the country in which he is resident or carries on the business to which the monetary obligation relates.[104] It is suggested that this more closely represents the intention of the parties and would represent a legitimate approach to

---

[100] It is necessary to emphasise this point.

[101] At 304, *per* Scrutton LJ.

[102] It is submitted that the English courts should only apply the *Ralli Bros* case, where the contract is governed by English law because the case deals with the implied terms of the contract or with the application of the doctrine of frustration. In other words, the case does not reflect any general principle of English private international law—see the discussion in Dicey and Morris (n 99 above) paras 32-141–32-148.

[103] This would have been the position in the *Ralli Bros* case, where the obligations for which payment was due had been performed.

[104] A further layer of complexity may arise if the creditor is resident or carries on business in a country which imposes a system of exchange control. However, in such a case, it would usually become incumbent upon the creditor to surrender the resultant foreign currency to the central bank against payment of the local currency at the official rate—see, eg, Exchange Control Act 1947, s 2, discussed in Ch 14 above. The obligation to surrender such currency is usually imposed by reference to the residence of the creditor, and not by reference to the place of performance. Consequently, the implied term suggested in the text should not be affected by the fact that the creditor is resident in a State which itself imposes a system of exchange control.

the interpretation of a contract governed by English law. Indeed, given that the place of payment is usually a matter of practical convenience and no more,[105] it may even be argued that a term should be implied to the effect that payment should be made to a place nominated by the creditor for these purposes, provided that the net cost to the debtor remains the same.[106] A term of this type is particularly apt in the context of a monetary obligation where settlement is to occur by means of cheque or bank transfer, and the place to which funds are to be remitted makes little difference to the debtor. It would also have to be an implied term that the obligation to pay would be suspended until the creditor had nominated the place of payment.[107] It may be objected that implied terms of this kind are far-reaching and may give a significant degree of control and discretion to the creditor in this type of case. That is, of course, true; but there are various factors which favour this approach. First of all, the justice of the case is clearly with the creditor, especially where he has already performed his side of the contractual bargain. Secondly, the debtor is protected by the proposed stipulation as to the costs involved in the revised method of performance. Thirdly, although the creditor is allowed a discretion as to the identification of the place of payment, the point will in practice only arise in a tiny fraction of cases. Fourthly, the implied term would deprive the debtor of an unwarranted windfall.[108] Finally, it is suggested that the implied terms here proposed would be entirely in harmony with legitimate commercial expectations, for neither party could have expected that the debtor could be discharged otherwise than by payment.[109]

---

[105] eg, payments through the banking system in US dollars or sterling will usually be required to be made in New York and London respectively, solely because the payments may most efficiently be cleared and redeployed there. The location of the place of payment usually has no deeper significance. In this context, it may be added that the decision in *Ralli Bros* is generally regarded as involving frustration as a result of supervening illegality—see, eg, Goode, *Payment Obligations in Commercial and Financial Transactions* (Sweet & Maxwell, 1983, (reprinted 1987)) 133. However, the doctrine of frustration cannot apply if the supervening events are dealt with by an implied term of the contract as here suggested.

[106] ie the debtor would be allowed to recoup any foreign exchange or remittance costs incurred as a result of performance in accordance with the implied term.

[107] The implied term suggested in earlier editions of this work was subjected to criticism by Goode, (n 105 above) 133–4. The revised formulation of the implied term in the text represents an attempt to overcome the difficulties which he mentions.

[108] It may be objected that the implied terms proposed in the text may result in hardship for the debtor where he is resident in the place of payment when the relevant exchange controls are imposed. Yet this cannot be a sufficient ground of objection, for English law pays no regard to exchange controls merely on the ground that the debtor is resident in the restricting State—*Kleinwort Sons & Co v Ungarische Baumwolle Industrie AG* [1939] 2 KB 678.

[109] It is necessary to emphasise that the present review is confined to the consequences of the *Ralli Bros* decision for obligations of a monetary character, and is in part based on the fact that

(c) At a more general level, it does appear that the principle laid down in the *Ralli Bros* decision is a rule of English domestic law (rather than a rule of English private international law).[110] On this basis, the English courts would enforce a foreign law contract which had been affected by supervening exchange controls in the place of payment,[111] but would decline to enforce a corresponding agreement governed by English law. In so far as the principle is designed to avoid conflicts between the English courts and the legal systems of foreign States, this distinction appears to lack any sensible rationale.

(d) Finally, it may be added that, so far as the Rome Convention is concerned, the law of the place of performance is merely to be taken into account in assessing the *manner* of performance. The place of payment thus now has a more limited role, and the courts should recognise its reduced status in this context.[112]

For these reasons, at least in so far as it would discharge the debtor from a monetary obligation, it is suggested that the decision in *Ralli Bros* ought to be overruled, when a suitable opportunity arises.[113]

16.39   However that may be, it is for the present necessary to consider how the *Ralli*

---

payment can readily be made in alternative jurisdictions. The continued application of the decision may well be appropriate in relation to obligations to deliver goods or to supply services, for the place of performance is, in that context, likely to be of greater significance to both parties.

[110]   On this point, see Dicey and Morris, *The Conflict of Laws* (Sweet & Maxwell, 13th edn, 2000) paras 32-141–32-148; Plender and Wilderspin, *The European Contracts Convention* (Sweet & Maxwell, 2nd edn, 2001) para 9-06. The same point was noted with apparent approval although without any decision on the issue in *Ispahani v Bank Melli Iran* [1998] 1 Lloyds Bank Rep 133.

[111]   Assuming, of course, that the contract remained valid under the applicable law in such circumstances.

[112]   See Art 10(2) of the Rome Convention. It should be appreciated that this point is made merely for the purposes of illustration. The discussion in the text considers the *substance* of performance of a monetary obligation. Strictly speaking, Art 10(2) is not in point since it is directed to the *manner* of performance.

[113]   It must, however, be acknowledged that the point will arise only rarely, for the reasons discussed by Dicey and Morris (n 110 above) para 32-148. Equally, it must not be forgotten that courts have occasionally ascribed a greater significance to the place of payment than that suggested in the text, eg in *Dalmia Cement v National Bank of Pakistan* [1974] 3 WLR 138, Kerr J remarked (at 152) that "to compel a Pakistani bank to pay a large sum in England is certainly not the same, and in my view also not to the same effect, as compelling it to pay such sum in India. The consequences to the bank of these two obligations may be entirely different, and the obligation itself is certainly different". It is submitted that this overstates the position—the effect is to discharge the obligation in each case, and the precise identity of the place of payment seems to make very little difference so far as the debtor is concerned. Finally, it must be acknowledged that the *Ralli Bros* principle was considered with apparent approval in *Ispahani v Bank Melli Iran* [1998] 1 Lloyds Bank Rep 133, albeit under circumstances rather different from those discussed in the text. It should be emphasised that the discussion in the text is limited solely to the principle illustrated by the decision in *Ralli Bros*. The separate line of authority—exemplified by the decision in *Foster v Driscoll* [1929] 1 KB 470 (CA)—prohibits the enforcement of a contract where both parties have actively conspired to evade the foreign exchange laws of a foreign State; it is not intended to cast any doubt on the latter principle.

Bros principle has been applied by other courts. Notwithstanding that the Court of Appeal in that case expressly proceeded on the basis of an implied term of the contract, it has subsequently been treated as a decision based on the doctrine of frustration.[114] In other words, supervening illegality under the law of the place of performance will result in the frustration of the contract.[115] It is fair to observe that the *Ralli Bros* principle is mitigated in certain respects. For example, it only applies where payment has been made *illegal* in the place of performance—it does not apply merely because payment has been *excused* under that law.[116] Furthermore, the principle will only apply where the supervening exchange restrictions are likely to be of a duration which seriously impedes or defeats the effective performance of the contract. Where the supervening regulations are likely to be of only a temporary nature, then the performance of the contract is merely suspended; frustration does not occur.[117]

Exchange controls and the mode of performance

Although monetary obligations can be settled in a variety of ways,[118] cash remains a significant means of performance in the context of monetary obligations. This, in turn, creates a particular set of problems, because many systems of exchange control prohibit both the import and the export of banknotes,[119] at any rate in the absence of a licence for that purpose. In such cases, the greater part of such banknotes of the restricting State as are situate outside its territory will have arrived there as a result of smuggling. Consequently, the value of such banknotes in terms of their exchange for other currencies will usually be significantly depreciated.[120] Yet, from a legal point of view, it remains the case that banknotes issued by but situate outside the restricting State nevertheless retain

16.40

---

[114] This, of course, provides a further reason for the belief that the principle applies only to contracts governed by English law because—consistently with Art 10(1) of the Rome Convention—the doctrine of frustration can only be applied to contracts governed by English law.

[115] For discussion, see Goode, *Payment Obligations in Commercial and Financial Transactions* (Sweet & Maxwell, 1983, reprinted 1987) 133. Cases which have applied the *Ralli Bros* principle include *AV Pound & Co Ltd v MW Hardy & Co Inc* [1956] AC 588; *Toprak Mahsulleri Ofisi v Finagrain Compagnie Commerciale Agricole et Financiere SA* [1979] 2 Lloyd's Rep 98. More recently, the principle has been cited without any hint of disapproval in *Mahonia Ltd v West LB* [2004] EWHC 1938 (Comm).

[116] *Jacobs v Credit Lyonnais* (1884) 12 QBD 589.

[117] On this point, see *Arab Bank Ltd v Barclays Bank (DC & O)* [1954] AC 495; cited with approval in *Libyan Arab Foreign Bank v Bankers Trust Co* [1989] QB 728; Goode (n 115 above) 134.

[118] On the various means of performance of a monetary obligation, see Ch 7 above.

[119] Under the UK's former system of exchange controls, only the export of sterling notes was prohibited. By way of further example, note the system of Spanish exchange control at issue in Cases C–163, 165, 250/94 [1995] ECR I–4821, *Criminal Proceedings against Sanz de Lera*.

[120] See Ciano, "The Pre-War 'Black' Market for Foreign Bank Notes" (1941) 8 *Economica* 378. This article answers some of the questions which were treated as unanswerable in *Rex v Haddock*. A.P. Herbert, *Codd's Last Case and other Misleading Cases* (London, 1952) 112.

the quality of lawful money; the fact that the practical possibilities of making use of the banknotes are necessarily reduced does not affect their status as money. Formal demonetisations of notes would require both an express provision of the *lex monetae* governing them and (in practice) some form of distinguishing mark. The restricting State's mere prohibition of the import or export of its currency to or from its territory does not of itself affect the legal tender quality of the notes.

16.41 Under these circumstances, it is necessary to address two points, namely:

(1) It has been noted that currency smuggled out of a restricting State may have a depreciated market or exchange value, ie where the notes are being purchased in exchange for some other currency. It is perhaps right to regard this as an economic (rather than a legal) consequence of the existence of the exchange control system in question. But it is suggested that the possibility that notes have been smuggled out of the restricting State does not usually have any consequences of a purely legal character.[121] A creditor cannot refuse to accept the notes on the basis that they must necessarily have been smuggled, because it will be possible to export notes under official licence; it will be equally impossible to distinguish between those notes which have lawfully been exported, and those which have not. In any event, smuggling has no "tainting" effect upon the performance of a contract unless it reflects a common intention of the parties jointly to commit an illegal act by reintroducing smuggled currency into the restricting State without licence.[122] The performance of the contract would not be "tainted" in this way merely because one party knew or suspected that the other may have been involved in smuggling.[123]

---

[121] In the present context, we are, of course, only concerned with the use of the notes as a means of satisfying a monetary obligation. We are not concerned with criminal sanctions or other questions which may arise within the restricting State itself.

[122] *Foster v Driscoll* [1929] 1 KB 470 (CA); *Marrache v Ashton* [1943] AC 311, 319 (PC).

[123] The statements just made rely upon *Foster v Driscoll* [1929] KB 470 (see in particular the formulation at 571) as approved and applied in *Reggazoni v KC Sethia (1944) Ltd* [1958] AC 301, a case which involved a deliberate attempt to circumvent Indian sanctions against South Africa. It may be noted that the German courts have likewise repeatedly decided that a contract designed to circumvent the public laws of a foreign State may be unenforceable on the grounds that it constitutes an "immoral contract" for the purposes of art 138 of the German Civil Code. In a case which bears some similarity to the decision in *Reggazoni*, the German Federal Supreme Court ordered a supplier of steel to pay compensation to the Thai buyer, on the grounds that the supplier had attempted to deliver steel originating from South Africa, in direct contravention of Thai sanctions against that country—German Federal Supreme Court, 20 October 1992, *RIW* 1993, 146, *IPRspr* 1992, No. 59. Similarly, a contract which violated US sanctions against members of the Warsaw Pact was held to contravene art 138 of the Civil Code. In another case, the Court of Appeal of Hamburg was confronted with a case involving a contravention of Nigerian exchange controls—6 May 1993, *RIW* 1994, 686 with a note by Mankowski or *IPRspr* 1993, No. 32. The court rejected arguments based on Art VIII(2)(b) of the Fund Agreement, and

(2) The circumstances under which the relevant banknotes left the restricting State cannot be taken to affect the application of the nominalistic principle. It thus remains the case that the creditor of a sum expressed in the restricted currency must accept whatever is legal tender under the *lex monetae* for the nominal amount of the debt. Performance remains possible in the agreed manner and under these circumstances the creditor cannot insist on a method of payment for which the parties have not contracted, nor may he make any complaint by reference to the (reduced) value of those notes as compared to other currencies.

As a general rule, it follows that the restricting State's banknotes can be used in **16.42** discharge of all debts which are expressed in its currency and payable outside its boundaries. This is plainly so where the obligation is subject to a legal system other than that of the restricting State. In such a case, the only connection between the contract and the restricting State is that the latter supplies the applicable legal tender legislation as the *lex monetae*, which will inevitably be silent on this subject. As a result, and in the absence of special terms, an English judgment for a sum of foreign money can be satisfied by the payment of foreign banknotes.[124] But even where the obligation is governed by the law of the restricting State, the result will be the same unless that law contains specific provisions which prohibit payment by means of banknotes.[125] Of course, it will be necessary in each case to interpret the contract to ascertain whether the parties envisaged payment in (devalued) banknotes delivered outside the restricting State. If, upon a proper construction of the contract, the place of performance is found to be within the restricting State itself, then the creditor will be entitled to receive "full value" notes, tendered to him in compliance with the local exchange regime—ie where payment is required within the restricting State itself, the obligation cannot be performed with notes unlawfully smuggled back into the country.[126]

---

also found that the contravention of Nigerian exchange controls did not offend against German notions of "good morals" under art 138 of the Civil Code, partly because (on the facts) the damage suffered by the claimant was not related to the alleged violation of Nigerian exchange controls, and partly because the imposition of those controls did not reflect international or generally accepted values.

[124] See *Mechanical & Electrical Engineering Contracts Co v Christy & Norris Ltd*, which has not been fully reported but is noted in (1984) NLJ 1017.

[125] This approach would now appear to be in accordance with the Rome Convention, Art 10(1)(b). It also reflects the decision in *Marrache v Ashton* [1943] AC 311, which probably renders *Graumann v Treitel* [1940] LQR 552, bad in law. See the commentary of Dr Mann (1940) 3 MLR 214, n 55.

[126] This point would appear to follow from an application of Art 10(2) of the Rome Convention. Alternatively, where a monetary obligation is to be performed in a particular place, it may be an implied term of the contract that the performance of the obligation is to be achieved in harmony with the law of that place. The term to be implied into a contract where performance has been rendered unlawful under that law has already been discussed.

D. Exchange Control and Rights of Property

16.43 The effect of foreign exchange controls upon rights of property (whether tangible or intangible and including related questions of ownership, transfer, and assignment) situate in England ought, in principle, to be capable of very brief description. This is because there exists "the simple rule that generally, property in England is subject to English law and none other".[127] This rule is firmly established[128] and will preclude foreign exchange legislation from changing title to, or restraining dispositions of, property situate in England. It may be added that this result does not involve an analysis of the public or confiscatory character of the legislation concerned; the foreign exchange controls do not fall for consideration at all, for whether or not English property has been transferred is an issue which must be determined solely by reference to English law. The English courts would thus disregard foreign exchange control laws which sought to impose controls upon the English property of persons who were once resident within the restricting State but have since emigrated;[129] indeed, given that English law claims the exclusive right to determine title to property situate in England, such laws should be disregarded even if the individual concerned remains resident in the restricting State. Likewise, it may be expected that foreign courts would have declined to give effect to those provisions of the Exchange Control Act 1947 which allowed the Treasury to vest certain property in itself, even if that property was situate abroad.[130] The question may cause particular difficulty in the context of an assignment of debts, partly because the contractual and proprietary aspects of a debt are inextricably intertwined.[131] Thus, suppose that a debtor, resident in England[132] owes money to a creditor resident in a restricting State under the terms of a contract which is governed by the laws of that State. The creditor then assigns the benefit of that by means of an assignment governed by English law. What is the position if the exchange control regulations of the restricting State prohibit the assignment[133] and render it void? A

---

[127] *Bank voor Handel en Scheepvaart v Slatford* [1953] 1 QB 248, 260. It should be noted that this decision applies both to tangible property (gold bars) and intangible property (book debts).

[128] See, eg, the discussion in Dicey and Morris, *The Conflict of Laws* (Sweet & Maxwell, 13th edn, 2000) ch 22.

[129] This was the position under s 55 of the German Foreign Exchange Act 1938, on which see Hahn, *Festschrift für Sir Joseph Gold*, 155.

[130] See ss 2(5), 24(2), 26(2), and 27(1) of the 1947 Act. In so far as they applied to foreign countries, these provisions involved an excess of international jurisdiction.

[131] See, in particular, *Raiffeisen Zentralbank Girozentrale v Five Star Trading Ltd* [2000] Lloyd's Rep 284.

[132] If the debtor is resident in England, then the debt will usually constitute property situate in this country—see Dicey and Morris (n 128 above) ch 22.

[133] ie on the grounds that the assignment deprives the restricting State of the benefit of the foreign exchange receipt.

strict application of Article 12 of the Rome Convention[134] would lead to the conclusion that the assignment is valid as between the creditor and the assignee, for it is governed by English law and its material validity is thus determined exclusively by reference to that law. On the other hand, the assignment would have no effect as against the English debtor, for his monetary obligation is governed by the laws of the restricting State and the laws of that State render the assignment ineffective as against him.[135] However, given that the property concerned is situate in England, it is suggested that the courts would instead apply the "simple rule" noted above. They may refuse to apply the prohibition contained within the applicable law on the straightforward ground that foreign law cannot be allowed to have any impact upon transfers of assets situate in England.

It might be thought both logical and desirable to extend the "simple rule" to questions of possession as well as title, for there seems no obvious reason for distinguishing between the two. At this point, however, it becomes necessary to consider the unfortunate decision of the House of Lords in *Kahler v Midland Bank*[136] which seems to allow the exchange control regulations of a foreign State significantly to interfere with the right to possession of property in England. In that case, the plaintiff, then resident in Prague, had deposited bearer securities with the Bohemian Bank in Czechoslovakia. The Bohemian Bank had in turn deposited those securities with the defendant bank in London.[137] The defendant bank was therefore in the position of a sub-bailee, and no contract subsisted between it and the plaintiff, who accordingly sought the return of the securities through proceedings founded in detinue. His claim succeeded at first instance but failed both in the Court of Appeal[138] and, by a bare majority, in the House of Lords.[139] The majority in the House of Lords held that the action in detinue could only succeed if the plaintiff had an immediate right to possession of the securities; his ability to recover the securities from Midland Bank depended on the terms of his contract with the Bohemian Bank.[140] That contract was found

16.44

---

[134] Article 12 of the Rome Convention provides that the mutual obligations of an assignor and an assignee are governed by the law applicable to the assignment. However, the consequences of the assignment for the debtor are governed by the law applicable to the debt itself.

[135] Some authority for this approach may be derived from the *Raiffeisen* case (n 131 above).

[136] [1950] AC 24. The companion case of *Zivnovstenska Banka v Frankman* [1950] AC 57 should also be noted, although it is of less general interest since the decision rests primarily upon the terms of the contract between the parties.

[137] At this point, the securities fell to be regarded as English property, because bearer securities are deemed to be situate in the country in which they are physically located—see Dicey and Morris, *The Conflict of Laws* (Sweet & Maxwell, 13th edn, 2000) para 22-040.

[138] [1948] 1 All ER 811, discussed by Mann (1948) 11 MLR 479.

[139] [1950] AC 24. A detailed discussion of the decision is provided by Mann, "Nazi Spoliation in Czechoslovakia" (1950) 13 MLR 206.

[140] ie he could have no better right of recovery against the sub-bailee than that which he enjoyed as against the original bailee.

to be governed by the laws of Czechoslovakia and it conferred upon the plaintiff the right to call for the securities at any time. However, exchange control regulations forming a part of the applicable law imposed a condition precedent (namely, the consent of the central bank) to the exercise of the plaintiff's right, and that consent had been refused. The relevant provisions of Czechoslovakian law were not penal or confiscatory in character, and the English courts accordingly had to apply them. It followed that (1) the plaintiff's claim to possession was subject to satisfaction of a condition precedent which had not been fulfilled and (2) the plaintiff's claim therefore had to fail. It is necessary to make the following points in relation to this decision:

(a) The plaintiff had been the victim of persecution in Czechoslovakia and it appears that the contract with the Bohemian Bank was executed under some duress. If the court had been able to disregard the contract on that ground, then it might have been able to hold that the plaintiff enjoyed the necessary right to immediate possession as against the bailee.[141]

(b) Secondly, in a monetary context, it has been noted earlier that exchange controls may deprive the debtor of the practical ability to pay but they do not affect the validity of the debt in question.[142] Likewise, the fact that the Bohemian Bank was doubtless prevented from redelivering the securities may have had *contractual* consequences; but this should not have affected the plaintiff's *possessory* or *proprietary* rights as against a sub-bailee in England, for these involve property situate in England and should accordingly be governed exclusively by English law.

(c) It is necessary to emphasise the House of Lords' conclusion that the Czechoslovakian exchange controls were not of a penal or confiscatory nature. From one perspective, it should be appreciated that, by refusing the requisite consent, the Czechoslovakian National Bank was allowed effectively to block dealings with property situate in England and to prevent its lawful owner from recovering it. On the face of it, the effect of the exchange control regulations was not only confiscatory but, for good measure, was also extraterritorial in character. Considerations of this kind should, it is suggested, have led the House of Lords to decide in the opposite sense. Yet no member of the House of Lords considered this position to be confiscatory. They merely concluded that foreign exchange control laws did not fall within the category of penal, revenue, or confiscatory laws which the English courts would decline to recognise. The treatment of this subject by

---

[141] It appears that the plaintiff's pleadings had effectively accepted the validity of the contract, with the result that the suggested course of action was not open to the court. The point is discussed in *Re Helbert Wagg & Co Ltd's Claim* [1956] Ch 323, 352.

[142] See *Contract and Trading Co (Southern) Ltd v Barbey* [1960] AC 244. The case has already been noted in Ch 14 above.

the House of Lords was too superficial, and is characterised by statements of a rather general character which are not directed to the facts of the case.[143] But whatever the merits of the decision, it must be acknowledged that foreign exchange controls may interfere with the right to possession of property in England and they would not (by reason only of that fact) be disregarded on the grounds of their confiscatory nature. This is a highly regrettable result. It has, on the whole, been avoided by the New York courts,[144] and by courts in South Africa,[145] and Austria.[146]

For reasons which are obscure, it does not appear to have been argued in the **16.45** *Kahler* case that a decision in favour of the bank would effectively amount to the enforcement of the Czech exchange control regime in England—a position which plainly should not have been allowed to arise.[147] This state of affairs greatly reduces both the scope and persuasiveness of the decision.

---

[143] In some respects, they are also at odds with the decision in *Zivnovstenska Banka v Frankman* [1950] AC 57 where it is acknowledged (at 72) that a foreign exchange control law may be disregarded in England if it is in fact used or administered as a means of confiscation. The point was later taken up in *Re Helbert Wagg & Co Ltd's Claim* [1956] Ch 323, 352.

[144] *Loeb v Bank of Manhattan* (1939) 18 NYS 2d 497; *Bercholz v Guaranty Trust Co of New York* (1943) 44 NYS 2d; *Marcu v Fisher* (1946) 65 NYS (2d) 892; *Re Liebl's Estate* (1951) 106 NYS 2d 705 and 715; cf also *Feuchtwanger v Central Hanover Bank and Trust Co* (1941) 27 NYS 2d 518 after 263 App Div 711, 31 NYS 2d 671, after (1942) 288 NY 342, 43 NE 434. There are, however, cases to the contrary effect, eg in *Re Muller's Estate* (1951) 104 NYS 2d 133, the New York courts recognised German exchange control rules which allegedly prevented a German resident from disclaiming a legacy which arose under a German will. This decision was followed in *Re Meyer* 238 (1951) Pa 2d 597 and in *Kent Jewelry Corp v Keifer* (1952) 119 NY Supp 2d 242. However, it appears that these cases rested upon a misunderstanding of the applicable German regulations—Supreme Court of Bavaria, 28 November 1952, *NJW* 1953, 944. In *Callwood v Virgin Islands National Bank* (1955) 221 F 2d 770, 775 the Court of Appeals (3rd Cir) held that a debt situate in the US could not be effectively assigned in Germany in contravention of German exchange control regulations. To the extent to which the decision rests on the view that the assignment was governed by German law, the decision is probably acceptable. However, the means by which the court identified the governing law are open to doubt. It must also be said that, against a factual background strikingly similar to that which arose in the *Kahler* case, a US court reached the same conclusion. In *NV Suikerfabrik Wono-Aseh v Chase National Bank of New York* (1953) III F Supp 833, an Indonesian company sought to recover securities held by a sub-custodian in New York, but in the absence of the required Indonesian exchange control approval, it was held that the sub-custodian had a good defence. The decision is thus open to objection on the grounds stated in the text, although it must be said that the case was complicated by various factors, eg the extent to which Dutch law continued to apply in Indonesia once the independence of the latter country had been recognised.

[145] *Standard Bank of South Africa Ltd v Ocean Commodities Inc* (1980) 2 South African LR 175, where the Full Bench of the Transvaal Provincial Division refused to follow the *Kahler* case on the primary ground that "the *lex situs* was ignored in it". Given that the *lex situs* was English law, this may be regarded as a telling criticism of the decision of the House of Lords.

[146] Supreme Court, 24 April 1968, *Juristische Blätter* 1969, 339.

[147] That the English courts may recognise, but should not positively enforce, foreign exchange control regulations has already been noted—see paras 16.09–16.15 above.

E. Exchange Control and Money Laundering

16.46   In the course of considering the former United Kingdom's system of exchange control, it was briefly noted that a contravention of the restrictions created by the Exchange Control Act 1947 constituted a serious offence. Naturally, this position will continue to apply in those countries which continue to impose a system of exchange control. There is nothing surprising about that position, and it might be thought that the fact that an offence may have been committed under those laws is of no particular consequence in England.

16.47   In broad measure, that conclusion has always been correct but the position has been clouded by recent initiatives designed to counteract the laundering of the proceeds of crime.[148] In an effort to cover their tracks, money launderers will frequently use the financial system in one country to launder the proceeds of a crime committed in another. Consequently, money laundering legislation both in the United Kingdom and elsewhere is aimed at the proceeds of crime, regardless of the location in which that crime was committed. The legislation in this country creates a series of "secondary" offences which are designed to ensure that money launderers cannot use the financial system here to disguise the origins of their funds. The offences are "secondary" in the sense that they are targeted at individuals working within financial institutions; they commit an offence if they *assist* a money launderer or aid him in the retention or utilisation of the proceeds of crime. Can it be said that money exported from a country in breach of its exchange control regulations constitutes the "proceeds of crime", such that a person in the United Kingdom may commit an offence if he renders assistance of the kind just described? In order to answer questions of this kind, it is necessary briefly to review the statutory provisions at issue.

16.48   In essence, a person commits an offence under the Proceeds of Crime Act 2002 if he conceals, disguises, or transfers criminal property, or if he acquires or uses such property or becomes involved in an arrangement which facilitates the acquisition, retention, or use of criminal property by another person.[149] The meaning of the expression "criminal property" is clearly the central feature in an analysis of the money laundering offences just described. In this context:[150]

   (a)   "Property is criminal property if . . . it constitutes a person's benefit from criminal conduct or it represents such a benefit . . . and the alleged

---

[148] A detailed survey of money laundering and the legislative framework designed to deal with it lies beyond the scope of this book. For a useful comparative survey, see Stressens, *Money Laundering—A New International Law Enforcement Model* (Cambridge University Press, 2000).

[149] For the details of these offences, see Proceeds of Crime Act 2002, ss 327–329.

[150] On the points about to be made, see Proceeds of Crime Act 2002, s 340.

offender knows or suspects that it constitutes or represents such a benefit . . ."; and

(b) conduct is "criminal conduct" for these purposes, if it "is conduct
which . . . constitutes an offence in any part of the United Kingdom or . . .
would constitute an offence in any part of the United Kingdom if it
occurred there".

It must follow that moneys held, obtained, or retained by an individual as a
result of a breach of the exchange control laws of a foreign country do not
constitute "criminal property" for the purposes of the 2002 Act, because evasion
of exchange controls does not "constitute an offence in any part of the United
Kingdom". The mere fact that the funds are derived from a breach of
such requirements in a foreign country does not mean that they are "criminal
property" for the purposes of the 2002 Act.

As a result, individuals working within a financial institution do not commit an **16.49**
offence as a result of receiving or processing funds for the account of a customer,
even though they may actually know that such amounts have been brought out
of the customer's home country in breach of local exchange control regulations.
The Proceeds of Crime Act 2002 does not condemn such proceeds as "criminal
property", with the necessary consequence that the money laundering offences
cannot apply to the ownership, transfer, or use of such funds. Of course, matters
will frequently be more complicated than these straightforward formulations may
at first suggest. For example, there may be grounds to suspect the commission
of other offences in the customer's home country; for example, the funds concerned may be the proceeds of fraud or corruption. In such a case, there may be
other grounds upon which the funds at issue may be regarded as "criminal
property" for the purposes of the 2002 Act.[151]

F. Foreign Exchange Control as an Unenforceable Prerogative Right

Exchange control is a field which has occasionally tempted States to assert **16.50**
extraterritorially their statutory rights of controlling, collecting, or retrieving
private property or other rights vested in them or their government agencies.
Such efforts are bound to fail, for by virtue of a firmly established and universally accepted principle of international law, no State is entitled directly or
indirectly to enforce outside its own territory its prerogative rights or public

---

[151] For a discussion of some of the difficult problems which can arise in the application of the
2002 Act, see *P v P (Ancillary Relief: Proceeds of Crime)* [2003] EWHC Fam 2260.

laws.[152] It is nevertheless necessary to examine the various attempts which have been made, and their consistency (or otherwise) with the principle just noted.

16.51   It seems that there is only one case in which the United Kingdom—in disregard of the general principle—tried to enforce by proceedings in New York, rights which it claimed to have acquired by virtue of a vesting order made under the Exchange Control Act 1947.[153] The case is reported only on a preliminary point of procedure, but the substantive action was bound to fail. The 1947 Act conferred upon the Treasury the right to vest in itself property which was affected by a breach in the exchange control regime, but the law of New York would not enforce such provisions—just as English law could refuse to do, in a converse case.[154] New York law in this area was subsequently reaffirmed by the Court of Appeals in *Banco do Brasil SA v Israel Commodity Co Inc*.[155] In that case, Brazilian exchange controls required a coffee exporter to surrender the US dollar proceeds of its sales to the central bank, against payment of 90 cruzeiros to the dollar. The central bank alleged that the exporter and the defendant had conspired so as to enable the exporter to obtain the free market rate of 220 cruzeiros to the dollar, and that the central bank had suffered loss as a consequence. An action in New York to recover that loss failed, on the grounds that the claim arose under a "revenue law" and that "one State does not enforce the revenue laws of another".[156] The fact that the claim was clothed in the form of an action for damages for conspiracy under New York law did not render the court oblivious of the substance of the matter, namely the assertion of an injury

---

[152] For some of Dr Mann's work in this particular area, see (1955) 40 *Transactions of the Grotius Society* 25 or *Studies in International Law* (1973) 124 and 492; *Rec* 132 (1971, i) 166; *Rec* 111 (1964, i) 141; *Further Studies in International Law* (1990) 355. The most prominent example to which the doctrine applies is taxation, but it applies equally to other laws of a public character— including exchange control. The most frequently cited English authority is *Government of India v Taylor* [1955] AC 491. More recent English cases include *Schemmer v Property Resources Ltd* [1975] Ch 273, where the court refused to allow enforcement of the US Securities Exchange Act 1934 by means of an action in England, and *QRS 1 ApS v Frandsen* [1999] 1 WLR 2169, which involved an attempt to recover moneys owing to the Danish Revenue Authorities.

[153] *Solicitor of the Affairs of HM Treasury v Bankers Trust* (1952) 107 NE 2d 448. See n 130 above.

[154] Difficulties of this kind are now recognised by legislation in this country. See, eg, Proceeds of Crime Act 2002, s 222, which effectively acknowledges that the recovery of criminal property situate abroad requires the co-operation of the foreign State concerned.

[155] (1963) 12 NY 2d, 371, 190 NE 2d 235 or 32 Int LR 371, discussed by Gold, *IMF Staff Papers* (1964) 468; Trickey (1964) 62 Mich LR 1232; Baker (1963) 16 Stanford LR 202; Anon (1963) 63 Col LR 1334. The law as stated in the text is also in harmony with Cass Civ, 2 May 1990, *Clunet* 1991, 137—a case of great general significance.

[156] In truth, of course, exchange control laws cannot be described as revenue laws at all—see in this sense *Regazzoni v KC Sethia Ltd* [1958] AC 301, 324. But revenue laws are only one example of a group of laws which are characterised by the fact that they confer prerogative rights upon the State and its instrumentalities. Foreign public laws of this kind are not enforced by the English courts. The New York court thus applied the correct principle, even if it erred in its terminology.

to the plaintiff's prerogative rights.[157] Subsequently, however, the New York Court of Appeals decided a rather less satisfactory case, where the factual background is less than completely clear.[158] In that case, a private bank in Brazil claimed damages for fraud and conspiracy arising from alleged violations of Brazilian exchange control regulations. It seems that the defendants improperly obtained from the bank US dollars in exchange for cruzeiros; it appears, however, that the official rate of exchange was used and the nature and extent of the losses claimed by the plaintiff are therefore by no means clear. However that may be, the plaintiff was seeking (albeit indirectly) to enforce a prerogative right of Brazil before the New York courts. The claim thus ran counter to the well-established principle of international law just described—namely, that one State will not enforce the public laws of another. As noted earlier, exchange control laws cannot be characterised as revenue laws; but they are nevertheless of a type with those many public laws which confer prerogative rights upon a State and which it cannot extraterritorially assert or enforce. Thus, whilst the IMF Agreement does not *prevent* a member from voluntarily lending assistance to another member in rendering effective the latter's exchange control regulations, nothing in the Agreement *requires* that they should do so.[159] Courts in the United States have generally adhered to this principle; for example, they have declined to enforce Canadian judgments for the recovery of taxes[160] or to give effect to Cuban currency regulations.[161]

Similar attempts to enforce exchange control regulations outside their country of origin have generally failed. For example:

16.52

(a) The Government of Indonesia claimed rights in respect of a Dutch bank account belonging to an Indonesian resident and established in contravention of its currency regulations. The Court of Appeal at Amsterdam rejected the claim and, in respect of the rights arising under the Indonesian legislation, the court observed that the plaintiff could not "exercise them in

---

[157] The court discussed at length Art VIII(2)(b) of the Bretton Woods Agreement, but neither this particular provision nor the Agreement as a whole had any bearing on the plaintiff's claim, which was plainly misconceived. The only surprising feature is that the decision of the Court of Appeals was arrived at by a majority of 4 to 3.

[158] *Banco Frances e Brasiliero v John Doe* (1975) 36 NY 2d 592.

[159] *J Zeevi and Sons Ltd v Grindlays Bank (Uganda) Ltd* (1975) 37 NY 2d 220—view of IMF Agreement.

[160] *Her Majesty The Queen in Right of British Columbia v Gilbertson* (1976) 597 F 2D 1161, where the Court of Appeals, Ninth Circuit, noted (at 1166) that "the revenue rule has been with us for centuries and as such has become firmly embedded in the law. There were sound reasons which supported its original adoption, and there remain sound reasons supporting its continued validity."

[161] *Menendez v Saks & Co* 485 F 2d 1355, where the Court of Appeals, Second Circuit, noted (at 1366) that "Currency controls are but a species of revenue law . . . As a general rule one nation will not enforce the revenue laws of another."

the Netherlands or maintain them any more than would be possible with respect to the rights and authority of a foreign Government in the field of military service, taxation, requisition of dwellings or expropriation".[162]

(b) The Swedish Supreme Court rejected an attempt by Bulgaria to enforce its exchange control legislation in Sweden.[163]

(c) Colombia failed in its attempt to claim luggage which had allegedly found its way into the United States in breach of Colombian exchange control.[164]

16.53 The extraterritorial enforcement of rights arising under exchange control legislation may take many forms; here as elsewhere it will be necessary to look to the substance, reality, and effect of that assertion. Thus, a claim may be made by a private person such as a Bank—possibly acting for the benefit or even at the direction of the State—or it may be made by way of defence, rather than attack. It is submitted that these features were present in *Kahler v Midland Bank*[165] and should have led to the failure of the bank's defence. The State itself could not have enforced in England any right of possession or ownership of the securities conferred upon it by Czech exchange control laws. By the same token, those currency laws should not be invoked in England to deprive the true owner of possession; and if the State itself could not rely on its currency laws in this regard, then they should not be capable of affording a defence to a bank or sub-bailee in England which has physical custody of the securities concerned. If the foreign State cannot rely on its currency laws to obtain possession, then this must involve, as a corollary, the true owner's right to recover possession without hindrance by the foreign government's obstruction.[166] There are, however, exceptional cases in which a private party who has been compelled to make payments to a foreign State (for example, by way of fine or penalty) may be able to claim an indemnity. The authorities appear to establish that where an individual has been compelled to pay taxes, customs duties, social security contributions, or a fine, he may under the applicable law be entitled to an indemnity or compensation from the person who was principally liable.[167] In so far as exchange control is concerned, such a case may have been the New York decision in *Banco Frances e Brasileiro v John Doe*,[168] to the extent of the penalty

---

[162] 9 April 1959, 30 Int LR 25.

[163] 21 March 1961 (*Bulgaria v Takvorian*) summarised by *Clunet* 1966, 437 and 47 Int LR 40.

[164] *Fontana v Regan* (1984)734 F 2d 944, 950.

[165] [1950] AC 24, HL.

[166] The submission in the text was accepted as a subsidiary ground of decision in *Standard Bank of South Africa Ltd v Ocean Commodities Inc* (1980) 2 South Africa LR 175, although a decision of a US District Court runs counter to this proposition—see *NV Suikerfabriek Wono-Aseh v Chase National Bank* (1953) 111 F Supp 833.

[167] See the cases collected at *Rec* 132 (1971, i) 167, n 5.

[168] (1975) 36 N 2d 592. The facts of this case have already been noted, above.

which, according to the majority,[169] "was levied by the Central Bank of Brazil and actually paid by the plaintiff". If this was a genuine penalty which had in fact been paid by the plaintiffs, then it may well be that they would be entitled to an indemnity under Brazilian law, which apparently governed the contract in question.[170] But if, as the dissenting judge put it,[171] penalties were "to be imposed", then the plaintiffs were no more than an instrument of Brazil to recover a possible fine and the New York courts thus allowed the indirect enforcement of exchange control regulations in the United States, under circumstances where this ought not to have been permitted. The difference between the two factual situations is significant. In the first type of case, the plaintiffs would be claiming the repayment of amounts paid to the State after what one must assume to be a proper assessment procedure. In the second type of case, the plaintiff would in substance be acting as a collection agent on behalf of the foreign revenue authorities concerned.[172] On this basis, doubts may exist over the decision in *Re Lord Cable deceased*.[173] The plaintiffs were beneficiaries of a trust established in India under Indian law, but which had significant assets in England. The defendant trustees intended to transfer these assets to India, both to pay local estate duty and to comply with Indian exchange control regulations. The plaintiffs sought an injunction to prevent the transfer. The court recognised that foreign prerogative claims could not be enforced in England but refused the requested injunction, on the grounds that—in the event of non-payment—the trustees could be made liable to serious penalties in India, including fines and imprisonment. However, it is by no means clear that a conviction would have followed from the Indian law in question,[174] and reasoning of this kind necessarily involves an element of speculation. Its effect was to enable India to obtain from English sources amounts to which it claimed to be entitled under its revenue and exchange control laws;[175] at the same time, the beneficiaries had no

---

[169] At 599.

[170] There must be some question, on the facts, about the genuine nature and character of the penalty.

[171] At 603.

[172] The distinction between the two types of case was clearly made by the British Columbian Court of Appeal in *Re Reid* (1971) 17 DLR (2d) 199, where executors who had paid UK estate duty were held to be entitled to an indemnity on the grounds that, in all earlier cases "success would have enriched the Treasury of the interested State" whereas, in the instant case "here the United Kingdom has nothing whatever to do with the respondent's claim to be indemnified" (at 205). See also *Scottish & National Orchestra Society v Thomson's Executors* [1969] SLT 199, holding that Scottish executors could not normally remit money abroad to meet estate duty liabilities arising under a foreign law, but that they could do so where payment of the duty was necessary in order to allow the payment of legacies due to legatees resident in the foreign State concerned.

[173] [1976] 3 All ER 417.

[174] The relevant law is set out on p 434 of the report.

[175] A position which is at odds with the landmark decision in *Government of India v Taylor* [1955] AC 491 (HL).

assurance that any net residue would be freely transferred and made available to them. This, therefore, is something very different from the defendants' actual liabilities properly incurred and discharged, which in fairness require reimbursement. And criminal liability in the country of a person's residence or nationality (if such liability exists when acting under the compulsion of an English court order) is not necessarily an argument for giving effect to a foreign legal system which, according to English conflict rules, has no application.[176]

16.54　In conclusion, it may be noted that Lord Denning appeared to share the doubts expressed above in relation to the *Kahler* case and *Re Lord Cable deceased*[177] and that courts in Commonwealth jurisdictions have acknowledged that cases in which payment has actually been made must be distinguished from those in which there is merely a *potential* liability.[178] On the other hand, it must be accepted that the decision in *Re Lord Cable deceased* has frequently been referred to with apparent approval.[179] For the present, it can only be said that the decision should be carefully reviewed if a similar situation should arise at a future date.

---

[176] At least in the present context, there are many illustrations of this principle, eg the Hungarian drawer of the bill in *Kleinwort Sons & Co v Ungarische Baumwolle Industrie AG* [1939] 2 KB 678 (CA) may have committed an offence in Hungary by arranging reimbursement to the acceptor without the necessary exchange control licence in that country. Yet this did not afford to it a defence in English proceedings.

[177] See comments in *A-G of New Zealand v Ortiz* [1984] AC 1, 24.

[178] See *Bath v British & Malayan Trustees* (1969) 2 NSWR 114; *Re Reid* 17 DLR (3d) 206 (1971) and *Jones v Borland* 1969 (4) SALR 114. These cases do not appear to have been drawn to the court's attention in *Re Lord Cable deceased*.

[179] See, eg, *Camdex International Ltd v Bank of Zambia (No. 3)* [1997] CLC 714; Dicey and Morris, *The Conflict of Laws* (Sweet & Maxwell, 13th edn, 2000) para 5-022.

17

SANCTIONS AND
MONETARY OBLIGATIONS

A. Introduction

The preceding chapters in this Part have demonstrated that a State has the right **17.01** to impose exchange controls to limit the outward flow of money, and that the existence of such controls is entitled to a degree of international recognition.

The present chapter will consider economic sanctions which, likewise, may seek **17.02** to impose restrictions on outward transfers.[1] They do, however, differ from exchange controls in terms of their extent. A legitimate system of exchange controls applies as against foreign countries generally, and is designed for the protection of the domestic economy of the imposing State. In contrast, economic sanctions are generally designed to harm the economy of another State.[2] The expression "economic sanctions" has been well defined[3] as "measures of an

---

[1] The whole subject of economic sanctions is, in legal terms, a very complex one; the present chapter will merely provide an overview of the applicable principles. For a more detailed and very helpful review, see Lowenfeld, *International Economic Law* (Oxford University Press, 2002) 701–64.

[2] This difference in objective means that laws forming a part of a sanctions regime imposed by a foreign State should not be entitled to the protection envisaged by Art VIII(2)(b) of the IMF Agreement, because they do not constitute part of a genuine system of exchange control of the kind envisaged by that Article.

[3] See Lowenfeld, *International Economic Law* (Oxford University Press, 2001) 698. Part of that text deals with the concept of "Economic controls for political ends" and provides a very useful discussion of the whole subject. The present discussion is, of course, limited to the *monetary* consequences of a sanctions regime. As Lowenfeld points out (at p 708) a sanctions regime will often also impose trade, travel, and other restrictions.

economic—as contrasted with diplomatic or military—character taken by States to express disapproval of the acts of the target State or to induce that State to change some policy or practice or even its governmental structure".[4]

17.03 In general terms, sanctions will usually involve a "freeze" over the assets of the target State, to the extent that such assets are held within the State or States which impose the sanctions concerned.[5] In a monetary context, this will mean that debtors resident in the imposing State will be barred from making payments which are otherwise due to the target State or to companies or individuals resident within it. Thus, so long as the sanctions regime remains in place, a bank branch situate within the imposing State will be unable to repay deposits or operate accounts for the benefit of the target State or any of its residents. The present chapter will proceed on the assumption that the relevant sanctions operate in the manner just described.

17.04 In line with the approach adopted in relation to exchange control, it is necessary to enquire whether the imposition of financial sanctions is consistent with international law. It is also necessary to consider the precise consequences of sanctions for domestic monetary obligations, and the extent to which a sanctions regime adopted by a foreign State is capable of recognition and application in English proceedings.

17.05 In order to cover this ground, it is proposed to consider the following matters:

(a) the consistency of a sanctions regime with international law;
(b) the effect of sanctions adopted by supranational organisations;
(c) the effect of sanctions unilaterally imposed by the United Kingdom; and
(d) the status of foreign sanctions before the English courts.

B. Sanctions and International Law

17.06 In view of the definition of "sanctions" provided above, it is apparent that measures of this kind are deliberately intended to harm the financial interests of the target State and its residents. As that definition contemplates, sanctions may even be intended to impel a country to change its entire political system.[6] In

---

[4] Other descriptions are offered by Proctor, *International Payment Obligations—A Legal Perspective* (Butterworths, 1997) 278–9; Malloy, *United States Economic Sanctions: Theory and Practice* (Kluwer Law International, 2001) ch 1. As will be noted at the end of this chapter, the distinction between the two forms of action is only partly recognised by the IMF.

[5] It should be added that, in more recent times, blocking and similar legislation has frequently been directed towards terrorist organisations, rather than States. One particular aspect of legislation which has been introduced for that purpose is considered in the final section of this chapter.

[6] Sanctions imposed against South Africa and Rhodesia clearly fall into this category.

view of this coercive element, it is necessary to ask whether the imposition of sanctions is consistent with international law. It must not be forgotten that every State has the right to select and to organise its own political and economic structures; this right is an attribute of the sovereignty and independence of the State.[7] As a result, no State has the right to intervene in the internal affairs of another State with a view to securing changes to its political ideology or outlook.[8] How, then, can the imposition of economic sanctions for political ends be reconciled with these principles?

The answer lies in the undoubted rule that an intervention into the internal affairs of another State only contravenes international law if it is "forcible or dictatorial or otherwise coercive", such that the target State is effectively deprived of its sovereign rights over the subject matter in question.[9] It seems to be accepted that a decision to terminate trading relations or to impose an economic embargo does not meet this threshold test, and thus cannot be taken to be contrary to customary international law.[10] Furthermore the imposition of a sanctions regime could not in any event contravene the rules of customary law, if it constitutes a proportionate response to an international wrong committed by the target State itself.[11]   **17.07**

For the purposes of this Chapter, and so far as rules of customary international law are concerned, it is thus necessary to rest upon the broad principle that the imposition of financial and economic sanctions will not amount to an international wrong by the imposing State.[12] As will always be the case, however, the general rules of customary international law must yield in the face of treaty   **17.08**

---

[7] On customary international law in the field, see *Oppenheim's International Law* (Longman, 9th edn, 1991) para 129.

[8] See in particular the *Military and Paramilitary Activities Case* [1986] ICJ Rep 15, where the International Court of Justice held unlawful the support given by the US to opposition forces in Nicaragua. The principle of non-interference is in some respects "codified" by Art 2(7) of the UN Charter.

[9] On this formulation, see *Oppenheim's International Law* (n 7 above) para 129.

[10] It seems to be accepted that a State is entitled to impose "blocking" legislation against another State without thereby infringing any rule of customary international law—see *Claim of Chobady; Claim of Mureson* and *Claim of Evanoff* reported in (1958) II Int LR 292, 294 and 301 respectively. In the same sense, see the practice of the French Foreign Claims Commission reported by Weston, *International Claims: Post-War French Practice* (Syracuse, 1971). Similarly, in the *Military and Paramilitary Activities* Case [1986] ICJ Rep 13, 126, where the International Court of Justice held that the *economic* measures taken by the US against Nicaragua (including a trade embargo and the termination of financial aid) did not violate the principle of non-intervention.

[11] See Article 22 of The International Law Commission's Articles on State Responsibility and see, eg, *Air Services Agreement of 27 March 1946 (US v France)* [1979] RIAA, Vol XVIII, 416.

[12] The importance of this point will become apparent when the public policy aspects of foreign sanctions fall for consideration later in this chapter.

engagements to the contrary.[13] Apart from any specific bilateral arrangements, two multilateral treaties merit specific mention in this context.

17.09   First of all, the Treaty constituting the European Community broadly prohibits national restrictions which would impede the free movement of capital and payments as between Member States.[14] Consequently, and regardless of any general principle of international law, no Member State could unilaterally impose economic sanctions against another Member State in a manner which contravenes the relevant treaty provisions.[15]

17.10   Secondly, economic sanctions are, by their very nature, discriminatory; by their very purpose, they are designed to treat the target State less favourably than others with which the imposing State maintains cordial relations. As will be seen elsewhere,[16] the "most favoured nation" provision in Article 1 of the General Agreement on Tariffs and Trade (GATT) prohibits discriminatory arrangements both in relation to imports and exports[17] and in relation to the international transfer of payments relating thereto. Likewise, Article XI prohibits quantitative restrictions on trade, and the application of economic sanctions would frequently be inconsistent with that Article. Nevertheless, the point appears to have been taken only rarely, no doubt for political reasons[18] and partly because of explicit exemptions provided by the Agreement. Article 21(b) allows that a State may, without thereby contravening GATT, take "any action which it considers necessary for the protection of its essential security interests . . . taken in time of war or other emergency, in international relations". Clearly, any action taken in reliance of this provision should be motivated by considerations of foreign policy, rather than commercial protectionism, but the provision has proved to be difficult to apply in practice.[19] Furthermore, Article 21(c) confirms that a State will not breach the Agreement if it joins in action taken pursuant to the UN Charter with a view to the preservation of international peace and security.

---

[13] An exception to this general statement applies where the treaty is at odds with a peremptory norm of international law—see Art 53 of the Vienna Convention on the Law of Treaties, and the discussion in Aust, *Modern Treaty Law and Practice* (Cambridge University Press, 2000) 257. It is unnecessary to pursue this point in the present context.

[14] See Arts 56–60 of the EC Treaty and the discussion on the subject at para 25.33 below.

[15] As noted below, the position may be different in the context of *multilateral* sanctions.

[16] See para 22.20 (d) below.

[17] The preamble to GATT stated that the Agreement was intended to secure "the substantial reduction of tariffs and other barriers to trade and . . . the elimination of discriminatory treatment in international commerce".

[18] On these points, see Lowenfeld, *International Economic Law* (Oxford University Press, 2001) 755–6.

[19] See Lowenfeld (n 18 above) 757.

As noted above, the discussion must accordingly rest on the assumption that the   **17.11**
imposition of economic sanctions for foreign policy reasons does not infringe
customary international law; it must also rest on the assumption that such
sanctions are not inconsistent with any treaty obligation of the imposing State.

C. International Sanctions

On the plane of international law, sanctions may be imposed against a State   **17.12**
under the terms of the Charter of the United Nations. Briefly, Articles 39 and
40 of the Charter allow the Security Council to make recommendations or
binding decisions to deal with any act of aggression or threat to international
peace and security. Article 41 then provides:

> The Security Council may decide what measures not involving the use of armed
> force[20] are to be employed to give effect to its decisions, and it may call upon the
> Members of the United Nations to apply such measures. These may include
> complete or partial interruption of economic relations and of rail, sea, air, postal,
> telegraphic, radio and other means of communication, and the severance of
> diplomatic relations.

Article 41 thus directly contemplates the use of economic sanctions as a means   **17.13**
of maintaining or restoring international peace and security. Any sanctions
applied against a State in compliance with the Charter plainly could not be
regarded as a contravention of any rule of customary international law.[21] It is,
however, unnecessary to pursue this point in depth because the preceding section has already concluded that the imposition of sanctions for foreign policy
reasons does not generally offend international law. But it is necessary to consider the consequences of a Security Council decision in the context of private
monetary obligations.

The status of the rules of international law in proceedings before the English   **17.14**
courts is a matter of some difficulty and debate.[22] Nevertheless, it seems clear
that a Security Council decision to impose sanctions cannot *of itself* affect the
content or enforceability of monetary obligations before the English courts;
rules of international law cannot be applied so as to defeat existing contractual

---

[20] Measures involving the use of armed force may be applied under Art 42 of the Charter.
However, that aspect is not relevant to the present discussion.
[21] It may be added that member countries are under the obligation to implement any sanctions
approved by the Security Council—see Art 25 of the UN Charter.
[22] See, eg, *Oppenheim's International Law* (Longman, 9th edn, 1991) paras 18–21; Brownlie,
Principles of Public International Law (Oxford, 6th edn, 2003) 41–7.

rights of a private or commercial character.[23] A domestic government with constitutional arrangements similar to those applicable in the United Kingdom thus cannot take steps to implement sanctions at a domestic level, unless and until the necessary local legislation has been put in place for that purpose.[24]

17.15   In most cases, however, this point will be of no more than theoretical interest. As noted above, the United Kingdom is under an obligation to give effect to the resolutions of the Security Council in this type of case; it will do so by means of secondary legislation introduced under the terms of the United Nations Act 1946.[25] In such a case, the sanctions regime forms a part of the English domestic law, and must naturally be applied by courts sitting in this country.[26]

17.16   In an international law context, it will sometimes become necessary to reconcile treaty obligations which may apparently conflict with each other. In the present case, there may be some friction between an obligation to impose sanctions and an obligation to ensure the free movement of capital and payments; a treaty obligation of the latter kind is created by Articles 56 to 60 of the EC Treaty.[27] In that instance, however, the conflict is resolved by Article 307 of the EC Treaty, which contains a "saving" for obligations under pre-existing treaties such as the UN Charter.[28] As a result, a person resident in the "target" country could not demand repayment of a frozen bank deposit in London on the grounds that the free movement of his capital is guaranteed by the EC Treaty; to the extent to which any such guarantee could be said to exist, it would have been overridden by the United Kingdom's domestic legislation implementing the UN sanctions.[29]

---

[23] See, eg, the English decision in *Commercial and Estates Co of Egypt v Board of Trade* [1925] 1 KB 271 (CA), the Privy Council decision in *Croft v Dunphy* [1933] AC 156, and the decision of the US Supreme Court in *The Paquette Habana* (1900) 175 US 677. Where, however, a contract has been made with the specific object of evading a sanctions regime, it may be that the English courts would refuse to enforce it on policy grounds by reference to the principles illustrated by *De Wutz v Hendricks* (1824) 2 Bing 314 and *Foster v Driscoll* [1929] 1 KB 470 (CA); the most direct illustration of this point is *Regazzoni v KC Sethia (1944) Ltd* [1958] AC 301. The existence of this principle has recently been reaffirmed by the decision in *Mahonia Ltd v West LB* [2004] EWHC 1938 (Comm).

[24] The point is well illustrated by the decision in the High Court of Australia in *Bradley v Commonwealth of Australia* [1973] 1 ALR 241; the government had acted unlawfully in severing links with Rhodesia in the absence of Australian legislation to that effect. This was so even though the Government was seeking to implement UN sanctions against that territory.

[25] eg, see the Serbia and Montenegro (United Nations Sanctions) Order 1992.

[26] The rules applicable in this context are considered in the next section.

[27] Those Articles are considered at para 25.33 below.

[28] The point is noted in *R v Searle* [1995] 3 CMLR 196 (CA).

[29] Nevertheless, EC law does effectively require that any such system of sanctions does not operate in a manner which is discriminatory as between Member States—see *R v HM Treasury, ex p Centro-Com Srl* [1997] All ER (EC) 193 (ECJ); *EC Commission v Hellenic Republic* [1994] ECR I–3037.

Equally, on occasion, there may be a conflict between the international obliga-   **17.17**
tion to impose sanctions and some provision of domestic law. So far as international law is concerned, the position is clear; a State cannot rely on its domestic
laws as a ground for non-compliance with an international obligation. So far as
domestic courts are concerned, there would usually be no obligation to give
effect to the international obligation, especially where the State has deliberately
elected to pass legislation which is inconsistent with that obligation.[30]

D. UK Sanctions

It is, of course, open to the United Kingdom to impose unilateral sanctions   **17.18**
against another State. This may happen when the foreign State is taking or is
likely to take steps which are detrimental to the economic position of the United
Kingdom.[31] The Treasury may make orders prohibiting the transfer of any
funds, gold, or securities at the request or direction of the relevant foreign State
or its residents. By way of an example, this power was used against Argentina in
the immediate aftermath of its invasion of the Falkland Islands in 1982.

What is the effect of a "blocking" order of the kind just described, or of any   **17.19**
similar legislation?[32] It is necessary to examine three different types of case where
different lines of reasoning may be required although, as will be seen, the
essential result will be the same.

In the first group of cases, the monetary obligation may subsist under the terms   **17.20**
of a contract governed by English law. It will be appreciated that the blocking
order forms a part of the same system of law and touches the substance of the
obligation at issue. Consequently, the debtor is relieved of his payment obligation for as long as the blocking order remains in force, although the obligation is
reinstated once the order is lifted.[33] The introduction of a sanctions regime thus

---

[30] See *Diggs v Schultz* 470 F 2d 461, cert denied (1972) 411 US 931, discussed by Lowenfeld,
International Economic Law (Oxford University Press, 2002) 714–15. For a wide-ranging discussion of US sanctions legislation in the wake of the Iran hostage crisis, see *Dames & Moore v Regan*
(1981) 453 US 464.

[31] Section 2, Emergency Laws (Re-enactments and Repeals) Act 1964, as amended.

[32] It should be noted that the European Community may on occasion introduce sanctions
against a particular State. Usually the regulations concerned would have direct effect in all
Member States; they would thus form a part of English law and would be applied in the manner
described in the text. For decisions of the ECJ in relation to the EC's sanctions against Serbia and
Montenegro, see Case 84/95, *Bosphorous Hava Yollari Turizm Ticaret AS v Minister for Transport*
[1996] 3 CMLR 257; Case C–177/95, *Ebony Maritime SA v Prefetto della Provincia di Brindisi*
[1997] 2 CMLR 24; and Case C–162/96, *Racke v Hamptzollamt Mainz* [1998] ECR I-3655. The
basis for legal sanctions of this kind is provided by Art 301 of the EC Treaty.

[33] See *Wahda Bank v Arab Bank plc* (1992) 137 Sol Jo LB 24; cf *Arab Bank Ltd v Barclays Bank
(DC & O)* [1954] AC 495 (HL).

has the effect of suspending the obligation and deferring the date on which the debtor is liable to make payment.[34] It must follow that, if payment is made when the sanctions are eventually lifted, the debtor is not in breach of his contract, with the necessary result that the creditor is not entitled to any damages or interest in respect of the delay.[35] Furthermore, since sanctions will invariably be imposed as a matter of high public policy, the imposition of a sanctions regime cannot be regarded as an unlawful deprivation of property for the purposes of the European Convention on Human Rights.[36] It should be added that sanctions do not normally operate to discharge contracts; rather they normally prohibit performance of obligations arising under affected contracts. This leads to the legally curious position that the contract remains alive and yet, according to the legislation, is permanently incapable of performance. However, in a case involving European Community sanctions against Iraq, the House of Lords held that the relevant regulations had permanently barred claims by Iraqi parties against non-Iraqi contractors and that this prohibition would remain in effect even if sanctions were subsequently lifted.[37]

17.21   In a second category of cases, an obligor in England may be obliged to pay moneys to the target State or one of its residents; the obligation is governed by a foreign system of law. In such a case, the substance of performance—including the date on which it is due—is in principle governed by the applicable law; in general terms, English law cannot vary or discharge an obligation created and governed by a foreign system of law. Nevertheless, it is clear that the English courts would not give effect to the foreign law in the face of the sanctions regime. Such sanctions are imposed as a matter of national policy and the application of those rules must be mandatory irrespective of the governing law

---

[34] In policy terms, the approach is acceptable because the imposition of sanctions is generally intended to address a political expedient of a temporary nature. It must, however, be accepted that this expectation is not always borne out by experience—US sanctions against Cuba have remained in place for several decades. It has been suggested that a monetary obligation is *initially* suspended by the imposition of sanctions, but that frustration may *subsequently* occur if the sanctions later assume a more permanent character—see *Libyan Arab Foreign Bank v Manufacturers Hanover Trust Co (No. 2)* [1989] 1 Lloyd's Rep 608. This proposition has some attraction, although the court would presumably be unable to make an effective award under the Law Reform (Frustrated Contracts) Act 1943, for the payment of any such award would likewise be prohibited.

[35] Of course, if the obligation is a bank deposit which is expressed to bear interest "until the date of actual payment", then interest may accrue during the blocked period. However, this would be referable to the terms of the contract itself and thus does not affect the general principle stated in the text.

[36] See *Al-Kishtaini v Shanshal* [2001] All ER (D) 295, CA.

[37] This result was in part driven by policy considerations because the objective of the regulations was to protect contractors within the Community from legal claims by Iraqi counterparties: see *Shanning International Ltd v Rasheed Bank* [2001] UKHL 31.

of the obligation.[38] It must likewise follow that—so far as the English courts are concerned—the debtor is not in breach of the obligation during the period in which the sanctions are effective, even though that result would obtain under the foreign law by which the obligation is governed. Of course, courts sitting in other countries which had not imposed similar sanctions would be very likely to reach the opposite conclusion.

A third set of cases may involve proceedings between a foreign national and the **17.22** target State or one of its residents, where the proceedings only take place in England because of an express, contractual submission to the jurisdiction of the English courts. It naturally becomes more difficult to justify the application of the UK sanctions regime to an obligation which is governed by a foreign law, which is to be performed abroad and which has no material nexus with the United Kingdom. In such a case, the blocking legislation would frequently be inapplicable, for the prohibition against payments to the target State can at best only apply to persons who are nationals or residents of the United Kingdom or who instigate or achieve the relevant payments through this country. There is no room for the view that the regulations can be applied to a foreign law contract by virtue of Article 7(2) of the Rome Convention, for by their very terms those regulations will have no relevance to the case before the court. Nevertheless, it is suggested that an English court would decline to enforce such an obligation in reliance on Article 16 of the Convention; it must be manifestly contrary to public policy for an English court to assist a creditor to obtain funds where the creditor is the target of a regime of sanctions imposed by this country.[39]

It is thus appropriate to conclude that, following the imposition of a sanctions **17.23** regime by the United Kingdom, the target State and its residents will receive no assistance from the English courts in enforcing payment of any debts owing to them. This conclusion will continue to apply even though the contract is governed by a foreign law, the place of payment is outside the United Kingdom or the debtor is a foreign resident, and even though the contract has no material connection with this country.

E. Foreign Sanctions

It is equally open to a foreign State to elect to impose sanctions against some **17.24** third State as a consequence of some political disagreement or other difficulty; as

---

[38] See the language employed in the Rome Convention, Art 7(2). The application of considerations of public policy in accordance with Art 16 of that Convention may lead to a similar result—see generally the discussion of these provisions in Ch 4 above.

[39] Although the case arose in rather different circumstances, it may be that the decision in *Regazzoni v KC Sethia (1944) Ltd* [1958] AC 301 (CA) offers some support for this proposition.

has been shown earlier in this chapter; such action will not generally be inconsistent with international law. Assuming that the regime of sanctions is essentially a "private" matter between the imposing State and the target State and that the United Kingdom has thus not imposed any parallel system of sanctions, how is the English court to respond when confronted with a case caught in the crossfire? In a case of this kind, it is necessary first to identify the law which governs the obligation at issue.[40]

17.25 If it is found that the contract is governed by English law—or by the law of any other country which is not itself the imposing State—then the legislation creating the sanctions will generally be irrelevant, for it does not form a part of the law which governs the obligation.[41] Regulations which form a part of the law of the imposing State cannot vary or discharge an obligation governed by English law or by any other foreign system of law. The obligation will thus be enforced in accordance with its terms, regardless of the blocking legislation.[42] This apparently straightforward position must, however, be made subject to a few observations:

(a) If the obligation is governed by English law and the place of performance is within the imposing State,[43] then the English courts will decline to enforce the obligation.[44]

(b) Where sanctions have been imposed by a State with which the United Kingdom has amicable relations and are intended to operate as a countermeasure in respect of a clear breach of international obligations on the part of the target State, it has been suggested that the English courts should give effect to those sanctions as a policy matter and thus decline to enforce the monetary obligation in question.[45] The point must, however, be regarded as doubtful. Public policy may offer grounds upon which the application of a foreign law may be refused,[46] but it does not afford a basis upon which

---

[40] On this process, see Ch 4 above.

[41] See Rome Convention, Art 10 and the general discussion in Ch 4 above.

[42] Although it was a complex case, this reasoning lies at the heart of the decision in *Libyan Arab Foreign Bank v Bankers Trust Co* [1989] QB 728. The factual background to the case has been discussed in the context of the performance of monetary obligations—see para 7.23 above.

[43] ie the creditor is contractually entitled to receive payment within that State. Thus, if under a contract governed by English law, the creditor is entitled to receive US dollars in London, the debtor cannot deny him payment on the basis that payment is illegal in the United States, where the funds transfer must ultimately be cleared, for the monetary obligation has but one place of payment, and that is London—see *Libyan Arab Foreign Bank v Bankers Trust Co* [1989] QB 728.

[44] This statement is based upon the decision in *Ralli Bros v Compagnia Naviera Sota y Aznar* [1920] 2 KB 287 (CA). For a discussion and criticism of that decision, see para 16.38 above.

[45] For a suggestion to this effect, see Mann, *Foreign Affairs in English Courts* (Clarendon, 1986) 158.

[46] See Art 16 of the Rome Convention.

effect may be given to a foreign law which is in principle inapplicable to the dispute at hand.[47]

(c) Where the contract at issue was made with the shared and deliberate objective of evading a sanctions regime imposed by a foreign State with which the United Kingdom has amicable relations, an English court should decline to enforce the contract, whatever its applicable law.[48]

(d) It has been argued by some that foreign sanctions legislation should be seen as a system of exchange control which should be recognised by the courts on the basis of Article VIII(2)(b) of the Articles of Agreement of the International Monetary Fund.[49] It is true that a Decision of the Fund[50] records that "Article VIII, section (2)(a), in conformity with its language, applies to all restrictions on current payments and transfers, irrespective of their motivation and the circumstances under which they are imposed. Sometimes, members impose such restrictions solely for the preservation of national or international security." The Decision then records that the Fund is not an appropriate forum for discussion of the political or military merits of such action, and invites a State to notify the Fund of any such measures. The member country may then assume that the Fund has no objection to such arrangements, unless notice to the contrary is given; that is to say, the approval of the Fund to the imposition of restrictions against transfers for current transactions is given for the purposes of Article VIII(2)(a) of the Fund Agreement. Although the point does not appear to have been decided, it is submitted that the approval of a sanctions regime for the purposes of Article VIII(2)(a) does not entitle those regulations to any degree of international recognition under Article VIII(2)(b). Apart from considerations of a more general nature, it has previously been noted that a contract which was lawful at its inception, cannot by virtue of subsequent legislation, be converted into an "exchange contract" for the purposes of Article VIII(2)(b).[51] Consequently, Article VIII(2)(b) could

---

[47] See Smedresman and Lowenfeld, "Eurodollars, Multinational Banks and National Laws" (1989) 64 New York University LR 733, 751.

[48] See *Regazzoni v KC Sethia (1944) Ltd* [1958] AC 301, where the court refused to enforce a contract which was intended to evade Indian sanctions against South Africa. The principle stated in the text can obviously only apply where the sanctions were already in force when the contract was made.

[49] See in particular, Carreau and Juillard, *Droit international économique* (Dalloz, 2003) para 1607; Edwards (1982) AJIL 870 and Gianviti (1980) *Rev Crit* 179, where blocking legislation is described as "a rough form of exchange control". Smedresman and Lowenfeld, "Eurodollars, Multinational Banks and National Laws" 64 NYU LR 733, 750, note that American banks involved in litigation over Iranian sanctions raised Art VIII(2)(b) by way of defence.

[50] *Decision No. 144 (52/51)* dated 14 August 1952.

[51] On this point, see the discussion of the meaning of "exchange contracts" at para 15.28 above.

not provide a defence in the English courts for a debtor who found himself unable to pay as a result of supervening sanctions legislation.[52]

(e)   A further set of problems may arise in countries whose system of private international law incorporates Article 7(1) of the Rome Convention or a rule similar to it. As noted previously, that provision allows the court to give effect to the mandatory laws of a country with which the contractual situation has a close connection.[53] The point arose in the 1980s in connection with the attempts of the US Government to prohibit participation by US commercial interests in the construction of the trans-Siberian pipeline; the US embargo applied to subsidiaries of US entities which were incorporated and carried on their business outside the United States. A Dutch subsidiary of a US corporation had agreed to supply equipment for the pipeline, but subsequently refused to do so, on the basis that it was bound by the export embargo. The mere fact that the Dutch company was a subsidiary of a US corporation was insufficient to create a close connection between the contract—which was found to be governed by Dutch law—and the mandatory sanctions regime imposed by the United States. Consequently, the Dutch subsidiary was liable for breach of contract in failing to deliver the equipment.[54]

17.26   Where the contract is governed by the law of the imposing State, the sanctions legislation would form a part of the body of law which governs the obligation.[55] In such a case, an English court would usually have to apply the terms of such legislation and hold that the payment obligation has been suspended or terminated, as prescribed by the relevant sanctions regime and the law applicable to the contract. Thus, in *Libyan Arab Foreign Bank v Manufacturers Hanover Trust Co (No 2)*,[56] the Libyan claimant held US dollar deposits with the New York head office of the defendant bank. When the US imposed sanctions against Libya, the English court held that the deposit contract was governed by New York law

---

[52] For further discussion of US sanctions against Iran in the specific context of the eurodollar market, see Carreau, *Deposit Contracts in "International Contracts"* (materials reprinted from the proceedings at the Columbia Law School Symposium on International Contracts, 1981, Matthew Bender & Co).

[53] Article 7(1) of the Rome Convention has already been discussed in the context of a private international law of exchange control—see para 16.08(4) above.

[54] *Cie européene des pêtroles SA v Sensor Nederland BV* (1983) 23 Int LM 66. The case is discussed by Dicey and Morris, *The Conflict of Laws* (Sweet & Maxwell, 13th edn, 2000) para 32-139.

[55] Article 15 of the Rome Convention. If the contract is governed by the laws of a third State, then the effect of the sanctions must be determined by reference to that system of law: see generally Art 20(1) of the Rome Convention.

[56] [1989] 1 Lloyd's Rep 608.

and was thus apparently prepared to hold that the obligation to repay had been deferred by the US Presidential Order.[57]

As noted earlier, there may also be cases in which the existence of foreign sanctions may have an impact upon proceedings in this country, even though the contract itself is governed by English law. For example, it is established that the English courts will not enforce a contract which is designed to circumvent sanctions imposed by a foreign State with which the United Kingdom had cordial relations.[58]   **17.27**

F. "Long Arm" Jurisdiction and Monetary Assets

The fight against terrorist activity has assumed a heightened importance in recent years, not least because of the events of 11 September 2001. It has been recognised that a major part of the war on terror has to be waged on a financial front; if terrorists can be prevented from using the financial system and thus be starved of funds, then it naturally becomes more difficult for them to mount their operations. Legislation has been introduced with a view to identifying and seizing funds which might support terrorist activity.   **17.28**

In the light of these developments, it is appropriate to consider the extent of a State's jurisdiction to confiscate monetary assets belonging to foreigners and held within its borders. It should be appreciated that this aspect of the discussion differs from that contained in the earlier part of this chapter. The previous sections have concentrated on "blocking" legislation, which will suspend obligations to make payments to the victim State or its residents, but will not normally deprive them of their contractual or proprietary rights; those rights may usually be resumed once the relevant political confrontation comes to an end and the sanctions are lifted. In contrast, the present section considers legislation of a confiscatory character, where the targets of the sanctions are permanently deprived of their assets.   **17.29**

Of course, no one can object to the confiscation of assets which are intended to be used to further a terrorist purpose, and the present text does not seek to challenge legislation which has been introduced for that purpose. But, as in the case of money laundering laws generally, rules which seek to counter terrorist   **17.30**

---

[57] On the evidence, however, it was found that the terms of the Presidential Order did not in any event prohibit the repayment of the particular deposit in question.

[58] See *Regazzoni v KC Sethia (1944) Ltd* [1958] AC 301 (CA), relating to Indian sanctions against South Africa. The decision is grounded on English domestic public policy. If the contract were governed by a foreign system of law, then it is likely that a similar result would be reached by an application of Art 16 of the Rome Convention.

funding activities can only operate effectively if a certain burden of compliance is imposed upon financial institutions, and if non-compliance is met with effective penalties. It then becomes necessary to enquire as to the permissible limits of any such legislation, especially in so far as it relates to the activities of foreign institutions operating outside the legislating State.

17.31   The question has recently assumed relevance in the light of the measures taken by the United States in the immediate aftermath of the attacks of 11 September 2001.[59] In order to place the discussion in its context, it is necessary to provide a brief summary of the legislative steps which immediately followed that atrocity.

17.32   First of all, the President of the United States signed Executive Order 13224, which prohibited dealings with persons and organisations deemed to be linked to terrorist actions and blocked the assets of those persons, to the extent to which those assets "are in the United States, or . . . hereafter come within the possession or control of United States persons".[60] The Executive Order was soon followed by the USA PATRIOT ACT,[61] which was passed at the end of October 2001. Title III of that Act creates the International Money Laundering Abatement and Anti-Terrorism Financing Act of 2001. In broad terms, Title III strengthens pre-existing money laundering legislation; it also requires US financial institutions to exercise a degree of diligence before allowing foreign financial institutions to open correspondent accounts, and thereby to gain access to the US banking and financial system.[62]

17.33   These general rules are supported by forfeiture provisions contained in sections 317 to 319 of the Patriot Act. Section 317[63] provides that, where a person has

---

[59] On the subject generally, see Alexander, "United States Financial Sanctions and International Terrorism" (2002) 2 JIBFL 80 and (2002) 5 JIBFL 213.

[60] Executive Order 13224, s 1(d). Section 3(c) of the Order provides that the term "United States person" is to include "any . . . entity organised under the laws of the United States (including foreign branches)". Consequently, the Executive Order purports to have extraterritorial effect and would require the blocking of accounts and other assets by the London branch of a US bank. The English courts would not give effect to such a blocking order: *Libyan Arab Foreign Bank v Bankers Trust Co* [1989] QB 728. However, the point is of limited practical importance because, in line with many other countries, the UK introduced a parallel set of sanctions against terrorist organisations.

[61] The title of the Act is "Uniting and Strengthening America by Providing Appropriate Tools Required to Intercept and Obstruct Terrorism (USA PATRIOT ACT) Act of 2001".

[62] Correspondent accounts are frequently accounts of smaller banks held with major institutions. The smaller bank will be using the facilities of the larger organisation to clear or settle transactions. The difficulty with these accounts flows from the fact that the smaller bank will be known to the correspondent bank, but the underlying customer will usually be unknown. Section 312 of the Act requires US financial institutions to establish procedures to identify the shareholders of privately held banks and to conduct "enhanced scrutiny" of such accounts in order to guard against money laundering. Similar obligations of scrutiny are imposed with respect to private bank accounts.

[63] Section 317 operates by way of an amendment to s 1956(b) of Title 18 to the US Code.

been involved in a financial transaction in the United States involving unlawful activity, he commits an offence and is liable for a penalty up to the value of the money or assets involved. For the purposes of forfeiture, section 317 allows the court to exercise "long arm" jurisdiction over foreign banks which have no connection with the United States, other than the fact that they maintain an account with a US financial institution, or have been involved in a relevant financial transaction occurring wholly or partly within the United States.

Section 319 of the Act—whilst pursuing the same broad objective—poses far more difficulties. Where funds are liable to forfeiture under section 317 and those funds have been deposited with a bank *outside* the United States, then a corresponding amount of money may be seized from an inter-bank account of the non-US institution held with a bank in the United States. The scope of the provision can perhaps best be understood if the relevant extracts are reproduced: 17.34

> For the purpose of a forfeiture under this section . . . if funds are deposited into an account at a foreign bank, and that foreign bank has an interbank account in the United States with a covered financial institution . . . the funds shall be deemed to have been deposited in the interbank account in the United States, and any restraining order, seizure warrant, or arrest warrant in rem regarding the funds may be served on the covered financial institution and funds in the interbank account, up to the value of the funds deposited into the account at the foreign bank, may be restrained, seized or arrested . . .

Section 317 thus creates "long arm" jurisdiction over money laundering offences involving the United States but committed by persons abroad, whilst section 319 allows for the assets of a foreign bank in the United States to be forfeit on the grounds that the foreign bank has accepted deposits from the person concerned through a branch outside the United States. It is not necessary for the US Government to demonstrate any link between the overseas money launderer and the funds held in the interbank account of the foreign bank.[64] The two provisions read together thus constitute a significant attempt to exercise extraterritorial jurisdiction, not merely over terrorists themselves but also over those within the financial system who do business with them.[65] Since the original depositor of the funds, rather than the foreign bank, is deemed to be the owner of the funds, it seems that the foreign bank has no standing to challenge a forfeiture order under the terms of the Patriot Act itself.[66] This is so, even 17.35

---

[64] Section 319 confirms that "it shall not be necessary for the Government to establish that the funds are directly traceable to the funds deposited into the foreign account".

[65] As noted above, money laundering legislation generally operates by targeting institutions which might deal with those seeking to enjoy the proceeds of their criminal activity; it is, perhaps, the most effective means of tackling the problem.

[66] Section 319 provides that "the *owner* of the funds deposited into the account of the foreign bank may contest the forfeiture order". The "*owner*" of the funds is usually the person alleged to have been involved in criminal activity, and not the bank itself.

though the moneys held in the interbank account are not directly traceable to the original overseas deposit.[67]

17.36   It has been observed that foreign banks may object to this provision on the basis that it deprives them of their property without due process of law.[68] Given their extraterritorial "reach", the provisions may also create difficulties in the context of international law. It must be remembered that section 319 of the Patriot Act allows the court to make a forfeiture order against funds held by a foreign bank in an interbank account within the United States, even though:

(a)   the bank itself has not been shown to be guilty of, or otherwise complicit in, the criminal activity;

(b)   no nexus has been demonstrated between the funds in the interbank account in the United States and the proceeds of the money laundering transaction; and

(c)   the foreign bank concerned will usually remain liable to reimburse its own customer under the law applicable to the primary account relationship.

It must be concluded that, in substance, the United States exerts jurisdiction over funds which are physically present in the United States in order to impose penalties on a foreign bank which has not necessarily been shown to be complicit in a money laundering offence and which will not necessarily have any legal right to deprive the suspect customer of his funds in the foreign jurisdiction concerned.

17.37   It may well be that section 319 will have beneficial effects, in the sense that foreign banks will have to take care to ensure that they do not deal with suspect individuals or organisations in their home jurisdictions; otherwise the funds standing to the credit of their interbank accounts in the United States may be jeopardised. It may also be said that draconian action was consistent with the Security Council Resolution which was passed in the immediate aftermath of the attacks on the World Trade Center;[69] that resolution called on all States "to work together urgently to bring justice to the perpetrators, organisers and sponsors of the terrorist attacks". The resolution also stressed that "those responsible for aiding, supporting or harbouring the perpetrators, organisers and sponsors

---

[67] It may be added for completeness that s 806 of the Patriot Act allows for the forfeiture of the assets of individuals or organisations involved in terrorist acts against the US. It is not proposed to review that provision in the present context.

[68] See Comisky and Lee, "The USA Patriot Act has Broad Implications for Financial Institutions" (May/June 2002) 15 (5) *Journal of Taxation of Financial Institutions* 23. Article XIV of the Constitution provides, so far as relevant "nor shall any State deprive any person of life liberty or property, without due process of law nor deny to any person within its jurisdiction the equal protection of the laws".

[69] UN Security Council Resolution 1368 of 12 September 2001.

of those acts will be held accountable"[70] and called on States "to redouble their efforts to prevent and suppress terrorist acts, including by increased co-operation and full implementation of the relevant international anti-terrorist conventions". There seems to be no doubt that the legislation seeks to assert a criminal jurisdiction, since forfeiture orders are made in support of proceedings relating to criminal activity; it is therefore necessary to ask whether, in terms of international law, the United States was entitled to pass and to enforce this legislation? It is true that the precise scope and territorial extent of a State's criminal jurisdiction is a matter of no small controversy.[71] Furthermore, it must not be forgotten that international law now accepts that a State may prosecute a non-national for certain crimes committed abroad; the established list includes war crimes and crimes against humanity, and it may well be that the principle could justifiably be extended to major acts of international terrorism.[72]

There nevertheless remains a certain conceptual difficulty in imposing criminal penalties against a bank which has not been shown to have committed a crime, or civil penalties against an institution which has not committed a tort.[73] The Patriot Act thus enables the US Government to forfeit the assets of an institution which may be entirely blameless and whose only connection with the United States is the holding of interbank accounts with US institutions. On the basis of the language employed, the legislation may thus be difficult to justify in terms of the international jurisdiction of the United States.[74] However, it must not be overlooked that the mere *existence* of legislation of this kind does not of itself infringe international law; such an infringement would only occur if an attempt was made to enforce the legislation in the manner just described.[75] If   **17.38**

---

[70] This language should be noted, in that it would extend to any financial institution which had knowingly assisted a terrorist organisation to conceal or to utilise funds. It is perhaps significant that the preamble to Executive Order 13224 echoes (although it does not reproduce) the language quoted in the text.

[71] Leading cases include the *SS Lotus Case (France v Turkey)* (1927) PCIJ Series A No. 9, Permanent Court of International Justice. For a discussion of this subject, see Brownlie, *General Principles of Public International Law* (Oxford University Press, 6th edn, 2003) ch 15.

[72] UN Security Council Resolutions 1269 (19 October 1999) and 1368 (12 September 2001) certainly lend some support to that view.

[73] In other words, the PATRIOT Act is open to objections which are in their essence similar to those which were levelled against the Iran and Libya Sanctions Act 1996 and the Cuban Liberty and Democratic Solidarity (LIBERTAD) Act 1996. This legislation is reviewed and cogently criticised by Lowe, "US Extra-territorial Jurisdiction" (1997) 46 ICLQ 378.

[74] The mere fact that the foreign bank holds funds in an account in the US does not, of itself, confer upon the US the international right to take action of this kind.

[75] By way of comparison, it should be remembered that the UK's Exchange Control Act 1947 was written in broad terms and certain of its provisions could have applied to the activities of non-residents abroad. However, the point did not arise because the Act was generally applied and administered in a manner which was consistent with international law. The 1947 Act has been discussed in Ch 14 above.

the use of the legislation is confined to cases in which there is real evidence that the foreign institution is complicit in money laundering and the foreign institution is, by some means, given access to the courts to challenge any forfeiture order, then it may well be that this apparently draconian legislation can be justified against the background of concerted international efforts to counteract terrorist activities and to restrict their sources of funding.[76]

---

[76] In other words, it may be argued that current and concerted action against terrorism is creating new norms of international law which can justify wide-ranging measures against terrorists and those who assist them. The precise scope of such norms, however, could not at present be formulated with great confidence and it is thus unclear whether they would be sufficient to justify the legislation which has been discussed in this section.

18

EXCHANGE RATES

A. Introduction

The existence of an independent monetary system creates two distinct problem **18.01** areas in terms of its relationship with other monetary systems. The first problem area concerns the question of making payments into areas covered by different currency systems. The ability to make such payments may be affected by the incidence of exchange controls or sanctions and these aspects have been considered earlier in this Part. It is now necessary to consider the second problem area, namely, the valuation of one currency in terms of another.

Monetary systems may be related to each other by two means of measurement, **18.02** the (nominal) par of exchange and the (real) rate of exchange. The par of exchange is now of very limited importance in a world in which currencies are "floating" and will therefore require only a few comments. On the other hand, the real rate of exchange gives rise to many and varied problems which will require more detailed discussion.

B. The Par of Exchange

The par of exchange is the equation between two money units, each based on a **18.03** fixed (usually metallic) standard. Where both currencies were based on the gold standard, each currency would have a value in terms of gold, by reference to a

469

fixed quantity or weight of gold. From the common element of these two equations (namely the relevant quantity of gold), it was possible to derive a third, which provided a par (or fixed) value between the two currencies concerned. The par of exchange sometimes represented an equality fixed by law. Thus the relationship between the US dollar and the pound sterling had long been fixed at US$4.44,[1] although this was bound to be of limited influence since both currencies were on the gold standard and the weight for weight par was apparently US$4.866. Under the Bretton Woods system as originally devised and as in force from 1946 until 1971, the par of exchange between most currencies was fixed by treaty, namely the Articles of Agreement of the International Monetary Fund.[2]

18.04   The *par* of exchange is independent of the *rate* of exchange of the day, and consequently it does not express the current value of a foreign money unit as resulting from general economic events or influences, or the impact of supply and demand. Moreover, if one country or both of the countries are on a purely paper standard, then the par of exchange either does not exist or becomes effectively meaningless, for there is no independently valued medium which provides a feature common to both monetary systems. With these considerations in mind, it is hardly surprising that, under present circumstances, the par of exchange is never resorted to—indeed, it does not even exist—when two currencies have to be valued in terms of each other for commercial purposes.[3] Even in a sovereign or governmental context, references to the par of exchange are rare. The par rate of exchange could be applied in valuing imported goods for customs purposes, and it was envisaged that the par value would generally be derived from the Bretton Woods Agreement; but in the absence of such a par rate, it was envisaged that a commercial rate of exchange would apply.[4]

18.05   In the context of legal proceedings, the question periodically arose whether, in valuing one currency as against another, it was appropriate to adopt the par of exchange or the rate of exchange. The question appears not to have arisen in continental Europe, but the correct choice appears to have caused some difficulty for US courts over a considerable period. At one time, it was thought that the choice depended upon the place of payment. If payment was to be made in a country with which the United States had an established par of exchange, then

---

[1] USA Revised Statutes, s 3565, repealed by s 403(d) of the Dye and Chemical Control Act 1921 (67th Congress, Ch 14).

[2] On this general subject, see Art IV of the Agreement, discussed at 22.15 below.

[3] During the twentieth century, the only material exception to this statement arose in the context of the calculation of a currency's gold content for the purpose of giving effect to a gold clause—see the discussion of this subject in Ch 11 above. But this exception, too, is now obsolete.

[4] For further details of these arrangements, see Art VII (4) of the General Agreement on Tariffs and Trade.

the nominal rate should be applied; in any other case, the real par (or commercial rate of exchange) would be used. This position is reflected in cases decided as late as the second half of the nineteenth century,[5] but there is now no doubt that courts in that country will apply the actual rate of exchange where a comparison between the value of two currencies is involved.[6]

In England, there was likewise some doubt whether the par or the actual rate of **18.06** exchange should be regarded as the proper indicator of the value of a foreign currency. Early cases did, however, tend to adopt the actual rate of exchange in the place of payment. In *Cockrell v Barber*,[7] legacies expressed in sicca rupees were payable in England and the court was invited to choose between (a) the East India Company's rate between India and Great Britain; (b) the East India Company's rate between Great Britain and India; and (c) the current value of sicca rupees in England. Consistently with the principle just outlined, the last solution was adopted. Likewise, in *Scott v Bevan*,[8] the English court was called upon to enforce a judgment given in Jamaica and expressed in the local currency. The question arose whether the amount in question should be converted at the nominal par or at the actual rate of exchange. The court applied the actual rate, on the basis that computation by reference to that rate "approximates most nearly to a payment in Jamaica in the currency of that island". This is surely the most cogent reason for the adoption of the actual rate, and yet the court reached this conclusion only with some hesitation.[9] Today, however, it cannot be doubted that the current rate of exchange in the place of payment is almost universally applicable.[10]

---

[5] See *Marburg v Marburg* (1866) 26 Maryland 8, a case which was quoted in many of the English decisions which precede the reform effected by *Miliangos v George Frank (Textiles) Ltd* [1976] AC 443.

[6] See, eg, *Nevillon v Demmer* (1920) 114 Mis 1, 185 NY Suppl 443; *Hicks v Guinness* (1925) 269 US 71; *Deutsche Bank Filiale Nurnberg v Humphreys* (1926) 272 US 517; but cf *Frontera Transportation Co v Abaunza* (1921) 271 F 199 (CCA 5th).

[7] (1810) 16 Ves 461; on this case, see Story, *Conflict of Laws* (8th edn, 1883) s 313.

[8] (1831) 2 B & Ad 78. Ses also *Delegal v Naylor* (1831) 7 Bing 460 and *Campbell v Graham* (1830) 1 Russ & NY 453, 461, affirmed sub nom *Campbell v Sandford* (1834) 2 CI & F 429, 450, where it appears that the par of exchange was applied.

[9] See p 85 of the report. It should be added that this case plainly concerned the application of the nominal or actual par of exchange—Negus 40 (1924) LQR 149 and Rifkind (1926) 26 Col LR 559, 562. The Court of Appeal in *Di Fernando v Simon Smits & Co Ltd* [1920] KB 409 (at 412 and 415) appears to have adopted the view stated in the text, although the decision in that case was overruled by the House of Lords in *The Despina R* [1979] AC 685. The decision in *Scott v Bevan* was heavily relied upon in other cases which were really concerned with the date (rather than the rate) of conversion—see, eg, *The Volturno* [1921] 2 AC 544, which, however, was also overruled by the decision in *The Despina R*.

[10] See note 92, para 7.31 above. See also *Re Tillam Boehme & Tickle Pty Ltd* (1932) Vict LR 146, 148 where the par of exchange was expressly rejected, in reliance on the decision in *Scott v Bevan* (1831) 2 B & Ad 78.

18.07 Perhaps the most clear illustration of the dominance of the actual rate of exchange is provided by the House of Lords decision in *Atlantic Trading and Shipping Co v Louis Dreyfus*.[11] The respondents were agents for a ship owned by the appellants. The respondents became entitled to the repayment of expenses incurred by them in Argentine dollars, and to the payment in sterling of dispatch money and commission. In payment they received from the appellants in Buenos Aires 66,727 = 30 Argentinean dollars, with the stipulation that any balance was to be returned to the appellants. In applying this amount in paying the sterling amounts owing to themselves, the respondents employed a rate of $5.04 to the pound sterling. There remained a surplus of $3,433, which the respondents paid to the appellants in sterling after having converted the surplus at a rate of $3.66 to the pound. The appellants contended that the first step in the accounting process should also have been effected at the $3.66 rate. It is necessary to explain that the $3.66 rate was the actual market rate of the day. In contrast, the $5.04 rate was fixed by an Argentine law of 1881, which had been passed to stabilise the relative value of the Argentine currency. For that purpose, it was decreed that the currency units in circulation in Argentina should be reckoned in terms of the British gold sovereign at a rate of $5.04 per sovereign.[12] It appears that British gold sovereigns were circulating in Argentina at the time of the 1881 law and this enabled the House of Lords to characterise such law[13] as "merely a legal tender law, fixing the parity at which certain gold coins then passing current in the Republic should be made legal tender with the national currency then recently established". In other words, the rate of the new Argentine paper money was stabilised in terms of a (nominal) par of exchange with certain gold standard currencies; the 1881 law regulated the parity of sovereigns with the Argentine currency, but could not affect international obligations or payment obligations governed by English law which were to be performed in England. In the present case, the contract was governed by English law and required payment to be made in England; it could therefore only be seen as an obligation to pay the "commercial equivalent of the sums, measured in sterling", and that equivalent had "to be ascertained not by a permanent legal tender law relating to currency, but by the current quotation for the exchange rate of sterling" at the relevant time.[14] It followed that the appellant shipowners were entitled to succeed in their claim.

---

[11] (1922) 10 Ll LR 477, 703, followed in *Ellawood v Ford & Co* (1922) 12 Ll LR 47 and in *Williams & Mordey v Muller & Co* (1924) 18 Ll LR 50.

[12] The sovereign was a gold coin having a nominal or face value of one pound.

[13] At 704

[14] On the points just made, see pp 703–5 of the report.

A similar point arose in *Lively Ltd v City of Munich.*[15] The case involved the conversion of a US dollar sum into sterling on 1 December 1973. The conversion was required to be effected for the purposes of Article 13 of the Agreement on German External Debts (1953), which provided for the rate of exchange to be "determined by the par values of the currencies concerned in force on the appropriate date as agreed with the International Monetary Fund" and "if no such par values are or were in force", the current rate for "cable transfers" was to apply. As has already been shown,[16] by 1 December 1973 the Bretton Woods par value system had collapsed although, on paper, par values still existed and even continued to be used for certain intergovernmental purposes. In a commercial context, the par values may have continued to exist but (for all practical purposes) they were not "in force" for the purposes of Article 13 of the 1953 Agreement. Since the rate of exchange was required in a commercial—as opposed to governmental—context, it was appropriate to ignore the nominally existing par value and to apply the commercial rate of exchange as to the date in question.[17]

18.08

The foregoing discussion has demonstrated that the par of exchange is of virtually no modern significance. It is thus now possible to concentrate on issues associated with the use of a market rate.

18.09

C. The Rate of Exchange

Whenever it is necessary to employ a rate of exchange for the purpose of converting a sum of money from one currency into another, four distinct problems are likely to arise. At the risk of repetition, these must be stated in a comprehensive manner, as follows:

18.10

(1) Where a payment is contractually required to be made in England, all questions as to the rate of exchange (including questions as to the identification of the applicable rate) should usually be governed by the law applicable to the contract.[18] As to payments which, under the terms of the contract, are required to be made abroad in a currency other than sterling, the need for conversion into sterling only arises where it is sought to

---

[15] [1976] 1 WLR 1004.

[16] See para 2.10 above.

[17] The rate of exchange was required to measure the amount payable by the City of Munich in respect of bonds issued on the London market. The ECJ also rejected an attempt to settle a fine in Italian lira on the basis of the Bretton Woods par values, when that system was in theory still in effect but had, for all practical purposes, broken down—see *Société Anonyme Générale Sucrière v EC Commission*, Cases 41, 43 and 44–73 [1977] ECR 445.

[18] This conclusion follows from the terms of Art 10 of the Rome Convention on the law applicable to contractual obligations.

enforce a foreign judgment in this country.[19] In such a case, questions touching the rate of exchange are governed by English law, since the enforcement of a foreign judgment is a matter of procedure, to be governed by the laws of the forum.[20] The following observations are thus aimed at providing a summary of English domestic law in this field.

(2) In an era of floating currencies, the date with reference to which the required rate of exchange is to be fixed assumes a considerable importance. Where the conversion is required for the purpose of proceedings, the rate prevailing as at the date of payment is now firmly established.[21] Outside

---

[19] ie because, where the proceedings are commenced in England, they may be expressed in the foreign currency concerned—see the discussion of the *Miliangos* case in Ch 8 above.

[20] See Dicey and Morris, *The Conflict of Laws* (Sweet & Maxwell, 13th edn, 2000) ch 14.

[21] See the discussion of the *Miliangos* decision in Ch 8 above. It must be observed that the courts in Germany have in recent years been confronted with some very difficult cases involving the date with reference to which the rate of exchange is to be established. The Court of Appeal of Hamm, 8 March 1991, *IPRspr* 1991, No. 78, had to decide a case involving a couple who were married in Tehran in 1967; they subsequently lived in Germany for many years and eventually obtained a divorce before a German court. Under the terms of their 1967 marriage contract, the husband had agreed to pay 500,000 rials to the wife in the event of their divorce. The wife, accordingly demanded payment of that sum, although it may be noted that the external value of the Iranian currency had suffered large-scale depreciation between 1967 and the date of the demand. Further, Iranian exchange controls allowed for the export of only 2,000 rials, so it was impossible for the husband to pay the entire amount owing in Germany. The court thus ordered the husband to pay in Deutsche marks and it thereupon became necessary to decide whether the rate of exchange to be applied should be that prevailing as at the date of the contract (1967) or as at the date of the proceedings (1991). The court selected 1991 as the relevant date, on the basis that the wife would have borne the risk of inflation had the parties remained in Iran, and it was inappropriate to shift that risk to the husband merely because the award now had to be made in a different currency. The decision was, perhaps, a little harsh from the wife's perspective, but it is consistent with the payment date rule noted in the text. In contrast, the Municipal Court of Aachen had to consider a very similar case but reached the opposite result: 7 February 2000, *IPRspr* 2000, No. 67. The parties had married in Iran in 1974, but had been permanently resident in Germany for a number of years. The Court does not seem to have considered whether the payment of the nuptial gift in rials would contravene Iranian exchange control laws, but it did find that Article 1082 of the Iranian Civil Code required the husband to adjust the payment for inflation which had occurred between the date of the marriage and the date of payment. In order to achieve this result, the court required the husband to pay in marks by reference to the exchange rate in 1974 (rather than 2000). Finally, in a slightly different vein, the District Court of Cologne had to deal with a claim by a German contractor who had built an airport in Iraq: 19 April 2000, *IPRspr* 2000, No. 122. As is frequently the case in such contracts, the claimants were to be paid partly in US dollars and partly in Iraqi dinars. The claimants successfully sought payment of the entire price in US dollars, on the basis that the original agreement to accept dinars had been frustrated by the subsequent UN embargo which rendered it impossible for the claimant to receive payment in dinars and, in any event, rendered them worthless in the hands of the contractor. The District Court held that this result was also consistent with Iraqi private law which contained a general principle of good faith and fair dealing. It is submitted that this decision cannot be supported, for Iraqi law could hardly require the substitution of a foreign currency for its own under such circumstances. On the other hand, it has been seen that the application of frustration or similar principles may be justified where the currency concerned has become worthless—see para 9.47(4) above.

proceedings, the appropriate date depends upon the construction of the contract, but again there exists a strong tendency to apply the payment-date rule.

(3) Rates of exchange may differ from place to place. As a result, the ascertainment of the legally relevant place may be important in some cases. That place may, of course, be expressly identified by the parties in their contract. But what is the position if the contract is silent? Whilst the point has not been explicitly decided, it is suggested that the rate of exchange in the place of payment should be applied for these purposes.[22] In other words, where the contract is governed by English law, it is an implied term of the contract that any required rate of exchange should be the rate prevailing in the place in which payment is contractually required to be made,[23] ie and not in the place (if different) in which payment is actually made. It is thus submitted that the general rule formerly applicable to bills of exchange is of general application.[24] The justification for this position lies in the fact that the application of a different rate would not necessarily secure to the creditor the amount which he is entitled to have at the agreed place of payment, rather than elsewhere. The rule suggested in the text—adopting the rate in the contractual, rather than the actual, place of payment—has thus been adopted in New York[25] and also receives some support in English case law.[26]

(4) The most troublesome problem of the rate of exchange has been that of identifying the particular rate of exchange to which resort is to be had for the purpose of effecting the conversion. This matter is investigated in the ensuing section of this chapter.[27]

---

[22] Once again, the place of payment may have been specified by the parties; if it has not, then the identification of the place of payment is governed by the principles discussed at para 7.84 above.

[23] Since this submission is derived from an implied term of the contract, it should be appreciated that this is a point of substance which would be derived from the contract in accordance with Art 10(1)(a) of the Rome Convention. Article 10(2) deals with the law of the place of payment in the context of the *mode* of performance. It is thus not in point in the present context.

[24] Bills of Exchange Act 1882, s 72(4), now repealed. However, note that the *actual* place of payment was formerly adopted in the context of the Merchant Shipping Act 1894, s 139.

[25] *Richard v National City Bank of New York* (1931) 231 App Div 559 248 NYS 113.

[26] See in particular *Marrache v Ashton* [1943] AC 411. See also *Manners v Pearson* [1898] 1 Ch 581, 592, where it is noted that "The amount of the English judgment or order must be based on the quantity of English sterling which one would have to pay here to obtain in the market the amount of the debt payable in foreign currency delivered *at the appointed place of payment*."

[27] The ensuing part of this chapter was originally based on Dr Mann's article, "Problems of the Rate of Exchange" (1945) 8 MLR 177, although extensive alterations were made to the original commentary.

D. Identifying the Rate of Exchange

The market rate

18.11 There does not at present exist on the London market any rate of exchange which can be described as official, in the sense that it is an exclusive rate or is conclusive and binding on contracting parties in the event of a dispute. The amounts transacted daily on the London Foreign Exchange Market represent vast sums and yet it is not an official market in any real sense.[28] Thus, the dealings which occur on a daily basis as between brokers and dealers in the major financial institutions do not produce what can be described as a uniform or generally acceptable or authoritative rate.[29] Banks will thus have their own rates for everyday transactions; but these may vary from day to day (and during the course of a day), and different rates may be negotiated for especially large transactions. For these reasons, loan agreements or other documents involving an exchange transaction should specify both (a) the institution whose rate is to be used[30] and (b) the date and time on which the relevant note is required to be ascertained.[31]

18.12 Where a rate of exchange is required in order to give effect to an agreement but none has been expressly stipulated, then it becomes necessary to deal with the point by way of implied term.[32] Inevitably, this analysis will depend upon the precise circumstances. However, a few general propositions may be suggested. Where a contract between a bank and its customer refers to a rate of exchange, it may be inferred that the rate quoted by that bank at the relevant time was

---

[28] In a world of "floating" currencies, the absence of an "official" rate can hardly be a surprising feature. Of course, the position was different under the par value system applied by the IMF, and may remain different in certain countries where rates of exchange continue to be fixed by the monetary authorities. But for the most part, the position remains as stated in the text.

[29] For a description of the London foreign exchange market see the (1980) Bank of England's Quarterly Bulletin 437.

[30] It should be appreciated that institutions will quote separate rates for the purchase or the sale of a particular currency and the appropriate rate should be identified. For example, the contractual language may require an amount in sterling to be converted into US dollars "By reference to the rate quoted by X Bank for the purchase of US dollars with sterling at 11 am on the business day in question", thus making it clear that it is the buy rate which is in question.

[31] It will be apparent from this discussion that there is no generally applicable rule of law which determines the type of rate of exchange to be used in all cases. The point has occasionally been dealt with in specific contexts. For example, s 72(4) of the Bills of Exchange Act 1882 formerly provided that the amount of a bill expressed in a foreign currency was to be converted into sterling "according to the rate of exchange for sight drafts". The same solution is adopted by Art 75(2)(b) of the UNCITRAL Convention on International Bills of Exchange and International Promissory Notes.

[32] It is submitted that a contract should fail for want of certainty on this ground in the most extreme or exceptional of cases.

intended to be used.[33] Equally, where a rate of exchange is to be ascertained in the context of a contract for the sale of goods, it may be possible to infer that the rate quoted by the seller's bank was intended to be used as the reference point, because the seller will be the recipient of the funds and will rely on his own bank to effect any necessary exchange. In each case, the appropriate rate is determined by the context in which the need for conversion arises, and by reference to any relevant contractual or statutory provisions at issue.

Types of exchange rate

The most frequently quoted rate of exchange is the spot rate, which involves immediate delivery of the currency concerned by means of a credit to the account of the buyer or to its owner. The rate for a sight draft, ie a cheque in the relevant foreign currency, has been used in various legislative contexts.[34] The rate for notes and coins is based on the spot rate, but is influenced by the fact that transactions are normally effected in small amounts (thus making the cost per transaction higher) and the need for the dealer to carry a stock of the currency concerned. It was only as a result of exchange control that the market for notes at times became enlivened, and led to quotations which were largely independent of the spot rate but were determined by the laws of supply and demand, expressing the opportunities for smuggling and resmuggling. In other words, the rate of exchange became detached from any objective attempt at the valuation of the currency concerned.

18.13

More sophisticated contracts may involve the sale and purchase of currencies at a fixed future date, usually for the purpose of hedging an obligation to pay a particular amount in a particular currency at that date. The rates employed in such contexts may differ significantly from the spot rate, and their pricing is a matter of some complexity. However, they will not usually have any legal relevance outside their own specialist field except perhaps where the parties to a contract will have contemplated that forward exchange contracts may have been executed as a means of hedging particular currency exposures, or where it might be reasonable to expect a party to enter into such a contract as a means of mitigating his loss.[35]

18.14

---

[33] The point may be important because, in a world of floating currencies, different banks may quote different rates for identical transactions. Competitive pressures will no doubt dictate that the differentials are usually small, but a small variation in rates may be significant in the context of a sizeable transaction.

[34] See n 31 above.

[35] eg, see, *Virani v Manuel Revert y Cia SA* (CA, 18 July 2003).

Multiple currency rates

18.15 Another concomitant of exchange control flows from the use of so-called multiple currency rates, ie a series of different rates to be applied, depending upon the circumstances of the transaction. These come under the heading of discriminatory currency practices, which are generally forbidden to members of the International Monetary Fund unless approval is obtained.[36]

18.16 Whatever the reasons for the introduction of a system of several rates of exchange may be,[37] their effect is nearly always the same. A country will have established a basic rate of exchange but (for example) it will pay a premium for the foreign exchange earned by exporters of certain goods or minerals; and it will charge a premium for the foreign exchange required to purchase overseas goods or assets.[38] The introduction of such a multiple currency practice may cause obvious difficulties where parties had previously contracted by reference to an "official rate of exchange" which had been assumed to be uniform.[39]

18.17 From a legal point of view it is conceivable that, in particular circumstances, it may become necessary to take note of and to apply a rate of exchange which is effective and legitimate but which is not the official rate. Such cases are bound to be rare, for they can in any event only arise where a system of exchange control is in operation: they have not yet occurred in British judicial practice.[40]

Pseudo-rates of exchange

18.18 While multiple currency practices lead to the establishment of a variety of genuine rates of exchange, another aspect of exchange control has produced

---

[36] See Art VIII(3) of the IMF Agreement. The subject is discussed in Ch 22 below. Arrangements of this kind would necessarily not be open to EC Member States, since the imposition of any form of exchange control is inconsistent with the terms of the EC Treaty—see para 31.45 below.

[37] See the IMF's *Annual Reports* and *Annual Report on Exchange Restrictions.*

[38] In the context of UK exchange control, see the description of the "dollar premium" in *Shelley v Paddock* [1980] 2 WLR 647. For a Survey of this type of arrangement, see the IMF Ancillary Report 1979 on *Exchange Arrangements and Exchange Restrictions*, 17–18.

[39] This problem arose in Israel following the Government's introduction of multiple exchange rates in March 1952. The problem (which necessarily included the contractual meaning of the term "Official rate") was considered in three cases—see *Aaranson v Kaplan* Jerusalem Post, 2 October 1955; *Levin v Esheg Ltd* Jerusalem Post, 24 May 1956; *Tillinger v Jewish Agency* Jerusalem Post, 22 April 1958.

[40] An interesting case was, however, decided in Canada: *Djamous v Alepin* (1949) Rapports Judiciaries Officials de Québec (Cour Supérieure) 354. The defendant received Syrian pounds in Syria and undertook to pay the corresponding dollar amount to the plaintiff. In order to effect such a transaction at the official rate, the permission of the Syrian Government was necessary but unobtainable. There existed, however, a free exchange market which was known to (and tolerated by) the interested governments. The court accordingly applied the rate quoted on that market. It is important to note that the market concerned was not an illegal one. Had it been illegal, then the "free" rate could not have been applied; as noted at the end of this chapter, it must be contrary to public policy for the courts to adopt a black market rate.

what can only be described as a pseudo-rate of exchange. It is incidental to exchange control that the accounts or credit balances of non-residents are blocked in the sense that they cannot be freely dealt with whether their use be absolutely prohibited or merely limited.[41] Outside the restricting country, such blocked accounts can frequently be sold at a discount which depends on the extent to which the buyer will in practice be able to make use of the funds concerned.[42] Where such a market exists, it should be emphasised that it does not lead to the creation of a rate of exchange in the legal sense of the term. In law, a price is being paid for the assignment of a chose in action; such a price is entirely different from the price at which the unit of account of one currency can be exchanged into a unit of account of another currency.[43] As a result, this type of pseudo-rate of exchange cannot normally be regarded as a rate of exchange for legal purposes.[44]

Contracts

Under the terms of a contract, a currency may be employed as a measure of an obligation (the money of account) which is in fact required to be discharged in a different currency (the money of payment).[45] In such a case, a monetary conversion or an exchange operation is a necessary incident to performance of the contract. In the absence of any contrary stipulation expressed in, or to be inferred from, the terms of the contract, the parties may be taken to have impliedly agreed upon the application of the spot rate (for example, as opposed to the rate for notes), because the spot rate is applied in the vast majority of commercial transactions and is thus likely to be the most familiar to the parties. In such cases, the spot rate is the "reasonable" rate which applies in the absence of an express term, just as the law imputes an intention to pay a reasonable price for goods if it has not otherwise been fixed.[46]

18.19

Thus, if a contract provides for "payment at the current rate of exchange", "at the rate of exchange of the day", or "at the rate of exchange in London", it is a matter of construction to ascertain the rate of exchange envisaged by the parties, but in default of special circumstances this will be the spot rate as the

18.20

---

[41] For the system of blocked accounts which applied under the UK regime, see the Exchange Control Act 1947, s 32 and Sch 3.

[42] It should be pointed out that such an arrangement would frequently be illegal under the law of the restricting State.

[43] For this reason, it appears that the Federal Reserve Bank fell into error in 1940 when it certified a "free" rate of US$3.45 to the pound sterling. The error was not appreciated by the Supreme Court when it decided *Barn v US* (1944) 324 US 83. For strong criticism of this decision, see Nussbaum (1945) 45 Col LR 412, 417.

[44] For further discussion of this point, see para 18.42 below.

[45] On the money of account and the money of payment, see Ch 7 above.

[46] Sale of Goods Act 1979, s 8(2).

commercially reasonable rate. The same effective position may apply where the money of account and the money of payment are identical, but some element of the case—usually, the quantification of the liability—will involve an exchange calculation. For example, a London bank may guarantee the liabilities of its customer up to a maximum of £500,000; if a call is made under the guarantee in respect of a liability expressed in US dollars, then the bank must pay in sterling and, in the absence of contrary stipulation, the amount payable will be the sterling amount required to purchase the amount of the US dollar claim at the spot rate on the date of payment. Likewise, if a London underwriter, by means of a policy expressed in sterling, reinsures[47] a foreign insurance company against its liability under a fire insurance policy on foreign property, the amount of his liability depends on the sum of foreign currency paid by the primary insurer to the assured. Again, the parties must be taken to have contemplated the conversion of the foreign monetary element into sterling at the spot rate. But the spot rate applies in such cases because it reflects the commercial intention of the parties. Cases of this kind do not involve the *settlement* or *performance* of an obligation in foreign money, nor do they even contemplate that a foreign exchange transaction will actually have to be effected by the parties; they merely contemplate a (notional) conversion or calculation, which is required in order to determine the amount payable in the currency in which the contract is expressed.

Debts

18.21   Where a debtor has promised to pay a liquidated sum in a particular currency, a conversion into sterling (or some other currency) may be required either for substantive or procedural reasons.

18.22   In the substantive arena, the problem may arise in a purely domestic context. A contract between X and Y (both resident in England) may provide for X to pay £10,000 in London, but he is entitled to deduct certain expenses which were incurred in US dollars. The determination of the sterling amount payable necessarily involves the conversion of the relevant US dollar amount. As has been shown, the construction of the contract will frequently lead to the conclusion that the spot rate should be applied.

18.23   The question may, however, also arise in a procedural context, and the contract may not always be available to assist in this type of case. A contract creating a debt expressed in US dollars may be the subject of a judgment in England and, as has been seen,[48] the English courts may give judgment expressed in that

---

[47] For this purpose it is assumed that the reinsurance contract stipulates for claims to be paid in sterling.

[48] See Ch 8 above.

currency. Consequently, the question of conversion into sterling only arises once the creditor takes steps to enforce the judgment against any English assets which the debtor may possess. Enforcement of the judgment raises questions of procedure, and it is thus not possible to refer to the original contract in this regard. It is therefore desirable to formulate a rule which is *prima facie* applicable to foreign currency debts in this type of situation.

The rate of exchange to be applied in such circumstances is the rate at the place **18.24** of payment for whatever is legal tender under the law of the currency in which the debt is expressed. Usually, this will be the rate for banknotes, because a promise to pay a given number of units of foreign currency is a promise to pay whatever may be legal tender at the time of payment in the State of issue of the currency concerned, and the debtor is entitled to discharge his obligation by payment in that manner.[49] Since the amount of sterling (or other currency) into which the foreign currency is to be converted should most closely correspond to the value of that which the debtor has promised to pay and which, if paid, would discharge the debt, the appropriate rate must be that for legal tender of the country concerned as at the date on which payment is made.[50]

It should be appreciated that this approach has only begun to enjoy support in **18.25** recent years, and earlier decisions adopted a different route. In *Graumann v Treitel*[51] the rate for notes was specifically rejected. The case involved a debt of approximately RM78,000 arising under a German law agreement made in Germany between individuals then resident in that country, but both of whom had subsequently moved to England. As a result, it was found that the place of performance had shifted to London.[52] On the London market, it was possible to purchase reichsmark notes at the rate of RM36 to the pound, but the official rate stipulated in Germany was RM12 to the pound.[53] The court accepted that the defendant could simply have purchased the necessary number of reichsmark notes on the London market and paid them to the plaintiff in

---

[49] These well-established principles have been discussed at para 9.03 above. That the rate for banknotes is to be applied is accepted by Dicey and Morris, *The Conflict of Laws* (Sweet & Maxwell, 13th edn, 2000) Rule 210, although it is noted that there is no specific authority on this point. It must be said that the use of the rate for notes lacks appeal in the modern context, yet it seems that it must be maintained in the light of the decision in *Libyan Arab Foreign Bank v Bankers Trust Co* [1989] QB 728.

[50] *Syndic in Bankruptcy of Khoury v Khayat* [1943] AC 507 (PC); *The Alexandra I* [1972] 1 Lloyd's Rep 399 (CA); *Barclays Bank International Ltd v Levin Brothers (Bradford) Ltd* [1977] QB 270; *George Veflings Rederi AS v President of India* [1979] 1 WLR 59 (CA).

[51] [1940] 2 ALL ER 188, followed in *Ginsberg v Canadian Pacific Steamship Ltd* [1940] 66 Ll LR 20.

[52] For criticism of this and other aspects of the decision, see Kahn-Freund (1940) 4 MLR 149.

[53] This state of affairs does, of course, emphasise both the impact which a system of exchange control may have in this field, and the importance of selecting the correct rate of exchange.

complete discharge of the debt. But despite this concession, the Court applied the German official rate of exchange, apparently on the basis that there was then no authority for applying a London market rate.[54] However, the necessary authority for the application of the market rate was subsequently supplied by the decision in *Marrache v Ashton*.[55] In that case, the debtor owed some 110,000 Spanish pesetas to the creditor. Both parties were resident in Gibraltar, the law of which governed the contract and where payment was to be made. At the date of the contract, gold and silver coins were legal tender in Spain. Prior to the date of payment, however, Bank of Spain peseta notes were made the only form of legal tender in Spain (apart from gold). Under Spanish law, it was illegal both to export and to import peseta notes. Yet there was a market for them in Gibraltar, London, and elsewhere. The "market" rate was approximately 132 pesetas to the pound, whilst the Spanish "official" rate was 53 pesetas to the pound. The debtor admitted liability for the sterling equivalent of the debt converted at the market rate, and the Privy Council held that payment on this basis did indeed discharge the debt. As the Privy Council noted:[56]

> All that the Court had to do was to ascertain what was legal tender in Spain for so many pesetas and then to inquire whether there was a market in Gibraltar for the sale and purchase of such currency and if so, what was the market rate. Bank of Spain notes were legal tender in Spain, there was a market for such notes in Gibraltar and the rate there prevailing was 132 pesetas to the pound sterling.

18.26 In both *Marrache v Ashton* and in *Graumann v Treitel* the place of payment was held to be outside the State which issued the money of account, ie Spanish pesetas were payable in Gibraltar and German reichsmarks were payable in London. However, the principle remains that one must look to the rate of exchange for notes in the place of payment; the general rule thus continues to apply where the place of payment is within the territory of the State which issues the money of account.

18.27 In the latter type of case, however, the application of the principle may lead to a radically different result where an exchange control system is in operation, because such a system will inevitably place a premium on the value of the domestic currency.[57] Odd though this may seem—and perhaps, at first sight,

---

[54] Although much criticised, it may be that the court was in some respects justified in its approach. The contract was governed by German law, which thus governed the substance of the obligation and which would plainly have applied the official (rather than the London market) rate.

[55] [1943] AC 311, discussed by Dr Mann (1943) 59 LQR 301. For a discussion of both cases mentioned in the text, see R Lachs (1943) 93 Law Journal 299, 307. Subject only to the point made in the preceding footnote, the Privy Council decision deprives *Graumann v Treitel* of its authority.

[56] At 319.

[57] See *Re Parana Plantations Ltd* [1946] 2 All ER 214, discussed below. The point made in the text is illustrated by the decision of a District Court in Florida in *Sun Insurance Office Ltd v Aranca*

unjust—the discrepancy between the two types of case may be justified by reference to the intention of the parties. They will, expressly or impliedly, have selected the place of payment; and it is a not uncommon feature of monetary obligations that decisive legal consequences are derived from the law of the place of payment.[58] Thus, in *Marrache v Ashton*, the debtor was obliged to pay a determined amount in Spanish pesetas in Gibraltar. The facts that Spanish law (as the *lex monetae*) imposed exchange control restrictions and stipulated for an official rate were thus entirely irrelevant considerations. Likewise, the fact that the creditor might have wished to take the money into Spain but could not lawfully do so were also irrelevant, for the performance of the debtor's obligation is in no way linked to the creditor's intended use of the proceeds. The position in terms of cost to the debtor would have been radically different had Madrid been the place of payment, for the creditor would there have been entitled to receive the same number of pesetas. The debtor could only have achieved this result by purchasing pesetas at the official rate, so that they could lawfully be tendered to the creditor in the place of payment. It must not be overlooked that the place of payment can be varied, and that in such a case, the rate of exchange prevailing as at the due date in the substituted place of payment will be decisive.[59]

In no case is there room for the application of the "rate" for foreign blocked **18.28** accounts (ie the pseudo-rate of exchange described earlier in this chapter). As has already been noted, the rate for blocked accounts represents the price at which an external buyer can purchase the debt represented by a blocked bank account held within a State which imposes exchange controls. The contrary

---

Fund (1948) 84 F Supp 516. In the course of 1940, an insurer became entitled to a payment in reichsmarks under a contract governed by German law and requiring payment in Germany. The insurer sought to obtain judgment in Florida with a view to enforcing payment against assets which the defendant held within the jurisdiction. The reichsmark sum had a nil value in terms of US dollars at the relevant time and, consequently, the insurer recovered nothing.

[58] It has been suggested at para 16.38 above that, if performance becomes *illegal* in the intended place of payment, then it should be an implied term of the contract that payment should be made elsewhere. That position should be distinguished from the present type of case, where no question of illegality arises.

[59] The place of payment may be varied by the operation of a rule forming a part of the law applicable to the contract or by virtue of an express/implied agreement of the parties to that effect. In *Graumann v Treitel* (above) the court rightly held that the place of payment had shifted to England, but (in applying the German "official" rate) failed to follow through the natural consequences of that finding. As to an agreement to vary the place of payment, see Dr Mann's paper at (1945) 8 MLR 177. It should be remembered that (a) great care will have to be taken in ascertaining the place of payment where it has not been explicitly agreed between the parties (see para 7.84 above), (b) that the expression, "place of payment", where it is a connecting factor in a conflict of laws rule, is always interpreted in accordance with English law, and (c) that a creditor under an English judgment, though residing abroad, has only the right to be paid in England: *Re A Debtor* [1912] 1 KB 53.

argument may be illustrated by reference to *Graumann v Treitel*, the factual background to which has already been noted (see para 18.25 above). Suppose that Berlin had been the place of payment in that case, and that the debtor had made payment in accordance with the contract. The funds would have been virtually worthless to the creditor, for he could only have extracted from Germany a fraction of the nominal amount paid by the debtor. As a result, the English courts should award only such amount as the creditor would have been able to *transfer* from Germany, had payment been made there. Why, so it may be asked, should the creditor be better placed if he sues for payment in England? He should surely receive the same benefit or value which he would have received had the debtor performed his obligation in accordance with the contract? This line of argument has a superficial attraction. However, the notions of damage and restoration are not germane to the present issue. The debtor who has to discharge a promise to pay a fixed sum of money is burdened with that obligation wherever he happens to reside, and regardless of changes in his place of residence.[60] The debtor's argument that the quantum of his obligation should be reduced as a result of extraneous circumstances (in this case, a change in the creditor's residence) is entirely without merit; it is incompatible with the nature of the bargain between the parties and the concept of debt. Consequently, it is not possible to subscribe to the theory underlying some of the New York decisions in the "ticket" cases which arose as a result of the outbreak of the Second World War.[61] In one case, the plaintiff—then resident in Vienna—paid to the defendant's Vienna agency the sum of RM420 to enjoy a credit of that amount on-board one of the defendant's ships bound for New York. The outbreak of war prevented him from boarding that ship, and he thus subsequently claimed repayment of the money in US dollars at the "official" rate of exchange. The action was dismissed. After an elaborate discussion of the German currency system, the court pointed out that the defendants were liable to refund the money in Vienna and that, if they discharged their obligation there, the plaintiff would have received emigrants' blocked marks:

> Such marks are not dealt in here or elsewhere outside of Germany and were not dealt in on January 26, 1940, the date of breach. They had no market value here on January 26, 1940, and the only way such Reichsmarks could be disposed of for dollars was to offer them for sale to the Deutsche Golddiskontbank in Berlin. That bank occasionally purchased such marks and in January 1940 paid in Berlin for such marks between 1.6c. and 2c. per mark . . . The restricted internal marks

---

[60] It must, however, be observed that the English courts have occasionally failed to appreciate or to apply this principle—eg in *Ralli Bros v Compania Naviera Sota y Aznar* [1920] 2 KB 287 (CA).

[61] See, eg, *Steinfink v North German Lloyd Steamship Co* [1941] AMC 773 (New York Supreme Court).

in which the excess board money deposit was repayable is without demonstrable foreign exchange value in dollars. The plaintiff cannot, therefore, recover dollars for them here.[62]

This reasoning was followed in other cases,[63] but does not appear to be accept- **18.29** able in the light of the principles discussed earlier. The price at which blocked accounts of a certain type can be sold and thus effectively transferred to a different holder in another country is something entirely different from the rate at which the blocked currency—a unit of account—can be converted into another currency. In the cases just discussed, the debt should have retained its essential character notwithstanding the creditor's change of residence; the loss or profit which the creditor would have made had the debtor paid at the agreed place of payment should be irrelevant in enforcing the payment of a debt obligation.[64] The Swiss Federal Tribunal expressed the matter with great clarity in a case involving an English resident plaintiff who was owed RM108,046.47 by a German resident defendant. The debt was payable in Berlin, but the plaintiff sought payment in Switzerland. According to the Tribunal, the object of the conversion is:

> . . . out of the defendant's Swiss property to make available to the plaintiffs so much monetary value in Swiss currency as is required to enable them to obtain with it RM 108,046 = 47 in Berlin . . . In this connection only an objective standard should be applied. It is, therefore, irrelevant whether it would perhaps have been impossible for the plaintiffs, for special personal reasons (as Jews, foreigners, non-residents) to accept or enforce payment in Berlin or to make use of the sum of Reichsmarks paid to them. . . There is no question of transferring German property to Switzerland (in which event the plaintiffs would certainly make a loss) . . .

The Tribunal thus selected the spot rate, thereby giving effect to the general **18.30** principles noted above.[65] The same approach seems to have been adopted by the German Restitution Courts in the aftermath of the Second World War, when they had to consider whether a sum (say) in sterling paid in London represented a fair price for property in Germany which had been sold by a victim of

---

[62] *Halpern v Holland-America Line* [1942] AMC 786. In the same sense see *Zimmern v Holland-America Line* [1941] AMC 954.

[63] *Freund v Laenderbank* (1949) 111 NYS (2d) 178 affirmed without opinion (1950) 277 App Div 770, 97 NYS 2d 549, on which see Cohn, 3 (1950) Int LQ 99.

[64] It should be re-emphasised that the present discussion is concerned only with debts. The position is different where (eg) a claim in damages is made for breach of an obligation to account for money held on a blocked, foreign account: *Hughes Tool Co v United Artists Corp* 279 App Div 417, 110 NYS 2d 383, affirmed without opinion (1953) 304 NY 942, 110 NE 2d 884 where, notwithstanding some unfortunate observations, it was correctly stated that "in evaluating foreign currency the circumstance that it is blocked is a factor of prime importance which makes it impossible to use the official rate as the sole standard".

[65] 27 June 1946, *BGE* 72 III, 100.

Nazi persecution and which necessarily fell to be valued in terms of the German currency. The Supreme Restitution Court determined that the necessary conversion should be effected by reference to the rate for those blocked mark accounts which could be freely bought outside Germany and used for the purchase of German real property.[66]

18.31 It will be apparent that the use of the rate for blocked accounts (or the "pseudo" rate of exchange) would result in a windfall gain for the debtor and, thus, an injustice to the creditor. The US Court of Appeals, 2nd Circuit, avoided these consequences in *Menendez v Saks & Co*,[67] where Cuban emigrants sued New York debtors for US dollar amounts which were assumed to be payable in Cuba in accordance with Cuban law. When paid in Cuba, the dollars would have had to be surrendered to the authorities in exchange for pesos, and would thus have become unavailable to the claimants. But the plaintiffs' claim was in debt and they were thus entitled to the dollar amounts. It was irrelevant that— had payment been made in accordance with the contractual terms—the plaintiffs would have been left with inconvertible pesos.

Damages

18.32 The appropriate rate of exchange for the conversion of damages or losses expressed in a foreign currency is a matter of some difficulty. Much seems to depend upon the precise circumstances, and different types of case may arise.

18.33 In one set of cases, the damages may really be a liquidated amount. This is so, for example, where the value of goods at a certain place is to be restored. For instance, a seller fails to deliver goods at an agreed foreign location, and is therefore liable to pay damages to the buyer, which will be measured by reference to the market value of the goods in that place. In a case of this kind, it seems that the rate of exchange should be determined by reference to the rules developed above in the context of debt claims.

18.34 In other cases, the level of damages may be at large, for example, as in the case of a motor accident abroad. At least where the claimant is resident in this country, an English court will probably assess damages in sterling, with the result that the problem of the rate of exchange will generally not arise.

18.35 In another category of cases, losses expressed in a foreign currency may have to be converted into sterling for the purpose of English proceedings. In such cases,

---

[66] This rate would be more favourable to the victim of persecution than the official rate or any rate which was tainted by persecution. These alternative rates were rejected by the court—13 July 1955, *RzW* 1955, 328; 11 April 1957, *RzW* 1957, 226.

[67] (1973) 485 F 2d 1355, 1365–1367.

the plaintiff's losses should be made good by reference to the rate of exchange for sterling at which the claimant is in fact compelled to purchase the required amount of foreign currency.[68] The decision in *Arcos Ltd v London & Northern Trading Co*[69] involved an English law contract between a buyer and a seller which were both incorporated in England. The contract involved the sale of a quantity of Russian timber, but the buyer failed to take delivery. In its claim for damages, the claimant alleged that it had incurred expense as a result of the need to store the timber in Russia; it claimed a sum of 40,000 roubles, which it translated into sterling at the spot rate of 7.42 roubles to the pound. The buyer asserted that this rate was wholly fictitious, in that the real value of the rouble in terms of sterling was infinitely smaller. The court, however, upheld the contention of the seller, holding[70] "that the great bulk of exchange transactions between this country and Russia as between roubles and sterling are carried out at that (ie the spot) rate". The court rejected the buyer's assertion that rouble notes could have been purchased much more cheaply on black markets in Berlin or Switzerland, partly because the rouble expenses had to be paid in Russia and the importation of such notes was prohibited by Russian law. The decisive question appears to be—at what rate did the seller actually purchase the roubles which it had to spend in Russia? That rate represents the seller's actual loss and should thus be applied unless it could be shown that the seller failed to mitigate its loss. It would seem that the buyers could only assert a different rate if it could be shown that (a) rouble notes which were legal tender under Russian law could have been obtained from a cheaper source and (b) those notes could lawfully have been sent to Russia to pay the storage expenses. It appears that the buyer may have been able to satisfy the first condition, but failed on the second. As a final alternative, the seller might have had roubles available to it in Russia, and might have used them to meet the expenses. If the seller wished to be indemnified in London, then the London value of a rouble credit in London would appear to be the appropriate measure of damages.

Special contexts

It is necessary briefly to refer to a selection of other cases in which the need for conversion has arisen (directly or otherwise). These cases merely serve to   **18.36**

---

[68] It is assumed for these purposes that the claimant operates in sterling, but the principle would apply even in cases where the claimant conducts his business by reference to some other currency—*The Texaco Melbourne* [1994] 1 Lloyd's Rep 473 (HL). It is also assumed that the claimant has been compelled to purchase the relevant foreign currency with sterling, with the result that a direct action expressed in the foreign currency is not appropriate. The whole subject is discussed at para 5.26 above.

[69] (1935) 53 Ll L R 38.

[70] At 47.

emphasise that the answer to particular problems may depend largely upon the context in which they arise, and it is not possible to draw any particular principle from these decisions:

(a) For the purposes of a claim for salvage, it is established that the salved value of the vessel is its value at the time and place where the services came to an end. In *The Eisenach*[71], the court had to ascertain the value of a German ship towed into Dover Harbour. Shortly afterwards, the owners sold the vessel for 550,000 reichsmarks. The official rate of exchange was RM12.20 to the pound, thus producing a sterling equivalent of £45,000. However, the court refused to accept this figure as the salved value of the vessel, on a variety of grounds. First of all, the owners of the ship were required to apply the proceeds in building new tonnage in Germany, and German law prevented the owners from converting the proceeds into sterling in any event. Furthermore, in the context of transactions involving the sale and purchase of a ship, the relative values of the mark and the pound were in a very fluid and uncertain state. Since there was no reliable standard for the conversion of the sale proceeds into sterling, the court felt justified in disregarding the consequences of the sale. Under these circumstances, no problem of conversion actually had to be addressed in a definitive manner.

(b) A similar latitude is enjoyed by those who have to estimate the sterling value of a debt which is expressed in a foreign currency and is payable in a foreign country at some future date. *Re Parana Plantations Ltd*[72] involved a German law contract under which the claimant (an individual then resident in Germany) paid approximately 20,000 reichsmarks in Germany to the credit of Parana Plantations, a company incorporated in England. As a result of the outbreak of war, the performance of the contract became impossible and the claimant (by now resident in England) accordingly became entitled to the refund of the moneys paid. The company went into liquidation in 1944. The court was thus required to value the claim for the purposes of the liquidation and effectively applied what is now rule 4.86 of the Insolvency Rules 1986; in making "a just estimate" of the claim, the liquidator was allowed to adopt the rate of RM40 to the pound, which was the rate at which British soldiers could purchase marks from the field cashiers when Germany was occupied in 1945. Again, the case is of limited value in this context, because the court was concerned with a "just estimate", as opposed to an actual conversion of the claim.

(c) For taxation purposes it is often necessary to express in terms of sterling the value of property situate abroad, or of an income stream expressed in a

---

[71] [1936] 1 All ER 155; (1936) 54 Ll LR 354.
[72] [1946] 2 All ER 214.

foreign currency. Taxation is concerned with value in terms of sterling and, therefore, it would often be misleading merely to ascertain the value of the property or income in the local currency and to translate it into sterling at the spot rate. The true question is—what is the sterling value of the property or income in the United Kingdom? Thus, in connection with inheritance tax, the "value" is the estimated price which the property would fetch if sold in the open market at the relevant time[73] and this must generally be taken to refer to the open market in this country. A similar rule should apply in relation to income tax. The point has not directly arisen in this country,[74] but two American decisions should be noted. In *Leder v Commissioner of Internal Revenue*,[75] the taxpayer was obliged to treat as his own the income of an investment company in Colombia, which was "blocked". The commissioner valued the Colombian pesos at the spot rate for US dollars. This method was rejected by the Circuit Court of Appeals, which suggested that the true test was to ascertain what "economic satisfaction" the taxpayer could have received in Colombia, and that it could perhaps be measured in terms of price indices. In a later case[76] the same court applied the "commercial" rate, ie apparently, the rate at which the Brazilian income in question could be disposed of in the United States.

(d) There are other cases in which justice demands that the real purchasing power of money should be taken into account and that, accordingly, a standard of measurement other than the rate of exchange should be used. Suppose, for example, that a husband resident in the United Kingdom is obliged to support a wife resident in the United States. It is not sufficient for the English court simply to divide the husband's income on a percentage basis, for this disregards the comparative cost of living in the two countries. For the same reason, the slavish application of a spot rate of exchange would not do justice as between the parties. Wherever a person's standard of living has to be ascertained or secured in a cross-border case of this kind, it is necessary to compare the relative purchasing power of the two currencies, and not merely their strict rate of exchange.[77]

---

[73] Inheritance Tax Act 1984, s 160.

[74] See Income and Corporation Taxes Act 1988, s 584. *Inland Revenue Commissioners v Paget* [1938] 2 KB 25 and *Cross v London and Provincial Trust Ltd* [1938] 1 KB 792 deal with different points, and the latter decision is superseded by s 582 of the 1988 Act.

[75] (1943) 138 F 2d 27; see Anon, "Taxation of Foreign Currency Transaction" (1952) 61 Yale LJ 1181. The problem arises everywhere and has proved difficult. On Germany, see the decision of the Federal Finance Court, 13 September 1989, *RIW* 1990, 75 and the survey by Hartung, *RIW* 1989, 879. See generally, Langenbucher, *Die Umrechnung von Fremdwährungsgeschäften* (1988).

[76] *Edmond Weil Inc v Commissioner of Inland Revenue* 150 F 2d 950.

[77] It may well be difficult to procure the economic or statistical evidence necessary to make the analysis adequately in individual cases but this does not detract from the general principle stated

(e) What is a specific price or value of an asset is sometimes erroneously described as a certain rate of exchange. Under a system of exchange control such as existed in the United Kingdom until 1979, certain foreign capital assets belonging or accruing to a resident of the United Kingdom could be sold to other residents at a "premium", ie at a price higher than that which could be obtained in the open market. The demand by residents for foreign investments was at times so strong that the premium reached more than 100 per cent. Thus, at a time when the rate of exchange was US$2.40 to the pound, a resident holding foreign assets of US$2,400 would receive far more than the £1,000 which—by reference to the rate of exchange—was equivalent thereto. The foreign asset thus had an inherent quality, namely a "premium value". But the rate of exchange in the legal sense was the same throughout and it was thus not correct in law to speak of a premium rate.[78] It is true that it was the existence of exchange control which created the market conditions under which the premium arose, but the premium did not alter the rate of exchange as between sterling and foreign currencies. The foreign asset merely acquired a higher value in the "premium market" which existed as between resident buyers and sellers. Nor was the premium a "profit or gain derived from the sale" of the foreign asset, for even before the sale, the value of the asset in the resident market included the possibility of commanding a premium over the price available in the general market.[79]

(f) Where a person is entitled to a share in, or to a proportion of a fund, no problem of conversion will usually arise on distribution. The participants will generally be entitled to distributions in specie, and thus will receive their pro rata payments in the currency in which the fund has been maintained. Where, however, one participant is entitled to a fixed sum expressed in a particular currency which differs from that of the fund, then questions touching the rate of exchange may arise. This may, for example, occur if a testator leaves a fund of €100,000 out of which £20,000 is to be paid to one relative and the balance is to be distributed to three other relatives. In

---

in the text. The point has arisen in two contexts in Germany. First of all, in cases involving the payment of maintenance as between a resident of the Federal Republic of Germany and the German Democratic Republic many (although by no means all) courts adopted a "shopping basket" or purchasing power approach. Likewise, the Federal Republic's legislation about compensation payable to victims of Nazi persecution required the victim's non-German income to be brought into account on the basis of purchasing power equivalents (ie as opposed to the rate of exchange). Cases of this type required statistical evidence and were consistent with the principle stated in the text. For further details, see the Fifth Edition of this work, 452.

[78] Although in ordinary usage, the term "dollar premium" was frequently seen—see *Shelley v Paddock* [1980] 2 WLR 647.

[79] In this sense, see the decision of the Privy Council in *Holden v Commissioner of Inland Revenue* [1974] AC 868.

such a case, it may perhaps be inferred that the spot rate as at the date of actual payment was to be applied, so that the first relative does indeed receive £10,000 and the others share whatever euro balance may remain. This question would, however, fall to be determined by reference to the law which governed the obligation concerned.

E. Absence of a Rate of Exchange

The absence of a rate of exchange indicating the relative values of two currencies may have either an absolute or a relative character.   **18.37**

Discontinuance of quotations may be absolute where dealings in a particular currency are suspended altogether. This would usually occur only in the course of a revolution or civil war when, at least temporarily, there is nowhere any market for the currency of the country concerned; for no one can be sure whether money issued by a former government will be respected by an incoming regime. What is the position of the creditor who (as a result of a contract entered into prior to the suspension) becomes entitled to a sum in sterling or dollars to be calculated by reference to the rate of exchange for the currency concerned? No rate of exchange will be available for the day in question, so the court must presumably adopt either (a) the rate which prevailed immediately prior to the suspension or (b) the rate in force on the day on which the suspension was lifted, if this has occurred. The first solution should probably be applied, because the law presumes that a particular state of affairs is continuing unless it has been proved to have changed. Thus, in one American case[80] it became necessary to determine the value of cotton at Barcelona on 6 October 1936 in terms of US dollars. However, due to the outbreak of the Spanish Civil War, no exchange rates were available between 22 September and 13 November 1936. On 21 September, the rate was $0.1365 to the peseta; when dealings resumed in November, the peseta was significantly depreciated. The court held that the rate of exchange as at 21 September should be applied, with the result that the cotton had (or was deemed to have) the same value in US dollars on 6 October as it had on 21 September.[81]   **18.38**

---

[80] *Pape Williams & Co v Home Insurance Co* 139 F 2d 131 and [1944] AMC 51.

[81] See also *Melzer v Zimmermann* 118 Misc (1922) Rep 407, 194 NYS 222, affirmed without opinion (1923) 198 NYS 932 and *Birge-Forbes Co v Heye* (1920) 251 US 317, 325. The difficulties caused by the absence of regular dealings caused practical difficulties as between the Federal Republic of Germany and the former German Democratic Republic. In one case, the Federal Supreme Court thought that the conversion should be effected on the basis of relative purchasing power: 10 July 1954, *BGHZ* 14, 212. However, it appears that the majority of later decisions adopted a rate of 1:1. See also Federal Supreme Court, 13 February 163, *RzW* 1963, 449.

18.39   Against that background, if a rate for the conversion of hostile currencies has to be found with reference to a date during the war, how is this to be achieved in the absence of direct market quotations between the two currencies at issue?

18.40   In some cases, specific legislation may provide the answer to this valuation question. Under Article 1(iv)(d) of the Trading with the Enemy (Custodian) Order 1939, the Treasury could determine the rate appropriate for payments to the Custodian of Enemy Property.[82] But in the absence of such a rate, the difficulties may become acute. However, since the currencies of both countries will be quoted in the markets of neutral States on the (wartime) date with reference to which the conversion is required to be made, it seems appropriate to use a cross-rate derived from that market. Thus, if a rate between the reichsmark and sterling was required on a date in 1943, it might have been fair to ascertain the number of (neutral) Swiss francs which could have been purchased in Zurich with the stated number of reichsmarks. The resultant number of Swiss francs would then be converted into sterling on the same basis. Although plainly not a perfect equation, this would probably have been the most objective means of effecting the comparison, and would therefore have operated fairly as between the parties.[83] Conversion through the currency of a neutral country is supported by the decision in *Pollard v Herries*,[84] from which it may be deduced that the court would have resort to "the indirect course of exchange". The solution also finds support in an analogy to be drawn from the sale of goods: where for the purpose of assessing damages it is necessary to ascertain the market value of goods at the place of delivery, but there is no available market at that place, the value at the nearest available place will usually constitute the measure of damages.[85] The solution does, however, only retain its attraction if the neutral market truly produces an independent rate; if that market effectively reflects official rates set by enemy legislation or action, then an English court would have to look for some other standard of valuation—for example, the pre-war rate which (as noted above) would be applied in the case of an absolute suspension of dealings.

---

[82] Such a rate may in practice be applied in a broader context where private debts are involved—see *Bank Mizrahi v The Chief Execution Officer, Tel Aviv* (1943) Palestine Law Reports 364.

[83] Courts in the US have instead tended to adopt the first rate available after the cessation of hostilities: *Sutherland v Mayer* (1926) 271 US 272; *International Silk Guild v Rogers* (1958) 262 F 2d 219; *Aratani v Kennedy* (1963) 317 F 2d 161. These cases appear to apply only where payment is to be made in the US. See also Cohn (1962) 50 Geo LJ 513. This solution is unattractive, in that it is arbitrary and lacks the fairness which would flow from the solution suggested in the text.

[84] (1803) 3 B & P 335.

[85] *Rodocanachi v Milburn* (1886) 18 QB 67, 76; *The Arpad* [1934] P 189 (*CA). The suggested approach is also supported by the practice of the Mixed Arbitral Tribunals—see Anglo-German Mixed Arbitral Tribunal in MAT iv (1925) 261 (*Catty v German Government*) and vi (1927) 17 (*Strauss v German Government*).

Notwithstanding the difficulties which may arise in the search for any form of   **18.41**
rate of exchange under these circumstance, it should not generally be permissible to apply a "black market" rate for these purposes, ie a rate arising from
transactions which are illegal under the local law.[86] There may be extreme cases
in which public policy may lead the English court to disregard the illegality
under the local law, although every country is allowed to regulate its own
currency and it is thus very difficult to envisage the circumstances under which
such laws could be disregarded.[87] Courts in the United States do not appear to
adhere to the foregoing principles and adopt an approach which some might
describe as more robust. Thus in *Cinelli v Commissioners of Internal Revenue*,[88]
4,314,000 Italian lire, representing the value of an Italian estate on 1 May 1942,
had to be assessed in terms of US dollars. The official rate (surprisingly held to
exist at that time) was 19 lire to the dollar. The so-called commercial rate (ie the
black market rate) was 719 lire to the dollar. It was held that the official rate
"had no relationship to actual value" and that the black market rate should thus
be applied. More recently, the problem arose in those cases in which customers
of the Saigon branches of American banks were allowed to recover Vietnamese
dong credits (into which the original Vietnamese piasters had been converted by
application of the recurrent link) from the head office in the United States.[89]
The courts treated the date of demand in the United States as the date of the
breach and, thus, as the date by reference to which a rate of exchange had to be
ascertained. In one case[90] there was in April 1975 no rate for the dong in
New York. The Court of Appeals, second Circuit directed that the District
Court should determine the "true value" of the piaster so as to provide "just
compensation" for the plaintiff. For this purpose, regard was to be had to "the
underground market for dollars in Saigon" or alternatively the value of the dong

---

[86] Thus, where a resident of Poland was entitled to maintenance, she was entitled to be paid in
Deutsche marks because it was illegal to import zlotys into Poland. When considering the rate of
exchange which necessarily had to be applied as a consequence, the court noted that "the creditor
cannot be expected to exchange the DM at the black market rate": Federal Supreme Court,
1 April 1987, *IPRspr* 1987, No. 66.

[87] On the sovereign rights of individual States in this area, see Ch 19, below.

[88] (1974) 502 F 2d 695.

[89] Two points may be observed in passing. First of all, if the obligation to repay the deposits
had been terminated under Vietnamese law (by which the banker-customer contracts were presumably governed) then the English courts would not have enforced the depositiors' claims—see
the Rome Convention, Art 10(1) and *Arab Bank v Barclays Bank DCO* [1954] AC 495 (HL).
Secondly, the American cases led to new legislation, which insulated US banks from this type of
claim in the absence of agreement to the contrary.

[90] *Vishipco Line v Chase Manhattan Bank* (1985) 754 F 2d 452, following upon (1981) 660 F
2d 854. This may not correspond to the payment date rule, which has been discussed at para 7.37
above. However, in the case of a bank deposit, it may be said that the claim to the US dollar
amount crystallised as at the date of demand, and that interest at US dollar rates would therefore
provide appropriate compensation for the continuing delay.

in Singapore or Hong Kong. In a similar case, the District Court for the Eastern District of Michigan held[91] that while there was an "effective rate of exchange" of 2.39 dong to the dollar in November 1980 (the date of the assumed breach), there was no New York market rate and therefore the proper rate was the unofficial or "black market rate" of 17 dong to the dollar, for the official rate was inapplicable "where currencies are blocked or when the official rate otherwise does not apply to the transactions at hand".

18.42 It is submitted that, in the absence of a rate for dongs in the United States, it would have been the correct solution to have resort to the rate prevailing in any other financial centre. No doubt, in the cases just described, the courts were striving to achieve justice between the parties under very difficult circumstances. But notwithstanding that worthy objective, it will in nearly every case be inappropriate to apply a rate of exchange which can only be obtained by means of criminal activity in the country in which the market is located; whatever the commercial or other merits of such a rate may be, it is suggested that a court should not give effect to a rate ascertained by reference to a domestic market which exists in defiance of the monetary sovereignty of the State concerned.

---

[91] *Trinh v Citibank* (1985) 623 F Supp 1526, affirmed without reference to the point (1988) 850 F 2d 1164.

PART V

PUBLIC INTERNATIONAL
LAW OF MONEY

INTRODUCTION

The role of the State in the creation and regulation of a monetary system has been considered in various contexts. The chapters comprised within Part V are intended to explain the framework of international law within which the State may exercise its monetary powers.

Intro.5.01

It has been noted on several occasions that a State enjoys sovereignty over its monetary affairs. Yet in the monetary field, as in any other, sovereignty is not unlimited. International law sets certain minimum requirements as to acceptable conduct in this sphere and these must be explored. Furthermore, concepts of sovereignty do not merely involve a collection of rights which a State may enjoy; they also connote a set of corresponding obligations which are owed to other States. If a State has the right to establish and to regulate a monetary system, then it must respect the right of other States to do likewise. Such rules of customary international law as may exist can, of course, be varied by treaty, and States can agree to submit to additional obligations by that means.

Intro.5.02

The present Part will therefore review the content of both the rights and obligations which international law confers and imposes on States with respect to their own currencies and those of other countries:

Intro.5.03

(a) Chapter 19 will accordingly consider the general nature and consequences of monetary sovereignty, and the extent to which the exercise of that sovereignty is subject to control by rules of customary international law;

(b) Chapters 20 and 21 review the extent to which a State is required to respect or even to protect the monetary systems and institutions of other States;

(c) Chapter 22 examines the extent to which States have agreed to regulate the conduct of their monetary affairs by means of bilateral and multilateral treaties; and

(d) Chapter 23 will consider the special questions which may arise in the context of monetary obligations incurred on an interstate basis.

19

MONETARY SOVEREIGNTY

A. Introduction

The State theory of money has been discussed in some detail earlier in this **19.01**
book.[1] The State theory proceeds on the assumption that every State is entitled
to create and define a monetary system and to issue money in pursuance of it. As
a result, money is an institution created by or under the authority of a domestic
legal system, and falls within the jurisdiction of the issuing State.[2] The present
chapter will consider the extent to which customary international law underpins
the national right to issue money and to organise a monetary system. It will also
consider the extent to which action taken in the monetary sphere may be open
to challenge on international or constitutional grounds.

---

[1] See Ch 1 above.

[2] As will be seen, even the creation of the euro is ultimately derived from an exercise of national
monetary sovereignty by the individual, participating Member States. On this point, see para
31.03 below.

B. The Principle of Monetary Sovereignty

19.02 The State's undeniable sovereignty over its own currency is traditionally recognised by public international law; to the power granted by municipal law there corresponds an international right, to the exercise of which other States cannot, as a rule, object.[3] In other words, if a State enjoys sovereignty over its monetary system, then no international wrong or any resultant claim can arise from any action taken by that State to control or manage that system. As the Permanent Court of International Justice noted,[4] "it is indeed a generally accepted principle that a state is entitled to regulate its own currency". Domestic courts have, on occasion, noted the same principle.[5] It follows that money, like tariffs, taxation, or the admission of aliens is one of those matters which *prima facie* fall within the domestic jurisdiction of individual States.[6]

19.03 It must also follow that, subject to such exceptions as customary international law[7] or treaties[8] have grafted upon this rule, the municipal legislator is free to define the currency of his country,[9] to decide whether or not it should be pegged to another currency,[10] to determine the means by which monetary and exchange

---

[3] This passage was approved by the Foreign Claims Settlement Commission of the US in *Claim of Boyle*, Annual Report of the Commission for 1968, p 81. For a brief but very useful discussion of monetary sovereignty under modern conditions, see Treves, "Monetary Sovereignty Today" in Giovanoli (ed) *International Monetary Law—Issues for the New Millennium* (Oxford University Press, 2000).

[4] *Serbian and Brazilian Loan Case* (1929) PCIJ Series A, Nos 20–21, 44.

[5] See, eg, *Naamloze Vernootschap Suiker-Fabriek "Wono-Aseh" v Chase National Bank of City of New York* (1953) 111 F Supp 833, 845—"control of the national currency and of foreign exchange is a necessary attribute of sovereignty".

[6] Article 2(7) of the Charter of the United Nations. States have, of course, limited their domestic sovereignty in all of these areas, through both bilateral and multilateral treaties. But this does not detract from the general rule of customary international law stated in the text. Further, it should not be thought that national monetary legislation is entirely immune from consideration at an international level, merely because the State possesses sovereignty in that field—see the *Case of Certain Norwegian Loans* [1957] ICJ Rep 9. This case is considered at para 19.19 below.

[7] The potential bases of challenge to monetary legislation are considered later in this chapter.

[8] See the discussion in Ch 22 below.

[9] Since the issue of a foreign currency would be a sovereign act of the foreign country concerned occurring within its own borders, the State concerned would be entitled to immunity before the English court in relation to that activity: State Immunity Act 1978, s 1. Alternatively, the subject matter of any dispute would be non-justiciable under the principles explained by the House of Lords in *Buttes Oil & Gas Co v Hammer (No 3)* [1982] AC 888. However, if the notes concerned were to breach a patent held by a third party, then it seems that, in that respect, the foreign State could not rely upon these protections. The claimant's proceedings would arise from the State's choice of printing materials, not from the exercise of its sovereign right to issue a currency: see State Immunity Act 1978, s 7 and *A Ltd v B Bank* [1997] 6 Bank LR 85.

[10] For further discussion of currency "peg" arrangements and their consistency with international law, see para 22.18 below. The structure of a currency pegging arrangement is discussed in para 33.14 below.

rate policies are to be defined and implemented, to devalue or revalue the currency,[11] to allow or prohibit the use of foreign currencies within its borders,[12] to impose exchange controls, or to take other measures affecting monetary relations. Customary international law does not normally fetter the municipal legislator's discretion in these matters or characterise his measures as an international wrong[13] for which he could be held responsible, just as it leaves him the freedom to decide whether he wishes to introduce a particular type of tax and whether he levies tax at a particular rate. And if a State enjoys sovereignty over its currency and monetary system, it must necessarily follow that, as a matter of international law, other States are bound to recognise that sovereignty and the consequences of its exercise.[14] Yet this statement, whilst perhaps attractive in its simplicity, may appear to overstate the position and some further examination of these principles thus becomes necessary.

In so far as the currency of an issuing State is concerned, it may be said that the **19.04** concept of monetary sovereignty exhibits features of both an internal and an external character. "Internal" sovereignty includes the rights to define the monetary system, to devalue the currency, and to operate a monetary policy; "external" sovereignty includes the right to impose a system of exchange control. In broad terms, the exercise of an internal monetary power cannot be questioned, and must be respected, by other States. For example, as has been shown, the obligation to recognise the monetary sovereignty of other States lies at the heart of the *lex monetae* principle.[15] There will thus generally be no basis upon which a State or its courts can impugn the decision of another State to withdraw or replace its currency or generally to reorganise its monetary system,[16] nor will the monetary policy of a particular State be open to legal challenge in another State. In contrast, the exercise of "external" monetary sovereignty—such as the

---

[11] On devaluation/revaluation, see paras 2.41–2.47 above.

[12] It must follow from this rule that a foreign State has no positive right to have its notes circulated in the UK, for such a right would be inconsistent with this country's sovereignty over its own monetary system. In principle, English law determines what may be done with foreign bank notes in this country: *A Ltd v B Bank* [1997] 6 Bank LR 85. This rule would, however, be inapplicable to the euro and other Community currencies, for the UK is under an obligation to permit the free movement of capital and payments. That particular subject is discussed at para 33.32 below.

[13] This sentence was approved by the International Court of Justice in the *Case concerning Rights of Nationals of the United States in Morocco*, [1952] ICJ Rep 176. The case is discussed at para 22.07 below.

[14] This rule may in some respects follow from the sovereign equality of States and the correlative duty of non-intervention. On the whole subject, see Brownlie, *Principles of Public International Law* (Oxford, 6th edn, 2003) ch 14.

[15] See Ch 13 above.

[16] For a possible exception to this statement in the context of a withdrawal from monetary union, see Ch 32 below. This exception, does, however, only arise because of specific treaty obligations undertaken by the issuing State.

imposition of a system of exchange control—necessarily has a greater impact upon other States and their nationals. It is thus perhaps unsurprising that international law pays greater attention to the precise scope of external monetary sovereignty, with the result that the purported exercise of such sovereignty may be more susceptible to challenge.[17] Nevertheless, the principle remains that a proper exercise of such sovereignty cannot be impugned before any domestic or international tribunal.[18]

19.05 The principle of monetary sovereignty becomes a little more obscure when one considers the ability of a State to determine the extent to which *foreign* monetary laws are to be applicable within the borders of that State.[19] There can be no doubt that (a) customary international law allows each State to devise its own system of private international law and (b) the extent to which foreign monetary laws may be applied is a matter which can legitimately be regulated by such a system. Yet it is suggested that such rules must, as a matter of public international law, demonstrate a sufficient degree of consistency with the principles of monetary sovereignty just discussed. The precise extent of that requirement is by no means clear, but a few general points may be made. First of all, if a State has the sovereign right to organise its monetary system, this must include the right to replace that currency and to specify the basis of conversion ("recurrent link") between the old and the new units; this position reflects the principle of nominalism, which has been discussed earlier.[20] Secondly, the obligation to recognise such a reorganisation is imposed by international law; it must thus have practical consequences which go beyond the mere recognition of a factual state of affairs. For example, in the view of the present writer, an obligation to recognise a change in the currency system of another country necessarily connotes a duty to recognise that contractual obligations expressed in the former currency remain valid when converted into the new currency at the rate prescribed by the recurrent link, and that they should be enforceable by judicial proceedings to the like extent; what is the practical value of the former obligation if the latter duty does not exist? It must therefore follow that customary international law requires that monetary relationships continue to be effective under these circumstances, and that a monetary substitution alone cannot be used as a basis for the termination of monetary obligations expressed in the

---

[17] See, generally, the discussion of exchange control regulation in Part IV above.

[18] Whilst it is hoped that statements of this kind may be found to be helpful, it cannot be overlooked that, in some respects, they beg their own question and are not necessarily of great assistance in the sphere of international law. The problem is noted by Brownlie, *Principles of Public International Law* (Oxford University Press, 6th edn, 2003) 290.

[19] In the exercise of its external monetary sovereignty, a State may be able to prohibit the use of foreign money within its own borders, but that is a different point—see, *A Ltd v B Bank* [1997] 6 Bank LR 85.

[20] See Part III above.

former currency units.[21] On the other hand, customary international law does not require other States to enforce the consequences of every financial adjustment made by an issuing State. This point is illustrated by reference to a revalorisation of debts; the legislator or judiciary of a particular State may take the view that the question of the revalorisation of a depreciated debt should be subject to the *lex monetae*, whilst in another State the same question may be determined by the law applicable to the debt.[22] Customary international law contains no rule which would prescribe the application of one or the other solution; it is thus open to a State and its courts to adopt either solution when formulating an appropriate rule as part of its system of private international law.

It must be said that the principle of monetary sovereignty has not always been unquestioned, and various attempts have been made to limit the obligation of a State to recognise the right of other States to regulate their currencies and to determine their monetary policy at their discretion. Thus: **19.06**

(a) in a case decided in 1688, an English court refused to give effect to the depreciation of the Portuguese currency, because this would reduce the effective value of a bill drawn in London and Portugal could not alter the value of property in England;[23]

(b) in 1800, the United States protested to the Spanish Government against the debasement of the Spanish currency, complaining that the value of debts expressed in that currency had thereby been significantly reduced;[24] and

(c) in France and countries influenced by its legal system, it is occasionally stated that "les lois monétaires sont strictement territoriales". Statements of this kind are easy to make but difficult to define and apply. Nevertheless, the Supreme Court of Syria held that a contract for the payment of "francs" made between the Syrian Government and an Egyptian firm was subject to an international rule by which legal tender legislation, enacted after the date of the contract, applied only within the territory of the legislating State and did not affect contracts with a foreigner.[25]

---

[21] In terms of English law, this means that a monetary substitution alone cannot be regarded as giving rise to the application of the doctrine of frustration. Since this particular point was of special importance in the context of monetary union, this subject is discussed in more detail in Ch 30 below.

[22] This is the position adopted in England. On the general subject of revalorisation, see para 13.09 above.

[23] *Du Costa v Cole* (1688) Skin 272. The case is noted in more depth in the context of the principle of nominalism—see para 13.07(e) above.

[24] Moore, *A Digest of International Law* (1906) vi, 754. On another case, the facts of which are not entirely clear, see p 279 of the same volume.

[25] Decision of 30 December 1931: *Annual Digest* (1931–2) Case No 151. To similar effect, see Dupuis, *Rec* 3 (1930, ii) 164.

19.07   Whilst these attempts to limit the international recognition of monetary changes are of historical interest, there can be no doubt that they are now obsolete, and—as already noted—that States are now under an international obligation to recognise the sovereignty of other States in the monetary field. It should not, however, be overlooked that the rules of customary international law will give way to any countervailing treaty obligations, and that in some respects the content of customary law may itself be shaped by international treaties which have won general acceptance. The EC Treaty provides an example of the former category[26] whilst the latter category is represented by the Articles of Agreement of the International Monetary Fund.[27] Subject to that reservation, however, the present chapter is principally concerned with general rules of customary international law.

19.08   Having defined the nature and scope of monetary sovereignty under international law, it is now proposed to illustrate the application of that principle in four particular types of circumstances.

Depreciation

19.09   As regards the international effects of an internal monetary depreciation,[28] it has been explained that all monetary obligations—whether expressed in the domestic or a foreign currency—are subject to the principle of nominalism.[29] The promise to pay 10,000 Swiss francs is satisfied by the payment of whatever are declared to be 10,000 Swiss francs by Swiss law as in effect at the time when payment falls due. This rule of municipal law is, for all practical purposes, universally accepted. In order to be consistent with it, public international law must follow suit; if under all relevant municipal systems, effect is to be given to the Swiss monetary law, then it must necessarily follow that Switzerland does not violate any international duty by the exercise of its sovereign powers over its own currency. The available authorities establish complete harmony between international and domestic law on this point by recognising a State's right to allow its currency to depreciate.[30] Thus in *Adam's Case*, a British subject held bonds issued by an American railway company and suffered a loss as a result of the issue of greenbacks and the consequent depreciation of the dollar; having

---

[26]   See the discussion on the European Community in the final part of this chapter.

[27]   See generally Ch 22 below. Those provisions of the Fund Agreement which seek to regulate the imposition of exchange controls have already been considered in Ch 15 above.

[28]   On the distinction between depreciation and devaluation, see Ch 2 above.

[29]   The principle of nominalism has been discussed in detail in Part III above.

[30]   In other words, customary international law does not impose an obligation to intervene in the markets in an effort to prevent the depreciation of the national currency. Obligations of this kind can, of course, arise under the terms of a treaty—see, eg, the discussion of the European Monetary System in Ch 25 below.

regard to the principles just noted, the fall in value of the dollar could not constitute the basis of a claim against the United States, for it had committed no international wrong.[31] Likewise, if a State elected to abandon the gold standard—thus causing a depreciation of the currency—persons holding bank-notes prior to the abandonment cannot claim against the issuing State for the resultant loss, for a State has the sovereign right to manage its currency in this way, and thus, no wrong was committed as a result of a decision to abandon the gold standard.[32] Finally, in a case which came before the Supreme Court of Germany, an Italian creditor whose German debtor had repaid a loan in depreciated German marks claimed to be entitled to payment on a gold basis. He alleged the existence of a rule of public international law to the effect that loans made by foreigners were invariably repayable according to their gold value. Such a rule would plainly fly in the face of the nominalistic principle. Referring to the practice in England and other countries, the Supreme Court summarily disposed of the creditor's manifestly absurd contention.[33]

Devaluation

It must follow from the points just made that, as a rule, a State is within its rights to bring about the (external) devaluation of its currency, for example, by varying its system of exchange controls such that the exchange value of the domestic currency is reduced, or by taking any other step which might achieve the same end. A State may not only allow its currency to depreciate; it may also take active steps to achieve that end, provided that it does not act in a discrimi-natory manner.[34] This right again flows from the universal acceptance of the principle of nominalism, and has been stated with great precision by the Government of Canada:[35] "Un principe bien établi en droit international exhonore les gouvernements de toute responsabilité pour les pertes dues à une devaluation de leurs devises, pourvu que cette devaluation s'accomplisse sans discrimination."

19.10

---

[31] Moore, *International Arbitrations* (1898) iii, 3066, a decision of the American-British Claims Commission established under the terms of a Treaty of 5 May 1871.

[32] *Muller v Germany* (1923) 2 *Receuil des decisions des tribunaux arbitraux mixtes* 32. In terms of private international law, this decision is reflected in such cases as *R v International Trustees for the Protection of Bondholders AG* [1937] AC 500 (HL) and in *Norman v Baltimore & Ohio Railroad Co* (1934) 294 US 240.

[33] 6 June 1928 *RGZ* 121, 203 and *Annual Digest* 1927–8, Case No 230.

[34] This general rule of customary international law would be subject to any treaty engagements to the contrary. For an example of such an obligation undertaken by the UK under the EC Treaty, see para 31.30 below.

[35] Statement of 7 December 1966 reported by Gottlieb (1967) *Canadian Yearbook of International Law* 268.

19.11   This rule seems to have been followed by the European Commission of Human Rights,[36] by the French Foreign Claims Commissions,[37] and repeatedly affirmed by the Foreign Claims Settlement Commission of the United States.[38] A few treaties which apply a different rule provide an insufficient basis upon which to vary the general customary rule just stated.[39]

Non-revalorisation

19.12   It is within a State's discretion to decide whether or not it should legislate with a view to revalorising debts which have arisen on the level of private law[40] and which, as a result of the depreciation of the State's currency, have become worthless or at least considerably reduced in intrinsic value. This follows from the apparent absence of any rule of customary international law which requires individual States to provide for the revalorisation of their currencies under these circumstances.

---

[36] Fawcett, *Application of the European Convention on Human Rights* (Clarendon Press, 2nd edn, 1969) 407–9. In *Kannapathipillai v Anuradhapura Preservation Board* (Court of Appeal of Sri Lanka, 2 October 1978), the court had to deal with a domestic contract with the Government of that country. During the course of the contract, the Government devalued the rupee by 20%, and the contractor claimed a compensating uplift in the contract price. Relying upon the decision in *Treseder-Griffin v Co-operative Insurance Society* [1956] 2 QB 127, the court reasserted the principle of nominalism ("a rupee is a rupee whatever its international value") and rejected any general right to a compensating payment, even though the contract had been made with the party responsible for the devaluation. However, on the facts, it was found that the Government had separately contracted to pay the uplift amount.

[37] B.H. Weston, *International Claims: Post-war French Practice* (Syracuse University Press, 1971) 135.

[38] *Claim of Tabar* (1953) Int LR 211. As noted in the text, the State may incur liability if it seeks to depreciate its currency in a manner which is discriminatory or deliberately injurious to foreigners or a particular class of them—see *Claim of Zuk* (1958) ii Int LR 284 which was followed in numerous subsequent cases such as *Claim of Mascotte*, ibid, 275; *Claim of Bondareff*, ibid, 286; *Claim of Malan*, ibid, 290; *Claim of Chobady*, ibid, 292; *Claim of Mureson*, ibid, 294; *Claim of Endreny*, ibid, 278.

[39] The Peace Treaties of 1920 provided that debts due to nationals of victorious nations were payable at the pre-war rate of exchange or in gold (Art 296(4)(d) of the Treaty of Versailles; Art 248 of the Treaty of St Germain; Art 176 of the Treaty of Neuilly; Art 231 of the Treaty of Trianon). In contrast, the Paris Peace Treaties of 1947 contain no such provisions; cl 14 of the Financial Agreement between the UK and Italy made in Rome on 17 April 1947 provides that the rate of exchange for the payment of live debts "will be that current when the debt became due". It should be added that Borchard, *State Insolvency and Foreign Bondholders*, Vol I (Beard Books, 1951) 137 suggests that a devaluation arising from "a deliberate act on the part of the debtor government" may be a ground for international responsibility even in the absence of discrimination against foreign nationals. Wortley, *Expropriation in Public International Law* (1959) 107 expresses approval. However, for the reasons given in the text, there is no justification for this view.

[40] The position may be different where a debt arises under the terms of a treaty or is likewise governed by international law. The point is discussed in Ch 23 below.

It is possible to state these views because the number of countries which have **19.13** taken care of the effects of monetary depreciation by revalorisation is small.[41] The number of countries which have objected to a failure to revalorise on the part of other States is even smaller; even the German Supreme Court—which can fairly be described as the foremost protagonist of the fundamental equities of revalorisation—refused to apply *ordre public* in favour of a German national who was entitled to payment of an old mark debt under a contract governed by the laws of Czechoslovakia, whose laws did not provide for revalorisation.[42] Likewise, at the end of the Second World War, several States in South-East Asia introduced legislation to revalorise debts which had been discharged by worthless Japanese military notes, but the decision of the Philippines not to take such a step was within the scope of the discretion afforded to it by customary international law, and thus could not constitute an international wrong.[43] A similar situation arose in relation to French franc securities issued in London by the French Government between 1915 and 1918.[44] At the time of the issue, the sterling equivalent of these obligations amounted to some £50 million, but the depreciation of the franc reduced this figure to £13.5 million by 1930. The British Government sought an "equitable measure of compensation" for the British holders, partly because of the special circumstances under which the securities were issued and partly because the French Government itself demanded payment in gold francs from its own debtor governments. The French Government declined to consider the matter, on the grounds that "The determination both of the financial policy of a State, so long as that policy is not disputed on grounds of law, and of any measures of equity which may be considered proper to take in connection with that policy, is entirely a matter for the State in question, *i.e.* in the present case, for France." This statement effectively asserts the broad national discretion in the monetary field which has already been described in this section, and it is perhaps significant that the British Government elected not to pursue the matter beyond this point. Certainly, the claim against France appears to have been based upon a general appeal to notions of fairness, rather than upon any specific rule of international law.

---

[41] See the discussion in Ch 9 above, in the context of nominalism and liquidated sums.

[42] 14 December 1927, *RGZ* 119, 259, see also 25 June 1926, *RGZ* 114, 171, a very special case.

[43] The Supreme Court of the Philippines rightly arrived at this conclusion in *Gibbs v Rodriguez* (1951) Int LR 661, following and developing *Haw Pia v China Banking Corp* (1951) Int LR 642. In "Concerning the Haw Pia Case" (1949) 24 Philippine LJ 141, C.C. Hyde asserts that the failure to revalorise constituted "internationally illegal conduct on the part of the Philippine Government which is productive of a solid claim for compensation on behalf of alien nationals or creditors who suffered loss as a direct consequence of such decision". For the reasons given in the text, it is suggested that the decision of the Philippines Supreme Court was plainly right, and that the criticism is therefore misplaced.

[44] On the correspondence, see Cmd 3779. See also H. Samuel, *The French Default* (1930).

19.14 It is true that a different result may be required in the very specific cases which the widespread practice of States treats in a privileged manner. This has occurred in the context of pensions. Thus, when the value of pensions payable to British pensioners of Argentine companies fell by some 60 per cent as a result of the devaluation of the Argentine peso in 1955, the Argentine Government substantially acceded to a British request for "an equitable solution".[45] Whilst this may reflect a rule of customary international law, it must be said that it has not always been applied consistently.

Exchange control

19.15 While it does not seem ever to have been seriously doubted that, in principle, a State is entitled to abrogate gold or similar protective clauses,[46] there is much authority in support of the further right to introduce exchange control with all its incidental ramifications.

19.16 The British Government,[47] the Government of Canada,[48] and the Government of the United States[49] have frequently stated their acceptance of this position. Thus, Canada "recognises the right of each country to control its foreign exchange resources, and restrictions of this nature, so long as they are not discriminating against Canadian citizens, cannot give rise to a claim".[50] The Foreign Claims Settlement Commission of the United States has propounded the same principle on a number of occasions.[51] Acceptance of this principle is also implicit in a number of treaties which have restricted or regulated the national right to impose exchange controls, for it would clearly be unnecessary to constrain the exercise of a right which did not exist.[52] It follows that national laws requiring the surrender of foreign currency,[53] imposing restrictions on the

---

[45] See *Hansard*, HC Deb, vol 552, col 72 (14 May 1956); E. Lauterpacht (1956) v ICLQ 426.

[46] Although, see Borchard, *State Insolvency and Foreign Bondholders*, Vol I (Beard Books, 1951) 138.

[47] See, eg, *Hansard*, HC vol 522, col 1633 (14 May 1956).

[48] See the two statements reproduced by Gotlieb "Canadian Practice in International Law", (1965) *Canadian Yearbook of International Law* 328.

[49] See, eg, Hyde (1945) i *International Law* 690–2. See also the statement of the Department of State (1 March 1961) noted in (1965) AJIL 165, which emphasises that "the right to regulate foreign exchange does not, however, include the right to discriminate against nationals of a particular country, or to deprive an owner of an account of all rights of ownership". See also the Report of the War Claims Commission set out in Whiteman, *Digest of International Law (1963–73)* viii, 981.

[50] See the materials mentioned in note 35 above.

[51] The main decision is *Claim of Tabar* (1953) Int LR 211. Later decisions are mentioned in the following notes.

[52] A major example is provided by the provisions in the EC Treaty dealing with the free movement of capital and payments. This subject is discussed in Ch 25 below.

[53] See, eg, Exchange Control Act 1947, s 2, discussed in Ch 14 above, and see *Maeyer v Federal Republic* Arbitral Commission on Property Rights and Interests in Germany, Collections of Decisions, iv, 173.

export of currency,[54] or modifying contractual terms in support of a system of exchange control[55] are not inconsistent with customary international law. The principle of national sovereignty likewise serves to legitimise sanctions against another State by means of blocking or freezing measures.[56] It should, however, be said that—so far as customary law is concerned—this particular aspect of monetary sovereignty does not entitle a State to exercise any degree of direct control over transactions which involve its currency but which occur abroad and are governed by a foreign system of law; this is so even though any payment made in respect of that transaction would ultimately have to be reflected by account movements on the clearing system which is operated within that State.[57]

Whilst the principles just discussed appear to be fairly clear, it is necessary to proceed with some caution in considering the applicable customary international law in this sphere. Treaties dealing with the imposition of exchange controls and similar matters have tended to be of a multilateral character[58] and are thus in themselves capable of altering the content of customary international law. As a result of these developments, it may now be said that customary international law recognises it as illegal to restrict transfers for current transactions, or transfers of capital in those cases in which capital has been introduced into a State's economy with its explicit approval and on terms providing for the retransfer of capital, profits, and any compensation.[59]   **19.17**

C. Monetary Sovereignty and International Legal Disputes

The fact that the regulation of its currency falls within the sovereign and domestic jurisdiction of a State does not mean that the subject matter is entirely   **19.18**

---

[54] See the two decisions mentioned by Whiteman (n 49 above) 988–9.

[55] See, eg, Exchange Control Act 1947, s 33, discussed in Ch 14 above; *Re Helbert Wagg & Co Ltd* [1956] Ch 323; *Kahler v Midland Bank* [1950] AC 24. *Claim of Kuhn*, decided by the American-Mexican Claims Commission (1948) and mentioned by Whiteman, *Digest of International Law* (1963–73) viii, 990.

[56] The consistency of a sanctions regime with international law is considered in Ch 17 above. Whilst the right to impose a system of exchange controls may be said to flow from the external *monetary* sovereignty of a State, the ability to implement a sanctions regime is perhaps derived from rather broader considerations of national sovereignty (ie the right to conduct foreign policy).

[57] Authority for this statement is provided by the decision in *Libyan Arab Foreign Bank v Bankers Trust Co* [1989] 1 QB 728, which is discussed in Ch 7 above. For another view, see Treves, "Monetary Sovereignty Today" in Giovanoli (ed) *International Monetary Law—Issues for the New Millennium* (Oxford University Press, 2000).

[58] Obvious examples include the Articles of Agreement of the IMF and those provisions of the EC Treaty dealing with capital and payments.

[59] The relevant provisions of the Articles of Agreement of the IMF are considered in Ch 22 below.

withdrawn from any control by international law. Monetary laws are fully capable of giving rise to legal disputes concerning international law within the meaning of Article 36(2) of the Statute of the International Court of Justice.

19.19 It would not be necessary to state so platitudinous a proposition, but for the failure to appreciate it which lies at the heart of some of the arguments presented to the International Court of Justice in the *Case of Certain Norwegian Loans*.[60] Before the First World War, both the State of Norway and various Norwegian undertakings issued bonds in various European financial centres. All of these bonds were alleged to contain a gold clause at the time of the issue, but Norway abolished the gold clause while the bonds were still outstanding. French bondholders denied the international validity of this measure, and the French Government took up their cause before the International Court of Justice. Norway took a number of objections to jurisdiction, which were ultimately upheld by the Court. One such objection was that the Court was confined to legal disputes concerning international law, but that the case presented by France required the court to pronounce on questions of the domestic law of Norway.[61] Yet there should be no doubt that France was justified in its assertion that an international dispute existed between France and Norway because of their disagreement over the nature and extent of the obligations created by the bonds.[62] As Sir Hersch Lauterpacht observed in his separate opinion,[63] "national legislation—including currency legislation—may be contrary, in its intention or effects, to the international obligations of the State. The question of conformity of national legislation with international law is a matter of international law. The notion that if a matter is governed by national law it is for that reason at the same time outside the sphere of international law is both novel and, if accepted, subversive of international law." It is thus possible to conclude that, although monetary legislation is of a domestic character,[64] as soon as its international effects are challenged by a foreign State, such State raises a legal dispute concerning international law, so that the jurisdiction of the International Court under Article 36(2) of its Statute is not open to question.[65]

---

[60] [1957] ICJ Rep 9.

[61] See *Rec* 96 (1959, i) 81, 82. It was only at a very late stage that France made some (insufficient) submissions on the cause of action under international law.

[62] *Pleadings* i, 172, 176 and 384.

[63] [1957] ICJ Rep 9, 37; see also Judge Reed at 87.

[64] The substance of this remark is not affected by the existence of a monetary union, for the creation of such a union must ultimately be traceable to the domestic laws of the members of the union—see the discussion of this subject in Ch 31 below.

[65] In accordance with the principles discussed under "Monetary Legislation as Confiscation", para 19.20 below, there seems to be no doubt that Norway was entitled to abolish the gold clause. However, the effect of that abolition on the bonds would fall to be decided by reference to the governing law of those instruments.

D. Monetary Legislation as Confiscation

What, then, are the causes of action upon which an attack against a State's **19.20** monetary legislation may be based? The main cause of action arises from the rule that it is contrary to international law to confiscate or take the property of an alien without payment of proper compensation or, perhaps, to deprive an alien of his property.[66] In view of the clear analogy with private law, however, it seems that monetary legislation will not normally infringe this principle.[67] A legislator who reduces rates of interest or renders agreements invalid or incapable of performance does not thereby take property. Nor does he take property if he devalues the national currency or allows it to depreciate, prohibits payment in foreign currency, or abrogates gold clauses.[68] Expectations relating to the continuing intrinsic or external value of a currency are, like favourable business conditions and goodwill, "transient circumstances, subject to changes";[69] they suffer from the "congenital infirmity"[70] that they may be changed by the competent legislator. They are not property, their change is not deprivation.[71] Yet there are certain features of monetary legislation which are so extreme that they come within the conception of confiscation[72] in the traditional sense of that term.[73]

Perhaps the clearest case is a Cuban law of 1961 which, among other unusual **19.21** provisions, declared all Cuban currency situate outside the country to be null

---

[66] For present purposes, this rule is taken to be established, although it should be appreciated that a taking of foreign property is only unlawful if the State concerned fails to offer prompt, adequate, and effective compensation. For discussion, see *Oppenheim's International Law* (Longman, 9th edn, 1991) para 407; Brownlie, *Principles of Public International Law* (Oxford University Press, 6th edn, 2003) 509–12.

[67] See *Knox v Lee* and *Parker v Davies* (1870) 12 Wall (79) US 457, 551–2.

[68] That a State has the right under international law to regulate domestic payments in, and the export of, foreign currency is implicit in the Articles of Agreement of the IMF; see also *Ling Su Fan v US* (1910) 218 US 320, 310. On the abrogation of gold clauses in this context, see *Norman v Baltimore & Ohio Railway Co* (1934) 294 US 240.

[69] *Case of Oscar Chinn* (1934) PCIJ Series A/B No 63, at 88.

[70] *Norman v Baltimore & Ohio Railway Co* (1934) 294 US 240, 308.

[71] This passage was approved by the majority of the Court of Appeals of New York in *French v Banco Nacional de Cuba* (1968) 23 NY 2d 46, 55, (considered below). Yet in *Sardino v Federal Reserve Bank of New York* (1966) 361 F 2d 111, the Court of Appeals (Second Circuit) held that US regulations freezing the New York property of a Cuban national resident in Cuba constituted deprivation within the meaning of the due process clause—"we find it hard to say there is no deprivation when a man is prevented both from obtaining his property and from realising any benefit from it for a period of indefinite duration which may outrun his life". The case does not seem to have been cited to the court in the *French* case (above). In the sense of the text see also the Foreign Claims Commission of the US in *Re Fürst* (1960) 42 Int LR 153.

[72] If the international rule condemns deprivation, then the monetary measures which may be inconsistent with international law will be more numerous for "deprivation" is inevitably a broader concept than "confiscation".

[73] See Fawcett, *Application of the European Convention on Human Rights* (1969).

and void. The Foreign Claims Commission of the United States rightly held that the holder of such currency had been deprived of his property, and that Cuba had been correspondingly enriched by being relieved of the liability represented by such banknotes.[74] In another case, the Romanian legatee, under a New York will, would have received in Romania about 12 Romanian lei to the dollar (or about twice the rate for commercial transactions), while in New York the rate was 32 lei to the dollar. The court held that the Romanian official rate was confiscatory although the decision must be very doubtful.[75] In *Re Helbert Wagg & Co Ltd*,[76] German exchange control regulations allowed a German debtor to discharge a sterling debt due to an English creditor by paying the equivalent amount of German currency to a German Government Agency for the creditor's account. The court concluded that these arrangements involved the confiscation of the property of the English creditor, but found that this did not offend either public international law or English public policy; this line of reasoning cannot be supported in the light of the remarks made in para 19.20 above. However, it is suggested that the premise of confiscation is incorrect; the German legislation at issue provided for a method of discharge of monetary obligations governed by German law, and thus affected rights of a contractual (rather than a proprietary) nature.[77] Similar facts led to the decision of the Court of Appeals (Ninth Circuit) in *West v Multibanco Comermex SA*.[78] The claimant had deposited dollars with the defendant Mexican bank. Subsequently, a Mexican law converted all dollar deposits into pesos. The claimant alleged that this was an unlawful confiscation of his property in breach of international law.[79] But this line of argument was rejected in a carefully reasoned judgment. In

---

[74] *Claim of Boyle*, Annual Report of the Foreign Claims Commission of the United States for 1968, p 81. For the proposition that banknotes represent a debt obligation of, or a claim against, the issuing central bank, see *Banco de Portugal v Waterlow & Sons* [1932] AC 452 (HL) discussed in Ch 1 above.

[75] *Re Greenberg's Estate* (1965) 260 NYS 2d 818, also 38 Int LR 142. The question was whether the legatee would have the "benefit, use or control of the money". It is difficult to see why the answer was in the negative, for the New York executor could have purchased lei in New York at the market rate (32 lei to the dollar) and remitted that sum to Romania.

[76] [1956] Ch 323.

[77] In the context of legislation affecting debts, it is often not easy to distinguish between laws which operate to adjust contractual obligations, and those which have the effect of confiscating property yet, for the reasons given in the text, it is important to do so. For a recent discussion of this distinction, see the decision of the Privy Council in *Wright v Eckhardt Marine GmbH* (14 May 2003, Privy Council Appeal No. 13 of 2002).

[78] (1987) 807 F 2d 820.

[79] The action of the Mexican Government within its own boundaries would normally be immune from review under the US Act of State doctrine, but it would become subject to such review if it was in breach of international law and, under the Hickenlooper Amendment, the Act of State doctrine would then not apply. On the Hickenlooper Amendment, see Mann, *Foreign Affairs in English Courts* (Oxford University Press, 1986) 172. The relevant provision reads "no court in the United States shall decline on the ground of the federal act of state doctrine to make a

accordance with accepted principles of conflict of laws, the contract created by the account would be governed by Mexican law[80] and the Mexican law thus varied the mode of discharge of the bank's obligation. As noted previously, this does not amount to the confiscation of property.

A much more difficult case is *French v Banco Nacional de Cuba*.[81] In June 1956, **19.22** six months after the inception of the Castro regime, the claimant acquired dollar certificates issued by the defendant central bank and by the Cuban Government's Currency Stabilisation Fund; these provided for payment by cheque in New York. In July 1959, the Cuban Government issued a decree suspending redemption of the certificates in order to stop the outflow of foreign currency. In 1968, the majority of the New York Court held that this was a breach of contract, not a taking of property. According to the minority, the decree "was in line with Cuba's consistent quest to acquire the last remnants of foreign private capital in the country"; by rescinding the Cuban Government certificates the Cuban Government "has simply added to its currency resources by this ploy" and added to "the great number of regulations enforced to implement the Cuban Government's policy of expropriating the property of foreigners".[82] It is this particular point which is a distinguishing feature of great weight, and there is much to be said for the minority opinion. The Cuban Government had not merely allowed its currency to depreciate, which would have been unobjectionable in accordance with the principles outlined above; rather, it had effectively cancelled obligations owing to foreign creditors.

Finally, it may be noted that the imposition of a system of exchange control may **19.23** in limited circumstances amount to a taking of property.[83] It would, however, be very difficult to substantiate such a claim, especially if the exchange controls at issue are maintained in a manner which is consistent with the Articles of Agreement of the International Monetary Fund.[84]

---

determination on the merits giving effect to the principles of international law in a case in which a claim of title or other right to property is asserted by any party including a foreign State . . . based upon a confiscation or other taking . . . by an act of that state in violation of the principles of international law". The provision effectively overturns the decision in *Banco Nacional de Cuba v Sabbatino* (1964) 376 US 398. For other challenges to this type of monetary legislation, see para 19.28 below.

[80] ie by the law of the place where the account was held. Dicey and Morris, *The Conflict of Laws* (Sweet & Maxwell, 13th edn, 2000) para 22-029.

[81] (1968) 23 NY 2d 46. See also *Nielsen v Treasury* (1970) 424 F 2d 833.

[82] At 83 and 93.

[83] See, eg, the dissenting opinion of Judge Mosk in *Schering Corp v Iran*, Iran-US Claims Tribunal Reports 5, 361 and in *Hood Corp v Iran*, Iran-US Claims Tribunal Reports 7, 36, at 51.

[84] See generally, Chs 15 and 16 above.

E. Fair and Equitable Treatment of Aliens

19.24 The foregoing discussion leaves the impression that the principle of monetary sovereignty and some of its incidents[85] are well established and accepted in general terms but that the application of the principle is limited or excluded in certain cases. Thus, the principle will not apply in respect of monetary legislation which discriminates against foreign nationals,[86] or which constitutes "arbitrary intervention".[87] On other occasions, the exception has been founded on the theory of denial of justice.[88] The doctrine of abuse of rights has likewise been invoked, ie the notion that legislation lacks "a reasonable relation to a legitimate end", or is being operated in a manner or for purposes repugnant to its accepted function.[89] Here as elsewhere, the formulation of a comprehensive yet precise principle is a difficult process.[90] Here as elsewhere, the descriptions of the international wrongs differ. But it is submitted (and for present purposes assumed) that whether one speaks of unjustifiable discrimination, deliberate injury, arbitrariness, denial of justice in a broad sense, or abuse of rights, the essence of the matter is always the same. It is fair and equitable treatment or, as it is sometimes put, good faith that every State is internationally required to display in its conduct towards aliens. It is the lack of equitable treatment, or good faith, that is the real and fundamental and, at the same time, the most comprehensive cause of action of which all other aspects of State responsibility are mere illustrations.[91] The difficulties lie in the application rather than the existence of a doctrine, the substance of which is hard to deny. There are few precedents such as judicial decisions, diplomatic incidents, or factual events from which the law may be developed and which may suggest legal conclusions. In the last resort, the matter will be one of degree: while normally the State is entitled at its discretion to regulate its monetary affairs, there comes a point at which the exercise of such discretion so unreasonably or so grossly offends against the alien's right to fair and equitable treatment, or so clearly

---

[85] These were discussed in the opening section of this chapter.

[86] See, eg, *Claim of Tabar* [1953] Int LR 211, and other cases mentioned at n 38 above.

[87] See the statement of the Government of Canada, noted at para 19.10 above.

[88] *Claim of Zuk* (1958, ii) Int LR 285.

[89] On the status of *abus de droit* in public international law and its specific application in the monetary field, see the *Barcelona Traction* case [1970] ICJ Rep 3 and (more particularly) the arguments presented on behalf of Belgium, *Oral Proceedings VIII* 55–109 and *X* 46–82. See also, Mann, *Rec* 96 (1959, I) 92–5.

[90] *Metliss v National Bank of Greece* [1959] AC 509, 524.

[91] The comment in the text cannot apply to negligence, which is a doubtful head of liability in the international context. It is plainly impossible here to develop the submission in the text, for the issue far transcends the specific sphere of monetary law.

deviates from customary standards of behaviour, that international law will intervene.[92]

The following are examples and exceptions which throw light upon the principle, and from which a firm and well-delineated rule may perhaps, in due course, be derived: **19.25**

(a) If a State deliberately used its monetary legislation or practice as a means of injuring the interests of foreigners generally, then this would amount to an international wrong. Thus, if it were true that, during the period from 1921 to 1923, the German Government deliberately created or at least aggravated the depreciation of the mark so that it assumed its well-known astronomic proportions with a view to eliminating the country's foreign indebtedness, then such a policy would stand condemned by international law.[93]

(b) Cases in which foreign nationals have become victims of unreasonable and unfair discrimination are better documented. An interesting case is that of the Tobacco Monopoly Bonds issued by Portugal. They carried an option of currency (*option de change*) in terms of escudos, sterling, Dutch florins, and French francs. In 1924, Portugal withdrew some of the foreign currency options but, as a result of British protests, it subsequently reinstated the sterling option for British holders. The United States protested that this measure unjustifiably discriminated against American holders, and Portugal thus further extended the reinstatement of the sterling option so as to cover American bondholders.[94]

(c) It is, however, necessary to emphasise that discrimination in this field may only amount to an international wrong if it is unjustifiable. There would be

---

[92] This passage was approved by the Court in *French v Banco Nacional de Cuba* (1968) 23 NY 2d 46.

[93] A suggestion to this effect has been made, for instance, by Rasba (1944) 54 Yale LJ 34, n 137. It has been pointed out that the German State was itself a major beneficiary from the inflation, in the sense that its domestic indebtedness was virtually wiped out, but that the inflation was not a deliberate governmental ploy; rather it seems to have resulted from a different view of the role of the central bank in the context of such a crisis. On these points, see Widdig, *Culture and Inflation in Weimar Germany* (University of California Press, 2001) 43–51.

[94] For details, see *Foreign Relations* (1926, ii), 880; Borchard, *State Insolvency and Foreign Bondholders*, Vol II (Beard Books, 1951) 383. For not dissimilar facts, see the Exchange of Letters which accompanied the Anglo–Egyptian Financial Agreement of 31 March 1949 (Cmnd 7675). The Egyptian Government claimed that Egypt's sterling balances held in London "should have the benefit of a gold clause identical to that granted to some other countries". It seems that this referred to the gold guarantees given, for instance, to Uruguay (Cmnd 7172), Argentina (Cmnd 7346, Art IV(e) and (f), and Cmnd 7735, Arts 21 and 26), Iran and Portugal (1949) 157 *The Economist*, 682. As a result of the devaluation of sterling in 1949, those guarantees were estimated to have cost the UK £68 million: see the article in *The Economist* just noted. In the circumstances, the Egyptian demand would appear to have been justified.

no actionable discrimination if inequality of treatment were the necessary result of a genuine system of exchange control; indeed in the nature of things, an exchange control system is *designed* to discriminate between different classes of persons.[95] Thus, the fact that the United Kingdom at one time permitted certain payments to be made to creditors resident in other parts of the sterling area but—in the absence of exchange control consent—prohibited corresponding payments to creditors in the United States was, in principle, unobjectionable in the context of the rules now under consideration.[96] Such discrimination as arose in that context was a necessary and justifiable ingredient of the exchange control system.

(d) The wrongful character of discrimination based on reasons of nationality, religion, race, or sex should no longer be open to question. Thus, when in 1918, Poland introduced in her newly acquired western provinces a substitution rate of one mark to one zloty for the conversion of mark debts into Polish currency, German courts rightly refused to apply the prescribed rate on the ground that the measure was specifically designed to injure German subjects.[97] Likewise, and as has frequently been decided, it was plainly abusive for Nazi Germany to persecute Jews, whether of German or foreign nationality and to compel them to leave the country, and yet at the same time to apply to them her stringent exchange control rules. Similar practices prevailed in certain countries of the former Communist bloc, and were objectionable for the same reasons.

(e) Though this did not fall to be dealt with on an international level, a striking case of abuse of monetary power was held to have occurred in 1935, when new German legislation provided that bonds issued outside Germany and incorporating a gold clause were redeemable only to the extent of the (devalued) currency in which they were expressed. At least where the bonds were governed by German law, it might be expected that foreign courts would give effect to the new German law, subject to any considerations of public policy.[98] But the Swiss Federal Tribunal refused to

---

[95] For reasons given below, a system of exchange control should only discriminate on the basis of the residence of the parties.

[96] Thus in the *Case of Certain Norwegian Loans* [1957] ICJ Rep 9, Danish and Swedish holders of Norwegian bonds were paid certain amounts due on their bonds, but French bondholders did not receive a similar payment. Although the case is in some respects obscure, it appears that the Swedish and Danish bondholders effectively received a preference as a result of the particular application of inter-Scandinavian exchange control regulations. As a result, the discrimination was justified. The point is to some extent dealt with by Judge Read, at 88–9.

[97] Berlin Court of Appeal, 25 February 1922, *JW* 1922, 398; 28 October 1922, *JW* 1923, 128; 2 November 1928, *JW* 1928, 1462.

[98] On these points, see Arts 10(1)(b) and 16 of the Rome Convention and *Re Helbert Wagg & Co Ltd* [1956] Ch 323. The subject has been discussed generally in Ch 4 above.

give effect to these provisions[99] on the grounds that the measures were aimed solely at foreign bondholders and were designed for the protection of German debtors. The Tribunal found that these "violent measures" were intended unilaterally to enrich Germany at the expense of foreign nationals, and refused to apply them on public policy grounds. On the basis that the Tribunal's analysis of the German legislation and its objectives is correct,[100] then the decision of the Tribunal is plainly right. An international tribunal would be equally justified in treating the German law as an international wrong.

(f) An international wrong would clearly be committed if, in a case of State succession, the successor State cancelled the rights of the holders of the predecessor State's currency at the time of succession. On the contrary, it is the clear duty of the successor State under international law to provide for the continuing validity of such predecessor's currency or to make arrangements for its exchange into the currency of the successor State at a reasonable rate.[101]

(g) There are occasions when a State's currency legislation may involve an excess of international jurisdiction. Thus, a State could not properly legislate to prevent the use of its currency as a contractual medium by foreigners outside its boundaries, for this would involve an attempt to regulate the conduct of foreigners abroad.[102] For this reason, the United States cannot lawfully control the eurodollar market, except in so far as activities within its own boundaries, or by its own nationals, are concerned; money has no nationality and the rule that a State may in certain circumstances control its nationals abroad cannot be invoked to justify an unusual and, it is submitted, internationally unlawful piece of domestic legislation.[103] Exchange control regulations may be vulnerable to attack on this basis

---

[99] 1 February 1938, BGE 64 ii 88, also *Bulletin de L'Institut Juridique International* (1938) 111. The relevant passages are in section 7 of the judgment.

[100] This point is not entirely free from doubt—see Weigert, *The Abrogation of Gold Clauses in International Law* (1940) 6.

[101] O'Connell, *State Succession*, I (Cambridge University Press, 1967) 191–2. On the corresponding monetary obligations of a belligerent occupant, see para 20.08 below.

[102] Two points should be emphasised in relation to the rule stated in the text. First of all, most transactions involving the currency of a country will usually fall to be settled through the clearing system operated in that country. As a result, a State may be in a position to control or influence transactions involving its currency, even though they take place abroad. To that extent, the point just made in the text is controversial; it must also be said that English courts did not allow US federal law any influence in this respect even though US dollars had to be cleared through New York—see *Libyan Arab Foreign Bank v Bankers Trust Co* [1989] 1 QB 728. Secondly, the text deals merely with contracts which refer to the currency of a foreign State. Different considerations may apply where a State wishes to *adopt* the currency of another State as its own unit; on this subject, ("dollarisation") see para 33.11 below.

[103] On this point, see Wengler, RGR Kommentar vi (2) 1296–7.

where they seek to control the activities of nationals abroad[104] and, for that reason, references to "nationals" in exchange control legislation should be read as references to nationals who are resident within the jurisdiction, for example, on the basis that criminal jurisdiction is of an essentially territorial character.[105]

(h) It has been shown that, as a general rule, a State has the right to impose a system of exchange control; international law will thus not generally object either to the creation or to the terms of such a system.[106] Nevertheless, both a domestic and an international tribunal "is entitled to be satisfied that the foreign law is a genuine foreign exchange law . . . and is not a law passed ostensibly with that object, but in reality with some object not in accordance with the usage of nations"[107] or, in other words, is not abusive. The German Moratorium Law of 30 June 1933 was held to be entitled to recognition in England, because it was found to have been passed for the genuine purpose of protecting the economy.[108] Had the Court reached the conclusion that the law was an instrument of economic warfare, a measure preparatory to war, or an instrument of discrimination or oppression, then it should plainly have declined to apply it on public policy grounds.

(i) Exchange control legislation represents a grave encroachment upon private rights and liabilities and may cause such serious prejudice, that good faith requires the restricting State to formulate and operate the law with due regard for the legitimate interests of aliens[109] and in a consistent manner. Thus, if an individual resident in England is unable to pay his debts because (1) all his money and assets are situate in a restricting State and (2) the restricting State refuses to allow for the transfer of assets in order to meet the debtor's obligations, then (consistently with that refusal) the restricting State must prohibit any execution against the debtor's local assets to enforce the monetary obligations which he is unable to meet. In other words, if the restricting State prevents the alien debtor from meeting

---

[104] An attempt to apply exchange control rules to *non-nationals* resident abroad would plainly constitute an excess of jurisdiction.

[105] For this reason, it is suggested that *Boissevain v Weil* [1950] AC 327 was wrongly decided. On this case, see Mann, *Rec* 111 (1964, i) 124 or *Studies in International Law*, p 108.

[106] On this point, see "The Principle of Monetary Sovereignty", para 19.02 above.

[107] In *Re Helbert Wagg & Co Ltd* [1956] Ch 323, 351–2.

[108] See the case mentioned in n 107 above. Whether this finding was in fact justified on the particular facts may be a matter for debate—see Mann (1956) 19 Mod LR 301. Nevertheless, on the basis of the view which the Court took of the Moratorium Law, it was clearly right to apply its provisions in the context of a contract governed by German law.

[109] This wording was approved by Mr Holtzmann in *Sea-Land Service Inc v Iran*, and by Mr Mosk in *Hood Corp v Iran*, Iran-United States Claims Tribunal Reports 6, 149, 209 and Tribunal Reports 7, 36, 49 respectively. Extracts of these cases are also reprinted in (1985) *Yearbook of Commercial Arbitration X*, 245 and 297 respectively.

his obligations voluntarily, then it should not subsequently compel him to do so on an involuntary basis.[110]

(j) Since exchange control is designed to protect a State's exchange resources, the mere refusal to allow the transfer of funds abroad could only rarely be impugned on the basis that it is a misuse of discretion or otherwise unfair or inequitable. Subject to the various qualifications noted in the preceding paragraphs, it will usually be lawful for a restricting State even to limit or exclude the internal use of the non-resident alien's internal funds. Inevitably, however, special circumstances may require different solutions. In the *Case of Barcelona Traction*,[111] Belgium alleged an abuse of rights committed by Spain's refusal to allow a Spanish debtor to apply available peseta sums in the discharge of peseta interest liabilities due from it to Spanish creditors even though the use of such funds for previous interest payments in respect of the same liabilities had invariably been permitted. If the refusal of consent had been motivated by the desire to bankrupt the Belgian entity and thus to deprive it of its Spanish investments, then this would plainly constitute a misuse of the exchange control system and thus constitute an international wrong.[112] Similarly, an abusive operation of exchange control occurs when the system is employed for purposes which are extraneous to it, for example, in order to inflict punishment upon an alien to secure tax claims or in an attempt to secure other advantages from the State in which the alien resides.[113] It also follows that the restricting State cannot refuse consent merely because the alien applicant refuses to answer queries on extraneous matters which are unconnected with the objectives of exchange control, nor may it so excessively delay its response to an alien applicant as to cause him damage or injustice. In short, "the right to accord or refuse permission is in all the circumstances interpreted not as one of absolute discretion but of controllable discretion, one which must be used reasonably and not capriciously, one which must be exercised in good faith".[114]

---

[110] A factual situation of this kind arose in the *Case of Barcelona Traction* [1970] ICJ Rep 3, although the line of argument noted in the text was not advanced on that occasion. Nevertheless, the existence of an obligation to treat alien nationals in a fair and equitable manner would appear to support the conclusion noted in the text. The inability of the debtor to access foreign assets in order to meet his obligations would not, of course, prevent an English court from giving judgment against him—see *Universal Corp v Five Ways Properties Ltd* [1978] 3 All ER 1131.

[111] [1970] ICJ Rep 3.

[112] Belgium made a number of other allegations about Spain's conduct and the case is far more complex than suggested by the brief statement in the text.

[113] The German Federal Constitutional Court has held that the State infringed the constitutional provisions on the protection of property and the rule of law when it refused permission to transfer assets for reasons of the kind described in the text, and not with a view to the protection of exchange resources: Decision of 3 November 1982, *BverfGE* 62,169.

[114] *Case of Right of Passage (Portugal v India)* [1960] ICJ 107.

19.26 The examples could no doubt be multiplied, but the fundamental principle is the same in every case, even if its application to particular factual situations necessarily involves a degree of appreciation. It is perhaps possible to conclude that monetary sovereignty is an incident of Statehood, and an exercise of monetary sovereignty is entitled to positive recognition by foreign States and their courts. This is, however, subject to the important qualification that recognition of a particular exercise of monetary sovereignty is only required where that exercise represents a legitimate use of that sovereignty for the purposes of which it is conferred. Monetary sovereignty cannot be used as a cloak for confiscation, discrimination, or other actions of a type generally condemned by international law.

F. Other Challenges to Monetary Legislation

19.27 Thus far, the present chapter has been concerned with monetary sovereignty in the sense of public international law. Nevertheless, it must not be forgotten that the concept of monetary sovereignty allows to a State the right to legislate in the monetary field and, although that legislation must be consistent with international law, such legislation is inevitably of a domestic character. Monetary laws are thus liable to challenge on various grounds; for example, because they are inconsistent with the constitution of the State concerned or because they infringe proprietary rights which are guaranteed by the local law.[115] These points are perhaps obvious and it may be thought that no further discussion should be required, especially in the context of a section principally concerned with international law. Yet, there have been a number of recent developments in this sphere, and it seems inappropriate to overlook them. The various cases to be discussed below emanate from very different systems of law and it is thus not possible to identify a common theme[116] but they nevertheless illustrate the difficulties which may arise in a domestic monetary context.

Argentina

19.28 The Supreme Court of Argentina gave judgment in *Province of San Luis v Banco de la Nacion Argentina* on 5 March 2003.[117]

---

[115] It will be recalled that the ability of the US to issue paper money was the subject of a series of cases before the US Supreme Court. The subject has been discussed in Ch 1 above.

[116] Save that the English and German cases discussed below both arose from the intended ratification of the Treaty on European Union.

[117] The present description of this case and the background to it draws upon two articles by Gomez, "Review of the San Luis Province Case" [2003] 7 JIBLR 298 and "Emergency Law and Financial Entities in Argentina" [2003] 10 JIBLR 397. For earlier proceedings, see *Smith v Banco de Galicia*, discussed in [2002] JIBLR N-21.

Since 1991, Argentina had maintained a "currency board" arrangement[118] **19.29**
under which the local peso was "pegged" to the US dollar on a one-for-one
basis. Each peso in circulation was thus required to be "backed" by one US
dollar of foreign reserves held by the central bank.[119] A financial crisis created a
general fear that the Government would devalue the peso, and this in turn
resulted in large-scale withdrawals of US dollars from the local banking system.
In the light of the monetary "peg" arrangements, the Government was unable to
devalue the peso and the central bank was unable simply to print additional
banknotes and to put them into circulation.[120] The authorities attempted to
stem the crisis by passing an Emergency Law (No 25,561) which abolished the
fixed peg system and also empowered the Executive to take urgent action.
Section 6 of the Emergency Law allowed the Government to introduce "measures intended to protect consumers who had deposited their savings at financial
institutions . . . by rescheduling the original obligations in a way consistent with
changes in the financial system's creditworthiness. This protection shall also
include all deposits in foreign currency." In the purported exercise of that
power, the Government introduced a rule[121] to the effect that "all deposits
denominated in US dollars or in any other foreign currencies existing in the
financial system shall be converted into pesos at the peso to US dollar ratio of
one peso and forty cents per US dollar, or its equivalent in any other foreign
currency. The financial entity shall return the amount denominated in pesos at
the above mentioned ratio."

The Supreme Court reviewed a number of leading authorities from other **19.30**
jurisdictions,[122] and held that the forcible and unilateral conversion of US
dollar deposits into pesos under the terms of the Executive Order exceeded the
scope of the powers delegated by the legislature to the Government. To that
extent, the Executive Order was unconstitutional and it thus appears that the
US dollar deposits would have to be repaid in the originally contracted currency. It is difficult for the English lawyer to comment further on a decision of
this kind, although it may be said that a reading of the Emergency Law and
the terms of the Executive Order does suggest that the latter did indeed go

---

[118] On these arrangements, see Ch 33 below.
[119] The "peg" was regulated by the Argentine Convertibility Law of 1991 (Law No. 23,928 as
amended by Law No 25,445).
[120] This discipline is, of course, one of the points often made in favour of the use of pegging
arrangements. But as the Argentinian difficulties demonstrate, that discipline may command a
very high price. The country suffered both rapid and serious political upheaval as a result of the
financial crisis described in the text.
[121] The wording about to be quoted is taken from Executive Order 214/2002, s 2, as reproduced
in the articles mentioned in n 117 above.
[122] Including the decisions of the US Supreme Court in *Perry v US* (1934) 294 US 330 and
Baker v US (1962) 369 US 186.

beyond the boundaries of the authority extended by the Emergency Law.[123] The case also serves as a reminder of a point which flows in part from the State theory of money,[124] namely that money derives its essential status from a domestic monetary system and is thus in all respects subjected to the laws of that system. In other words, money is the subject of the law; it cannot be its master.

The European Convention on Human Rights

19.31 Constitutional guarantees of the right to own and retain property might also provide a ground upon which legislation of a monetary character may be challenged in appropriate cases. A typical example of such a guarantee is provided by Article 1 of the First Protocol to the European Convention on Human Rights.[125] It is perhaps useful to reproduce the provision in full:

> Every natural or legal person is entitled to the peaceful enjoyment of his possessions. No one shall be deprived of his possessions except in the public interest and subject to the conditions provided for by the law and by the general principles of international law.

> The preceding provisions shall not, however, in any way impair the right of a state to enforce such laws as it deems necessary to control the use of property in accordance with the general interest or to secure the payment of taxes or other contributions or penalties.

19.32 It seems clear that rights to money or to a monetary claim are to be treated as "possessions" (or property) for the purposes of Article 1 of the First Protocol.[126] In a case involving monetary rights, it would be necessary to ascertain (a) whether legislative or governmental action in the monetary field amounted to a "deprivation" of the rights of the holder and, if so, (b) whether any of the

---

[123] It should be added that the decision of the Supreme Court was reached by a majority of 5 to 3. However, the minority did not uphold the propriety of the Executive Order; they merely held that further proceedings and evidence were necessary in order to determine a case of considerable importance and complexity. The Supreme Court subsequently reversed its view, holding that the peso substitution was lawful in *Bustos v Estado Nacional* (26 October 2004). The decision has attracted much criticism.

[124] On the State theory of money, see Ch 1 above.

[125] As is well known, certain provisions of the Convention—including Article 1 of the First Protocol—have effect in the UK by virtue of the Human Rights Act 1998. To this extent, the Convention may be regarded as a part of British constitutional law.

[126] Property such as shares and the benefit of a legal claim fall within the scope of the provision—see *Bramelid and Malmstrom v Sweden* (1982) 29 DR 64, EComHR and *National Provincial Building Society v UK* (1977) 25 EHRR 127, ECtHR, paras 69–70. There is no reason to suppose that monetary claims should be approached on a different basis.

exemptions in Article 1 applied. It will be seen that Article 1 effectively comprises three related but distinct rules,[127] namely:

(1)   the individual's right to peaceful enjoyment of property;
(2)   the right not to be deprived of property, except in accordance with national laws which conform to internationally accepted standards; and
(3)   the right of the State to control the use of property in accordance with the general interest or to secure the payment of taxes or other amounts owing to the State.

In a monetary context, it is possible to conceive of various causes of action which could deprive an individual of the right to peaceful enjoyment of property, in the form of his monetary assets. First of all, the State could elect to introduce a new currency or to replace all money currently in circulation, but then allow only an unreasonably short period for the surrender of old currency in return for new notes and coins, with the old ceasing to be available for any purpose at the end of that period. Alternatively, a State could simply block, on an indefinite basis, the repayment of bank deposits owing to foreign residents. The effective demonetisation of the existing currency may contravene the first rule described above, because the holder has been deprived of the effective benefit of his property.[128] In the second case involving the blocking of bank deposits, it would be necessary to invoke the second rule. Whilst there has been no "deprivation" of property in the sense of a formal expropriation, nevertheless the measures taken by the State rendered the depositor's ownership rights effectively useless; this may amount to a "deprivation" for the purposes of the second rule even though formal title to the bank deposit continues to rest with its original owner.[129]   **19.33**

It may be concluded from the above discussion that, as a general principle, property consisting of monetary assets is protected by Article 1 of the First Protocol, on a basis similar to the protection afforded to other forms of property. Yet, as is not infrequently the case, it will be the exceptions to the general principle which will assume the greatest importance in practice. For example: **19.34**

---

[127]   This formulation was originally adopted by the European Court of Human Rights in *Sporrong and Lönnroth v Sweden* (1985) 5 EHRR 35, para 61 and has been adopted in numerous subsequent cases; see, eg, *James v UK* (1986) 8 EHRR 123; and *Immobiliare Saffi v Italy* (2000) EHRR 756. For details of this aspect and of the First Protocol generally, see Lester and Pannick, *The European Convention on Human Rights* (Butterworths, 2001), ch 4.

[128]   See *Stran Greek Refineries v Greece* (1994) 19 EHRR 293, ECtHR, para 68 and the discussion of that case in Lester and Pannick, (n 127 above) para 4.19.8. In a slightly different context, it has been held that legal tender legislation which allowed for the use of banknotes to discharge preexisting contractual obligations did not amount to a deprivation of property or an unwarranted interference with contractual rights—see *Knox v Lee* and *Parker v Davis* (1870) 12 Wall (79) US 457.

[129]   This result follows from the national rule that the Convention is intended to guarantee property rights which are "practical and effective"—see the discussion in Lester and Pannick (n 127 above) para 4.19.9.

(a) If the repayment of bank deposits held by foreign residents were blocked as part of a *general* scheme of exchange control, then it would seem that any deprivation of property thereby occasioned would conform to international law, and thus no breach of the First Protocol would occur.[130]

(b) As has been shown elsewhere,[131] and subject to any treaty engagements to the contrary, a State has a right to devalue its currency. Since this right is recognised by international law, a decision to devalue would not amount to "deprivation" of property for the purposes of the First Protocol, even though the external value of monetary assets may have been very significantly reduced as a consequence.

(c) Likewise, Article 1 cannot be invoked as an effective safeguard against the ravages of inflation. An individual may be severely affected by a fall in the value of his money, but this would not amount to a "deprivation" for the purposes of the Convention. The point is expressed by a series of decisions of the European Court of Human Rights, which have rejected the notion that Article 1 creates any right to the indexation of bank deposits or savings accounts.[132]

(d) Measures imposing a withholding tax on interest paid in respect of bank deposits are designed to prevent the loss of tax revenues and thus plainly fall within the third rule set out in para 19.32 above.

(e) States may occasionally impose economic or trading sanctions against other States in times of severe political tension.[133] While these sanctions are imposed as part of an international initiative sponsored by the United Nations, States will usually be obliged to implement those sanctions in compliance with Articles 25 and 41 of the Charter of the United Nations. There can thus be no doubt that such sanctions are compliant with international law and that the consequent freezing of assets belonging to the target State and its nationals does not constitute a deprivation of property

---

[130] See the second rule outlined above. The statement in the text assumes that the system of exchange control at issue was imposed consistently with the Articles of Agreement of the IMF, as to which see Ch 15 above. This would obviously involve a detailed examination of the system of exchange control involved. Whilst some restrictions on foreign remittances may be acceptable, an outright and definitive ban on the repayment of foreign-owned deposits almost certainly would not.

[131] See para 19.03 above. For the reasons there noted, the concept of "official devaluation" is now of very limited concern. However, an official decision to intervene in the markets with a view to depreciating the currency would be treated on the same footing.

[132] See *Rudzinska v Poland* (1999) ECHR-VI 45223/97; *Gayduk v Ukraine* (2002) 45526/99, ECHR 2002–VI; *Appolonov v Russia* (2002) 67578/01 (29 August 2002); and *Ryabykh v Russia* (2003) 52854/99 [2003] ECHR. As the Court expressed matters in the *Rudzinska* case, "the applicant complains that, as a result of inflation her savings . . . lost their purchasing power . . . the Court is of the view that a general obligation on States to maintain the purchasing power of sums deposited with banking or financial institutions by way of a systematic indexation of savings, cannot be derived from Article 1 of Protocol 1".

[133] For a general discussion of this subject, see Ch 17 above.

which infringes the terms of the First Protocol or any similar constitutional protection. In many such cases, such deprivation of property as may occur will also fall within the "public interest" exemption noted in the third rule set out in para 19.32 above. The point is well illustrated by the decision of the Court of Appeal in *Al-Kishtaini v Shanshal.*[134] In that case the claimant sought repayment from the defendant of DM113, 569. The obligation to repay that money arose from a transfer originally made to the defendant, who was resident in Iraq at the time of the Iraqi invasion of Kuwait in August 1990. The Court thus found that the transaction at hand was tainted by illegality, because it involved a transfer to a person resident in Iraq in contravention of the system of sanctions imposed against that country.[135] The claimant sought to argue that the application of the doctrine of illegality had the effect of depriving him of the benefit of his claim, and this infringed Article 1 of the First Protocol. As the court observed, it must be very doubtful whether a claim for restitution can be regarded as a "possession" for the purposes of Article 1; even if it were, the public interest in securing compliance with sanctions imposed by the international community would outweigh the requirement for the protection of individual property rights.[136]

The European Community

It may be appropriate at this point to mention litigation which arose in the context of the European single currency.[137] In cases involving the Member States of the European Community the issues which may arise are of a rather different order. The Member State will not be passing monetary legislation in the usual sense; instead, it will be introducing legislation to transfer its monetary authority to an international organisation. In essence, the court may be asked whether the Member State concerned is constitutionally in a position to transfer national monetary sovereignty to the Community and, if so, whether it has observed the procedures which are necessary for that purpose. The answer to those questions

19.35

---

[134] [2001] All ER (D) 295.

[135] In the UK, those sanctions formed part of the domestic law by virtue of the Control of Gold, Securities, Payments and Credit (Republic of Iraq) Directions 1990, SI 1990/1616. The case includes some interesting commentary on the temporal application of those Directions and the consequences of a change of residence occurring after the date on which they came into effect. However, those questions are beyond the scope of the present discussion.

[136] It may be wondered why the Court did not find it necessary to rely on the undoubted fact that the 1990 Directions were introduced in conformity with the requirements of public international law. The reason must be that the claimant was resident in the UK; the principles of international law can only be invoked in the context of property owned by foreigners: see *James v UK* (1986) 8 EHRR 123, ECtHR paras 58–66 and *Lithgow v UK* (1986) 8 EHRR 329 ECtHR paras 111–119.

[137] The present discussion is brief because the larger subject of monetary union is considered in detail in Part VI below.

will plainly depend upon the constitutional law of the Member State in question, and different considerations may therefore apply in each country. Matters touching upon the sovereignty of the State have tended to be controversial, and the issues frequently fall upon an awkard boundary line between politics and the law. In one Irish case involving the Single European Act, it was decided that the transfer of authority in the field of foreign affairs could only be achieved with the authority of a referendum, on the basis that the Treaty involved an outright transfer of sovereignty as opposed to an exercise of it.[138] But in England, the decision to ratify Title V of the Treaty on European Union, establishing a common foreign and security policy could not be challenged on the basis that it was an abandonment of the Crown's prerogative in the field of foreign affairs; on the contrary, the Treaty represented an exercise of that sovereignty.[139] The German Federal Constitutional Court likewise held that Germany could ratify the Treaty on European Union.[140] Interestingly, however, both the English and the German courts rested their decisions at least in part on the ability of the State to denounce that treaty and—even though acting in breach of its terms—to disclaim its obligations thereunder;[141] it may be thought that this is not an especially appealing basis for major constitutional decisions of this kind.

19.36   The decision of the German Constitutional Court in *Brunner v The European Union Treaty*[142] perhaps deserves the most attention in the present context, for the Court dealt specifically with the consistency of economic and monetary union with the terms of the German Constitution itself. The Court ruled inadmissible a complaint to the effect that the citizen's basic rights under the Constitution were infringed by the prospective replacement of the German mark by the euro. Article 88 of the Constitution had been specifically revised to allow for the transfer of the functions and powers of the Bundesbank to the European Central Bank within the framework of the European Union. The proposed monetary union and the associated transfer of powers were thereby explicitly recognised by the Constitution itself; it thus could not be argued that monetary union could infringe the basic rights created by that document.[143] The other criticisms of monetary union under the terms of the Treaty focused on the fact that the Bundestag would be transferring its powers under the terms of the Treaty which lacked a degree of certainty in its terms. These were rejected

---

[138] *Crotty v An Taoiseach* [1987] 2 CMLR 666. The decision does, of course, pre-date the Treaty on European Union, and questions of monetary sovereignty thus did not arise.

[139] *R v Secretary of State for Foreign and Commonwealth Affairs, ex p Rees-Mogg* [1994] 1 All ER 457. The English and Irish courts thus adopted different approaches to the subject.

[140] *Brunner v The European Union Treaty* [1994] 1 CMLR 57.

[141] See the judgment in *Rees-Mogg* at p 469; *Brunner* at para 55.

[142] [1994] 1 CMLR 57.

[143] See para 11 of the judgment.

on the grounds that the Treaty set out clear criteria to qualify for participation in monetary union, and the path to the beginning of the Third Stage could be supervised by the national parliament by reference to the convergence criteria. Furthermore, once the euro had been created, price stability would remain the key objective of monetary policy; in addition, Member States would be subjected to the excessive deficit procedure and other constraints in the context of their domestic fiscal policies. The Court thus concluded that "the fear that efforts towards stability will fail to materialise, with the consequence that the Member States could make further concessions of financial policy, is insufficiently plausible to ground the conclusion that the Treaty is legally uncertain".[144] In so far as it relates to the technical question of legal certainty, this statement may well be accurate. However, the statement as a whole discloses a degree of optimism which has perhaps not been borne out by subsequent experience.[145] Nevertheless, the Federal Constitutional Court sent a clear signal that German participation in monetary union was conditional upon a proper observance of the convergence criteria, and that such participation could only constitutionally be justified on that basis,[146] but the Court did concede that the decision to enter into a monetary union had an essentially political, rather than constitutional, flavour.[147] This is no doubt correct and certainly reflects the position which would apply in the United Kingdom, should any legal challenge be made to any eventual decision to join the single currency.

It may perhaps be concluded from this section that legislation of a monetary character may be open to objection on constitutional or monetary grounds in the State concerned. But money is central to the conduct of the national economy, and its all-pervasiveness will inevitably mean that the courts will be very reluctant to uphold a challenge to legislation of this kind. **19.37**

---

[144] See para 89 of the judgment.
[145] See the discussion of the Stability Pact and the events of November 2003 at para 26.16 below.
[146] On the observance of the convergence criteria, see para 26.11 below.
[147] See para 93 of the judgment.

20

THE PROTECTION OF FOREIGN CURRENCY SYSTEMS

A. Introduction

It has been shown that States are under a general international duty to recognise **20.01** the monetary systems of other States. In large measure, this flows from the broader duty to recognise a State's exclusive jurisdiction over its own internal affairs.[1] In private law, this obligation manifests itself in the *lex monetae* principle, which lies at the heart of monetary law.[2] It is now necessary to ask whether there are duties beyond mere recognition; does the State have a broader obligation to *protect* and *defend* the monetary systems of other States?

B. The General Principle

To what extent is a State under an international obligation to afford any form of **20.02** protection to the monetary system of a foreign country? A State's duty to protect the monetary systems of other States may arise from treaties or even from an informal network of arrangements such as used to characterise the

---

[1] This general subject has been discussed in Ch 19 above.

[2] Although the the the *lex monetae* principle is essentially a private law concept, it has been shown that its application derives from international law, which binds both the State itself and the courts which sit within it. The point has been discussed in Ch 13 above.

sterling area.[3] As has been seen,[4] certain aspects of an exchange control system are entitled to a degree of protection by other States by virtue of Article VIII of the Articles of Agreement of the International Monetary Fund, and other duties of protection may arise under bilateral treaties.

20.03   However, apart from treaties, it would at present not be possible to maintain that customary international law imposes upon a State any *general* duty of affording protection to the monetary systems of other States.[5] The existence of such a duty could only be asserted if the development of international law had progressed so far as to outlaw all activities injurious to a foreign State or even to demand the adoption of measures to safeguard the interests of a foreign State. It hardly needs to be stated that customary international law has not arrived at this utopian position.

20.04   But if it is not possible to go that far, it may nevertheless be observed that a State is under a duty to prevent the commission within its territory of unlawful acts injurious to foreign States.[6] The duty is usually discussed in the context of terrorist or similar activities; a State must take measures to prevent its territory from being used as a base for the planning and launching of terrorist activities against another State. It is by no means inconceivable that monetary or financial practices may acquire a character which would likewise justify international law in demanding their suppression. Thus, when the Hungarian revolutionary Louis Kossuth had banknotes printed in England with the avowed object of introducing them into Hungary upon his return to that country, and had them inscribed: "in the name of the nation: Louis Kossuth", the Emperor of Austria sought an injunction from the English courts.[7] He alleged, and the Court found, an infringement of his proprietary rights, but it is significant that the Court also referred to a broader ground for the decision[8] namely "that in an English Court of Justice, the manufacturing in England of such notes for such a purpose . . . cannot be defended"; if it were permitted, this would justify diplomatic protests. The banknotes were being printed as part of a scheme to overthrow the recognised government of a foreign State; the United Kingdom thus

---

[3] On the sterling area, see Ch 33 below.

[4] See Ch 15 above.

[5] In the same sense, see Carreau, *Souveraineté et co-opération monétaire international* (Cujas, Paris, 1970) 31. Gold, *Special Drawing Rights* (Washington, 1969) 2, disagrees with the view expressed in the text, but does not provide evidence in support of his position.

[6] For explanation and discussion of this duty, see *Oppenheim's International Law* (Longman, 9th edn, 1991) paras 121 and 122. For an illustration of its operation in a different context, see the *Corfu Channel* case, [1949] ICJ Rep 244.

[7] *Emperor of Austria v Day* (1861) 3 DeG F & J 217. From a strictly legal point of view, the Emperor's case was by no means free from doubt—see Mann (1955) 40 *Transactions of the Grotius Society* 25, 37 or *Studies in International Law* (Oxford University Press, 1973) 505.

[8] At 236.

came under an international obligation to suppress this activity. Especially in the context of the modern (and relatively open) financial and money markets, concerted action or speculation specifically designed to undermine the international value of a foreign currency could be held to constitute acts of hostility which—in accordance with the principles just discussed—the host State may be under an international obligation to prevent. Yet such actions could only attract international responsibility if they were motivated by a desire to undermine the issuing State or its government; a simple desire on the part of private financial institutions to profit from the declining currency of a foreign State could not engage the responsibility of the State within which those institutions were operating.[9] In the nature of things, cases of this type will be exceptional and will have to be judged by reference to their own unique circumstances; as noted above, it may be possible to deal with such cases within the parameters of existing principles of public international law.

Leaving aside these exceptional cases, it should be emphasised again that there exists no *general* duty to protect foreign monetary systems. It thus becomes necessary to consider whether international law imposes any such duty in *specific* types of case.   **20.05**

C. Prevention of Counterfeiting

One particular duty has become firmly established in public international law in this context: it is the responsibility of every State to prevent and punish the counterfeiting of a foreign State's currency.[10] This rule, apparently first propounded by Vattel,[11] was judicially recognised by the Supreme Court of the United States in 1887:[12]   **20.06**

---

[9] A State would not generally be responsible under international law for the activities of such institutions—on the attribution of conduct to a State for these purposes, see generally, Arts 4–11 of the International Law Commission's Articles on State Responsibility. Consequently the UK had no grounds for complaint against other States when dealings by their financial institutions seriously damaged both the value and credibility of sterling on 16 September 1992 ("Black Wednesday"). For the background see the discussion of the European Monetary System in Ch 25 below.

[10] It may be noted that, on the facts, the printing activities in the *Emperor of Austria* case (n 7 above) were hostile to the interests of the plaintiff, but it was not a case which involved counterfeiting of the Hungarian currency. On the contrary, the notes were very distinctly separate from those then in circulation in Austria, and were intended for use only once the existing government had been overthrown.

[11] *The Law of Nations* (translation by Fenwick 1916) 46.

[12] *US v Arjona* (1887) 120 US 479, 483. See also *US v Grosh* (1965) 342 F 2d 141 or 35 Int LR 65.

The law of nations requires every national Government to use "due diligence" to prevent a wrong being done within its own dominion to another nation with which it is at peace or to the people thereof; and because of this, the obligation of the one nation to punish those who, within its own jurisdiction, counterfeit the money of another nation, has long been recognised.

There was scarcely adequate existing authority for this statement at the time it was made, but the correctness of this far-sighted pronouncement is not now open to doubt. The Convention for the Suppression of Counterfeiting Currency, concluded under the auspices of the League of Nations in 1929,[13] has substantially become the law of many countries, and has formalised the broad principles of modern public international law on this point. There may be differences of detail but they are of limited significance so long as the practice of States conforms to the rules established by the Convention.

20.07 The principles just discussed appear to apply as between States which are at peace. It is thus necessary to enquire whether it is a legitimate means of warfare to counterfeit the enemy's currency for the purpose of destroying his monetary system and credit. A few cases of such counterfeiting appear to be on record,[14] but they seem to have attracted little attention, and still less condemnation. Consequently, it cannot at present be said that counterfeiting activities of this kind, conducted in the prosecution of a war, are contrary to international law.

D. Duties of a Belligerent Occupant

20.08 On the other hand, the duties of a belligerent occupant towards the currency of the occupied territory have become more clearly defined.[15]

Methods of currency management

20.09 There are three main courses of action open to the belligerent occupant. It may allow the territory's existing currency to remain in circulation; it may create a new currency; or it may introduce its own currency for use in the occupied territory. A combination of these three methods may be appropriate in some

---

[13] Hudson, *International Legislation*, Vol iv, 2692 (1928–1929, Carnegie Endowment for International Peace).

[14] For alleged German attempts at forgery during the Second World War, see Murray Teigh Bloom, *Money of their Own* (1957) 234.

[15] For a comprehensive discussion written in English, see Skubiszewski, *Jahrbuch für Internationales Recht*, 9 (1959–60). See also Carreau (1982) 19 San Diego LR 233 and McNair and Watts, *Legal Effects of War* (Oxford University Press, 4th edn, 1966) 391–2. In view of some of the points about to be made, it may be helpful to point out that the concept of the "belligerent occupation" is not limited to enemy forces in time of war—see Brownlie, *Principles of Public International Law* (Oxford University Press, 6th edn, 2003) 369.

cases. The decision to be made in such situations is not governed by any monetary law considerations; rather, the decision should be guided by the terms and spirit of the Hague Convention IV and the annexed Regulations respecting the Laws and Customs of War on Land, particularly Article 43 which requires the occupant to "re-establish and ensure, so far as possible, public order and safety, while respecting, unless absolutely prevented, the laws in force in the country".

At first sight, this provision speaks in favour of the retention of the existing currency system, for Article 43 looks to the stability and continuity of the fundamental structures which formerly underpinned the occupied territory. If the original currency is preserved during the initial phase of the occupation, the occupant may also introduce a replacement currency system at a later stage, if public order so requires.[16]   **20.10**

But the retention of the existing currency system will often be impracticable. Between 1914 and 1918, Belgium was occupied by German forces but the printing plates for the local currency had been removed abroad; the Germans were thus compelled to introduce a new currency and the German Supreme Court later held that this action was justifiable by reference to Article 43 of the Hague Regulations.[17] Similar difficulties may arise where the assets which supported the currency—such as foreign reserves or gold—have been taken abroad or are otherwise outside the actual control of the occupying State.[18] Under circumstances of this kind, it seems that the introduction of an entirely new currency cannot be regarded as unlawful; the new currency—and obligations expressed in it—should be recognised as valid.[19] If this route is taken, then the   **20.11**

---

[16] Thus, the Constitutional Court of the Federal Republic of Germany (3 December 1969, *BverfGE* 27, 253, 279) held that in 1948 the Allies were entitled to substitute the Deutsche mark currency for its reichsmark predecessor, and that such measure did not offend against the obligation of the occupying Powers to protect private property. The general principle is clearly correct, although it is doubtful whether the Hague Regulations applied to Germany during this period. The right of the occupying Powers to reorganise the German monetary system on a rational basis was also recognised in *Eisner v US* (1954) 117 F Supp 197 or [1954] Int LR 576. In the context of the occupation of Iraq in 2003, the pre-existing currency was initially allowed to remain in circulation, although plans were made to replace it at a later stage—see n 21 below.

[17] 22 April 1922, *JW* 1922, 1324; 20 December 1924, *RGZ* 109, 357, 360.

[18] On this point, see Art 53 of the Hague Regulations, which allows the belligerent occupant to take possession of cash, securities, and other assets which are strictly the property of the occupied State. Title to such assets may in any event be disputed—see, eg, the first instance decision in *Dollfus Mieg & Co v Bank of England* [1949] 1 Ch 369, 392 where it was decided that that gold in the possession of the UK, the US, and France was held for public purposes within the meaning of the rules on State immunity, even though it admittedly belonged to the claimants at the time of its seizure by the Germans and may still have belonged to them at the date of the writ. The decision of the House of Lords rests on different grounds: [1952] AC 582.

[19] At least this should be so in the context of transactions of a private character—see *Thorrington v Smith* (1869) 75 US 1 and the decision of the Supreme Court of the Philippines in *Haw Pia v The China Banking Corp* [1951] Int LR 642.

occupant must take some care in establishing the rate of exchange (or "recurrent link") for the purposes of obligations expressed in the former currency; the introduction of an occupation currency with a rate of exchange disadvantageous to the inhabitants may infringe the occupant's obligation to respect private property under Article 53 of the Hague Regulations.[20] Subject to these considerations, the introduction of a new currency by the occupant is not itself unlawful.[21] Consequently, Germany did not act unlawfully during the First World War (1914–18) when it entrusted the printing of a new currency to the Société Générale and introduced a law which conferred the status of legal tender on those notes. The real problem in this type of case is not the legality of issue but rather the source of the cover; where should the occupant find cover for the new issue? In the Belgian situation just described, the Germans covered the new notes by opening at the Reichsbank a mark credit in favour of the Société Générale. This deposit amounted to 1,600 million marks, but it subsequently became worthless as a result of the massive depreciation of the mark. The ensuing

---

[20] *G v H* (1951) 18 Int LR 198. Where the legality of the occupation currency falls to be considered by domestic courts within the territory concerned and after the end of the occupation, it is perhaps unsurprising that opinions may differ. For example, Japanese occupation currency issued in the Philippines at par with the local unit was subsequently held to have been lawfully issued—see the decision of the Philippines Supreme Court in *Haw Pia v The China Banking Corp* [1951] Int LR 642, as explained by the Supreme Court in *Gibbs v Rodriguez* [1951] Int LR 661. For decisions of the Philippines Court of Appeal to similar effect, see *Madlambayan v Aquino* [1955] Int LR 944 and *Singson v Velosa* [1956] Int LR 800. See also the decision of the District Court of Utah in *Aboitz & Co v Price* (1951) 99 F Supp 602. In contrast, the Burmese Supreme Court found that the Japanese occupation authorities had no power to issue a parallel currency. Consequently, the notes so issued lacked any monetary status: *Dooply v Chan Taik* [1951] Int LR 641.

[21] The introduction of a new currency under these circumstances may amount to a political statement, as much as a matter of monetary policy. This was transparently the case where a new currency was introduced in Iraq following the occupation in 2003 and was substituted for the former Iraqi dinar on a one-for-one basis. In cases of this kind, where a transfer of power back to locally created authorities is one of the short-term objectives of the occupying powers, it may be difficult to determine whether the currency is created by the occupants or by newly emerging authorities within the occupied States; in the case of Iraq, the new issue appears to have been sanctioned by the Coalition Provisional Authority. It seems that, following removal of the Taliban regime in Afghanistan, the former monetary system continued in force but—partly for political and partly for practical reasons—the former notes were withdrawn and replaced by a new and more durable version and the unit of account was revised to take account of the effects of inflation under the former regime; for that purpose, one "new" afghani replaced 1,000 "old" afghanis. This appears to have operated as a measure of revalorisation, rather than as an outright replacement of the former monetary system. On these developments, see the Washington File Fact Sheet (7 July 2003), "New Iraqi Dinar to be released in October"; "Dollars replace dinars while Iraq awaits new currency", *The Guardian*, 16 April 2003; "Afghanistan shores up new currency", BBC World News Release, 26 October 2002.

controversy was only settled by a Convention of 13 July 1929,[22] whereby Germany undertook to pay certain annuities to Belgium by way of indemnity.

But what was the true legal position? It has been shown that Germany did not commit an international wrong by issuing an occupation currency. If a wrong occurred, it must in some way be identifiable by reference to the selected cover. It cannot be said that a wrong occurred merely on the grounds that—several years later and for reasons unconnected with the occupation—the mark suffered massive depreciation. The legality of Germany's action in providing the cover must be judged at the time that the cover was provided. If there was a wrong, it must therefore subsist in the very selection of mark assets as cover. But the alternative would have been to use Belgian assets as cover, and in practical terms this could well prove to be a more damaging solution for the occupied territory. Moreover, Allied practice following the Second World War not only confirms the legality of introducing an occupation currency but also indicates a method of providing cover which is essentially similar to that adopted by Germany in the Belgian case just described. The Allies issued Allied Military Currency denominated in the currency of the occupied territory[23] (reichsmarks, lire, or schillings) and gave it the force of legal tender. At least in the case of Allied Military lire, both the British and the US Governments caused the equivalent amounts (in sterling and dollars respectively) to be credited to special accounts to provide for the contingency of the lire in future becoming a charge against the occupying Powers. This suggests that the belligerent occupant may indeed lawfully cover the new currency with its own credit. Of course, this is to view the subject matter in its narrowest terms, for the belligerent occupant may place itself in a position where it has little choice as to the manner of cover; for example, because it has stripped the territory's central bank of its assets as part of a general scheme to deprive the territory of its resources and correspondingly to enrich those of the occupying power.[24] Activities of this kind are plainly prohibited by international law.

20.12

---

[22] *Nouveau Recueil general de traités* (1931) 3W Series 24, 527. The parties concluded the treaty without settling the problems just described; the treaty is in any event of limited value in this context because it settled a number of issues outstanding between the two countries and was not restricted to the monetary law issues. The further history of the Convention is described in Cmd 8653, p 23.

[23] See generally Kemmerer, "Allied Military Currency in Constitutional and International Law" in *Money and the Law, Supplement to the New York University Law Quarterly Review* (1945) 83; Fraleigh, 35 (1949–50) Corn LQ 89, 107.

[24] Whilst an occupying power may be able to requisition property required for its war effort, private property rights must generally be respected—see Arts 46 and 47 of the Hague Regulations. However, it would appear that funds and securities held locally by the central bank and other authorities could be used to provide cover for the new currency—see Art 53 of the Hague Regulations, to which reference has already been made in n 18 above.

20.13 The third method, ie the use of the occupant's own currency, is frequently a necessary practice, especially during the early stages of an occupation; it must accordingly be regarded as lawful. It must likewise be lawful for the occupying power to introduce local legislation to confer upon its own currency the status of legal tender within the territory concerned.

The question of responsibility

20.14 From the question of the legality of the currency system adopted by the occupant for the occupied territory it is necessary to distinguish clearly the problem of responsibility. Where the occupant introduces his own currency, it would seem clear that it is itself responsible for the use and redemption of that currency; for this reason, an occupant will normally discontinue using its own currency as soon as possible. Where, however, the occupant introduces military notes, it does not engage its own credit but that of the occupied territory. This was the view taken by the Allies in regard to the military currencies issued by them in the latter stages of the Second World War, but it is remarkable that Japanese war notes issued as legal tender at par with the peso in the Philippines were stated to be guaranteed by the Japanese Government "which takes full responsibility for this usage having the correct amount to back them up". From a practical point of view, the problem is of very limited significance because the victorious belligerent will usually obtain an indemnity from the defeated enemy. The duty of redemption will thus be imposed upon the defeated occupant—as happened, for example, in the context of the Armistice with Italy,[25] in the Treaties of Peace concluded with Italy, Romania and Hungary in 1947,[26] and in the State Treaty with Austria.[27]

The operation of the currency system

20.15 Whichever type of monetary organisation is adopted by the occupant and whatever answer is given to the question of responsibility, it remains necessary to define the occupant's duties in relation to the operation and management of the territory's monetary system. The question may be elusive to the lawyer because questions of valuation and quantum may become involved. Nevertheless, it is perhaps possible to formulate a few general rules of conduct in this area. First of all, it appears that an occupant which introduces its own, or a new, currency can only do so to such extent as is required to satisfy military needs or to supplement

---

[25] Clause 23.

[26] Article 76(4) of the Treaty with Italy; Art 30(4) of the Treaty with Romania; Art 32(4) of the Treaty with Hungary.

[27] Cmd 9482, art 24(4). Where British Military notes were issued in Allied territory, the Government of the latter usually assumed responsibility; see, eg, the Treaty with Greece of 7 March 1955 (Cmd 9481), para 13(a).

an inadequate amount of circulating local currency.[28] Moreover, where the occupant establishes a rate of conversion as between the military and the local currencies, it must carry out a process of valuation which requires a high degree of objectivity and disinterestedness, with a view to ensuring that the economic position of the occupied territory is not unduly disadvantaged as a result of the currency situation.[29] Finally, the occupant will commit a breach of duty if it allows an extraordinary increase in the quantity of circulating money or if it promotes (or does not take steps to prevent) rapid inflation and the consequent depreciation in the value of money. The occupant cannot be made responsible for economic or other circumstances which are beyond its control[30] but, subject to that reservation, international law forbids the occupant to make it possible for the debtor to take advantage of its creditors by the satisfaction of a debt through a greatly depreciated and practically worthless currency.[31] It will, of course, be difficult to apply these general principles in particular cases, for each case will depend upon its own peculiar facts and the economic conditions at hand. The lawyer will have to keep in mind the principle which underlies the law of belligerent occupation, which allows the belligerent to make war support war, but does not permit it to exceed the functions of an "administrator and usufructuary";[32] within the limits of military need, the occupant must act for the public benefit of the inhabitants.

E. Duties of the Legitimate Government

As has been shown, the Hague Regulations and other sources provide some **20.16** guidance as to the duties of a belligerent occupant. In contrast, there does not as yet exist a rule of international law defining the duties of the legitimate government which, upon its restoration, it is expected to take in order to deal with the previous management of the currency by the belligerent occupant. In the absence of retrospective legislation, notes issued by the occupant must be recognised as having been legal tender during the period of the occupation, and thus as having been capable of discharging debts—even those incurred prior to the

---

[28] See the decision of the District Court of Luxembourg, 20 June 1951 (1951) Int LR 633.

[29] The formal requirement outlined in the text may be derived from Art 43 of the Hague Regulations.

[30] The substance of this reservation is emphasised by Fraleigh in (1949) 35 Corn LQ 89, 107, at 113.

[31] The suggestion in the text is made by Professor Hyde in "Concerning the *Haw Pia* case" in (1949) 24 *Philippine Law Journal* 141, 144. The point may perhaps be derived from Art 46 of the Hague Regulations, which requires the preservation of property rights.

[32] See the language of Art 55 of the Hague Regulations.

occupation.[33] Although the legitimate government will usually provide for the conversion of the existing stock of occupation currency into the lawful money of the country, it is a question of private law (as opposed to public international law) as to what extent the discharge of pre-occupation debts by the payment of occupation money should be recognised and revalorisation of debts repaid in greatly depreciated military currency is necessary or advisable; these are thus questions for (retrospective) legislation, for the possibilities of judicial revalorisation are very limited.

20.17   In most cases, the legislator will no doubt intervene. Following the Second World War, legislation was introduced in Malaya which confirmed the validity of contracts made during the period of the occupation and provided for the revalorisation of debts incurred in that currency, so as to protect the creditor against the consequences of its depreciation.[34] But any failure on the part of the liberated State to effect legislative or judicial revalorisation will not amount to an international wrong on its part. This conclusion is in harmony with the view that a State has a discretion whether or not to revalorise private law debts which have been affected by a major depreciation of the currency.[35]

---

[33] *Haw Pia v The China Banking Corp* [1951] Int LR 642, followed in *Madlambayan v Aquino* [1955] Int LR 994 and by the District Court in Utah in *Aboitz & Co v Price* (1951) 99 F Supp 602. Courts in Burma took a contrary view: *Dooply v Chan Taik* [1951] Int LR 641.

[34] See the Debtor and Creditor (Occupation Period) Ordinance (42 of 1948). Similar legislation was enacted in the other British territories in the Far East which had been subject to Japanese occupation. In *Ooi Phee Cheng v Kok Yoon San* (1950) 16 MLJ 187, a Malaysian debtor had borrowed a sum in Japanese occupation notes and undertook to repay in "British or Allied Currency". At the time of the loan, the identity and value of the post-war currency could not be known, so both the amount of the obligation and the money of account were unknown at the time. The 1948 Ordinance did not apply, and the court directed that the amount to be repaid should be ascertained by an inquiry into the value of the Japanese occupation currency in terms of commodities at the relevant time. The Ordinance enacted in Sarawak fell for consideration in *The Chartered Bank of India, Australia and China v Wee Kheng Chiang* [1957] Int LR 945 (PC).

[35] On this aspect of monetary sovereignty, see Ch 19 above.

21

THE PROTECTION OF FOREIGN MONETARY INSTITUTIONS

A. Introduction

As was emphasised by Dr Mann on a number of occasions, this is a book about money.[1] It may, of course, be debated whether a chapter on monetary institutions is therefore appropriate in the present context. But it has been shown that the existence of a monetary system relies upon the State, which must authorise its issue and define its unit of account and other characteristics. It therefore seemed that the institutions responsible for the issue of physical money and the conduct of monetary policy on behalf of the State were worthy of at least some examination in the present context; in part, this view was taken because recent developments have emphasised that (a) such institutions enjoy a particular role within a national economic system and (b) that role may affect the attitude of foreign courts in their approach to cases involving such monetary institutions.[2]

21.01

---

[1] See in particular his preface to the Third Edition of this work.

[2] Since the present section is concerned with international questions, the discussion is solely concerned with the position of foreign monetary institutions before a domestic court. In a purely domestic context, monetary authorities may enjoy special immunities from suit, but these are purely matters of national law. On the subject generally, see *Three Rivers DC v Bank of England* [2000] 3 All ER 1 (HL). The subject is discussed by Proctor, "Financial Regulators: Risks and Liabilities" (2002) 1 JIBFL 15 and (2002) 1 JIBFL 71.

B. Central Banks and Monetary Institutions

21.02   Every modern State has some form of monetary institution which is responsible for the issue of its currency. They will frequently include the term "central bank" or "monetary authority" in their corporate titles, and their essential functions will be broadly similar.[3]

21.03   There exists no satisfactory *legal* definition of a central bank.[4] Certainly, so far as the United Kingdom is concerned, the legislation establishing the Bank of England defines its functions, but does not attempt a broader philosophical definition of the role or purpose of a central bank.[5] The State Immunity Act 1978 confers immunity on foreign central banks in defined circumstances, and yet does not attempt a formal definition of "central bank".[6] We must therefore be content with a definition which focuses on certain features and functions of a central bank:[7]

(1)   a central bank will usually be wholly owned by the State concerned or will form a part of the machinery of government;[8]

(2)   a central bank will usually be a legal entity in its own right;[9]

(3)   the central bank will usually be recognised as the institution which stands at the apex of the monetary and banking system of its home country, and will be required to perform, as best it can in the national economic interest, the functions described in points (4) to (9) below;

---

[3]   The expression "currency board" refers to an authority charged with the administration of a monetary peg or similar arrangement—for a discussion of this subject, see Ch 33 below. A currency board will usually be the principal monetary authority in the State concerned and will thus fall to be treated as a "central bank" for present purposes.

[4]   This must necessarily be so, because the precise role of central banks varies from country to country; furthermore, that role and the status of a national institution will vary over time. This point and many others are made by Fox, *The Law of State Immunity* (Oxford University Press, 2002) 360–6.

[5]   For the legislation, see the Bank of England Act 1694 (as amended), the Charter of the Bank of England 1694, the Bank Charter Act 1844, the Bank of England Act 1946, the Charter of the Bank of England Act 1988, and the Bank of England Act 1988.

[6]   The relevant aspects of the State Immunity Act will be discussed at para 21.16 below.

[7]   The description about to be given draws on Silard, "Money and Foreign Exchange" *International Encyclopaedia of Comparative Law*, vol XVII (1975) 9 and on Blair, "The Legal Status of Central Bank Investments under English Law" [1998] CLJ 374.

[8]   In the case of the Bank of England, see the Bank of England Act 1946, s 1.

[9]   In the case of the Bank of England, see The Charter of the Corporation of the Governor and the Company of the Bank of England, 27 July 1694. Central banks in some countries have been incorporated under the general company law, but this would not have any impact on the points made in this chapter.

(4) the central bank will usually enjoy a monopoly in relation to the issue of banknotes and coin;[10]

(5) it will be responsible for the conduct of monetary policy and the control of credit, although the government may have various powers to intervene or to give directions to the central bank;[11]

(6) the central bank will hold and manage the State's foreign reserves and will perform general banking and paying agency functions for the government;

(7) a central bank will frequently be entrusted with the administration of the national system of exchange control;[12]

(8) it may act as custodian of the cash reserves of commercial banks, and will enter into rediscounting or other arrangements with them; and

(9) it will usually perform the role of lender of last resort.[13]

It may be added that a central bank may have other functions. In some juris- **21.04** dictions the central bank is responsible for the prudential supervision of the banking sector, whilst in other countries a separate agency is established for this purpose.[14] But these additional features do not add to (or detract from) an entity's legal status as the central bank of a given country. The present Chapter will therefore work on the basis that an institution which broadly displays the characteristics described in points (1) to (9) above and forms part of the machinery of the State[15] should be treated as a "central bank" for the purposes

---

[10] The Bank of England enjoys such monopoly only in relation to notes. It was required to keep the issuing function separate from its general banking business by the Bank Charter Act 1844, s 1.

[11] The Statutes of the Bank for International Settlements focus on this aspect; Art 56(a) describes a central bank as "the bank in any country to which has been entrusted the duty of regulating the volume of currency or credit in that country" or "a banking system [which] has been so entrusted". The latter expression was no doubt included with the US Federal Reserve in mind. In the case of the Bank of England, the Treasury was formerly entitled to give directions as to the conduct of monetary policy—see Bank of England Act 1946, s 4(1). The Treasury's power in this area was, however, terminated by the Bank of England Act 1998, which established a Monetary Policy Committee. That Committee is responsible for the formulation of monetary policy within the guidelines laid down by the Treasury. The Treasury may now only give directions with respect to monetary policy if the Treasury is "satisfied that the directions are required in the public interest and by extreme economic circumstances". On the various points just made, see the Bank of England Act 1998, ss 10, 11, 12, 13, and 19.

[12] The Bank of England carried out this function until 1979—see Ch 14 above.

[13] This role involves the provision of liquidity to the financial markets, as opposed to any obligation to rescue financial institutions which find themselves in difficulty.

[14] In the UK, the Bank of England was formerly responsible for banking supervision, but these functions were transferred to the Financial Services Authority under Part III of the Bank of England Act 1998. An entity which carries out the supervisory function but which does not perform the other functions just described will not constitute a "central bank" for present purposes.

[15] In other words, it seems that the central bank must have an established position within the apparatus of the State concerned—this seems to follow from the decision in *Banco Nacional de Cuba v Cosmos Trading Corp* [2000] 1 BCLC 813.

of the present discussion. It should be added that most central banks are incorporated under the domestic laws of the countries which they serve; for legal purposes, this may be regarded as the typical model. However, it should not be overlooked that a central bank which operates within a monetary union (ie such that two or more States are involved) will usually be established as an international organisation. The main example is the European Central Bank which was established following the Treaty on European Union. Other examples include the Eastern Caribbean Central Bank and the central banks established for the purposes of the African monetary unions. Likewise, the conduct of central banking functions may be entrusted to a group of institutions, such as the Federal Reserve System of the United States. The nature of such institutions will be discussed elsewhere,[16] but they are mentioned here because the mode of their establishment gives rise to certain issues in the context of their entitlement to immunities. This point will be discussed in the next section.

C. Status of Monetary Institutions before Domestic Courts

21.05 The foregoing section has provided a broad description of a central bank and its activities. It is now proposed to consider (a) the procedural immunities of such institutions; (b) the procedural immunities of central banks established by treaty; and (c) the position of exchange control authorities.

National central banks

21.06 It is necessary to establish a functional definition of a "central bank" as a necessary precursor to any discussion on the immunities of such institutions. But what are these "immunities" and why are they conferred? Historically, it may be said that all States were to be treated as equal, and thus no State could claim jurisdiction over another—in other words, each sovereign enjoys immunity from proceedings before the courts of each other's sovereignty. In modern times, it may be said that a State should not use its immunity as a means of avoiding liability in the context of commercial transactions, but it is still appropriate that a court should not seek to sit in judgment on the public or sovereign activities of a foreign State.[17] This distinction between sovereign acts (*acta jure imperii*) and actions of a commercial character (*acta jure gestionis*) lies at the heart of the law

---

[16] In relation to the Eastern Caribbean Central Bank and the central banks of the African Monetary Unions, see Ch 24 below. On the European Central Bank, see Ch 27 below.

[17] Since State immunity is derived from international law, it will be appreciated that the rules about to be discussed apply only where a court has to consider the position of a *foreign* central

of State immunity.[18] In essence, a foreign State is immune from the adjudicative jurisdiction of courts in the United Kingdom, unless an exception to that immunity applies in the particular circumstances of the case; exceptions generally apply in cases of a commercial character.[19] In the present context, it is important to appreciate that the immunity also extends to the government and the departments of that State.[20] The immunity also extends to entities which are separate from the State itself, provided that the court proceedings relate to actions taken in the exercise of sovereign authority and the State itself would have been immune in corresponding circumstances.[21] It has already been noted that a central bank is established as a separate body corporate under its local law; it will therefore only qualify for immunity from adjudicative jurisdiction in the United Kingdom if it can satisfy the tests just described.[22]

A central bank is an institution of a State.[23] In the issue of money,[24] the conduct **21.07** of national monetary policy, the administration of a system of exchange control, and the management of a country's foreign reserves,[25] it plainly discharges functions of a peculiarly sovereign nature. It is thus unsurprising to find that they are generally entitled to immunity from proceedings before the English

---

bank. Any immunity enjoyed by a central bank before the courts of its own country are thus entirely a matter of domestic procedural law. Those points are effectively recognised by State Immunity Act 1978, s 4(1), which notes that "the immunities and privileges . . . apply to any foreign or Commonwealth State *other than the United Kingdom*" (emphasis added).

[18] For a full discussion of the theoretical basis of State immunity, see Fox, *The Law of State Immunity* (Oxford University Press, 2002) chs 1–3.

[19] This is the starting point adopted by the State Immunity Act 1978, s 1. For exceptions to the immunity, see ss 2 and 11 of the 1978 Act.

[20] See s 14(1) of the 1978 Act.

[21] See s 14(2) of the 1978 Act. For previous discussion of the subject by the present writer, see "Central Banks and Sovereign Immunity" (2000) 3 JIBFL 70 and, for a corresponding discussion under German law, see Krauskopf and Stephen, "Immunity of Foreign Central Banks under German Law" [2000] 4 JIFM 138.

[22] It may be added that, at the outset, the institution concerned would have to prove that it is a central bank by adducing evidence for that purpose. State Immunity Act 1978, s 21 allows the Executive to certify various matters, but the section does not extend to the existence or status of a foreign central bank. For a case in which this general evidential point is discussed, see *New England Merchants National Bank v Iran Power Generation and Transmission* (1980) 502 F Supp 120.

[23] Since the central bank will almost invariably have been established as a separate corporation, it will usually follow that the foreign State is not itself liable for the engagements of the central bank, nor vice versa. For an exceptional occasion on which the Supreme Court elected to "pierce the corporate veil" in a case involving a foreign trade bank, see *First National City Bank v Banco Para El Comercio Exterior de Cuba* (1983) 462 US 611 discussed by M.M. Christopher (1985) 25 Virginia JIL 45. See also *First City Texas-Houston v Rafidain* Bank (US Court of Appeals for the Second Circuit, 16 July 1998).

[24] See *Camdex International Ltd v Bank of Zambia (No. 2)* [1977] 1 All ER 728.

[25] See *Crescent Oil & Shipping Services Ltd v Banco Nacional de Angola* [1997] 3 All ER 428; a similar view was taken in *De Sanchez v Banco Central de Nicaragua* (1985) 770 F 2d 1385, although the decision was not supportable on the particular facts of the case. The decision was disapproved in *Republic of Argentina v Weltover* (1992) 504 US 607.

courts, in any event so far as the conduct of their sovereign functions is concerned.[26] Of course, it is relatively easy to state that a central bank enjoys immunity in respect of its sovereign acts; it is much harder to determine whether a particular act should be classified as sovereign or commercial. In this context it is the *nature* of the particular activity, rather than the underlying *purpose* which will be relevant. The issue of a letter of credit is thus a commercial activity, even though this is done at the request of the government in support of a public works project.[27] Likewise, the issue of a promissory note is a commercial activity; this is so even though the note was issued by a central bank in the context of an inter-governmental agreement to foster trade and friendly relations between the Socialist States and thus reflected underlying obligations of an essentially sovereign or political character.[28] Perhaps the clearest illustration of this point in the monetary field is provided by the decision of the US Supreme Court in *Republic of Argentina v Weltover*.[29] In that case, the Argentine Government had agreed to cover the risk that its currency would depreciate against the US dollar, thus helping the Argentine borrowers to raise funding in the dollar market. The Government was unable to meet its obligations, and issued US dollar bonds in substitution therefor. It was subsequently unable to meet those bonds, and passed a Presidential Decree which further extended the time for payment. All of these steps were taken with a view to stabilising the Argentinian currency, and the Government thus argued that it was immune from suit in respect of them. However, it was found that the decision to default was of a *commercial nature*, because such a decision could equally have been made by a private issuer of debt securities. The underlying purpose of the default was of a sovereign character,[30] but this could not affect the Court's decision; the Government was thus liable to repay the bonds in accordance with the original terms. A foreign central bank will thus generally find it difficult to rely upon the plea of State immunity where the claim against it is based upon a contractual obligation of a kind which could be incurred by a non-State financial

---

[26] State Immunity Act 1978, s 1, read together with s 13(1)–(3) and s 14 (4) of that Act. The position is essentially the same in the US—see the Foreign Sovereign Immunities Act, s 1611. In accordance with the principles discussed in the text, a foreign central bank is amenable to the adjudicative jurisdiction of the English Courts in the context of any commercial activities which it may carry out. For recent examples, see *Trendtex Trading Corp v Central Bank of Nigeria* [1977] QB 529; *Verlinden BV v Central Bank of Nigeria* (1983) 461 US 480; *Central Bank of Yemen v Cardinal Financial Investment Corp (No. 1)* [2001] 1 Lloyd's Rep 1 CA; *Banca Carige SpA Cassa di Risparmio di Genova e Imperio v Banco Nacional de Cuba* [2001] 3 All ER 923; and *Banco Nacional de Cuba v Cosmos Trading Corp* [2000] 1 BCLC 813.

[27] *Trendtex Trading Corp v Central Bank of Nigeria* [1977] QB 529.

[28] *Central Bank of Yemen v Cardinal Financial Investment Corp* [2001] Lloyd's Rep 1 (CA).

[29] (1992) 504 US 607.

[30] ie because Argentina was seeking to control the external value of its currency and to regulate its economy.

institution. It should be appreciated that a successful plea of State immunity amounts to a procedural bar which prevents a court from hearing the case on the merits; a foreign State or central bank is not deprived of its immunity merely because it may incur a liability in respect of the same subject matter before its domestic courts,[31] where a plea of sovereign immunity will plainly not be available.

Whilst foreign central banks may be amenable to the *adjudicative* jurisdiction of **21.08** the English courts in cases of a commercial character, their assets nevertheless remain immune from *enforcement* proceedings, unless they have given their written consent thereto.[32] The privileged treatment so extended to central banks is said to recognise their special position as guardian of the foreign reserves of the State concerned.[33] Whatever the justification and merits of this status, it must be acknowledged that a number of States have adopted legal provisions similar to those which insulate central banks from enforcement proceedings in the United Kingdom and the United States.[34] It will thus be apparent that foreign central banks enjoy an immunity position which is in some respects superior to that of the State itself; given that the immunity may have the effect of depriving a judgment creditor of his remedy, it might be thought that the courts would tend to apply central bank immunity on a restrictive basis and to construe doubtful cases against the central bank. Yet the opposite has proved to be the case; the English courts have in recent times, adopted a general attitude

---

[31] For an example of this position in relation to a central bank, see *Renato E Corzo DC Ltd v Banco Central de Reserva del Peru* (US Court of Appeals for the 9th Cir, 12 March 2001).

[32] State Immunity Act 1978, s 14(4), read together with s 13(3) and (4). In this sense, central banks are placed in a privileged position because their assets are only vulnerable to attachment if they have expressly consented thereto; in contrast, the assets of other State entities may be subjected to execution proceedings if those assets are held for commercial purposes. The position is similar (although not identical) in the US—Foreign Sovereign Immunities Act 1976, s 1611(b)(i) on which see *Banque Compafina v Banco de Guatemala* (1984) 583 F Supp 320; *Electronic Data Systems v Social Security Organisation of the Government of Iran* (1979) 610 F 2d 94) (discussed by Assiedu-Akiofi (1990) *Canadian Year Book of International Law* 263); *Weston Compagnie de Finance et d'Investissement v La Republic del Ecuador* 823 F Supp 1107 (SDNY 1993) and Fox, *The Law of State Immunity* (Oxford University Press, 2002) 365.

[33] To this it may be added that the credibility and external value of the currency issued by the central bank is in some respects dependent upon its holdings of foreign reserve assets; the provision may thus indirectly reflect a desire to ensure that enforcement proceedings in this country would not have an adverse impact upon the currency or economy of the State concerned. At least in general terms, this view finds expression in the *Camdex* litigation which is discussed below. At a more basic level, it must be acknowledged that the State Immunity Act 1978 and the Foreign Sovereign Immunities Act 1976 were, at least in part, designed to encourage foreign central banks to place their reserves in the UK and the US and thus to secure the respective positions of London and New York as major international financial centres. For criticism of the special status thus accorded to central banks, see Mann, *Further Studies in International Law* (Oxford University Press, 1990) 303.

[34] See, eg, Canadian State Immunity Act 1982, s 12(4).

which is protective of foreign central banks. As will be seen, they have in some respects extended the privileged position of such banks even beyond that required pursuant to the State Immunity Act 1978. At least in part, this has been achieved through the recognition that the monetary functions and status of foreign central banks are relevant factors which must be taken into account in deciding whether to grant enforcement remedies, which are at the discretion of the court. Although the case law in this particular field is not vast, it is suggested that the following analysis will justify the general proposition just stated.

21.09 It is necessary at the outset to consider *Camdex International Ltd v Bank of Zambia*.[35] In that case, Camdex was the assignee of a deposit placed with the Bank of Zambia. The transaction was thus of a commercial character, and the Bank of Zambia accordingly enjoyed no immunity from the adjudicative jurisdiction of the English courts.[36] As a result, summary judgment had been awarded against the central bank. Furthermore, the deposit contract included an express consent to the execution of a judgment against the property and assets of the Bank of Zambia, with the result that it was also amenable to the *enforcement* jurisdiction of the English courts.[37] A freezing order was granted in respect of the assets of the Bank of Zambia.[38] Although this was subsequently varied so as to apply only to assets within England and Wales, the order continued to cause significant difficulties for the Bank of Zambia. It happened that, at the time of the proceedings, rapid inflation was eroding the value of the Zambian currency (the kwacha). It had therefore been decided to issue new kwacha notes in much higher denominations, in order to facilitate domestic transactions in cash and thereby (it was hoped) to stimulate domestic economic activity. The new notes had been printed by a security printer in England and it appears that title to the notes had passed to the Bank of Zambia, but the notes remained physically present in England pending their shipment to Zambia. The notes were thus caught by the freezing order. However, on the application of the central bank, the Court of Appeal decided that the notes should be released from the order so that they could be put into circulation in Zambia.

21.10 There were three main grounds for this decision:

(1) Although the physical kwacha notes were an asset of the Bank of Zambia, they did not acquire any monetary value until they were issued by the

---

[35] The present commentary considers the Court of Appeal decision reported at [1997] 1 All ER 728. Other aspects of the case also reached the Court of Appeal and are reported at [1996] 3 All ER 431 and [1997] CLC 714. The latter decision raises various issues in the context of the administration of an exchange control system and it is thus considered in the final section of this chapter.

[36] See State Immunity Act 1978, s 2.

[37] ibid, s 13(3), discussed at n 32 above.

[38] The course of events is described in the Court of Appeal decision at [1997] 1 All ER 728.

central bank to commercial banks within Zambia itself. In England, the value of the notes was virtually nil.[39] Since the purpose of a freezing order was to preserve assets of potential value to the creditor, it was inappropriate to extend the order to assets which had no intrinsic or monetary value.[40]

(2) There was evidence that the Zambian economy would suffer serious damage if the new notes were not introduced, because this would result in severe constraints upon the supply of money and, consequently, in a reduction in economic activity.

(3) A central bank is responsible for the management of the State's foreign exchange resources. This will involve both the public and the international obligations of the central bank and the State and it is inappropriate for an English court order to interfere with these functions.[41]

The above considerations were summarised in the leading judgment, in terms which should be reproduced in full:[42]   **21.11**

> Of course one agrees with the judge, without qualification, that a judgment debt should, in the ordinary way and in the ordinary situation, be paid. It is, however, relevant that the defendant is a body to whom the ordinary procedures of bankruptcy and winding up are not available. The situation is one in which, on the evidence, severe national hardship to the people of Zambia would follow if the State defaulted in its international obligations. It would seem to me that the defendant, grievously short of funds as it plainly is, cannot be at fault if it seeks to pay its creditors on a pro-rata basis, even if that means that each of them recover very little. It must be a legitimate concern of the defendant to try and ensure that the repayments due to the World Bank and the International Monetary Fund are not the subject of default . . . the learned judge did fall into error in failing to recognise this new dimension of the problem with which he was confronted.

The *Camdex* litigation was clearly of a very unusual nature.[43] However, it is clear that the status of the Bank of Zambia—both as note issuer and as an institution   **21.12**

---

[39] In other words—prior to their issue by the Bank of Zambia—the notes were merely paper and ink and had no value as money. This may be contrasted with the situation which arose in *Banco de Portugal v Waterlow & Sons* [1932] AC 452, where the notes concerned had been put into circulation in Portugal (albeit, unlawfully) and had thus acquired a monetary value. That case has been discussed in Ch 1 above. It should be added that in the absence of the waiver of immunity given by the Bank of Zambia, the banknotes would plainly have been immune from execution proceedings.

[40] It may be relevant to add that—once issued—the banknotes would represent a *liability* of the central bank, rather than an *asset*.

[41] It must be said that this point is more clearly made by the Court of Appeal in the later *Camdex* case reported at [1997] CLC 714.

[42] [1997] 1 All ER 728, 732 *per* Sir Thomas Bingham MR.

[43] The general theme of the judgment reproduced above has, however, been echoed in other cases—eg, in *Banca Carige SpA Cassa di Risparmio di Genova e Imperio v Banco Nacional de Cuba* [2001] 3 All ER 923, where the court refused to entertain an allegation of dishonesty against a foreign central bank partly on the grounds that it had "adopted a consistent approach to all its foreign creditors, treating them equally".

at the centre of the national economy—lies at the heart of the Court of Appeal's decision on this aspect of the case.[44] The same may perhaps be said of a decision of a US court, which was asked to prohibit the Republic of Iran and its agencies from transferring certain property. The court made the requested order but declined to extend it to the foreign reserve assets of Bank Markazi (the central bank) held with the Federal Reserve Bank in New York.[45]

21.13 Further evidence of the treatment extended to foreign central banks is provided by the Court of Appeal decision in *Banco Nacional de Cuba v Cosmos Trading Corp.*[46] In that case, Banco Nacional de Cuba (BNC) had functioned both as the central bank of Cuba and as a commercial bank; it owned a controlling interest in Havana International Bank Ltd (HIB), which was incorporated in Great Britain and was authorised to carry on a deposit-taking business in this country. In 1997, Cuba undertook a general economic restructuring, and Banco Central de Cuba (BCC) was established as its new central bank. As a part of these arrangements, the controlling stake in HIB was transferred to BCC. Cosmos was a creditor of BNC; it sought an English winding-up order against that entity.[47] In general terms, the court will only exercise its discretion to make such an order if some positive benefit will accrue to creditors as a consequence. Cosmos asserted that such a benefit could accrue, because the sale of the HIB shares had allegedly been transferred at a significant undervalue and could be set aside by the court, with the result that these shares would become available to the liquidator and creditors of BNC.[48] However, the Court of Appeal refused to make the requested order, partly on the following grounds:

---

[44] A central bank is thus treated differently from other creditors, because it is required to use its assets to discharge the public obligations which it owes to the State and its nationals—see Blair, "The Legal Status of Central Bank Investments under English Law" [1998] CLJ 374. As pointed out in that article, the Court of Appeal returned to this theme in a later hearing—*Camdex International Ltd v Bank of Zambia (No. 3)* [1997] CLC 714 (CA). Camdex sought a garnishee order in respect of foreign currency funds payable by a Zambian commercial enterprise to the central bank in accordance with local exchange control legislation. The application failed for a number of reasons, but the Court of Appeal again noted some of the wider issues. For example, in the absence of evidence, the court could not be certain that the Bank of Zambia would be beneficially entitled to the moneys paid to it under the exchange control system. Further, the Bank would be required to use its foreign exchange receipts in accordance with its duties as a central bank, and a payment to Camdex in priority to a distribution to the co-operating creditors was unlikely to be consistent with those duties. Under these circumstances, the Bank's duty to use its foreign exchange resources for public purposes would defeat the application for a garnishee order.

[45] *Electronic Data Systems Corp Iran v Social Security Organisation of the Republic of Iran* (1979) 610 F 2d 94.

[46] [2000] 1 BCLC 813.

[47] The English courts have a discretion to wind up foreign companies which are unable to pay their debts—see Insolvency Act 1986, s 222(1), read together with ss 222 and 224 of that Act.

[48] On the powers of an English court to set aside such transactions, see Insolvency Act 1986, ss 238 and 423.

(a) In order to recover the HIB shares, the BNC liquidator would have to take proceedings against BCC, which was now the Cuban central bank. Even if an order for the restoration of the HIB shares could be obtained, BCC would remain immune from any proceedings to enforce that judgment.[49] Likewise, it would be impossible for the English courts to make a winding-up order against BCC, for it would enjoy immunity in the context of such proceedings.[50] It followed that no assets would become available to a liquidator of BNC in the course of English winding-up proceedings.

(b) Quite apart from the formal immunity issues, the Court of Appeal thought it "inconceivable" that the English courts could exercise their discretion so as to make a winding-up order against the central bank of a foreign State. Such an order would interfere with the conduct of the sovereign and international functions of the central bank, and it would thus be inappropriate for the English court to intervene in this manner on behalf of individual creditors. It is submitted that this line of reasoning is plainly correct and reinforces the views expressed by the Court of Appeal in the earlier *Camdex* decision.

It is apparent from these cases that the courts are sensitive to the special role **21.14** which central banks fulfil, both within the domestic economy[51] and within the context of the international obligations of the State concerned. As a result—and even where a formal plea of State immunity is not available—the courts will seek to exercise any discretions available to them so as avoid orders which might adversely affect the functions of a central bank or which might impact upon the external monetary obligations or relationships of the State concerned.

It may be objected that the rules just described may leave the creditor without a **21.15** remedy and may provide an undeserving central bank debtor with an entirely unwarranted defence. This may well be true in some cases,[52] but the policy which underlies these rules appears to be generally accepted. The International Law Commission draft Articles on Jurisdictional Immunity of States and their Property contemplate that central banks and monetary institutions should enjoy adjudicative immunity in the context of their sovereign functions and should

---

[49] Under the State Immunity Act 1978, s 13(2)(a), "relief shall not be given against a state by way of . . . order for the recovery of land *or other property*". The benefit of this provision is extended to central banks by s 14(4) of the 1978 Act. For a decision of the US Supreme Court which displays features similar to the present case, see *First National City Bank v Banco Para el Comercio* (1983) 462 US 611.

[50] State Immunity Act 1978, s 14(2).

[51] ie both as the issuer of the national currency and as the guardian of the country's foreign reserves.

[52] In the exercise of its discretion, the court would clearly have to determine whether the central bank was genuinely facing financial difficulty, or whether it was merely attempting to avoid its obligations.

continue to enjoy immunity from proceedings by way of execution.[53] Further-more, the European Court of Human Rights has held that the granting of such immunities is consistent with international law and that the procedural obstacles thereby created cannot be impugned on the basis that they deprive a creditor or claimant of his right to a fair trial in the context of a civil claim.[54]

Treaty organisations as central banks

21.16 In so far as it confers upon central banks immunity from enforcement or attachment proceedings, the State Immunity Act 1978 adopts a fairly tradi-tional approach to the notion of a central bank. In particular, it assumes that a central bank is an emanation of a single State, and that each State has its own central bank.[55] As has been pointed out elsewhere,[56] the European Central Bank (ECB) presents certain difficulties of classification. The ECB is created by the terms of the EC Treaty and is thus an international organisation rather than an agency of a particular State.[57] On the other hand, the functions of the ECB[58] are very much those of a central bank as traditionally understood. This point is of some importance in practical terms, at least so far as English law is concerned. If the ECB is classified as a "central bank", then it will enjoy State immunity in English proceedings, to the extent which has already been described. On the other hand, no such immunity is available if the ECB is characterised as an "international organisation", for such entities have no general entitlement to State immunity. Such privileges and immunities as these organisations may

---

[53] On these points, see Articles 1(b)(iii), 5 and 21(1)(c) of the draft Articles. The draft is discussed in the *Report of the Ad Hoc Committee on Jurisdictional Immunities of States and their Property* (Official Records of the General Assembly, Fifty-eighth Session, Supplement No. 22(A/58/22)).

[54] See in particular, *Waiter v Germany* [1999] 6 BHRC 499 and *NCF and AG v Italy* [1995] 111 ILR 154. These decisions were accepted and applied by the House of Lords in *Holland v Lampen-Wolfe* [2000] 1 WLR 1573.

[55] See State Immunity Act 1978, s 14(4), which refers to "property of a *State's* central bank or monetary authority" (emphasis added).

[56] See, eg, Fox, *The Law of State Immunity* (Oxford University Press, 2000) 361. For a further discussion, see Proctor, "The European System of Central Banks—Status and Immunities" (2001) 1 JIBFL 23.

[57] The ECB must be recognised as an independent and separate juridical person by courts sitting within the UK—see Art 107(2) of the EC Treaty. The ECB's entitlement to such recogni-tion is an "enforceable Community right" for the purposes of European Communities (Amend-ment) Act 1993, s 1, read together with European Communities 1972, s 2(1). The rights and liabilities of the ECB are to be regarded as vested in the ECB itself rather than its constituent governing bodies, and it is to be regarded as distinct from the Community itself and the Member States. On these points, see respectively Case 7/56 *Algera v Common Assembly of the ECSC* [1957] ECR 39; Case 168/82 *ECSC v Liquidator of Ferriere Saint Anna* [1983] ECR 1681. See also para 27.14 below.

[58] Including, eg, the establishment and implementation of monetary policy and the holding of foreign reserves. The functions of the ECB are discussed in more detail in Ch 27 below.

possess are governed by the treaties which created them, and not by customary international law.[59]

So far as English law is concerned, it seems reasonably clear that the ECB would **21.17** not be entitled to the procedural protections and privileges created by the State Immunity Act 1978. As a narrow matter of construction, it seems that the ECB cannot be the central bank "of a State" for the purposes of the 1978 Act.[60] More broadly, however, the United Kingdom is a party to the treaty which created the ECB, and its courts are thus bound to extend to the ECB the specific immunities created by that treaty. Whilst the ECB is amenable to the adjudicative jurisdiction of the domestic courts in the context of contractual or tortious matters,[61] no proceedings by way of enforcement can be issued against it except with the sanction of the European Court of Justice.[62] It cannot have been the intention to confer upon the ECB two parallel sets of immunities under English law. Since the United Kingdom is bound by treaty to extend the latter set of immunities, it must follow that the ECB does not fall within the scope of the 1978 Act.

This, however, cannot be the end of the matter, for it has already been seen **21.18** that—whatever its formal classification—the ECB does in fact *perform* the functions of a central bank. Indeed, its status as the institution responsible for the definition and implementation of monetary policy throughout the eurozone confers upon it a unique role in the economic lives of all the eurozone Member States. Under these circumstances, it is suggested that an English court could not seek to review or impugn decisions taken by the ECB in relation to the issue of banknotes, the conduct of monetary policy, or other functions of a sovereign character. This conclusion flows not from any formal immunity, but from the restraint which the courts will exercise in reviewing the internal conduct of foreign States,[63] and, hence, the restraint which they will likewise exercise in considering the activities of international organisations which exercise sovereign

---

[59] On the position of international organisations created by treaty in relation to State immunity, see Fox, *The Law of State Immunity* (Oxford University Press, 2000) 467–73; Rheinsch, *International Organisations Before National Courts* (Cambridge University Press, 2000) 347.

[60] See the discussion of s 14(4) of the 1978 Act in n 26 above.

[61] See Art 288 of the EC treaty.

[62] See the Protocol on the Privileges and Immunities of the European Communities annexed to the Treaty establishing a single Council and a Single Commission for the Communities. The provisions of that Protocol were extended to the ECB by means of a further Protocol annexed to the Treaty on European Union. It should be appreciated that the procedural immunities conferred upon the ECB are only available to it to the extent necessary for the performance of its tasks—see Art 40 of the Statute of the European System of Central Banks.

[63] See the House of Lords decision in *Buttes Gas Oil & Gas Co v Hammer (No. 3)* [1982] AC 888 (HL).

power on behalf of a group of States.[64] The result is that the ECB is treated as a central bank for some purposes, but not for others.[65] But if this position is a little untidy, it is by no means impracticable; the English courts will respect the functions and the role of the ECB, and they will accord to it the immunities conferred upon it by the EC Treaty, rather than the more general form of State immunity.

21.19 Yet matters cannot end here. As has been shown, the procedural protections afforded to the central banks are essentially derived from customary international law. The obligation to grant such immunities is imposed by international law; consequently, a central bank may expect to enjoy broadly similar immunities in any country in which proceedings might be instituted against it. The same cannot be said about immunities conferred upon international organisations by treaty. Such immunities are derived solely from the treaty and, whilst naturally binding on the contracting parties, third States are under no obligation either to confer or to respect such immunities.[66] It is thus necessary to ask—to what extent would the ECB enjoy any form of immunity from the jurisdiction of courts sitting *outside* the European Community?

21.20 Inevitably, the answer to this question will depend upon the domestic laws of the State in which such litigation happens to arise. Some countries—no doubt recognising that the creation of an international organisation by treaty amounts to a pooling of the national sovereignty of the individual member countries— have extended the entitlement to State immunity to entities which are jointly owned by a group of States;[67] such language is, of course, apt to include an international organisation such as the ECB. In the United States, the Foreign Sovereign Immunities Act extends the entitlement to immunity to an entity "a majority of whose shares or other ownership interests is owned by a foreign State". Although the approach adopted by the US courts in this sphere has not been entirely consistent,[68] it seems that an entity which is jointly controlled by a group of States will qualify for sovereign immunity under this definition, even

---

[64] In so far as this statement relates to international organisations, it is suggested that it is justified by the decision in *Westland Helicopters Ltd v Arab Organisation for Industrialisation* [1995] QB 282.

[65] It is suggested that essentially similar considerations would apply in relation to the Eastern Caribbean Central Bank and those African institutions which preside over a common monetary unit. These institutions are discussed in Ch 24 below.

[66] It seems that customary international law has not developed to a point at which it requires States to respect the immunities of an international organisation of which it is not a member—see Rheinsch, *International Organisations Before National Courts* (Cambridge University Press, 2000) 245.

[67] See, eg, the Australian Foreign States Immunities Act 1985, s 3.

[68] For a discussion and additional references, Rheinsch (n 66 above) 154–7.

though no individual State has a controlling interest.[69] In other words, US courts recognise that foreign States may "pool" their sovereignty by delegating governmental authority to an international organisation such as the ECB, and will extend entitlement to sovereign immunity to that organisation on that basis.[70] Although the point would plainly cause little difficulty in relation to the ECB, it would be incumbent upon it to demonstrate that it in fact performs the sovereign functions of a central bank.[71] If the US courts are prepared to treat the ECB on the basis that its creation involved a pooling of sovereignty among Member States, then it should in principle be entitled to those adjudicative and enforcement immunities which are afforded to national central banks of the more traditional kind.

Quite apart from formal questions of sovereign immunity, it seems that courts in the United States will not enquire into the actions taken by the ECB within the eurozone and within the sphere of its sovereign functions.[72] Principles of this kind will not, however, prevent US courts from determining disputes of a purely contractual or commercial nature, for no deference to sovereign sensitivities is involved.[73]   **21.21**

Whilst the ECB will thus enjoy those immunities conferred upon it by the EC Treaty in so far as proceedings within the Member States are concerned, its immunity position in external jurisdictions is less clear; it appears that a plea of sovereign immunity may be available in some countries.   **21.22**

---

[69] *Re Air Crash Disaster near Roselawn, Indiana* (1996) 96 F 3d 932 (7th Cir); *Re EAL Delaware Corp* (1977) 107 ILR 318. Consistently with principles which have been discussed earlier, it seems that immunity may only be extended to entities which perform functions of an essentially sovereign nature—see the tests described in *Edlow International Co v Nuklearna Elektrana Krsko* (1977) 63 ILR 101 and *Williams v The Shipping Corp of India* (1980) 63 ILR 363.

[70] See, eg, *Le Donne v Gulf Air Inc* (1988) 700 F Supp 1400.

[71] See *New England Merchants National Bank v Iran Power Generation and Transmission* (1980) 502 F Supp 120. It should be added that, in defined cases, certain immunities can be conferred upon treaty organisations under the terms of the International Organisations Immunities Act. The application of the concepts of "pooled" sovereignty to such entities in the context of sovereign immunity thus tends to blur the distinction between States and international organisations for these purposes. However, this detailed question is beyond the scope of this work.

[72] This involves the application of the Act of State Doctrine in the Supreme Court decision in *Banco Nacional de Cuba v Sabbatino* (1964) 376 US 98 to the affairs of international organisations; for further cases on that principle, see *First National City Bank v Banco Nacional de Cuba* (1972) 406 US 759 and *Kirkpatrick & Co Inc v Environmental Tectonics Corp* (1990) 493 US 400. It is true that the principle adopted in *Sabbatino* was reversed in so far as it related to the expropriation of property by means of the Second Hickenlooper Amendment, on which see Mann, *Foreign Affairs in English Courts* (Oxford University Press, 1986) 172; Brownlie, *Principles of Public International Law* (Oxford University Press, 6th edn, 2003) 483–4; and Fox, *The Law of State Immunity* (Oxford University Press, 2002) 483–4. Nevertheless, the broader principle in many ways mirrors the approach adopted by the English courts as explained in the *Buttes Gas* case—see para 21.18 above.

[73] *Alfred Dunhill of London Inc v Republic of Cuba* (1976) 425 US 682.

Administration of exchange control

21.23 Exchange control as a general subject has been discussed earlier in this work.[74] A system of exchange control was broadly defined as a system designed to regulate outward transfers of monetary resources. An exchange control authority may thus be described as the entity or body charged with the administration of such a system. Frequently, the exchange control authority will also be the central bank, but there is no requirement that this must be the case.[75] In any event, since the supervision of exchange control is a distinct function, it is convenient to examine it separately from other central bank activities. It is thus necessary to ask—to what extent does the function of administering a system of exchange control attract any form of immunity before the English courts?

21.24 The relevant principles in this context are well illustrated by the first instance decision in *Crescent Oil and Shipping Services Ltd v Banco Nacional de Angola*.[76] Briefly, Crescent had agreed to sell a consignment of refined soya bean oil to Importang, an Angolan State entity involved in the purchase of foodstuffs. Under the terms of the contract between the buyer and the seller, payment in US dollars was to be made by means of a letter of credit to be opened by Banco Nacional de Angola (BNA), which functioned both as a commercial bank and as the central bank of Angola. In the latter capacity, BNA also operated as the country's exchange control authority. When Importang approached BNA to request the opening of the credit, BNA (allegedly on the instructions of the Angolan Ministry of Commerce) indicated that it would be unable to accede to that request; this left Importang unable to make the required US dollar payment. Crescent thereupon issued proceedings against BNA and the Ministry of Commerce, apparently on the bases that (a) the BNA and the Ministry had together decided that Angola had other priority requirements to which foreign exchange resources should be directed and (b) by refusing to allocate the necessary US dollar resources, BNA had wrongfully interfered in the contractual relationship established by the Crescent/Importang sale and purchase agreement. The claimant's application failed for a number of reasons, but only the following are relevant in the present context:

---

[74] See Part IV above.

[75] In this context, it may be recalled that the UK's system of exchange control was to be administered by the Treasury, but in fact this function was delegated to the Bank of England. On this point, see Ch 14 above.

[76] [1997] 3 All ER 428. It should be emphasised that the proceedings involved an application for permission to serve proceedings outside the jurisdiction. Consequently, the Court worked on the basis that the factual position alleged by the claimant was accurate, without making any specific findings in that regard.

(a) BNA had not entered into any commercial contract (or, indeed, any contract of any kind), nor had it submitted to the jurisdiction of the English
courts in connection with the proceedings.[77] As a result, BNA would be
immune from the proceedings if the actions alleged to have been taken
were of a sovereign character and Angola itself would have been immune
under corresponding circumstances.[78] Now, governmental decisions as to
the allocation of (necessarily limited) foreign exchange resources are of an
essentially sovereign or public character.[79] It followed that BNA enjoyed
state immunity in relation to these proceedings.

(b) Quite apart from the formal State immunity position, it is reasonably well
established that the English courts will not review the actions of a State or
State entity if those actions are carried out in the exercise of governmental
authority within the territory of the State concerned.[80] This principle was
of direct application in the present context, with the result that the English
court could not assume jurisdiction over BNA.

It remains to conclude that—at least in the context of their public or sovereign   **21.25**
functions—foreign central banks enjoy extensive protection from actions before
the English courts. That protection stems partly from the specific position of
central banks as entities which are entitled to State immunity in the formal
sense. But their position is further enhanced by the more general recognition
that central banks play a key role in the management of a national economy, and
that the English courts should tread warily in interfering with the discharge of
those functions. As has been shown, the position of the ECB and similar institutions is more ambiguous. Nevertheless, it is suggested that the courts should
recognise that the functions of the ECB play an important role within the
eurozone economies, and would decline to make any order which might interfere
with those functions.

---

[77] It may be noted in passing that had BNA proceeded to issue the requested letters of credit,
those arrangements would have been of a commercial nature, and BNA would not have enjoyed
adjudicative immunity—see State Immunity Act 1976, s 3 and *Trendtex Trading Corp v Central
Bank of Nigeria* [1977] QB 529, which have been noted earlier in this chapter.

[78] State Immunity Act 1978, s 1, read together with s 13(4).

[79] See *Pan-American Tankers Corp v Republic of Vietnam* (1969) 296 F Supp 361; *Republic of
Argentina v Weltover* (1992) 504 US 607, 614; and *Renato E Corzo DC Ltd v Banco Central de
Reserva del Peru* (US Court of Appeals for the 9th Cir, 12 March 2001).

[80] On this principle, see *Buttes Gas and Oil Co v Hammer (No. 3)* [1982] AC 888; *Kuwait
Airways Corp v Iraqi Airways Co* [1995] 3 All ER 694. For discussion, see Mann, *Foreign Affairs in
English Courts* (Oxford University Press, 1986) 69–71.

22

INTERNATIONAL RULES OF MONETARY CONDUCT

A. Introduction

The present chapter considers the impact of public international law in relation **22.01** to the monetary conduct of States.[1] It should be explained that "monetary conduct" in this context refers to the manner in which a State may seek to exercise its monetary sovereignty, for example, by seeking to fix the exchange rate of its own currency by reference to the unit of account of another State or by imposing exchange controls. The rules of public international law to be discussed in this chapter will be those rules which either circumscribe or facilitate the exercise of national sovereignty in this area. In the main, the discussion will focus on relevant treaty provisions, but there will also be some reference to the rules of customary international law.

---

[1] For a very helpful discussion of the many issues considered in this chapter, see Carreau and Juillard, *Droit international économique* (Dalloz, 2003) paras 1453–1514.

22.02   In general terms, rules of monetary conduct which arise from treaties in principle apply only as between the States which are parties thereto.[2] It would therefore generally be wrong to assume that any such treaties express universally binding duties.

22.03   In some cases, it is true, treaties which have consequences for the monetary or financial conduct of States may merely repeat an obligation which is imposed by customary international law. Thus, for example, a treaty obligation to "accord fair and equitable treatment" to each other's nationals,[3] and which in law is unlikely to amount to more than an obligation to act in good faith, and to refrain from abuse or arbitrariness; in other words, such treaties merely require States to comply with the general principles of international law in the specific context of their monetary legislation and activities. It is, of course, also true that the common practice of States, reflected through the terms of treaties which they have concluded, may lead to the formation of rules of customary international law which are thus binding upon all members of the international community. The point at which such a rule of customary law may come into effect as a result of a series of bilateral or multilateral treaties involves a high degree of appreciation and the difficulties in this area are by no means confined to the monetary sphere.[4] In general terms, it is submitted that bilateral treaty practice in the monetary field has not reached a level at which it is possible to deduce from it any specific rules of customary international law.

22.04   It is, of course, obvious that multilateral treaties are much more likely to create or give expression to customary rules of international law. But even here, much caution is necessary. As will be seen elsewhere,[5] the Treaty establishing the European Community now contains a number of provisions on monetary matters and seeks to regulate the conduct of Member States in the economic sphere—this position applies even to those Member States which currently remain outside the eurozone. But these rules are designed to support a monetary union, which is a discrete form of monetary organisation; consequently, despite the number of States which are party to it and its obvious significance within the

---

[2] This natural starting point is enshrined in Art 34 of the Vienna Convention on the Law of Treaties. The rule has recently been confirmed in the context of monetary obligations contained in an inter-governmental agreement between the US and Korea—see the decision of the US Court of Appeals in *Kang Joo Kwan v US* (27 November 2001).

[3] The phrase is to be found in Art 1 of the American Treaties of Friendship, Commerce and Navigation, and in numerous agreements for the provision and Protection of Investments concluded by the US. These arrangements are further considered at para 22.51 below.

[4] For general discussions of this subject, see *Oppenheim's International Law* (Longman, 9th edn, 1991) para 11; Brownlie, *Principles of Public International Law* (Oxford University Press, 6th edn, 2003) 12–15, discussing the *North Sea Continental Shelf Cases* [1969] ICJ Rep 3. Treaties of this kind are usually referred to as "law-making treaties".

[5] See generally, Part VI below.

monetary field generally, it is submitted that the EC Treaty cannot provide a source for newly emerging norms of customary international law in the monetary sphere.[6] A lesser degree of caution is perhaps required when one considers the position of the International Monetary Fund (IMF), where the vast majority of States are members.[7] Thus, if the members of the Fund grant to each other the right "to regulate international capital movements",[8] then it is possible to suggest that such a right is recognised by customary international law. As a result, the imposition of capital controls—even by a State which is not a member of the Fund—could not be regarded as a wrongful act within the context of customary international law.[9] The point has been acknowledged by the General Counsel to the Fund, who has noted that Article VI(3) of the Fund Agreement—allowing members to impose controls on capital movements—is merely declaratory of pre-existing customary international law.[10]

The position of the IMF Agreement may be regarded as exceptional in this context and various aspects of the agreement are considered below. Apart from that particular case, it is necessary to maintain a clear distinction between treaty law and customary international law. **22.05**

B. Enforcement of Treaty Rules

The right to enforce treaty provisions dealing with monetary conduct is generally vested in the contracting parties. Thus, whether or not the nationals of a contracting State or a third State can derive rights or benefits from a treaty is a **22.06**

---

[6] Indeed, in some respects, the opposite is true. The euro was created by treaty but relies for its recognition in other States upon the *lex monetae* principle, which itself reflects an established rule of customary international law—see in particular the discussion at para 30.34 below. The comments in the text would apply equally to other treaties creating a monetary union.

[7] For an illuminating historical and functional description of the Fund, see Lastra, "The International Monetary Fund in Historical Perspective" (2000) *Journal of International Economic Law* 507.

[8] Article VI (3) of the Articles of Agreement of the IMF. The substantive point has been discussed in Ch 15 above in the context of exchange control.

[9] In 1997, Malaysia imposed controls on the repatriation of capital by foreigner investors. These controls provoked significant controversy at the time. But whatever the economic or political objections may have been, it seems plain that the imposition of these controls did not involve a breach of international law. For further discussion of this subject in the context of exchange controls, see para 22.42 below.

[10] See Gianviti, "Member's Rights and Obligations under the IMF Articles of Agreement, the Role of Practice in the Interpretation of an Organisation's Charter" in Efros (ed) *Current Legal Issues Affecting Central Banks*, Vol III (IMF, 1995) 3; the point is also noted by Treves, "Monetary Sovereignty Today" in Giovanoli (ed) *International Monetary Law: Issues for the New Millenium* (Oxford University Press, 2000) 115.

question governed by the general law.[11] So is the important question thrown up by the Articles of Agreement of the IMF, namely whether a duty laid down by the Articles exists only as between the member States and the Fund, or also as between the member States themselves. A review of the Articles of Agreement does not provide an unequivocal answer.[12] It is true that the Articles provide the Fund itself with certain sanctions against the member State in default, but this does not necessarily lead to the conclusion that other member States are deprived of the rights and remedies usually available to them following the breach of a treaty by another party.[13] It may, for example, be argued that the Fund needed to have treaty-based sanctions at its disposal, for otherwise it would have had none; on the other hand, it was unnecessary to confer specific remedies on the member States themselves, for remedies such as counter-measures were already available to them under international law.[14] It may also be argued that membership of an international organisation involves a mutuality of rights and obligations among the member States, which should themselves be enforceable by the members individually.[15] It should be added that the point may assume importance where, for example, a member State restricts current payments in contravention of Article VIII(2)(a) of the Fund Agreement; does the errant State thereby become liable only to such sanctions as may be imposed by the Fund, or does it also breach an obligation separately owed to all of the other member States? It is suggested that the wider interpretation should be adopted, such that member countries are entitled to enforce their mutual obligations under the Agreement, should the occasion ever arise.[16]

Treaty law and treaty purposes

22.07 All treaties establishing rules of monetary conduct pursue specific purposes which are usually defined and of which those mentioned in the first Article of

---

[11] Third States can acquire rights under treaties in limited circumstances—see Art 36 of the Vienna Convention on the Law of Treaties. The provision is considered by Brownlie, *Principles of Public International Law* (Oxford University Press, 6th edn, 2003) 598–600.

[12] This may be contrasted with the position which prevails under the EC Treaty, where Member States are allowed specific enforcement rights as against each other—see Art 227 of that Treaty.

[13] eg, the right to apply proportionate countermeasures against the party in default. On this subject, see Art 49–54 of the ILC Articles on State Responsibility and the commentary in Crawford, *The International Law Commission's Articles on State Responsibility* (Cambridge University Press, 2002) 47–56, 281–305.

[14] Remedies of this kind were available only to States, and not to international organisations such as the IMF itself.

[15] This argument is based upon an analogy with the position of shareholders in a private company, who acquire contractual rights as against each other by virtue of the constitution of the company in an English context, see Companies Act 1985, s 14.

[16] Since the duty not to restrict current payments is to be found in a multilateral treaty to which numerous member countries are party, it may well be that a corresponding duty will also form a part of customary international law.

the constitution of the International Monetary Fund are probably representative. They include, in particular, the promotion of international monetary co-operation, the stability of exchanges, the creation of a multilateral system of payments, the elimination of exchange restrictions and of any disequilibrium in the international balance of payments. Such statements provide a valuable aid to the interpretation of the substantive provisions of the treaty, but they should not themselves be treated as laying down any legally binding rights and duties. It would, therefore, be wrong to derive from the very broad terms of Article 1 of the International Monetary Fund Agreement any specific legal duties which are not reflected in the express terms of the treaty.[17]

A similar example is provided by the Treaty establishing the European Community. Thus, the introductory provisions refer to the desire "to promote . . . a harmonious and balanced and sustainable development of economic activities . . . sustainable and non-inflationary growth [and] a high degree of competitiveness and convergence of economic performance".[18] These provisions represent a statement of intention or objectives; they provide a useful backdrop to the rest of the Treaty but they are not themselves capable of creating independent rights or obligations.[19] Substantive rights and duties of a legal character only become apparent as the Treaty develops its theme, for example, by imposing upon Member States a positive obligation to conduct their economic policies in accordance with guidelines developed by the Council in that area.[20]

22.08

Duties of co-operation and consultation

Even where a treaty includes the promotion of international monetary co-operation amongst the express obligations of the contracting States,[21] the precise extent of any legal obligation thereby created is very doubtful. It is necessary to reach this conclusion because, in the nature of monetary and economic matters,

22.09

---

[17] It should be mentioned that the International Court of justice inferred substantive treaty rights of "economic liberty without any inequality" from the treaty in issue in the *Case Concerning Rights of Nationals of the United States of America in Morocco* [1952] ICJ Rep 176, when the relevant expression was found only in the preamble and in an article addressed only to one specific field. Such passing references should not be regarded as the source of firm and legal duties. This case has also been noted in a different context—see para 19.03 above. For a general discussion of the purposes and objectives of the Fund from a Swiss perspective, see Nobel, *Swiss Finance Law and International Standards* (Kluwer, 2002) ch 3.

[18] EC Treaty, Art 2. For further discussion of this provision, see Ch 28 below.

[19] The ECJ frequently refers to these general introductory statements as an aid to the interpretation of the operative provisions of the EC Treaty. For a recent example which arose in the context of a monetary institution, see Case 11/00, *Commission v European Central Bank* [2003] ECR–I 7147.

[20] EC Treaty, Art 98.

[21] ie as opposed merely to a general statement of objectives in the introductory sections of the Treaty.

the ultimate objective is likely to consist of subject matter which is not readily amenable to judicial consideration. Thus, for example, the members of the IMF are placed under an obligation to "consult with the Fund" in relation to that country's exchange rate policies, and to allow the Fund to exercise "firm surveillance over the exchange rate policies" of its members.[22] Member countries are also placed under a duty to "collaborate" both with the Fund and other members "in order to ensure that the policies of the member with respect to reserve assets shall be consistent with the objectives of promoting better international surveillance of monetary liquidity".[23]

22.10   The duty to "consult" or to "collaborate" is one of uncertain legal quality. Furthermore, the ultimate objective of that collaboration is understandable in general terms but wholly abstract in legal terms. The same remarks must apply to duties of "co-operation" and similar obligations. Thus, where actions in the field of exchange control to be taken under the Fund Agreement conflicted with the terms of earlier international engagements, the affected parties were required to "consult with one another with a view to making such adjustments as may be necessary".[24] Provisions to similar effect were found in the original text of the EC Treaty. Article 105 provided that "Member States shall co-ordinate their economic policies" with a view to ensuring the equilibrium of their overall balance of payments and to maintain confidence in each Member State's currency; for that purpose they were to "provide for co-operation between their appropriate administrative departments and central banks". Provisions of this kind are doubtless required to be performed in good faith,[25] and this requires genuine co-operation or consultation with a view to arriving at a result; the States concerned are under an obligation to conduct themselves such that the co-operative or consultative process is designed to be a meaningful one.[26]

22.11   Whilst duties of consultation and collaboration are thus clothed with some legal substance, it is nevertheless necessary to conclude that there is no obligation on the parties to reach a solution by means of the co-operative or consultative process and (even if there were) the required objectives tend to be stated in a manner which would preclude any meaningful judicial examination. An obligation to co-operate with a view to achieving a particular objective does not impose an obligation to achieve that objective. The duty to negotiate is not an

---

[22] Fund Agreement, Art IV(3)(b).

[23] ibid, Art VIII(7).

[24] ibid, Art VIII(6).

[25] In the context of treaties generally, see Art 26 of the Vienna Convention on the Law of Treaties. In a Community context, see Art 10 of the EC Treaty, which both reflects and expands upon the general duty of good faith.

[26] These propositions are derived from remarks made by the International Court of Justice in the context of a "duty to negotiate" in the *North Sea Continental Shelf Cases* [1969] ICJ Rep 1, 47.

onerous one, and can be discharged with relative ease.[27] These conclusions are no doubt entirely unsurprising, and the general points which have been made are by no means confined to treaties addressing monetary or economic issues. Whilst all will, of course, depend on the precise terms of the treaty at hand, it seems that obligations to co-operate or to consult in the monetary sphere will usually have only limited legal content. This view is only reinforced by the undoubted fact that intensive consultation between governments in a monetary field could only act as a spur for market speculation and rapid movements of capital, both of which may have destabilising economic consequences; the secrecy of such consultations will therefore be vital to all parties. Where such a duty of consultation exists, there is accordingly every reason for limiting both its scope and its duration. It is for this reason that the failure of the British government to consult with the IMF prior to the 1949 devaluation of sterling is perhaps understandable, if not necessarily defensible on a strict view of the Articles of Agreement.[28]

Obligations of consultation and co-operation thus impose only minor constraints on a State's freedom of action in the monetary field. It is thus necessary to conclude that treaty provisions of the type here discussed have only a very limited impact on the monetary sovereignty of the contracting States.[29]   **22.12**

---

[27] See Lauterpacht, *First Report on the Law of Treaties (International Law Commission), 5th Session*, UN Doc A/CN 4/63, p 25; Lauterpacht, *Second Report on the Law of Treaties (International Law Commission), 6th Session*, UN Doc A/CN 4/87, p 5.

[28] An obligation to consult the Fund under these circumstances was imposed by Art IV(5)(b) and (c) of the original Agreement. Such "consultation" as did occur took place on a Saturday, when financial markets were closed, against the background of news leaks from the Executive Board session. For a description of these events, see Triffin, *Europe and the Money Muddle* (Greenwood (reprint), 1976) 119. On the sterling devaluation of 1967 and international law, see Carreau *et al*, "Annuaire Français de Droit International", (1968) 597.

[29] Whilst it is submitted that the statement in the text represents the true legal position, it is important to emphasise that obligations of co-operation and consultation are by no means without value. If nothing else, they give pause for thought before a course of action is finally decided upon; and it may well be that more may be achieved by efforts to co-operate on equal terms, rather than by insistence upon rigid legal positions. But frequently, matters will go further than that; the *legal* obligation to consult may result in a political need to reach a mutually acceptable solution, and *political* impetus may provide a greater spur to action than any formal, legal obligation. As has been noted in the text, treaty provisions of this kind do create a legal obligation, but it is at best, a relatively shallow one. It may therefore be appropriate to categorise such provisions as a form of "soft law". The whole subject of soft law is considered, albeit in a slightly different context, by Giovanoli "A New Architecture for the Global Financial Market: Legal Aspects of International Standard Setting" in (Giovanoli (ed) *International Monetary Law* (Oxford University Press, 2000). Of course, other aspects of the Fund Agreement create legally binding obligations which are thus "hard law", eg, the duties to pay subscriptions and to impose exchange control restrictions only in a manner which is consistent with the Fund itself.

C. Stability of Exchange Rates

22.13 A clearly defined and self-standing legal duty to maintain stable currencies does not at present exist; under current monetary conditions and bearing in mind the international character of the financial markets, it is difficult to imagine that State practice will even begin to suggest the existence of such an obligation under customary international law.

22.14 Such obligations as exist in the field of exchange rate stability tend to involve general statements of intention or duties of co-operation/consultation, which are inevitably subject to the difficulties which have just been described.[30] Thus, the members of the Organisation for Economic Co-operation and Development (OECD) have merely undertaken to "pursue policies designed to achieve . . . internal and external financial stability".[31] A Member State of the European Community which remains outside the eurozone is under an obligation to "treat its exchange rate policy as a matter of common interest", but this by no means affects the "floating" status of the currency concerned.[32] The Exchange Rate Mechanism of the European Monetary System attempted to achieve a degree of exchange rate stability, but even this formal arrangement only required currencies to be valued within permitted "margins of fluctuation".[33]

22.15 On the other hand, one of the main purposes of the Fund was to "promote exchange stability, to maintain orderly exchange arrangements amongst members and to avoid competitive exchange depreciation".[34] In seeking to give effect to that objective, the original rules of the International Fund imposed very specific duties on the United Kingdom and other members which had established a par value for their currencies. Such members were under a duty to maintain the par value and they were not to change it except in accordance with the terms of the Agreement; furthermore, member States were not allowed to propose a change in the par value of their currency, unless this was required to correct a fundamental disequilibrium.[35] This system broke down in 1971 and is now only of

---

[30] See the discussion of Art IV(3)(b) of the Fund Agreement, above.

[31] OECD Agreement, Art 2(c).

[32] EC Treaty, Art 124. This provision is discussed in more depth at para 31.30 below.

[33] The ERM and its history are discussed in Ch 25 below.

[34] See the original Art 1(iii) of the Articles of Agreement of the Fund. For a discussion of the history, see Gold, *Legal Effects of Fluctuating Exchange Rates* (IMF, 1990) ch 1.

[35] These obligations were set out in Art IV of the original version of the Agreement. Although the par value arrangements lay at the heart of the Bretton Woods system, it seems that other States had no remedy for the loss in value of their external holdings in the event of an unauthorised devaluation—Gold (n 34 above) 139.

historical interest as an experiment in the international management of money, which operated reasonably successfully for about 25 years but which was unable to withstand an economic crisis caused by the abrogation of the dollar convertibility into gold.

When the Second Amendment to the Articles came into effect on 1 April 1978,[36] member countries were allowed a choice of exchange rate regimes.[37] They could maintain the external value of their currencies by reference to the Special Drawing Right or the currency of another member country; they could maintain that external value by co-operative arrangements with one or more other members of the Fund,[38] or they could adopt "other exchange arrangements of a member's choice" (for example, a freely floating currency). These open-textured provisions were accompanied by the members' undertaking "to collaborate with the Fund and other members to assure orderly exchange arrangements and to promote a stable system of exchange rates". This obligation was explained[39] by a number of additional provisions which are open to the objections noted in para 22.15 above. Members were required to "endeavour" to direct their economic and financial policies towards the objective of orderly economic growth; they were obliged to "seek to promote" orderly economic conditions and monetary systems which did not tend to produce "erratic disruptions"; and they were required to follow exchange policies which were compatible with these very general obligations. Perhaps the most substantive obligation required member countries to "avoid manipulating exchange rates . . . or the international monetary system in order to prevent effective balance of payments adjustments or to gain an unfair competitive advantage over other members".[40] At the same time, the Fund has the duty to "oversee the international monetary system to ensure its effective operation" and "the compliance of each member with its obligations" just mentioned. In particular, the par value system has disappeared and the prospects of its reintroduction must be remote in the extreme.[41]

22.16

---

[36] See Art IV of the current version of the IMF Agreement.

[37] See Art IV(2)(b).

[38] The European system offers an example of this type of arrangement. On the EMS, see para 25.11 below.

[39] See Art IV(1) of the IMF Agreement.

[40] See Art IV(1)(iii) of the IMF Agreement. The main effect of this provision is to prohibit a competitive devaluation of a member's currency. To that extent, it is suggested that the legal effect of Art IV(1)(iii) is essentially similar to that of Art 124 of the EC Treaty, which has been noted above.

[41] The Agreement provides for the reintroduction of the par value system by an 85% majority of the Fund's total voting power. On this provision, and the effective veto which it conferred upon the US, see Gold, *Legal Effects of Fluctuating Exchange Rates* (IMF, 1990), 8.

22.17   It is thus plain that there is at present no positive treaty or other obligation on States to ensure the international stability of currencies, nor does the creation of any such obligation appear to be at all likely.[42]

D. Floating Exchange Rates, Monetary Pegs, and Dollarisation

22.18   If there is no positive duty on States to maintain the stability of relative exchange rates, then it might instinctively be thought that the question of floating exchange rates does not arise for consideration. If a State is not under an obligation to maintain a stable rate of exchange, other States can scarcely complain if it allows its currency to float.

22.19   But the recent emergence of a dispute centred on the renminbi, the currency of the People's Republic of China, raises another question. Is a country under an *obligation* to allow its currency to float under any circumstances? Or, to express matters another way, can other States object if a particular State elects to fix or "peg" the value of its currency to the currency of another country? The nature of such arrangements, including the institutional and other means by which they can be achieved, will be considered at a later stage.[43] The present discussion is concerned solely with the consistency of such arrangements with international law.[44]

22.20   Since 1995, China had maintained a pegged currency, such that the rate of exchange with the US dollar was maintained at r8.28 : US$1.00. Tensions began to surface in the second half of 2003,[45] with the allegation that the exchange rate was artificially depressed in a manner which gave an unfair advantage to Chinese imports into the United States. Could it be argued that either the initial creation or the continued maintenance of the "peg" was in any sense inconsistent with any international obligations of China, such that it was thereby placed under an effective obligation to terminate the peg and to allow its currency to float on the international markets or, alternatively, to re-fix the peg at a rate which would effectively allow for a more balanced level of trade

---

[42] It should not, however, be thought that governments have entirely ceded control to the markets. Examples of efforts to maintain a degree of exchange rate stability include the EMS—see Ch 25 below—and the US Omnibus Trade and Competitiveness Act 1988, which authorised the President to seek to negotiate international agreements with a view to long-term exchange rate stability.

[43] See Ch 33 below.

[44] Of course, if the country of the currency which is used as the "peg" explicitly consents to the arrangement, then no difficulties can arise in relation to that State. But the pegging of a currency can clearly affect the economic interests of any State which engages in trading or financial relationships with the State whose currency provides the peg.

[45] See, eg, "China rejects US plea for renminbi revaluation", *Financial Times*, 19 October 2003.

between the two countries? The point does not appear to be the subject of any direct decision or precedent, and it is thus possible only to make a few comments of a general nature. The following may be noted:

(a) Subject only to the point noted in (b) below, there is no evident principle of customary international law which would prevent a country from establishing a "peg" or fixed exchange rate by reference to another currency.[46] As will be seen, a "peg" usually operates by means of a requirement that all physical money in circulation should be "backed" by assets in the reference currency held by the monetary authority of the pegged currency.[47] If the country which issues the reference currency chooses to allow that currency to be used and traded internationally and without restriction, then it is difficult to see any ground for objection if other countries seek to peg their national units against that currency as part of a broader economic policy.[48] No doubt, in the normal course of financial and diplomatic affairs, a country which proposed to establish such a peg would usually seek the consent of the country which issues the reference currency, or would at least notify it of the proposed arrangements before they were brought into effect. But there is no positive obligation to do so.

(b) Under international law, States are to be regarded as both independent and equal. As a result, customary international law requires States to refrain from intervention in the affairs of other States.[49] Would this principle of non-intervention prohibit China (or any other country) from linking its currency to the US dollar as part of its broader economic policy?[50] In other words, does the implementation of the currency peg by China constitute unwarranted intervention in the affairs of the United States? It is suggested that this question must plainly be answered in the negative. First of all,

---

[46] On the contrary, as noted above, Art IV(2)(b) of the Article of Agreement of the IMF specifically contemplates that members may maintain the external value of their currencies by pegging them to that of another member.

[47] For further discussion of this point, see Ch 33 below.

[48] It is necessary to emphasise the closing words of this sentence. If a peg were adopted as a deliberate means of harming the interests of the country which issues the reference currency, then this might constitute a "discriminatory monetary practice" (on which see para 22.24 below) and might also be objectionable on other grounds. For example, Art 32 of the Charter of Economic Rights and Duties of States 1974, provides that no State may use economic, political, or other measures *as a means of coercion* in order to obtain from the latter the subordination of the exercise of its sovereign rights. On this general subject and for further references, see *Oppenheim's International Law* (Longman, 9th edn, 1991) para 129.

[49] This principle is in some respects mirrored by Art 2(7) of the Charter of the United Nations, which provides that: "Nothing in the present Charter shall authorise the United Nations to intervene in matters which are essentially within the domestic jurisdiction of any State . . .". On the subject generally, see Brownlie, *Principles of Public International Law* (Oxford University Press, 6th edn, 2003) 290–4.

[50] Once again, it is necessary to emphasise the last few words.

action taken by a State will only constitute "intervention" for these purposes if it is "forcible or dictatorial, or otherwise coercive, in effect, depriving the State intervened against of control over the matter in question. Interference, pure and simple is not intervention."[51] The establishment of a currency peg for general economic objectives cannot possibly meet these criteria, for such an arrangement does not detract from the internal sovereignty of the United States. Furthermore, the establishment of the peg will only amount to unlawful intervention if it bears "on matters in which each State is permitted by the principle of State sovereignty, to decide freely".[52] Now it has been shown that a State enjoys sovereignty in the monetary field, but the extent of that sovereignty is necessarily limited. In particular, a State cannot by means of domestic legislation, control the price which others will pay for its currency on foreign markets, or otherwise control the use of its domestic currency outside its borders.[53] It follows that China's decision to introduce and to maintain a peg of its domestic currency to the US dollar cannot be impugned on the ground of international customary law.

(c) In the absence of any relevant principle of customary international law which would inhibit currency pegging, any legitimate objection must be derived from multilateral treaties to which both countries are party. So far as the US-China situation is concerned, this would seem to include the Agreement establishing the World Trade Organization (WTO)[54] and the Articles of Agreement of the IMF.[55] It is necessary to consider each of these possibilities. For immediate purposes, the questions arising from the WTO Agreement will be considered; the issues arising under the IMF Agreement are discussed below.[56]

(d) Article 1 of the General Agreement on Tariffs and Trade (GATT) 1947[57] provides that "with respect to customs duties and charges of any kind imposed on or in connection with importation or exportation *or imposed on the international transfer of payments for imports or exports* . . . any advantage, favour, privilege or immunity granted by any contracting party to any product originating in or destined for any other country shall be accorded

---

[51] *Oppenheim's International Law* (Longman, 9th edn, 1991) para 129.
[52] *Military and Paramilitary Activities Case* (1986) ICJ Rep 14, 108.
[53] On the nature and scope of monetary sovereignty, see Ch 19 above. Of course, a State may impose exchange controls which limit the availability of its currency outside its borders.
[54] China joined the WTO in December 2001.
[55] China rejoined the Fund in 1980.
[56] See "Manipulation of Exchange Rates", para 22.23 below and "Discriminatory Currency Arrangements", para 22.24 below.
[57] The General Agreement falls under the "umbrella" of the arrangements for which the WTO is responsible.

immediately and unconditionally to the like product originating in or destined for the territories of all other contracting parties".[58] Now it has been noted elsewhere that treaties dealing with exchange controls do not normally affect the imposition of tariffs and that likewise, treaties dealing with tariffs do not normally affect the sovereign ability of a State to introduce exchange controls or otherwise to regulate its currency in the general sense.[59] This rule of thumb is useful but it must, of course, give way to the specific terms of the treaty concerned; a treaty may deal with both subjects, and the provision reproduced above is clearly a case in point. However, in this context, Article 1 applies to "charges of any kind imposed on the international transfer of payments for imports or exports". It is true that Article 1 is intended to prohibit discrimination among products originating in or destined for different countries[60] and that the Article is directed to any form of discrimination, however achieved (ie and not merely to discrimination achieved by means of legal rules). It is also true that the discrimination which results from the measures at issue may be objectionable under the Agreement even though the discriminatory purpose is not apparent from the face of the measure or is otherwise not overt.[61] But there would appear to be no basis upon which a currency pegging arrangement could be regarded as a "charge" on the international transfer of payments, and it is difficult to see how the other requirements of Article 1 could be met. It is thus necessary to conclude that the Agreement does not confer any general jurisdiction over exchange rate systems adopted for general economic ends.[62] It seems to follow that Article 1 of GATT does not offer any ground

---

[58] Emphasis added. Art III(2) and (4) prohibit the imposition of "internal taxes or other internal charges" on imported goods in excess of those applicable to domestic goods, and other forms of differentiation between local and foreign goods. However, the language of these provisions (in particular, the references to "taxes" or "charges") is not apt to embrace the difficulties which exporters to a particular country might face in consequence of the general exchange rate policy of that country. It is suggested that very clear language would have been required to reflect such an objective.

[59] See para 19.03 above.

[60] See the discussion of Art 1 in *Canada-Autos*, Appellate Body Report on Canada Autos case, para 78.

[61] See *Canada-Autos* (n 60 above) para 84.

[62] In the present context, the point is in some respects confirmed by the Protocol on the Accession of the People's Republic of China (23 November 2001, WTO Doc ref WT/L/432). By para 7 of the Protocol, China undertook to eliminate certain non-tariff measures; the list of such measures is lengthy, but no reference is made to China's monetary arrangements. Other provisions of the Protocol deal very indirectly with monetary and financial issues (eg para 9, Price Controls; para 11, Taxes and Charges), but none of this is sufficient to suggest that China's admission to the WTO was in any way conditional upon the adoption of any particular exchange rate system. Indeed the opposite intention may be inferred from para II(2)(a) of Annex IA to the Protocol which merely requires that China "provide information as required under Article VIII, section 5 of the IMF's Articles of Agreement" (which deals with statistical information relating to the member countries).

of complaint against any country's general exchange rate policy, for this cannot be regarded as discriminatory in relation to any particular member of the WTO.[63]

(e) Inevitably, however, matters do not end there. It has been seen that Article 1 of GATT prohibits the imposition of tariffs such as custom duties and similar charges. If a country takes steps to maintain its currency at a deliberately low value as compared with the currency of another country,[64] then the effect of that action is to create a subsidy for its exports whilst creating a barrier to imports—the latter may be said to have an effect which is similar to that of a customs duty or charge.[65] At this point it is necessary to consider Article XV of GATT, which provides a link between the WTO and the IMF. Article XV(1) provides that the members of the WTO shall seek to co-operate with the IMF so as to pursue a co-ordinated approach to exchange questions. Rather more substantially, Article XV(4) states that "Contracting Parties shall not, by exchange action, frustrate the intent of the provisions of this Agreement nor, by trade action, the intent of the provisions of the Articles of Agreement of the International Monetary Fund." In principle, there is an obvious logic to this provision. The supply of goods and services (on the one hand) and the means of payment (on the other) are merely two sides of the same coin, and Article XV(4) seeks to recognise this reality. But what, precisely, is its meaning and legal effect? In some respects, the provision merely gives effect to the principle that treaty obligations must be observed and performed in good faith. It has been asserted that countries should allow the value of their currencies to be determined solely by market forces,[66] but this must reflect an economic preference rather than a positive rule. Article XV(4) has not been the

---

[63] The point was inferentially made by Jin Renqing, Governor for the Bank of the People's Republic of China, when he said that "a country's foreign exchange regime should be determined by its economic development stage, its financial regulatory capacity, and the solvency of enterprises"—see his statement to the Joint Annual Meeting of the IMF/World Bank (IMF Press Release No 16, 23 September 2003). Critics of the exchange rate arrangements would have to demonstrate that these arrangements were intended to damage US interests by undermining US manufacturers and providing a corresponding advantage to Chinese exporters. This assertion has been made in some quarters—see "China hits record $6bn trade surplus" (*Financial Times*, 14 November 2003).

[64] It should be emphasised that the present discussion is concerned only with cases involving a single reference currency. Where a country seeks to manage the exchange rate against a more broadly based "basket" of currencies, the points made in the text could only arise in the most exceptional of cases.

[65] A case to this effect is made by William Primrosch of the US National Association of Manufacturers, in evidence to the Congressional Executive Commission on China (24 September 2003).

[66] See, eg, the Communiqué issued by the G–7 member countries following their meeting in September 2003.

subject of any decision, and it is thus difficult to comment on its scope. The provision does seem to recognise that exchange rates may have a distortive effect upon free trade and does not, in terms, object to that position; it merely objects to deliberate exchange action which is specifically designed to have that effect. Whilst it is impossible to be entirely confident in such matters—not least because of the levels of factual and economic analysis which would in practice be involved—it is difficult to see how Article XV(4) could prohibit the establishment and maintenance of a currency peg as a normal part of a country's economic and foreign exchange policies. Once established, it is in the nature of a currency peg that it should remain fixed, even during periods when the precise rate may seem inappropriate— the very object of a peg is to impose disciplines of this nature.[67] The disadvantages of a periodically inappropriate exchange rate may be said to be off-set by the advantages of long-term certainty in that sphere. It has also been shown that the establishment of a peg is consistent with customary international law.[68] In the absence of explicit terms, Article XV(4) should not be construed so as to deprive States of that right.

The process of "dollarisation"—the wholesale adoption of another country's currency in substitution for one's own—raises problems of a rather different order. If a State adopts another currency in this way, then its entire banking and financial system must be based upon that currency. This must necessarily lead to the consequence that the issuing State is in some respects deprived of some of its sovereign control over its own monetary policy, for large numbers of institutions will be operating in that currency but will be outside the jurisdiction of the issuing State. It is perhaps for this reason that the European Central Bank adheres to the view that a non-eurozone State should only adopt the euro as its currency with the explicit consent of the Community and under the terms of an agreement which would presumably deal with the concerns just noted.[69] It is understood that the United States takes a more relaxed attitude to the adoption of its currency by other States. In terms of international law, it may well be that the adoption of another country's currency would constitute an unlawful interference in the affairs of the issuing State, in that it may impede the sovereign

22.21

---

[67] See the discussion of this type of arrangement in Ch 33 below.

[68] See para 22.18 above.

[69] For the position of the ECB on this subject, see, eg, Recital (4) to the ECB's opinion on a proposed agreement concerning the monetary relations with the Principality of Andorra (CON/ 2004/12) [2004] OJ C88/18, and see the views expressed in *Official Dollarisation/Euroisation: Motives, Features and Policy Implications of Current Cases*, ECB Occasional Paper No. 11 February 2004. For the view that the consent of the issuing State is not required in order to achieve dollarisation, and for a discussion of the US International Monetary Stability Act 2000 which would encourage that process in other countries, see Gruson, "Dollarisation and Euroisation" in *Current Developments in Monetary and Financial Law*, Vol 2 (IMF, 2003) ch 31. Similar views are persuasively expressed by Gianviti, "Use of a Foreign Currency under the Fund's Articles of Agreement" (17 May 2002), relying in part on para 20.03 above.

ability of the issuing State to conduct an independent monetary policy. The issuing State would, however, presumably have to demonstrate that its monetary sovereignty had been diluted in a meaningful and practical (as opposed to a purely theoretical) fashion.

22.22   At this point, it becomes appropriate to return to the "Institutional theory of money", which was discussed at an earlier stage.[70] If, in accordance with that theory, international law requires that the monetary system of each State is built around a central bank which is entitled to control monetary policy, then it becomes possible to reinforce the case against unilateral dollarisation, for the central bank of the parent State will not have adequate control of monetary policy if the activities of banks outside its jurisdiction are affecting the money supply.[71] Consequently, dollarisation could only lawfully be achieved if appropriate arrangements are agreed between the central bank of the issuing State and the authorities of the other country. In the case of the euro, the arguments become even more persuasive. The Member States of the eurozone were only able to acquire that status by satisfying the Maastricht Criteria and agreeing to subscribe to various budgetary and other restrictions which were designed to support the currency.[72] If other States unilaterally adopt the euro without going through this pre-qualification process, then this may well constitute an unwarranted interference in the internal affairs of the eurozone States.[73]

E. Manipulation of Exchange Rates

22.23   Under the terms of Article IV(1) of the Articles of Agreement of the IMF, all member countries are required "to collaborate with the Fund and other members to assure orderly exchange arrangements and to promote a stable system of exchange rates". Provisions of this kind do not of themselves create legal obligations of any great significance[74] but, in the present case, the provision is reinforced by an obligation to "avoid manipulating exchange rates of the

---

[70] See para 1.27, n 93 above.

[71] Difficult though this line of argument may, at first sight, appear, it becomes more attractive if one recalls that "it is indeed a generally accepted principle that a State is entitled to regulate its own currency"—see, *Serbian and Brazilian Loan Case* PCIJ Series A, Nos 20–21, 44. Action taken by another State which interferes with that right in a meaningful and substantive way must thus constitute a breach of customary international law.

[72] It is, perhaps for this reason that the President of the ECB indicated that "adoption of the euro outside the treaty process would not be welcome"—see the President's speech "The ECB and the Accession Process", European Bank Congress, Frankfurt, 23 November 2001.

[73] It may be doubted whether the principle of non-interference is really directed to this type of case. Yet there is a logic to its application if action by the adopting State diminishes the sovereignty of the issuing State over its own monetary affairs.

[74] This general point has been discussed at para 22.09 above.

international monetary system in order to prevent the effective balance of payments adjustment *or to gain an unfair competitive advantage over other members*";[75] members are also required to follow exchange rate policies which are compatible with the provisions just described.[76] Now, it seems clear that a disproportionately large devaluation designed to secure a competitive advantage over neighbouring States with no broader objective in view will constitute a breach of these obligations. Thus, when Sweden devalued its currency by 16 per cent in order to restore confidence in the krona and to improve conditions for Swedish industry, it seems to have been accepted that Sweden had acted in breach of the obligation just described.[77] But this line of reasoning can only apply where a member country takes specific action to obtain a competitive advantage by means of a devaluation. Consequently, when China adopted a stable exchange rate regime for the renminbi in 1997 in an attempt to enhance both its own financial stability and that of the Asian region as a whole, its action was not open to criticism under Article IV(1), because it was not thereby seeking to gain an unfair competitive advantage.[78] Nor can it subsequently be criticised for retaining the same exchange rate policy after the Asian financial crisis had abated, for passive inaction can scarcely be characterised as "manipulation", at least until a very significant period of time has elapsed from the crisis which gave rise to the exchange rate policy at issue.

F. Discriminatory Currency Arrangements and Multiple Currency Practices

22.24 Article VIII(3) of the IMF Agreement lays down positive legal duties when it provides that, in the absence of Fund approval, no member may engage in "any discriminatory currency arrangements or multiple currency practices".

22.25 The meaning of the term "discriminatory monetary practices" is by no means clear, and has only occasionally been considered.[79] The term perhaps refers to arrangements (including bilateral treaties, unilateral action, or administrative

---

[75] Emphasis added. The language is of importance in the context of the position of China, which is discussed below.

[76] These obligations are set out in Art IV(1) of the Fund Agreement.

[77] This incident is described by Lowenfeld, *International Economic Law* (Oxford University Press, 2002) 536–7.

[78] Many Asian economies were in the midst of a very serious financial crisis at this time. For the Chinese position on the renminbi exchange rate during this period, see the address of Jin Renqing, para 22.20, n 63 above.

[79] See Gold, *The International Monetary Fund and Private Business Transactions* (IMF, 1965) 14. The subject is also discussed by the same writer in *Legal Effects of Fluctuating Exchange Rates* (IMF, 1990) ch 7.

practices) which are directed against a particular currency and are thus intended to discriminate against it;[80] bilateral payment agreements allowing for favourable exchange arrangements between two countries are likely to constitute discriminatory arrangements for these purposes because of the impact they will have on the exchange rate of the currencies of other countries. However, essentially for the reasons given earlier in this chapter, an economic decision to "peg" the value of a national currency with reference to the currency of another State should not generally constitute a "discriminatory currency arrangement" for these purposes.[81]

22.26   On the other hand, the nature of "multiple currency practices" can more readily be ascertained, even though the IMF Agreement does not contain a formal definition.[82] Such practices involve offering different rates for foreign currency according to the way in which it has been earned, ie according to the goods or services which it is intended to buy.[83] Many variations are possible; the legal difficulty is to distinguish between a currency practice and a quantitative restriction, such as a concealed tariff or an export subsidy.[84]

22.27   Thus, if a central bank levies a tax or premium when selling currency to be used for payment for a specific type of goods, that activity is rightly regarded as a multiple currency practice. In one case, Greece had granted a concession and, to the extent to which this involved imports into Greece, the agreement provided that these were to be free from any taxes or duties of any kind, including customs and similar charges. Greek law required the payment of a premium over and above the official rate of exchange where funds were required to pay for

---

[80]   Certain forms of discriminatory practice can, however, be directed against the currencies of other member countries generally. On this subject, see Gold, *Legal Effects of Fluctuating Exchange Rates* (IMF, 1990) 280.

[81]   See the discussion of the episode involving China under "Floating Exchange Rates, Monetary Pegs, and Dollarisation", paras 22.19 and 22.20 above.

[82]   On the whole subject, including the interpretation of the term and the Fund's practices in this area, see the Decisions of the Fund on Multiple Currency Practices, reproduced by Gold (n 80 above) end of ch 7.

[83]   The essential characteristic of a multiple currency practice is the existence of two or more exchange rates which are independent of each other and which apply to different categories of exchange transaction—see Gold (n 80 above) 257. However, the existence of such rates will only contravene the relevant prohibition if they result from legislative or other official action—see n 86 below.

[84]   That the provision is aimed solely at currency practices (rather than tariffs) is apparent from the whole scheme of the Agreement. The point is perhaps further emphasised by the language of Article VIII(3), which requires that the "fiscal agencies" (eg the central bank or treasury) of a member country should not engage in practices of this kind. Nevertheless, it appears that multiple currency practices were prohibited because they could be used as an instrument for discrimination in trade relationships—indeed, Nazi Germany had adopted such measures as a means to political ends, and this must have been a relevant consideration when the Articles of Agreement of the Fund were prepared in 1944.

certain imports. The majority of the arbitrators held that this was a monetary measure, and was therefore not prohibited by the concession, which only contemplated the payment of import duties and similar charges.[85]

The IMF itself refers to surcharges in respect of applicable customs duties, **22.28** import deposits, exchange taxes, and taxes on travel, and seems to suggest that such measures may involve multiple currency practices. Similarly, arrangements to encourage exports, such as tax rebates, cash subsidies, interest rate subsidies, and even official export credit insurance seem capable of coming within the Fund's definition of that term.[86] This may well be so, but in each case the test must be whether the restriction or practice affects or is concerned with the currency and its characteristics, such as the rate of exchange, ie the price of the currency, rather than the price or value of the goods. Thus, the United Kingdom's Customs (Import Deposits) Act 1968 created a customs duty or tariff, as opposed to a currency practice; it is a clear example of legislation which cannot be affected by treaty obligations with respect to exchange restrictions.

G. Convertibility for Current International Transactions

Those member States of the IMF which no longer enjoy the protection of the **22.29** transitional period under Article XIV of the Fund Agreement are under an obligation not to "impose restrictions on the making of payments and transfers for current transactions".[87] This rule is supplemented by Article VIII(4), according to which a member State shall buy gold or foreign balances of its own currency which are held by another member and result from current transactions. In other words, member countries are under an obligation to maintain the convertibility of their national currencies, to the extent required to support current transactions of this kind.[88]

The provisions dealing with current transactions may be contrasted with those **22.30** applicable to transfers of capital; Article VI(4) confirms that "members may

---

[85] *Société Générale Hellénique SA v Greece* (1951) 4 *Revue Hellenique de droit International* 373.

[86] International Monetary Fund's Annual Report (1979, 1980, and 1987) on *Exchange Arrangements and Exchange Restrictions*, 8, 17, and 27 respectively. It should be emphasised that Article VIII(3) prohibits a member country or its fiscal agencies from engaging in multiple currency practices. The existence of different rates for the same currency which flow from market forces (eg different rates will apply for spot, forward, and other transactions) will thus not involve a contravention of Article VIII(3).

[87] The obligation is imposed by Art VIII(2)(a). The Fund may approve particular restrictions on a case-by-case basis.

[88] This provision appears to have been respected by Argentina during the course of its financial crisis in 2001. Executive Order 1570/2001, s 2 provided that foreign transfers could only be made with the approval of the Central Bank. However, payments in respect of foreign trade transactions were specifically excluded from this requirement.

exercise such controls as are necessary to regulate international capital movements".[89] It appears to follow that member countries are under no general obligation to ensure the convertibility of capital which an investor may wish to remove from the country.[90]

22.31   Against this general background it is proposed to consider four issues in the context of convertibility for current transactions, ie: (1) the types of transaction which may be considered "current" for the purposes of the Fund Agreement; (2) the nature of any "restrictions" which might infringe Article VIII(2)(a); (3) the general effect of the duty of convertibility; and (4) the relationship between exchange restrictions and import restrictions.

Payments for current transactions

22.32   Since the rules about to be discussed apply only to current payments, it is necessary to attempt a description of that term. The definition of "payments for current transactions" is supplied by Article XIX of the Fund Agreement. The term:

> . . . means payments which are not for the purpose of transferring capital and includes, without limitation,
>
> (1)   All payments due in connection with foreign trade, other current business including services, and normal short term banking and credit facilities;
> (2)   Payments due as interest on loans and as net income from other investments;
> (3)   Payments of moderate amount for amortization of loans or for depreciation of direct investment;
> (4)   Moderate remittances for family expenses . . .

---

[89] Whether the term "necessary" is to be construed subjectively or objectively is a matter of some difficulty. Presumably, a member State would be allowed a certain margin of appreciation, but any measure taken to control capital flows would have to be taken in good faith, and not for some ulterior motive of a purely political character. Furthermore, both on general principles and because of the terms of Art VIII(3) of the Agreement, it would seem that Art VI(3) would not allow the use of discriminatory or multiple currency practices as a means of capital control—see Fawcett (1964) *British Yearbook of International Law* 46. However, in view of the open-ended language employed in Art VI(3), this point cannot be entirely free from doubt.

[90] There have, however, been numerous developments in the field of international investment—for a very helpful discussion, see Lowenfeld, *International Economic Law* (Oxford University Press, 2002), chs 13, 14, and 15. It may be that, as a matter of international law, foreign investors are entitled to fair and equitable treatment at the hands of the host government; such investors may also be entitled to non-discriminatory treatment. But in the absence of other factors, these principles appear insufficient to impose a positive duty of convertibility upon the host government. It may be that customary international law will develop to a point at which an obligation of convertibility will be imposed, but for the present, such obligations as do exist find more direct expression in bilateral expression investment treaties. The subject is thus discussed in more detail at para 22.54 below.

Given the importance of the definition, its terms may perhaps be regarded as a **22.33**
little loose and lacking in detail. The distinction between capital and current
transactions is in some respects dependent upon subjective elements[91] and it is
impossible to establish a uniform test applicable in all cases. Article XIX introduces further complications through a certain lack of consistency. For example,
payments for the amortisation of loans are, in accounting and business terms,
regarded as capital transfers, yet paragraph (3) of the definition classifies them as
current payments. Furthermore, paragraph (3) of the definition refers to "payments for . . . depreciation of direct investment", yet depreciation is not usually
a payment at all; it is merely a book entry or charge.

Nor must it be overlooked that a transaction may constitute a capital transac- **22.34**
tion for one party and yet be treated as a current transaction for the other. A
New York art dealer who sells a valuable painting in the course of his business to
an overseas client is engaging in a current transaction for the purposes of his
trade; but the purchaser may be acquiring that painting for investment, so that
the transaction is, from his perspective, of a capital nature. In cases of this kind,
it is suggested that the transaction would have to be categorised from the viewpoint of the buyer, since Article VIII(2)(a) is concerned with the ability of the
buyer to transfer payment. Thus, in the example just given, a restriction or
restraint on payment imposed in the buyer's country would not infringe Article
VIII(2)(a), in view of the *capital* nature of the transaction at hand.[92]

It should be emphasised that "current transactions" must necessarily have an **22.35**
international character if Article VIII(2)(a) is to apply to them; the Fund
Agreement is not directed towards payments or transactions of a purely
domestic nature. Deciding whether or not a transaction is to be categorised as
"international" or "domestic" is, of course, frequently very difficult and will
involve questions of degree. Given the objectives of the IMF Agreement, it is
suggested that a transaction is "international" for the purposes of Article
VIII(2)(b) if the payment of the purchase price will affect the exchange
resources of a country other than the one in which the seller carries on business.

---

[91] Mann (1945) BYIL 251.

[92] It may be noted that the Fund has power to "determine whether certain specific transactions
are to be considered current transactions or capital transactions"—see Art XIX(i) of the Fund
Agreement. But even this provision may not be especially helpful where, as in the example given
in the text, a single transaction would attract different classifications from the perspective of the
seller and that of the buyer.

Restrictions under Article VIII(2)(a)

22.36   The Articles of Agreement of the IMF aim at "the elimination of foreign exchange restrictions which hamper the growth of world trade".[93] They do not anywhere require the abolition of an existing regime, nor do they prohibit the introduction of new systems of exchange control. They merely require that any system of exchange control should be administered and applied in a manner which is consistent with the terms of the Agreement. This is confirmed by the co-existence of Article VIII(2)(a) and Article VI(3).[94] If a member State is effectively to exercise its right to restrict capital movements, then it must be entitled to monitor current transfers as well; how else can it draw the necessary distinction in relation to particular transfers and thus secure compliance in relation to restrictions involving capital movements?[95] This difficulty is explicitly acknowledged by the language of Article VI(3). Consequently, when Article VIII(2)(a) generally precludes the imposition of restrictions on current payments, it only contemplates measures which *in fact* prevent or limit payments. It does not deny the legality of such requirements as the completion of forms, the submission of applications, the production of supporting evidence, and similar matters which are the inevitable requirements of any system of exchange control.[96] The Articles of Agreement thus condemn factual obstacles to current payments, rather than a legal machinery which seeks to monitor such payments and may as a result *retard* and *burden* them, but which does not *restrict* them in the broadest sense.

22.37   It should be added, for completeness, that many treaties may require that current payments be liberalised to an even greater extent—the current version of the EC Treaty is a case in point. The United Kingdom has a general right to impose a system of exchange control under (and consistently with) the terms of the Fund Agreement. At least in terms of international law, the United Kingdom thus retains that right in relation to the rest of the world but has agreed to forgo it

---

[93] Article I(iv) of the Agreement.

[94] Article VIII(2)(a) provides that, subject to various exceptions, no member country may impose restrictions on the making of payments and transfers for current international transactions. Article VI(3) provides that member countries "may exercise such controls as are necessary to regulate international capital movement, *but no member may exercise these controls in a manner which will restrict payments for current transactions or which will unduly delay transfers of funds in settlement of commitments*" (emphasis added).

[95] The point was made by the Radcliffe Committee, Cmnd 827, para 727. See also the discussion in *Shanshal v Al-Kishtaini* [2001] EWCA Civ 264, paras 35–37.

[96] A similar position arose in a Community context, where restrictions on current payments were lifted at a more rapid rate than restrictions on capital movements. But the continued existence of the latter meant that a member State retained the right to monitor (if not to prohibit) payments falling within the former, liberalised category—see Case 203/80 *Re Casati* [1981] ECR 2595.

specifically in relation to the other EC Member States.[97] A State may thus—on a bilateral or on a multilateral basis—accept obligations in this field which are more onerous than those created by the IMF Agreement, but member countries cannot (of course) derogate or detract from their obligations under that Agreement.

Effect of the duty of convertibility

Convertibility[98] or transferability in the factual sense just discussed is guaranteed by Article VIII(2)(a) for the benefit of non-residents. The duty of convertibility does not apply where a resident trader is to be paid by another resident for the sale of goods or property abroad, for this is not an international transaction which falls within the scope of the Fund Agreement. A member State could thus impose restrictions on payments for such transactions, without infringing the Agreement.[99] On the other hand, and although the text is silent on the specific point, the privilege is guaranteed only to members of the Fund.[100]

22.38

Moreover, convertibility is only achieved within the meaning of Article VIII(2)(a) if any *partial* restrictions are abolished. Thus, convertibility is not accomplished if, as a result of multiple currency practices, payments are only transferable at a discount. Nor is it consonant with the Articles to limit convertibility to transfers to certain countries or in certain currencies. A non-resident creditor can require payments for current transactions to the country of his residence or anywhere else, and it would not be the function of the authorities in the transferor country to ensure observance of any restrictions imposed by a foreign country. "The guiding principle in ascertaining whether a measure is a restriction on payments and transfers for current transactions under Article VIII(2) is whether it involves a direct governmental limitation on the availability or use of exchange as such."[101]

22.39

---

[97] It should, however, be appreciated that the imposition of exchange control even as against third States would in many cases result in a contravention of the EC Treaty itself—see Art 56 (2) of that Treaty.

[98] On this term, see Sir Joseph Gold's "The Fund's Concept of Convertibility" (1971) and *Rec* (1982, i) 174, 263.

[99] eg, under the terms of the UK's Exchange Control Act 1947, a payment in US dollars between two residents of the UK could only be made with the consent of the Treasury for, quite apart from any other consideration, the payer would have been under an obligation to offer any such foreign currency held by it for sale to an authorised dealer—see s 2(1) of the 1947 Act, which has been considered in more detail in Ch 14 above. For the reasons given in the text, the existence of this provision was not inconsistent with the UK's membership of the Fund.

[100] This position may be said to follow from Art 1(iv), according to which the Fund "aims at a multilateral system of payments in respect of current transactions *between members*" (emphasis added). Nevertheless, for the reasons noted in the introduction to this chapter, it may equally be argued that Art VIII(2) now represents a rule of customary international law which would thus be binding on all States, regardless of their membership of the Fund.

[101] *Selected Decisions of the Executive Directors* (1987) 298 (Decision No. 1034 of 1 June 1960). See also para 15.31 above.

22.40   Difficult problems may arise from the possibility of the Fund approving restrictions. Presumably, the decision to grant or withhold consent must turn upon questions associated with the balance of payments of the applicant Member State, and not upon any extraneous issues. It is, for example, entirely unsurprising that the Fund does not consider itself a suitable forum for the discussion of political or military issues leading to monetary restrictions which are related to the preservation of national or international security; the Fund is prepared to approve such restrictions at least by silence, thus implicitly accepting that member States retain the right to impose restrictions for non-economic reasons.[102]

22.41   Article VIII(2)(a) is concerned only with the *making* of payments and transfers. If exporters are allowed to sell only particular foreign currencies to the exclusion of others, this is not contrary to the provision,[103] though such a rule may be caught by Article VIII(3) which, as we have seen, prohibits discriminatory arrangements and multiple currency practices. Nor does Article VIII(2)(a) affect the fate of payments after receipt; member States are thus free to impose the duty upon exporters to surrender foreign currency received by them.[104]

Exchange restrictions and import restrictions

22.42   As has been pointed out earlier,[105] import restrictions are generally distinguishable from exchange restrictions, so that provisions dealing with the former do not extend to the latter and vice versa.[106] Thus, when the Treaties of Friendship, Commerce and Navigation concluded by the United States provide[107] that "Neither Party shall impose restrictions or prohibitions on the importation of any product of the other Party . . . unless the importation of the product . . . of all third countries is similarly prohibited", exchange restrictions are not thereby prohibited as between the Parties.

---

[102] *Selected Decisions of the Executive Directors* (1987) 292 (Decision No. 144 of 14 August 1952). Where a State elects to impose sanctions against another State for political, military, or other reasons of national security, it is submitted that these cannot be regarded as a system of exchange control for the purposes of the IMF Agreement because they are not imposed for the purpose of protecting national monetary reserves. See para 17.25 (d) above.

[103] See Fawcett (1964) BYIL 44.

[104] Again, therefore, the obligation created by Exchange Control Act 1947, s 2 (mentioned in n 99 above) thus did not infringe the Fund Agreement.

[105] See para 15.31 above.

[106] As noted earlier, a general observation of this kind is inevitably subject to a review of the terms of the treaty at issue.

[107] See, eg, Art XIV(2) of the Treaty with the Federal Republic of Germany of 29 October 1954 (UNTS, 273, 3).

Although the specific issue is now of historical interest only,[108] it is appropriate **22.43** to note that this point seems to have been overlooked by the European Court of Justice. Where Article 28 of the EC Treaty prohibits "quantitative restrictions on imports and all measures having equivalent effect", the Court held that this prohibited any measures which, were "likely to hinder directly or indirectly, actually or potentially imports between Member States".[109] This formulation would have prohibited the introduction of exchange controls which might have rendered the import/export process more difficult and (to that extent) the formulation is unacceptable.[110]

On the other hand, where a treaty prohibits exchange restrictions, that treaty **22.44** does not affect the imposition of import controls. Thus, Article VIII(2)(a) of the Fund Agreement does not prevent the introduction of import controls, because such controls do not involve "a direct governmental limitation on the availability or use of exchange as such".[111] So far as English law is concerned, the point is perhaps inferentially confirmed by the decision in *Fielding & Platt Ltd v Najjar*.[112] In that case, English manufacturers sued for the price of an aluminium press to be exported to a buyer in Lebanon; the buyer resisted the action on the ground that the import of such goods into Lebanon would have contravened local import restrictions. The seller's claim succeeded on various grounds, but the buyer did not attempt to raise any defence based upon the consistency of the import controls with Article VIII(2)(b) of the Fund Agreement.

H. Bilateral Arrangements

It will be apparent from the foregoing discussion that—at least when viewed **22.45** from a modern perspective—the Articles of Agreement of the IMF are of relatively limited scope in so far as they seek to regulate the introduction and administration of exchange controls. The sovereign powers of the member States in this area are left largely intact. The whole field of capital transfers is largely untouched by the terms of the Agreement[113] and, in relation to current

---

[108] The point to be discussed is of historical interest because the individual Member States of the European Community are no longer entitled to impose any system of exchange control—on this point, see para 31.45 below.

[109] Case 8/74 *Procureur du Roi v Dassonville* [1974] ECR 837. The quoted language is to be found in para 5 of the judgment. The decision has been followed on subsequent occasions, notably in Case 120/78 *Cassis de Dijion* [1979] ECR 649.

[110] It may be added that the ECJ's approach seems to overlook the word "quantitative" which appears at the beginning of Art 28.

[111] See the Fund's persuasive definition, noted at n 101 above.

[112] [1969] 1 WLR 257 (CA).

[113] Although see Art VI(3), which prohibits undue delay in the discharge of commitments.

transactions, a number of member States still maintain restrictions and even the remaining members may apply for approval to new restrictions.[114]

22.46   Under these circumstances, and subject only to the limitations just described, it remains open to the member States—either on a bilateral or multilateral basis—to agree further restrictions to their sovereign rights to impose exchange controls. Multilateral treaties would tend to deal with this subject in a direct sense and may prohibit the introduction of exchange controls or may seek to regulate the manner in which such controls are operated. The most obvious and well-known provisions are those contained in Article 56 of the EC Treaty, which prohibit restrictions on the movement of capital and payments. As will be noted elsewhere, the introduction of any effective system of exchange control by an individual Member State would almost invariably contravene these rules.[115] On the other hand, bilateral treaties are less likely directly to require the mutual repeal of exchange controls, no doubt because the abolition of exchange control merely as between two countries is perhaps unlikely to have a great impact on trade or the economy. Rather, such treaties are more likely to require—in very broad and general terms—fair and non-discriminatory treatment of the nationals of the other contracting State, and may thus have an impact upon the adminis-tration of exchange control, as opposed to its continued existence. Whether particular provisions do in fact have an impact in the field of exchange control must inevitably be a matter of interpretation of the treaty itself, but it is possible to state a few general points.

Most-favoured-nation/national-treatment clauses

22.47   Is it possible to derive a requirement for equality or non-discrimination from a most-favoured-nation/national-treatment clause? A broad and general clause[116] which confers upon the nationals of the contracting States the right to the benefits and privileges granted by either State to the nationals of a third State or to its own nationals, is unlikely to afford any meaningful protection against the implications of exchange control, for it will probably have to be so construed as to condemn discrimination only on the grounds of nationality. The operation of all systems of exchange control is necessarily characterised by discrimination between residents and non-residents, for the very purpose of such systems is the preservation of currency resources within a particular monetary area. It is residence rather than nationality of a country which indicates the legally definable and relevant connection with a currency area. In contrast, a

---

[114]   On these points, see Arts VIII(2)(a) and XIV of the Fund Agreement.

[115]   See para 31.45 below.

[116]   On most-favoured-nation clauses generally, see McNair, *The Law of Treaties* (Oxford University Press, 1961) ch 15.

most-favoured-nation clause will generally preclude discrimination on the grounds of *nationality*, rather than *residence*.[117] As a result, most-favoured-nation clauses, expressed in a general sense, will usually have little bearing upon the practice or effects of exchange control. Nevertheless, it must be observed that a State which operates a system of exchange control consistently with the Articles of Agreement of the IMF will not thereby be taken to have infringed a "most-favoured-nation" clause dealing with mutual rights of property and inheritance as between nationals of the contracting States.[118]

Some treaties have, however, dealt with the subject of exchange control more directly. They have attempted to deal with exchange control in more depth but, in the absence of a uniform approach, it is only possible to note some general points.[119] In particular, the many Treaties of Friendship, Commerce and Navigation concluded by the United States since the end of the Second World War contain provisions of the following type: "Nationals and companies of either Party shall be accorded national treatment by the other Party with respect to the assumption of undertakings for, and the making of payments, remittances, and transfers of money and financial instruments."[120]

22.48

One might have thought that such a provision would have a greater impact in the present area than the broadly written, general provisions which were noted above. Yet this proves not to be the case, for such a provision is only designed to preclude discrimination against nationals and companies on a nationality basis in the application of foreign exchange regulations.[121] On the other hand, there is no rigid rule that such treaties must apply by reference to a *nationality* test; they may, on proper interpretation, apply by reference to *residence*.[122] An example is provided by the Anglo-Greek Treaty of Commerce and Navigation of 16 July 1926;[123] in the event that Greece introduced exchange control, the terms on which foreign currency was to be made available to pay for imports from Britain "shall be not less favourable in any respect than the corresponding

22.49

---

[117] See generally, the *Case of Oscar Chinn* A/B No. 63 (1934) 88; Mann (1959, i) *Rec* 96. For a different view, see Kewening (1966–7) 16 Buffalo LR 377, 391.

[118] This appears to be the effect of the decision of the US Supreme Court in *Kolovrat v Oregon* (1961) 366 US 187.

[119] The General Agreement on Tariffs and Trade contains a "multi-lateral" most favoured nation clause. The consequences of this provision in a monetary context have been considered earlier in this chapter—see para 22.47 above.

[120] This example is taken form Art XII(I) of the Treaty with the Federal Republic of Germany of 29 October 1954.

[121] See para 14 of the Protocol to the Treaty referred to in n 120 above.

[122] ie the Treaty may be intended to apply for the benefit of those in a particular geographical area, as opposed to those bearing a particular nationality—see Hyde, *International Law* (Little Brown, Boston, 2nd edn, 1945) 1504–6.

[123] Cmd 2790, Art 11.

conditions under which foreign currency may be made available to pay for imports the produce or manufacture of any other foreign country". This provision appears to apply for the benefit of this country as an economic area; consequently a breach of this provision could have occurred even if the relevant discrimination was not based upon considerations of nationality. Given the context of a commercial treaty of this kind, this would seem to be a wholly sensible result although, as has been shown, it will frequently be a utopian one.

Fair and equitable treatment clauses

22.50 The preceding section has demonstrated that a standard of equality based upon nationality will generally fail to provide protection against discrimination in the field of exchange control. It thus becomes necessary to ask whether a treaty requirement for fair and equitable treatment is likely to be more effective for these purposes.

22.51 An obligation of fair and equitable treatment in relation to the allocation of exchange, has been laid down in a number of treaties. Once again, the Treaties of Friendship, Commerce and Navigation concluded by the United States supply some examples:[124]

(. . .)

3. Neither Party may, with respect to the other Party, in any manner impose exchange restrictions which are unnecessarily detrimental to or arbitrarily discriminate against the claims, investments, transportation, trade or other interests of nationals and companies of such other Party or their competitive position. Should either Party impose exchange restrictions with respect to the other party, it will remove them as rapidly as it is able to do so considering its economic position.

4. The two Parties, recognising that the international movement of investment capital and the returns thereof would be conducive to the full realisation of the objectives of the present Treaty, are agreed that such movements shall not be unnecessarily hampered. In accordance with this mutually agreed principle, each party undertakes to afford to nationals and companies of the other Party reasonable facilities for the withdrawal of funds earned by them as a result of making or maintaining capital investments as well as for the transfer of capital investments . . .

5. The term "exchange restrictions" as used in the present Article includes all restrictions, regulations, charges, fees, and other requirements imposed by either Party, which burden or interfere with the assumption of undertakings for, or the making of payments, remittances, or transfers of money and financial instruments . . .

---

[124] The present extract is taken from the Treaty with Germany—see n 120 above.

This network of bilateral treaties thus creates the duty not to apply exchange **22.52**
restrictions[125] so that they are "unnecessarily detrimental to or arbitrarily discriminate against" the interests and competitive position of nationals of the
other Party. There is a further duty to afford "reasonable facilities" for the
transfer of capital movements and the income derived from them. It appears
that discriminatory conduct may infringe these provisions even though such
discrimination is not based upon nationality.[126] It is also noteworthy that provisions of the type reproduced above extend to capital transfers; they thus restrict
national monetary sovereignty in that area to a far greater extent than the
corresponding provisions to be found in the Articles of Agreement of the IMF.

Provisions of the kind reproduced above are by no means free from difficulty. **22.53**
For example, the first sentence of paragraph 3 above contemplates that neither
party will impose exchange restrictions, whilst the second sentence contemplates
that they may do so, apparently in times of economic emergency. Equally, terms
such as "*unnecessarily* detrimental" and "*reasonable* facility" pose obvious
difficulties of interpretation and appreciation. Yet, whatever these difficulties
may be, it is suggested that the American precedents provide a satisfactory
recognition and affirmation of the principle of customary international law
which requires States to afford fair and equitable treatment to aliens, ie to act in
good faith, reasonably, without abuse, arbitrariness, or discrimination.

Bilateral investment treaties

It is, finally, necessary to refer to the growth of bilateral investment treaties. **22.54**
There are now more than 1,100 such treaties.[127] The treaties apply for the
benefit of the nationals (rather than the residents) of the contracting parties, and
thus suffer from some of the difficulties to which reference has already been
made. Typical provisions would include:

(1) an obligation to guarantee to nationals or companies of the other party
    both the transfer of the invested capital and of the returns upon it;[128]
(2) an obligation to pay compensation in the event of expropriation; and

---

[125] It is possible that the definition of exchange restrictions employed in these treaties is not
entirely satisfactory—see Mann *Rec* 96 (1959, i) 53.

[126] On this point, see Kewening, (1966–7) 16 Buffalo LR 377.

[127] For this and other statistics, and for an informative overview of this class of treaties, see
Lowenfeld, *International Economic Law* (Oxford University Press, 2002) 473–88. For a very
detailed review, see Dolzer and Stevens, *Bilateral Investment Treaties* (Brill Academic Publishing,
1995).

[128] Article 4 of the Treaty between the Federal Republic of Germany and Pakistan
of 25 November 1959 provides: "Either Party shall in respect of all investments guarantee to
nationals or companies of the other Party the transfer of the invested capital, of the returns and, in
the event of liquidation, the proceeds of such realisation."

(3) an undertaking to ensure that payment of any amounts owing pursuant to the obligations described in (1) and (2) above "shall be made without undue delay and at the rates of exchange applicable to current transactions on the date the transfer is made".[129]

22.55 The large number of these agreements may ultimately lead to the acceptance of a broad principle of customary international law to the effect that a government which has approved or accepted the importation of investment of capital must permit both the payment of interest, dividends, or other returns on that capital, and must allow the re-export of that capital upon sale or liquidation of the investment.[130] For the present, however, such a conclusion may be a little premature. The IMF Agreement still empowers member countries to impose capital controls, and it is difficult to see how this right could readily be overridden by the development of customary international law. Furthermore, Malaysia's decision to introduce capital controls in 1998 was criticised particularly on economic (rather than legal) grounds,[131] thus suggesting that those controls were not open to challenge by reference to principles of international law.

---

[129] The language is taken from Art 6 of the Treaty between the Federal Republic of Germany and Pakistan (see n 128 above). The language implicitly confirms that the investor is entitled to receive his return in the currency of his "home" country, and that there is to be no discrimination between current and capital transactions in terms of the rate of exchange to be applied.

[130] For a discussion of the British practice in the field of bilateral investment treaties, see Mann, "British Treaties for the Promotion and Protection of Investment" (1981) 52 BYIL 241. This article notes that the paramount duty of States is to observe and act in accordance with the requirements of good faith and provides various arguments in support of the principle of customary international law stated in the text. For a competing view, see Guzman, "Why LDCs Sign Treaties that Hurt them: Explaining the Popularity of Bilateral Investment Treaties?" (1989) 38 Virginia JIL 639. The competing views are discussed by Lowenfeld, *International Economic Law* (Oxford University Press, 2002) 486.

[131] See para 15.23 above.

23

THE MONETARY LAW OF
INTERSTATE OBLIGATIONS

A. Introduction

Monetary obligations arising under public international law will normally **23.01**
involve obligations arising between international persons (such as States or
organisations created by a treaty made between States). Although the respective
contexts may be very different, the types of difficulty with which the lawyer will
be concerned are likely to be similar to those which arise under a domestic contract—for example, What is the money of account; What is the money of
payment; What interest rate is to apply; may late payment result in liability for
interest, damages, or other remedies?

But two complications must be borne in mind. First of all, international **23.02**
practice in this field has developed over a long period of time and it is difficult to
discern any uniformity or consistency of approach; it is thus difficult to formulate
with confidence any applicable rules of customary international law. Secondly,
the international legal order lacks any currency of its own, with the necessary
result that questions touching both the measure and the means of performance
of international obligations require recourse to national currencies. The resulting

587

interplay of international and municipal law creates problems which involve peculiar difficulties.

23.03　The absence of an international currency caused limited practical difficulty where international law could resort to the device of adopting an independently defined unit of account. Thus, during the first seven decades of the twentieth century, numerous multilateral treaties were concluded on the basis of the gold franc of 100 centimes weighing of a gramme and of a fineness of 0.900[1] or the gold franc containing 65½ milligrammes of gold of a fineness of 900/1,000[2] or of European Monetary Units of account.[3] In these and similar cases,[4] the definition is identical with that of a national unit of account as constituted at the material time, ie the French franc or the US dollar, yet by incorporating the full definition in their text these treaties achieved more than they could have done by a mere reference to the national unit of account or the mere adoption of a gold clause; they effectively created an independent monetary system which could not be affected by purely domestic legislation. As a result of the "demonetisation" of gold and the volatility of its value, references in most of these cases have been replaced by references to Special Drawing Rights (SDRs)[5] or European Currency Units (ECUs)[6] with the result that international practice works with monetary standards which are even more susceptible to fluctuations in value.

---

[1] See, eg, the Universal Postal Union of 1964 (Cmnd 3141), Art 7; Convention on the Transport of Goods by Rail 1961 (Cmnd 2810), Art 57; Convention on the Transport of Passengers and Luggage by Rail 1961 (Cmnd 2811), Art 57.

[2] See, eg, Art 9 of the Convention relating to the Carriage of Passengers and their Luggage by Sea 1974 ((1975) Int LM 945 or Cmnd 6326). See also the Convention relating to the Limitation of the Liability of Owners of Sea-going Ships 1957 (Cmnd 353); the Convention was adopted by the Merchant Shipping (Liability of Shipowners and Others) Act 1958. Section 1(3) of the Act allowed the Minister to define the sterling equivalent of the gold franc; this he did by SI 1958/1725. On the effect of these Orders, see *The Abadesa* [1968] P 656 and *The Mecca* [1968] P 655.

[3] See, eg, Art 1, Protocol No. 7 to the Convention between the EEC and the African States, (1970) Int LM 485. The European unit of account was defined as a unit of account of 0.88867088 gm of fine gold—see Art 24 of the European Monetary Agreement of 5 August 1955. This was up to 1972 the par value in terms of gold of one US dollar.

[4] The Statutes of the Bank for International Settlements provided that the authorised capital of the Bank shall be 500 million Swiss gold francs equivalent to 145,161,280.32 gm of fine gold (Cmnd 3766), Art 5. This example is, strictly speaking, not on the same footing as those discussed above, because reference is made to the *Swiss* franc. The SDR was substituted for the gold franc as the unit of account of the Bank with effect from 1 April 2003—see the Bank's Press Release of 10 March 2003.

[5] An SDR represents a credit in the books of the IMF. The value of an SDR in terms of its currency composition is determined by the Fund—see Art XV(2) of the Articles of Agreement.

[6] In accordance with the principles discussed at para 9.03 above, treaty references to "European Currency Units" should now be read as references to the euro. Given that States had contracted by reference to the ECU, they must be taken to have selected Community law as the source of the *lex monetae* for their treaty obligations.

B. Determination of the Money of Account

Debts

As noted previously,[7] it may occasionally be difficult to ascertain the money of account in the context of a private law contract; if the parties have referred to "dollars", does this refer to US dollars or to Canadian dollars, or to one of the several other currencies which use that name? When entering into treaties, States will usually take care of questions of this kind. In those few cases in which the money of account has not been defined with sufficient clarity, the intention of the parties will have to be deduced from the construction of the treaty or from the circumstances attending its conclusion. As in the case of private contracts, it is difficult to offer any general rules in this area. However, the following comments may offer some guidance in cases of doubt: **23.04**

(a) There is no general presumption that the money of account is that of the country in which the treaty is signed. Thus, where a treaty was executed in Switzerland, the fact that France was a signatory (whilst Switzerland was not) suggested that references to "francs" involved French francs, rather than the Swiss unit.[8]

(b) Likewise, it has on occasion been suggested that debts arising under public international law are expressed in the currency of the creditor State. However, this appears to lack any foundation and would in any event be of no assistance where debits and credits may accrue separately to the parties throughout the life of the agreement.

(c) The purpose of the payment may provide an indicator of the money of account. If the payment is intended to meet the cost of maintaining the seat of an international organisation, this may tend to suggest that the money of account is the currency of the country in which the seat is located. Thus, in the pre-euro era, a requirement to contribute to administrative expenses in "francs" would probably have been a reference to French francs if the headquarters were located in Paris; or to Belgian francs if the seat of the organisation was situate in Brussels.

Attempts at clarification have occasionally had the opposite effect. Under the terms of a 1967 treaty,[9] France undertook to pay a sum of "163 million French **23.05**

---

[7] See Ch 5 above.
[8] Convention concerning the Régime of the Straits, 20 July 1936, see Hudson International Legislation VII, No. 449, p 401.
[9] See Art 2 of the Convention printed in Cmnd 6457.

francs (132 million DM)" and Germany undertook to pay "43 million French francs (35 million DM)". It would seem that the French franc was the money of account, and that the reference to Deutsche marks was solely for information purposes. The European Court of Justice had to decide a similar problem, in a case in which it had expressed a fine in terms of "80,000 units of account (FF 444,235.20)". The Court found that the French franc was the money of account for the purposes of its order, and that it had merely wished to demonstrate that the amount of the fine had been derived from the unit of account used by the Community for budget purposes.[10]

23.06 There are relatively few cases in which an international tribunal has had to determine the money of account in the context of a debt claim. One case[11] arose out of events in April 1941, where Greek vessels had taken on various cargoes from the United States and the United Kingdom—the former having been purchased for US dollars and the latter for sterling. The vessels were then diverted to ports outside Greece, where their cargoes were taken over by the British authorities for use against the common enemy. In February 1942, Greece and the United Kingdom agreed[12] that the Greek Government would prevent the cargo owners from making a claim against the British Government and that the latter would credit the Greek Government with the fob cost of the cargoes. The parties were agreed that, even in respect of goods purchased in the United States, credit was to be given to Greece in terms of sterling.[13] The issue was the rate of exchange at which the fob value of the goods of American origin was to be converted into sterling. Not unnaturally, the British Government contended for the pre-September 1949 rate of US$4.03 to £1, whilst the Greek Government argued for the post-September rate of US$2.80 for £1. Now, no question arose either as to the money of account or as to the money of payment, for both were admittedly sterling. The case thus involved only the question of which rate of exchange was to be employed, and this was plainly a question of the construction of the treaty concerned. The arbitrator concluded that the treaty of 1942 "created a single account in a single currency, and it was a credit in pounds sterling that the British Government undertook to give . . . to the exclusion of any other currency". The award in this case is thus authority for the (perhaps self-evident) proposition that the determination of the money of

---

[10] Case 41/73 *Générale Sucrière v Commission of EEC* [1977] ECR I–445, followed in Case C–196/99, *Aristrain v Commission*. For a similar difficulty encountered by the Court in a case involving a fine expressed in ECU but which only became payable following the introduction of the euro, see Case C–49/92P *Commission v ANIC Partecipazione* [1999] ECR I–4125.

[11] *Case of Diverted Cargoes* [1955] Int LR 820.

[12] The treaty is printed in Cmnd 9754.

[13] This followed from the Terms of Reference set out in Cmnd 9754.

account and the identification of any required rate of exchange are, in public international law no less than in private law, a matter of construction.[14]

Damages

The problem of determining the money of account in which unliquidated **23.07**
damages are to be expressed is familiar to international practice.[15] In some cases, the Convention creating an international tribunal has specified the currency to be employed for the assessment of damages. Any ambiguity surrounding the precise meaning of any such treaty provision must, of course, be resolved by a process of construction. In the absence of any express directions, tribunals must search for other indications in the relevant treaty. A process of construction is still involved, albeit perhaps from a different starting point. In the Mexican arbitrations, those indications were frequently found in the provisions according to which any *balance* due from one to the other government after the disposal of all claims shall be paid "in gold coin or its equivalent to the Government of the country in favour of whose citizens the greater amount may have been awarded".[16] In view of this provision, the United States-Mexico General Claims Commission adopted the practice of rendering awards in US dollars, apparently on the basis that this would avoid any future uncertainties with respect to the rate of exchange and was consistent with the underlying purpose of Article IX of the Convention concerned.[17] And yet, this arbitrary approach necessarily also involved an exchange operation (or calculation) and gave rise to difficulties in other contexts.[18] It may be added that this practice was not followed by the other Mexican Claims Commissions, all of which awarded damages in gold pesos.[19]

---

[14] It will be necessary to return to this case in the context of the rate of exchange to be applied—see para 23.57 below.

[15] See, eg, Brownlie, *State Responsibility* (Oxford University Press, 1995) 230.

[16] See, eg, United States of America and Mexico General Claims Commission, Convention of 25 September 1924 (Art IX); Great Britain and Mexico Claims Commission, Convention of 19 November 1926 (Art 9).

[17] On these points, see Feller, *The Mexican Claims Commissions 1923–1934* (Periodicals Service Co (reprint), 1935) 313; De Beus, *The Jurisprudence of the General Claims Commission United States and Mexico* (1938) 272.

[18] See, eg, *United States of America on behalf of Socony-Vacuum Oil Co Inc v The Republic of Turkey*, in Neilsen, "America—Turkish Claims Settlement" (1932) 369. The case was related to the assessment of the value of property requisitioned without compensation in Turkey. The Tribunal said: "The claimant in the present case and other claimants have as a general rule converted Turkish money into American money at rates understood to prevail at the time of the taking of the property." This practice was approved.

[19] See, eg, Great Britain and Mexico Claims Commission, Award of 19 May 1931, *Re Watson* (AD 1931–2, Case No. 113). See also the discussion by Feller, *The Mexican Claims Commissions 1923–1934* (1935) 314, discussing the approach adopted by the British–Mexican, French–Mexican, German–Mexican and Spanish–Mexican Claims Commissions.

23.08   Where the tribunal can find no express or implicit guidance in the Convention from which it derives its existence, then a different approach becomes necessary. In *The Wimbledon*[20] Germany had wrongfully refused to allow a French vessel to pass through the Kiel Canal. The Permanent Court of International Justice determined that damages should be paid in French francs because "this is the currency of the applicant in which his financial operations and accounts are conducted and it may therefore be said that this currency gives the exact measure of the loss to be made good". Similarly, in the *Corfu Channel* case,[21] the International Court of Justice assessed damages in sterling where the claimant State (the United Kingdom) was awarded damages for the loss of a destroyer. This principle appears to be sound, both in the sense that it seeks to identify as closely as possible the losses suffered by the claimant, and in that the principle has a parallel in private law.[22] Nevertheless it cannot be said that this principle has been consistently applied; furthermore, it cannot be appropriate to every case and, consequently, is not of general validity.[23] Thus the value of a house destroyed in the course of a rebellion, and for the loss of which the respondent government has to indemnify the owner, can only be assessed in terms of the currency of the country in which the property is situate.[24] Similarly, when Greece wrongfully took over lighthouses operated by a French firm following the premature termination of a concession, the Arbitration Tribunal was fully justified in determining the value of the concession by calculating the annual profit in terms of the Greek drachma;[25] both the income derived from the

---

[20] PCIJ Series A, No. 1, 32.

[21] [1949] ICJ Rep 244.

[22] See *The Texaco Melbourne* and other cases discussed in the context of money of account and unliquidated claims in Ch 5 above.

[23] In *Lauritzen v Chile* [1956] Int LR 708, 753, the Supreme Court of Chile, applying international law, held that Danish shipowners whose ships had been requisitioned by Chile during the war, were entitled to compensation in terms of US dollars, partly because this had become international practice and partly because dollars were "used as an international medium of exchange". Similarly, *Withall v Administrator of German Property* [1934] BYIL 180 concerned the charge imposed by the Treaty of Versailles upon German assets to secure British claims for the destruction of property in Turkey. It was decided that the money of account must be the Turkish currency, although sterling was the money of payment; the rate of exchange to be applied for those purposes was that prevailing as at the date of the Treaty of Versailles.

[24] It should perhaps be emphasised that a three-stage process is involved in this type of case. First of all, it is necessary to identify the currency in which the property or its value is expressed. Secondly, the date and manner of assessment of the value must be determined. Thirdly, it is necessary to determine whether compensation should be paid in a currency which differs from the valuation currency. If so, it is only at this stage that a rate of exchange (including the date of its ascertainment) falls for consideration.

[25] *Lighthouses Arbitration between France and Greece*, Reports of International Arbitral Awards xii 155, at 247. The English translation is to be found at [1956] Int LR 301 (although unfortunately not published in consecutive order). The award is closely reasoned and illuminating on monetary law. Only that part relating to interest is unconvincing and likely to be incorrect.

concession and the expenses incurred in earning it would have been expressed and paid in that currency.[26]

The various views just expressed would appear to be consistent with the International Law Commission Articles on State Responsibility (2001), although those Articles do not explicitly deal with the money of account in this context. Where a State is responsible for an international wrong, it is placed under "an obligation to compensate for the damage caused thereby, insofar as such damage is not made good by restitution".[27] Any such compensation "shall cover any financially assessable damage including loss of profits insofar as it is established".[28] This language makes it plain that a State which improperly terminates a concession agreement may be ordered to compensate the concessionaire, and that the damages must include an assessment of the value of any likely future profits over the unexpired period.[29]   **23.09**

The process of identifying the money of account may be assisted if it is remembered that compensation is awarded where (and to the extent to which) restitution is not available for some reason. In practice, monetary compensation may well be the preferred solution of the parties. It may be the only available solution in others, for example, where the claim relates to the destruction of property. But the primary status of the requirement for restitution should not be overlooked.[30] Article 35 of the ILC Articles records the obligation of a State responsible for an intentionally wrongful act "to make restitution, that is, to re-establish the situation which existed before the wrongful act was committed, provided and to the extent that restitution . . . is not materially impossible". Herein lies the clue; compensation must, as nearly as possible, place the claimant in the position in which it would have been, had restitution been possible. The compensation must be fixed so that it will correspond to the value which restitution would otherwise have provided; where appropriate, this may mean that different   **23.10**

---

[26] The first aspect of this formulation is certainly true, in the sense that the contract provided for payment in the Greek unit. The second aspect is less clear, in that the French firm presumably operated in French francs and may have felt its loss in that currency. However, the actual decision is justifiable if the contract was effectively self-financing, such that the French firm did not have to use its domestic currency to purchase Greek drachmas. It should be appreciated that this commentary refers to the money of account in the *calculation* of damages. In the context of the money of payment, the case is further considered at para 23.55 below.

[27] Article 36(1). Restitution is an important subject, but will not be dealt with in detail here, since we are concerned principally with questions of monetary compensation. On the ILC Articles generally, see James Crawford, *The International Law Commission's Articles on State Responsibility—Introduction, Text and Commentaries* (Cambridge University Press, 2002).

[28] Article 36(2).

[29] Article 36(2) is thus in conformity with the decision in the *Lighthouses Arbitration* (n 25 above).

[30] On the relationship between restitution and compensation, see Brownlie, *Principles of Public International Law* (Oxford University Press, 6th edn, 2003) 445–6; Crawford (n 27 above) 218.

heads of damage may be compensated by awards in different currencies and each currency award may bear interest at different rates.[31]

23.11 As a result, where the claim relates to real property which has been wrongfully destroyed or confiscated, its value will initially have to be ascertained in the currency of the country in which the property was situate.[32] Where the claim relates to moveable property, however, a more flexible approach seems to be necessary; it should perhaps be valued in the currency of the country in which such chattels were most frequently used. In the case of an improperly terminated concession or similar agreement, restitution would have required both parties to continue with the performance of their respective obligations; consequently, the compensation payable to the disappointed concessionaire should be calculated in the currency or currencies in which his profits would have been accrued under the contract.[33]

23.12 It should not, however, be overlooked that the above discussion is concerned with the calculation of compensation, ie with the money of account. The money in which such compensation must be paid (ie the money of payment) is considered below.[34]

Interest

23.13 Questions touching the payment of interest may arise in a variety of ways. A treaty may explicitly provide for the payment of interest on amounts owing under its terms. The money of account will plainly be a matter of construction in such a case; in the absence of any explicit statement, it may perhaps be inferred that interest accrues in the currency in which the relative principal sum is outstanding.

23.14 Where a State seeks compensation in respect of an internationally wrongful act of another State, then, under the terms of Article 38 of the International Law Commission's Articles:

(a) interest shall be awarded when this is necessary to ensure full reparation;

(b) if interest is awarded, then it should run from the date when the relative

---

[31] For judicial articulation of these principles, see the decision of the Permanent Court of International Justice in *Factory at Chorzow, Merits* [1928] PCIJ Series A, No 17, 47. The principle has been applied on many subsequent occasions—see, eg, the decision of the International Tribunal for the Law of the Sea in *The M/V "Saiga" No. 2*, 1 July 1999, para 170 and other cases cited by Crawford (n 27 above) 219. The formulation does, of course, reflect corresponding rules in the private law of damages.

[32] This is the first step in the three-stage process mentioned in n 24 above.

[33] Once again, this leads to the conclusion that the provisions of the ILC Articles are, in this respect, consistent with the decision in the *Lighthouses Arbitration* (n 25 above).

[34] See para 23.54 below.

principal sum should have been paid until the date on which it is actually paid; and

(c) the rate of interest and the mode of its calculation shall be fixed with a view to ensuring full reparation for the claimant.

In general terms, a claimant State is entitled to interest if the compensation awarded to it is assessed (say) by reference to the value of property as at a date which precedes the award, but not if the value is assessed as at the date of the award itself.[35] Where interest is payable, it will generally be necessary for the rate to reflect the likely cost to the claimant of borrowing the relative principal amount with effect from the date on which it ought to have been paid, for only in this way can the principal of full reparation be satisfied.[36] The funding cost will usually have been met in the currency in which the relative principal amount was owing, so that the money of account for interest will "follow" the money of account for the primary claim. There is, however, a lack of consistency in the approach adopted as to the place by reference to which the rate of interest is to be ascertained. Some cases have adopted the rate of interest prevailing in the territory of the debtor State,[37] whilst others have awarded the claimant a rate of interest reflecting the return on commercial investments in his home country.[38]

23.15

C. Nominalism and Treaties

Application of principle

Treaties providing for the payment of a sum of money have become a matter of almost daily occurrence; for many centuries, treaties of peace have imposed obligations of monetary indemnity upon the vanquished party;[39] in more modern times, the EC Treaty creates many financial obligations and examples could be multiplied. The present section is therefore concerned with the principle of nominalism and its application to liquidated obligations found in a treaty.

23.16

It has been noted elsewhere that the principle of nominalism applies only to liquidated obligations;[40] it has no general application to claims which sound in

23.17

---

[35] On this subject, see the *Lighthouses Arbitration* (1956) xii RIAA 155, 252 and other cases discussed by Crawford (n 27 above) 235.

[36] The point seems to have been accepted in *The Wimbeldon* (1923) PCIJ Series A, No 1, 32. Different rates of interest may therefore be appropriate to differing classes of claimant—see Crawford (n 27 above) 235.

[37] See *Senser's Claim* (1953) 20 Int LR 240.

[38] *Sylvania Technical Systems v Iran* (1986) 80 AJ 365. On the award of compound interest, see the ICSID award in *Middle East Cement Co v Egypt* (Art 99/6, Award dated 12 April 2002).

[39] See the materials collected by Feilchenfeld and Kersten, "Reparations from Carthage to Versailles" (1957, i) *World Polity* 29.

[40] See para 10.01 above.

damages. This distinction must apply (for the same reasons and with equal force) in the context of obligations arising under public international law.

23.18 This proposition does, however, require further examination. Is there any basis upon which the principle of nominalism could be set aside as a result of some peculiar characteristic of treaties or the identity of the parties which may enter into them? For example, given that the parties will be sovereign States, should it be assumed that monetary references were intended to be insulated from the vagaries of national legislation, such that a gold clause or similar protective provision should be implied? It is suggested that there was never any basis for the implication of any such clause; had the parties so required, they could have stated it expressly. There is certainly no room for the implication of a gold clause into treaties entered into following the collapse of the Bretton Woods system of parities.[41]

23.19 Under these circumstances, the principle of nominalism must apply to liquidated obligations arising under public international law. It follows that the debtor State is bound (and entitled) to pay the nominal amount of the agreed currency, irrespective of its intrinsic value—in terms of purchasing power or some other currency—as at the date of payment. By contracting on the footing of a specific national currency, States incorporate into their treaties the monetary legislation of the country concerned and, to that extent, those treaties contain a *renvoi* to the *lex monetae*. The problem is always one of construction; when a treaty refers to a national monetary system, the contracting States are aware that such system is created by a municipal system of law, and that monetary obligations can only be defined by reference to that system. To that extent, their treaty necessarily adopts *pro tanto* that national monetary legislation. In a private contract which is subject to English law and which stipulates for the payment of a sum of foreign money, the system of law which regulates that money effectively becomes a part of the law applicable to the contract.[42] It is for this reason that the definition of what the stipulated unit of account means is referred to as the *lex monetae* by a universally followed rule of the conflict of laws. It is for the same reason that monetary obligations under public international law are subject to the *lex monetae* in so far as the definition of the unit of account is concerned.

---

[41] On this subject, see para 23.43 below. As Sir Joseph Gold observed, customary international law does not include any general principle requiring that a State must compensate others for a decline in the value of their holdings of the first State's currency—see Gold, *Legal Effects of Fluctuating Exchange Rates* (IMF, 1990) 137. The absence of such a liability is derived from the application of the principle of nominalism in the international sphere and thus reinforces the more specific rules stated in the text.

[42] See para 4.11 above, and see *Re Chesterman's Trusts* [1923] 2 Ch 466.

On this basis, the further question arises of whether the reference to the **23.20**
lex monetae envisages (a) the particular law of the currency as it exists at the time
of conclusion of the treaty or (b) such law of the currency as it may be amended
from time to time. As has been shown,[43] nominalism has the latter meaning in a
private law context. Once again, the reasoning which underlies this rule must
apply equally to interstate monetary obligations. If the parties have merely
referred to a domestic currency without using some indexing or similar protective measure, then they must be taken to have contracted by reference to that
currency as a measure of value from time to time. No "value maintenance" or
similar provision can be implied in such a case.

Thus far, the stated conclusions display a pleasing symmetry with the solutions **23.21**
adopted in corresponding private law situations. Yet the analogy cannot be
entirely complete, for this reason: whilst private parties do not control the
monetary system and thus contract by reference to a currency over which they
have no control, a State has the sovereign power to adjust and replace its own
national currency.[44] Where a treaty involves monetary obligations expressed in
the national currency of one of the contracting parties, it thus becomes necessary to ask whether the *lex monetae* should be rigidly applied during the lifetime
of the treaty. In general terms, it is suggested that the principle of nominalism
should be applied equally in such a case—*unless* it can be shown that the
devaluation has been effected either in defiance of some general international
obligation or in breach of some (express or implied) term of the treaty in
question. It is necessary to consider these two possibilities in turn:

(a) If a devaluation were effected in breach of a general principle of international law,[45] then an international tribunal would be compelled to disregard the relevant legislative or executive action in determining the
amount payable under the treaty. The debtor State would thus have to pay
such amount as will ensure that the creditor State receives the value which
it would have received, had the devaluation not occurred.[46]

(b) Even in the absence of specific "value maintenance" provisions in the treaty

---

[43] See para 9.03 above.

[44] On this aspect of monetary sovereignty, see para 19.02 above.

[45] eg because the devaluation fell to be regarded as confiscatory in accordance with the principles discussed at para 19.20 above, or because the devaluation disregarded obligations formerly
imposed upon member States under the Articles of Agreement of the IMF. It must be said that, in
view of the collapse of the par value system, States no longer have the power to effect an official
devaluation. It may be that some points in the text may equally apply if a State intervened in the
financial markets with a view to reducing the value of the creditor's claim. Such a state of affairs is,
however, very unlikely to arise in practice.

[46] Seeking to apply the parties' intentions in this context, the *renvoi* to private law is unlikely to
comprise the consequences which are considered unlawful under public international law. For an
express and unique revalorisation provision, see Art IV of the Payments Agreement between Sierra
Leone and Guinea, (1965) Int LM 337.

concerned, it may be argued that (1) the promisor State's monetary legislation must be ignored by public international law on the grounds of its inconsistency with the principle of *pacta sunt servanda* and (2) a waiver of the right to rely on municipal legislation must accordingly be read into the treaty. A State cannot, by means of its own national legislation, reduce indebtedness which it has contracted under international law; likewise, it should be unable to reduce the effective value of its indebtedness by means of a devaluation effected pursuant to such legislation.[47] To put matters another way, the debtor State—by contracting in its own currency—cannot be allowed the effective and unilateral right to devalue its own monetary obligations.[48]

23.22 These arguments have a certain attraction when the matter is viewed from the angle of public international law, but it is submitted that they cannot be accepted as sound. The quality and extent of the protection which public international law affords to a treaty are necessarily impaired to the extent to which the treaty incorporates or refers to municipal law. Monetary obligations in particular are "subject to the constitutional power of the government over the currency, whatever that power may be, and the obligation of the parties is therefore assumed with reference to that power".[49] Consequently, when States enter into treaties on the basis of the promisor's money of account and no special protective clauses are included, it must be assumed that the promisor retains its sovereign right to devalue its currency—there is no basis for reading into the treaty an implied waiver of such a fundamental feature of monetary sovereignty.[50]

23.23 Although slightly different lines of reasoning are involved in each case, it appears to follow that—both in private law claims and in the context of debt claims

---

[47] It is an accepted principle that a State cannot alter its international obligations by means of its domestic legislation, or rely on such legislation as a defence to the performance of such obligations. In some respects, this principle is now enshrined in Art 3 of the ILC Articles on State Responsibility on which see Crawford *The International Law Commission's Articles on State Responsibility—Introduction, Text and Commentaries* (Cambridge University Press, 2002) 86–90. In the context of treaty obligations, the same point is made in Art 27 of the Vienna Convention on the Law of Treaties. The point arises again in the context of exchange control and its impact on interstate obligations—see para 23.63 below.

[48] Such a position was described as "an absurdity" in *Murray v Charleston* (1877) 96 US 432, 445; see also *Hartman v Greenhaw* (1880) 102 US 678 and cf *Perry v US* (1935) 294 US 330.

[49] *Knox v Lee* and *Parker v Davies* (1870) 12 Wall (79) US 457, 548.

[50] On the right to devalue, see para 19.10 above. In the *Diverted Cargoes* case (1955) Int LR 820, 836, the arbitrator noted that "the creditor is entitled to reject, in so far as it would affect the substance of his claim, the effect of any action taken by the debtor State itself to devalue its currency". In so far as this remark applies to claims governed by international law (ie where the creditor is also a State) this statement cannot be accepted for the reasons just given in the text. In so far as it relates to private law claims, it is likewise inaccurate in the light of the nominalistic principle.

governed by international law—the creditor takes the risk of a devaluation in, or a depreciation of, the money of account.

Effect of catastrophic depreciation

In a private law context, it has already been seen that the principle of nominalism may give way in the face of a catastrophic devaluation of the currency.[51] It is necessary to ask whether the same position should prevail in the context of a treaty obligation governed by public international law. Older cases dealing with the depreciation of pensions due to employees of international organisations[52] are of limited assistance in this area since they involved devaluations or depreciations which (on the facts) could not be described as catastrophic. It is therefore necessary to consider the present question in the absence of direct and relevant authority.

23.24

So far as private law obligations are concerned, we have seen that a State is not subject to any general international duty to revalorise debts whose effective value has been diminished as a result of a massive depreciation in the value of the national currency.[53] But does a State owe a particular duty to pay "value" in relation to its own international financial obligations to other States? There are arguments which would support the existence of such a duty. In particular, a State must perform its treaty obligations in good faith[54] and this may of itself support an international rule of revalorisation. The French doctrine of *imprévision* may be regarded as an analogy to which an international tribunal could turn. On the whole, however, it is felt that international law should not require revalorisation in the context of monetary obligations created by treaty because:

23.25

(a) There are many factors which may lead to a collapse in the value of the national currency. These do not necessarily imply a lack of good faith on the part of the debtor State.

(b) The imposition of a duty of revalorisation in the context of treaty obligations would effectively confer upon State creditors an advantage over private creditors who enjoy no such right of revalorisation. There seems to be no equitable consideration which requires that treaty creditors should be favoured in this way; and

---

[51] See para 9.23 above

[52] eg *Desplanques v Administration Board of the Staff Pension Fund of the League of Nations* AD 1941–2, Case No. 132; *Niestlé v International Institute of Intellectual Co-operation* [1955] Int LR 762, 764. In the case of *Harpignies* (1974) *Annuaire Francais de droit international* 376, the Administrative Tribunal of the UN refused the adjustment of a pension on the grounds of the devaluation of the dollar, because there was no principle of law which required payment obligations to be increased in line with changes in the cost of living.

[53] On this point, see para 19.12 above.

[54] On this point, see the Vienna Convention on the Law of Treaties, Art 26.

(c) when entering into a treaty, a creditor State will usually be well placed to stipulate for payment in some external currency, or to require some other form of "value maintenance" mechanism. If the creditor elects to enter into a treaty based on the monetary laws of the debtor State and without any additional protection, then it does so in full knowledge of the attendant dangers—indeed, the State creditor may usually be assumed to have a greater familiarity with such dangers than a private creditor may possess.[55] It is neither necessary nor appropriate for international law to provide for rights of revalorisation where the creditor State could have negotiated such a right, but elected not to do so.

23.26   On this basis, it may be tentatively concluded that, in the absence of specific treaty provisions, international law does not impose a general duty of revalorisation upon a debtor State following a catastrophic collapse in the value of its own currency. But as is the case in the context of private debts, questions of fact and degree will inevitably be involved, and there may come a point at which it would be unconscionable to allow the debtor State to rely upon the rules just described.

Post-maturity depreciation

23.27   The last two sections have considered the extent to which the creditor State is effectively required to take the risk of the contractual currency until the date on which payment falls due. But what is the position if payment is delayed and the currency depreciates during the period of the delay? Does international law require the creditor to bear that further risk of depreciation during that extended period? In this context, it appears that international law requires the debtor to make good the damage flowing from his delay (*mora*).

23.28   The oldest case on the point is perhaps *Pilkington v Commissioners for Claims on France*,[56] which may well be considered as an international case. In the course of the Napoleonic War, the French Government had confiscated moneys due to the English claimants; subsequently, it provided a fund for compensation. The Privy Council held that the wrong done by the French Government must be completely undone, and that if the wrongdoer "has received the assignats at the value of 50d, he does not make compensation by returning an assignat which is worth only 20d; he must make up the difference between the value of the assignats at the different dates". In other words, monetary compensation must

---

[55] In other words, as noted above, the creditor State contracts by reference to the *lex monetae* principle.

[56] (1821) 2 Knapp 7, 20. The case has previously been noted in the context of nominalism in relation to private law obligations—see para 9.34 above.

be adequate and effective, and the underlying principle of restitution must be firmly kept in mind.

In another case, the Colombian business of an Italian claimant had been wrong-   **23.29**
fully confiscated and (as a result) it was determined that he was entitled to an indemnity against debts which he had personally incurred in connection with that business. Subsequently, a creditor for an amount expressed in Colombian pesos obtained an Italian judgment against the claimant; although the peso was greatly depreciated, the creditor had obtained judgment for some 181,000 lire. It was apparently held that the claimant was entitled to a full indemnity against this judgment, on the grounds that, so far possible, he was to be restored to the financial position which prevailed immediately prior to the confiscation of his business.[57] A similar result followed in three arbitrations between Germany and Romania. In the first case, an estate wrongfully expropriated in 1914 was found to have a value of 1,000,000 lei at that time. As a result of a currency reform in 1929, this had become 32,000,000 lei but, bearing in mind the depreciation of the leu since that time, the arbitrators awarded 64,000,000 lei.[58] In the second case, a Romanian entity owed £16,818 to a German bank in 1914; allowing interest at the rate of 5½ (five and a half) per cent the arbitrators awarded in 1940 a sum of £40,867 "valeur —or" and thus eliminated the effect of the devaluation of sterling.[59] In the third case, Romanian buyers had in 1914 paid a sum of marks to Berlin sellers. In 1921, the buyers received an indemnity against one-sixth of the sum so paid, and in 1929 an arbitrator awarded them compensation for the remaining five-sixths.[60] The Greek-Bulgarian Mixed Arbitral Tribunal had to deal with a claim to some 14,000 leva which was due to the claimant under a judgment of 1911. The First World War brought about long delays as well as a severe depreciation of the Bulgarian currency. Applying a broad approach rooted in fairness, the Arbitrators in 1929 awarded 100,000 leva.[61]

The decisions in these cases demonstrate a clear attempt to do justice as between   **23.30**
the parties, although it is not always clear whether the arbitrators were requiring the revalorisation of a debt expressed in a catastrophically depreciated currency, or whether they were seeking to assess damages for late payment.[62] But in the

---

[57] *Cerruti's Case* (1912) 19 *Revue générale de droit international public* 268, 273. See also the decision of the US-Peru Claims Commission in the *Montano* case, Moore, *Digest of International Law* (1906) vii 51; *International Arbitrations* (1898) ii 1638, 1645, 1649.

[58] *Affaire Junghans* (1928) iii RIAA 1885.

[59] *Affaire Deutsche Bank* (1940) iii RIAA 1895.

[60] *Goldenberg's Case* (1928) ii RIAA 901, 909, where some general remarks will be found; the award itself rests on the specific provisions of the Treaty of Versailles.

[61] *Fontana v Bulgaria, Receuil des Décisions des Tribunaux Arbitraux Mixtes* ix, 374.

[62] No doubt this state of affairs is attributable to the more general approach adopted in an international law context, where narrower, private law distinctions are not always drawn.

Lighthouses Arbitration between France and Greece,[63] the Tribunal held that, as a result of the devaluation of the drachma, "an adjustment based on good faith" was required. The devaluation had disturbed the financial equilibrium of the concession arrangements, and the debtor State thus came under a "good faith" obligation to ensure that the concession could be continued on equitable terms.[64] This case perhaps provides the clearest statement that revalorisation is required where the relevant currency depreciates significantly between the due date and the actual date of repayment. On the other hand, in 1961 the Swiss Government delivered an opinion in relation to a case in which Swiss owners of French property had become entitled to a French franc payment in 1935. When finally paid in 1951, it represented less than five per cent of the gold value in 1935. The Swiss Government expressed the view that France was liable to pay the difference, stating that there existed a generally accepted practice under which the claimant should be indemnified for losses accruing as a result of monetary depreciation which occurs between the date of the wrongful act and the date on which compensation is ultimately paid.

23.31 Although the precise foundation of this monetary law analysis remains some-what obscure, it is perhaps necessary to conclude that, in the event of a delayed payment, the creditor is entitled to be compensated for the loss of monetary value between the due date and the date of actual payment. It may be that the right to an adjustment flows from an obligation on the debtor State to revalorise its obligations—and thus to make an appropriate, upward adjustment in such a case. However, it is perhaps more likely that the creditor's rights in this case would flow from the fact that the debtor is in breach of his obligations, and is under an obligation to provide adequate compensation.[65] Given that there seems to be no general obligation to revalorise debts following a catastrophic depreciation, it seems unattractive to impose a *specific* duty of that kind merely in those cases in which a breach has occurred. It seems more appropriate that the adjustment should be required by way of compensation for the debtor's wrong.

D. The Calculation of Damages

23.32 It has previously been noted that the principle of nominalism has no application in the context of an award of damages or similar compensation. When, on account of the respondent State's international responsibility, the claimant State is entitled to compensation for property taken from, or to damages for a wrong

---

[63] (1956) xii RIAA 155, 224–8; (1956) Int LR 342, 345–6.

[64] The case related to a tariff rather than a liquidated sum, but this factor would not appear to affect the general principle.

[65] See Art 36(1) of the ILC Articles.

done to, itself or its nationals, international law again takes a broad view of the monetary implications and approaches them without undue concern for conceptualist refinements or subtle distinctions.[66] The need to treat aliens fairly and equitably and consistently with the demands of good faith precludes results which would allow the respondent State to benefit from delay or jeopardise the principle of the effectiveness of any award. International law has emphasised that principle,[67] and should therefore not find it difficult to award such sums of money as will effectively take care of changes in monetary value from which, in fairness, the claimant should not be required to suffer.

Accordingly, international law can compensate the injured party for any currency depreciations which may have occurred since the date of the wrongful act in question.[68] However, having stated the general principle, it is necessary to consider four types of case in which this issue has arisen.   **23.33**

There are in the first place, cases in which no harm is done by assessing the value as at the date of the taking or the wrong. This is so where no subsequent change in monetary value occurs, or where any such change as has occurred can be taken into account by way of damages for delayed payment. Such circumstances were envisaged by the Permanent Court of International Justice in the *Chorzow Factory* case.[69] The Court noted that—had Poland enjoyed the right to expropriate the factory—then damages would have to be limited to the value of the factory at the date of dispossession and interest to the date of payment. No further award of damages could be made, because the wrongful act would consist solely of the failure to pay at the point of expropriation. However, damages could not in fact be limited in this way, because the very taking of the factories in the first instance had been found to be unlawful. Germany was thus entitled to compensation because the original action of the Polish Government had been unlawful.[70]   **23.34**

In the second set of cases, changes in monetary value do occur but it is impossible or inconvenient to effect the valuation as at a date later than that of the   **23.35**

---

[66] For recent discussions of the alien's right to compensation for the expropriation of property, see Lowenfeld, *International Economic Law* (Oxford University Press, 2000) 480–4; Brownlie, *Principles of Public International Law* (Oxford University Press, 6th edn, 2003) 509–12.

[67] On the requirement for "effective" compensation, see *Oppenheim's International Law* (Longman, 9th edn, 1991) para 155. The principle is in some respects encapsulated by Art 34 of the ILC Articles on State Responsibility which refers to "full reparation".

[68] The suggestions in the text were expressly approved in the opinion of the Swiss Government referred to above, and by Judge Holtzmann in his separate opinion in *INA Corp v Iran* (1985) 75 Int LR 595. Without any discussion of this problem, the majority assessed the compensation for nationalisation in terms of dollars rather than rials, and applied the rate of exchange ruling on the date of nationalisation.

[69] PCIJ Series A, No. 17.

[70] The right to compensation would now arise in accordance with Art 36 of the ILC Articles.

taking or the wrong, and the tribunal succeeds in neutralising those changes by converting the amount of the valuation into a stable currency. Such a procedure was adopted in an arbitration between Greece and Bulgaria.[71] This approach was rejected by the Arbitral Commission on Property, Rights and Interests in Germany,[72] but enjoys the sanction of the award in the *Lighthouses Arbitration between France and Greece*.[73] In that case, the Tribunal found that the concession had been wrongfully revoked in 1929, that the indemnity due to France was to be determined in terms of drachmas, and that the value of the concession had to be determined as of 1929. The tribunal stated that:

> . . . the injured party has the right to receive the equivalent at the date of the award of the loss suffered as the result of an illegal act and ought not to be prejudiced by the effects of a devaluation which took place between the date at which the wrongful act occurred and the determination of the amounts of compensation. To this end, the tribunal must as far as possible use as a medium a stable currency, and as such it accepts . . . the United States dollar.

23.36   Having used the US dollar as a medium through which the losses suffered by the claimant could be protected from the depreciation of the drachma, the Tribunal considered whether the final award should be expressed in drachmas or in francs. It opted for the French franc, on the basis that the claimant undertook its business and kept its accounts in that currency.

23.37   In a third set of cases, the property concerned is valued as at the date of the award (rather than the date of the unlawful act). This method recognises that restitution should be the primary form of relief and if that is not available, compensation should, as nearly as possible, place the claimant in the same position.[74] This approach was adopted in the *Corfu Channel* case[75] where a destroyer built in 1943 at a cost of £554,678 became a total loss in 1949. It was held that the injured State must be put in a position to effect its replacement, and was consequently entitled to the cost of building a similar vessel as at the date of the award.[76] This approach to the assessment of compensation is in some

---

[71] *Affaire des Forêts du Rhodope Central, Reports of International Arbitral Awards* iii, 1391, particularly at 1434.

[72] *Rousseau v Germany*, Decisions of the Arbitral Commission on Property, Rights and Interests in Germany iii, 297 or 29 Int LR 329.

[73] [1956] Int LR 299, 302.

[74] See the *Chorzow Factory* case, (1928) PCIJ Series A, No. 17, 48 and 50.

[75] [1949] ICJ Rep 244.

[76] cf the decision of the international tribunal constituted in 1933 under the chairmanship of M.J.G. Guerrero in order to make arrangements between Hungary, Austria, and Yugoslavia for the exploitation and reorganisation of two railway systems which, in consequence of the First World War, extended across the new frontiers. Although in many respects amounts expressed in the old Austrian currency had to be considered in these complicated cases, the tribunal, making "une équitable évaluation" or "une juste appréciation des circonstances" based in 1934 its decision upon the old gold franc of the Latin Monetary Union: *Affaire du Chemin de Fer de Barcs-Pakrac*,

respects now supported by Article 36 of the International Law Commission's Articles on State Responsibility, which requires compensation "for the damage caused . . . insofar as such damage is not made good by restitution". For that reason, the question of monetary compensation should now be dealt with in the manner here suggested—although the difference between the second approach and the present one may have limited practical impact.

A fourth and somewhat arbitrary method was adopted in the arbitration **23.38** between *Aminoil v Kuwait*.[77] The arbitrators took account of inflation by awarding a sum increased at an annual overall rate of 10 per cent. In similar vein, the European Court of Human Rights made the familiar (if inexcusable) mistake of treating interest "as providing some shelter against inflation during the period from then until the date of payment".[78] It should be repeated that interest compensates for delay in payment, and not for loss in value attributable to inflation.[79]

E. Protective Clauses

In view of the tentative nature of some of the conclusions drawn in the preced- **23.39** ing sections, it is perhaps unsurprising that States have frequently sought to protect themselves against the consequences of monetary depreciation. An early example[80] is provided by the Treaty dated 30 April 1803, whereby the United States of America acquired Louisiana from France.[81] The purchaser agreed to pay 60 million francs by creating US$11,250,000 6 per cent Redeemable Stock. By Article III of the Treaty, the parties agreed "that the dollar of the United States specified in the present Convention shall be fixed at five francs 3333/10.000 or five livres eight sous tournois". It must be inferred that the issuer of the stock would have been required to pay the necessary additional amounts in US dollars, had that currency at any time fallen in value as compared to the franc.

International Arbitral Awards iii, 1571, 1577 et seq; *Affaire des Chemins de Fer Zeltweg-Wolfsberg et Unterdrauburg-Woellan*, ibid iii, 1797, 1806 et seq. It is remarkable that a judgment was expressed in a currency which never existed as such and which by 1934 certainly had lost all vestiges of existence. It is even more remarkable that the judgment did not provide for conversion into some existing currency.

[77] (1982) Int LM 976 or 66 Int LR 518. See paras 168–171 and 178 of the award. The case was discussed by Mann (1982) BYIL 976 or *Further Studies in International Law* 252.

[78] *Lithgow v UK* (1986) 75 Int LR 439, 493.

[79] The same point has been discussed in other contexts—see para 9.36 above.

[80] For earlier examples, see Feichenfeld and Kersten "Reparations from Carthage to Versailles" in (1957) I *World Polity* 38, n 3.

[81] Malloy, *Treaties, Conventions, International Acts, Protocols and Agreements between the USA and Other Powers (1776–1909)* (1910) i, 511.

23.40 In the type of case just described, it will be seen that the amount of the payment obligation is linked to the currency of the creditor State—thereby providing a very significant measure of protection against a devaluation in the currency of the debtor State. In another set of cases, the parties may choose a neutral currency as their benchmark. Thus in a Treaty of 3 March 1935, Japan agreed to purchase the Chinese Eastern Railway from the USSR for 140 million Japanese yen, payable by instalments. By Article VIII the parties agreed that, should the yen rise or fall by more than 8 per cent in relation to the Swiss franc, the amount of any instalment should be increased or reduced (as the case may be) "so that the value in Swiss francs of the instalment shall be the same as it is at the date of the coming into force of the present agreement". The Treaty also contains detailed provisions dealing with any alteration in the gold parity of the Swiss franc and with the suspension of its convertibility into gold.[82] Likewise, in a Convention dated 29 November 1947, Italy agreed to pay France the sum of 1,500 million lire in consideration of the release of Italian property from the charge imposed by Article 79 of the Treaty of Peace of 1947. Such sum was subject to a dollar clause at a fixed rate, such that the amount due had to be equivalent to US$28,965,117. Techniques of this kind are not dissimilar to those which have occasionally been adopted in a private law context.[83]

23.41 A further and perhaps more modern approach is provided by the Agreement concerning an International Trust Fund for Tuvalu dated 16 June 1987. The Agreement refers to the "real value" of payments which (according to Article 14) fall to be defined and adjusted by reference to movements in the Australian Consumer Price Index.[84] Similarly when member States agree to contribute to the resources of an international institution, they will frequently undertake to maintain the value of such amounts.[85]

23.42 Historically, however, the most common form of protection against monetary depreciations was the use of a gold clause. For obvious reasons the use of this type of provision has now been discontinued, but a brief review of the older materials remains appropriate for two reasons. First of all, the very fact that States felt it necessary to protect themselves against the consequences of monetary depreciation is in itself cogent evidence that the principle of nominalism was believed to apply in the context of payment obligations created by treaty, and that there was no general obligation on a State to revalorise its debts following

---

[82] *Nouveau Récueil Générale*, 3rd Series No 30, 649.

[83] See in particular the discussion of *Multiservice Bookbinding Ltd v Mardon* [1979] Ch 84 discussed at para 12.13 above.

[84] Cm 735.

[85] See, eg, Art V(11) of the IMF Articles of Agreement or Art V(3) of the Agreement relating to the Inter-American Development Bank (Cmnd 6271).

the devaluation of its currency.[86] Why, otherwise, would such provisions have been thought desirable? Secondly, the international law which developed around gold clauses is, as in private law, at least valuable as a paradigm, or as a basis for comparison with other techniques which may be employed in an effort to avoid the effects of nominalism[87]—for example, the use of the Special Drawing Right or by means of a reference to a major international currency.

As in the case of private law, it was necessary at the outset to consider whether **23.43** the terminology employed by the parties was sufficient to bring a gold clause into existence. On the one hand, the existence of a gold clause cannot generally be implied or presumed,[88] and some form of express provision is thus required. On the other hand, given the broad interpretative approach to be adopted in the context of a treaty, a simple reference to "gold" would by itself frequently be sufficient to create a binding gold clause.[89] Although a well-drawn gold clause would include more detailed definition—for example, as to the gold's weight and fineness—this was not necessary and matters of this kind were frequently not addressed.[90] In such cases, it should usually be inferred that the parties were contemplating the monetary conditions which existed at the time when the treaty was made.

The best known controversy about the existence of a gold clause in a treaty arose **23.44** in connection with the Boxer Indemnity, which was extracted by the Western Powers from China following an uprising against the foreign presence in that country. By a Protocol of 7 September 1901,[91] China undertook to pay the Western Powers over a forty-year period an aggregate sum of 450 million Haikwan taels which were to "constitute a gold debt calculated at the rate of Haikwan tael to the currency of each currency" as indicated in a Schedule according to which a Haikwan tael was equal to 0.742 gold dollar, three shillings

---

[86] The application of the principle of nominalism to treaty obligations has been discussed earlier in this chapter.

[87] The present discussion will be brief—further details may be found in the Fifth Edition of this work, 548–53.

[88] In the first *Pious Funds* case (Scott, The Hague Court Reports, p 48) an 1875 award was made in Mexican gold dollars, apparently without discussion of the gold clause. In 1902, the second *Pious Funds* case came before the Arbitral Tribunal ((1902) ix RIAA 1), where the point was considered. The Tribunal noted that the silver dollar was legal tender in Mexico and that, under those circumstances, it would only be possible to claim payment in gold by virtue of an express term in the treaty to that effect. This perhaps goes a little far, but it illustrates the point made in the text.

[89] In other words, the court or tribunal would have to construe the reference to gold, rather than ignore it—a position taken by the Permanent Court of International Justice in the case of *Brazilian Loans* (1929) PCIJ Series A, No. 21 115–16.

[90] eg see the materials about to be discussed in the context of the Boxer Indemnity.

[91] Article VI. See, eg Malloy, *Treaties* (n 81 above), ii, 2006.

in sterling, 1.796 Dutch florin, and so on.[92] It was also provided that capital and interest should be paid in gold or at the rates of exchange corresponding to the dates at which the different payments fell due. Notwithstanding its elaborate character, the clause left room for doubt and China made a number of payments in silver. The dispute which thus arose gave rise to diplomatic correspondence and was ultimately settled by the Protocol of 2 July 1905,[93] under which China recognised that "the sum of 450 million taels constitutes a debt in gold; that is to say, for each Haikwan tael due to each of the Powers, China must pay in gold the amount which is shown in Article VI" of the 1901 treaty. China also undertook to pay a lump sum of 8 million taels in settlement of arrears and to make future payment "either in silver . . . or in gold bills or telegraphic transfers at the choice of each Power". Fresh difficulties arose during and after the First World War, when China proposed to pay some of the creditor States in their depreciated national currencies.[94] In February 1923, the creditor States informed China that the 1901 and 1905 arrangements established that the indemnity was to be paid in gold—ie that for every Haikwan tael owed to each Power, China should pay the equivalent amount in gold ascertained pursuant to Article VI. China responded that "in gold" was merely a reference to the respective gold currencies of the creditor States, in contrast to the Haikwan tael which was on a silver standard. In other words, "gold" referred not to gold metal but simply to gold currencies. It is submitted that this position was untenable; the Chinese interpretation would have deprived the word "gold" of any effective meaning. The dispute was ultimately settled in 1925 by the adoption of the US dollar as a medium of exchange in relation to the remaining payments.[95]

23.45 It should not be thought that the problems here discussed are unique to gold clauses and thus of purely historical interest. The learning derived from them continues to apply to other forms of protective clauses to be found in more recent treaties. The establishment of international organisations tends to be an expensive and often highly political activity, and the member countries will be careful to ensure that financial contributions are made on an appropriate basis. It is thus entirely unsurprising that issues of this kind should have been carefully addressed in the establishment of international financial institutions. The Statute of the European Investment Bank[96] offers a modern example. The share capital

---

[92] This massive indemnity was intended to be met from maritime customs, native customs, and the salt monopoly; it placed a huge burden on Chinese financial resources.

[93] *Foreign Relations of the United States* 1905, 145 (the correspondence) and 156 (the Protocol).

[94] On the points about to be discussed, see the correspondence reproduced in *Foreign Relations of the United States* 1972, i, 809; 1923, i, 592, 593, 600 and 1924, i, 564.

[95] *Survey of International Affairs* 1925, ii, 358, 368–70.

[96] The Statute is set out in a Protocol to the EC Treaty.

of the Bank was expressed in ECUs, but Member States were entitled to provide a proportion of their subscription moneys in their own national currencies. Fluctuations in the values of national currencies against the ECU could result in a shortfall (or excess) of the Bank's paid-in capital. Article 7(1) and (2) of the Statute thus provide for a "topping-up" payment by a Member State whose currency declines in relation to the ECU, and for a refund to a Member State whose currency appreciates against that unit.[97] It should be added that these provisions have not become wholly "spent" as a result of the introduction of the euro, because non-eurozone Member States are shareholders in the Bank.

A similar point could also have arisen in relation to international institutions **23.46** whose share capital was expressed in ECU but which were not an integral part of the European Community. The prime example is provided by the European Bank for Reconstruction and Development (EBRD). The EBRD was established by an Agreement dated 29 May 1990. Although the European Community and a number of its Member States are parties to the Agreement, other shareholders include the United States, Russia, and numerous other States from around the globe; consequently, the EBRD does not exist within a framework of Community law. Nevertheless, its share capital was expressed in ECUs, a "basket" unit of account which ceased to exist upon the introduction of the euro as the single currency of the participating Member States. How were references to "ECU" in the EBRD Agreement to be construed after the creation of the single currency? It is true that Community law stipulated that "every reference in a legal instrument to the ECU . . . shall be replaced by reference to the euro at a rate of one euro to one ECU",[98] but this mandatory provision plainly could not apply to or override the provisions of the EBRD Agreement, which is governed by international law. Further, there is an added difficulty in applying the *lex monetae* principle to obligations expressed in ECUs, because that unit was not the lawful money of any State and was thus not entitled to the international recognition which lies at the heart of that principle.[99] It is also difficult to read into the EBRD Agreement any intention on the part of the contracting States that the euro would in due course be substituted for the ECU, because the Agreement was executed in 1990, when the single currency project was still at a very early stage and by no means certain to reach fruition. In spite of these

---

[97] In general terms, provisions of this kind are designed to ensure that the organisation maintains its capital and is thus able to fulfil its functions. At the same time, they ensure that a State's commitment to the organisation is not increased as a result of an appreciation in its currency. A further example of this type of arrangement is offered by the original Articles of Agreement of the IMF; that subject is considered by Gold, *Legal Effects of Fluctuating Exchange Rates* (IMF, 1990) 140.

[98] Council Regulation 1103/97, Art 2(1), discussed in more detail at para 29.08 below.

[99] On this general subject, see para 30.49 below.

difficulties, however, the substitution of the euro for the ECU in the context of the EBRD Agreement appears to have been accepted without demur.[100]

23.47 It remains to consider which system of law would govern the existence and effect of a gold or other protective clause; for by extension, that system of law will also govern the consequences of the abrogation of such a gold clause. The point would become relevant where a State had entered into treaties which included a clause, but has subsequently declared such provisions to be contrary to the public policy of that State. This, of course, was precisely the position which arose in the United States in 1933, when a Joint Resolution of Congress declared the gold clause to be contrary to the policy of the US municipal law. Two competing views may be put forward in this context:

(a) First of all, it may be argued that the substance of a treaty obligation is governed by public international law.[101] On this basis, the continuing validity and effect of a gold clause in a treaty would be governed by international law, and the abrogation of a gold clause under domestic law would have no effect.

(b) By way of contrary argument, it has been shown that treaty references to a particular currency necessarily import a reference to the *lex monetae*. If the gold or other protective clause is also to be regarded as governed by the *lex monetae*, then the abrogation of the protective provision under the domestic law would also have effect in relation to treaties expressed in that currency.

23.48 Although the abrogation of the gold clause fell to be regarded as a measure of monetary policy and although there is perhaps something inherently unattractive in the submission of a single clause to different systems of law, it must probably be regarded as decisive that the very purpose of a gold clause—or any other protective provision—is to protect the creditor against the principle of nominalism as it applies to the currency in which the obligation is expressed. As a result the parties must have intended that the gold clause should be governed by international law (as opposed to the *lex monetae* itself). The parties to a treaty are essentially contracting against a background of public international law and thus cannot be presumed to extend their reference to municipal law—necessitated by the use of a national currency—any further than the terms of the treaty appear strictly to require. It follows that questions touching both

---

[100] The financial statements of the EBRD are now compiled in euros. In any event, it is difficult to see how any other solution could be entertained; the acceptance of the substitution would appear to be consistent with the requirement of good faith which has to be observed in the context of treaty obligations.

[101] Just as the substance of a contractual obligation is referred to the law applicable to it.

the existence and abrogation of gold clauses contained in a treaty must be determined by reference to public international law.

This point assumed practical importance—although it was not finally decided—in the context of Article 14 of the Convention for the construction of the Panama Canal of 18 November 1903,[102] whereby the United States undertook to make to Panama an annual payment of US$250,000 in gold coin of the United States. As noted earlier, in 1933 the United States declared gold clauses to be contrary to public policy and thereupon accordingly refused to pay more than the nominal amount of the annuity in US dollars. For the reasons discussed above, it is submitted that the treaty contained a valid gold clause which was governed by international law; domestic legislation could not vary or abrogate that clause, and the attitude adopted by the United States was therefore unjustifiable within the framework of the treaty. Panama disputed the actions of the United States on this basis; the matter was subsequently settled on the basis that the United States would pay an annuity of 430,000 balboas, ie the currency of Panama, the gold content of which was simultaneously reduced.[103]

23.49

F. The Payment of Interstate Debts

A variety of issues arise in the context of the payment of interstate debts. Many of these issues mirror the corresponding questions which may arise under arrangements governed by private law, although the solutions are not necessarily identical. It is proposed to consider each of the relevant issues in turn.

23.50

Place of payment

Some treaties will contain express provisions dealing with the place in which the creditor is entitled to receive payment of moneys owing to it. For example, the Agreement establishing the European Reconstruction and Development Bank specifically empowers the Bank unilaterally to determine the place in which it is to receive the proceeds of any call on its shares.[104] The precise legal effect of any such provision is, of course, a matter of construction.

23.51

In the absence of express provisions in the relevant treaty, where is a sum of money due from one international person to another to be paid? It is suggested

23.52

---

[102] Malloy, *Treaties, Conventions, International Acts, Protocols and Agreements between the USA and Other Powers (1776–1909)* (1910) ii, 1349; *Noveau Récueil Générale* 2nd Series, No. 31, 599.
[103] (1940) 34 AJIL, *Supplement* 139 and the note on p 157. On the Convention, see Wolsey (1937) 31 AJIL 300.
[104] See Art 6(6) of the Agreement establishing the EBRD dated 29 May 1990.

that the strong tendencies prevailing in private law[105] and the requirements of reasonableness and justice favour the rule that payment is to be made in the capital (or, where different, the financial capital) of the creditor State.[106] This approach also entitles the creditor State to receive payment in the most effective manner, ie within its own jurisdiction, and free of any conditions or restrictions as may be imposed by some third State in which payment might otherwise be made.[107]

Manner of performance

23.53 How is the debtor State to perform its monetary obligations to another State? It has been seen that, so far as private law is concerned, tender is to be made in cash or (more precisely) in that which constitutes legal tender according to the *lex monetae*,[108] although this rule can be displaced with the greatest of ease. In public international law, which will usually be concerned with very large sums, such a rule is clearly inappropriate. In the absence of any express or contrary stipulation, the proper method of payment will be by means of transfers as between the central banks of the debtor and creditor States. This, of course, leads to a result which is consistent with the points made above in relation to the place of payment.[109]

The money of payment

23.54 In which currency does public international law require an interstate debt to be discharged? The debtor State may no doubt usually perform his obligation by payment of the requisite amount of the currency in which the debt is expressed.

---

[105] On this subject, see para 7.84 above.

[106] The decision in *Swiss Confederation v German Federal Republic* (1958) 1 Int LR 25, 33 discussed the meaning of the term "place of payment" in the context of the London Agreement on German External Debts (Cmnd 8781). So far as international law is concerned, it was held that the place of payment was the place at which the creditor State was actually entitled to receive the funds due to it. This was an accurate statement of the principle, although (in holding that Switzerland was the place of payment) it is less clear that the Tribunal correctly applied that principle to the facts of the case. On this decision, see Johnson (1958) BYIL 363.

[107] In the modern financial markets, it is perhaps attractive to assume that payment should be made in the financial centre of the currency of payment—a formulation frequently adopted in the context of international loans. However, this may be significantly affected by the political climate of the times, eg at certain times, a Libyan creditor might have preferred to receive a credit of US dollars in London rather than New York; cf the position in relation to a private law debt which arose in *Libyan Arab Foreign Bank v Bankers Trust Co* [1989] QB 728.

[108] On this rule, see para 9.03 above.

[109] This line of reasoning cannot apply where the creditor is an international institution whose membership will comprise a number of different States; in such a case, it may be that payment should be made in the country in which the institution has its headquarters. For an example of a treaty provision which seeks to address this issue, see Art 6(6) of the Agreement establishing the EBRD, n 104 above.

But does it have the option of paying in the currency of the place of payment, if the money of account is not in circulation there?[110] If, for example, Switzerland undertakes to pay hundreds of millions of Swiss francs to the United States in New York, does it pay in Swiss francs or in US dollars?[111] In the former case, the creditor State would have the burden of collecting the draft in Switzerland and arranging for the amount to be remitted to the United States; it would not receive effective payment in the place of performance on the due date. As a result, it is suggested, though with some hesitation, that the "local currency" option granted to the debtor in a private law context should equally be recognised by international law in favour of the debtor State.[112]

Questions touching the money of payment are in some respects addressed by the Agreement establishing the European Bank for Reconstruction and Development. The share capital of the Bank was expressed in ECUs;[113] members could meet their obligations either by means of an ECU credit or by payment "in any fully convertible currency . . . which is equivalent on the date of payment . . . to the value of the relevant obligation in ECU".[114] This leaves the question of construction as to the meaning of the expression "fully convertible currency", but the general import of the provision is clear.

It may well be, however, that international law allows for a much broader rule   **23.55** which may entitle the creditor State to receive payment in its own currency— perhaps partly recognising the inconvenience to the creditor of receiving payment

---

[110] This option, well known in a private law context, has been discussed at para 7.30 above.

[111] See, eg, the treaty between the Allied Governments and Switzerland made in Washington in 1946, whereby Switzerland undertook to pay "250 million Swiss francs payable on demand in gold in New York", Cmd 6884, clause II(2). By a treaty of 25 May 1959, Japan undertook to pay US$1,175,000 to Denmark, payment to be "remitted in US dollars to the Danish Ministry of Finance, Copenhagen" [1960] *Japanese Annual of International Law* 203.

[112] It should be appreciated that this type of problem will only arise where there is no explicit agreement about the mode of payment. A relatively recent example is afforded by the Statute of the European System of Central Banks (ESCB), which forms a Protocol to the EC Treaty. Article 28.1 provides that the capital of the European Central Bank (ECB) was to be ECU5,000 million, to be subscribed by Member States in set proportions. Given that the ECB was established within the framework of the EC Treaty, it may perhaps be inferred that payment had to be made by means of an ECU credit and there was no option for Member States to pay an equivalent amount in their national currencies, which continued to exist as at the date on which the capital was called up. In contrast, Art 30 of the Statute required Member States to transfer to the ESCB foreign reserve assets up to an amount *equivalent to* ECU50,000 million, but specifically prohibited the use of ECUs or the currencies of participating Member States for that purpose. Consequently, the figure of ECU50,000 million, represented a measure of the financial obligations of the Member States, but the performance of those obligations could be achieved by transferring any currency (other than ECU and the prohibited national currencies) which could properly be regarded as a foreign reserve asset. The transferor Member States were thus left with a measure of discretion in relation to the money of payment.

[113] See Art 6(3) of the Agreement establishing the EBRD.

[114] ibid, Art 6(8).

in some other currency, as just described. This solution was adopted in the *Lighthouses Arbitration between France and Greece*.[115] Having found that various amounts were to be credited to each party and one important item was to be calculated in terms of a "third" currency (US dollars) the arbitrators thought it necessary to convert the total amounts to be awarded to the parties into one single currency. The candidate currencies for this purpose were the Greek drachma and the French franc—ie the respective currencies of the debtor and creditor States. The Tribunal adopted the French franc, since the ultimate balance favoured a French entity which undertook its operations and maintained its accounts in that currency. This case did, however, involve the computation of damages or compensation for breach of a concession agreement;[116] it is not entirely clear how far the same analysis can be applied to a liquidated debt obligation arising under international law.

The rate of exchange

23.56　If, in accordance with the rules just discussed, the money of account and the money of payment are to differ, it becomes necessary to identify the date with reference to which the rate of exchange is to be ascertained.

23.57　In the absence of any contrary indication in the treaty concerned or other special circumstances, it seems that the day of actual payment should be the reference point for the ascertainment of the rate of exchange. The reasons are similar to those which apply in a private law context.[117] In the *Case of the Diverted Cargoes*,[118] the arbitrator expressed the view that the payment-date rule constituted a general principle of international law. At the time it was made, this statement could not be justified[119] but subsequent developments render it possible to suggest that the payment-date rule should now be accepted in this context. The rule is founded on obvious considerations of justice, although it must be equally understood that damages for default and delay may also be awarded.[120]

---

[115] (1956) xii RIAA 155; [1956] Int LR 342.

[116] Although again involving a claim for an unliquidated sum and involving an individual (rather than a State) claimant, it may also be appropriate to note the case of *Ringeisen* (1973) 56 Int LR 501 where the Republic of Austria was ordered to pay damages to an individual resident in the Federal Republic of Germany. The European Court of Human Rights ordered that both the money of account and the money of payment should be Deutsche marks and that the Federal Republic of Germany should be the place of payment. These factors lend support to the principles outlined in the text.

[117] See para 18.10 above.

[118] [1955] Int LR 820. This case has already been noted at para 23.06 above.

[119] See in particular [1957] BYIL, 43.

[120] There are, however, various decisions of the US-Mexican Claims Commission in which conversion was ordered to take place by reference to the rate of exchange on the date on which the claims originally arose. See *Case of George W Cook* (1927), *Case of Moffit* (1929), and *Case of George W Cook* (1930) reported in Neilsen, *International Law applied to Reclamations*, respectively at 195, 404, and 500.

There may be special circumstances in which the payment-date rule cannot **23.58** realistically or fairly be applied. For example, in the *Lighthouses Arbitration between France and Greece*,[121] the arbitrators ordered that the amount payable under the definitive award should be converted into French francs on the day on which that award was published. This may be the most appropriate solution where—as in that case—the award of compensation had to be a balancing sum derived from the conversion of several different currencies.

When it had to calculate compensation for the confiscation of property in Iran **23.59** by reference to the local currency and to convert the resultant amount into US dollars, the Iran-United States Claims Tribunal applied the official rate in force as at the date on which the property was taken, provided that the claimant would, in the normal course, have repatriated the funds had they been received on the due date.[122] It is submitted that this is an unwarranted and in some respects arbitrary approach, which is not directed to ensuring that the claimant receives proper compensation as at the date of the award.[123]

The type of rate of exchange

When public international law requires the conversion of a monetary obligation **23.60** or amount, what type of rate of exchange is to be used? Current treaty practice frequently refers merely to "market rates" and the precise definition of that term will clearly be a matter of construction in each case. Where the treaty relates to the establishment of an international financial institution, it is submitted that "market" refers to a major institutional market for the currencies concerned (ie and not merely to the market in which the institution happens to have its headquarters). Thus, when the Agreement establishing the European Bank of Reconstruction and Development stipulates for the payment of US dollars or Japanese yen in satisfaction of an ECU obligation "on the basis of the average exchange rate of relevant currency in terms of the ECU for the period from 30 September 1989 to 31 March 1990" it would appear that this refers to the London rates, because London is the major financial market in the European arena in which the Bank is to operate, and in which its headquarters are located.[124]

---

[121] RIAA xii, 155; (1956) Int LR 342.

[122] *Starrett Housing Corp v Iran* Iran-US Claims Tribunal Reports, 16, 223.

[123] For further criticism and for discussion of other aspects of this case, see Carten, Daems and Robert (1988) xxi *Revue Belge de Droit International* 142.

[124] Of course, it may be that rates are unlikely to differ materially across different markets, but that is an entirely separate matter. On the point made in the text, see Art 6(3) of the Agreement establishing the EBRD. Likewise, Art 7(3) of the Statute of the European Investment Bank refers to the use of "market rates" for the conversion of national currencies into ECUs and vice versa, but does not elaborate upon the precise "market" to which it is intended to refer.

23.61   In cases involving the payment of compensation (ie by reference to an unliquidated claim, as opposed to a liquidated sum), it is tentatively suggested that the principle of effective compensation should require the use of the relevant rate of exchange prevailing in the place of payment. Yet in certain circumstances, the incidence of exchange control leads to some difficulty for a State which espouses a claim originally vested in one of its nationals. As has been seen, where the national is entitled to damages or compensation for the destruction or taking of property situate within the territory of the debtor State, his claim is in general expressed and measured in terms of the currency of the debtor State,[125] except where there exists an international market for investments of the type in question; no other solution is practicable. The real problem arises only in the context of convertibility and transferability; is the amount due to be converted at all and (if so) should this be done at an official rate or at the (presumably less favourable) rate which would have been applied had the debtor State made payment direct to the private individual? In regard to compensation for the taking of property, it has been suggested that the law should operate so as to put the alien investor in a better position than he would have occupied if his property had not been taken; "once he has lost his investment it would be inequitable to require him to keep his funds in the territory of the State that has deprived him of it".[126] But this argument is not convincing; in the absence of treaty protection, it is hard to see why the foreign investor should be allowed to derive positive advantage (as opposed to just compensation) from the respondent State's international wrong. It would seem safer to find the solution in the principle of effectiveness of compensation and payment, which international law clearly recognises and which has frequently been laid down.[127]

23.62   The Treaties of Friendship, Commerce and Navigation concluded by the United States since 1945 express the point in a form which is likely to correspond to customary international law; the compensation is required to be paid promptly and "in effectively realisable form",[128] and where there are exchange restrictions

---

[125] See para 23.11 above.

[126] Comment on s 190 of the Foreign Relations Law of the United States (1965); s 712(1) and Reporter's Note 3 of the Revised Edition (1987) is less clear. A similar thought underlies the suggestion by Brandon "Legal Aspects of Foreign Investment" (1958) xviii *Federal Bar Journal* 316, according to which "compensation must be effective in the sense that it should be payable in the currency in which the original capital was imported into the nationalising State".

[127] See s 190 of the 1965 Law (n 126 above), which requires that compensation must either be paid in the currency of the State of which the alien is a national, or it must be both convertible into that currency and freely transferable. See also Art 3 of the draft Convention on the Protection of Foreign Property of 12 October 1967 prepared by the OECD ((1969) vii Int LM 117) according to which compensation representing "the genuine value of the property" must be "transferable to the extent necessary to make it effective for the national entitled thereto".

[128] eg see Art VI(3) of the Treaty of Japan (29 August 1953, UNTS 206, 143); Art IV(2) of the Treaty with Iran (15 August 1955, UNTS 284, 93); and Art V(4) of the Treaty with Germany (29 October 1954, UNTS 273, 3).

"reasonable provision for the withdrawal in foreign exchange in the currency of the other Party" must be made, the rate of exchange being that approved by the International Monetary Fund or, alternatively, such rate as is "just and reasonable".[129] It is true that treaty rules of the kind just described primarily envisage the legal rights of the alien investor himself. But the State espousing his claim cannot be in a worse position; indeed, as the ensuing section will show, the State is, in some respects, in a superior position.

G. The Effect of Exchange Control

Domestic exchange control legislation cannot, as a rule, have any impact upon interstate monetary obligations.[130] This applies even where the claimant State espouses the national's claim, which will almost of necessity be derived from municipal law; as a result of the debtor State's wrong and the espousal by the claimant State, it becomes an international claim vested in the claimant State, even though it does, of course, comprise only the damage actually suffered. The reason for this rule is that a State cannot rely upon the provisions of its internal law as a justification for a failure to comply with its international obligations except (in the case of a treaty obligation) to the extent to which the terms of the treaty itself specifically allow it to do so.[131] Consequently, the United Kingdom could not rely upon its own exchange control legislation as a ground for refusing or delaying payment in respect of any obligation governed by international law.

23.63

---

[129] See, eg, the Treaty with Japan, Art XII(3);Iran, Art VII (2).

[130] Many treaties, particularly those relating to international financial institutions, provide expressly for freedom from exchange restrictions. The Agreement establishing the Inter-American Development Bank of 8 April 1959 (Cmnd 6271) includes elaborate provisions exempting the Bank's resources from such provisions. Article 22(2) of the Statute of the European Investment Bank (as set out in a Protocol to the EC Treaty) states that the Bank "may borrow on the capital markets of a Member State . . . in accordance with the legal provisions applying to internal issues". A provision of this kind would in theory exempt the Bank from any need to obtain local exchange control approval when raising funds in any particular Member State, although the point is now academic in the light of the abolition of exchange control by the EC Member States.

[131] In the context of treaty obligations, see Art 27 of the Vienna Convention on the Law of Treaties; in the context of other obligations, see Art 32 of the ILC's Articles on State Responsibility (2001). For an example of the application of this principle, see the *Peter Pazmany University Case* [1933] PCIJ Series A/B, No. 61, 208, where the Permanent Court of International Justice specifically required that property to be restored to the claimant should be returned to it free of any compulsory measures of administration or sequestration. For an important discussion of the principle by the Privy Council, see *A-G for Canada v A-G for Ontario* [1937] AC 326. On the specific application of this principle in the context of exchange controls, see the "US State Department Memorandum in relation to Iranian Foreign Exchange Control Regulations" (1984) 23 Int LM 1182.

This was so even though the relevant legislation was expressed to be binding on the Crown itself.[132]

23.64 The above discussion does, however, presuppose that the relevant relationship is governed by public international law. Thus, if a State has a sum of money standing to the credit of an account with a bank (even the central bank) in a foreign state, the debt obligation thereby created is very likely to be governed by private law, with the result that the local exchange control regulations may be applicable.

23.65 Inevitably, however, there may be marginal cases. For example, by a treaty of 25 November 1958[133] the United Kingdom agreed to lend a sterling amount to Turkey by paying the necessary funds "to a transferable account in the United Kingdom to be designated by the Government of the Turkish Republic". Clearly, the United Kingdom could not have relied upon the provisions of the Exchange Control Act 1947 to exempt itself from the obligation to make the advance. That obligation would, however, be discharged by payment into the designated account within the United Kingdom. At that point, the funds would represent a Turkish claim against a British bank, which could not then have been paid in the absence of the necessary approval;[134] in other words, at the point of credit, the arrangements could thereon have become subject to the domestic exchange control legislation of the United Kingdom. However, it is suggested that the point would not, in fact, have arisen; the use of the word "transferable" in the quoted treaty language would be sufficient to impose upon the United Kingdom an obligation to grant such exchange approvals as were necessary to enable Turkey to remove the funds from the account and to use them abroad as required.

---

[132] See Exchange Control Act 1947, s 35. The system of exchange control formerly operated in the UK has been discussed in Ch 14 above.

[133] Cmnd 615.

[134] On this point, see Exchange Control Act 1947, s 16.

Part VI

MONETARY UNIONS AND
OTHER FORMS OF
MONETARY ORGANISATION

INTRODUCTION

There is no doubt that the completion of Economic and Monetary Union in Europe is the major monetary development since the Fifth Edition of this work was completed in 1991. This achievement directly challenges the traditional notion that individual States must create and organise their own, independent monetary systems. In past times, it had been taken for granted that a State must have its own currency, just as it had its own territory and its own constitution. Yet, radical though the introduction of the euro may appear to be, monetary union drew upon many accepted tenets of monetary law, including the State theory of money, the *lex monetae* principle, and the accepted rule that monetary sovereignty rests principally with the State. The completion of the union also highlighted the crucial role of central banking institutions in the creation of a monetary system, and the importance of a regime for the regulation of the economic policies of the participant States. Questions of this kind were previously thought to be inappropriate to a text which is intended to focus on the law of money, but they can no longer be ignored. **Intro.6.01**

In view of the points just made, it is tempting to think that monetary union was a high-level project which requires analysis in terms of Community and international law. But it must not be overlooked that the introduction of the euro had the effect of changing the money of account in every contract which subsisted on 1 January 1999 and which was expressed in one of the participating currencies. The single currency project thus also had far-reaching consequences for private law obligations. **Intro.6.02**

Under these circumstances, it is perhaps unsurprising that the present Part adds greatly to the length of this work; but the nature and scope of monetary union requires detailed analysis not only for its own sake, but because future such unions are likely to draw upon the European experience. **Intro.6.03**

With these general considerations in mind: **Intro.6.04**

(a) Chapters 24 and 25 consider pre-existing monetary unions and the background to the creation of the euro;

(b) Chapters 26 to 29 consider the treaty framework for the single currency and the institutional framework which was put into place to support the euro;

(c) Chapter 30 considers the consequences of monetary union for contracts which were expressed in the participant currencies;

(d) Chapter 31 reviews the impact of the euro in relation to the monetary sovereignty of participating Member States;

(e) Chapter 32 considers the interesting theoretical questions which would arise in the wholly unlikely event that a participating Member State attempted to withdraw from the eurozone; and

(f) finally, Chapter 33 considers certain alternative forms of monetary organisation.

24

THE NATURE AND HISTORY OF
MONETARY UNIONS

A. Introduction

In the preface to the Fifth Edition of this work, Dr Mann noted the efforts then **24.01** being made to establish a monetary union or a single currency in Europe. From the language he employed, it is perhaps fair to infer that Dr Mann (along with many others) did not find this proposal entirely to his taste. Nevertheless, in the years which have elapsed since the last edition, a project which was at times uncertain and, to many, ill-advised has now come to fruition; the euro was established as the single currency of eleven, participating Member States with effect from 1 January 1999. Greece became a participating Member State on 1 January 2001, bringing the current total to twelve. The eurozone has considerable potential for further growth; three Member States (the United Kingdom, Sweden, and Denmark) elected to remain outside the zone and could join at a later date. Equally, the recent enlargement of the European Union may create a number of additional candidates for eurozone membership if the requisite degree of economic convergence is achieved.

Economic and monetary union thus requires detailed examination, not only for **24.02** its own sake but also because the euro is in some respects unique.[1] For example, the euro was the single currency of the eurozone States from 1 January 1999,

---

[1] It should be said that the present writer has previously published work in this area—see *The Euro and the Financial Markets—The Legal Impact of EMU* (Jordans, 1999).

623

and yet euro notes and coins did not come into circulation or become legal tender until 1 January 2002. Furthermore—even though not currently a participating Member State—the United Kingdom is a party to the Treaty on European Union, which was the principal catalyst for the creation of the single currency. It is necessary to determine, both for English and EC law purposes, the consequences of these particular states of affairs. These topics—and many others—will be considered in this Part. In keeping with the overall character of this book, the discussion will, so far as practicable, be confined to issues which are germane to money or monetary obligations. Inevitably, however, a broader treatment will at times be required in order to place matters into context.

B. Definition and Consequences

24.03   First of all, what is a monetary union? Dr Mann defined[2] a "monetary union" to mean "a monetary system common to several independent States and characterised by a single currency issued by or on behalf of a single central bank and being legal tender in the States of the Union". He therefore noted that the creation of a central bank was a key feature of this type of arrangement and that the following powers were the "indispensable ingredients" of a monetary union:[3]

(a)   the *exclusive* power to issue those notes and coins which are to enjoy the status of legal tender throughout the union;

(b)   the power to determine the interest rate for the single currency;

(c)   the power to effect the reduction or expansion of credit; and

(d)   the power to take control of the external reserves of Member States and to effect the discharge of their external debts, ie foreign reserves *and liabilities* would be pooled.[4]

24.04   This approach perhaps rightly focuses on the central bank, which lies at the heart of a monetary union. But before this stage can be reached, the Member

---

[2] See the Fifth Edition of this work, 505 reflecting Gold, *Encyclopaedia of Public International Law*, 8, 405. It should be said at the outset that the Delors Report on Economic and Monetary Union suggests (at p 19) that a monetary union can exist without a single currency. In truth, however, such an arrangement would be a system of fixed parities, rather than a monetary union in its fullest, legal sense. Subject to certain comments made below, it may be appropriate to emphasise that the definition of a monetary union presupposes that its member countries will continue to exist as separate States. Consequently, England and Scotland never constituted a monetary union, because the adoption of a common unit of account was merely a part of a broader arrangement for the union of two countries into one. In this context, Art XVI of the Treaty of Union (1707) provided that "*from and after the Union*, the coin shall be the same standard and value throughout the United Kingdom" (emphasis added).

[3] See the Fifth Edition of this work, 505.

[4] In so far as this criterion suggests a pooling *of liabilities* it will be necessary to return to this point at a later stage—see para 26.15(e) below.

States of the union must achieve a degree of economic harmonisation and conditions must be created in which funds can flow freely among the Member States of the union. As Dr Mann noted,[5] the abolition of both overt and covert exchange control is a prerequisite to the creation of a monetary union. In a European context, it will therefore be necessary to consider the rules on the free movement of capital now contained in Articles 56 to 60 of the EC Treaty.[6]

It will be appreciated that this definition of a monetary union—focusing as it does on the institutional structure of the single currency—is in some respects rather narrowly based. In practical terms, the treaty which creates a monetary union will also deal with a number of other matters. In particular, the treaty will impose at least some degree of restraint upon the economic policies and financial conduct of the participating Member States.[7] It may also be necessary to stipulate that the institutions of monetary union are to act independently of Member States' control. Matters of this kind will become apparent from the discussion throughout this Part. Nevertheless they deserve emphasis at this point. It is no accident that the Treaty on European Union referred not merely to a "monetary union" but to an "economic *and* monetary union" for in practical terms the two concepts are inextricably linked—indeed, as will be shown, economic union is in some respects the master, whilst monetary union is its servant. For that reason, a purely legal definition of a monetary union alone is bound to be unduly narrow and thus unsatisfactory in some respects. In order to place matters in their context, some attention must thus be given to the economic provisions of the Treaty.   **24.05**

As to the legal *consequences* of a monetary union, Dr Mann stated[8] that "there cannot . . . be any doubt that a monetary union presupposes a constitutional organisation which is or approximates that of a single (federal) State". This statement could doubtless generate extended (and heated) debate. As a matter of international law, the Member States within the eurozone continue to be recognised as independent, sovereign States despite their participation in monetary union. Ultimately, the existence of an independent State rests upon its recognition by other States.[9] It is true that the transfer of sovereign powers to an   **24.06**

---

[5] Fifth Edition of this work, 505.

[6] See para 25.33 below.

[7] For a useful contribution in this area, see Southard (1978) 4 *North Carolina Journal of International Law & Commercial Regulation* 1, who rightly observes (at p 16) that where countries have a common currency, "there must be a reasonable amount of co-ordination and uniformity of policy and regulation in fiscal, financial, trade and other economic matters among the participants if, over time, the common currency is to be maintained. For example, it would not be feasible for one participant to run a heavy fiscal deficit or to expand credit to a much greater extent than were the other participants."

[8] Fifth Edition of this work, 509. Similar views are also expressed on p 53 of that Edition.

[9] *Oppenheim's International Law* (Longman, 9th edn, 1992) paras 38–40.

international organisation (such as the European Community) may ultimately deprive the transferring State of its independent statehood and thus of its continuing existence. This, of course, depends upon the circumstances of the case, including in particular the scope and extent of the rights and powers which are transferred, and on the revocability of the transfer,[10] and these are inevitably matters of degree and appreciation.[11] In any event, a transfer of monetary sovereignty does not of itself, deprive a State of its independent existence—as matters stand at present, the continued international statehood of the EC Member States is not in question.[12] Nevertheless, this issue remains at the heart of the debate on the United Kingdom's (non-)membership of the eurozone, and it will therefore be discussed in more detail at a later stage.[13]

24.07   Finally, it is perhaps appropriate to ask whether this attempt to define monetary union—and to describe its consequences—is of particular assistance or value? The lawyer, naturally enough, tends to pay particularly close attention to matters of definition, and a description of the common features (especially the single central bank and the role which it plays within the union) is perhaps of some help in outlining the type of institutional structure upon which a monetary union must rest. The definition is also of value in that it helps to distinguish other forms of monetary arrangements which are fundamentally different and ought not properly to be labelled as "monetary unions" at all; this can be of assistance in the sense that the necessary *consequences* of a monetary union[14] only apply to monetary unions as strictly so defined, and not to other forms of monetary arrangements. But beyond those limits, it will be unsafe to generalise, and an analysis of the union will depend upon a close reading and evaluation of the instruments which created it.

C. Other Monetary Unions

24.08   The foregoing section has determined the nature and character of a monetary union, in the legal sense of that term. Monetary union in Europe is a large subject, and will be dealt with separately in the ensuing chapters.

---

[10] On this subject, it will be seen that monetary union in Europe is expressed to be "irrevocable" but such a provision is by no means an essential ingredient of a monetary union. As will be seen, withdrawal is allowed both in the context of the African and Eastern Caribbean monetary unions, which is discussed below.

[11] On the points just made, see Oppenheim (n 9 above) para 37.

[12] This point is made by Oppenheim (n 9 above) para 37, although admittedly with reference to the law as it stood in January 1991.

[13] See generally Ch 31 below.

[14] On other forms of monetary arrangements, see Ch 33 below.

It is, however, necessary to retain a sense of perspective and to appreciate that **24.09** earlier attempts at monetary union have been made; the present section will consider two such other unions which continue to operate—namely, the monetary unions established in Africa and in the Eastern Caribbean. Moreover, the importance of monetary union as a concept is perhaps better understood if it is borne in mind that plans for further such unions are under active discussion in various parts of the world. A brief discussion of these developments has accordingly been included at the end of this section.

Monetary union in Africa

Monetary union has been established in parts of Africa by reference to the CFA **24.10** franc (ie the franc of the Communauté Financière Africaine).[15] The structure of the CFA franc zone in fact involves two monetary unions:

(a) the Central African Monetary Union[16] comprises Chad, Cameroon, the Central African Republic, Congo, Gabon, and Equatorial Guinea;[17]

(b) the West African Monetary Union[18] comprises the Ivory Coast, Benin, Burkina Faso, Niger, Senegal, Togo, and Mali.[19]

These two unions were established with the co-operation of France in the post- **24.11** colonial era.[20] In both cases, the CFA franc is the unit of account. The documentation creating the unions thus includes: (a) a monetary union treaty between the African States concerned, and (b) a Treaty of Monetary Co-operation and an Operations Account Agreement with the French Treasury. The

---

[15] For copies of the treaties and other materials about to be discussed, see the annexes to Yansané, *Contrôle de l'activité bancaire dans les pays africains de zone franc* (Nouvelles Editions Africaines, Paris, 1984). The first chapter of this book describes the evolution and structure of the French franc zone.

[16] The Central African Monetary Union was originally established in 1960 and is now constituted by a Treaty dated 23 November 1972.

[17] Equatorial Guinea joined the Union in 1984.

[18] The West African Monetary Union was originally established in 1962 and is now constituted by a treaty dated 14 November 1973.

[19] Mali joined the Union in 1984.

[20] It is suggested that this statement is correct in so far as it relates to the formalities of the monetary unions. However, the origins of the unions lie earlier in the twentieth century, when France instituted a form of monetary arrangement under which its colonial currencies were multiples of the French franc itself, and thus "shadowed" its fluctuations; free convertibility was also established between the colonial and the "parent" currency. For discussion, see *Zone Franc— Du Franc CFA à la monnaie unique européene*, Sandretto (ed) (Paris, 1994) chs 1 and 2. This text includes additional chapters on devaluation, international debt crises, and other factors which have had an impact upon the CFA franc. For earlier materials, see Neurrisse, *Le franc CFA* (1987); contributions by Burdeau and Carreau in *Festschrift F.A. Mann* (1977) and Djuemo Henri, a doctoral thesis entitled *La zone franc (l'organisation monétaire en Afrique Centrale)* (University of Sorbonne, 1976–7). The arrangements which link the CFA franc to France itself—and ultimately to the euro—are considered at para 33.29 below.

latter treaty was not essential to the establishment of a monetary union in the general sense; rather, it was necessary because the CFA franc was to enjoy a fixed parity with the French franc in this particular instance.[21]

24.12   The African monetary unions in many ways conform to the general scheme of a monetary union as it has been described above. For example:

(1)   Both treaties establish a central bank as the main financial institution of monetary union—the *Banque des Etats de l'Afrique Centrale* (for the Central African Union) and the *Banque Centrale des Etats de l'Afrique de l'Ouest* (for the West African Union).[22]

(2)   The member States transferred to the respective central banks the exclusive right to issue notes and coins which would constitute legal tender within their territory.[23]

(3)   The pooling of foreign exchange reserves is also addressed by the treaties. The member States of the Central African Union were required to transfer their foreign reserves to the central bank, while in the West African Union, the central bank has the right to require such transfer.[24]

(4)   In order to ensure the effectiveness of the unions, the member States are required to harmonise their policies in a number of areas, including (a) the control of their external financial relations, (b) the control of lending, (c) the distribution of credit, and (d) the counterfeiting of money.[25]

(5)   In support of the concept of monetary union, transfers of funds between member States are to be free of any exchange controls or other restrictions.[26]

(6)   Various provisions seek to insulate the central bank functions from control by individual member States. In the case of the West African Union, for example, it is explicitly provided that no obligations or restrictions can be placed upon the central bank beyond those provided for in the treaty and the bank's statutes.[27] Similarly, neither central bank can grant to any member State credits of an amount in excess of 20 per cent of the national fiscal receipts in the last financial year.[28]

---

[21]   This aspect of the arrangements is considered in more detail at para 33.30 below.

[22]   On the establishment of these institutions, see respectively Arts 1 and 7 of the Central African Treaty and Art 15 of the West African Treaty.

[23]   Article 8 of the Central African Treaty; Art 15 of the West African Treaty.

[24]   Article 10 of the Central African Treaty; Art 20 of the West African Treaty.

[25]   Article 14 of the Central African Treaty; Art 22 of the West African Treaty.

[26]   Article 13 of the Central African Treaty; the point is implicit in Art 18 of the West African Treaty.

[27]   Article 17 of the West African Treaty.

[28]   Article 22 of the Statutes of the Central Bank of the Central African Union; Art 16 of the Statutes of the Central Bank of the West African States.

(7) The treaties also created further institutional structures. The Central African Union includes a Monetary Committee charged with the supervision of the effective application of the treaty,[29] whilst the West African Union provides for a Council of Ministers which is placed in charge of monetary and credit policy.[30]

(8) In each case, the CFA franc is the unit of account, and it was to enjoy a fixed parity with the French franc.[31]

(9) The fixed parity between the CFA franc and the French franc was recognised by France under the Monetary Co-operation Agreements with the member States of the Central African Union (23 November 1972) and the member States of the West African Union (4 December 1973). Under the terms of these agreements, France assured the free convertibility of the CFA franc as against its own currency, whilst the foreign exchange resources of member States were required to be deposited with the Banque de France. These arrangements were supported by the opening of operational accounts with the French Treasury.

An examination of these features demonstrates that the African structures do constitute genuine monetary unions within the scope of the working definition; in particular, they include a central bank enjoying the exclusive right to issue banknotes and coins within the territory of the union. They also include a number of other provisions which are a common (if not a *necessary*) feature of such unions.   **24.13**

In view of points which will be made later[32] it should be noted that the African monetary unions were constituted with a clear recognition that a delegation of monetary sovereignty was involved; in the context of newly independent States emerging from the colonial era, it is perhaps unsurprising that the point received some attention. Thus, for example, the first paragraph of the Central African Treaty refers to the desire of the member States to promote "une coopération monétaire mutuellement profitable, dans le respect de leur souveraineté nationale". More substantially, each member State is entitled to reclaim its   **24.14**

---

[29] Article 4 of the Central African Treaty.

[30] Article 12 of the West African Treaty. Article 5 of the treaty provides that a Conference of Heads of State is the "supreme authority" of the union which (amongst other things) is to decide any question which the Council of Ministers has been unable to resolve.

[31] Article 9 of the Central African Treaty; Art 14 of the West African Treaty. In 1994, it was found necessary to devalue the CFA franc by some 50%. On the economic consequences of this episode, see Clément, Mueller, Cossé, and Le Dem, *Aftermath of the CFA Franc Devaluation* (IMF Occasional Paper 138, 18 June 1996).

[32] See the discussion on the consequences of a withdrawal from monetary union for national sovereignty in Ch 32 below.

sovereignty in this area by electing to withdraw from the relevant treaty.[33] It must follow that in strict law, the States of the two African unions merely pooled their monetary sovereignty on a temporary basis, for that sovereignty can be reclaimed by the individual member States without the consent of any other party.[34]

Monetary union in the Eastern Caribbean

24.15 Another monetary union has existed since 1965, in the Eastern Caribbean.[35] Its current members are Anguilla, Barbuda, Dominica, Grenada, Montserrat, St Kitts and Nevis, St Lucia, and St Vincent and the Grenadines. The union is at present governed by an Agreement between its member territories dated 5 July 1983. Once again, it is fair to say that these arrangements constitute a "monetary union" within the working definition of that term. The Eastern Caribbean Central Bank (ECCB) is an international organisation established under the terms of the 1983 Agreement;[36] it has the exclusive right to issue the Eastern Caribbean dollar, which is the sole legal tender within the union.[37] The central bank holds the external assets of the participating governments, and is responsible for the establishment of interest rates.[38] The 1983 Agreement contains a number of other provisions which may be expected to be found within the context of a monetary union but which are not determinative as to the legal existence of such a union. For example, the 1983 Agreement regulates the ECCB's financial relationship with the participating governments; the central bank may only make advances to participating governments in limited circumstances, and even then only up to an amount representing a pre-set percentage of government revenues;[39] the central bank must generally maintain an external reserve equal to 60 per cent of the currency issued by it;[40] the business of the

---

[33] Withdrawal from the Central African Union is permitted on notice to that effect—see Art 17 of that Treaty. Article 3 of the West African Treaty permits withdrawal on 80 days' notice.

[34] It is necessary to contrast this position with the approach adopted in the European Union. In the latter case, there are no provisions for withdrawal and monetary union is stated to be "irrevocable", although this position may change if the proposed EC Constitution is adopted. On this point, see para 32.06, n 7 below.

[35] For an analysis of the consequences of this union in the context of the local banking system, see Polius and Samuel, "Banking Efficiency in the Eastern Caribbean Currency Union: an examination of the structure—conduct-performance paradigm and the efficiency hypothesis" (2002) (Jan–June) *Money Affairs* 75.

[36] The corporate status and capacities of the ECCB are set out in Arts 3 and 4 of the 1983 Agreement. For a detailed account of the institutional framework, see van Beek, Rosales, Zermeno, Randall, and Shepherd, *The Eastern Caribbean Currency Union: Institutions, Performance and Policy Issues* (IMF Occasional Paper 195, 11 August 2000).

[37] See Art 18 of the 1983 Agreement.

[38] See respectively, Arts 25 and 34 of the 1983 Agreement.

[39] Articles 39 and 40 of the 1983 Agreement.

[40] Article 24 of the 1983 Agreement.

central bank is run by a board of directors, under the supervision of a Monetary Council of Ministers.[41]

Once again, the member territories have retained the right to withdraw from the union.[42] Consequently, the delegation of monetary sovereignty may be revoked and ultimate control of such sovereignty thus rests within the individual member territories, as opposed to the union itself.[43]

24.16

D. Future Monetary Unions

Plainly, a monetary union cannot be created on short notice; a great deal of detailed planning is required and the prospective members of the union must achieve a satisfactory degree of economic convergence. Despite these obstacles, other monetary unions are under active consideration, and it is necessary to briefly describe these developments.

24.17

The monetary unions which exist in Africa, based upon the "zone franc", have already been considered. However, the Economic Community of West African States (ECOWAS) has announced plans for a monetary union embracing Ghana, Guinea, Nigeria, Sierra Leone, and Gambia, with a view to promoting economic growth across the region.[44] The area is known as the West African Monetary Zone, and its institutional structure clearly draws upon the experience acquired in the context of monetary union in Europe.[45] For example, a West African Monetary Institute has been established by the terms of an Agreement among the ECOWAS States dated 15 December 2000. The objectives of the Institute include the co-ordination of monetary policy with a view to achieving price stability; monitoring compliance with agreed convergence criteria; developing an exchange rate mechanism; and making the preparations necessary for the launch of the West African Central Bank, which will be responsible for the new currency upon its introduction[46]—the Institute may

24.18

---

[41] See respectively, Arts 7 and 8 of the 1983 Agreement.

[42] Article 52 of the 1983 Agreement. The procedure for withdrawal envisages a settlement of accounts, having regard to (a) the amount of notes and coins in circulation in the territory concerned, (b) any amounts owing by the Government concerned to the ECCB, and (c) the withdrawing Government's imputed share in the ECCB's general reserve.

[43] It should be added that the so-called Latin Monetary Union was not in fact a monetary union in the sense now under discussion. Consequently, that arrangement is considered in Ch 33 below.

[44] For an analysis of the prospects for a broader African monetary union, see *Zone Franc—Du Franc CFA à la monnaie unique européene*, Sandretto (ed) (Paris, 1994) p 255 and Masson and Pattillo, "A Single Currency for Africa?" *Finance and Development* (December 2004), p 9.

[45] On the institutions created in a Community context, see Ch 27 below.

[46] The new unit is to be known as the ECO. On the points to be made in the text, see Art 4 of the Agreement of 15 December 2000.

thus be regarded as a transitional organisation. It was originally hoped that the monetary union would come into existence on 1 January 2003. However, assessments undertaken during the course of 2002 revealed an insufficient degree of macro-economic convergence amongst the participating States. Accordingly, it was decided to defer the launch of the single currency until 1 July 2005.[47]

24.19 In addition, the members of the Gulf Co-operation Council (GCC)[48] have announced plans to achieve a monetary union by 1 January 2010 with a new currency which will be pegged to the US dollar. Progress in this area included (a) a decision officially to link individual currencies to the US dollar by the end of 2002,[49] and (b) a decision to adopt, by 2005, the economic convergence criteria which would be necessary to support monetary union. It has been pointed out that the creation of an effective monetary union in this region will depend upon the establishment of a common central bank; the adoption of clear criteria for fiscal convergence; the pooling of foreign reserves; and the determination of a common exchange rate policy.[50] Once again, this position is entirely consistent with the definition of a monetary union adopted for the purposes of this work. The importance of this prospective monetary union should not be under-estimated; the creation of such a union amongst the members of the GCC would involve a region which, in 2001, had a combined GDP of some US$335 billion and which boasts a very significant portion of the world's oil and natural gas reserves.[51] Further momentum towards a common unit of account is becoming apparent, and the concept of "regional currencies" involving a monetary union is gaining support in some quarters.[52]

24.20 This chapter has, hopefully, served to emphasise that monetary union, as a concept, is not new; nor is it a concept which has been discredited by experience.

---

[47] This decision was taken at the summit of Heads of State and Governments of the West African Monetary Zone at their meeting in Conakry, November 2002. For an informative discussion of the merits of the proposed union, see Masson and Pattillo, *Monetary Union in West Africa: An Agency of Restraint for Fiscal Policies?* (IMF Working Paper WP/01/34).

[48] The GCC comprises Bahrain, Kuwait, Oman, Qatar, Saudi Arabia, and the United Arab Emirates. The proposals about to be discussed were formulated at a GCC Summit Meeting held at the end of 2001.

[49] All members of the Council complied with this obligation by the end of 2002 or in the early part of 2003. Most of the GCC currencies had formerly been linked to the SDR. On this subject, see Fasano, *Monetary Union among Member Countries of the Gulf Co-operation Council* (IMF Occasional Paper 223, 28 August 2003).

[50] These points are emphasised by Fasano and Zubair Iqbal in "Common Currency" (December 2002) 39 (4) *Finance & Development.*

[51] For these and other statistics, see the materials mentioned in n 50 above.

[52] See, eg, Beddoes, "From EMU to AMU—The Case for Regional Currencies" (1999) 78 (4) (July/August) *Foreign Affairs* 8.

On the contrary, current indications suggest that the influence of this form of monetary organisation is likely to increase. Monetary union in Europe is the most ambitious project thus far, and it will be discussed in depth in the ensuing chapters.

25

HISTORICAL BACKGROUND TO EMU

A. Introduction

As will be recalled, the creation of the euro was not a short-term project; many **25.01** years of preparation were necessary before the single currency could come into being. As is almost invariably the case, a complete understanding of the present situation can only be achieved if the historical background is explained. Consequently, it is necessary to explain—it is hoped, not in excessive detail—some of the milestones on the road to European Monetary Union (EMU), and to examine some of its foundations.[1]

B. Origins of Monetary Union

For these purposes, it is necessary to return to the very origins of the European **25.02** Community. The Treaty establishing the European Economic Community was signed by the six original Member States on 25 March 1957. Under Article 2 of the Treaty, the objective of the Community was "to promote throughout the Community a harmonious development of economic activities, a continuous and balanced expansion, an increase in stability, an accelerated raising of the

---

[1] For other discussions, see Usher, *The Law of Money and Financial Services in the European Community* (Oxford University Press, 2nd edn, 2000) chs 2 and 8; Craig and de Búrca, *EC Law—Texts, Cases and Materials* (Oxford University Press, 3rd edn, 2003) ch 15; Sideek Mohammed, *European Community Law on the Free Movement of Capital and the EMU* (Kluwer Law International, 1999).

standard of living and closer relations between the States belonging to it". This objective was to be achieved "by establishing a common market and progressively approximating the economic polices of Member States". With these objectives in mind, the activities of the Community included (a) "the abolition, as between Member States, of obstacles to freedom of movement for persons, services and capital";[2] (b) the abolition of rules which restricted the right to establish branches, agencies, or subsidiaries in other Member States;[3] and (c) "the application of procedures by which the economic policies of Member States can be co-ordinated and disequilibria in their balances of payments remedied".[4]

25.03 In terms of a purely legal analysis, and against the background of the Treaty framework, it is apparent that monetary union is principally concerned with the free movement of capital and payments[5] and the conduct of economic policy throughout the Member States. In this context, the key provisions of the 1957 Treaty, and Directives issued pursuant to it, included the following requirements:

(a) Member States were required progressively to abolish as between themselves all restrictions on the movement of capital belonging to persons resident in Member States and any discrimination based on the nationality or on the place of residence of the parties or on the place where such capital was invested; however, this requirement only applied "to the extent necessary to ensure the proper functioning of the common market".[6] Current payments (for example, payments of interest) in connection with a movement of

---

[2] Article 3(c) of the EC Treaty (in its original form).

[3] The freedom of establishment was created by Arts 52–58 of the EC Treaty (in its original form).

[4] Article 3(g) of the EC Treaty (in its original form).

[5] The rules on free movement of capital and payments are a necessary adjunct to the other freedoms established by the Treaty. It would be pointless to provide for the free movement of goods and services, and the right of establishment, if the means of paying for those goods and services or the investment of the necessary capital could be restricted by national regulations. But it is equally apparent that treaty provisions requiring that monetary or capital flows should be unimpeded do not deal with the entire problem. For example, investment in another Member State necessarily involved the expense of purchasing the currency of the investee State, and in terms of the investor's "home" currency, the possible returns on the investment could be significantly affected by exchange rate fluctuations. Factors of this kind would, in practice, tend to make investors more reluctant to exercise the treaty freedoms in the first place. Despite the controversy which surrounded monetary union, it is nevertheless fair to observe that the introduction of the single currency was not an end in itself; rather it was a means to achieving broader Community objectives and to support the freedoms created by the Treaty. Indeed, no exchange rate system can of itself deliver or guarantee economic growth; it is merely one part of a broader set of economic policies.

[6] Article 67(1) of the EC Treaty (in its original form).

capital were to be freed from national restrictions[7] and—to the extent to which national systems of exchange control remained in force—Member States were required to be "as liberal as possible" in granting any authorisations required in relation to capital movements and the connected current payments which fell within the scope of the Treaty.[8] Finally, Member States had to "endeavour to avoid" the introduction of any new or more restrictive rules against the movement of capital or associated current payments.[9] The language of these provisions was deliberately equivocal; they allowed some scope for discretion and value judgment as to the manner and precise extent of their implementation. Indeed, in purely legal terms, provisions of this kind hardly impose definite obligations of any kind. As a result, these Treaty rules were found not to create rights which were directly enforceable by individuals in the context of domestic legal proceedings within a Member State.[10]

(b) Articles 104 to 109 of the Treaty contained various rules on the balance of payments of Member States in the context of overall economic policy. At a general level (and, to some extent, foreshadowing the more detailed provisions which would later be inserted by the Treaty on European Union), each Member State was required to "pursue the economic policy needed to ensure the equilibrium of its overall balance of payments and to maintain confidence in its currency" and to "treat its policy with regard to rates of exchange as a matter of common concern".[11] Provisions of this kind create obligations of an inter-governmental nature, and are thus incapable of creating rights directly enforceable by individuals.[12] More substantively, however, each Member State undertook to authorise payments to creditors in other Member States (in the currency of the creditor's home country), where such payments were connected with the movement of goods, services, or capital or any transfers connected therewith, to the extent to which these movements had been liberalised pursuant to the terms of the Treaty.[13] Of course, until the free movement of capital was fully liberalised, it necessarily followed that these treaty provisions could not have direct effect in

---

[7] Article 67(2) of the EC Treaty (in its original form). Subject to various conditions, a Member State could restrict the movement of capital if this was leading to disturbances in the functioning of the domestic capital markets within that Member State. The details are set out in Art 73 of the EC Treaty (in its original form).

[8] Article 68(1) of the EC Treaty (in its original form).

[9] Article 71 of the EC Treaty (in its original form).

[10] Case 203/80 *Re Casati* [1981] ECR 2595.

[11] On these points, see Arts 104 and 107 of the EC Treaty (in its original form).

[12] On this point, see Case 9/73 *Schlüter v HZA Lörrach* [1973] ECR 1135.

[13] Article 106(1) of the EC Treaty (in its original form).

Member States.[14] By way of derogation from these provisions, Member States were allowed to restrict the free movement of capital when faced with serious balance of payment difficulties.[15]

(c) The early 1960s saw the issue of a series of Council Directives which gradually gave substance to the principle of free movement of capital; for example, Member States were required to provide authorisation for payments to residents of other Member States for services rendered, and for the investment of capital as between the Member States.[16]

C. The Werner Report

25.04 Matters virtually rested here until 1970 when, at a meeting at the Hague, the Member States determined to establish an Economic and Monetary Union, and commissioned the Prime Minster of Luxembourg, M. Pierre Werner to produce a report on the subject. Very briefly, the Report[17] noted the following key points:

(a) Economic and monetary union would allow the Community to create a geographical area in which goods, services, persons, and capital could circulate freely, without competitive distortions and without giving rise to structural or regional imbalances.[18]

(b) The creation of a monetary union would necessarily involve the complete liberalisation of capital movements, the final abolition of exchange control regimes, the elimination of margins of fluctuation in exchange rates, and the consequent fixing of parity rates. It will be apparent from the final part of this statement that the Werner Report did not necessarily contemplate

---

[14] Cases 286/82 and 26/83 *Luisi and Carbone v Ministero del Tresore* [1984] ECR 377. On this case, see Smits, "The end of claustrophobia: European Court requires free travel for payments" (1984) 9 (3) ELR 192. See also Case 157/85 *Brugnoni and Ruffinengo v Casa di Risparmio di Genova e Imperia* [1986] ECR 625, discussed by Smits, "Free Movement of Capital and Payments: A further step on the road to liberalisation?" (1986) 11 (5) ELR 456.

[15] For the details, see Arts 108 and 109 of the EC Treaty (in its original form).

[16] A detailed analysis of these Directives is beyond the scope of this book. For a clear and concise description of the progress which was made, see Usher, *The Law of Money and Financial Services in the European Community* (Oxford University Press, 2nd edn, 2000) 13–22.

[17] For the text of the Werner Report, see EC Bull, Supplement 11, 1970.

[18] It has been pointed out by at least one writer that the very concept of a common market implies a single internal market and the abolition of restrictions on the free movement of money. Since the very existence of different currencies creates practical restrictions against the free flow of capital, a single currency is a necessary prerequisite to the existence and functioning of a common market in its fullest sense. See van Themaat, "Some Preliminary Observations on the Inter-governmental Conferences: The Relations between the Concepts of a Common Market, a Monetary Union, an Economic Union, a Political Union and Sovereignty" (1984) 28 CML Rev 291, noting Case 15/81 *Gaston Schul* [1982] ECR 1409, para 33.

the establishment of a monetary union in the strict sense of the working definition formulated earlier.[19] Nevertheless, the Report did assert that the ultimate creation of a single Community currency would be "preferable".

(c) Economic and monetary union would involve the transfer of national sovereign powers to new, supra-national institutions which would be established within the framework of the Community. In particular, these institutions would become responsible for monetary policy; policies affecting the capital markets; and public budgets (including the available methods of financing those budgets).

(d) The co-ordination and approximation of economic policies were necessary prerequisites to the achievement of a monetary union. The Report also notes (perhaps a little optimistically) that the convergence of economic and monetary policies would have the practical effect of fixing exchange rates at appropriate levels, without the need for national governments themselves to adjust exchange rate parities.

A review of the Werner Report does serve to emphasise that a monetary **25.05** union—whether or not within the strict definition of that term—will not normally be an end in itself. It will usually play a supporting role (albeit a crucial one) in attempts to create a geographical area in which economic and monetary policies are to converge and to be harmonised.[20] This can be a difficult point for the lawyer to grasp, yet it is vital that he should do so, for the Treaty provisions dealing with monetary union must be interpreted in the light of Community objectives;[21]

Unfortunately, the Werner Report was published when the world was on the **25.06** brink of a period of serious monetary instability. Stable exchange rates were supported by the Bretton Woods system of parities and perhaps represented one of the main assumptions upon which the Report had been based, but that system was to break down barely a few months after the publication of the Report.[22] Difficult economic conditions and inflationary problems plagued the 1970s, with the result that it would have been extremely difficult to progress the necessary harmonisation of national economic policies—even had the political will to do so existed. It must also be accepted that the Werner Report suffered from

---

[19] See para 24.03 above. As there noted, the Delors Report likewise argued that a single currency was not a necessary prerequisite for monetary union.

[20] A point recognised by the Council and the Representatives of Member States in their resolution accepting the Report—[1971] OJ C28/1. For judicial discussion of the monetary and exchange rate consequences of this resolution, see Case 9/73 *Schlüter v HZA Lörrach* [1973] ECR 1135.

[21] This important point was occasionally overlooked in technical discussions in the City of London during the pre-euro period—see the discussion of monetary union and its consequences for monetary obligations in Ch 30 below.

[22] On the breakdown of this system, see para 2.10 above.

various deficiencies, which perhaps undermined its value as a guide to possible future developments. For example, the ultimate structures put in place for the euro are heavily dependent upon the institutional arrangements; the working definition of a monetary union[23] demonstrates a similar such dependence. Unfortunately, the Werner Report—with its emphasis on economic policies, exchange rates and like matters—was too superficial in its consideration of the establishment and the role of the required institutions. In a foretaste of later debates it was acknowledged that monetary union would involve a significant transfer of sovereignty to new institutions, but the Report did not go into depth on the structures required in order to create and sustain such a union.[24]

25.07 The Werner Report was thus in part a victim of changing macro-economic circumstances, and in part a victim of certain inadequacies within the Report itself. But it would be quite wrong to dismiss the Report out of hand, for it was in many respects the first major step towards monetary union, and it may also have influenced some of the other progress which was made in later years. Perhaps the Report's most important lasting achievement was to highlight both the objectives and value of a monetary union;[25] such a union would enable the Community to create "an area within which persons, goods, services and capital may move freely and without distortion of competition". Once again, this serves to emphasise that monetary union—whilst a very important development in itself—is intended to play a supporting, rather than a leading, role in the achievement of Community objectives.

25.08 The Werner Report also made it clear that a stable exchange rate environment or a single currency would help to drive economic growth. Despite the adverse conditions of the 1970s, various steps were thus taken both in the monetary field and in the context of the convergence of economic policies. Since these developments may be said to have their origins in the Werner Report,[26] it is appropriate to describe them briefly.

25.09 First of all, a European Monetary Co-operation Fund began to operate in 1973.[27] The stated purpose of the Fund was to facilitate the creation of an

---

[23] See para 24.03 above.

[24] On these and other factors which limited the influence of the Report, see Baer and Padoa-Schioppa, "The Werner Report Revisited". This Paper is attached to the Delors Report, which is discussed below.

[25] A point recognised by the Council and representatives of Member States in their resolution on the Report—[1971] OJ C28/21.

[26] It should also be said that the essential conclusions of the Werner Report—namely that immutable fixed rates, or preferably a single currency, should be achieved within the Community—were also mirrored in the Delors Report some 19 years later.

[27] Regulation 907/73 [1973] JO L189/2. The decision to establish the EMCF had been announced following a Conference of the Heads of State (Paris, 21 October 1972).

economic and monetary union between Member States, whether on the basis of a single currency or through the use of fixed exchange rate parities. Bilateral central rates applied as between each of the currencies within the system, and the Fund was to promote intervention in the foreign exchange markets in an effort to control the margins of fluctuation between the currencies of the respective Member States.[28] The system of controlling margins of fluctuation was referred to as the "currency snake" or simply, "the snake". The snake provided for currency fluctuations within a band of 2.25 per cent. As will be seen, this figure acquired a remarkable durability in the European monetary context. The fortunes of the snake itself were less marked; continuing tensions in the foreign exchange markets precipitated a number of departures from the system and only five Member States remained within it by 1977; by that time, the system effectively functioned as a mini-Deutsche mark zone.[29] Perhaps fore-shadowing later events, the pound only remained within the snake for a matter of weeks, and the membership of the French franc had to be terminated and renewed on two occasions.

Secondly, Community institutions adopted various measures on the con-   **25.10**
vergence of economic policies, economic stability, and short-term monetary support.[30] Whilst the original aspiration of achieving monetary union by 1980 was not destined to be achieved,[31] it is nevertheless possible to discern from these early developments the outline of the institutional and economic arrangements which were later to be put in place to underpin the euro.

D. The European Monetary System

Although the "snake" ultimately came to grief, the Community did not abandon   **25.11**
the quest for a more stable exchange rate environment. As a consequence, the European Monetary System (EMS) was established on 1 January 1979, and commenced operation on 13 March 1979.[32] As Dr Mann noted in the Fifth

---

[28] See Arts 2 and 3 of Reg 907/73 [1973] JO L189/2.

[29] On this point, see Usher, *The Law of Money and Financial Services in the European Community* (Oxford University Press, 2nd edn, 2000) 172.

[30] For the details, see the Council Decision on the convergence of economic policies (74/120 [1974] JO C20/1, a Directive on economic stability, growth and full employment (74/121 [1974] JO L63/19) and a Resolution on short-term monetary support ([1974] JO C20/1). Short-term monetary support was intended to assist Member States encountering balance of payment problems.

[31] On this aspiration, see the Paris Final Communiqué mentioned in n 27 above.

[32] For helpful discussions of the EMS and a number of the other matters about to be discussed, see Jean-Jacques Rey, "The European Monetary System" (1980) 17 CMR 7; Lowenfeld, *International Economic Law* (Oxford University Press, 2002) 640; and Mehnert, *User's Guide to the ECU* (Graham & Trotman, 1992). It should be noted that the UK—along with all of the other

Edition of this book, the EMS was not established by a single and comprehensive document and some of the obligations apparently created by the documentation are not readily understood by a lawyer.[33] Nevertheless, it is important to attempt an analysis, partly because the EMS arrangements were an important forerunner of monetary union itself, and partly because they provide a valuable illustration of interstate co-operation in the field of monetary affairs.

25.12 The primary documentation establishing the EMS consisted of:

(a)   a Resolution of the European Council made on 5 December 1978;[34] and

(b)   an agreement amongst the central banks of the Member States.[35]

Consistently with the earlier initiatives which have already been discussed, these arrangements were intended to create a durable and effective scheme for closer monetary co-operation between Member States with a view to creating a greater measure of monetary stability and economic convergence within the Community; although the point was perhaps not much noted at the time, the creation of the EMS was also intended to provide "fresh impetus to the process of European Union".[36]

25.13 The EMS was operated under the supervision of the European Monetary Co-operation Fund. The new system involved[37] the creation of (a) the Exchange Rate Mechanism (ERM) and (b) the European Currency Unit (ECU).

Member States—was a founder member of the EMS itself. However, this had no material consequences for the UK until it elected to join the ERM on 8 October 1990. The position of the UK in this respect is discussed below. The terms of the European Council Resolution specifically contemplated that some of the Member States might not join the ERM at the outset, but allowed them to do so at a later date—see Art 3.1 of the agreement amongst central banks of the Member States. It may thus be said that in the context of European monetary affairs, the UK has something of a history of "opt-outs", hesitation, and deferred membership—on the UK's opt out from monetary union itself, see para 31.31 below.

[33] See Dr Mann's comments on this subject in the Fifth Edition of this work, 503. For a discussion of the slightly uncertain legal basis of the EMS within the framework of the EC Treaty, see Usher, *The Law of Money and Financial Services in the European Community* (Oxford University Press, 2nd edn, 2000) 173–6. Indeed, the precise status of these arrangements seems to have caused some confusion at the Community level—see the decision of the ECJ (an appeal against a judgment of the Court of First Instance) in Case C–193/01 P *Pitsiloras v Council and the ECB* [2003] ECR I–4837. The case concerned access to the Basle/Nyborg Agreement on the Reinforcement of the Monetary System, to which further reference is made below.

[34] EC Bull 12, 1978.

[35] A copy of the agreement is annexed to the Resolution of the European Council just noted. The texts are set out in a 1979 EC publication entitled *Texts concerning the European Monetary System* (Cmnd 7419); they are also reproduced in Appendix A to Mehnert, *User's Guide to the ECU* (Graham & Trotman, 1992).

[36] See the introduction to the Conclusions of the Presidency of the European Council, Brussels, 4 and 5 December 1978.

[37] In addition to the matters about to be mentioned in the text, the EMS involved certain credit and other financing measures, and arrangements to assist the less advanced economies within the system. However, these aspects fall outside the scope of the present work.

The ECU formed the cornerstone of the ERM itself. This unit was originally   **25.14**
defined by reference to stated amounts of the national currencies of the Member
States, and provision was made for the "basket" composition to be adjusted at
five-yearly intervals, if necessary.[38] In 1989, the system was changed so that the
composition of the ECU was determined by reference to percentages or
"weights", ie as opposed to fixed amounts of the currencies within the basket.
The final readjustment of these weightings was effected by Council Regulation
1971/89[39] as subsequently restated by Council Regulation 3320/94.[40] Thus,
with effect from the 1989 realignment, the respective weights attributed to the
ECU were as follows:

German mark	30.1%	Spanish peseta	5.3%
French franc	19.0%	Danish krone	2.45%
Pound sterling	13.0%	Irish punt	1.1%
Italian lira	10.15%	Greek drachma	0.8%
Dutch guilder	9.4%	Portuguese escudo	0.8%
Belgian franc	7.6%	Luxembourg franc	0.3%

What, then, was the purpose of this artificial unit, or "basket" of currencies? Its   **25.15**
functions are outlined in the European Council Resolution already noted. The
ECU was to lie "at the centre of the EMS"; it was to serve as the denominator
for the ERM, as the basis for a divergence indicator, as the denominator for
intervention and credit mechanisms and as a means of settlement between
monetary authorities within the EC.[41] Each currency within the ECU basket
was to have an ECU-related central rate, which was used to establish a "grid" of
bilateral exchange rates. Currencies were allowed a fluctuation margin of plus/
minus 2.25 per cent (or 6 per cent in the case of floating currencies). The
intention was to reduce the permitted bands of fluctuation when economic
conditions so permitted[42] but in fact this never proved to be practicable. Indeed,
circumstances compelled a widening of the bands on certain occasions.[43] It may

---

[38] At its inception, the ECU was substituted for the European Unit of Account by reference to
the same value and currency composition—see Council Regulation 3180/80, [1978] OJ L379/1
and para 2.1 of the Resolution of the European Council on the establishment of the EMS
(Brussels, 5 December 1978). For present purposes, it is not necessary to trace the history of the
EUA but for a discussion, see Usher (n 33 above) 160–2.

[39] [1989] OJ L189/1.

[40] [1994] OJ L350/27. This proved to be the final adjustment because further variations in the
ECU basket were prohibited under Art 118 of the EC Treaty (as inserted by the Treaty on
European Union).

[41] On these points, see para 2.2 of the European Council Resolution. It should be said that the
ECU never gained the credibility required for it to fulfil its intended function as a denominator
for the ERM and, in practical terms, the Deutsche mark assumed that mantle. It was thus the
inability of sterling to "shadow" the mark which led to its departure from the system on "Black
Wednesday"—see below.

[42] On these points, see para 3.1 of the European Council Resolution.

[43] Thus, when sterling entered the ERM on 8 October 1990, it did so at a rate equivalent to
DM2.95 and a fluctuation "band" of 6% was agreed. Even this, however, proved to be insufficient

be added that an "early warning mechanism" was also built into this aspect of the System. If a currency crossed its "threshold of divergence" (stated to be 75 per cent of the maximum permitted divergence), then this created a "presumption" that the national authorities would take "adequate measures" to correct the situation—for example, by way of diversified intervention or adjustments to monetary or economic policy.[44]

25.16   In order to preserve the System, intervention[45] was stated to be "compulsory" when the limit of the fluctuation margins had been reached.[46] Crucially, it is not stated precisely who was responsible for such intervention. It must necessarily have included the central bank of Member State whose currency had reached the limits of the permitted margins, but it is not explicitly stated that other central banks were under an obligation to support these operations and (if so) to what extent.[47] It would seem to follow that each individual central bank was primarily, but not exclusively, responsible for the market operations which might prove necessary to ensure that its national currency observed the fluctuation margins prescribed by the System. The central bank responsible for the weaker currency thus had to sell its reserves of the stronger currency, to the intent that its own currency would appreciate. If that central bank had insufficient reserves in the stronger currency, then it could borrow them from the central bank which issued that currency on a short-term basis. Furthermore, the central bank of the stronger currency was expected to sell its own currency against the weaker currency, thus depreciating its own national currency as against the weaker unit. Finally, the System included provisions for financial support from the European Monetary Co-operation Fund to a Member State which was attempting to ward off speculation against its currency. The most frequently used facility was the Very Short Term Financing Facility.[48] There

---

to maintain sterling's membership of the system—see para 25.17 below. It has been pointed out that the realignments within the EMS were inevitably necessary from time to time, and that the stability of the System thus depended in many respects upon the management of such realignments consistently with market expectations—see Chen and Giovannini, *The Determinants of Realignment Expectations under the EMS—Some Empirical Regularities* (1993) CEPR Discussion Paper No 79, London Centre for Economic Policy Research.

[44] See paras 3.4 and 3.5 of the European Council Resolution.

[45] ie the sale or purchase of the currency concerned with a view to maintaining its value within the prescribed margins of fluctuation.

[46] See para 3.4 of the European Council Resolution. It may be added that, in financial terms, the obligation to intervene in the markets was unlimited once the compulsory intervention rates had been reached—see Article 2.2 of the agreement amongst the central banks of the Member States. In practice, this intervention proved to be beyond the resources of both the Bank of England and the Banca d'Italia in the circumstances which confronted them on "Black Wednesday".

[47] The point is only partially clarified by Art 2 of the Agreement of the Central Banks referred to in n 46 above.

[48] The other available options were Short Term Monetary Support and Medium Term Financial Assistance.

were various practical difficulties with these arrangements. First of all, the Very Short Term Financing Facility was originally available for a maximum period of 45 days, which was found to afford insufficient flexibility during a period when Community law required the progressive dismantling of restrictions on the movement of capital and payments and thus rendered currencies more vulnerable to attack by market speculators. This problem was partly addressed by the Basle/Nyborg Agreement on the Reinforcement of the European Monetary System, which was endorsed by Community Finance Ministers on 12 November 1987.[49] More fundamentally, once the final margin of fluctuation was reached, intervention was in theory obligatory and without limit. As has been shown, however, this position was not always respected in practice; it was, in any event, plainly unsustainable in the context of a serious monetary crisis. It would also be unpalatable for the central bank of the stronger currency to support the weaker currency on an open-ended basis and this tends to reinforce a point made earlier, ie that the responsibility to intervene in the markets fell mainly upon the central bank of the currency under attack. Thus, when sterling came under pressure in the days leading up to "Black Wednesday", 16 September 1992, the agreement apparently did not impose upon other central banks within the system an effective or enforceable duty to purchase sterling in order to assist the Bank of England in its (ultimately fruitless) attempt to remain in the System.[50]

Although the history of "Black Wednesday" is well known, it is appropriate to provide a brief account, because the episode illustrates the limitations of exchange rate systems of this kind.[51] Towards the end of August 1992, sterling went into decline on the foreign exchange markets, and the Bank of England began purchasing the currency in order to prevent it from falling through the ERM "floor". The Italian lira was suffering a similar fate. Perhaps unwisely,

25.17

---

[49] On this Agreement, see the *Pitsiloras* decision mentioned in n 33 above.

[50] For discussion of "Black Wednesday" and its consequences, and for a general view of the problems encountered within the EMS, see Johnson and Collignon, *The Monetary Economics of Europe: Causes of the EMS Crisis* (Associated University Press, 1994) and Collignon, *Monetary Stability in Europe: From Bretton Woods to Sustainable EMU* (Routledge, 2002). On the decision of the Bundesbank to support the French franc (but not sterling or the Italian lira) during this period, see the paper by Smaghi and Fern, *Was the Provision of Liquidity Support Assymetric in the ERM? New Light on an old issue*. The slightly ambiguous position of the Bundesbank in relation to its intervention obligations in respect of the EMS is discussed by Collignon, Bofinger, Johnson and de Maigret in *Europe's Monetary Future* (Thompson, 1994) 23. It may be that the system had been intended to function differently—see Mehnert, *User's Guide to the ECU* (Graham & Trotman, 1992) 28, where it is suggested that the central banks of other States within the system may be obliged to co-operate in any necessary corrective action. It is, however, perhaps more realistic to assume that each central bank was individually and solely responsible for any intervention which became necessary—see Lowenfeld, *International Economic Law* (Oxford University Press, 2002) 641.

[51] Of course, some of the weaknesses inherent in such systems had already been demonstrated by the collapse of the Bretton Woods system of fixed parities—see para 22.15 above.

the Community Finance Ministers decided to announce that a realignment of the central rates within the EMS would not be considered as a solution to the evident strains within the system. The markets then placed sterling and the lira under further pressure, and vast sums were expended by the two central banks in attempting to defend their currencies at the required rate. When it became apparent that intervention in the foreign exchange market would not prevent sterling falling below its ERM "floor", the Government increased sterling interest rates from the then current rate of 10 per cent to 15 per cent within the space of a single day. Leaving aside political considerations, this may have represented an attempt to comply with the United Kingdom's duty to bring sterling back within the permitted threshold of divergence by means of "measures of domestic monetary policy [and] other means of economic policy".[52] When even this measure failed to stem the tide, the Government (in a move mirrored by Italy) announced that it was suspending this country's membership of the ERM. This may have constituted a breach of the terms of the documents establishing the System,[53] but other Member States accepted the position. In spite of the announcement previously made by the Community Finance Ministers, other countries found it necessary to devalue their currencies so that they could remain within the ERM. Subsequently, the French franc came under market pressure but the Banque de France was able to prevent the French franc from falling through its ERM "floor", in part because the Bundesbank itself intervened significantly to support the franc. In view of the points made in the previous paragraph, the decision of the Bundesbank to support the efforts of the Banque de France must have been a matter of policy, rather than of legal obligation.

25.18   Pressure on the system resumed in mid-1993 when, in order to remain within their permitted margins of fluctuation, several countries had been forced to raise their interest rates even though the state of their economies suggested that rates should be moving in the opposite direction. Despite central bank intervention, the French franc tested its "floor" ERM rate and other currencies began to fall. It was apparent that the fluctuation margins could no longer be sustained in the face of market pressure and on 2 August 1993, it was announced that the margins of fluctuation would be extended to 15 per cent (although, by way of minor exception, the permitted margin as between the German mark and the Dutch guilder remained at 2.25 per cent). Such wide margins amounted to an effective suspension of the system, although it was essential to retain the system

---

[52] See para 3.6(b) and (d) of the European Council Resolution. An attempt to comply with this requirement by raising interest rates to such an extent on a single day must be described as either heroic of foolhardy, depending on one's point of view.

[53] Neither the European Council Resolution nor the agreement amongst central banks of Member States contained any reference to a right of suspension or withdrawal.

in some form; by this time the Treaty on European Union had been signed and membership of the ERM was one of the entry criteria for the euro.[54]

As noted earlier, amongst other functions, the ECU was to serve as a means of settlement of obligations within the Community. For this purpose, central banks of Member States within the system were required to deposit 20 per cent of their gold reserves, and 20 per cent of their dollar reserves in return for a credit expressed in ECUs.[55] Despite its role as a means of settlement, it should be appreciated that the ECU was not "money" in a legal sense because (apart from other considerations) it was never intended to serve as the general means of exchange in any country,[56] nor was the unit subject to institutional control by a monetary authority. Despite these difficulties, it may be noted that the US Securities and Exchange Commission accepted that the ECU was a "foreign currency", and that the SEC thus had jurisdiction to allow the trading of options on the ECU.[57] Rather, it was a measure of value which was denominated by reference to (and served as) a unit of account. Payments in ECUs could only be made in the form of a bank or similar credit, for no ECU notes/coins were ever issued with the intention that they should be exclusive legal tender throughout the Community.[58]

25.19

So far as English law is concerned, the ECU may not have constituted "money" in a legal sense,[59] but it did in fact enjoy the status of a *de facto* currency, and other systems of law might have adopted a more positive approach in its formal status. In particular, the position in the United States was likely to be different, at least in some contexts, for "money" is there defined as "a medium of exchange authorised or adopted by a domestic or foreign government and includes a monetary unit of account established by an international organisation or by an agreement between two or more nations".[60]

25.20

---

[54] On this point, see para 26.12 below.

[55] See para 3.8 of the European Council Resolution. During the period leading up to monetary union, the European Monetary Institute was responsible for the administration of this system—see Art 6.2 of the Statute of the European Monetary Institute, as set out in the Fourth Protocol to the EC Treaty. On the Institute itself, see para 27.06 below

[56] See the definition of "money", at para 1.35 above. For further discussion, see Brown, *L'ECU devant les juges: monnaie ou unité de compte?* (Europargnes, 1985).

[57] SEC Release No 22853. The episode is discussed by Gold, *Legal Effects of Fluctuating Currencies* (IMF, 1990) 394.

[58] For completeness, it should be noted that certain Member States did issue ECU coins, but these became collectors' items, rather than a form of money, and their formal status as legal tender was confined to the issuing State. For further discussion of this point, see the consideration of the "private ECU" in Ch 30 below and Mehnert, *User's Guide to the ECU* (Graham & Trotman, 1992) 133–4.

[59] In particular, it was not a unit of account which was defined by a State as part of its monetary system, nor did it serve as a generally accepted means of exchange in any State.

[60] Uniform Commercial Code, s 1-201(24)

25.21   It may be noted in passing that, in 1990, the British Government proposed the introduction of the so-called "hard ecu". The unit would have enjoyed the status of legal tender throughout the Community and would have circulated as a "parallel" currency, to the intent that it would have gradually replaced national currencies as a result of market and consumer acceptance. Plainly, this would have significantly enhanced the status of the ECU; however, the proposal did not find sufficient support and is now a matter of history.[61]

25.22   It will be apparent that the EMS in some respects circumscribed the monetary sovereignty[62] of Member States. A Member State was required to ensure that the external value of its currency remained within the fluctuation margins prescribed by the System; it would thus have to pursue monetary, fiscal, and economic policies which were designed to secure that end.[63] To that extent, the measure of discretion available to individual Member States in the exercise of their monetary sovereignty was inevitably reduced by the constraints of the System.[64] In addition, the *discretion* to intervene in the markets to support the national currency could be converted into an *obligation* to do so, where the intervention margins were reached. Factors of this nature may have deterred the United Kingdom from joining the EMS until 8 October 1990, and may help to explain its reluctance to rejoin the System following sterling's ignominious departure from the System on 16 September 1992.[65]

25.23   Thus far, it may be said that developments in the field of monetary co-operation had been of considerable importance—especially for the United Kingdom—

---

[61] On this subject, see *Positive Hard ECU Proposals*, British Treasury Release, 12 November 1990.

[62] On the incidents of monetary sovereignty in a general sense (including the right to issue a currency and to control interest rates), see Ch 19 above. On the subject of monetary sovereignty in a Community context, see Ch 31 below.

[63] The obligations of intervention and the requirement to adopt other measures of monetary and economic policy in order to support ERM membership have already been noted.

[64] The exercise of that discretion is inevitably constrained by domestic and international economic conditions, but that is an entirely different matter.

[65] It should be added that a revised exchange rate mechanism (ERM II) was created by means of an agreement amongst the ECB, the eurozone central banks, and the non-eurozone central banks, dated 1 September 1998 ([1998] OJ C345/6). The euro naturally constitutes the reference currency for the system, and the agreement provides for a fluctuation margin of plus or minus 15%. As was formerly the case, intervention at the margins is, in principle, both unlimited and automatic. Significantly, however, Art 3.1 of the Agreement allows for the suspension of intervention if its continuation could conflict with the overriding requirement of price stability. In this sense, the ERM II agreement departs from the terms of the predecessor agreement. The UK has not yet elected to participate in the new exchange rate mechanism. It may be added that the agreement was revised in order to accommodate the accession of new Member States on 1 May 2004. The agreement of 29 April 2004 is reproduced at [2004] OJ C135/3 For a general consideration of ERM II and its consequences for acceding Member States, see *The Acceding Countries' Strategies Towards ERM II and the Adoption of the Euro: An Analytical Review* (ECB Occasional Paper 10 February 2004).

and yet they were of a somewhat technical nature. However, this was to change, for monetary union was to become more clearly associated with objectives of a more overtly political character, including the movement towards a closer union between Member States.

E. The Single European Act

The process of European integration gained considerable impetus following the signature of the Single European Act in 1986.[66] Under the terms of Article 7(a) of that Act,[67] the Community was to "adopt measures with the aim of progressively establishing the internal market over a period expiring on 31 December 1992 . . . The internal market shall comprise an area without internal frontiers in which the free movement of goods, persons, services and capital is ensured in accordance with the provisions of this Treaty". Whilst this provision was declared[68] to express the "firm political will" of the Member States—as opposed to a legally binding commitment—the Single European Act clearly contemplated that the free movement of capital was to become a priority area.

25.24

Moving from policy matters to questions of implementation, the Single European Act allowed the Council (after following the applicable co-decision procedures laid down by the Treaty) to adopt measures (a) which were intended to approximate or harmonise the laws, regulations or administrative practises of Member States and (b) which were intended to facilitate the establishment and functioning of the single market, in accordance with the objectives outlined in the preceding paragraph.[69]

25.25

After many years of relatively slow progress, the Single European Act 1986 demonstrated that further European integration was possible, and provided the momentum which was necessary for that purpose.[70] The Single European Act contains only limited references to monetary union, but the progression of the single market initiative perhaps inevitably gave some further momentum to the notion of a single currency area.

25.26

---

[66] HMSO Cmnd 9578. The Single European Act was signed on 17 February 1986 and (following ratification by Member States) came into force on 1 July 1987.

[67] See now Art 14 of the EC Treaty.

[68] See the Declaration relating to Art 7(a), annexed to the Single European Act.

[69] This provision is now to be found in Art 95 of the EC Treaty. It should be noted that there are several areas of procedural and other difficulty surrounding the "single market" provisions contained in Art 14 and 15 of the Treaty, but these fall outside the scope of the present work. For a discussion, see Craig and De Búrca, *EC Law, Text, Cases, and Materials* (Oxford University Press, 3rd edn, 2003) 1115–24.

[70] For a discussion of the limited scope of integration prior to 1986, see Craig and de Búrca, (n 69 above) 1170–6.

F. Council Directive 88/361

25.27 Council Directive 88/361[71] was introduced with a view to the progressive abolition of national restrictions on capital movements. The Directive required Member States to abolish restrictions on the free movement of capital between persons resident in Member States, and to achieve this objective by 1 July 1990.[72] Member States were also required to ensure that transfers in respect of capital movements and current payments were made on the basis of the same exchange rates.[73] The Directive thus originally enshrined the principle of free movement of capital as an effective and enforceable part of Community law. Although the Directive has now been superseded by the provisions of the EC Treaty (as amended by the Treaty on European Union), the terms of the Directive remain useful because they seek to provide a non-exhaustive classification or definition of capital movements for present purposes.[74] These included:

(1) direct investments in branches/subsidiaries in other Member States;

(2) investments in real estate;

(3) investments in bonds, shares, and other securities;

(4) loans and other credits granted by or to residents of other Member States;

(5) guarantees and security interests granted by or to residents of other Member States; and

(6) the deposit of funds with financial institutions in other Member States.

25.28 As a general rule, it follows that Member States could not impose rules which would inhibit or impede capital flows of the kind just described. The general principle was inevitably subject to exceptions, but these were in many respects similar to the provisions subsequently introduced into the EC Treaty by the Treaty on European Union. These issues—and the other consequences of the liberalisation of capital movements—will therefore be discussed at a later stage.[75]

---

[71] [1988] OJ L178/5. This directive was found to have direct effect in Member States—see Cases C–358/93 and C–416/93 *Bordessa and Mellado* [1995] ECR I–361, and the discussion in Usher, *The Law of Money and Financial Services in the European Community* (Oxford University Press, 2nd edn, 2000) 23–7.

[72] See Art 1(1) of the Directive, read together with Art 6.

[73] See Art 1(2) of the Directive.

[74] See Annex I to the Directive. The terms of the Directive have been used for guidance purposes even in cases decided after the Treaty on European Union came into force—see Case C–222/97 *Trummer and Mayer* [1999] ECR I–1661 and Case C–464/98 *Westdeutsche Landesbank Girozentrale v Stefan* [2001] ECR I–173.

[75] See para 25.33 below.

G. The Delors Report

It has been shown that the Single European Act 1986 indirectly provided the **25.29** basis for further work in the field of monetary union. The subject was picked up by the European Council at its Hanover Meeting in June 1988. It appointed a committee under the chairmanship of M. Jacques Delors—then President of the European Commission—to prepare a report on the subject which would be considered at the European Council meeting in Madrid the following year.

The Delors Report[76] adopted the broad definition of a monetary union which **25.30** had formerly appeared in the Werner Report. The Delors Report noted[77] that a monetary union "constitutes a currency area in which policies are managed jointly with a view to adopting common macroeconomic objectives"; sadly, the lawyer must content himself with the working definition proposed earlier and which, by comparison, can only be described as mundane. The Report further observed that a monetary union would involve:

(a) the assurance of total and irreversible convertibility of currencies, coupled with the elimination of margins of fluctuation and (as a consequence) the irrevocable locking of exchange rate parities;

(b) the complete liberalisation of capital transactions;

(c) the full integration of the financial markets, such that loans, deposits, and investments could be made on a Community-wide basis, free of any restrictions of a purely national character;[78] and

(d) the creation of an institutional structure which would be charged with the formulation of a common monetary policy for the eurozone.[79]

Whilst the Delors Report did not assert that a single currency was a *necessary* feature of a monetary union,[80] it was nevertheless, seen to be a *desirable* feature.

The Delors Report suggested that the ECU could be transformed from a **25.31** currency basket into the Community's common currency.[81] The Report further made the point that monetary union would not be durable unless it were sustained by a sufficient harmonisation of economic policies of the individual

---

[76] Luxembourg, Office for Official Publications of the European Communities, 1989.

[77] On the points about to be made, see para 22 of the Report.

[78] In part, conditions of this nature were already being met by measures such as the Second Banking Directive ([1989] OJ L386), which allowed banks authorised in one Member State to provide services in other Member States without further approval.

[79] See para 32 of the Report.

[80] See para 23 of the Report. Based on the working definition noted at para 24.03 above, the lawyer would have to take a different view.

[81] See para 46 and 58 of the Report.

Member States,[82] and noted that fiscal policy (government taxation and spending) would have to be subject to some degree of co-ordination or control at the Community level;[83] clearly, inflationary policies adopted in one participating Member State could have an adverse impact on the single monetary area as a whole. These points have, of course, been made on a number of occasions, but the present work will consider these aspects from a purely legal perspective.[84] But the difficulties inherent in economic convergence, and the time required to achieve it, led the Delors Committee to propose a "three-stage" approach to the achievement of monetary union. These proposals were broadly implemented by the Treaty on European Union, and they will thus be considered when the monetary provisions of that Treaty are reviewed in depth.

H. The Treaty on European Union

25.32 The various steps and events described in this chapter ultimately led to the Treaty on European Union, which was signed at Maastricht on 7 February 1992; this may be regarded as the key political event on the road to monetary union. The Treaty came into force on 1 November 1993, following the delivery of the final ratification by Germany. Ratification had been delayed as a result of a challenge on constitutional grounds.[85]

25.33 For reasons given earlier, the creation of a monetary union necessarily involves the elimination of exchange control and the abolition of restrictions on the free movement of capital and payments.[86] As a result, Article 56 of the (amended) EC Treaty provided that "all restrictions on the movement of *capital* between Member States and between Member States and third countries shall be prohibited" and "all restrictions on *payments* between Member States and third countries shall be prohibited".[87] The terms "capital" and "payments" are not

---

[82] See ch II and para 42 of the Report.

[83] See para 30 of the Report.

[84] On the regulation of economic policy, see para 26.15 below.

[85] See *Brunner v European Union Treaty* [1994] 1 CMLR 57. The German Federal Constitutional Court dismissed two further complaints against euro entry in 1998; in the first case, it rejected the complaint on the basis that it was evidently unfounded; in the second case, the Court merely referred to and followed its two earlier judgments: 31 March 1998, *NJW* 1998, 1934; 22 June 1998, *NJW* 1998, 3187. For another challenge to the Treaty on domestic and constitutional grounds, see *R v Secretary of State for Foreign and Commonwealth Affairs, ex p Rees-Mogg* [1994] QB 552 (UK), although the arguments in this case were not in any sense founded upon questions touching the single currency or monetary sovereignty. On the ratification procedure, see Art 52(2) of the Treaty on European Union.

[86] See the working definition of a monetary union at para 24.03 above.

[87] Emphasis added. It may be inferred from this language that capital and payments are now subject to identical provisions, such that the distinction between them is no longer of importance. But in fact, this is not the case; Art 57(1) "grandfathers" certain restrictions on capital movements

defined. However, as noted above, the European Court of Justice will pray in aid the detailed categories set out in Council Directive 88/361 in identifying those transactions which involve a movement of capital. In addition, the Court has noted that a movement of "capital" involves a transfer of funds for investment purposes, whilst "payments" connote transfers of a current nature, such as payments of interest or payments for goods and services.[88]

Although they are stated to be subject to various exceptions, the rules contained **25.34** in the revised Article 56 are clear and unambiguous, and are mandatory in their terms. As a result, the European Court of Justice decided in the *Sanz de Lera* case[89] that Article 56 had direct effect in Member States and was thus capable of creating individual rights. It followed that a Spanish law which (in the absence of official approval) prohibited the export of peseta notes could not stand, because it was inconsistent with the obligation of Member States to ensure the free movement of capital.[90] Likewise, an Austrian requirement that mortgages over land could only be registered in the Austrian Schilling was found to be inconsistent with Article 56, because it would deter non-Austrian lenders from providing loans secured on real estate in Austria.[91] At a fairly obvious level, a Member State could not impose a general restriction on the transfer of funds outside the country,[92] nor could a Member State prohibit its own nationals from subscribing for eurobonds issued by its own government.[93] The European Court

---

which were in existence on 31 December 1993, whilst Art 57(2) allows the Council to adopt various measures in relation to the flow of capital between Member States and third countries. Furthermore, Art 59 allows the Council to take certain safeguard measures with regard to third countries if exceptional transfers of capital threaten the stability of economic and monetary union. There are no corresponding provisions which apply to payments. For a discussion of these provisions, see Peers, "Free Movement of Capital: Learning Lessons or Slipping on Split Milk?" in (Barnard and Scott (eds) *The Law of the Single European Market* (Hart, 2002).

[88] The point was made by the ECJ in Joined Cases 26/83 and 286/83 *Luisi and Carbone v Ministero del Tresoro* [1984] ECR 377. It has already been shown that a similar distinction is of significant importance in relation to the Articles of Agreement of the IMF which contains detailed restrictions on exchange control regimes affecting current payments but does not deal with controls on capital transfers—see para 22.29 above. It may be thought that the principle of free movement of capital and payments would embrace virtually any kind of monetary transfer. Yet, from the language employed in the text, it is clear that this is not so. It would, eg, remain open to Member States to restrict transfers by way of gift or upon inheritance, although in practice the point does not arise.

[89] Case 250/94 *Criminal Proceedings against Sanz de Lera* [1994] ECR I–4821.

[90] For a decision to similar effect, see Joined Cases C–358/93 and C–416/93 *Criminal Proceedings against Bordessa* [1995] ECR I–361.

[91] Case C–222/97 *Trummer and Mayer* [1999] ECR I–1661, followed (on very similar facts) in Case C–464/98 *Westdeutsche Landesbank Girozentrale v Stefan* [2001] ECR I–173. On the decision in *Trummer and Mayer* see Sideek Mohammed, "A Critical Assessment of the ECJ Judgment in Trummer and Mayer" (1999) JIBFL 396.

[92] Case 194/84 *Commission v Greece, Re Blocked Accounts* [1989] 2 CMLR 453.

[93] Case C–478/98 *Commission v Belgium* [2000] ECR I–7857. For a more recent decision to similar effect, see Case C–242/03, *Ministre des Finances v Weidert* (15 July 2004).

of Justice has, however, decided that matters should not be taken too far—a domestic rule will only be taken to infringe Article 56 if there is a serious likelihood (as opposed to a remote possibility) that the rule will impede inflows or outflows of capital.[94]

25.35   It is true that Member States are allowed various derogations in this context— for example, in the context of the administration of their system of taxation, in order to ensure enforcement of certain national laws, and on grounds of public policy or public security. However, any such national rules must not be used as a means of arbitrary discrimination or as a disguised restriction on the free movement of capital and payments.[95] Furthermore, the relevant national measures must be of a reasonable scope, bearing in mind the principle of proportionality.[96] It is apparent that Member States will encounter considerable difficulty in relying upon these exemptions, which will be narrowly construed.[97]

25.36   At this point, the discussion moves away from a purely historical analysis, for the Treaty on European Union and the measures adopted under it continue to govern the eurozone to this day. A review of those provisions which directly address monetary union is thus reserved to the next chapter.

---

[94] Case C–412/97 *ED Srl v Italo Fennochio* [1999] ECR I–3845.

[95] On these aspects, see EC Treaty, Art 58.

[96] On the principle of proportionality, see Protocol No 30 annexed to the EC Treaty, and the discussion on this topic in Craig and De Búrca, *EU Law, Text, Cases, and Materials* (Oxford University Press, 3rd edn, 2003) ch 8.

[97] For illustrations of this general comment, see Case C–478/98, *Commission v Belgium* [2000] ECR I–7587; Case C–439/97 *Sandoz GmbH v Finanzlandesdirektion für Wien* [1999] ECR I–7041 and Case C–35/98 *Staatssecretaris van Financiere v Verkoojen* [2000] ECR I–4071. For a recent decision which illustrates the same point, see Case 319/02 *In the Matter of Manninen* (7 September 2004).

26

EMU AND THE TREATY ON EUROPEAN UNION

A. Introduction

The present chapter, like the previous one, deals with a number of issues which **26.01** may not be regarded as questions of monetary law in the strictest sense. Nevertheless, a review of those issues is necessary in order to create an understanding of the legal rules and structures which are required to underpin a monetary union.

As previously noted, the Treaty on European Union was signed at Maastricht on **26.02** 7 February 1992. The Treaty dealt with a number of areas in which it was hoped to expand the degree of co-operation amongst Member States, for example, in the fields of foreign and security policy, justice, and home affairs. These are outside the scope of the present discussion.[1] In the present context, the Treaty was significant because it brought monetary union to centre stage.[2] Article 2 set out the objectives of the Union. The first of these[3] was stated to be:

> . . . to promote economic and social progress and a high level of employment and to achieve balanced and sustainable development, in particular through the

---

[1] On these and other issues, see Titles V and VI of the Treaty.

[2] In spite of this comment, it is important to recall that monetary union plays a supporting role to the achievement of broader Community objectives. This point has already been made above at para 25.03, n 5, and it will be necessary to return to it from time to time.

[3] The text of Art 2 as a whole is reproduced in the form in which it has subsequently been amended, but the language dealing with monetary union remains in the form originally introduced by the Treaty on European Union.

creation of an area without internal frontiers, through the strengthening of economic and social cohesion and through the establishment of economic and monetary union, ultimately including a single currency in accordance with the provisions of this Treaty . . .

26.03 The language reproduced above continues to suggest that a monetary union can come into being *before* the goal of the single currency is achieved. This is a view which cannot be accepted from a purely legal perspective, in the light of the working definition of a monetary union.[4] However that may be, the general theme of Article 2 is carried through in the revisions which were introduced into the EC Treaty itself. Article 2 of that Treaty now provides that:

> . . . The Community shall have as its task, by establishing a common market and an economic and monetary union . . . to promote throughout the Community a harmonious and balanced and sustainable development of economic activities . . . sustainable and non-inflationary growth, a high degree of competitiveness and convergence of economic performance . . . and social cohesion and solidarity among Member States . . .

In order to achieve these objectives, Article 3 of the EC Treaty required the Member States to adopt "an economic policy which is based on the close co-ordination of Member States' economic policies . . . and conducted in accordance with the principle of an open market economy with free competition".

26.04 It is tempting for the lawyer to view such statements of high policy with a somewhat cynical eye. Yet this temptation must be resisted, for if questions concerning economic and monetary union fall to be considered by the European Court of Justice, the Court will have to consider the Treaty as a whole and the context in which the disputed provisions appear; it will then interpret and apply those provisions in a manner designed to further their apparent objective.[5] Whatever may be the merits of economic and monetary union,[6] the Court of Justice would look to these provisions as a guide to the interpretative process. What could the Court legitimately discern from them?

26.05 First of all, it is suggested that the Court must conclude from Article 2 of the Treaty on European Union that the establishment of a monetary union is in itself a key objective which has been introduced in support of the internal market. From the corresponding provisions in the EC Treaty, it is apparent that monetary union is intended to provide a catalyst for a high degree of

---

[4] See para 24.03 above.

[5] On the Court's approach to questions and interpretation, see Craig and de Búrca, *EU Law, Text, Cases, and Materials* (Oxford University Press, 3rd edn, 2003) 96–100.

[6] For discussions, see (amongst many others) Craig and de Búrca (n 5 above) 691–4; C. Johnson, *In with the Euro, Out with the Pound* (Penguin, 1996); and *The euro*, Paul Temperton (ed) (Wiley, 1997).

competitiveness and for the convergence of economic performance amongst Member States. It would appear to follow from these provisions that the Treaty rules on the free movement of capital and payments must now be enforced with particular rigour, because any impediment to the movement of capital must ultimately detract both from the internal market and from the principle of free competition. Secondly and as a necessary corollary, it must follow that those Treaty provisions which provide exemptions in these areas must be narrowly construed, such that they do not materially affect the free flow of funds within the Community area.[7] It has already been shown that issues of this kind are most likely to arise in the context of capital and payments, partly because the introduction of the euro is most closely associated with that particular freedom.

B. The Stages of Monetary Union

As explained in Chapter 25, the introduction of a single currency necessarily required a degree of economic convergence amongst the participating Member States; such convergence could only be achieved over a period of time. As a result, the Delors Report recommended a three-stage approach to European Monetary Union (EMU), and this recommendation was adopted when the Treaty on European Union was signed. It is instructive to note that the Treaty thus provided an accelerating momentum towards the ultimate goal of a single currency. **26.06**

The first stage of economic and monetary union was deemed to have begun on 1 July 1990 and ended on 31 December 1993.[8] Since the commencement of stage one pre-dates the Treaty on European Union, it will be apparent that the steps taken during that stage were based on powers which then existed in the EC Treaty—including in particular those provisions introduced by the Single European Act. Stage one thus involved the completion of the internal market and the establishment of procedures to monitor economic conditions and policies.[9] **26.07**

---

[7] The views just expressed can only be reinforced by a review of the existing case law in this area—see para 25.34 above. They are further supported by the view of the ECJ that economic and monetary union was already a Community objective even before the Treaty on European Union had been signed—*Opinion 1/91* [1991] ECR I–6079. This view reflected provisions contained in the Single European Act.

[8] The commencement date was fixed by the European Council meeting in Madrid in June 1989; the end date necessarily followed from the fact that the second stage was required to begin on 1 January 1994 pursuant to Art 116 of the EC Treaty.

[9] See Decision 90/141 on the attainment of progressive convergence of economic policies and performance during stage one of economic and monetary union [1990] OJ L78/23.

26.08 The second stage began on 1 January 1994.[10] It is unsurprising that matters began to accelerate at this point, partly because the Treaty on European Union had now come into effect, and partly because the introduction of the single currency was, by then, a maximum of five years away.[11] This process of acceleration is illustrated by a description of some of the steps which were required to be taken during this period:

(1) Member States were under a continuing obligation to conduct their economic policies with a view to achieving monetary union and other Community objectives. To that end, Member States had to regard their economic policies as a matter of common concern and to continue to co-ordinate them with the Council.[12]

(2) Member States were required to treat their exchange rate policy "as a matter of common interest", taking account of experience acquired in the context of the European Monetary System.[13]

(3) Member States were placed under an obligation to "endeavour to avoid" excessive government deficits.[14] Procedures were introduced to monitor such deficits from the beginning of the second stage but, at that time, no sanctions could be applied to an errant Member State.[15]

(4) At the institutional level, Member States were required to take certain legislative steps to ensure that the independence of their central banks was enshrined within their domestic legal systems.[16] Furthermore, the European Monetary Institute (EMI) was established to strengthen the co-ordination of national monetary policies and to carry out numerous technical and preparatory functions leading up to the beginning of the third stage.[17] The EMI was of a transitional character and was effectively the forerunner of the European Central Bank. The EMI was wound up when the ECB was established and it is thus not now necessary to undertake a detailed examination of the functions of this institution.[18]

---

[10] Article 116(1) of the EC Treaty.

[11] It was provided that the third stage of EMU would start, at the latest, on 1 January 1999—see Art 121(4) of the EC Treaty.

[12] On these obligations and the procedures involved, see Art 98 and 99 of the EC Treaty.

[13] Article 124 of the EC Treaty. Since this provision continues to apply to the UK, its effect is considered in para 31.36(5) below.

[14] Article 116(4) of the EC Treaty.

[15] This conclusion follows from Art 104 of the EC Treaty, read together with Art 116(3).

[16] On this point, see EC Treaty, Arts 108 and 116(5). The requirement for central bank independence is discussed at para 27.14 below.

[17] On the establishment of the EMI and for a list of its functions and powers, see Art 117 of the EC Treaty and the Statute of The European Monetary Institute which is set out as a Protocol to the Treaty.

[18] For a very brief discussion of the role of the EMI, see para 27.06 below. On the dissolution of the EMI, see Art 123(2) of the EC Treaty. The assets and liabilities of the EMI were, upon its liquidation, automatically vested in the ECB—see Art 23 of the Statute of the EMI.

(5) Towards the end of the third stage, the list of Member States which would be included within the eurozone at the outset was identified.[19]

The third stage of economic and monetary union began on 1 January 1999.[20] Only at this point did the single currency of the eurozone come into existence. In the context of a book on the law of money, this aspect necessarily requires detailed consideration and analysis, but it is convenient to deal with the details of the single currency at a later stage.[21] For immediate purposes, the primary consequences of the commencement of the third stage were as follows: **26.09**

(a) the euro became the single currency of the participating Member States—whilst national notes and coins continued to circulate, they were merely subdivisions or representations of the euro itself;

(b) the respective rates at which the former national currencies were to be substituted by the euro were fixed;

(c) the European Central Bank and the European System of Central Banks took up their functions and responsibilities associated with the new currency;[22] and

(d) participating Member States became subject to an absolute obligation to avoid excessive government deficits and the terms of the Stability and Growth Pact came into operation.[23]

Developments within the eurozone thus broadly equated to a "monetary union" within the working definition proposed earlier.[24] At this juncture, however, there existed no notes or coins which constituted legal tender throughout the entire eurozone; this was only achieved on 1 January 2002, upon expiry of a three year transitional period.[25] **26.10**

---

[19] Article 121(3) of the EC Treaty.

[20] ibid, Art 121(4). The third stage could have begun at an earlier date had the necessary conditions been met, but ultimately this proved not to have been the case—see Council Decision 96/736 ([1996] OJ L335/48). The conditions to the commencement of the third stage are discussed at para 26.11 below. Although the point is now of historical interest only, it may be noted that Art 121(4) stipulated that, in the absence of an earlier starting date, "the third stage shall start on 1 January 1999". Perhaps understandably, the treaty does not address the difficulties which would have arisen had no Member State satisfied the preconditions to the adoption of the single currency. The German Supreme Court held that the stipulated starting date of the third stage "must be understood as a target rather than a legally enforceable date"; the Member States were required by Community law "to make serious efforts to achieve the date in the Treaty [but] the purpose of setting target dates according to established Community tradition tends to be to encourage and accelerate the integration process, rather than to realise it within the time limit in all circumstances"—see *Brunner v European Union Treaty* [1994] 1 CMLR 57, para 83. This view conflicts with the plain terms of Art 121(4) itself, although the analysis is no doubt politically realistic.

[21] See Ch 29 below.

[22] On this aspect, see para 27.07 below.

[23] See para 26.16(b) below.

[24] See para 24.03 above.

[25] On the nature and consequences of the transitional period see para 29.16 below.

C. The Maastricht Criteria

26.11 Thus far, occasional references have been made to the fact that Member States had to be selected for participation within the eurozone. The need for the convergence of economic policies as a condition to the creation of that zone has also been noted. It is thus entirely unsurprising that the necessary selection process was governed and determined by tests of an essentially economic character. These tests became generally known as the "Maastricht Criteria", named after the location in which the Treaty on European Union was signed. These criteria and the manner of their application must be summarised briefly.

26.12 In essence, it was for the Council (meeting in the composition of Heads of State or Government) to decide whether or not a majority of Member States fulfilled the conditions for participation in the single currency and whether it was appropriate for the Community to move to the third stage.[26] The Council was required to undertake this task on the basis of reports from the Commission and the European Monetary Institute on the progress made by Member States in fulfilling their treaty obligations in respect of EMU.[27] At a technical level, these reports were to indicate whether Member States had conferred upon their central banks the degree of independence required in order to enable them to participate in the European System of Central Banks.[28] The remaining criteria attracted a rather greater degree of attention at the time. The reports were required to examine, in relation to each Member State, "the achievement of a high degree of sustainable convergence" by reference to the four criteria set out in the treaty,[29] ie:

(1) the achievement of a high degree of price stability—this involved a "sustainable" price performance and a rate of inflation comparable with that of the best performing States;

(2) the sustainability of the government's financial position—this requirement would be met so long as the relevant Member State was not the subject of

---

[26] The text only provides a brief overview of the procedures involved. For the details, see Art 121(2) and (3) of the EC Treaty.

[27] Article 121(1) of the EC Treaty. Member States which did not fulfil the Maastricht Criteria could not become members of the eurozone and were referred to in the Treaty as "Member States with a derogation". This meant that they were not required to move to the third stage of EMU and, for the most part, were excluded from the rights and obligations arising from the completion of monetary union. See Art 122(1) and (3) of the EC Treaty.

[28] See Article 108 of the EC Treaty and the discussion at para 27.14 below.

[29] The criteria are set out in Art 121(1) of the EC Treaty, with further details included in a Protocol on the Convergence Criteria annexed to the EC Treaty.

an "excessive deficit" determination by the Council at the time when the reports were prepared;[30]

(3) the observance of the normal fluctuation margins provided for by the Exchange Rate Mechanism (ERM) for at least two years, without devaluing against the currency of another Member State—the ERM and the applicable margins of fluctuation have been discussed earlier;[31]

(4) the durability of the convergence achieved by the Member State and of its participation in the ERM being reflected in long-term interest rate levels— this was to be tested by reference to the interest rates applicable to long-term government debt issued by the Member State concerned; the rate so achieved had to stand comparison with the rates of the best performing Member States.

This is not the place to discuss some of the accounting methods adopted by Member States which proved to be controversial in the context of their attempts to meet the Maastricht Criteria. Nor is it necessary to observe that several Member States were the subject of "excessive deficit" decisions which had to be revoked in order that this particular criterion could be met or that one Member State (Italy) had not participated in the ERM for a two-year period prior to the preparation of the report. From a purely legal perspective, however, it is only important to highlight a particular drafting point; the assessment of qualification for membership of the eurozone was required to be made "by reference to" the four criteria just discussed—ie the Maastricht Criteria provided a starting point for the assessment of process; they did not provide the rigid rules which had to be met in order to gain entry to the eurozone.[32] In other words, "sustainable convergence" was the key test for membership; the Maastricht Criteria were essentially guidelines, with all of the scope for flexibility which that term implies. The report and recommendation published by the Commission on 25 March 1998 indicated that eleven Member States fulfilled the criteria necessary to move to the third stage of EMU; Greece did not fulfil those criteria and the United Kingdom, Denmark, and Sweden would not participate by virtue of "opt-outs" or for other reasons.[33] No attempt was made to mount a legal

26.13

---

[30] On the determination as to an "excessive deficit" in relation to a Member State, see Art 104(6) of the EC Treaty and the discussion at para 26.16(b) below. It should be noted that the existence of an excessive deficit at the time of the preparation of the reports did not necessarily involve a breach of the treaty; during the second stage, Member States were only under an obligation to "endeavour to avoid" excessive deficits—see para 26.08(3) above.

[31] See para 25.16 above.

[32] This particular point may assume some importance in the event that the UK seeks to move to the third stage—see para 31.32 below.

[33] The Report and Recommendation were published by the Office for Official Publications of the European Communities. It may be observed that Greece was subsequently found to have met the Maastricht Criteria and thus became a eurozone member with effect from 1 January 2001— see Council Decision of 19 June 2000 (2000/427/EC) [2000] OJ L167/19. See para 32.35, n 78 below.

challenge either to the report or the recommendation, and indeed it appears that any such challenge would necessarily have failed.[34] Nor was any successful attempt made to challenge subsequent Council Regulations made in relation to the single currency[35] and, once again, it is difficult to identify any basis upon which such a challenge might have succeeded.

26.14 Of course, it is one thing to bring about the conditions necessary to create a monetary union, it is quite another to sustain that monetary union once it has been brought into existence. It is now necessary to examine the treaty provisions which are designed to nurture and preserve the union over the longer term.

D. The Regulation of Economic and Fiscal Policies

26.15 As noted earlier, the cohesion of a monetary union depends upon a sufficient degree of convergence between the economic policies of the Member States of the union—it is thus by no means a mere coincidence that the Treaty provisions deal with both economic and monetary union as virtually inseparable concepts.[36] This point received a great deal of attention in the years leading up to the beginning of the third stage. Thus, for example, the European Council emphasised that sound government finances, budgetary discipline, and national economic policies supporting a stable monetary environment would be crucial requirements during the third stage.[37] Likewise, it was felt that a detailed framework had to be put in place in order to ensure that compliance with these high economic objectives could be monitored and enforced. In this context, the German Government put forward a proposal for a Stability Pact[38] which was subsequently rebranded as the "Stability and Growth Pact". Furthermore, it has already been noted that the Treaty on European Union introduced new provisions dealing with excessive government deficits.

---

[34] A recommendation is not reviewable by the ECJ under Art 230 of the EC Treaty. The report itself is probably likewise immune from judicial inquiry, not only for procedural reasons but because it was required to assess ". . . The achievement of a high degree of sustainable convergence *by reference to*" the Maastricht Criteria (emphasis added). Assessments of this kind are not readily amenable to judicial challenge.

[35] On these Regulations see Ch 29 below. On the attempts made to challenge these regulations in the context of the adoption of the "euro" name, see the *Berthu* litigation, discussed at para 28.13 below.

[36] This point has already been noted in considering the definition of a monetary union—see para 24.03 above.

[37] See the introductory paragraph of the Resolution of the European Council (Amsterdam, 17 June 1997) [1997] OJ C236/l. It should be noted that *monetary* policy is in the hands of the ESCB. This aspect is accordingly considered in the ensuing part of this chapter.

[38] See "Stability Pact for Europe" presented by the German Ministry of Finance to the ECOFIN Council, November 1995.

Against this rather general background, it is proposed to consider some of the **26.16** specific provisions of the Treaty and the actions which have been taken pursuant thereto.

(a) In the context of economic convergence, Article 99 of the EC Treaty requires Member States to regard their economic policies as a matter of common concern, to ensure that those policies conform with broad guidelines formulated by the Council,[39] and to co-ordinate these policies with the Council. Member States are required to keep the Commission informed of these policies, and the Council was empowered to make regulations to provide a detailed framework for the multilateral surveillance procedure which would be required for these purposes. In this context, a Council Regulation on the strengthening of the surveillance of budgetary provisions and the surveillance and co-ordination of economic policies (hereafter the "Surveillance Regulation") was introduced.[40] The Surveillance Regulation requires eurozone Member States annually to submit a "stability programme", providing their medium-term objectives for a balanced budget and the steps to be taken to achieve that end.[41] If a Member State fails to adhere to the broad guidelines laid down by the Council, or if economic policies may jeopardise the proper functioning of economic and monetary union, then the Council may issue recommendations to the Member State concerned and may elect to publish those recommendations.[42]

(b) Reference has already been made to the excessive deficit procedure. From the beginning of the third stage, eurozone Member States were placed under an *absolute* obligation to avoid excessive government deficits.[43] This general rule is supplemented both by a Protocol on the Excessive Deficit

---

[39] These "broad guidelines" were intended to be developed into an effective instrument for the convergence of economic policies, although the steps required to achieve convergence were required to be taken at a national (rather than Community) level. On these points, see paras 3 and 4 of the Resolution of the European Council on Economic Policy Co-ordination (Luxembourg, 13 December 1997).

[40] No 1466/97 [1997] OJ L209/1. The Surveillance Regulation was made pursuant to Art 99(5) of the EC Treaty. The subject is further developed by the *Code of Conduct on the Content and Format of the Stability and Convergence Programmes*, which was approved by the ECOFIN Council on 10 July 2001.

[41] The purpose of this procedure is to ensure the maintenance of sound budgetary positions and price stability, which are regarded as the key features of the eurozone. It may be noted that Member States remaining outside the eurozone are required to submit similar materials, but in their case this is referred to as a "convergence programme", and the objective of the procedure is to ensure the pursuit of national policies aimed at a high degree of sustainable economic convergence. The provisions applicable to non-eurozone Member States thus both reflect and emphasize the fact that they are members of an *economic* union, even if they have not yet graduated to a *monetary* union. On the points just made, see paras (8) and (9) of the preamble to the Surveillance Regulation, together with Arts 4 and 8 of that Regulation.

[42] See Art 99(4) of the EC Treaty.

[43] ibid, Art 104(1).

Procedure annexed to the EC Treaty itself and by a Council Regulation[44] on speeding up and clarifying the implementation of the excessive deficit procedure (hereafter, the "Excessive Deficit Regulation"). As might be expected in such an area, both the Treaty and the Excessive Deficit Regulation contain a significant amount of detail and definition for these purposes; there are also intricate procedural and institutional steps which must be followed before a final decision can be made as to the existence of an excessive deficit in any particular Member State. Bearing in mind the context of this work, it is not necessary to examine these areas in depth. It may suffice to note that an excessive deficit may exist in a given Member State if its government incurs a deficit exceeding 3 per cent of gross domestic product, or if government debt exceeds 60 per cent of gross national product. A system of sanctions—including substantial cash deposits, fines, and non-financial penalties—may be applied to an errant Member State.

(c) The Surveillance Regulation and the Excessive Deficit Regulation thus provide the core of the arrangements which became known as the Stability and Growth Pact.[45] This essentially *legal* and *economic* framework was supported by a *political* commitment to its terms. A Resolution of the European Council[46] on the Stability and Growth Pact contained confirmation on behalf of various parties concerned with economic and monetary union. Member States undertook to abide by their respective stability and convergence programmes; the Commission undertook to initiate action in a manner which would ensure the "strict, timely and effective" operation of the Stability and Growth Pact. For its part, the Council confirmed its commitment to the Pact and its intention to enforce the system of financial deposits and penalties thereby created. In practical terms, it is fair to say that these high-level objectives and commitments have not always been borne out by experience. Adverse economic conditions in Europe have made it difficult for some Member States to adhere to the Pact in its fullest rigour. Furthermore, the authority of the Pact was perhaps not greatly enhanced by the difficulties encountered in attempting to apply the Pact to some of the major eurozone Member States (including Germany, which originally provided the impetus for the Pact), nor by the decision of the President of the European Commission to label the Pact as "stupid".[47]

---

[44] No 1467/97, [1997] OJ L209/6. The regulation was made pursuant to Art 104(14) of the EC Treaty.

[45] The title perhaps suggests that the Pact is an independent arrangement but, as has been shown, the Pact is in many respects a gloss on provisions which had already been introduced into the EC Treaty by the Treaty on European Union.

[46] Amsterdam, 17 June 1997, [1997] OJ C236/1.

[47] See "EU haunted by spectre of pact no one will let die" and "Eurozone loses its fear of economic torture chamber", *Financial Times*, 3 July 2003, p 8.

Perhaps most damaging was the decision of the Council to hold the excessive deficit procedure "in abeyance" for both France and Germany. This led the Commission publicly to record its deep regret that the Council had failed to apply both the spirit and the rules of the Stability and Growth Pact.[48] The Commission subsequently commenced proceedings against the Council in respect of its alleged failure to abide by the terms of the Treaty, and the matter was brought before the European Court of Justice with some expedition. Although the resultant decision raises no direct issues of monetary law, it does demonstrate that the excessive deficit and surveillance procedures designed to underpin the single currency do enjoy a degree of legal force, and to that extent the decision is of some interest. In *Commission v Council*,[49] the Commission brought proceedings against the Council in respect of the Council's failure to impose sanctions against France and Germany after those countries had incurred excessive government deficits. Procedures leading up to the imposition of sanctions had been commenced but the Council elected to defer any formal findings against the two countries concerned. The Council was entitled to hold the excessive procedure "in abeyance" if the relevant Member State had acted in accordance with recommendations or notices given to it by the Council with a view to correcting the situation.[50] The Commission recommended that the Council give notice to France and Germany to take measures to reduce their deficits but, at its meeting on 25 November 2003, the Council failed to adopt those recommendations. Instead, the Council accepted "public commitments" from the Member States concerned to take measures with a view to reducing their deficits; in return the Council agreed to hold the excessive deficit procedure in abeyance. The Court held that the acceptance of these undertakings fell outside the scope of the Treaty; the Council was only entitled to hold the excessive deficit procedure "in abeyance" if the Member States concerned had acted in compliance with recommendations or notices given to them, and this condition was plainly not met.[51] The Court explicitly rejected the argument that the Council's conclusions were of a purely political nature which did not entail consequences of a legal character.[52] However, whilst the Council was unable to suspend the Stability

---

[48] On the point just noted, see the Minutes of the 2546th Meeting of the Council (Brussels, 25 November 2003). The ECB also condemned the failure to enforce the Pact—see the ECB Press Release on the ECOFIN Council conclusions regarding the Excessive Deficits in France and Germany (25 November 2003).

[49] Case C–27/04, 13 July 2004.

[50] See Arts 104(7) and 104(9) of the EC Treaty, read together with Arts 3(9) of the Council Regulation (EC) No 1467/97, [1999] OJ L209/6.

[51] Paragraph 54 of the Judgment.

[52] ibid, 37.

and Growth Pact in this way, there was no obligation upon them to accept or to adopt the specific recommendations placed before it by the Commission.[53] The details of this judgment are less important than the essential principle established by the case to the effect that the rules of financial and economic conduct designed to support the single currency are not merely statements of aspiration, but do have a meaningful effect within a strictly legal framework. In the longer term, this decision may provide an incentive to Member States to comply with the budgetary disciplines which the Treaty seeks to impose, and may thus play a role in ensuring the long-term success of the EMU project.

(d) The decision of the European Court of Justice in the case just noted might have been expected to lead to more rigorous enforcement of the Pact. In practical terms, however, it seems more likely to lead to revisions either to the Pact itself or to its intended mode of application; indeed a more flexible interpretation of certain aspects of the Pact had already been announced in 2002.[54] But the present work is not concerned with the details of such matters or with the disputes to which they gave rise; it is merely necessary to note that the Pact and its associated treaty provisions illustrate the type of economic and budgetary framework which must be put in place to support a monetary union. It is apparent from experience thus far that the credibility and durability of such a framework depends upon a genuine political commitment to its terms, as opposed to its purely legal content.

(e) It is now necessary to review three further articles which are included under the "Economic Policy" heading in the EC Treaty. These are designed to reinforce the budgetary disciplines imposed upon the Member States by limiting the sources and modes of finance available to them. Subject to various exceptions, neither the European Central Bank nor the central banks of Member States may grant overdraft or other credit facilities to Community institutions or to central, regional or other governmental bodies, or public authorities; likewise neither the Community nor national governments may avail themselves of any form of "privileged access" to financial institutions.[55] These rules prevent a Member State from financing its deficit by means of recourse to its own central bank. Such a deficit must be financed on commercial terms from other sources and since the funding costs would presumably be higher, these provisions create a further incentive

---

[53] ibid, 36.

[54] See the speech of Pedro Solbes to the European Parliament (21 October 2002), announcing a revised strategy for the implementation of the Pact to take account of cyclical developments.

[55] On these points, see Arts 101 and 102 of the EC Treaty. On the meaning of "privileged access" and other matters of definition for these purposes, see Arts 1 and 3 of the Council Regulation 3604/98, [1998] OJ L332/4.

to fiscal prudence. The Treaty prohibits[56] the Community from assuming liability for the commitments of Member States; it also confirms that "A Member State shall not *be liable* for or assume the commitments of central governments, regional, local or other public authorities, other bodies governed by public law, or public undertakings *of another Member State*" (emphasis added). This provision—occasionally described as a "no bail out" clause—is intended to ensure that each Member State must take responsibility for its own budgetary and fiscal position; it cannot look for support either from the Community itself or from any other Member State which (for whatever reason of high policy) might otherwise have chosen to assist it.[57] These apparently technical rules do, however, have an important consequence; whilst the participating Member States pool certain of their foreign reserve *assets* as a consequence of monetary union,[58] the same cannot be said of their liabilities; these remain the separate liabilities of individual Member States.[59] It follows that, to the extent to which the working definition of a monetary union[60] referred to a pooling of liabilities, that definition must be viewed with a considerable degree of caution. Indeed, any guarantee or other contractual arrangement entered into by a Member State or any of its public authorities in contravention of the rules just described would not be enforced by the English courts because (a) it would contravene Article 103 of the EC Treaty and (b) the provisions of that Article have direct effect in the United Kingdom, because they are clear and unconditional, and no further action is required for their implementation at a national level.[61] Arrangements made in contravention of these provisions would be illegal under English law, and their enforcement

---

[56] On the points about to be discussed, see Art 103 of the EC Treaty. The general rules are subject to exceptions in relation to the financing of arrangements for specific projects.

[57] It should, however, be noted that a Member State confronted by severe difficulties caused by exceptional circumstances beyond its control may receive financial assistance from the Community. The Council may grant such assistance by unanimous vote (or, in the case of difficulties arising from a natural disaster, by a qualified majority) on a proposal from the Commission—see Art 100(2) of the EC Treaty. The precise scope of this Article has not been determined and, presumably, assistance would not be given where a Member State was in difficulty as a result of a deliberate failure to adhere to the Community economic guidelines laid down in accordance with Art 99 of the Treaty.

[58] As will be seen, this is achieved by means of the financial provisions applicable to the ECB—see para 27.08 below.

[59] This particular point has been emphasised by the ECOFIN Council—see para 6 of the Declaration accompanying the Council's Recommendation of Member States participating in EMU (Brussels, 3 May 1998).

[60] See the definition at para 24.03 above.

[61] On the direct effect of treaty provisions in proceedings before national courts, see the line of cases beginning with *Van Gend en Loos v Netherlandse Administratie der Belastingen* [1963] ECR 1. For discussion of the principle, see Craig and de Búrca, *EC Law – Texts, Cases and Materials* (Oxford University Press, 3rd edn, 2003) 179–89.

would be thus contrary to public policy.[62] It must therefore be concluded that the treaty rules prohibiting the "pooling" and assumption of liabilities would be respected and enforced by national courts sitting in individual Member States.[63]

(f)   Questions touching monetary and exchange rate policy are also addressed by the EC Treaty. Given that the conduct of monetary policy falls within the exclusive remit of the European System of Central Banks, this subject will be considered in an institutional context.[64] Exchange rate policy forms the subject matter of Article 111 of the EC Treaty, which carries the hallmarks of difficult negotiation and awkward compromise. In essence, the Council may enter into formal exchange rate agreements involving non-Community currencies, but only on a recommendation from the Commission or the European Central Bank and after following a consultation procedure. In addition, the Council must endeavour to act consistently with the overall objective of monetary policy—ie the preservation of price stability.[65] In the absence of any such formal agreements, the Council may (again, subject to institutional procedures) formulate "general orientations" for exchange rate policies in relation to external currencies. Again, however, they must act in a manner consistent with the objective of price stability.[66] Ultimately, however, the external value of the euro will depend upon the success of Community policies in economic and monetary fields. The European Council has acknowledged this reality, and has confirmed that the power to formulate general orientations for exchange rate policy should only be exercised in the event of a clear misalignment of exchange rates or in other exceptional circumstances.[67]

(g)   It is finally necessary to consider fiscal policy. Broadly, fiscal policy determines (1) the levels of government spending and (2) the levels and burden of national taxation. The EC Treaty does not directly address these issues with the result that the conduct of fiscal policy remains a matter for individual Member States. In practice, however, matters are less straightforward. Although levels of government *spending* are not regulated by the

---

[62]   See, eg, *Garden Cottage Foods Ltd v Milk Marketing Board* [1984] AC 130.

[63]   In relation to the application of Article 103, certain matters of detail and definition are set out in Council Regulation 3603/93 ([1993] OJ L332/1), but it is unnecessary to consider that regulation for present purposes.

[64]   See para 27.10 below.

[65]   On monetary policy and price stability, see para 27.13 below.

[66]   For further discussion of these provisions, see Usher, *The Law of Money and Financial Services in the European Community* (Oxford University Press, 2nd edn, 2000) 245–8.

[67]   See para 8 of the Resolution of the European Council on Economic Policy Co-ordination (13 December 1997). These provisions assume some importance in the context of monetary sovereignty and the eurozone, and it will thus be necessary to return to them at a later stage—see Ch 31 below.

Treaty, the level of government *deficit* is controlled under the terms of the Stability and Growth Pact. A restriction on the level of government deficits clearly has the effect of placing a limit on government spending. It may be observed that the EC Treaty does not directly seek to regulate national tax systems; indeed, Member States have been keen to preserve their freedom of action in this area. Nevertheless, as has been shown[68] the Treaty does restrict national powers of taxation in a variety of ways, largely in support of rules relating to the free movement of capital. Since the rules are an essential aspect of economic and monetary union,[69] it may be said that the EMU project has tended indirectly to limit the scope of the sovereign discretion enjoyed by individual Member States in the field of fiscal policy.

It is perhaps fair to conclude that the EC Treaty and the regulations made under it provided a legally robust framework for the conduct of economic policies in a manner which is designed to support the single currency. However, the lack of growth endured by a number of eurozone Member States in recent years has led to political obstacles to the enforcement of those rules and a consequent decline in their credibility. From the point of view of the present work, however, it is only necessary to observe that some form of framework for the conduct of economic policy is in practice a necessary feature of a monetary union, even if the detailed rules may have to be varied from time to time in the light of experience. **26.17**

---

[68] See the discussion at paras 25.33–25.35 above.
[69] See para 25.33 above.

27

THE INSTITUTIONAL FRAMEWORK
OF MONETARY UNION

A. Introduction

A review of the institutional structures established for monetary union perhaps **27.01** tests the permissible boundary lines of the present work on the law of money. Yet the working definition[1] of a monetary union is heavily dependent upon the need for a single central bank which issues the sole currency constituting legal tender within the territory of the union; it thus remains appropriate to review the institutional arrangements for the performance of the central banking functions and the issue of the currency within the eurozone.[2]

---

[1] See para 24.03 above.

[2] The most comprehensive work in this field is Smits, *The European Central Bank: Institutional Aspects* (Kluwer, 1997). Another detailed work which post-dates the establishment of the ECB is Zilioli and Selmayr, *The Law of the European Central Bank* (Hart Publishing, 2001). The latter text is a compliation of three major articles by the same authors, these are: "The External Relations of the Euro Area: Legal Aspects" (1999) CML Rev 273; "The European Central Bank, its System and its Law" [1999] Euredia 187 and [1999–2000] YEL 348; and "The European Central Bank: An Independent Specialised Organisation of Community Law" (2000) CML Rev 591. For criticism of some of the views there expressed, see Torrent, "Whom is the European Central Bank the Central Bank of?" [1999] CML Rev 1229 and Smits, *The European Central Bank in the European Constitutional Order* (Eleven International Publishing, 2003). For another approach to the institutional arrangements, see Louis, "A Legal and Institutional Approach for Building a Monetary Union" (1998) CML Rev 33. For other discussions on this subject, see Andenas *et al* (eds), *European Economic and Monetary Union: The Institutional Framework* (Kluwer Law International, 1997), in particular chs 15 (Rosa Maria Lastra) and 16 (de Haan and Gormley); and Usher, *The Law of Money and Financial Services in the European Community* (Oxford University Press, 2nd edn, 2000) ch 10.

27.02 With these considerations in mind, it is proposed briefly to consider the institutional history. Thereafter, it will be necessary to consider the establishment, structure, and functions of the European Central Bank and the European System of Central Banks.

B. Institutional History

27.03 It has been shown that monetary union itself was by no means a bolt from the blue; rather, it represented the culmination of a number of developments within the Community over a period of years.[3] Essentially the same remark may be made in relation to the monetary institutions of the eurozone.[4]

27.04 Indeed, the development of monetary institutions may legitimately be traced back to the Treaty of Rome in its original form. Article 104 of that Treaty required Member States to "pursue the economic policy needed to ensure the equilibrium of its overall balance of payments and to maintain confidence in its currency, while taking care to ensure . . . a stable level of prices". In order to promote the co-ordination of policies in the monetary field, Article 105 established a Monetary Committee. That Committee was required to keep under review the monetary and financial situation of the Member States and to deliver reports and opinions on that subject. The Monetary Committee had advisory status only, and had a right to be consulted in various areas.[5] It is thus possible to trace back the need for monetary institutions to the very origins of the Community itself. The Monetary Committee ceased to exist once the third stage of EMU began but it was replaced by an Economic and Financial Committee which enjoys similar (although not identical) consultative powers.[6]

27.05 If, however, one seeks the precise forerunner of the present monetary institutions, then one must look to the Committee of Governors of the Central Banks,

---

[3] See Ch 25 above.

[4] It may also be observed in passing that money is a creation of the law, and the same applies to monetary institutions. A central bank can only exist as a separately incorporated entity if that status has been conferred upon it by law. This obvious and straightforward point is entirely followed through by the institutional structures established for monetary union. Yet matters have not always been so straightforward. The US Constitution did not deal with the establishment of a central bank in explicit terms, but it was found that the Federal Government had the power to found such an institution because both "the happiness and the prosperity of the nation" depended on it. See *McCulloch v Maryland* (1819) 17 US (4 Wheaton) 316. In more modern times, greater reliance may perhaps be placed on the second part of this formulation.

[5] eg in the context of certain issues arising from exchange rate adjustments and balance of payments difficulties, see Arts 107(2), 108(1), and 109(3) of the EC Treaty, in its original form. The Committee also had a consultative role in various contexts involving the free movement of capital—see Arts 69, 71, and 73 of the original Treaty.

[6] See Art 114(2) of the EC Treaty.

which was formed in 1964 to promote the co-ordination of monetary policy.[7] In 1972, the Committee of Governors was tasked with the management of the European Monetary Co-operation Fund.[8] In 1979, the Committee assumed responsibility for the operation of the Exchange Rate Mechanism[9] and it was later required to promote monetary policies aimed at the achievement of price stability, so as to support the operation of the European Monetary System.[10]

The Committee of Governors was dissolved at the start of the second stage of
27.06
European Monetary Union (EMU), when the European Monetary Institute (EMI) was established.[11] Naturally enough, the functions of the EMI reflect its status as a transitional institution which was intended to accelerate the movement towards the third stage of monetary union. Apart from various consultative and reporting roles, the EMI took over responsibility for the operation of the European Monetary System and the co-ordination of national monetary policies with the objective of price stability; it was required to establish the procedures for the conduct of monetary policy following the creation of the single currency, and to promote the efficiency of cross-border payment systems. The EMI was also involved in the preparation of reports designed to assess whether Member States had met the "Maastricht criteria" in order to qualify for membership of the eurozone.[12] It will be observed that the EMI (in common with its predecessors) was responsible for the *co-ordination* of monetary policies. This was necessarily the case, for the individual Member States retained their separate national currencies and the actual *selection* and *conduct* of monetary policy thus remained a national responsibility. This position was to change on 1 January 1999, with the creation of the single currency.[13]

---

[7] On the original establishment and functions of the Committee of Governors, see Council Decision 64/300, [1964] JO P77/1206. On the general subject discussed in the text see, Usher, *The Law of Money and Financial Services in the European Union* (Oxford University Press, 2nd edn, 2000) 212–16. As will be seen, the Governors of the national central banks remained in control of both the EMI and the ECB.

[8] The European Monetary Co-operation Fund has already been considered at para 25.09 above.

[9] On this mechanism, see para 25.15 above.

[10] See Council Decision 90/142, [1990] OJ L78/25.

[11] On the establishment and tasks of the EMI, see Art 117 of the EC Treaty; further details are given in the statutes of the EMI, which are set out in a Protocol to the Treaty. In accordance with Art 123(2) of the EC Treaty, the EMI went into liquidation upon the establishment of the ECB; a detailed examination of its functions is therefore unnecessary. However for a description of the preparations made by the EMI for the creation of the euro, see Sainz de Vicuña, "Institutional Aspects of the European Central Bank" (1991) 1 *Current Developments in Monetary and Financial Law* (IMF) 291.

[12] See Art 121 of the EC Treaty. On the Maastricht Criteria, see para 26.11 above.

[13] On the conduct of monetary policy during the third stage of monetary union, see para 27.13 below.

C. The European Central Bank and the European System of Central Banks

27.07   The European Central Bank (ECB) and the European System of Central Banks (ESCB) provide the core of the institutional structure upon which the euro depends.[14] This structure came into existence on 1 June 1998 upon the appointment of the Executive Board of the ECB, although it could clearly assume responsibility for monetary policy only when the single currency was established on 1 January 1999.[15] Both the ECB and the ESCB are required to act within the scope of the powers conferred upon them by the Treaty and the Statute of the ESCB.[16] Given the limited objectives of the present survey, it is perhaps sufficient to note a series of key points which will provide an overview of the two organisations. It will also be necessary to comment briefly on the role of the national central banks within the ESCB.

The ECB

27.08   The ECB is an international organisation created by treaty, and it has separate legal personality.[17] The ECB can thus acquire rights and become subject to liabilities; it may sue and be sued in its own name; it is to have the most extensive legal capacity accorded to corporations under the national laws of each Member State.[18] The resources available to the ECB originally consisted of

---

[14] For a discussion of the internal management arrangements, see Sáinz de Vicuña, "Recent Developments in the European Central Bank" (2003) 2 *Current Developments in Monetary and Financial Law* (IMF) 79. It should be added that the Finance Ministers of the eurozone Member States have been accustomed to meet to discuss issues arising in relation to the single currency. In some respects, these arrangements must be regarded as informal, in the sense that the EC Treaty does not provide for meetings of this kind. A "Protocol on the Euro Group", annexed to the Draft Treaty establishing a Constitution for Europe, would provide recognition for this grouping and confer upon the Commission and the ECB the right to participate in such meetings.

[15] On these points see, Art 123 of the EC Treaty and the Decision appointing the President, the Vice-President and the other Members of the Executive Board of the ECB—Decision 98/345, [1998] OJ L154/33.

[16] Article 8 of the EC Treaty. The Statute of the ESCB is set out in a Protocol to the Treaty. It should be appreciated that a protocol to a treaty will usually enjoy the same legal force as the treaty itself; in the context of the EC Treaty, the point is confirmed by Art 311. The laws which create both the ECB and the ESCB are thus a part of primary Community law—see Zilioli and Selmayr, *The Law of the European Central Bank* (Hart Publishing, 2001) 54. It should further be added that the proposed Treaty establishing a Constitution for Europe would revise the legal framework applicable to the ECB and the ESCB—see in particular Art 29. However, this would not appear to affect the general substance of the matters discussed in the text.

[17] Article 107(2) of the EC Treaty.

[18] On this point, see Art 9.1 of the Statute of the ESCB. For an English decision which considers a treaty provision of this kind, see *JH Rayner (Mincing Lane) Ltd v Department of Trade and Industry* [1990] 2 AC 418. The UK was thus placed under an obligation to secure the

(a) subscriptions to its share capital by the national central banks of the euro-zone Member States[19] and (b) substantial foreign reserve assets transferred to the ECB by the same central banks.[20] The profits and losses accruing to the ECB are allocated amongst the participating central banks.[21] In principle, therefore, the assets and liabilities of the ECB are entirely separate from those of the Community itself; it thus enjoys independence in the conduct of its financial and monetary operations. Nevertheless, it must not be overlooked that the ECB was created by the EC Treaty to serve an objective of the Community—ie the creation of a monetary union. Consequently, the ECB exists within the Community framework and is bound by Community law, to the extent applicable to it. In particular, the independence of the central bank cannot be invoked so as to exempt the ECB from the requirements of the EC Treaty itself.[22]

The ECB enjoys the exclusive right to authorise the issue of euro banknotes and coins; these constitute the sole form of legal tender within the eurozone.[23] This general subject will be considered in more detail at a later stage.[24]   **27.09**

The decision-making bodies of the ECB are the Governing Council and the Executive Board.[25] The Governing Council comprises (a) the members of   **27.10**

---

recognition of the legal personality of the ECB within this country. This was achieved by means of s 1 of the European Communities (Amendment) Act 1993, read together with s 2(1) of the European Communities Act 1972.

[19] See Art 28.1 of the ESCB Statute. It should, however, be appreciated that the national central banks do not "control" the ECB by virtue of their status as shareholders. For example, they cannot alter the objectives of the ECB, for they are enshrined in the Treaty itself. Likewise, they cannot remove those in executive positions, for these appointments are the prerogative of the Member States—see Zilioli and Selmayr (n 16 above) 72–3.

[20] Article 30 of the ESCB Statute.

[21] See Art 33 of the ESCB Statute. Article 32 of that Statute deals with the income of the participating central banks in so far as that income is derived from activities within the framework of the ESCB. The percentage ratios for the subscription of the ECB's capital were amended upon the accession of further Member States on 1 May 2004—see the ECB Decision on the national central banks' percentage shares in the key for subscription of the ECB's capital (ECB/2005/5), [2004] OJ L205/5.

[22] The point is clearly made in proceedings concerning the relationship between the ECB and the European Anti-Fraud Office—see Case C–11/00 *Commission v European Central Bank* [2003] ECR I–7147, paras 113–145, relying in particular on *Commission v European Investment Bank* [1988] ECR 1281 and Case C–370/89 *SGEEM and Etroy v European Investment Bank* [1992] ECR I–6211.

[23] On these points, see Art 106 of the EC Treaty.

[24] See para 29.24 below.

[25] Article 107(3) of the EC Treaty. It should be added that Art 45.1 of the ESCB Statute adds a third body, namely the General Council. The General Council includes (amongst others) the governors of the central banks of all the Member States, whether or not they are eurozone participants. As a result, it is entirely unsurprising that the General Council performs relatively limited functions, eg it performs various transitional tasks and makes preparations for the admission of new Member States to the third stage of EMU—see Art 4 of the Statute of the ESCB read together with Arts 47.1 and 47.3.

the Executive Board and (b) the governors of national central banks within the eurozone.[26] The Governing Council has a range of powers and functions, but it is primarily charged with the *formulation* of monetary policy for the eurozone (including decisions relating to intermediate monetary objectives, interest rates, and the level of reserves within the ESCB).[27] The Governing Council may adopt guidelines and decisions for these purposes, and may take any step necessary to ensure compliance by national central banks within the ESCB.[28]

27.11   The Executive Board comprises the president,[29] the vice-president, and four other members.[30] The principal task of the Executive Board is the *implementation* of the monetary policy determined by the Governing Council although, to the extent possible, this should be achieved through the activities of the national central banks within the ESCB.[31]

The ESCB

27.12   The ESCB comprises the ECB itself and the central banks of the Member States of the Community[32]—it should thus be appreciated that the ESCB as such does not have an independent or composite legal personality. Even the central banks of non-eurozone Member States with a derogation[33] are members of the ESCB, although in practice they are excluded from most of the material rights and obligations which arise within the framework of the system,[34] and references to the ESCB should accordingly be read in that light. As noted earlier, the ESCB is governed by the decision-making bodies of the ECB itself;[35] the Governing Council may require national central banks to comply with the guidelines and decisions of the ECB.

---

[26] Article 112(1) of the EC Treaty and Art 10.1 of the Statute of the ESCB. National central banks of Member States outside the eurozone are excluded from participation in the Governing Council—see Art 43.4 of the Statute of the ESCB.

[27] Article 12.1, Statute of the ESCB.

[28] ibid, Art 14.3.

[29] The President is the representative of the ECB to the outside world—see Art 13.2 of the ESCB Statute.

[30] For the appointment procedure, see Art 112(2) of the EC Treaty and Art 11.1 of the ESCB Statute.

[31] See Art 12.1 of the ESCB Statute.

[32] Article 107(1) of the EC Treaty.

[33] ie Member States which have not satisfied the Maastricht criteria—see Art 122(1) of the EC Treaty.

[34] See generally Arts 43 and 44 of the Statute of the ESCB. The central banks concerned were, however, required to pay up a "minimal percentage" of their capital in the ECB by way of a contribution to its operating costs—see Art 48 of the Statute.

[35] As has been pointed out, the dominance of the ECB within the euro system in some respects follow from the fact that the ECB has legal personality whilst the ESCB does not—Zilioli and Selmayr, *The Law of the European Central Bank* (Hart Publishing, 2001) 64.

What, then, are the objectives and functions of the ESCB? The primary objective **27.13**
is the maintenance of price stability.[36] The ESCB must thus both formulate and
implement monetary policy with a view to creating a low-inflation environment. It also conducts foreign exchange operations and is required to promote
the smooth operation of payment systems.[37] Perhaps more importantly from
the point of view of the working definition of a monetary union, it is required
to hold and manage the official foreign reserves of the particular Member
States.[38]

Finally, it should be observed that, in carrying out their functions within the **27.14**
ESCB, both the ECB and the national central banks are required to act
independently both of Community institutions and of national governments.[39] It is said that central bank independence insulates monetary policy
from temporary governmental or political expedients, which may have an
inflationary impact. Consequently, monetary policy should be conducted
independently of the government itself. It is not necessary here to record the
various arguments for and against the concept of independent central banking.[40] It is merely necessary to note that the principle of independence was
adopted and applied by the Treaty and was reinforced in various ways, and
that some have argued that the principle leads to a lack of accountability.[41]
The requirement for central bank independence necessarily implies a considerable degree of central bank autonomy. Thus, it will be noted that the
ECB can make regulations and issue decisions within its sphere of competence
without any requirement to consult with any other Community organs.[42] To

---

[36] Article 105(1) of the EC Treaty, repeated in Art 2 of the Statute of the ESCB. Without
prejudice to that objective, the ESCB is also required to support the Community's general
economic objectives.

[37] On the TARGET payment system operated by the ESCB, see para 33.44 below.

[38] Article 105(2) of the EC Treaty.

[39] This principle is clearly expressed both in Art 108 of the EC Treaty and in Art 7 of the
Statute of the ESCB. It may be more accurate to state that the central bank must enjoy autonomy
within the Community structure, rather than *from* it—see Smits, *The European Central Bank
Institutional Aspects* (Kluwer, 1997) 154, and materials there noted. Whilst it is really beyond
the scope of the present text, it may be noted that the precise legal nature of these institutions
and their status within the Community have provoked considerable debate. The arguments are
summarised by Smits, *The European Central Bank in the European Constitutional Order* (Eleven
International Publishing, 2003) 10–24. He concludes that the ESCB is "the central bank of
the European Community", ie it is independent *within* the framework of the Community,
rather than from it. This view is consistent with the later decision in Case C–11/00, *Commission v
European Central Bank* (see n 22 above).

[40] For discussion, see the materials mentioned in n 39 above.

[41] Issues of this kind are beyond the scope of this work. For discussion, see Gormley and de
Haan, "The Democratic Deficit of the European Central Bank" (1996) ELR 95; Zilioli and
Selmayr, *The Law of the European Central Bank* (Hart Publishing, 2001) 47.

[42] See Art 110 of the EC Treaty and Art 34 of the ESCB Statute.

this extent, it may be said that the ECB has become a new and independent source of monetary law.[43]

The National Central Banks

27.15   Since the structure of the ESCB is relatively novel,[44] it may be helpful briefly to outline the position of the national central banks which operate within it.

27.16   To the extent to which the individual national central banks engage in operations involving foreign reserve assets which belong to the ECB,[45] it might well be thought that those central banks act as agent for the ECB in carrying out those activities.[46] This impression is confirmed by various provisions within the Treaty itself. The ESCB Statute itself confirms[47] that "the national central banks are an integral part of the ESCB and shall act in accordance with the guidelines and instructions of the ECB". This is by no means merely a statement of intention, for the ECB has power to take proceedings before the European Court of Justice in the event of an alleged failure by a national central bank to perform its obligations under the Statute.[48] Further support for this position may be derived from an ECB Guideline, which makes it clear that each national central bank acts as the agent of the ECB when conducting foreign reserve operations and must therefore subordinate its own interests to those of the ECB itself.[49] The agency nature of the relationship is further reinforced by the financial arrangements which govern the operation of the system. Monetary income derived from foreign exchange operations is not retained by the individual central banks concerned; instead, it is effectively required to be pooled and shared amongst all the central banks within the system.[50]

---

[43] On this general subject, see Nierop, "A New Corpus Juris Monetae for Europe" (2000) 5 JIBFL 157.

[44] Comparable examples are perhaps offered by the early history of the US Federal Reserve System and the Bank of the German States, which operated between 1948 and 1957. However, the ESCB operates on a much more centralised structure and, as has been shown, the operations of the ESCB are governed exclusively by the decision-making bodies within the ESCB itself. For further discussion of these points and the precedents just noted, see Zilioli and Selmayr (n 41 above) 63–70.

[45] On the original and continuing obligations of the national central banks to credit the ECB with such assets, see Art 30 of the ESCB Statute.

[46] Although the relationship between the members of the system is derived from a treaty, it is nevertheless suggested that the private law analogy is appropriate.

[47] See Art 14.3 of the ESCB Statute.

[48] For the procedure, see Art 35.6 of the ESCB Statute.

[49] See Arts 2.1 and 2.2 of ECB Guideline dated 3 February 2000 (ECB/2000/1 [2000] OJ L207/24); the relevant provisions are headed "Agency Status of the NCBs". This Guideline was amended by further Guidelines dated 21 June 2001 (ECB/2001/5, [2001] OJ L190/26) and 27 September 2001 (ECB/2001/9 [2001] OJ L276/21), but these amendments are not material to the points made in the text.

[50] See Art 32 of the ESCB Statute.

In the light of these provisions, it is necessary to conclude that the ECB itself is **27.17** responsible as principal for the contractual obligations and other liabilities which the national central banks may incur in the course of their activities on behalf of the ESCB.[51]

---

[51] For further discussion of this subject, see Proctor, "The European System of Central Banks—Status and Immunities" (2001) 1 JIBFL 23. A broadly similar conclusion is stated by Zilioli and Selmayr, *The Law of the European Central Bank* (Hart Publishing, 2001) 72–80, where the whole subject is naturally discussed in more depth.

28

THE SINGLE CURRENCY AND ITS TREATY FRAMEWORK

A. Introduction

It is now proposed to consider the provisions established for the creation of the **28.01** euro pursuant to the terms of the Treaty on European Union. It will also be necessary to consider certain initiatives—in particular, the so-called "Madrid Scenario"—which followed the ratification of the Treaty. However, purely as a matter of convenience, the Council Regulations which were introduced pursuant to the relevant Treaty provisions will be held over to the next chapter.

It was noted earlier that any change in the nature or denomination of a national **28.02** monetary system involves the establishment of a legal basis for the conversion of debts expressed in the former currency into its replacement.[1] This position necessarily followed from the role which the State and its legislative processes must play in the definition of a monetary system.[2] In addition, it has been shown that notes and coins can only enjoy the status of legal tender if it has been conferred upon them by legislative act.[3] It will be seen that the creation of monetary union reflected and respected these requirements. Although the use of the ECU as the foundation of the single currency does cloud this point in some respects, it should not be allowed to obscure it.[4]

---

[1] See the discussion of the "recurrent link" at para 2.34 above.
[2] On the State theory of money and the role of the State in this area, see para 1.15 above.
[3] See para 2.24 above.
[4] See para 28.13 below.

B. Treaty Provisions

28.03   It is now necessary to identify those provisions which were introduced into the EC Treaty pursuant to the Treaty on European Union and which may be said to be of a wholly or partially monetary character.[5] On this basis, only three of the provisions inserted into the EC Treaty may be considered to have a monetary character.[6] These will be considered in the chronological order of their relevance for the creation of monetary union (ie as opposed to the order in which they appear in the EC Treaty).

28.04   First of all, Article 118 of the EC Treaty provides that:

> The currency composition of the ECU basket shall not be changed.
>
> From the start of the third stage, the value of the ECU shall be irrevocably fixed in accordance with Article 123(4).

28.05   In accordance with suggestions originally made in the Delors Report, the ECU was to form the monetary cornerstone of the EMU project; indeed, subject to its rebranding as the "euro", the ECU *is* the single currency of the eurozone.[7] It has also been shown that—under the arrangements applicable to it—the composition of the ECU basket could be revised on a five-yearly basis; the last review had occurred in 1989.[8] But if the ECU was to provide the foundation of the new monetary unit, then it was necessary to ensure that the foundation was a solid one which could command the confidence of the financial markets. It should be recalled in this context that the Treaty on European Union was signed on 7 February 1992[9] and that a five-yearly adjustment of the composition of the ECU basket would otherwise have occurred in 1994; in the interests of certainty and stability, a further review was thus precluded by the first sentence of Article 118. This did not merely have the effect of prohibiting a *realignment* of the currencies then within the ECU basket; it also prevented the *admission* to the basket of those Member States (ie Austria, Finland, and Sweden) which joined

---

[5] Institutional, economic, and other provisions associated with the single currency have been discussed at para 26.15 and Ch 27 above. It may be noted in passing that Economic Policy, Monetary Policy, and the Institutional Provisions are respectively marked out in Title VII of the EC Treaty as chs 1, 2, and 3. In contrast (and with the sole exception of Art 106), the core monetary rules fall under the heading of "Transitional Provisions" in ch 4. This may be thought to understate the importance of some of the provisions about to be discussed.

[6] Under the circumstances, this must be noted as a quite remarkable fact, although it is true that one of these provisions did allow for delegation of much of the detailed and technical work.

[7] This point will be reinforced (below) in the context of the review of Art 123 of the Treaty.

[8] On this point and on the weightings of the currencies within the basket, see para 25.14 above.

[9] It will be recalled that the Treaty came into force on 1 November 1993, following its ratification by Germany—see para 25.32 above.

the Community at a later date. The second sentence of Article 118 appears to have no independent legal significance, in that it merely cross-refers to the fact that the value of the ECU will be irrevocably fixed at the beginning of the third stage in accordance with the provisions of Article 123(4). It is thus appropriate immediately to move to a consideration of that Article.

Article 123(4) of the EC Treaty reads: **28.06**

> At the starting date of the third stage, the Council shall, acting with the unanimity of the Member States without a derogation, on a proposal from the Commission and after consulting the ECB, adopt the conversion rates at which their currencies shall be irrevocably fixed and at which irrevocably fixed rate the ECU shall be substituted for these currencies and the ECU will become a currency in its own right. This measure shall by itself not modify the external value of the ECU. The Council acting by a qualified majority of the said Member States, on a proposal from the Commission and after consulting the ECB, shall also take the other measures necessary for the rapid introduction of the ECU as the single currency of the Member States. The second sentence of Article 122(5) shall apply . . .[10]

This provision requires rather more detailed analysis.[11] In monetary terms, it **28.07** will be seen that Article 123(4) had three consequences:

(1) It provided for the euro[12] to become "a currency in its own right". Thus was the creation of the euro clothed with the required legal force. It is true that the currency was created from a pre-existing "basket" of currencies which could not itself properly be called "money", but this cannot in any way affect the status of the euro as the currency of the eurozone. At a later stage, it was felt necessary to confirm that contractual and other references to the "basket" ECU would be replaced by references to the euro on a one-for-one basis.[13] Yet in fact this was not strictly necessary, for under the terms of Article 123(4) of the Treaty, the ECU *itself* became the single currency of the eurozone Member States. The subsequent decision to rename the unit was—at least from a legal perspective—simply a rebranding exercise, and it did not result in the creation of a new monetary unit which was separate from the ECU itself. The requirement that references to the ECU should

---

[10] Article 122(5) describes the applicable voting procedure. The text is reproduced as amended by the Treaty of Nice.

[11] It should be noted that Art 123(5) of the Treaty contains essentially similar provisions and procedures which are to apply where a hitherto non-participating Member State is to join the eurozone (or, in the language of the Treaty, where "it is decided . . . to abrogate a derogation"). These provisions have thus far been applied only to Greece—see para 29.31 below. In view of the similarity of Arts 123(4) and 123(5), it is not considered necessary to review the latter provision in any depth.

[12] On the ECU/euro terminology, see the discussion of the "Madrid Scenario", para 28.11 below.

[13] See Art 2(1) of Council Regulation 1103/97, discussed in more detail at paras 29.03 et seq below.

be replaced by references to the euro on a one-to-one basis thus had the same effect as (say) a provision requiring one pound to be substituted for another. There was only one monetary unit, not two, so the question of substitution did not strictly arise.[14] This explanation may help to clarify that the theory of "recurrent link" does not apply as between the basket ECU and the euro, for the latter is merely a "continuation" of the former under a different guise and with full monetary status under the law;[15] there is no "link" between them because they are the same unit. Rather, the "recurrent link" subsists as between the former national currencies of the eurozone Member States (on the one hand) and the euro (on the other).

(2) Article 123(4) also provided for the adoption of the conversion rates at which the ECU (euro) would be substituted for the participating national currencies. Once again, this is entirely reflective of the "recurrent link" theory, which anticipates that the legislator will make provision for the rate at which debts expressed in the old currency must be restated and settled in the new unit. It must also be observed that the terminology adopted by Article 123(4) is that of "substitution" (rather than "conversion"), thus emphasising that the introduction of the euro did not involve any form of foreign exchange transaction between the euro and any of the participating national currencies.[16]

(3) Finally, it is provided that the substitution of the euro for national currencies "shall by itself not modify the external value of the ECU". This phrase is at first sight somewhat obscure, and requires explanation. In essence, the provision confirmed that the substitution rates for each individual participating currency had to be equal to the value of the ECU basket as at the beginning of the third stage (ie on 1 January 1999)—although the provision refers to the "external value" of the euro, the process of irrevocable fixing could only relate to those currencies which it actually replaced. As a result it was not possible to determine the rates at which individual currencies would "converge" into the euro before the beginning of the third

---

[14] It must, however, be accepted that the later renaming of the single currency was liable to cause confusion when examining the Treaty provisions, and the attempt to clarify the position in the later Council Regulation does not result in any harm from a monetary law perspective.

[15] On the theory of the "recurrent link", see para 2.34 above. There may be some difficulty in applying this theory to the ECU basket for (as we have seen) the ECU basket was not "money" in any traditional sense. This specific point is considered at para 30.52 below.

[16] This (unexpressed) consideration—and the resultant view that consumers should not bear a cost where a bank carries no foreign exchange risk—perhaps lies at the heart of a series of Commission Recommendations (98/286, 98/287, and 98/289) issued on 23 April 1998 ([1998] OJ L130/22). The first recommendation expressed the view that no banking charges should generally be levied by financial institutions when dealing with payment transactions as between the euro and the participating national currencies. Following the introduction of the euro notes and coins and the redenomination of bank accounts at the end of the transitional period, this recommendation is now "spent".

stage, although it was possible to announce bilateral convergence rates between participating currencies ahead of that time.[17]

Finally, it is necessary to turn to Article 106 of the Treaty. In many respects, this Article reflects features both of the State theory of money and the working definition of a monetary union, for it provides both the legal underpinning for the issue of banknotes and coins, and confers an effective monopoly on the ECB in this area. Article 106 reads as follows: **28.08**

1.   The ECB shall have the exclusive right to authorise the issue of bank notes within the Community. The ECB and the national central banks may issue such notes. The bank notes issued by the ECB and the national central banks shall be the only such notes to have the status of legal tender within the Community.

2.   Member States may issue coins subject to approval by the ECB of the volume of the issue. The Council may, acting in accordance with the procedure referred to in Article 252 and after consulting the ECB, adopt measures to harmonise the denomination and technical specifications of all coins intended for circulation to the extent necessary to permit their smooth circulation within the Community.

It will be noted that Article 106 refers to the issue of coins by "Member States", and provides that euro banknotes are the only notes which will constitute legal tender within "the Community". At the risk of stating an obvious point, the Article in fact applies only to participating Member States within the eurozone.[18] Thus, whilst euro banknotes may be accepted as a matter of practice in non-participating Member States and indeed, non-Member States, they do not there enjoy the status of legal tender. It is self-evident that non-participating Member States will continue to issue their own national currencies and thus retain their own powers with respect to the conduct of national monetary policy.[19]   **28.09**

The second part of Article 106(2) deals with questions touching the denomination and technical specifications to be complied with in the production of euro coins.[20] Apart from these details, Article 106 contains some core monetary provisions. The ECB itself may issue banknotes; although national central banks within the ESCB may also *issue* banknotes, they may only do so with the *authorisation* of the ECB itself.[21] In contrast, the power to issue coins is   **28.10**

---

[17] See the Joint Communiqué on the determination of the irrevocable conversion rates for the euro (2 May 1998). The bilateral central rates may also be found in *Practical Issues Arising from the Introduction of the Euro* (Bank of England, Issue 9, September 1998, p 8).

[18] See Art 122(3) of the EC Treaty.

[19] The point is, however, confirmed by Art 43(2) of the Statute of the ESCB.

[20] For the provisions made pursuant to this power, see Regulation 975/98, [1998] OJ L139/6.

[21] The provisions dealing with the issue of banknotes are mirrored in Art 16 of the Statute of the ESCB.

delegated to the Member States themselves, although they could clearly fulfil this function through any national agency. Once again, however, the volume of the issue will in each case be subject to the prior approval of the ECB. It follows from these provisions that the ECB has control over the issue of all *physical* money within the eurozone, and that it thus helps to ensure that monetary union in Europe conforms to the working definition of a monetary union.

C. The Madrid Scenario

28.11 The Treaty on European Union—and the resultant amendments to the EC Treaty—came into force on 1 November 1993. This may have been somewhat later than originally hoped, partly because of political opposition to the Treaty and partly because of various legal and constitutional challenges in some Member States.[22]

28.12 Once the political momentum for a single currency had been established, it became necessary to turn to the detailed technical and management work which was essential to such a large-scale project. The burden of this work naturally fell upon the Community institutions. It is nevertheless fair to observe that various financial market associations played a significant role in promoting the preparatory work. From their perspective, it was important to achieve legal certainty as to the consequences of the introduction of the single currency; it must be remembered that, in the mid-1990s, institutions found themselves entering into long-term financial arrangements expressed in a currency which would probably have ceased to exist by the maturity date. Their quest for clarity is therefore entirely understandable.[23]

28.13 The process of technical preparation essentially got under way with the publication by the Commission of "One Currency for Europe", a Green Paper on the practical arrangements for the introduction of the single currency.[24] This paper provided the initial framework for progress on the technical aspects, and this work was taken up by the Presidency Conclusions published following the meeting of the European Council held at Madrid on 15/16 December 1995.[25]

---

[22] See *Brunner v European Union Treaty* [1994] 1 CMLR 57 (Germany); *R v Secretary of State for Foreign and Commonwealth Affairs ex p Rees-Mogg* [1994] QB 552 (UK).

[23] On the other hand, some organisations pressed for UK legislation confirming the continuity of contracts which would be re-expressed in euros as a result of the introduction of the single currency. For the reasons given in Ch 30 below, it is the view of the present writer that such an approach underestimated the ability of English law to cope with the substitution of the euro in a commercially sensible manner.

[24] COM (95) 333, 31 May 1995.

[25] The "Madrid Scenario" comprises both the Presidency Conclusions of the Madrid European Council and an Annex which addresses the more detailed points.

As noted previously, this became known as the "Madrid Scenario" for the single currency. This document should be described in some depth since it set the tone for the two Council Regulations which will be discussed at a later stage,[26] and provided the basis upon which the Commission and the European Monetary Institute were to take forward their preparations in this area. The main, monetary matters addressed by the Madrid Scenario are as follows:

(1) It was determined that the single currency would be known as the "euro". This name had been selected because the new currency had to "symbolise" Europe, and it was believed that the revised name would help to secure public acceptance for the new currency.[27] No doubt, in presentational terms, the adoption of the new name may be regarded as a rebranding exercise *par excellence*, but it is not easy to reconcile with the terms of the EC Treaty itself. Article 123(4), it will be recalled, states that "the ECU will become a currency in its own right". To the casual reader, it might thus appear that the name of the single currency had been settled by the Treaty itself; certainly the Treaty did not delegate any specific power to determine or to revise the name of the new unit. The European Council was doubtless troubled by this point, for the Madrid Scenario states.[28] that the "euro" was to be the *specific* name for the new currency, whilst the Treaty merely utilised the term "ecu" in a generic sense. Whether this ingenious approach to interpretation would withstand close scrutiny must be doubtful, but the fifteen Member States were of the opinion that this represented "the agreed and definitive interpretation of the relevant Treaty provisions". The decision to adopt the term "euro" in place of the "ecu" was challenged, both as a proposal and when ultimately incorporated into a Council Regulation, but these challenges both failed for Community law reasons unconnected with the legal means by which the new name had been adopted.[29]

(2) Paragraph 9 of the Madrid Scenario confirmed that the euro would become a currency in its own right and that the official ECU basket would cease to exist. The ECU would necessarily cease to exist *as a currency basket* because, under the terms of the Treaty, the ECU was itself to become a currency.[30] It should be appreciated that this aspect of the Treaty was indeed applied in

---

[26] See Ch 29 below.

[27] No doubt for the same reason, it was made clear that "euro" would be the sole name of the currency, and would be used in all of the EU's official languages. Individual Member States would not be able to add additional words (eg France could not call the currency "euro franc"). These points were subsequently reiterated in para (2) of the preamble to Reg 974/98, discussed below.

[28] See paras 8 and 14 of the Madrid Scenario.

[29] See Case T–175/96 *Berthu v Commission* [1997] ECR II–811 and Case T–207/97 *Berthu v Council* [1998] ECR II–509.

[30] Article 123(4) of the EC Treaty.

accordance with its terms—the ECU did become a separate currency, and it had merely been relabelled as the euro.

(3) It was confirmed that national currency notes/coins would remain legal tender within the respective issuing Member States pending the introduction of euro notes/coins.[31]

(4) It was confirmed that a Council Regulation would be made[32] to provide a sound legal framework for the use of the new currency.

(5) There would be a three-year "transitional period" (ie 1 January 1999 to 31 December 2001) for the introduction of the new currency. As has been noted earlier,[33] the euro became the single currency of the participating Member States with effect from 1 January 1999, but the separate, national currency notes and coins were to remain the sole form of legal tender during that period.[34] The legal framework would clarify this rather confusing state of affairs by confirming that the various national currencies would become "different expressions" of the single euro unit. As a consequence, there would be a "legally enforceable equivalence" between the national currencies and the euro. It would follow that, during the transitional period, the separate national currencies could not fluctuate against each other or against the euro. This must, of course, be the case, because all of the national currencies and the euro were but different expressions of the same currency unit; and a single currency plainly cannot fluctuate in value against itself.

(6) The legal framework would confirm[35] that obligations expressed in ecu would be translated into euro on a one-for-one basis. It may be added that this provision was an inevitable consequence of the rebranding exercise noted above. The ecu was to become the single currency, and it had merely been relabelled as "euro". It necessarily followed that a one-to-one basis had to be used—otherwise, it would have been necessary further to amend the EC Treaty itself.

(7) The Madrid Scenario also established what became known as the "no compulsion-no prohibition" principle. Parties would be allowed to use the euro as a means of payment during the transitional period, but they would generally not be obliged to do so. For the most part, national currency units

---

[31] In this context, see paras 9, 12, and 13 of the Madrid Scenario.

[32] In the event, for reasons described below, it proved necessary to introduce two separate Regulations for these purposes.

[33] See point (3) above.

[34] The transitional period and its legal consequences are discussed in more detail at para 29.16 below. The use of a three-year transitional period appears to have been motivated by considerations of a purely practical character; the task of printing the volume of banknotes/coins for the eurozone was a very large one, and it was not felt possible to complete it by 1 January 1999.

[35] See the Madrid Scenario, para 9.

(within their territorial limits) would continue to be used throughout the transitional period. This had to be the case, given that no euro notes/coin were available during the transitional period.

(8) The Madrid scenario confirmed[36] that the introduction of the euro would not result in the termination of contractual obligations expressed in the former national currencies, nor would it affect the continuing operation of stipulations for fixed rate interest.

(9) Finally, the Madrid Senario contained various statements as to the conversion of tradeable securities into euros.[37]

As noted above, the Madrid Scenario was designed to create a sound basis to enable the Community, Member States, financial institutions, and many others to make appropriate preparations for the introduction of the single currency. Before leaving this subject, however, it may be noted that many of the points made in the Madrid Scenario are in fact necessary inferences from the EC Treaty itself, or are derived from pre-existing rules of monetary law. For example, the terms of the treaty refer to the "ecu" as the single currency: if the single currency was to be renamed the "euro" without any amendment to the substantive terms of the Treaty, then this could only be achieved consistently with the EC Treaty if ecu obligations were translated into euros on a one-for-one basis.[38] Equally, if national currencies were to continue in circulation for a period, then the "legally enforceable equivalence" as between the national currencies themselves and in relation to the euro was a necessary consequence of the introduction of a single currency under the terms of the EC Treaty.[39] In similar vein, the confirmation as to the continuing effectiveness of contractual obligations (including fixed interest rates) expressed in a legacy currency merely reflected existing legal principles.[40] Thus, whilst the Madrid Scenario fulfilled a very valuable function in that it provided a "road map" for the establishment of the single currency and provided a degree of legal certainty sought by the financial markets, it should not be overlooked that, in a number of significant areas, it merely applied existing and well-established legal rules to the introduction of the euro.

28.14

The process which began with the Madrid Scenario ultimately led to the creation of a comprehensive legal framework which catered for the introduction of the euro. It is now necessary to consider the Treaty basis for that framework, and thereafter to examine the Council Regulations involved.

28.15

---

[36] ibid, para 10.
[37] ibid, para 11.
[38] See para 28.13(1) above.
[39] See para 28.13(5) above.
[40] On the continuity of contracts generally, see Ch 30 below.

29

THE EURO REGULATIONS

A. Introduction

The preceding chapters have considered the consequences of the Treaty on   **29.01**
European Union and other questions of a relatively "high level" nature. It is now
necessary to focus on the more detailed legal framework for the introduction of
the single currency.

It has been noted earlier that, ultimately, two separate Council Regulations   **29.02**
were made in order to provide the initial framework for the use of the euro.
Plainly, it would have been preferable if the required "code" for the single
currency could have been set out in a single document. It is therefore pertinent
to ask—why was this unfortunate division of labour found to be necessary? In
order to answer this question, it is proposed to consider the two regulations in
chronological order.

B. Council Regulation 1103/97

The first Regulation—Council Regulation 1103/97[1] came into effect in June   **29.03**
1997.[2] The Regulation was made under Article 308 (formerly Article 235) of
the EC Treaty. It may be helpful to remember that Article 308 reads as follows:

---

[1] [1997] OJ L162/1.
[2] See Art 6 of that Regulation.

If action by the Community should prove necessary to attain, in the course of the operation of the common market, one of the objectives of the Community *and this Treaty has not provided the necessary powers* the Council shall, acting unanimously on a proposal from the Commission and after consulting the European Parliament, take the appropriate measures.[3]

29.04 This immediately gives rise to two questions. First of all, why was it necessary to introduce a Regulation dealing with the euro some eighteen months before the single currency was due to be created? Secondly, why was it necessary to invoke Article 308, when Article 123(4) of the Treaty[4] already contained a power to issue regulations for the rapid introduction of the single currency? The latter point assumes a certain importance when it is borne in mind that Article 308 cannot be used where an explicit and appropriate Treaty provision is available to deal with the matter in hand.[5]

29.05 As to the first question, it was felt necessary to provide legal certainty so that financial institutions and other organisations involved in or affected by the changeover could plan their preparations well in advance.[6] Proper advance planning would allow for a more smoothly conducted changeover when the single currency came into being. The nature and extent of the legal certainty actually provided by this Regulation will be discussed below.

29.06 Whilst the answer to the first question is therefore founded mainly on practical considerations, the answer to the second lies in a more technical approach to the terms of the EC Treaty. Article 123(4) of the Treaty allows the Council—acting on a proposal from the Commission and after consulting the European Central Bank[7]—to issue the necessary measures *with the unanimity of the Member States without a derogation*. Now, as noted earlier,[8] a Member State which did not qualify for single currency membership at the beginning of the third stage of European Monetary Union (EMU) was referred to in the Treaty as a "Member State with a derogation". However, the identities of the participating and

---

[3] Emphasis added.

[4] The text of Art 123(4) is reproduced at para 28.06 above.

[5] A point emphasised by the decision in Case 56/88 *UK v Council* [1989] 2 CMLR 789. Article 308 can only be used to further the objectives of the Treaty—see *Opinion 2/94 on the Accession of the Community to the ECHR* [1996] ECR I–1759. However, this particular limitation clearly posed no difficulty in the present context, for the achievement of economic and monetary union is expressed to be one of the basic tasks of the Community in accordance with the terms of Art 2 of the EC Treaty.

[6] This general point has already been mentioned but specific reference to it is made in para (4) of the preamble to Council Regulation (EC) 1103/97.

[7] It may be noted that the ECB had not come into existence at this point, and consequently the consultation process instead involved the European Monetary Institute in accordance with Art 117(8) of the EC Treaty.

[8] See para 26.13, n 27 above, discussing Art 122(1) of the EC Treaty.

non-participating Member States had not been ascertained in June 1997 when Regulation 1103/97 was to be made. Indeed, those Member States were only finally identified on 3 May 1998, and consequently the power to make regulations conferred by Article 123(4) could not be exercised until that date; only at that point would it become possible to name these Member States "without derogation" whose "unanimity" was required for these purposes. Turning to considerations of a rather more national character, it should be said that much of the pressure for legal certainty in this area emanated from the London financial markets, which feared for the sanctity of contracts whose effectiveness spanned the changeover period.[9] Yet, by this time, it was tolerably clear that the United Kingdom would not participate in monetary union. Even if it had been possible for the Community to invoke Article 123(4) as a basis for the regulation at that stage, this would still have been of no assistance to the London markets, for regulations issued under Article 123(4) have no application in this country for so long as the United Kingdom remains outside the eurozone.[10] This particular point has consequences for the status of the euro in the United Kingdom, to which it will be necessary to return. But the present discussion has hopefully demonstrated that Article 308 provided the only basis upon which a regulation dealing with the euro could then be made in a manner which would be legally effective in *all* Member States, whether or not they would ultimately move on to the Third Stage of EMU.[11]

29.07 It follows that the legal basis of Regulation 1103/97 is secure, even if perhaps derived from an unexpected source. But what did the Regulation achieve? In broad terms, the Regulation is directed to three main issues upon which early clarification had been sought, namely (a) the consequences of monetary union for the ECU; (b) the continuity of transitional contracts which "spanned" the introduction of the euro; and (c) the calculation and rounding of applicable conversion rates.

---

[9] On this point see the discussion on continuity of contracts in Ch 30 below.

[10] This follows from para 5 of the Protocol on Certain Provisions relating to the United Kingdom of Great Britain and Northern Ireland, as annexed to the EC Treaty. This Protocol contains the UK "opt out" from monetary union, and will be discussed at para 31.30 below. It should perhaps be explained that neither Art 123(4) nor regulations made under it have effect in the UK so far as the terms of the EC Treaty itself are concerned. As will be seen, certain provisions of Art 1103/97 will have effect in the UK by virtue of the *lex monetae* principle, but that is an entirely separate matter.

[11] This point is highlighted in para (5) of the preamble to Regulation 1103/97. It may be argued that the points noted in the text highlight the inadequacy of the rule-making power embodied within Art 123(4) of the Treaty, but that would be an inappropriate conclusion. It was hardly likely that the UK would have agreed to the extension of that power to this country, given that the Government had negotiated its "opt-out" from monetary union.

29.08 Some of the points addressed in the Regulation[12] will be considered in greater depth in more specific contexts, but it is appropriate here to provide a brief description of the main provisions:

(1) It is confirmed that references in any legal instrument[13] to the ECU are to be replaced by a reference to the euro on a one-for-one basis.[14] As noted previously, in accordance with the terms of the Madrid Scenario, the ECU was merely being renamed "euro" and as a result, the one-for-one basis had necessarily to follow. Where a legal instrument referred to the ECU without further explanation, it was presumed that this referred to the "official" ECU, although this presumption was rebuttable if the parties had a contrary intention.[15]

(2) It is confirmed that the introduction of the euro will not result in the discharge of any legal instrument, nor will it alter any of the terms of such an instrument or create any unilateral rights of termination. Parties were, however, allowed to include in their contracts any provision specifically allowing for termination of the contract, if they wished to do so.[16]

---

[12] Consistently with the points noted above in the context of Art 308, it should be noted that Reg 1103/97 is directly applicable in all Member States, whether within or outside the eurozone. On this point, see Art 6 of the Regulation. The terms of the Regulation thus form a part of English law.

[13] "Legal Instrument" is broadly defined in Art 1 of the Regulation to include legislative and statutory provisions, court orders, contracts, unilateral payment obligations, payment instruments (other than banknotes and coins), and other instruments with legal effect. At first sight, it may appear curious that a regulation dealing with a monetary substitution should not apply to banknotes and coins. Yet this exclusion was necessary to support the rules that *national* banknotes and coins were to represent euros during the transitional period but that they were to enjoy the status of legal tender only within the boundaries of the issuing State. These rules are discussed below in the context of Council Reg 974/98.

[14] Article 2(1) of Council Reg 1103/97. The ECJ has had occasion to apply this rule in a number of cases when assessing debts or damages in the context of contractual claims, eg, see Case C–127/03 *Commission v Trendsoft (Ireland) Ltd* (8 July, 2004) para 27.

[15] Article 2(1) of Council Reg 1103/97. The difficulties posed by the "official"/"private" ECU distinction will be considered at para 30.49 below. Interestingly, the presumption noted in the text was found to have been rebutted in the context of a decision of the Commission to impose a fine. In Case C–49/92P *Commission v ANIC Partecipazione SpA* [1999] ECR I–4125, a Commission decision of 23 April 1986 imposed "a fine of 750,000 ECU or ITL1,103,695,500". By making specific reference to the countervalue of the Italian lira on the date on which the decision was made, the Commission had explained its decision in terms of the lira, and the presumption that the ECU obligation should be substituted by a euro obligation on a one-for-one basis thus could not stand. When the ECJ thus gave its judgment on 8 July 1999 (shortly after the introduction of the euro), it followed that ANIC was required to pay the euro equivalent of ITL1,103,695,500. Since the lira had been replaced by the euro at a rate of one euro to 1,936.27 lire, this resulted in a fine of €570,011. Had the one-to-one presumption applied then, of course, the fine would have been €750,000. The Commission's practice of expressing fines both in ECU (or, formerly, the EUA) had previously caused difficulties of this kind—see Cases 41, 43, and 44/73 *Société Anonyme Générale Sucrière v EC Commission* [1977] ECR 445.

[16] These points are set out in more detail in Art 2 of Reg 1103/97. The effect of this provision is discussed in more depth at para 30.25 below.

(3) Finally, certain rounding and conversion points are addressed. In particular, (a) the conversion rates to be adopted on 1 January 1999 were to be expressed as one euro compared to a set amount of the relevant legacy currencies;[17] (b) the conversion rates were not to be rounded or truncated when making calculations, since this would inevitably lead to distortions;[18] (c) for the same reason, conversions between separate legacy currencies had to be achieved "through" the euro, and the use of inverse rates or alternative methods of calculation were prohibited (unless they produced the same results);[19] and (d) provision was made for rounding of odd amounts to the nearest cent.[20]

It should be said that paragraph (3) above represents a fairly simplistic description of a set of conversion/rounding rules which could be relatively difficult to apply in practical situations.[21] However, the detailed mathematics are fortunately

29.09

---

[17] Article 4(1) of Council Reg 1103/97. Conversion rates were also to be adopted with 6 significant figures, ie 6 figures counting from the first non-zero figure on the left, disregarding the decimal point. See para (12) of the preamble to Reg 1103/97.

[18] Article 4(2) of Council Reg 1103/97.

[19] ibid, Art 4(3) and (4).

[20] ibid, Art 5. Oddly enough, the rounding rules have given rise to litigation. Article 5 provides that "Monetary amounts to be *paid or accounted for* when a rounding takes place after a conversion into the euro unit pursuant to Article 4 shall be rounded up or down to the nearest cent" (emphasis added). In Case C–19/03, *Verbraucher-Zentrale Hamburg v O2 Germany GmbH* [2004] All ER (D) 81 (Sept), the tariffs published by the defendant mobile phone company were expressed in Deutsche marks. Upon the introduction of euro notes and coins, the company revised its tariffs by expressing them in euros and rounding up the figures to the nearest cent. Since the tariff itself merely provided a *basis for calculation* of the customer's final invoice, the figures in the tariff did not constitute amounts which were to be "paid or accounted for" for the purposes of Art 5. It followed that the mandatory rounding rules could not apply to those figures. However, Article 5 did not *prohibit* the rounding of figures in other contexts—indeed, para 11 of the preamble to Reg 1103/97 provided that the rounding rules "do not affect any rounding practice, convention or national provisions providing a higher degree of accuracy for intermediate computations". The Court accordingly concluded that the tariff could be rounded up on conversion into the euro, provided that the cumulative effect of the intermediate rounding process did not have a real impact on the price to be paid. If there were such a material impact, then this would have the effect of revising the contract without the consent of the debtor and would consequently be inconsistent with the principle of continuity of contracts.

[21] Some of the problem areas are considered in *Euro Papers (No 22)* "The Introduction of the euro and the rounding of Currency Amounts". Without addressing the point in great detail, it may be appropriate to note one point which troubled certain market practitioners and the Department of Trade and Industry—see in particular the DTI Consultative Document *The Euro: Redenomination of Share Capital* (January 1998). Certain companies in the UK had outstanding share capital expressed in the national currencies of participating Member States. Concerns were expressed that, if the rounding rules operated to round an amount *down* to the nearest cent, this would amount to an unlawful reduction of capital under Companies Act 1985, s 135. It is respectfully submitted that this concern was wholly misplaced. Leaving aside company law objections to this line of reasoning, it overlooks a point which is fundamental to the rounding process. When an amount is rounded up or down in accordance with these rules, it neither increases nor decreases the amount payable; rather, the rounding rules are applied as a means of determining the euro *equivalent* of the amount expressed in the participating national currency. For these reasons, the substitution of the euro could not under any circumstances result in the reduction of a company's capital.

not of concern in a book of this character. Rather, it is more relevant to note that these rules—taken together with the substitution rates adopted by further regulations with effect from 1 January 1999—provide the "recurrent link" between the respective legacy currency and the euro.[22] To those of a conservative mind-set, it is, perhaps, reassuring to note that a project as vast and as revolutionary as monetary union in Europe still had to have recourse to long-established principles and precedents.[23]

C. Council Regulation 974/98

29.10   It has been noted that Council Regulation (EC) 1103/97 applies to all Member States, even if they currently remain outside the eurozone. By contrast, Council Regulation (EC) 974/98 applies only within the participating, eurozone Member States.[24] It will be necessary to return to this distinction in other contexts.[25] First of all, however, the key contents of the Regulation must be described. As will be seen, a number of its provisions must be regarded as the *lex monetae* of the eurozone Member States. Indeed, the opening sentence of the introductory preamble states that "this Regulation defines monetary law provisions of the Member States which have adopted the euro". Community law accordingly now provides the *sole* source of the monetary law of participating Member States, since the delegation of monetary sovereignty to institutions created by the EC Treaty is complete, unconditional, and irrevocable.[26]

29.11   The Regulation came into force on 1 January 1999;[27] it includes four main operative parts dealing with the substitution of the euro, the transitional period, the introduction of euro notes/coin, and certain final provisions applicable from the end of the transitional period. Each of these areas must be examined separately.

---

[22] On the theory of the recurrent link, see para 2.34 above.

[23] For completeness, it should be noted that Council Reg 1103/97 subsequently had to be amended, since it contemplated the position of Member States which joined the eurozone at the beginning of the third stage of EMU but failed to cater for those which joined later, eg by virtue of the abrogation of a derogation pursuant to Art 123(5) of the Treaty. The problem became apparent when Greece later moved to the third stage, and the necessary technical changes were made by Council Reg 2595/2000, [2000] OJ L300/1.

[24] For the reasons noted above, the limited territorial scope of Reg 974/98 was an inevitable consequence of Art 123(4) of the EC Treaty. However, the point is also explicitly recognised in Art 17 of that Regulation.

[25] See, in particular, para 31.30 below.

[26] On monetary union and national sovereignty, see Ch 31 below, where a possible qualification to the statement in the text is considered.

[27] This was, of course, the day on which the euro came into existence, being the first day of the third stage of EMU.

Substitution of the euro

Part II of the Regulation comprises Articles 2, 3, and 4 and deals with the **29.12**
substitution of the euro for the currencies of the participating Member States. It
is appropriate to reproduce Articles 2 and 3 of Regulation 974/98 in full:

Article 2

*As from 1 January 1999 the currency of the participating Member States shall be
the euro. The currency unit shall be one euro. One euro shall be divided into
one hundred cent.*

Article 3

*The euro shall be substituted for the currency of each participating Member State at the
conversion rate.*

These straightforward provisions—expressed with great clarity and admirable **29.13**
brevity—lie at the heart of monetary union. They emphasise that the euro has
been the *sole* currency of the participating Member States since 1 January 1999,
even though no euro notes/coins were available in physical form at that time,
and even though, as a necessary consequence, the available forms of legal tender
differed across the various parts of the eurozone.[28]

It may be inferred from Article 3 that, whilst *national* notes/coins continued to **29.14**
circulate, these so-called "legacy currencies" would merely "represent" the euro
at the substitution rates ascertained, and irrevocably fixed pursuant to the provisions of the EC Treaty and regulations made under it.[29] The same point is,
however, reinforced by Article 9 of the same Regulation.[30]

Article 4 of the Regulation confirms that the euro is the unit of account both of **29.15**
the ECB itself and of the central banks of the eurozone Member States.

Transitional period

Articles 5 to 9 of Regulation 974/98 contain transitional provisions, dealing **29.16**
with the initial introduction of the euro and its relationship to legacy currencies
which were to be substituted by the new unit. Perhaps the most important
aspect is the creation of a "transitional period".

---

[28] As a matter of detail, it may be recorded that the euro was also to become the currency of
San Marino (Council Decision 1999/97/EC, [1999] OJ L30/33), the Vatican City (Coun-
cil Decision 1999/98/EC, [1999] OJ L30/35) and Saint Pierre-et-Miquelon and Mayotte
(Council Decision 1999/98/EC, [1999] OJ L30/29). On the details of these arrangements, see
Strumpf, "The Introduction of the euro to States and territories outside the European Union"
[2003] 28 ELR 283.

[29] These rates were fixed by Reg 2866/98 and (in the case of the Greek drachma) by 1478/
2000. The relevant rates are reproduced at para 29.29 below.

[30] Article 9 is noted under "Transitional Period", para 29.16 below.

29.17   The transitional period was the three-year period beginning on 1 January 1999 and ending on 31 December 2001.[31] At the beginning of this period, the euro came into being; at the end of it, euro banknotes and coins were brought into circulation. Had these two events occurred on the same day, then the task of recalculating prices and the simultaneous introduction of new, physical currency across the entire eurozone would have placed an enormous burden on banks, businesses, governments, central banks, and many others. In the absence of Herculean efforts, it would have been quite likely that the introduction of the new currency would have been accompanied by scenes of chaos; scarcely an auspicious beginning for such a major project. Consequently, a period of three years was interposed between these two events. This perhaps serves to emphasise that a monetary system is something of an abstract notion, related to but distinct from the more physically apparent concept of legal tender for obligations expressed in that money.[32] It may be noted that neither the Treaty on European Union nor the revised version of the EC Treaty contemplated any form of transitional period, still less a period of such duration.[33] Nevertheless, it was clearly felt that Article 123(4), allowing the Council (after following various procedural requirements) to "take the . . . measures necessary for the rapid introduction of the ECU as the single currency" formed a sufficient legislative basis for this aspect of Regulation 974/98. For present purposes, it is perhaps unnecessary to enquire whether the three-year period was justified in terms of the Treaty, for that period is now spent.[34] It is, however, necessary to ask—what were the consequences of the transitional period for the monetary laws of the participating Member States?

29.18   In the longer term, it has already been shown that the euro became the single currency of the participating Member States on 1 January 1999, and that the euro is divided into one hundred cents; but for the purposes of the transitional period, the euro was also divided into the national currency units of the legacy currencies, and any subdivision of those legacy currencies was to be maintained.[35] In other words, the German mark, the French franc and other legacy currencies

---

[31] See the definition of "transitional period" set out in Art 1 of Reg 974/98.

[32] Considerations of this kind perhaps help to justify the revised approach to the definition of money adopted in Ch 1 above, which places less reliance on cash in its physical form.

[33] The proposal for a transitional period only seriously emerged in the context of the Madrid Scenario—see para 28.13 above. But in themselves, these Presidency Conclusions could not provide a formal legal basis for a transitional period—this could only be derived from the Treaty itself.

[34] The point might, of course, arise at a later date if a transitional period is adopted in relation to any other Member States which elect to move beyond the third stage. But in the light of the decisions in the *Berthu* cases which have been noted earlier, it is perhaps unlikely that the device could successfully be challenged.

[35] See Art 6(1) of Council Reg 974/98.

would continue to exist as "expressions" of the euro. What did this mean in practice? The essential consequences were as follows:

(a) With effect from 1 January 1999, national currency notes/coins were merely subdivisions or "representations" of the euro according to the appropriate conversion rates. This had necessarily to be the case, for the euro was now the *sole* currency of all of the participating Member States. If the old notes/coins continued to circulate, they could only constitute legal tender if they represented a subdivision of the euro in the manner just described, for legal tender must necessarily represent the monetary system of the State concerned.

(b) Part of the purpose of the transitional period was to allow businesses and consumers to accustom themselves to the new currency over an extended period. As a result, it had to be anticipated that parties would continue to contract by reference to the legacy currencies even after the transition period had begun. It was thus important to ensure that contracts written in legacy currencies and in the euro were treated on the same basis. For this purpose, it was provided that a contractual reference to national currency units "shall be as valid as if reference were made to the euro unit according to the conversion rates".[36]

(c) Leaving aside interbank and other financial markets, which generally moved to dealing in euros with effect from 1 January 1999, these arrangements also allowed many consumers and businesses operating in a purely domestic environment effectively to ignore the creation of the euro, up until the end of the transitional period. Prices continued to be quoted in the legacy currencies and obligations could be settled by payment of the corresponding amount in the notes/coins of the national currency concerned or, where appropriate, by a cheque or bank transfer denominated in that currency. Since the conversion rates as between the euro and the legacy currency had been irrevocably fixed, the parties could continue to agree prices and to settle them in the relevant national currency. There was no need to engage in a conversion exercise, because the quantum of the obligations expressed either in a legacy currency or the euro was legally equivalent to the corresponding amount in the other unit. As a result, parties may have been entering into contracts expressed in legacy currencies during the transitional period, and may have regarded themselves as entering into obligations by reference to those currencies. Yet, for the reasons given in (a) above, they were in fact undertaking obligations by reference to the euro unit itself.

(d) As a result of the above, a curious state of affairs prevailed during the

---

[36] Article 6(2).

transitional period. The euro was the sole currency of the participating, eurozone Member States, and yet no notes/coin expressed in euros were available during this period. By the same token, notes expressed to be denominated in German marks, French francs, and other legacy currencies continued to be used within their respective national boundaries,[37] even though the countries concerned had ceased to have an independent monetary system. In other words, the euro was the single currency of the participating Member States; national notes/coins continued to circulate, but only constituted *legal tender* because of their status as representations of the euro;

(e) This situation, in turn, gave rise to a further curiosity in that, during the transitional period: the monetary system of the participating Member States was governed by the Community laws which had created the euro but the identification of the chattels which constituted legal tender for such monetary obligations remained a matter for the national law of each individual eurozone Member State.[38] Likewise, rules relating to the identification of the national currency unit (and any subdivisions of it) remained in effect. In these narrow senses, it may be said that those individual States retained a degree of national monetary sovereignty up until the end of the transitional period. Thus, although French franc notes represented the euro, they did not become legal tender in Germany, even though the euro had also become the currency of the latter Member State.[39] Although a curious position, this was necessary to ensure that the euro could be introduced smoothly on 1 January 1999. Many practical difficulties would have ensued if each legacy had been made legal tender in all eurozone Member States. Nevertheless, the state of affairs described in this paragraph can only reinforce points made earlier in this work, namely, that the State theory of money can no longer depend upon the existence of a uniform system of physical notes and coins expressed in the currency concerned.[40]

(f) Given their uniform status as subdivisions and representations of the euro, it followed that the legacy currencies could not fluctuate in value against each other during the transitional period, even though the physical indicia of those separate currencies continued in circulation. In practical terms,

---

[37] The position stated in the text is confirmed by Art 9 of Reg 974/98.

[38] To this extent, a degree of monetary sovereignty rested with the participating Member States during the transitional period. This was the effect of Art 6(1) of Council Reg 974/98, which provided that "subject to the various provisions of this regulation the monetary law of the participating Member States shall continue to apply". This provision must have been directed, at least in part, towards the identification of legal tender.

[39] This point is confirmed by Arts 6(1) and 9 of Council Reg 974/98, which specifically allowed for the continuing application of national law in this area.

[40] On the State theory of money, see Ch 1 above.

it remained possible to purchase French francs with German marks throughout the transitional period; indeed, given the "territorial" status of the national currencies discussed in (d) above, it was frequently necessary to do so for travel and other purposes. But the rate of exchange between French francs and German marks could not fluctuate, and merely represented the cross-rate between these two currencies and the euro.[41] The "single currency" status of the different national notes was reinforced by the requirement for central banks to ensure that national currencies emanating from other eurozone Member States could be exchanged at their "par values", ie at the conversion rates adopted pursuant to the treaty, without any margin or spread between buying and selling rates.[42]

(g) As a result of the provisions summarised above, all cash transactions to be settled during the transitional period had to be settled in the notes/coins which represented the relevant legacy currency in the place of payment. In many senses, the euro itself was a form of money which could only be uniformly used across the eurozone in the form of a bank account or account transfer. At that time, there existed no banknotes representing the euro which could be used across national borders within the eurozone, and an exchange transaction thus remained necessary in order to meet such an obligation in cash.

Given that the legacy currencies effectively represented the euro during the transitional period,[43] it is also necessary to ask—which unit was to be used for the settlement of monetary obligations during the transitional period? The following points are relevant in this context: **29.19**

(1) the starting point was the "no compulsion-no prohibition" principle, which has already been discussed.[44] It was accepted that any positive obligation to use the euro unit could only be imposed by Community legislation.[45] Equally, however, Member States and contracting parties were free to use

---

[41] This point is noted in para (b) of the preamble to Reg 974/98, which refers to the "absence of exchange rate risk either between the euro unit and the national currency units or between those national currency units". See also Art 4 of Reg 1103/97, which deals with the calculation of national currency equivalents "through" the euro. This provision has already been noted at para 29.08(3) above.

[42] Guideline of the ECB on the implementation of Art 52 of the Statute of the European System of Central Banks and of the European Central Bank (ECB/1998/NP10), [2001] OJ L55/69.

[43] Or, to adopt the language of para (16) of the preamble to Council Reg 974/98, "the euro unit and the national currency units are units of the same currency".

[44] See para 28.13(7) above.

[45] See para (16) of the preamble to Reg 974/98, read together with Art 8(5) of that Regulation. An obligation to use the euro unit could only be imposed sparingly, given that no euro notes/coins were available during the transitional period.

the euro unit on a voluntary basis, whether in any legislation, contract, or other legal instrument.[46]

(2) As a result, it was generally expected that obligations which had been contracted (whether before or after 1 January 1999) by reference to a legacy currency unit would be settled by payment in that unit until the end of the transitional period. This position was reinforced by confirming that the substitution of the euro for participating currencies would not of itself alter the "denomination" of contracts which were in existence on the first day of the transitional period.[47] Thus, a contract entered into before the transitional period and expressed in French francs would remain denominated in francs during the transitional period itself, even though the franc had by then become a subdivision of the euro itself.

(3) Consistently with this position, a contract stipulating for payment in a legacy currency—whether entered into before or during the transitional period—would fall to be settled by payment in the national currency units concerned.[48] Equally, where a contract stipulated for payment in euros, the obligation had to be performed in euros and not in a legacy currency.[49] The parties were, however, to be free to use whichever means of settlement they chose, and the above rules would thus yield to any contrary provision agreed by the parties.[50]

(4) Despite the difficulties involved (bearing in mind the absence of physical euro notes/coins), there was nevertheless a desire to promote the use of the euro during the transitional period, to the extent possible as part of a process designed to familiarise the public with the new currency. In the absence of physical euro notes and coins it was clearly not possible to encourage the use of the euro in the context of cash transactions. Two specific means were therefore adopted (see points (5) and (6) below) in seeking to raise the profile of the new currency.

(5) The first method involved the use of the euro in transactions to be settled by way of bank transfer. Where a debtor was obliged to pay an amount expressed in legacy currency by crediting a bank account of the creditor within the issuing Member State, he had the option of remitting that amount either in the legacy currency concerned or in euros. Equally,

---

[46] See paras (10) and (11) of the preamble to Council Reg 974/98.

[47] Article 7 of Council Reg 974/98.

[48] ibid, Art 8(1), first sentence.

[49] ibid, Art 8(2), second sentence. Where parties had contracted by reference to the euro and payment was to fall due prior to the end of the transitional period, then (notwithstanding the difficulties with such a term discussed at para 7.10 above), it must have been an implied term of the contract that payment should be made by means of a bank transfer, for no physical euro banknotes/coins existed at that point.

[50] Article 8(2) of Council Reg 974/98.

however, where the obligation was expressed in euros and payable by credit to a bank account within a Member State, the debtor could remit either euros or the legacy currency of the Member State concerned. In either case, the receiving bank had to credit the relevant account in the currency in which it was denominated. Obviously, all of the transactions described in this paragraph had to be effected at the prescribed conversion rates.[51] It may be added that these provisions applied only where the debtor was obliged to discharge his obligation "by crediting an account of the creditor", so that no action was required on the part of the creditor; it was merely necessary for the debtor to procure the transfer of funds to the account concerned. It follows that this provision did not apply where payment was made by cheque delivered to the creditor, because further action on the creditor's part would be necessary to complete the payment. He would have to present the cheque to his bank for collection. Accordingly, where payment was to be made by cheque, the debtor had to draw the instrument on an account expressed in the unit in which the debt itself was expressed. The option to pay either in euros or the relevant legacy currency was thus not available in this type of case.

(6) The securities market was used as a more obvious means of raising the public profile of the new currency. Each participating Member State could redenominate its public debt, so that it would cease to be expressed in the relevant legacy currency and would instead be expressed in euros. Once a Member State had taken this step, then any entity which had issued debt in the relevant legacy currency could likewise generally redenominate its debt into euros.[52] The options were exercisable unilaterally by the debtors concerned, without reference to, or the consent of, the creditors in question.[53]

(7) Finally, it was confirmed that netting, set-off and similar arrangements applicable under the domestic law of individual Member States would apply to monetary obligations expressed in the euro or in a legacy currency.[54] In other words, an obligation expressed in French francs could be set off against a countervailing obligation expressed in euros, applying the relevant substitution rates. Once again, these consequences should follow naturally from the fact that the euro and the legacy currencies were but expressions or subdivisions of the same currency.

---

[51] On the points made in this paragraph, see Art 8(3) of Council Reg 974/98.

[52] On these points, see ibid, Art 8(4).

[53] In many cases this will have resulted in odd amounts following conversion. Individual Member States thus provided for the rounding of such amounts in such cases. For further discussion of some of the issues arising in this area, see Proctor, *The Euro and the Financial Markets—The Legal Impact of EMU* (Jordons, 1999) ch 7 and Bank of England, *Practical Issues arising from the Introduction of the Euro* (No 9, September 1998) 46–7.

[54] Article 8(6) of Reg 974/98.

29.20 It will be apparent from the above discussion that the three-year transitional period created a number of curiosities and anomalies. Yet these were perhaps inevitable given that a fairly lengthy transitional period was adopted, and no criticism of the transitional provisions is intended. On the contrary, the transitional rules appear to have worked well in practice and allowed for a timed and orderly introduction of the single currency throughout the eurozone Member States.

Euro banknotes and coins

29.21 With effect from 1 January 2002, the European Central Bank (ECB) and the central banks of participating Member States put into circulation euro-denominated banknotes.[55] Subject to short-term arrangements relating to the withdrawal of the legacy currencies, the euro banknotes became the only notes which could enjoy the status of legal tender within the eurozone Member States.[56] It should be appreciated that, whilst national central banks could issue euro banknotes, they could only do so with the prior consent of the ECB, which has the exclusive right to authorise such issues.[57] A decision of the ECB provides that eight per cent of banknotes should be issued by the ECB itself, whilst the national central banks issue the balance *pro rata* to their capital in the ECB.[58]

29.22 By contrast, coins denominated in euros and cents were to be issued by the Member States themselves, although once again this right was subject to prior authorisation by the ECB as to the volume of the issue. With a view to ensuring the smooth circulation of coins within the eurozone, it was necessary to pre-scribe, at the level of Community law, both the denominations and technical specifications of such coins.[59]

29.23 It may be appropriate to pause at this juncture, and to reflect that the transfer of national monetary sovereignty to the ECB had essentially become complete as

---

[55] The logistical arrangements for the issue of notes and coins were complex. They are dealt with in a Guideline of the ECB adopting certain provisions on the 2002 cash changeover (ECB/2001/01), [2001] OJ L55/80 and the Guideline of the ECB adopting certain provisions on the frontloading of euro banknotes outside the euro area (ECB/2001/8), [2001] OJ L2257/6.

[56] Article 10 of Reg 974/98.

[57] Article 106(1) of the EC Treaty and Art 16 of the Statute of the ESCB. It has rightly been pointed out that the Treaty does not define what is meant by "banknote issue", but that it must involve the issue of paper which: (a) creates a liability on the part of the issuing institution; (b) acts as a store of value; (c) represents the official unit of account; and (d) serves as a means of discharging debts—see Weenink, "The Legal Nature of Euro Banknotes" [2003] JIBLR 433.

[58] ECB Decision 2001/15, [2001] OJ L337/52.

[59] On this point, see Art 106(2) of the EC Treaty and Council Reg 975/98, which provides for coins in a range of denominations from one cent to two euros and includes the technical specifica-tions for such coins. It may be added that, subject to minor exceptions, no one is obliged to accept more than 50 such coins as part of a single payment—see Art 11 of Reg 974/98.

at 1 January 2002. Every participating Member State had lost the right to create or reorganise a national currency system with effect from 1 January 1999 and with it had lost the corresponding right to control monetary policy.[60] Now, it had lost the right to issue any form of money, except with prior authorisation from the ECB. This subject will be discussed in more depth in the context of monetary sovereignty.[61]

In the present context, it is necessary to consider the precise legal nature of the **29.24** euro banknotes and coins which have been put into circulation. This gives rise to questions of a more conceptual nature, which are by no means easy to answer. It has been noted elsewhere[62] that banknotes are to be regarded as a form of promissory note, with the consequence that the Bills of Exchange Act 1882 will apply to them, so far as appropriate. In a European context, however, it is necessary to treat such statements with some care. Writers in France, Germany, and the Netherlands have reached a different conclusion. Banknotes are not negotiable instruments in a private law sense; rather they are tokens of money exclusively governed by public monetary law which prescribes the form of legal tender. Accordingly, banknotes should be regarded as unique instruments which embody claims which are created and governed by public monetary law.[63] It is entirely unsurprising that English law should differ from the civil law approach to these matters; it is probably also fair to observe that the issue and legal effect of banknotes ought properly to be a matter of public law, and should not depend upon the terms of a statute which was essentially designed for the protection of rights of a private and commercial character. Nevertheless, these divergent theories do reveal a common thread; a banknote does represent a form of monetary claim. This naturally begs a further question; if the holder is a creditor in respect of a claim, then who is the debtor? In the case of a sterling note issued by the Bank of England, the question admits of no doubt. But which institution is the issuer of euro banknotes? The EC Treaty answers this question only indirectly. It provides that the ECB "shall have the exclusive right to *authorise* the issue of banknotes within the Community" but that "The ECB and the national central banks *may issue* such notes."[64] The Treaty thus

---

[60] This point is perhaps emphasised by the fact that eurozone central banks required an authority from the ECB to continue issuing their own, national currency notes during the transitional period. They were, however, given a general authorisation to continue issuing those banknotes in accordance with national practice—see the Guideline of the ECB on the authorisation to issue national banknotes during the transitional period (ECB/1999/NP11, [2001] OJ L55/71).

[61] See, generally, Ch 31 below.

[62] See para 1.56 above.

[63] On the points made in the last sentences, and for further references, see Weenink, "The Legal Nature of Euro Banknotes" [2003] JIBLR 433, 436–7.

[64] Article 106(1) of the EC Treaty, emphasis added.

contemplates that, subject to approval from the ECB, the national central banks of participating Member States may separately issue euro banknotes. If these banknotes represent liabilities of *separate* institutions, then how can the euro be regarded as a *single* currency?[65] A decision of the ECB on the issue of euro banknotes seeks to deal with this subject.[66]

29.25   The ECB Decision refers to Article 106 of the EC Treaty and the corresponding provision in the ESCB Statute, and rightly notes that "Community law has foreseen a system of plurality of issuers of banknotes". It then states that "the ECB and the NCBs shall issue euro banknotes".[67] Perhaps conscious of the conceptual difficulty noted above, the Decision then states that "Euro banknotes are expressions of the same and single currency and subject to a single legal regime."[68] The Decision warms to its single currency theme, noting that "No distinction is to be made between banknotes of the same denomination"[69] that "all euro banknotes should be subject to identical acceptance and processing requirements by the Eurosystem members irrespective of which put them into circulation".[70] and that "euro banknotes are legal tender in all participating Member States, will freely circulate within the euro area [and] will be reissued by members of the Eurosystem".[71] The Decision then acknowledges that the liabilities in respect of issued banknotes should be allocated between the ECB and the Eurosystem central banks; it provides that the ECB will issue eight per cent of the notes in circulation, and that the balance will be issued by the national central banks pro rata to their shares in the issued share capital of the ECB.[72] Each central bank thus separately shows in its balance sheet as a liability the total face amount of euro banknotes issued by it.[73] It may thus become tempting to suggest that the euro is not a *single* currency in the strict sense, because it is separately issued by different central banks. But this point is satisfactorily addressed by Article 3 of the Decision, which provides for all central

---

[65] That the euro should be so regarded is obvious, and was the major objective of monetary union. The point is made apparent in various provisions of the Treaty—see, eg, Art 121(3).

[66] Decision of 6 December 2001 (ECB/2001/15, [2001] OJ L337/52). It should be mentioned that details of this Decision were amended by a further ECB decision amending Decision ECB/2001/15 on the issue of euro banknotes (ECB/2004/9, [2004] OJ L205/17), but the revisions are not material in the present context.

[67] See Recital (1) to the Decision.

[68] ibid, Recital (2).

[69] ibid, Recital (4).

[70] ibid, Recital (5).

[71] ibid, Recital (7).

[72] ibid, Recital (7) read with Art 4 of the Decision.

[73] On the accounting implications of these arrangements, see Weenink, "The Legal Nature of Euro Banknotes" [2003] JIBLR 433, 435.

banks within the Eurosystem to accept euro banknotes at the request of the holder, regardless of the identity of the issuing institution.[74]

Finally, it is necessary to add a few points about counterfeit notes.[75] Article 12 of **29.26** Regulation 974/98 requires participating Member States to ensure adequate sanctions against counterfeiting and falsification of euro notes and coins. Although the requirement is in terms directed only to *participating* Member States, the obligation has in effect also been extended to the United Kingdom and other "out" Member States by regulations made in reliance on Article 308 of the EC Treaty.[76] Now, it has been noted previously,[77] that States are generally subject to an international obligation to punish those who (within the boundaries of that State) seek to counterfeit the currency of another State. The scope of that obligation is reasonably clear, but it was nevertheless felt necessary to introduce a defined Community-based legal framework to address the problem. No doubt, this was in some measure due to official sensitivities surrounding the introduction of euro notes and coins, and was partly due to the opportunities for counterfeiting presented by the introduction of a new currency over such a large geographical area. It is unnecessary to examine the relevant legal framework in great depth; much of it deals with the establishment of agencies involved in supervising the fight against counterfeit currency[78] and for the co-ordination of the separate efforts of Member States in this area.[79] Notably, Member States were requested to ensure that banknote design benefited from copyright protection under national law.[80] Credit institutions, bureaux de

---

[74] Article 3(2) of the Decision provides that "NCBs shall accept all euro banknotes on the request of the holder for exchange against euro banknotes of the same value." whilst Art 3(3) requires that the NCBs "shall treat all euro banknotes accepted by them as liabilities and process them in an identical manner". This requirement—coupled with the legal tender status of all euro banknotes throughout the Community—leads to the conclusion that all euro banknotes form a part of a single currency system, regardless of the identity of the particular Eurosystem central bank which issued them.

[75] On the whole subject, see Weenink (n 73 above) 276.

[76] See Council Reg 1338/2001 and 1339/2001, reflecting a Council Decision to the effect that effective criminal sanctions were required in this context—see [2000] OJ L140/1. The Regulations are implemented in the UK by The Protection of the Euro against Counterfeiting Regulations, 2001 (SI 3948/2001).

[77] See Ch 21 above.

[78] eg the Counterfeiting Analysis Centre established by the ECB Guildeline of 26 August 1998, on certain provisions regarding euro banknotes, as amended on 26 August 1999, [1999] OJ L258/32.

[79] See, eg, Arts 7, 8, and 9 of Council Reg 1338/2001. See also the co-operation agreement between the ECB and the European Police Office (EUROPOL) dated 13 December 2001, [2003] OJ C23/9.

[80] See the Recommendation of the ECB regarding the adoption of certain measures to enhance the legal protection of euro banknotes (ECB/1998/7, [1999] OJ C11/13). For a case in which a commercial organisation unsuccessfully argued that the use of the euro symbol infringed trade marks registered in the name of that organisation, see Case T–195/00 *Travelex Global and Financial Services v EC Commission* [2003] ECR II–1677.

change, and other entities are required to withdraw from circulation any euro notes/coins believed to be counterfeit, and to hand them over to national authorities.[81] In closing on this topic, it may be noted that the anti-counterfeiting framework seeks to take advantage of some pre-existing procedures in international law, through Article 12 of the Convention for the Suppression of Counterfeiting Currency (1929).[82]

Final provisions

29.27   The closing Articles of Council Regulation (EC) 974/98 address two substantive issues, and one technical provision also dealt with the withdrawal of the legacy currencies. Dealing firstly with the two substantive issues:

(1)   With effect from the end of the transitional period, it will be appreciated that all new contracts involving a monetary obligation should be expressed in euros (as opposed to a legacy currency). A reference to "French francs" in a contract made on or after 1 January 2002 would plainly be inappropriate, since France no longer possesses a *lex monetae* which is independent of that of the other participating Member States and the French franc had at that point ceased to be a subdivision of the euro.[83] Whilst the *lex monetae* principle could no doubt be applied in the usual way in relation to legacy currency contracts executed *before* 1 January 2001, it was nevertheless felt appropriate explicitly to state this point in the legal framework itself. Consequently, it is confirmed that a reference to a legacy currency in a legal instrument in existence before 1 January 2001, will be read as a reference to the euro at the appropriate substitution rate.[84]

(2)   It has been noted earlier that Regulation 974/98 was made in reliance on Article 123(4) of the EC Treaty, and that this provision applied only to *participating* Member States. The Regulation acknowledges this point and confirms that its territorial scope is similarly limited.[85]

29.28   The technical provisions dealing with the physical withdrawal of the legacy currencies are now of essentially historical interest. National banknotes/coins could remain in circulation until 30 June 2002 and could continue to be used in accordance with the respective national law until that point; but in practice,

---

[81]   See Art 6 of Council Reg 1338/2001. Member States were required to impose sanctions on organisations which failed to comply with this requirement. The UK has complied with this obligation through the introduction of The Protection of the Euro against Counterfeiting Regulations 2001 (SI 3948/2001).

[82]   Reference has already been made to this Convention—see para 20.06 above.

[83]   The combined effect of Arts 5 and 6 of Reg 974/98 was to confer upon the legacy currencies the status of a subdivision of the euro, but only until the end of the transitional period.

[84]   See Art 14 of Reg 974/98.

[85]   See Art 17 of Council Reg 974/98.

Member States undertook to complete the changeover by 28 February 2002.[86] In addition, central banks and other issuers were to continue to accept the banknotes and coins previously issued by them in accordance with the laws of the Member State concerned.[87]

D. Council Regulation 2866/98

The final major legal step in the creation of the euro came on 31 December 1998, with the fixing of the rates at which the euro would be substituted for the participating currencies. As noted previously, in fixing the rates, the Council was required to act on a proposal from the Commission and after consulting the European Central Bank.[88] The substitution rates prescribed by Article 1 of the Regulation are as follows:

29.29

one euro =	40.3399	Belgian francs
	1.95583	German marks
	166.386	Spanish pesetas
	6.55957	French francs
	0.787564	Irish pounds
	1,936.27	Italian lire
	40.3399	Luxembourg francs
	2.20371	Dutch guilders
	13.7603	Austrian schillings
	200.482	Portuguese escudos
	5.94573	Finnish marks

Article 2 of the Regulation states that it "shall be binding in its entirety and directly applicable in all Member States . . .". Yet this statement is only accurate in so far as it relates to the participating Member States. Apart from the other considerations, the legal basis of the Regulation is Article 123(4) of the Treaty and, as we have seen, this provision does not apply in the United Kingdom.[89] Nevertheless, the United Kingdom and its courts are bound to recognise both the creation of the euro and the prescribed substitution rates.[90] The present regulation thus defines the conversion rates to be used in applying the theory of the "recurrent link".

29.30

---

[86] On these points, see ibid, Art 15.

[87] ibid, Art 16.

[88] For the opinion of the ECB, see [1998] OJ C412/1.

[89] See para 29.06 above.

[90] This follows from the application of the *lex monetae* principle. On the application of this principle in the present context, see para 30.03 below. In view of these points, it would seem that the court of first instance in *Virani Ltd v Manuel Revert y Cia SA* (CA, 18 July 2003) may have fallen into error when it remarked that "the original contract stipulated a price in pesetas. The peseta of course is no longer currency which is in use since Spain joined the single currency at a

29.31　It may be added that, subsequently, Greece was found to have satisfied the "Maastricht Criteria" for admission to the eurozone.[91] Regulation 2866/98 was thereupon amended to provide that one euro should also equal 340.750 Greek drachmas.[92] In accordance with these arrangements, Greece thus became a eurozone Member State with effect from 1 January 2001.

29.32　The legal basis for the creation of the euro and its consequences have been reviewed in some depth. It is now necessary to consider in more detail the impact of the single currency on contractual obligations of a monetary character.

---

fixed euro [rate] . . . The sale . . . was expressed in euros. There is to some degree a difficulty in making a practical conversion between pesetas at the time when it was fluctuating and its equivalent in euros after Spain joined the EU." The last reference should clearly be to the eurozone rather than the EU. In the light of the points made in the text, there should have been no difficulty in establishing the peseta/euro substitution rate. It may be, however, that the court was in fact referring to the difficulty of identifying the appropriate exchange rate between those two units and the US dollar, which was also relevant to the case before the Court.

[91] See Council Decision of 19 June 2000, [2000] OJ L167/19. See also para 32.35 n 78.

[92] For the amending Regulation, see Council Reg 1478/2000 of 19 June 2000, [2000] OJ L167/1. On a proposal to consolidate the regulations dealing with the conversion rules, see an Opinion of the ECB dated 31 March 2004 (CON/2004/10, [2004] OJ C88/20).

30

MONETARY UNION AND
MONETARY OBLIGATIONS

A. Introduction

It has been noted earlier[1] that a monetary obligation cannot be frustrated; **30.01**
performance of such an obligation may be suspended in certain cases[2] but it
cannot be rendered objectively impossible, even if the monetary unit in which it
was originally expressed has ceased to exist. It is, however, to be noted that
monetary union in Europe involved the effective disappearance of eleven
national currencies with effect from 1 January 1999[3] As noted earlier, the physical indicia of those currencies remained in circulation until the early part of
2002, but during this transitional period, they were "subdivisions" or "representations" of the euro. The substitution of the euro thus involved a very large
economic area and was achieved in the context of advanced economies and
against the background of very sophisticated financial and banking systems.
Whilst, ultimately, the question was for certain purposes resolved by legislation,

---

[1] See para 3.06 above.

[2] eg by means of legislation or a moratorium which (in each case) forms a part of the law
applicable to the obligation itself.

[3] As noted previously, a twelfth currency, the Greek drachma, was subsumed into the euro with
effect from 1 January 2001.

it is appropriate to consider whether the substitution of so many convertible and internationally traded currencies could have had the effect of frustrating or otherwise terminating contracts which were expressed in the legacy currencies, and which had been entered into before the creation of the single currency had been contemplated or agreed.[4] This point was of significant importance in the international bond markets, where obligations may frequently be contracted with maturities of twenty or more years—bonds issued during the 1980s or even during the early 1990s would not have contemplated the introduction of a substitute currency within such a relatively short time frame. But the point could be of equal importance in the context of any long-term contract expressed in a legacy currency and which "spanned" the introduction of the euro; and matters were further complicated by the existence of certain types of contract which were intended to create a "hedge" between different participating currencies, and which could thus be said to presuppose the continuing availability of the separate national currencies. Apart from the issues which are specific to the single currency itself, the episode carries lessons which are of general relevance in the context of currency substitutions.[5]

30.02 Whilst monetary union offered many important lessons in this area, it is important to retain a sense of proportion about the scope and extent of the principles about to be discussed. For the most part, these would apply only to contracts entered into before 1 January 1999 and which contained payment obligations which had to be performed after that date. In other words, the present discussion is principally concerned with legacy currency contracts (hereafter, "transitional contracts") which spanned the changeover period. It should not, however, be thought that the points about to be discussed are of purely historical interest; they will become relevant again as and when further Member States move to the third stage of economic and monetary union, and their national currencies are thus subsumed into the euro. Against this background, it is proposed to consider the following matters:

(a) the termination of contracts before the English courts;

---

[4] In view of the remarks contained in the opening paragraph of this chapter, the answer to this question should, in principle, be in the negative. However, the scale of the EMU project requires that the point be investigated and verified.

[5] It may be added that the impact of monetary union on monetary obligations generated much discussion during the period leading up to the creation of the euro but, so far as the present writer is aware, the debate was principally driven by market practitioners. The wider question appears to have generated limited academic interest which is perhaps unsurprising but is nevertheless disappointing, for a clear analysis of the issues might have laid to rest any fear that the introduction of the euro might lead to the termination of contractual obligations. In his illuminating book, *The Law of Money and Financial Services in the European Community* (Oxford University Press, 2nd edn, 1999), Professor Usher deals in detail with the transition from national currencies to the euro (ch 7) but unfortunately only briefly considers the contractual issues (p 166).

(b)   the termination of contracts before foreign courts;

(c)   the impact of the euro on fixed and variable interest rates; and

(d)   the position of obligations expressed in the private ECU.

B. Termination and the English Courts

As noted elsewhere, every State enjoys sovereignty over the organisation of its national monetary system. As a result, it may change the unit of account and provide for a "recurrent link" between the old and the new currencies, ie it may stipulate that debts *expressed* in the old currency may be restated and *settled* in the new currency at a stated rate of conversion. These rules are ultimately derived from the *lex monetae* principle, under which questions touching the identity of the currency, its status as legal tender, and the substitution of the national monetary system are ascribed to the law of the issuing State.[6] Since the *lex monetae* principle enjoys universal recognition, it follows that the English courts must give effect to those provisions of the euro legal framework[7] which provide for the creation of the single currency, which ascribe to it the status of legal tender, and which provide the conversion rates for participating national currencies. However, provisions dealing with the continued enforceability of contracts do not form part of the *lex monetae*; such questions must be dealt with by reference to the law applicable to the contract.[8] It has been suggested in some quarters that the creation of the euro has in some respects broadened the scope of the *lex monetae* principle, and that the Community provisions for the enforceability of contracts should thus be recognised and applied by foreign courts even when the contract concerned is governed by a third system of law.[9] This position cannot be accepted; whether or not a contract remains enforceable following a change in circumstances is a question which all systems of private international law ascribe to that system of law which governs the obligation as a whole.[10]

30.03

Nevertheless, it must be recognised that monetary union in Europe was a major initiative in the monetary field. It involved a number of States whose currencies

30.04

---

[6]   On the *lex monetae* principle, see para 13.03 above.

[7]   The relevant EC Regulations have been considered in Ch 29 above.

[8]   As noted earlier, the contractual continuity provision in Art 3 of Council Reg 1103/97 forms a part of English law by reason of this country's membership of the European Community.

[9]   This attempt is perhaps reflected in para (8) of the preamble to Council Reg 1103/97 which reads:

> Whereas the introduction of the euro constitutes a change in the monetary law of each participating Member State; whereas the recognition of the monetary law of a State is a universally accepted principle; whereas the explicit recognition of the principle of continuity should lead to the recognition of continuity of contracts and other legal instruments in the jurisdiction of third countries.

[10]   This principle is reflected in Art 10(1)(d) of the Rome Convention on the law applicable to contractual obligations.

were (to a greater or lesser extent) freely traded on international markets. Monetary union also occurred at a time when financial contracts of a fairly sophisticated nature—including derivatives, currency, and interest rate options—were created and traded in many centres on a daily basis. Under these circumstances, it was necessary to ask whether the substitution of the euro for so many major currencies might have broader or deeper consequences than those which had applied in the context of earlier monetary changes. In particular, there was a fear that contracts of an essentially financial character might be frustrated or otherwise terminated by the introduction of the euro.[11]

30.05 Against this rather general background, it is necessary to consider a variety of issues which the English courts would have to decide if a party sought to claim that the substitution of the euro for the participating national currencies had the effect of terminating a contract which was expressed in one of the legacy currencies or which had assumed the continuing and separate existence of those currencies. In particular, it would be necessary to consider (a) which system of law governs the contract at hand and (b) the consequences of the introduction of the euro under that system of law, be it English or a foreign system of law.

The applicable law

30.06 The terms and effect of the Rome Convention on the law applicable to contractual obligations have already been considered.[12] It is thus not necessary to repeat the process which the court must undertake in order to identify the law applicable to a particular contract. It is merely necessary to record that:

(a) whether or not a contract has validly come into existence is a question essentially to be determined by reference to the applicable law;[13]

(b) if a contact has come into existence, then the question of the extinction or termination of that contract is likewise governed by the applicable law.[14]

30.07 How, then, could the introduction of the euro affect contracts, entered into before the beginning of the third stage of monetary union, which are expressed in a legacy currency and contain monetary obligations to be performed after the beginning of that third stage? In broader terms, it would appear that the *validity*

---

[11] The point was an early and serious concern for the Bank of England in planning for the introduction of the euro and its consequences for the financial markets—see *Bank of England, Practical Issues arising from the Introduction of the Euro No 2* (September 1996). For reasons which will be discussed in this section, it is suggested that the fears expressed by the Bank of England and other financial market associations were largely unfounded; the legal principles required to deal with monetary union in a contractual context were already embedded in English law.

[12] See Ch 4 above.

[13] Rome Convention, Art 8(1).

[14] ibid, Art 10(1)(d).

of the contract might be challenged on the basis that the continued and separate existence of particular legacy currencies was a fundamental assumption of the parties. The *continuity* of the contract may be challenged on the basis that the introduction of the euro constituted a fundamental change of circumstances, with the result that the parties should not be held to their bargain. The resolution of both of these questions is assigned to the law applicable to the contract.

English law—general principles

What, then, is the position if the court finds the transitional contract to be governed by English law? It seems that a party could seek to impugn the essential *validity* of the contract on the basis that it was concluded on the footing of a common mistake or misapprehension, ie that the relevant legacy currency would continue to exist. The *continuity* of the contract may be attacked on the grounds that the introduction of the euro is a new and supervening event, which ought to lead to the frustration of the contract. **30.08**

As to the first possibility, it must be said that the law on the subject of common mistake is by no means free from difficulty.[15] But it does seem clear that a contract governed by English law is to be treated as void *ab initio* if (a) it was entered into on the basis of a particular contractual assumption; (b) that assumption was fundamental to the validity of the contract or was a foundation of its existence; and (c) that assumption proves to have been untrue.[16] Could the continued existence of a particular legacy currency be said to constitute a fundamental assumption upon which the contract was based? In virtually every case, this question must necessarily be answered in the negative. Money provides both the measure of an obligation and the means by which that obligation may be satisfied. Where a reorganisation of the relevant monetary system occurs during the lifetime of a contract, the *lex monetae* principle is applied so that the contractual obligations can be redenominated, recalculated, and performed as appropriate. To put matters another way, the parties may have assumed that France will have a lawful currency and that monetary obligations may be settled in Paris; but the assumption that such currency would at all times be labelled the "French franc" cannot be regarded as fundamental.[17] It follows that the **30.09**

---

[15] See, eg, *Chitty on Contracts* (Sweet and Maxwell, 29th edn, 2004) ch 5.

[16] The leading decision in this area remains *Bell v Lever Brothers Ltd* [1932] AC 161. For later examples, see *Associated Japanese Bank International Ltd v Credit du Nord SA* [1989] 1 WLR 255; and *The Great Peace* [2003] QB 679.

[17] This discussion assumes that the monetary aspects of the contract refer exclusively to money as a means of payment. It will be necessary to revisit this point (below) when considering specific forms of financial contract although, as will be seen, the essential result is the same.

introduction of the euro could not have formed the basis of a challenge to the initial validity of a contract on the grounds of common mistake.

30.10   A contract expressed in a legacy currency was thus valid and binding from the outset; but could the introduction of the euro have the effect of terminating the contract? Could the English law doctrine of frustration apply to a transitional contract, solely because of the substitution of the euro for the legacy currency or currencies in which that contract was expressed? In order to answer this question, it is necessary to formulate the tests which must be met in order to invoke the doctrine, and then seek to apply those tests to a transitional contract. In considering this subject, it is necessary to remember that English law sets great store by the enforceability of the contractual bargain.[18] Whilst the doctrine of frustration exists in order to mitigate the injustice which might follow from the literal enforcement of contracts in changed circumstances and thus reach a fair and reasonable result as between the parties, nevertheless the doctrine should not be lightly invoked and must be confined within narrow limits.[19] In other words, the doctrine of frustration should be applied with restraint, because it detracts from the sanctity of the contractual bond. These formulations perhaps set out the state of mind with which one should approach the subject, but it is now necessary to examine the specific tests in more detail.

30.11   The modern law on the subject of frustration was outlined by the House of Lords in *Davis Contractors Ltd v Fareham UDC*.[20] A contract may be frustrated[21] if all of the following criteria are met:

(1)   a change in circumstances relevant to the contract has occurred since the date on which the contract was made;

(2)   the change in circumstances is outside the control of the parties;

(3)   the contract does not provide for the changed circumstances which have arisen;

(4)   the change in circumstances was not anticipated or foreseen by the parties at the time of the contract; and

(5)   as a result of that change, performance of the contract in accordance with

---

[18] "It is of paramount importance that contracts should be observed", *Bell v Lever Brothers Ltd* [1932] AC 161, 224 *per* Lord's Atkin.

[19] On these points, see the speech of Bingham LJ in *J Launtzen AS v Wijsmuller BV (The Super Servant Two)* [1990] 1 Lloyd's Rep 1.

[20] [1956] AC 696. The tests formulated in that case have subsequently been upheld by the courts on a number of occasions—see, eg, *Paal Wilson & Co A/S v Partenreederei Hannah Blumenthal* [1983] 1 AC 854 and cases there noted.

[21] As a general rule, it should be appreciated that the doctrine of frustration operates to terminate a contract in its entirety; it cannot be applied merely to individual obligations within that contract. This conclusion is inferentially supported by the language of s 1 of the Law Reform (Frustrated Contracts) Act 1943. On this general subject, and on the possibility of "partial" frustration, see *Chitty on Contracts* (Sweet and Maxwell, 29th edn, 2004) para 23-064.

its stated terms would be unlawful or impossible or would otherwise be radically different from that contemplated by the parties when the contract was originally made.

If a contract governed by English law is found to have been frustrated, then the contract is terminated automatically and neither party is obliged to perform any of the obligations expressed to arise after the occurrence of the frustrating event.[22] If necessary, the court can order various payments as between the parties in an effort to secure fairness in their respective positions.[23] This point is, however, noted purely for the sake of completeness. As will be seen, in the view of the present writer, the doctrine of frustration could not have been invoked in relation to any transitional contract merely as a consequence of the substitution of the euro for the participating national currencies.   **30.12**

Returning, then, to the basic theme—could the criteria listed in points (1) to (5) of para 30.11 above be said to be met in the context of transitional contracts? The points noted in points (1), (2), (3), and (4) can be disposed of rapidly, and we will then return to the more crucial test noted in point (5).   **30.13**

First of all, the test outlined in point (1) above would inevitably be met in the case of a transitional contract. Such a contract involves monetary obligations expressed in a legacy currency which would cease to exist in consequence of the introduction of the euro. The creation of the single currency is clearly a supervening event which is relevant to the bargain originally made between the parties.   **30.14**

As far as point (2) is concerned, the doctrine of frustration can apply only if the introduction of monetary union was beyond the control of the contracting parties. In other words, a contracting party which is itself responsible for the relevant change in circumstances will not be able to invoke the doctrine.[24] This test will so obviously be met that it is hardly necessary to explore it further. Even where an individual, participating Member State is party to the contract concerned, it cannot be argued that it bears *sole* responsibility for the creation of the single currency   **30.15**

The test outlined in point (3) above is self-explanatory. Occasionally, parties may anticipate a possible change in circumstances and will provide for it in their   **30.16**

---

[22] On this point see, eg, *J Lauritzen AS v Wijsmuller BV (The Super Servant Two)* [1990] 1 Lloyd's Rep 1.

[23] See the Law Reform (Frustrated Contracts) Act 1943, discussed in *Chitty on Contracts* (Sweet and Maxwell, 29th edn, 2004) para 23-072.

[24] See, eg, *Bank Line Ltd v Arthur Capel & Co* [1919] AC 435; *Joseph Constantine SS Line Ltd v Imperial Smelting Corp Ltd* [1942] AC 154; and *J Lauritzen AS v Wijsmuller BV (The Super Servant Two)* [1990] I Lloyd's Rep 1.

contract. Provided that, on a proper interpretation, the contract covers those circumstances, then the contract will not be frustrated—it will remain in effect, to be performed in accordance with the terms agreed by the parties.[25] During the period leading up to monetary union, there was much uncertainty concerning the EMU project and many doubted the political will to see the project through to completion. Equally, many were doubtful about the likely external value of the euro. As a result of these concerns, some transactions completed during this period specifically provided that the legacy currency obligation would be converted into a third currency (usually US dollars) if the euro came into existence. Sophisticated contractual clauses were created in order to deal with these requirements. Whether these were necessary or desirable may be a matter for debate, but there seems to be no doubt that the English courts would enforce such a contractual provision in accordance with its stated terms.[26]

30.17 The application of the test noted in point (4) above is rather more problematical. If the introduction of the euro was foreseeable at the time the parties entered into their contract, then the subsequent introduction of the single currency could not have the effect of frustrating the contract. The key question, then is—at what point of time did the introduction of the euro become foreseeable for these purposes? Given that we are here concerned with contracts governed by English law *and* which were expressed in a legacy currency, it is perhaps safe to assume that the parties have sufficient knowledge of the European political scene.[27] On that basis, at what point of time did the creation of the euro become a foreseen event? The point would be important because contracts entered into *after* that date could not be frustrated on the grounds that the single currency was indeed subsequently created. It could be said that the publication of the Delors Report in 1989 gave adequate advance notice of the single currency for these purposes. However, this must be doubtful because the Delors Report did not specifically require the creation of a single currency; it contemplated that separate national currencies could continue to exist within the framework of a monetary union.[28] The Delors Report was thus not a sufficiently unequivocal signal for these purposes.[29] Likewise, it may be argued that the

---

[25] On this point, see *Joseph Constantine SS Line Ltd v Imperial Smelting Corp Ltd* [1942] AC 154.

[26] In any event, Council Reg 1103/97 specifically preserves the principle of freedom of contract in this context, and thus allowed parties to agree such contractual provisions as they may have thought appropriate—see in particular the final sentence of Art 2(1) of that Regulation. It will be recalled that this Regulation forms a part of English law, notwithstanding the UK's opt-out. On this subject, see para 29.03 above.

[27] The test of a foreseen event appears to be subjective to the parties as opposed to an objective test—see *Chitty on Contracts* (Sweet and Maxwell, 29th edn, 2004) para 23-058.

[28] On these aspects of the Delors Report, see Ch 29 above.

[29] This conclusion is only reinforced when one considers the fate of the predecessor report produced by M. Pierre Werner.

introduction of the euro became foreseeable on 7 February 1992, when the Treaty on European Union was signed and the broad framework for the single currency project was thus established. However, in the view of the present writer, the correct date for these purposes would be 30 November 1993, at which point the Treaty on European Union came into effect following its ratification by all Member States. At that point, aspiring eurozone Member States had agreed to make the transfers of national monetary sovereignty which would be necessary to achieve monetary union. Although the analysis would inevitably be subject to factual situations arising in particular cases, it is thus suggested, in the most general terms, that (a) the creation of the single currency was an event which contracting parties would have foreseen from 30 November 1993 and (b) on that ground, contracts entered into after that date were not amenable to the doctrine of frustration as a result of the creation of the single currency. One cannot, however, dismiss the application of frustration to transitional contracts generally on this ground, partly because the foregoing conclusions are of a tentative nature and partly because some contracts would pre-date whichever event is chosen for "foreseeability" purposes.

It thus remains to consider the test outlined in para 30.11, point (5)—did the introduction of the single currency render the performance of a transitional contract either unlawful, impossible, or radically different from that contemplated by the parties? Given that the criteria listed in points (1), (2), (3), and (4) have been met or have been assumed, in certain cases, to have been met, it follows that a transitional contract could have been affected by the doctrine of frustration, if the point (5) criterion were also met. **30.18**

So far as English law is concerned, the introduction of the euro plainly did not render the performance of a transitional contract unlawful. On the contrary, English law was required to respect and give positive effect to the introduction of the euro, for the reasons described later in this section. Likewise, it cannot be said that the performance of the monetary obligations arising under a transitional contract became "impossible" as a result of the substitution of the euro for the legacy currencies. It may be that this involved a decision as to the amount required to be paid in the single currency, but the substitution rates were clearly set out in the relevant legislation,[30] and a purely mathematical calculation is all that is required. The theory of the "recurrent link" is clearly applicable in this type of case.[31] **30.19**

It thus remains to ask—did the introduction of the single currency render **30.20**

---

[30] The legal framework for the introduction of the euro has already been discussed in Ch 29 above.

[31] On the "recurrent link", see the discussion at para 2.34 above.

the performance of the contract "radically different" from that originally contemplated by the contracting parties? Whilst it was relatively easy to decide whether performance had become "unlawful" or "impossible"—because those tests involve a significant degree of objectivity—the application of the "radically different" test poses rather more difficulty. Whilst still, in theory, an objective test, the application of this test is rather more difficult since it involves a large measure of appreciation.

30.21   Viewed against this background, it is suggested that the substitution of the euro for national currencies could not result in the operation of the doctrine of frustration, because performance of the monetary obligation in euros would not be "radically different" from payment in the legacy currency concerned. There are several reasons for this view, including the following:

(a)   Perhaps most fundamentally, a contractual obligation to pay a given amount in a specific currency connotes an obligation to pay the nominal amount of the debt in those units of account which constitute legal tender under the *lex monetae* on the date on which payment is due to be made. This reflects the principle of nominalism, which has already been discussed in some detail.[32] Now, there can be no doubt that the provisions for substitution of the euro in place of the legacy currencies[33] would constitute a part of the *lex monetae* of the participating Member States. Those provisions are directly applicable in those Member States;[34] they operate to define the entirely new monetary system which was introduced throughout the eurozone Member States. Following the introduction of the euro, a payment obligation expressed in a legacy currency can be settled by payment of the corresponding amount in euros at the prescribed conversion rate.[35] Based upon this analysis and bearing in mind that the principle of nominalism operates as an implied term of the contract,[36] it becomes apparent that the Court—by ordering payment in euros—would be enforcing the contract *in accordance with its terms*. Not only has performance of the monetary obligation *not* become "radically different", it remains, in law, the *same* monetary obligation. It necessarily follows that the substitution of the euro for national currencies could never cause the frustration of a transitional contract.

(b)   Given the conclusion noted in point (a) above, it is unnecessary to consider

---

[32] See, generally, Part III above.
[33] See in particular Council Reg 974/98, Arts 2, 3, and 8(i) and Council Reg 2866/98, Art 1, prescribing the applicable substitution rates. Similarly, Council Reg 1478/2000 prescribing the substitution rate for the Greek drachma, would form a part of Greek monetary law.
[34] See Council Reg 974/98, Art 17, and Council Reg 1103/97, Art 6.
[35] The prescribed conversion rates have been noted at para 29.29 above.
[36] On this point see para 9.23 above.

other points in great depth. However, there are various other considerations which would prevent the frustration of a contract expressed in a legacy currency under these circumstances. First of all, international law obliges the United Kingdom (including its courts) to recognise the monetary sovereignty of other States, including their right to substitute their national currency units.[37] That obligation must have substance and must go beyond the mere passive acknowledgement that a country has changed its monetary unit; in order to fulfil that obligation, the courts must give effect to the monetary substitution by reference to the recurrent link established by the legislator.[38] It would be curious if the English courts claimed to "recognise" the monetary substitution whilst at the same time holding that such substitution led to the frustration of obligations expressed in the former unit— this would in effect amount to denial of the monetary sovereignty of the first State.[39] In other words, if the court recognises the currency substitution on the basis of the *lex monetae* principle, then the possibility of invoking the doctrine of frustration in reliance upon that substitution is effectively foreclosed. In the view of the present writer, the English courts would be acting inconsistently with the international obligations of the United Kingdom, were they to hold that a contract was frustrated as a result of the substitution of the legacy currency in which it was expressed.[40] Secondly, even if it could be established that the introduction of the euro rendered performance of a contract more expensive—a highly doubtful factual proposition[41]—a mere increase in cost is not a supervening event sufficient to frustrate a contract.[42] Finally, the introduction of the euro may affect the *mode of performance* of a legacy currency obligation, but it does

---

[37] On this point, see the *Serbian and Brazilian Loans Cases* (1929) PCIJ Series A, Nos 20–21, discussed at para 19.02 above.

[38] The general point has already been discussed at para 2.34 above.

[39] It is true that the monetary laws invariably have a public character but their recognition and application cannot be denied on the basis that the well-known principle in *Government of India v Taylor* [1995] AC 491 for the continued enforcement of a monetary obligation which has previously been contracted does not equate to the enforcement of the foreign public law. The point has previously been discussed at para 13.05 above.

[40] A foreign monetary law (like any other foreign law) can be disregarded by the English courts on cogent grounds of public policy—see para 4.22 above. But, given the UK's membership of the Community, the public policy arguments run entirely in the opposite direction.

[41] Indeed, for reasons given below, it is suggested that the English courts could not even embark upon a line of enquiry designed to show that a legacy currency was over-or undervalued as compared with the euro.

[42] *Davis Contractors Ltd v Fareham UDC* [1956] AC 696 HL. The position appears to be, the same in the US—see, *Transatlantic Financing Corp v US* (1996) 363 F 2d 312. Of course, the cost of performance cannot be completely divorced from performance itself, and there will be a point at which the increase in such cost leads to the frustration of the contract—*Asphalt International Inc v Enterprise Shipping Corp* (1981) 667 F 2d 261, but this point can have no application in the present context.

not affect the *substance* of the obligation. The doctrine of frustration does not generally apply under such circumstances.[43]

It follows that—applying well-established principles—transitional contracts governed by English law could not be frustrated solely as a result of the substitution of the euro for the legacy currency in which contractual obligations were originally expressed.

30.22　In view of the conclusions just stated, it would be possible to close the present discussion at this point. However, given the Community context of the present subject, it is perhaps appropriate to note that other, broader considerations would have prevented the English courts from applying the doctrine of frustration to this type of case.

30.23　Although not (yet) a participant in monetary union, the United Kingdom is a member of the European Community and was a party to the Treaty on European Union. Since that Treaty is the ultimate source of the single currency, it might be anticipated that the United Kingdom has some obligations in relation to it. This expectation is borne out by an examination of the Treaty on European Union and the amendments which it made to the EC Treaty.

30.24　In specific terms, the United Kingdom acknowledged[44] that the intention to create the single currency was "irreversible"—a statement which appeared optimistic when the Treaty was signed on 7 February 1992 and for a number of years thereafter, but which nevertheless proved ultimately to be justified. The United Kingdom also undertook to "respect the will for the Community to enter swiftly into the third stage" and therefore the United Kingdom would not prevent the commencement of the third stage. It may be inferred from these provisions that neither the United Kingdom nor its courts could take any action which called into question the process of monetary union or the progression to the third stage; to do so would be inconsistent with the spirit (if not the letter) of the provisions just noted. In this context, it should be recalled that Member States—including, to the extent of their jurisdiction, the national courts of Member States—are under a Community law obligation to facilitate the achievement of the tasks of the Community and to abstain from measures which would jeopardise the fulfilment of the objectives of the Treaty.[45] For this reason, an English court which—in the context of a contractual claim—sought

---

[43] See, eg, *Ocean Trading Tankers Corp v V/O Sovfracht* (1964) 2 QB 226; *Palmco Inc v Continental Ore Corp* [1970] 2 Lloyd's Rep 21.

[44] On the points about to be made, see the Protocol annexed to the EC Treaty on Transition to the Third Stage of Economic and Monetary Union.

[45] On these points see, Art 10 of the EC Treaty, as interpreted and applied in Case 14/83 *Von Colson and Kamann v Land Nordrhein-Westfalen* [1984] ECR 1891; see also Case C–168-94 *Criminal Proceedings against Luciano Arcaro* [1996] ECR I–4705.

to examine the relative value of legacy currencies and the euro or the economic merits of the substitution thereby effected would clearly be acting in breach of the EC treaty itself.[46] The English court is therefore left in the position that (a) it must recognise and give effect to the legal equivalence between the euro and the legacy currency concerned; (b) since the obligation expressed in euros is legally equivalent to the legacy currency obligation, it must follow that there has been no radical change in the nature or scope of the obligation; and (c) accordingly, there is no room for the application of the doctrine of frustration.[47]

Finally, it has already been noted that part (if not all) of the regulatory framework created for the euro is applicable in the United Kingdom, even though it currently remains a non-participant.[48] Article 3 of the Council Regulation (EC) 1103/97 states that, subject to any contrary agreement between the parties "the introduction of the euro shall not have the effect of altering any term of a legal instrument or of discharging or excusing performance under any legal instrument, nor give a party the right unilaterally to alter or terminate such an instrument". Given that this Regulation is directly applicable in the United Kingdom, it must be taken to form a part of English contract law. It follows that the substitution of the euro for a participating national currency cannot be treated as a ground for frustration of a transitional contract.[49] Whilst this particular provision may therefore be helpful in terms of legal certainty,[50] it was not strictly necessary, because English law would doubtless have adopted this attitude in any event.[51]

30.25

---

[46] Such an attempt would no doubt also fail on many other grounds, eg because such a line of enquiry would intrude upon the sovereign activities of the eurozone Member States and because there are no judicially manageable standards which could be applied in order to resolve such an issue—see, eg, *Buttes Gas and Oil Co v Hammer (No 3)* [1982] AC 888.

[47] To express matters in a different way, the doctrine of frustration could not be used to circumvent the court's obligation to give effect to the *lex monetae* and the recurrent link.

[48] In this context, it will be recalled that Council Reg 1103/97 is directly applicable in the UK, whilst Council Reg 974/98 is not. On this point, see para 29.10 above.

[49] It may be added that the relevant provision prevents the operation of doctrines akin to frustration, where a contract may be terminated against the wishes of one of the parties, but it does not restrict contractual freedom. Consequently, parties could *mutually* agree to terminate their contract. As stated in the text, the operation of Art 3 of the Regulation is explicitly stated to be subject to any specific agreement between the parties.

[50] The provision was inserted into the Regulation at the request of various financial market associations which, in the view of the present writer, took an excessively cautious approach to this subject. Nevertheless, it may be that the volume of contracts affected by the monetary substitution justified the desire for a very high degree of certainty. The provision is perhaps of most value in the specialist area of interest rate and currency swaps; the subject is considered in paras 30.27 and 30.28 below.

[51] It may be added that the contractual continuity provision has been considered by the Court of Justice in the context of proceedings involving the rounding of euro amounts following conversion from the legacy currencies: Case 19/03 *Verbraucher-Zentrale Hamburg v O2 Germany GmbH* [2004] All ER (D) 81, para 31.

English law—specific contracts

30.26   The principle discussed in paras 30.08 to 30.25 above will no doubt suffice for the vast majority of transitional contracts. They remain valid and binding in accordance with their terms; obligations expressed in a legacy currency are now to be performed in euros, at the prescribed substitution rate. There is no basis upon which such contracts could be said to be amenable to the doctrine of frustration (or any similar principle) as a result of the introduction of the single currency. Thus far, however, the text has been concerned with contracts involving money purely as a medium through which monetary obligations can be *defined and settled*. But it must be said that the modern financial markets have developed more sophisticated forms of contract in which the role of money goes beyond the traditional and narrower range just described; indeed, money may form the very subject matter of the contract itself, in the sense that both parties undertake obligations of a purely monetary character. Contracts of particular concern in the present context would include currency swaps and interest rate swaps.

30.27   A currency swap may serve one of two essential purposes; it may be designed to hedge against the risk of losses flowing from exchange rate fluctuations, or it may be intended as a means of profiting from anticipated movements as between the two currencies concerned.[52] In such a case, it may be said that the contract has been entered into on the fundamental assumption that two separate currencies existed and would continue to exist throughout the entire life of the contract; the contract presupposed the existence of exchange rate volatility between two different units of account. Suppose that the two currencies concerned were (say) the Deutsche mark and the French franc; should not the contract have been frustrated on 1 January 1999, when the two currencies were substituted by the euro? A single currency plainly cannot fluctuate against itself;[53] the essential foundations of the contract (ie the existence of separate currencies and the resultant possibility of fluctuations) were swept away at that point. Yet, in spite of these important factors, it is suggested that the doctrine of frustration could not apply to such a contract and it therefore remained enforceable notwithstanding the introduction of the single currency. There are two main reasons for this view:

(1)   The irrevocable fixing of the substitution rates between the Deutsche mark/euro and the French franc/euro naturally prevented any further fluctuation

---

[52] The element of speculation involved in the latter form of contract suggested that such arrangements might be void in consequence of the Gaming Act 1845, s 18. However, the validity of such contracts entered into between market participants has been expressly preserved by the Financial Services and Markets Act 2000, s 412.

[53] As has been shown, to the extent to which the legacy currencies retained a separate legal status during the transitional period, this was merely as a subdivision and representation of the euro.

between the currencies named in the contract. The payment obligations of the party which had undertaken to pay a fixed amount in French francs could now be quantified as a stated amount in euro, and the same conversion process could be achieved in relation to the other party and the Deutsche mark obligations which it had undertaken. As a result, the amount of all future payments required under the contract could be calculated with certainty with effect from 1 January 1999. In all probability, one party would effectively be obliged to pay an ascertained net amount in euro over the remaining life of the contract. But despite the absence of separate currencies and the absence of volatility, it is suggested that the contract continued to perform its original purpose because it still created an effective hedge between the value of money in France and the value of money in Germany. Indeed, the fixing of the relative values of the two currencies by the substitution of the euro helps to achieve (rather than to defeat) the purpose and objectives of a contract which has been entered into for the purpose of hedging currency risk.

(2) It may be objected that, in a case of this kind, the introduction of the single currency does not merely involve the mechanical or mathematical substitution of the euro for the legacy currency. The volatility which was a feature of the contract has gone, and the possibility of profits from future exchange rate fluctuations is likewise lost. The economics and the profits potential of the contract have thus been disrupted. In the view of the present writer, considerations of this kind would not have led to the frustration of a currency swap, since the considerations outlined in (1) above would have been sufficient to preserve it from that fate. However, this conclusion is reinforced by Article 3 of Council Regulation (EC) 1103/97,[54] which provides that "the introduction of the euro shall not have the effect of . . . discharging or excusing performance under any legal instrument". It seems that this provision must be vigorously applied even where (as in the present context) the *quantum* or *value* of the payments required to be made may themselves have been varied as a result of the creation of the euro. In other words, Article 3 must be applied in the broadest sense—it is not restricted only to cases in which a mathematical substitution of monetary amounts is involved. Article 3 thus requires that parties accept any adverse financial consequences, including the loss of any anticipated profits, which may have flowed from the creation of the single currency in the context of specialised contracts of this kind.[55]

---

[54] This Regulation has been discussed in detail in Ch 29 above.

[55] It may be added that the mere fact that the changed circumstances may have imposed additional financial burdens on one of the parties does not of itself provide a basis upon which a contract can be frustrated—see the cases mentioned in n 42 above.

30.28 Interest rate swaps give rise to a slightly different set of issues, which may perhaps be best illustrated by an example. A borrower of a long-term French franc loan may have been obliged to pay interest by reference to a floating rate which varied (say) by reference to the applicable London interbank offered rate. The borrower wished to know that the effective cost to it of servicing that loan would not exceed 6 per cent per annum. Accordingly, it entered into an interest rate swap with its bank under the terms of which (a) the borrower would pay to the bank amounts equal to 6 per cent per annum calculated by reference to the principal amount of the French franc loan and (b) the bank would pay to the borrower corresponding interest amounts calculated by reference to the floating rate. The borrower would thus suffer no loss if French franc interest rates rose above the 6 per cent threshold. What would be the fate of such obligations upon the introduction of the euro? In relation to the fixed, 6 per cent payments, it is clear that the borrower would continue to pay 6 per cent calculated on the amount of the loan in euros, ascertained by applying the fixed conversion rate.[56] In relation to the floating rate payments, it must be remembered that a contractual reference to "French francs" connoted the lawful currency of France as it existed from time to time. Consequently, where a contract provided for interest to be calculated by reference to a floating rate for French francs quoted by a particular provider of (usually screen-based) information to the financial markets, this would be read as a reference to the corresponding floating rate for the euro with effect from the beginning of the third stage. Alternatively, it will be an implied term of the contract that the most nearly corresponding rate from similar price source will be applied.[57] As a result, the substitution of the euro did not provide grounds for the frustration of an interest rate swap of the type just described.

---

[56] This point is confirmed by para 7 of the preamble to Council Reg 1103/97, which notes that "in the case of fixed interest rate instruments the introduction of the euro does not alter the nominal interest rate payable by the debtor".

[57] See *Bank of Credit and Commerce International SA v Malik* [1996] BCC 15. For a view similar to that expressed in the text, see *Economic and Monetary Union—Continuity of Contracts in English law* (Financial Law Panel 1998). The need to identify corresponding price sources for these purposes was discussed by the Commission in *Impact of the Introduction of the euro on Capital Markets* (Euro Paper No 3). The same theme was taken up by interested market associations—see, eg, *EMU and outstanding eurobonds—a guide for issuers* (International Primary Markets Association, Spring 1998) and *Overview of Price Sponsors' Intentions* (International Swaps and Derivatives Association, 25 November 1998): It may be noted that a US court has held a contract to be frustrated where the stipulated price source ceased to be available to calculate obligations arising under the contract concerned—see *Interstate Plywood Sales Ltd v Interstate Container Corp* (1964) 331 F 2d 4499. However, it is suggested that the principle of this case should not apply where, as in the present context, suitable alternative price sources are readily available.

Foreign law contracts

An English court may have to consider a transitional contract governed by a **30.29** foreign system of law and, in such a case, the applicable law would generally determine whether a contract has been terminated—whether as a result of frustration, *force majeure*, or similar doctrine. What would be the position in the unlikely event that the applicable law[58] stipulated for the termination of a legacy currency contract in consequence of the substitution of the euro? In the normal course, questions touching the termination of a contract fall to be governed by its applicable law.[59] Would the English court be required to give effect to such a conclusion under the current and very specific circumstances? It is suggested that it would not. There are several reasons for this view but it may suffice to mention two of them.

First of all, a rule which forms a part of a foreign system of law will not be applied **30.30** by the English courts "if such application is manifestly incompatible with the public policy ('ordre public') of the forum". This formulation is contained in the Rome Convention and reflects established conflict of law principles.[60] Now, English public policy must be taken to embrace the public policy of the Community as a whole.[61] The recognition that transitional contracts will continue to be enforceable—both under domestic legal systems within the Community and under external systems—must clearly be a fundamental tenet of Community public policy.[62] The introduction of the euro was a major Community initiative;[63] it would thus be contrary to Community policy if that project could have precipitated the termination of existing commercial arrangements. As a consequence, the English courts would enforce such a transitional contract in accordance with the terms of the applicable law, but disregarding those rules which would otherwise have the effect of terminating the contract on the grounds that the euro had been substituted for the legacy currencies.

---

[58] This contention could not arise if the contract is governed by the law of another EC Member State, because the legal framework for the introduction of the euro (including the "continuity" provision contained in Art 3 of Council Reg 1103/97) forms a part of the domestic law of that State. For all practical purposes, therefore, references to foreign systems of law have comprised the systems of non-EC Member States.

[59] ie in accordance with the Rome Convention, Art 10(1)(d).

[60] See Rome Convention, Art 16 and *Vervaeke v Smith* [1983] 1 AC 45.

[61] On this point, see the Giuliano-Lagarde Report and its discussion of Art 16 of the Rome Convention.

[62] In the context of Community legal systems, the effect of the "continuity" provision in Art 3 of Council Reg 1103/97 has already been noted. Paragraph (8) of the preamble to that Regulation anticipates that the continuity of transitional contracts will also be recognised by external legal systems.

[63] If authority be required for this statement, the point is implicitly recognised by the EC Treaty, Art 4(2).

30.31   Secondly, it is suggested that the contractual continuity provision[64] constitutes a rule of English law, the application of which is intended to be mandatory "irrespective of the law otherwise applicable to the contract". If that is the case then the English court would have to apply the mandatory rule in any event.[65] It is suggested that the contractual continuity provision is a rule of mandatory application for these purposes, because the provision is intended to apply to all types of contracts, irrespective of the manner in which they are created.[66] In addition, a failure to give effect to the contractual continuity provisions under these circumstances would place the United Kingdom in breach of its treaty obligation to support the process of monetary union.[67] Considerations of this kind lead to the conclusion that the contractual continuity provision is of mandatory application for these purposes.[68]

30.32   It follows that transitional contracts could not be found to be frustrated or otherwise terminated solely by reason of the substitution of the euro for the legacy currency in which such contract was originally expressed. Given that these views are based upon relevant provisions of the Rome Convention on the law applicable to contractual obligations, this conclusion should apply in any proceedings in the United Kingdom or in any other Member State, regardless of the system of law which governs the contract concerned.

C. Termination and the Foreign Courts

General considerations

30.33   What is to be the position if a transitional contract falls to be considered by a domestic court sitting outside the European Community? The legislative framework created for the euro plainly cannot apply as part of the domestic legal system of the foreign State concerned. If an external court has to consider a legacy currency contract governed by its own, domestic system of law, how should it respond to the argument that the contract has been terminated as a result of the introduction of the euro? In accordance with generally applicable principles of conflicts of law, questions concerning the continued validity of the contract will be determined by reference to the system of law which governs it.

---

[64]   ie Council Reg 1103/97, Art 3. This provision has already been discussed at para 29.08(2) above.

[65]   Rome Convention, Art 7(2).

[66]   eg whether orally or in writing, or by any other means. This wording clearly includes any form of binding agreement, whether subjected to a domestic or a foreign system of law. On this point, see para 9 of the preamble to Council Reg 1103/97.

[67]   On the treaty obligations of the UK in this regard, see para 32.25(5) below.

[68]   On this line of argument, see *Corocraft Ltd v Pan American Airways Inc* [1969] 1 QB 616.

Inevitably, it is difficult to generalise as to the approach which foreign courts **30.34** might adopt in this arena. However, it has been noted earlier elsewhere[69] that all States—and their courts—are under an international obligation to recognise the sovereignty of other States over their domestic monetary systems, including the right to reorganise those systems. Equally, States must recognise the right of other States to "pool" their monetary sovereignty and thus create a common currency; a decision to delegate or to pool sovereignty is nevertheless an exercise of that sovereignty, which is entitled to international recognition on the same footing as an exercise of that sovereignty.[70] It follows that other States are likewise under an obligation to recognise the substitution of the euro for the legacy currencies, and to give effect to the substitution rates prescribed in accordance with the provisions of the EC Treaty. In other words, the consequences of an external delegation of monetary sovereignty must be recognised on the same basis as an internal exercise of that sovereignty. Save in cases amounting to expropriation,[71] a foreign court could not enquire into the economic merits or fairness of the respective rates at which the euro had been substituted for the various legacy currencies; to do so would place the State concerned in breach of its obligation to respect the monetary sovereignty of the eurozone Member States. If the foreign Court could not properly enquire into the financial or economic merits of the currency substitution, then it must follow that there can be no grounds to support the application of any local law concepts akin to the doctrine of frustration. An obligation to "recognise" a change in monetary arrangements must have some substantive meaning and require the recognising State and its courts to give some positive meaning to such recognition. As noted previously, an intolerable inconsistency would arise if the courts were permitted merely to acknowledge that a change of currency had occurred and yet to use that fact as a ground for terminating obligations expressed in the former currency. As a result, the international duty to recognise monetary sovereignty coupled with the *lex monetae* principle in themselves virtually preclude the application of domestic rules which might otherwise terminate the contract by operation of law or allow one party a unilateral right of termination under these circumstances.[72]

---

[69] On the international obligation to recognise the monetary sovereignty of other States, see Ch 19 above.

[70] On this point, see *R v Secretary of State for Foreign and Commonwealth Affairs ex p Rees-Mogg* [1994] QB 552. Of course, the delegation of sovereignty may be subject to *internal* constraints under the domestic constitutional arrangements of a particular State, see eg *Crotty v An Taoiseach* [1987] 2 CMLR 666. But that does not detract from the principle of international law stated in the text.

[71] As to which, see para 19.20 above.

[72] There is, of course, nothing to prevent parties from explicitly agreeing to vary the terms of their contract, or to change the currency in which a payment is due, should they wish to do so. As noted previously, the autonomy of the parties in this area is explicitly recognised by the contractual continuity provision contained in Council Reg 1103/97, Art 3.

Position in the United States

30.35   It is perhaps unsurprising that the substitution of the euro for the national currencies of participating Member States caused particular concern in the large financial markets in the United States of America, although even there it is suggested that a careful analysis of the legal position would have allayed any fear that the introduction of the euro might lead to the termination of contracts expressed in legacy currencies. Nevertheless, New York and other States elected to pass legislation addressing the issue, and it is thus appropriate to make a few remarks on this subject.

30.36   Whilst it is not practicable for the present writer to deal with issues of New York law in great depth, it is nevertheless possible to note that New York courts were under a general obligation to recognise the substitution of the euro for national currencies by reference to the theory of the recurrent link. Likewise, and for reasons discussed earlier, the monetary substitution could not be invoked as a ground for the frustration or termination of contracts.[73] The Supreme Court has recognised that the creation and control of the US dollar is within the constitutional power of the Government,[74] and that Congress may therefore establish the conversion date (recurrent link) to be applied where a formerly independent country becomes a part of the United States.[75] Whilst those matters have fallen for decision in an essentially domestic context, the courts in the United States have applied the same principles when dealing with foreign currencies. Those courts have recognised the right of an issuing State to define (and to redefine) its monetary system, and to adopt the applicable substitution rate; actions of this kind represent an exercise of monetary sovereignty by the issuing State, and effect must therefore be given to them, regardless of the law applicable to the contract as a whole.[76] Indeed, New York courts have applied these rules rigidly, even where this has resulted in hardship or loss to one of the parties.[77]

30.37   If the present writer's views on this subject are accepted, then it is already possible to exclude the possibility that contracts may be terminated as a result of currency substitution. However, even if those views are not accepted, the same

---

[73] See the discussion at para 30.21 above in the context of English law.

[74] See *Knox v Lee* and *Parker v Davis* (1980) 12 Wall (79) US 457, and other cases noted at para 1.20 above.

[75] See *Succession of Serrales v Estri* (1906) 200 US 103. For a discussion of this case, see Lenihan, *The Legal Implications of the European Monetary Union under US and New York Law*, EC Commission, January 1998, pp 42–3. This very detailed and carefully researched publication provides a useful analysis of relevant case law in this area.

[76] See, eg, *Dougherty v Equitable Life Assurance Society* (1934) 266 NY 71, 193 NE 897; *Sternberg v West Coast Life Insurance Co* (1961) 16 Cal Rep 546.

[77] *Dougherty v Equitable Life Assurance Society* (1934) 193 NE 897; *Dougherty v National City Bank of New York* (1941) 118 F 2d 631.

result can be achieved by other means. New York contract law incorporates a doctrine of frustration, which is essentially similar in purpose and scope to the corresponding English doctrine. It has been decided that a fluctuation in the comparative value of two separate currencies does not of itself lead to the frustration of a contract governed by New York law.[78] If that is so, then it is very difficult to see how a mere, internal currency substitution could lead to the operation of the doctrine. Equally, a contract may be terminated if its performance becomes impossible, or if it becomes "commercially impracticable".[79] Given that the New York courts recognise the *lex monetae* principle, there can be no scope for the argument that performance of the monetary obligation has become either impossible or commercially impracticable; the arrangements for the substitution of the euro render the performance of such monetary obligations perfectly feasible. Nevertheless, as noted earlier, the New York legislature felt it necessary to provide specifically that obligations expressed in participating national currencies or the ECU could henceforth be performed in euros at the appropriate rate, and that none of the arrangements surrounding the introduction of the euro would have the effect of discharging or excusing performance of an obligation governed by New York Law.[80] It may be regretted that New York believed it to be either necessary or appropriate to introduce legislation which effectively recognised the right of the eurozone Member States to substitute their national currencies; this should have been wholly unnecessary in the light of the principles of international monetary law to which reference has already been made.[81] However, given that the European Community itself felt it necessary to introduce contractual continuity legislation,[82] it is scarcely possible to criticise the New York authorities for adopting an essentially parallel approach.

Other States have adopted the Uniform Foreign Money Claims Act.[83] Where a **30.38** contract stipulates for payment in a particular currency and, prior to payment, a

---

[78] *Bank of America NT & SA v Envases Venezolanos* (1990) 740 F Supp 260; affirmed (1990) 923 F 2d 843.

[79] Article 2-615 of the Uniform Commercial Code. In a case which would seem to be highly relevant in this context, the US Court of Appeals for the 10th Circuit held that performance of a contract between an American importer and a Swiss exporter payable in Swiss francs did not become commercially impracticable merely because the US dollar suffered severe depreciation in relation to the Swiss franc over the life of the contract—see *Bernina Distributors Inc v Bernina Sewing Machine Co* (1981) 646 F 2d 434.

[80] The New York legislation inserted a new Title 16 into Article 5 of the General Obligation Law in order to deal with this subject. Similar steps were taken in other States of the Union, including Illinois, California, Pennsylvania, and Michigan.

[81] It should, however, be said that the New York legislation does not explicitly address questions touching on the monetary sovereignty of the eurozone; it confines itself to the contractual consequences of the creation of the euro.

[82] See Art 3 of Council Reg 1103/97, which has been considered at para 29.08 above.

[83] It should be mentioned that this Act is framed in general terms and was not introduced with specific reference to the creation of the euro.

new currency is substituted therefor, then the relevant obligation is deemed to be substituted by the new unit of account at the conversion rate specified by the monetary law of the issuing State.[84] This provision constitutes a very clear statutory confirmation of the *lex monetae* principle.[85] A contract affected by the monetary substitution will continue in force in accordance with its terms.[86] Furthermore, the application of this rule is mandatory, regardless of the system of law which governs the contract as a whole.[87]

Other jurisdictions

30.39 Once again, it is only possible for the present writer to comment in outline terms on the legal status of the euro under the laws of other jurisdictions, although the *lex monetae* principle reflects international law and should thus be binding in each case.

30.40 Much research on the subject—naturally focusing on major financial centres—was undertaken by the Financial Law Panel. In relation to Japan and Switzerland,[88] it was concluded that local courts would recognise the introduction of the euro and that contracts would continue to be enforceable notwithstanding any perceived economic disadvantage to one party. A report with similar conclusions was also published in relation to Singapore but that country elected to introduce local legislation to deal with the "continuity" question.[89] Hong Kong, likewise introduced local legislation on the subject.[90]

---

[84] Uniform Foreign Money Claims Act, s 2(b). This provision reinforces the prior decision in *Sternberg v West Coast Life Insurance Co* (1961) 16 Cal Rep 546.

[85] It is particularly apposite in the context of the creation of the euro, for s 1(7) of the Act defines "foreign money" to include "a medium of exchange for the payment of obligations . . . authorised or adopted by *inter-governmental agreement*" (emphasis added).

[86] This point is not explicitly stated, but is implicit in s 12(a) of the Act, which provides for the substitution of the new currency for the old.

[87] Uniform Foreign Money Claims Act, s 2(b). The requirement to respect a foreign monetary substitution thus forms a mandatory law of the forum. This differs from the approach adopted in England, where a reference to a foreign law currency implies a choice of the law of the relevant currency to govern certain monetary issues. The requirement to respect the currency substitution thus forms an integral part of the *lex monetae* principle itself—see the discussion at para 30.03 above. Cases governed by the Uniform Foreign Money Claims Act would thus require a different analysis in a private international law context, but the ultimate result would appear to be identical.

[88] The Financial Law Panel's reports on these two jurisdictions were published in July 1997 and May 1998 respectively.

[89] The Financial Law Panel's report was issued in July 1998. For the relevant statutory provisions, see s 9 of the Civil Law Act (Ch 43) of Singapore.

[90] See The Introduction of the Euro Ordinance 1998 (ch 543).

D. Fixed and Variable Interest Rates

Fixed interest rates

Thus far, the text has been principally concerned with the consequences of the **30.41** euro substitution for the payment of set amounts contractually expressed in legacy currencies. But it must not be overlooked that many such obligations would in addition be expressed to bear interest. How were such legacy currency interest obligations to be calculated after the substitution of the euro? Could a borrower claim that it was no longer possible to calculate the applicable rate? Or could that borrower claim to be materially disadvantaged to the extent that the doctrine of frustration might apply? As will be seen, the legal framework for the establishment of the euro contained only passing reference to the consequences of the currency substitution for interest rate obligations. Nevertheless, as this section will seek to demonstrate, the absence of specific provisions in this area does not pose any difficulty in practical terms.

Dealing first of all with fixed interest rates, it was noted earlier that (a) a **30.42** monetary obligation contained in a legacy currency contract became a euro obligation with effect from 1 January 1999 and (b) that the precise amount of the monetary obligation expressed in euros was to be ascertained according to the prescribed substitution rates. Subject only to the necessary change in the money of account, the legacy currency contract continues in effect in accordance with its terms. There should be no difficulty in applying the contractual, fixed interest calculation provisions to the contract following the introduction of the euro.[91] However, since the interest rate arises in respect of a euro obligation, it is submitted that the correct sequence of events should be (1) the translation of the legacy currency principal amount into euro and (2) the calculation of the fixed interest payable by relevance to the resultant euro amount.[92]

Although the point is now perhaps purely theoretical, would it have been open **30.43** to either contracting party to prove that (a) the contractual fixed rate was appropriate when originally agreed in the context of the relevant legacy currency and (b) in relation to the euro, that the fixed rate is excessive?[93] It seems clear that a legacy contract involving a fixed interest rate could not be frustrated on

---

[91] Paragraph 7 of the preamble to Council Reg 1103/97 confirms that the principle of contractual continuity implies that the introduction of the euro does not affect fixed interest rates.

[92] In view of the effect of rounding rules, slight differences might arise if the interest was calculated by reference to the legacy amount and the resultant interest obligation itself was converted into euros.

[93] The lender or intended recipient of the interest might seek to assert that the rate has become too low.

this basis. The contractual continuity provision[94] requires that agreements remain in force notwithstanding the introduction of the euro and, as noted previously, the doctrine of frustration cannot be applied merely on the grounds that a fixed interest rate renders the contract uneconomic for one of the parties.

Variable interest rates

30.44 The position for floating interest rates is—at least in some cases—slightly more complex, but nevertheless some workable solutions may be found. Of course, it is always necessary to refer to the specific terms of the contract for these purposes, but a clause providing for a floating rate of interest will usually involve either (a) a right conferred upon the lending bank to vary the interest obligation by reference to the base rate from time to time quoted by the lender or (b) a provision for the rate to be ascertained by reference to an independent price source, eg an interbank rate quoted by a provider of information to the financial markets.

30.45 The first type of case causes little difficulty, because it involves a unilateral right for the lender to stipulate the interest rate applicable to the currency concerned. From 1 January 1999, contractual references to legacy currencies were replaced by references to the euro, and banks have quoted rates for loans in euros since that date. Consequently, unilateral, interest fixing provisions of this kind can be operated in accordance with their terms.

30.46 The second type of clause requires more detailed consideration. Legacy currency contracts of this kind may require an interest rate to be calculated by reference to the London Interbank Offered Rate (LIBOR) for funds in the legacy currency concerned for the necessary calculation period.[95] Providers of information to the financial markets will usually quote LIBOR by averaging out the rates obtained from several institutions operating in the relevant currency market, and loan contracts will stipulate for the legacy currency screen rate made available by a particular provider to govern their interest calculation arrangements. What was to be the position when screen rates expressed in that legacy currency ceased to be available as a consequence of the euro substitution?

30.47 In the context of a loan or similar financial contract, it plainly cannot be said that the legacy currency contract as a whole has been frustrated nor can it be

---

[94] ie Art 3 of Council Reg 1103/97.

[95] It may be noted that LIBOR itself is not an objectively ascertainable rate. The rate at which banks lend to each other is not inflexible but (apart from market conditions) will vary according to the perceived credit standing of the particular borrowing bank concerned. It may become an objectively identifiable rate if the parties agree on a particular pricing source from which the rate is to be taken, as described in the text.

said that the obligation to pay interest alone has been terminated.[96] Given that the contract remains effective, a means must be found to ascertain the interest rate following the currency substitution. Where the legacy currency contract is governed by English law, then the mechanism of the implied term offers the necessary solution.[97] In essence, it will be an implied term of the contract that (following the substitution of the euro for the legacy currencies) interest will be calculated by reference to the most closely corresponding pricing mechanism or source of funding.[98] Thus, where a legacy currency contract provided for a French franc loan to carry interest at London interbank rates, it would follow that the London interbank rate for euros would apply following the currency substitution. Equally, if the interbank rate were required to be ascertained from a particular price source, then the post-euro rate would have to be ascertained from the most closely corresponding price source.[99]

As a final point, it might be noted that it will frequently be unnecessary to have **30.48** to resort to implied contractual terms in order to ascertain an interest rate under these circumstances. For example, where a credit agreement stipulates for the calculation of interest rates by reference to the lender's publicly quoted rate for advances in (say) French francs, then the reference to francs is to be read as a reference to the lawful currency of France from time to time—and would thus be read as a reference to the euro with effect from 1 January 1999. The principle just mentioned is well established both by the terms of the legal framework for the euro[100] and by decided cases.[101]

---

[96] Generally speaking, the doctrine of frustration can only apply to a contract as a whole, and not to individual parts of it—see *Kawasaki Steel Corp v Sardoil SpA (The Zuiko Maru)* [1977] Lloyd's Rep 552 and *J Lauritzen A/S v Wijsmuller BV (The Super Servant Two)* [1990] 1 Lloyd's Rep 1. This approach is also supported by the language of s 1(1) of the Law Reform (Frustrated Contracts) Act 1943. On this point, see the discussion in *Chitty on Contracts* (Sweet & Maxwell, 29th edn, 2004) para 23-064. It may be noted that a US court has held a contract to be frustrated where a pricing source ceased to be available—see *Interstate Plywood Sales Ltd v Interstate Container Corp* (1964) 331 F 2d 4499. See also para 30.28 above.

[97] No doubt a similar or equally effective solution could be identified under most other systems of law.

[98] See *Bank of Credit and Commerce International SA v Malik* [1996] BCC 15.

[99] For a similar view, see *Economic and Monetary Union—Continuity of Contracts in English Law* (Financial Law Panel, January 1998). In practical terms the need to identify the appropriate successor sources of funding/price mechanisms was taken up by the Commission—see *The impact of the introduction of the euro on capital markets* (Euro Papers, No 3). The same theme was then pursued by various financial market associations—see, eg, *EMU and outstanding eurobonds—a guide for issuers* (International Primary Market Association, Spring 1998) and *Overview of Price Sponsors' Intentions* (International Swaps and Derivatives Association Inc, 25 November 1998).

[100] See, in particular, Arts 6(2) and 14 of Council Reg 974/98.

[101] This statement reflects the *lex monetae* principle, which has been discussed in depth in Ch 13 above.

E. Private ECU Obligations

30.49 The possible application of the doctrine of frustration or similar principles gave rise to particular questions on the context of obligations expressed in the so-called "private ECU". In order to explain these issues, it is necessary to provide a brief outline of the private ECU and what may properly be described as its quasi-monetary status in the financial markets.

30.50 Reference has been made earlier to the *official* ECU and its status as the forerunner to the euro itself.[102] It has been noted that the official ECU was calculated by reference to a "basket" of currencies of EC Member States, was originally intended to function as a denominator for the European Monetary System, and was used as a means of payment only in transactions among EC institutions. However, in a parallel development, banks and other commercial entities began to deal in the ECU independently, and developed the so-called "private" ECU.[103] This was achieved by placing deposits and issuing securities expressed in the ECU but in fact consisting of the appropriate proportion of all the underlying currencies comprised within the ECU basket. Despite issues concerning the formal legal status of the private ECU which will be discussed below, the financial markets treated the unit as "money" for all practical purposes. The use of the unit became popular, partly because its external value against other currencies tended to be strong—the "basket" nature of the currency insulated it from some of the fluctuations which from time to time affected the individual component currencies. Dealings in the private ECU market were spurred by the establishment of a system for payment and settlement of private ECU obligations in 1986. This was known as the ECU Clearing System and the existence of these arrangements encouraged the rapid growth of a two-way market in deposits and loans denominated in ECUs. It may be added that the label "private" ECU was entirely justified in this context, for the ECU Clearing System was operated by a number of commercial banks, essentially without any official (or "public") supervision. The Bank for International Settlements was a member of the System, but effectively acted as the ultimate clearing agent for the System; it did not carry out any formal supervisory or similar central banking functions in relation to the System.[104]

30.51 It will be apparent from the above discussion that dealings in the private ECU were essentially confined to the financial markets—the unit never attained any

---

[102] See in particular para 25.11 above.

[103] For the historical background to the development of the private ECU market, see Mehnert, *User's Guide to the ECU* (Graham & Trotman, 1992) 82–4.

[104] For further details on the structure and operation of the system, see Mehnert (n 103 above) 134–8.

real status as a means of payment in ordinary commercial transactions, no doubt partly because the unit did not enjoy the formal status of "money" and partly because of a lack of familiarity with the unit outside financial circles. Nevertheless, and despite these limitations, it became apparent to corporations conducting business with a number of EC Member States that the use of the private ECU could have a number of advantages. In particular, the ECU basket facilitated the management of currency risk, in that the corporation concerned could simply raise funds in ECUs rather than in the numerous different currencies of the various Member States. Furthermore, as already noted, a basket currency implies a natural hedge against fluctuations in the external value of an individual currency, and thus offers a degree of protection to creditor and debtor alike.[105] Similar considerations prompted the use of the private ECU Market by international financial institutions such as the European Investment Bank.[106] Thus, although the use of the private ECU was confined to a relatively narrow range of activities and market participants, the absolute amounts involved were huge.

Financial markets deal in deposits and loans, and it was thus perhaps natural **30.52** that the private ECU should have been treated as "money" once the ECU Clearing System had become available. But regardless of the practicalities, it must be said that the unit was *not* money in the legal sense.[107] There are several reasons for this view. First of all, the ECU was merely a yardstick or measure of value expressed by reference to a series of national currencies; it was not a form of currency issued under the authority of any State.[108] Furthermore, the ECU never served (nor was it intended to serve) as the universal means of exchange within any State; no notes or coins were issued which had the status of legal tender *throughout the Community* for obligations expressed in ECUs.[109]

---

[105] It should be appreciated that "basket" currencies do not, of course, provide an absolute guarantee that external values will be maintained; they merely provide that degree of stability which is inherent in the averaging process which is necessary to create a basket currency in the first instance. This point has already been noted in relation to the use of the SDR as a means of mitigating the effect of the principle of nominalism—see para 11.35 above.

[106] On the establishment and function of the European Investment Bank, see Arts 266–267 of the EC Treaty.

[107] If the State theory of money formulated in this work is accepted, then it is clear that the private ECU could not constitute "money" because it lacked the necessary imprimatur of a State. The same conclusion would appear to follow from an application of the Institutional theory, which was noted at para 1.27, n 93 above.

[108] Indeed, the absence of a single State (or central bank) having jurisdiction over the *private* ECU may have been perceived as one of its advantages.

[109] It is, however, fair to observe that many countries (usually in the context of their systems of exchange control) treated the private ECU as a *de facto* foreign currency, even if it could not generally attain this status *de jure*—for the position in individual Member States see Mehnert, *User's Guide to the ECU* (Graham & Trotman, 1992) 157–64. Certain individual countries within the Community issued ECU coins which were expressed to have the status of legal tender, but

30.53 Why did this divergence between the strict legal analysis and the practice of the financial markets matter in this context? The answer is that, if the ECU was not "money", then it had to follow that the *lex monetae* principle could not apply to it.[110] There is logic to this position; since the ECU was not issued by a State, other States could not be under an international obligation to recognise the substitution of that unit—and it will be remembered that international law and considerations of monetary sovereignty provide the foundations of the *lex monetae* principle. But as a result of this analysis, the lawyer is deprived of one of the key tools which enabled him effectively and comprehensively to deal with the substitution of the euro for the legacy currencies. What, then, was to be the fate of obligations expressed in the private ECU on 1 January 1999, when the single currency came into being? In order to answer this question, it is necessary to consider the manner in which the ECU could be used to create a quasi-monetary obligation.

30.54 It must be remembered that a simple reference to the "ECU" did not refer to a national currency created by a domestic system of law. As a consequence, the implied reference to a single system of domestic law available in the context of individual currencies was not available in the present context.[111] At the risk of stating the obvious, it follows that the substance of the debtor's obligation must be governed solely by the law applicable to the contract concerned, *without* any implied reference to the law of a currency. It was therefore necessary to examine the terms of the particular contract in order to identify the nature of the debtor's obligation in the post-euro period.[112]

30.55 An examination of the terms of the contract would lead to one of three possible conclusions:

(1) The document may stipulate for the payment of (say) ECU10,000 as defined by the relevant Community legislation from time to time. Although the contracting parties were necessarily dealing in the *private* ECU market, it is nevertheless plain from the language employed that they intended to "mirror" the *official* ECU, and to track any periodic changes in

---

only within the individual State of issue. For a description of these developments, see Mehnert (above) 133–4. Of course, under the terms of the State theory of money as adopted in the present edition of this work, the existence of notes and coins is not, in principle, essential to the creation of a monetary system.

[110] On the *lex monetae* principle, see Ch 13 above.

[111] eg, a reference to US dollars implies a reference to US law; a reference to yen implies a reference to Japanese law, and so on. This point has already been discussed in Ch 4 above, in the context of the Rome Convention and monetary obligations.

[112] In other words, the nature of the ECU obligation fell to be determined by reference to the law of the contract, without the aid of the *lex monetae*.

its composition.[113] Consistently with the parties' intentions, an obligation to pay ECU10,000 became an obligation to pay €10,000 on and with effect from 1 January 1999. The point is explicitly confirmed by Art 2(1) of Council Regulation (EC) 1103/97, which forms a part of the domestic legal system of all Member States.[114]

(2) The document may merely stipulate for the payment of ECU10,000, without any further definition of the "ECU" for those purposes. In most cases, it will be fair to imply—if only by default—that the parties intended to contract by reference to the Community definition of the ECU. Again, this expectation is borne out by Article 2(1) of Regulation 1103/97; in the case of a "bare" reference to the ECU, there is a rebuttable presumption that the parties intended to contract by reference to the official ECU.[115] It may be repeated that this provision forms a part of the domestic law of all Member States, with the result that an ECU obligation expressed in this manner was presumed to be converted into euro on a one-for-one basis, with effect from 1 January 1999; and

(3) The parties may have expressed the relevant obligation in the "ECU", but they may have made it plain that their *private* ECU arrangements were not to be affected by subsequent changes in the composition of the *official* ECU. Since the private ECU was essentially a contractual invention, it was quite open to the parties to conclude their contract in this way. Given that the *official* ECU and the *private* ECU were, strictly speaking, separate and distinct, there seems to be no consideration of public policy which would strike down the parties' bargain in this respect. In such a case, the rebuttable presumption noted in (2) above would indeed be rebutted. As a result, the private ECU obligation would *not* have been substituted by a euro obligation on a one-for-one basis, and a court would be left to enforce the contract in accordance with its stipulated terms—whatever they may happen to be.[116] In practical terms, it is believed that relatively

---

[113] On the occasional changes in the composition of the *official* ECU basket, see para 25.14 above. It should be added that, in the experience of the present writer, the type of position described in this paragraph (point (1)) was the most commonly adopted in practice, eg see the prospectus dated 23 February 1989 for the Kingdom of Belgium ECU150,000,000 Bonds due 1994 (reproduced by Mehnet, *User's Guide to the ECU* (Graham & Trotman, 1992) 314); see also Louis and De L'Honeux, "The Development of the Use of the ECU: Legal Aspect" [1991] CML Rev 335.

[114] See Art 6 of the Regulation.

[115] Whether the presumption was in fact rebutted in such a case would be a question of contractual interpretation. It would accordingly have been governed by the law applicable to the contract—see, Art 10(1)(a) of the Rome Convention.

[116] This would probably have involved a calculation by reference to the respective currency amounts stipulated in the contractually agreed currency basket. Since those currencies had themselves been substituted by the single currency, an obligation expressed in euros would be the likely result in any event, but it might not have precisely reflected the one-for-one basis.

few cases will have fallen into the residual category discussed in this paragraph.

30.56 It has already been noted that the rules just discussed form a part of the domestic legal systems of all Member States. Consequently, courts sitting within those Member States would give effect to these conclusions where the contract is governed by the laws of any Member State.[117] Given the importance of these rules in the overall context of monetary union, it is perhaps likely (although not entirely free from doubt) that courts within Member States would have to apply these rules to contracts governed by a foreign system of law, where the application of that foreign law would otherwise produce a different result.[118]

30.57 It follows from the above discussion that contractual obligations expressed in ECUs would, for the most part, have involved an obligation to pay euros on a one-for-one basis from the beginning of the third stage. As a result, it would seem clear that the introduction of the euro could not result in the frustration or termination of ECU-denominated contracts.[119] Nevertheless in view of the particular nature of the ECU and the role which the official unit played in the context of monetary union, it is instructive to outline some of the issues which were debated before the legal framework for the transition was finalised.

30.58 It was occasionally suggested that the economic character of private ECU obligations was altered in consequence of the adoption of the single currency, because (a) as noted above, the private ECU usually "mirrored" the composition of the official ECU; (b) the private ECU thus reflected the weighted value of twelve separate national currencies; and (c) it was quite likely that the currencies comprised within the basket would not be representative of those Member States which would progress to the third stage of monetary union.[120] In other

---

[117] ie in accordance with Art 10(1) of the Rome Convention. Where a contract is governed by English law, it will be remembered that this refers to English law as in force from time to time—see *R v International Trustee for the Protection of Bondholders AG* [1937] AC 500 and *Re Helbert Wagg & Co Ltd's Claim* [1956] Ch 323. As a consequence, Art 2 of Council Reg (EC) 1103/97 would apply to any contract governed by English law, even though the contract was made before the Regulation came into force.

[118] ie Art 2(1) of Council Reg (EC) 1103/97 creates rules which are of mandatory application, irrespective of the law otherwise applicable to the contract—see Art 7(2) of the Rome Convention and the discussion at para 4.21 above.

[119] See the contractual continuity provision in Art 3(1) of Council Reg (EC) 1103/97, discussed at para 29.08(2) above. That Article applies to ECU contracts, just as it applies to agreements expressed in a legacy currency.

[120] In the events which happened, both Austria and Finland moved to the third stage of EMU, even though their respective national currencies had never comprised a part of the official ECU basket. Likewise, sterling and the Greek drachma formed a part of that basket, but neither the UK nor Greece progressed to the third stage when the euro was created on 1 January 1999. As noted earlier, however, Greece moved to the third stage on 1 January 2001.

words, the euro did not supersede the private or the official ECU in a precise, economic sense.

Whilst these statements may be factually accurate, they do not in law provide **30.59** grounds upon which an ECU-denominated contract could be frustrated. First of all, the legal framework for the single currency confirmed that obligations expressed in the private ECU were generally to be converted into euros on a one-for-one basis, and that the contract in question would remain in effect. Secondly, as noted earlier, a variation in comparative monetary or other values to be paid or given under a contract would not usually lead to the frustration of the parties' agreement.[121] Finally, the conversion of the ECU into the single currency of the eurozone Member States was not to result in any immediate variation in its external value against other currencies.[122] At the point at which the euro came into being on 1 January 1999, it thus had a value equivalent to that of the private ECU on its last dealing day. Consequently, even had a court been able to engage in a comparative economic assessment of the value of the private ECU and the euro, it would have come to the conclusion that the values of the two units were essentially similar, with the result that there was no "radical change" in the debtor's obligation which could support an application of the doctrine of frustration.[123]

---

[121] See *Tresden-Griffin v Co-operative Insurance Society Ltd* [1956] 2 QB 127 and other cases discussed at para 9.19 above.

[122] See Art 123(4) of the EC Treaty. It will be recalled that the terms of the Treaty itself refer to the ECU as the single currency, and that the term "euro" was only adopted subsequently.

[123] For reasons essentially similar to those discussed at para 30.21(b) above, it is suggested that a court could not in any event have embarked upon such a line of enquiry.

31

THE EURO AND MONETARY SOVEREIGNTY

A. Introduction

The process of monetary union has, without question, resulted in the transfer **31.01** of national monetary sovereignty from Member States to entities subsisting within the framework of the EC Treaties. Indeed, the perceived desire to preserve sovereignty in this area lies at the heart of the continuing political debate about the United Kingdom's (non-)membership of the eurozone. It has, however, been shown that monetary sovereignty is not a single and indivisible concept; apart from any other classifications which might be adopted, monetary sovereignty comprises both certain internal and certain external aspects.[1] Given that monetary sovereignty is divisible in this way, it follows that it may be partly retained and partly transferred; or different aspects of monetary sovereignty may be transferred to different recipients. Equally, a State may retain its monetary sovereignty and yet enter into arrangements which may limit or restrict the extent to which such sovereignty may be exercised in particular circumstances.

---

[1] On this subject, see Ch 19 above.

743

31.02 The treaty arrangements for the introduction of the single currency exhibit all of the features just described. With this in mind, the present chapter will consider the following matters:

(a) the *transfer* of monetary sovereignty by the eurozone Member States;

(b) the *exercise* of monetary sovereignty within the eurozone;

(c) monetary sovereignty and the ECB;

(d) monetary sovereignty and the Community;

(e) monetary sovereignty and external relations;

(f) the position of the United Kingdom and its own monetary sovereignty;

(g) monetary sovereignty and the federal State; and

(h) monetary sovereignty and exchange controls.

B. Member States and the Transfer of Sovereignty

31.03 It is easy to assume that the transfer of monetary sovereignty by the eurozone Member States occurred on 1 January 1999, when the single currency came into being. This is in many ways a natural conclusion, but it overlooks the point that monetary sovereignty is divisible and that, in fact, the Member States had been accepting limitations to that sovereignty over a period of years. A few examples may serve to illustrate this point.

31.04 First of all, the operation of the Exchange Rate Mechanism (ERM) within the European Monetary System (EMS), has previously been noted, and it has been shown that this involved an effective obligation on Member States to ensure that their national currencies remained within certain permitted margins of fluctuation.[2] This, in turn, inevitably placed limits upon a Member State's ability to devalue its currency and to adopt particular interest rates as part of its national monetary policy.[3]

31.05 Secondly, it has been noted that—subject to various exceptions—Article 56 of the EC Treaty required Member States to abolish all restrictions on the free movement of capital and payments; this provision was found to have direct effect in Member States.[4] It might perhaps be anticipated that a requirement to liberalise capital movements and the making of payments would of itself have the effect of limiting the national monetary sovereignty of the individual Member States and indeed this has been borne out by experience in a variety of

---

[2] See para 25.11 above.

[3] On the general rights of a State in this field, see para 19.02 above.

[4] On this subject, see para 25.34 above. The point cannot, however, be regarded as absolute, and certain qualifications to this rule are discussed under "Monetary Sovereignty and Exchange Controls" at para 31.45 below.

ways. It has been seen that Member States could no longer apply any system of exchange control; indeed, the very existence of a monetary union implies the abolition of all forms of such control, at the very least, as between the constituent territories.[5] This, however, was not the limit of the matter. The concept of national monetary sovereignty would, in general terms, allow a State to require that transactions occurring within its borders should be settled exclusively by payment in the national currency.[6] The case law of the European Court of Justice demonstrates that this feature of national monetary sovereignty was likewise being eroded by Article 56 of the EC Treaty and by earlier directives which sought to establish the free movement of capital as a general principle of Community law.

The above point is perhaps best illustrated by the Court's decision in *Trummer and Mayer*.[7] In that case, Mayer was resident in Germany but owned a property in Austria. He sold a part share in the property to Trummer, but agreed that the price could be left outstanding for a period on the basis that it was secured by a mortgage over Trummer's share. No doubt Mayer conducted his financial affairs by reference to the Deutsche mark, and did not wish to accept any exchange rate risks in the context of future fluctuations between that currency and the Austrian schilling. For that reason, and notwithstanding that the property was situate in Austria, the price and the amount secured by the mortgage were expressed in the Germany currency. The transaction between them ran into difficulty; the Austrian authorities refused to register the mortgage because (a) the document secured a debt expressed in German marks and (b) the registration of a mortgage infringed the Austrian currency law unless the amount secured was denominated in Austrian schillings or determined by reference to the price of fine gold.[8] Having held that loan transactions involving a mortgage or similar security constituted "movements of capital" and thus fell within the scope of Article 56, the Court was required to consider whether the Austrian currency law had the effect of restricting such movements. In this context, the Court correctly pointed out that the effect of the currency law:

31.06

> . . . is to weaken the link between the debt to be secured, payable in the currency of another Member State, and the mortgage whose value may, as a result of subsequent currency exchange fluctuations, come to be lower than that of the debt

---

[5] On this subject and for possible qualifications to this statement, see para 31.45 below.

[6] On this point, see Ch 19 above. This right is, in effect, an aspect of the general right to control the use of the national currency.

[7] Case C–222/97 [1999] ECR I–1661. The decision was followed on the very similar factual situation which arose in Case C–464/98, *Westdeutsche Landesbank Girozentrale v Stefan* [2001] ECR I–173.

[8] From this formulation, it is perhaps unsurprising that the relevant Austrian law was one of some antiquity and had apparently fallen into disuse. However, this point does not detract from the general principle discussed in the case.

secured. This can only reduce the effectiveness of such a security and thus its attractiveness. Consequently, those rules are liable to dissuade the parties concerned from denominating a debt in the currency of another Member State, and may thus deprive them of a right which constitutes a component element of the free movement of capital and payments . . .

As a result, the Austrian requirement that security arrangements had to be expressed in the national currency was incompatible with Article 56 of the EC Treaty.[9] Plainly, the facts of this particular case could not arise again as between the eurozone Member States themselves. But the case serves to emphasise that the national monetary sovereignty of the individual Member States was subjected to Community law limitations even before the euro came into existence.[10]

31.07 Thirdly, provisions introduced into the EC Treaty to regulate the second stage of EMU likewise served to restrict national sovereignty in various ways.[11] There are two main illustrations of this position. Article 124(1) of the Treaty required Member States to treat their exchange rate policies "as a matter of common interest". Whilst it would be possible to debate the precise scope of the obligations created by this provision, there seems to be little doubt that it operates as a restriction upon the external monetary sovereignty of the individual Member States.[12] More substantive restrictions on exchange rate policy were imposed by the "Maastricht Criteria" set out in Article 121 of the Treaty. If a Member State wished to qualify for eurozone membership, then the necessary report would assess (amongst other things) whether the national currency of that Member State had remained within the normal margins of fluctuation provided for by the ERM for a period of at least two years and without devaluing against the currency of any Member State.[13] This provision is framed as a condition precedent to eurozone membership, rather than as a positive obligation on Member States. Nevertheless, it thereby indirectly placed further limitations on

---

[9] It should be appreciated that Article 58 of the EC Treaty allows Member States certain derogations from Article 56. In particular, Member States may apply tax laws which may differentiate between taxpayers resident in different jurisdictions or who have invested capital in different locations; likewise, there are exemptions from regulations designed for the supervision of the financial system or which are justified on grounds of public policy or security. However, any such measures must be of a non-discriminatory character—see Art 58(3) and Case C–439/97 *Sandoz v Finanzlandesdirektion für Wien* [1999] ECR I–7041.

[10] For further discussion of this subject, see Craig and de Búrca, *EC Law—Texts, Cases and Materials* (Oxford University Press, 3rd edn, 2003) 680–4; Proctor, "Taxation, Investments and the Free Movement of Capital" (September, 2001) *Butterworth's Journal of International Banking and Financial Law* 363.

[11] It will be recalled that the second stage of EMU spanned the period 1 January 1994 to 31 December 1998—see Art 116 of the EC Treaty.

[12] Since this provision continues to apply to Member States which remain outside the eurozone, the meaning of Art 124 is considered at para 31.36(5) below in relation to the UK.

[13] The Maastricht Criteria have been considered at para 26.11 above.

the conduct of exchange rate policy by those Member States which aspired to join the eurozone.

Finally, it may be observed that the conduct of monetary policy by Member **31.08** States was effectively constrained (if not overtly restricted) during the second stage. Without imposing positive obligations in this regard, the Maastricht Criteria set out in Article 121 of the EC Treaty achieved this result in two ways. The reports prepared in connection with progression to the third stage had to examine the extent to which each Member State had achieved "a high degree of price stability". This would effectively be evidenced by a rate of inflation comparable to that of the three best-performing Member States in this area. In addition, the reports had to assess the durability of the convergence achieved by each Member State, and this had to be reflected in long-term interest rate levels. Conditions of this kind circumscribed the freedom of aspiring eurozone Member States to reduce interest rates if the consequences were likely to be inflationary.

The transfer or limitation of national monetary sovereignty was thus something **31.09** of a gradual process. But the process was taken to its furthest extreme on 1 January 1999, when the euro was created. The introduction of the single currency had many obvious consequences for the national monetary sovereignty of the participating Member States,[14] in particular:

(a) the substitution of the euro for participating national currencies was stated to be irrevocable,[15] and as a result, the eurozone Member State lost the right to create, define, and reorganise a national monetary system;

(b) it necessarily followed that the right to conduct an independent monetary policy was lost, for this can only be achieved by a State or institution which controls a monetary system—the point is in any event made explicit by the EC Treaty, which entrusts the conduct of monetary policy to the ESCB;[16]

(c) the creation of the single currency also implied the loss of the sovereign right to impose exchange control or similar restrictions.[17]

---

[14] It may be noted that, as a matter of public international law, the conclusion of a treaty is seen as an exercise of (rather than a derogation from) national sovereignty, for "the right of entering into international engagements is an attribute of State sovereignty": *The Wimbledon* PCIJ Series A, No. 1, p 25. However, the ECJ views matters in a different light and has held that the Treaty does limit the sovereign rights of Member States in the field covered by the terms of the Treaty— see in particular, Case 26/62 *Van Gend en Loos* [1963] ECR 1; and Case 6/64 *Costa v ENEL* [1964] ECR 585.

[15] See, eg, Art 123(4) of the EC Treaty.

[16] ibid, Art 105(2), which imposes on the ESCB the task of both defining and implementing "the monetary policy of the Community" (ie of the eurozone). The provision is repeated in Art 3 of the Statute of the ESCB. The quoted language serves to emphasise that the creation of the eurozone necessarily connoted a single monetary policy.

[17] See para 31.05 above.

31.10   In effect, therefore, all national powers of legislation and action in the monetary law field came to an end when the euro was introduced in the participating Member States.[18] To the very minor extent to which Member States or their central banks continue to conduct monetary functions, these are effectively delegated back to them under the terms of the EC Treaty.[19] It is, however, necessary to highlight one final area in which it may be said that the eurozone Member States have indeed retained a degree of monetary sovereignty. As noted previously, the ability to define, organise, and replace a monetary system is a key aspect of national monetary sovereignty. It has already been shown[20] that the organisation and definition of the eurozone monetary system is now a matter of Community law.[21] But what of the power to *replace* the euro and to substitute therefor an entirely new monetary system? Does that aspect of monetary sovereignty now rest with the Community, or does it remain with the individual Member States? There is no question but that this aspect of monetary sovereignty originated in the Member States; it is thus necessary to ask whether it has been transferred by them to the Community under the terms of the EC Treaty. It is to be noted that the Treaty states that the creation of the euro is "irreversible" and "irrevocable". Partly for that reason, and no doubt for reasons of high policy, the Treaty does not contemplate that the euro might be replaced by a

---

[18] Of course, the accuracy of this statement depends upon the meaning of "monetary law field" for these purposes. In essence, it refers to those national competencies which were described as the attributes of monetary sovereignty in Ch 19 above. The German Supreme Court has acknowledged that the ability of Germany and its institutions to influence monetary policy "have no doubt been taken away almost completely in so far as the European Central Bank has been made independent as regards the European Community and Member States" but this was held to be justifiable under the terms of the German Constitution because "it takes account of the special characteristic . . . that an independent central bank is a better guarantee of the value of the currency"—see *Brunner v The European Union Treaty* [1994] 1 CMLR 57, paras 95 and 96. It may be added that it is not open to an individual participant Member State to introduce national legislation to revalue or adjust debts expressed in euros, because this would be a monetary law matter where competence now resides with the Community. Compare the decision of the German Federal Court (20 July 1954, *BVerfG* 4, 60) in which it was held that an attempt by an individual *Land* to allow for the revalorisation of debts affected by a currency reform could not be upheld; it formed a part of the monetary system and thus fell within the exclusive jurisdiction of the Federal State. It is submitted that this analysis would likewise be applied in a Community context even though, in a narrower private law context, revalorisation affects *debts* rather than *money*, and is thus to be regarded as a part of the law of obligations, rather than monetary law. Nevertheless, the notion that individual Member States could separately revalorise debts expressed in the euro would seem to be inconsistent with the notion of a monetary union.

[19] eg in relation to the production of notes and coins at the national level, see Art 106 of the EC Treaty. Member States retain certain limited competences in the design and issue of coins—see Zilioli and Selmayr, *The Law of the European Central Bank* (Hart Publishing, 2001) 215.

[20] See Chs 28 and 29 above.

[21] This would be so even to the extent that individual Member States may have introduced parallel domestic legislation dealing with currency questions—see Case 34/73 *Variola SpA v Amministrazione delle Finanze* [1973] ECR 981.

substitute, single currency.[22] The "irrevocable" fixing of the substitution rates between legacy currencies and the euro[23] negates any suggestion that the Community has inherited the sovereign power to *replace* the currency system. That power must thus remain with Member States, with the result that an amendment to the EC Treaty would be required if it were desired to introduce a new monetary system to replace the euro itself.[24]

C. Monetary Sovereignty in the Eurozone

If participating Member States have largely foregone their national sovereignty   **31.11**
in the monetary field, who may now be said to be in possession of the corresponding rights? It is tempting merely to state that monetary sovereignty has been transferred to the Community, and yet this would be to oversimplify matters. In very broad terms, this statement is acceptable but it will be seen that monetary sovereignty has been transferred in a fragmented fashion and different monetary functions are exercisable by different bodies. It is fair to say that questions touching the external relations of the euro area and the competence of the Community and the ECB in this field have provided a certain amount of debate.[25] It is not proposed to repeat those arguments in great depth, for to do so would be to stray beyond the confines of the present work. It is, however, necessary briefly to consider the extent to which different aspects of monetary sovereignty have been attributed to different bodies under the terms of the Treaty. For these purposes, it is proposed to consider (a) monetary sovereignty and the ECB; (b) monetary sovereignty and the Community; (c) the exercise of external monetary sovereignty and the euro; and (d) the residual monetary sovereignty of the Member States. The first two issues are essentially issues of Community law whilst public international law has some influence on the last two issues.

---

[22] The substitution of the "euro" for the "ECU" was merely a rebranding exercise—see para 28.13 above.

[23] See in particular the language employed in Art 123(4) of the EC Treaty.

[24] In the light of the view that a Treaty amendment would be required, it must follow that the generalised legislative power contained in Art 308 could not be used as a basis for the introduction of a replacement currency: see *Opinion 2/94* [1996] ECR I–1759 and the discussion in Craig and de Búrca, *EC Law, Text, Cases and Materials* (Oxford University Press, 3rd edn, 2003) 125–7.

[25] See, in particular, Zilioli and Selmayr, "The External Relations of the Euro Area: Legal Aspects" (1999) 36 CML Rev, 273; R. Torrent "Whom is the ECB the Central Bank of? Reaction to Zilioli and Selmayr" (1999) 36 CML Rev 1229; Zilioli and Selmayr, "The European Central Bank, An Independent Specialised Organisation of Community Law" (2000) 37 CML Rev 591; and C. Herrmann, "Monetary Sovereignty over the Euro and External Relations of the Euro Area: Competences, Procedures and Practice" (2002) 7 EFAR 1. The materials produced by Zilioli and Selmayr have been consolidated and updated in their book, *The Law of the European Central Bank* (Hart, 2000) and are considered by Smits, *The European Central Bank in the European Constitutional Order* (Eleven International Publishing, 2003).

D. Monetary Sovereignty and the ECB

31.12 It will be recalled that the European Central Bank (ECB) has legal personality and thus exists as a separate legal entity;[26] the legal personality is not unlimited or unconditional but is linked to the functions which the ECB was established to perform.[27] It will be remembered that the European System of Central Banks (ESCB) comprises both the ECB itself and the national central banks of the Member States of the Community.[28] The ESCB itself does not have independent legal personality; rather, it is governed by the decision-making bodies of the ECB itself.[29] The national central banks within the ESCB are required to act in accordance with the guidelines and instructions of the ECB itself.[30]

31.13 It will be apparent from this discussion that the ESCB cannot readily be described as the recipient of any aspect of national monetary sovereignty from the eurozone Member States. The ESCB is not a legal person and the exercise of any form of right is difficult in the absence of such personality; in any event, the national central banks within the ESCB lack the decision-making power which is a necessary ingredient or incident of sovereignty, for they are required to comply with the instructions of the ECB. On this basis, it is difficult to argue that monetary sovereignty has been vested in the ESCB.

31.14 It is thus necessary to consider whether the ECB can be said to have received a transfer of any aspect of national monetary sovereignty from the eurozone Member States. It is suggested that the search for an answer to this relatively high-level line of enquiry must be limited to the Treaty itself, partly because it constitutes the primary source of Community law and partly because any assertion that national sovereignty has been transferred must ultimately derive its legitimacy from the Treaty itself, even if some of the detailed arrangements are later completed by means of secondary legislation. It must also be remembered that the right to *exercise* sovereign powers as a matter of Community law is *not* parallel to the ownership of such rights so far as international law is concerned.[31]

---

[26] Article 107(2) of the EC Treaty.

[27] The extent to which international organisations enjoy legal personality under both domestic and international law is a particularly complex topic. For discussion, see Brownlie, *Principles of Public International Law* (Oxford University Press, 6th edn, 2003) ch 30; White, *The Law of International Organisations* (University of Manchester Press, 1996) ch 2; Seidl-Hohenveldem, *Corporations in and under International Law* (Grotius, 1987).

[28] Article 107(1) of the EC Treaty.

[29] ibid, Art 107(3).

[30] Article 14.3 of the Statute of the ESCB.

[31] By way of comparison, the Bank of England is entrusted with the implementation of monetary policy under the domestic law of the UK, but this does not detract from the position under international law, namely that monetary sovereignty rests with the UK itself. To put matters

With these general considerations in mind, it is necessary to turn to the provisions of the Treaty itself.

Article 105(1) of the EC Treaty[32] states that the "primary objective" of the ESCB **31.15** is the maintenance of price stability, ie the preservation of a low inflation environment. Without prejudice to that core objective, the same provision establishes ancillary objectives requiring the ESCB to support the general economic policies of the Community with a view to contributing to the achievement of the overall objectives of the Community as set out in Article 2 of the Treaty; the ESCB is also required to act in accordance with the principles of an open-market economy with free competition, in accordance with the principles set out in Article 4 of the Treaty. It will thus be seen that the overriding task of the ESCB is to ensure continuing price stability. A reading of Article 105 suggests that this is an independent objective of the ESCB which stands apart from the policies of the Community itself; yet this cannot be the case, for the promotion of "sustainable and non-inflationary growth" is one of the key tasks of the Community as a whole.[33] The primary objective of the ESCB thus implicitly supports Community objectives; the ancillary objectives of the ESCB explicitly do so.

Article 105(2) of the Treaty[34] thereafter lists the functions (or "tasks") which **31.16** are to be carried out through the ESCB. These are:

(a) to define and implement the monetary policy of the Community;
(b) to conduct foreign exchange transactions consistently with Article 111 of the Treaty;[35]
(c) to hold and manage the official foreign reserves of the Member States (but without prejudice to the holding and management of foreign exchange working balances by the governments of individual Member States; and
(d) to promote the smooth operation of payment systems.

Point (a) of the above list should be particularly noted in the present context. **31.17** The ESCB is required both to define and to implement monetary policy but it is explicitly stated that this is the monetary policy *of the Community*. Thus,

---

another way, whether or not a State possesses monetary sovereignty is a matter of international law; the allocation of functions which flow from the existence of that sovereignty are a matter for the internal law of the State concerned. It should be emphasised, however, that analogies of this kind are not always appropriate in a Community context—see Zilioli and Selmayr, *The Law of the European Central Bank* (Hart, 2000) 8, noting Case C–359/92, *Germany v Council* [1994] ECR I–3681 and stressing the *sui generis* character of Community law.

[32] The provision is repeated in Art 2 of the ESCB Statute.
[33] See EC Treaty, Art 2.
[34] The provision is repeated in the ESCB Statute, Art 3.
[35] Article 111 allows the Council to enter into exchange rate agreements and to formulate general orientations for exchange rate policy. Article 111 is considered at para 31.20 below.

although the ECB, the ESCB, and the members of their decision-making bodies are required to act independently of the Community and Member States for these purposes,[36] nevertheless, it is made clear that the ESCB is exercising an internal Community law competence. Likewise, it will be seen from point (b) of the list that the central banks within the ESCB are entitled to conduct foreign exchange operations. No doubt any such operations must be consistent with the primary objective of price stability. However, more importantly in the present context, they must also be consistent with any exchange rate agreements entered into by the Council or any exchange rate orientations formulated pursuant to Article 111 of the Treaty; the tasks of the ESCB are in some respects subordinated to actions taken by the Council under Article 111. It must follow from considerations of this kind that neither the ECB nor the ESCB has received the benefit of, or the entitlement to, the monetary sovereignty which has been transferred by the Member States. It is therefore suggested that, whilst the ECB and the ESCB are responsible for the exercise of certain powers which are a necessary consequence of monetary sovereignty, they have not inherited it. This conclusion would appear to be supported, if only inferentially, by an analysis of other Treaty provisions. For example:

(a) Article 105(4) of the Treaty confers upon the ECB a right to be *consulted* on any Community act or proposed national legislation which falls within its fields of competence. This provision of itself suggests that the ECB's competence in the monetary field is limited to the types of "internal" functions described above.[37]

(b) Article 106(1) confers upon the ECB "the exclusive right to authorise the issue of bank notes within the Community". The Article immediately continues "the ECB and the national central banks may issue such notes". It follows that strictly speaking, the ECB requires *authorisation* from itself if it wishes to exercise its right to *issue* banknotes. If that is the case, then this suggests that the right to authorise the issue of banknotes is effectively exercised on behalf of the Community.[38] In other words, the *exercise* of

---

[36] On this point, see Art 108 of the EC Treaty. The position is mirrored by Art 7 of the ESCB Statute.

[37] Currency matters, means of payment and payment/settlement systems are amongst the areas where Member States may be required to consulted the ECB—see Council Decision 98/415 on the consultation of the ECB by national authorities regarding draft legislative provisions [1998] OJ L189/42.

[38] This may seem to be a strained interpretation, but it seems necessary to work on the basis that the ECB is acting in the dual capacity just described. Otherwise, it is difficult to understand the provision. Further, if monetary sovereignty had been transferred to the ECB itself, then it would have been clear that the ECB could issue banknotes and Art 106 would not have been necessary.

monetary sovereignty in relation to the printing of banknotes has been delegated to the ECB; but the *entitlement* to that sovereignty does not rest with the ECB itself.[39]

This brief analysis of the *internal* aspects of monetary sovereignty thus confirms that the ECB and the ESCB exercise numerous functions in relation to the euro, but that they are not the outright beneficiaries of the corresponding transfers of sovereignty which were made at the beginning of the third stage of EMU; since the ECB and the ESCB carry out tasks of the Community, they must be regarded as organs of the Community entrusted with the achievement of Community objectives. Whilst acting independently *within* the Community, they are not independent from it. Since the ESCB as a whole carries out the functions of a central bank in relation to the euro, it must be seen as the "central bank of the Community", even though it lacks separate legal personality.[40] It is difficult to see what other conclusion is possible.[41] The status of a central bank may be consistent with the exercise of monetary sovereignty, but it is not consistent with the *ownership* of it. That aspect of the discussion has in a sense served only to prove a negative proposition; but a positive proposition must follow in that internal monetary sovereignty must thus have been transferred to the Community itself. It is difficult to see what other conclusion could be possible.

31.18

---

[39] This impression is reinforced by the legal framework for the single currency itself. As we have seen, the currency was created by the EC Treaty itself and the power to take the necessary steps for the introduction of the currency was conferred upon the Council, rather than the ECB. On these points, see para 28.06 above.

[40] See Smits, *The European Central Bank in the European Constitutional Order* (Eleven International Publishing, 2003).

[41] It may be argued that the point is decisively answered by Art 105(2) of the EC Treaty, which makes it plain that the ESCB must be an agent or organ of the Community, for it is required "to define and implement the monetary policy of the Community"; not, it may be added, the monetary policy of the ECB or of the ESCB itself. Yet even this formulation is not entirely satisfactory, because the Community is not synonymous with the Member States which participate in the monetary union; it does seem odd that the ESCB should be described as the central bank of the Community when a number of Member States are not a part of the single currency zone. In practice, however, the Treaty addressed the point by excluding "out" Member States from the decision-making process in relation to monetary matters; see, eg, Arts 122(3), (4), and (5) of the Treaty. Likewise, the central banks of the "out" Member States are excluded from most of the material rights and obligations relating to the ESCB—see Art 43 of the ESCB Statute. The practical effect is that monetary policy and other functions conferred on the ESCB are exercised by the ECB and the national central banks of the participating Member States. Although it has no formal Treaty basis, this grouping has become known as the "Eurosystem"; on this subject, see Zilioli and Selmayr, *The Law of the European Central Bank* (Hart Publishing, 2001) 166–7. In view of the points just made, it was not unreasonable to state that "the Eurosystem is the central bank of the euro area"—see Paddoa-Schioppa, Introductory Statement at the Sub-Committee on Monetary Affairs, European Parliament, 17 March 1999.

E. Monetary Sovereignty and the Community

31.19 If *internal* monetary sovereignty now rests with the Community, what of the *external* aspects of the sovereignty? It has been shown that external sovereignty includes the right to impose exchange controls, enter into exchange rate or similar agreements, and generally to regulate monetary relationships with third States. In contrast to the question of internal monetary sovereignty, it may be observed that the external issues just noted are directly addressed by the terms of the EC Treaty.

31.20 First of all, Article 111(1) allows the Council, acting unanimously, to "conclude formal agreements on an exchange rate system for the ECU [euro] in relation to non-Community currencies". This provision appears to refer to international agreements similar to the type established by the Bretton Woods Agreement.[42] Significantly, the Council may act on a recommendation emanating from either the ECB itself or from the Commission. Whatever may be the political realities, the formal position thus remains that the initiative for the conclusion of an exchange rate agreement does not necessarily involve the concurrence of the ECB. It is true that the ECB must in any event be consulted with a view to reaching a consensus consistent with the objective of price stability; but it is clear that this is a right of consultation only and the Council may conclude an exchange rate agreement without the approval of the ECB.[43] Save that the Council is permitted to act by a qualified majority for these purposes, the same initiation procedure applies if the Council is to adopt, adjust, or abandon the central rate of the euro within such a system. It is therefore apparent that the Council may enter into and regulate formal exchange rate agreements without the concurrence of the ECB; such agreements would be binding on the participating Member States.[44]

31.21 The remainder of Article 111 may be said to deal with "lower level" arrangements concerning the euro and its relationship with non-Community

---

[42] On this point, see, C. Herrmann, "Monetary Sovereignty over the Euro and External Relations of the Euro Area: Competences, Procedures and Practice" (2002) 7 EFAR 1. On the Bretton Woods Agreement generally, see Ch 22 above.

[43] For the sake of completeness, it should be added that the European Parliament also has a right to be consulted under Art 111(1) in so far as it relates to the conclusion of formal exchange rate agreements.

[44] It may be emphasised that such agreements would not be binding on the non-participating Member States. On this point, see para 31.37 below and Usher, *The Law of Money and Financial Services in the European Community* (Oxford University Press, 2nd edn, 2000) 246–8.

currencies.[45] Nevertheless, these provisions serve to emphasise that, in relation to the eurozone, external monetary competence rests with the Community itself.[46] Thus:

(a) Article 111(2) allows the Council, acting by a qualified majority, to formulate "general orientations" for exchange rate policies in relation to particular non-Community currencies. Both the Commission and the ECB have a right to initiate such policies. If the initiative comes from the Commission, then the ECB has the right to be consulted, but no more. The ECB is required to effect exchange transactions in a manner which is compliant with these orientations,[47] but these orientations are expressly stated to be subordinate to the primary objective of price stability. As a result, it seems that the ECB could decline to give effect to these orientations for the exchange rate policy if this may have inflationary consequences; subject only to that reservation, however, the ECB is effectively bound by such orientations in accordance with Article 105(2) of the Treaty.[48] This formulation does, of course, illustrate the difficulty or impossibility of achieving a particularly satisfactory or complete separation of exchange rate policy from the conduct of monetary policy. The compromise nature of this position is further emphasised by the understanding that the power to formulate guidelines for exchange rate policy will only be exercised in the event of a clear misalignment of exchange rates or in other exceptional circumstances, and even then the Council will be required to respect the independence of the ESCB and the objective of price stability.[49] Nevertheless, it is clear that the ECB only has a right to intervene or object on the sole ground of price stability.

(b) Article 111(3) deals with the conclusion of monetary or foreign exchange agreements with other States or international organisations. The Council

---

[45] It may be added that the term "non-Community currencies" means precisely what it says. Consequently, Art 111 does not entitle the Council to conclude an exchange rate agreement or other arrangement in relation to sterling or the currency of any other Member State which remains outside the eurozone. Currencies of such Member States may be covered by ERM II, if they elect to participate in that system. Otherwise, the conduct of such Member States in the monetary field is to some extent constrained by the Treaty itself—see para 31.36 below.

[46] For further discussion of some of the points about to be noted, see C. Herrmann, "Monetary Sovereignty over the Euro and External Relations of the Euro Area: Competences, Procedures and Practice" (2002) 7 EFAR 10–13.

[47] See Art 105(2) of the EC Treaty.

[48] This point is by no means free from difficulty—see the discussion in Lowenfeld, *International Economic Law* (Oxford University Press, 2002) 658 and Hahn, "European Union Exchange Rate Policy?" in Giovanoli (ed) *International Monetary Law: Issues for the New Millennium* (Oxford University Press, 2000) 195.

[49] On these points, see para 8 of the Resolution of the European Council on Economic Policy Co-ordination in the Third Stage of monetary union (Luxembourg, 13 December 1997) [1998] OJ C35/1.

may negotiate and conclude such agreements on a recommendation from the Commission and after consulting the ECB. Once again, the ECB is confined to a consultative role, and it should be noted that Article 111(3) refers to the negotiation of monetary agreements "by the Community", thus again conveying the impression that external monetary sovereignty rests with the Community itself.

(c) Article 111(4) allows the Council, acting on a proposal from the Commission and after consulting the ECB, to decide on the position of the Community at international level in relation to matters of particular relevance to economic and monetary union. Once again, the dominance of the Council is apparent from the language of the provision.

(d) Article 111(5) allows individual Member States to negotiate in international bodies and to conclude international agreements. However, this right is expressed to be subject to Community competences and Community agreements in the field of economic and monetary union. On the face of it, this provision appears to reserve a degree of monetary sovereignty to the participating Member States in their individual capacities. But in reality this cannot be so for, as has been shown, both internal and external monetary sovereignty were fully transferred to the Community with effect from the beginning of the third stage.[50] The provision thus effectively reserves to Member States the power to enter into agreements dealing with economic matters in such areas as remain outside Community competence.

31.22 The ESCB does, of course, play a major role in the external representation of the euro area. The ECB may participate in international monetary institutions.[51] But the Treaty provisions which are relevant in this area also tend to emphasise that the ESCB is required to exercise monetary functions on behalf of the Community as the primary transferee of national sovereignty. For example, the ESCB Statute provides[52] that "In the field of international co-operation *involving the tasks entrusted to the ESCB*, the ECB shall decide how the ESCB shall be represented."

31.23 It follows from this discussion that, as between the Member States and the Community, external sovereignty in the monetary field now rests with the Community itself.

---

[50] This observation is subject to the relatively minor points discussed under "Monetary Sovereignty and Exchange Controls", para 31.45 below.

[51] Article 6(2) of the ESCB Statute. Eurozone central banks may likewise participate, subject to the approval of the ECB.

[52] Article 6(1), emphasis added.

F. Monetary Sovereignty and External Relations

The preceding sections have considered the consequences of the transfer of **31.24** monetary sovereignty and its implications for the Member States, the Community, the ECB, and the ESCB. It is now necessary briefly to consider the corresponding consequences in dealings with third States and international organisations.

For present purposes, it is necessary once again to distinguish between the **31.25** internal and the external aspects of monetary sovereignty. In so far as the substitution of the euro for participating national currencies is concerned, it has been seen that States are subject to an international obligation to recognise the effect of that step. However, recognition of the euro did not require any positive step on the part of third States at the beginning of the third stage; recognition in a positive sense was merely required as and when the occasion arose (for example, where a national court was confronted with a monetary obligation which was contractually expressed in a legacy currency). Furthermore, the obligation of recognition was probably owed—at least in the first instance—to the individual Member States, rather than to the Community itself.[53]

Recognition of external monetary sovereignty poses rather different issues. As **31.26** noted earlier, the exercise of external sovereignty may involve the conclusion of exchange rate and monetary agreements and the representation of the Community in international financial institutions.[54] But the Community may only conclude such agreements with third States or participate in international monetary organisations if (in each case) those States will recognise that the Community can indeed exercise that sovereignty as a matter of international law or, more likely, under the terms of the treaties or other instruments which establish the organisation concerned. Whilst the Community itself has established guidelines for the representation of the eurozone in its external dealings,[55] the practice of third States and other international organisations is more complex.

This state of affairs has given rise to some difficulties and anomalies in relation **31.27** to the main international institution of interest in this area, namely, the

---

[53] It is difficult to see how other States could owe the obligation to the Community, because the Community and the eurozone are not identical. Further, the eurozone is not in itself an international organisation or legal person, so it is difficult to see how it can enjoy rights or incur obligations for its own account.

[54] See the above discussion in relation to Art 111(1), (3), and (4) of the EC Treaty.

[55] See Padoa-Schioppa, *The External Representation of the Euro Area*, Introductory Statement at the Sub-committee on Monetary Affairs of the European Parliament (17 March 1999); The ECB's Relations with International Organisations and Fora, *ECB Monthly Bulletin*, January 2001, p 57.

International Monetary Fund (IMF).[56] The Articles of Agreement of the Fund stipulate that membership is only open to "countries".[57] The Agreement was, of course, negotiated in 1944 at a time when individual States were unquestionably the bearers of their own monetary sovereignty; the Agreement imposes obligations upon the member countries which presuppose the existence and retention of that sovereignty.[58] Member States of the Community remain members of the IMF in their separate capacities, yet they now lack the individual power to comply with these aspects of the IMF Agreement. The Community may itself have power to comply with the IMF Agreement, but it cannot become party thereto since it is not a "country"; under the terms of the IMF Agreement as it stands at present, the Fund can only "co-operate" with the Community within the strict terms of the Fund Agreement itself.[59] Under these rather unsatisfactory circumstances, the ECB has obtained "observer status" within the IMF and thus attends meetings of the latter's Executive Board[60] and the eurozone Member States are obliged to ensure that a common position is adopted, representing the eurozone as a whole.[61]

31.28 Finally, it might be argued that the eurozone Member States have become subject to an obligation to seek the renegotiation of the IMF Agreement such that the Community itself could be admitted as a member. It may be said that the IMF Agreement is incompatible with the EC Treaty, on the bases that:

(a) so far as Community law is concerned, the Community is the bearer of the external monetary sovereignty which formerly rested with the eurozone Member States; and

(b) the IMF Agreement is not in harmony with the position, because it continues implicitly to ascribe such monetary sovereignty to those Member States in their respective capacities of individual members of the IMF.

---

[56] For a discussion of some of the problems about to be discussed, see Martha, "The Fund Agreement and the Surrender of Monetary Sovereignty to the European Community" (1993) 30 CML Rev 749; and Lowenfeld, *International Economic Law* (Oxford University Press, 2002) 661–3.

[57] See Art II of the Articles of Agreement. This difficulty was recognised by the European Council, which called for "pragmatic arrangements" to ensure that Community positions would be presented in IMF fora—see para 10 of the Resolution of the European Council on Economic Policy Co-operation in Stage 3 of EMU, noted above. The Resolution also deals with representation of Community interests at G7 meetings and certain other matters.

[58] See, eg, Art IV(1)(iii), which requires a member country to refrain from the manipulation of exchange rates.

[59] See Art X of the IMF Agreement. The Community presumably falls to be regarded as a "general international organisation" for the purposes of that Article.

[60] The subject is discussed by Padoa-Schioppa (n 55 above).

[61] For a similar situation which arose in a Community context, see *Opinion 2/91* [1993] ECR I–1061.

Under these circumstances, the EC Treaty may require Member States to seek to **31.29** renegotiate the IMF Agreement so as to eliminate the areas of incompatibility.[62] This suggestion is, however, only put forward in a tentative manner, for it may be that the degree of incompatibility between the two documents is implicitly acknowledged and accepted by the terms of the EC Treaty itself.[63]

G. Monetary Sovereignty and the United Kingdom

It has been noted previously that questions touching the national sovereignty of **31.30** the United Kingdom have been at the heart of the euro debate in this country. Naturally, this is not the place to engage in a discussion of the political merits of the arguments and counterarguments which have been put forward in this area. Rather, it is proposed to examine the relationship of the United Kingdom with the eurozone and to consider the implications (if any) of that relationship for the monetary sovereignty of this country.[64]

The position of the United Kingdom in this area is conveniently set out in a **31.31** Protocol annexed to the EC Treaty (as inserted by the Treaty on European Union).[65] Paragraph 1 of the Protocol allowed the United Kingdom to notify the Council whether or not it intended to move to the third stage of economic and monetary union with effect from its commencement on 1 January 1999. In October 1997, the United Kingdom advised the Council that it would remain

---

[62] On this obligation, see Art 307 (second paragraph) of the EC Treaty and, for an example of its application, see Case C–197/96 *Commission v France* [1997] ECR I–1489, where Member States were required to denounce particular provisions of an ILO Convention found to be inconsistent with Community legislation in the same field. It should, however, be noted that Member States which comply with their separate obligations as members of the Fund cannot thereby commit a breach of the EC Treaty—see Art 307 (first paragraph).

[63] eg it may be possible to draw this conclusion from Art 111(4), which provides for the formulation of a Community position on international matters affecting EMU. It may then be inferred that Member States are thereafter required to support that position in international organisations of which they are separately members. However, it is not possible to express a definitive view in this area.

[64] It should be added that, until the accession of new Member States on 1 May 2004, Sweden and Denmark were the only other Member States which are not eurozone participants. The positions of all three States differ in various aspects. In particular, the positions of the UK and Denmark are dealt with in separate Protocols to the Treaty which are drafted in different terms, whilst Sweden is (in the language of Art 122 of the Treaty) a "Member State with a derogation". Despite these differences of detail, the common factor is that none of the Member States have progressed to the third stage. The effective position of all three is therefore broadly the same for these purposes.

[65] These provisions have usually been referred to as the UK's "opt-out" from monetary union. For reasons which will become apparent, they might more accurately be described as an "opt-in", at least from a legal perspective.

outside the eurozone at that time. This, of course, remains the position at the time of writing.

31.32 The United Kingdom now has the right to become a member of the eurozone, by giving notice to the Council to that effect. The only precondition is that the United Kingdom must qualify for membership under the "Maastricht Criteria" which have been discussed earlier.[66] If the United Kingdom gave such notice, then the following procedures would apply:[67]

(1) The Commission and the ECB would report to the Council on the progress made by the United Kingdom in fulfilling its "stage two" obligations with respect to economic and monetary union.[68] The report must also include an assessment of (a) the degree of economic convergence achieved by the United Kingdom with reference to the Maastricht Criteria and (b) the compatibility of the UK legislation with the terms of the EC Treaty and the Statute of the ESCB.[69] As noted earlier,[70] the national legislation of the eurozone Member States must secure the independence of the central bank and must also enable that institution to operate as a member of the ESCB. No doubt many detailed legislative changes would be required for these purposes—for example, the Bank of England's monopoly on the issue of banknotes constituting legal tender within the United Kingdom would

---

[66] See para 26.11 above. Leaving aside compliance with the other economic tests comprised within the Maastricht Criteria, the principal difficulty for the UK in this area is its absence from the ERM; a two-year period of stable membership of that mechanism is stated to be one of the criteria in Art 121 of the EC Treaty. Whilst the two-year period was not rigidly applied in relation to all the existing eurozone Member States, it must be said that they had all been within that system for a period prior to their movement to the third stage. Sweden, likewise, is not a member of the ERM, and thus has an effective veto over its own membership of the eurozone—see the Sveriges Riksbank publication, *The Euro in the Swedish Financial Sector—Situation Report 5*, 7. It should be said, however, that on a strict reading of the Treaty, there is no positive requirement to join the Mechanism; the reports to be prepared in relation to a Member State seeking to join the eurozone are merely required to state whether the Member State has achieved "a high degree of sustainable conference *by reference to*" the Maastricht criteria (emphasis added). In other words, the key criteria is economic convergence; it is not necessary to comply with the strict details of each of the criteria. On the details of the ERM during the third stage, see para 25.22, n 65 above.

[67] On the points about to be made, see para 10 of the Protocol on Certain Provisions Relating to the United Kingdom of Great Britain and Northern Ireland. As is well known, the present Government has prescribed a series of conditions (including a positive referendum vote) which must be met before any such notice should be given. Those conditions are of a political character and it is thus unnecessary to discuss them here. It is only necessary to observe that any domestic legal step designed to prevent the giving of such notice would almost certainly fail. By way of comparison, see *R v Secretary of State for Foreign and Commonwealth Affairs ex p Rees-Mogg* [1994] QB 552.

[68] On these obligations, see para 26.08 above.

[69] On these points, see Art 121 of the EC Treaty, read together with Arts 108 and 109.

[70] See para 27.14 above.

plainly be incompatible with Article 106 of the EC Treaty, which confers upon the ECB the exclusive right to authorise the issue of banknotes within the eurozone; similarly, provisions dealing with the conduct of a purely national monetary policy would have to be repealed. If the United Kingdom elects to move to the third stage, then political considerations may lead the Government to introduce primary legislation to deal with that state of affairs and such legislation could doubtless deal with the matters of the type just described which—important though they may be to the lawyer—are of an essentially technical or consequential nature. Whilst primary legislation might therefore be the preferred route for these purposes, it is nevertheless suggested that the necessary domestic legislative framework could be achieved by Order in Council or statutory instrument under the terms of the European Communities Act 1972. Section 2(2) of that Act states that provision may be made "for the purpose of implementing any Community obligation of the United Kingdom. . .or of enabling any rights enjoyed or to be enjoyed by the United Kingdom under or by virtue of the Treaties to be exercised". This provision is reinforced by section 2(4) of the Act, which confirms that any instrument or Order made under section 2(2) may make provision similar to that which may be made by Act of Parliament. This, of course, includes the power to repeal any legislation which is inconsistent with the United Kingdom's progression to the third stage. It may be added that it would be inappropriate for the United Kingdom directly to legislate on matters covered by the Treaties or by the Regulation which the Council would introduce in order to cater for the introduction of the euro as the currency of the United Kingdom.[71]

(2) Following the submission of the report, the Council, meeting in the composition of the Heads of State or Government, would have to determine whether the United Kingdom met the conditions for eurozone membership.[72]

(3) If the United Kingdom were found to have met the conditions for movement to the third stage, then the Council would adopt the rate at which the euro would be substituted for sterling. The substitution rate requires the

---

[71] On the necessary Council Regulation, see point (3) below. Member States are under a Community obligation not to introduce national measures which reproduce Community regulations and which thus confuse or obscure the legal source of the Community measures—see Case 34/73 *Variola SpA v Amministrazione delle Finanze* [1973] ECR 981. Member States may, however, introduce legislation which properly falls within the field of the law of obligations, as opposed to monetary law in its purest sense. Member States in fact exercised this right upon the introduction of the euro; eg see the German Act on the Introduction of the Euro (2 April 1998) and, in France, Law 98-546 (2 July 1998).

[72] The Council must act on a proposal from the Commission and after consulting the European Parliament; for the procedure, see Art 122(2) of the EC Treaty.

unanimous consent of the United Kingdom itself and of the existing Member States.[73] The Council would also introduce a regulation dealing with the introduction of the euro as the currency of the United Kingdom.[74] In addition, the Bank of England would assume full membership of the ESCB. It would accordingly become obliged to pay up its subscribed capital in the ECB and to transfer to it foreign reserve assets in the required amount.[75]

31.33 Quite apart from the Treaty provisions just described, a number of practical and logistical issues would have to be addressed. For example, arrangements would have to be made for the withdrawal of sterling and the introduction of euro banknotes/coins within the United Kingdom. Financial institutions would need to make the necessary changes to their systems,[76] and arrangements would have to be made for the display and quotation of prices in the new currency. No doubt the United Kingdom would draw on the experience acquired in other Member States, both upon the creation of the new currency on 1 January 1999 and the subsequent introduction of euro notes and coins in 1 January 2001. These are issues of considerable practical importance but they are of limited interest from a legal perspective.[77]

31.34 The above discussion outlined the choices available to the United Kingdom and the procedures which will apply should it elect to move to the third stage. In terms of the monetary sovereignty of this country, membership of the eurozone would place the United Kingdom in exactly the same position as all of the other participating Member States, for the exemptions currently available to it in the context of monetary union would cease to apply.[78]

31.35 It thus remains to consider the monetary sovereignty of this country whilst it remains outside the eurozone. In this context, the overriding principle is set out in paragraph 4 of the UK Protocol, ie that "the United Kingdom shall retain its

---

[73] On these points, see Art 123(5) of the EC Treaty. The Council is required to act on a proposal from the Commission and after consulting the ECB.

[74] See, Art 123(5) of the EC Treaty.

[75] On these points, see Arts 28–30 of the ESCB Statute. These provisions have already been noted at para 27.08 above.

[76] On this subject, see Yeowart, "Creating the Legal Framework in the Financial Markets for UK Euro Entry" (March 2003) *Butterworth's Journal of International Banking and Financial Law* 81.

[77] It may be added that some of the issues raised at the time of the original creation of the euro—such as contractual continuity price, sources and similar matters which have previously been considered in Ch 30 above—would arise again in the context of sterling entry. However, the answers provided in Ch 30 would again apply.

[78] On this point, see para 10 (final sentence) of the UK Protocol noted earlier. The monetary sovereignty of eurozone Member States has been discussed at para 31.03 above, and the same comments would apply to the UK in the third stage.

powers in the field of monetary policy according to national law". This apparently straightforward statement is, in fact, less clear than it appears on first examination. In particular, if the United Kingdom is expressly stated to retain national powers in the field of *monetary* policy, what is its position in the context of *exchange rate* policy, which is not mentioned? Is it to be inferred from the quoted wording that the United Kingdom's freedom of action in the latter area has in some way been surrendered to the Community? Two points should be made here. First of all, paragraph 4 of the UK Protocol is limited to monetary policy as properly understood. Secondly, external monetary sovereignty is addressed in other paragraphs of the Protocol.

Leaving aside paragraph 4, the remaining provisions of the UK Protocol deal **31.36** with a variety of matters which are essentially the necessary consequences of the decision to remain outside the eurozone or which deal with the external monetary sovereignty of the United Kingdom. The points of interest in the present context include the following:

(1) In so far as the activities of the Community include the creation of the single currency and the introduction of a single monetary policy, the United Kingdom is exempted from those activities.[79]

(2) The United Kingdom remains subject to the (second stage) obligation to *endeavour* to avoid excessive government deficits,[80] whilst the eurozone Member States are under an *absolute* obligation to avoid such deficits.[81]

(3) Broadly speaking, both the United Kingdom and the Bank of England are exempted or excluded from those provisions of the EC Treaty dealing with monetary policy and the role played by the ESCB in that perspective.[82] This, of course, is the natural consequence of the United Kingdom's absence from the eurozone and the retention of its own monetary competences.

(4) It has been noted previously that external monetary sovereignty with respect to the euro is vested in the Community, in the sense that the Council enjoys primacy in such matters by virtue of Article 111 of the Treaty.[83] However, any action taken under those provisions is not binding on the United Kingdom.[84] Subject to the point noted in the next paragraph,

---

[79] See para 5 of the UK Protocol, read together with Art 4(2) of the EC Treaty.

[80] Article 116(4) of the EC Treaty, read with para 6 of the UK Protocol. It should not be forgotten that the UK is a participant in *economic* union even though, for the time being, it remains outside *monetary* union. Consequently, it continues to be bound by provisions associated with the economic aspects of the union.

[81] See Art 104(1) of the EC Treaty. For confirmation that this provision is not applicable to the UK, see para 5 of the UK Protocol.

[82] See paras 5 and 8 of the UK Protocol.

[83] See para 31.21 above.

[84] See para 5 of the UK Protocol.

it follows that the United Kingdom retains its external monetary sovereignty, in the sense that it may determine its own exchange rate policy without reference to Treaty constraints.

(5) The United Kingdom is required to treat its exchange rate policy "as a matter of common interest".[85] This provision can be traced back to the EC Treaty in its original form.[86] It is not easy to define the precise scope of meaning of a provision of this kind, but as a minimum, it would probably prevent the United Kingdom from taking deliberate steps designed to depreciate its currency with a view to securing a competitive advantage over other eurozone Member States.[87] However, a decline in the relative value of sterling as a result of external or market factors would not involve a breach of this provision.[88]

(6) In common with all other Member States, the United Kingdom is subject to the EC Treaty rules on the free movement of capital and payments.[89] As a result, the United Kingdom is unable to impose any form of exchange control system which would be inconsistent with those provisions. Unlike other Member States, however, the United Kingdom remains entitled to take unilateral protective measures in the event of a sudden crisis in its balance of payments, or to enlist the assistance of the Commission in the case of less serious difficulties.[90]

31.37 In summary, it appears that the United Kingdom retains internal monetary sovereignty in respect of the conduct of monetary policy. The position in relation to external monetary sovereignty is a little more complex. The United Kingdom retains its external monetary sovereignty in the sense that it may determine its own exchange rate policy, although this is to some extent constrained by the "common interest" provision which has been discussed above. This country's ability to impose a system of exchange control is effectively

---

[85] Article 124 of the EC Treaty, read together with para 6 of the UK Protocol. If further confirmation were needed, it is clear from this provision that the UK retains competence in the field of its sterling exchange rate policy, subject to the constraints imposed by the Treaty.

[86] Article 107(1) of that Treaty, adopting slightly different language, described exchange rate policies as "A matter of common concern."

[87] This interpretation is perhaps reinforced by other provisions of the Treaty, eg the acknowledgement that the Community's movement to the third stage was "irreversible" (see Protocol on the Transition to the Third Stage of Monetary Union) and the duty of Member States to abstain from any measure which might jeopardise the achievement of Treaty objectives (Art 10 of the Treaty).

[88] By way of comparison, see *Chobady Claim* (1958) 26 Int LR 262; *Mascotte Claim* (1957) 26 Int LR 275.

[89] See Arts 56–60 of the EC Treaty, discussed at para 25.33 above.

[90] On these points, see Arts 119 and 120 of the EC Treaty, read together with para 5 of the UK Protocol.

nullified by the terms of the EC Treaty, although that position is attributable to the rules on free movement of capital and payments, as opposed to the monetary union provisions themselves.

In effect, therefore, the United Kingdom's membership of the European Community and its position in the second stage of economic and monetary union involves a partial limitation on its external monetary sovereignty. Transition to the third stage will involve the complete transfer of national monetary sovereignty to the Community, subject only to the minor reservations discussed earlier.[91]   **31.38**

H. Monetary Sovereignty and the Federal State

In the Fifth Edition of this work, Dr Mann commented[92] that: **31.39**

> . . . the transfer of functions to a monetary union involves the corresponding decline of the powers of the States who become its constituent members. It does not matter whether the union is equiparated to a federal State or whether the members continue to be called States . . . What matters is that numerous functions traditionally vested in the nation State are transferred to the union and that such transfer has far-reaching direct and indirect financial, economic, budgetary and fiscal consequences for the Member States . . . There cannot . . . be any doubt that a monetary union presupposes a constitutional organisation which is or approximates that of a single (federal) State . . .

It is necessary to re-examine this statement in the light of monetary union in Europe and the experience acquired since those words were written.

In so far as they relate to the transfer of national sovereignty, Dr Mann's observations have proved to be accurate. As noted earlier, transition to the third stage of monetary union involved the transfer to the Community of virtually all aspects of monetary sovereignty, both internal and external. It has also been shown that the sovereign discretion of eurozone Member States in the economic, budgetary, and financial fields has been constrained both in terms of the need to comply with the Maastricht Criteria for admission to the zone and in terms of the ongoing fiscal and budgetary requirements imposed by the Treaty and the Stability and Growth Pact.[93] But in view of the sensitivities which surround the question of national sovereignty, it is also necessary to ask whether monetary union has created a constitutional structure akin to that of a federal State. In other words, is the Community a "State" in international law, such that   **31.40**

---

[91] See "Member States and the Transfer of Sovereignty", para 31.03 above.
[92] At pp 508–9.
[93] See para 26.15 above.

the current Member States are relegated to the role of mere constituent parts of that State? If so, does that consequence follow from the transition to the third stage of monetary union? These are not straightforward questions, but these issues are raised periodically and it seems appropriate to attempt a response based upon a purely legal analysis of the current position.[94]

31.41 A federal State has been defined as a union of several sovereign States which has organs of its own and is vested with power, not only over the member States, but also over their citizens. The union is generally established by means of an international treaty between the member States, but is subsequently based upon a jointly accepted constitution. A federal State is said to be a State which exists side by side with its member States, because the organs of the federal State have direct powers over the citizens of the member States.[95] At this point, it is fair to observe that the Community exhibits certain features of a federal State—even disregarding the consequences of economic and monetary union—for regulations and certain provisions of the EC Treaty itself will have direct effect in Member States.[96] No further, domestic legislative action or intervention is required in order to clothe those measures with legal effect.

31.42 Nevertheless, it is suggested that the Community must continue to be seen as an international organisation, and not as a State. The legal personality and capacity of the Community continues to depend upon the terms of the treaty between the Member States[97] and this seems to be inconsistent with the notion that the Community can exist as a State in its own right. In other words, the Community has not yet satisfied the second test for the creation of a federal State—it has not yet adopted an agreed form of constitution.[98]

---

[94] It may well be argued in particular, that the term "federal State" is merely a label and it does not greatly matter whether that label can be attached to the present Community arrangements; what matters is the extent to which powers of a sovereign character are transferred to, or retained by, the individual Member States and the consequences of that division. So far as the internal relationship between Member States and Community is concerned, the present writer would have some sympathy with that view, although it must be said that labels of this kind can have a peculiar cogency in the domestic political context. However that may be, the point would clearly be important from the perspective of international law; if the Community were a State (rather than an international organisation), then it would assume a very different set of rights and obligations on the plane of international law. Apart from other considerations, it would become eligible for admission as a member country of the IMF under Art II(2) of the IMF Agreement—see the discussion at para 31.27 above.

[95] These points are drawn from *Oppenheim's International Law* (Longman, 9th edn, 1991) para 75.

[96] See the discussion by T.C. Fischer and S. Neff, "Some thoughts about European 'Federalism' " (1995) 44 ICLQ 904.

[97] See Arts 281 and 284 of the EC Treaty.

[98] Of course, it must be noted that a proposal for a Constitution for the European Union has been agreed by Member States, but it remains subject to ratification.

It is also necessary to note various matters from the perspective of a Member **31.43** State. First of all, whether or not the transfer of sovereign powers is so extensive as to prejudice the continued existence of a Member State under international law must necessarily depend upon the scope of the rights and powers transferred to the Community and on the extent to which those transfers may be revocable.[99] Secondly, it should be noted that a State exists in international law if (amongst other things), it enjoys the independent capacity to enter into relations with other States.[100] Despite the provisions on a common foreign and security policy introduced by Arts 11 to 28 of the Treaty on European Union and despite the power of the Community to enter into international agreements which are binding on Member States,[101] it seems clear that Member States retain the necessary degree of independence in the conduct of their foreign relations. It follows that the individual Member States thus remain "States" on the plane of international law; it necessarily follows from that conclusion that the Community itself cannot be a federal State.[102] It may be noted that the existence of a State on the plane of international law is in significant measure a matter of recognition by other States,[103] and the individual Member States continue to be recognised as such by the international community. Certainly, the German Constitutional Court regarded Germany as a State, albeit existing within a "federation of States, the common authority of which is derived from the Member States". As a result, Community law would "only have binding effects within the German sovereign sphere by virtue of the German instruction that its law be applied".[104] The Court went on to note that, despite its Community

---

[99] On this point, see Oppenheim (n 95 above) para 37, where it is noted that the continued Statehood of the individual members of the Community is not in doubt.

[100] See, Brownlie, *Principles of Public International Law* (Oxford University Press, 6th edn, 2003) 70; and Oppenheim (n 95 above) para 34.

[101] Article 300 of the EC Treaty. On this subject generally, see McGoldrick, *International Relations Law of the European Union* (Longman, 1997); McLeod, Hendry, and Hyett, *The External Relations of the European Court of Justice: A Manual of Law and Practice* (Oxford University Press, 1996); Dashwood and Hillion (eds), *The General Law of EC Relations* (Sweet & Maxwell, 2000); and Craig and de Búrca, *EU Law, Text, Cases, and Materials* (Oxford University Press, 3rd edn, 2003) 127–32.

[102] It may be added that, according to *Oppenheim's International Law* (Longman, 9th edn, 1991) para 7, the pooling of sovereignty involved in the membership of the Community may, in the final analysis, be regarded as temporary so long as the possibility of withdrawal from the Community remains open. This view may well have been acceptable when the last edition of that text was prepared in 1991. However, it is more difficult to support this view following the ratification of the Treaty on European Union. It must also be remembered that the EC Treaty provides no general right of withdrawal, although such a right is included in the text of the proposed European Constitution.

[103] On the recognition of States generally, see Oppenheim (n 102 above) paras 38–44.

[104] See that Court's decision in *Brunner v European Union Treaty* [1994] 1 CMLR 57, para 55. For the wider context of the decision and further materials, see Craig and de Búrca (n 101 above) 293.

membership, "Germany . . . preserves the quality of a sovereign State in its own right".

31.44 If this was the position prior to the introduction of the euro, has it changed as a result of the commencement of the third stage? Certainly, the transfer of monetary sovereignty itself does not necessarily deprive a State of its independent Statehood under international law, for the power to organise and control the monetary system is an incident or a consequence of Statehood, and not a condition precedent to its existence. The loss of the independent right to define and control a monetary system is thus not fatal in this regard; as noted earlier, it is merely one of the factors to be taken into account in determining whether a particular territory is no longer able to function with a sufficient degree of independence on the international plane. However, it does seem possible to assert that the creation of a monetary union does not *of itself* lead to the conclusion that the Member States have foregone their separate Statehood, nor that the Community has become a federal State.[105]

I. Monetary Sovereignty and Exchange Controls

31.45 It has been noted elsewhere that the provisions of the EC Treaty generally prohibit the imposition of restrictions against the free movement of capital and payments and that, accordingly, the creation of a system of exchange control would thus be inconsistent with the terms of that Treaty.[106] Yet, inevitably, this broad statement cannot be presented without qualification. On the contrary, it is necessary to observe that the EC Treaty specifically contemplates that exchange controls can be imposed in limited circumstances.[107] The concept of exchange control is perhaps a surprising one in the context of a single monetary area[108] and, given that the subjects of exchange control and monetary union are central to the present work, it is necessary to explore the subject in more depth.

31.46 As noted elsewhere,[109] all restrictions on the movement of capital and the

---

[105] It should, however, be noted that Professor Smits argues very cogently for a different conclusion—see *The European Central Bank in the European Constitutional Order* (Eleven International Publishing, 2003).

[106] See para 31.05 above.

[107] It should be emphasised that the EC Treaty does not employ the language of exchange control, but that is the substance and effect of the provisions about to be discussed. It may be added that some of the points about to be made are considered in the paper "Capital Movements in the Legal Framework of the Community", which is set out as an Annex to *The EU Economy: 2003 Review* (EC Commission, November 2003).

[108] It was noted in the context of a definition of a monetary union that all forms of exchange control would generally have to be prohibited—see para 24.04 above.

[109] See para 25.33 above.

making of payments—both as between Member States themselves and between Member States and third countries—are now prohibited by Article 57 of the EC Treaty. That provision is directly applicable within Member States. It is, however, subject to the explicit exemptions contained within Articles 56–60 and is also subject to other overriding provisions of the Treaty. Some of these exemptions have already been noted, but the following points are of particular relevance when considering the imposition of exchange control:

(a) Article 58(1)(b) of the Treaty confirms that, despite the terms of Article 56, Member States may "take measures which are justified on grounds of public policy or public security". The free movement of capital and payments may thus be restricted on this ground. It is true that such measures cannot be used as a means of arbitrary discrimination or as a disguised restriction on the free movement of capital and payments;[110] it is equally true that, in other contexts, the use of public policy and public security exemptions has been tightly controlled and restricted by the European Court of Justice.[111] Nevertheless, within that framework, Member States must retain some margin of appreciation in determining when restrictions on the movement of capital and payments should be restricted in reliance upon its own policy or security considerations. It is possible to envisage that a Member State might seek to impose a system of exchange control if it is confronted by a very serious domestic financial crisis. If necessary, such a system could apply equally to transfers and payments to other Member States as it does to third countries.[112] It may, however, be assumed that any such system of exchange control would have to be abolished once the policy or security considerations had ceased to be of concern.[113]

(b) Member States outside the eurozone may take "protective measures" in the event of a serious balance of payments crisis,[114] and this must include the ability to impose a system of exchange controls where appropriate.[115]

(c) In another class of cases, the Council is authorised to take "safeguard measures" for a period not exceeding six months to protect the operation of economic and monetary union, or to take "urgent measures" to restrict the

---

[110] See Art 58(2) of the EC Treaty.

[111] See para 25.35 above.

[112] The language of Art 58(1)(b) does not discriminate between Member States and third countries in this regard.

[113] This conclusion may be justified on a number of bases, eg by reference to the language of Art 58(1)(b) and by reference to the general principle of proportionality.

[114] The relevant procedures are detailed—see Arts 119 and 120 of the EC Treaty.

[115] Under Art 120(1) of the EC Treaty, which may be taken to reflect the principle of proportionality, any such measures "must cause the least possible disturbance in the functioning of the common market and must not be wider in scope than is strictly necessary to remedy the sudden difficulties which have arisen".

free movement of capital and payments to third countries. An individual Member State may adopt measures of this kind in urgent cases, with the result that the imposition of exchange controls may, in limited cases, occur both at the Community level or in relation to individual Member States.[116] It can be noted that the Council may in some cases take safeguard measures by means of a qualified majority vote, with the result that Member States could be required to administer a system of exchange control which they did not support.

31.47 Whilst these instruments remain available to Member States in extreme cases, it is to be hoped and expected that they will remain a matter of purely theoretical interest. Nevertheless, the above discussion serves to demonstrate that Member States retain a residual degree of external monetary sovereignty, in the sense that they may introduce forms of exchange control under limited and defined circumstances.

---

[116] The points made in this paragraph represent a very brief summary of Arts 59 and 60 of the EC Treaty. Article 60 deals with measures taken in support of the common foreign and security policy, and thus does not contemplate a general system of exchange controls.

32

WITHDRAWAL FROM THE EUROZONE

A. Introduction

There can be no doubt that the introduction of the euro must be seen as a **32.01** highly successful exercise. The single currency came into being on 1 January 1999, precisely in accordance with the terms of the EC Treaty. Upon their introduction at the beginning of 2002, physical notes and coins were distributed across the eurozone very rapidly and smoothly indeed, and national notes and coins were withdrawn from circulation even more quickly than had originally been contemplated. Given both the enormous implications and the scale and complexity of the single currency project, it must be accepted that its implementation represents a very considerable achievement on the part of all of the institutions involved.

Against that background, it is not the function of a legal text to speculate on the **32.02** likelihood that the single currency ideal will come to grief, or to comment on the possible causes of such an occurrence. If a Member State withdrew from the eurozone, then the *causes* of that decision would be of a political nature which are not an appropriate subject for discussion in a work of this kind; the *consequences* of such a decision may, however, give rise to questions which would require resolution in legal terms. It is thus necessary to emphasise that a withdrawal from the eurozone is very difficult to imagine and almost impossible to achieve in political terms, especially bearing in mind the interdependence of the eurozone's financial systems. It is perhaps no coincidence that, in the period leading up to the introduction of the single currency, there was considerable speculation about the possibility that a Member State might, for a variety of reasons, be compelled to withdraw from the eurozone at a later date.[1] But, following the successful introduction of the single currency, a distinct silence has fallen upon that particular debate. The present discussion is therefore motivated by the present writer's view that such a withdrawal would give rise to questions of a relatively complex nature which may be instructive in the fields of monetary law and monetary sovereignty; the discussion is therefore of an essentially theoretical nature.[2] Nevertheless, there is growing interest in single currency areas as a form of monetary organisation[3] and it cannot necessarily be assumed that all will be equally successful. It may therefore be that the present discussion will be of practical relevance at some point in relation to a single currency area and that the eurozone offers a convenient medium through which the present issues can be considered.

32.03 What then, is the nature of the legal issues which might flow from a withdrawal from the eurozone? In some respects, these resemble the issues discussed earlier[4] in the context of the identification of the money of account and subsequent uncertainty; it will therefore be necessary to cross-refer to the earlier commentary from time to time. But as will be seen, a withdrawal from the present monetary union arrangements within the eurozone would raise issues of a broader and deeper nature, partly because the monetary union was created by treaty between all EC Member States (including the United Kingdom and others not currently participating in the union). As a result, a departure from the eurozone by one or more participating Member States would have consequences at two levels. First of all, it would have a clear impact on the position of the affected Member State under the EC Treaty. Secondly, it would create difficulties in the context of monetary obligations expressed in euros. As will be seen, it is the view of the present writer that these two consequences cannot be viewed entirely separately but are, in some important respects, interrelated.

32.04 The legal consequences which would flow from a withdrawal from the eurozone appear to depend in some measure upon the manner in which such withdrawal is achieved, ie whether it results from (a) amendments to the EC Treaty negotiated with other Member States or (b) a unilateral decision by one or more

---

[1] See, eg, Paul Mortimer-Lee, "Could EMU break up?" in Paul Temperton (ed) *The Euro* (John Wiley & Sons, 2nd edn, 1998); and *Financial Times Survey on Economic and Monetary Union* (23 March 1998).

[2] Once again, the present writer would wish to emphasise the point which has just been made.

[3] See generally, Ch 24 above.

[4] See Ch 6 above.

participating Member States.[5] It is therefore proposed to deal with the subject matter under those two headings.

B. Negotiated Withdrawal

Treaty consequences

If a participating Member State succeeded in negotiating its withdrawal from the eurozone then three related events would have to occur. First of all, the euro would cease to be the currency of the Member State concerned. Secondly, the monetary sovereignty of the relevant Member State would be restored to it.[6] Thirdly, the Member State would have to create a new, domestic currency. With this broad framework in mind, how would a negotiated withdrawal have to be effected ?

32.05

It will be remembered that the substitution of the euro for each national currency is stated to be irrevocable, and that the process of monetary union was declared to be irreversible.[7] As a necessary consequence, the Treaty does not contemplate or make provision for withdrawal by a participating Member State. It follows that the EC Treaty would have to be renegotiated in order to permit the withdrawal of the participating Member State concerned. The Treaty can, of course, be amended with the consent of all signatories even though the original

32.06

---

[5] For the purposes of a legal discussion of a necessarily hypothetical state of affairs, this is inevitably a somewhat simplistic classification. The approach to problems of this kind could clearly be affected by the number of Member States seeking to withdraw from the eurozone and the circumstances which impelled them to do so. As a result, the views expressed in this chapter are of a tentative nature. It should be added that the present discussion will proceed on the basis that a single Member State wishes to withdraw from the eurozone. However, many of the issues about to be discussed would arise in an essentially similar form in the event of a multiple withdrawal from the eurozone. Indeed, as will be show below, the same essential principles would apply in the event of an outright dissolution of the eurozone.

[6] It will be recalled that the creation of monetary union involved a transfer of monetary sovereignty by the Member States concerned—see para 31.03 above.

[7] On these points see Art 123(4) of the EC Treaty and Protocol 24 on the Transition to the Third Stage of monetary Union. These points have already been noted and considered at para 31.10 above. It should be added that, if ratified, Art 59 of the Treaty establishing a Constitution for Europe would confer a right of withdrawal from the Union upon individual Member States. It would then be unnecessary to seek the consent of the Member States for that purpose, although the detailed terms of withdrawal would have to be negotiated. Article 59 does not specifically deal with the particular difficulties which might arise if the withdrawal involved a eurozone Member State, although the ECB has indicated that it should be "fully associated" with any such withdrawal process—see para 18 of the Opinion of the European Central Bank on the draft Treaty establishing a Constitution for Europe (CON/2003/20), 19 September 2003. The withdrawal procedure is discussed generally by Friel, "Providing a Constitutional Framework for the Withdrawal from the EU: Article 59 of the Draft European Constitution", 53 ICLQ 407.

text declares monetary union to be irreversible.[8] It should be appreciated that the approval of non-participating Member States (including the United Kingdom) would also be required in this context. The "out" Member States have the right to participate in monetary union[9] at a later date, subject to meeting the necessary criteria for that purpose. The EC Treaty cannot be amended so as to deprive them of that right, unless they have agreed to that arrangement.[10]

32.07 At present, the monetary law of the participating Member States is established by Community law, rather than by national law.[11] But, as noted earlier, monetary sovereignty could be restored to the withdrawing Member State by means of a subsequent revision to the EC Treaty. In many respects, this aspect may be regarded as a purely technical matter, as once it has been agreed that a participating Member State is to withdraw from the eurozone, then the restoration of its national monetary sovereignty is a necessary consequence of that agreement—it would follow as a matter of course. Much more difficult problems would flow from the institutional structure put in place for the single currency. It will be recalled that the central bank of each Member State became a member of the European System of Central Banks (ESCB); each national central bank was required to subscribe for a proportion of the share capital of the European Central Bank (ECB) and to transfer to it very substantial foreign reserve assets.[12] The central bank of the relevant Member State would presumably cease to be a member of the ESCB upon the withdrawal of that Member State from the

---

[8] Article 39 of the Vienna Convention on the Law of Treaties. The Vienna Convention can be applied in a Community context where it is appropriate to do so—see, eg, Case C–27/96 *Danisco Sugar AB v Allmäna* [1997] ECR I–6653 and Case T–115/94 *Opel Austria GmbH v Council* [1997] ECR II–11. It has been suggested that the irrevocable character of monetary union, as expressed in the EC Treaty, would prevent Member States from seeking an exit from monetary union—see Zilioli and Selmayr, "The European Central Bank, An Independent Specialised Organisation of Community Law" (2000) 37 CML Rev 591. The point is repeated by the same authors in *The Law of the European Central Bank* (Hart, 2001) 12–13. If this proposition were correct, then this would prevent a renegotiation of the EC Treaty now contemplated. However, it is suggested that the right of Member States to renegotiate the Treaty is not subject to any legal impediment, whatever the practical problems may be. The Treaty subsists within a framework of international law and the Member States thus remain the masters of the treaties—on these points, see in particular Case 26/62 *Van Gend en Loos* [1963] ECR 1 and *Brunner v European Union Treaty* [1994] 1 CML Rev 57.

[9] ie in a monetary union which *includes* the Member State which (in the supposed example) now desires to withdraw. Whilst this point is not explicitly stated, it appears to follow from the context of the Treaty as a whole. On the UK's right to "opt-in" to monetary union, see para 31.32 above.

[10] See Art 41 of the Vienna Convention on the Law of Treaties.

[11] A point confirmed in para 8 of the preamble to Council Reg 1103/97, which states that the introduction of the euro changes the monetary laws of the participating Member States. Articles 2 and 3 of Council Reg 974/98 make it abundantly clear that Community law is now the source of the monetary laws of the participating Member States. These provisions have already been discussed at para 29.12 above.

[12] See Arts 28–30 of the ESCB Statute, which have been discussed at para 27.08 above.

eurozone, and would accordingly cease to be represented both on the Governing Council and the General Council.[13] The most difficult aspect would be the settlement of the financial consequences of the withdrawal. The outgoing central bank would no doubt seek the repayment of its capital contribution to the ECB, and a *pro rata* return of its share of the foreign reserve assets then held by the ECB. The allocation of outstanding profits and losses of the ECB would also have to be addressed.[14] No doubt these figures could be calculated objectively with relative ease,[15] but the remaining eurozone Member States are under no obligation to consent to the departure of the Member State concerned; depending upon the circumstances of withdrawal, they might be inclined to extract a price for agreeing to withdrawal. The withdrawing State would also seek the return of foreign reserves to provide support for its newly created national currency,[16] and similar considerations would apply.

But returning to the main, monetary law issues, the essential consequences of a withdrawal from the eurozone would be as follows: **32.08**

(1) national monetary sovereignty would be restored to the withdrawing Member State;[17]

(2) in reliance upon its newly reacquired sovereignty in this area, the Member State concerned would create and issue a new currency, denominated by reference to such units of account as it may select;

(3) the central bank concerned would once again become subject to purely national jurisdiction[18] and would presumably again resume responsibility for the conduct of monetary policy and associated matters;[19] and

---

[13] These aspects of the ECB institutional structure have already been discussed at para 27.10 above.

[14] See Arts 32 and 33 of the ESCB Statute, discussed at para 27.08 above.

[15] ie by application of the key ratio most recently ascribed to the relevant Member State under Art 29 of the Statute of the ESCB.

[16] This discussion does, of course, presuppose that the initiative for withdrawal comes from the Member State concerned. It could equally be the case that withdrawal occurs under pressure from the remaining Member States, eg where the economy of the individual State has ceased to be comparable with that of the eurozone as a whole, such that it threatens the effective conduct of monetary policy and the cohesion of monetary union itself. In such a case, the balance of negotiating power may shift to the withdrawing Member State, producing results which may differ from those suggested in the main text. The difficulties which may arise when a territory leaves a currency area and needs to create a new currency unit were the subject of some discussion when the secession of Quebec from Canada was under consideration—see, eg, D. Laidler and W. Robson, *Two Nations, One Money? Canada's Monetary System following a Quebec Secession* (C.D. Howe Institute, Toronto, 1991).

[17] The Treaty and regulatory framework for the euro described in Chs 28 and 29 above would cease to apply to that Member State.

[18] That is to say, the "independence" requirements imposed under the terms of the EC Treaty and discussed at para 27.14 above would cease to apply.

[19] On the delegation of these powers under the EC Treaty, see para 31.03 above.

(4) the withdrawing Member State would, by national legislation, establish the rate at which the new currency is substituted for the euro.[20]

32.09 It is necessary at this point to make some observations about the practical aspects of this admittedly highly unlikely process. Even if a Member State is permitted to withdraw from the eurozone, it would remain bound by the other provisions of the EC Treaty, including those involving the free movement of capital.[21] It has been noted earlier[22] that Member States cannot impose restrictions on the movement of banknotes across borders, or any other forms of exchange control which would restrict transfers of funds through the banking system. Under these circumstances, it may be very difficult to manage the process whereby the new currency is introduced and exchanged for the euro in the withdrawing Member State. As an example of the difficulties, large amounts of physical cash and bank money could be drained out of the withdrawing Member State if it were thought that the new currency was likely to be substituted for the euro on unfavourable terms.[23] Conversely, euro funds could flow into the withdrawing Member State if its new currency was thought likely to be substituted on attractive terms. This could result in significant financial imbalances, with an excess of liquidity in parts of the eurozone, and liquidity shortages in others. It may well be fair to conclude that an attempt to withdraw from the eurozone will create problems of a magnitude even greater than those which such withdrawal seeks to solve. Practical considerations of this kind render a withdrawal very difficult to contemplate, thus perhaps ensuring that the present discussion remains in the realms of the purely theoretical.

Consequences for monetary obligations

32.10 The substitution of the euro for the former national currencies of the participating Member States was discussed at an earlier stage.[24] Although the introduction of the euro was surrounded by a number of legal, technical, and logistical issues,

---

[20] This, of course, reflects the theory of the "recurrent link", which has been discussed in more detailed terms at para 2.34 above.

[21] The free movement of capital rules have been discussed at para 25.32 above. The present discussion does, of course, assume that a Member State is withdrawing from the eurozone but is to remain a Member State of the European Community. In strict legal terms, this arrangement is, of course, perfectly possible in the context of a negotiated withdrawal. Whether it would be possible in political terms is an entirely different matter and would clearly depend upon the circumstances giving rise to the withdrawal.

[22] See the discussion at para 25.33 above on the free movement of capital, the direct effect of the relevant provisions of the EC Treaty and cases such as Case C–250/94 *Sanz de Lera* [1995] ECR I–4821.

[23] ie if the rate established under the theory of the recurrent link was expected to be less favourable to holders than the anticipated market exchange rate once the new national currency has come into being.

[24] See para 26.09 above.

there was at least a conceptual neatness and simplicity to the entire process. Diversity was being replaced by uniformity; eleven separate independent monetary systems were replaced by a single currency. It was thus clear that an obligation expressed in any legacy currency would be redenominated in euros as a consequence of the introduction of the single currency. In the absence of some special contractual term, the conversion of monetary obligations into euros was inevitable; there was nowhere else to turn.

In the present situation, plainly the opposite problem would arise—uniformity **32.11** is to be replaced by diversity. As will be seen, this creates a completely different set of legal issues. The key difficulty arises, of course, because the euro itself will continue to exist and a new currency will have been created in the withdrawing Member State. The question thus arises—in which of the two currencies are outstanding monetary obligations then to be performed? This already difficult issue is further complicated by the fact that courts in different countries may be compelled to come to different conclusions in identical factual situations.[25]

It is difficult to consider the present subject in a purely abstract manner, and it **32.12** is thus necessary to construct a purely hypothetical example for illustrative purposes.[26] In this context, let it be assumed[27] that:

(a) Belgium has negotiated its departure from the eurozone. It intends to introduce a new currency (the "New Belgian franc" or "NBF"). Belgian law provides that the NBF will be substituted for the euro on a 2:1 basis, thus providing the necessary "recurrent link" between the euro and the NBF.

(b) X Bank is a Belgian-incorporated bank based in Brussels. It has issued two guarantees in respect of the obligations of a customer which is, likewise, incorporated in Belgium. The first guarantee, issued in 1996, covered an obligation of 1,000,000 "old" Belgian francs.[28] Under the terms of the first guarantee, in the event of a demand, payment is to be made by credit to the beneficiary's account in Brussels. The second guarantee was issued in 2003, and covered an obligation of €2,500,000. If a demand is made under the

---

[25] See, in particular, the discussion at para 6.31 above.

[26] Once again, let it be emphasised that the example has been constructed purely for the purpose of illustrating some theoretical questions of monetary law. It is not intended to reflect upon the possibility that a particular Member State may elect to seek an exit from the eurozone.

[27] The chosen example works by reference to a bank guarantee, but it is suggested that similar considerations would apply to most forms of monetary obligation. The example of a guarantee is used principally because the monetary obligation does not stand alone but is linked to an underlying contract or obligation which may in turn be governed by a different system of law. The selected example thus illustrates some of the most difficult problems which would arise should a Member State ever seek an exit from the eurozone.

[28] ie the obligation was incurred prior to the introduction of the euro, and was thus expressed in Belgium's legacy (or pre-euro) currency.

second guarantee, payment is to be made in euros to an account of the creditor in London.

(c) The two guarantees are expressed to be governed by English law, and it is assumed that the beneficiary may take proceedings either in England or in Belgium. The beneficiary of the two guarantees is a company incorporated in England.

(d) The customer of the Belgian bank has now defaulted in respect of the covered obligations, and the beneficiary has made demands under both the 1996 and the 2003 guarantees.

32.13 It is necessary to ask—in which currency would the English[29] and Belgian courts express their respective judgments? The point may be of no small significance, given that Belgian law prescribes a fixed recurrent link but, in the foreign exchange markets, the euro and the NBF may fluctuate in value against each other. It may be observed that this feature distinguishes a departure from the eurozone from the more simple case where a State simply decides to introduce one monetary system in substitution for another. In the latter case, no question of market value fluctuation can arise, because the old currency is entirely extinguished; the only connection between the old and the new currency in terms of value is that provided by the recurrent link which will have legal force. In the present case, Belgian law will provide a recurrent link, but the "old" currency (the euro) will continue separately to exist.

32.14 It is appropriate to begin by considering the position of Belgian courts in this matter. It may be safe to assume that the new Belgian monetary law creating the NBF will be of mandatory application in proceedings in Belgium, regardless of the system of law which governs the contract as a whole.[30] However, the extent to which the Belgian monetary law is mandatory, and the scope of the obligations to which it applies, will of course involve the interpretation of that law. Thus, if the monetary law seeks to apply its mandatory rules[31] only where (a) the debtor is established or resident in Belgium *and* (b) the obligation is required to be discharged by payment in Belgium, then:

(1) In the case of the first (1996) guarantee, the obligation would (so far as the

---

[29] On the general power of the English courts to give judgments expressed in foreign currencies, see Ch 8 above.

[30] On rules of mandatory application, see Art 7(2) of the Rome Convention discussed in Ch 4 above.

[31] ie the "recurrent link" applies only in the circumstances about to be described. It is necessary to observe that some form of territorial or other limitation must be expressed or implied into the new Belgian monetary law. Whatever the legislation may apparently purport to provide, it is obvious that cannot simply convert *all* outstanding euro obligations into NBF obligations. Some form of limitation is plainly necessary, so that it is possible to distinguish between those obligations which are converted into the NBF and those which remain outstanding in euro.

Belgian court is concerned) fall to be discharged by a Belgian corporation in NBF, and judgment would be given accordingly. Both of the stated preconditions to the application of the monetary law would be met in these circumstances, and its application would be mandatory, regardless of the fact that the obligation is governed by English law. In applying the theory of the recurrent link, the Belgian court would first of all convert the legacy currency obligation (ie the "old" Belgian franc amount stated on the face of the 1996 guarantee) into euros at the rate appropriate[32] to "old" Belgian francs. It would then convert the resultant euro amount into NBF, by applying the substitution rate stipulated in the new Belgian monetary law.

(2)   The case of the second (2003) guarantee would pose greater problems, in the sense that the Belgian monetary law does not apply in these circumstances. That law recognised that the euro would continue to exist, and the scope of the new Belgian monetary law was restricted accordingly. Since the place of payment is London, the Belgian law does not apply. How, then, should the Belgian court approach this situation? In such a case, it is suggested that the Belgian court should construe the guarantee, and require that it be interpreted and performed in accordance with English law, as the law applicable to the contract.[33] English law would continue to view this as a euro obligation, because that currency continues to exist and the obligation can be performed in accordance with its stated terms. Belgian law cannot alter the terms of an obligation governed by English law. It follows that the Belgian court should accordingly give judgment under the second guarantee in euros.

It will be seen that the Belgian court is effectively asked to decide whether the monetary obligation meets the terms of the Belgian monetary law, ie whether the debtor is resident in Belgium *and* Belgium is the place of payment. If it does, then the euro obligation is converted into an NBF obligation. The Belgian court must apply this rule, regardless of the governing law of the contract or any other consideration. But in cases falling outside the scope of that mandatory law, the usual processes should be applied and effect should be given to the rules forming part of the law which governs the contract.   **32.15**

How would the position differ if proceedings were taken in England? In order to answer this question, it is necessary to examine the status of the Belgian monetary law before the English courts. In this context: **32.16**

(a)   The position under the first guarantee involves a review of the link with the "old" Belgian franc, in which that guarantee was originally expressed. It will

---

[32] That is in accordance with Council Reg 2866/98, which has been considered at para 29.29 above.
[33] See Art 10(1)(a) and (b) of the Rome Convention.

be recalled that English law recognised the substitution of the euro for the former Belgian currency on 1 January 1999.[34] Should the English courts recognise the further, purported substitution of the NBF for the euro? It is not sufficient simply to assert that the court should apply the *lex monetae* in this type of situation, for this begs a question—should the court apply the *lex monetae* of Belgium, or the *lex monetae* of the remainder of the eurozone? This, in turn, leads to a question of contractual interpretation, which must be governed by English law,[35] and that question is: by reference to which currency did the parties intend to make their contract? As noted previously,[36] this is an entirely artificial question, but the question can only be answered by reference to the inferred intention of the parties and it is plainly necessary to find an answer in order to give effect to the contract. In essence, it is suggested that the following question should be asked—did the parties *specifically* intend to contract by reference to the currency in circulation in Belgium? If so, then Belgian law must supply the *lex monetae*, and the English Courts should give judgment in NBF. If, however, the question is answered in the negative, then the obligation remains in euros, and judgment should be given accordingly. In the case of the first guarantee, it seems clear that the parties intended to contract by reference to Belgian money. The guarantee was originally expressed in "old" Belgian francs and Brussels was the contractually nominated place of payment.[37] These factors suggest that Belgian law supplies the *lex monetae* under the terms of the first guarantee. It follows that the guarantor can discharge his obligation by payment of the appropriate amount in NBF calculated by reference to the new Belgian monetary law[38] and any judgment on the guarantee should thus be given in that currency.

(b) In the case of the second guarantee, it will be noted that the obligation was originally expressed to be contracted in euros, the place of payment is London, and the beneficiary is established in the United Kingdom. The mere fact that the guarantor/debtor is a Belgian entity will not be sufficient to demonstrate that both parties intended to contract exclusively by

---

[34] See para 30.03 above.

[35] ie in accordance with Art 10(1)(a) of the Rome Convention.

[36] See, generally, Ch 6 above.

[37] As noted in Ch 5 above, there is a weak presumption that obligations are expressed in the currency of the place of payment—see *Adelaide Electric Supply Co v Prudential Assurance Co* [1934] AC 122; *Auckland Corp v Alliance Assurance Co* [1937] AC 587; and other cases there cited.

[38] It should not be forgotten that the Belgian monetary law will not merely identify the new currency but must also supply the "recurrent link", ie the rate to be applied in translating obligations expressed in the old currency into new currency obligations—see para 2.34 above. This rule can only be displaced if the new monetary law can be said to be confiscatory, as to which see para 19.20 above.

reference to the currency circulating in Belgium, for the contract is of an inherently "international" nature. The result must be that the English courts would not apply the Belgian monetary law; the obligation must thus be settled in euros and judgment should be given in that currency, if necessary.[39]

Thus far, the text has considered the problems which might arise if one Member **32.17** State departs from the eurozone. Although this situation has already highlighted a certain degree of complexity, one factor has helped to facilitate the analysis. As has been seen, it has been necessary to ask whether the law of the departing Member State supplies the *lex monetae* in relation to the obligation concerned. If so, then that law applies. If it does not, then—effectively by default—the *lex monetae* will be that applicable to the euro. Plainly, however, the relative simplicity of this approach would be lost if the eurozone were to suffer a total dissolution, such that the euro would cease to exist and all of the formerly participating Member States would create a new currency.[40] How would the courts resolve such a situation? In order to answer this question, it is necessary to revert to the two guarantees discussed above and the examples thereby provided.

In the case of the first guarantee, it was shown that the Belgian courts would **32.18** find the guarantee to be expressed in NBF, because the application of the new Belgian monetary law would be mandatory before the courts of the forum. The English courts would likewise hold that the obligation would be expressed in NBF, but they would do so on the basis that Belgium supplied the *lex monetae* in relation to the contract between the parties. Courts in both countries will thus reach the same conclusion, albeit by a different process of reasoning. In relation to the first guarantee, it follows that the Belgian monetary law will apply in any event; this conclusion would accordingly continue to apply even in the context of a multilateral withdrawal from monetary union.

The second guarantee would, however, pose far greater difficulty. As noted **32.19** earlier, both the Belgian and the English courts (again, for their different

---

[39] It should be emphasised that these examples are given purely for the purpose of illustration and—given that the object of the exercise is to ascertain the contractual intention of the parties— a much deeper analysis of the factual matrix would be required, which might lead to different results. For example, if it could be shown that the second guarantee had a particular nexus with the first (eg both guarantees were given to support different stages of the same, long-term commercial contract), then it *may* be possible to demonstrate that the parties in fact had in mind the continued application of Belgian monetary law. In such event, obligations arising under the second guarantee would also have to be discharged in NBF. This does, perhaps, serve to emphasise that, ultimately, one is seeking to ascertain the parties' intentions in a matter to which they will never have addressed their minds—an elusive process, even under the most favourable of circumstances. The possible permutations also highlight the sensitivity of the analysis which would be required, should such an unlikely state of affairs ever arise.

[40] It should be emphasised that we are still working on the assumption that the dismemberment of the eurozone is achieved by means of a treaty to that effect with the consent of all

reasons) would have concluded that the new Belgian monetary law would not apply and thus—by default—the guarantee continued to constitute a euro obligation. But the refuge of the euro is not available in the context of a multi-lateral dissolution of monetary union, for that currency will no longer exist. A more disciplined approach is thus required in relation to the second part of the required analysis.

32.20   For these purposes, it is necessary to recall the admittedly weak presumption that the law of the place of payment supplies the money of account in this situation.[41] Unfortunately, this presumption cannot be used in relation to the second guarantee—whilst the contractual document is expressed in euros, the place of payment is London,[42] and the United Kingdom was not a participating Member State at the time of the dissolution of the union.[43] It is plain that sterling cannot supply the money of account, because the parties clearly never intended to contract by reference to the currency in circulation in the United Kingdom. Equally, it is difficult to assert that the new Belgian law should supply the *lex monetae* in this situation because that law does not purport to apply to euro obligations to be settled in London, nor does it purport to provide a recurrent link for those purposes. The ascertainment of the parties' (presumed) intention as to the money of account would thus require a broader examination of the underlying circumstances. Thus, for example, if the guarantee covered primary obligations expressed in euros and incurred by an Italian customer of the guarantor, then this may suggest that the parties intended to contract by reference to the *lex monetae* of Italy—in that event, the obligation would now be expressed in the new Italian currency, and the recurrent link or substitution rate provided by Italian law should be applied.

Member States. The wholesale dissolution of the eurozone is, of course, an event which it is impossible to contemplate; but that does not detract from the points of theoretical interest to which such a hypothetical situation gives rise.

[41] See para 5.12 above. The presumption is, in any event, not a particularly strong one.

[42] It may be noted in passing that it is perfectly possible to maintain a euro account (and to clear euro payments) in the UK, despite its absence from the eurozone.

[43] At least, this is the factual assumption for the purpose of the illustrations now under discussion. It may be added that, had the place of payment been Paris, instead of London, then the presumption just noted would (in the absence of any cogent, countervailing factors) lead to the conclusion that the new French currency—introduced upon disintegration of the union—would henceforth be the money of account. The substitution rate (recurrent link) provided by the relevant French monetary law would therefore be applied. It may, however, be repeated that this presumption will readily give way to contrary indications. As the present example demonstrates, it may be especially difficult to apply in the context of a guarantee, where an examination of the money of account of the primary obligation will also be required.

C. Unilateral Withdrawal

Treaty consequences

Thus far, the text has considered the creation of new national currencies **32.21** following a renegotiation of the EC Treaty. The earlier discussion has established the approach which a court should adopt in identifying the money of account of a financial obligation following a withdrawal from, or the dissolution of, monetary union. In this context, it has also been established that the English courts would reach conclusions which are in some respects similar to those which would apply in the courts of the departing Member State —even if different lines of reasoning have to be adopted in each case.

How does this situation change if a participating Member State *unilaterally* **32.22** withdraws from the eurozone, without securing the consent of the other Member States or a revision of the EC Treaty for that purpose? Such a course of action plainly constitutes a breach[44] of its Treaty obligations on the part of the withdrawing State.[45] The withdrawing Member State would not acquire any right to the repayment of the capital or reserves contributed by it to the ECB and would thus lack the resources necessary to instil confidence in its newly established currency. For this reason, amongst countless others, a unilateral withdrawal from the eurozone would be very difficult to contemplate in practical terms. The fact that such a withdrawal would take place in contravention of the

---

[44] The text works on the assumption that unilateral withdrawal would indeed be a breach of the EC Treaty. There seems to be little doubt that this assumption is justified; a State cannot simply resile from its treaty obligations, and there is a general presumption against any right of withdrawal—see McNair, *Law of Treaties* (Clarendon Press, 1961) 493–500; the point is confirmed by Art 42 of the Vienna Convention on the Law of Treaties. It has been noted that Art 59 of the Treaty establishing a Constitution for Europe creates a unilateral right of withdrawal, subject to various procedural matters. In its commentary on that Article drafting the Convention's Presidium commented that "many consider that it is possible to withdraw [from the Union] even in the absence of a specific provision to that effect"—see the European Convention Doc CONV 724/03 at p 135. For the reasons just given, this must be a highly doubtful proposition. The same point is made by Smits, *The European Central Bank in the European Constitutional Order* (Eleven International Publishing, 2003) 44, note 246. In any event, even if Art 59 came into effect, it would still be possible for a unilateral withdrawal to constitute a breach of the Treaty if the applicable procedures had not been followed.

[45] A breach of an international obligation does not, however, necessarily constitute a breach of the domestic law of the offending State. For example, if Germany elected unilaterally to withdraw from the Community, it appears that the German courts would give effect to that state of affairs, even though the withdrawal was wrongful in terms of international law. In *Brunner v European Union Treaty* [1994] 1 CMLR 57, the Court noted that Germany remained a sovereign State and, even though the treaties were established for an unlimited period, Germany could revoke its adherence by domestic legislative action to that extent (see, in particular, para 55).

Treaty necessarily adds to the level of complexity involved, and certain aspects are thus considered in another context.[46]

Consequences for monetary obligations

32.23   What, then, would be the consequences of a unilateral withdrawal in the context of financial obligations arising under a contract? For this purpose, it is necessary to return to the two Belgian bank guarantees and the examples outlined earlier. The assumed factual matrix remains identical, save that Belgium has unilaterally departed the eurozone, without the consent of the other Member States.

32.24   So far as the Belgian courts are concerned, it is probable that they would continue to reach the conclusions earlier stated to be applicable in the context of a negotiated withdrawal. The application of the new Belgian monetary law would be mandatory in its stated sphere, and would be applied by the Belgian courts accordingly. Where the new law does not apply, then the relevant obligations would continue to be expressed in euros. It might well be argued that the legal framework for the euro—as created by the Treaty and applicable regulations—has direct effect and thus should be applied by the Belgian courts, regardless of conflicting national laws. So far as Community law is concerned, the Belgian courts should give effect to the supremacy of Community law because "the transfer by the Member States from their domestic legal system to the Community legal system of the rights and obligations arising under the Treaty carries with it a permanent limitation of their sovereign rights, *against which a subsequent unilateral act incompatible with the concept of the Community cannot prevail*", ie the doctrine of the supremacy of Community law should be applied.[47] However, whatever the merits of such a line of argument,[48] in the present context it is almost inconceivable that a national court sitting in the withdrawing Member State would apply this principle in its fullest rigour because of the immense practical difficulties which this would create; apart from other considerations it would, in the hypothetical situation now under consideration, deprive the newly issued Belgian currency of its status as legal tender within its own national boundaries.[49] For all practical purposes, a Belgian court would thus be compelled to recognise the realities of the situation, and apply the new Belgian monetary law in accordance with its terms.

---

[46] This subject is further considered under "Position of the Withdrawing Member State", para 32.29 below.

[47] Case 6/64 *Costa v ENEL* [1964] ECR 585—emphasis added.

[48] As a matter of Community law, the argument would appear to be conclusive.

[49] It will be recalled that, so far as Community law is concerned, the euro is the *sole* currency of the eurozone, and thus there is no scope for the issue and circulation of a "parallel currency".

It is, however, suggested that very different considerations would apply before an **32.25** English court; in particular, it is suggested that the unilateral nature of Belgium's withdrawal would have a very significant impact in this context. Why should this be the case? It will be remembered that the United Kingdom is under an international obligation to recognise the monetary sovereignty of other States, to recognise changes in the monetary systems of those States, and to give effect to the substitution rates prescribed for these purposes.[50] Further, the United Kingdom is not a member of the eurozone, and it is thus not immediately obvious why the English courts should have to pursue a separate agenda or adopt a different line of reasoning. Nevertheless, in the present context, it is suggested that the English courts would be compelled entirely to disregard the introduction of the NBF, and to hold that obligations expressed in euros must so remain, irrespective of the contents and intended effect of the new Belgian monetary law. This conclusion may appear both harsh and unrealistic, but it is suggested that it is justifiable as a matter of principle. In particular:

(1) In accordance with general conflict of law principles, the English courts will refuse to give effect to a particular rule of a foreign legal system if its application would be manifestly incompatible with English public policy.[51]

(2) For these purposes, the public policy to be taken into account by the English courts must include Community public policy. This comment may again have general application, but its importance is specifically confirmed in the case of contractual obligations, by Article 16 of the Rome Convention and the commentary on that Article to be found in the Giuliano-Lagarde Report.[52] Given that the establishment of monetary union was one of the primary objectives of the Community,[53] it must follow that the application of the new Belgian monetary law flies in the face of Community public policy. The English courts should decline to give effect to the Belgian law on that ground.

(3) Although the United Kingdom is not currently a member of the eurozone, it is of course a party to the EC Treaty. Subject to various conditions, the United Kingdom has the right to join monetary union, and is subject to certain obligations to the eurozone Member States.[54] Although there appears to be very little English authority which is directly in point, it is suggested that the English courts should—again, on grounds of public

---

[50] This general subject has been discussed in Ch 19 above.

[51] The general subject has been discussed at para 4.22 above.

[52] Article 16 allows a Court to decline to give effect to a foreign rule if its application would be manifestly incompatible with the public policy (*ordre public*) of the forum. Given that the Rome Convention was itself intended to further Community objectives, it is unsurprising that Community public policy is to be taken into account in giving effect to Art 16.

[53] See Art 4 of the EC Treaty.

[54] On these points, see para 31.32 above.

policy—refuse to give effect to a foreign law which is manifestly inconsistent with the terms of a treaty to which the United Kingdom and the relevant foreign State are party.[55]

(4) A decision to disregard the new Belgian monetary law would also recognise that Belgium has irrevocably delegated its monetary sovereignty pursuant to the EC Treaty, and cannot legislate in a field which has been taken up by the Community.[56]

(5) It might be added that this approach would also be consistent with other, more general principles of Community law. For example, the United Kingdom (and, by extension, its courts) are under an obligation[57] "to facilitate the achievement of the Community's tasks [and to] abstain from any measure which could jeopardise the attainment of the objectives of [the] Treaty". Equally, the United Kingdom was placed under an obligation to respect the process of monetary union, even though it was not itself an initial participant.[58] A decision by the English courts to give effect to the new Belgian monetary law clearly could not be reconciled with the principles just mentioned. This would place the United Kingdom in breach of its obligations to the other Member States—a position which the courts will generally strive to avoid.[59]

32.26 As noted earlier, it is suggested that considerations of this kind should justify the English courts in declining to recognise the new monetary law discussed in our example. But it has to be admitted that the matter is by no means clear cut. Counterarguments—in favour of recognition and application of the Belgian monetary law—include the following:

---

[55] One of the few authorities in this area is *Royal Hellenic Government v Vergottis* (1945) Lloyd's Rep 292. This part of the decision is stated to be "plainly right" by Mann, *Foreign Affairs in English Courts* (Clarendon Press, 1986) 133. It must, however, be accepted that the authority of the case for the present proposition is not incontestable, because the Court also cited a number of other grounds for its decision.

[56] See, eg, Case 60/86 *Commission v UK* [1988] ECR 3921; Case C–35/88 *Commission v Greece, re KYPED* [1992] I CMLR 548 and Case 24/83 *Gewiese v Mackenzie* [1984] ECR 817.

[57] See Art 10 of the EC Treaty.

[58] All Member States acknowledged that the monetary union process was "irreversible"—see Protocol 24 to the EC Treaty, on the Transition to the Third Stage of Economic and Monetary Union.

[59] A Member State cannot avoid liability for a breach of Community law, merely on the grounds that the relevant action was taken by a court or other constitutionally independent authority—see, eg, Case 301/81 *Commission v Belgium* [1983] ECR 467 and Case C–128/78 *Commission v UK* [1979] ECR 419. The same principle would apply to judicial decisions which are inconsistent with Community law, although it seems that in such a case, a breach only occurs if a court makes a deliberate decision to disregard relevant Community law—see the remarks of the Advocate General in Case 30/77 *R v Bouchereau* [1977] ECR 1999.

(a) If the English court wishes to disregard the Belgian monetary law, it can only do so by holding that Belgium is in breach of the EC Treaty. It should not be open to a domestic tribunal in England to determine that another Member State is in breach of its Community law obligations—such a decision should be reserved to the European Court of Justice.[60] Nevertheless whilst an English court may naturally be reluctant to express a view on such a sensitive matter, it is suggested that it should be prepared to do so in a plain and obvious case.

(b) In similar vein, it may be argued that the procedures created by Articles 226 and 227 of the EC Treaty—allowing the Commission or a Member State to take proceedings against a delinquent Member State before the European Court of Justice—are exclusive, in the sense that these are the only available procedures which may lead to a ruling that a Member State is in breach of its Treaty obligations. As a result, it is thus not open to a national court in one Member State to find that another Member State is in breach of its obligations under the Treaty. However, Articles 226 and 227 allow for proceedings as between Member States and the Commission. Accordingly they should not prevent the Community law issue being raised and decided in domestic proceedings between private parties.

(c) Generally speaking, the English courts will not seek to sit in judgment on the conduct of foreign governments within their own borders.[61] As a result, the English courts will not usually seek to analyse the merits of a domestic monetary law introduced in another State.[62] Likewise, the English courts cannot rule upon or enforce the obligations of foreign States under treaties to which they are party.[63]

Whilst arguments of this kind will inevitably cause some difficulty, it is tenta- **32.27**
tively suggested that the English court would be justified in refusing to recognise or give effect to the new Belgian monetary law. The introduction of that law and the unilateral creation of a new national currency within a eurozone Member State would plainly be contrary to Community (and thus English) public policy.

---

[60] cf the rule that a measure adopted by Community institutions can only be vitiated by the ECJ, and not by a domestic court within a Member State. The jurisdiction of the ECJ in this area is exclusive by virtue of Article 230 of the EC Treaty—see Case 314/85 *Foto-Frost v HZA Lübeck Ost* [1987] ECR 4199; Case C–27/95 *Woodspring DC v Bakers of Nailsea Ltd* [1997] ECR I–1847.

[61] See, eg, *Duke of Brunswick v King of Hanover* (1848) 2 HL Cases 1; *Underhill v Hermandez* 168 US 250 (1897); *Buttes Gas and Oil Co v Hammer (No 3)* [1982] AC 888 (HL); and *I Congress del Partido* [1983] 1 AC 244 (HL).

[62] It has been noted earlier that courts may not inquire into the economic merits or effects of foreign monetary laws—see para 30.21(b) above.

[63] eg see *Republic of Italy v Hambros Bank Ltd* [1950] Ch 314; *JH Rayner (Mincing Lane) Ltd v Department of Trade and Industry* [1990] 2 AC 418 (HL); and *Westland Helicopters Ltd v Arab Organisation for Industrialisation* [1995] QB 282.

That, it is suggested, would be the decisive factor in the extremely unlikely event that a case of this kind should ever arise. It would follow that the English courts would enforce all outstanding euro obligations by means of a judgment expressed in euros, notwithstanding that the relevant monetary obligation would have fallen within the scope of the new Belgian monetary law and even though Belgium would otherwise have supplied the *lex monetae* in the case at hand.[64]

32.28 In conclusion, it will be seen that a unilateral withdrawal from the eurozone could have far-reaching consequences in the context of the recognition of the new foreign monetary law and the position of contracts affected by it. The precise means by which withdrawal is achieved would have far-reaching consequences for private monetary obligations.

D. Position of the Withdrawing Member State

32.29 Thus far, the text has stated some tentative conclusions about the consequences of a participating Member State withdrawing from the eurozone, whether as a result of negotiations or as a result of unilateral action; but that discussion has been limited to the *contractual* and *monetary* implications of such withdrawal. It is now necessary to consider the legal position of the withdrawing Member State itself, including any potential liabilities which it might incur. In this context, it must be borne in mind that a withdrawal from the eurozone has far-reaching consequences not only for the Member States themselves but also for commercial organisations and individuals within the Community. For example, bank customers holding euro deposits in the withdrawing Member State may find that their holdings are converted into a new currency which depreciates rapidly in terms of its relative market value to the euro.

32.30 Where withdrawal occurs as a result of negotiated amendments to the EC Treaty, the withdrawing State would clearly have to comply with any penalties or other conditions imposed upon it under the revised Treaty. Apart from that consideration, however, the withdrawing Member State would incur no particular liability to the other Member States, for its withdrawal occurs in accordance with the terms of the revised Treaty. In the absence of a breach, the withdrawing Member State plainly incurs no liability to the other parties to the Treaty.

---

[64] Since this view is ultimately founded in Community public policy, it follows that national courts sitting in other Member States should in principle arrive at the same conclusion. Of course, if some form of political accommodation were subsequently made with the withdrawing Member State, then the policy considerations preventing the recognition of the new currency would fall away.

If there can be no liability to other Member States, what would be the position   **32.31**
of companies or individuals whose holdings of bank deposits or other monetary
assets fall in terms of their external value as a result of their conversion into the
new currency? May they establish some form of claim against the withdrawing
Member State in that respect? It seems clear that this question must be answered
in the negative. The withdrawing Member State is not in breach of its revised
treaty obligations, and the political or other grounds upon which a government
may decide to undertake or revise particular treaty obligations are not matters
which are capable of review by a domestic court.[65] As a result, a person who is
adversely affected by the consequences of a treaty revision cannot acquire a
claim in damages against the State concerned.

How would these conclusions change if a Member State elected unilaterally to   **32.32**
withdraw from the eurozone? It has been seen that the creation of the single
currency was stated to be irrevocable, and that the Community's progress to the
third stage of EMU was irreversible. Unilateral withdrawal would thus constitute the plainest breach of the terms of the EC Treaty. Proceedings could thus be
initiated against the withdrawing Member State either by the Commission or
another Member State; given that the withdrawing Member State would presumably not be in a position to remedy its breach, an unlimited penalty or fine
could ensue.[66] Furthermore, the central bank of the withdrawing Member State
would remain a shareholder of the ECB; it would be unable to recover its capital
contribution because the Treaty creates no express right of withdrawal and no
such right can be implied.[67]

It is also necessary to ask whether the withdrawing Member State might incur a   **32.33**
liability to compensate those who suffer loss as a result of the diminution in the
external value of their euro-denominated monetary assets, as a result of their

---

[65] At least, this is the position in England, where the conclusion of treaties remains a matter
within the scope of the royal prerogative and is not capable of judicial review—see, eg, *Blackburn
v A-G* [1971] 2 All ER 1380 (CA); and *R v Secretary of State for Foreign and Commonwealth Affairs
ex p Rees-Mogg* [1994] QB 552.

[66] On these points, see Arts 226, 227, and 228 of the EC Treaty.

[67] On this point, see White, *The Law of International Organisations* (Manchester University
Press, 1996) 62–3. It may be added that the text proceeds on the assumption that the Member
State withdrawing from the eurozone would nevertheless remain within the Community—a
position which is by no means conceptually impossible, given that other Member States currently
remain outside the zone. However, even if a Member State unilaterally withdrew (or purported to
withdraw) from the Community, it seems that the ECJ would retain jurisdiction to deal with
matters arising in consequence of the breach. For a comparable decision arising in a different
context, see *Appeal Relating to the Jurisdiction of the ICAO Council* [1972] ICJ Rep 46. The new
right of withdrawal to be found in Art 59 of the proposed EU Constitution has already been
mentioned at para 32.06, n 7 above.

conversion into the new national currency.[68] Although a breach of the Treaty is involved, it seems that this would not constitute sufficient grounds for a private claim for damages against the Member State concerned. It is true that a Member State may incur liability to individuals for a serious failure to give effect to Community law provided that (a) the result prescribed by Community law entailed the grant of rights to individuals, (b) the content of those rights can be identified from the Treaty provisions concerned and (c) there is a causal link between the breach of the Member State's obligations under the Treaty and the losses suffered by the claimant.[69] But it seems that these criteria could not be met in the present case. In particular, it should be remembered that the single currency was introduced with a view to encouraging economic growth and convergence between the Member States,[70] a formulation which suggests that the Treaty provisions dealing with the single currency were not intended to confer private rights on individuals. This impression is further reinforced by the fact that the relevant section of the Treaty appears under the heading "Economic and Monetary Policy". This part of the Treaty deals with government deficits, the Maastricht Criteria, and similar matters, thus placing the relevant provisions firmly in a macro-economic context. It is true that certain rights accrued to individuals as a result of the introduction of the single currency—for example, a right to discharge legacy currency obligations by payment in euros—but matters of this kind were merely incidents of the broader EMU project.[71] For these reasons, it is suggested that a breach of the Treaty framework for the single

---

[68] On the possibility that a currency substitution might amount to an expropriation and the consequences of such a situation, see para 19.20 above. The present section considers the matter solely from a Community law viewpoint.

[69] The principles stated in the text are derived from Cases C–6/90 and C–9/90 *Francovich and Bonifaci v Italy* [1991] ECR I–5357. It should be stated that this and similar cases considered the question of Member State liability for the non-implementation of Directives. However, it is assumed that essentially similar principles will apply to breaches of those provisions of the Treaty itself which are intended to have direct effect and otherwise satisfy the criteria just mentioned, for the Court noted (in paragraph 37) that "it is a principle of Community law that the Member States are obliged to pay compensation for harm caused to individuals by breaches of Community law for which they can be held responsible". For further cases and discussion of the general principle of State liability for breach of Community law, see Craig and de Búrca, *EC Law, Text, Cases, and Materials*, (University Press Oxford, 3rd edn, 2003) 257–74.

[70] See Art 2 of the EC Treaty.

[71] In any event, given the "legal equivalence" between legacy currencies and the euro (on which see para 28.13(5) above) the right to discharge a legacy currency obligation in euros was effectively a matter of form, rather than substance. For a case in which the House of Lords considered the extent to which an EC Directive dealing with banking supervision could create a right of action against the regulation following the collapse of a supervised institution, see *Three Rivers District Council v Bank of England* [2000] 2 WLR 1220. The House of Lords concluded that the Directive was intended to liberalise the financial markets, and thus did not confer upon individuals a right to a particular level of regulatory supervision in this area. The general tenor of that decision appears to support the position adopted in the text, and the decision of the Court of Justice in Case C–222/02 *Peter Paul v Germany* (12 October 2004) is to similar effect.

currency would not entitle an individual suffering resultant financial loss to seek compensation from the withdrawing Member State. As a general matter, it may be added that any attempt to obtain compensation from the withdrawing Member State would necessarily have to be pursued through the courts of that Member State. Quite apart from other jurisdictional considerations, the English courts could not entertain proceedings against the withdrawing Member State because:

(1) as noted earlier, the English courts cannot generally rule on matters touching the breach of the treaty obligations of another State, nor could they award damages in respect of any such breach;[72] and

(2) the reorganisation of its domestic monetary system by the withdrawing Member State would plainly constitute a governmental or public act on the part of the Member State concerned. Consequently, that State would be entitled to sovereign immunity in respect of any proceedings which sought to impugn those actions.[73]

E. Position of the Community and the ECB

The potential position and liabilities of a Member State which seeks to with- **32.34** draw from the eurozone have been considered above. It thus remains to consider whether the Community or the ECB could incur any possible liability if one or more Member States were to withdraw from the eurozone.

The only apparent basis for any such liability is provided by Article 288 of the **32.35** EC Treaty, which requires the Community to make good any damage caused by its institutions in the performance of its duties.[74] Article 288 imposes a corresponding liability on the ECB itself in the context of the performance of its own functions, and provides that non-contractual liability shall be imposed "in accordance with the general principles common to the laws of the Member States". The European Court of Justice has exclusive jurisdiction in relation to such matters.[75] Although the outcome will inevitably depend upon the precise factual circumstances, it appears unlikely that the Community or the ECB

---

[72] See, eg, the cases mentioned in n 61 above.

[73] See State Immunity Act 1978, s 1.

[74] On the whole subject of Community liability, see Craig and de Búrca, *EC Law, Text, Cases, and Materials* (Oxford University Press, 3rd edn, 2003) ch 13. It should be mentioned that Art 288 does not render the Community responsible for damage caused by the ECB, because the latter is not a "Community institution" for these purposes—see Art 7 of the EC Treaty. The point is also implicit in the language of Art 288 which contemplates that the liability of the ECB is separate from that of the Community itself.

[75] See Art 235 of the EC Treaty.

would incur any liability for losses which any person may suffer as a result of the withdrawal of a Member State from the eurozone. The following reasons are offered in support of this view:

(a) Monetary union was created by the EC Treaty, which was in turn created by the Member States. Similarly, a withdrawal from the eurozone would occur as a result of the actions of all of the Member States (in the context of a negotiated withdrawal) or of the Member State concerned (in the case of a unilateral withdrawal). Article 215 does not render the Community liable for the actions of the Member States.[76]

(b) Any losses incurred by a potential claimant will thus not have resulted from action taken on behalf of the Community, and the Community cannot incur non-contractual liability in the absence of a causal link between the conduct of the Community and the loss or damage in respect of which the claim is made.[77]

(c) Finally, neither the Community nor the ECB can incur any non-contractual liability in the absence of some unlawful act on their part.[78] It cannot be unlawful to renegotiate the Treaty in the context of a consensual withdrawal from the eurozone, and the Community cannot be taken to have acted unlawfully merely on the grounds that an individual Member State unilaterally, and in breach of the Treaty, elects to withdraw from the eurozone.

---

[76] See, eg, Case169/73 *Compagnie Continental de France v Council* [1975] 1 CMLR 578; Joined Cases 31 and 35/86 *Laisa and CPC Espana v Council* [1988] ECR I–2285; Case T–113/96 *Edouard Dubois et Fils SA v Council and Commission* [1998] 1 CMLR 1355.

[77] Case T–175/94 *International Procurement Services v Commission* [1996] ECR II–279; Case T–336/94 *Efisol v Commission* [1996] ECR II–1343; Case T–113/96 *Edouard Dubois et Fils SA v Council and Commission* [1998] 1 CMLR 1355.

[78] Case 59/83 *Biovilac NV v Commission* [1984] ECR 4075; Case 26/81 *Oleitici Mediterranei SA v EEC* [1982] ECR 3057. The ECJ has accordingly held that a measure of a legislative nature taken in the sphere of economic policy cannot generally give rise to any non-contractual liability on the part of the Community: Case 54/76, *Compagnie Industrielle et Agricole du Comte de Loheac v Council and Commission* [1977] ECR 645. As a footnote to this Chapter as a whole, it may be possible to consider whether a eurozone Member State could be compelled to withdraw from the zone on the basis that it had provided misleading statistical information in order to gain admission in the first instance. The point arose too late for consideration in this edition, but see the Commission Press Release IP/04/1431 (1 December 2004): "Commission Reports on Greek Statistics, Starts Infringement Procedure".

33

OTHER FORMS OF
MONETARY ORGANISATION

A. Introduction

The present Part of this book has thus far considered monetary unions in the **33.01** strict sense of the definition which was formulated for that purpose. Earlier chapters[1] have considered the State theory of money and some of the issues associated with it. As a result, this book has thus far placed a focus on what may be described as the two extremes of the monetary spectrum. At one end, one finds a State which issues its own currency and exercises exclusive sovereignty over its own monetary system. At the other end, one finds the eurozone Member States which have irrevocably transferred their monetary sovereignty to the Community.[2] As is well known, the political desire to stand at one extreme or the other has provided much fertile ground for the debate over the merits (or otherwise) of a monetary union in the context of the national sovereignty of the participating Member States. But between these two extremes lie a number of different types of monetary organisation or arrangement which may have differing degrees of impact on the national monetary sovereignty

---

[1] See, in particular, Ch 1 above.
[2] This statement must be read subject to the reservations noted in Ch 31 above.

of the States concerned.[3] In this context, it is proposed to examine the following subjects:

(a) international monetary institutions;
(b) the common organisation of monetary systems;
(c) dollarisation;
(d) currency boards;
(e) monetary areas; and
(f) monetary agreements.

B. International Monetary Institutions

33.02   In the present context, monetary institutions are international organisations the principal and specific object of which is the initiation and implementation of monetary policies and facilities. In terms of characterisation, it is thus necessary to exclude various types of organisation from the present discussion. At one end of the spectrum, it is necessary to exclude institutions such as the International Bank for Reconstruction and Development (the World Bank),[4] the International Finance Corporation, and the European Investment Bank; such institutions are involved in the borrowing and lending of money, but their activities lie outside the field of monetary policy. At the other end of the spectrum, it is necessary to exclude institutions whose objectives are of an essentially economic nature and which may therefore have an incidental impact upon issues of monetary policy. A significant illustration of this type of institution is provided by the Organisation for Economic Co-operation and Development (OECD), which was established by a treaty of 14 December 1960.[5] Given the relatively limited scope of the current line of enquiry, it is perhaps also necessary to exclude the Bank for International Settlements, which accepts deposits from, and carries out other transactions on behalf of, many central banks and also

---

[3] For a very helpful discussion of this subject, see Jean-Victor Louis, "Common Currencies, Single Currency and other Forms of Currency Arrangements" in *Current Developments in Monetary and Financial Law* Vol 2 (IMF, 2003) ch 33.

[4] This exclusion is necessary even though the World Bank was created contemporaneously with the IMF.

[5] Cmnd 1646. The principal aim of the OECD is stated in Art 1 to be the achievement of "the highest maintainable economic growth". As part of that objective, the Member States agreed (in Art 2(d)) "to pursue their efforts to reduce or abolish obstacles to the exchange of goods and services and current payments and maintain and extend the liberalisation of capital movements". It is perhaps difficult to derive firm legal obligations from this type of language, but its broad objective is clear. Furthermore, the obligation provides evidence in favour of the view that customary international law imposes an obligation not to obstruct payments of that kind. On that obligation, see para 22.29 above. It may therefore be that the treaty is of some value in the monetary field, but it nevertheless remains the case that it was designed primarily for economic ends.

plays a funding role in certain situations. It also provides a forum for the development of common standards in the field of bank supervision and capital adequacy. These roles have great practical importance for the international financial system but they are not directed towards the monetary policy of its Member States.[6]

In the strictly monetary sphere, paramount status doubtless attaches to the **33.03** International Monetary Fund (IMF), an international organisation currently comprising some 184 member countries.[7] The Fund was conceived at Bretton Woods 1944; it came into existence on 27 December 1945 and has been in operation since 1 March 1947. It is suggested that the Fund was established to fulfil three broad functions.

First of all, the Fund is required to promote "international monetary co- **33.04** operation through a permanent institution which provides the machinery for consultation and collaboration on international monetary problems".[8] No doubt much could be read into this provision, but it implies in particular the expansion of monetary trade, the promotion of exchange stability, and the creation of a multilateral system of payments. Secondly, as a method of carrying out these objectives, the Articles of Agreement imposed a system of par values for currencies, allowing for only a limited "spread" in the relevant exchange rate. Both the creation and the collapse of this system have been discussed earlier.[9] With effect from 1 April 1978, the Second Amendment to the Articles of Agreement substituted an inherently weaker exchange regime, requiring the Fund to exercise "firm surveillance" over the exchange rate policies of member countries and to "adopt specific principles for the guidance of all members with respect to those policies".[10] In the important field of exchange rate stability, it thus follows that the Fund has no substantive legal rights with respect to the exchange rate policies of its members and, correspondingly, the member countries have very few obligations with respect thereto. Thirdly, in order to increase their liquid international reserves, member countries are allowed access to the Fund's pool of currencies. Originally, this was derived from the subscriptions of

---

[6] For a general description, see Lowenfeld, *International Economic Law* (Oxford University Press, 2002) 622–4; for a more detailed description, see Giovanoli, "The Role of the Bank for International Settlements in International Monetary Cooperation and its Tasks Relating to the ECU" in Robert C. Effros (ed) *Current Legal Issues affecting Central Banks*, Vol I (IMF, 1992) 39.

[7] Several books and other publications on this subject were contributed by the late Sir Joseph Gold, who was for many years General Counsel to the Fund. See in particular *Legal and Institutional Aspects of the International Monetary System, Selected Essays*, Vol II (1984); reviewed by Professor Hugo J. Hahn (1986) XXXIV (3) AJCL. For a more recent discussion of the legal aspects of the Fund and its Articles of Agreement, see Lowenfeld (n 6 above) chs 16 and 17.

[8] See Art 1 of the Articles of Agreement.

[9] See para 2.07 above.

[10] See Article IV(3) of the Articles of Agreement.

member countries. Such access was available for certain transactions with the Fund, for example, for the purchase of another member's currency either for gold[11] or in exchange for the purchasing member's own currency;[12] in addition, a member is at certain intervals obliged to repurchase certain holdings of its own currency in exchange for gold or convertible currencies.[13] These transactions gave rise to many difficulties of interpretation[14] and they failed to ensure an adequate measure of international liquidity. As a result, the Articles of Agreement were amended in 1969 (the Second Amendment) to provide for a system of Special Drawing Rights (SDRs), which some may think has resulted in an even more obscure set of provisions.[15]

33.05 An SDR is simply a book entry, namely a credit in the books of the International Monetary Fund in favour of participating members, in respect of which the Fund pays interest in terms of SDRs at a rate determined by it.[16] The value of an SDR was originally 0.888671 grammes of fine gold, ie equal to the gold value of the "classical" dollar.[17] From the summer of 1974—without any amendment to the Articles of the Fund—the SDR was based on the "standard basket measure of valuation" comprising sixteen major currencies.[18] Since the date of the Second Amendment to the Fund's Articles of Agreement, the value of the SDR has been determined by the fund itself.[19] At first, the determination was again based on upon sixteen currencies, but various changes were subsequently made. In July 1978, the Saudi Arabian riyal and the Iranian rial were substituted for the Danish krone and the South African rand—the latter no doubt for political rather than commercial reasons. From 1981, the SDR was the sum of the value of five currencies, namely, the US dollar, the Deutsche mark, the French franc, the Japanese yen, and the pound sterling. The weightings were adjusted in January 1986, with the US dollar then representing 42 per cent of the basket. Since the creation of the euro, the SDR basket has necessarily

---

[11] Art V(6) of the Articles of Agreement.

[12] ibid, Art V(3).

[13] ibid, Art V(7).

[14] See, generally, Triffin, *Europe and the Money Muddle* (New Haven, 1957; Greenwood Press (Reprint) 1976) 111, 128; Gold, "The Reform of the Fund" (1969) 32; (1963) 12 ICLQ 1, (on Stand-by Agreements) and (1967) 16 ICLQ 320 (on Borrowing and Standby Agreements).

[15] The relevant provisions are set out in Arts XV–XXV of the Articles of Agreement. For literature on this subject, see Gold, in particular, *Special Drawing Rights* (IMF Pamphlet No 13, 1970); *Floating Currencies, Gold and SDRs* (IMF Pamphlet No 19, 1976); *SDRs and Gold* (IMF Pamphlet No 22, 1977); *SDRs, Gold and Currencies* (IMF Pamphlet, No 26 1979; No 33 1980; No 36, 1981); (1976) IMF Staff Papers xxiii 295; (1981) 16 *George Washington Journal of International Law and Economics* 1.

[16] Article XX(1)–(3).

[17] See Art XXI(2) of the original version of the Articles of Agreement.

[18] The basket valuation comprised various percentage weightings of those currencies with the weightings reflecting the relevant country's share of the world trade at the time.

[19] Article XV(2), which sets out the procedures involved in such a valuation.

been reduced to four currencies, weighted as follows: US dollar (45 per cent); euro (29 per cent); Japanese yen (15 per cent); pound sterling (11 per cent). The value of the SDR in terms of currencies is published in the financial press and is thus readily ascertainable.[20] The SDR has been used as a unit of account in many international treaties, no doubt because its "basket" nature implies a natural hedge against currency fluctuations and because it displays a (limited) degree of independence from individual national currencies.[21]

It should be noted that the creation and allocation of SDRs is a matter for the Board of Governors of the Fund.[22] In practice, the necessary level of agreement has been difficult to obtain, and no new allocation of SDRs has been made since 1981; the SDR represents only one per cent of the world reserve of assets.[23] When it is decided to allocate SDRs, the amount of the allocation is distributed pro rata to all Member States which are participants in the Fund's Special Drawing Rights Department, according to their respective Fund quotas.[24] A participant Member State which subsequently wishes to use SDRs notifies the Fund; in effect, an SDR entitles the participant to obtain an equivalent amount of foreign currency from other participants which are selected by the Fund itself.[25] The SDR has also been used in the context of international bond issues and similar transactions. However, it must be said that the private use of the SDR never mirrored the degree of success attained by the private ECU.

33.06

It will be apparent from this discussion that the SDR is not "money" within the State theory discussed earlier.[26] Apart from other considerations, it does not derive its existence from a delegation of monetary sovereignty and is not intended to serve as a generally accepted means of exchange. Nevertheless, and despite the relatively limited allocations, it is plainly recognised as a standard of

33.07

---

[20] At the time of writing, the value of one SDR is approximately US$1.46.

[21] For a discussion of some of the treaties which have employed the SDR, see the publications of Sir Joseph Gold mentioned in n 15 above.

[22] See Art XV(1), read together with Art XVIII(4) of the Fund Agreement.

[23] On these points, see Lowenfeld, *International Economic Law* (Oxford University Press, 2002) 520.

[24] A Fund member may become a participant in that Department by delivering to the Fund an undertaking to comply with the applicable obligations under the Articles of Agreement—see Art XVII(1) of the Fund Agreement.

[25] See Art XIX(2)(a) and XIX(4) and (5) of the Fund Agreement. The latter provisions explain the criteria to be applied by the Fund in identifying the participants which are to provide the required foreign currency, and provide a cap on the maximum extent of the liability of the participants so called upon. There was originally a requirement upon the utilising participant to replenish a proportion of the SDRs which it had used, but this is not currently in effect. On this point, see Art XIX(6) of the Fund Agreement. This subject and the possibility that the SDR system could be used as a source of development assistance, are discussed by Lowenfeld (n 23 above) 521–2.

[26] On the State theory of money, see Ch 1 above. The statement in the text remains valid even though the State theory of money has in some respects been diluted by modern developments.

value and is treated as a reserve asset—a point emphasised by the fact that SDRs could be comprised within the foreign reserves to be made available to the European Central Bank upon its foundation.[27]

33.08 The International Monetary Fund thus creates a narrowly based and limited form of monetary organisation, based upon a "basket" currency which is available for utilisation by States in the context of their dealings with the Fund.[28]

C. Common Organisation of Monetary Systems

33.09 Independent monetary systems may occasionally be organised on a common basis. This happened in the case of the Latin Monetary Union which, it should be emphasised, was not a "monetary union" in the sense in which that term has been defined for the purposes of the present work.[29] The union was formed between France, Belgium, Switzerland, Italy, and Greece "pour ce qui regarde le titre, le poids, le diametre et le cours de leurs espèces monnayes d'or et d'argent". The union subsisted with effect from 1865 and formally came to an end in 1921.

33.10 Efforts to standardise coinage across a number of States are of very limited value, for no single currency is involved and the arrangements do not involve any economic convergence or harmonisation of monetary policies. It will therefore be apparent that arrangements of this kind do not have any material impact upon the monetary sovereignty of the States involved.

D. Dollarisation

33.11 On occasion, a State may elect to adopt the currency of another State as its sole currency. An arrangement of this kind[30] has for many years existed in

---

[27] See Art 30.1 of the ESCB Statute. In this context, as noted above, SDRs are allocated to individual States. However, the Fund may prescribe that SDRs may also be held by the central bank of a monetary union—see Art XVII(3) of the Articles of Agreement.

[28] Essentially similar remarks could be made in relation to the ECU, which has been considered at para 25.14 above.

[29] See para 24.03 above.

[30] The adoption by one country of the currency of another as its sole currency is frequently referred to as "dollarisation". On this subject, see W. Max Corden, *Too Sensational: On the Choice of Exchange Rate Regimes* (MIT Press, 2002) 22 and 67. In view of the developments noted below, the expression "euroisation" has also come into use. It may be added that, in some cases, a country has elected to adopt a foreign unit as an alternative to its own currency, rather than as a substitute. Thus, in Panama, the US dollar circulates alongside the local baloa under the terms of Law No 84 of 28 June 1904. Prior to the introduction of the euro, a similar arrangement applied in

Liechtenstein, where the Swiss franc circulates as the sole currency.[31] More recently, Ecuador has adopted the dollar as its sole currency. The process of dollarisation in that country involved three stages. First of all, during the 1990s, businesses voluntarily substituted deposits and other investments in the local currency (the sucre) with their dollar equivalents. Secondly, the government announced the formal adoption of a dollarisation scheme on 9 January 2000, fixing the value of the sucre at 25,000 to the dollar. The statute endorsing this arrangement (the "Economic Transformation Law") was signed into law on 9 March 2000. Finally, on September 2000, sucre notes and coins ceased to be legal tender.[32] El Salvador and East Timor likewise adopted the US dollar as their sole currencies, whilst Kosovo and Montenegro adopted the euro.

Dollarisation differs from a monetary union in various respects.[33] In particular, **33.12** no treaty arrangements are necessary;[34] the "subsidiary" country merely needs to

---

Luxembourg where Belgian francs were legal tender as well as the local unit. This resulted from a treaty between the two countries: 547 UNTS 141–7. The risks and benefits involved in dollarisation are considered by Balino, "Dollarisation: A Primer" in *Current Developments in Monetary and Financial Law*, Vol 2 (IMF, 2003) ch 30.

[31] See the Monetary Treaty of 19 June 1980 and the Message of the Swiss Federal Council of 12 November 1980. Although there was no treaty at that time, Liechtenstein had previously adopted the Swiss currency by a statute of 20 June 1924. The 1980 treaty was concluded "without prejudice to Liechtenstein's monetary sovereignty" but Liechtenstein nevertheless undertook not to issue banknotes, submitted to certain Swiss legislation, and, in particular, recognised the authority of the Swiss National Bank. In the context of the euro, similar arrangements had to be established in dependent territories which had previously used the national currencies of their "parent" States. That subject has already been considered at para 29.13, n 28 above.

[32] It may be added that dollarisation in Ecuador was controversial at a number of levels. The first victim was the President who announced dollarisation on 9 January 2000; he was overthrown in a coup which occurred just 12 days later, by plotters whose motives were no doubt complex but which included a desire to reverse the process of dollarisation. For general discussion, see Schuler, "The Future of Dollarisation in Ecuador" a paper presented to the Instituto Ecuatoriano de Economia Politica, Guayaquil (August 2000); Emanuel, *Dollarisation in Ecuador: a definite step towards a real economy*, Andean Community Documents (Documents on Andean Community Integration, February 2002).

[33] It should be emphasised that the text is concerned with dollarisation as a formal, legally supported process such that the State concerned ceases to issue any currency of its own. In some countries, the effective adoption of the US dollar as a local medium of exchange may occur through popular action as opposed to legislative measures. On this subject, see Quispe, "Monetary Policy in a Dollarised Economy" in (July–December 2000) Monetary Affairs 167. See also the BIS Paper No 17, *Regional Currency Areas and the Use of Foreign Currencies*.

[34] Whilst not *necessary* in strict legal terms, the process of dollarisation *may* of course be formalised by means of a treaty—see, eg, the Swiss arrangements mentioned in n 31 above. It should be added that the absence of any requirement for the consent of the issuing State is a controversial topic and is by no means free from doubt. This aspect of the subject has been considered at para 22.21 above. It should, however, be noted that in each of the cases mentioned in para 33.11 above, none of the States which adopted the dollar or the euro entered into any bilateral arrangements with the issuing authority. On this subject, see *Official Dollarisation/ Euroisation: Motives, Features and Policy Implications of Recent Cases* (ECB Occasional Paper No 11, February 2004) 40. For a discussion of the economic distinctions between unilateral and

introduce domestic legislation adopting the "parent" currency and conferring upon it the status of legal tender.[35] Secondly, the parent country necessarily remains in charge of its own monetary and exchange rate policies; the subsidiary State necessarily has no (formal) influence in that regard. Where no treaty is involved, the subsidiary State cannot be said to have diminished its monetary sovereignty in terms of international law although in practical terms the *exercise* of that sovereignty is clearly very restricted so long as the arrangements remain in force; it could in theory revoke the arrangements and reintroduce its own currency at any time.[36] Nevertheless, for reasons given in the preceding sentence, the freedom of action of the subsidiary State in the field of monetary affairs is necessarily very limited; it will, for example, clearly have no representation within the central bank of the parent State in relation to monetary policy discussions.[37]

33.13 It should be appreciated that the foregoing discussion considers only those cases in which the dollar is adopted as a local currency by virtue of legal measures taken in the adopting State and which confer upon the dollar the status of legal tender within the boundaries of that State. Of course, there may be occasions in which the residents of a particular State lose confidence in the local unit such that the dollar is adopted as a means of exchange by general consent.[38] In countries which operate a system of exchange control along the lines of the United Kingdom model, it is fair to point out that such a "voluntary" process of dollarisation must be unlawful, because residents holding foreign currencies must generally surrender them to authorised dealers or to the central bank.[39]

---

bilateral dollarisation in the context of an ultimately abortive dollarisation proposal in Argentina, see Velde and Veracierto *Dollarisation in Argentina* (Policy Issues, Federal Revenue Bank of Chicago, March 2000) 24.

[35] In contrast, it has been seen that a monetary union must necessarily be concluded by treaty—see para 24.05 above.

[36] In terms of its domestic constitutional law, it is noteworthy that Ecuador has—notwithstanding dollarisation—retained Art 264 of its Constitution, which enables the central bank to issue the currency, subject to limitations imposed by the Government. In spite of this position, the Government has suggested that dollarisation is for all practical purposes irreversible—see the materials mentioned in n 32 above.

[37] This may be contrasted with the arrangements for monetary union in Europe, where the central bank of each participating Member State is represented in the context of the formulation of monetary policy for the euro—see, generally, Ch 27 above.

[38] In passing, it should be noted that this phenomenon may offer some support to the Societary theory of money, which was considered in Ch 1 above. Dollarisation which occurs as a result of the practices of a particular society is usually driven by high rates of inflation affecting the local unit; on the general subject, see Guidotti and Rodriguez, *Dollarisation in Latin America: Gresham's Law in Reverse?* (IMF, September 1992) Staff Papers Vol 39, No. 3. It is, however, fair to say that legal or "official" attempts at dollarisation have likewise been seen as a means of dealing with inflation and the problems created by it.

[39] On this obligation, see the discussion of the former UK system of exchange control in Ch 14 above. Similar points are made by Kapeta, "Devaluation and Dollarisation of the Malawi Economy" in *Comparative Law Yearbook of International Business* (Kluwer, 1999) 281.

E. Currency Boards

In essence, a currency board is a monetary authority which issues a domestic **33.14** currency which is convertible into a reserve currency at a fixed rate and on demand. The reserve currency (or "anchor currency") will be an external currency which is expected to remain stable and which is internationally acceptable, thus lending credibility to the local currency unit.[40] In order to support these arrangements, a currency board will hold low risk assets denominated in the reserve currency which must (at the fixed rate of exchange or "peg") be at least equal to the face value of the domestic monetary base.[41]

A currency board is an essentially domestic form of monetary organisation; the **33.15** creation or existence of a currency board will not depend on a treaty or any other form of international arrangement.[42] A currency board may be broadly defined as a monetary regime based on a legislative or administrative commitment to exchange domestic currency for a specified foreign currency at a predetermined exchange rate. In order to secure compliance with this obligation, the issuer of the local currency will only be able to issue its domestic currency against a deposit of foreign currency assets, thus ensuring that banknotes and currency in circulation remain "backed" by the foreign currency concerned.[43] This type of arrangement—frequently described as a "peg"—is clearly a step short of dollarisation because the State concerned continues to issue its own currency. For the same reason, currency board arrangements do not resemble a monetary union in the terms in which it was defined for the purposes of this work. Nor is it similar to a monetary area for (at least in formal terms) a peg may be established without the approval of the country which issues the reference currency. But in the absence of some specific strain on the "pegging" arrangements, the market will effectively treat the two currencies as essentially equivalents at the pegged rate.

---

[40] It will be apparent that the currency board structure bears some resemblance to the gold standard, where a central bank was under an obligation to deliver a stated amount of gold in exchange for its own notes.

[41] The "monetary base" for these purposes will be defined by the applicable legislation. In practice, currency boards are usually required to hold in excess of 100% in reserve currency assets, to provide a margin against a fall in value of the external assets so held.

[42] The Dayton Peace Agreement on Bosnia and Hezegovina contemplated a currency board arrangement for that country but this may be regarded as exceptional; even then, the currency board was to be created under that country's Constitution, and was thus essentially a domestic entity.

[43] For this definition, see Yu Syue-Ming, "The Role of the Central Bank in a Crisis Environment: The Experience of Hong Kong and Taiwan, 1997–99" in Giovanoli (ed), *International Monetary Law—Issues for the New Millennium* (Oxford University Press, 2000) 280.

33.16   Currency boards have at various times existed in about seventy countries or territories,[44] but this form of monetary organisation went out of fashion for a period. However, currency board structures enjoyed something of a revival during the 1990s, largely in response to specific monetary problems.[45] It is thus necessary to provide a brief general description and to outline some of the legal provisions which may be necessary to underpin a currency board structure.

33.17   The very existence of a currency board connotes full and complete convertibility between the domestic currency and the anchor currency at the fixed rate. This implies that the State concerned cannot impose exchange controls or similar restrictions affecting the exchange of the domestic currency.

33.18   In contrast to the more traditional central bank model, currency boards play no role in monetary policy, the control of interest rates or attempts to regulate levels of inflation. The function of a currency board is to exchange its notes and coins for the reserve currency at the "pegged" rate. It is a feature of a currency board that it may not lend to its home State government[46] or to anyone else; this prohibition is designed to ensure that government expenditure is financed solely through taxation or borrowing, ie and not through the (inflationary) printing of money. Likewise, a currency board does not regulate interest rates through the establishment of a discount rate. Instead, the fixed rate of exchange should ensure that local interest rates are comparable to those prevailing in the State which issues the reserve currency. These features in some respects reflect one of the main attractions of a currency board arrangement—it demonstrates that the country concerned is determined to have a sound monetary system with a secure, anti-inflationary strategy.

33.19   The history of currency boards has something of a colonial flavour. The West African Currency Board was established in 1912, covering Nigeria, Ghana, Sierra Leone, and the Gambia. A similar model was thereafter adopted in many parts of the British Empire, but—as these countries achieved independence— currency boards tended to be replaced by central banks along more traditional

---

[44] Some of the historical and descriptive material which follows relies upon (a) a paper dated 17 June 2002, *Introduction to Currency Boards* by Kurt Schuler; (b) an article entitled "Are Currency Boards a Cure for all Monetary Problems?" by Enoch and Gulde (1998) 35(4) *Finance & Development*; and (c) *Currency Boards for Developing Countries: A Handbook* by Hanke and Schuler (ICS Press, San Francisco, 1994). It should be appreciated that the present discussion is framed in very general terms for local economic and political conditions will inevitably dictate variations on the general theme.

[45] Apart from those countries which do retain a currency board system, other countries debated the possibility of establishing such a board, eg Russia (see Hanke, "Create a Currency-Board Law for Russia", *The Wall Street Journal*, Europe, 7 September 1998).

[46] cf the corresponding rules applicable to the ECB discussed at para 26.16(e) above.

lines. The British influence can perhaps be detected in the facts that the Hong Kong Monetary Authority now offers the main example of a currency board, and that other currency boards exist in territories such as Bermuda,[47] Gibraltar, Brunei, and the Cayman Islands; the Eastern Caribbean Central Bank[48] may also be regarded as a currency board.

If a currency board is to achieve the objectives which have been described above, **33.20** then there must clearly be public confidence that the peg will be appropriately maintained. This, in turn, demands that the peg must be enshrined in the legal system of the country concerned, or must be adequately secured in some other way. It is therefore appropriate to provide a brief overview of the statutory provisions which have been adopted for currency boards established in the modern era.

Perhaps the most durable currency board of recent times has been that operated **33.21** by the Hong Kong Monetary Authority; despite inevitable and periodic strains,[49] the Hong Kong dollar has been pegged at US$1 = HK$7.80 since 1983 when the creation of the peg was prompted by a loss of confidence in the Hong Kong currency. Under the arrangements operating there, the local currency is fully backed by foreign assets or gold[50] and the assets within the Hong Kong Exchange Fund are available for the purpose of backing the exchange value of the Hong Kong dollar.[51] Under the terms of a Convertibility Undertaking issued by the Hong Kong Monetary Authority in 1998, the Monetary Authority provides an unconditional undertaking to licensed banks that it will on request convert their local currency holdings into US dollars at the pegged

---

[47] The point is made clear by s 10 of the Bermuda Monetary Authority Act of 1969, which provides that "the parity of the Bermudian dollar shall be equivalent to such amount of sterling or any other national or international currency, or gold, as the Governor . . . may by order . . . prescribe".

[48] The ECCB is also discussed in another context—see para 24.15 above.

[49] It may be observed that Hong Kong succeeded in defending the "peg" arrangements even during the course of the Asian financial crisis in 1997—see the Hong Kong Monetary Authority Annual Report, 1997.

[50] For a description of these arrangements, see Balino and Enoch, *Currency Board Arrangements: Issues and Experiences* (IMF Occasional Paper 151, August 1997) 151; "The Currency Board Account and other Fine-Tuning Measures to Strengthen the Currency Board Arrangements in Hong Kong" (1999) 5 *Hong Kong Monetary Authority Quarterly Bulletin*.

[51] As to this Fund, see the Hong Kong Exchange Fund Ordinance (Cap 66). Under the terms of the Ordinance, the Exchange Fund may be used to support the external value of the Hong Kong dollar, to maintain Hong Kong's status as an international financial centre and for certain other purposes (see s 3). The issue of banknotes in Hong Kong is undertaken by certain financial institutions and, when they do so, they must pay to the Financial Secretary a covering amount in foreign currency in return for a certificate of indebtedness (see s 4(1) of the Ordinance). It is this discipline which (at least in legal terms) prevents a "printing press" approach to the issue of money and thus preserves confidence in the Hong Kong dollar.

rate. Although it does not explicitly refer to a currency board arrangement, it should be noted that the constitution of the Special Administrative Region of Hong Kong does specifically require that the local currency must be fully backed by a reserve fund.[52]

33.22 Argentina likewise established a currency board pursuant to its Convertibility Law of 1991. The currency board system was placed under the management of an independent central bank, and the local peso was fixed on a one-to-one basis against the US dollar.[53] The Convertibility Law allowed Argentine nationals to hold and use foreign currencies, and contained the necessary central bank undertaking to pay US dollars against the peso at the stated fixed rate. In order to guarantee the conversion arrangements, the central bank was required to back the peso monetary base with assets denominated in US dollars or freely convertible currencies. As a result of these arrangements, the free convertibility of the peso itself was likewise assured and the peso and the dollar both circulated on a "par" basis within Argentina itself. In January 2002, in the midst of an economic crisis the Convertibility Law was repealed, thus ending the guarantee arrangements described above and effectively depriving peso holders of their right to claim the US dollar reserves held by the central bank.

33.23 For completeness, a few other examples of the currency board regimes should be given. The Dayton Peace Agreement on Bosnia and Herzegovina specifically referred to the creation of a central bank operating as a currency board. Annex 4 to the Accords set out the Constitution of Bosnia and Herzegovina; Article VII(1) of that Constitution provided that for the first six years after it came into effect, the central bank "may not extend credit by creating money, operating in this respect as a monetary board". The position is buttressed by Article 02.1 of the Central Bank Law (1997), which provides that "the objective of the Central Bank shall be to achieve and maintain the stability of the domestic currency by issuing it according to the rule known as a currency board". In Bulgaria, the Law on the Bulgarian National Bank requires the Bank to maintain foreign exchange reserves sufficient to cover its monetary liabilities, and provides for the currency to be pegged to the German mark.[54] The "currency board" label is not used, but these arrangements plainly exhibit the necessary features of such a board. Other variants of the currency board are to be found in

---

[52] See Art 111 of the Basic Law. The Article does not, however, stipulate that the reserve fund must comprise particular types of asset.

[53] For a description of the system, see W. Max Corden, *Too Sensational: On the Choice of Exchange Rate Regimes* (MIT Press, 2002) ch 11.

[54] On these points, see Arts 28.1 and 29 of the Law on the Bulgarian National Bank.

Estonia,[55] Lithuania,[56] and Latvia.[57] In each of these cases, it may be said that the States concerned have sought the benefits of fixed exchange rates and stable money, without introducing a system of exchange controls.[58]

It remains to observe that a currency "peg" is not an entirely uniform concept. **33.24** The peg may be fixed, in the sense that the relevant rate of exchange for banknotes and coins is fixed by law.[59] Alternatively, the arrangement may be a "crawling peg" under which the local unit is to be allowed to depreciate against the reference currency over a period of time.[60] A further variation on the theme involves the pursuit of an exchange rate policy based upon a "basket" of reference currencies.[61] Finally, the peg may not be set by reference to a fixed rate but may operate within a permitted band of comparative values.[62] In other words, the type of exchange rate arrangements now under discussion may vary between a fixed and legally binding commitment to a particular fixed rate and a relatively flexible exchange rate policy which allows for a certain degree of latitude. Many different shades of arrangement exist between the two extremes.[63] The lawyer is likely to be concerned only with those arrangements which imply a degree of legally effective commitment on the part of the issuing State concerned.

---

[55] Estonia established its currency board in 1992. Article 1 of the Law on the Security of the Estonian Kroon requires that the monetary liabilities of the central bank must be secured by gold and convertible foreign currency reserves, whilst Art 2 stipulated that the currency would be pegged against the German mark.

[56] Lithuania established a currency board system in 1994. Article 7 of the Law on the Bank of Lithuania states that its principal objective is "to achieve the stability of the currency of the Republic of Lithuania". This is supported by Art 3 of the Law on the Credibility of the litas, which provides that "the official exchange rate of the litas shall be established against the currency chosen as the anchor currency". The US dollar was originally chosen for this purpose, but the euro was substituted with effect from February 2002.

[57] Latvia established a currency board in 1994, and elected to adopt the SDR as the anchor unit, with a view to taking advantage of the spreading of risk which is implicit in the use of a "basket" unit. On the adoption of currency boards in the Baltic States following their independence from the Soviet Union, see Knöbl and Haas, *The IMF and the Baltics: A Decade of Cooperation* (IMF Working Paper WP/03/241).

[58] On this point, and for further details of the arrangements described in this paragraph, see the short but illuminating article of Professor Tsang Shu-Ki, "Legal Frameworks of Currency Board Regimes" (1999) 8 *Hong Kong Monetary Authority Quarterly Bulletin* 50.

[59] For examples of fixed peg arrangements involving the euro, see "The Eurosystem and the EU enlargement Process" (February 2000) *ECB Monthly Bulletin* 29.

[60] On "crawling pegs", see W. Max Corden (n 53 above) 74–6. For examples of crawling pegs maintained against the euro, see *ECB Monthly Bulletin* (n 59 above) 104.

[61] For examples involving the euro, see *ECB Monthly Bulletin* (n 59 above) 103.

[62] See, eg, the arrangements created by the ERM of the European Monetary System and "ERM II" discussed at para 25.11 and para 25.22, n 65 above.

[63] For a classification, see W. Max Corden (n 53 above) 63. On the arrangements for the use of the South African rand and the "rand zone", see Grandes, "Macroeconomic Convergence in Southern Africa: The Rand Zone Experience" (OECD Working Paper No. 231).

F. Monetary Areas

33.25 Monetary areas are characterised by the fact that restrictions on monetary transfers within the area are abolished, or much reduced. In other words, each of the States within the area maintains a system of exchange control, but applies this system less rigorously to countries which are fellow members of the monetary area. Certain resources, such as foreign exchange or gold, may be pooled.

The sterling area

33.26 The most important area for many years was the sterling area.[64] It comprised the territories which section 1(3) of the Exchange Control Act 1947 described as the "scheduled territories" listed in the First Schedule to the Act[65] as amended from time to time and within which payments and transfers could freely be made. The sterling area ceased to exist for all practical purposes on 23 June 1972;[66] the complete abolition of exchange control in 1979 has perhaps further propelled the sterling area into the realm of history, but a brief review nevertheless remains appropriate.

33.27 The sterling area did not depend upon any specific treaty arrangements between the territories within the area. Whilst each territory had an independent monetary system and maintained parity with sterling, this was formally maintained through the exchange rate arrangements of the International Monetary Fund. Perhaps as evidence of the reciprocal and domestic nature of the arrangements, each country had its own system of exchange control and, in many cases, the local legislation was based upon the model provided by the UK Exchange Control Act 1947.[67] Subject to certain exceptions, the legislation would not apply to transactions effected with other territories within the sterling area and, in principle, each territory had the right to hold and manage its own resources as it wished. Despite the lack of uniform organisation, the sterling area existed as a fairly homogenous unit, relying largely on informal undertakings and on ties of

---

[64] For literature see, A.R. Conan, *The Sterling Area* (Macmillan, 1952) and W.M. Scammell, *International Monetary Policy* (Macmillan, 1975) 242. For more recent assessments of these arrangements, see Aldcroft, *The Sterling Area in the 1930s; A Unique Monetary Arrangement?* (Earlybrave Publications, 2000); Hinds, *Britain's Sterling Colonial Policy and Decolonisation, 1939–1958* (Greenwood Press, 2001).

[65] This point has been noted earlier in the context of UK exchange control—see para 14.11, n 18 above.

[66] See SI 1972/930. The sterling area effectively came to an end at that point because exchange control restrictions were extended to nearly all of the territories which were formerly within the sterling area. For details, see Exchange Control Notice EC 83.

[67] Elements of the Exchange Control Act 1947 can still be seen, eg, in the Exchange Control Act of Malaysia, and in the corresponding legislation in Ghana, Zambia, and South Africa.

a financial, commercial, and historical character. As a result, it was only on rare occasions that the lawyer had to concern himself with the sterling area as such; he was much more likely to be concerned with issues arising under the domestic system of exchange control. An attempt was made to terminate the internal, dollar-pooling arrangements in force within the sterling area under the terms of the Financial Agreement between the United States and the United Kingdom on 6 December 1945, but the attempt failed.[68]

Despite the informal origins of the sterling area, however, it was perhaps inevitable that formal agreements would become necessary as time passed. Thus, for example, the pooling arrangements were both relaxed and regulated by agreement between the United Kingdom and Ceylon. Under the heading of Monetary Co-operation, the two governments recognised that "Ceylon is at all times free to dispose of her currency savings abroad"; the United Kingdom agrees that "Ceylon may retain from that surplus an independent reserve of gold or dollars" which, during the period to 30 June 1950 should amount to no more than US$1 million, and that "subject to this, Ceylon intends to contribute her surplus dollar earnings to the foreign exchange resources of the scheduled territories".[69] An even more significant step towards formal regulation occurred in the period following the Second World War. The essential problem arose from the extent of the sterling balances, namely, the liabilities of the United Kingdom towards foreign States and their nationals. Most of these liabilities accrued during the war to pay for local supplies and services; by December 1947, those liabilities amounted to more than £3,600 million. The subject was first addressed by the Anglo-American Financial Agreement of 1945, to which reference has already been made.[70] It was subsequently regulated by a large number of treaties which provided for a release of the balances over a period of years.[71] The final development resulted from the devaluation of the pound in November 1967 which "was, of course, a shock to the sterling system" because the great majority of the 39 countries forming part of the sterling area did not devalue; as a result, they suffered loss "not only in terms of dollar purchasing power but . . . in terms of their own currency also".[72] As a result, the United Kingdom entered

33.28

---

[68] Cmd 6708. Clause 7 provided that "The sterling receipts from current transactions of all sterling area countries . . . will be freely available for current transactions in any currency area without discrimination with the result that any discrimination arising from the so-called sterling area dollar pool will be entirely removed and that each will have its current sterling and dollar receipts at its free disposal for current transactions anywhere." On the problem generally, see Richard N. Gardner, *Sterling—Dollar Diplomacy* (Oxford University Press, 1956).

[69] Cmd 7766, and see Cmd 8165. For a reference to the gold reserves of the sterling area, see the Anglo-Egyptian Financial Agreement of 31 March 1949 (Cmd 7675) Letter No 1.

[70] Cmd 6708. See Richard N. Gardner (n 68 above) 204 and 326.

[71] See, eg, treaties with Ceylon (Cmd 8165), Pakistan (Cmd 8380), India (Cmd 8953), Egypt (Cmd 7675), Uruguay (Cmd 7172), and Iraq (Cmd 7201).

[72] Cmnd 3787; the quotations in the text are taken from para 7.

into formal treaties with the sterling area countries, guaranteeing to maintain the dollar value of 90 per cent of their official sterling reserves, while these countries in turn undertook to maintain an agreed proportion of their reserves in sterling. Nine-tenths of the sterling area's official sterling reserves were secured by a dollar clause.[73]

The French franc area

33.29 The French franc area or the Operations Account Area, as it was technically but unattractively renamed on 1 February 1967,[74] is much more closely organised. The area comprises France itself, and the countries of the West African and Central African Monetary Unions. Although the French franc area thus comprised two monetary unions,[75] it should be appreciated that the French franc area was not itself a monetary union, because France retained its own currency which was separate from that of the union States. The legal status of the French franc area was originally derived from the treaties such as that between France and the West African Monetary Union of 12 May 1962.[76] The French Republic allowed to the Central Bank of the West African States "la dotation de 500 millions"[77] and guaranteed the convertibility of the CFA franc into French francs.[78] For this purpose, the French Treasury opened "un compte d'opérations" in favour of the Central Bank, the terms of which were the subject of a separate Convention. Article 4 then provided that "Les États prendront toutes dispositions utiles pour que soient centralisés au compte d'opérations les avoirs extérieurs de l'Union Monétaire". This important provision in substance creates the legal obligation to pool foreign exchange resources.[79]

33.30 These arrangements necessarily required review in the context of monetary union in Europe, for France would now be called upon to ensure the convertibility of the CFA franc into the euro and this state of affairs might, in turn, have an impact upon price stability within the eurozone as a whole. Thus, in a sense,

---

[73] The guarantee invariably read that the UK undertook "to maintain the sterling value in terms of the United States dollar of the balances". What would have been the effect of a devaluation of the dollar? It is submitted that, notwithstanding the wording of the guarantee, there would have been no reduction in the sterling value of the balances.

[74] For the details, see the IMF *Annual Report on Exchange Agreements and Exchange Restrictions* (1979) 159.

[75] These unions have been discussed in more detail at para 24.10 above.

[76] *Clunet* 1963, 868, as amended by a Convention of 21 February 1963, *Clunet* 1964, 267.

[77] Article 2. The reference was presumably to French francs.

[78] It should be added that a similar guarantee of convertibility had been given with respect to the Comorian franc under the terms of a Convention originally entered into on 23 November 1979. These arrangements were, likewise, adjusted in accordance with the terms of the Council Decision about to be discussed.

[79] For some of the later treaty materials, see the general discussion of the African monetary unions at para 24.10 above.

the fulfilment of the guarantee of convertibility ceased to be an essentially domestic matter for France; in view of the arrangements for the introduction of the single currency, it became a concern for the eurozone as a whole. But it must be observed that the continuation of such arrangements constituted a matter of fiscal (as opposed to monetary) policy, and France retained its competence in fiscal matters notwithstanding its progression to the third stage of EMU.[80] Furthermore, the guarantee was given by the French Republic, and not by the Banque de France; consequently, the guarantee did not impinge upon the latter's role and functions as a member of the European System of Central Banks.[81] Nevertheless, in view of the indirect consequences to which reference has already been made, France gave an assurance that these arrangements had no major financial implications for France and its economy and as a result, would not have a material impact upon the goal of price stability. The Council accepted the position, although it wished to monitor the situation and approval would be required before the relevant agreements could be amended in any way.[82] It may be noted in passing that the Council Decision on the subject appears to be based on Article 111(3) of the Treaty, which allows for the negotiation of monetary or exchange rate agreements by the Community. This seems to be misguided, since the CFA Agreements were binding on France but not on other members of the Community.[83]

Freedom of internal transfers

It has been suggested earlier that freedom of internal transfers of currency is one **33.31** of the characteristics of a monetary area; it ought to follow that the import and export of goods within the same area should likewise be free. It is the corollary of this situation that the control of currency transfers to persons outside the monetary area of necessity implies the control of imports into the area.

---

[80] On fiscal policy and national competence, see para 26.16(g) above.

[81] On this subject, see the discussion of the institutional arrangements for EMU in Ch 27 above.

[82] Council Decision 1998/683/EC, concerning exchange rate matters relating to the CFA franc and the Comorian franc [1998] OJ L320/58. The Council was clearly concerned to emphasise that the continuation of arrangements for the CFA area did not impose any obligation upon the ECB or any member of the ESCB—see para (7) of the preamble and Art 2 of the Decision. For discussion, see Strumpf, "The introduction of the euro to States and territories outside the European Union" [2003] 28 ELR 283. Although not directly relevant in the present context, it may be convenient here to note that France also retained the right to issue currency (the CFP franc) in its overseas territories and to determine its parity rate—see the Protocol on France, annexed to the EC Treaty.

[83] It may be noted here that Portugal had also maintained a similar agreement which was designated to ensure the convertibility of the Cape Verdi escudo. Portugal was to continue that agreement following the introduction of the euro, on the basis that it remained solely responsible for its implementation—see Council Decision 1998/774/EC, [1998] OJ L358/109.

33.32   It is suggested that these views are logical, both in legal and economic terms, yet they are not supported by the difficult decision of the International Court of Justice in the *Case Concerning Rights of Nationals of the United States of America in Morocco*.[84] The background to the case and the issues which arose are very complex, and must be summarised briefly. Under the Act of Algeciras of 7 April 1906, citizens of the United States were entitled to the benefits of the principle of "economic liberty without any inequality".[85] On 9 September 1939, Morocco promulgated a law which banned the import of all goods other than gold and provided for exceptions to be made by means of regulations. On the same day, a regulation was made which provided a complete exemption for goods of French origin; they were to be admitted into Morocco without further formality. On 10 September 1939, Morocco passed a further law which created a system of exchange controls; once again, a regulation was introduced on the same day which allowed for payment to French suppliers on a more favourable basis than those which applied generally. During an interim period, other regulations were put into force but the decrees and regulations passed on 9 September 1939 were reinstated by a further decree of 30 December 1948. Did these arrangements for France have the effect of creating a prohibited "inequality" so far as citizens of the United States were concerned?

33.33   France put forward a number of arguments; in particular, it asserted that the decree of 9 September 1939 was a decree relating to exchange control, and nothing in the treaty prohibited the imposition of such a system. The Court dismissed this argument because, on the face of it, the decree of 9 September related to import control or quantitative restrictions, rather than exchange control. France's attempt to classify the 9 September decree as an exchange control measure thus failed, but this may be because no sufficient attempt was made either (a) to link it with the system of exchange control which was introduced on the following day or (b) to demonstrate that import control and exchange control are in fact inseparable emanations of a single system of economic planning.[86]

33.34   However that may be, it is unfortunate that a different line of argument—based upon the existence of the "zone franc"—may have been open to France but it was not even put forward. It was well known to all parties that Morocco was part of the monetary area known as the "zone franc" and it appears that the United States had not at any time objected to Morocco's membership of that

---

[84] ICJ Reports [1952] 176.

[85] This, at any rate, is the conclusion reached by the International Court of Justice. In fact, the principle was only noted in the preamble and in Art 105 of the Act, and it must be very doubtful whether the alleged general principle was in fact established by the treaty. Nevertheless, the discussion must proceed upon the basis of the Court's ruling on this point.

[86] For criticism, see Labaudère (1952) 6 *Revue Juridique et Politique de l' Union Française* 429.

zone. The United States must likewise have well understood the point made earlier, namely that the existence of a monetary zone implies a geographical area within which money and goods circulate freely; certainly, it must imply *some* monetary and trading preferences for the members of the area, for otherwise its existence has no meaning. Under these circumstances, as a result of its acquiescence in Morocco's membership of the zone franc, the United States must have accepted that its citizens could not be entitled to commercial equality with the members of the zone; the standard of equality had thus to be measured by reference to the treatment extended to other States *outside* the zone.

G. Monetary Agreements

For the purposes of the present discussion, monetary agreements are treaties or other arrangements which regulate exclusively monetary matters, but which do not seek to create a separate institution for that purpose. Such agreements either have an essentially political character or, otherwise, are of a highly technical nature. **33.35**

Political agreements

Agreements of a political nature have tended to focus on the objective of exchange rate stability and the economic damage which can be caused by excessive fluctuations. The present section will therefore focus on agreements of this kind. **33.36**

An example is provided by the Declaration establishing the "gold bloc" which subsisted between 1933 and 1936 among France, Belgium, Italy, the Netherlands, Switzerland, and Poland. These States confirmed "their intention to maintain the free functioning of the gold standard in their respective countries at the existing gold parities and within the framework of existing monetary laws". The States concerned asked their respective central banks to keep in close touch to give the maximum efficacy to this Declaration.[87] In 1936, a more overtly political Declaration was made by the United States, France, and Great Britain; Belgium, Switzerland, and the Netherlands subsequently adhered to it. These States reaffirmed their intention to continue their monetary policies "one object of which is to maintain the greatest possible equilibrium in the system of international exchanges and to avoid to the utmost the creation of any disturbance of that system by [unilateral] monetary action". The participating **33.37**

---

[87] *Documents on International Affairs* (1933) 45. The Declaration was supported by a Protocol of 20 October 1934 (*Hudson, International Legislation* V, No 396), where some literature will also be found.

States also extended an invitation to other nations "to realise the policy laid down in the present Declaration".[88] Declarations of this kind are essentially statements of intent; it is submitted that they do not place any formal restrictions upon the States' sovereignty in monetary matters.[89]

33.38 The demise of the network of fixed rate parities established by the Bretton Woods system has been noted on a number of occasions. A world of floating exchange rates—where rates are in large measure determined by market forces—has been broadly accepted for many years. Yet there can be no doubt that exchange rate fluctuations can seriously distort business planning and expectations, and can have a very damaging effect on national economies.[90] Whilst floating rates have been accepted as a reality, the question of relative exchange rate stability has necessarily received a great deal of governmental attention.[91]

33.39 In an effort to limit the damage which may flow from exchange rate fluctuations, governments have from time to time entered into arrangements designed to ensure that their currencies may float only within limited margins.[92] On occasion, the permitted margins of fluctuation have been made known to the markets. This has not always had positive consequences, since the foreign exchange markets may speculate against a currency which appears to be in danger of crossing the permitted thresholds.[93] In other cases, the precise extent

---

[88] *Documents on International Affairs* (1936) 668.

[89] It may be argued that such a position involves an obligation on a State not deliberately to seek to manipulate exchange rates to its own advantage. But this would be very difficult to achieve in practice in any event, and is very unlikely to occur. This may be contrasted with the "common interest" provision contained in the EC Treaty and addressing the exchange rate policy of non-participating Member States. As has been seen (see para 31.36(5) above), it is possible to attribute some substantial legal meaning to that provision. However, this is because the provision is found within a detailed treaty dealing with the creation of a new currency; it is not merely a political statement of the type described in the text.

[90] This state of affairs does, of course, provide one of the main arguments in favour of monetary unions amongst States which are close trading partners.

[91] Apart from specific arrangements such as the ERM of the EMS (see para 25.11 above), the subject of exchange rate stability seems, at least in recent times, to have received relatively limited attention from legal writers (although for an exception to this statement, see Gold, *Legal Effects of Fluctuating Exchange Rates* (IMF, 1990)). No doubt this is because there is now no general international obligation which requires a State to maintain the external value of its currency at any particular level (see para 22.13 above). In contrast, and as one might expect, the economic literature is enormous. Shorter articles which may provide useful background for the lawyer include Coeuré and Pisani-Ferry, "The Case Against Benign Neglect of Exchange Rate Stability" (September, 1999) *Finance & Development* 5; Sarno and Taylor, "Official Intervention in the Foreign Exchange Market: Is it Effective and, If so, How does it Work?" (September, 2001) XXXIX *Journal of Economic Literature* 839.

[92] Such arrangements are often referred to as a "managed float".

[93] A prime example is offered by the UK's participation in the ERM and the events of "Black Wednesday"—see para 25.17 above.

of obligations undertaken by the governments concerned will be less clearly defined, but the overall objective may be clear.[94]

Examples of arrangements falling within the latter category would include the **33.40** Plaza Agreement and the Louvre Accord. In September 1985, the Group of Five[95] met at the Plaza Hotel, New York, and agreed collectively to intervene in the market to lower the value of the US dollar, which was perceived to have been too high during the early years of the 1980s. The Plaza Agreement appears to have had the desired effect; the value of the US dollar fell over the ensuing period although significant official intervention was required to assist in that process. In February 1987, the Group of Six met at Louvre and announced that the dollar had reached a level which was consistent with underlying economic conditions; future market intervention would therefore only occur when required to ensure exchange rate stability.[96] The Louvre Accord again appeared to work well for a period, although once again, significant market intervention was required.[97] However, political shocks, including German reunification and the invasion of Kuwait, weakened commitment to the Louvre Accord, and by 1993 the arrangement was, to all intents, at an end.[98] Whilst governmental intervention in foreign exchange markets is by no means excluded,[99] the governmental appetite for such intervention appears to have waned. Thus, for example, following its meeting in Boca Raton in February 2004, the Group of Seven issued a Press Statement[100] noting that "exchange rates should reflect economic fundamentals. Excess volatility and disorderly exchange rates are undesirable for

---

[94] The benefit of an ill-defined objective is, of course, that it only provides to the markets a rather more elusive target.

[95] The Group of Five (G5) countries are the US, the UK, Germany, France, and Japan. The Group of Six (G6) comprises the Group of Five plus Canada, whilst the Group of Seven (G7) also includes Italy.

[96] It was agreed that the dollar should be stabilised within informal "reference ranges", although precise target zones were apparently not established (or perhaps, not published). In this context, the official press release of the Louvre Accord noted that "the substantial exchange rate intervention since the Plaza Agreement will increasingly contribute to reducing external imbalances and have now brought their currencies within ranges broadly consistent with underlying economic fundamentals . . . Further substantial exchange rate shifts among their currencies could damage growth and adjustment prospects." See, generally, Sarno and Taylor (n 91 above).

[97] On intervention following the Plaza Agreement and the Louvre Accord, see Obstfeld, "*The Effectiveness of Foreign Exchange Intervention: Recent Experience 1985–1988*" in Branson, Frenkel and Goldstein (eds) *International Policy Co-ordination and Exchange Rate Fluctuations* (University of Chicago Press, 1990).

[98] The point is made by Coeuré and Pisani-Ferry (n 91 above).

[99] The central banks of the G7 countries intervened in the markets in a concerted way on 22 September 2000 in order to support the euro, which had been the subject of persistent depreciation against the US dollar since the introduction of the single currency in January 1999: see Sarno and Taylor (n 91 above).

[100] The Press Statement merely adds some detail to the statement which had been issued following a similar meeting in Dubai, in September 2003.

economic growth. We continue to monitor exchange markets closely and co-operate as appropriate." This statement in some respects signals a retreat from market intervention, in the sense that it merely includes confirmation that the major nations will co-operate where necessary; no target ranges are established for the US dollar or any other currency. This impression is only reinforced if it is borne in mind that this Statement was released at a time when the declining value of the US dollar was a matter of international concern.

33.41   The success of the Plaza Agreement, the Louvre Accord, and similar arrangements can best be described as mixed, although they are perhaps likely only to be of short-term validity and, as has been shown, they may easily be overtaken by other political or economic events. Arrangements of this kind are necessarily open-textured, and are perhaps more successful in creating an agenda for political action than in laying down any enforceable guidelines; this view is proved by the extracts from the various statements and agreements which have been reproduced. It must follow that—important though they may be in other contexts—they must be taken to lack any legally relevant content. This merely serves to reinforce the views expressed earlier[101] to the effect that international law knows of no general obligation to maintain exchange rates at particular levels, and that obligations of consultation and co-operation have limited legal force in the monetary sphere.

Technical agreements

33.42   Technical agreements are not usually intended to make a contribution to the development of an international monetary system; rather, they establish a (temporary) expedient or machinery to deal with a particular difficulty. For example, they may aim at facilitating the transfer of funds from one country to another so as to maintain the balance of payments in a state of reasonable equilibrium. Such was the object of the clearing system which was widely used up to the end of the Second World War, particularly by Switzerland, but also by the United Kingdom in their dealings with Romania, Italy, Turkey, and Spain.[102] However, the system could only operate effectively if private traders strictly observed the regulations designed to ensure that payment for all goods covered by the agreement should be made exclusively to the Clearing Office—a condition which was liable to cause much hardship to creditors. As a result, the

---

[101] See para 22.13 above. This view would, of course, give way to any clearly expressed treaty obligation to the contrary.

[102] So far as the UK is concerned, the system depended on a series of statutory instruments made under the Debts Clearing Office and Import Restrictions Act 1934.

use of the system gave rise to litigation in various countries, but it only fell to be considered in one case in England.[103]

A monetary agreement of a technical nature, but with much extended scope, **33.43** was the European Payments Union, which existed during the ten years ended in December 1958 and constituted an International Clearing Union involving "the full and automatic offsetting of all bilateral surpluses and deficits incurred by each participating country with all others".[104] It was succeeded by the European Monetary Agreement[105] which again provided for a multilateral system of settlements.

The most important cross-border technical agreement established in recent **33.44** times is that established to support the creation of the euro. It was recognised that the smooth transfer of funds across the eurozone would be a necessary prerequisite to the proper functioning of monetary union and the full realisation of the benefits of the single currency area; accordingly, amongst its other tasks, the European System of Central Banks was required "to promote the smooth operation of payment systems".[106] This resulted in the establishment of a real-time gross settlement system[107] known as TARGET.[108] The system is used for the settlement of transactions between central banks and large value interbank transfers. TARGET does, in fact, consist of the real-time gross settlement systems of the Member States.[109] which are linked together through the ECB's

---

[103] In *Fischler v Administrator of Roumanian Property* [1960] 3 All ER 433, the question was whether a credit balance standing in the books of the Anglo-Roumanian Clearing Office in London was "property, rights or interests" of the Romanian exporter or his Romanian bank to whose credit the payment had been made. The House of Lords answered in the former sense. The legislation creating the clearing office was complex but in the final analysis, it merely created a mechanism for collection and control; it did not have the effect of transferring beneficial ownership to the claim involved. The Romanian bank was involved in the transaction to ensure compliance with Romanian exchange control, but it did not become the "beneficiary" of those funds in the true legal sense.

[104] This definition is used by Triffin, *Europe and the Money Muddle* (New Haven, 1957; Greenwood Press (Reprint) 1976) 168–9. For literature on the union—now a matter of the past—see Mann *Rec* 96 (1959, i) 28–30.

[105] For details, see Mann, *Rec* 96 (1959, i) 30–1. On economic and financial aspects, see Graham L. Rees, *Britain and the Post-War European Payments System* (1963). The Agreement came to an end on 31 December 1972.

[106] The obligation is contained in Art 105(2) of the EC Treaty and is repeated in Art 3.1 of the ESCB Statute.

[107] One of the features of such systems is that transfers of funds are settled immediately and are thus not held in the system pending settlement on a "net" basis at the end of the business day.

[108] To give the system its full name, the Trans European Automated Real-time Gross Settlement Express Transfer System.

[109] In the UK, the RTGS system is known as CHAPS euro.

own payment mechanism.[110] The system has been designed to provide safe and reliable mechanisms for the settlement of high-value euro payments and to enhance the efficiency of cross-border payments made in the single currency. Payments are settled in central bank money, with the security and finality which that term implies.[111] Since payments through the system are intended to be final—in the sense that they cannot be recalled by a liquidator or other insolvency official—it has been necessary to require Member States to introduce national legislation which achieves that objective.[112]

33.45   Finally, it may be anticipated that TARGET will have to cope with ever increasing levels of activity, not least because many of the new Member States which joined the European Union on 1 May 2004 aspire to become eurozone members as well. The ECB is working on a system known as TARGET 2, which will cater for these eventualities but which will continue to be based upon the general principles which have been described above.[113] TARGET has operated successfully but the continuing development of the system will no doubt be work in progress for the foreseeable future.

---

[110] The establishment of TARGET as a system which links together the separate payment systems of the Member States may be regarded as consistent with Art 12.1 of the ESCB Statute, which requires the ECB to have recourse to the national central banks to carry out operations which form part of the tasks entrusted to the ESCB. It may be added that TARGET is intended for high-value payments, but the efficiency of a single currency area also depends on the smooth transfer of retail payments. For that purpose, the ECB has been promoting a "Single Euro Payments Area", which is in part designed to ensure that payments can be made across the eurozone on the same basis as purely domestic transfers—see generally *Towards a Single Euro Payments Area—Progress Report* (ECB, June 2003).

[111] TARGET operates under the terms of a Guideline of the ECB of 26 April 2001 (as amended), [2001] OJ L140/72. It should be added that, since the ESCB includes non-eurozone Member States which would not be bound by the ECB Guideline, it has been necessary to enter into a TARGET Agreement, which essentially imposes equivalent obligations upon the central banks of the "out" Member States. This and many other instructive points are noted by Nierop, "The TARGET System of the European System of Central Banks" in *Current Developments in Financial Law*, Vol 2 (IMF, 2003) ch 37.

[112] In view of the very high value of payments which may be settled through TARGET, the system might be placed in jeopardy if a liquidator had a right to reclaim payments which had passed through the system immediately prior to the insolvency of the transferor. The point is beyond the scope of the present discussion, but see Directive 98/26/EC of the European Parliament and the Council of 19 May 1998, on settlement and finality in payment and securities settlement systems, [1998] OJ L166/43.

[113] For details, see *The long-term evolution of TARGET*, ECB Press Release, 24 October 2002.

INDEX

821

The Cambridge Illustrated History of

THE MIDDLE AGES

The Cambridge Illustrated History of

THE MIDDLE AGES

I 350–950

Edited by

ROBERT FOSSIER

Translated by

JANET SONDHEIMER

*The right of the
University of Cambridge
to print and sell
all manner of books
was granted by
Henry VIII in 1534.
The University has printed
and published continuously
since 1584.*

CAMBRIDGE UNIVERSITY PRESS

Cambridge

New York   Port Chester

Melbourne   Sydney

Published by the Press Syndicate of the University of Cambridge
The Pitt Building, Trumpington Street, Cambridge CB2 1RP
40 West 20th Street, New York, NY 10011, USA
10 Stamford Road, Oakleigh, Melbourne 3166, Australia

© Cambridge University Press 1989

First published 1989
Reprinted 1990

Printed in Great Britain at The Bath Press, Avon

British Library cataloguing in publication data

The Cambridge Illustrated History of the Middle Ages.
1: 350–950
1. Civilization. Medieval
I. Fossier, Robert   II. Le Moyen Age. *English*
909.07   CB351

Library of Congress cataloguing in publication data

Moyen Age (Armand Colin Firm). English.
The Cambridge Illustrated History of the Middle Ages.
Translation of: Le Moyen Age.
Bibliography: v. 1. p.
Includes index.
Contents:- 1. 350–950.
1. Civilization. Medieval. I. Fossier, Robert.
II. Title.

CB351.M7813 1988 909:07 85-21268

ISBN 0 521 26644 0

SE